THE COMPLETE SHOOTER

By Sam Fadala

DBI BOOKS, INC., NORTHFIELD, ILL.

Staff

EDITOR
Robert Anderson

COVER PHOTOGRAPHY
John Hanusin

PHOTOGRAPHY AND RESEARCH
Nancy Fadala

PRODUCTION MANAGER
Pamela J. Johnson

PUBLISHER
Sheldon L. Factor

ABOUT OUR COVERS

The "Good Old Boys" of Omark Industries grace the front and back covers of The Complete Shooter. We are, indeed, proud to show our readers products from RCBS, Speer, CCI and Outers.

On our front cover you'll see CCI 38 Special Blazer and CCI Mini-Mag rimfire ammo (the latter all done up in CCI's new blue and silver packaging). Next to that ammo you'll find Outers new, multipiece, brass, Imperial cleaning rod for both rifle and pistol. Also seen is a copy of the 10th Edition of the *Speer Reloading Manual* —a long-time favorite with handloaders. Hanging on the wall is Speer's well known Bullet Board which displays the full Speer lineup of pistol and rifle bullets.

Our back cover continues the "Good Old Boys' theme with the centerpiece being an RCBS Reloader Special 2 O-frame, lightweight press designed for the reloading of all popular centerfire rifle and handgun calibers. In back of the RS-2 press you'll see and RCBS Powder Scale, to the right of which is the well known RCBS Case Trimmer. Also seen is a selection of Blazer/CCI ammo, Speer bullets, RCBS reloading dies, Outers Targets, an Outers handgun carrying (lockable) case and a can of Crud Cutter™ aerosol degreaser—it's Outers latest entry in the gun-care and maintenance field. Guns courtesy of the Fix-It Shop, Northfield, Ill. Photos by John Hanusin.

DEDICATION

This book is dedicated to Nick Fadala, John Kane, Gene Thompson, Dean Zollinger, Admiral Schneider and the rest of my shooting friends.

Copyright © MCMLXXXIV by DBI Books, Inc., One Northfield Plaza, Northfield, Ill. 60093. Printed in the United States of America. All rights reserved. No part of this book may be reproduced, stored in a retrieval system or transmitted in any form or by any means, electronic, mechanical, photocopying, recording or otherwise, without prior written permission of the publisher.

The views and opinions of the author expressed herein are not necessarily those of the publisher, and no responsibility for such views will be assumed.

Since the author, editor and publisher have no control over the components, assembly of the ammunition, arms it is to be fired in, the degree of knowledge involved or how the resulting ammunition may be used, no responsibility, either implied or expressed, is assumed for the use of any of the loading data in this book.

Arms and Armour Press, London, G.B., exclusive licensees and distributors in Britain and Europe; Australasia; Nigeria, South Africa and Zimbabwe; India and Pakistan; Singapore, Hong Kong and Japan.

ISBN 0-910676-65-8

Library of Congress Catalog Card #84-071763

Contents

Contents

Chapter 1
The Modern Shooter

THIS IS a practical shooting book. It is written for the shooter who enjoys his firearms at the grass roots level, a shooter who is following in the footsteps of the first American marksmen, who not only depended upon their firearms as important tools in everyday life, but who also enjoyed those guns the way we do today, as instruments of skill, to be admired or as works of art. The practical shooter might be called an "average" shooter, but that would be missing the mark. There is nothing average about the American shooter. He can do it all.

He is a self-sufficient marksman—man, woman, youth—he is capable of much more than average skill, being able to chew the X-ring out of the bull's-eye one day and cleanly harvest a fine piece of venison the next. This book is a self-help guide for that shooter, the shooter who wants to involve himself more fully in his sport, who wants to select his firearms based upon function and design, who wants to better understand ballistics, practice more effectively, load his own ammunition from scratch to target quality, take advantage of many branches of the shooting sport from simple plinking to the most serious safaris.

The complete shooter must be able to accomplish far more than the hitting of a mark. He *knows* his guns. He *understands* them. He wisely selects the proper one for the task at hand, the one best suited to the occasion. When he's harvesting his own meat, be it the winged or hooved variety, his loads are correctly chosen. He can shoot fast in the brush. He can shoot far on the plains. He knows how to hit, and as important, he knows why he missed. He knows ballistics. He can pattern a shotgun for himself. His major love of firearms is in the shooting, but he's probably a collector of sorts, from simply putting a few guns away to pass on to a son or daughter, to seeking, finding, sometimes restoring and keeping valuable arms of both the past and the present.

When he fashions his own metallic cartridges or shotshells, he does so as a scientist. He reloads for economy, but he would reload even if there were no savings, for he has learned to squeeze the most versatility possible from both cartridge and shotshell. He likes performance, and he understands how to get the most from the firearms he has chosen for his battery.

Marksmanship has always been a tradition in America and today's shooter is no exception to the rule. He wants to gain the most from his activity.

John Fadala tries his very first rifle, a 22-caliber. He will experience no recoil problems here and he will get off to a good start. Starting the shooter off on the right foot is paramount for future success and future safety.

This book is dedicated to the American shooter from the southern border to the great northlands, from the eastern seaboard to the western coast. It's dedicated to you, the modern practical shooter. Your main interest is in arms of contemporary design, yet 5 million of you also shoot black powder muzzleloaders, firearms outdated before the invention of the telephone. Yes, you have a rifle. But you also have a shotgun, and at least one handgun. There are about 26,000,000 of you in this land, and though you are a good marksman, your deepest interest lies in your own personal shooting in the field and on the range instead of the formal target. Although you know a lot about guns, you always want to learn more. You read about firearms and you have a library of firearms texts. You would be better at trap and Skeet than you think, but when you pick up your shotgun, it's for quail or ducks or small game. You are the modern practical American shooter, the *complete shooter,* and this is your book.

This book begins with the wonderful world of the 22 rimfire. Who among us can forget the almost unbelievable speed apparent of those wonderful 22 rimfire rounds after we had been shooting the BB gun in our youth? And for those newer shooters who are about to graduate to the 22 rimfire, remember that nothing has been spared. The 22 rimfire in both rifle and handgun form are more accurate than even necessary to accomplish their intended purposes. And then we move into the realm of the deer rifle. Who can explain the thrill and honor of harvesting your own venison? Many are the firearms intended for this important task. Deer, the white-tailed deer first and his cousin the mule deer second, are the most popular and populous of America's big game.

But there is the larger-than-deer category of big game, and even though we may not find ourselves in that field often, it is part of the complete shooter's knowledge to know and understand those arms intended for the big, heavy animals which still walk the quiet places. And of course, there is the all-around rifle. This has been the somewhat elusive firearm and cartridge, that do-it-all rifle capable of deer on Saturday and bull elk on Sunday. It's a rifle which shoots flat and far, and it delivers more energy at long range than many of its brother rounds acquire at the muzzle. And yet, it will push relatively heavy bullets as well. The all-around rifle and round is here, and it's discussed for the complete shooter.

The modern shooter has a wide variety of firearms to select from. Here, Bill Fadala enjoys firing the Weatherby Mark XXII 22 rimfire autoloader, a very accurate rifle. Considering past out-of-manufacture firearms as well as current models, today's shooter has a tremendous variety to choose from.

Your shotgun is just as important to you as your rifle, even if America is the land of the rifleman. Many of us will put a great deal of ammunition through a shell-shucker in a year, and this book reveres the smoothbore and discusses its worth. Some of you will learn to fire at very small targets very far away with a specialized rifle. It's the varmint rifle, and it is also a part of our complete shooter's battery in many cases. The 22 rimfire sidearm has really come into its own. The very day before putting these words on paper, I took the sitting position at the range with my own Ruger 22 semi-auto target model pistol and managed to score 6 out of 10 hits on a target no more than 6 inches

A record head need not be harvested in order to build a good memory. Take a game animal from the terrain in accord with game management policy and you will obtain some fine meat for the table. Kenn Oberrecht poses with a small mule deer buck he took with one shot from a 30-06 rifle. The complete shooter is not always a hunter, to be sure, but many a modern shooter takes some form of game from time to time.

Although we have the finest modern arms ever offered to the shooting public, today's complete shooter also has a wide range of muzzleloaders to choose from. Estimations reveal a total muzzleloader shooting body of more than 5 million. This step backward has been a step forward for many shooters in many ways and the black powder trend is a definite and strong part of modern shooting.

high and 3 inches wide—at 100 yards distance. That is accuracy, for this particular shooter is no champion with the one-hand gun.

Of course, there has been another addition to the world of shooting. It's not really new, and yet it is new. The big game handgun has been around for a very long time, even before shooters recognized its potential. But it is today's complete shooter who has a chance to own truly big game sidearms, from the revolvers of 44 Magnum and similar cartridge stature to break-open and bolt-action pistols chambered for powerhouse rounds which also ''shoot flat'' to a couple hundred yards or more. Of course, there is the firearm intended for the personal defense of home and life.

There is no doubt that it is air-propelled missiles which the shooter first sends downrange. And today, the air gun is so advanced that it has earned its way into national competition and even international competition. Better and better accuracy has been the byword, but along the way, the makers of air powered guns did not forget power. The ''pellet gun'' is more powerful today than ever before, caliber for caliber, although it's quite true that the larger bore air guns of the past were of warfare authority!

Black powder is more than alive and well today. It has a following of dedicated shooters to its credit. The complete shooter may well own a smokepole, for it is the very foundation of his modern battery, the forerunner, the basic firearm which preceded the guns we enjoy today. The man, woman or youth who has mastered the charcoal burner has managed to tame and control one of the most challenging and rewarding of all guns.

At 14 years of age, this hunter (John Fadala) is preparing himself for a lifetime of outdoor enjoyment in a wise-use way. Using firearms with safety is an important part of that outdoor knowledge and the complete shooter has a very broad base of information to work from. He knows how to use many different types of firearms, and he has an appreciation for them all.

Owning a fine battery is not enough for the modern complete shooter. He wants to understand how to hit the mark more often, and our chapter on shooting stance with mini-lessons is geared for the caring marksman who wants to get better and better until he can truly call himself "expert." Following the lessons is a chapter on practice, for we all have to stay in tune. Being good with a gun means being polished and in order to achieve and retain that status, it takes practice. The complete shooter must understand the aiming devices which guide the missile to the target, and that is why we have a chapter on sights. As part of the process of sending a tiny projectile downrange with accuracy is an understanding of its trajectory, and trajectory is the topic of an important chapter, a chapter which gives the shooter a working knowledge of how to sight in to strain the most from the potential of his firearm.

Factory ammunition is remarkably good. It was always good, but this chapter shows just how precise today's factory fodder has become. The manufacturers have proved how much they care, for they have continued to upgrade their product. Nobody who shoots factory ammo need concern himself about its reliability. And yet, the complete shooter is also a handloader, and the book dedicates itself to this maker of ammunition in reloaded form, taking him from the empty case or hull to a professionally handcrafted product of great accuracy and pattern potential. Today's shooter, in a tradition begun in the time of the frontloader, can also make his own missiles.

The complete shooter needs to understand the wildcat round as well, for it has been the wildcatter who has provided us with a number of today's most successful cartridges. Wildcatting is not for everyone, but it is for every shooter's understanding. And the pros and cons of owning and shooting a wildcat round are discussed at length. The big game bullet has come a very long way from the first round lead projectiles of bygone days, which are still fired now as a challenge to the modern shooter. Our chapter on big game bullets will reveal to the reader just how well off we truly are, and why, and how to select the correct bullet for the job at hand, for the range of fine bullets in both factory form and handloaded proposition is a range of great variety and depth.

What about the brushbusters? The modern complete shooter wants to know the capability of his ammo not only for long-range shooting, but also for a type of shooting which is accomplished all over this land from east to west, shooting in the brush. Our study will show the shooter what he is dealing with and will give a basis for treating the "brushbuster" in a very specific manner. The rifled slug is discussed, too, not only for its wonderful potential, but also for its limitations, for knowing the limitations of a load is just as important as knowing its potential.

Understanding ballistics is the foundation for much shooting, and basic but sometimes profound facts in the realm of ballistics occupy an entire chapter of the book. It is a deserving topic, because the complete shooter is both artist and scientist. He shoots with artistic ability, but understands his arms with scientific precision. He can pattern his own shotgun, this complete shooter, and our chapter on the subject will enhance his ability to accomplish this important task with assurance and skill. And as our shooter's interest grow, he may find himself at the door which leads to the custom rifle, a handmade firearm meant personally just for him. How does a shooter go about selecting this important firearm? What should he watch out for, so that the rifle ends up being a keepsake for life, and not just another rifle? Our chapter on the subject deals with this important aspect of gun ownership.

It is also important to know about the actual fit of a firearm and how to alter that fit for our own personal stature and shooting style. Storing and transporting firearms correctly is also of importance and is treated briefly, but with deference. Proper gun care and cleaning are a part of the complete shooter's knowledge and are treated here, as is shooting safety. Getting the new shooter started is also discussed, and so is the interesting realm of shooter's accessories, for there are many important accoutrements which attend the great sport of shooting. Safety is touched on, too and so is the area of gun collecting as an investment.

The ladies are not left out in modern shooting. Women are well represented in today's shooting circles and they prove themselves to be fine marksmen and good hunters.

Cindy Zollinger, wife of gunmaker Dean Zollinger, poses with nice antelope buck she took with a custom 7×57 rifle. Clean quick harvests are the desire of every good hunter, and the complete shooter knows how to use his firearms for just that purpose.

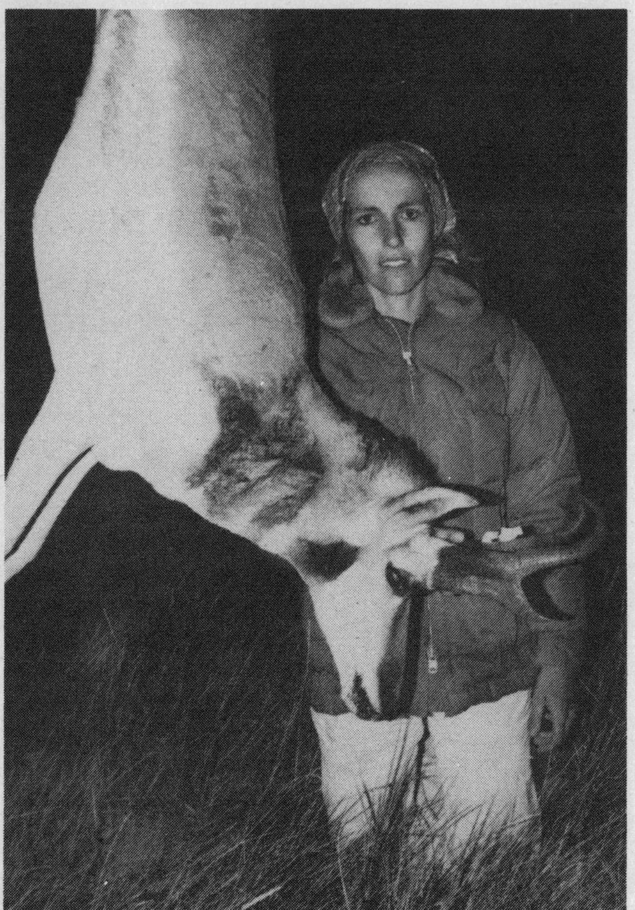

Firearms are so valuable we insure them, but how does a shooter go about doing that wisely? Our chapter on gun collecting offers a few ideas on the subject. The all-encompassing shooting game is looked at from various angles with varying depth in this book, for it was the intention from the opening sentence to the closing remark to aid the shooter in achieving a goal, the goal of delving into this fascinating world of the firearm from the surface to the depths. The complete shooter already has plenty of hard knowledge backing him up, and it is the task of our book to enhance that knowledge and to add to it where we can.

The purpose of the book is fulfilled if the shooter uses the information presented here to guide him to a fine battery of guns chosen upon the basis of understanding and knowledge. If the shooter increases his appreciation of his own firearms, then another aim of the book will be satisfied. And along the way, he may gain insight into many aspects of the sport of shooting which may have lain fallow until now. This is a great time for the shooter. He has some of the finest arms ever built since the days of the harqebus. And his choice has widened and deepened to the point of our being able to select the *correct* shooting tool for any occasion. This book is dedicated to the wise use of those superb firearms.

Chapter 2

The 22 Rimfire Rifle

CLOSE TO THREE BILLION 22 rimfire rounds are fired annually in the United States. That fact in itself reveals the immense popularity of the 22 rimfire cartridge and its firearms. Certainly, the 22 is the beginner's choice in many instances, though air-power is more likely to claim that "first-experience" status. The progression, as I see it, is 22 rimfire and then deer rifle, with handguns and shotguns falling in right along with that deer rifle choice. In areas where deer must be hunted, by law, with shotguns, the deer rifle is pushed aside for the scattergun.

The evolution itself is not that important. What is important is the fact that the 22 rimfire is never outgrown. Our complete shooter generally starts off with a 22 rimfire at an early age and continues shooting one in some form for the rest of his life. The 22 rimfire maintains its popularity for many reasons. Its best attributes, besides shooting economy, are its potential accuracy, extreme shooting pleasantness and its low-cost operation. After all, if 22 ammo were free, but ineffective, few shooters would have anything to do with the stuff. Furthermore, the 22 rimfire is, in fact, a specialty round. It seems so mundane to us that we often fail to realize that 22 rimfire ammo is highly sophisticated and so are the arms which fire it.

Just because the 22 becomes a part of a shooter's life at, usually, an early stage, does not mean the ammunition or firearms in this caliber are simplistic. Too many people get the idea that selecting a 22 rimfire is a less weighty matter than seeking out a big game rifle. It isn't. Overall, I wonder just how many thousands of 22 rimfire rounds are fired in comparison to the number of big game cartridges fired in the lifetime of that so-called "average" shooter. I think the ratio would be hundreds- if not thousands-to-one.

The history of self-contained ammo, cartridges in other words, really begins with the 22 Short round as far as America is concerned. In commercial terms, it was the 22 Short cartridge which was offered, ready to fire, to the American shooting public before any other round. In 1851, at the London Expedition, Louis Flobert showed the public a small-sized rifle which he had designed for what he would call "plinking" today. The caliber was 22, or 22/100ths of an inch. And the little rifle used ammo which was self-contained, not loaded from the muzzle (muzzle-

The little 22 rimfire rifle has given many millions of hours of pleasure to shooters since its beginning. Greg Thompson returns with a cottontail rabbit taken with his Remington 22 rimfire slide-action rifle. Good food and healthy outdoor recreation are afforded with 22 rimfire shooting.

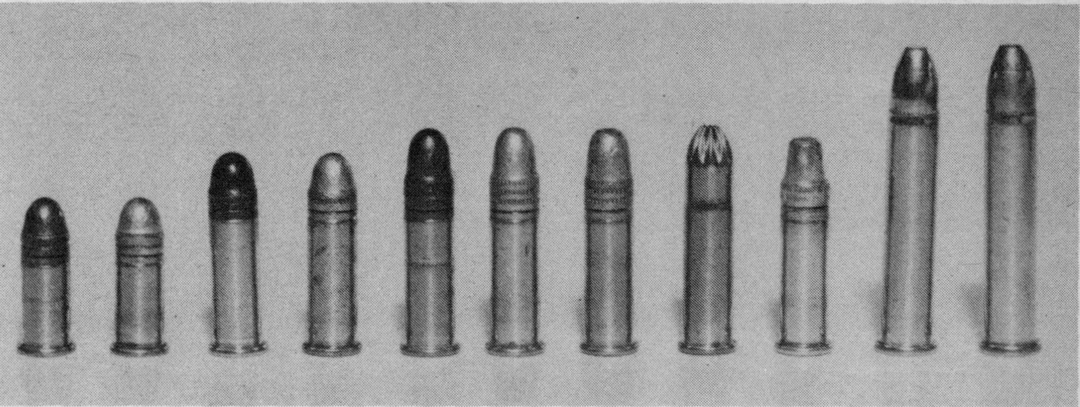

Modern 22 rimfire ammunition has followed the tradition of offering many different loads for the shooter. On the far left is a CB Cap, a very low velocity load for quiet close-range plinking and dispatch of small pests or small game. The 22 Short is next in line and to its right is the 22 CB Long with the regular 22 rimfire Long next to it. Then we have a standard velocity 22 Long Rifle without the copper coating and next to it a 22 Long Rifle with the copper coating. Next in line is another 22 Long Rifle, but this one is the hollow point offering and to its right is a 22 Long Rifle shot cartridge, loaded with a few No. 12 pellets for very close-range work on tiny pests of mouse size. Next is a Federal 22 Long Rifle Spitfire. On the far right we have two 22 Magnum loads, the full metal jacket and the hollow point.

(Left) The common 22 Long Rifle round is in fact quite an accomplishment. The components are loaded with a remarkable degree of accuracy. Weighed bullets and powder charges have proved amazingly consistent. Note the priming charge surrounding the rim of the round (arrow), hence "rimfire."

loader) but rather from the breech (breechloader). The difference was that there was a case, the bullet being held in the mouth of the case. In the case there was no powder. And more than that, the shooter did not have to employ a percussion cap or a pan/flint/frizzen combination because the ignition system was also self-contained. No powder in the case? True. There was no powder in the Flobert case; the primer was the force which expelled the bullet from the barrel. And it was a rimfire round, with the priming compound located all around the internal rim of the case, as per Robert's patent (France) in 1831.

What Flobert had was a BB Cap, as per his invention in 1845. What the world had was the forerunner of the 22 rimfire. In 1857 Smith & Wesson developed its own rimfire round, the still-famous 22 Short. Apparently Horace Smith and Daniel Wesson were on hand at the London Exposition because the Flobert design certainly influenced the development of the 22 Short. It seems somewhat ludicrous now, but the 22 Short was probably intended as a self-defense round, with Smith & Wesson chambering it in a self-defense firearm, the S&W First Model revolver. At the time, S&W did not call the 22 a Short. That would be akin to finding coins dated "B.C." But the S&W 22 rimfire was only the beginning. The rest is history, a history which is still being written. In recent times we have added a few new 22 rimfire loadings.

22 Rimfire Ammo Today

Today, we have sifted the virtually dozens of 22 rimfire rounds down to a comparative few, especially if we look at only the popular numbers. The 22 Extra Long is gone. The 22 Winchester Auto is very hard to find, even in larger gunshops or from ammo dealers. And many larger-than-22 rimfires are also defunct, though I believe some of them to be of value to this day. We no longer have the 25 Short, 32 Extra Long, or a host of other similar calibers, though to be sure, ammo can at times be located for these. As a matter of conjecture, if not fact, I wonder if that old 32 Extra Long, with a 90-100-grain bullet at modest velocity, would not have been quite a good close-range wild turkey cartridge.

22 BB Cap

In fact, here we have, for all practical purposes, Flobert's cartridge. It is still with us in a very limited way. The "BB" stands for "bulleted breech," in reference to the breech-loading quality of the round. One can scarcely find BB Cap ammo these days, though the German firm, RWS, does load this round-ball caliber. This may suggest the round's worthlessness, but I do not agree with the assessment at all. I'd like to buy a box of 22 BB Caps now and then just for quiet close-range plinking purposes. Nonetheless, the complete shooter of today can just about forget the BB Cap.

22 CB Cap

The BB Cap fired a little round ball. Therefore, when someone decided to alter the BB Cap to fire a conical bullet, CB was added to the name, standing for "conical bullet or ball." Remember, "ball" in shooting terms does not

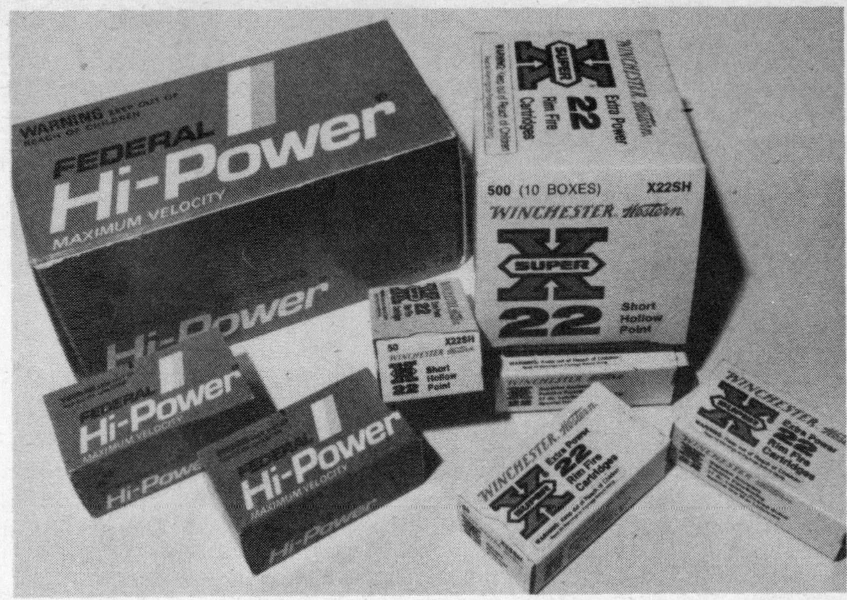

Twenty-two rimfire ammunition is better than ever. It is uniform, accurate and reliable. One can purchase 22 ammo by the "brick," a brick containing 10 boxes, or 500 rounds. Here are two bricks of 22 Short hollow point ammunition, the author's favorite for cottontail rabbits and squirrels under close-range conditions.

always mean a *sphere of lead*; a ball can be *conical* in shape. It can be confusing. But there is nothing confusing about the CB Cap. It was not a transitional design leading to the 22 Short but rather a more powerful version of the BB Cap. German RWS CB Caps can still be purchased. While the 22 BB Cap pushed a little 18-20-grain ball at under 800 fps MV (feet-per-second muzzle velocity), the CB Cap would fire a 29-30-grain bullet at 750 fps MV.

22 CB Short

As I write this, I am looking at a box of Winchester brand "22 CB Short Low Velocity Rimfire Cartridges." These are loaded 250 rounds to the box, in the loose form, and the bullet is 29 grains, the same grain weight as a 22 Short bullet. This bullet leaves the muzzle at about 650 fps. I buy the Winchester 22 CB Short for special-purpose shooting, mostly around-the-backyard pest control in out-of-town situations, especially in winter when rabbits can destroy expensive vegetation. The little low-noise, short-range 22 CB Short is just right for close-range rabbit shooting, or for shooting rats at the dump.

22 Mini-Group

This is a Short in all areas of specs; however, it is another low-velocity round and is offered by the CCI company, Omark Industries. The bullet is once again the standard 22 Short bullet of 29 grains weight, and the MV is about 835 fps in my tests out of a 22-inch barrel. It serves about the same purpose as the above round, but with a little bit higher velocity.

22 Short

This ever-famous round is still with us in high numbers, and well it should be. The Short comes in many loadings, actually, far too many to list here. A lead bullet is available in 29 grains weight as the primary projectile for the Short, but in the Target load the MV is about a flat 1000 fps, while the high-velocity rounds best this MV by about 100 fps, or roughly 1100 fps average. In fact, my favorite 22 rimfire round for cottontail rabbit hunting is the 22 Short hollow point version. This round is almost perfect because of its low-noise level and superb results on game at short range. On squirrels, with short-range shots in the 20- to 50-yard category, the 22 Short hollow point is again just right in my book. By its lack of popularity in my area—I cannot buy 22 Short hollow point ammo in my neighborhood gun stores very often—I would say that there are few 22 rimfire fans who feel the way I do about the round. But I will not change my mind. I have too many years of top-notch service from this round to abandon it. Obviously, head shots are the rule on small game with the 22 rimfire though I have found that up to 50 yards, a chest-hit rabbit or squirrel taken with the 22 Short hollow point is in the bag.

22 Long

This little fellow is catching it from all sides these days. Almost everyone who writes about 22 rimfires ends up saying that the 22 Long is worthless. In fact, that's a pretty fair assessment when one considers that the 22 Short offers close to the same ballistics, and the 22 Long Rifle offers better ballistics than the 22 Long. However, I hope the 22 Long lives on if only for those shooters who own older arms which seem to chamber and fire the Long when the Long Rifle or Short will not work as well. Rare is this circumstance, but I have seen it.

The 22 Long is, in fact, a special loading. Generally, the Longs I have tested end up with a MV of about 1200 fps, give or take a few fps. However, the CCI 22 Long Mini Cap is another story. Here we have the 29-grain bullet

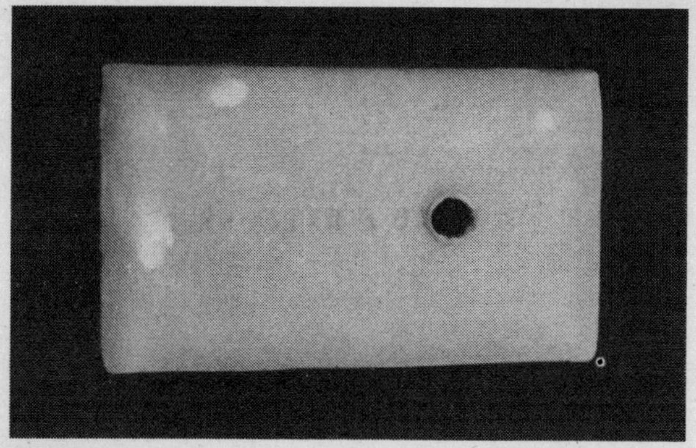

The hollow point design is used very effectively with 22 rimfire ammunition as this bar of soap demonstrates. Hit with a single 22 Long Rifle hollow point, the exit hole (below) is quite impressive. A 22 rimfire hollow point bullet is considered correct for varmints and for small game hunting where head shots are uncertain. Also, the author uses the 22 Short hollow-point for close-range squirrel and rabbit hunting. He finds that little meat is wasted by the Short, even in the hollow point style.

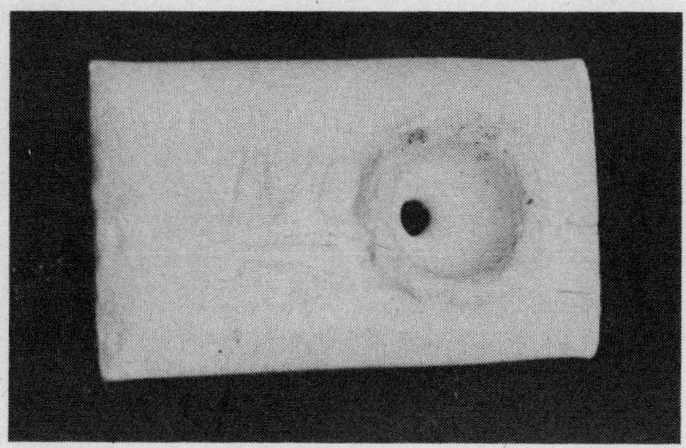

again, which is standard in both the Short and the Long, but the MV is only 600 fps. It serves the same purpose as the aforementioned low-velocity loadings, with one big difference—the 22 Long Mini Cap chambers in some rifles which do not digest Shorts too well. Also, it prevents a situation which bothers some 22 shooters a great deal, the erosion of the throat of the firearm.

When a pile of 22 Short ammo is fired in what is actually a 22 Long Rifle chamber, the Short can erode the upper part of the chamber so that a 22 Long Rifle fails in proper ejection. In short, the chamber has been eroded from 22 cartridge gases. But if the Long is used, the longer case (in fact the same exact dimensions as the 22 Long Rifle case) does not affect the upper part of the chamber and all is well. It takes a lot of 22 Shorts to damage a chamber, but to ease the minds of the shooters who do not like firing Shorts in a LR (Long Rifle) chamber, this round is the answer. All in all, however, the 22 Long is an in between cartridge with very little good to say about it.

22 Long Rifle

This is the king of the rimfires. No doubt about it. There are, once again, so very many variations on this theme that it would be nearly impossible to list them all. Surely, something would be left out, and if not, then an ammo company would offer a new loading while this book was going to print. However, we can look at some *categories* of 22 Long Rifle ammo. The match ammo is just that, high-class ammunition meant to group tightly. Mainly, it falls into the 1100 fps MV arena, but there will be some brand-to-brand differences in velocity. In terms of standard deviation from the mean velocity, I have seen as low as 4 fps. However, I have also seen as high as 25 fps with match ammunition in the 22 LR rimfire mode. I would like the reader to hold that last figure in his mind.

Next, we have the standard velocity 22 LR round. I have found this ammo to be very much like target or match ammunition, with low standard deviations from the mean velocity and about the same range of muzzle velocities. In fact, with certain lots of ammo, I'd not be afraid to head for the target range, even for an important match.

The high-velocity 22 LR offers the shooter about 1200-1250 fps, about 100 to 150 fps more than the standard velocity. The quality of this ammunition can be excellent, and generally is. I have tested high-velocity 22 rimfire LR loads which gave near match standard deviation figures, and proved themselves very accurate on the target. All in all, however, the standard velocity and target/match 22 rimfire ammunition does render a little more accuracy. I have to admit that I sometimes select standard velocity ammo for hunting purposes when I am more interested in bullet placement than striking power. In one old 22 rifle of mine, a long outdated H&R target model which only accepts 22 LR ammo, I always pick standard velocity for hunting because the accuracy is slightly better than it is with high-velocity, but only slightly better. Accuracy with high-velocity 22 rounds is fine.

How about the 22 LR hollow point? It's good, the very best when a hunter feels the need to drop his game with maximum authority from a standard rimfire loading. I always use the 22 LR hollow point ammo on jackrabbits, as these larger hares are tough. Up to 75, even 100 yards once in a great while, I'll drop the jacks cleanly with a 22 LR high-velocity hollow point bullet.

The latest 22 LR high-velocity ammo that I have on hand are those which fall into the "hyper-velocity" domain. Hyper-velocity ammo is 22 LR in format. A good example of the hyper-velocity cartridge would be Federal's "Spitfires," Remington's Yellow Jackets or CCI's Stingers. All three of these will crack out of the muzzle at well over 1400 fps. I have no complaints with the accuracy levels of hyper-velocity ammo, since its use would be confined to hunting anyway, mainly hunting for smaller varmints at modest range, where explosiveness is advantageous. The bullet is lighter in the hyper-velocity load, part

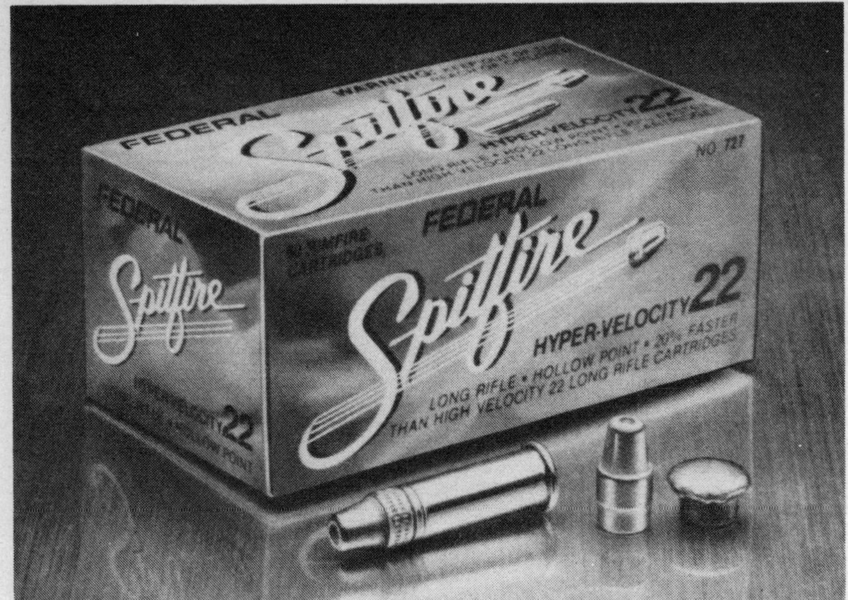

Hyper-velocity 22 ammunition is here to stay. These Spitfires use a 33-grain hollow point bullet. They are copper plated for cleanliness, and they mushroom very uniformly, as seen by the recovered bullet in the photograph.

Rimfire ammunition has been packaged in various ways over the years, and can be found currently in various containers. CCI's Mini Mag 22 Long Rifle cartridges are shown here in a handy plastic container of 100 count. The sliding lid allows the shooter to expose the rounds five at a time. Tipping the box then drops five rounds into the hand—or as many as the shooter desires in five-round-at-a-time fashion.

of the reason for its extra MV, and in fact, we have a slightly heavier 22 Short bullet loaded into the LR case. But isn't that what a 22 Long is? Yes, the 22 Long could be interpreted in the same way, but the hyper-velocity ammo does have a hotter powder charge, and though the bullet may weigh in between the Short and LR bullet (33 grains in the Yellow Jacket, for example), this is still most definitely not a 22 Long in performance.

22 Magnum Rimfire

The 22 Magnum Rimfire is very much like the old, and well-liked, WRF load. The WRF, Winchester Rim Fire, offered a 45-grain solid bullet at a MV of about 1400-1450 fps. Remember that the 22 Long Rifle, with its 40-grain bullet at about 1250 fps, is worth about 139 foot-pounds of muzzle energy. The 22 WRF, also called the "22 Remington Special," (the same cartridge) gained a ME (muzzle energy) of 210 foot-pounds, this with the 45-grain bullet at 1450 fps. That is a considerable gain. But the newer 22 Magnum Rimfire does better yet. I chronographed the Winchester ammo at about 1900 fps MV with a 40-grain bullet for an energy figure of 321 foot-pounds.

How about accuracy? I disclaim the statements I have read about a lack of accuracy in the 22 Magnum Rimfire round. I have obtained 1-inch groups at 100 yards with this type of ammunition. Remember those standard deviation figures I asked to hold in mind, being a low of 4 fps to a high of 25 fps? These were for the match-grade ammo which I tested in 22 LR. In testing a batch of Winchester 22 Magnum Rimfire ammunition, I ended up with a low of 9 fps and a high of 19 fps, and these figures were gathered over extensive shooting runs, not one-time trials. In fact, here are a couple of relatively standard results for 22 Magnum Rimfire hollow point and full metal jacket ammunition which I personally tested:

Winchester 22 Magnum Rimfire

	MV	Spread	Avg. MV	Standard Deviation
40-gr. HP	1875/1926	51	1906	18
40 gr. FMJ	1839/1876	37	1861	15

In other words, with the 40-grain hollow point, the lowest MV was 1875 fps, the highest 1926 fps, with a spread of 51 fps, an average MV of 1906 fps and a standard deviation of 18 fps. The solids offered a standard deviation of 15 fps. In both cases, the figures are for 5-shot strings.

The question one must ask before buying into the 22 Magnum Rimfire is this: what will I use this caliber for? My answer is based upon my own experiences with a Marlin lever-action 22 Magnum Rimfire. I find the rifle to be excellent for varmints up to 150 yards. I think the solid, where allowed by law, is a very good wild turkey taker, though I have a few other rounds I like better for that chore. While the 22 Magnum Rimfire is not cheap to shoot, neither is it expensive to shoot when one considers the cost of factory centerfire ammunition. And the round is *effective*. The hollow point version will cleanly drop modest-sized varmints up to fox-size and even coyote-size out to 150 yards. I do not believe in using the 22 LR for these animals at that range. Therefore, the 22 Magnum Rimfire is unique. It has its niche. It is a better 22 WRF, and its jacketed bullets offer a shooter extra penetration in the solid form, and plenty of explosiveness in the hollow point form. I saw the 22 Magnum Rimfire used on white-tailed deer in Mexico, these being the much smaller Coues variety, and though no deer were lost that I know of, I consider the round too small for anything larger than a coyote.

I do not feel that the caliber is a necessarily correct choice for small game hunting. In an effort to give the "average" shooter extra leeway, some experts will invite shooters to use rounds such as the 22 WRF or 22 Magnum Rimfire on edible small game. It will work. The solid will certainly do a good job on cottontails without destroying the entire rabbit, and a head shot, even with the hollow point version, will put a bunny in the bag with meat intact. But nobody needs that much punch for squirrels or rabbits if he will hunt, stalk, take good shots and pass up bad ones. I prefer the standard 22 LR or 22 Short hollow point for my own small game hunting, leaving the larger 22 Magnum Rimfire for game up to and including *javelina* (peccary) if the shooter is willing to make *close-range, well-placed* shots.

That wraps up a brief overview of 22 rimfire ammunition. I believe it is important for the shooter to recognize that in the 22 rimfire he has a wide range of ammo choices. These choices help make the 22 rimfire very versatile, much more versatile than first meets the eye.

Choosing the 22 Rifle

We will take a brief look here at the right 22 rifle for the task at hand, which is the key to selection—what do you need a 22 rimfire for? Our survey of 22 rimfire ammunition shows that there is a wide range of applications for rimfire 22s, from serious international competition right down to putting small game in the freezer or plinking for shooting practice. The rimfire fan can shoot a quiet 22 Long Mini Cap on one end of the spectrum, taking out dump rats, perhaps, or harvesting bunnies under conditions unsuitable to LR shooting, or he can go all the way up to the 22 Magnum Rimfire round, which is legal in some areas for game up to the size of *javelina*.

But what rifle? It is the rifle's action which determines, primarily, how that rifle is going to "behave" in the hands of the shooter. And the 22 rimfire comes in many different action styles, from single shot to semi-auto. Nobody can dictate to the shooter what he ought to have in 22 rimfire style, but there are some hard and fast laws which do pertain to the various actions, and we can look at these without offending anyone's personal choice.

The Single Shot

The only reason I would ever select a single shot 22 rimfire rifle is for compactness. My young daughter is going to begin her powder-pushed bullet shooting with the very small "Chipmunk" single shot rifle, but not because it is a single shot. She's going to start with that fine little rifle because it will *fit her*. It is sometimes very wise to begin a new shooter with a single shot, teaching him or her the value of that precious first round out of the barrel. You know, even on targets, I have succumbed to the lure of that fast second shot available from a repeater, and instead of concentrating on the bullet in the chamber, I was in fact

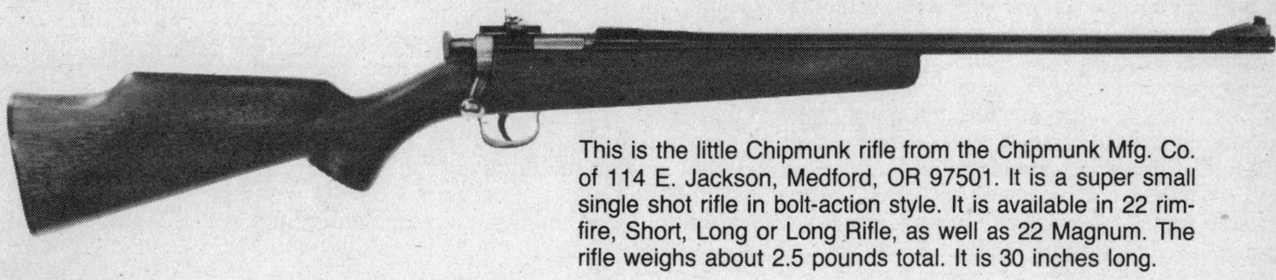

This is the little Chipmunk rifle from the Chipmunk Mfg. Co. of 114 E. Jackson, Medford, OR 97501. It is a super small single shot rifle in bolt-action style. It is available in 22 rimfire, Short, Long or Long Rifle, as well as 22 Magnum. The rifle weighs about 2.5 pounds total. It is 30 inches long.

The little Savage-Stevens Model 72 Crackshot 22 is typical of the lightweight 22 rifles offered years ago and still available today. This is a falling block type action, a sporty little single-shot rifle for small game hunting, as well as plinking.

The little single shot bolt-action rifle has been a beginner's first line 22 rifle for many years. It is priced very reasonably, and it is a safe and accurate design. The single shot seen here is a Marlin "Glenfield" Model 10.

thinking about the next round to come. That is no way to make a bull's-eye. However, many repeaters can be singly loaded with no trouble at all. A 22 semi-auto, the Weatherby model, has a single shot mode, in fact, and there is no problem feeding one round at a time in a bolt-action repeater.

The single shot, then, shines in one area, and that area is size. I truly admire those old-time single shots, such as the Remington rolling block series or the newer Chipmunk model. The comparatively new comeback of the Stevens single shot is another example of compactness. There is no doubt that the single shot can get the job done, all the way from targets to small game. But it is still a single shot, and the enjoyment of repeated fire is lost, (though I am never in favor of fast shooting just for the sake of hearing the rifle go rat-tat-tat and having shiny 22 cases raining down all around me).

In truth, I'd not buy a single shot 22 rifle as my *only* rimfire. I would want to have a single shot, however, as a compact, neat, easy-to-handle, ultra-light rifle for carrying hither and yon. There isn't anything neater than these tiny single shots when it comes to small size while retaining accuracy and reliability.

The Bolt-Action

On the one hand, chambering a bolt-action rifle in 22 rimfire is like driving a tack with a jackhammer. There is no reason in the world to use a bolt-action in rimfires except that shooters find them so wonderful! Accuracy? Sure, in a match rifle, go with the bolt-action. But I have fired a

The Kleinguenther K-22 22 Long Rifle rimfire bolt-action rifle is the only rifle of its type sold with guaranteed accuracy. Before each rifle leaves the plant it *must* put three shots in 1/2-inch at 50 yards.

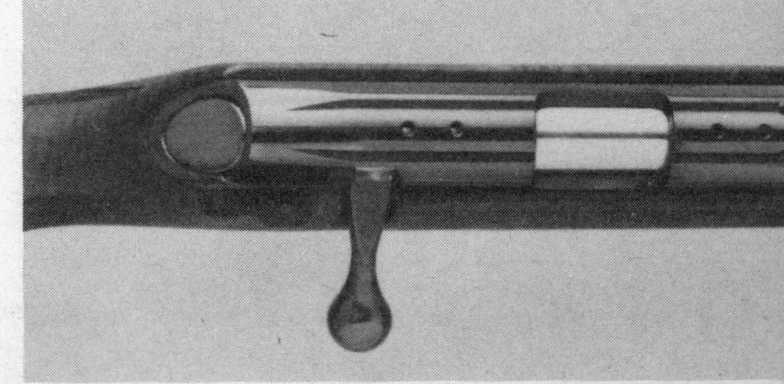

(Right) The clean lines of a bolt-action are enjoyed by many serious 22 rimfire shooters. Here is the fine bolt system on the Kleinguenther 22 rimfire rifle.

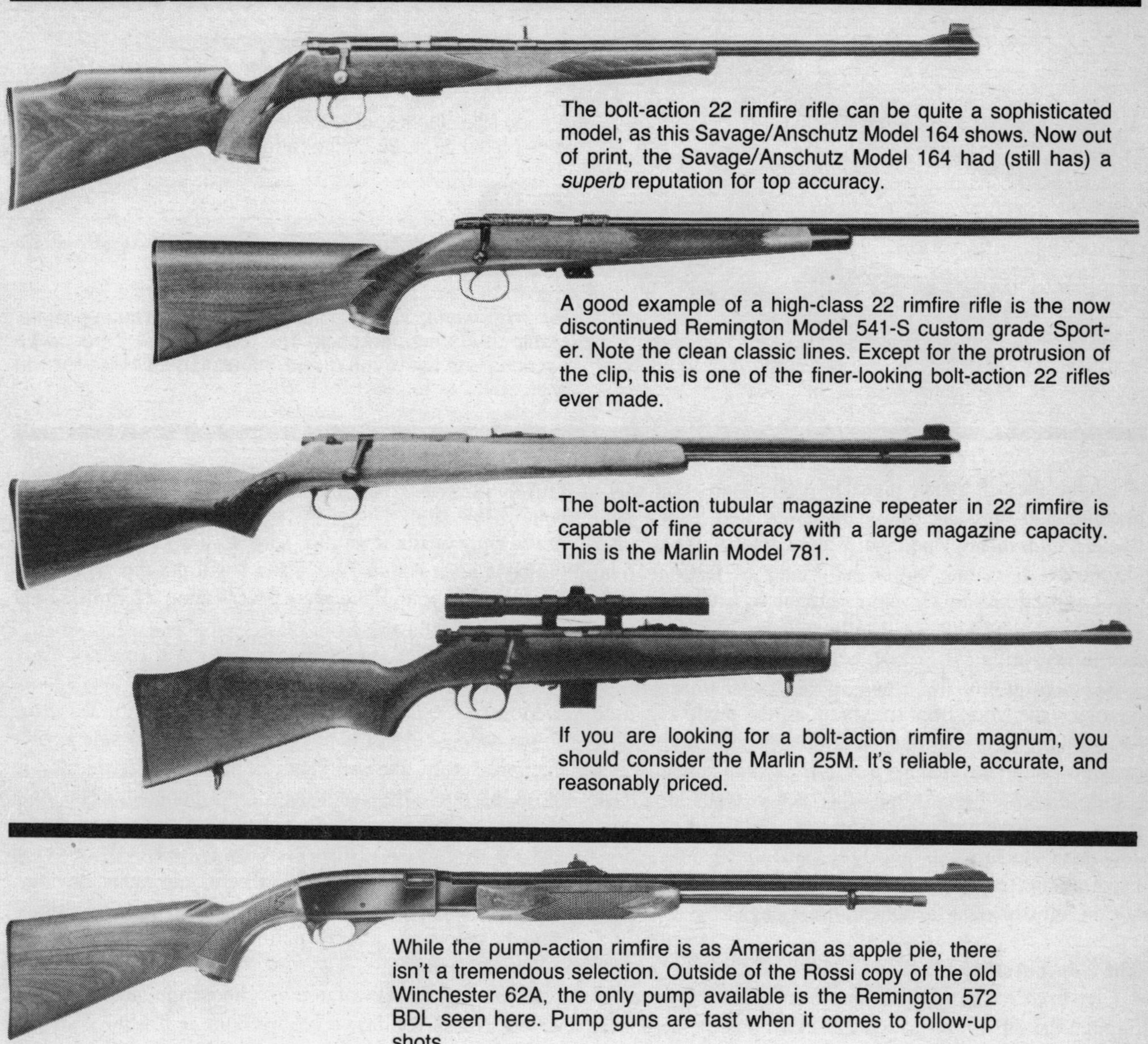

The bolt-action 22 rimfire rifle can be quite a sophisticated model, as this Savage/Anschutz Model 164 shows. Now out of print, the Savage/Anschutz Model 164 had (still has) a *superb* reputation for top accuracy.

A good example of a high-class 22 rimfire rifle is the now discontinued Remington Model 541-S custom grade Sporter. Note the clean classic lines. Except for the protrusion of the clip, this is one of the finer-looking bolt-action 22 rifles ever made.

The bolt-action tubular magazine repeater in 22 rimfire is capable of fine accuracy with a large magazine capacity. This is the Marlin Model 781.

If you are looking for a bolt-action rimfire magnum, you should consider the Marlin 25M. It's reliable, accurate, and reasonably priced.

While the pump-action rimfire is as American as apple pie, there isn't a tremendous selection. Outside of the Rossi copy of the old Winchester 62A, the only pump available is the Remington 572 BDL seen here. Pump guns are fast when it comes to follow-up shots.

22 Weatherby on the range in its semi-auto mode along with some fairly fine 22 rimfire bolt-actions, the result being equal group sizes with the same ammunition.

The bolt-action fits in because it is king among today's riflemen. It is reliable, but so are the other action styles. It is accurate, but so are the other action styles. And in terms of fire power, the slide or semi-auto (also called simply "auto") will beat it. Having pointed all of this out to a son who was in line for a 22 rifle, I allowed him to use several of my 22s in order to see which action type he liked best.

After a season of shooting a semi-auto, a pump and a single shot, as well as a bolt-action repeater, John went with the bolt, without so much as a moment's hesitation when the moment of truth arrived. He simply liked it better than the other styles.

I own a bolt-action 22 rimfire rifle, an older H&R target model, and I know I would not trade it away easily. So let there be no mistake. This shooter is not anti-bolt-action when it comes to 22 rimfires. My particular model is clip fed, this one featuring a 10-shot clip. I like the clip better than the tube magazine in a bolt-action 22. I like the idea of having an extra clip on hand, all loaded up and ready for use. It is also very easy to unload.

The Slide-Action

The sales on slide-action 22 rimfires is nowhere near that of autos or bolts. That about tells what is going on in America with this action style in 22 rimfire. But I don't care. I still like the pumpgun a lot. I have two on hand. They have been positive feeders, and I like the flat sides and easy-packing feel of these rifles. Of course, those qualities are also inherent in the lever and semi-auto, neither of

A good little single shot in the lever-action design is the Stevens Model 89, a 22 rimfire model.

While the world of lever-action rimfires is not a large one, the Marlin 39A leads the pack. The 39A has been around for decades and has a top-drawer reputation for reliability and accuracy.

which has the bolt handle protruding. The pump is smooth-handling and slick and fast. With a Model 61 Winchester, I won a little money one time, betting another shooter that I could get 10 rounds out of that Model 61 faster than he could expel 10 rounds from his semi-auto. I not only won; I won hands down! It was hardly a contest. The pumpgun can be fast-firing.

Although any of the action styles can be fired without removing the stock from the shoulder, the pump is a little handier here than a bolt-action, I think, and a little behind the auto. All in all, making a case for a slide-action rifle is a little difficult because the other action types also have many positive attributes. Given a shotgun, however, American shooters will quickly respond to the slide-action. I like pump 22s. So do many other shooters, but they are not the most popular actions in use today.

The Lever-Action

I have no recollection of how many rounds I have put through the three lever-action 22s I have had in the house, but it's a lot. I have never, to date, had a round hang up in the levergun. I owned a tube-loading 22 bolt-action which occasionally gave me feeding problems, and I've even had my pumpgun balk once or twice. But the lever-action 22s, in my experience, have been *totally* reliable. As for features which better the other actions, I am not sure there are any. The pumpgun is flat in profile and so is the levergun as well as many of the semi-autos. In short, a flat-sided rimfire rifle easily fits into tight places; they're handy to pack. The lever-action 22 is very good because it works, just as the other action types work, faithfully.

I imagine that the popularity of the lever Marlin or Winchester has quite a bit to do with the fact that America's top deer rifle has been the lever-action, if one considers the entire picture of deer hunting from the late 19th century to the present. Perhaps the bolt-action will take over, but right now the romance rifle is the lever, and there are two things that seem to promote this situation. One is the western movie. Seldom will you see a western film bereft of a lever-action rifle. The other factor is clearly the top notch proficiency of the levergun. Day in, day out, hand me an old-style lever-action 30-30, and I will put the venison on the table for you. Hand me a lever-action 22 rimfire, and I'm content with it.

The Semi-Auto

Modern technology is, perhaps, left out with all of the above actions, even the boltgun, when one considers automation. Surely, the semi-auto is the action of the day in terms of our advanced state of development. The only problem is that shooters do not live by technology alone, and the rimfire auto rifle is not always selected, not even selected most of the time. Its benefits are rather obvious. Again, it can be made slender, meaning few protrusions. And it shoots by merely pulling the trigger, *again* and *again* and *again*.

Given that a rimfire fan must choose the most advanced action style of the day, it has to be the semi-auto. I already alluded to the accuracy potential of this action type, and I can, any day, fire 10 shots into the bull's-eye with my Weatherby or Remington semi-autos—even the fellow with a top-grade bolt-action 22 is going to be hard-pressed to better the groups made by these two popular rifles. Some say that the use of a semi-auto leads to sloppy shooting. That can be true. I have succumbed to that phenomenon myself. But it does not have to be the case. It's a matter of shooter management. The shooter manages the rifle instead of letting the rifle manage him. Just because a semi-auto will spew lead out faster than a popcorn machine does not mean that the shooter has to empty the magazine every time he picks up the rifle. It's a matter of learning to live with the semi-auto mode.

When I want a bag full of cottontails and my time is limited, I turn to my semi-auto, wearing a low-powered scope sight. Many a rabbit has been put into the bag, even on the run, when this little rifle does its magic. The speed of firing is not always a plus, but it is a plus when an appropriate situation presents itself. I've missed a sitting rabbit, only to harvest that rabbit before he could dive into his nearby hideout. I could scarcely have gotten a shot off without at least a pumpgun, and though I can shoot a pump fast, when talking about keeping those repeated shots on the money, there is no doubt that the auto is the answer.

Which Action for You?

While it is a matter of common sense to select that action type which suits the situation best, pump or auto for running shots, a fine bolt-action with a good scope for longer range work, a tiny single shot to carry in tight places, and so forth, the bottom line of 22 rimfire action selection rests with the desires of the shooter. What looks good to him? What fits him well? What action type does he work best? My suggestion is for the shooter to try the various actions for himself, choosing the one which seems right *for him*.

The Used 22 Rifle

Go ahead and buy a used 22 rifle if you want to. That is my advice because of one major fact—a lifetime of shooting will not wear out a 22 rimfire. In fact, it's my guess

(Right) An interesting 22 rimfire rifle for the rabbit hunter and plinker is the Remington 552 semi-auto, with capability of firing 22 Short, Long or Long Rifle ammunition interchangeably. With a good scope, such as this Leupold 3×, this rifle is excellent for fast-moving targets.

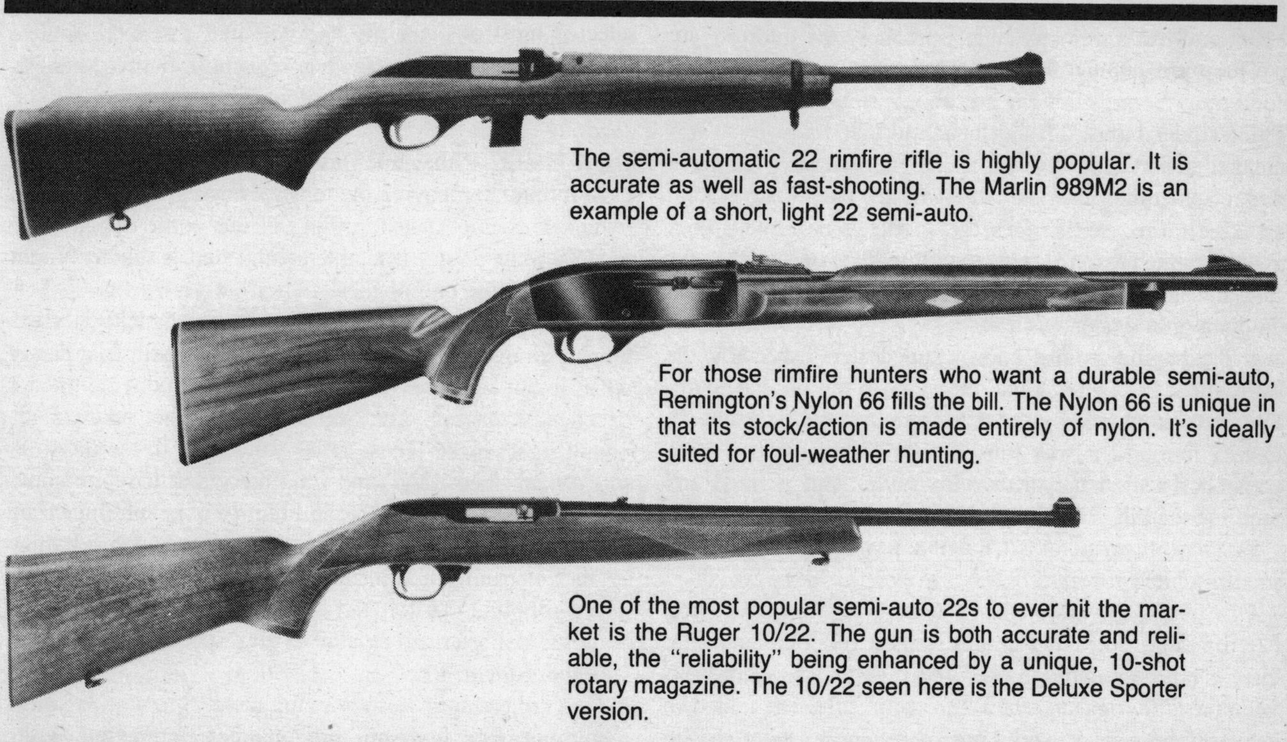

The semi-automatic 22 rimfire rifle is highly popular. It is accurate as well as fast-shooting. The Marlin 989M2 is an example of a short, light 22 semi-auto.

For those rimfire hunters who want a durable semi-auto, Remington's Nylon 66 fills the bill. The Nylon 66 is unique in that its stock/action is made entirely of nylon. It's ideally suited for foul-weather hunting.

One of the most popular semi-auto 22s to ever hit the market is the Ruger 10/22. The gun is both accurate and reliable, the "reliability" being enhanced by a unique, 10-shot rotary magazine. The 10/22 seen here is the Deluxe Sporter version.

Gene Thompson employs a Remington pump 22 rimfire with a good Bushnell telescopic sight to harvest cottontail rabbits. Where the rabbits are not too wild to stalk, the 22 rimfire, especially when fitted with a scope sight, is a very fine tool for filling the game bag.

that most 22 rimfires are worn out by improper cleaning or outright neglect, but not by shooting. I have seen estimates which suggest that a 22 rimfire could last for a half-million rounds. Considering the small powder charge, soft lead bullet and lower velocity, that's probably the truth.

There are always plenty of 22 rimfires for sale in used condition. Some of them are about as good as new. A shooter may buy a 22 and then find that he really wants another action type instead, so in goes the new 22 for a trade. Sometimes a shooter will want the latest state-of-the-art 22 rimfire, so in goes the hardly used ''old'' one. Whatever the reason, I have seen hundreds of used 22s for sale not only in the ever-present hock shop, but also from the local gun dealer.

I like buying from a known gun dealer, especially the local gunshop. I have a real-life story to tell on that score. I recently purchased a used rifle from my local gunshop. It looked fine and it was fine, but the firing pin had been chipped. I called my dealer. He said, ''Get it fixed and send me the bill.'' And that was the end of the story. I had a like-new firearm, and I did not pay extra to have the small problem repaired.

Obviously, there are bound to be problem-ridden used 22s for sale, too, and I do not suggest for a moment that there is no risk in buying used items, be they rifles or cars. Sometimes the reason that a 22 rimfire rifle was traded in is simply because it would not shoot worth a hoot. All in all, however, I have no qualms with looking for a used 22 rimfire. On that score, I do have one piece of advice perhaps worth listening to—buy the 22 rimfire rifle *you* really want. A small loan is worth the sacrifice in order to end up with that special rifle. If a shooter breaks the cost down on a per-month basis for life, he will find that a 22 rimfire rifle is a great big bargain, even for those deluxe versions with price tags that remind one of big game rifles.

Old-Time 22 Rimfire Rifles

Before totally leaving the topic of buying a used 22 rifle, I think it is important to point out that some of the older models were unique and interesting, and a shooter might consider adding one of these oldies but goodies to his battery. The little Remington Rolling Block Model 7, for example, weighed but 4 pounds. It was and still is a dandy when it can be found in at least very good condition if not excellent condition. The Stevens Little Scout was a 2.75-pound lightweight. These rifles were born in the days before ''man-sized 22s,'' and I am sorry that they are gone. Somebody got the idea that in order to mate and match up the 22 rimfire to the whims of the modern shooter that the 22 had to handle like a big game rifle. Gratefully, things never got quite that far, but a lot of today's 22 rifles could be lighter, shorter and smaller in all respects. And men can still shoot them, too.

Gun collecting is not my main game. Shooting is. But I would not trade away my long-outdated Remington Model 12, 22 rimfire pump rifle. Watch the classified ads in the local newspaper or shopper's guide. Take a look at the local gunshop or hockshop. Read the popular gun-value books. This type of search will reveal not only some interesting 22 rimfires for keeping and shooting, but will also give you a ballpark price range for these guns.

Scopes for 22 Rifles

The standard "22 rimfire scope" is all right, and if the budget allows for no more than this range of cash outlay, then such a purchase is a good one. I prefer the "big game" type scope on a 22 rifle, or one of the nice new compact models, but still in the big game rifle domain—preferably parallax free at 50 yards. A good 22 rimfire rifle is deserving of an equally good scope. I speak in terms of optics and field of view. One of our 22 rifles wears a Bushnell 2.5x scope meant for a big game rifle. Another wears an older Leupold 3x scope taken from a big game rifle which was given a new variable. Another has a 4x compact from Burris. But, I hastily add that two of our rifles enjoy Redfield 22 type scopes. However, these are constructed in big game scope fashion, the optics being bright and clear. In short, put a *good* scope on that 22 rifle. It deserves it.

Sighting In

Simply, a 22 rimfire rifle should be sighted to strike the bull's-eye dead on the money at 12 to 13 yards distance from the muzzle of the gun. If so sighted, that rifle will be about on at 75 yards and a little low at 100, which is just about the limit in range for the 22 LR rimfire round on small game. By sighting in up close first, a lot of time and ammo is saved, because "getting on the paper" is easier than it is from longer range. After a good group is established at 12 to 13 yards, then the shooter can back off to 75 yards, using a solid benchrest. Here, refinements are made until the 22 rifle smacks the bull's-eye dead center.

Wind Drift

While the 22 LR is not nearly as susceptible to the ravages of the wind as air guns, wind can play havoc with any light bullet driven at modest velocities. A 10-mile-per-hour breeze can blow a 22 rimfire bullet 4 or 5 inches off course at 100 yards and a 20 mph wind can double that. Interestingly, I like to teach newcomers how to dope the wind by handing them a 22 rifle and having them shoot in a breeze at an object with lots of space around it. A good example would be a tin can against a sandy backstop. New shooters are usually amazed when they see the bullet blow off course. "But it's so fast!," they protest, disbelieving their own eyes when the bullet strikes a half-foot off target. The 22 rimfire, with its low report and negligible recoil, allows the shooter to actually watch the bullet strike in the scope sight picture. This enables the new shooter to compensate not only for wind deflection, but also for drop.

Hunting with the 22 Rimfire

We have already stated that the 22 rimfire round is just about right for close-range small game hunting and varmints of modest size. While comparing foot-pounds of energy with larger calibers makes the 22 rimfire look puny, it's got enough punch for small game. The 22 LR is going to deliver a muzzle velocity of about 1250 fps, as a rough average. In fact, a test run of Federal Lightning Long Rifle ammo rendered an average MV of 1244 fps out of a 24-inch barrel. In the same rifle, Remington Thunderbolt 22 LR ammo averaged 1230 fps, or about the same for all practical purposes. These figures are typical. Given a shorter barrel, MV will pick up a little, due, no doubt, to the fact that the powder charge is used more efficiently in about 16 to 17 inches of bore length. Additional bore (barrel length) only serving to add drag to the slug, but I

TABLE OF WIND ALLOWANCES

22 L.R. Super-Speed and Super-X . . . Deflection of Bullet in Inches and Minutes

Distance	Wind Velocity (Miles Per Hour)	1, 5, 7, 11 o'Clock Winds		2, 4, 8, 10 o'Clock Winds		3 and 9 o'Clock Winds	
		Inches	Min.	Inches	Min.	Inches	Min.
50 Yards	5	0.33	0.66	0.57	1.14	0.66	1.32
	10	0.67	1.33	1.15	2.31	1.33	2.66
	15	1.00	1.98	1.72	3.45	1.99	3.98
	20	1.34	2.66	2.30	4.61	2.66	5.32
100 Yards	5	1.25	1.25	2.17	2.17	2.50	2.50
	10	2.50	2.50	4.33	4.33	5.00	5.00
	15	3.75	3.75	6.50	6.50	7.50	7.50
	20	5.00	5.00	8.67	8.67	10.00	10.00
200 Yards	5	4.28	2.14	7.42	3.71	8.56	4.28
	10	8.56	4.28	14.84	7.42	17.12	8.56
	15	12.84	6.42	22.26	11.13	25.68	12.84
	20	17.12	8.56	29.69	14.84	34.24	17.12

wouldn't buy a short barrel for any reason other than to enjoy its handier length. In the 22 rimfire, the slight increase in MV is hardly worth bothering over.

If one were to summarize a long list of *dos* and *do nots* for the rimfire hunter, the list would boil down to a few simple rules. Do not shoot beyond 75, possibly 100 yards on small game with the 22 LR round, and probably not past 50 yards with the Short. Do get close to your quarry. Hunt in such a way as to earn that close shot, by looking intently instead of simply walking through the small game coverts. Use binoculars where appropriate. I have found many small game edibles with the glass, thereby allowing a careful stalk, approaching from the proper angle so as not to be seen by the game.

Do not expect rapid fire to take the place of careful aim. Do pick a specific spot on a game animal rather than simply trying to hit it somewhere. The head shot is best because it is humane and because it does not ruin edible meat. (Remember, harvesting of small game is entirely appropriate and totally game management wise. Small game of the rabbit class will expire at a rapid rate whether hunted or not. Simply put, it's better to harvest the meat to table than feed it back to mother earth during a winter kill.) A head shot will also harvest game on the spot. A lung shot will, admittedly, kill any squirrel or rabbit. However, small game animals are usually only a hop or short burst away from a den of some sort and, a lung-shot squirrel or rabbit will usually get away from the hunter. Small game must be, and can be, dropped on the spot with the head shot.

The 22 rimfire is a fine close-range varmint-taker. Bill Fadala has removed a prairie dog from the range of a rancher who was in need of help concerning these rodents. Bill used an old, but fine, Remington Model 121 pumpgun.

Unfortunately, there are times when head shots are not possible. That's when you should turn to the high-speed hollow point bullet in either Short or LR. The hollow point will disrupt more heart/lung tissue than the solid, imparting greater shock. Do move quickly to fallen small game. Do not approach so slowly that the animal can recover and make it into a den. Even when head-shot, a rabbit, for example, can kick its way down into a den from shear nervous reaction.

As for varmint hunting, the 22 LR high-speed hollow point is a viable round if the circumstances are right. Shooting at over 100 yards at a member of the rodent clan is truly not advised. Once again, do get close. Do not shoot from long range on varmints. At 50 yards, a head shot on a woodchuck is possible, and it is the only shot conscionable on such a sturdy animal when using a 22 rimfire. I prefer a stronger round for rockchuck or woodchuck hunting, but have taken many prairie dogs, which are much smaller, at up to 50 and occasionally 75 yards with head shots.

Target Shooting

There are many phases of 22 rimfire target shooting. At the lower end of the list is plinking, but by lower, I do not mean without class and respect. Plinking is a word without much distinction, but I have enjoyed many hours of practical practice plinking. My brother and I got pretty good with a 22 rimfire rifle by playing a plinking game, which was merely to draw a circle in the sand with a safe backstop behind the circle, tin cans being placed in the circle itself. The idea was to expel the tin cans from the circle with a specific number of shots. We learned to ping the rims of the cans, sending them flying through the air. Water-filled cans make interesting targets, too, and will "explode" dramatically, especially if hollow point 22 LR ammo is used. Water balloons or just plain balloons also make good targets, as do clay pigeons, all plinker's delights, but at the same time, extremely good practice.

Then, of course, there are the more "serious" competitions, where medals and honors await the winners. The world of competitive 22 rimfire shooting is complete and deep, and certainly worth looking into for any shooter serious about competing. My advice to the would-be competition rimfire shooter is short and to the point—get to an NRA affiliated club. At this sort of shooting club, there will be formal meets and there is something else. There is help. Competitive shooting seems to differ from some other forms of organized sports, for I have seen shooters carefully and wisely advise others on the range. I saw this

ACCURACY CHART

Group Size Chart For Various Guns and Ammo

(10 shots fired from bench rest at 25 yards)

	Charter Arms AR-7 Explorer	Browning BAR-22	Ithaca Model 72 Saddlegun	Marlin Model 39A	Marlin Model 39M	Mossberg Model 377 Plinkster	Remington Model 541-S Custom Sporter	Remington Nylon 66	Ruger 10/22 Sporter	Weatherby Mark XXII	Winchester Model 9422
Federal .22 Long Rifle Power-Flite high vel.	1⅛	⅜-⅝	7/16	⅜-9/16	11/16-1¼	½-⅞	7/16	⅝-1	¾-1¼	½-¾	*5/16-13/16
Remington .22 Long Rifle Rifle Match standard vel.	¾-1⅜	½	½	½	½	½	⅝	½	½	5/16-⅝	*¼-5/16
Winchester .22 Long Rifle Super Match Mark III standard velocity	1⅝	5/16	½-1⅜	½	½-13/16	9/16	½	½-13/16	11/16	9/16	*5/16-⅜
Winchester .22 Long Rifle Super-X Dynapoint high velocity	1 1/16	½-9/16	7/16-9/16	½	⅝	¾	5/16-7/16	⅜-11/16	¾-1⅛	5/16-½	*¼-⅝
Federal .22 Long Rifle Semi-Hollow Point Power-Flite high vel.	¾-1	⅝-¾	⅜	½-13/16	1-1⅛	9/16-¾	¼-½	½	1-1 5/16	7/16-¾	*5/16-¾
CCI .22 Long Rifle Stinger high vel.	1¼	⅜-½	5/16-½	⅝-¾	⅝-15/16	¾-1	⅝	11/16	⅝	⅜	*⅜-⅝
Winchester .22 Long Rifle Super-X Xpediter		1⅜-1⅝					⅝-1⅛			¾-1⅜	9/16-1¾

Unless otherwise specified, the first measure represents main body of 10-shot group.
The second measure (if any) represents widest spread including any fliers.

*First measure is horizontal, second is vertical.
**5 shots only.
***10 shots.

RIMFIRE CARTRIDGES–BALLISTICS

Cartridge Type	Bullet Wt. Grs.	Bullet Type	Velocity (fps) 18½" Barrel Muzzle	50 Yds.	100 Yds.	Energy (ft. lbs.) Muzzle	50 Yds.	100 Yds.
22 CB Short (CCI & Win. only)	29	Solid	727	667	610	34	29	24
22 CB Long (CCI only)	29	Solid	727	667	610	34	29	24
22 Short Standard Velocity	29	Solid	1045	—	810	70	—	42
22 Short High Velocity (Fed., Rem., Win.)	29	Solid	1095	—	903	77	—	53
22 Short High Velocity (CCI only)	29	Solid	1132	1004	920	83	65	55
22 Short High Velocity HP (Fed., Rem., Win.)	27	Hollow Point	1120	—	904	75	—	49
22 Short High Vel. HP (CCI only)	27	Hollow Point	1164	1013	920	81	62	51
22 Long Standard Vel. (CCI only)	29	Solid	1180	1038	946	90	69	58
22 Long High Velocity (Fed., Rem., Win.)	29	Solid	1240	—	962	99	—	60
22 Long Rifle Stand. Velocity (CCI only)	40	Solid	1138	1046	975	115	97	84
22 Long Rifle Stand. Velocity (Fed., Rem., Win.)	40	Solid	1150	—	976	117	—	85
22 Long Rifle High Vel. (CCI only)	40	Solid	1341	1150	1045	160	117	97
22 Long Rifle High Velocity (Fed., Rem., Win.)	40	Solid	1255	—	1017	140	—	92
22 Long Rifle High Velocity HP (CCI only)	37	Hollow Point	1370	1165	1040	154	111	89
22 Long Rifle High Velocity HP (Fed., Rem., Win.)	36-38	Hollow Point	1280	—	1010	131	—	82
22 Long Rifle Yellow Jacket (Rem. only)	33	Hollow Point	1500	1240	1075	165	110	85
22 Long Rifle Spitfire (Fed. only)	33	Hollow Point	1500	1240	1075	165	110	85
22 Long Rifle Viper (Rem. only)	36	Solid	1410	1187	1056	159	113	89
22 Stinger (CCI only)	32	Hollow Point	1687	1300	1158	202	120	95
22 Winchester Magnum Rimfire (Win., Fed.)	40	FMC or HP	1910	—	1326	324	—	156
22 Winchester Magnum Rimfire (CCI only)	40	FMC or HP	2025	1688	1407	364	253	176
22 Long Rifle Pistol Match (Win., Fed.)	40	Solid	—	—	—	—	—	—
22 Long Rifle Match (Rifle) (CCI only)	40	Solid	1138	1047	975	116	97	84
22 Long Rifle Shot (CCI, Fed., Win.)	—	#11 or #12 shot	1047	—	—	—	—	—
22 Winchester Magnum Rimfire Shot (CCI only)	—	#11 shot	1126	—	—	—	—	—
22 Short Match (CCI only)	29	Solid	830	752	695	44	36	31
22 Long Rifle Silhouette (Fed. only)	40	Solid	1150	—	976	117	—	85
22 Long Rifle Super Silhouette (Win. only)	42	Solid	1220	—	1003	139	—	94
22 Long Rifle Super-Max (Win. only)	34	Hollow Point	1500	1250	1081	170	118	88

Please note that the actual ballistics obtained in your gun can vary considerably from the advertised ballistics. Also, ballistics can vary from lot to lot even within the same brand.

very thing happen but a week past at a local benchrest shoot where one competitor told another what he thought was preventing a tighter group. He was right, too. I know, because my groups next time out were markedly improved.

Match shooting with the 22 rimfire means a host of events. The NRA has guidelines for these events, and local clubs generally have access to the specific and precise rules which must be followed in each competition. Also, the shooter should buy some practice targets and spend many hours learning to score high at the specified ranges.

Everyman's Rifle

The 22 rimfire is for everyone. It is a teaching tool. It is a competitor's dream. The 22 rimfire can help a person spend some wonderful days outdoors harvesting small, delicious edible meat to the table. The rimfire rifle is a delight for practice, and it does not cost much to shoot either. It is not noisy, and the recoil is too light to shoo away a housefly. There is accuracy in the round, and there is enough punch to make it a hunter's round up to modest-sized varmints at close range. While the rimfire case cannot be reloaded, the round is one of pure convenience at the same time, requiring no more than its modest purchase in order to enjoy its virtues at a small cost.

Lucky is the shooter who recognizes early the concept of building a good battery, for he will seldom end up with two firearms which perform exactly the same function. But luckier still is the shooter who has several 22 rimfire rifles in his battery, for he has learned that the little round is much more versatile than most shooters think. And he will find that what one style of 22 rimfire rifle does best, another may not accomplish quite so well, but that rifle will be better for another task. I have seldom come across a 22 rifle I didn't like. And I have come across even fewer which were not just about perfect for one shooting job or another. If suddenly there were no 22 rimfire rifles on the planet, shooters would be missing out on one of the key arms in any complete firearms battery.

Chapter 3

Your Deer Rifle

The winter-kill skull next to the hunter is typical of areas in which deer hunters cannot or do not crop a full compliment of deer during the hunting season, followed by a harsh winter. Scouting such areas can pay off, the hunter not only learning the lay of the land, but also getting a fairly good idea of where the bucks were on the winter range. In this case, bucks were found right in the same area as shed antlers and winter-kills, for their movement here was quite limited from season to season.

BIG GAME to an American hunter means deer. The deer is far and away America's most important big game species, and the deer rifle is among the most important shooting tools in the complete shooter's battery. The problem in picking that one perfect deer rifle is that there is no such thing, nor will there ever be. Since deer roam almost all general areas of the United States, it is impossible to come up with a rifle that is perfect for hunting this game animal nationwide. If a particular rifle is perfect in upstate New York, then it would be just so-so in the big canyon country of Idaho, where instead of a woods shot at 50 yards, the hunter could be looking at a 200-yard shot, and sometimes legitimately much longer.

Books have been filled with advice on deer rifles and calibers. A lot of that advice has been quite good. Some of it has been excellent for one region, but somewhat misplaced in terms of another area with different shooting conditions. One writer I know has all but made a living writing about the perfect deer rifle. By now he has about 20 rifles of various sizes, shapes and calibers, all, apparently, perfect for deer hunting. Those of us who live around firearms tend to grow excited over new calibers, new stock shapes, new metals, new scopes, new slings, new anything when it comes to rifles meant to harvest venison.

There isn't anything wrong with that. It is genuine interest which spurs us to make declarations of undying devotion to various firearms, and then later on switch camps to another caliber, another rifle style. It's not fickleness. It's excitement. And the problem lies in another valley, too—it's easy to find more and more perfect deer rifles because there are dozens of styles which work on deer to near perfection, not only in the actual makeup of the rifle, but also in the caliber. All the same, I do believe that a deer hunter owes it to himself to search out many avenues in *his* quest for a perfect deer rifle, applying as much logic as well as a little bit of emotion to the subject.

There are all kinds of experts. Before my time there were men who shot deer for market. They had hundreds of times more deer hunting experience than today's sportsman. I have read into the few good works pertaining to that age of deer hunting in our land, and I learned a great deal from my search.

Those old hunters were mighty interested in calibers, all right, and they all had their favorite deer rifles, too. Just like today's experts, they did not agree with each other down the line. One hunter may have preferred the 44 Winchester (44-40), considering that round perfect for deer, while another couldn't wait to get his hands on a different rifle so he could get away from the 44 WCF. Something else rings true from these hunters of yesteryear—when they hunted properly, got decent shots and put the bullet where it belonged, there was never a complaint about cartridge performance. Sometimes I think we try to leave the hunt out of hunting today, looking to a caliber which will take the place of good careful hunting, stalking and bullet placement. Well, there is no substitute for good hunting and careful shooting. A deer hit in the leg with the latest magnum is still no more than a deer hit in the leg, while on the other side of that coin, a deer taken directly in the shoulder with even a 44-40 is meat in the pot if the range is not too great for the old round.

Criteria for the Deer Rifle

The only criteria for the deer rifle which amount to anything much are two, how the rifle handles and caliber. First, you have the actual handling of the rifle itself: how it feels at the carry; how it mounts to the shoulder; how it fits the individual shooter; where the sight picture presents itself when that rifle is quickly sighted on a target that does not always sit there like a hunk of paper with a black circle on it. In the same vein, we need to look at how a rifle functions. How does it work? And this, in fact, leads us into the variety of modern deer rifles available to us—in other words, we have to look at the action styles.

The second big criterion for the deer rifle is caliber. But I feel we have made way too much on that score, and I will explain my position. In the 30 years plus that I have pursued venison in North America, I have had a chance to use many, many different calibers. I do not for a moment wish to give the impression that calibers do not matter. They do. A lot! I am against tiny 22 hotrock varmint calibers for deer and see no point in the big bores either.

Credentials

If a person wants to get on the soap box and talk deer rifles and calibers, he should state his credentials somewhere along the line and then the reader or listener can make up his own mind as to the level of credence and stock he wishes to place in the fellow doing the talking, or the writing. I don't have the experience amassed by those late 19th century/early 20th century market hunters. There is no way I could have. But in the past 30 years I have hunted four countries, three of them for deer and the fourth for game of deer-size. As a young man, I bought hunting licenses for Mexico. At the time, a fellow could hunt with that license not only in the state of his choice, such as Sonora, but also in one adjacent state. In some areas, three deer were allowed, plus three on the other side of the line in that adjacent Mexican state. Three seasons of this and you had 18 deer harvests under your belt.

Among deer hunters the lever-action has been the king for a long, long time. The Winchester Model 86 was (and still is, to some degree) very popular with deer hunters. Chambered for rounds like the 45-70, the old '86 was potent medicine in the deep woods.

Deer always interested me a lot. So I extended my hunting. This season, I will hold a license for Mexico, Arizona, Montana, Colorado and Wyoming. We love the meat. We take good care of it. And we hunt all we can. The "we" is my family of five hunters. I have had a chance to add their experiences to my own, since I started them all in the field. Friends, too, have joined me, and added to my own experience. And yet, the market hunter of yore still had more deer to his credit. E. N. Woodcock, in *Fifty Years a Hunter and Trapper,* writings compiled from the pages of *Hunter, Trader, Trapper (Fur-Fish-Game* now), 1903 to 1913, had this to say about late 19th century deer hunting in the Northeast: "People at that time [1870-1900], hunted more for profit than sport and their forte was the slaughter of deer. In those days it was nothing uncommon to see sleigh loads of deer pass every day on the way to market." These men found that the larger-bored rifles of black powder cartridge chambering were fine for deer, but they turned away from these in favor of the smokeless numbers, mainly the 30-30 Winchester. We have grown numb to the big splash made by the 30-30 and its smokeless powder brothers of the same era. In fact, Woodcock felt the 30-30 was simply *more than necessary for deer!* Wouldn't he have a laugh on us today? I just read the book of one gunwriter who claimed that the 30-30 was no good on deer past 45 yards. Maybe deer have learned to wear flak jackets today. Woodcock said of his caliber choice:

> Another reader asks what kind of a gun he shall take with him to hunt deer, as he is contemplating going on a deer hunting trip next fall. Now I would say any kind of a rifle that suits you. But if you should ask me what kind of gun I use, I would not hesitate to say that I prefer the 38-40 and black powder. This gun shoots plenty strong to do all the shooting as to the distance or penetration that the deer hunter will require, and there is not near so much danger of shooting a man or domestic animal a mile away that the hunter knows nothing of, as is the case with a high-power gun. Besides, from an economical point, the ammunition for the 38-40 black powder gun costs only about one-half that of the smokeless or high-power guns. However, if the hunter thinks he must have a high-power gun in order to be a successful deer hunter, he will find the 30-30 or similar caliber good for large game, and it is not heavy to handle.

Things have changed. I admit that. Hunters are strapped, rightfully so, by rules and regulations. Hunters cannot go forth when they feel ready, taking what game they come across. They have short seasons to obey and strict limits on game. One deer tag is generally the limit in an area, though in my state a hunter can get two tags by purchasing a second non-antlered or non-buck tag. The old 38-40 black powder cartridge loved by Woodcock will still take a deer down quickly, but I don't recommend it. However, it is interesting that the lever-action in which that old 38-40 cartridge was chambered is as viable today as it was so very long ago.

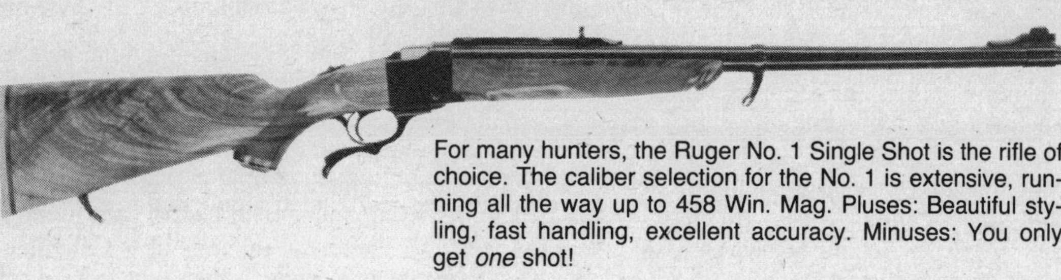

For many hunters, the Ruger No. 1 Single Shot is the rifle of choice. The caliber selection for the No. 1 is extensive, running all the way up to 458 Win. Mag. Pluses: Beautiful styling, fast handling, excellent accuracy. Minuses: You only get *one* shot!

Handling Characteristics

Handling characteristics for deer rifles can be more important than handling characteristics for rifles used for other big game hunting. As a perfect example, I recall being on a ledge at about 12,000 feet above sea level in the Rocky Mountains. A band of bighorn sheep was feeding below. I did not have to mount my rifle and shoot with amazing speed. In fact, the rifle did not even have to fit very well, because I would have had time to squirm myself into the stock. Antelope hunters can get by with rifles which do not handle like silk. I've seen mountain goats, caribou, moose and many other game animals in terrain which did not call for that fast sure shot.

But deer are another story. Even in the so-called wide open West, I want handling ability in that deer rifle. Only two seasons ago I was working a series of canyons in Idaho that looked like huge jagged teeth on some mythical monster. The best a person could do was work slowly along one steep side and glass and search out the other side. Then, no more than 30 yards in front of me, on my side of the canyon, a big-bodied buck broke cover and charged straight ahead of me. By the time I got that long-stocked rifle to my shoulder, the deer had faded into the woods. Had I my little carbine along, I would have put a round through his neck before he took two bounds. I corrected that problem with a compromise rifle, somewhat short, very light, modest length of pull, variable scope, long-range caliber . . . fast handling, but with ballistics to reach across the canyon as well as handling ability for the quick shorter shot.

But that's a deer for you. Even in so-called long-range country, a deer can be expected to burst from underfoot like a rabbit. That is why the first criterion I insist upon in a deer rifle is *fast-handling action*. And that is a combination of many individual factors. Each factor must be looked at alone, and then the hunter should seek out a compromise combination of those characteristics which make the deer rifle handle as a deer rifle should, fast but steady in the hand.

The Action

The first consideration for the deer hunting rifle is its action style. Once again, we have the single shot, the bolt, the pump, lever and semi-auto. Each type deserves at least a quick handshake to familiarize ourselves with its attributes and, I suppose, its shortcomings.

The single-shot can be made up into a short and light rifle. Therein lie its virtues. The Ruger Number One, for example, may have an overall length of just 42 inches, even with a 26-inch barrel. The H&R 158 with a 22-inch barrel is but 37 inches long. Since the action is short in a single shot, so is overall length. And we can dispense with the double rifle right here, for it is, in effect, two single shot

The Remington Model 700 bolt-action rifle in the Classic design is a favorite among modern shooters who appreciate the fine lines of this style rifle. Offered without iron sights, since the shooter is going to install a scope, it makes a fine deer rifle for any part of the country.

Ruger's Round Top M-77 comes complete with iron sights—a plus for scope users who want a back-up set of sights.

Sako's line of bolt-actions have long been popular with deer hunters. They are reliable and *accurate.*

Colt offers their Colt/Sauer bolt-action in a broad range of deer calibers.

barrels on one frame. The double, either side-by-side or over/under, is a useful deer hunting rifle style, but Americans have never gone overboard for it. Advantage—two quick shots instead of one, but from a short firearm, handy, quick to mount, and fast-pointing if built correctly.

The bolt-action repeater is no doubt *the* upcoming deer hunting firearm. In the West, one sees little else these days, though the back-East hunter still clings oftentimes to the fine lever-action model. The bolt is strong. Therefore, the hunter seeking a high-intensity round has always gravitated to the bolt-action. Well, this was perhaps more necessary once, than it is now. There are and have been some wonderfully powerful deer hunting rounds chambered in other types of actions, to include all of the actions mentioned here, *all of them*. One can get even a big magnum cartridge chambered into a semi-auto, as the BAR (Browning Automatic Rifle) proves.

The bolt-action offers the deer hunter the option of many calibers, more than any other rifle action type, if we include the vast array of wildcat rounds, most of which were designed around a bolt-action rifle. We are told that the rigid and stiff bolt-action allows the handloader an opportunity to get more life from cases. It's true. But it matters not at all. Nobody is going to shoot enough at deer to make economy of ammunition an issue in modern day hunting.

So we have an extremely popular action style and a good one. There is nothing wrong with the boltgun. I own several and will own more. But in terms of a deer rifle, the selection of the bolt is really made on this basis—it is chambered for rounds deer hunters seem to feel they want. It operates quickly enough for second shots; it makes up into classically beautiful rifles; and it is popular.

The semi-automatic is not as popular as the bolt, but a lot of deer hunters love this style of firearm. Its advantage? It shoots fast, and it can be made up into a very smooth-handling, trim firearm like the Model 4 Remington.

The slide-action can be made to feel and look just like an autoloader. The only difference is that the forearm is pulled back in order to eject an empty cartridge case and slid forward to chamber a new round. It's fast, very fast. The slide-action does not have the camming power of the bolt, and it suffers a little more case stretch. So, for the handloader, what does this mean? It means full-length resizing the case (which I always do for hunting rounds anyway), and it might mean slightly less case life. I say don't worry about it. If the slide-action feels right, buy it and shoot it.

The lever-action is still with us in various rifle brands and chamberings. The lever-action is fast, and all those tales

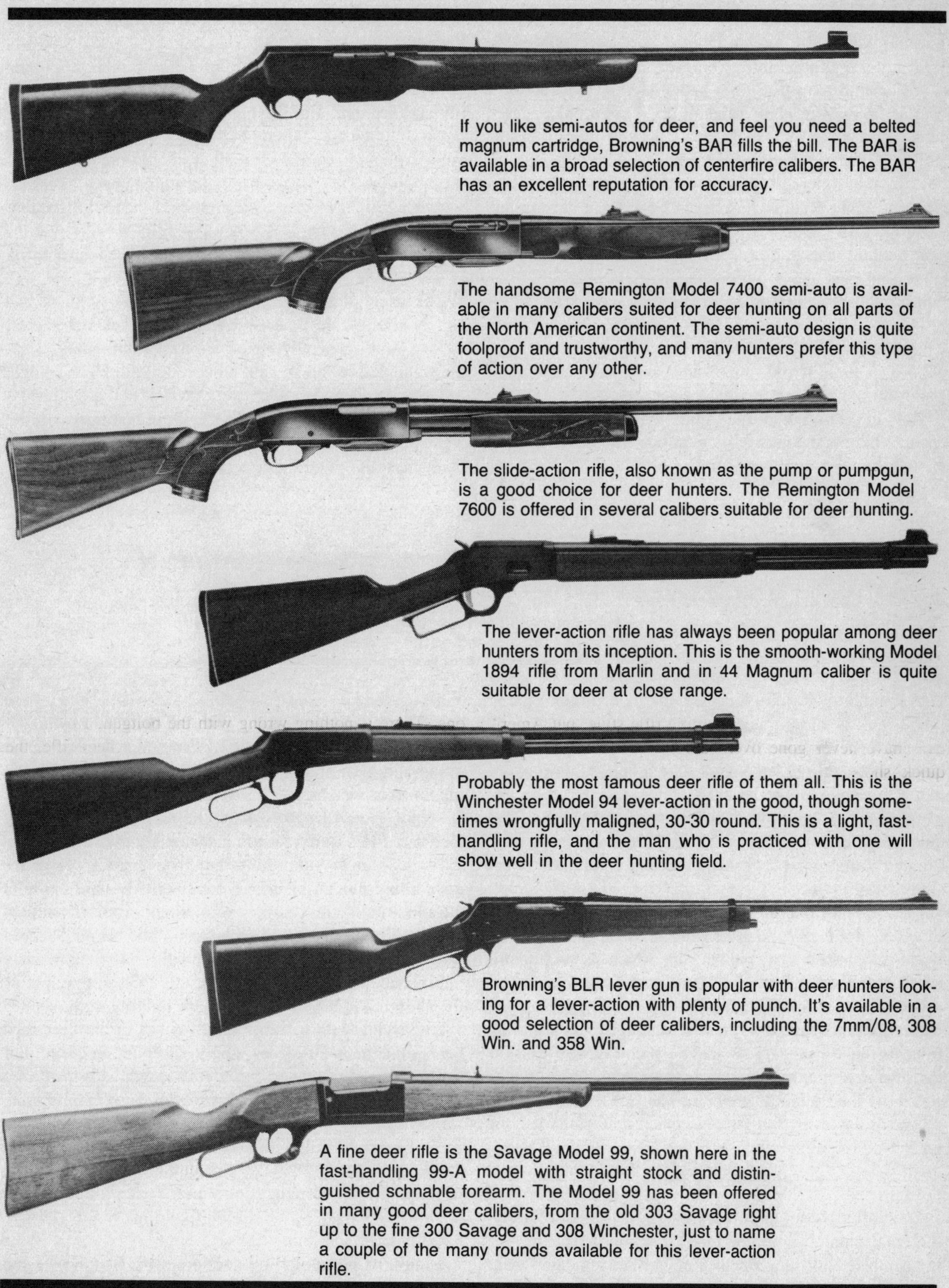

If you like semi-autos for deer, and feel you need a belted magnum cartridge, Browning's BAR fills the bill. The BAR is available in a broad selection of centerfire calibers. The BAR has an excellent reputation for accuracy.

The handsome Remington Model 7400 semi-auto is available in many calibers suited for deer hunting on all parts of the North American continent. The semi-auto design is quite foolproof and trustworthy, and many hunters prefer this type of action over any other.

The slide-action rifle, also known as the pump or pumpgun, is a good choice for deer hunters. The Remington Model 7600 is offered in several calibers suitable for deer hunting.

The lever-action rifle has always been popular among deer hunters from its inception. This is the smooth-working Model 1894 rifle from Marlin and in 44 Magnum caliber is quite suitable for deer at close range.

Probably the most famous deer rifle of them all. This is the Winchester Model 94 lever-action in the good, though sometimes wrongfully maligned, 30-30 round. This is a light, fast-handling rifle, and the man who is practiced with one will show well in the deer hunting field.

Browning's BLR lever gun is popular with deer hunters looking for a lever-action with plenty of punch. It's available in a good selection of deer calibers, including the 7mm/08, 308 Win. and 358 Win.

A fine deer rifle is the Savage Model 99, shown here in the fast-handling 99-A model with straight stock and distinguished schnable forearm. The Model 99 has been offered in many good deer calibers, from the old 303 Savage right up to the fine 300 Savage and 308 Winchester, just to name a couple of the many rounds available for this lever-action rifle.

about the action design being weak are just that—tales. The old Model 88 was chambered very successfully by Winchester in at least three "hot" calibers. The Browning is still chambered up in lever-action style in hot calibers. And as far as deer hunting rounds go, I know of no lever-action offered today which cannot handle more ballistic authority than required for deer.

I can almost hear the reader say, "But you haven't said anything about accuracy!" I haven't because I have tested all of the above action styles and for taking venison within deer hunting ranges, each action style offers sufficient accuracy, in most cases more than sufficient accuracy. The bolt is probably the most accurate, but I have seen plenty of leverguns and autos shoot well within the limits of even long-range accuracy. My old 30-30 can keep five shots in a 2.5-inch circle at 100 yards, and when I shoot better, that group shrinks to 2 inches—with *iron sights!*

Pick an action based upon what you like, and give it a chance. I know shooters who prefer one type of action over another because they consider that other type "clumsy to operate." Give yourself a chance. Practice with a borrowed bolt-action before you declare it clumsy. For example, if a shooter rolls the knob of the bolt handle in the palm of his shooting hand as he operates the action, the unloading-loading cycle will be faster and smoother. (Pinching the bolt between thumb and forefinger is the slower way to go.)

I am not trying to get out of anything here by failing to offer the reader a solid statement in favor of one action type over another. I say pick the one which seems smoothest to operate, but more than that, go for the overall feel and handling of the rifle. If a rifle feels bulky, it may be wrong for day in and day out deer hunting. If getting away from the bulk means trying another action type, try it. For my own deer hunting, there have been two actions which somehow end up in my gun rack. The first is the bolt. The second is the lever. But I feel I could successfully use the other types as well.

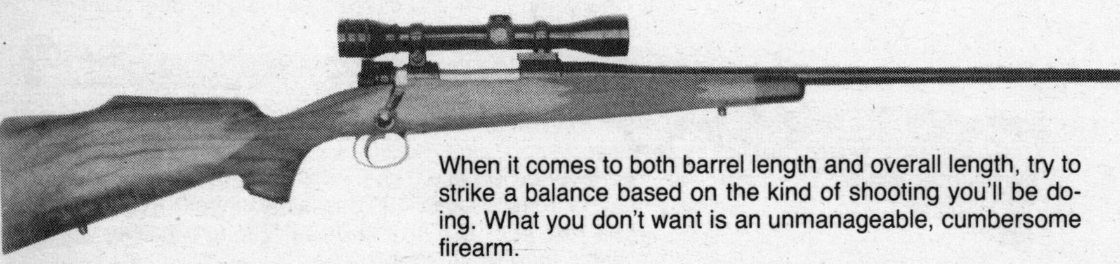

When it comes to both barrel length and overall length, try to strike a balance based on the kind of shooting you'll be doing. What you don't want is an unmanageable, cumbersome firearm.

Length of Rifle

Deer rifles do not have to be long. The length of a barrel, for example, should be based upon the round the rifle is chambered for and whether or not sight radius means anything to the shooter. As for barrel length and caliber, it's somewhat pointless to buy a 300 Magnum and then try to cut the barrel to 20 inches. No, all of the velocity advantage will not be lost. I once cut a 270 Winchester barrel down to 20 inches and lost less than 125 fps according to my chronograph. But the big case burns a lot of powder; noise will increase. Muzzle blast will increase. Some of the velocity in a big cartridge can be lost when the barrel is cut back. Therefore, I like a barrel length of about 22 inches with the 270-30/06 class caliber and 24 inches for the bigger magnum numbers. Whenever a lot of powder is to be burned in a case, regardless of the caliber, the longer barrel is likely to help burn that powder.

The term "sight radius" pertains only to iron sights and simply refers to the distance between front and rear sights. A long barrel generally means a longer sight radius. Also, the sight picture can be a bit more clear with a longer sight radius, especially for older eyes where visual accommodation (the ability of the eye to focus from rear sight to front sight to target simultaneously), is somewhat impaired as compared with youthful eyes. Also, a long barrel "hangs" very nicely. I have found that I can shoot better offhand groups, in most areas, with longer barrels due, I think, to the up-front weight.

As for overall length, I like a modest figure. Two truly nice deer rifles were recently made up for my wife and me by two different gunmakers, but to our specs. They are quite alike, though of different caliber. My wife's rifle is ultra-light, 284 caliber, very slim, slight pistol grip (European style) and though a bolt-action is still but 40.5 inches long with its 22-inch barrel. My rifle is a 6.5mm on a blown out 7mm Mauser case, and it's the same weight as the above 284, but longer due to its longer length of pull.

By staying with a barrel of 22 inches in the deer calibers, sometimes 20 inches, and by keeping length of pull shorter instead of longer, the overall length is *controlled*. I would not allow a deer rifle to grow long and cumbersome for some almost mythical gain in fps MV, and I would take care to keep the length of pull *shorter* than most shooters think they require. They don't require it. They simply have not tried the shorter length of pull.

Length of Pull

Length of pull is the distance from the buttplate to the trigger, or at least that is the popular measurement for this figure. I had to learn about proper length of pull the hard way. My own rifles were built with as much as 14.5 inches length of pull. My "reach," the distance from fingertip-to-fingertip with arms outstretched, is about 76 inches, so I have always tended to move toward a rifle with a long length of pull.

I learned about the disadvantages of long length of pull the hard way. I am convinced I failed to get my rifle into shooting position a couple of times due to overly long rifle stocks. In too many cases, hunters forget that they might be wearing a hunting coat in the field. My long stock more than once hung up on my coat. In shooting my wife's rifle one time, I found that I could mount the rifle much faster than I could my own. I had some of my rifle's stock cut off. I now prefer a rifle with 13⅞ inches length-of-pull. Most factory rifles are made about right in terms of length of pull, but the shooter owes it to himself to see if he can actually mount the rifle without hanging it up anywhere along the line on its journey from the carry position to the shooting stance.

buck is about to go out of sight.

The shooter should insist that comb height and style are right for him, so that when the rifle is mounted the sight picture is *right there*. He should not have to go looking for it by bending himself to fit into the stock.

The Forearm

Shooters get the idea that a forearm should be a nice fat beavertail affair that rests solidly in the hand and allows for a good firm grip. To the contrary, I want my forearm to be slender and tiny, and not one I can grab. A large forearm is a curse for fast-handling. You want your hand to merely caress the forearm, not strangle it. A white-knuckle grip causes the shooter to lose control, not gain control. The idea is to gently support the forearm with the hand. A strangle grip badly curtails the smooth motion of the rifle. For a benchrest or varmint rifle. I don't mind a fat forearm, but I would not think of it on a deer rifle where flow of motion and grace of movement is often paramount to getting off a well-aimed shot.

When it comes to actual "gun-handling," the author prefers a rifle with a classic or slim forearm. Beavertail forearms are for varmints, not deer.

The Comb

The comb is that upper crest of the buttstock against which we rest our cheek when we aim. Today, the Monte Carlo type comb is in popular use. I am not in love with the looks of the Monte Carlo; I like the straighter Classic American style. A classic stock can still be had with a comb that is high enough to put the eye in line with the scope. Therein lies the importance of the comb. Comb height dictates eye level when the rifle is mounted to the shoulder. To test for proper comb height try this: Mount your deer rifle with your eyes closed. After pulling the rifle up to the ready, open your eyes and see where you are really looking. Sometimes the shooter will find he is looking right over the top of his iron sights or perhaps underneath the center of his scope sight. Both problems of comb height primarily, and it should be corrected. Why try the closed-eyes trick? Because you may have learned to adjust to an improper comb height by moving your head rapidly, squirming on the stock in order to see the sights. Sure, that's OK, but it means a loss in time, valuable time if a

The shooter can test this for himself. Stand up and shoot at a bull's-eye at 100 yards, offhand, first strangling the forearm to see what that group looks like. Then shoot again, controlling the forearm with gentle pressure, but using the buttstock to truly support the rifle.

Trigger Pull

Trigger pull in the deer rifle must be as smooth as possible. Therefore, a trigger which requires a hefty pull is to be avoided. Trigger work is for professional gunsmiths. It is up to the expert to make any internal adjustments to a trigger. In fact, an expert smith just smoothed up the trigger pull on my older Model 94 30-30 rifle.

My favorite trigger is the "multiple-lever" design, often referred to as "double-set" trigger. This type of trigger is popular on muzzle-loading rifles which I use frequently for my own deer hunting. Once mastered, the two-trigger arrangement is superb. If a deer jumps "under your nose," you can simply pull the front trigger and fire the rifle. If there is any time at all, and I am speaking of mere seconds,

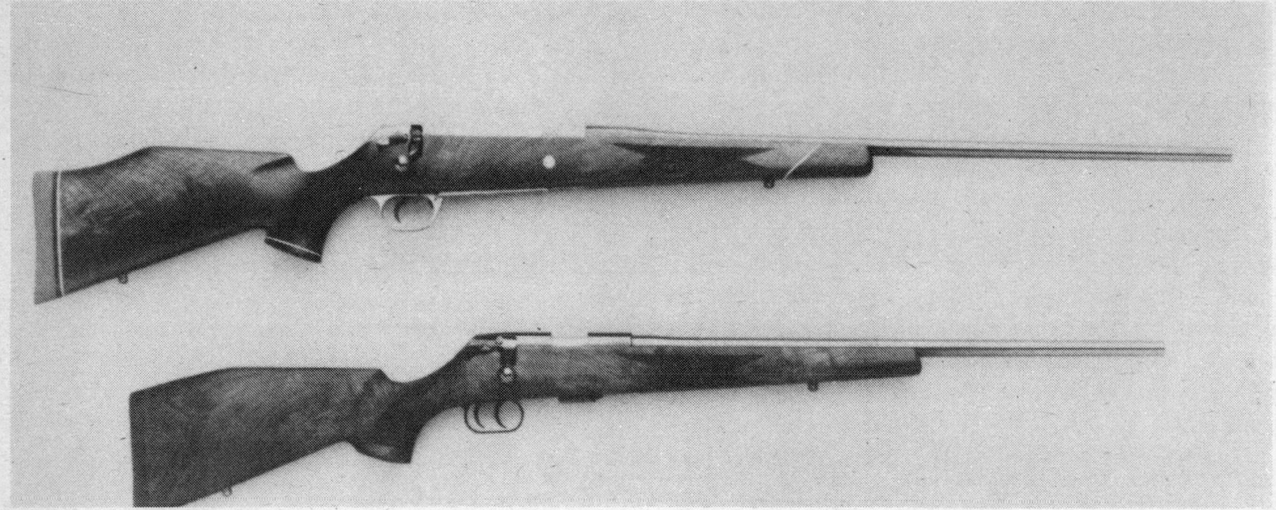

Triggers are always of utmost importance on any type rifle meant to do accurate work. The double set trigger has been around for a very long time, and it offers a multiple lever system so that the "hair" trigger releases with extremely light touch, yet the system is safe when properly constructed and properly handled.

the trigger can be set using the rear trigger. Now the front trigger has a pull of only a few ounces instead of pounds. This means when the sight picture is just right, we "touch her off." I know I have made some shots on deer which would have been more difficult without at least a good if not great trigger pull. On my single-stage triggers, I like a 2-pound pull, *if it is safe for that specific trigger design*. My double trigger rifles, mostly on muzzleloaders but also on a Bishop custom rifle, enjoy a letoff of about 6 to 8 *ounces*. No, I don't condone walking through the woods with a double-set trigger fully "set"—that's asking for an accident.

Incidentals

Slings, sights and many other incidental features can change the handling qualities of a deer rifle. You can easily find out if you have any semi-hidden gremlins on your own deer rifle by mounting the rifle many times in succession and noting any irregularity in how the rifle feels. If, as an example, you find that your left hand butts up against a sling swivel or that a line in the stock hits your face in the wrong way or that a scope is mounted too far forward or too far back, you'll have an opportunity to correct the situation *before* you head for the woods.

Cartridges

What must a deer rifle do? It must drop a buck cleanly and swiftly, preferably with one shot. And what does it take to do that? In my eyes, all of the charts and figures in the world mean little when it comes to determining how many foot-pounds of energy are minimum for deer-taking force. Even when we compute striking energy, the number of foot-pounds at the target itself, we may still have only a dim picture of "killing power."

A fellow gunwriter told me he demands an arrival ener-

The mule deer can attain very decent body weight. Even this young and small-racked buck weighed, field-dressed, 170 pounds. In the West, in some of the big canyon country, such a buck can be often encountered across open reaches for very long-range shooting. When this is the situation, the larger-cased ammunition, such as the 270, 30-06, 7mm Magnum, and similar rounds, are not out of place.

The range of modern cartridges for deer hunting is somewhat overwhelming. This is a very small representation of rounds. From right to left: the 243 Winchester; the 308 Winchester; the 270 Winchester with 130-grain bullet; the 270 again, but with the 150-grain bullet; the 30-06 and a 150-grain bullet; the 30-06 with a 180-grain bullet; the 300 Winchester Magnum with 180-grain bullet; the 160-grain 7mm bullet; and on the far left the 7mm Remington Magnum round.

The 25-06 is considered one of the better long-range deer cartridges and many western hunters have turned to it, especially since it has been standardized by Remington. It used to be a wildcat number only.

The 257 Roberts cartridge is a fine deer round. Many hunters have used it with success over the years. The 257 Roberts was put on the back burner when the 243 Winchester and 6mm Remington came on the scene, but some would argue that neither are better than the fine 257 Roberts.

gy of 1500 foot-pounds for his deer rifle. I don't mind. But I don't believe it. If that is true, then the dozens of deer which dropped to one shot from my 54-caliber muzzleloader and its round lead ball must have expired from pneumonia from the hole made by the projectile. In fact, I have taken a goodly number of deer, the actual count lost a long time ago, at about 100 yards with a round ball. Out of my own 54, the remaining energy at 100 yards would be in the neighborhood of about 675 foot-pounds. And yet, with that much force, a lead round ball of 230 grains weight has often penetrated both sides of the chest cavity.

In fact, I think the shooter should put the horse before the cart, and that means selecting the rifle for deer hunting which fits, which he *likes* (important) and which seems right for him. Then worry about the caliber. I could spend the next several pages of this book naming calibers which are capable of cleanly harvesting deer. There are countless numbers of them, especially if one includes the wildcat rounds. Choose the deer rifle. Then worry about the deer rifle caliber.

I don't want to give the idea that I am totally liberal on the subject of deer calibers. Sure, a hunter can take a deer with a 22 Short, but that does not make the 22 Short a deer caliber. A fellow I hunted with in Mexico, Don Gustavo, used 22 LR rimfire ammo for whitetail hunting. He had nothing else for which he had ammo. He got deer by stalking to 20 yards and pipping them in the head with the 22, but he often had to hold off entirely and let the deer go because he had learned the hard way that you don't hit a deer just anyplace with that rabbit caliber and get your quarry. I learned that Don Gustavo owned a 30-30, and I asked the *patron* of the ranch if I could present the old foreman with a few rounds of ammo. He said yes, and on my next hunt I had two boxes of 170-grain soft-point ammunition as a gift for the hunter. He was pleased. So was I. I don't think the 22 rimfire is right for anything bigger than a woodchuck, and then only at very close range to boot.

I don't like the 222, 223, 220 or any of the fast-stepping varmint rounds for deer. In one state, it is legal to shoot a deer with a 22-caliber rifle, and a friend of mine prides himself in using a 22-250 for deer. He has never lost one either. I am aware of things like this. But I think you have to look at the deer caliber story in full perspective. And that means keeping things appropriate. I saw a 60-grain bullet from a hotrock 22 varmint rifle wound a deer which had to be followed up. The same shot with a "deer caliber" would have taken that buck down on the spot.

The full range of rounds from the 243/6mm clan to the 35s is useful for deer. The high-velocity pills are fine for open country, with the larger caliber rounds better, I think, for up-close shooting, though I have precious little faith in many rounds "getting through brush."

So I am not going to list a *parcel* of rounds, giving the

theoretical advantage of each one. I have some favorites, but am quick to admit that these rounds fit my set of prejudices and that's about all. I know full well that the 30-30 class is just fine for close range, and medium range, too, as I will point out soon. I like the 7mm/08 for deer, but only because I have shot the round and like how it shoots, and because I know of a couple deer cleanly dispatched with it. Pick your own caliber, *after* you find that rifle you like.

Recoil Factors

We are often predisposed to recoil problems. That is, we learn and are conditioned to flinch during rifle practice and during sighting-in periods. I am sure that no shooter ever remembers feeling the recoil of a rifle during that "moment of truth" when he is firing at game. Even rifles of high recoil energy fail to bother a shooter in the field. But sit at a bench and that's another story. The reasons are several, but two stand out. First, a shooter is more conscious of recoil when target shooting, practicing or sighting-in because he is concentrating not on game, but on the shooting the rifle itself. Second, when seated at the bench especially, shooters are in a position to absorb the maximum effect of recoil.

I bring up the recoil factors because I think it pointless to pick a deer caliber/firearm combination which is going to make a flincher out of the hunter. But, if the effects of recoil are hardly felt in the field, then why worry about choosing a more mild caliber for deer hunting? The reason is conditioned response. We may not consciously think about being "kicked" when shooting at a deer, but I know full well that we do indeed flinch in the field, even though we do not *remember* being whacked by the rifle when we were shooting at game.

Once, I was with a fellow whose rifle failed to pick up a round from the magazine when he worked the bolt. He was shooting a hot wildcat caliber in what I would call the elk/grizzly/moose range, but he believed in lots of punch, even for deer. We spotted a feeding buck and moved in on it. When close enough, we stopped, took several deep breaths and whispered a little, mainly to briefly get his mind off of the deer. He looked calm. He steadied the rifle, and when the empty gun went *click!*, my buddy

This buck was taken with a 25-06. The 25-06 is a good deer round and it has also been used for game larger than deer. One friend hunts elk with the 25-06 on a regular basis. He's a good shot and a good hunter, however, and he spends a great deal of time in the outdoors. His load is the 120-grain bullet using H-870 powder, 64.0 grains, for a MV of 3200 fps and an energy rating of 2729 foot-pounds. This is the load we now use exclusively in our own 25-06 for big game.

The little 6mm/222 wildcat round chambered up in this Frank Wells custom rifle has accounted for a great number of one-shot kills. It is a very effective rifle for deer at ranges up to 200 yards.

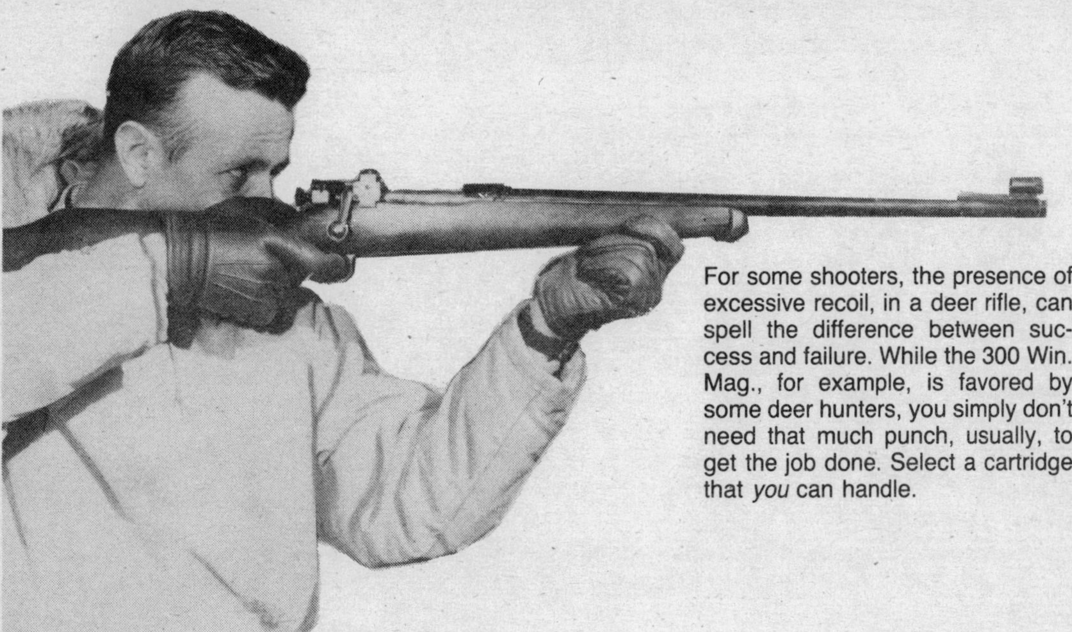

For some shooters, the presence of excessive recoil, in a deer rifle, can spell the difference between success and failure. While the 300 Win. Mag., for example, is favored by some deer hunters, you simply don't need that much punch, usually, to get the job done. Select a cartridge that *you* can handle.

backed up as if he'd been hit by an invisible force. He'd flinched. He had learned to fear the recoil of his rifle. The moral is to choose an appropriate deer round, one you can handle without flinching. Even for long-range shooting, one does not need a 300 Magnum to drop a deer. Pick a sensible deer caliber, a more balanced one.

Remember that recoil is more complex than we might consider at first glance, and one factor of recoil has to do with the powder charge itself. This is why some of those bigger rounds kick pretty hard compared with what they have to deliver. I'm not knocking big powerful rounds—they have their place. I am pointing out that one does not need over 3000 fps with a modest bullet for even long-range deer hunting. Don't believe it? Turn to the chapter on using the trajectory table and see what is actually gained with a couple hundred fps MV in a load, going from 3000 to 3200 fps. Oh, there is a gain. And since foot-pounds depends upon the square of the velocity in the formula, the gain looks rather impressive on paper as far as "power" is concerned.

I have hunted deer and deer-sized game for a good many years with a degree of faithfulness to the involvement, and I guarantee the hunter that if he will use a correct big-game style bullet, he will find that even at 300 yards a round such as the ancient 7mm Mauser will down a deer with one shot, provided the placement is reasonably decent. One does not even need as much punch as the 30-06 has, though surely the 30-06 is a fine cartridge when it comes to deer. The rounds I look at for deer are mainly in three broad categories. There is the 243/6mm class. The only time I do not care for this cartridge class is in a cross-canyon situation. Then I like more bullet mass. I have hunted in a few (rare) places where a 300+-yard shot was not uncommon, and where the mule deer were simply the largest in body weight that I had ever seen. Here, I'd want more penetration than a 90- or 100-grain bullet might deliver for the sake of insurance. The 243/6mm clan can drop a big buck at well over 300 yards but I'm talking about insurance now, having that extra punch.

The second class is a broad band of rounds. I would call it the 30-30 group, but those who use the 7mm/08 and similar rounds, to include the 308 Winchester and 300 Savage may object. In fact, my 30-30 handload has more punch at 200 yards than anything which can be put through a 243 Winchester or 6mm Remington. Therefore, I look at this branch of cartridges as all-inclusive, beginning with the 30-30 types, the 307 Winchester, 7mm/08, 300 Savage, 308 Winchester and the rest of the "mediums" of this type.

The third group I classify as the 270/30-06 class, represented here by the 270 Winchester, 280 Remington, 30-06 and a host of similar rounds. At longer ranges, these do what the mediums do up close. We might artificially stuff all of those so-called short-range "brush-busters" into this category, too, such as the 356 Winchester, 358 Winchester, 375 Winchester, 35 Remington and so forth. They do at modest range what the bigger case capacity calibers do at longer ranges.

Any of the rounds in these three make-believe pigeon holes will harvest deer, and I do not mean incidentally, or under ideal circumstances only. I am speaking of a deer harvest under *normal* or "average" hunting circumstances.

I say again, pick the rifle you like, and then worry about the caliber. The criteria set down above concerning deer rifles mean a lot more than some almost theoretical difference between two cartridges. Warren Page, the respected gunwriter, once said that reports he compiled showed as many one-shot kills with a 30-30 on deer at close range as

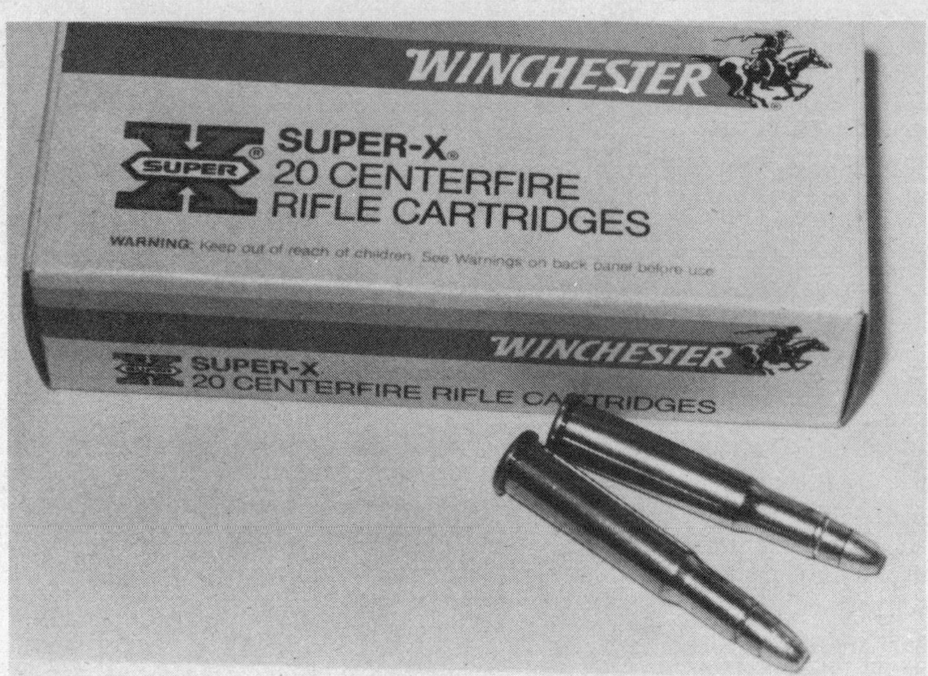

The old 30-30 Winchester round has improved quite a bit over the years. Now it is one of the most accurate in terms of factory ammunition. The 30-30, when fired from a solid bolt-action rifle, such as the Model 54 Winchester, fixed with good glass sighting, is very accurate. The author has fired 1/2-inch groups at 100 yards with such an arrangement. But most of all, the 30-30 is a good short to medium range deer-taker.

with any other caliber, including a 300 Magnum. The reason was clear then. The reason is clear now. The 30-30 at close range has enough energy to harvest a deer.

Deer Rifles East/Deer Rifles West

In my travels east, I see a preponderance of what America use to call a "deer rifle." These Marlin or Winchester lever-actions and Remington pumps are chambered for calibers such as the 30-30 or the 35 Remington.

A prominent leader of an ammunition company provided a special deer hunt in the Northeast for his daughter and new son-in-law. Part of the honeymoon present consisted of two rifles, both bolt-actions, both in modern up-to-date calibers. On the hunt, however, the two felt almost out of place as they gathered around the lodge to shelve their rifles; every other firearm in the rack was a lever-action.

Apparently, the guided hunters found those "deer rifles" just right for their needs in an eastern woods setting. Out West, however, if a person will post himself along a highway in my state during the deer season, he will see many pickup trucks with gunracks in the rear window, and in almost every case that gunrack will contain a bolt-action scope-sighted rifle. In fact, there has been a change in the "deer rifle" as far as the western hunter is concerned. When I was growing up in the 1950s and 1960s, "deer rifle" out West meant lever-action, probably in 30-30 or 300 Savage. Today, it means 270 Winchester, or similar round, chambered in a bolt-action rifle wearing a scope.

In truth, eastern hunters can find long-range shooting on deer, and western hunters, if they actually pace off each and every deer harvest they make, will find that most of their 200-yard shots turn out to be closer, sometimes a lot closer. Still, I will buy the general concept of longer-range rifles for the West. However, there are days when I want venison and prefer to take a lever-action rifle in 30-30. Though I hunt mostly in the "wide open spaces" I have not found a "brush rifle" that much of a handicap.

America's Sweetheart—the 30-30

About 8,000,000 30-30s have been sold since the round was offered to the public in 1895. About 5,000,000 of these are Model 94 lever-action rifles or carbines. Though not all of those have been chambered for 30-30, it's fair to say the majority of them have been. Marlin has turned out more than 3,000,000 lever-action rifles, most of them in 30-30 caliber. Savage has made a number of 30-30 rifles. Mossberg has, too. So have others. In spite of the backhanded treatment the 30-30 gets in print from the modern gunwriter, millions of hunters seem to ignore all of the lofty facts thrown at them from the printed page. They simply go on providing tons of good-eating venison with their 30-30s. And I cite Warren Page once again. He felt that the 30-30 was a "balanced round." Page was right.

I am obliged to give the 30-30 a special little section in this analysis of deer calibers because the American hunter has insisted upon it. Also, you will find that in spite of the often-stated idea that handloading for the 30-30 is more or less a waste of time (since the round will not gain from the personal handloading process), there is strong evidence that thousands of shooters still handload for the old 30-30. In the all-time best selling list for dies, RCBS lists the 30-30 as number 6 in 1977, number 5 in 1978, same in '79, up to number 4 in 1980! The 1983 list shows the 30-30 dropped to "only" number 7 on a list of the 30 most popular handloaded rounds.

Once again, the American hunter has been smart enough to know what works for him, and the 30-30 *works.* It is not a long-range round, though back in 1895 it startled those hunters used to the trajectories of the standard black powder loads, the 30-30 "shooting flat" to well over 150 yards. Teddy Roosevelt and his contemporaries turned to the 30-30 for some of their plains hunting because of its flat trajectory. Today, however, it has been far outstripped by dozens of rounds. So be it. But the 30-30 is alive and well. Bigger and "better" rounds have come—and some of them have *gone,* but the 30-30 presses on. There is a reason. It works.

My Personal Deer Rifles

I suppose if someone is going to stand up and advocate, then he should have the courage of his convictions, revealing his own personal equipment. I hunt many different areas. Therefore, I have different deer rifles. But there are three rifles in my battery which seem to get the most work when it comes time to put venison in the pot. First, I have a 54-caliber muzzleloader. I love hunting with black powder. And with a 230-grain round ball at close to 2000 fps MV, my 54 will cleanly harvest a deer at close range, certainly up to 125 yards, and probably farther, but I do not advocate shooting much beyond 125 yards considering the muzzleloader's trajectory. (The ball in the above 54-caliber rifle load is 6 inches low at 125 yards, for example.)

Second, I own a couple of Winchester 30-30s. One is pre-'64 with a 26-inch barrel, and the other a pre-'64 carbine with a 20-inch barrel. Give me just about any deer terrain, and I will find the old 30-30, especially with my handloads, quite certain for taking deer. The 30-30 class of cartridge falls in between for me. It's a lot more than a muzzleloader in terms of actual range. But it does not match the long-range rounds in flatness of trajectory.

My third rifle is a wildcat caliber, but in truth, the round is duplicated by several factory calibers. The thrust of this rifle is its weight, or lack of it. The rifle goes about 7.5 pounds with scope sight. The caliber is 6.5 DGS, which stands for Dale's Gun Shop. It is, in fact, a 7mm Mauser case necked to 6.5-caliber (.264-inch). In a 22-inch barrel, the 129-grain bullet is pushed at 3100 fps MV. I can get 2900 fps with a 140-grain bullet with no problem at all. The blown out case with its sharp shoulder seems to burn powder efficiently.

The rifle is built on the fine Remington Model 700 action, with slim stock, blind magazine and a 2.5-8x Bushnell scope atop the receiver. It handles like a dream and it is accurate. In fact, with a 140-grain Speer bullet at 2900 fps, I'd never fear hunting elk with the little rifle. This is my long-range number. It has enough remaining energy at long range to cleanly drop a deer. Yet, it is no problem to carry around the hills. Gunmaker Dale Storey built the rifle to my specs.

I hunt with many, many other rifles because I am often testing a firearm and will use it on deer to see how it does. I have also used two other deer rifles which happen to be in my home, and they both might interest the deer hunter. One is my wife's 6mm/222 that pushes an 85-grain bullet at a bit under 2900 fps MV. This little gem was built around a Sako action by gunsmith Frank Wells. It is also a lightweight, and we have never had the least problem cleanly dropping deer with it. The other rifle also belongs to my wife, a 284 Winchester on a Ruger 77 action, built by Dean Zollinger. With turned down barrel, we have another lightweight "mountain rifle." It has plenty of power, too.

If I were forced to stay with only one rifle for deer, I suppose it would have to be my 6.5 DGS or my wife's 284, both very light to carry, both workable in brush, though intended for open country shooting.

Your Deer Rifle

If you have a deer rifle which works well, let no one talk you out of it. Of course, keep an open mind. I have had hunters, who were totally adamant about their own deer rifles, shoot our 6.5 DGS or 284. They changed those made-up minds quickly, asking themselves why they were carrying all that bulk for ballistics no better than what we were getting in our "mountain rifles."

The deer rifle turns out to be somewhat personal in nature. I have found the deer rifle so personal and so important to me, that I have gone to custom-crafted deer rifles in a couple of instances. I have never been sorry for the move. Owning and shooting these gems has proved their worth to me. But I would be able to harvest deer joyfully with any of dozens of over-the-counter rifles as well. If I were to go with such a rifle, it would be one of the featherweights, probably in bolt-action, but not necessarily. I could use the rifle east or west, and it would wear a 2.5-8x scope sight, with the scope set on the lower power for stillhunting, and turned up in magnification for shots across a western canyon or from hill-to-hill in a Pennsylvania wooded setting.

But I would not want to live with one deer rifle alone. I have had too many hours of deep reward from packing a muzzleloader in the field. I have found my old 30-30s too fine to abandon them. And then, for real "business" hunting, that long-range round in the scope-sighted bolt-action rifle has proved itself more than worthy. The deer rifle is no one rifle. It could never be. The deer rifle is a medium-powered firearm with good hunting accuracy. Most importantly, the deer rifle is that which is best handled and most accurately fired by its owner.

Chapter 4

The Rifle for Larger Than Deer Game

Roy Weatherby has been a fan of high velocity for many years and his fine trophies have proved that his theories are correct, but we should look at those theories with accuracy. Roy's famous line of cartridges does not deal in high velocity alone, but rather *good bullets of substantial mass* at high velocity! For example, his famous 300 Weatherby Magnum, favorite round of many hunters, pushes a 180-grain bullet at 3200 fps MV. Yes, we have high velocity. But we also have a bullet of 180 grains weight as well.

LARGER THAN DEER GAME, in terms of American hunting, generally means the elk. However, there are a number of North American big game animals which qualify for the larger than deer category, to include the moose, the grizzly bear, black bear and the caribou of the northlands. In fact, the latter, on the barren grounds, will fall between a big mule deer in size and a bull elk in weight. The bison is actually the largest of our indigenous game, much bigger than a moose or even a brown bear (coastal grizzly or ''Kodiak'' bear). But the bison is seldom hunted in fair chase, though he can be in Utah and parts of Canada.

The complete shooter might want to have at least one larger-than-deer caliber in his battery of firearms. But which one should he have? And why should he have it? As with all matters of shooting, the answers are varied with as many different hues as a patchwork quilt. But the problem is well worth examining. The dedicated hunter wants to use the correct tools for each type of game harvested. That is why he concerns himself with matters of caliber and ''power.'' And, let's admit it—the complete shooter has a great interest in firearms and enjoys mastering various levels of cartridge power and lethality, as evidenced by the comparative popularity in America of the 458 Winchester and the old 45-70. Nothing on this continent requires the punch of a 458 Winchester to bring it down. And the 45-70, when loaded in a rifle such as the Ruger Number One with a 500-grain bullet at about 1800 fps MV, also has more authority than necessary for any game in our land. Exceptions? You bet there are. I am friends with two professional Alaskan guides, both of whom have had to stop the charge of an enraged grizzly. While neither owns a 458, both admit that at times this caliber would have served them better than the 338s and 375 H&Hs they were carrying. One of the men told me that he felt an ideal caliber for coastal Alaska, where the bears resemble King Kong, is the 450 Alaskan, a 45-caliber based on a blown-out 348 Winchester case and chambered in the old Winchester lever-action Model 71.

When I was in the Yukon on an extensive trip, I made it my business to talk to as many hunters as possible. Professional trappers in the main, they used what they had. They

A bull bison can weigh *ten times* more than a mule deer buck. The old saying concerning "where you hit 'em that counts" is quite correct, but an animal of this size also suggests that *what* you hit 'em with does count for something. Such game is the reason for larger-than-deer cartridges.

were generally not imbued with firearms knowledge, but they certainly had a lot of practical shooting experience to draw from. I found that many of them used the 30-06, and just about as many owned rifles chambered for the 303 British or the 30-40 Krag. One fellow told me, "I take the 30-06 with me a lot, but I don't really like to carry it much, and when I need game, such as a moose, I always grab my Model 94 30-30 for that. I sometimes have to hit a moose twice with it, but usually one shot is enough."

How about bears? He had taken a couple grizzlies, but it was always with the 30-30 which he had had no problem with at all. I asked him what he thought an ideal rifle for grizzlies would be, and the trapper, a man of 60 years who had spent all of his life in the Yukon, suggested that the 30-06 would be more than enough. He had good luck, he added, with the 180-grain Silvertip bullet on a couple moose and felt that its good penetration and hang-together characteristics would serve well on bear also. All of this was interesting because while in Whitehorse I collected newspaper articles documenting grizzly bear attacks and also spoke with a few of the authorities around the area. By the time I left I was convinced that if I lived there and moved in the same circles with grizzlies on a daily basis, I might chance getting by with a 30-06, perhaps even a smaller round. But, if I were to hunt with clients, I would want insurance. And that insurance would come in the form of a bigger caliber, at least a 338, possibly a Marlin 45-70 or a 450 Alaskan. I read one account of two trappers in the Yukon found dead, killed by a grizzly. The grizzly was killed, too, but not before he managed to dispatch both trappers. The bear had been hit in the vitals several times; both trappers had rifles, both in the same caliber—30-06.

I relate these stories because there is endless controversy over larger-than-deer calibers. Just about everyone who shoots has a comment to offer on the best caliber to use. And his partner has an equally powerful story to refute the use of that caliber in favor of the one he holds closest to his heart. We may not be able to clear up the matter totally here, but at least we can look at it systematically. We can study the larger-than-deer calibers step-by-step. And then, as with all shooting problems, each of us will have to individually decide which path to follow in the quest for a rifle/caliber with which to cleanly harvest those big game animals.

The Nature of the Beast

Briefly, it's wise to put down a foundation before trying to build a case for any larger-than-deer caliber. That foundation starts with the size of the game itself. Unfortunately, game sizes and weights vary within a species not unlike human sizes and weights. If one asked, "How much does a human weigh?," he would certainly be up against the impossible in terms of one answer.

With game we tend to exaggerate the weight though not with the intention of telling "fish stories." Most of us just don't know any better. One fellow told me that he got a mule deer buck in Colorado that *dressed out* at just shy of 600 pounds. I asked him if he tagged that buck with his elk ticket (600 pounds is more in the elk class than mule deer class). But it happens to us all. One season I got what I thought was a huge black bear. However, the professional bear hunting guide I was with told me the bear probably went only 400 pounds at most.

A good bull elk will easily dress out at 600 pounds. And a moose can be much larger, especially the Yukon variety, which might weigh as much as 1200 pounds on the hoof. Dressed out, that 1200-pound moose will weigh in at around 800 pounds. Some sources say that a mature brown bear (or coastal grizzly) can weigh perhaps 1650 pounds live-weight. A bison can weigh as much as 3000 pounds "on the hoof."

One thing is sure, the larger-than-deer clan do gain formidable mass, and therein lies part of our need for a powerful caliber to cleanly drop this sort of game. When an animal is big, and tough, it requires more energy to put him away cleanly. This rudimentary fact must underly any question of caliber for larger-than-deer game. A 30-caliber bullet through the chest cavity of a deer will generally disrupt sufficient tissue to end that buck on the spot, provided, of course, that the velocity is high enough to "upset" the bullet and create a large wound channel. Putting the same bullet into the chest cavity of an elk may create a very similar wound channel, but it does so in a much greater mass of tissue, hence the result is a comparatively *smaller* effect. However, selection of caliber must also depend on the nature of the beast. My experience with moose is limited, but from what I have seen, a good solid hit with any caliber in the 30-06 range will put a moose down quickly. A bull elk, a smaller animal by a good measure, may go on for miles with the same strike. There is a difference between the natures of these two animals.

(Right) Larger-than-deer game such as this waterbuck require either a more potent load or correct bullet placement. Whereas a deer will fold fairly rapidly with a slightly-off-the-mark hit using a bigger caliber, such as the 270 Winchester or 30-06, the tenacity of the waterbuck requires either more cartridge or good bullet placement. This one was taken with one shot from a 264 Winchester with a 140-grain bullet at about 3000 fps. The bullet hit spine/neck.

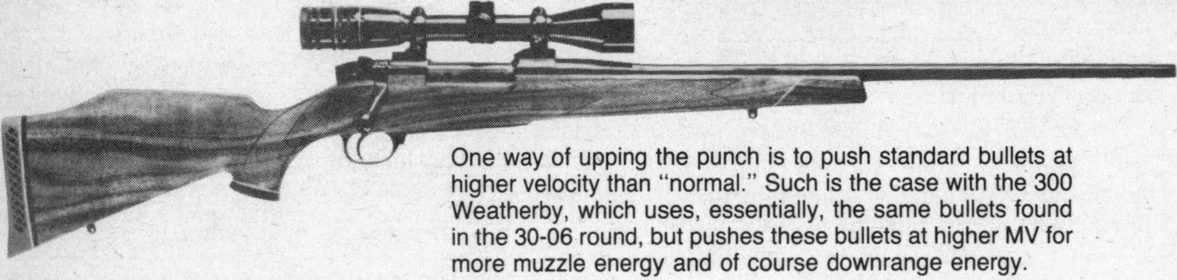

One way of upping the punch is to push standard bullets at higher velocity than "normal." Such is the case with the 300 Weatherby, which uses, essentially, the same bullets found in the 30-06 round, but pushes these bullets at higher MV for more muzzle energy and of course downrange energy.

As you can see, dropping a big game animal requires some thought on the part of the hunter before the hunt begins. You must consider the physical size of the animal to be hunted and that animal's ability (reputation) or lack of it to absorb lead and keep moving. The answers to these two considerations will be the basis upon which you make your caliber selection.

It's Not What You Hit 'Em With, . . .

Talk about calibers for big game and someone will certainly pipe up with the old saying, "It's not *what* you hit 'em with, it's *where* you hit 'em that counts." That's all very well indeed, and the statement carries much truth. The only problem is that no hunter can guarantee he will always place that projectile "just right" under fair-chase hunting circumstances. It is not going to happen. Granted, if I am always offered a standing neck shot on a bull elk at 50 yards, I will take a 243/6mm class rifle and do the job every time. But don't expect the same results with that

When it comes to downing elk, the hunter must select his cartridge, as well as bullet type and weight, wisely. Yes, elk have been taken with less-than-suitable calibers; however, that's a less-than-sporting approach when it comes to harvesting valuable game.

(Right) Weighing in at about 1000 pounds, a bull moose can be unpredictable. When you shoot a moose, that bullet *must* be able to drive through a tremendous amount of flesh and bone, fully penetrating the vitals, hopefully dropping the bull cleanly. Select your cartridge, and bullet, carefully.

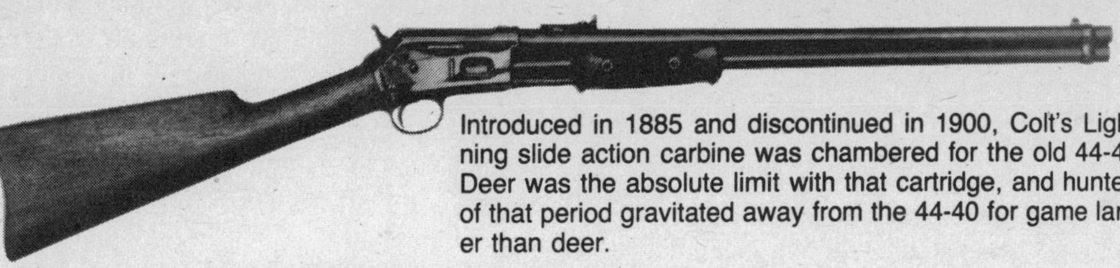

Introduced in 1885 and discontinued in 1900, Colt's Lightning slide action carbine was chambered for the old 44-40. Deer was the absolute limit with that cartridge, and hunters of that period gravitated away from the 44-40 for game larger than deer.

caliber on a chest shot; it's too small.

While we are talking about stories, there is another one that always pops up when talking larger-than-deer calibers. This is the one about how old Uncle Jim shot 15 elk with 15 shots from a 25-20, and that goes to prove that you don't need more than a 25-20 for elk. Sure it does. Now Jim may have gotten 15 elk with 15 shots from a 25-20, but if the story is investigated fully, chances are the circumstances were unique. The fellow may have taken every elk under ideal circumstances at some little-known watering spot where the shot was from 20 yards at an always-sedentary animal. Yes, bull moose have been dropped with 22 Short rounds, and the Eskimo has taken more than one Polar bear with the 222 Remington, but none of this has any bearing when it comes to choosing a caliber for our own larger-than-deer hunting.

What the Old-Timers Used

It's interesting and informative to look at what the old-timers used for larger than deer game. In the days of the muzzleloader, caliber was king. Caliber is still king for those who wish to hunt big game with muzzleloaders under modern conditions. The reason is simple. One cannot achieve high velocity as we know it with the use of black powder. Therefore, what we cannot gain in velocity, we try to make up for in projectile mass. And it does work out quite well. Given a 50- or 54-caliber round ball at a decent MV, I am totally confident of dropping a big mule deer buck at 125 yards.

When the 44-40 was born, it was born small. Even though quite ample, the bullet only weighed 200 grains, less than my own .535-inch round ball for my current muzzleloader, and it was lucky to achieve a MV of 1200 fps. Hunters found the round effective, if the shot was placed "just so." But if they loved the 44-40 for hunting, they certainly did not show it for they gravitated away from it and went to the 40-60, 45-70, 45-90 and many other larger calibers before smokeless arrived on the scene.

In fact, plenty of old-timers stayed with the big bore black powder numbers even after the advent of the smokeless round. In about 1895, the 30-30 was on the scene, and it was well-loved, too. It still is. Most of the hunters found

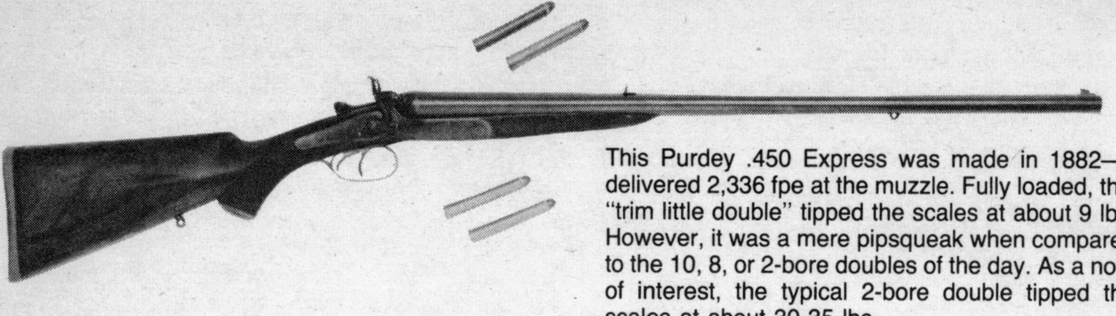

This Purdey .450 Express was made in 1882—it delivered 2,336 fpe at the muzzle. Fully loaded, this "trim little double" tipped the scales at about 9 lbs. However, it was a mere pipsqueak when compared to the 10, 8, or 2-bore doubles of the day. As a note of interest, the typical 2-bore double tipped the scales at about 30-35 lbs.

While the 25-06 is a very fine cartridge, it was not selected as an all-around caliber due to the fact that it does not offer the larger weight bullet for the elk/moose animal size. However, the 25-06 has, of course, harvested game of this dimension.

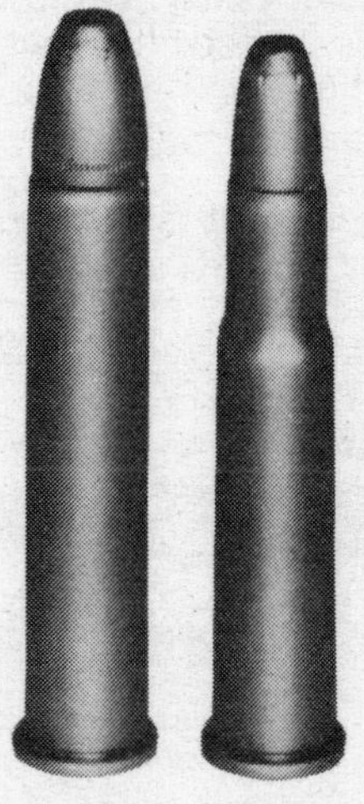

The 375 Winchester round on the left is compared with the old standard 30-30 Winchester. Firing a bullet of 250 grains, this round will handle larger-than-deer game at close range.

it better than what they had been using, for it shot flatter and apparently did the job nicely on game of the deer class and even larger. As we look back now, we have forgotten that many hunters turned to the 30-30 for larger-than-deer game. If one reads Frank C. Hibben's reports of bear hunting, the 30-30 will present itself often. And the well-known hunter, William Hornaday, used a 303 Savage for his collection of grizzly bear specimens.

Samuel Baker, before the time of smokeless powder, used a round ball and sometimes a conical, from rifles of 4-bore to 10-bore dimension. The 4-bore rifle weighed 21 pounds and burned 16 drams of black powder, or to us about 435 grains weight. Another rifle of note was a 2-bore made by William Moore of London. This rifle was no mere 21-pound strippling. It weighed 33 pounds. Instead of burning a minuscule 435 grains of black powder, the Moore rifle burned 800 grains of black powder (Fg) for a MV of 1500 fps. The bullet was conical. It weighed 3500 grains. This means that the Moore rifle delivered a muzzle energy of 17,491 foot-pounds! The terribly powerful 460 Weatherby, with its 500-grain bullet at 2650 fps MV gains a muzzle energy of 7799 foot-pounds. The Moore beats the 460 by almost 10,000 foot-pounds.

But the problems of power soon surface. Sure, that Moore rifle is a dandy one—to talk about. But not to shoot. And Sir Samuel Baker's big guns were also very nice. However, as we shall soon discover, recoil is not merely a factor of the rifle's muzzle energy, and those huge powder charges helped to create very uncomfortable recoil factors in Baker's rifles. The old-timer had to answer the problem of big punch with a very big caliber and a lot of bullet. And this worked, too. I doubt that we have any caliber today which will drop big game faster with the same bullet placement than Baker's 4-bore.

Big Bore vs. Small Bore

One of the greatest gun arguments in history is the famous big bore *vs.* small bore controversy. Two schools of thought developed, one in favor of bores large enough to house a colony of bats, the other in favor of velocity high enough to turn a bull moose into steaks on the spot. In my opinion, both schools lost out to a compromise. But before looking at that compromise, I think we should admit that there is a strong chain of truth binding both of the extremes above. Given terribly high velocity with good bullets, game can be dropped quickly. And given a monstrous bullet, game can be floored, too. It is painfully obvious that a combination of the two is the most powerful of all, a big bullet at high speed.

For the curious, let's examine one caliber in terms of what happens when we add velocity. Given a 25-caliber, we can shoot an 87-grain bullet at 1800 fps MV for a muzzle energy of 626 foot-pounds. If we up the MV to 2200 fps, the energy rises to 935 foot-pounds. At a flat 3000 fps we have the factory 250 Savage load and a muzzle energy of 1739 foot-pounds. And finally, let's boost that MV to 3600 fps. If we do that, the energy rises to 2504 foot-pounds. These very facts make the heavy bullet boys go mad. Here's why: that 87-grain bullet at 3600 fps, with its over 2500 foot-pounds of muzzle energy is "better" on paper than many of the buffalo cartridges. The famed 45-120 Sharps generally threw a bullet of about 500 grains weight at about 1500 fps for an energy rating of 2499 foot-pounds, no better than the little 25-caliber with its fast 87-grain bullet. And the tests I have run with the

45-70 show a 500-grain bullet at about 1200 fps for a muzzle energy of only 1599 foot-pounds.

Now comes the moment of truth—the hunter has stalked a grizzly bear and he stands 100 yards from the animal. He is hunting with a friend who is carrying one of his rifles while he himself carries the other. One rifle is a 25-caliber with an 87-grain bullet at 3600 fps MV; the other is a 45-caliber with a 500-grain bullet at 1500 fps, both offering about the same "paper ballistics." Which one does he choose to drop the grizzly? This *dilemma* is the epitome of the big bore *vs.* small bore controversy. In my opinion if the 87-grain bullet tears up plenty of lung area, it will do all right. But if bones are to be broken, give me the 500-grain bullet at lower velocity.

The Compromise

The big bore school still exists. So does the small bore school. The latter says that a 220 Swift will cleanly drop a deer every time. The former feels that a 7mm Remington Magnum is a good gopher gun, but sadly lacking in punch for game much more than deer-sized. And then there is that vast majority of shooters who comprise the backbone of American shooting. In their sensible way, they have taken to the middle ground. They use modest calibers shooting bullets of medium weight at medium velocity. The grand old 375 H&H Magnum is of this type. We see here no 500-grain bullet. We see here no 3600 fps MV. Instead, we have a bullet of perhaps 300 grains with a MV in the 2500 fps domain. It's a compromise. The 338 Winchester leans a bit more toward speed, but if we take a close look at the 338 round, we find bullets in the 250-grain domain at MV figures of around 2700 fps.

I believe we can cease our general glance at larger-than-deer calibers by believing in the compromise and then looking at some specifics. The object here is to list a few rounds which actually do make sense for hunters today, under today's hunting conditions on today's larger-than-deer game. Sure, any good shot with a lot of time to hunt for that perfect situation can bag big game with modest calibers. I do not refute that. Given the time and right conditions, my companion rifle, an old Model 94 30-30 loaded with various projectiles, such as the 190-grain Silvertip, will fill my hands on just about any hunt for any North American big game, with a few exceptions. I know that with my handload and the 190-grain Silvertip I can penetrate both shoulders of a bull elk at close range. But let's talk about the calibers which are more suited *by design* to do the work of harvesting larger-than-deer game.

Class-One Calibers

For the sake of pigeon-holing the rounds, let's divide the big game calibers into classes. I would call Class One that range of cartridge power which belongs to the 270/30-06 clan. Obviously, these are the in-between calibers, and by calibers we mean, of course, cartridge types. A lot of elk have been taken with 270/30-06 rounds. A lot of moose have, too, though certainly not as many as harvested by the

(Right) The caribou is not as large as an elk, nor as tenacious, but it is an animal which is bigger than a deer. This one took two 160-grain Nosler bullets from a well-loaded 270 Winchester before dropping.

(Right) Larger or tougher animals often require extra ballistic authority. This warthog was taken with a 308 Winchester round because the hunter had no other rifle at the time of the encounter with the boar and he wanted the trophy and meat. It took several shots to down the animal.

mundane 30-30. At one time, the world record polar bear was held by a man who used the standard 270 Winchester rifle. I believe he collected that bear with one shot, but I am going by memory on that score. Hosea Sarber, the well-known Alaskan hunter, dropped many bears and other big game animals with his 270 Winchester rifle. The 30-06 was the favorite round of record head hunter Grancel Fitz.

Without going into reams of explanation, I think we can summarize the status of the 270/30-06 class of cartridge for game larger than deer as all right, OK, serviceable, useful and acceptable. In the hands of a seasoned rifleman, these calibers become more than "all right," of course, and enter the domain of downright deadly. The handloader can turn both the 270 and 30-06 into more powerful rounds by reloading, too. An example is the 270 with a 160-grain Nosler bullet at 2900 fps MV, a load I used in Alaska satisfactorily. And our 30-06s have harvested elk with no problem using a 165-grain Speer bullet at 2900 fps or the 180-grain Hornady Interlock at 2800 fps MV.

The 270 Winchester and 30-06, both rightfully popular and even famous, serve well for game larger than deer. There is no doubt about it. Selection of the right bullet is important to the clean harvest of game in elk/moose class with these rounds, considering an everyday shooting situation where perfect bullet placement is not always possible. I like the 150-grain Sierra and 160-grain Nosler in the 270 for larger-than-deer game, and I think 30-06 handloads with strong bullets of the 165- to 180-grain weight are also very good. Jack O'Connor reported shooting totally through a large boar grizzly bear with a 180-grain 30-06 bullet and a common load in the 2700 fps MV range. Up close, where even more penetration is desired, special bullets up to 250 grains and more can be used in the 30-06.

Class-Two Calibers

This class contains all of the "hotter" 7mm Magnum types, mainly the popular 7mm Remington Magnum and its ilk. In Class One, we spoke of the 270 and the 30-06; however, these were representatives of a clan, a group of rounds, and the 280 Remington and a series of wildcat rounds also fit the same picture. The same goes for this grouping. Anything which throws a bullet of about 7mm diameter at about 3000 fps MV is to be considered a Class Two round for our purposes. My friend, John Kane, a big game guide who has taken many elk and seen many more harvested by his clients, believes strongly in the 7mm Magnum with handloads. He likes the 7mm Remington Magnum round loaded with a 175-grain Hornady Interlock bullet and a charge of H-870 powder for a chronographed MV of over 3000 fps.

Even so, John says that few elk hit with the 270/30-06 class of round, or the 7mm Magnum, drop on the spot with one shot, unless the neck or spine (same effect) is struck. On the other hand, he has never had to trail an elk very far after it had met up with a 7mm Magnum bullet of about 175 grains. Interestingly, he feels that a host of other calibers do just as well at up to 200 yards, but the 7mm Magnum takes over after that range and up to 300 yards or so (as far as he will shoot at elk or allow his clients to shoot). "At under 200 yards," John says, "the old 7mm Mauser and 7mm Magnum do the same on an elk with a chest hit. They both get your elk for you."

Actually, how much stronger is the 7mm Magnum over the old 270 or 30-06 load? Here is a fair and honest comparison, using the 180-grain 30-06 handload against the 7mm Magnum's 175-grain handload. We chose to show the reader two good strong handloads which illustrate the true potential of these two rounds. I am sorry to say that not all factory loadings for these two are up to par in the power department. I tested one factory 30-06 load which pushed a 150-grain bullet at just a bit over 2850 fps, certainly all right, but not nearly as powerful as a safe handload using the same 150-grain bullets and chronographing at over 3000 fps MV. One 7mm Remington Magnum load

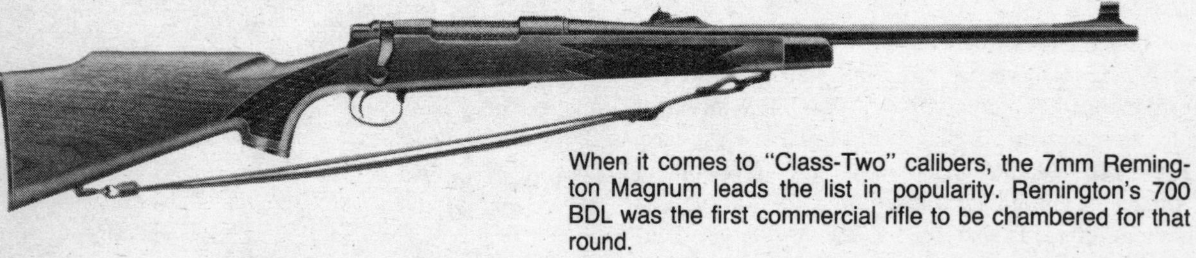

When it comes to "Class-Two" calibers, the 7mm Remington Magnum leads the list in popularity. Remington's 700 BDL was the first commercial rifle to be chambered for that round.

Handloads for the 30-06 and 7mm Rem. Mag.

Caliber	Bullet Wt. Grs. Type	Powder Wt. Grs. Type	Primer	Case	MV (fps)	ME (fpe)	MV (300 yds)	ME (300 yds)	Rifle Bbl. Length
30-06 Spring.	180 Hornady SP	56.0 IMR4350	9½ M Rem.	Win.	2812	3134	2250	2024	24″
7mm Rem. Mag.	175 Hornady SP	80.0 H870	9½ M Rem.	Win.	3041	3594	2400	2239	24″

These loads were taken from the *Hornady Handbook of Cartridge Reloading,* Volume II. They were chronographed in the author's own rifle. SP—Spire Point

The powerful 300 Winchester Magnum (left) and the 375 Holland & Holland have a worldwide reputation for dropping big game, *quickly.* Both cartridges also have superb reputations for accuracy.

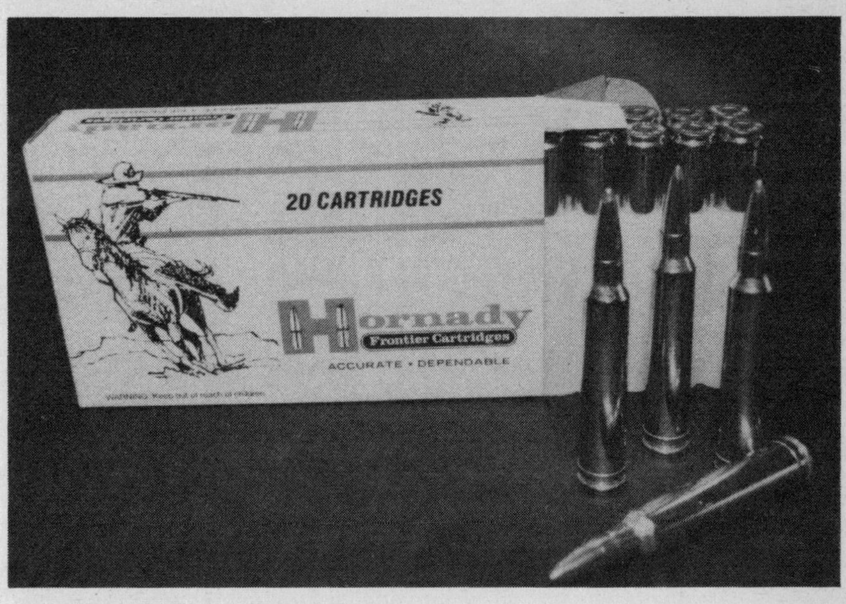

One excellent cartridge for larger-than-deer game is the 300 Winchester Magnum. These factory rounds are loaded with the 190-grain boat-tail spire point Interlock bullet. This particular bullet is ideal in the 300 Winchester Magnum because of its ability to hold together and penetrate deeply on large game.

pushed a 150-grain bullet at 2900 fps MV, which to me is a 30-06, not a 7mm Magnum. So we have turned to a couple of stout handloads, safe but up to par. Incidentally, not all factory fodder for the 30-06 and 7mm Remington Magnum turned up anemic figures. Some, however, did.

Over a range of 300 yards, using handloads in both the 30-06 and the 7mm Remington Magnum, with both loads chronographed, one can see that the 7mm Magnum is ahead of the 30-06 in "power" using these loads only, of course, by a margin of 215 foot-pounds. In my 7mm Remington Magnum rifle, using a 139-grain Hornady bullet, I have achieved a muzzle velocity of just over 3400 fps for a muzzle energy of 3569 foot-pounds. The remaining energy at 300 yards of this load is about 2160 foot-pounds. I offer this as a comparison between the 139- and 175-grain bullets.

I can sight in for a 3-inch high strike at 100 yards with the 175-grain 7mm Magnum load and be just about on the money at 275 yards and about 3 inches low at 300 yards. The 30-06, using the 180-grain load above, is sighted 3 inches high at 100 yards also, and is on at about 260 yards or so and perhaps 4 inches low at 300 yards. The tentativeness of the figures lies in the fact that it is sometimes difficult to determine the exact drop at longer ranges. Some of that "drop" is inherent in the actual group size. In other words, sighted right on at 100 yards, a 1-inch group means that some of the bullets will actually strike *below* the line of sight, even at the sighted-in distance.

But the figures are good enough to show the reader something. The 30-06, the old tired round that it may be, is still a lot of cartridge and certainly in the same circle of power occupied by the newer 7mm Remington Magnum. The latter has an advantage in that a 175-grain 7mm bullet is ahead of a 180-grain 30-caliber bullet in terms of ballistic coefficient. Using bullets of the same style, we find a Hornady 175-grain Spire Point worth .520 in terms of ballistic coefficient, while the 180-grain Hornady Spire Point is worth .431. This translates to, most likely, a little more penetration for the 175-grain 7mm bullet, at least in theory. In point of fact, using good handloads, the 7mm Remington Magnum ends up with a ballistic edge of about 10 percent over a range of 300 yards.

Class-Three Calibers

The "hot 30s" fill the bill here, and a perfect example is the 300 Winchester Magnum. We need not labor long to see where this cartridge lies in the scheme of things, for it compares very easily with the standard 30-06, since both use precisely the same bullets. From a 24-inch barrel, using the same 180-grain bullet which registered an average MV of 2812 fps in the above handloads, the 300 Magnum, using Winchester cases, Remington 9½M primers, and 71.5 grains of IMR 4350 powder, obtained a flat 3100 fps average MV for a muzzle energy of 3842 foot-pounds. At 300 yards, the 180-grain bullet is still churning along at a retained velocity of about 2450 fps for an energy rating of 2400 foot-pounds. The 300 Magnum has about a 15 percent edge over a range of 300 yards with this load as compared with the above 180-grain 30-06 load.

Sighted in to strike the target about 3 inches high at 100 yards, the 180-grain bullet is on at about 275 yards and a couple inches low at 300 yards. Certainly, this is flat-

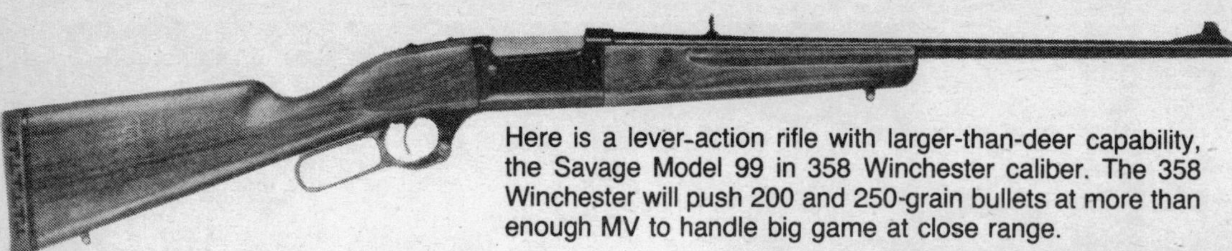

Here is a lever-action rifle with larger-than-deer capability, the Savage Model 99 in 358 Winchester caliber. The 358 Winchester will push 200 and 250-grain bullets at more than enough MV to handle big game at close range.

shooting. And with a 220-grain bullet, the 300 Winchester Magnum registers about 2700 fps MV for a muzzle energy of 3562 foot-pounds. Such a bullet will penetrate well. Such a bullet, when properly constructed, will certainly reach the vitals of a big game animal.

The 300 Weatherby Magnum is about 100 fps ahead of the 300 Winchester Magnum all the way. The 308 Norma Magnum is, for all practical purposes, in the same boat with the 300 Winchester Magnum. And a host of wildcat rounds in 30-caliber are also much the same in power as the above rounds. One sees on the surface very little difference between any of the numbers we have looked at so far. But I do not want to leave the impression that 10 percent means nothing in the case of the 7mm Magnum *vs*. the 30-06. It means something. It means 10 percent, and 10 percent is 10 percent. . . . We can say the same for the 300 Winchester Magnum and its 15 percent edge over the 30-06. Maybe 15 percent does not sound worthwhile. But many shooters feel that it is. No one can say for sure, but there must be times when 15 percent can make a difference on a big game animal which may not have been struck just right.

Federal offers the 338 Winchester round for larger-than-deer game. This is the Premium™ line of Federal ammo, and the 338 is loaded here with the 210-grain Nosler Partition bullet.

Class-Four Calibers

The larger-than-30 calibers dominate here, and that means the "third-of-an-inch" range, the 33s. The 33s are nothing new. Wildcat 33 calibers based on the 30-06 necked up and some of the magnum cases were known years ago. In fact, Winchester also had a rather fine 33 in its 33 Winchester, a round used by the famous bear and lion hunter, Ben Lilly. Our major concern, however, is with the 338 Winchester and its larger cousin the 340 Weatherby. The 338 Winchester can drive a 250-grain bullet at 2700 fps MV for a muzzle energy rating of 4048 foot-pounds. This is formidable punch. The same bullet is pushed out of the 340 Weatherby at a MV of 2850 fps for an energy rating of 4510 foot-pounds. Lots of punch.

I believe that we can see a true and realistic jump in "power" in Newtonian terms in the 338 Winchester over the standard 30-06. I have good friends who live in Alaska and hunt at least in part for their living, and who live by the 338 Winchester. They love it. They believe it to be almost as effective as the 375 Magnum on bears. The hunter who wants added punch over the 30-06 should think about the 338 Winchester. But he must also consider the big 30s, for they have proved themselves on game larger than deer for a very long time. Both the hot 30s and the 33s offer a hunter a true larger-than-deer cartridge.

Class-Five Calibers

There are many 35-caliber cartridges around, some actually in the deer/black bear realm. I think of the 35 Remington in this manner. Then there are the larger-than-deer 35s,

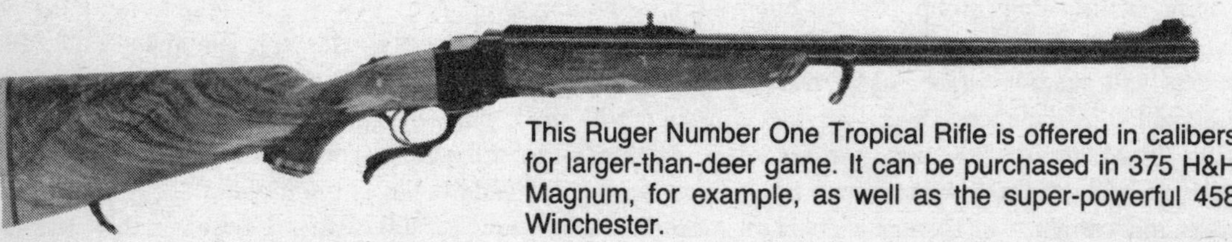

This Ruger Number One Tropical Rifle is offered in calibers for larger-than-deer game. It can be purchased in 375 H&H Magnum, for example, as well as the super-powerful 458 Winchester.

Val Forgett III poses with his Cape buffalo taken with a 375 H&H Magnum and a 416 Rigby. The 400-grain solid of the 416 made it through only a few inches of the buff before the jacket broke up. But an RWS solid from the 375 remained intact.

and I have used but one of these, the 358 Winchester. In my opinion, the 358 Winchester with the 250-grain bullet at about 2300 fps MV is entirely capable of breaking the shoulder on a moose or elk at reasonable ranges. The wildcat 35 Whelen (simply the 30-06 necked up to accept 35-caliber bullets), pushes the same 250-grain bullet at about 2500 fps MV. While the 358 load above earns a muzzle energy rating of 2937 foot-pounds, the Whelen with the same bullet at 2500 fps gains an energy rating of 3470 foot-pounds.

Then we have the larger 35s, those based on magnum brass. A perfect example is the 358 Norma Magnum with its 250-grain bullet at 2800 fps for a muzzle energy of 4353 foot-pounds. There can be no doubt that the 35s are capable of harvesting larger-than-deer game. They are, in the larger brass at least, ahead of the 30-06 clan in energy. In addition, the bigger bullet can mean more in terms of bone-breaking and long wound channels, especially the former.

Class-Six Calibers

The famous 375 H&H Magnum is in a class almost by itself. I used a 375 H&H in Africa and found it very good, though I was not terribly overcome by its performance on some of the game we got with it. I saw a 375 H&H Magnum down a large old Cape buffalo. Penetration was excellent, but the big bull did not fall in a heap from the first blow even though the shot was nicely placed in the shoulder area. I dropped a very large eland which the white hunters felt weighed a ton, and yet it did not crumble at the first blow from the 375. I think that the 375 H&H is to African and Asian hunting what the 30-06 is to American hunting, a versatile and useful caliber, capable of getting the job done very nicely, but in the back seat when it comes to other calibers. Most of the white hunters I spoke with felt that the 375 H&H was a wonderful round, but all agreed that for stopping the charge of a beast which was bent on making a lunch of the hunter, a 458 was indeed a better choice.

The 378 Weatherby Magnum is a 375 only more-so. While the 375 H&H drives its 300-grain bullet at a muzzle velocity of about 2600 fps for an energy of 4504 foot-pounds, the bigger 378 pushes the same 300-grain bullet at 2900 fps MV for an energy rating of 5604 foot-pounds. For game larger than deer, the 375s are basically more than is normally necessary, but the standard 375 H&H is often considered ideal for Alaska brown bear hunting and some hunters feel it is none too large for these bears. Harold Schetzle, professional Alaskan hunter, fired into a charging brown bear at only a few yards distance. His client also fired with the same caliber from the same distance. The bear simply crumpled, though the spine was intact. Both

The eland is a large and strong African antelope. This one took three 300-grain bullets from a 375 Weatherby out of a rechambered Model 70 Winchester. There was absolutely no external loss of body fluids from any of the three hits, all using soft-point bullets. Such an animal would be better hit *in the shoulder,* rather than in the chest itself.

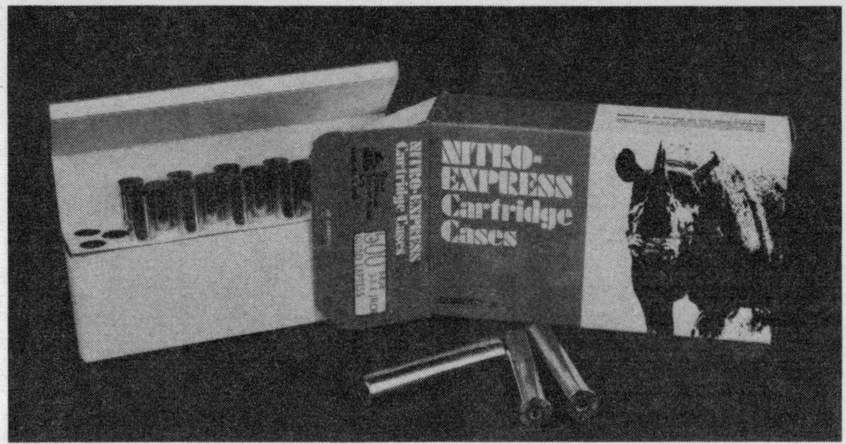

The B.E.L.L. Company offers brass for some of the big rounds, such as the 500 Nitro Express. The African hunter long ago found that there was no substitute for large, strongly constructed bullets at modest velocity, usually in the 2000 to 2400 fps range. Of course, when these big bullets are driven faster, such as seen in the 460 Weatherby, even more energy is derived.

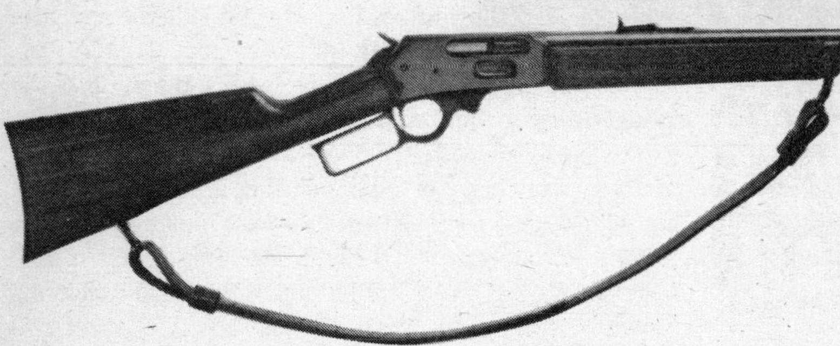

This Marlin Model 1895 rifle is chambered for the 45-70 round. It will fire a 500-grain bullet, and is definitely a candidate for larger-than-deer game.

men felt that the 375 was just right for this work. Neither felt it was too large as they saw the bear bolting toward them.

Class-Seven Calibers

These are the 45s, and I will speak briefly of only two of the many 45 calibers still available in one form or another to the shooter. First, we have the old, but revived, 45-70. In its original form, with a 500-grain bullet at about 1200 fps, it was not a powerhouse in paper terms, but many a hunter was very happy with its performance. In my research, I found that a good number of sportsmen also liked its bigger brother the 45-90. In the modern loading for modern updated firerarms, the 45-70 turns out to be a short-range powerhouse. I have owned three 45-70s, and I found them all to be ballistically very strong and somewhat limited as to actual application in the modern hunting field, at least in my hunting field. But I would own another without complaint if I were to live where larger-than-deer game abounded and I was in touch with that game on a regular basis. In short, the 45-70 in the Marlin Model 1895 rifle will push a 400-grain bullet at over 1800 fps MV for an energy of 2878 foot-pounds. The big-bullet shooting fans again feel somewhat cheated by the Newtonian formula here, for they consider the 400-grain to 405-grain bullet at 1800 fps a much more powerful ballistic force than paper shows.

They may be right. I have seen the work of a 400-grain bullet on game at close range, and it proved to be much more formidable than any 180-grain, 30-caliber bullet at velocities up to and including the magnum range. But the 45-70 is certainly no long-range round, so we have to consider that fact in our discussion of it. In the Ruger Number One rifle the 500-grain bullet will attain 1800 fps MV for an energy of 3598 foot-pounds. Again, I have seen this load at work. It's powerful at close range. I would prefer it over any hot-rock magnum round for close work. But American game is not always taken at close range, the high-velocity numbers continuing to reign supreme in the eyes of the American sportsman.

The 458 is mentioned because it is much more popular than anyone can account for; that is, popular among American shooters. I have one. I do not know why I do. I just do. A couple of my shooting friends own 458s. I imagine they are also at a loss to say why. But the 458 is a very fine round. It will push a 500-grain bullet out of the muzzle at 2150 fps for an energy rating of 5133 foot-pounds. The 458 is loved in Africa. All of the hunters I spoke with found the cartridge very useful on the largest of game, to include elephant.

My good friend David Drummond, born in South Africa, now a resident of Zimbabwe, Africa, has hunted native large game all of his adult life. He has total faith in the 458 against the charge of a Cape buffalo. Of course, even with the 458, the shot must break the animal down or pierce the brain. While David will not speak at length of his own adventures in the bushveld, his friends have told me many tales of his exciting encounters with buffalo and elephants, the 458 coming through every time—in the hands of this excellent and cool shot.

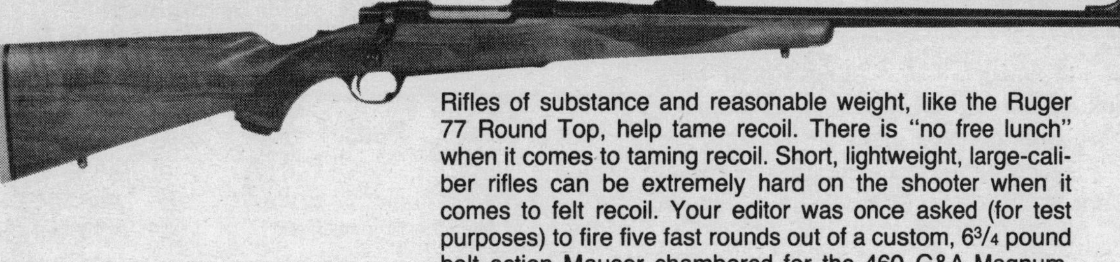

Rifles of substance and reasonable weight, like the Ruger 77 Round Top, help tame recoil. There is "no free lunch" when it comes to taming recoil. Short, lightweight, large-caliber rifles can be extremely hard on the shooter when it comes to felt recoil. Your editor was once asked (for test purposes) to fire five fast rounds out of a custom, 6¾ pound bolt action Mauser chambered for the 460 G&A Magnum. The recoil was *brutal.*

The big 8mm Remington Magnum is a powerhouse round meant for game larger than deer. It is not an all-around caliber, but rather a specialized cartridge.

And All the Rest

Obviously, we have not attempted to name and rank each popular caliber (round) being used today by the American hunter. But I think our pigeon-hole classes give a good idea of the larger-than-deer cartridges available today. There are many rounds which come close to duplicating each other. We did not cover the 308 Norma Magnum, but it is a fine round, about a 300 Winchester Magnum ballistically. The wildcat 8mm/06 is a strong one. So is the 8mm Remington Magnum.

The larger-than-deer cartridge serves a purpose all right, that added authority which can mean a little better results on the bigger game. We do not achieve an actual proportional upgrading of ballistic punch as we enter the domain of these rounds, for that is virtually impossible. For example, a nice buck deer may dress at 200 pounds, while an elk dresses at 600 pounds, three times as heavy. But we do not have rounds which readily offer up three times more energy when comparing deer cartridges with larger-than-deer cartridges.

Therefore, we settle for an increase in the 10 percent realm, or in the 15 percent realm when looking for a round which we think of as more at home in the larger-than-deer fields of hunting. And they do the job for us. In the hands of a truly cool shot, one must admit that these rounds are not a necessity. A hunter I know uses a 7 x 57 Mauser on brown bear in Alaska. He has certainly never lost a bear and is still alive to tell of his adventures. But he's a pro. I truly like the 7 x 57, but I'd prefer something larger for brown bear if I had my choice.

I also know a man who has taken several bull elk with special handloads out of a 30-30 rifle he enjoys carrying. He has never lost an elk. He has not even trailed one for more than a few yards after placing one of those well-loaded bullets on target. Tell him a 30-30 is too small for elk, and he will laugh out loud. But in the hands of a hunter who may not get into the field as often as this fellow does, I'd prefer seeing at least a 30-06 type round for elk, and maybe even a tad larger.

Over the years I have taken a fairly large number of game animals with muzzleloaders. Their remaining energies make modern calibers look like cannons. Yet, I have lost nothing nor have I chased anything down on a long trail after it was struck. The reason is that I have lived with the limitations of the black powder rifle, getting close and placing the ball in the right spot. Ah, bullet placement again, right? Of course, but I stick to my guns, if the pun will be excused, when I say that bullet placement is not always a clear-cut matter of fact. That is why people invented larger-than-deer calibers in the first place.

No Free Lunch

There is no free lunch, however, and the hunter who employs the round which transcends the power normally associated with the deer caliber is going to have to pay at least a small price for doing so. Sure, today there are many nice light magnum rifles around. Good strong stocks make them possible. But going too light in magnums means a lot of recoil. And recoil is a very important shooting topic, one the complete shooter should have grasped firmly in hand and clear in his head. The big rifle is wonderful in terms of what it will do to stop dangerous game or cleanly harvest any larger animal. But shooting the larger numbers is not always pleasant. Recoil can be tamed in many ways, of course, but before the shooter can deal with this problem he has to understand it.

Recoil Defined

Newton's Third Law of Motion fairly well defines recoil. The law states that, "for every action there must be an opposite and equal reaction." Given a force, we have a motion. Or, we can say that a force causes a motion. A force applied to any body is always met with a force *from* that same body. This sort of thinking can get cloudy on us, for we have to remember that when we are pushing on a wall, the wall is "pushing back" on our hand. In spite of the minimal elasticity in that wall, it is, in terms of physics, pushing back.

Rockets would not function if it were not for the facts inherent in Newton's law. We may sometimes think that a rocket works because its expelled gases push against the atmosphere. This is not so. If this were true, a rocket would fail to work at all in space. Yet it does work in space. Why? Because of Newton's Third Law of Motion.

If we have two objects of identical mass, one going 100 fps striking an object which is motionless, the second object will "take off" at 50 fps and the first one will be reduced from 100 to 50 fps. So we now have two objects at 50 fps. Remember this general concept, for it helps in understanding recoil, even though it is *not* a model we can directly apply to recoil theory. But the firing of the gun does produce energy, and it does give us an equal force in two directions. The bullet speeds away at X velocity, but the rifle does not take off at the same X velocity because it has so much more mass than the bullet. Even a 500-grain bullet for elephant hunting is but a tiny fraction of the weight of the lightest featherweight rifle.

Before the gun is fired, the gun and the projectile have zero momentum (momentum is mass times velocity). The tremendous forward momentum of the bullet must be compensated for by the backward momentum of the gun, which equals *recoil*. Recoil velocity of the gun is far less than the velocity of the projectile because of the unequal mass already alluded to above. The gun, in short, is a heck of a lot heavier than the bullet so it cannot be shot away at the same speed the bullet left the muzzle.

Recoil Energy 30-06 Springfield
Bullet: 180-grain/MV: 2800fps/Powder: 56.0 grains IMR 4350

6-Pound Rifle*	Recoil Energy:	32 foot-pounds
7-Pound Rifle	Recoil Energy:	27 foot-pounds
8-Pound Rifle	Recoil Energy:	24 foot-pounds
9-Pound Rifle	Recoil Energy:	21 foot-pounds

*This is not an invented figure. Dale Storey of DGS, Inc. of Casper, Wyoming has built a 30-06 featherweight which weighed 6 pounds.

Recoil Energy 458 Winchester
Bullet: 500 grains/MV: 2150fps/Powder: 80.6 grains W748

7-Pound Rifle**	Recoil Energy:	86 foot-pounds
10-Pound Rifle	Recoil Energy:	60 foot-pounds

**This is the actual weight of a 458 Winchester rifle fired by the author in Africa and owned by a gentleman from New Jersey.

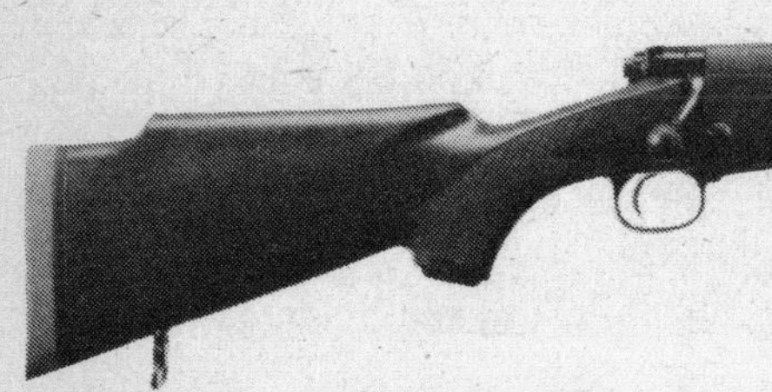

Here is the big Winchester Model 70 Super Express Magnum rifle, offered in 458 Winchester for game really larger than deer, right up to elephants and Cape buffalo and charging lions. The larger-than-deer round should be coupled with a heavy rifle like this one if the cartridge is a truly high recoil proposition, but many of the larger-than-deer rounds do not "kick" that badly in modest-weight rifles.

I think it is very important for the modern complete shooter to be able to quickly compute his recoil energy. It is useful because the shooter may be thinking about buying a particular rifle or having a rifle made up, especially a lightweight rifle. He should be able to determine quickly and easily just how much that rifle will "kick" him. The formula presented here is quite simple. Its explanation can be wordy, but mainly the figures are constants which work over and over again, and that is all the reader needs to work with in order to fully determine the recoil energy of his own rifle or a rifle he wishes to add to his battery.

Steps to Figuring Recoil Energy.

1. Multiply 1.75 times the weight of the powder charge in grains.
2. Add the product to the weight of the bullet.
3. Multiply the resulting figure times MV (muzzle velocity).
4. Divide the result by the weight of the gun in pounds.
5. Divide this figure by 7000 to reduce from grains to pounds so we can have the familiar foot-pounds of recoil figure to work with. This is not yet foot-pounds at this point in the formula but it will be. (It is recoil velocity at this stage.)
6. Now multiply the recoil velocity figure times itself.
7. Multiply the result by weight of gun in pounds.
8. Divide this product by 64.4 in order to obtain *recoil energy in foot-pounds*.

This is an important little formula and though it is a bit long, it's very easy to manage. With the resulting figure, the shooter can determine the actual foot-pounds of recoil of a given gun. It gives us a gauge to work with. Take a look at our recoil chart, and it will be easy to see why some guns kick a lot harder than others. Then take your own

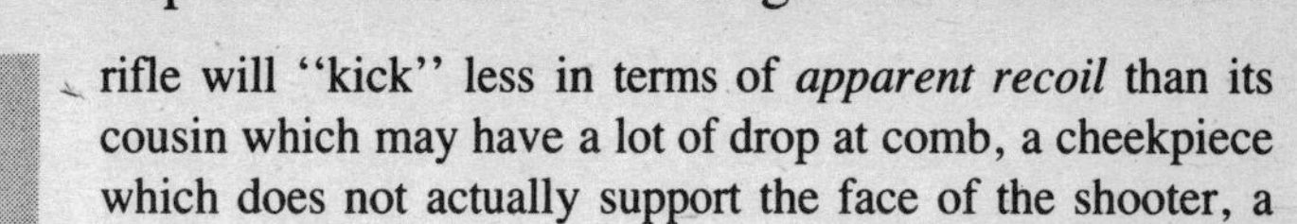

From left to right: 270 Win., 7mm Rem. Mag., 30-06 and the 300 Win. Mag. All of these rounds have been successfully used on the North American continent to down larger-than-deer size game.

hard kicker and use the formula to determine how much actual recoil energy it has. Remember, this is recoil energy. There is still *apparent recoil,* not so scientific but still very useful, which must be considered, too.

Felt Recoil vs. Recoil Energy

It is imperative that the shooter understand the difference between actual foot-pounds of recoil energy and "felt" recoil. The latter is sometimes called "apparent recoil." Examine this situation: You are standing in a boat. You have an oar in your hand. You want to toss the oar to someone on the bank. When you toss the oar toward the bank, the boat moves away from the direction the oar took. That movement of the boat was produced by recoil energy. In a rifle, we might have 20 foot-pounds of recoil energy. That is Newton's Third at work.

But how we *feel* that recoil is another matter. For example, we have two rifles. Both are in the same caliber using the same load and they weigh exactly the same. Recoil energy will be equal in both rifles. But felt recoil may not be. Let's assume that the first rifle has a generous buttplate with a recoil pad attached, a fairly straight stock, a stock which fits, no lines in the stock which will "up and smack the shooter in the face," and a good balance overall. This rifle will "kick" less in terms of *apparent recoil* than its cousin which may have a lot of drop at comb, a cheekpiece which does not actually support the face of the shooter, a narrow buttplate of steel, and so forth. I do not think we have to belabor this. However, we can see clearly that though both of these rifles deliver the same in foot-pounds of recoil energy, they will not *feel* the same when fired.

Other Important Factors

There is also noise to consider. I recently fired a 300 Magnum which was cut down to a 20-inch barrel. It barked like a ship's cannon and at dusk the flame from the muzzle could light a cigarette at 20 paces. The rifle was heavy, however, and the stock was well-constructed to offer recoil absorption. Yet, that rifle *seemed* to kick like an angry mule. Its high noise level was translated by the shooter's senses into a very negative and abusive "felt recoil." Sight is also a factor in apparent recoil. I am convinced that part of the reason shooters think a black powder rifle is a real kicker (and some of them are, partly due to the large powder charge) is the volume of smoke produced by the gun. It "looks" formidable. And the senses balk at such a sight.

In a way, it is our sense of well-being which is attacked when a firearm "goes off." It is, of course, a controlled explosion and explosions tend to scare us. But we learn to manage ourselves. We learn to stand steady, squeeze the trigger, and follow through in shooting. We convince ourselves of the truth—very few firearms will actually *hurt* us when they go off. They may tend to offend our senses, but they do not break our arms or give us nose bleeds, though there are some rifles which can do both.

We can wrap this up by advising the reader to approach recoil in those rifles chambered for larger-than-deer cartridges with an open mind, remembering that there are two types of recoil to consider, foot-pounds of recoil energy, or real recoil, and apparent or felt recoil, which is also very important. And we train ourselves to master both of these. Calibers in the range suitable for game larger than deer need not belt us in the chops if chambered up in the right rifle styles, meaning stocks that fit properly. We must remember that much of the recoil we think is taking a toll on our bodies is in fact taking a toll on our *senses*. We are not really being bodily damaged.

The Efficiency of Cartridges

One soon learns that as the cartridge case gets bigger and bigger, efficiency tends to fall off, caliber-for-caliber. In other words, if we have a 25-caliber case which holds a set amount of powder and we double that capacity, we certainly do not double our MV. In fact, as the powder charge goes up and up, efficiency generally goes down and down. And yet, adding powder may certainly be worth it, especially in those cartridges which we want to use on game larger than deer. I only bring up cartridge efficiency here because I believe the shooter should be aware that as he looks to those powerhouse rounds, he may not at all "buy" what he thinks he is attaining. He will get a lot more recoil, a lot more noise, a lot more blast and *maybe* enough additional MV to make all of these negatives worth the bother.

I see cartridge efficiency on three planes. There is an extreme in which actual performance is lost in the name of efficiency. Then there is the other extreme in which efficiency is tossed out the window so that a shooter can *think* he is gaining a lot of power just because he is getting banged around, both on the shoulder and in the ears. Third, there is that golden middle ground in which true cartridge efficiency does mean something. I want to pose an example of these three extremes.

Using the 270-caliber, I can think of three cartridges which serve as examples of the three conditions described above. First, there is the wildcat 270/300 Savage round. This is simply a 300 Savage case necked down to shoot .277-inch diameter bullets. It is more efficient than the standard 270 Winchester, but it is also a situation of giving up performance in the name of efficiency. I fully realize that some shooters opted for this wildcat so that they could fire .277-inch diameter bullets from the fine Model 99 Savage lever-action rifle, but I know of at least one case where the fellow chambered a Remington bolt-action in 270/300 Savage in the name of efficiency.

In our tests, the best we ever arrived at in terms of MV with a 130-grain bullet was 2700 fps in the 270/300 Savage. That is a far cry from the standard 270 Winchester. In the standard 270, I have been able to obtain 3125 fps MV with the 130-grain bullet. Now steps in a 270-caliber on the 7mm Mauser case. In my own chronographed tests, using the wildcat 270/7mm Mauser as produced in a custom rifle by Dale Storey, velocity with the 130-grain bullet was 3100 fps at the muzzle and case life was fine with nil case head expansion or primer pocket expansion, if you prefer that way of looking at pressure problems. Using about 10 grains less powder, the 270/7mm Mauser produced about the same MV as the standard 270 Winchester.

Overbore capacity is an often-used term and I don't always agree with the results given. Sometimes the theory is eclipsed by other factors. The 270 Winchester is slightly overbore capacity. That is, the 270 case will in fact hold or contain a bit more powder than will *efficiently* burn behind a .277-inch bullet. Naturally, burning rates of powders can offer help in an overbore capacity situation, but the condition exists all the same. I have seen a 270-caliber built on a 7mm Mauser case with no change in shoulder or capacity of the 7 x 57 in which the smaller case was right on the heels of the 270 Winchester. But this was in the 22-inch barrel for the 270/7mm Mauser and for the 270 Winchester. Given a 26-inch barrel, the 270 Winchester could not be duplicated by the 270/7mm Mauser.

Also, we can change a few other factors and have varying results. If the 270 Winchester is overbore capacity, then the 270 Weatherby Magnum is surely moreso. However, out of a 26-inch barrel the 270 Weatherby can gain 3300 fps MV using a 130-grain bullet. However, the rate of twist has been changed from the 1:10 of the 270 Winchester to the 1:14 of the Weatherby, thereby reducing bore friction and allowing a bit more powder to be used. Also, some freebore helps here. Pressure rises when the bullet engages the rifling prior to firing. This is why we are careful to handload our rounds so that they are of the proper length and not stuck into the beginning of the rifling lands prior to firing. If the throat is reamed so that it has freebore —a longer unrifled piece of bore so that the bullet does not contact the rifling for a greater length-again, greater powder charges can be utilized with resulting higher velocity.

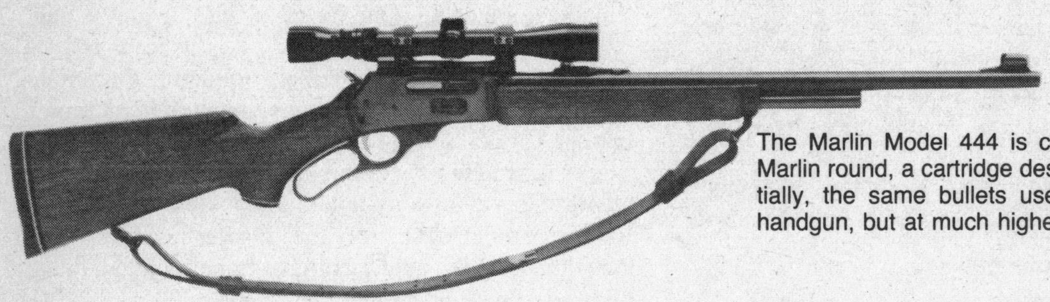

The Marlin Model 444 is chambered for the 444 Marlin round, a cartridge designed to shoot, essentially, the same bullets used in the 44 Magnum handgun, but at much higher velocity.

Finally, to look at one more example, we have the 264 Winchester Magnum round. In actual tests, using a 24-inch barrel in both cases, I have managed to come within 100 fps MV of the 264 Magnum with a 30-06 case necked to 264-caliber! And in both rifles, our best loads were used. There was no fudging as is sometimes the case when shooters try to make their point. Furthermore, my own 6.5 DGS (6.5mm Dales Gun Shop), a wildcat based on a blown-out 7mm Mauser case, pushes a 129-grain bullet at 3100 fps MV, which is to say, 270 Winchester performance or a bit better considering the higher ballistics of a 6.5 (.264-inch) 129-grain bullet as compared with a 130-grain. .277-inch bullet.

The Rifle

We have talked at length about cartridges for larger-than-deer game, but have not given a single statement concerning the rifle used to contain this cartridge. That was not an oversight. The reason I did not dwell on the actual rifle used for hunting game larger than the common deer is simply the fact that I do not think the rifle style matters very much. If the shooter can manage the rifle in the field and shoot it accurately, then we can ask for no more.

If I needed a rifle for extensive bear hunting, a situation which certainly does not exist these days anyway, I would think about picking up an old Model 71 Winchester lever-action and converting it to a blown-out case of one sort or another, or rechambering it to 450 Alaskan. On the other hand, there would certainly be nothing wrong with a good bolt-action rifle in 338 Magnum or 358 Norma caliber. Nor would I balk the slightest at the ownership of a Marlin Model 1895 in 45-70 or the similar 444 Marlin round.

When I was in Zimbabwe for the period of about a month, two persons were killed by Cape buffalo. Having hunted this species, I might suggest that a repeater of a large caliber would be in order. But that is Africa and African big game. I met a man who had been tossed by a buffalo. He was lucky. The old dame wheeled with the intent of coming back to tap dance on his hide, but the fellow got stuck in a thorn tree instead of coming back to earth; there he remained, scratched but safe.

No, I might opt for a 458 Winchester on such game, a repeater at that, maybe even a double barrel rifle. All in all, however, for American hunting, where elk would be the main game animal in the larger-than-deer class, even a single shot would suffice, and in fact work quite well. Pumpgun? The fine Remington slide-action is available in our Class-One cartridge domain. Semi-auto? Try a Browning or the Remington. I think any of these would be very good for the larger-than-deer rifle.

Many hunters will wonder about the exclusion of some of the larger-bored calibers which may seem to deserve status as rounds for bigger-than-deer game. The 44 Magnum is a good caliber, and many hunters use it. And yes, I am well aware that elephants and Cape buffalo have been dropped with 44 Magnum handguns let alone rifles. But we are talking the norm here, the average, the day in and day out situation, and I will add one more thing—the fellow who takes on a Cape buffalo or elephant with a handgun should have another fellow nearby, armed with a rifle, a big rifle, a *stopper*.

The arguments will rage on forever, it seems, concerning which caliber is best for what game. And the worn-out cliche, "It does not matter what you hit them with; it only matters *where* you hit them," will live on long after all of us have departed. But there is more to the cartridge story than bullet placement. Make no mistake—where you hit 'em is still the most important factor of all, and I would always vote for the firearm which can be handled and fired accurately over any round from any rifle which cannot be managed properly by the shooter. However, the reason various cartridges have been invented over the years is *suitability*. And the larger-than-deer rounds do have a purpose in the world of shooting.

Chapter 5

The All-Around Cartridge and Rifle

THE COMPLETE SHOOTER has spent a good deal of time, at least in this century, looking for a specific cartridge to be chambered in a specific rifle with which to hunt a great variety of game from varmints to moose. The cartridge is supposed to fit into something called "The All-Around Rifle." Some experts contend that the all-around rifle (and cartridge) is a myth, a butterfly of the imagination which goes flitting around in the heads of gunwriters and shooters alike. Actually, the all-around rifle and its round exist. A shooter can buy one rifle chambered for one of a select few cartridges and with that one rifle he can shoot for pleasure, punching holes in paper, or he can harvest game from rabbits and woodchucks to grizzly bears. In short, he can hunt any furred game in North America (and much of Africa's game, too) with this all-around rifle.

The only problem with an all-around rifle is the fact that it is very much like the worker who is called a "jack-of-all-trades," a fellow who can fix a car, paint a house or build a cabinet, all tolerably well, but who is an expert at nothing specific. So too the all-around rifle. It will get the job done on anything from long-range varmints to putting a moose into the freezer. But other calibers are better suited for varmint taking, and still other calibers are better suited for moose hunting than is this all-around number. What must our all-around rifle do? What tasks must it perform to qualify for that most coveted place in the American shooter's gun cabinet, the "all-around rifle slot?"

Attributes of the All-Around Caliber

Power

The all-around rifle must be chambered for a cartridge which has a very broad *range* of power. With this rifle, a shooter should be able to cleanly dispatch a cottontail rabbit at 30 paces without undue destruction of valuable meat, remove a woodchuck from a farmer's field at more than 300 yards, and then turn around and drop a bull moose at 30 paces in the deep forest. A lot to ask? You bet it is. But is it possible? Absolutely!

Trajectory

While the all-around rifle must serve well for close-range shooting, as well as that middle ground where most actual field shooting does take place, it must also qualify as a flat-shooting rifle, meaning that the exit velocity simply has to be high. None of the big bore heavy-bullet rifles qualify here. The all-around rifle must project its bullet over a parabola which offers the shooter "flat" trajectory out to at least 300 yards, meaning minimal hold-over or hold-under from zero to 300 yards or better.

Versatility Through Bullet Selection

The third major criterion for the all-around cartridge is a wide selection of bullet weights and shapes which can handle all of the demands asked of the all-around rifle. A cartridge which offers one bullet weight or two, such as the 348 Winchester, just to pick an example, is not going to qualify for our all-around rifle spot, even though it is a marvelous round for certain important shooting tasks.

The 7mm Remington Magnum

The 7mm Remington Magnum is the best all-around cartridge in the world, not because I say so, not because its fans say so, but because its ballistics prove the point. Obviously, its close brothers qualify equally for this honored position. By the way, this does not mean to imply that a shooter must run out and buy a 7mm Remington Magnum,

The 7mm Remington Magnum has, since its introduction in 1962, won the hearts and minds of hunters worldwide. It's the author's first choice as an all-around cartridge.

Where the use of a rifle is legal, turkeys can be taken with cast bullet squib loads out of a 7mm Rem. Mag. Meat destruction will be minimal.

or a 7 x 61 Sharp & Hart, or a 7mm Weatherby Magnum. Not at all. But we are talking about the all-around cartridge, and these hot 7mm cartridges prove themselves in this arena. Remember, too, the 7mm Remington Magnum is like that jack-of-all trades, adequate for many jobs, not necessarily perfect for any of them.

But with a 7mm Rem. Magnum a person can go out on Monday and put cottontail rabbits in the pot (with the handloads I will soon mention), and turn around Tuesday and drop a bull elk across a western canyon, all with the exact same rifle. That is versatility. It is the type of versatility gained from the now very popular family of 7mm Magnums.

Small Game and Wild Turkeys

The 7mm Remington Magnum will handle small game and wild turkeys with several squib loads. The *Lyman Reloading Handbook,* 44th Edition shows a load for the cast lead #287405, which weighs 154 grains in No. 2 Alloy. Yes, that seems to be, and is, a heavy bullet for small game, but at about 1600 fps MV, using 18.0 grains weight of Hercules 2400 rifle powder, this load shoots with total pleasantness, mild report and sufficient accuracy for any small game or wild turkey hunting. If a shooter prefers using a jacketed bullet for small game hunting, he can. Using a 120-grain jacketed bullet and 12 grains weight of SR 7625 rifle powder, the velocity will be not much more than the 22 Long Rifle, and since the 120-grain jacketed bullet is made tough enough to withstand muzzle velocities in the 3500 fps domain, it will not blow up at low velocity, meaning it will not destroy as much good edible meat as one may at first think. Or, a shooter can load a 123-grain cast bullet with gas check, such as the Lyman #287448 if he wishes a lead projectile. It's up to him. But I know for a fact that small game can be harvested cleanly with the above loads without undue meat destruction. I know because I have done it.

Eastern Deer/Black Bear/Boar

If I were to strike off on an eastern deer hunt, or a hunt for black bear, boar or other game in the eastern woods, I would not hesitate to carry a 7mm Remington Magnum on the hunt. I would load it with a 175-grain round-nose bullet but would not opt for the full velocity potential capable with that bullet. Instead, I'd probably load 46.0 grains weight of H-380 for a muzzle velocity of about 2400 fps. That would be a mild load, but more than adequate for close-range woods shooting on whitetail deer, black bear or boar. In fact, we have all but duplicated the actual ballistics at close range of the 30-30, which can fire a 170-grain bullet at about 2300 fps with handloads. And if the hunter/handloader wants a bit more *oomph* for his eastern woods hunting, he need only take advantage of the stronger, safe powder charges easily found in the popular handloading manuals.

Western Deer/Antelope/Sheep/Goats

These animals are sometimes taken at long range, especially in certain types of western terrain, though most can be stalked for close-range shooting as well. I have taken some of this game at various ranges with the 7mm Remington Magnum using two loads. These are a 139-140-grain bullet and 71.0 grains of H-4831 rifle powder, and the 160-grain bullet with a maximum charge of 80.0 grains weight of H-870 powder. The 139-140-grain bullet leaves the muzzle of my custom 7mm Rem. Mag. rifle at an average of 3400 fps with the above load, while the 160-grain bullet manages 3140 fps average from the same rifle, chronographed of course.

Other rifles may vary, but I tested a rifle belonging to a friend, Dean Zollinger, and Dean's 7mm Remington Magnum produced the same results as stated here. Think of it—a 139-140-grain bullet at 3400 fps MV. If one prefers to tame that load a little, he can reduce the charge a "mere" 3200 fps MV with this class of bullet, still entirely

An all-around rifle took this big buck for Dean Zollinger, who builds rifles of custom quality. Dean used a 7mm Remington Magnum to harvest this deer in big canyon country where long shots across the canyon were the only shots obtainable. In such situations, even the 7mm Magnum is not too terribly large for the task at hand.

When it comes to larger game like elk, moose or grizzly, the 7mm can be quite effective, especially with 160- or 175-grain bullets. The latter slug, backed by 80 grains of H-870 provides a muzzle velocity of over 3000 fps. This translates into a flat shooting round with excellent penetration. (Photo courtesy of the Wyoming Game & Fish Dept.)

adequate for the big game considered here. The 160-grain bullet may be an even better choice; it penetrates well and still shoots with a very flat trajectory.

Elk/Moose/Grizzly

The 7mm Remington Magnum can be used on this class of game with the above 160-grain load. Or, the 175-grain bullet can be put into play. I have used a maximum charge of 80.0 grains of H-870 rifle powder behind the 175-grain bullet for a MV of over 3000 fps. This means flat shooting, but it also means a bullet of good sectional density for deep penetration. Also, 175 grains, as modern bullets go, is about middle of the road in weight. Want a heavier bullet? Go to the Barnes 195-grain projectile. Barnes shows this bullet with a 2750 fps MV using 75.0 grains of H-870.

Varmints

No, the 7mm Remington Magnum is no varmint cartridge. But it will do the job if the shooter does his part. A 120-grain bullet can be pushed from the muzzle at 3500 fps. This sort of muzzle velocity with a bullet which is far less sensitive to wind drift than the littler hot shot 22 calibers, means high potential for long-range success in varmint hunting. The all-around round is that jack-of-all-trades, yes, and the 7mm Remington Magnum has too

Given its wind-bucking ability, 120-grain 7mm Rem. Mag. slugs are ideal for larger varmints at longer ranges. In the eyes of most, the 7mm Remington Magnum isn't a "1st choice" when it comes to varmints; however, it must be said that the cartridge can get the job done rather neatly. (Photo courtesy of the Wyoming Game & Fish Dept.)

much recoil and too much muzzle blast to make it ideal for varminting, but it will work. It will perform. It will do the job.

Summary of 7mm Remington Magnum Attributes

Power Range

In the well-loaded 7mm Remington Magnum we have a very wide range of power. There is the little 120-grain bullet at perhaps 1400 fps MV for a muzzle energy of 522 foot-pounds and the 160-grain bullet at more than 3100 fps MV for a muzzle energy over 3400 foot-pounds. Any round which can go from the 500 foot-pound category all the way up to the 3400 foot-pound category simply has to be called *utilitarian*. At 300 yards the 139-grain bullet can have *over a ton* of energy left.

Trajectory

With the 120-grain bullet at about 3500 fps MV, a 7mm Remington Magnum can be sighted to strike the target about 2.5 inches high at 100 yards. With this sighting, it will be about 3.5 inches high at 200 yards and about on the money a full 300 yards from the muzzle. At a full 400 yards distance, the bullet will drop only 8.5 inches, less than the standing height of some varmints. In effect, the 7mm Remington Magnum "shoots flat" out to 300 and even 400 yards for all practical purposes, requiring no creativeness whatsoever in hold-over on large game until after 400 yards. You can't ask for much more.

But you will get more if you want it. Think about the 160-grain bullet for a moment. Sighted 3 inches high at 100 yards, it is on target at about 280 yards, and if firing at game of deer size, we can, again, aim about "on" up to 350 yards, even 400 yards depending upon the size of our quarry. The 139-grain bullet at 3400 fps MV sighted 3 inches high at 100 yards is about 3.5 inches high at 200 yards and right on the money a full 300 yards from the muzzle. At 400 yards, this bullet with the above starting velocity strikes only about 8.5 inches low. On a big mule deer buck, a shooter could hold high on the center of the chest and still make a hit low in the chest from a distance of 400 yards. I do not know what more we could ask for in flat-shooting performance.

Versatility Through Bullet Selection

The 7mm Remington Magnum is capable of accurately firing bullets from as light as 120 grains up to 195 grains weight. Certainly, this is an adequate selection as far as projectile versatility is concerned.

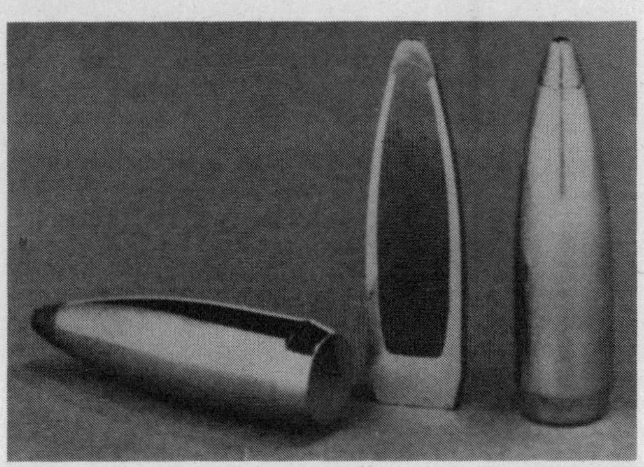

(Left) The all-around rifle caliber picked by the author is the 7mm Remington Magnum, and here is but one of the many bullets available for this versatile cartridge. It is the Nosler solid base 7mm 120-grain Spitzer, a good deer bullet.

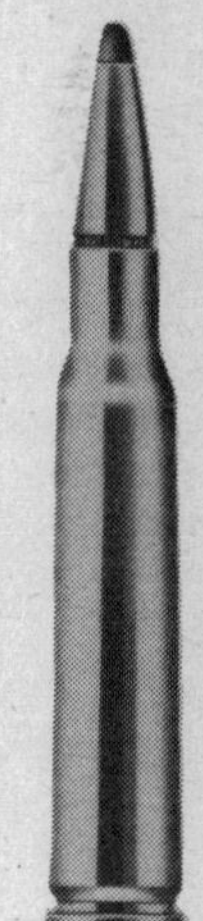

The very old 7mm Mauser was selected as an all-around caliber by the author. Although this cartridge appears to be almost too small for larger-than-deer sized game, it has a long track record on big game animals. Some veteran shooters feel it is sufficient for game of elk and moose size due to its mild recoil and consequent ease of handling in the field even in a lightweight rifle.

Other Choices

There are going to be many shooters who prefer other cartridges for their own all-around rifles. I am not at all locked into the 7mm Rem. Mag. as the only all-around cartridge for North American shooting; therefore, we will take a look at *some* of the other contenders for the coveted title of "all-around cartridge." Furthermore, experience is indeed a wonderful teacher, and this fact applies strongly to hunting and shooting. With experience backing him up, a shooter/hunter may tend to be more cool in the big game field, more steady in small game or varmint shooting, and because of these pluses, he may be able to sift a lot of performance from some of the following rounds, which someone else might consider less than perfect for the job. This is not to take away from the few "other choices" listed here, for all of them are time-tested and superb.

7mm Mauser (7 x 57mm)

The very old 7 x 57mm has taken game from rabbits to elephants in the hunting fields. Many famous hunters found the 7 x 57 adequate on a variety of game. The nice thing about this round is its mild recoil and report, while seeming to get so much "work" accomplished. Very light, handy and neat rifles can be built in 7mm Mauser caliber, whereas our aforementioned 7mm Remington Magnum may require just a bit more heft to overcome its tendency to recoil with authority. That point can be argued either way, of course. Some shooters, including this one, would say that recoil during the act of shooting at big game is a factor disregarded by the shooter. I have never consciously felt the recoil of a rifle when I was firing at game. Flinching, I think, is generally learned during practice sessions or sighting in phases of shooting. There's a moral here: use light loads for practice and benchrest shooting.

Small Game and Wild Turkeys

The 7mm Mauser is at home in the small game field. The 123-grain cast bullet, from a #287448 Lyman mould using No. 2 Alloy, and a charge of 17.0 grains of Hercules 2400 will give you about 1700 fps. Once again, one may use the 120-grain jacketed bullet for less disruption of tissue, but with head shots, this economical and accurate cast bullet will do nicely. It will not badly tear a wild turkey with correct bullet placement in the pinion area (where wing joins body), or in the lower abdomen, though the bird should be retrieved by the hunter and eviscerated immediately if the latter shot is used. Wild turkeys can be tough. I saw one try to run off after being hit with a 243 Lynx bullet.

Eastern Deer/Black Bear/Boar

The 7mm Mauser can be loaded to its normal safe maximum status for all of this game. A typical load would be the round-nose 175-grain bullet normally used for woods hunting, though one may question any advantage here in "brush bucking," at about 2500 fps MV. Many powder charges will deliver this sort of MV out of the 7 x 57mm round, one example being 38.5 grains of IMR 4895 rifle powder. With this load and its muzzle energy of over 2400 foot-pounds, the 7mm Mauser is entirely adequate for the above-mentioned game. Another load which has worked well for me in the 7 x 57 (and I did own a rifle in this caliber) was 50.0 grains of Winchester 760 with the 154-grain bullet for a muzzle velocity of a flat 2700 fps. With a muzzle energy just shy of 2500 fpe, this load is entirely adequate for woods whitetails and the black bear.

Western Deer/Antelope/Sheep/Goats

The 139-140-grain 7mm bullet can be driven at about 2900 fps with a maximum charge of 53.0 grains of IMR 4350 rifle powder. This load offers sufficient flatness of trajectory with enough remaining energy to take the above game at the longer ranges. Remember that one of the factors in recoil was the amount of powder burned. Of course, this is also a factor in muzzle blast, and the little 7 x 57 case with its modest powder charges offers good MV and energy without undue recoil or noise. One will find that even in a light rifle, the 139-140-grain bullet and the above maximum charge will be pleasant to shoot. It's a very fine load. I am convinced that the 7mm Mauser, with this load, is good for deer, antelope and similar game up to 300 yards, even beyond, taking decent bullet placement as a foregone conclusion.

Elk/Moose/Grizzly

The 7 x 57 would not be my number one choice for these game animals, but any all-around cartridge is a *compromise*, and as such, we simply have to make up for any shortcomings through more careful hunting and bullet placement. I know of a person who hunts "Kodiak" bear with a 7 x 57 using 154-grain bullets, and he is satisfied with the results. I'd want more on these bears for a day-in-day-out out hunting situation, but obviously the 7 x 57 can do the job with good bullet placement.

The 7 x 57 can push a 160-grain bullet at about 2700 fps MV with a charge of 49.0 grains of Winchester 760 powder. I have chronographed 2700 fps with IMR-4320, too, using 42.0 grains of that rifle powder. However, the latter was out of a 26-inch barrel, the former from a 22-inch barrel. Either way, we do have a very fine bullet at a reasonable MV with good downrange trajectory and remaining energy. The 175-grain 7mm bullet leaves the muzzle of a 22-inch barreled 7mm Mauser at about 2500 fps using a maximum charge of 47.0 grains of Winchester 760 rifle powder.

Varmints

The venerable 7 x 57 will scoot a 120-grain bullet from the muzzle of a long barrel at 3100 fps using 45.0 grains of IMR-4064 rifle powder. Obviously, this is sufficient velocity to insure relatively flat trajectory. Of course, we always think of varmint hunting as super long-range work, and that is what we generally make of it, primarily for the sake of marksmanship. However, some varmint hunting is for ranch or farm protection, and it is surprising how many varmints are bagged with the 30-30 annually. The 120-grain bullet at 3000-3100, obviously, is no also-ran for varmints, even though this load would not constitute my idea of a truly fine varmint-taker. But remember—compromise; it's the name of the all-around cartridge game.

Summary of 7mm Mauser (7 x 57mm) Attributes

Power Range

We have 120- to 123-grain bullets in the mild 500 foot-pound category for small game, wild turkey or other similar application. And on the other end of the 7mm Mauser continuum is a 160-grain bullet at a MV of 2700 fps for an energy rating of almost 2600 foot-pounds. The 175-grain bullet at a MV of 2500 fps out of a 22-inch barrel earns an energy tally of about 2429 foot-pounds. At 300 yards from the muzzle, the 139-140-grain bullet which began its journey at 2900 fps with 2615 foot-pounds of energy is still cranking along at a little over 2200 fps with an energy of approximately 1500 foot-pounds. *That's not bad.*

Trajectory

With the 139-140-grain bullet at 2900 fps MV, the 7mm Mauser can be sighted to strike the target 2 inches high at 100 yards, and it will be back in the black at about 225 yards and about 6 inches low at 300 yards. Therefore, from zero to about 325, possibly 350 yards, no appreciable holdover is required for a chest strike on a deer. I think this puts the 7mm Mauser in the all-around category trajectory-wise.

Versatility Through Bullet Selection

No need to labor here. The 7mm Mauser shoots the same bullets already listed for the 7mm Remington Magnum. This list shows us many different offerings, not only in bullet weights (from at least 120 to 175 grains), but also in bullet types, such as the 130-grain Speer Spitzer, the 154-grain Hornady Interlock, and Sierra's 150-grain Matchking. Incidentally, Speer makes a 115-grain hollow point which would be a good one for varmint hunting. In a 22-inch barreled rifle, the 115-grain bullet has been chronographed at just short of 3100 fps MV using a maximum charge of 55.0 grains of Norma 204 rifle powder.

270 Winchester

The 270 Winchester has been a favorite cartridge of mine since boyhood days when I got lucky and took my first big whitetail buck with one at the outlandish range of about 30 paces. The cartridge has been used on all manner of big game all over the world. In fact, as I recall, the world record polar bear was at one time held by a man who took the trophy with one shot from a 270 Winchester. Russell Annabel felt that the 270 was fine for Alaska, and he bagged many a moose with it. The great Colonel Townsend Whelen used the 270 and spoke highly of it. I believe the 270 was the top favorite of that fine writer John Jobson. And certainly the late Jack O'Connor did more to promote the 270 Winchester than any other gunwriter. There has been great controversy, however, among 270 lovers and 270 haters. Be that as it may, the record speaks clearly—the 270 Winchester is an all-around cartridge.

Small Game and Wild Turkeys

The 270 fires a .277-inch bullet—a bit smaller than the 7mm .284-inch bullet. In my opinion, this allows for some interesting 270 squib loads. A 117-grain cast bullet, using Alloy No. 2 in a #280468 mould, can be pushed along at a MV of about 1500 fps with a charge of 10.0 grains of SR-7625 rifle powder. Here is good close-range ammunition for the wild turkey, and for small game. A shooter could also use a 100-grain jacketed bullet with the same charge for similar MV. With proper placement of projectile, the fine meat of turkey or small game need not be unduly lost.

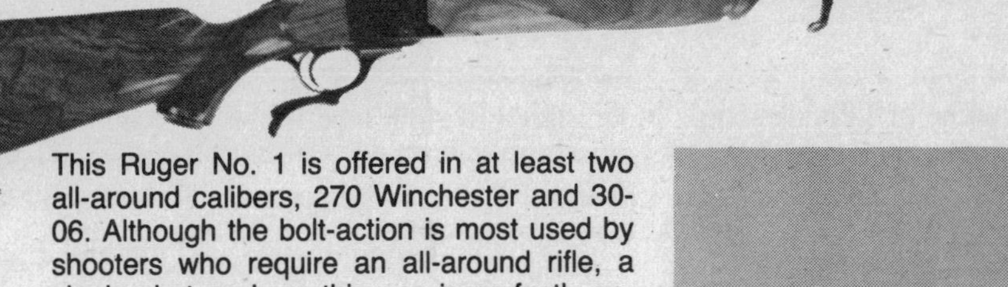

This Ruger No. 1 is offered in at least two all-around calibers, 270 Winchester and 30-06. Although the bolt-action is most used by shooters who require an all-around rifle, a single shot such as this one is perfectly acceptable for the job.

(Right) When it comes to high-country sheep or plains-roaming antelope, the 270 Winchester has what it takes, sufficient velocity and flat trajectory. The 270 has developed an excellent reputation for handling western game. Wyoming Game & Fish employee Al Langston took this nice antelope with his Ruger 77 in 270.

A favorite of the legendary Jack O'Connor, the 270 has developed a great following since it was introduced in 1925. O'Connor felt it was the best elk medicine ever made available to the shooting public.

Eastern Deer/Black Bear/Boar

We do not think of the 270 Winchester as a "back-East" rifle/cartridge, but it can be, using our sense of compromise with our investigation of the all-around rounds. A 170-grain bullet at about 2600 fps MV using 54.0 grains of H-4831 is just fine for woods hunting of deer, black bear and boar. Without the availability of this bullet, one can select the 160-grain slug, pushing it out at about 2600 fps MV with 50.0 grains of IMR-4831 rifle powder. No bullet eats brush in spite of what we may tend to think, a point easily proved to anyone's satisfaction if he will try to hit a target which lies behind a good screen of bushes. So I find the 270 feasible for the woods.

Western Deer/Antelope/Sheep/Goats

The 270 Winchester excels here. It is most at home in the West on the above game. The recoil, in spite of the 270's slightly overbore nature, is not bad, and it can be shot accurately with a flat trajectory and good remaining energy. The time-tested 130-grain bullet is a very good one for deer/antelope "out West," and my old handload is 60.0 grains of H-4831 rifle powder for about 3100 fps out of a 24-inch barrel. Another good bullet is the 140-grain boat-tail at a flat 3000 fps, which can be obtained with a maximum charge of 58.0 grains of H-4831 powder. This is a round well-suited for long-range work. No one can go wrong with it on deer and similar western game.

Elk/Moose/Grizzly

On the one hand, I don't think of the 270 Winchester as ideal for elk or moose or grizzly, but apparently a good many hunters have achieved success with the 270 on such game. I have taken caribou at rather long range with the 270 Winchester, using both the 130- and 160-grain bullets on this game animal. The latter (a Nosler offering) is better for caribou at 300 yards or so. Loaded with 57.0 grains of H-4831 for close to 2900 fps MV, the 270 with its 160-grain bullet did a good job on caribou to well over 300 yards. A MV of almost 2900 fps was gained with 54.0 grains of IMR-4831.

For a very long period of time, I used the 150-grain Sierra boat-tail bullet in the 270 Winchester with a lot of success, top accuracy and good penetration on game. I purchased several boxes of this bullet at one time, and I have always felt that this particular lot of slugs had harder jackets; the bullet proved itself more than adequate on larger-than-deer game. The 150-grain Speer was used in a 270 by a friend who bagged several elk without a single complaint about bullet or cartridge performance.

Varmints

Of the rounds mentioned thus far, as well as the ones yet to come in our brief encounter with a few all-around cartridges, the 270 shines brightest in the varmint field. The 270 can use a 90-grain hollow point bullet at a MV of about 3600 fps, one good load being 54.0 grains of IMR-4064. I have shot this load a number of times. Accuracy was good. Trajectory was flat. The 100-grain bullet can be driven along at a MV of about 3400 fps. A maximum load of 54.0 grains of H-380 will do this. I also like the 110-grain hollow point at 3300 fps MV, a load which is easily achieved with 57.0 grains of Winchester 760 powder. The 110-grain load shoots very flat and is not nearly as sensitive to wind as the 22-caliber varmint calibers, though I still like the latter better than the 270 for most varminting.

In the wide open spaces of the West, the 270 toting deer hunter can easily sharpen his skills on off-season varmints. With the right load, the 270 can be dandy on varmints.

Summary of 270 Winchester Attributes

Power Range

With its 117-grain cast bullet at a MV of 1500 fps, the 270 delivers a light 585 foot-pounds on the low end of the power scale. On the upper reach of the 270's punch, the 150-grain bullet at 2900 fps is worth a muzzle energy rating of 2800 foot-pounds, while the 160-grain Nosler bullet at close to 2900 fps MV gains an energy of just shy of 3000 foot-pounds. Furthermore, I have chronographed the 150-grain bullet at a flat 3000 fps which would give a muzzle energy of about 3000 foot-pounds. The 150-grain bullet at a MV of about 3000 fps is moving at about 2350 fps for a retained energy at 300 yards of about 1840 foot-pounds, the better part of a long ton.

Trajectory

The 270 Winchester is a flat-shooting number. With the 130-grain bullet at a MV of 3100 fps, the 270 can be sighted 3 inches high at 100 yards. It will land on the target about 4 inches high at 200 yards, on the money again at about 275 yards and about 3 inches low at 300 yards. I have tested this many times, the above figures being about average. The 150-grain bullet at 3000 fps MV is sighted for very much the same range. For varminting, using the 110-grain Hornady hollow-point, for example, the 270 shooter can sight his rifle 3 inches high at 100 yards, and it will be on at 300 yards, about 10 inches low at 400 yards. Varmints can be taken, certainly, up to 350 yards with the 270 varmint load.

Versatility Through Bullet Selection

The 270 Winchester is extremely versatile in its bullet offerings. Several cast bullets can be made for this caliber. We have bullets in jacketed style from a mere 90 grains up to 160 grains and even 170 grains and more in special-order propositions. There are 150-grain round nose bullets for those who would like to load the 270 for close-range work using a round-nose bullet (the 30-30 ballistics can be just about duplicated in the 270 using 40.0 grains of IMR-4064 and a 150-grain slug for about 2400 fps MV). The 140-grain bullet at 3000 fps MV, for example, is a compromise which lands right in between the 130- and 150-grain bullets. I used 140-grain MGS bullets (no longer made) in the 270 back in the late 1950s when I was first becoming serious about hunting for trophy white-tailed deer and found this bullet weight fine in the 270 Winchester.

The all-around rifle must be capable of harvesting the thin-skinned smaller big game species as well as the larger, tougher animals. A rifle such as the 7mm Remington Magnum or 30-06 can be counted on for long-range shooting of game in the antelope size, and yet both can be loaded for moose as well.

(Right) Be they turkeys, rabbits or squirrels, all have been taken with cast bullet squib loads for over 75 years. The '06 can be easily tamed down to 32-20 velocities for the taking of small game.

30-06 Springfield

Many shooters will insist that it is the 30-06 which deserves the accolades for "number one all-around cartridge." I'd not truly argue very long and hard on the subject, for my heart wouldn't be in it. I, too, love the 30-06 round and consider it extremely versatile. I will stick to the 7mm Remington Magnum, however, as my *number one choice*; for nothing which can be put through a 30-06 comes up to *quite* the authority of the 7mm Remington Magnum, and the latter is also flatter-shooting, a better varmint number, and a slightly better long-range big game taker as well. The 7mm Remington Magnum simply has the ballistic edge, at least on paper.

But the 30-06 *is* a "wonder cartridge." There have been reams of paper written on the '06, and also written on the long-standing controversy concerning the 30-06 *vs* the 270. I have had my share of fun with this fight myself. It's an enjoyable matter to ruminate over, and one which writers and shooters have had fun with almost from the first day the 270 came out, in about 1925. I would take either the 270 or 30-06 on just about any North American hunting trip with full confidence in either cartridge. But I guess if one wants to stick to the chronographs and charts and ballistics, the 30-06 comes up a slight winner over the 270 all-around.

Small Game and Wild Turkeys

The 30-06 can be made to duplicate the old 32-20, a round many of the old-timers thought was just right for wild turkey hunting. I think these old hunters may have been right about the 32-20, and if so, then the 30-06 squib loads must also be fine for the big birds. To be specific, how about a 125-grain cast bullet with a gas check, #311465, cast in Alloy No. 2, Lyman mould, and using 10.0 grains of PB for about 1500 fps MV? Surely, this load would do well for small game with head shots as well as for Benjamin Franklin's bird.

The 30-06 certainly qualifies as the all-around caliber, even though, for very specific and small reasons the author picks the 7mm Remington Magnum as the apex in all-around rounds. Here, Bill Fadala poses with a "stag" buck taken with his 30-06, a rifle which just happens to come up with groups as small as 1/2-inch for three shots at 100 yards. Bill likes a strong 165-grain bullet for most of his 30-06 hunting.

Given the excellence of today's specialized .308-inch game bullets, the old '06 is more than capable of handling high-country sheep and goats. (Photo courtesy of the Wyoming Game & Fish Dept.)

Eastern Whitetail/Black Bear/Boars

It's no trick to load the 30-06 to 300 Savage or 30-30 ballistics. In fact, one can use the 170-grain 30-30 bullet in the 30-06 if he so desires. With a charge of 42.0 grains of IMR-4895 rifle powder, muzzle velocity in a 24-inch barrel will be about 2350 fps, whereas a top-end load with the same bullet out of the 30-30 with a 20-inch barrel will achieve about 2300 fps. Nobody can argue against the use of the 30-06 for eastern woods hunting, not only in special handloads but also with good factory fodder. How about a 180-grain round nose from the factory, for example? It's a good one, as are many other loads.

If a hunter feels more at home with a heavier bullet for close-range work, there is nothing wrong with the 220-grain bullet in either factory form or handload. A 220-grain bullet can be pushed along at a modest MV too, for those shooters who do not feel the need for the top end of power from the 30-06 for deer hunting in the woods where shots are likely to be under 100 yards. Such a load is 41.0 grains

Marmots like this western rockchuck are more than manageable with a 30-06, especially when the ammo is loaded with 100- or 125-grain hollow point bullets. It's bullet selection that makes the venerable '06 so versatile. It will handle everything from varmints to venison—easily.

of IMR-4064 for a MV of about 2100 fps out of a 24-inch barrel.

Western Deer/Antelope/Sheep/Goats

Much to the surprise of those who begin a study of the 30-06, it is quite capable of flat shooting. The 150-grain bullet is a good one for this cartridge, and those who think that a .308-inch projectile in 150 grains weight is quite inferior (ballistically) are wrong. On paper, the 150-grain bullet shows a sectional density of .226, not terribly impressive, but in a sharp profile, spitzer or spire point, this bullet "carries up" quite well in fact. The 150-grain bullet can be driven from a 30-06 case with roughly the same muzzle velocity given the 130-grain bullet out of the 270 Winchester case, 3100 fps. Using 63.0 grains of Winchester 760, we in fact achieved 3115 fps MV out of our own 30-06 with a 24-inch barrel and 150-grain spire point bullet.

But hold on. With a 165-grain Speer boat-tail and 60.0 grains of the same Winchester 760 powder, the same 24-inch barreled rifle achieved a MV of a flat 3000 fps average. The latter has become my favorite load out of the 30-06 for western hunting. The sectional density of a 165-grain .308-inch bullet is .248 and Speer shows a ballistic coefficient of .477 for this bullet. There is no reason for anyone to shy away from the 30-06 cartridge for western hunting for game of the deer, sheep, antelope and goat variety.

Elk/Moose/Grizzly

The 180-grain .308-inch bullet comes out of a 24-inch barreled 30-06, in our 30-06 at least, at an average MV of 2812 fps. This is with 56.0 grains of IMR-4350 rifle powder. A charge of 58.5 grains IMR-4831 delivers the same velocity with the same 180-grain bullet in the same rifle. If the hunter finds that too little in terms of bullet weight for his own preference, he can elect for a 200-grain bullet at about 2700 fps MV using 57.0 grains weight of IMR-4831 rifle powder. If still more bullet mass is desired, there is the standard and easy-to-find 220-grain bullet, leaving the muzzle at a 2600 fps rate with 54.5 grains of IMR-4350 pushing it; the same can be achieved with a maximum load of 57.5 grains of IMR-4831 powder.

Varmints

No round we have spoken of here is a truly fine varmint number when one considers the recoil factor and excessive power inherent in these all-around cartridges. In my opinion, the 30-06 is no varmint round. But in the sense of compromise, it will get us by. One can load a 110-grain bullet at 3400 fps using 62.0 grains of Winchester 748 powder. That bullet will maintain a trajectory flat enough for varmint shooting, though I must contend that due to the 110-grain slug's rather low sectional density, the 130-grain bullet at 3300 fps MV, also achieved with Winchester 748 powder, a 58.5-grain charge, will carry up better and offer good windbucking ability. The 30-06, in short, can be used for varmint hunting.

Summary of 30-06 Attributes

The 30-06 has long been considered king in the all-around caliber field, though I can show that the 7mm Remington Magnum is a step, albeit a small step, ahead of this round in terms of total versatility. However, anyone who owns a 30-06 can be perfectly comfortable with his choice of all-around caliber. It is a fine round. I guess it always will be as long as powder is available to push projectiles from gun barrels.

The 30-06 is one of the very best of the all-around rounds. Here is a Remington factory round using the fine 165-grain Core-Lokt bullet.

The all-around cartridge is one which uses a variety of bullet weights at many different velocities. The 30-06, shown here in the Winchester factory load, does well with a 165-grain bullet, so well that the factory now offers this bullet weight to the shooter. This is the 165-grain Winchester Pointed Soft Point load.

Power Range

The 125-grain lead bullet at 1500 fps MV is worth 625 foot-pounds. Of course, this is far more than is necessary for small game hunting or wild turkey taking, but we once again plead that in the name of versatility we accept this load as useful for the smaller quarry. At the other end of the story the 165-grain bullet at a flat 3000 fps gains a muzzle energy of 3298 foot-pounds. What's more, that bullet is still kicking along at 2300 fps a full 300 yards out for a whopping 1939 foot-pounds of energy, darn near a full ton. That is power. Of course, just to continue my defense of the 7mm Remington Magnum as the all around champ, I must point out that its 175-grain pointed profile bullet is doing a bit over 2400 fps at 300 yards for 2239 foot-pounds of remaining energy, not a lot more, but *more*.

Trajectory

With a 150-grain bullet at about 3100 fps MV, the 30-06 can be sighted in 3 inches high at 100 yards, and it will be back on target at about 260 to 270 yards and maybe 4 inches low at 300 yards. That's pretty flat shooting. The 165-grain bullet beginning at a flat 3000 fps MV falls just a bit short of this trajectory flatness, but certainly it is entirely adequate in terms of trajectory for shots on deer-sized game to as much as 350 yards and perhaps a bit farther. Again, in the interest of explaining why the 7mm Remington Magnum was given the crown, we find that the "Big 7" does shoot a little flatter than the '06, with its 139-grain bullet especially.

Versatility Through Bullet Selection

I would have to call all of the 30 calibers the winners in this category. The 30-06 can use bullets from as light as 90 grains, and I suppose even lighter (I have seen some 30-caliber bullets of about 85 grains weight). And, yes, you can go on up to the big 220-grain bullet (and even heavier numbers from special sources). I have read of a special 30-caliber bullet which weighed 300 grains, but I have never tested any, nor have I even seen one. As far as bullets go, the 30 calibers are certainly rich, not only in weights, but in all types of styles, from full metal jackets to hollow points and just about everything in between.

300 Winchester Magnum

The 300 Winchester Magnum round is our last selection; however, anything said here about that cartridge can be applied as well to the 300 H&H Magnum, 308 Norma Magnum and the 300 Weatherby Magnum. In fact, these cartridges would probably fall first in ranking in our all-around category but for the fact that one must consider them somewhat in the specialty area because of their great power. While there is no doubt in my mind that this group of "Big 30s" outclasses the 7mm Remington Magnum and the 30-06 in the elk/moose/grizzly category, the smaller rounds are indeed more suited to the needs of the complete shooter on a day-to-day basis.

Therefore, we are not going to run through the features of the "Big 30s," but I will say that I have tested my own Bishop custom 300 Winchester Magnum and found it quite a powerhouse, while at the same time more versatile than thought previously. For example, the 150-grain bullet from the 24-inch barrel screamed out at just a few fps short of 3400 fps using 76.0 grains of IMR-4350 rifle powder. That means a muzzle energy of over 3800 foot-pounds. At 300 yards this bullet is still hopping along at about 2575 fps for a retained energy of over 2200 foot-pounds, a slight edge over the 139-grain 7mm Remington Magnum load.

Using a 180-grain bullet in my 300 Win. Mag., a MV of 3100 fps was obtained with 71.5 grains of IMR-4350 for a muzzle energy of 3842 foot-pounds. At 300 yards the 180-grain bullet is still going about 2450 fps for a retained energy of about 2400 foot-pounds. That is indeed long-

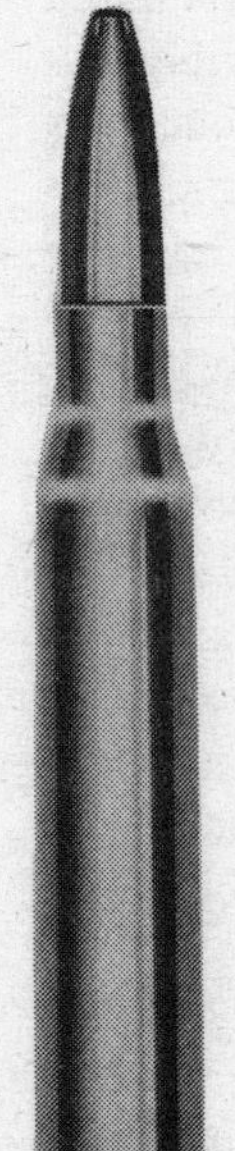

The 280 Remington round is a fine all-around cartridge and very much like the 270 Winchester in the scope of game it will harvest under normal hunting conditions. It is an all-around cartridge.

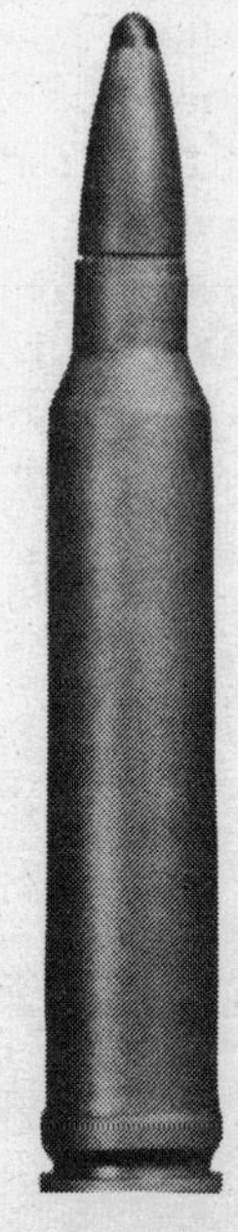

The big 300 Win. Mag., by virtue of its .308-inch bore diameter, is blessed with a large selection of bullet weights and types. It's a favorite with many experienced hunters.

range power. If the 150-grain bullet, at 3400 fps from the muzzle, is sighted to hit 3 inches high at 100 yards, it will be on again at 300 yards. That is flat-shooting indeed, much the same pattern obtained by the 139-140-grain 7mm Remington Magnum load. And all of the array of 30-caliber bullets belonging to the 30-06 also belong to the 30-caliber magnum clan.

Still, we hand the title to the 7mm Remington Magnum, and with great admiration list the other rounds here. They are all superb really, and in the hands of a practiced rifleman they are indeed worthy of being called all-around cartridges. Naturally, we have left out many rounds which could also fit the picture, and if the reader's favorite is not here, he must forgive a lack of space for the exclusion. The 280 Remington is, of course, a contender for the crown in the all-around arena. It's very much like the 270 Winchester in ballistics. The 284 Winchester, while not popular today, is very good all the same. My wife has a custom rifle in this caliber, a featherweight made by Dean Zollinger, and it shows fine ballistics. We have achieved 3100 fps in her rifle using 57.0 grains of IMR-4350 powder and a 139-grain bullet.

The 264 Winchester Magnum is another good round, though since it is overbore capacity I have found that the 6.5-06 creates ballistics on par with this magnum caliber and my little 6.5 DGS on a blown-out 7mm Mauser case also gives fine performance as well, shooting .264-inch bullets. Of course the 270 Weatherby is a good all-around cartridge for obvious reasons. And though we sort of set a minimum with the 7 x 57mm, the little 7mm-08 is also a very nice round.

But if I had to pick only one cartridge with which to hunt all North American big game from the forests of Maine to the mountains of Montana and up into the tundra home of the grizzly bear or coastal regions of the same species in Alaska, I would opt for the 7mm Remington Magnum. It's a jack-of-all-trades, and as such is whipped in each category by other rounds. I would far rather have a 22-250 for varmint hunting. I would be quite content with a 270 or my little 6.5 DGS for deer or antelope, sheep and goats, too. If moose in the forest were my aim, I'd as soon have something in the 300 Winchester Magnum range, or perhaps a 338 Winchester Magnum. If I were aiming to put a white-tailed deer in my freezer in a brush setting, my old 30-30 would suit me just fine. For small game I like a 22 rifle. When rifle hunting is appropriate and legal for wild turkeys, a 22 rimfire magnum is all right with me, or a 25-20 or 32-20. But when a need to feel a sense of the past enters my shooting, I turn to my muzzle-loading firearms for the hunt.

But the all-around rifle, and its cartridge, constitute a compromise and the rounds discussed here are compromise calibers. They do many things exceedingly well, but they are bested in each specific shooting category by some other specialty round.

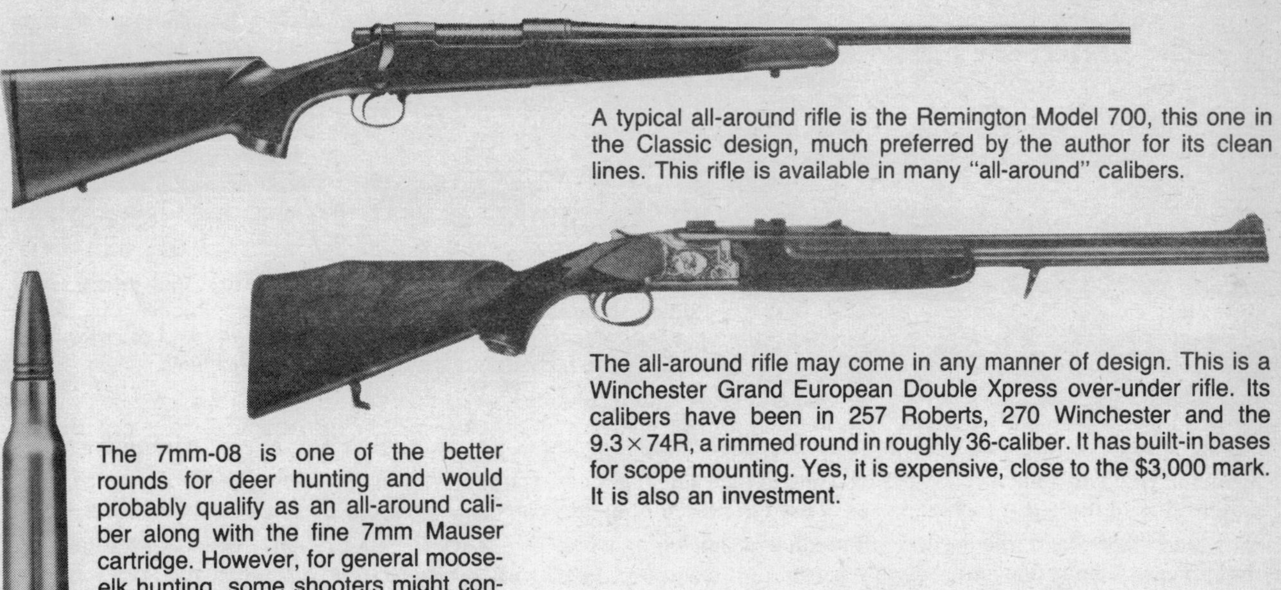

A typical all-around rifle is the Remington Model 700, this one in the Classic design, much preferred by the author for its clean lines. This rifle is available in many "all-around" calibers.

The all-around rifle may come in any manner of design. This is a Winchester Grand European Double Xpress over-under rifle. Its calibers have been in 257 Roberts, 270 Winchester and the 9.3×74R, a rimmed round in roughly 36-caliber. It has built-in bases for scope mounting. Yes, it is expensive, close to the $3,000 mark. It is also an investment.

The 7mm-08 is one of the better rounds for deer hunting and would probably qualify as an all-around caliber along with the fine 7mm Mauser cartridge. However, for general moose-elk hunting, some shooters might consider it just on the border in power, except of course for that perfectly placed shot.

The All-Around Rifle

Now for the rifle. It won't take long to capture and hold onto the correct rifle in which to chamber that all-around cartridge with its variety of loads. Your all-around rifle is going to be a bolt-action model with a scope sight and a 22-inch barrel, maybe a 24-inch tube. I am not advocating now. I am simply pointing out the fact that the all-around cartridges are most popular in bolt-action rifles. Any other action will indeed do, providing it will handle the selected cartridge. We have already looked at the fact that good calibers are offered today in lever-actions, semi-autos, slide-actions, single-shots and double guns.

Attributes of the All-Around Rifle

Accuracy

Of course that all-around rifle must be accurate. But I dismiss this criterion quickly because the rifles one can obtain today are accurate, plenty accurate for big game hunting as well as the occasional varmint work and even some small game hunting which the all-around rifle may be called upon to perform. Accuracy is primarily a factor of a quality bullet exiting the muzzle of a precision barrel with the bullet stabilized with the correct RPS (revolutions per second), i.e., a correct rifling twist rate and exit velocity. All-around rifles are going to be accurate. It's generally not an area of concern with today's quality barrels and actions.

Weight

I think the weight of the rifle matters considerably in the all-around rifle category. Today, the featherweight rifle is mounting a comeback, not that it was ever gone, but it certainly was quiet for a while. The name is changed to "mountain rifle" in some circles, but lightweight or featherweight it is all the same. I like the trend. I used to preach with a loud voice that a rifle needed heft to allow a shooter to hold it still. That is true. A heavy rifle is better in steadiness than a light one. But after a while an older shooter learns to carve away at the negative and add on to the positive and while a light rifle can be a shaky one, it does not have to be.

Proper stock fit will definitely help a shooter hold a lighter rifle with precision. The correct use of a sling is also a big factor in getting field accuracy from a light rifle. Taking correct shooting positions in the field adds to the steadiness of the shot, too. Using a rest when possible is another means of making a lightweight rifle behave a bit more like a heavier model. My all-around rifle, even if it's a caliber in the 7mm magnum class, will be somewhat lighter than heavier, though extremes are to be avoided.

My own all-around rifle these days, in terms of modern arms, is generally a little jewel which is not really at the upper reaches of the all-around cartridge list. It's that little custom featherweight Model 700 with the small octagon barrel, caliber 6.5 DGS (Dales Gun Shop), a round made on the blown out 7mm Mauser case. A 129-grain bullet at 3100 fps makes it a 270 Winchester in power, though with smaller powder capacity it's not much of a kicker. I also have my fine Frank Wells 7mm Magnum, a rifle I'll never part with. When I want that long-range authority, she will come along with me into the field.

The Scope

The all-around rifle these days will wear a scope sight. Remember, we are not talking about a specialty rifle here. We are talking about a rifle meant to function under almost any circumstance and this means a scope sight. My scope for my own all-around rifle is going to be a variable of high optical resolution and mechanical reliability. My favorite range of power is the 2.5x-8x. At the 2.5x setting, I can get on a game animal in the timber or brush, fast. On the plains I can carry the scope on a middle of the road power, such as 4x. When the shot is long, and I want to put that projectile in an exact target spot, then the power will be switched upward toward the 8x setting. The variable makes sense when the rifle is going to be called upon under so many different circumstances, from close-range fast action to long-range precision shooting.

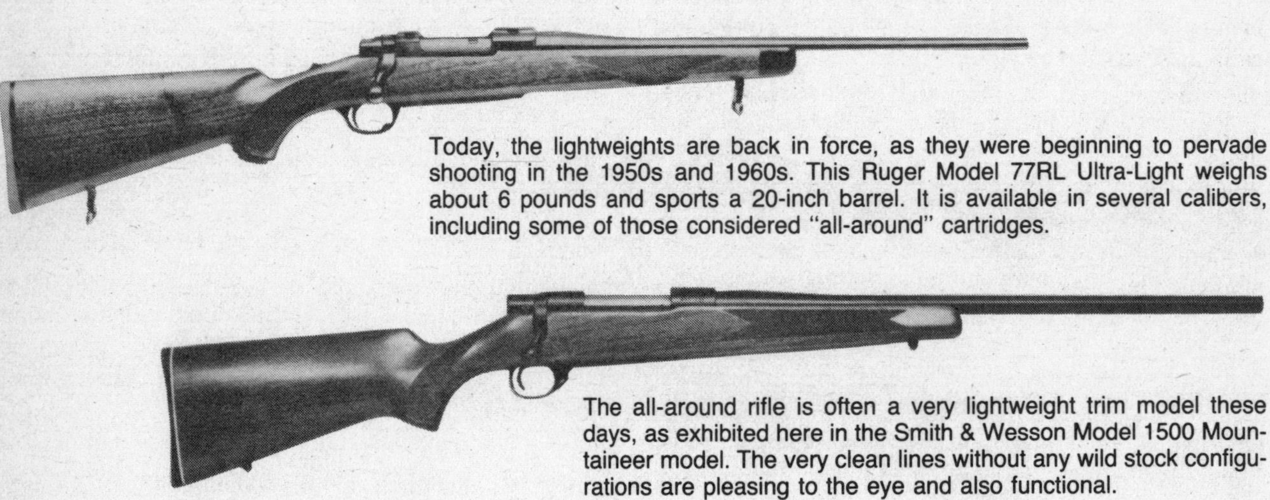

Today, the lightweights are back in force, as they were beginning to pervade shooting in the 1950s and 1960s. This Ruger Model 77RL Ultra-Light weighs about 6 pounds and sports a 20-inch barrel. It is available in several calibers, including some of those considered "all-around" cartridges.

The all-around rifle is often a very lightweight trim model these days, as exhibited here in the Smith & Wesson Model 1500 Mountaineer model. The very clean lines without any wild stock configurations are pleasing to the eye and also functional.

The Action

I already admitted that the all-around rifle is going to be a bolt-action. But there are a few additional reasons, other than the obvious fact that the all-around calibers are offered mostly in bolt-action models. The all-around rifle sees use. It's an all-arounder because the shooter wants a single rifle with which to do a lot of different work. And the bolt-action rifle will allow a *maximum* of accuracy under all

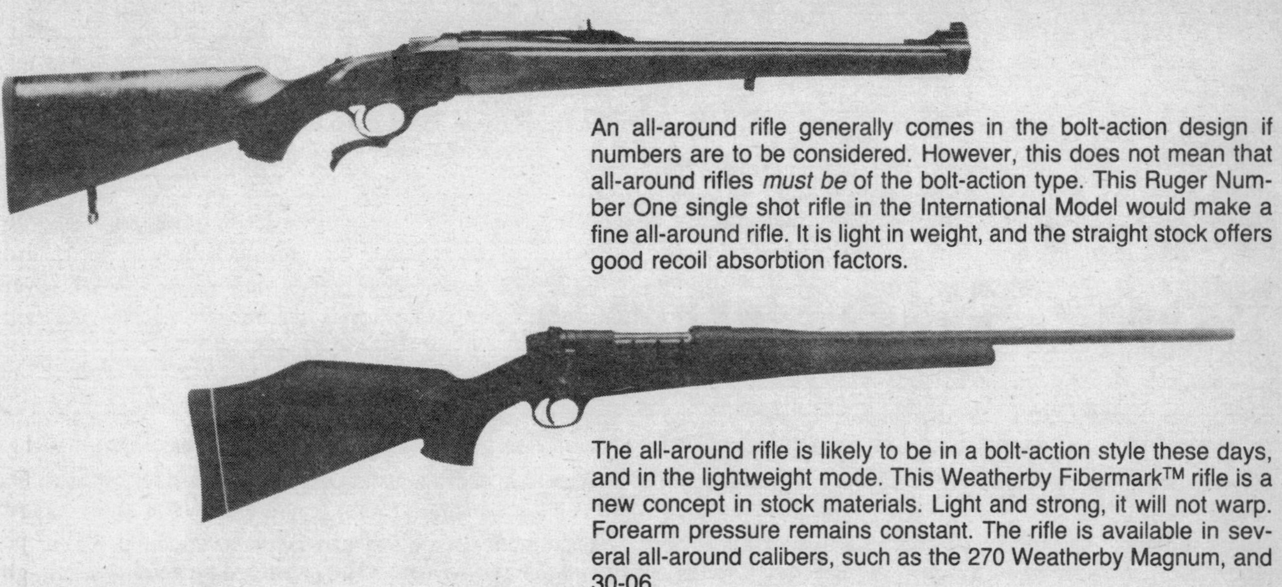

An all-around rifle generally comes in the bolt-action design if numbers are to be considered. However, this does not mean that all-around rifles *must be* of the bolt-action type. This Ruger Number One single shot rifle in the International Model would make a fine all-around rifle. It is light in weight, and the straight stock offers good recoil absorbtion factors.

The all-around rifle is likely to be in a bolt-action style these days, and in the lightweight mode. This Weatherby Fibermark™ rifle is a new concept in stock materials. Light and strong, it will not warp. Forearm pressure remains constant. The rifle is available in several all-around calibers, such as the 270 Weatherby Magnum, and 30-06.

hunting and shooting circumstances and it treats cartridge cases with tenderness when it comes to multiple reloadings.

I like the various action styles for various reasons. But in the all-around rifle, I think the bolt-action is probably the way to go, unless the shooter simply prefers some other style. Then he is certainly free to pursue that choice. After all, good all-around calibers are offered in all of the different action types.

Making Your All-Around Rifle Work for You

The all-around rifle is a reality. It's here, has been for a long time, and is better than ever. But the shooter still owes it to himself to take advantage of the fine points inherent in the all-around rifle. First, he should choose his rifle with thought and care. It should fit. It should be chambered in the type of caliber which will be called upon most often. In other words, the fellow who might hunt elk twice in a lifetime but deer every year should consider, perhaps, an all-around rifle in a milder caliber, with a loaner for that once or twice elk hunt.

That all-around rifle should be sighted in for the most gain of the cartridge's potential. I have seen many a 270 Winchester sighted in for a short 100 yards. That's like buying a race horse and tying his legs together. And the all-around rifleman might as well make up his mind that in order to strain all of the super versatility possible from his round that he is going to have to be a handloader, a thoughtful and creative handloader at times. By handloading, he can often make a fire-breather out of a pussycat, or a pussycat out of a fire-breather. He can also learn to build that exact load which that individual rifle prefers for accuracy.

The all-around rifle and its cartridge are versatile, but that versatility is commanded and controlled by the man behind the gun. It is up to him to gain the most potential from his rifle and its cartridge. And the process is one of the most enjoyable in the vast world of modern shooting. The all-around rifle matches the complete shooter. They have a lot to offer each other.

Chapter 6

Your Shotgun

A SHOOTING BATTERY without a shotgun would be like a canoe without paddles. The scattergun is the most versatile tool in the family of firearms. You can hunt deer with a shotgun, but somehow a 30-30 is out of place on quail. The pioneers of early America knew the shotgun was the all-around king. When a settler reached up to grab Old Betsy from its pegs over the fireplace, you can bet he was reaching for a shotgun. To this day, a hunter could procure meat on the backtrail with only a shotgun, and that meat could range from cottontail rabbits and squirrel to grouse and right up to moose if the need presented itself.

I do not want to paint a picture of the scattergun as only a tool, for it is much more than that and always has been. The shotgun has been a work of art for centuries, and a challenge to shooters for just as long. The uninitiated think of the shotgun as a "can't-miss-with-it" proposition. "You have all those little pellets," I have heard them say, "so how in the world can you miss?" A fast cure for that sort of thinking is to usher the accuser to the trap range and allow the little clay birds to teach him a lesson. While the shotgun is a most amazing paragon of virtues, it is most certainly not a sure-hit gun. It never was. But in the hands of the practiced shot, it can be very effective. There is something almost poetic about the great shotgun-shooting feat, a smooth flow of the body, a proper handling of the gun itself, and that ability to place the string of shot not where the target used to be, but where the target is going to be when the shot gets there.

The Shotgun Types

The Single Shot

When I was 16, a neighbor came by holding a 16-gauge single shot break-open shotgun cradled in his arm. "Thought you might like to try this old 16 on dove and quail this year," he offered. He had taken possession of a new pumpgun and the 16 was gathering dust. I borrowed it. With a modified choke, the ultra-light, single shot 16 was extremely smooth-handling and fast-pointing; I did

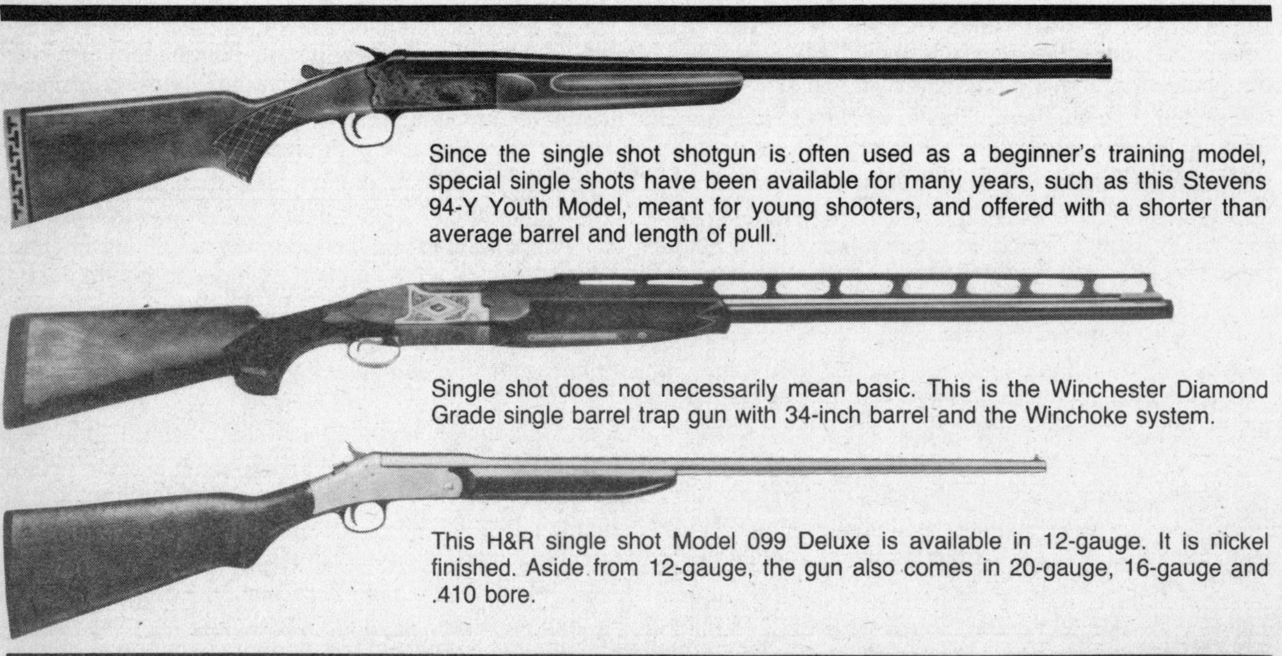

Since the single shot shotgun is often used as a beginner's training model, special single shots have been available for many years, such as this Stevens 94-Y Youth Model, meant for young shooters, and offered with a shorter than average barrel and length of pull.

Single shot does not necessarily mean basic. This is the Winchester Diamond Grade single barrel trap gun with 34-inch barrel and the Winchoke system.

This H&R single shot Model 099 Deluxe is available in 12-gauge. It is nickel finished. Aside from 12-gauge, the gun also comes in 20-gauge, 16-gauge and .410 bore.

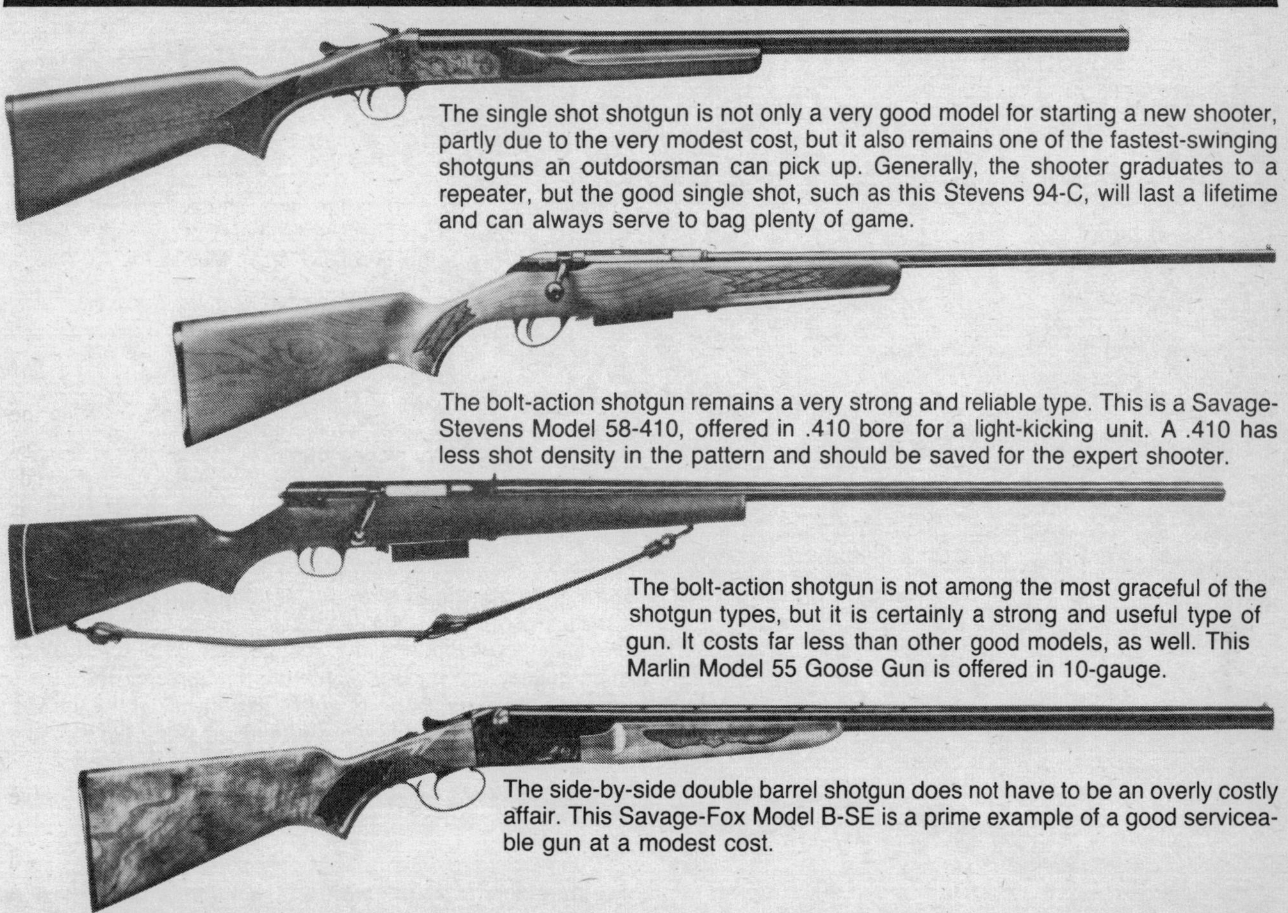

The single shot shotgun is not only a very good model for starting a new shooter, partly due to the very modest cost, but it also remains one of the fastest-swinging shotguns an outdoorsman can pick up. Generally, the shooter graduates to a repeater, but the good single shot, such as this Stevens 94-C, will last a lifetime and can always serve to bag plenty of game.

The bolt-action shotgun remains a very strong and reliable type. This is a Savage-Stevens Model 58-410, offered in .410 bore for a light-kicking unit. A .410 has less shot density in the pattern and should be saved for the expert shooter.

The bolt-action shotgun is not among the most graceful of the shotgun types, but it is certainly a strong and useful type of gun. It costs far less than other good models, as well. This Marlin Model 55 Goose Gun is offered in 10-gauge.

The side-by-side double barrel shotgun does not have to be an overly costly affair. This Savage-Fox Model B-SE is a prime example of a good serviceable gun at a modest cost.

well with it. I had hunted birds a little bit, using a rather heavy bolt-action .410 bore gun, and found the 16-gauge a much better tool for dove and quail.

The single shot is considered a beginner's gun, except for the those superb trap guns of single shot design. I like the single shot and still use one now and then. But for much of my hunting one shot is not enough, especially when the covey is on the rise or the ducks have decided to pass the blind within range. However, on certain long hunting trips, I still tote a single shot. It will break down neatly into a small package (generally) and, let's face it, modest single shots are not as costly as double-barrels, pumps or semi-autos. If lost, the loss is less financially painful.

Having a good little single shot around the house is a sensible addition to the shooter's battery. Beginning with a single shot also makes sense. Using the single shot where a less expensive gun is needed, for fear of damage or loss, also proves satisfactory. For a lifetime of shotgunning, however, I think the American complete shooter needs to expand his battery; he must look to the repeaters

The Bolt-Action

A bolt-action shotgun flows like molasses on a cold rock. It looks like a miscarriage of design and feels like a war club found in an archaeological dig. Yet, there is a place for a bolt-action shotgun. That place is wherever there is need for a repeater at a modest price. Some shooters can master the bolt-action shotgun with more than rudimentary success. I watched a fellow shooter take ducks out of the air with a long-barreled bolt-action and certainly could not fault his shooting ability. I would rather have another type of repeater most of the time, but in certain conditions, the solid, reliable, strong, plain and not-too-expensive bolt-action shotgun is a jewel in uncut form. There is a place for it, and it has survived the test of time.

The Side-by-Side

I once had myself convinced that a side-by-side was not for me. In fact, I could only hit with the left barrel. The right barrel might as well have been attached as a drain pipe for all the good it did me. That was a borrowed 16-gauge shotgun, and I was too new to shooting to realize that it was not the double barrel configuration which was the problem, but rather something else. I will never know what, now. Perhaps the stock fit was all wrong. Today, I have two side-by-sides, one a percussion in 10-gauge and the other an older utility grade 12-gauge which belonged to

Sometimes the big 10-gauge is a shooter's best choice, such as in the goose blind when the honkers might be 50 yards out. This is the Richland Arms Model 711 10-gauge Magnum double.

(Left) The short barreled 12-gauge Armsport Model 1212 hammergun is just right for fast-jumping quail and similar upland game at very close range.

Here is a fine side-by-side double barrel shotgun, the Winchester Model 23 in the Lightweight model. It weighs approximately 6¾ pounds in 12-gauge and about 6¼ pounds in 20-gauge. Three-inch chambers are standard. Barrels are 25½ inches, tapered, with ventilated rib, choked improved cylinder and modified in the 20-gauge, a true upland game gun.

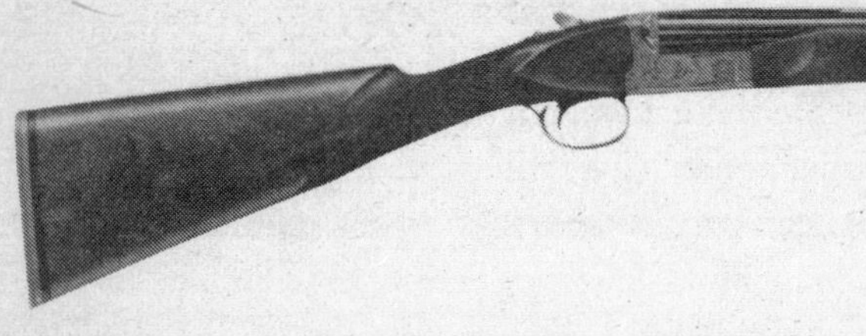

a good friend of mine who bought the shotgun in the early years of this century.

With a strong wind blowing, and in the trees to boot, I once harvested 16 doves in a row with a side-by-side, and though I can't shoot that well all the time, it showed me how wrong I had been in thinking that I could not do well with a two-barreled shotgun. The side-by-side points as well or maybe better than any other type of shotgun, is shorter than a pump gun with the same length barrels because of its shorter action, and can be made up into a very lightweight gun. The sighting plane is broad and rather easy to point with.

Futhermore, any quality double gun will print its patterns together at normal shotgunning ranges. In a double rifle, the barrels are made to shoot close to one another. This is called "regulation," and the barrels of a good double shotgun are also, in a way, regulated. The notion that a double will toss one pattern to the right of the aiming point, while the other barrel delivers its pattern to the left of the aiming point is totally wrong. The double is fast, easy to swing, often lightweight (not always), good-pointing and all in all a very fine style of shotgun. I could get by with a side-by-side for all of my shotgunning if I had to. For those who wish to consider a shotgun for investment as well as for practical shooting, the side-by-side is a fine choice.

Many years ago, I was putting pennies in the old piggy bank for a Winchester Model 21 side-by-side. Before the pennies amounted to dollars, the gun's price had gone up and finally the gun itself was gone, out of manufacture. This lesson I pass on to the shooter. A small loan would have secured that Model 21 for me. The money would have been forgotten, but the shotgun would have delivered a lifetime of reward to its owner. Have your eye on a fine shotgun? Buy it. You won't regret the purchase. If it happens to be a side-by-side, all the better.

The Over/Under

My own Winchester 101 is a fast-pointing, beautifully balanced shotgun and a firearm of grace and beauty. The over/under is the rival of the side-by-side. Both are double barrel guns, of course, with the big difference supposedly lying in the trimmer sighting plane of the over/under. I used to buy the notion that this sighting surface was superior to the side-by-side. I don't believe it any longer. I do my very best shooting with a side-by-side in spite of the "fatter" view over the barrels.

Another feature attributed to the over/under is recoil in a straight line, through the buttstock. The idea is that both barrels recoil the same, albeit one barrel is underneath the

The over/under shotgun is exceedlingly clean of line and fast in the hand. The author's own over/under is a Model 101 Winchester like this one. Many shooters prefer the single sight plane of the over/under. Although the author holds the over/under in high esteem, he does not believe that the single sight plane is necessary to good shotgunning.

The over/under shotgun, broken open here to show the chambers, offers many different options in terms of ejection, including non-ejector types. Author's wife has a Model 333 Savage such as this one in 20-gauge. It is the non-ejector type. This type is easier to break, because there are no ejectors to cock.

A little over/under 20-gauge is at home when fast-handling is necessary. Author keeps eye on bird, knees breaking so that the body will flow. It is the body which will aim at bird, or point at it, along with the shotgun.

other, while the side-by-side does not "kick" straight back. I can't prove or disprove the theory. The over/under seems to recoil with a slightly more mild effect, gauge-for-gauge, in comparison with the side-by-side. In the field, even at trap, I do not think the differences here are going to be truly measurable. But in one very informal look at the recoil differences (felt recoil, not foot-pounds) two 20-gauge lightweight shotguns were fired numerous times and by several different people using identical loads. The guns were within a few ounces of each other in mass weight. All of us decided that the over/under rendered slightly less felt recoil than the side-by-side. This, however, does not take into account variables such as length of pull, drop at comb, and individual shooting variations, such as stance, physical build and so forth.

The over/under is slimmer looking than the side-by-side. I suspect some shooters buy over/unders because of this factor. Moreover, the over/under is every bit as good as the side-by-side in all measurable factors. My lifelong record seems to point to a side-by-side as my best bet in hitting a target, especially an upland game bird. But I do all right with an over/under, too, and I own a good one and have every intention of continuing its use.

The Pump

The slide-action has to be America's favorite style of repeating shotgun. Reading information on shotguns, one finds that the English consider a side-by-side their major action choice, but on this continent the pumpgun gets the nod. The original draw for American shooters who went to the trombone action was cost. A pump of quality can be made for less money than a side-by-side of high quality. Futhermore, the slide-action was more than a two-shot affair. In fact, I suspect that the capacity of shells offered by the pump was a big factor in its takeover in America.

Today, the advantage of multiple shots is less pronounced, because of federal regulations concerning waterfowl and some state regulations concerning upland gamebirds. In short, federal regulations (and some state regulations) rule out a magazine capacity greater than two shells. So the pumpgun has to be "plugged" to hold only two shells in the magazine, making the gun a three-shot affair. Those regulations do not apply to all shotgun hunting, however, and the shooter should check the laws in his own area concerning shell capacity. He will probably find that he can hunt rabbits or deer with a shotgun capable of firing more than three shots. Of course, laws vary area-to-area and the individual hunter must take the responsibility of learning the rules for his locale.

The pump, with its long action, becomes a rather long

The Marlin 120 Magnum shotgun is an example of the ever popular pump model. Its long barrel with good swinging properties makes it a fine duck gun.

The pump-action shotgun remains an American favorite. Bill Fadala used a pumpgun to account for these sage hens. With interchangeable barrels or multiple choke system, the pump is very versatile.

(overall length) shotgun. For upland gunning, I do not consider that fact a plus. But in a duck blind, the length (and generally greater heft) of the pump is welcome. I have seen some superior marksmanship on all game from shooters using the pump. I have an old Remington Model 870 12-gauge in the long-discontinued Sungrain style, with a Skeet choke barrel and a full-choke barrel. It is a marvelous piece of machinery offered at a rather small price in its day. In all the years that I have owned this shotgun it has *never jammed once*.

The pump is as American as Old Glory. It is a reliable and effective hunting tool, and of course is more than supreme on the trap range. The pump will shuck shells in and out at a rapid firing rate and will feed less-than-perfect ammo with somewhat remarkable regularity. No shooter can go wrong choosing the pump shotgun. While it does not exhibit the *apparent* simplicity of the double barrel shotgun, if one studies the composition of the pump and a fine double, I think the pump will actually win in the "simplicity-of-design" department.

The Semi-Auto

Everything noted about the pumpgun applies to the semi-auto. It is very popular in America, though not as popular as the pump. Of course, it, too, offers more than two shots, and obviously the shooter need merely squeeze the trigger again and again in order to empty the magazine. Also, due to the fact that some of the recoil energy may be used up in working the action, the semi-auto may deliver less "kick" at the shoulder. In fact, some semi-autos are especially noted for this, and a lady shooter of my acquaintance uses a Model 1100 Remington mainly because of reduced recoil effect.

The semi-auto is reliable. And with today's fine reloading tools, one can prepare excellent shotgun ammo which will feed through the semi-auto with reliability. At the same time, if we must choose between the pumpgun or auto in terms of total reliability, the pump would get the nod, a small nod, just a shake of the head and no more. A non-ejector double gun would probably have to hold first place in a tie with the pumpgun for year-in and year-out reliability, but the semi-auto would be right in there close to both these styles.

Why pick a semi-auto? Shooters like the rapidity of fire, the ease of operation, the sleek lines, the reduced recoil effect and the reliability. It is a good choice. But it is an individual choice. I am a great fan of the shotgun, and I own a couple of side-by-sides, an over/under and a pump-

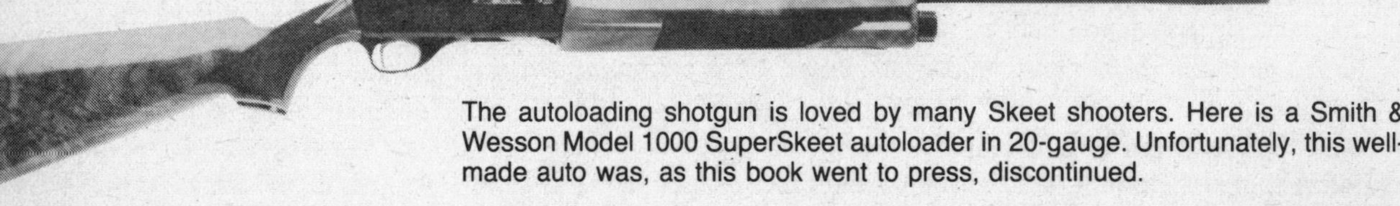

The autoloading shotgun is loved by many Skeet shooters. Here is a Smith & Wesson Model 1000 SuperSkeet autoloader in 20-gauge. Unfortunately, this well-made auto was, as this book went to press, discontinued.

The shotgun has meant a great deal to American shooters over the years. Author poses with a vizsla and two shotguns, a Remington Sungrain pump 870 model and a short-barreled hammergun, the Model 1212 from Armsport, very different shotguns for very different uses.

gun. But I do not own a semi-auto. I have gotten along fine with my guns, but at the same time, there are thousands of shooters who think semi-auto when they think shotgun, and nobody can fault them for their choice. There are gas-operated autos and mechanically operated autos, and both are viable. I can actually *feel* the operation of the "long-recoil" type of auto. When I shoot a long-recoil operated shotgun, what I *feel* is a two-motion, back-and-forth shuffling of the action. I believe gas-operated autos to be smoother, though there are short-recoil autos which also feel smooth in follow-through.

Which Action Style to Pick?

You do not pick a shotgun based upon its action style alone. You pick a shotgun for an intended purpose. Shotguns are as individual as automobiles in their application. I want a short, light and fast-pointing shotgun for upland gunning, but I'd as soon have a steady, longer, heavier gun in the duck blind. In my opinion, the reason many shooters gravitate toward the pump is the fact that it is versatile. In my own pumpgun, there is a heavy steel unit which is inserted in place of the plug, this adding weight for reduced recoil and steadiness in the duck blind.

Of course, there are also lightweight pumpguns for the upland field. I have witnessed one of my shooting partners, John Doyle, as he dropped three quail on the rise with three shots from an old .410-bore Model 42 Winchester pump. It is impossible to say that a pumpgun is not an upland bird getter when shooting of this caliber can be accomplished. But I would prefer a light side-by-side or over/under, for day-in and day-out quail shooting. The pump points like an accusatory finger, all right, but the double is swifter in the hand than a sparrow on the wing.

I can feel what I need to know in a shotgun without taking it afield, though the actual shooting is the proof of the pudding, of course. I can feel litheness. I can feel slothfulness, too. And if the grammarian wants to take exception to my chosen words, let him. A shotgun feels alive or defunct in the hand. Any shooter can feel it. You pick it up, mounting the gun quickly to the shoulder. She snaps to position like a good dog on point, or she lumbers up to the shoulder like a log, or something in between. Sometimes I shut my eyes, mount the shotgun and then open my eyes to see where she's pointing in relation to the imaginary target I previously picked out. I also want to see how much barrel I am looking at, too. Some shotguns will jump to the shoulder in an almost self-pointing way for the shooter; others will not.

Naturally, we are talking about more than action style now. We are talking about more than the weight of the shotgun or its length. We are now getting into *shotgun fit*. Obviously, the subject has two major parts—how the gun is built, and how the shooter is built. When the two are matched, watch out! Some good shooting is in order. Personal fit should dictate the choice of shotgun. If a shooter is comfortable with the semi-auto, he should choose it. The same goes for the double gun and the pump. But in any case, the gun has to fit the shooter and the shooter has to fit the gun. That last part is also important. Our bodies bend. They can be trained to adjust to minor variations in the shotgun's makeup. But they should not have to bend too much, just a little here and there to forgive a slight lack of perfection in the hand/glove fit which we would all like to feel in the shotgun/shooter relationship.

Shotgun Fit

Good shotgun shooting hinges on a flow, the flow of the gun and the shooter's body. If the gun does not fit, the flow is halted. It is balky. It is jerky. It is a matter of the human body having to bend too much in order to fit into the shotgun. All of this is lost motion. We don't point a shotgun, really. We point our body and the shotgun follows. More on this later when we discuss a few practical shooting lessons.

Length of Pull

The first criterion of shotgun fit is length of pull. Given a length of pull which is too short (and remember that length of pull is the distance from the trigger to the plane of

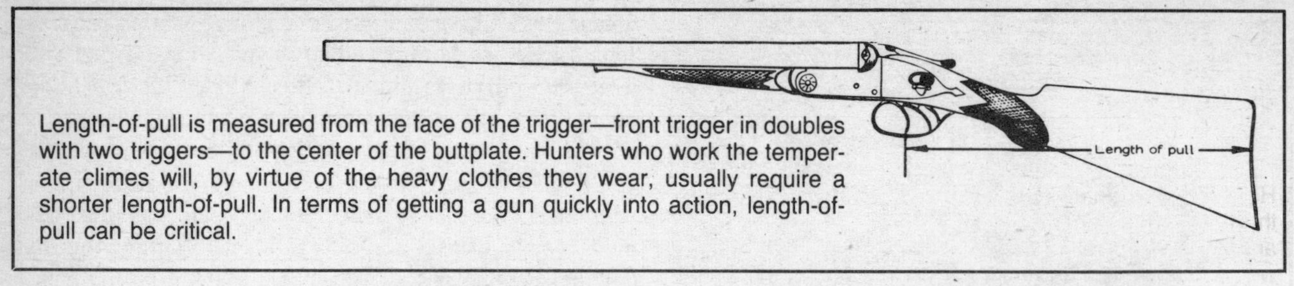

Length-of-pull is measured from the face of the trigger—front trigger in doubles with two triggers—to the center of the buttplate. Hunters who work the temperate climes will, by virtue of the heavy clothes they wear, usually require a shorter length-of-pull. In terms of getting a gun quickly into action, length-of-pull can be critical.

The old Savage 333-T over/under was designed to be a trap model. Its length of pull is longer than most field type shotguns. The stock is quite straight. This type of shotgun is at home in the duck blind as well as on the trap range.

the butt), a shooter can often live with it. Given a length of pull which is too long, a shotgun will be very difficult to shoot correctly. My own length of pull measures out at over 14 inches, but I have decided that, at least for me, I can do better with a shorter pull. Generalizing this fact is probably dangerous, but I'll do it anyway. I think that most shotgunners will do better with a length of pull very slightly below (shorter) than what would normally be called for by strict measurement. The slightly shorter length of pull not only allows for faster mounting to the shoulder, it also facilitates positioning the face properly on the stock. Instead of the face hitting the stock in only one fixed position because of the limitations imposed by the length of pull, the face is more relaxed and can more naturally assume its location on the stock. In short, the face comes to rest on the comb with grace and ease because the neck does not have to be stretched out.

Length of pull, of course, can be too short. This means that the face and thumb almost touch, or perhaps do touch. If the nose is just about touching the thumb when the shotgun is mounted, the length of pull is too short. Length of pull is too long, however, when the buttplate gets hung up on the shooting vest or jacket. I used to think that by holding a shotgun with the finger on the trigger and then placing the buttstock along the forearm, a fellow could determine if the gun was the correct length of pull. When I do this, I come up with, about, 14.5 inches. I know that's wrong for me. I think the best way to determine length of pull is to try mounting various shotguns. When a particular gun mounts swiftly to the shoulder without catching on clothing and the face touches the comb where it should so that a nice "sight picture" is present, that length of pull is correct for you. Sight picture in this sense is not the same as the sight picture when target shooting with a rifle. I mean the picture a shooter gets when his face touches the comb. He sees a bit of the tip of the barrel, but not the middle of the barrel and of course, the barrel is not missing altogether. Except on trap guns, where the gun is already mounted when the target presents itself, I prefer a comfortable length of pull which allows smooth, fast mounting of the gun with cheek touching comb correctly.

Drop at Comb

The comb of the gun can be either high or low in relation to where the shooter's face strikes it. When the comb is too high, we see a lot of barrel, too much barrel. The gun is, in effect, pointing up in the air. Not very conducive to good shooting, though a little bit of this condition is good for upland birds which are often on the rise. It helps the shooter push that shot out in front of that rising bird, in other words. The comb that is too low does not offer that "sight picture" spoken of earlier. Either condition takes away from good shooting.

The comb of a shotgun does not progress in a straight line out to the buttplate or heel of the stock. It has drop, and that drop is appropriately known as "drop at comb." If the comb does not suit the shooter, his head will not be positioned correctly on the stock, and if his head is positioned in the wrong place, how can he point that barrel correctly? He can't. If a shooter draws an imaginary line down the plane of his gun barrels and extends it back to the buttplate, that line will be straight, of course. The less the distance between the comb and the imaginary line, the greater the tendency to shoot high. The more the distance between comb and imaginary line, the greater the tendency to shoot low. On a rifle the front and rear sight or scope will require correct head placement on the stock, and drop will only affect shooting comfort not shooting accuracy. On a shotgun however, positioning the head in relation to the line of sight will directly affect accuracy as the eye is acting as the rear sight of the shotgun. Ideally the shotgunner's eye should be on the same plane as the imaginary line.

Drop at comb is measured in inches. Obviously, we do not have a ready figure for where our eye will be located

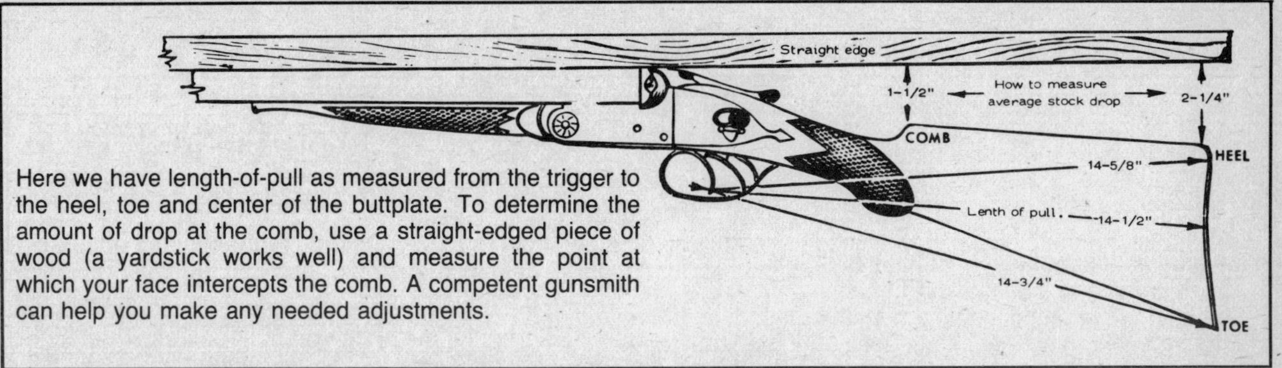

Here we have length-of-pull as measured from the trigger to the heel, toe and center of the buttplate. To determine the amount of drop at the comb, use a straight-edged piece of wood (a yardstick works well) and measure the point at which your face intercepts the comb. A competent gunsmith can help you make any needed adjustments.

on different stocks with different drops of comb since this depends upon where the face actually touches the stock and how the individual's face is built. But we can say that a straight stock delivers the recoil in a straight line and that as the stock is more and more "bent," the recoil changes in effect. A little drop at comb is enough, however. We want the stock to be somewhat straight for recoil deliverance.

Pitch

Pitch is another term associated with the stock. Consider a shotgun with the butt resting firmly on the floor. If there were no pitch, the barrel would point straight up into the air. Pitch, then, is an *angle*. We might consider it the angle which the buttplate makes. If the buttplate or recoil pad is mounted so that it in effect lengthens the heel of the stock (the top of the buttplate), the gun will pitch downward in the barrel. Of course, the reverse is true. If the bottom of the buttplate (the "toe") is made longer, then this makes the muzzle tip "back."

Pitch is important because it dictates (in part) how the buttplate settles into the shoulder. The toe and heel of the buttplate will not offer a perpendicular line with the muzzle of the shotgun although it can be made to do just that. The gun will be pitched up or down. Remember, we have a drop at comb which makes a drop at the heel of the stock. Pitch should match this drop so that the buttplate rests comfortably into the shoulder and the shooter sees the right sight picture over the gun.

All of this seems overly complicated and maybe it is, too. The real point is this: do not *worry* about shotgun stock dimensions. Rather, be *aware* of shotgun stock dimensions. An aware shooter can then ask intelligent questions of a shooting coach or a gunsmith. He can help these experts ascertain what is right for him, the individual shooter. As a general rule, we often find a shotgun from the factory with a length of pull of about 14 inches, a tad longer than the average rifle stock's length of pull. This should handle most of us, but I suggest a shooter be *aware* that it may not be the right length of pull for *him*. The drop at heel may be just right with 1.5-inch drop at comb. But it may not be, too. And the pitch of the gun may also be just right for the shooter. But he can mount the gun, decide how it feels against the shoulder, and then ask a competent gunsmith, "This stock does not seem to nestle into my shoulder correctly. Do you think the pitch is right for me?"

What Gauge?

Suppose we have made a selection here. The shotgun is a side-by-side, to be used for upland gamebirds. What gauge is right? Today, we have everything from a .410 bore on up to 10-gauge. Yes, there are larger and smaller bores and gauges. But the aforementined is the standard range, and it encompasses about all we will ever need for any modern shotgunning chore. The .410 is not a gauge measurement because gauge began as a counterpart of "bore." A 12-bore gun was one which fired a spherical lead ball, the 12 representing the number of balls suitable in size for the 12-bore that could be cast from 1 pound of lead. A 12-gauge was used as a term for the same thing but in modern usage is not identical in size to the old 12-bore. The .410 is more a caliber than a gauge. It means 410/1000 of 1-inch diameter, just as a 30-caliber means 30/100 of 1-inch diameter. The .410 is a 41-caliber, then.

With the .410 being the smallest we are dealing with here, the next popular gauge is the 28-bore. We can go back for a moment and think of the 28-gauge as a size which takes 28 balls of pure lead to make 1 pound of weight. Or we can look at it his way: A 28-gauge is .550-inch in bore size, a 55-caliber. The 20-gauge is .615-inch, between a 61-and 62-caliber. The 16-gauge is .662-inch in diameter, a 66-caliber. The 12-gauge is .729 inches in diameter, or about 73-caliber. And the 10-gauge is .775-inch diameter or between 77- and 78-caliber.

Various sources of information will alter the above figures. But this makes no difference to us. We can think in calibers if that is more comfortable, and this always gives a clear picture of just what a 12-gauge size is. It *is* about 73-caliber. And that is really all we need to know in order to work with a comparison unit.

Which is best? Of course, there is no answer to that question until we ask—for what purpose? But even that

Browning's Invector screw-in choke system is a handsome unit in that it is all but invisible to the eye and this is true both when shooting the gun and simply studying its lines. It fits flush with the muzzle. The system comes with full, modified and IC choke tubes. Cylinder and Skeet chokes are also available.

demand requires another thought. We can go up and up in gauge, but we will not, choke-for-choke, spray the landscape with more and more *pattern* as we increase in gauge. In other words, a full-choke 20-gauge will pattern about 70 up to maybe 80 percent of the shot into a 30-inch circle at 40 yards. A full-choke 12-gauge will pattern 70 to 80 percent of its shot charge into a 30-inch circle at 40 yards also.

The difference here is one of *density*. Since the 12-gauge load can toss more shot than a 20-gauge load, the 12-gauge will land more pellets on the target than the 20-gauge will. Is this necessary? It is nice at the longer ranges. It is useful because of another truth. Shotguns are going to deliver *about* the same muzzle velocity from one gauge to the next. So the 12-gauge is not going to deliver more individual pellet energy than the 20-gauge, *pellet for pellet*.

Now how do we go about choosing gauge? We choose gauge by determining how far it is we want to shoot and at what type of target. The large gauge is going to put more shot on target than the smaller gauge, albeit with about the same energy per each individual pellet. But if we take a rabbit at 40 yards with a 12-gauge, we are, if the pattern is centered, going to hit the rabbit with more shot if we are using that 12- over a 20-gauge. Next question: Do I really need a dense pattern at 40 yards? I will answer the question as I answered it for myself when I was out to pick a gauge for quail hunting. I knew by experience that most of my quail shooting would be within 20 yards of the muzzle. I chose a 20-gauge. I could have gotten by, probably, with a 28-gauge. I'm not good enough as a wingshot to merit a little .410, with its less dense pattern, and I do not need a big 12-gauge to drop a quail at 20 paces.

For waterfowling, where the birds are big and tough, ducks and geese in other words, I like a 12-gauge and in some cases a 10-gauge would be just right. On rabbits in thick cover, I prefer a 20-gauge. I like the 20 for quail and dove, too, unless the latter is a pass-shooting, 40-yard situation. Then give me the density of the 12-gauge. How about the 16-gauge? What a perfect compromise, right? Maybe. But the 16 is and has been much neglected. The 20-gauge loading has gone to 3-inch hulls and the 16-gauge has been left behind.

Today, the general choice lies between the 20 and the 12, and I choose the 20 for upland birds and closer ranges and the 12 for ducks, some pheasant shooting, sage hens and similar targets. The 12 is used at trap, too. If the 12 is so good, why have a 20-gauge? The reason is gun size. The actual heft and dimensions of the gun can grow petite and lithe by heading for the 20-gauge hull. And at the same time, the 20 has, as I have stated, gone to a possible option of the 3-inch hull. What does this mean?

When I was a kid, a stout load for the 2¾-inch 12-gauge shell was 1¼ ounces of shot. In the 1950s, when I was a teenager, we considered the 1¼-ounce 12-gauge load a duck-taker of premium quality. Today, the 20-gauge 3-inch shell is capable of holding 1¼ ounces of shot. It is, essentially, a 12-gauge of days gone by. Of course, there are some differences in the actual delivery of shot because as we go to a smaller diameter "tube" for that shot, the shot string has a tendency to stretch out longer. More on that in a moment. Nonetheless, the 20-gauge is a really fine shotgun shell. It is a fine choice for today's shotgunning on upland birds and the like. The 12-gauge is still an all-around master of all trades, however, not a jack-of-all-trades. A good 12-gauge can about do it all, from light loads in the upland field to heavy charges of shot for waterfowl. If I were to pick but one gauge, it would still be a 12, in spite of the fine properties of the modern 20-gauge hull.

Choke

It is hard to believe that when choke was first invented, many shooters argued that it was no improvement over the standard cylinder bore, where the bore was of the same dimension from breech to muzzle. W. W. Greener discusses choke, and is often credited with its success. He knew early on that choke was the answer to *controlling* the shot string. Today, we have several different chokes, and just as there are minor variations in measurement for other shooting dimensions, choke is also measured in different ways. The following is how I look at choke size, if "size" is a term we both can live with.

Extra Full Choke	80 percent or higher
Full Choke	70 - 79 percent
Improved Modified Choke	65 - 69 percent
Modified Choke	55 - 64 percent
Improved Cylinder I	50 - 54 percent
Improved Cylinder II*	45 - 49 percent
Cylinder	under 45 percent

*This is the usual Improved Cylinder choke. Improved Cylinder I is *strong* or *quarter* choke.

What does all of this mean? It means that if we pace off 40 yards from a big sheet of paper and fire into the center of the paper with a shotgun, we will find as much as 80 percent of that shot charge contained by a 30-inch circle at that distance. Or, only 20 percent of the shot will be outside of that 30-inch circle to look at the reverse. This is a standard measure and when we talk about patterning, 40 yards and 30-inch circles will be the norms.

We will not go into all of the chokes. Obviously, if we again stand 40 yards from the pattern sheet and fire, gauge notwithstanding, we can expect a Modified choke if 55-64 percent of the shot lands within the confines of that 30-inch circle. I am sure the reader knows we have set up a standard here to work with. That upper end of the Modified choke, being 64 percent, is somewhat nitpicking as a figure. If we obtained a 65 percent pattern, we would have to recognize that the pattern is on the "low end" of the Improved Modified choke.

The big differences come in *density* of the pattern. And this means the *amount* of shot contained in the load. The handloader has some interesting options, and we have a chapter that discusses shotgun shell reloading for that reason. A good example is the 16-gauge hull. Remember when we said the 12-gauge load of 1¼ ounces of shot was considered a strong duck load in days gone by? Well, a handloader can put 1¼ ounces of shot out of a 16-gauge hull of standard 2¾-inch length. In other words, the handloaded 16-gauge can toss as much shot as the handloaded 3-inch 20-gauge hull.

But let's compare the more popular 12- and 20-gauge loadings. In the 12-gauge 2¾-inch hull, we can fit a full 1½ ounces of shot. A good powder charge will propel this shot at about 1250 fps MV. In the 2¾-inch 20-gauge hull, a good stout load gives us 1⅛ ounces of shot. The muzzle velocity here will be about 1235 fps MV, or about the same as with the 12-gauge. We shoot at 40 yards. The individual pellet energy for the 12-gauge and 20-gauge will be close to the same at 40 yards, for the pellets began at about the same muzzle velocity.

But . . . the 1½ ounces of shot in the 12-gauge load will deliver a lot more pellets on target than will the 1⅛ ounces of shot out of the 20-gauge. Pattern density is in favor of the 12-gauge, of course. In 1½ ounces of No. 7½ shot, we have a total individual pellet count of 525 pellets. In 1⅛ ounces of No. 7½ shot size, there are about 394 pellets. At 40 yards, if a 12-gauge 1½-ounce load delivers a full choke pattern of 75 percent, the number of pellets which land in the 30-inch circle will be 393 pellets. The 20-gauge full choke with the 1⅛-ounce charge of No. 7½ shot will put 295 pellets into that 30-inch circle.

Actually, both seem quite good in terms of the number of pellets striking the 30-inch circle. But we have to adjust our thinking a little bit. First, all of the pellets do not arrive *at the same time*. If a bird is in that pattern, it is not going to receive full benefit of the shot charge delivered on a piece of paper which is not in motion. Second, few birds are going to present a target of 30 inches in diameter. Now, our increase of shot charge density does take on more meaning, and the 12-gauge charge of 1½ ounces of shot at 40 yards does offer a real advantage over the 20-gauge charge of 1⅛ ounces of the same shot size.

Another way to look at this pattern density is to consider that as the range increases, the smaller gauge offers less and less pellets to target in terms of a given area. No pattern is perfect, either. There are "holes" in shotgun patterns. If the quality of a pattern in a 12-gauge is the same as the quality of the pattern in a 20-gauge, the 12-gauge will have less gaps in the pattern as the range increases, meaning more mathematical opportunity to score a hit and more chance for a clean harvest on game.

We have made the 12-gauge very appealing in this analysis. But we must go back to our original story regarding choice of gauge, which was the actual intended use of the shotgun. While the 12-gauge does offer the capability of delivering more shot on target (denser patterns) as the range increases, we in fact find that a 20-gauge is entirely adequate for many and varied shotgunning circumstances. Given close-range shooting on upland birds, as our example used previously, and ranges of 20 or even 30 yards, the

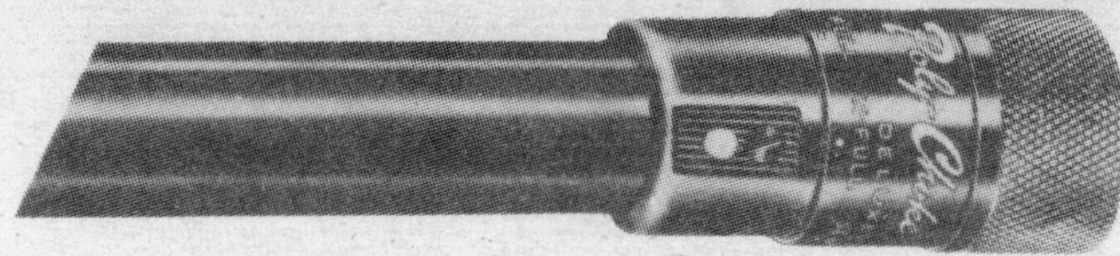

The Poly-Choke has been a very famous multiple choke system and it operates by twisting the body of the choke to switch from one choke setting to another. This Poly-Choke has an Extra Full setting.

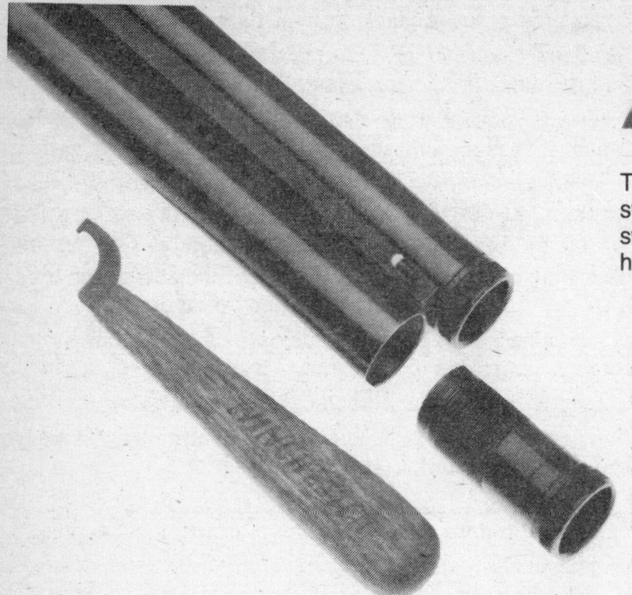

Here is a view of the Winchester Winchoke in the beautiful Model 23 Winchester side-by-side double barrel shotgun. The screw-in chokes offer the entire gamut of shotgun patterning, and this Model 23 comes with six Winchoke tubes in the 12-gauge chambering, and four in 20-gauge. The special wrench shown here makes choke tube change fast.

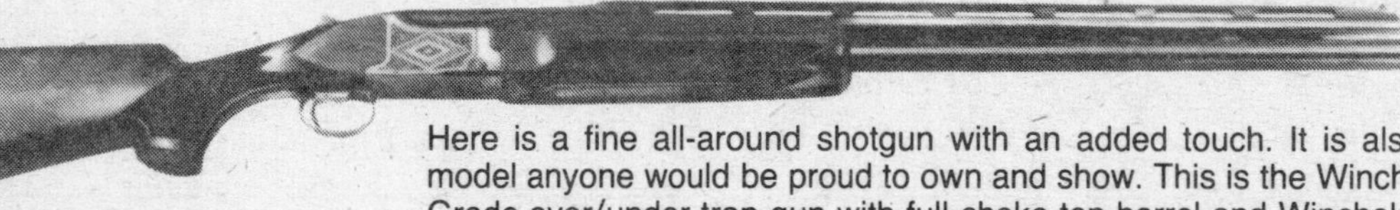

Here is a fine all-around shotgun with an added touch. It is also a handsome model anyone would be proud to own and show. This is the Winchester Diamond Grade over/under trap gun with full choke top barrel and Winchoke under barrel. It is made for trap shooting, but would serve in the duck blind as well, and in some upland bird gunning, too.

20-gauge is a good choice because it offers us a lighter, smaller, fast-in-the-hand gun. Meanwhile, the 12-gauge is better where the targets are farther away. And, it's like the story of the good little man and the good big man. The latter is likely to win the contest.

So it is with the 12-gauge. If held to but one shotgun, the 12-gauge can do it all. It can accept light charges in the 1 ounce of shot category, or it can push 1½ ounces of shot from the 2¾-inch hull. The 3-inch 12-gauge shell delivers as much as 1⅞ ounces of shot as this is written. Where choke is concerned, and we simply must talk choke and gauge at the same time in order to really have a full picture, we match the choke to the task just as we match the gauge to the task.

Full-choke is certainly very fine when the shots are far away. But up close, full-choke means, often, too much pattern density. A quail centered in a 12-gauge full-choke hailstorm of shot is going to be hit all too hard and valuable meat destroyed when the range is but 20 yards. Given a range that is much longer, the density will have diminished and the bird would be dropped but not destroyed. Since quail are usually taken at 10 yards, maybe 20 yards in some cases, the choke should *not be full,* not even for a 20-gauge. Improved Cylinder would be, and is, better here.

For a goose 40 yards out, the Extra Full choke is none too full, and the modified range of choking seems to offer us the compromise area. Choking is not a big mystery, being, in effect, the constriction of the barrel at some point, generally toward the muzzle. But this simple constriction, done in many and various ways, has changed shotgun shooting from a true "scattergun" condition to a rather sophisticated level of control. The cylinder bore is not only antiquated, it is also outclassed by choke boring. My tests show better patterns out of some sort of choke, even with buckshot. (Buckshot of all sizes patterned better in choked guns over cylinder bored guns.)

Adjustable Chokes and Choke Devices

Quite some time ago, someone came up with the idea of offering a series of chokes in one barrel. The feat was accomplished in at least two ways. First, different choke tubes could be screwed in and out of the muzzle, thereby offering a shooter a range of chokes. After all, choke is bore constriction, and the tubes would be constricted to various degrees to deliver various choke settings. Another means of varying the choke would be a collet, the collet either closed down for full-choke patterns or opened up for Skeet/Improved Cylinder patterns.

Poly-Choke is a name still well-known in the field of collet type choke devices, and the Lyman Cutts Compensator, along with the Weaver Choke, remain known as tube-type choke devices. These devices work or have worked rather well. We have in our home an older Model 870 Remington which has a variable choke device attached to it.

The value of such a unit is self-evident. In one shotgun, all of the general choke settings are available to the shooter. In fact, especially with the collet-type choke device, a shooter could simply turn the "nozzle" on the muzzle and change from open bore to tighter choke as his field conditions changed. He could actually shoot Skeet and trap with the same gun. It was wonderful. But the American shooter shunned these devices in time. The popularity of the many-choked gun device fell off badly. Why?

I think I know. There are two reasons for the variable choke losing favor with shotgunners. First, the addition of the device gave the muzzle of a shotgun barrel a nose not unlike W. C. Fields rather bulbous proboscis. It was ugly. Second, when a person sighted with the device in place, the picture looked like a lump of mud stuck on the end of the shotgun. Certainly, not all shooters felt this way. In fact, I read of at least one shooter who proclaimed better pointability with the device in place for it was big and easy to point with. Most shooters did not agree.

So, for lack of aesthetics, plus a loss of sight picture (theoretically), the multi-choke device waned in popularity. Then Versalite came along. This was Winchester's name for a multi-choke device which was offered on their Model 59 shotgun. The Versalite was, to my knowledge, the first screw-in type choke modifier. No more lump. The little "pipes" which screwed in and out of the Model 59 muzzle changed choke very effectively without changing the configuration of the barrel, or at least without any "obtrusive" change.

Unfortunately, the Model 59 was not the most popular shotgun in the world. Therefore, the variable-choke device did not really have a chance to excel. Later on, however, the Versalite spawned another choke device, Winchester's Winchoke. One gun, all chokes, and pretty, too. The screw-in type choke simply had few to no problems, actually. Yes, barrel wall thickness was increased modestly so that the interior of the bore could be threaded for the tubes, but this wasn't so bad. Besides, just the end of the barrel needed this beefing up, not the entire length of the bore. The screw-in choke device could be obtained on a bolt-action shotgun, a pumpgun, a semi-auto, even a double barrel. (That latter inclusion was *really* something and still is.)

Not only did the double-gun shooter have an instant choice of two different chokings, as he always had with a double, he now had the option of switching the pattern in either barrel for just about any shooting condition he could think of. In a thickly vegetated field, he could have an Improved Cylinder gun, and as he approached the open terrain, he could take a few moments and with his little wrench in hand, switch to a tighter choke boring. The little choke tubes did not cost an arm and leg, either. In the range of $10 each, subject to change of course, a shooter could add different choke tubes to his collection. At 10 times less than the cost of a new barrel, the tube was (and is) a bargain.

Custom outfits began to offer screw-in chokes added to an individual's shotgun. In one instance, a lady shotgunner took a Savage over/under which had bore damage near the muzzle, cut the barrels shorter, which was a big boon to her shooting in the first place, and then she had the screw-in choke added. The lines of the shotgun remained excellent, and she now had open- to full-choking all in one nice-handling shotgun.

Another big advantage of the screw-in chokes, although the advantage actually existed with the predecessors of the screw-in as well, was the near instant matching of shot size with choke. If a shooter would simply take a little time, he could pattern his own shotgun with the various tubes, using various shot sizes and loads. As a crude rule of thumb, we find that some of the larger shot sizes, such as BB, will actually pattern as tightly, even tighter, from a Modified choke as from a Full choke. On the other hand, the smaller shot, such as 7½ and 8, usually pattern tighter from the Full choke tube. Once the shooter learned which his choke device preferred in the way of shot size per pattern, he had it made. He could then switch not only his choke tube, but actually *his pattern* at will. Also, slug shooters generally find that Improved Cylinder works well for slugs (though in a couple of guns I found Modified and even Full just as good). When using slugs, the owner of the screw-in choke device could insert the appropriate tube for best accuracy.

Generally, a shooter can expect to receive from four to six tubes with his screw-in choke unit. He can often have Skeet, Improved Cylinder, Modified, Improved Modified, and Full, sometimes Extra Full, too. He might range all the way from 45-percent patterning to 80-percent patterning, all in one familiar gun and all with the employment of a little wrench and some tubes. The screw-in device will continue to undergo some changes, I am sure. But it is already a very wisely designed instrument and one worthy of looking into for the shotgunner who wants a lot of different choke possibilities, all in one gun, and without any lumpy projections at the muzzle.

Shot

If we treat shot for exactly what it is, a round lead ball with all of the same properties of a lead round ball used in the muzzle-loading firearm, then we can gain some solid understanding of another very important topic in shotgunning, which is the mental image of a shot string and how it acts. Shot is, then, a round ball, and we have applied numbers to indicate sizes. When we talked about gauges, we found that a little number meant a big gauge due to the fact that gauge originally meant the number of balls it took to make up a pound of weight. As the number grew smaller, such as 4, we had a very big gauge. It only took four round balls in 4-gauge to make up 1 full pound of weight.

Shot sizes also follow a system of "larger meaning smaller." In other words, No. 7½ shot is much smaller than No. 2 shot. In fact, when this system got to zero with 0-size Buck, additional zeroes were added to designate even larger ball sizes. Hence, we had 00 Buck and 000 Buckshot. That's no news. But I think it is important to think of each pellet as one round ball. If we do this, we can easily see why larger shot "carries up" better than smaller shot. It is a matter of *mass*. With a round ball the mass goes up way out of proportion to the diameter. Given a No. 8 size shot, which is about .09-inch in diameter, *in pure lead,* the weight of this individual pellet would be 1.1 grains. Remember, there are 7000 grains weight in a pound. So, 1.1 grains is indeed a very small weight.

Shot Size Chart

No.	12	11	10	9	8	7½	6	5	4	2
DIAMETER IN INCHES	.05	.06	.07	.08	.09	.095	.11	.12	.13	.15
APPROXIMATE NUMBER OF PELLETS TO THE OUNCE	2385	1380	870	585	410	350	225	170	135	90

	Air Rifle	BB	No. 4 Buck	No. 3 Buck	No. 1 Buck	No. 0 Buck	No. 00
DIAMETER IN INCHES	.175	.18	.24	.25	.30	.32	.33
	NUMBER TO THE OUNCE		APPROXIMATE NUMBER TO THE POUND				
	55	50	340	300	175	145	130

A No. 4 pellet is .13-inch in diameter. In fact, it is 13-caliber, if we want to look at it that way. A No. 4 pellet will weigh 3.3 grains. Again, that may not seem like much, and it isn't, but it's three times the weight of the No. 8 shot! No wonder No. 4 shot retains its original pellet energy better than No. 8 shot as the range increases. The only problem, of course, is the fact that it is shotgun pattern we must be concerned with here. Even with Full choke, a quail at 20 or 30 yards might escape through a "hole" in a pattern made by No. 4 shot.

So we end up with a compromise when we talk about shot choices for different duties. We also end up with a mini-war on our hands, because there are two different schools of thought on the subject of shot size effectiveness. One says to heck with big shot. Hit the birds with several small shot and the harvest is clean and fast. The other says nix on this. Hit the bird with one or two big pellets which will drive deeply into or even through the bird and then you have a real force. It is a tough argument. I have two friends who use No. 8 shot on geese over decoys. Their shooting distance is about 20 to 25 yards and in all the time these fellows have been using No. 8 shot, not one single bird has gotten away. The dense pattern of No. 8 shot made head shots not too difficult on geese at 20 yards or so.

I hunted pheasants in very dense cover one day using No. 8 shot and every bird dropped instantly when hit. But these are special, *highly unusual circumstances*. I think we should use a commonsense approach. Given ducks at 40 yards, No. 5 or No. 4 shot seems a much better choice to me than any load of No. 8 shot. Western Ammunition Company did a study using mallard ducks. The study concluded that it took five No. 4 pellets in the body of a large mallard to quickly and humanely dispatch the bird.

Circumstances dictate shot choice as well as the size of the game hunted or the target to be "busted." Ducks over decoys are game easily taken with No. 7½ shot. I have done it many times without ever losing a bird. No. 6 shot is also good here. But in pass-shooting at ducks, I like No. 5 shot the best and also use No. 4 shot when No. 5 is not readily attainable. On big sage grouse, which are large birds but soft-feathered, I also use No. 5 shot. In fact, No. 5 is my favorite all-around shot size for rabbits and ducks and pheasants and other game of this size range.

But on a fast-rising quail, give me the dense pattern of No. 8 shot from a somewhat open choke, such as Improved Cylinder. I would use No. 5 shot even on a goose, providing decoy placement meant 20- to 24-yard shooting. But give me No. 2 shot, even BB size, if the birds are 40 yards out. On a wild turkey, if I could be guaranteed a head shot at 20 paces, I'd use No. 7½ shot in order to gain that dense pattern. But in normal turkey hunting, I will take No. 4 at least, with No. 2 a better choice if it patterns well in my shotgun. I have also used BBs on turkeys and have no complaint with that size. Give me BBs for fox, too.

Shot size, then, is not too much of a mystery in terms of choosing the appropriate shot for the task at hand. As the target grows larger and tougher, so does the shot size, unless the range is very close. As distances increase, the use of heavier shot also means better penetration. But pattern must be considered, too. Solid hits in a dense pattern are more meaningful than one large pellet misplaced on the game.

Finally, the hardness of shot is important. I hunt sage hens annually, but it's a short season and I can count on no more than 12 birds grand total for the year. This is not much shooting, and I use reloads featuring nickel-plated

No. 5 shot with total satisfaction here. Sure, that's expensive shot. I certainly would not want to use nickel-plated shot for warm-ups! But a few ounces expended on a fine game bird certainly dictate the added expense to me.

Hard shot means more than penetration advantage. In fact, we will find that in using metals *less dense* than lead, penetration falls off per pellet size, at longer ranges. In short, steel shot, size for size, will not penetrate as well as lead shot on longish shots. While ''steel'' shot (actually ''iron,'' in composition) is *harder* than lead shot, it doesn't have the *density* of lead shot. As a result, lighter weight steel shot loses velocity quickly and, therefore, doesn't have the ''power'' to penetrate well at long range. That is in my mind, what the shot string *probably* looks like as it flies through the air. I know this helps me make hits.

I have spoken with many shotgunners who have given me *their* mental image of a shot string. They see a cloud of shot, a blanket of shot, a sheet of shot, a bunch of shot, a mass of shot, a lump of shot . . . but mostly, the first couple of images, ''blankets'' or ''sheets'' of shot.

I think of shot as a short burst of water from a garden hose. I think of shot strings as strings, longer than shorter, strung out. A tube, such as a hose or shotgun barrel, is likely to push out a column of liquid or shot. It strings it out, the shotgun barrel does, and we call it just that, a shot *string*. It is not a blanket or a cloud.

Aside from the over-anxious dog breaking point, we see a straigh-away shot about to be made with the bird being centered in the pattern. The pheasant is moving straight away from the shooter, and since he has an image in his mind of that shot string, he is going to "black the bird out" visually and send his shot somewhat ahead of and over the bird for it to collide with the pattern.

my experience as well as stated theory. So, we hope for a hard shot, but a dense shot at the same time. Hard high-antimony lead shot (hard lead shot) generally means better patterns and penetration because it deforms less, meaning less ''fliers'' (individual pellets which zip off course on their own routes). Flatten a pellet and you have a flying saucer, a little frisbee. Hard shot flattens less readily. But hard shot costs more. I don't use it on dove, quail or rabbits.

The Philosophy of the Shot String

I know the word is wrong. There is no ''philosophy'' of a shot string. But I want to use it to put across one of the most important ideas in shotgunning: How we *envision* the shot string can mean a great deal when it comes to hitting with the shotgun, a great deal indeed. When I go hunting with a shotgun I always do a little mental exercise before hitting the field. I think about the shot string. I try to see,

I think of a shot string as a *three dimensional* pattern. It is not a cloud with height and width. It is height, width and *depth*. It is a string of shot. Sure, modern factory and handloaded shotgun shells have short columns, comparatively, but still we have a column, a string. And if we *think* of the shot as coming out in that manner, we can use the *shape* of the shot string to much better advantage. This is what I call a ''philosophy'' of shot strings. Imagine a bird, a dove, for example, winging along at a right angle to the shooter.

The shooter leads that bird too little. The first part of the shot string misses the bird. If the first shot pellets miss, under these circumstances, you can forget any possible ''hit'' with the rest of the string. It is not even there yet! The rest of the string is behind the first runners in the pack, so when those first pellets miss, the ones yet to come will also miss the mark. Remember, all of the shot does not strike a given target at the same *time*, not even if the target is a big piece of paper used for patterning. Some of the shot gets there before other pellets in the string.

Now let's take another look at the above hunter and his cross-flying dove. This time he leads a bit too much. The first part of the string flies harmlessly in front of the dove. But wait. There is more to come. There is more shot on the way. He may hit that bird, unless he has given the bird so much lead that even the last pellet reaches the spot where the bird *will be* before the bird reaches that spot.

Think of shot strings as three dimensional. Because they are.

Angles

Another way to think of a shot string is to equate the string with a ball on a pool table. Not that we are going to "bounce" shot off of things in order for the pattern to strike a target, of course, but we need to recognize that hitting a bird is a matter of angles, just as bouncing an eight ball off the cushion is a matter of angles. If a bird is flying directly away from us, it would be pointless to aim to the right of it. Yet, if a bird is flying to our right, it will be hopeless to aim right at it and pull the trigger. When the shot gets there, the bird will have departed that part of the sky.

If a bird is on the rise, we shoot high, hoping to put the string over the bird so it will fly into the pattern. If the bird is going precisely straight away from us, we "blot the bird out" with the muzzle of the gun, visually, because we want the shot string to take precisely the same course in flight being taken by the bird. And so forth. The same angles pertain in Skeet or trap shooting. The shotgun is a matter of angles, bisecting angles, with shot and target coming together, hopefully, even though the angle each is taking is different.

Drop

Round balls lose velocity rapidly. It is their nature. And a shot charge is nothing more than a bunch of round balls. A shot charge loses velocity pretty rapidly, especially as the mass of each individual pellet decreases, just as a bullet drops over the course of its journey through the air from muzzle to target. Yet, we seldom think of shot as dropping. This is because our ranges are short and the string of shot does have "body." So there is some built-in leeway for drop. But I know I have cleanly harvested birds, even dove and quail, at 40 yards and more because I included drop in the picture.

It is a tiny factor and not one to worry about, just one to give a small consideration to. There is drop in the string of shot from muzzle to target, even at 40 yards and especially beyond. The shooter can satisfy himself of this by shooting at pattern sheets up to 75 yards or so.

Your Shotgun

Your own shotgun, then, is a self-selected tool, with the action style which suits you, in the gauge you prefer for the shotgunning you do, with the appropriate choke and shotshell load. It's a wonderful instrument in the hands of a practiced user, but it is not a haphazard piece of equipment. The so-called spray of shot is, in fact, non-existent. The mastery of the shotgun is a challenge. And good wingshots can be proud of their achievements.

Chapter 7
The Varmint Rifle

An important aspect of varmint hunting is the use of tools which are similar to those employed in the big game field. Here, Bill Fadala carries a Winchester 72A 22 rifle equipped with a Bushnell variable power telescopic sight.

ANY RIFLE from an air gun all the way up to a 300 Magnum or larger could be used to dispatch varmints. However, it takes a very specialized tool to meet the criteria of a true varmint rifle. The criteria are many, and the list varies according to the listmaker. I see a varmint rifle as small in caliber, very flat shooting, delivering light to modest recoil, highly accurate and topped with a good glass sight of high or variable power. Just as specific as the rifle's ballistic ability is the rifle itself. It is a stable firearm, carefully bedded, of medium to heavy barrel weight (some lightweight barreled varmint rifles are also accurate) and capable of top-rated accuracy.

The varmint rifle is so specialized that it deserves separate mention in our look at the complete shooter. What's more, not all varmint rifles are fired at varmints. Many shooters have enjoyed long-range target shooting with flat-trajectory firearms which would certainly qualify as varmint-takers. Yet, the object was not the clearing off of a few varmints, but rather the grouping of bullets on paper at long range. Long range, I think, is the key to classifying a varminting firearm. If the trajectory of the bullet is not "stretched string" in nature, then we do not have a varmint rifle.

Varmints, What Are They?

In the dictionary, we might find that varmints are, "Any obnoxious or pestiforous animal." Generally, the varmint is exactly that, harmful to the animals man has singled out as important to him, domestic or wild, and destructive of a situation. In the first sense, the coyote would classify as a varmint. In some areas, as many as 90 percent of the antelope kids dropped by pronghorn mothers in late spring may be eaten by coyotes. Since man determines that the antelope is important to him, then the eating of antelope fawns by the coyote places that canine in the varmint category.

Millions of dollars in damage to man's crops, buildings or landscape is done by pestiforous animals or birds classified as varmints. Rats and mice are good examples though we do not generally find rats and mice pursued by hunters. We do often, however, find woodchucks, ground squirrels and rockchucks as targets of the varmint hunter.

John Fadala, author's son, uses a 20× spotting scope to study a varmint. We have a strong transfer value of skills, for the shooter who learns how to truly master such optics as the spotting scope on varmints. He can then use that same skill in the big game field.

We might break down wildlife into three classes: game, non-game and varmints. Game is easy enough to distinguish from the other two. It has a season, is usually edible and carries a bag limit. The non-game animal is neither varmint nor game; it includes song birds and other creatures which are not hunted for food nor considered damaging to man's situation. The varmint generally does not have a season as such, and often may be hunted all year around. The varmint does not generally have a bag limit. Are foxes varmints? That all depends. When classified as a fur-bearing animal, the fox must be removed from the varmint class.

There is no point in making all of this complicated, and pigeon-holing wild animals is often very difficult to do. The coyote is a fur-bearer, but its tremendous predation on sheep, other domestic stock and wild game animals places the coyote into the varmint class. Many rodents are varmints. Some birds (feral pigeons come to mind) are also varmints. Is a bear a varmint? No, it is a big game animal, but there are, in fact, certain special hunters who make part of their annual living pursuing and dispatching those black bears that have made a habit of eating livestock belonging to ranchers and farmers. We think of the woodchucks and rockchucks as varmints as well as the prairie dog, ground squirrel, gopher, crow, jackrabbit, coyote and many other wildlife species which prey upon or damage those parts of civilization which we hold as valuable.

Should Varmints Be Hunted?

As long as we are speaking of a specialized form of rifle meant to remove varmints, it is appropriate, I feel, to discuss this question briefly. A true story may be in order. During a class I was attending in Flagstaff, Arizona, a professor lamented the fact that varmint hunters were shooting in a prairie dog village not far from town. He considered the shooting senseless. Less than 6 months after his speech, a group of developers went into the area. The group decided to use the land. Since the land was undermined by the prairie dogs, and since the presence of the rodents would mean more of the same excavation, the animals were poisoned, gassed and gotten rid of summarily. And that was that.

In another instance, a rancher in Wyoming asked me if I knew of any varmint hunters who would be willing to help thin the population of prairie dogs in a couple of his pastures. He had suffered the loss of some livestock from legs broken in prairie dog holes. I simply could not locate any varmint hunters at the time. The gentleman ended up gassing and poisoning the rodents. I believe that we face a matter of priorities in varmint hunting, and the priorities far transcend hunting or no-hunting attitudes. Non-hunter and hunter alike stipulate a value system and ranking of animals. Even the anti-hunter who would watch a herd of antelope devoured by a coyote population would probably opt to control that population of "wild dogs." Those making a living from the land, or providing food for the masses regard the removal of certain varmints as crucial to the welfare of the crops, both animal and vegetable.

Within the framework of game laws, then, the varmint is hunted. After consideration by the experts, certain animals and birds are placed on the varmint list with open seasons and generally no bag limits. It is not really a question of hunting or not hunting, but rather a question of the expert game manager making a decision based upon his years of knowledge and experience. Varmints are so classified, then, by game biologists, not by hunters in the field as laymen. And varmints are classified in that category due to the entire picture at hand, not a small part of the picture.

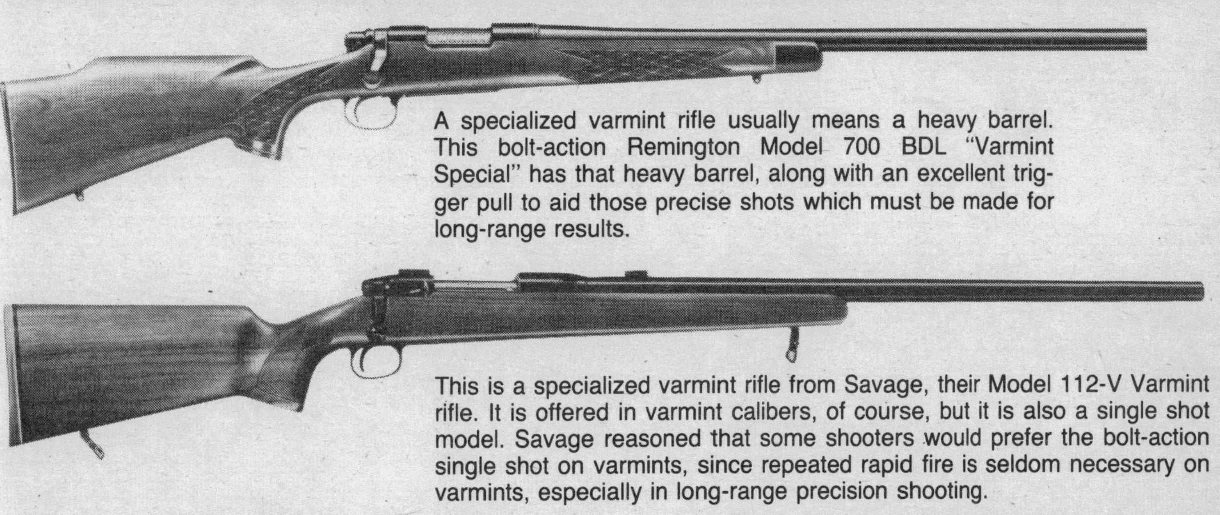

A specialized varmint rifle usually means a heavy barrel. This bolt-action Remington Model 700 BDL "Varmint Special" has that heavy barrel, along with an excellent trigger pull to aid those precise shots which must be made for long-range results.

This is a specialized varmint rifle from Savage, their Model 112-V Varmint rifle. It is offered in varmint calibers, of course, but it is also a single shot model. Savage reasoned that some shooters would prefer the bolt-action single shot on varmints, since repeated rapid fire is seldom necessary on varmints, especially in long-range precision shooting.

Varmint hunters stand out because they overtly reduce populations of varmints. Sometimes, they are chastized for this removal. While they are being chastized, no one even questions the many thousands of "varmints," rodent, insect or otherwise, which are removed scientifically for the growing of oranges, beets, carrots or peas.

The growth of varmint hunting as an individual endeavor has placed on the scene a most interesting rifle, a very specialized tool, a very precise tool, and one which requires understanding and appreciation, as well as ballistic knowledge.

The Characteristics of the Varmint Rifle

The varmint rifle itself is a stable, accurate piece. Weight does not matter much in most cases, depending upon the hunting style of the shooter. Generally, varmint hunting with true, heavy-weight varmint rifles means long-range work, and this precludes long hikes. Rather, the hunter finds a suitable safe varmint hunting area, such as a field or other open place, and he sets himself up to stay awhile. Naturally, there are many different methods of taking varmints, other than staking out a particular spot and hoping for long-range shots. Cruising for varmints is another means of getting many shots, especially in the West where one may go from one pasture to the next by vehicle, stopping long enough to do some shooting at specific spots along the way. And there is varmint calling as well. Here, the hunter will find a likely spot to call from, hoping to bring the varmints to him, usually coyotes, but also other animals and birds ranked in the varmint class.

But one factor seems rather universal in specific varmint shooting with specific varmint rifles, and this is the factor of distance. Even though by driving around from field to field a hunter may get a very close-range shot at a varmint, or may call a varmint in to virtually shotgun range, the varmint hunter generally considers long-range *potential* paramount to his activity. His rifle must meet the requirements of accurate long-range shooting.

The specialized varmint rifle can have a medium- to heavy-weight barrel because most of the shooting will take place from "stands" of one sort or another. Again, there are several lightweight rifles in varmint caliber for those who prefer to hike and hunt varmints in the field, but the long-range varmint rifle is very likely to enjoy the benefits of a heavier barrel, meaning more shots in succession before the barrel gets hot enough to change point of impact. A medium to heavy barrel, in part due to its very mass, heats more slowly. It also cools more slowly, but the varminter does not mind because he does his shooting, exhausts a particular locale, and then moves on. Meanwhile, during transportation, the barrel cools again.

The specific varmint rifle, then, can enjoy a heavier barrel than a model meant for packing in the field. This factor includes overall weight as well. When carrying the rifle is not an issue, then added weight is welcomed. The varmint rifle can also have a longer length of pull, in my opinion, since it is seldom used for fast shots and it won't hang up on clothing when brought to shoulder. Also, it need not have a slim forearm. I don't like beavertail forearms on any firearm which is going to be used on moving targets because there is a tendency to strangle the forearm with a tight grip, thereby reducing the flow of motion in the rifle. But a varmint rifle is not generally used for running targets, and it can have a wide, flat forearm. All the better for a rested shot if it presents itself.

The varmint rifle is also equipped, ideally, with a sensi-

Varminting is sometimes a matter of using a lighter rifle instead of a heavier one. This Ruger Number One single shot Light Sporter is available in varmint-taking calibers, such as the 243 Winchester. The barrel is 22 inches long and total weight is about 7¼ pounds without scope.

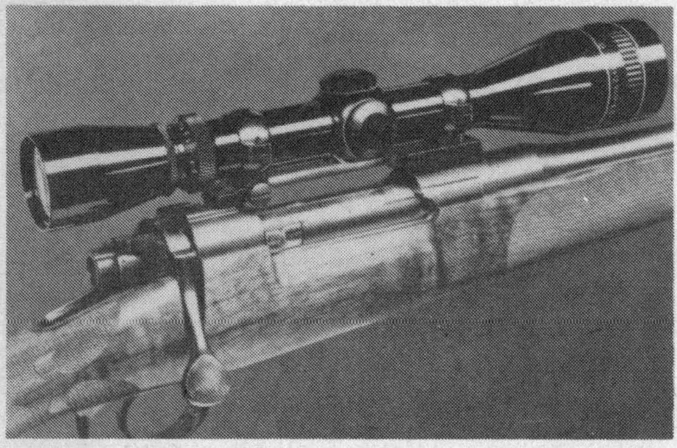

The varmint rifle in the varmint/deer calibers such as the 6mm Remington and 243 Winchester can be equipped with a 4×-12× variable scope to meet both deer hunting requirements and varmint hunting requirements. This is the Leupold 4×-12× with adjustable objective.

The varmint rifle is a precision instrument, as this Sako bolt-action rifle conveys. It is chambered for the 22-250 cartridge and fitted with a 4×-12× Burris scope sight.

tive trigger. I prefer good snappy trigger pulls on any rifle; however, if ever there was good reason to employ a light letoff and crisp trigger pull, it is on the varmint rifle. Single set triggers are good here, or even double triggers.

Sights for the long-range varmint rifle mean one thing to me—scopes. I can't imagine any other sight on a specialized rifle for taking varmints. Due to the more sedentary nature of the target and the more deliberate aiming process used in varminting, the scope can be of high magnification. There is nothing amiss in a 10x telescopic rifle sight (or higher magnification) on a varmint rifle. If the rifle is to be used in the field, carrying the rifle about looking for varmints under varying conditions, a variable scope is just right. The variables of the past were not always as stable as the fixed-power models. Today this is not the case. We have some fine varmint scope choices such as the 6x to 12x range, in the variable mode.

The varmint scope need not be elaborate. The regular internal adjustment found on most of today's scopes is just fine for the sophisticated varmint rifle. I ran several tests with scopes of various manufacture in terms of where the point of impact moved when the "clicks" were applied. They moved where they were supposed to go, and with fine precision. Scope adjustment will be fully discussed in the chapter on aiming devices. However, one of the features of the varmint rifle is its sights, and there is only one type of sight for this rifle—the glass sight.

Finally, the varmint rifle is chambered for a varmint cartridge and sighted-in to take full advantage of the potential flatness of trajectory offered by the proper varmint round. In a later chapter, specific sighting-in measures are dealt with in full. But the varminter will do no better than his scope sight allows him to see, and he will do no better than his knowledge of "where to hold" allows him to hit. Proper sighting-in is part of the chain of success which leads to high scores on varmints.

The Varmint Cartridge

All of this would be for naught without the proper cartridge, for you can have the most accurate, stable, well-sighted, scoped, fine-triggered varmint-type rifle in the world and do no good at long range if it's chambered for the wrong round. As with all other phases of shooting, there are many choices to be made on the road to the best varmint round for the job. As always, the key is compromise. We must compromise between the flatness of trajectory, mildness of report and recoil, explosiveness of the bullet, the bullet's ability to buck some wind, the actual delivered energy at the target, which may often be well beyond 300 yards, and other factors. The varmint round should be at least somewhat mild to shoot, yet sufficiently powerful for varmints at long range, flat of trajectory, accurate (by our definition), and explosive enough to quickly and humanely dispatch the target, while at the same time explosive enough to destroy itself when it makes contact with the ground. The latter is important for the varminting done in farm fields where a ricochet would be most unwanted. The fast and somewhat fragile varmint bullet should self-destruct if it makes a landing next to, instead of on, the target.

Accuracy

Accuracy is a factor which combines many sub-factors, the bedding of the rifle, precision of the scope, delicacy of the trigger and other nuances of the rifle. But most of all, accuracy is good bullets out of good barrels. Make no mistake, cartridge design, for all its worth, is nil without good bullets and good barrels. It is always a big surprise for someone to shoot a bolt-action 30-30, such as the old Model 54, using a fine scope sight. The surprise often comes in the form of 1 inch or less, center-to-center groups at 100 yards. Yes, there are some inherent factors in a cartridge which help make it accurate, such as the proper capacity of powder for the hole in the barrel (balance), but mostly, I repeat, accuracy is a matter of *good* bullets out of *good* barrels.

A varmint round is no more accurate than any other round. I recently read that, unlike the 30-30 and other hunting rounds, varmint cartridges were very carefully put together at the factory, with more than tender love and care, while the big game ammo was more or less crafted with decent, but not spectacular accuracy in mind. I don't find this to be the case. In fact, I find that *both* factory varmint ammo and big game ammo are well made. (I recently tested several brands of 30-30 ammo and found standard deviations from the mean velocity in the range of a few feet per second, often only 5 or 9 or 10 fps, in fact. *That* is hardly slipshod ammo.)

But we often think of varmint rounds as more accurate than big game ammunition, and I do not wonder why. The why is answered in somewhat heavier rifles, scopes of higher magnification and cartridges that do not "kick" much, thereby allowing the shooter to concentrate on shooting instead of thinking about being belted in the chops by recoil. However, let's not be lulled into thinking that varmint ammo and factory rifles are made with more skill and devotion than big game numbers. A recent test of an out-of-the-box Remington Model 700, in 30-06 caliber—the rifle belongs to my hunting partner Gene Thompson—revealed 1/2-inch groups at 100 yards using my handloads practice loads), the 180-grain bullets doing about 2500 fps from the muzzle.

A Rundown of Currently Popular Varmint Cartridges

It is valuable to look at several popular varmint rounds, because there is often much confusion over what the best varmint cartridges are in terms of overall design and efficiency. The best way to sort this out, I believe, is to look at the attributes of a number of these rounds so that the reader learns how to evaluate his own varmint cartridge, or how to pick his next one. We are not going to rank any of the rounds according to accuracy. Every one of them is accurate with the right load out of a good barrel.

Before we go any further, let's get something out of the

Bill Fadala, author's older son, concentrates the view of his binoculars on a prairie dog village. His goal is to discover a route to stalking the village for close shots. The use of binoculars for varmint hunting transfers directly to big game hunting. The person skillful at locating varmints in the distance with the binocular will also be skillful in finding big game with the glass.

way: the 22 Long Rifle is not a round suited for long-range varminting. It is not fast enough, flat enough, nor powerful enough at long range to qualify. Nor is its bigger rimfire brother, the 22 Magnum. These rounds are wonderful for their own balliwick. But, again, they are not suited at all to long-range varminting.

The First Centerfire "Varmint" Rounds

Initially, a move was made to present the shooter with longer-range potential for smaller wild animals. The rounds normally associated with this move are the 25-20 and 32-20. I find both of these cartridges useful to this day, but not for long-range varminting. They both came in fast-operating rifles bearing iron sights and no doubt were very exciting to own when compared with some of the cartridges of more looping trajectory of the day. In fact, they were both offered in bolt-action arms as well as lever-action models and pumps.

In old advertisements, I have seen the 25-20 touted for its effectiveness on varmints, and I have seen ads proclaiming the 32-20 a combination varmint/deer round. No way. The 25-20 is a fun round, light of recoil, and just fine for varmints at up to 150 yards and maybe even a little bit farther. Compare it, however, with a 22-250 and it will be seen immediately to be outclassed in terms of true, long-range potential. A 60-grain .257-inch bullet at 2200 fps is *not* a long-range varmint round, and that is the 25-20 in top form. An 80-grain .311-inch bullet at 2250 fps is good, maybe up to 200 yards, for varmints, but it is not a long-range varmint round. The 25-20 is best sighted to hit on target at 150 yards. It drops over 7 inches by the time it gets to 200 yards. It is wrong for long-range varmint shooting, but nice to pack around in a handy rifle and just fine for wild turkeys and similar game.

The 17 Remington

In a class by itself, many of us have wondered why this varmint cartridge was given life in the first place. I have always considered it terribly wind sensitive. Before I fired a rifle chambered for this round, I figured accuracy would be none too good with a tiny 17-caliber 25-grain bullet bursting forth at over 4000 fps MV. Of course, there are some negative factors pertaining to the 17-caliber, all right, but there is definitely a place in modern varmint shooting for this round.

The two factors I do not care for in shooting the 17-caliber are its wind-sensitive qualities and the fact that the bore seems to foul after about 10 shots or so. I learned, however, that the fouling problem was really quite minimal. Using 24.0 grains of IMR-4895, for example, accuracy was still good after 20 shots. A simple swab-out with Outer's NITRO solvent followed by a touch-up with Outer's Tri-Lube, took care of any fouling problem I might have experienced.

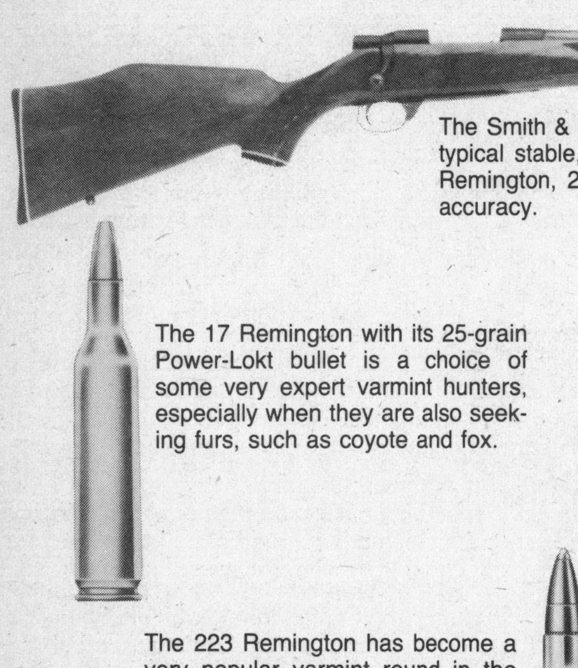

The Smith & Wesson Model 1500 Deluxe Varmint rifle is a typical stable, heavy barreled (medium weight) rifle in 222 Remington, 223 Remington and 22-250. It offers first rate accuracy.

The 17 Remington with its 25-grain Power-Lokt bullet is a choice of some very expert varmint hunters, especially when they are also seeking furs, such as coyote and fox.

The 223 Remington has become a very popular varmint round in the past few years. It is a fine round, though it does not appreciably excel over the standard 222 Remington. Military cases are available for the 223, however.

Second, though a strong wind will play hob with the little 25-grain bullet, it will not take it off course at closer ranges. Even where I live, in windy country, I could hit a jackrabbit-sized target at 300 yards in a breeze using the 17 Remington. Mostly, I came to respect the little caliber because my friend Jim Osborne, who was actually making a living as a full-time trapper, used the rifle with great success on coyotes. The little 25-grain pill dropped the coyotes instantly at well over 300 yards in many cases, and the pelt was undamaged by the little bullet, which entered and blew up on the inside of the animal, rather than creating a huge exit hole.

The 17 Remington I tested produced fine accuracy at full throttle using 24.0 grains of IMR-4895. Of almost equal accuracy in my tests was another load, however. This was

25.0 grains of IMR-4320. Using 25.0 grains of IMR-4320 with the Hornady 25-grain bullet, MV reached over 4100 fps, and accuracy was consistently good—under 1 inch for five-shot groups at 100 yards. This was a clean load, too, in terms of bore fouling. The 17 Remington can be made with a very light barrel in an easy-to-carry rifle for the roaming varmint hunter, too. In the Remington 700, with its 24-inch barrel and a 1:10 twist, accuracy is really quite fine.

The 22 Hornet

The 22 Hornet is a good little round. It is a medium-range varmint cartridge, which is to say it is better suited to neat little rifles than to big bolt-action rifles which could just as easily be chambered for the larger and flatter-shooting varmint cartridges. For example, in the Ruger No. 3, with a 22-inch barrel, the little Hornet round generates about 2800 fps MV with a 50-grain bullet. This makes the load very workable for varmints up to 250 yards and maybe 300 in the hands of a good shot.

The Hornet round goes back to 1930. It was good then. It is good now. Many shooters call it an accurate cartridge. It is accurate, but mainly because it is mild and can be chambered into many fine rifle styles. It was even available in the Winchester Models 54/70 rifles. Today, one can obtain the Hornet round in beautiful bolt-action rifles and handy single shots from Kimber and Ruger, respectively. It has a definite place in the varminter's world in spite of the fact that it is soundly whipped in terms of bullet velocity by many of its bigger brothers.

The Federal Cartridge Company offers a 55-grain boat-tail hollow point bullet for this varmint cartridge, a 223 Remington round. Federal suggests this load for super accurate long-range shooting where explosiveness of projectile is desired.

The 218 Bee

Still around because of some fine old rifles chambered in this caliber, the Bee is not any more than a 22 Hornet in actual load performance. Anyone who owns a rifle chambered in 218 Bee can reload for it quite successfully, but the round is really not much above the 22 Hornet.

The 222 Remington

I owned a 222 Remington for years. The cartridge was chambered into a heavy-barreled Sako and 1/2-inch groups at 100 yards were the byword. It was quite capable of taking varmints out at 300 yards, and on a calm day it was really no trick to hit at 350 yards with the high-power scope sight I had mounted on that rifle. The 222 Remington has been around since 1950, and it has always been a winner. In lightweight rifles, as well as in the heavier models, its smaller capacity case yields plenty of velocity without much fanfare.

The 222 Remington round is pleasant to shoot in any of its chamberings, in other words, and very easy to hit with. I truly admire the little round, especially when packaged in a light rifle. While true hardball varmint shooting may indeed mean heavy barreled, stable rifles for sedentary long-range work, I also enjoy the concept of lighter, more pleasant-to-carry varmint rifles as well. Out of a little 20-inch barrel, the 222 Remington will drive a 55-grain bullet at a MV of 3100 fps. I like the 222 Remington.

The 223 Remington

This is the 222 Remington Magnum all over again with ballistics out of the same length of barrel nearly identical. However, the 223 has the advantage of popularity, and I would recommend it over the 222 Remington Magnum for that reason alone. The military took the 223 on as its own, and this has meant lots of cheap, surplus brass for shooters who want to buy once-fired military 223 cases and reload them. The 223 is a very good round, of course. It is a shade ahead of the 222 Remington in terms of performance and a near twin brother of the 222 Remington Magnum. Due to its widespread popularity, I would buy the 223 over either the 222 Remington or 222 Remington Magnum today, but not because it is that far ahead of the former nor that different from the latter.

The 222 Remington Magnum

This is a slightly lengthened version of the 222 Remington and if a shooter has to have the name "magnum" attached to his cartridge, he should buy a 222 Remington

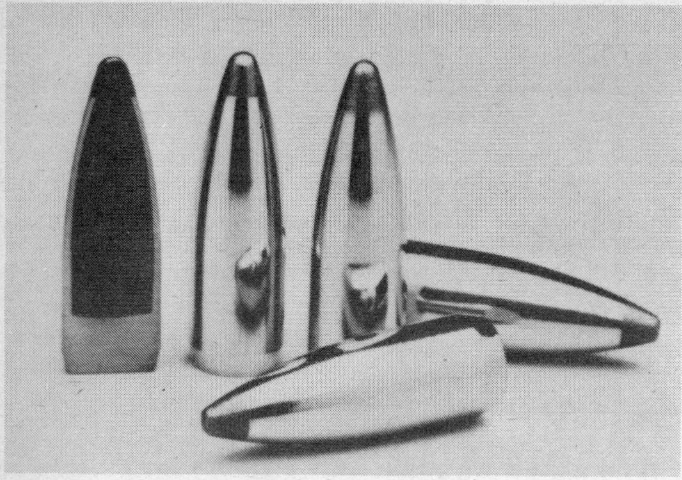

A 52-grain, .224-inch Nosler Solid Base soft nose bullet is meant for varmint hunting. This boat-tail type bullet has a thin jacket which means faster mushrooming.

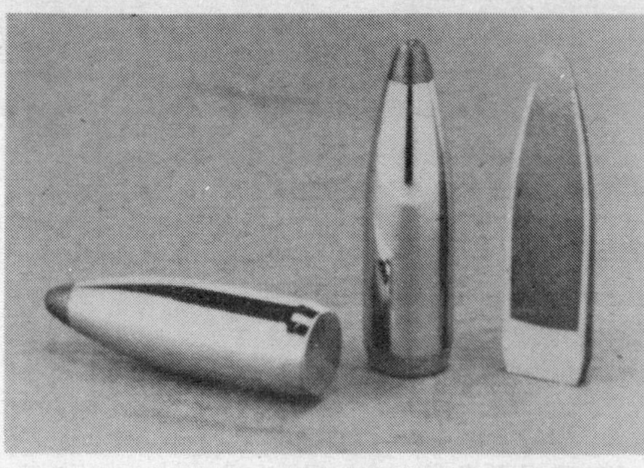

There has been a wide acceptance of the 60-grain bullet in 22-caliber for varmint hunting, the attempt being to increase sectional density and ballistic coefficient, hence remaining velocity and energy at long range. These 60-grain 22-caliber bullets are the Nosler Solid Base Spitzer design.

Magnum. However, in point of fact, the 222 Remington Magnum produces only slight advances in MV and trajectory over its smaller brother if the same barrel lengths are used for both rounds in a head-on test. I am not knocking the 222 Remington Magnum. It will do everything the 222 will do and just as well. It will push the heavier bullets in the 55- to 60-grain weight class a bit faster than the standard 222 Remington. The only problem with the 222 Remington Magnum is the fact that it's a bit difficult, these days, to procure (easily) ammo or brass.

The 225 Winchester

This is a semi-rimmed cartridge. It drives bullets in the 55-grain class at muzzle velocities of 3600-3700 fps, and is quite deadly at ranges of 300 yards and more. In fact, on calm days a shooter who is practiced can strike varmint-sized animals of the jackrabbit class at up to 400 yards with a good degree of regularity. If I were looking for a single shot varmint rifle, the 225 might be a possible choice but at this time the 225 is not chambered in any commercially available rifle. It is also whipped by other rounds in its niche.

The 224 Weatherby Magnum

With ballistics about on par with the 22-250 Remington, this is a strong varmint round for those who will be buying a Weatherby rifle. With a 26-inch barrel, the 55-grain bullet leaves the muzzle at 3700 fps or better. The 22-250 will beat that a bit. There is no doubt that this is a serious varmint cartridge for the varminter who is looking for something different. It's the only 22-caliber varmint cartridge that wears a belt. It's ideally suited for the handloader as brass and ammo are available from only one source—Weatherby.

The 220 Swift

Riflemaker Dean Zollinger owned a 220 Swift he made up, and we experimented with the round extensively. It's an interesting cartridge, and certainly deserves to be recognized as the round which excited varminters to truly long-range shooting. The Swift made its fame by offering a factory loading which drove a bullet at over 4000 fps—quite an achievement. Of course, the Swift still does the same thing today. In a 26-inch barrel, the handloader can gain 3900 fps with several powders. We drove a 50-grain bullet at 4100 fps MV using 40.0 grains of IMR-4064 powder.

With our hotter loads, case stretch was a minor problem and case life itself was not too fantastic. Accuracy was good in our rifle, but not spectacular. We had a medium-weight, air-gauged barrel to work with, and I maintain my position that this accuracy, or the lack of it, is less a matter of case design than other factors. All in all, the 220 Swift was and is a great cartridge. It has been around since 1935 and has been chambered into some very fine rifles. However, the Swift has been upstaged in the popularity charts by another cartridge—the 22-250 Remington.

The 22-250 Remington

This round was wildcatted back before I was born. In the 1930s, 250-3000 Savage cases were necked down to fire 22-caliber bullets, and there was the 22-250. I fired one for a few years when it was still a wildcat round, long before Remington began loading for it in 1967. I think the 22-250 is the current king of the 22-caliber specialized varmint rounds. It is very slightly behind the 220 Swift in out-and-out muzzle velocity, but we could always load the 22-250 to within 100 fps of the big Swift and the 22-250 seemed to give better barrel life and definitely gave us better case life.

I'd go for it today if looking for a hot varmint number.

Saying all of this, I must add that I'd not throw away a 220 Swift just to go out and buy a 22-250. Also, the fine little rifles which can be chambered for the 223 Remington round make that cartridge very useful for varmints, too, though I can load the 22-250 to equal the 223; the reverse is not true. About the highest velocity we obtained in our own 22-250 was 3900 fps MV with a 50-grain pill. No load we ever worked up gave us 4000 fps, as we found in the Swift, but in practical terms, the 22-250 proved itself as effective as the Swift. We loaded 41.5 grains of Winchester 760 powder for excellent accuracy with close to 3900 fps MV out of a 24-inch barrel.

The 22-250, by the way, can be chambered into a handy rifle. The single shot Thompson/Center Model TCR-83 is a prime example of this fact. The overall length of this rifle is 39 inches, and it weighs under 7 pounds. The Ruger Model 77 RSI International is a rifle with an 18.5-inch barrel, and it, too, is chambered for the 22-250. Anyone buying a rifle for the purpose of varmint hunting in the long-range "steady-rest" tradition should look carefully at the 22-250 chambering. For those who wish to varmint hunt on the move, this round also fills the bill in rifles similar to the last two mentioned above. This is a fine round, and I applaud it as the king of 22 centerfire long-range high-velocity numbers.

The 6mm Clan

I wish to lump all of the faster 6mm rounds here, such as the 6mm Remington, 243 Winchester and 240 Weatherby Magnum. All of these are, and always have been, compromise rounds, serving the function of both long-range varminting and deer hunting. This versatility is not merely a paper whim. It is a fact. Except for a few rare conditions, I would feel (and have felt) perfectly comfortable with any of the 6mm clan using 80- to 100-grain bullets for deer. There is an advantage in using these rounds for a long-range varmint hunting. That advantage is stability of the bullet in a breeze. Simply, the heavier 6mm bullet is less prone to blow off target than its lighter 22-caliber cousins.

If I were intent on long-range coyote shooting, for example, in very serious situations, I would as soon have a 6mm in a heavy barrel with a high-power scope sight than anything else. But this is talking about a special situation. I like the 6mms very much. But in the world of specialized varmint hunting using specialized rifles, I think the hotshot 22 centerfire rounds are the most appropriate, not always the best in all ways, but the most viable all-around.

Varmint Loads in Big Game Rifles

All of the big bores have varmint-load potential. This is easy enough to see by looking through the bullet lineup for any of the larger calibers, larger than 6mm, that is. The 25-caliber group has, for example, a 75-grain jacketed hollow point offering. For deer? Hardly. This is a varmint bullet. The 6.5mm (.264-inch) group is not blessed with as many choices, but a 100-grain bullet from any of the hotter 6.5s, such as the 6.5/06, my own 6.5 DGS and the 264 Winchester Magnum round, will all push bullets of the 100-grain class in the 3400-3600 fps MV domain, and that

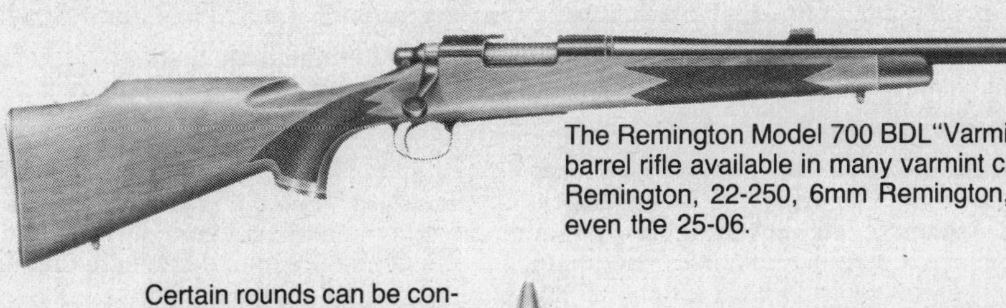

The Remington Model 700 BDL"Varmint Special" is a heavy barrel rifle available in many varmint calibers, to include 222 Remington, 22-250, 6mm Remington, 243 Winchester and even the 25-06.

Certain rounds can be considered both varmint and deer numbers. The 25-06 is much more a deer and antelope cartridge than a varmint round, but some shooters do use this fast number for varmints. Its bullets do comparatively well in the wind.

A fine varmint/deer cartridge is the 6mm Remington. It is entirely adequate for deer under most hunting situations, and yet it does make a fine wind-bucking long-range varmint round.

This 6mm caliber Nosler Solid Base boat-tail bullet would be useful on varmints out of any of the fast 6mm/243 caliber rifles. It is a perfect example of the varmint bullet in a compromise rifle. Of course, this bullet would also serve on deer, but Nosler makes other 6mm bullets specifically for deer hunting.

means *very flat* shooting for long-range work.

The 270-caliber offers bullets in the 90-100-grain weight class, and velocities of 3400-3500 fps are not that hard to obtain, showing another example of varmint bullets in big game cases. The 7mm group has its varminters, too, such as the 115-120-grain weight bullets. My own 7mm shoves a 120-grain bullet out of the 7mm Remington Magnum case at 3500 fps MV for flat-shooting of the highest order. The 30-caliber line is replete with varmint bullets, to include spire or spitzer 110-grain numbers as well as a 130-grain hollow-point. The standard 30-06 pushes a 110-grain varmint bullet faster than 3350 fps MV, and out of my custom Bishop 300 Winchester Magnum, we have clocked the 110-grain bullet at 3700 fps MV!

After 30-caliber, the varmint bullet syndrome falls away, as should be the case. However, what about all of these light bullets from big game cartridges? Are they any good? Of course they are good, but I do not see them as part of our story here at all. None is right in terms of *specialized* varminting, and though performance can be spectacular, some of the criteria we set up for a specific varmint round are not met by these bigger cartridges.

First, I consider a specialized varmint rifle one chambered for a round which offers mild recoil so that many shots can be fired on a given day with comfort. After the 6mm clan, we can forget that true mild recoil, and even in some of the 6mm loadings, firing 30 or 40 times (or more) is not as pleasant as we would wish for in a specialized varmint rifle. Second, a special varmint rifle/cartridge should offer high explosiveness for two reasons: 1) it should hit the varmint with a great deal of shock; 2) the slug should self-destruct when it strikes the ground. Yes, many of the bigger calibers with their thinner-skinned varmint weight bullets do offer good bustup characteristics, but nothing like the hotrock 22s.

While the crack from a high-speed centerfire 22 rifle is quite loud, louder than one might at first expect, it is not as noisy as most of the high-speed varmint loads in the big game caliber. I believe that a rancher or farmer who knows anything about firearms can tell the difference between a big booming 30-06 and a 22-250 that's being fired in his pasture. It's my guess that he's going to be a little happier with the 22-250. Additionally, it is seldom that we actually build a big game rifle for varmint rifle use. I'm speaking of a rifle with plenty of barrel weight and a big scope sight. Yes, there are some fine varmint rifles, already alluded to, which are light, short and sweet to carry. But in terms of +300-yard shooting from a sedentary position, give me a specialized varmint rifle, heavy in weight, stout of barrel, slim of caliber and topped with plenty of high-powered glassware.

In short, the varmint rifle is mainly chambered for a hot centerfire 22-caliber round, capable of putting a bullet out at high speed with consequent flat trajectory and high energy delivery at long range. The latter, of course, is in terms of varmint-sized game. We are not suggesting that the energy level of the 22 centerfire is going to challenge the delivered energy of a good big game load. A final note: I have learned more about shooting at long range by using a varmint rifle, than I have with any other type of rifle. Varmint rifles have also served well to educate me as to wind deflection and drop. It's my opinion that any shooter who wants to enjoy all aspects of the shooting sports should look into some form of varmint rifle for his own use.

And now, a brief comparison of loads we have tried in some of the 22 varmint cartridges.

Comparisons of Selected Varmint Rounds*

Cartridge	Bullet Wt.Grs.	MV(fps)	ME(fpe)	300-Yard Velocity(fps)	300-Yard Energy (fpe)
17 Rem.	25	4100	933	2465	337
22 Hornet	50	2800	871	1690	317
218 Bee	50	2800	871	1690	317
222 Rem.	50	3300	1209	2050	467
222 Rem. Mag.	50	3400	1284	2120	499
223 Rem.	50	3400	1284	2120	499
225 Win.	50	3800	1604	2425	653
224 Wthby.	50	3900	1689	2500	694
220 Swift	50	3900	1689	2500	694
22-250 Rem.	50	3900	1689	2500	694
243 Win.	75	3500	2041	2500	1041
6mm Rem.	75	3600	2159	2590	1117
For Comparison:					
30-06 Spgfld.	110	3500	2993	2330	1326
300 Win. Mag.	110	3700	3345	2490	1515

*(See chapter on trajectory charts for proper sightings.)

Note: With the 22-250 and the 50-grain bullet sighted 3 inches high at 100 yards, the bullet will be back on target at about 290-295 yards and close to 9 inches low at 400 yards.
With a 110-grain bullet from the 30-06 at a MV of 3500 fps, sighted to hit 3 inches high at 100 yards, the bullet is back on again at about 300 yards and about 10.5 inches low at 400.

Chapter 8
The Rimfire Sidearm

The small caliber sidearm is just about perfect for close-range varmint hunting. Author took this jackrabbit with a 22-caliber Ruger semi-auto target model at a range of about 50 yards.

THE 22 RIMFIRE HANDGUN is one of the most important pieces of shooting equipment in the battery of the complete shooter. Its cost is generally and comparatively low, as is the ammo it uses. But its uses are many. Having owned a few rimfire sidearms over the years, it was actually my backpacking trips into the no-road country which convinced me of a 22-caliber handgun's high value. These days, I always pack the pistol into the outback. But I also practice with my 22 semi-auto now and then, and I also employ it as a camp companion.

General Uses for the 22 Handgun

As already stated, my number one use for the 22 rimfire sidearm is on the backtrail. Where I do much of my big game hunting and country exploring, there are mountain grouse and cottontails, as well as snowshoe rabbits, all in season during the big-game harvest. It is entirely legal (in my area) to hunt those birds and rabbits using the 22 rimfire sidearm. Many times, I have found myself in a situation where a small supply of fresh meat would be welcomed, not only by me, but by hiking companions as well. The 22 rimfire handgun has most often supplied that meat.

Certainly, there are underloads for big game rifles which can also take small game edibles on the trail. I often carry a Pre-'64 Winchester Model 94 rifle in 30-30 caliber, and take with me some squib handloads which are excellent for potting camp meat. But no matter the rifle, an outdoorsman usually has little to no time to remove the big game load from the chamber and replace it with the light load. This does not make the light load useless, for there are many other times when big game hunting is set aside and the big game rifle is loaded with small game rounds. But most of the time, it's a matter of reaching into the holster and pulling out the little 22 rimfire handgun when it's important to make meat on the trail.

With this function in mind, the reader will understand why my personal 22 handgun is a target model. The head of a mountain grouse, cottontail or snowshoe is no huge target, and though the shooting ranges are usually very short, accuracy must be of the highest order. Now and then, I have taken small game or small varmints with the 22 rimfire handgun using the offhand stance, but most of the time, I try to steady myself as much as possible. My own 22 semi-auto, from a rested position, will put its rounds into a 1-inch group, center-to-center, at 25 yards; that's with me shooting the pistol, not an expert handgunner with formal target shooting experience.

While the backtrail is my favorite environment for the rimfire sidearm, another good function is in camp. A camp gun is a useful tool to have along, for many reasons—from plinking fun, where the noise will not disturb others, to small game getting to informal varminting at close range. The low recoil 22 can be used with effectiveness by most shooters if they will practice. The noise level is not too alarming, and the blast effect is minimal. The 22 sidearm is easy to master in comparison with the big bore one-hand guns for protection purposes or big game hunting.

Small game hunting is another viable use for the 22 sidearm. While campouts, backcountry hiking and big game hunting all merit the use of a 22 rimfire to collect small game as an incidental part of the trip, there is also a lot of challenge in using the 22 sidearm as a firstline small game hunting firearm. Hunters must check on the legalities before embarking on a small game hunt with pistol or revolver, but it is quite legal where I go, and I have put a number of cottontails in my fry pan with the 22 handgun. It is also useful in squirrel hunting situations. Yes, it does take both stalking skill and shooting skill to be a successful 22 rimfire handgunner of small game, but the activity can be mastered without that much effort.

Another good use for a 22 rimfire handgun is practice. It is much cheaper, generally speaking, to practice with a 22 rimfire sidearm than with a big bore. Not only that, but I believe a lot can be learned about the mastery of the handgun through shooting the light-recoil rimfire. All aspects of shooting the sidearm, from stance to body control to trigger squeeze, can be achieved first in the 22 rimfire sidearm and then transferred to the large-bore handgun. Shooting the 22

The 22 rimfire sidearm can be used to take smaller varmints such as prairie dogs. This Ruger Mark II is an example of a target model which is used in the field. The author likes the accuracy level and the good sights, as does his son, John Fadala, posing with his "catch" here.

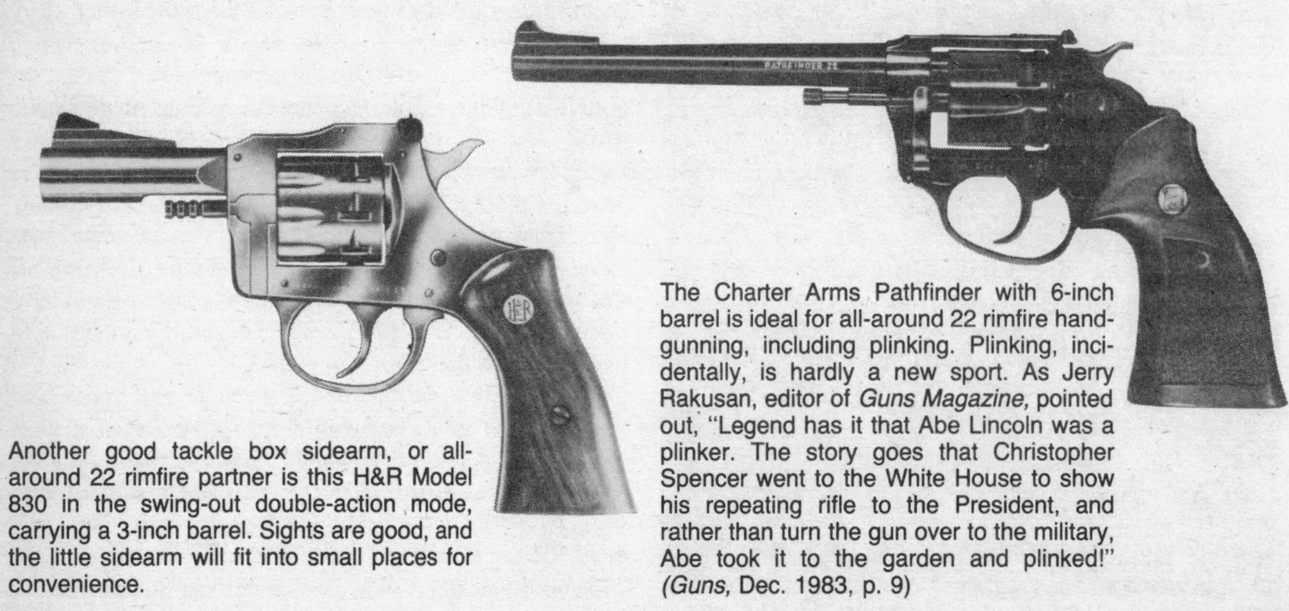

The Charter Arms Pathfinder with 6-inch barrel is ideal for all-around 22 rimfire handgunning, including plinking. Plinking, incidentally, is hardly a new sport. As Jerry Rakusan, editor of *Guns Magazine,* pointed out, "Legend has it that Abe Lincoln was a plinker. The story goes that Christopher Spencer went to the White House to show his repeating rifle to the President, and rather than turn the gun over to the military, Abe took it to the garden and plinked!" *(Guns,* Dec. 1983, p. 9)

Another good tackle box sidearm, or all-around 22 rimfire partner is this H&R Model 830 in the swing-out double-action mode, carrying a 3-inch barrel. Sights are good, and the little sidearm will fit into small places for convenience.

The 22 rimfire handgun may be king of all plinking arms. Here are a couple of Colt single-action six-shooters, both with good sights. The single-action design is generally a bit slower-loading, but this factor is of little to no consequence to the modern plinker.

rimfire for practice is about as natural and sensible as getting in out of the rain.

Plinking is another method of practicing with the 22 rimfire sidearm. But there is a difference. Plinking is far less structured, and while a shooter certainly can learn a lot about shooting when he is just rolling a tin can, the major value of plinking is entertainment and relaxation with a good safe backstop and some "mobile" targets. Plinking with just about any sort of firearm is acceptable, but plinking with the 22 rimfire handgun has its own special charm, and once again the economy angle has to be recognized here.

It stands to reason that if practice sessions and plinking games are 22 rimfire handgunning activities, then formal target shooting with the smallbores is of equal or even, to some shooters, greater merit. The 22 rimfire handgun is given its own matches, and there is no one who can argue with the excellence of the sport. Many schools have pistol clubs in which the 22 rimfire is the mainstay firearm, and there are good indoor ranges all over the country suited to serious target shooting with the 22 handguns.

While it may at first seem incredulous, the 22 rimfire is also a pretty good tackle box tool for the fisherman, where it is legal to secure a firearm within a tackle box. Fishermen sometimes find themselves in need of some form of firepower and the 22 is often enough to get the job done, be that task one of making supper of a small game animal or dispatching a small pest on the bank.

Semi-Auto Pistol or Revolver, Which Is Best?

I don't know which is best and nobody else knows either because both serve so admirably. All I can do is relate how I made my own personal choice in the matter and quickly add that my two sons, at the same time, and after long contemplation, went the other way. For my own 22 rimfire sidearm I selected the 22 semi-automatic pistol. Here is why. I liked the availability of 10 shots without reloading. Ten shots, even from a 22 rimfire, can be terribly discouraging to any form of attacker from rabid coyote to even larger forms of danger to the outdoorsman.

I also liked the fact that I could, if desired, buy an extra clip for my semi-auto, meaning I could carry 20 shots with me on the trail as handy as you please. Furthermore, I found the 22 semi-auto very pleasant to shoot and very accurate. In addition, its profile is flat. Unlike the revolver, the semi-auto has no cylinder, and therefore packs flatter on the hip than the revolver. Small nitpicking point? It might be. But when I have a packframe lashed onto my body, it's very nice keeping other items I am packing down to a minimum, not only in weight, but also in bulk. And the flat-sided 22 rimfire semi-auto pistol clings to the hip like a tight-fitting pair of pants. I also like the positive feeding of the semi-auto though I don't mean to suggest it feeds better than the revolver's cylinder. Yet, I have had the cylinder pin foul up a bit on a revolver but, to date, have not experienced a malfunction with my 22 semi-auto.

Both of my sons weighed my arguments, tossed each of my ideas into the bush with a casual air, and selected 22 revolvers for their own backtrail sidearms, plinking guns, fishing trip companions and small game getters. They reasoned, and not wrongfully, that they could not get the option of 22 rimfire magnum use in the semi-auto. They found the revolver totally reliable, without any problems whatever. Accuracy was also good, pretty close to my tar-

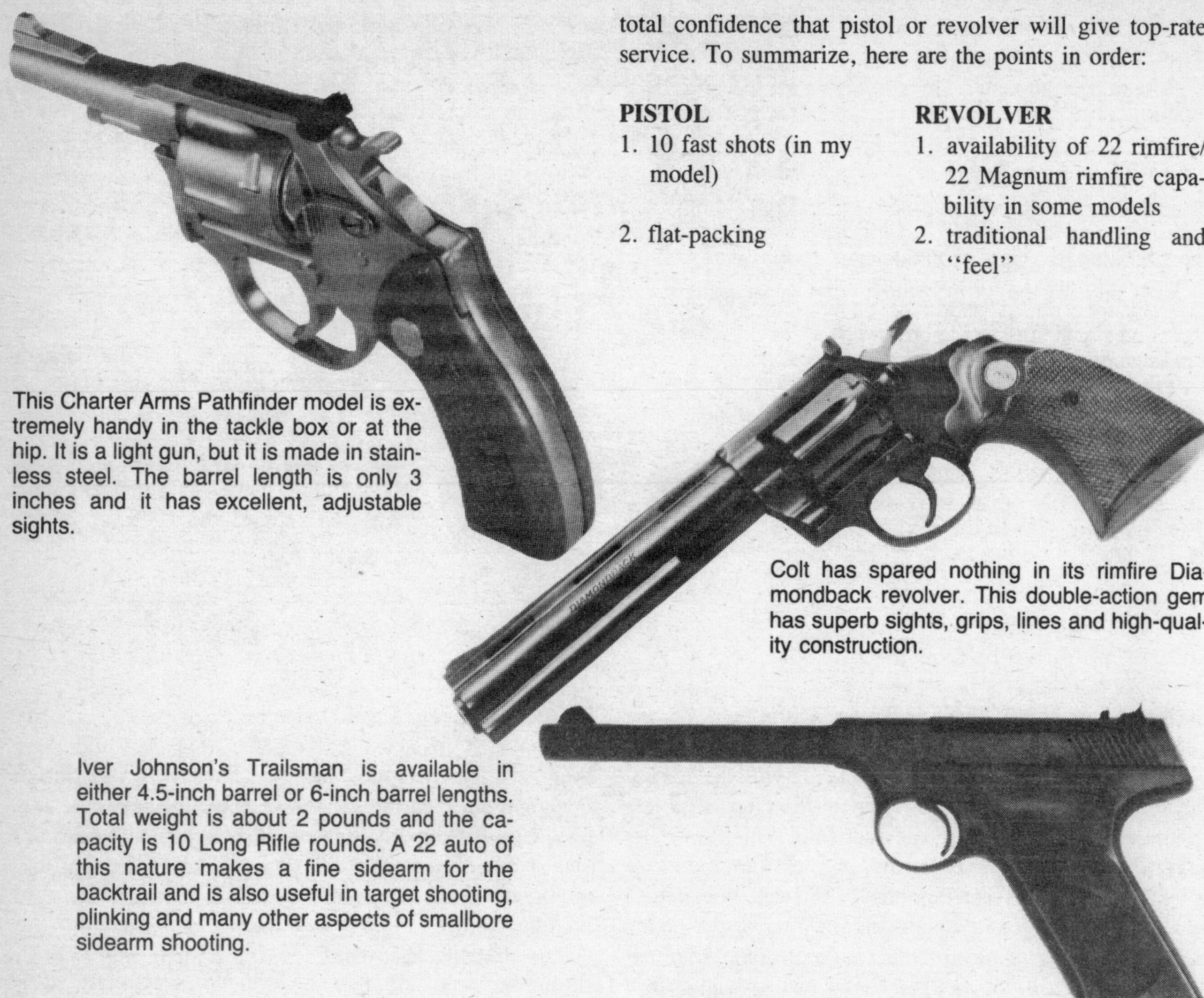

This Charter Arms Pathfinder model is extremely handy in the tackle box or at the hip. It is a light gun, but it is made in stainless steel. The barrel length is only 3 inches and it has excellent, adjustable sights.

Colt has spared nothing in its rimfire Diamondback revolver. This double-action gem has superb sights, grips, lines and high-quality construction.

Iver Johnson's Trailsman is available in either 4.5-inch barrel or 6-inch barrel lengths. Total weight is about 2 pounds and the capacity is 10 Long Rifle rounds. A 22 auto of this nature makes a fine sidearm for the backtrail and is also useful in target shooting, plinking and many other aspects of smallbore sidearm shooting.

get model semi-auto, though not quite on par with it, but certainly good enough to get the job accomplished (the revolvers were not to be used in formal target shooting matches).

They also liked the feel and overall "looks" of the revolver more than that of the semi-auto, though the aesthetics of either is a personal matter of course. They felt it was no more trouble to reload the revolver than to reload the pistol, unless the pistol was using a spare clip, obviously. Most of all, however, they were convinced of their choice because of the duplex nature of their revolvers.

The choice between revolver or pistol really is a toss-up. I chose the pistol. It is best for what I want it to do. But I could get by with a revolver just fine, and there have been times, admittedly, when the thought of dual cylinders loaded with 22 rimfires and 22 Magnum rimfires was appealing to me. Furthermore, the 22 revolver will use 22 Short, Long or Long Rifle ammo, while the 22 semi-auto is held to the use of Long Rifle ammo only. The complete shooter can add either 22 rimfire handgun type to his battery with total confidence that pistol or revolver will give top-rate service. To summarize, here are the points in order:

PISTOL	**REVOLVER**
1. 10 fast shots (in my model)	1. availability of 22 rimfire/22 Magnum rimfire capability in some models
2. flat-packing	2. traditional handling and "feel"
3. extra clip for ease of reloading	3. reliable
4. reliable	4. can use 22 Shorts, Longs and LR ammo
5. accurate	5. accurate

Sights for the 22 Sidearm

A close friend owns a fine little 22 revolver. It is compact, neat and about the best looking little 22 revolver anyone could ask for. I would not have it on a bet, for free, with a big pink bow tied around it. I have watched my friend unlimber that little jewel and attempt to put a small game edible in the pot with it. Left, right, up, and finally, *plunk!*, a low hit. He does not shoot the little revolver that way all the time, just most of the time. One afternoon he burned off about four cylinders full in order to collect one snowshoe rabbit.

That little pistol had a notch in the topstrap for a rear sight. Therein was its fault. I want a 22 rimfire sidearm with excellent adjustable sights. I purchased my own 22 sidearm because of its target sights, as well as bull barrel. I want fully adjustable rear sights with front sights that complement the rear sight notch for as clean a sight picture as possible. Remember, as with any sight, a frame of reference must be possible in order to draw a good "bead" on the target, and the target-type adjustable sights found on many 22 rimfire handguns allows for that.

By frame of reference, I mean a sight picture where there is a little bit of light on either side of the front sight as it rests optically in the rear sight notch. In this way, a shooter can be certain that he has given the front sight the proper placement in lining it up in the rear sight notch. I am well aware that a good shot can produce decent results with the "fixed sights" on some revolvers. I have a black powder revolver which is very sure-pointing, and I can hit a tin can with it almost every time at about 10 to 15 paces.

But for fine shooting and grouping of projectiles, sights are the answer, meaning adjustable, target-type sights of high sophistication. The 22 sidearm is not generally for close-range, life-saving use. It is not a mainstay self-defense firearm. It is not for pointing, in other words. It is for accurate shooting. I could get by very well with revolver or pistol, but I cannot and will not attempt to get by with a 22 rimfire sidearm which has sights that fall short of near-target or target quality. I own a 22 rimfire for *hitting,* not for fast-point-plinking or rapid fire capability to see if I can luck-out on a tin can by tossing lots of lead at it instead of being able to fire one well-aimed shot.

How to Sight In

I am not a long-range expert with a handgun, nor do I have an interest in shooting a 22 at more than 25 to a maximum of 50 yards from the target. I have taken a few jackrabbits with my 22 semi-auto at about 75 yards, but was in the company of a rifleman who was my backup; otherwise I would not have fired. Therefore, sighting in to hit point-of aim at only 25 yards is all right for me. I take many cottontails and mountain grouse as well at even closer ranges. On the backcountry trail, where I do a lot of my own 22 rimfire sidearm shooting, there is not a need for long-range shots. The game is usually taken at very close range.

Therefore, my 22 rimfire pistol is sighted in for a flat 25 yards. I would not sight a hunting handgun of the big-bore variety for this range, nor is 25 yards necessarily ideal in terms of gaining the most from the trajectory of the 22 rimfire round, even with handgun muzzle velocities. The chapter on trajectories shows how to sight in the 22 for maximum long-range advantage but I have chosen to ignore this since a majority of my shooting is within 50-yard limits.

Sighted to hit dead on at 25 yards, my 22 semi-auto puts the bullets a couple inches low at 50 yards, giving me a pretty good "hold-right-on" ability with my 22. This gives me the trajectory to aim right on target from a few feet away to 50 yards without concern for doping out hold-under or hold-over. While the 25-yard sighting is not perfect in terms of 22 potential, it serves me well in this case.

Accuracy

My 22 semi-auto target model with its heavy barrel will put 10 shots into 1 inch, center-to-center, at 25 yards from the muzzle, provided a good solid benchrest is used. I cannot shoot that type of group in the field, but that's not the pistol's fault. In many cases, I have fired 10 shots into *less* than 1 inch at 25 yards when conditions were just about perfect in terms of lighting, lack of wind, calmness of the shooter and rigidity of the benchrest setup.

My sons' revolvers will place five shots into about 1.25 inches at 25 yards under the same conditions described above. Using another revolver, we were able to group five shots into an average more like 1.75 inches at 25 yards, so the guns do vary in accuracy potential. However, I think there is even more variation in the exact sight picture obtained by the shooter and of course variation in the shooter himself, the atmospheric conditions, range conditions and benchrest conditions.

In brief, however, the shooter should consider a five-shot group of 1.5 inches at 25 yards as accurate in terms of the 22 rimfire handgun. I certainly would be satisfied and could do very well on small game with that degree of accuracy to work with. That my target model shoots closer than 1.5 inches most of the time, if I do my part from a benchrest, is conducive to some pretty good field shooting.

Trigger Pull

Lacking a trigger-pull gauge, the reader may find it difficult to do little more than guess at the weight of his gun's trigger pull. However, a trigger-pull gauge is not necessary to determine the *kind* of trigger your rimfire 22 sidearm has, be it good, bad or just all right. One of the reasons I chose the semi-auto pistol as best for my own 22 rimfire sidearm work, was its trigger pull. The trigger pull on my sons' revolvers averages out at about 5 pounds, whereas the release on my semi-auto is only 3 pounds, and I like that better. Furthermore, the trigger on my semi-auto has a backlash stop. It truly is a fine trigger all-around. However, the shooter should understand that as long as the trigger pull is *crisp* as opposed to creepy, it can be lived with. I have done reasonable field shooting with 5-pound trigger pulls on 22 rimfire handguns, even if I do feel that the 3-pound pull on my 22 is better because it is lighter. If the trigger on your particular rimfire sidearm is not to your liking, see a competent gunsmith. He should be able to cure the problem.

Safety

Some shooters feel that the revolver is a safer design than the semi-auto, and therefore opt for the revolver. The new-style revolvers with their modern safety design fea-

Browning's Challenger III semi-auto rimfire is noted for its fine trigger and reliable performance. This model comes with fully adjustable sights.

The Standard Auto Ruger semi-automatic pistol, in all its forms, has been a great favorite for many years. It offers the shooter repeated shots as fast as the trigger can be pulled. It's reliable and accurate. Seen here is the new new Mark II Target Model complete with adjustable sights and bull barrel.

tures are superb. Ruger uses a transfer bar in their revolver design and this bar comes between hammer and firing pin upon cocking the gun. The transfer bar is connected to the trigger mechanism and the bar transfers the energy of the hammer to the firing pin. This is an excellent safety feature on any revolver.

The semi-auto also has good safety features in all of the models I looked at. In fact, the semi-auto can be carried without a round in the chamber and still be rapidly operated so that a sedentary small game animal or mountain grouse is not going to get away while the shooter is working a round into the chamber. I carry my own 22 semi-auto (a Ruger) with an empty chamber but can slip a round in the chamber as quick as a wink. All that need be done is a short tug and release of the bolt. I do not think that either type beats the other in safety. Both are designed with strong safety features these days, and each is just as safe as its operator. Obviously, any sort of misuse cancels any built-in safety feature.

Ammunition and Ballistics

A 22 rimfire bullet in LR form gains its best muzzle velocity when barrel length is between 16 and 17 inches. This is as close as I can come in terms of the firearms I have chronographed. Given a 24-inch barrel and a 16-inch barrel on a 22 rimfire rifle using 22 LR ammo, the shorter barrel will have a slightly higher muzzle velocity. Theoretically, if not a 100 percent provable fact, the reason for this is the small charge of powder burning out in about 16 inches of bore length, the longer barrel only adding more drag on the bullet.

If 16 to 17 inches of barrel length is ideal in terms of optimum muzzle velocity from the 22 rimfire LR round, then it only stands to reason that 22 handguns will deliver less muzzle velocity and energy than 22 rifles. Of course, this is quite true. But it isn't so bad. In my tests with a 20-inch barreled rifle, most of the 22 LR ammo I chronographed averaged out *about* 1250 fps. In my handgun tests, the chronograph showed this same ammo to be doing about 1050 fps MV from the 5½-inch barrel.

At 1250 fps, the 40-grain 22 LR bullet delivers a muzzle energy of 139 foot-pounds. In my 5½-inch barrel with the same bullet doing 1050 fps, the muzzle energy would amount to 98 foot-pounds. Less, to be sure, but then a 22 rimfire handgun is fired at close range, often less than 30 or 40 yards. The effect of that 22 ammunition out of the revolver is quite adequate for its intended purpose. The Stinger will obtain about 1675+fps or so out of a 20-inch barrel for 200 foot-pounds of muzzle energy from its 32-grain bullet. The CCI Stinger will achieve about 1400 fps out of my 5½-inch barrel for a muzzle energy of 139 foot-pounds.

The Stinger and other hyper-velocity 22 ammo worked well in my own semi-auto, incidentally, and the bullets upset nicely at 15 yards from the muzzle in wet pack tests. Penetration with the hyper-velocity ammo from the pistol/revolver was very fine. When hunting varmints of the smaller variety at close range, the 22 rimfire handgun loaded with the hyper-velocity round is not a bad choice at all.

In my own case, I have turned to the 22 rimfire LR

The unique Charter Arms Explorer SII pistol is offered in 22 rimfire caliber. It has optional 6- and 10-inch barrels. Of course it is in the semi-auto mode. Note quick-switch barrel arrangement.

For those who want a little "beef" in a rimfire handgun, the Colt Trooper Mark III is the way to go. It's heavy (4- or 6-inch barrel) but beautifully made—not a bad choice for the man who wants to sit under a tree and snipe bushytails. The Trooper Mark III is available in either Long Rifle or Magnum persuasion.

standard velocity round in my 22 semi-auto. I use this round because it works for me, but have no qualms with anyone who would find the Long Rifle hollow-point a better choice. I find that a solid placed in the right spot (head shots in other words) will dispatch a small edible very nicely. Should the shot go slightly off target, there seems to be plenty of energy at 20 or 30 yards to anchor small game and mountain birds.

My all-time favorite small game close-range 22 rimfire round for the rifle is the 22 Short hollow point, and I have seen this round do good work at close range out of the rimfire revolver. Muzzle velocity will drop to a bit under 900 fps out of a 5½-inch barrel, but all the same, at 20 or 30 yards, the little 27-grain 22 Short hollow point bullet does the job well. I do not use it in my semi-auto because the 22 Short will not function. (Score "one" for those who prefer revolvers!)

Looking at a Few Models

A sample review of a few models will give the reader a very good idea of the *types* of features available in the 22 rimfire handgun. This little off-the-wall selection is not necessarily a recommendation on my part. It is a short survey only. Hopefully, the shooter will get a good idea of what is available if he has not yet familiarized himself with the 22 rimfire handgun.

Browning Challenger III/Sporter

This is a 22 semi-auto pistol using a 10-shot magazine. The Sporter has a 6¾-inch barrel, and its counterpart, the Browning Challenger III Auto Pistol has a heavy 5½-inch barrel. Either model features hardwood grips. Sights are adjustable. And these are well-finished, blued steel models. The action has the hold-open feature after the last shot is fired.

Charter Arms Explorer II Pistol

This semi-auto rimfire model wears an 8-inch barrel. Its magazine holds 8 shots. There is a blade front sight and the rear sight is adjustable for elevation. This model is priced in the very modest range and has interchangeable barrels. An extra 6-inch or 10-inch barrel is available.

Ruger Mark II

The Mark II is available in a Standard Auto Pistol or the bull barrel target model. The standard has a 4¾-inch barrel, which I would prefer for packing on the backtrail, or a 6-inch barrel. Good hard rubber grips complement these models and both hold 10-shot magazines. There is a hold-open device on the bolt. The target model has fully adjustable sights, which I like very much. Stainless steel versions of this handgun are just hitting the market.

Colt Trooper Mark III

Here is a standard high-class revolver in 22 Long Rifle chambering, six-shot. Barrel length options are 4, 6 or 8 inches. Checkered walnut grips. Rear sight is adjustable. Fixed ramp front sight. This is a nice-handling firearm and representative of the full-sized handguns of revolver style on large frames. They are stable and functional.

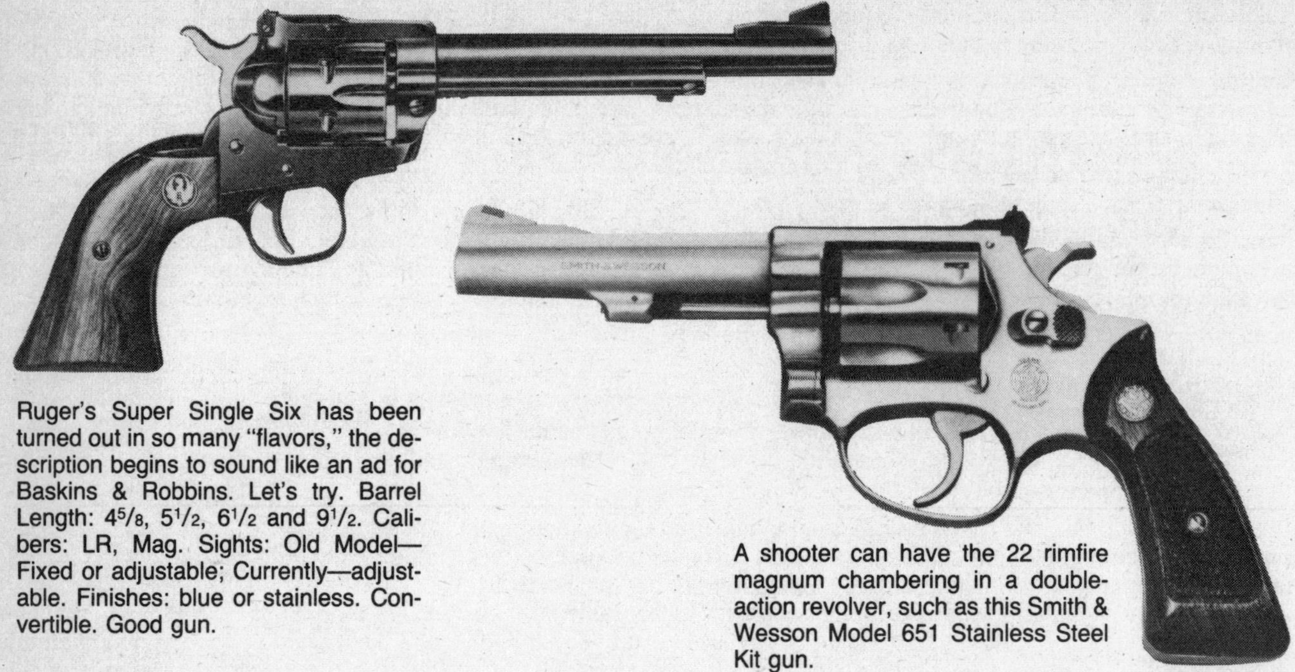

Ruger's Super Single Six has been turned out in so many "flavors," the description begins to sound like an ad for Baskins & Robbins. Let's try. Barrel Length: 4⅝, 5½, 6½ and 9½. Calibers: LR, Mag. Sights: Old Model—Fixed or adjustable; Currently—adjustable. Finishes: blue or stainless. Convertible. Good gun.

A shooter can have the 22 rimfire magnum chambering in a double-action revolver, such as this Smith & Wesson Model 651 Stainless Steel Kit gun.

Smith & Wesson Model 650/651 Magnum Kit Gun

Here is another full-sized revolver very much like the Models 34 and 63, except that it is designed to chamber the 22 rimfire magnum round, the 22 WMR. The Model 650 has a 3-inch barrel. The Model 651 has a 4-inch barrel. The 650 has a round butt and fixed sights. The 651 has a square butt, adjustable sights and is the one I would choose of these two models. Both are made of stainless steel. I list this sidearm because of the 22 WMR chambering, but the fine Model 34 22/32 Kit Gun is actually a favorite rimfire of mine, complete with a 4-inch barrel and a micro click, adjustable rear sight.

Ruger New Model Super Single Six Convertible Revolver

Reminiscent of the frontier-type six-gun, this Ruger offers plenty of rimfire versatility. You get two cylinders—one for the 22 Short, Long or Long Rifle, the other for the 22 Winchester Magnum Rimfire chambering. Barrel lengths are offered in 4⅝, 5½, 6½, and 9½ inches. The rear sight is fully adjustable and I applaud that. This is one of the many Rugers which has the transfer bar system, a very safe, durable design. The Super Single Six can be had in either blue or stainless form.

These are merely a tiny sampling of the myriad 22 rimfire handguns available to the complete shooter. The choice is not only wide, but deep in terms of excellent, well-constructed models. I believe that today's shooter has more superb choices in the 22 rimfire sidearm field than he has ever had in the past. I would not want to be without mine.

Getting the Most From Your Own 22 Rimfire Handgun

The steps to gaining the most from a 22 rimfire sidearm are several, beginning with selection. One selects a style of handgun based upon its intended use. In truth, the revolver/pistol choice is not the crux of the problem of choice. It is actually deeper than that. If I were to use a 22 rimfire for target shooting, obviously I would buy a 22 target model, of which there are many fine ones, such as the Hammerli, High-Standard, Heckler & Koch, Ruger, Smith & Wesson, and more.

For my own purpose—backpack companion with meat provision at the top of the list—I find the 22 semi-auto a good choice, but would do fine with a revolver, too. For plinking, there are many excellent and very inexpensive rimfire handguns around, guns which serve well on the trail and on the hunt as well as on the plinking range.

After selection, I would suggest you purchase at least a few different types of 22 rimfire ammo and fire a number of benchrest groups with that ammo. The shooter is likely to find that several brands and loads work just fine for his 22 handgun, but you never know. You could quickly discover that *one* specific brand of rimfire fodder will provide you with top groups. It is worth looking into and not very costly. Next, I would sight in with utmost care. There is no point in having superb accuracy potential unless that potential is realized through proper sighting in. A 22 rimfire handgun can be sighted to hit 1 or 2 inches high at 25 yards, and it will be back on in the 50-yard domain, or the shooter can elect to sight in for 25 yards and do most of his firing at that range.

Finally, success will be insured by practice. The chapters on shooting stance and practice will help the complete shooter with his 22 rimfire handgun proficiency. Most of us will never be *amazingly* proficient with a handgun, perhaps, but it is surprising how well we can do with a properly sighted 22 rimfire sidearm. No tiny can is safe at 25 yards when I have mine in hand, and many fine edibles have been feasted upon due to its accuracy. This is a very honorable harvest, for these species are short-lived and taking a few squirrels, rabbits or mountain gamebirds for food does not touch the overall population, as game managers will attest.

The Holster

Though we have a chapter on accessories, it is wise to put in a word here regarding the holster for the 22 rimfire handgun because I think the carrying method is very important. There are many good holsters, and it matters not one jot which one the shooter chooses. But I see the holster as a safety measure as well as a carrying tool, and like the type of holster which securely holds on to the handgun. To pack my semi-auto I use an Uncle Mike's Sidekick/holster because of the topstrap design and its non-scratch material. The handgun slides out of this holster with ease and never binds up in any way. Furthermore, the holster is waterproof, and will not wear out, even after years of heavy service. But there are many other good holsters, too. This one happens to be my choice, a light strong holster for the backcountry, where my little 22 semi-auto sees the most use.

Care

Talk about long-lasting, a well-cared-for 22 rimfire handgun will certainly fire thousands of rounds before any appreciable wear is noticed. I have heard of 50,000 rounds fired in a test rimfire handgun without any real wear showing, and I suspect that 100,000 rounds would not totally wear the 22 rimfire down. After all, the soft bullet at modest (low, actually) velocity using but a small powder charge is conducive to easy wear and tear. Cleaning and maintenance will be dealt with in the chapter on that subject, but let it suffice to say that the 22 rimfire requires only that attention given any fine tool and it will last a very long time.

In Closing

The best recommendation I can think of for the 22 rimfire handgun is an account of a hunt I took a few years ago. The game was mule deer and the terrain was definitely the outback. I had come into the area on an old cross-country road and had left the road a few miles behind me before I reached my first camp. During the deer season in that area, mountain grouse were open to hunting and the 22 rimfire was legal for taking this game. But I had enough food, I thought, to last me, so when I first encountered a few "fool hens" I simply let them pass me by.

Two days later, I found myself in an area I wanted to stay in for a while. I had 2 more days, possibly 3, before I had to return to civilization, but I had short-changed myself on food, and food to me is not only sustenance, but also a big part of any outing. I had some staples left, salt, some margarine, a few pounds of flour and the like, but my solid main-meal edibles were gone.

My little sidearm, however, brought me gourmet meat dishes every day in the form of cottontail mountain rabbits and gamebirds. If there need be any greater testimony to the value of the 22 rimfire, I don't know what it would be, but I think most shooters of the little soft-recoiling and not-too-noisy sidearms would say that their own rimfire one-hand guns are useful to them in other ways, for serious target work, hunting of small game, the taking of a close-range varmint now and then, and plenty of practice and plinking sessions.

The 22 rimfire sidearm may not be the most important tool in the complete shooter's battery, but it certainly makes sense to thousands of us and a shooting outfit bereft of the 22 rimfire handgun is like a hot dog without mustard. You just know something is missing.

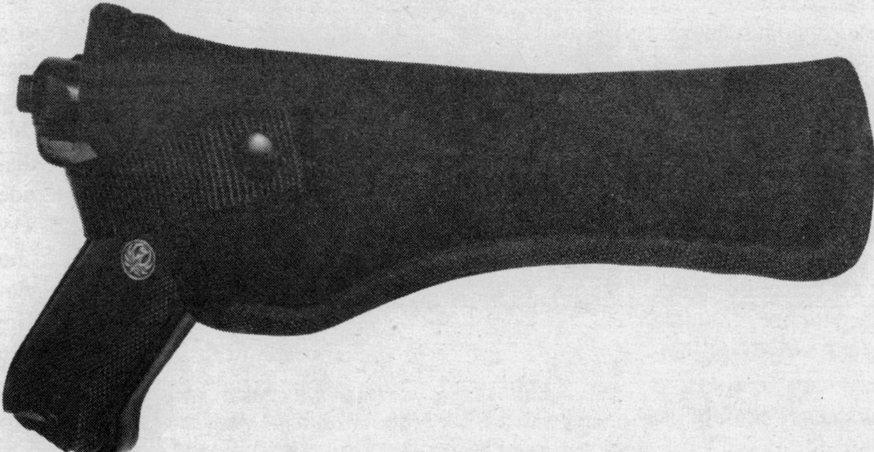

The author carries his personal 22 rimfire sidearm in an Uncle Mike's holster. He especially appreciates the non-scratch surface and interior of the holster and its high quality at small cost. Note top strap for added safety.

Chapter 9

The Big Game Handgun

THE HANDGUN is perhaps the most interesting firearm on the branch of the shooting family tree because of the subtle but important innovations blossoming annually. In a way, nothing truly new has been added. Certainly, there is nothing new about a break-open pistol. Those were around a long time ago. (In a 1932 gun catalog I have, several break-open pistols are shown for sale.) The revolver is certainly not new and the pistol in the semi-auto phase goes way back. But there have been changes.

These changes have made the most impact, I think, in the big game hunting handgun. Never before has the shooter had such variety before him in so many fine firearms. Never before has the shooter been able to enjoy truly big power in so many different models. The hunting handgun probably slipped in through the back door. I truly doubt that many shooters were interested in taking big game with the black powder handgun, though today that adjunct of big game handgunning is totally viable. I have fired more than one black powder pistol capable of harvesting big game.

The sidearm, however, was not originally intended for big game hunting. The handgun was a compact means of carrying power on the hip, or for that matter tucked into a belt or sash about the waist, or in holsters attached to a saddle. There was ample force available to the owner to take care of close-range trouble. It wasn't long before shooters realized that the handgun was capable of long-range effectiveness, however. The Harper's Ferry 58-caliber pistol, circa 1855, had a leaf sight which could be used for 300-yard shooting. That muzzleloader's 500-grain bullet, even at very meager velocity, was still effective in terms of soldiery at 300 yards. Captain Walker's modification of the Colt Dragoon is another example of long-range punch. The Colt Walker, a six-shot revolver in caplock black powder style, could hold as much as 60 grains of black powder in each of its chambers, giving the shooter six powerful loads to work with.

In spite of this strength in sidearms, the hunter of yesterday used the shotgun and rifle to procure meat, in the main. But the handgun was ever-present and some, certainly not all, of its owners were very capable shots. It was, I suppose, inevitable that outdoorsmen, certainly the roamers of the West, took a game animal now and then

This small 8-point whitetail was taken at a distance of 45 yards with a S&W Model 629 in 44 Mag. Big game handgunning should be confined to under 100 yards.

Legal in many areas for big game hunting, the black powder caplock revolver is capable of taking big game animals if the range is not too great and the shooter is capable of placing his ball in the right spot on the game animal. The Ruger 44-caliber Old Army fires a .457-inch round ball which weighs 143 grains and can be driven at just short of 1100 fps MV.

In years gone by, hunting big game with a handgun was a non-reality. It can be said that the lengendary Elmer Keith is directly responsible for today's big game handgunning success. It's modern hunters like the one seen here that have reaped the benefits of Keith's expertise in the field of big game handgunning.

with their sidearms. Certainly, power grew and reliability grew with it. A good example of this power and reliability came in the form of the old Colt six-gun. In the Frontier model or the Bisley or the Peacemaker, or any nuance thereof, those six-shooters were not too bad for big game hunting at close range.

We may not be impressed today, since we have surpassed the loading power of those old guns, but they were indeed a bit more than feeble in punch. The Colt could be obtained in 44-40 caliber, for example. This meant a 200-grain bullet, slow to be sure in terms of muzzle velocity, but no toy. Its smaller brother was the 38-40, but in spite of a slightly lighter bullet, this round was also quite strong for very close-range shooting. The 44-40 threw a 200-grain bullet at 918 fps MV from a 5½-inch barrel back then, and the 38-40 fired a 180-grain bullet at 985 fps MV from a 5½-inch barrel. The muzzle energies were 374 foot-pounds for the 44-40 with this load and 388 foot-pounds at the muzzle for the 38-40 in the 5½-inch barrel. Then there was the 45 Colt. We like to call this one the 45 "Long" Colt, as the designation helps to separate that round from others. However from a nomenclature standpoint, the correct designation for this round will always be the 45 Colt. I made up some factory duplicate black powder loads in an original 45 Colt Single Action Army with a 7½-inch barrel. The results were good. I used a 255-grain lead alloy bullet at 773 fps MV using 38 grains weight of GOEX FFg black powder. The muzzle energy was only 338 foot-pounds, down to 302 foot-pounds at 50 yards, but with proper bullet placement a 255-grain projectile is still a force to be reckoned with.

Incidentally, just for reader interest, the smokeless powder load for the 45 Colt gave a muzzle velocity of 790 fps from a 5½-inch barrel. This was also with a 255-grain bullet, and the muzzle energy was rated at 353 foot-pounds. Of course, there were many different loads in days gone by, and this last is simply one of them. In terms of energy, none of the three Colt chamberings above seems very effective to us today, since all have been badly outstripped by modern loads in the same cartridges and by new handgun rounds as well. But they got the job done, and they were the forerunners of today's fine big game handgun.

At any rate, the cowboy, miner, homesteader and general traveler in the West had a handgun. It took a very long time for the tradition to die, and we might conclude that it

Much has been done in recent years to provide the big game handgunner with the proper tools. Seen here is Mag-Na-Port's "Stalker," a customized Ruger Super Blackhawk in 44 Mag. It features Mag-Na-Porting, non-reflective finish, sling and swivels, 2× Leupold scope, complete action job and more.

is not yet dead. In the fall of 1983 I was walking in the hills with my wife, Nancy, and then 4-year-old daughter when a rattler stuck its head up out of the grass a few feet in front of Nancy's boot. I do not make war on the rattler and would have happily retreated but for the snake's hostility. It reared back and was apparently ready to strike, being within hitting distance of my wife. I picked my little girl up into my arms, but we were still in a standoff situation. Our first thought was to back out in a very slow and humble way and leave the place to Mr. Rattler, but I was afraid to have Nancy budge. In short, there was only one thing to do, considering the fact that we were 45 miles from the nearest hospital where snakebite could be treated. I shot the rattler with my sidearm. There are still sufficient "wide open spaces" in the world where the carrying of a sidearm is not unrealistic.

The growth of handgun big game hunting simply had to be precipitated by the fact that strong handguns were on the horizon. Even the 38-40, 44-40 and 45 Colt left a lot to be desired in factory loads and black powder loads of earlier times, though all three have improved considerably with modern smokeless powders, especially in strongly constructed firearms. In my opinion, it was Elmer Keith, the late gun writer, who launched modern handgun big game hunting, and he did so by giving us a load which would qualify on big game. I had the privilege of being in Keith's home twice. The gentleman told me that he had always wanted to take big game with the sidearm, and in the early days of Idaho and Montana hunting, where Keith roamed, it was often totally legal and prudent to drop big game with the sidearm.

Keith began to look at various handgun calibers, such as the 45 Colt, with an eye for improvement in terms of big game hunting. It was, however, the 44 S&W Special round which was to be boosted into big game power by Keith. His now famous 44 Special load of Hercules 2400 behind the Lyman No. 429421-moulded bullet is legendary. Keith's load produced about 1200 fps out of a 6-inch barrel for a muzzle energy of 800 foot-pounds with the 250-grain alloy bullet. Later on, in 1935, the 357 Magnum came along. The big difference here was more in the firearm than in the round. The round was quite simply a longer 38 Special (since 38 Special was actually a .357-inch caliber, the new cartridge was called a 357 Magnum). The Smith & Wesson handgun originally made for that cartridge was designed to hold together at up to 40,000 PSI, or about the same amount of pressure a Model 94 Winchester rifle was supposed to be good for on a day-in, day-out basis.

In the longer barrel lengths, the 357 Magnum is capable of driving a 158-grain bullet at about 1400 fps. I owned a 357 Magnum, taking two big game animals with it, both with 160-grain bullets which were moving between 1350 and 1400 fps MV from a 6½-inch barrel. The 158-grain bullet at 1400 fps would be worth a muzzle energy of 688 foot-pounds, so Keith's 800 foot-pound 44 Special load was still the way to go for the serious big game handgun hunter.

A decade after the introduction of the 357 Magnum, in 1955, another round for the big game handgun hunter was born. This was the famous 44 Magnum. We called it the 44 S&W Magnum for Smith & Wesson. Today, it is better known as the 44 Remington Magnum, but both firms, plus a lot of help from Elmer Keith, cooked up the round. My own 44 Magnum Model 29 Smith & Wesson gains a MV of 1350 fps+ with the 240-grain bullet and 25.0 grains of Hodgdon's H-110 powder for a muzzle energy of 971 foot-pounds. However, I have also achieved the same 1350 fps MV using a 265-grain Hornady bullet for a muzzle energy of 1,073 foot-pounds. The 44 Magnum, in other words, is a big game hunter's round.

Now there was no excuse for the serious big game hunter who wanted to employ the handgun to leave that tool out of the picture. In between the 357 Magnum and the 44 Magnum, there was the 41 Magnum round for those who did not care for quite as much recoil the 44 Magnum but who still wanted more punch than the 357 Magnum. Hunters such as the late Al Georg began to do truly remarkable work with the hunting handgun. Al bagged all sorts of game with all sorts of handguns, including black powder revolvers. One gentleman took himself off to Africa and bagged game up to and including elephant with a 44 Magnum.

Today's Handgun Big Game Rounds

Today, there are a number of big game cartridges offered in quite an array of firearms for the handgun hunter. In no case, not even in the huge 454 Casull Magnum, does the handgun exceed the more powerful rifles, but some handgun rounds are on par, energy-wise, with a number of rounds used in rifles for big game hunting. When seeking a big game hunting cartridge, I lean toward looking at the rifle first, because just about any rifle style today is offered in a cartridge which is perfectly suitable for big game hunting. I am not inclined to say the same about handgun cartridges. I think it could be wiser to look at the cartridge selection first and then decide first upon the round for the task at hand and second the sidearm which chambers that round.

Here is a list of rounds offered to the reader for his evaluation. The list is constructed upon the basis of my own experience, coupled with what I have found out from the *field knowledge* of several other handgun hunters. There are exceptions to what I say about the rounds, because there are exceptions among handgun hunters. I have one friend who laments the fact that his old 32-20 revolver is illegal for deer where he lives. He thinks it should be legalized as a deer cartridge. I don't. In his hands, he can no doubt *prove* that the cartridge is capable of taking a deer, but I prefer to look at the hard facts instead of the isolated incidents of shooters doing various things with various cartridges. The 32-20, and I love the round and wish it greater and extended popularity, fires a 115-grain jacketed bullet at a muzzle velocity of 925 fps using 5.9 grains weight of Unique for a muzzle energy of 219 foot-pounds, less than the old black powder load for the 38-40 or 44-40.

A fine big game revolver is shown here in the Colt single-action New Frontier model in 357 Magnum. The single-action, lacking the swingout cycliner, is a bit slower loading than a double-action revolver; however, to the big game hunter this is generally a factor of no consequence.

The 357 Magnum

This round is about the minimum for big game hunting, and then only in the hands of a cool shot. My friend Russell Sprung of Tucson, Arizona uses the 357 Magnum in a six-gun with telling effect on big game, but Russell is not exactly your ordinary hunter. He was raised in the mountains and could stalk for that close shot, and when he got close, he was capable of putting the bullet precisely where he wanted it placed.

In my 357 Magnum, the fine lead-alloy bullet, one of the better big game type bullets, would lead the bore so badly that I could remove lead strips from the bore. I turned to jacketed bullets right away, and I did bag two big game animals with the 357, neither harvest impressing me very much. About all we can actually hope for ballistically here is a 160-grain bullet at 1350 fps MV for a muzzle energy of 648 foot-pounds, not bad, certainly, but not a 44 Magnum either.

I tend to compare things when trying to make up my mind about harvesting power. My black powder rifle, which shoots a patched round ball, is often scoffed at by some shooters who think it too small in actual punch for big game hunting, and yet it drives a 230-grain round ball at 1975 fps MV for a muzzle energy of 1,993 foot-pounds. Another 54-caliber muzzleloader I own, the Ozark Mountain Arms Hawken, pushes a 224-grain round ball, .530-inch diameter, at 2025 fps MV for a muzzle energy of 2,040 foot-pounds. These round balls lose velocity and power rapidly, but even at 100 yards they have about as much punch as the 357 Magnum has at the muzzle. I relate these facts just to give the reader some food for thought.

The 44 S&W Special, shown here with the 200-grain Silvertip hollow point factory load by Wincester, may have started quite a bit of our present handgun hunting for big game. Elmer Keither took this round, and with a stout handload, gave us a powerful big game taker.

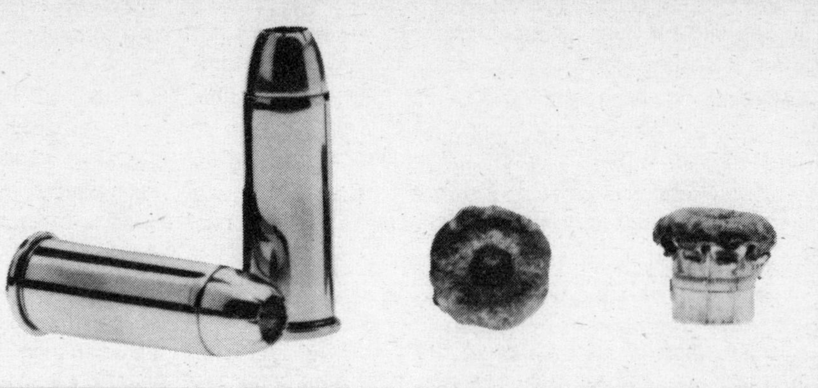

Without a doubt, the 357 Magnum is a fine cartridge and it is going to do all right on deer and other game if the shooting is good. One major point in favor of the 357 Magnum is that for a hunting round it is really quite mild in recoil, and very accurate shooting can be accomplished even if the shooter is somewhat sensitive to heavy recoil. Another plus factor in favor of the 357 Magnum is the broad choice of excellent handguns in this caliber. If the shooter is willing to practice, willing to wait for the close shot, then the 357 Magnum will do the job on big game, but not with sloppy shooting.

The 41 Magnum

The 41 Magnum is really quite a good cartridge, better, I think, than we tend to give it credit for. The 210-grain bullet, for example, is heavy enough for big game, and it can offer some good penetration quality. At 1450 fps MV, the muzzle energy for the 41 Magnum, pushing the 210-grain bullet is 981 foot-pounds, is more than Keith's original heavy load for the 44 Special. I also owned a 41 Magnum, but I never did take any game with it and cannot give a personal account of the round on big game in my hands.

But I have several friends who are 41 Magnum fans, and they have effectively taken big game with their 41s. Interestingly, the 41 Magnum with a 210-grain bullet at 1400 fps MV and the 44 Magnum with a 240-grain bullet at 1400 fps MV, both end up at 1082 fps remaining velocity at 100 meters, so the two rounds are not that far apart at the longer ranges, though a 44 Magnum is most certainly the most powerful round, especially with big-bullet reloads. All in all, however, anyone who hunts handgun style for big game is going to do fine with the 41 Magnum. It's a good and effective round for big game at close range.

The 44 Special

There are not all that many quality 44 Special handguns around these days, and there is no point in delving deeply into this cartridge. Let it be said that the 44 Special is still a fine handgun round. It will push a 255-grain gas check bullet (Thompson #429244) at 1025 fps MV using 9.0 grains of Unique power for a muzzle energy of 595 foot-pounds, or there is the more famous Keith load of Hercules 2400 powder behind the 250-grain bullet for 800 foot-pounds of muzzle energy. It will still take big game cleanly.

The 44 Remington Magnum

This is my favorite big game handgun cartridge out of a revolver using standard factory ammo. I recently chronographed my own Smith & Wesson Model 29, 44 Magnum, with the Federal 220-grain Metal Case Bullet at an average muzzle velocity in excess of 1500 fps. At a flat 1500 fps, the muzzle energy of this load is just shy of 1100 foot-pounds. The same load made over 1550 fps out of a 7½-inch barrel. That is power. Accuracy was very good at 25 yards, with groups of 1 inch or less for five shots.

If a shooter insisted upon deep penetration, he could select the Hornady 265-grain bullet, driving it at 1300 to 1350 fps. This is a very hard bullet intended for use in the 444 Marlin round, and it will not upset very much upon impact. But it will penetrate. At 1350 fps MV, with the 265-grain bullet, the 44 Magnum delivers a muzzle energy of 1073 foot-pounds. Sighted in for 50 yards with the 240-grain bullet at 1400 fps, the drop is less than a half-foot at 100 yards; excellent trajectory for big game hunting.

The 44-40 Revolver

The 44-40 round is still alive and well with firearms currently being chambered for this cartridge. With modern handloads, the 44-40 does all right for itself and cannot be overlooked as a big game handgun round. Using 9.3 grains of Unique, the 44-40 will push a 240-grain cast bullet at a muzzle velocity of 935 fps. This creates a muzzle energy of 466 foot-pounds, not too terribly exciting after looking at the 44 Magnum, but adequate due to good bullet weight and caliber, provided the shooter will get close and never shoot from very far.

45 Colt

Out of a Colt single action with a 5½-inch barrel, this old round did some fine work. Muzzle velocity with a 250-grain gas check bullet was 1100 fps using 22.0 grains of

H-4227 powder. That gives a muzzle energy of 672 foot-pounds, again nothing when compared with the 44 Magnum, but with the good bore size and adequate entry wound and channel, plus penetration, the old 45 Colt is useful in big game hunting.

The Single Shot

Now enter the Thompson/Center pistol, and with it a whole different group of rounds, as well as many of the standby numbers. We will talk about this and a few other big game hunting sidearms soon. For now, let's concentrate on some of the big game hunting rounds available for this good gun.

The 30 Herrett

Made from 30-30 brass, we get the 30 Herrett—meaning case alteration is necessary in order to obtain the finished product. But when the case is formed, a big game handgun hunter has a fine round capable of pushing a 150-grain .308-inch bullet at 2000 fps MV using 23.0 grains of Winchester 680 powder. This velocity is achieved from a 10-inch barrel. The muzzle energy is 1,333 foot-pounds. Furthermore, due to the fine ballistic shape of the 150-grain spire point or spitzer bullet, the energy is retained at longer ranges. At 150 yards from the muzzle, this bullet will still be doing over 1700 fps for an energy rating of 963 foot-pounds.

The 30-30 Winchester

This famous rifle round is also chambered in the T/C offering. It drives the 150-grain bullet at 2000 fps, just as the Herrett round does for the same muzzle energy and retained energies downrange. This is accomplished with about 22.5 grains of 2400 out of a 10-inch barrel. Of course, there is no case forming. The 30-30, however, is not quite right as a cartridge for the pistol-length barrel and accuracy is generally better with the Herrett round.

The 357/44 Bain & Davis

Here is a .357-inch caliber based on a 44 Magnum case, necked down. A 158-grain bullet is driven at 2100 fps for a muzzle energy rating of 1,548 foot-pounds. This is a good round, but the blunter 159-grain bullet will not keep up with the more streamlined .308-inch bullets of the 30 Herrett. Still, it makes a fine big game number from a handgun using 24.5 grains of Winchester 296 powder with the 158-grain bullet.

The 357 Herrett

This is the same proposition as the 30 Herrett in that cases must be formed from 30-30 brass. I cannot see that it improves upon the 357 Bain & Davis. It is a good round, of course, and the 158-grain bullet is given a muzzle velocity of 2000 fps using 25.0 grains of Winchester 296 powder.

The 44 Magnum

The longer 14-inch barrel of the Thompson/Center pistol allows for some impressive MV figures from the 44 Magnum round. A 240-grain bullet achieves a muzzle velocity of 1750 fps using 25.0 grains of H-110 powder for a muzzle energy of 1632 foot-pounds. That is certainly good big game power. And yet, perhaps, this is a good place to pause for an important statement. We sometimes tend to lose sight of hard facts in our shooting because no matter what we may say, shooting is still a very romantic activity.

I simply wish to point out that even with this powerful load and a muzzle energy rating of over 1600 foot-pounds,

The big Thompson/Center single shot can be had in myriad calibers. Conversion from one caliber to another only requires barrel replacement. Simple. Effective. Powerful.

we are still talking about *handgun power,* not rifle power. Therefore, when we reach the place where hunting style is mentioned and the suggestion is to get close and place the bullet with care, it should be kept in mind that these fine loads are still *handgun* loads. Let's keep things in perspective.

The 35 Remington

Another useful round in the Thompson/Center Contender is the 35 Remington, as is, no change in the round at all. In the T/C's 14-inch barrel, the 200-grain bullet reaches 1800 fps MV for an energy of 1439 foot-pounds. The gun weighs 3½ pounds and recoil energy (remember that we figured recoil energy when talking about big game cartridges for rifles) would be in the 24-pound class.

Handguns for Handgun Hunters

We are not going to spend much time running down each and every possible model which might be used by today's successful big game handgun hunter, but a look at a few possible choices might be helpful for the complete shooter who is trying to add a big-game sidearm to his battery. Basically, we are looking at the revolver in both single-action and double-action style. And then there is the single shot pistol, such as the Remington, which is a bolt-action model, as well as the Thompson/Center, a break-open model.

I suggested that we look at calibers before deciding on a big-game handgun because now the shooter has a focal point from which to operate. If the hunter simply must have a 7x45mm Ingram, which is actually a 223 Remington case opened to 7mm (.284-inch bullet) and improved through fire-forming (see the chapter on wildcats for fire-forming), then he must go with the pistol at the moment. Specifically, the bolt-action Remington XP-100 will be the pistol of choice. But more of that in a moment.

The Single-Action Revolver

Any of the fine single-action revolvers will make a wonderful big game hunting sidearm. This would include the Colt and the Ruger, of course, but also some of the other models now on the market, such as the Abiline Single Action, which is chambered for the 357 Magnum, the 44 Magnum and the 45 Colt. There is the F.I.E. single-action in many styles and hunting calibers and the EMF Dakota in 44-40, 45 Colt or 357 Magnum. The single-action is a fine revolver style and entirely useful for big-game hunting. To say more would be to add weight without substance.

The Freedom Arms 454 Casull Magnum is unique, and we are obliged to discuss this big single-action revolver separately. The Casull is a big single-action in that it weighs 50 ounces in the 7½-inch barrel model which goes 14 inches in overall length. It is a five-shot, not a six-shooter. You will currently pay around 700 American dollars for the big 454 Magnum, but you'll get a lot for your money. The revolver is made of stainless steel with a non-fluted cylinder. The reason for the five-shot capacity is simple—strength; the five-shot cylinder allows for thicker cylinder walls with a space of about .130 inch between the webs.

The gun will withstand pressures in the 55,000 PSI area,

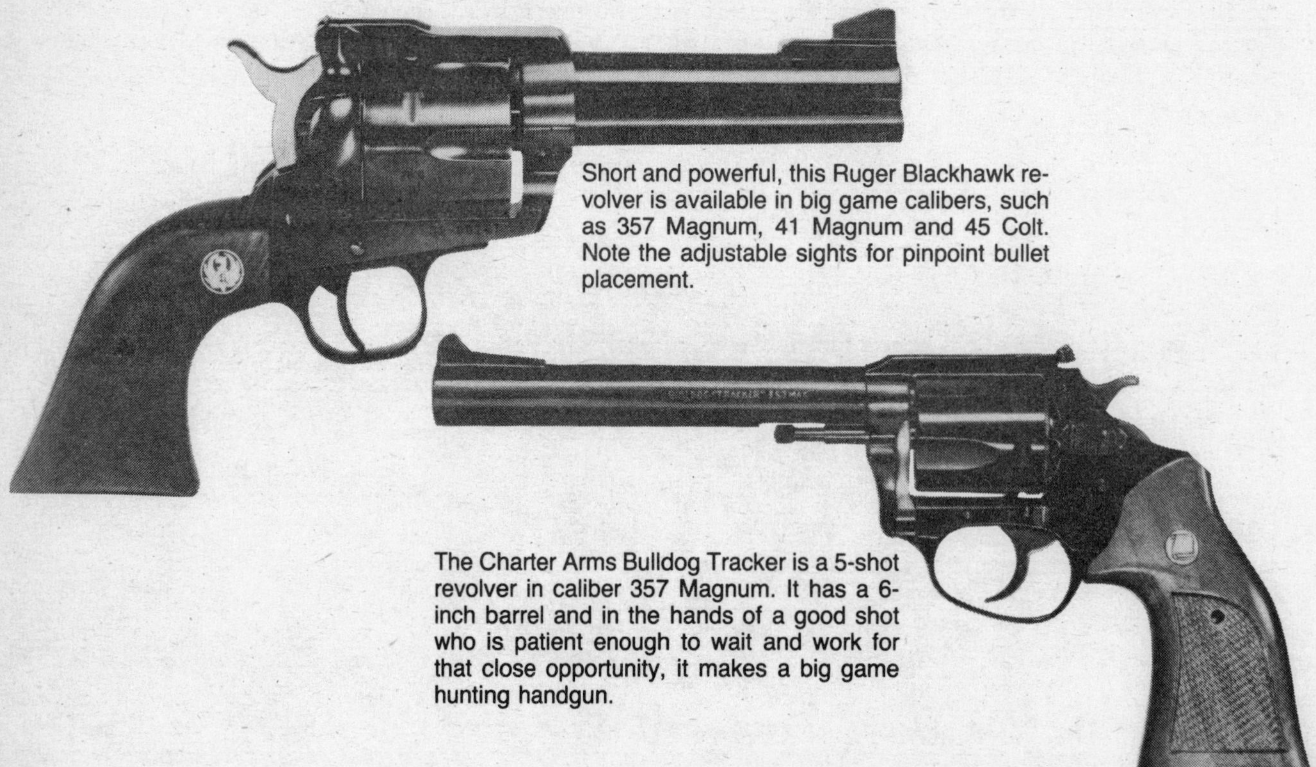

Short and powerful, this Ruger Blackhawk revolver is available in big game calibers, such as 357 Magnum, 41 Magnum and 45 Colt. Note the adjustable sights for pinpoint bullet placement.

The Charter Arms Bulldog Tracker is a 5-shot revolver in caliber 357 Magnum. It has a 6-inch barrel and in the hands of a good shot who is patient enough to wait and work for that close opportunity, it makes a big game hunting handgun.

and the round is rather remarkable. It is much like a 45 Colt, but longer by about .1-inch so that it cannot be tossed in a standard revolver chambered for the 45 Colt round. A 225-grain jacketed hollow point bullet has been clocked from the muzzle at 1980 fps for an energy rating of 1,959 foot-pounds. All of that power in a handgun spells recoil, of course, but this is a factor which can be reckoned with. One does not practice, for example, with full-throttle loads.

If ever there was a big game hunting revolver, the Casull is it. In fact, I can see no other reason for the big gun. The Casull offers a lot to the handgun hunter, and it remains a handgun in size. I need to emphasize that. It does come with a 10-inch or 12-inch barrel if the shooter wishes, but it is easily packed on the hip.

The Double-Action Revolver

I have never used the double-action feature on my own pet Model 29 S&W hunting revolver, but neither has it hurt my shooting in any way, and if the need for very rapid shooting did present itself, my double-action would offer shot-after-shot, six in a row, with the mere pulling of the trigger. There are many fine double-action revolvers around chambered for hunting-type cartridges. As an example, there is the Colt Python in 357 Magnum caliber. I would probably like a tiny bit more punch in a big-game revolver, but this Colt offers a few wrinkles which make up for the lack of a bigger caliber offering.

The Colt Python comes totally ready for hunting use. It is fitted with a 2x scope made by Leupold for Colt. The barrel is 8 inches long, so we will gain what potential the 357 Magnum has as a handgun number. The fine aluminum case which houses the Python has ammo holding capacity, too. So the hunter has it all in "one box," a fine revolver of the double-action class complete with scope, and case. It's a good package.

The Llama Super Comanche Revolver is also double-action. It is offered in 44 Magnum with 4-, 6- or 8½-inch barrels. It's a six-shot, of course, and has good target-type sights. The Ruger Redhawk is another fine 44 Magnum double-action revolver with all of the highlights we expect in a hunting revolver. It is easily scoped, too. In fact, it can be purchased with Ruger stainless steel scope rings. Smith & Wesson has the fine Model 57 revolver in 41 Magnum caliber, or the equally good Model 29 in 44 Magnum. And Dan Wesson has its Model 41V and Model 44V in 41 Magnum and 44 Magnum chamberings.

All of these double-action revolvers are more at home in the big game hunting field. They are positive, accurate and they bear good hunting sights. They can be scoped, too, as can the single-action models. That there is definite advantage to the double-action style for big game hunting is questionable, but there is certainly no detriment either, and the ability to fire rapidly is certainly available.

The Single Shots

In an attempt to gain high velocity with high ballistic coefficient, or in other words, "pointed" bullets, the single-shots have come on the scene. The Thompson/Center model is very popular today and is offered in many differ-

The fine Remington Model XP-100 pistol is a single shot bolt-action model which can be chambered for long-range big game rounds. Naturally, as with all handguns, top rifle power is not available; however, the good shot can do a fine job of big game hunting with an accurate pistol like this one. However, he should also answer the handgun big game hunting challenge by getting as close as possible to his quarry.

(Right) Here is the Colt Python in its aluminum case, entirely ready for the hunting field. With the excellent scope sight, this handgun is a good big game outfit, though the author considers the 357 Magnum round more toward the lower limits of power for big game hunting. With good bullet placement, however, the 357 Magnum has proved quite adequate in the big game field. This is handgun compactness at its best.

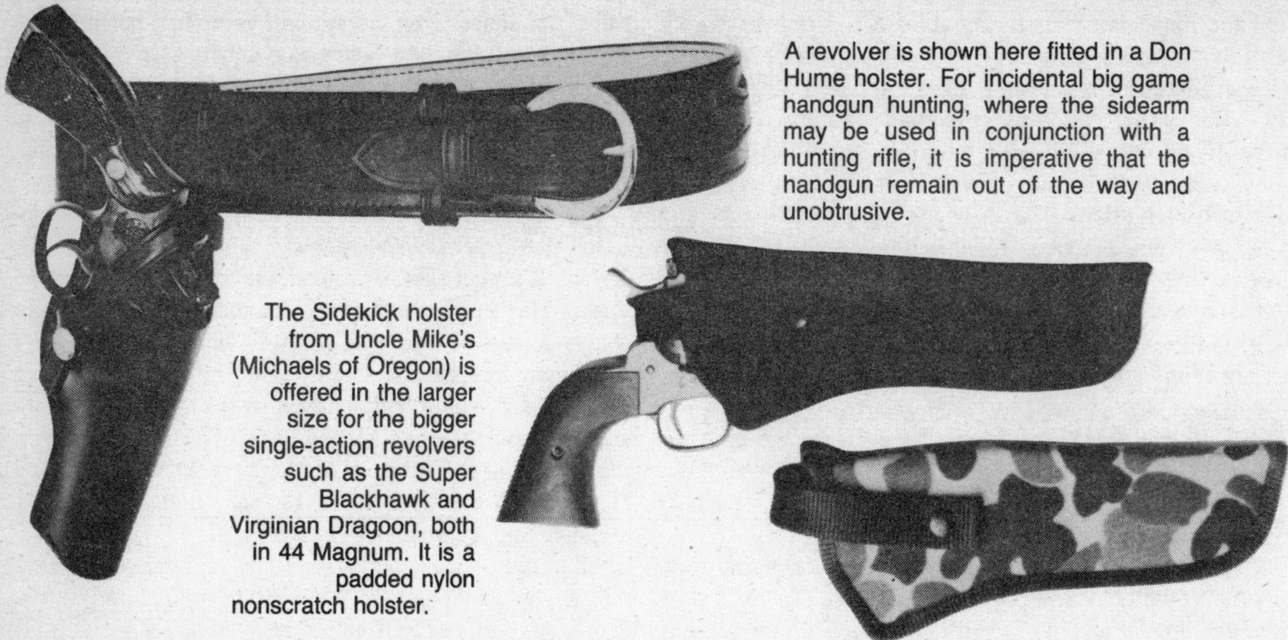

A revolver is shown here fitted in a Don Hume holster. For incidental big game handgun hunting, where the sidearm may be used in conjunction with a hunting rifle, it is imperative that the handgun remain out of the way and unobtrusive.

The Sidekick holster from Uncle Mike's (Michaels of Oregon) is offered in the larger size for the bigger single-action revolvers such as the Super Blackhawk and Virginian Dragoon, both in 44 Magnum. It is a padded nylon nonscratch holster.

ent calibers, as alluded to earlier. There is the 10-inch barrel and the 14-inch barrel. The Super 14 is available not only in the good 30 Herrett, 30-30 and 35 Remington, but also in the 7mm TCU round, which is the 223 case necked up to 7mm (.284-inch bullets). In the 14-inch barrel, the 7mm TCU will achieve about 2100 fps MV using the 130-grain bullet. Trigger pull in the T/C Contender is adjustable, and pull weights of only 2.5 pounds are possible.

Another popular single shot is the Merrill Sportsman's model which is available in many calibers, to include 357/44, 30-30, 30 Herrett and more. The barrel length may be 9 inches, 10¾ inches or even 14 inches. The Sterling X-Caliber Single Shot comes in either 357 or 44 Magnum for the big game hunter and has 8- or 10-inch barrels. The Remington Model XP-100, originally in 221 Fireball caliber, is a bolt-action pistol, not a break-open design. With a barrel length of 14⅞ inches, this pistol may be obtained in the 7mm Remington Bench Rest caliber, and this means ballistics in the 2300 fps range with a 120-grain bullet. The round is not a factory number, but in fact a wildcat. It is made from special 308 cases. Interestingly, the case features a small rifle primer pocket not Large Rifle or Large Pistol. What really intrigues me about the 7mm Remington Benchrest round out of the XP-100 is the fact that a 140-grain bullet can be pushed out at over 2100 fps, and a 160-grain bullet will achieve a muzzle velocity of about 1980+ fps. A spitzer bullet in 7mm with a weight of 160 grains is excellent for a long-range carry-up (retention of initial velocity).

How to Make a Choice

As I said earlier, handguns are extremely exciting today, especially in the hunting models. Not until recently has a 454 Casull been available, for example, and a bolt-action pistol is certainly unique and worthwhile. There are so many choices, in fact, that it no longer becomes a matter of wondering if a suitable big game handgun can be located, but rather it becomes a matter of finding the specific model and cartridge chambering that the hunter feels he wants and needs. Here are some things to consider:

Picking the Round

Unlike our advice in selecting a rifle which was to choose the action and then worry about the round, for handgun selection I like the idea of finding the cartridge which is "just right" for the task at hand and then looking for the gun to house it. For example, if the shooter wants a long-range outfit firing pointed bullets, he might opt for the above-mentioned 7mm Remington Bench Rest round. As a result, the Remington XP-100 pistol will be his choice.

Or a hunter may wish to use the time-tested 44 Magnum cartridge. Then his selection is very wide, for the single-action, double-action and single shot are all chambered in 44 Magnum. But it's really a simple matter of asking a few questions: **A.** Do I like the western style single-action or the more modern double-action best? **B.** Which shoots best for me? (Try each at the range if you can.) **C.** If I opt for the 44 Magnum, do I want the most ballistics I can possibly obtain from the round? If so, the single shot with the longer barrel is probably the way to go.

Price Range

Although it is always wise to buy the best, and hang the price, we do have to recognize that as the complete shooter builds a battery, he has to make some choices as to cash outlay. A serviceable 44 Magnum may cost a bit less than a special single shot model, for example. Therefore, price is another consideration.

Use

If I were going to hunt the woods, and only the woods, most certainly I would opt for a caliber of "larger" rather than "smaller" dimension, shooting heavier rather than lighter bullets. I am not speaking of the mythical idea of driving bullets through trees and brush and into the game, but rather the notion that a big, soft-point bullet at close range is hard to beat in putting game down quickly. In short, at 30 yards or so, that 44 Magnum with a 240-grain bullet is probably more at home than a 150-grain bullet at 2000 fps MV. But it is up to the hunter. Given a close-range shot, the 150-grain bullet at 2000 fps MV is certainly going to do great.

All in all, however, I had to decide what I wanted to carry on my hip for the *part-time use* of big game hunting. I knew that I would not turn to the handgun for all of my big game hunting, but I wanted something to use as a back-up to my rifle and something which would be *legal* on big game. I decided that the 44 Magnum would fill the bill, for *my uses*. Had I wanted a long-range big game sidearm, I may have opted for a single shot in a smaller, faster round, with a scope sight fitted. Oh, the choices are difficult when there are so many good ones.

Handle and "Feel"

All of these handgun styles and types handle in a different manner; they *feel* unique in the hand of the individual shooter. Fortunately, the actual feel of the handgun can be determined in the gunshop. Unfortunately, the handling characteristics cannot be ascertained without shooting the sidearm with hunting loads. The arc of recoil will vary with each handgun, and there may be minor aspects of the gun which either fit or do not fit the hand of the shooter. Obviously, we cannot demand to fire a brand new handgun before buying it. Once upon a time, the gunshop may have been so situated that a buyer could try a new firearm before the purchase, but even if a shop has an underground range today, new means *new,* and trying the hunting handgun before laying out the cash is usually not allowable.

What to do? If a shooter is lucky enough to know another shooter who has the hunting handgun he is interested in, he may be able to shoot that model. Also, if a handgun does not feel just right to the shooter a change in grips is possible. One may also use the Mag-na-port system in order to reduce apparent recoil. This system diverts gas which can act to minimize the felt recoil in terms of *how* that recoil pushes on the hand of the shooter.

Aesthetics

The complete shooter is seldom a person of such total practicality that he ignores the "looks" of a firearm. The firearm is more than a tool. If it were not, it would never have been embellished with engraving and carving. One does not carve on the handles of picks and shovels or engrave the head of a hammer. So the overall design, line, color and appearance of the handgun do count for something when the shooter selects his personal model for hunting or any other form of handgunning. Of course, we all see out of different eyes when it comes to aesthetics. I find the old Colt Bisley model a beautiful thing to behold, while others would prefer the flat clean lines of a GI 45 auto.

Barrel Length

Selecting the hunting handgun means looking at barrel length very carefully. Even the handgun rounds in the 44 or 41 Magnum realm pick up considerably more velocity as the barrel length increases. The reason for this is that these rounds and many others as well have a large enough powder capacity that the extra bore length is useful in burning the powder charge. Longer barrels can often allow for somewhat slower burning powder as well, meaning that (in

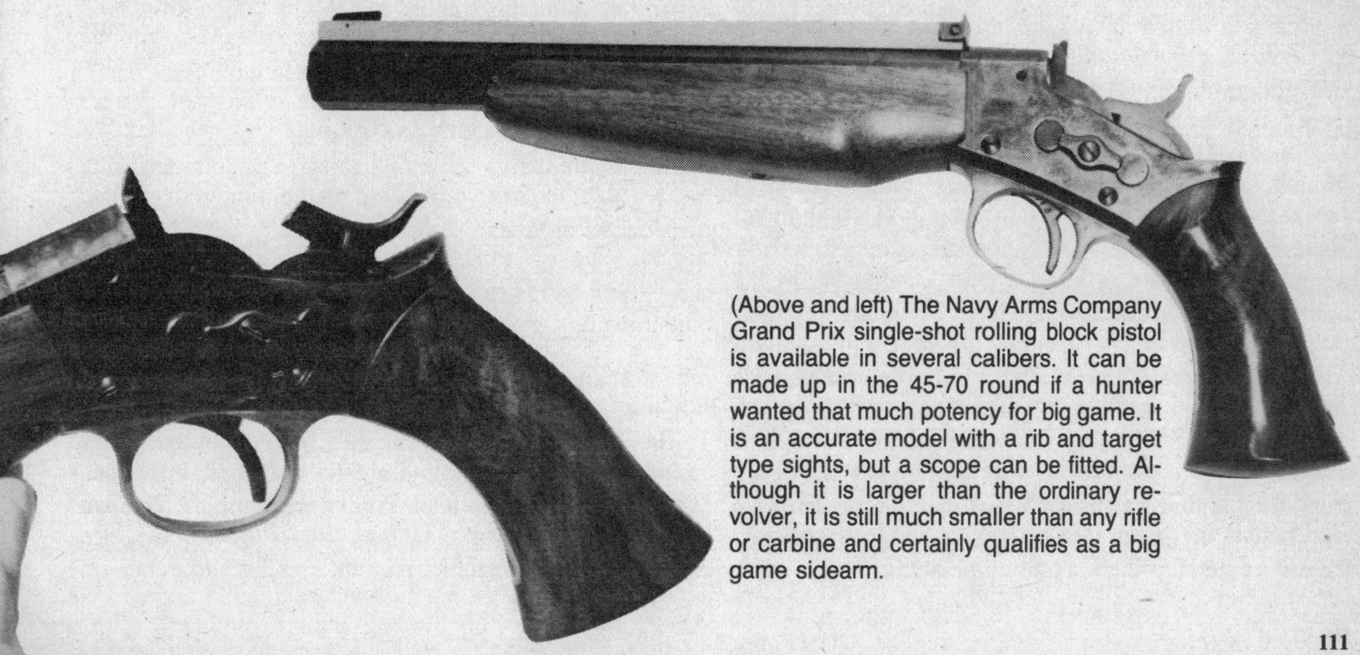

(Above and left) The Navy Arms Company Grand Prix single-shot rolling block pistol is available in several calibers. It can be made up in the 45-70 round if a hunter wanted that much potency for big game. It is an accurate model with a rib and target type sights, but a scope can be fitted. Although it is larger than the ordinary revolver, it is still much smaller than any rifle or carbine and certainly qualifies as a big game sidearm.

many cases) loading density is increased. One hundred percent loading density is the condition of having the cartridge case full of powder with, theoretically, all of the charge working toward giving the projectile velocity.

But there is another consideration. A handgun, by all standards, should be short enough in overall length to be carried easily. After all, if we don't mind an 18-inch barrel and a firearm of over 3 feet in overall length, we can simply buy a rifle (carbine). I see this problem as broken down into two distinct categories. First, there is the true handgun mode, a firearm packed on the hip, in a holster. Second, there is the short gun which is probably too long to be carried in a holster, but certainly not of rifle length. This gun can be carried on a short sling. It is still relatively light and handy, but it is not a real "sidearm." Which to take?

If the handgun hunting is going to be casual, I'd suggest a sidearm which fits in a holster and is carried on the hip. My 44 Magnum sidearm is a legal, powerful big game *option*. This season I filled one of my antelope doe tags with a 44 Magnum round, having several extra antelope tags as part of an important pre-winter harvest. I had a close shot, and I opted to take it with the 44 Magnum. I will also carry my 44 Magnum on backcountry big game hunts where the rifle is my first line hunting tool. If the notion strikes me, I will stalk for a handgun shot. So with this type of handgun hunting in mind, make my model one which fits at my side.

On the other hand, I would not at all mind packing a 14-inch barreled handgun carried on a strap such as the Uncle Mike's carrying unit. With this handgun, I would consider myself all set for big game hunting, the sidearm acting as my main tool of the harvest. I would not have a rifle with me, and would be hunting "handgun style" as well, looking for that close shot.

If I am going to carry a handgun as an incidental part of the big game hunt, I prefer modest weight. This means a sidearm that packs easily in a holster without making its presence known over the long haul. I do not mind packing 3 or even more pounds of handgun at my hip, but when the sidearm weighs over 5 pounds, it becomes a mainline (not secondary) tool of harvest.

There is another big factor to consider when looking at hunting handgun weight—recoil. The recoil formula in Chapter 4 used the weight of the gun as a major input. Therefore, I do not want a 44 Magnum packed into a lightweight revolver. Recoil is made more manageable by the mass of the firearm; therefore I want sufficient weight to overcome a portion of Newton's Third Law of Motion. Also, the handgun with some heft to it settles better, holds steadier, up to a point (that point being where the gun weighs so much the shooter cannot hold it out steadily), and the heavier handgun also rests across a log or another outdoor makeshift rest better than a light model. Give me just enough weight for steady shooting and modest recoil, without so much bulk that I am ill at ease.

Sights

A big game hunting handgun simply must wear sights which allow the hunter to group his bullets on target. If a handgun is going to wear a fixed-type sight for hunting, that is fine, provided the gunmaker can prove that his sidearm can be sighted in *precisely*. I have no use for a "point-at-'em" type handgun which is supposed to be used for big-game hunting. The idea is to place the bullet with utmost care. Even the most powerful sidearms do not match the power of big-game rifles. Bullet placement is essential in all big-game shooting, but super punch can make up somewhat for a hit which is not perfect.

Scopes make good sense on handguns. These days there is no excuse for wanting a scoped handgun and not having it. The chapter on aiming devices will show the reader some handgun glass options he might want to consider. The scope does a lot more than magnify the target. It allows for simple alignment by merely insuring that the vertical crosswire is straight up and down. When shooting without the scope, the hunter must make certain he is not canting the handgun too much to the left or right, which can be a little tricky in the field. The scope takes the trick out of it. Also the scope gives a single, flat sight picture. Squeeze off when the crosswires mark the target and good bullet placement is highly likely.

Bullets for Handguns

We have a chapter on big game bullets and there is no sense repeating here what is said there. However, there is one point worth remembering for the big game handgun hunter, and that is the fact that the cast, lead-alloy bullet is very formidable as a projectile on thin-skinned game, such as deer. The high molecular cohesion of lead allows the bullet to hang together and this means better penetration. When a bullet fragments, it gets lighter and this loss of mass decreases penetration ability. A pure lead bullet would be all right, except for leading problems. So it is the alloy bullet which is used for big game hunting.

While it is true that the cast bullet is excellent for big game hunting, I would in no way suggest that the jacketed bullet is inferior as a hunting missile, and on truly big game I would prefer it from what my information, tests and experience discloses. In short, if I were to hunt elk with a handgun, I would like a harder bullet for better penetration. In my own 44 Magnum, a handload with the 265-grain cast bullet would be welcomed.

How to Hunt with the Handgun

Handgun hunting is on par with bowhunting and black powder hunting. It means a greater challenge, of course. This challenge makes for a greater reward in the harvest. But big game handgun hunting is like bowhunting and muzzle-loading in another respect. *You have to get close.*

Oh, sure, there is plenty of deer-killing power left at 200 yards out of some of the single shot loads already discussed. But I still say *get close*. By getting close, bullet placement becomes a much more surefire situation. And bullet placement, important in all hunting, is even more important when the handgun's power (or lack of it) is in use.

In my book *Successful Deer Hunting*, (DBI Books Inc., Northfield, IL 60093) I outline several means of getting close to game. Mainly, it's a matter of using optics where possible in hopes of locating that big game animal before it sees you. Then a stalk is planned. The stalk puts the hunter close to his game. It is also a matter of *thinking* about being close to game by using the terrain correctly, taking advantage of the lay of the land, keeping the wind in our faces instead of allowing the breezes to signal our approach.

In harvesting game with the handgun, one of the prime rules is to take the proper sight picture. I try to follow the principles outlined in the chapter on shooting stances when I am shooting at any game, large or small, with the sidearm. The sight picture should be maintained constantly, with the trigger finger "sneaking" into the picture and gently nudging the trigger until the piece "goes off." No "snapshooting"please, whatever that truly is. Yes, snapshooting can mean a good fast shot, but there is only aimed shooting or unaimed shooting, and though firing without delay is sometimes very necessary, unaimed shots are pointless.

Get close to the game. I am not good enough with a handgun to take a deer much past 100 yards with iron sights. I would much prefer a range of 50 yards. I use a rest when I can for any form of hunting which will allow it—regardless of the type of firearm being used. A handgun is easily rested in the field, sometimes easier than the rifle. A hunter can kneel down and get a pretty good rest by putting his right elbow on top of his left knee for a right-handed shooter, for example. Making use of natural rests by placing a hat and/or gloves on a rock or tree branch and resting the handgun on that setup can also be conducive to steady shots. Get close; hold that sight picture and squeeze the trigger, all with the handgun rested. It's a hitting proposition.

Follow-Up

Please follow up after a shot.

One sunny afternoon in Arizona, a friend of mine took a crack at a white-tailed deer. He was using a 41 Magnum, plenty of punch for a small deer less than 50 yards away. But at the sharp crack of the revolver, the deer bolted and was gone in a flash of his tail. I thought my buddy missed. So did he. But as a general principle, we take a look after we fire on something. We took a look where the deer had stood; no sign of a hit.

However, we followed the tracks, easy enough to see in the sand, and we decided to stay on them as long as we could. About 100 yards down the draw, there was the buck, piled up like a heap of sausages. The bullet had passed completely through the chest cavity, but the exit wound was small, hence the lack of a blood trail. My friend was using a jacketed bullet; I don't think it was a hollow point type. At any rate, the slower striking velocity of the handgun bullet can sometimes mean less tissue disruption and a game animal may not instantly act as if hit. Take a good look after shooting. It's worth doing, and it is the right and humane thing to do besides.

The Laws

State-by-state hunting laws dictate the legality of the sidearm for big game hunting. It is a very simple matter to obtain the laws pertaining to big game handgunning by picking up a set of rules from the game department, or from the local gunshop, which often has proclamations available for the hunter. In a survey I made, I was somewhat surprised to find just how much handgun hunting for large game is available. Most states allow the handgun on deer and similar game. The reader should check the laws not only for handgun legality, but also for cartridge acceptance. In my own state, the laws state which handgun rounds are legal for big game hunting. The lower powered numbers are clearly illegal here. Though this is a good law, it becomes somewhat sticky in actual application. For example, this state had to add certain cartridges to its list, for it was clear that a few rounds which do not often see the field these days are still adequate for taking deer, especially with handloads in a strong sidearm.

Meeting the Challenge

The shooter chooses his big game handgun cartridge based on power and dictates of the law—no point in selecting a cartridge disallowed by the game rules—and he picks the sidearm he likes best which shoots that round. Then he practices with his correctly sighted piece until he is good with it. In the field, he looks a lot, and he hunts with great care, always stalking for the close shot when possible and letting the long shots go by.

Today, we have the finest revolvers and pistols ever assembled for big game hunting in cartridge chamberings adequate to get the job done cleanly. About the only thing standing between the hunter and big game handgunning is the everpresent challenge of the hunt itself. That challenge can be met when the hunter is dedicated to picking the right sidearm for big game and learning how to use it, not only on the range, but in the field, with the application of sound hunting principles leading the way to success.

Chapter 10
Powered By Air

John Fadala enjoyed collecting a brace of cottontail rabbits with his RWS Model 45 break-open single shot air rifle. Today's air rifles are well matched to the small game hunting opportunities which often present themselves in areas of somewhat dense human population.

A BOOK outlining all the various firearms types available to the shooter would not be complete without a discussion of air-powered rifles and pistols. Almost every shooter started his involvement and lifetime interest in firearms with an air gun of one sort or another. We can all remember the first gun in our lives, and that gun is generally a rifle, and most usually an air rifle. In my own case, there was a Daisy Red Ryder Carbine, purchased for me by an aunt who admonished that she did not necessarily care for guns and had thought a long while before buying a "BB gun" for me, but concluded, in words something like this, "I guess every boy raised out West ought to know how to shoot." I wrapped the priceless air rifle in a clean old sheet and tucked it under my bed, along with a few Red Ryder books. I was ready to become a marksman.

For some reason, many of us think of an air-powered gun as a fairly recent invention, at least a 20th century concept. It's not. The famous Lewis and Clark carried an air-powered gun on their expedition with them to explore the vast unknown territory of what is now the western half of the United States back in the years 1804 to 1806.

In my desire to study current air gun interest, and there is indeed a great deal of that going around these days, I first turned to a 1932 Stoeger's catalog. On page 97, I found a Webley "Junior" and a "Mark I," both air pistols. (I was especially interested in those Webleys because I own a Webley smoothbore Junior in .177-caliber, which I have had since my youth.) On page 98, there was a Webley Air Rifle featured, the price of which was $33, and for an additional $15, a shooter could buy an interchangeable barrel thereby having both .177-and 22-caliber in one piece.

Consider the price. In the very same catalog, a Winchester Model 61 Take Down pump-action 22 rifle was listed at $25.35, and the famous Model 94 lever-action 30-30 rifle was only $36.30. I mention all of these facts because it is evident that air guns were considered viable, important "grown up" shooting tools, even in the last century in this country. The Webley Air Rifle was offered with a 19-inch barrel, had an overall length of 35 inches and ran, 5¼ pounds in weight. In those days one could buy a Webley pellet trap for $5, allowing indoor shooting in a safe area

The pellet is still a very inexpensive missile for the target shooter.

of the home. Pellets were $1.50 per thousand in the .177-caliber size and $2.25 per thousand for the 22-caliber pellet. Such were those dollar-strong days of yesteryear.

Today's complete shooter has many reasons for owning a modern, air-powered gun. Modern air guns serve not only as a beginner's starting arm, but also as precision tools for the advanced shooter. In fact, looking at the air-powered gun, many important reasons for their very existence rise up before us.

Economy

Air gun shooting has always been economical. Today, shooting a ''pellet gun'' can cost a penny a shot, but that is not prohibitive. In fact, one can usually locate pellets ''on sale'' which insure true bargain shooting. The air gun lasts a very long time and requires very little maintenance. I have owned several different brands and found all to be ruggedly constructed and reliable. Pellets of soft-lead manufacture should remain economical to shoot. In fact, there is good reason to consider the air-powered gun as the most economical of all the shooting sports.

All-Weather Shooting, Practice and Fun

There are no bad days for air gun shooting. Neither rain, nor snow, nor heat of summer can thwart the air gun fan. Few are the firearms which can be used indoors, but the air gun can be fired in the basement, on the porch, in an attic —in any spot where a strong safe backstop is available. Investing in a simple pellet trap and locating that trap in a safe spot in the home is all that is required in order to enjoy shooting any day of the year.

Keeping in tune is very important to the shooter who cannot make it out to the range all the time. The air gun is a ''real'' shooting instrument, not a toy, and the new ones I have tested are capable of providing superb accuracy. The current crop of quality air guns usually come with excellent triggers and sights, oftentimes quality telescopic sights. Learning trigger squeeze and control, maintenance of a

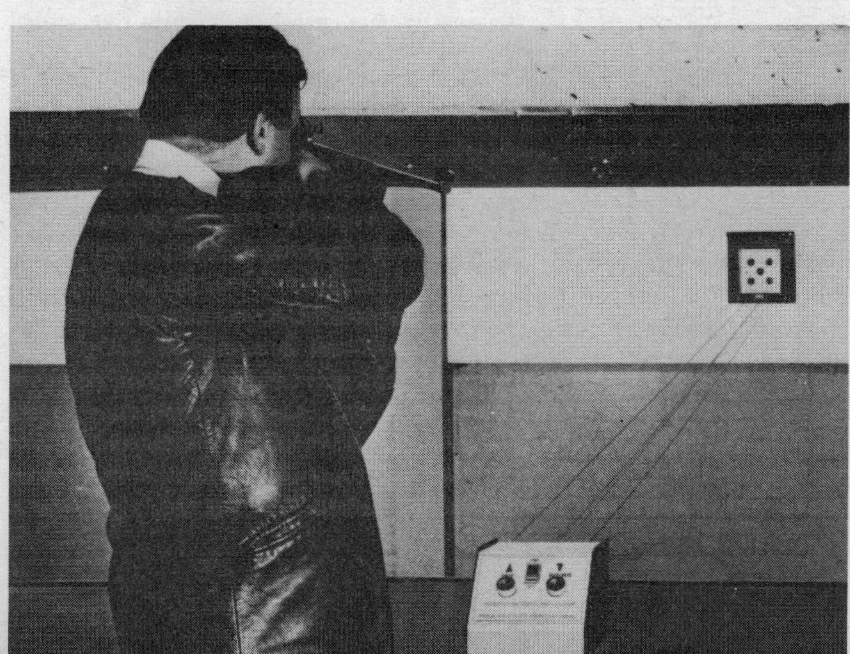

Using an air rifle, a shooter gains extremely important practice which can be a boon to him later on during the deer season. The air rifle allows for basement shooting without undue noise and in safety with proper backstop materials.

sight picture, mastery of stance and any other aspect of good shooting are all possible through air-gunning. While I am strongly in favor of "dry-fire practice," a method which will be described later, I have to admit that I enjoy shooting a "pellet gun" a lot more than dry-firing any other type of shooting tool.

There's another plus to air guns—they're fun to shoot! Friendly games of competition are possible, and so are many hours of quiet practice, competing against ourselves just for the fun of working toward higher and higher scores. When you consider that a good air rifle is capable of making one ragged hole in a bull's-eye at 30 feet, it is easy to see that these guns are more than capable of giving enjoyment to the shooter who insists upon accuracy as part of the shooting game. Shooting is most often for enjoyment, and the high-quality air gun of the day makes it possible for a shooter to go for high scores every day of the year, inside and outside of the home.

Pest Control

Small vermin, such as mice and rats, can be eliminated with pellet power. In fact, some modern pellet rifles have so much punch that they can be used to control even larger animals. My own RWS rifle has sufficient penetration to drop a rockchuck or woodchuck. I do not recommend this practice because the animal will probably make it to his lair, though indeed he is finished with a chest strike. I only relate the fact to point out that the modern air rifle is capable of significant force, and it must be used with all of the safety rules which pertain to any shooting tool. The accuracy level is so high that sparrows in the garden, or garden gophers can be dispatched with efficiency.

Small Game Hunting

I have taken small game up to the size of the western jackrabbit with the pellet rifle. When I was about 6 years old, an uncle returning from World War II brought a pellet rifle back for me. It was a finely made piece of shooting machinery if ever there was one. The stock was of high-grade walnut and the metalwork was flawless. Obviously, the manufacturer considered air-powered shooting as quite sophisticated. The rifle, a Diana, used the same hinged barrel cocking which my current RWS Model 45 enjoys.

I admired the fine figure in the wood even as a boy, as well as the blued steel of the rifle. When I was old enough to handle the rifle, I was allowed to use it for small game edibles, such as cottontail rabbits. Rabbit hunting was but a 5-minute walk from the house, and I learned that I could enjoy success if I stalked to 10 yards or so and placed the .177 pellet perfectly, usually aiming for the head, sometimes behind the shoulder.

Several years later, I was still using the Diana, and as a high school student my spare time was spent walking out along a canal area near our home, taking enough small game to make the walk worth the while. I could fill my game bag with the pellet rifle—the limit being 10 cottontails. I took no running shots, and I only used the body shot when I felt I could positively place it. I never lost a rabbit with that Diana. In fact, the little .177 pellet generally exited the target. I relate these facts because I believe in small game hunting with air power under the *right circumstances*. No air rifle I know of will take the place of a 22-caliber rimfire on small game, but there are places and circumstances when the "pellet rifle" is just right. It can humanely harvest small game if the shooter will get close.

Low Noise Level

Because of the low report of the air gun, it can be shot without disturbing others, even when that shooting takes place in the house. Of course, some air guns are more quiet than others, and a person trying to read the evening paper may take exception to the *crack!* of an air rifle too close by. All in all, however, air gun shooting is pretty quiet shooting. As an example, I have taken a couple rabbits as they sat in close proximity to one another. A noisier rifle would have no doubt sent the rabbits running instantly. I have also missed a head shot, reloaded and then improved my luck on the second try, again because of the low noise level of the air-powered gun. A noisier rifle, even a 22 rimfire, would most likely have frightened the rabbit away with the miss, especially from only 30 or 40 feet.

Recoil

The air gun has no noticeable recoil. This very positive attribute allows a shooter to fire away without any disturbance in terms of bothersome recoil. A shooter, developing a flinch with his big game rifle, or even handgun, should spend a few weeks with an air gun, firing several thousand shots in an attempt to reinforce the good habit of steady holding and follow-through. Shooter's form can also be learned from scratch with an air-powered gun. I think lack of noticeable recoil is one of the reasons for this truth. Of course, the 22 rimfire is also recoilless, but with the pellet gun a shooter can practice and enjoy himself right in his own home or backyard, and quietly at that.

A Beginner's Gun

The air gun is an excellent beginner's tool. Of course, no air gun should be used as a toy. Guns are tools, not toys—regardless of whether they're powered by powder or air. And beginning with an air rifle means enjoying the lack of muzzle blast associated with larger-bore firearms, as well as a quietness that not even a 22 rimfire can boast. No matter how many plus-features air guns have, they would be of small value without one attribute—*accuracy*. Because of accuracy, the newcomer can learn to shoot. Because of accuracy, a shooter will never outgrow air-powered pellet guns. Those 10-shot groups at 10 yards, which create one-hole results, tell the shooter that when he misses at close range, it was *his* shooting, not a lack of firearm accuracy which caused the miss. Missing or producing oversized groups at close range tells the shooter that he is doing something wrong, and that he must correct his stance, aim and control if he wishes to improve.

Camp Use

I am sure other hunters feel the same way I do—when I am in a big game camp, I prefer peace and quiet over noise. Needless camp shooting is bad manners if camps are close to one another. I am not so bothered by the idea of game being frightened away, and put only small stock in this happening. However, when a nearby camp is alive with 22 rimfire practice, that can be annoying and dangerous. However, there is nothing wrong with camp shooting if there is a safe backstop and if that shooting will not bother anyone. The obvious quietness of the air gun allows for this type of enjoyment. The nearby camp will never even hear the air-powered arm ''go off.''

Air power is often the means used in getting the young shooter started and started right, with safety always in the forefront of any instruction. The old Daisy BB gun, foreground, is in the famous Red Ryder model—note saddle ring with leather thong tied through it. The air rifle in the background is a 17-caliber Diana model from pre-war Germany.

This is the gun that "started it all" for millions of adult shooters—the Daisy Red Ryder repeater. It's still available.

Selecting an Air Gun

The BB Gun

The BB gun is here to stay. Millions of boys and girls have owned a BB gun as part of their growing up in America. Properly managed, the BB gun is a safe and instructive shooting system. I doubt that many serious shooters of our adult world have lost memory of their own BB gun somewhere back in the beginning of their personal shooting history. I remember mine. It was a Daisy Red Ryder. The Daisy Red Ryder is still available today.

In 1888 Daisy got its start, except the company was not called Daisy, nor did it build air rifles. It was the Plymouth Iron Windmill Company and that company made the first Daisy air rifle more as a premium for windmill customers than for outright sale. However, the customers wouldn't have it that way. By 1889 the windmills were gone but the Daisy BB gun was still being made, although now in serious full-time form. By 1895 the Plymouth Iron Windmill Company changed its name, too. It became the Daisy Manufacturing Company.

There have been many different Daisy models. I suppose the Red Ryder model, named for a famous comic book character (and films, too) will always come to my mind whenever I think of a BB gun. But in fact, it's a Daisy Model 499 which is used in competition shooting today—more on that in a moment. The Daisy 1894 Spittin' Image Carbine, I understand, has outsold the Red Ryder. It really is a replica-type rifle, and it does look like the famous Model 94 Winchester.

The BB gun, as such, is generally a smoothbore. The lack of rifling does mean that accuracy is not usually up to a strong comparison with the modern target ''pellet rifle,'' but all the same, at close range the BB gun is quite accurate. Usually, it's a repeater. But there are single shot BB guns as well. And there are pistols as well as rifles. Daisy has a Model 188 BB/pellet pistol, a spring-action model with 24-shot capacity. The Daisy Model 179 Six Gun is a 12-shot BB gun. Crosman has a Model 1600 BB Pistol with 17-shot capacity and it's a CO_2-powered handgun.

The rifles are many, to include the Crosman Model 66

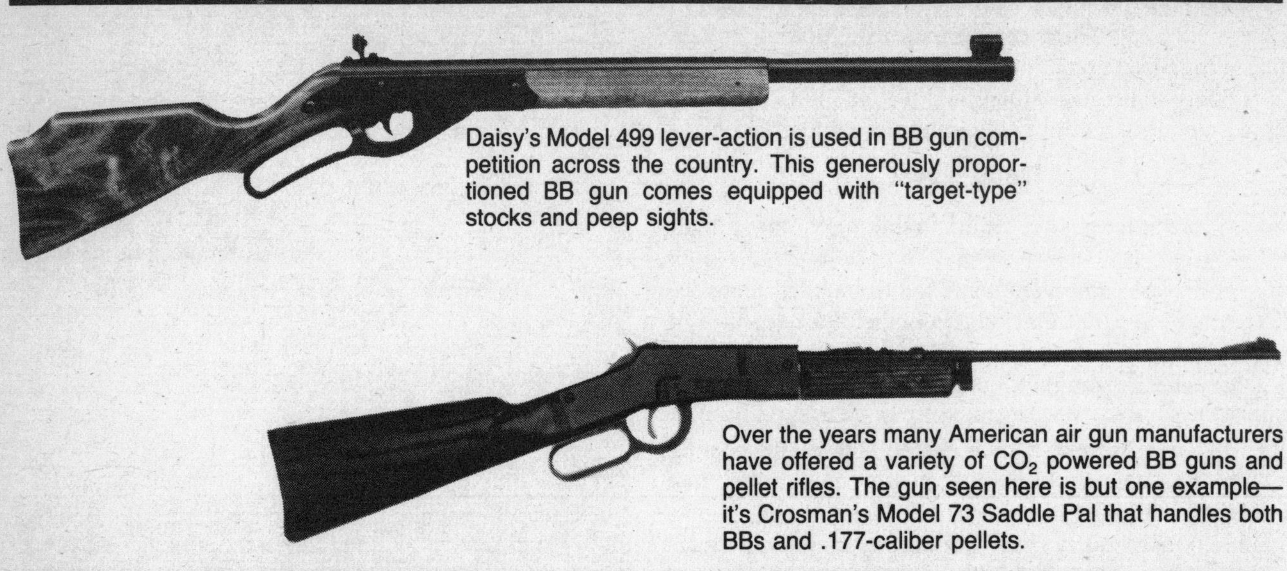

Daisy's Model 499 lever-action is used in BB gun competition across the country. This generously proportioned BB gun comes equipped with "target-type" stocks and peep sights.

Over the years many American air gun manufacturers have offered a variety of CO_2 powered BB guns and pellet rifles. The gun seen here is but one example—it's Crosman's Model 73 Saddle Pal that handles both BBs and .177-caliber pellets.

Powermaster BB rifle, which also fires pellets. But whatever the BB gun, it shoots a BB, and this means a copper-coated sphere of .177-inch diameter. A tiny round ball missile in fact. Because the little pill is round and so light in weight, partly because it is a sphere and partly because it is not pure lead, the BB does not fare well in a wind, nor is it for anything remotely resembling long range air guning.

But it can be a fine practice gun. And the practice can turn into pretty serious competition. There is, in fact, a BB Gun World Match, sponsored by Daisy, but coordinated by the Jaycees. The event has been carrying on for 18 years, and there has never been an accident. In fact, the U.S. Safety Council awarded the match for its fine record of safety. Boys and girls ages 8 to 14 are eligible and each state has its own championship. As stated earlier, the Daisy Model 499 is the only gun used in this match. And the targets are very tiny, just mere dots on paper at a range of 5 meters.

The competitor shoots 40 rounds at the target, 10 from each of four shooting positions, prone, sitting, kneeling and offhand. And they are doing this shooting with a regular BB through a smoothbore barrel. There is no sophistication in the projectile, or the bore, above the ordinary. While this event is of world stature, I can safely say that there is a great deal of BB gun practice going on all over the country which is much more informal. Sure, this shooting demands rules and regulations, too. And the careful parent is going to provide that supervision just as he or she provides supervision for the use of any other tool.

The BB gun is very much like the other air-powered shooting instruments of our time, quite economical and effective within the scope of its intention. The BB gun has remained an important item in many young person's bag of growing up experiences because it has always been functional. Yes, good advertising hasn't harmed the fame of the BB gun, but if these air-powered guns did not work, they would have been extinct a long time ago. Today's BB gun is a product of the modern age, of course, it serves a sophisticated youth. It has to be reliable. And it has to achieve sufficient close-range accuracy to make it interesting to use. The BB gun of now does boast of reliability, and it does have accuracy enough for its intended work.

Air power has been around for a very, very long time. Air power remains perfectly sufficient for many shooting tasks of the hour, and therefore is indeed going to continue. The trend may be toward further development of range and accuracy, but it's most likely that the latter is going to dominate as the BB gun grows in sophistication. The pellet rifle is going to gather momentum in both fields, punch and accuracy. Both will continue to serve the shooter, not only as a beginner's device, but also as a lifetime shooting tool, especially in the case of the target quality air rifles of the time.

The Pellet Gun

Today's sophisticated pellet gun is state-of-the art in quality and accuracy. I purposely tried some older air guns. They were good. But the new ones were better. By better, I mean two things: power was up and so was accuracy. Today's pellet gun is an investment, lifetime-lasting tool. You should approach your purchase with that fact uppermost in your mind. Since you will not outgrow the modern air rifle or air pistol, think about spending a little more because the use-per-dollar is very high.

There are basically three types of air guns—the pneumatic, CO_2 and spring models, the latter being either under-lever in design or hinged barrel. The pneumatic pellet gun works from air pressure stored in the chamber. The air

The modern air rifle is of adult size and adult power. This model, the RWS Model 45, proved more than adequate on small game as well as on the target range.

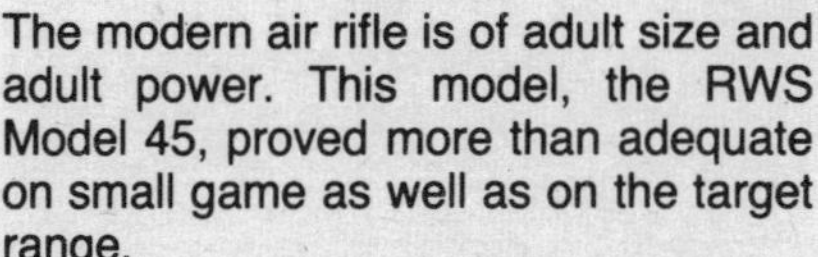

is forced into the chamber through pumping. As a result, the power is variable, depending upon how many times the gun is pumped. Over-pumping past chamber limitations is, of course, counter-productive.

The CO_2 models use cylinders pre-filled with liquid carbon dioxide. The rifle may have a chamber which is filled with CO_2, or it may use disposable CO_2 cartridges. The release of CO_2 gas propels the pellet, just as the release of compressed air does in the pneumatic model.

The spring-piston type, which may be hinged-barrel or lever-action in design (if lever, generally an under-lever as opposed to a side-lever), functions by cocking a strong spring with one stroke. Power is not variable. When the trigger's sear is released, the compressed spring-piston returns to its original position and in doing so pushes air in front of it with great force. Yes, we are using compressed air again, but in this case the compressed air is not created until the gun is "fired."

This RWS Model 45 air rifle is of the break-open design, using the spring-piston mode of compressing air. A simple cocking of the barrel compresses the interior spring for the rifle's power.

Advantages of the various styles are several. The advantage of the pump- or pneumatic-gun over the other two types is the variability of power. If a shooter wants to "blip" a pellet out for close-range shooting, he can do so. Generally, he will have to pump the gun a specific number of times, as a minimum, but the range is great. One pump-gun I tested required a minimum of three strokes for accuracy, but could be pumped eight times for more velocity. Another advantage is the fact that there is no jarring effect when the gun is shot; there is no powerful spring being released. Sharing a plus factor with the spring-piston pellet gun, the pneumatic is cheaper to shoot than the CO_2 model; one need not buy cylinders of CO_2 or charge the chamber.

The spring-piston model is also economical, and though it does have a jarring effect when shot, the "recoil" is not detrimental to accuracy. Unlike the CO_2 or pneumatic air guns, one need not worry about a leaking chamber as the spring-piston grows older, for no air is stored in the chamber in a compressed manner. The spring-piston model is rather simple in design, and yet very accurate.

The CO_2 model has a big plus factor, and that is total convenience. One need not pump nor cock the CO_2 air gun. But in my own tests to date (and things are changing all the time) the CO_2 was not quite as powerful as the spring-piston models. In fact, the latter achieved the highest velocity at the time of testing. Things change, and this factor may be reversed in the future, but for now, the spring-piston offers the highest velocity of the models tested.

Which type is best? Obviously, that depends upon the whims of the individual shooter, but I prefer the spring-piston at *at this time*. It is simple to operate, and it is cheap to shoot. Certainly, economy is a big factor in pellet gun operation. More than that, spring-piston models are highly accurate and, at the same time, *powerful*. The rifle itself is also economical to purchase as well as to shoot. I give the nod to the spring-piston air gun but as advances are made, *I could* be persuaded to change my mind.

Accuracy

Air gun competition is now an Olympic event. Certainly, the air gun must be accurate and consistent in that accuracy or such a lofty status could not have been at-

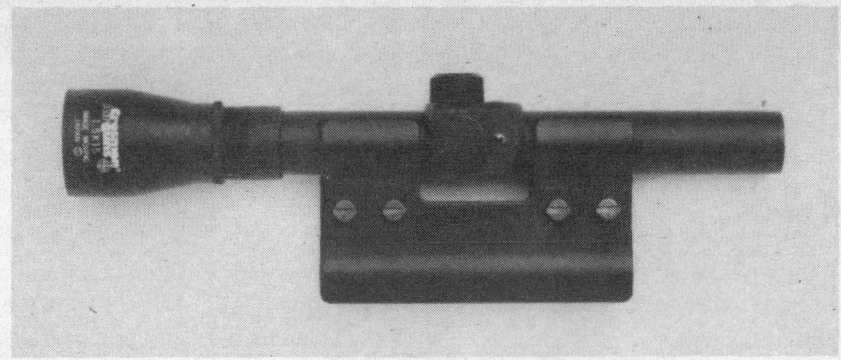

Pistol scopes have found their way into the air gun growth pattern. Here is the Crosman Model 457 Pistol scope with 1.5 power and a 15mm objective lens.

(Below) The sophisticated air gun has brought about sophisticated sightware in air gun design. The Beeman Rhino-hide Scope is an example of the current trend in adult air guns. The scope is coated with tough rubber, optics are quality and power is 4× or 3×-9×.

At this juncture Sheridan is the only American air gun company offering a 20-caliber (5mm) pellet rifle. The pump-up model seen here is the "Silver Streak."

Cottontail rabbit hunting with the pellet rifle of today is very feasible. The new air rifle has ample power for small game at close range. John Fadala found that the accuracy of the new air rifle afforded easy head shots up to 20 yards and even farther.

tained. In my own testing, I produced many groups at 10 yards which were no more than a ragged hole about .300-inch in some cases, and I was not attempting Olympic marksmanship. At about 20 yards, I found that with my RWS M45 I could count on a head shot for small game or rodents.

Of course, good projectiles are as important in the world of air gun accuracy as they are in any other form of shooting. Many companies provide quality pellets. I ran a few cursory tests on RWS pellets, using four of their offerings, the Diabolo, Superpoint, Hobby and Meisterkugeln. All four produced tight groups at 30 feet. Since the Meisterkugeln was supposed to be for target shooting, I decided to weigh a small sample of these pellets. The results of five pellets, pulled at random from the box and individually weighed, were that each tipped the scales at 8.2 grains. The weight of the Meisterkugeln is advertised as 8.6 grains, incidentally; however, my samples, weighed on two different scales, turned up at 8.2 grains each, a matter of no consequence. The important fact is the pellet-for-pellet consistency. With five random samples weighing 8.2 grains each on a scale good for 1/20 of 1 grain weight variation, the shooter has reason to believe that precision is the byword here. Naturally, a small sample from one population is not a statistically powerful statement, but I doubt that anyone can fail to admire such consistency all the same.

Which Caliber?

In my home, there are three air rifles and one air pistol at the moment. The little Webley Junior .177-caliber air pistol is a smoothbore and not intended for target accuracy,

Aiming the single shot scope-sighted air rifle, John Fadala uses the excellent RWS telescopic sight to put a .177-caliber pellet on target. The modern air rifle is of good balance and usually adult-size and adult power.

though for close-range plinking it has served us well. It has a fine trigger, and valuable handgun practice is possible with it. My youngest son has a 20-caliber air rifle. My oldest son has a 22-caliber model. And I have a .177-caliber rifle. One would surmise that of the three, the 22-caliber is the more stable, due to the greater mass of the projectile. One would further surmise that the 22-caliber is best on small game and vermin because of this added mass. After several years of shooting, however, I do not find this to be the case.

All three test calibers were accurate in their respective rifles, but I found the .177-caliber to shoot a bit flatter than 20- or 22-caliber. Also, while wind drift is in favor of the 20 and 22, none of the pellets faired very well in a breeze measured at 15 miles per hour. All were blown well off course. The tiny pellet is not a good projectile for windy conditions and wind drift is going to be great in all calibers. Penetration on small game was in favor of the .177-caliber as far as we could tell under field conditions. Obviously, the .177-caliber, being lighter in weight made the most in terms of muzzle velocity.

In conclusion, I would opt for the .177-caliber. It's cheaper to shoot than its larger cousins, and it does very well both on targets and in the field. If one wishes to be ultra-critical of the matter, it is a fact that the 20 or 22 calibers would have a slight mechanical advantage in pure width of projectile on a target, but again, I found no *practical* advantage in target shooting with the 20 or 22 over the .177-caliber. For most of the work demanded of a pellet gun, the .177 is a very sensible size.

Regardless of the caliber, the shooter should be very careful to sight in with the pellet of his choice and stay with that pellet for the intended purpose, be it target or small game/pest shooting. I say this because I found a very marked difference in point of impact between the various pellets of the same caliber. In my own .177-caliber rifle, each pellet style found a different point of impact on the target, all being pushed by the same air power of course. Naturally, we have a variation in actual weight from one pellet brand (and style) to another, and therein lies the big problem. My advice? Try all of the brands and styles you want in your new air rifle or air pistol, but once you have settled on a favorite, remember that switching from that pellet to another may *vastly* change your point of impact on the target.

Power

My own RWS M45 air rifle has driven an 8.2-grain pellet at a muzzle velocity of 900 fps. This is excellent velocity from an air gun, and is one of the higher velocities obtained to date in any air gun. But as one would suspect, there is no way to end up with much energy. As a result, we must treat the air gun as a short-range tool only, especially if used on any live target. I have hunted recently with a modern air rifle and can attest to the fact that a cottontail can be put down as far as 40 yards from the muzzle on a calm day when "guesstimation" of wind drift is not necessary. But I don't shoot that far as a rule. I like 20 yards better, and try for 10-yard shots whenever I can get them. When squirrel hunting or hunting cottontails in my part of the country, 10-yard shots are possible with a bit of stalking. I do realize that this is not always possible in all areas. The shooter must decide on the lethality of the air gun for small game hunting under the specific conditions in his area.

A pellet of 8.2 grains weight is certainly not hefty. Remember, there are 7,000 grains in a pound, 437.5 grains weight in a single ounce. The 8.2-grain pellet at 900 fps MV (muzzle velocity) is worth 15 foot-pounds of muzzle energy. Even compared with a 22 Short cartridge, that "ain't much." A 22 Short hollow point, with a 27-grain bullet at a muzzle velocity of 1150 fps, would enjoy 79 foot-pounds of ME (muzzle energy). This simple compari-

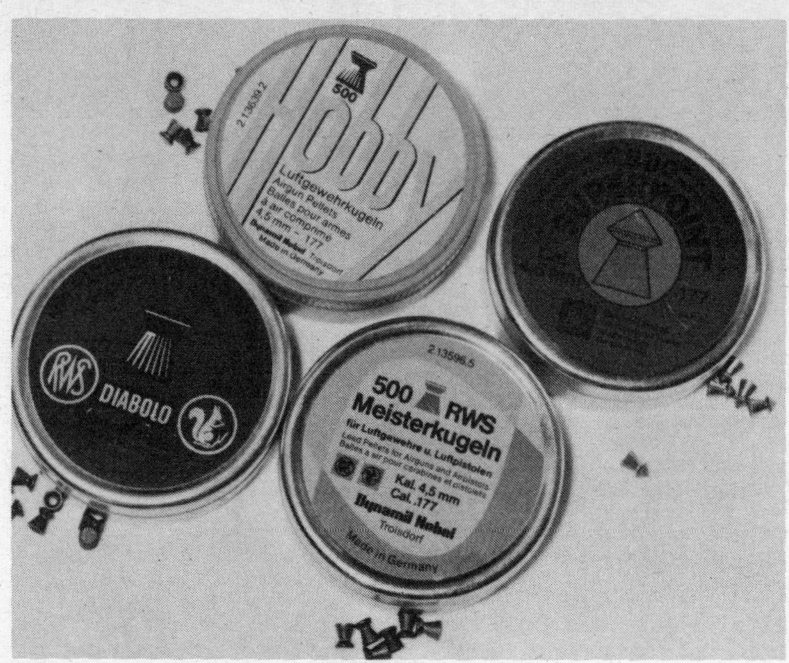

Today's offering of air gun ammunition means special pellets for special jobs. These pellets are from the famous RWS company, and they are offered to the shooter to fill various air gun functions. The Hobby style is an economical and accurate pellet. The Superpoint is meant for hunting, and it is a stronger pellet offering good penetration qualities. The Diabolo is a fine all-around pellet for both hunting and target work, and the Meisterkugeln is a pellet designed for competition shooting.

These three pellets are all of the same brand and type, RWS Superpoint. The pellet in the center was collected from a rabbit which it harvested. Note that while there is some deformation of the pellet, it is not flattened out. Penetration was almost complete in the small game animal, in fact.

son between the above .177-caliber air rifle and 22 Short rimfire round is telling in terms of hunting small game with a pellet gun.

This is why I prefer 10- and 20-yard shots on small game with air-powered rifles. Going up in caliber did not change the power situation in the pellet rifles I tested. For example, the RWS Model 45 in 22-caliber, pushing a 13.8-grain pellet at 700 fps was also worth 15 foot-pounds of ME. Yes, the heavier 22-caliber pellet may "carry up," or retain its energy better than the lighter weight .177 pellet, but at the same time, it loses in terms of trajectory.

The all-lead pellet does have a virtue. It retains its original mass quite well, as do pure-lead round balls or conicals in the world of black powder shooting. This is a function of high molecular cohesion for lead. I tried the four pellet, offerings from RWS mentioned earlier, in various media, and even extracted a few from defunct rabbits. Full or excellent retention of original weight was the rule. In an attempt to gain some "bust-up" of the pellets, I fired several of each type into a harder substance, in this case large department store catalogues with their compact "slick" pages.

I pre-weighed each pellet before shooting and then carefully retrieved the fired pellet from the catalogue. Incidentally, the pellets "mushroomed" or "upset" in the catalogue about as they had on game. We have illustrations of pellets taken from rabbits for the reader's interest. Another point—not only did the pellets upset, they also penetrated quite well, far deeper than I had expected before shooting them and to about the same depth. I think this is a function of the flattening of the soft-lead pellets. Energy is given up in the process of shape change during penetration. And, obviously, energy is necessary for penetration, so when the energy was used up, penetration halted. In all four cases, the pellets made it about 1/2-inch into the strong catalogue material. Here are the results of the collected RWS pellets, before shooting and after recovery, illustrating grain weight retention for each of the four pellet brands:

Meisterkugeln

Before: 8.2 grains
After : 8.2 grains

Diabolo

Before: 7.8 grains
After : 7.6 grains

Hobby

Before: 6.9 grains
After : 6.9 grains

Superpoint

Before: 7.5 grains
After : 7.0 grains

Though the power of an air gun is not impressive when compared with powder-burning firearms, the pellet gun is no *toy*. It never was, but some of the marginal performers of the past gave the impression of toys since they offered extremely low velocities and consequent poor performance. Also, some of those older models were far less accurate than the air guns of today. However, when one gets over 900 fps, there is not only the potential for short-range small game hunting and pest control, but also the potential for hazards through improper handling.

Of course, shooters want a certain ballistic force from any given class of gun, and pellet shooters are no exception to this rule. However, I found that with my personal air rifle the 900 fps level with a .177-inch pellet was sufficient for my air gun needs. In my opinion, the watchword for buyers should be accuracy first and power second. Here is a statement from the RWS catalogue which came with my rifle, and it is enlightening on the subject of air gun power. The paragraph reads:

> In the late 1700s, powerful pneumatic guns even found their way into the ranks of the military. The Austrian Army had an entire regiment armed with 44-caliber repeating air rifles. All surviving accounts indicate that the Austrians used those air guns with deadly effectiveness against Napoleans's soldiers, to the point that any Austrian soldier captured with an air rifle was summarily executed as an assassin!

After testing several modern air guns, I suggest that the trend should be toward increasing velocity to a modest level, while working harder in the areas of quietness and pleasantness in shooting, as well as ultimate accuracy. Speed, however, sells things in our land, and I imagine the pellet-gun makers will be working hard toward creating air-powered arms of top velocity. The advertisement which can honestly say, *''Fastest Air Rifle in the World''* will sell products. That's not all bad. Imagine a future pellet rifle capable of driving a heavier missile, perhaps 20 to 25 grains in weight, at about 1000+ fps. On small game, that rifle would work well. But . . . there have already been very powerful air guns in the past, as our previous quote stated, and I like to think that the goals of the air gun makers will not be high velocity alone.

The pellet-gun race will continue, with economy of shooting being one of the larger reasons for a surge in air rifle popularity. It is the cheapest form of shooting.

Cleaning and Maintenance

The air rifle is quite capable of years of service without a lot of worry and fuss. However, as with any mechanical tool, it does require a minimum level of care if the shooter expects a long life from his pellet shooter. First, it is a good idea to keep the air rifle or pistol clean. Newcomers to air gun shooting do not always observe this rule, because they do not think an air-powered arm can really get dirty. After all, there is no powder residue. While there is no powder residue, the air gun does get dirty. Internally, friction-reducing oil attracts and holds dirt. Externally, especially with those cocked by hand, the gun is subject to oils from our skin as well as ordinary dust. The air gun companies have provided cleaning kits for their products, and shooters should faithfully use those kits according to manufacturer's instructions.

Maintenance also means oiling of the internal piston on spring-piston guns and the working parts. Oil is imperative to continued, proper air gun function. *Warning*—any old oil will not do for air guns; they require a special lubricant to prevent the oil from becoming gummy. I recommend using the oils put out by the air gun companies and applying the oil per the manufacturer's instructions. They are priced low enough to warrant their purchase, and they are formulated specifically for air guns. How often to oil? I go by the number of pellets shot in my own air rifle. When I have used up a box of 500 pellets, it's time to oil her up.

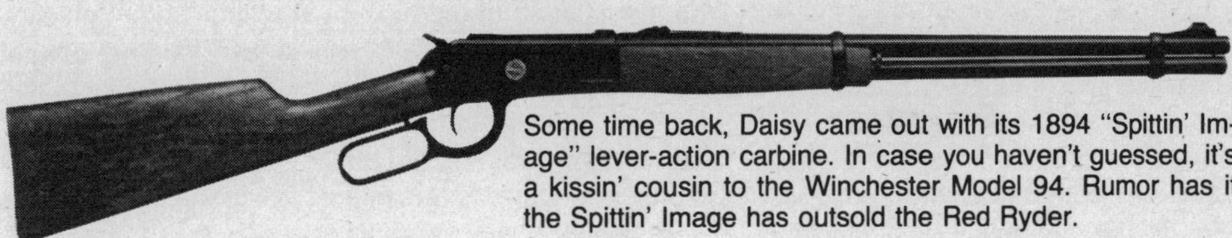

Some time back, Daisy came out with its 1894 "Spittin' Image" lever-action carbine. In case you haven't guessed, it's a kissin' cousin to the Winchester Model 94. Rumor has it the Spittin' Image has outsold the Red Ryder.

Sheridan continues to offer its Pelletrap, at a suggested retail price of $19. Use of the Pelletrap allows the shooter to practice indoors. For the avid pellet gun fan, a unit like the Pelletrap will prove to be a good investment, providing years of indoor shooting fun.

Safety

Closing this chapter on the subject of safety is akin to telling someone what you have already told him; however, the new, modern, air gun makes it impossible for us to gloss over the safety aspects of air-gunning. Some people still believe that air-powered arms are more for youngsters than serious shooters—toys, if you will. As for me, I'm still surprised at the punch inherent in today's air gun. And though I would recommend safety measures even if the air gun were not powerful, the actual lethality therein means we must be very watchful of *who* uses air guns and *where* those air guns are used, as well as how they are handled.

Also, there are a few secondary factors worth considering. First, even though it is safe to shoot a pellet gun in the home, it is only safe when a proper range has been prepared. Thousands of shooters are using air-powered guns inside of buildings with 100 percent success in the safety department. But backstops are required. Even with a good pellet trap, it is paramount to use a backstop because of splash-back. The modern high-speed air rifle can cause its pellets to all but disintegrate on the pellet trap. The distance from shooter to pellet trap should be at least, in my opinion, 30 feet or more so that any fragments of lead coming back at the shooter will be slowed down should they strike. Also, as in all shooting sports, eye protection is a good idea. Bystanders should be warned that shooting is a serious pastime and that they should maintain a position behind the shooter, well back in the room, if indoors, so that pellet fragments will not harm them. Eye protection is strongly advised for bystanders as well as for shooters.

Second, though a pellet gun is relatively quiet, when compared with powder-burning arms, there can still be a noise factor to think about, and ear protection can be in order, especially indoors where sound is confined. Simple earplugs will work fine.

Further, the proper ammo is necessary for safety purposes. Today, there are some pellets which are extra hard, or even contain non-lead hard alloys as a part of the pellet. These should not be shot at the pellet trap. They should be saved for outdoor shooting, especially small game. Target pellets should be soft lead projectiles which will smash on impact with most if not all of the debris being retained by the trap. Of course, even with these softer pellets, a backstop is necessary as there can still be flying particles of lead.

A Worthwhile Addition to the Arms Battery

The air-powered firearm, handgun or rifle, is a very worthy addition to the modern shooter's battery of arms. Although the air gun has been with us for a long time, as far back as 1500 AD, it has never been this sophisticated. And in the small, economical calibers, it has never been so fast in terms of muzzle velocity nor so powerful. The precision air gun is a serious tool to be enjoyed by shooters of beginning stature, yes, but also shooters of many years of experience.

When it is inconvenient, if not impossible, to get out and shoot the powder-burners, the sensible alternative is air-power. When super economy is useful, the answer is air. Today's air gun is an adult's practice arm, small game getter and pest control tool. It is also a very viable beginner's gun as well. The precision air gun is here to stay.

Chapter 11

The Home Defense Firearm

THE LEGAL aspects of firearms ownership and *use* has been given its own chapter. I refer you to it. In this chapter, we will only address the weapons used for self-defense. Can the use or presence of a firearm, under the right circumstances, save a life? I'll answer by saying that the National Rifle Association has compiled thousands of documented cases of citizens saving their own lives or the lives of others through the use or presence of a firearm in the act of self-defense. Obviously, a self-defense gun can be just about any type of shooting instrument from a 22 rimfire pistol on up to a big game rifle. However, there are definite limitations in trying to turn any hunting arm into a self-defense tool. The shooter must be concerned not only with defending his life with this firearm, but he must also be very concerned with where the projectile goes after the gun is fired. A bullet from a high-powered rifle fired in a neighborhood could make its way through a wall or door of your home and strike someone in another home, a block away. The same can be said for the magnum handgun.

High crime rate areas indicate a need for protection, however, and a compromise must be struck when legally selecting a firearm for the home. There must be sufficient ballistic authority to stop an intruder bent on personal harm and at the same time, the gun must be manageable. Naturally, the management of a given firearm depends upon the skill and experience of its owner, as well as the level of training that person has with the gun in question.

It is difficult, therefore, to say that one type of firearm will suit *every* person in *every* situation. If a self-defense gun must be transported on a person licensed to carry it, then the gun will surely be a pistol or revolver. But for the home, neither of these may be right. There are some obvious attributes of handguns and shotguns as home-defense firearms. This chapter will explore some of the high and low points of both, as well as discussing the old but still viable argument existing between those who favor the revolver and those who prefer the pistol as a self-defense/home-defense gun.

The most effective self-defense firearm is the shotgun. Although this double barrel shotgun, the Armsport 1212 hammer-gun, would not spread its shot widely at very close range, it is still extremely effective, even with smaller shot.

The Shotgun

Single Shots

Eliminate the single shot model, even though it is certainly effective, especially with the barrel sawed off to a

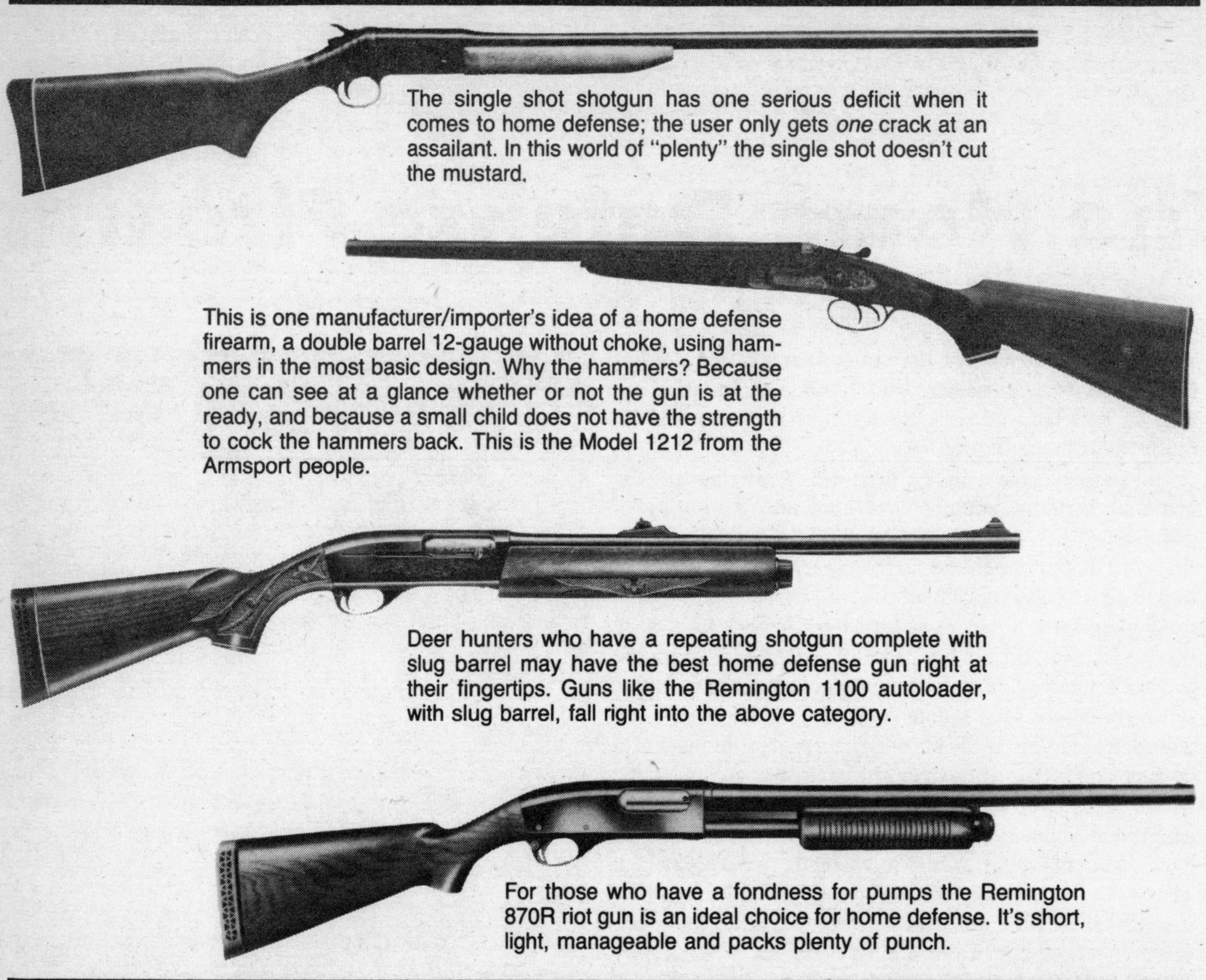

The single shot shotgun has one serious deficit when it comes to home defense; the user only gets *one* crack at an assailant. In this world of "plenty" the single shot doesn't cut the mustard.

This is one manufacturer/importer's idea of a home defense firearm, a double barrel 12-gauge without choke, using hammers in the most basic design. Why the hammers? Because one can see at a glance whether or not the gun is at the ready, and because a small child does not have the strength to cock the hammers back. This is the Model 1212 from the Armsport people.

Deer hunters who have a repeating shotgun complete with slug barrel may have the best home defense gun right at their fingertips. Guns like the Remington 1100 autoloader, with slug barrel, fall right into the above category.

For those who have a fondness for pumps the Remington 870R riot gun is an ideal choice for home defense. It's short, light, manageable and packs plenty of punch.

manageable, legal (18-inch) length. Manageable length means an overall length from buttplate to muzzle which will allow the shooter to wield the firearm quickly and with ease. Hallways are often quite narrow. Trying to maneuver down a hallway with a shotgun which wears a 30-inch barrel can be awkward at best.

While the sawed-off, single shot shotgun is ballistically as effective as any other type of shotgun, there is a rub—*one shot*. If a need arises for a fast second shot, it will not be there, obviously. And a need *could* arise. There may be more than one intruder, for example. Or a homeowner may want to fire a warning shot followed up by another shot if needed. One does not shoot away his only round as a warning shot. Therefore, the single shot shotgun is eliminated as a contender for a home-defense firearm.

Doubles

The double barrel shotgun has been a home defense tool for a very long time. The pioneers and settlers "out West" often counted on the double barrel shotgun hanging on its wall pegs to do the job when the home had to be defended. Of course, the example is like playing with a stacked deck. The only other choice of shotgun style would have been a single shot in those days because there was no pumpgun or semi-auto to select from. But the point is this: The double gun worked then and it can work now.

A double barreled shotgun has the same advantage of a double rifle, such as used in the hunting of dangerous game. And that advantage rests with *two* quick shots. I am fully confident that I can get two shots off from a double gun faster than I can get two shots off from a semi-automatic shotgun. There is, however, another point in favor of the double barreled shotgun, and that is overall length. Even with a very short barrel, the semi-auto and pumpgun will be longer than a double because of the action length of the last two. A double has a very brief action and even with normal sporting barrels can be quite short in overall length.

I have an Armsport Model 1212 hammer gun which is

kept handy in the house. The total length of my 12-gauge is 38 inches, and that is with the normal factory barrels, not sawed-off barrels. The hammer aspect is one of safety. The hammers cannot be cocked by a small child. At the same time, any adult can easily understand the function of this rebounding hammergun.

I think that another plus for the double gun is the "scare" factor. Its side-by-side (or over/under) barrels are formidable-looking. No person would lack respect when looking into the business end of a double gun. The double has always been thought of as *big medicine*. It has always had a "press" which admired its authority, be it a modern concept or the old-time stagecoach man "riding shotgun" with a double barrel side-by-side for an enforcer.

Pumps and Semi-Autos

The pumpgun is very familiar to American shooters because it is our basic shotgun these days and has been for a long time. It is typically American, in fact. Therefore, it is a familiar style to many shooters and even to nonshooters who wish to purchase a firearm for home-defense. In "riot gun" form it is short and handy. For example, the Smith & Wesson Model 3000 Police shotgun goes about 42 inches in overall length. This open-bore pump is typical of the riot gun form, and it is available with a hardwood stock or a folding stock, as well as a pistol grip and no actual buttstock.

The pump is entirely reliable. This is not to say that semi-autos are not reliable. They are. But there are rare instances of reloaded ammo hanging up in an auto-shotgun when the pump would have shucked 'em in and shucked 'em out. However, this is not an attempt to compare the reliability of the pump over that of the auto. Use nice new factory ammo for home defense or reloads with like-new hulls and the semi-auto will shoot them as fast as you can pull the trigger. Another plus factor of the pumpgun is the fact that it can be reloaded while still loaded.

In other words, one need not "break the action open" to insert fresh ammo. You just load the ammunition through a loading port while the pump is still fully ready to go. A double is inoperable when being reloaded, as is the single shot. Of course, this plus factor is shared by the semi-auto shotgun. Shoot. Shoot again. Then if you want to load in another shell, just pop it through the loading port. There are numerous good riot guns on the market today, such as the Mossberg M500, the Savage M69-RXL, the Remington 870, Marlin 120, the S&W M3000 already mentioned, the Winchester 1200 and others.

The semi-auto has two big advantages. First, repeated fire is accomplished by pulling the trigger with no other manipulation. Second, recoil is somewhat softened by the actual working of the action, which takes energy, but the energy is not a loss to power ballistically. So the semi-auto is not only fast-shooting, but also somewhat less bothersome in the recoil department.

Shotguns: The Best Home-Defense Guns

I feel that the shotgun is the best *home* defense gun of them all. It is impossible for me to take sides with the pump or double or semi-auto because the choice of action becomes personal. I have a double gun, already mentioned. It is short, handy and open-bored. I find it excellent as a tool not only for home protection but also for the camp. It is very easy to pack into small places, too. The big 12-gauge punch is good, but any style of shotgun can be acquired in 12-gauge, so that point is moot. However, I do like the exposed hammers. They are very hard to cock for a child, but no problem for an adult.

The double is not better than a pump or semi-auto riot gun, however, though I would much prefer it over a standard pump or semi-auto shotgun because of its short length. My suggestion is for the buyer to at least handle the three major types of home defense shotguns—double, pump and semi-auto—and then make up his mind on the basis of how these guns handle for him. I would, however, insist upon a riot gun barrel length for the pump or auto and a short barrel for the double gun. Long barrels have no place in a home defense shotgun.

The Winchester Stainless Police model is an ideal home defense firearm. It comes in 12-gauge.

Gauge

If the shotgun is the best home-defense gun, then what is the best gauge to buy? I stated that I was happy with the 12-gauge mentioned above, but I did not say why. The why is not power. I do not opt for a 12-gauge shotgun for home defense. I chose a 12-gauge shotgun because my model doubles for other uses in the field. I carry it for some backcountry hunting, and I like the versatility of the 12-gauge for these multi-purpose uses. But if possible, I would pick a 20-gauge for home-defense. I say "if possible," because the bulk of the riot gun styles come in 12-gauge, with the exception of a few models, such as the Winchester Defender Pump Gun, also offered in 20-gauge.

The 20-gauge in my opinion, is big enough for home-defense purposes. Police departments have a different set

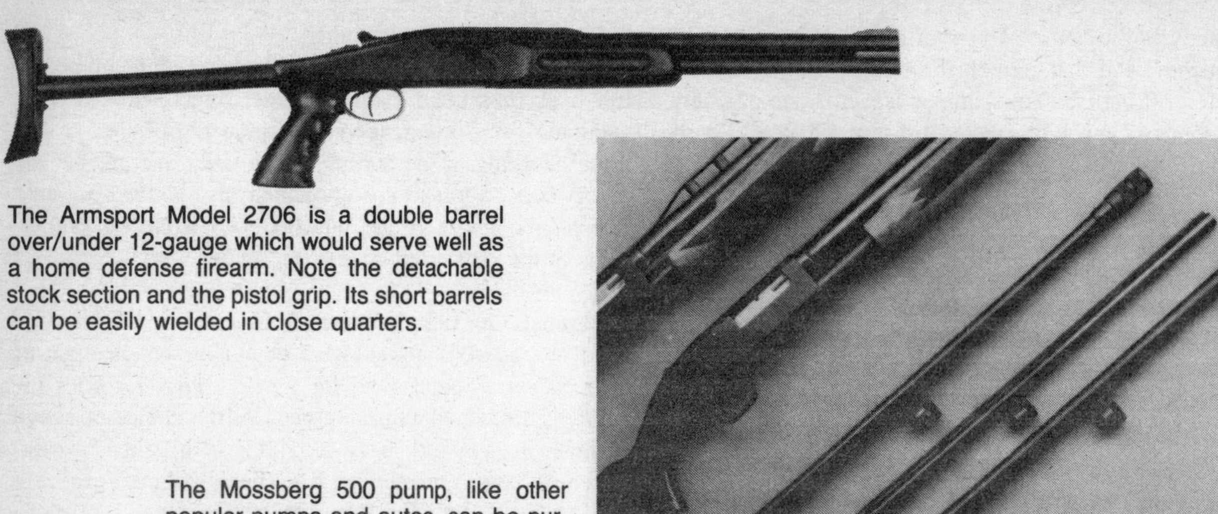

The Armsport Model 2706 is a double barrel over/under 12-gauge which would serve well as a home defense firearm. Note the detachable stock section and the pistol grip. Its short barrels can be easily wielded in close quarters.

The Mossberg 500 pump, like other popular pumps and autos, can be purchased complete with spare barrels. The hunter/homeowner would be wise to purchase a spare riot or slug barrel for his own repeater. It makes sense from a home defense standpoint.

of circumstances to work with and their selection of 12-gauge riot guns is a good choice. In fact, Ithaca makes a 10-gauge for police work or other heavy-duty defense operations. This is the Ithaca Mag-10 Roadblocker, and it comes in the Magnum 3½-inch chambering of the 10-gauge round. The barrel is 22 inches long, cylinder bore, and the gun weighs 10¾ pounds.

I like the 20-gauge because it allows for a smaller gun to be built overall. In fact, the 20-gauge seems almost ideal to me. In the 3-inch chamber, which the Winchester Defender does have, the charge could be a full 1¼ ounces. I doubt that this much load is needed. An ounce of shot equals a mass projectile weight of 437.5 grains weight, and at close quarters, such as normally encountered in the home-defense situation, all of the pellets, or almost all, will strike the target.

The 20-gauge is my choice for someone setting out to buy a new home-defense shotgun *provided* the shotgun can be purchased in that gauge. The 20 has enough power for the normal home-defense situation.

Can You Handle It?

While it is comforting to consider the terrific power of the shotgun at very close range, and while I still consider the shotgun the ideal tool for home defense, we truly do have to think about another pertinent question—can you handle it? I fired a Winchester Pistol Grip Pump Security Shotgun in 12-gauge and found that I *could* handle it. In fact, it would be a top consideration as a home-defense tool, though in 20- not 12-gauge.

But the gunowner simply has to ask himself that big question, and he must answer it with cold logic. Not everyone enjoys shooting a standard 12-gauge or 12-gauge with short barrel and modest weight. Sure, in a situation of defending life, that recoil would be of no consequence in actually *feeling* it, but a shooter may have predisposed himself to bad habits while practicing with that shotgun so that he, under the stress of action, simply cannot do well with the gun in terms of aiming and firing, especially if that second and even third shot might be necessary. The once-in-a-while shooter may wish to think about a shotgun for home defense in terms of recoil and he should make certain that he can handle the gun before depending upon it under emergency circumstances.

Shot Size

Buckshot of the 0, 00 and 000 variety is not needed in a home defense shotgun. Of course, there are as many arguments as there are experts in the field of gunning and a close friend-writer of mine considers 000 buck just right for the job. I don't. That heavy shot will just penetrate more than is necessary. I also dislike bird shot. Bird shot is for the birds. Sure, an ounce or more of No. 8 shot will discourage all but the most zealous from continuing in their beligerent ways, but we are talking "stopping" here. That is the key to the whole thing. *Stopping*. We are trying to stop someone who is bent upon dealing out damage to us or to other loved ones.

Something in the middle is about right, and I say No. 4 Buckshot is about best. There are 340 No. 4 Buckshot to the pound. This means 21 No. 4 Buck per ounce or about 24 to 25 of these pellets in a 1¼-ounce load for the 3-inch 20-gauge hull or the 2¾-inch 12-gauge hull, depending upon the wad system used. No. 4 Buck offers good penetration, but is not as bad as 0, 00 or 000 Buckshot in over-penetration. And anyone can prove for himself that No. 8 shot will also penetrate the usual sheetrock used in home construction. From 20 feet the wad and all will normally go through at least one and maybe two of these, meaning a whole wall in a home. It is always a danger to fire off any load under the home-defense circumstances, and even birdshot will not make the event safe.

The reader has a right to ask how many intruders I have deterred with No. 4 Buck, and the response is *none*. I base this commentary on tests and on the fact that I have taken game with No. 4 Buck at close range and the effect was considerably more pronounced than birdshot. I have not, at this time, dropped a charging bull elephant either, but my ballistic experience tells me that a 458 Winchester round would be more appropriate than a 225 Winchester. Also, my interview with law enforcement officials summarizes to a medium-sized shot as being correct for home defense.

Use birdshot instead of Buckshot if these are the only two choices, but give something like No. 4 Buck a chance on test materials from your shotgun and see if it works for you. Pattern is not the problem with any size Buck or with smaller shot because we are talking in feet distance in the home-defense situation, not yards. The pattern will be small no matter the shot used, since 20 or 30 feet is the probable range of fire.

The Handgun

For home defense, a handgun is acceptable in the hands of a person who knows how to shoot it. This means practice, of course. There is no sense in having a handgun on the shelf if the prospective user of that gun hardly knows how to load it, let alone shoot it. It takes a lot more practice to shoot a handgun with accuracy than it takes to point a shotgun across the room and let fly with a charge of pellets.

But the shotgun is not the obvious choice for self-defense in a situation where the gun is to be carried on the licensed owner or perhaps in an automobile.

Revolver or Auto?

Both have distinct advantages and disadvantages. Because of this, I have built a list of plus and minus factors concerning the choice of the handgun style, revolver or auto pistol. The reader can now turn to this list on the next page and begin to draw his own conclusions as to the values of each type.

In the trend of high power for home and self-protection, the 45 Auto has been in the foreground for a very long time. This Colt Government Model in 45 Automatic delivers a great deal of authority up close with multiple shots as fast as the trigger can be pulled.

A compact pistol is the Detonics 9MM Parabellum with its 7-shot magazine. It has a 2-inch barrel, and it weighs 22 ounces (empty). The sights are fixed, which is certainly fine for close-range self-protection or home defense work.

The Colt Agent is another of the personal defense sidearms available today. It comes in 38 Special caliber. Of course, it is double-action in design.

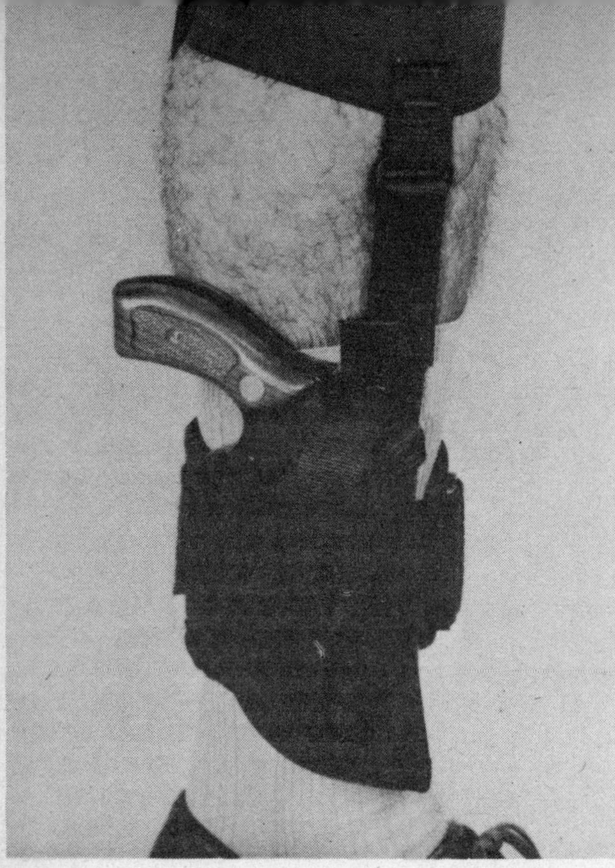

The Uncle Mike's Sidekick™ ankle holster will hold a handgun for those who have a permit to carry a concealed firearm. It is ultra light in weight, made of nylon, and will form to the contour of the individual's anatomy when worn.

In my opinion, the choice is a matter of personal preference coupled with the shooter's willingness to involve himself in his shooting. I fully subscribe to the revolver for those shooters who are going to buy a handgun, fire it only now and then. The auto, with its more complicated handling characteristics, requires more practice and more involvement—in my opinion. Of course, we are speaking of the big bore semi-auto here, not the little 22 rimfire auto, which does not normally carry multiple safeties.

On the other side of the coin, a person willing to practice, who enjoys handgunning, should well consider the auto. I like the flat-sidedness of the auto pistol, though that factor is only of value to those who need to pack or store the pistol in a compact place. I do like the firepower and the ease of inserting a fresh magazine. And the auto, given the proper caliber, is plenty powerful enough for self-defense. Having, perhaps, as many as 15 shots to work with could come in handy if a person finds himself faced with multiple antagonists.

The shooter should try both revolver and auto before he decides. Perhaps a local gun club will provide the would-be handgun buyer with an opportunity to try both the revolver and auto. That experience will help him decide between the two. If a revolver is selected for defense, I say it should be a double-action, even though I admire the single-action very much. A double-action allows the shooter to simply pick up the gun and pull the trigger.

Advantages and Disadvantages/Revolver *vs* Auto Pistol

Revolver

1. Extremely reliable. Not ammo sensitive.
2. No safety to fool with.
3. Does not require as much practice as the auto, in terms of understanding mechanical operation.
4. Quite accurate.
5. Bulky in larger calibers, and especially bulky in terms of the "lump" a cylinder makes.
6. Lacks firepower. (However, the FBI claims that most gun battles end in 2 to 3 shots.)
7. Fair to good pointability.
8. Grip angle sometimes feels "wrong."
9. Generally simpler to operate, load, unload, etc. Not complicated. More familiar to the general public.
10. Cannot be reloaded as rapidly as the auto.

Auto Pistol

1. Reliable, but sometimes very fussy concerning the ammo used.
2. Some autos have several safeties to deal with.
3. Does require more practice, but many shooters fire the auto more accurately than they shoot a revolver, and recoil is often much less in an auto.
4. Quite accurate.
5. Flat, compact, even in some of the larger calibers.
6. Has plenty of firepower, with some autos holding 15 rounds or so.
7. Good to excellent pointability.
8. Grip angle feels better on the auto.
9. Generally more difficult to operate, load, unload when in the hands of a shooter unpracticed in its use.
10. A fresh magazine can be inserted quickly.

Cartridge Selection for the Handgun

Underpower: Any of the 22 rimfires is underpowered for defense, though I quickly admit that the 22 rimfire can deter a criminal from attacking, and of course, people have expired having been struck by the 22 rimfire class cartridge. The 22 Short, Long, Long Rifle, even the 22 Magnum lack stopping power. That is the key here, *stopping* power, not necessarily killing power. The person interested in offering his family protection in the form of firearm defense must understand what he is up against. Today, many crimes are drug related, and individuals who are under the influence of narcotics can do remarkable things in terms of damage after being struck by a bullet.

We all know of the almost unbelievable cases of superhuman strength appearing in times of stress. In one instance, during the tragic earthquake in Alaska, a mother moved a power pole that was pinning down her child. I do not know the exact size of the pole, but the report stated the woman could not have possibly lifted it under normal circumstances. A person coming at you with destruction in mind may not be hyped up with drugs, but he could be experiencing that yet-to-be-understood phenomenon of human superstrength.

Another round I put in the category with the 22 rimfires is the 25 ACP, and the 32 ACP is not much stronger as far as I am concerned. Sure, the 32 ACP is better than nothing. It has a bullet of 71 grains and a muzzle velocity in the 975 fps domain—not much. The bullet is full metal jacket in my factory loads, though there is a cast bullet available for the 32 ACP. My verdict—forget it. The 32 ACP, like the 25 ACP, just doesn't have the stopping power.

Defense of the home can be accomplished with a tool of this sophistication, the Bushmaster Pistol from Bushmaster Firearms. It fires 223 Remington ammo in semi-auto mode, and it has a 30-round magazine. Obviously, the power and firepower of the model are both more than adequate for protection of one's home.

There are many different types of firearms meant for home/self-protection, as this unique design shows. It is the Advantage Arms Model 422, top-break, 4-shot, double-action, in 22 LR or 22 Magnum. Rimfires however, may not be the best choice when it comes to home/self-defense.

The American Derringer Corp. offers this stainless steel 25 Auto pistol. Although the 25 Auto round is not a strong one, many shooters feel that the small size of a 25 Auto pistol justifies its use as a self-defense tool. It's a matter of choice.

Adequate Power: Man is very susceptible to shock. When it comes to gunshot wounds, two types of shock come into play. There's "medical" shock, which stems from the loss of blood, and "hydrostatic" shock. It is the latter which blows a water-filled can apart when it is struck by almost any type of bullet with even modest velocity. During WWII, story had it that a man hit so lightly as in the hand by a 45 auto round was down, if not for good, at least stopped for the moment, but it took a fairly centered strike with the German 9mm Luger round to stop a soldier.

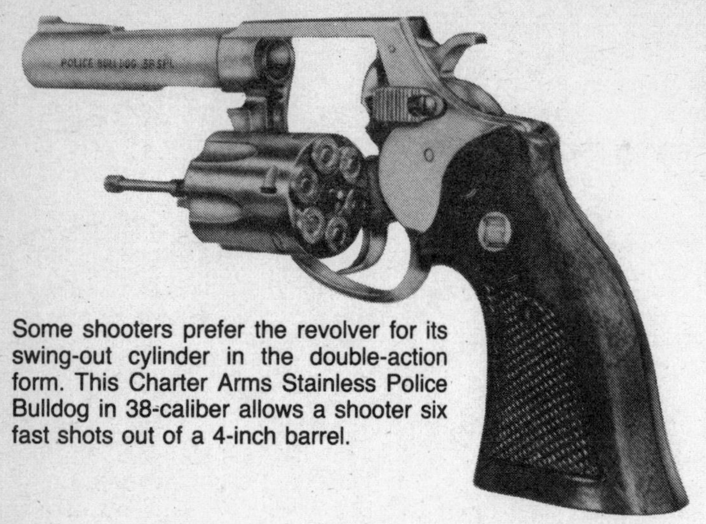

Some shooters prefer the revolver for its swing-out cylinder in the double-action form. This Charter Arms Stainless Police Bulldog in 38-caliber allows a shooter six fast shots out of a 4-inch barrel.

Something new in the handgun industry is nothing new. Innovation is always the byword. Here, we see the good Charter Arms Police Undercover handgun in 32 H&R Magnum. This round fires a 95-grain bullet at a muzzle velocity of 1030 fps. Muzzle energy is 224 foot-pounds. At 50 yards, the velocity is 940 fps for an energy of 186 foot-pounds. Ballistics campare favorably with the 38 Special, but the round allows for small handgun design.

The round which fits the niche of adequate power just about perfectly is the 38 Special. Do not misunderstand. This is not to say that it is the *perfect* defense caliber. It means to say that the 38 Special, with some loads, is adequate. It will stop an attacker if the bullet is fairly well placed, but it is not a marvel of stopping power either. I like a 158-grain lead hollow point bullet at maximum safe velocity out of the 38 Special. The 125-grain jacketed hollow point is also good. Shock is imparted by the wave in front of that bullet, and that wave grows large as the nose of the bullet expands. In short, the expanding type bullet is *generally* best for defense.

The 357 Magnum also fits the category of adequate. With a 125-grain hollow point bullet, the 357 is very powerful, although I did read of a case in which a police officer struck an assailant in the chest with a couple hits from a 357 Magnum, only to have the man continue coming on. But the article did not mention the load. The 140-grain bullet (in hollow point) from a 357 Magnum is a powerful force with the right powder charge behind it, too. For my money, solid lead bullets in the 357 only serve to leave deposits of lead in the bore that I am not fond of. And they lack expansion, which is desired in terms of defense.

The 9mm Luger is OK, but that's about it. Along with the 38 Super, it is adequate. And it is a round used in the auto, so multiple strikes are certainly possible.

Here is a flat-sided semi-automatic pistol from Smith & Wesson, their Model 659. It is a 15-shot pistol in 9mm caliber. Such firepower makes this handgun formidable in the hands of a trained marksman.

Big Punch: Although the following rounds have lots of power, they are not all ideal in terms of defense. Remember—there is more to a defense tool than super force. We mentioned where the self-defense encounter may take place, namely the home, even a condominium or apartment dwelling. Fire a big 44 Magnum under such circumstances and an innocent bystander could be hit several rooms away from the shooter. Walls are often thin, made of plaster board, and a 44 Magnum thinks plaster board is onion skin typing paper.

There are many handgun rounds which offer big punch.

The Charter Arms Bulldog in 357 Magnum, 5-shot, is a 2½-inch barreled revolver in double-action mode which would fit into the broad spectrum of home defense handguns. It has fixed sights, but for close-range shooting, this is all right.

This Randall 45 auto shows the relationship of the magazine to the firearm itself. High capacity is the byword for the semi-automatic pistol. Whereas a revolver in the big bore class usually holds six shots, a semi-auto can double that capacity and more.

The Randall 45 auto is a stainless steel model. It is made on the basis of meeting, and in some areas, exceeding military specs for the 45 auto. Every part of the Randall is stainless steel, including springs and pins. Also offered in 9mm and 38 Super.

The 44-40 is strong with handloads. The 44 Special is powerful, too. So is the 41 Magnum. The 45 Colt is plenty strong enough, and the 45 ACP will do the job in spades. I personally like the last one very much. It has adequate power, but a lot less recoil than some of the aforementioned rounds, in spite of the fact that it is thought of as a real "kicker" in the lighter pistols. A 45 ACP is a *stopper*. And stopping is the name of the self-defense game. Professionals, policemen in other words, often state that firepower is vital in selecting a protection handgun. If so, the 45 ACP meets that criterion while at the same time offering one-shot, human knockdown power. Remember, we are not talking about harvesting deer. The 357 Magnum is more powerful than the 45 ACP, all right, but several policemen told me they felt the 45 was a better stopper in self-defense terms.

This big Model 629 Smith & Wesson 44 Magnum would seem quite out of place in home defense, perhaps, but there are some experts who feel that a very powerful handgun is best, for the situation may demand *stopping* the intruder.

Bullet Design

In my tests, it seems to me that the lead hollow point bullet and the jacketed hollow point bullet in the big bore handgun rounds are best for self-defense. The semi-wadcutter is good, too, but I think inferior to the hollow points in tissue destruction and the delivery of shock, hence stopping power. A jacketed soft point can be quite good if it upsets enough to cause a large wound channel. A round nose in lead form usually provides minimal upset. I do not think them right for defense, and I don't care for the full metal jacket if other bullet design choices are available to the individual.

My Selection

I like the 45 ACP round. If I were to carry a handgun for self-defense purposes, this round would be high on my list. Today, there are a number of 45 ACP autos available in compact models. The 45 ACP round is powerful, but does not have the objectionable recoil of the larger cartridges of the 44 Magnum class.

In the semi-auto pistol, 45 ACP caliber is very strong and can be counted on to stop an attack with anything like decent bullet placement. This pistol, the 45-caliber Detonics, is a full-scale 45, weighing 41 ounces empty, and it is $8^3/_4$ inches in length. It has the 5-inch heavy weight match barrel with recessed muzzle and can be purchased with a 6-inch barrel. It would make a good home protection firearm in the hands of a practiced shot.

The Rifle

Little attention is given to the rifle here because it is not usually selected for home-defense or for self-defense, although one can find individuals who do like the rifle for such purposes. One police officer told me that in a rural area the Model 94 Winchester 30-30 was a good choice as a firearm for both protection and law enforcement, and many law enforcement agencies in this country and in Canada still have a few Model 94s around, though most have been replaced with semi-auto rifles now.

A Model 94 in the short Trapper version, with its 16-inch barrel and 30-30 chambering, might be a consideration for a home-defense rifle, but I believe the original statement above still holds up—choose a shotgun to defend the home and the camp, and look to the handgun when the self-defense firearm must be carried.

Training

The shooter interested in a self-defense arm can find suitable training to learn its use. This training may be available from many different places, such as NRA sponsored programs, a personal coach, an off-duty policeman, a police-sponsored school, shooting clubs, combat handgunning organizations and many other avenues. One who handles some of these shooting situations well will be quite ready for the event of protecting his life or the lives of others. I especially like professional programs for two big reasons: First, true experts are most likely going to be the teachers. Second, the pros will explain the whole story, giving the person valuable attitudes as well as arms know-how.

Practice with a pistol such as this Detonics 45 Auto means a very competent homeowner in terms of home protection. In 45 ACP (Automatic Colt Pistol) the Detonics uses a 6-shot magazine. In 9mm, the clip holds seven shots, as it does in 38 Super. Firepower, the ability to shoot fast with several shots, is in favor of a handgun like this.

Practice

No matter the defense gun, the shooter should practice with it at least now and then. And the gun should be sighted in—properly. Even with fixed sights, which are fine on the close-range gun, it is wise for the shooter to truly know where the gun hits. Practice is a *must,* then, in order for the shooter to know the mechanical function of his arm and in order to stay sharp with it. The gun will do the shooter no good if he has forgotten how to load it, or how to get the safety off.

Chapter 12
Modern Black Powder Shooting

BLACK POWDER SHOOTING never died. Nor did it fade away. It merely fell into the shadows when smokeless powder came along, for smokeless was much more efficient. The 30-40 Krag round burned smokeless powder, and that excited the shooting world to a degree. But it was the 30-30 which made Americans smokeless powder cartridge shooters. The 30-30 was the first *sporting* cartridge to use smokeless powder. Some arms scholars feel that the 30-30 was actually built for black powder to begin with, feeling that the second ''30'' in its name proves the point. Not so. The 30-40 Krag also features the powder charge designation at the tail end of its moniker, and it was not a black powder round.

No, smokeless powder was not an afterthought, and the small calibers, represented in the 25-35, 30-30 and 30-40 Krag, were of value to the modern shooter because of one major factor—speed. The 30-30 was offered with a 160-grain bullet (some experts say it was a 165-grain bullet) at 1970 fps muzzle velocity. That was fast. It doesn't seem fast to us today because even a commercial round which was born in 1935, the 220 Swift, broke the 4000 fps MV barrier. But the 30-30 was fast all right. I have chronographed some of the old-time black powder cartridge loads, and 1300 fps MV is quite common among them, in spite of case capacity, it seems. The 44-40 left the muzzle in the 1300 fps domain, and so did the 45-70. The big 45-120 Sharps of buffalo days was said to do better, and it probably did. However, the velocity depended upon the exact strength of the black powder. With modern black powder, which is probably as powerful a black powder as we have ever had, I have achieved about 1500 fps out of the 45-120.

So there is no doubt that the smokeless powder round was ''better'' than the black powder round, *better in muzzle velocity,* that is. Not all shooters immediatley believed this. Here is what one old-time hunter had to say about deer cartridges. This is from *Fifty Years a Hunter and Trapper,* a *Fur-Fish-Game* publication still available. It contains information printed in the original *Fur-Fish-Game* magazine before it was called that, dates being 1903-1913. The author, E. N. Woodcock, stated the following concerning deer cartridges from pages 242 and 243 of my copy:

Here is the 50-caliber Hatfield rifle in percussion style. This rifle is light in weight, well-balanced and accurate, a good choice for the deer hunter, as well as target shooter who wants the stability of the 50-caliber ball.

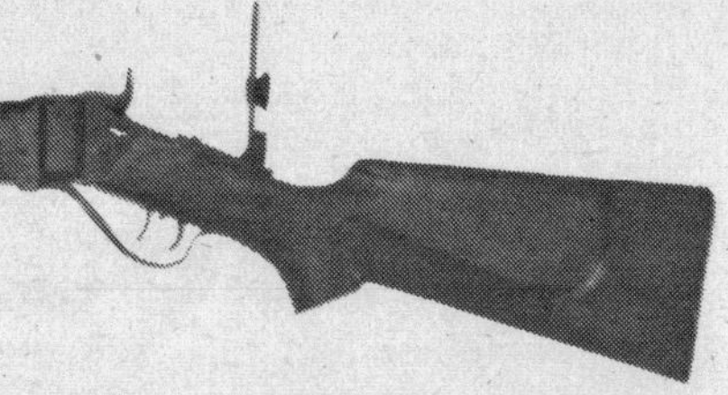

This Sharps replica from the C. Sharps Company of Big Timber, Montana, offers black powder shooters a chance to try the big metallic rounds of the buffalo-hunting era. This is the 45-120 shown here, also available in 50-140.

The black powder hunter must get close. And he can get close through dedication and practice. This nice antelope buck was approached to within 50 yards.

> Another reader asks what kind of a gun he shall take with him to hunt deer, as he is contemplating going on a deer hunting trip next fall. Now I would say any kind of a rifle that suits you. But if you should ask me what kind of a gun I use, I would not hesitate to say that I prefer the 38-40 and black powder. This gun shoots plenty strong to do all the shooting as to distance or penetrations that the deer hunter will require, and there is not near so much danger of shooting a man or domestic animal a mile away that the hunter knows nothing of, as is the case with a high power gun. Besides, from an economical point, the ammunition for the 38-40 black powder gun costs only about one-half that of the smokeless or high power guns. However, if the hunter thinks that he must have a high power gun in order to be a successful deer hunter, he will find the 30-30 or similar calibers good for large game, and it is not heavy to handle.

How things have changed. We have become accustomed to big power in high speed, and the words of Mr. Woodcock seem strange to us. He thought of the 30-30 as a high-power rifle and used the 38-40, which fired a bullet of about 180 grains in that 1300 fps MV area. Today we have "experts" who claim that the extreme effective range for a 30-30 on deer is about 50 yards. Yes, things have changed. Mr. Woodcock was worrying about the 30-30 in terms of extreme range, an unfounded worry if the hunter is in the woods or if he observes any backstop in his shooting, while modern arms writers often downgrade the 30-30 for lack of range.

But the smokeless round, the 30-30 especially, did catch fire, and its light outshone all of the black powder burners. Teddy Roosevelt, our hunting president, was certainly in awe of the smokeless powder fast-stepper. He took a 32 Winchester Special, a carbon copy of the 30-30, to Africa with him and reportedly did quite well with it. Imagine the near amazement of being able to shoot "flat" out to a couple hundred yards when the old black powder trajectory had been so looping in nature that the projectile would be a couple feet low at that distance. Roosevelt describes his first smokeless powder harvest in *Outdoor Pastimes of an American Hunter,* his book printed in 1923 by Charles Scribner's Sons. Teddy relates an adventure of 1896.

> In the fall of 1896 I spent a fortnight on the range with the ranch wagon. I was using for the first time one of the new small-calibre, smokeless-powder rifles, with the usual soft-nosed bullet. While travelling to and fro across the range we usually moved camp each day, not putting up the tent at all during the trip; but at one spot we spent three nights. It was a creek bottom, bounded on either side by rows of grassy hills, beyond which stretched the rolling prairie. . . .
>
> The last shot I got was when I was out with Joe Ferris, in whose company I had killed my first buffalo, just thirteen years before, and not very far from this same spot. We had seen two or three bands [of antelope] that morning, and in each case, after a couple of hours of useless effort, I failed to get near enough. At last, toward midday, after riding and tramping over a vast extent of broken sun-scorched country, we got within range of a small band lying down in a little cup-shaped hollow in the middle of a great flat. I did not have a close shot, for they were running about 180 yards off. The buck was rear-most, and at him I aimed; the bullet struck him in the flank, coming out of the

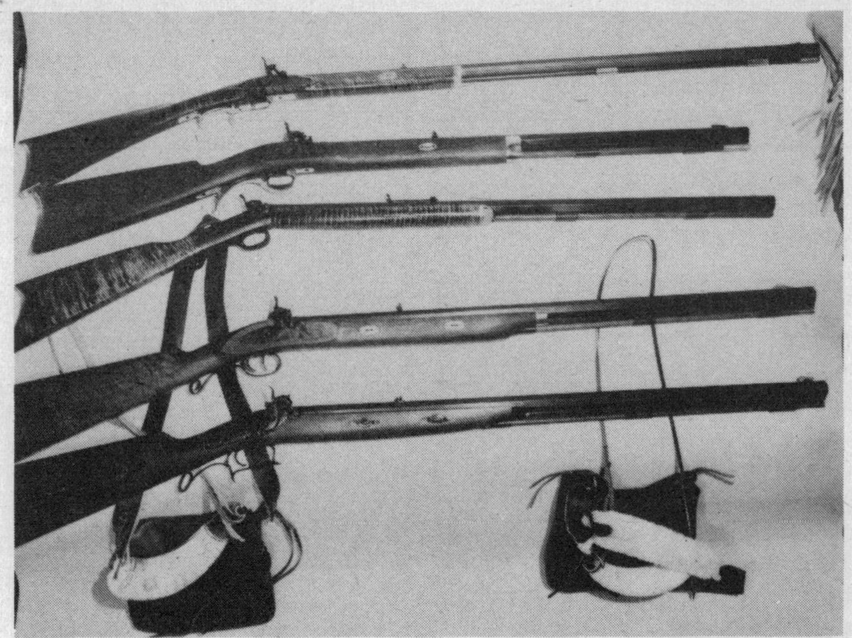

An array of deer rifles for the black powder hunter shows a 40-caliber Muskrat rifle at the top. The 40 is for the expert hunter only, one who will pass up all but the best shots and who will always place his shot carefully. This handsome rifle is offered by the Ozark Mt. Arms Co. Beneath it is the 50-caliber Lyman Trade Rifle, a good mule deer caliber. Then we have a 54-caliber all-steel Mowrey rifle with its beautiful tiger stripe maple stock, followed by the 53-caliber Santa Fe Hawken from the Lee Fire Arms Co. This 53 generally takes a .520-inch ball, though some will accept a .526-inch ball. Finally, there is the Armsport back-action 54, which can use a bore-diameter .530-inch ball and a .010-inch patch. The latter rifle is called the Try-on Trailblazer and is quite accurate. The shooting bags are by Uncle Mike's. The horn on the left is a custom by Vince Poulin. The horn on the right is a K-W model, a good choice.

> opposite shoulder, and he fell in his next bound. As we stood over him, Joe shook his head, and said, 'I guess that little rifle is the ace;' and I told him I guessed so too.

Then we come to Nessmuk, who was actually George W. Sears, a prominent outdoorsman and writer of his day. Nessmuk was gone by the time smokeless powder was in full force. However, he was certainly around when black powder cartridges took over. Yet Nessmuk stayed with a muzzleloader instead of turning to the self-contained load in a repeater. Why would he do this? Why would anyone elect to go with an obsolete system? The reason is very clear for there are over 5,000,000 shooters in this country who fire black powder in some form. Shooting is a challenge, and when all of the challenge is gone, gone, too, will be the reward.

Think not? Imagine this: Let us suppose that a new rifle has been developed. In essence, it fires a "guided missile." The bullet can never miss dead center on the bull's-eye. All of the shots are 10s. The X-ring of the target is eaten out by one perfect hole. What about a rifle like that? It would bore me to distraction. I would not shoot it, with the exception of course of some special situation. But this type of rifle would not thrill me. I don't think it would thrill very many shooters.

Nessmuk may have felt a little that way about the modern repeater of his day. Here is what this famous old-time shooter and outdoorsman had to say about his own firearm, taken from the pages of *Woodcraft and Camping,* the reprint Dover edition, page 82.

> My rifle was a neat, hair-triggered Billinghurst, carrying sixty balls to the pound [about a 43-caliber], a muzzle-loader of course, and a nail-driver. I made just three shots in ten days [on a cross-country deer hunt], and each shot stood for a plump young deer in the 'short blue.'

Hunting with the muzzleloader can provide some of the most interesting of experiences and long-lasting memories. This fine antelope buck was taken with a custom 54-caliber long-rifle.

I do not see the muzzleloader as a take-over proposition. I certainly would never put my modern arms aside for front-loaders, but on the other hand I would grieve at the loss of those firebreathers, for they have given me more shooting thrills than any other type of firearm. However, there is plenty of room in the battery of the complete shooter for a couple of smoke-belchers, and I think the shooter who leaves these totally out of the picture is dealing with a black-and-white landscape. Muzzleloaders add the color.

Getting Started in Black Powder

There are several important choices to be made before diving into black powder smoke. Many shooters could enjoy a lifetime of involvement with the smokepole if only they would make the right initial choices and learn the correct procedure for loading and handling their muzzleloaders to begin with. Instead, they buy the wrong guns (for them) and fail to learn the correct basics. The result: the black powder firearms are finally used as ornaments over fireplaces, or they are relegated to a dark closet to collect dust.

It is the muzzleloader hunt which has given the most impetus to the black powder revival. Here, elk hunters search the high country for the wapiti. It will take a close shot to cleanly harvest the big elk, but careful hunting can bring that close shot.

Quality

The bitterness of buying an inferior muzzleloader remains as an unpleasant aftertaste long after the savings of dollars has been forgotten. I urge the shooter to buy the very best he can afford. If a small personal loan is necessary, it's worth it. The money, as I say, will be forgotten, but the gun will still be around. If a muzzleloader is not accurate, it's a lousy muzzleloader. If it won't fire, it's an inferior product. If you must fear for your safety because of its design or materials, the gun is no good. I state with 100 percent conviction that the *properly constructed* muzzleloader is accurate, reliable and safe when handled safely and loaded with black powder only, and with the maximum charge recommended by the gunmaker. Buy the best. When an inferior muzzleloader is purchased, the shooter ends up doing one of two things. He either trades up later, meaning lost money, or he quits shooting frontloaders. The first is too bad. The second is a real pity.

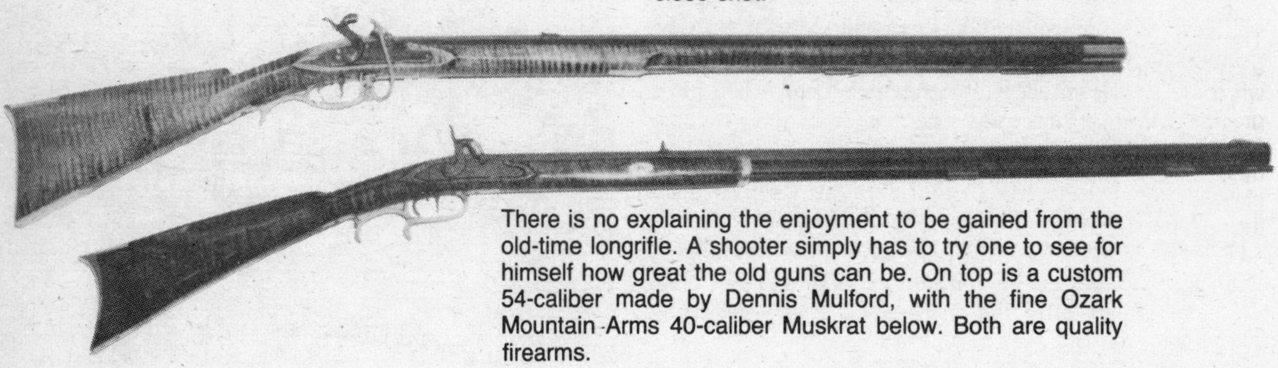

There is no explaining the enjoyment to be gained from the old-time longrifle. A shooter simply has to try one to see for himself how great the old guns can be. On top is a custom 54-caliber made by Dennis Mulford, with the fine Ozark Mountain Arms 40-caliber Muskrat below. Both are quality firearms.

But how does one find a truly *good* muzzleloader? Go with reputation. I urge any newcomer to black powder shooting to join a black powder club. For some reason, muzzle-loading seems to attract a fine class of human beings, and I have seen veterans to the sport offer plenty of good advice to newcomers as well as a chance to try the firearms they prefer. Sure, some of the old-time shooters deal in the fairytales of the past, giving bad advice instead of good. But if the shooter talks with several veteran shooters, he will soon be able to separate the chaff from the wheat.

Function

The next step is for the shooter to figure out what he wants a muzzleloader for. If he wants to hunt deer, he'd best buy a deer rifle. If he wants to hunt small game, he should look at a smallbore. If plinking and general shooting fun are the goals, then a medium caliber, such as a 40 to 45 is in order. He may like handguns better than rifles. He may wish to hunt upland game with a sootbelcher, and if so, then obviously the shotgun is the way to go. But the question must be asked and then answered, "What do I want *to do* with a muzzleloader?"

Flint or Percussion?

If the flintlock were as chancy as many modern gunwriters seem to think, every mountain man coming to the Far West would have been scalped or eaten by a grizzly. The Lewis and Clark expedition which started the whole thing was a party of flintlock shooters. Certainly, the caplock, another word for the percussion system, did take over, the "Hawken" type rifle of the Mountain Men being a caplock. But the bad press on the flintlock is really misplaced. Flintlocks are not bad, but there are some bad flintlocks. Frankly, what we said about quality goes triple in flinters. If you can't afford a good flintlock, do not buy one at all. You are bound to be disappointed.

Yes, there will be some misfires, even with a good flinter. My Hatfield flintlock, a 36-caliber squirrel rifle, and a beauty with the grace of a high-blowing cloud and the feel of a fine violin, will "go off" just about every shot, provided it is clean and correctly loaded. It will balk sometimes. I don't mind. That is part of the flintlock challenge. The flinter is very romantic, and there are dedicated modern black powder shooters who will have only this system in their personal batteries.

The flintlock works because a flint, held in the jaws of the hammer, formerly called the "cock," scrapes bits of hot metal from the face of the frizzen, these bits of molten metal igniting fine black powder in the pan, thereby creating a flash. The flash must dart through a small hole in the side of the barrel. That hole, called the *vent* or *touchhole,* leads to the main powder charge in the breech, setting it off. The lineup of the hammer must be correct so that the flint will strike the frizzen squarely. The mainspring has to be properly strong to get the job done, too, and the flint itself has to be of top quality. I have tried some flints which would hardly serve to strike a match. Buy good flints. They are worth it.

(Right) Flintlock or percussion—it's the reader's choice, and both work very well. The percussion is the most popular ignition style today. Both rifles are Navy Arms Hawkens (Ithaca).

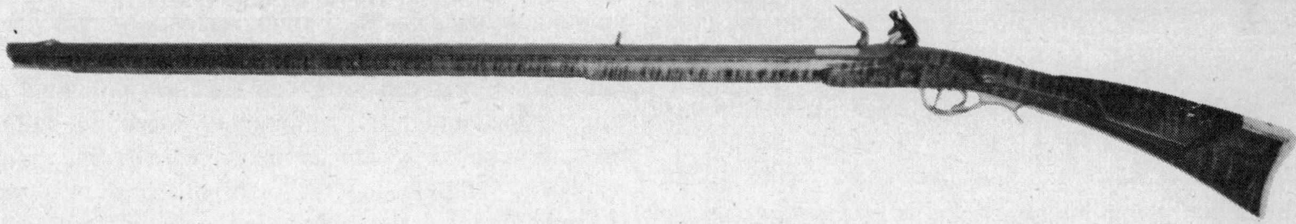

The beautiful Hatfield flintlock rifle is available in 50-caliber, a good one for deer. This is a very accurate rifle and one which will deliver excellent performance for the hunter. The graceful lines are enjoyable to any hunter who appreciates firearms and the long sight radius, with the back sight mounted well forward on the barrel flat, offers a clear sight picture even for older eyes which cannot function as well as they used to in terms of visual accommodation.

While I do like the flinter, the percussion system is more popular and on my big game hunts I will use this style more often than not. It is truly reliable, though again the design of the firearm must be correct. I have never had a misfire on game with a caplock since turning to the better made rifles. The percussion is recommended for the general shooting audience, although I still like to have at least one flinter around for the fun of shooting it.

Final choice? I would say the caplock wins. The so-called average shooter will probably find the percussion system his cup of tea. It is highly reliable and requires no special touchy tricks to make it work all the time, though, as I warn, some of the lower-quality caplocks have slower lock time and less reliability than the best flinters.

Style

There are two ways to go. There is the true replica muzzleloader and then the muzzleloader which loosely adheres to some older style, but replicates nothing from the past. In my opinion, the shooter should go with his desire. Some of the dyed-in-the-buckskin boys will turn their noses up at the sight of a non-authentic muzzleloader, but that should bother no one. A copy of an original is nice for historical reasons, but the shooter doesn't have to have one of these in order to enjoy his muzzle-loading activity.

This buck was taken on a special black powder only hunt, the rifle being a custom 54-caliber and the buck harvested with a round ball.

The Smallbore

Overlooked for a long time by the modern downwind shooter, the smallbore muzzleloader may be the most enjoyable firearm in the black powder lineup. Smallbore, for our purposes, means calibers 32, 36, 38 and 40. There have been smaller smallbore muzzleloaders, but these have been special-order models only so far. I know of one 20-caliber smallbore which used a .190-inch round ball, that ball only weighing about 10 grains. It was billed a "mouse rifle," though it would actually harvest squirrels and rabbits, too, with good shooting.

The 32-Caliber

The 32-caliber is a very wise choice. It is extremely cheap to shoot. In fact, I recently set out to see just how cheaply I could shoot a 32-caliber caplock rifle. In this case, I was given the lead, and I cast my own round ball with it for zero cents per ball. But that is somewhat unfair in favor of the 32, so I called a hide and fur establishment in the area and they had a sale on lead at 50¢ per pound. A pound of lead will make 155 32-caliber lead balls. This means that the ball cost a third cent each in this case. Even if the lead costs more, the little 32 ball is economical to cast.

As for the powder charge, I found black powder for as little as $4.50 per can, with $7 per can being the current retail in my locale. Using the higher figure, this would mean a cent a shot for powder. There are 7000 grains weight in a pound of powder, and a mere 10 grains volume will give the 32-caliber ball about 22 Long Rifle muzzle velocity. As for caps, I made my own, using the Forster Tap-O-Cap unit, a device which turns aluminum beverage cans into the body of the percussion cap. Then children's toy caps are inserted into the shell and a percussion cap is born. The children's toy caps cost me only a cent for several. As for patching, I obtained some pillow ticking at the local mattress factory for nothing. They were happy to have me pick up some scraps. Lube? Saliva is cheap, but even if a good quality lube is purchased, it takes so little to shoot a 32 as to be almost negligible.

All the same, just to be fair, let's call the toy caps, patching and lube a half-cent per shot. This gives us a third cent for the ball, a cent for the powder charge and a half-cent for the rest of the load chain. We still have under 2 cents per shot. Pyrodex P can also be used in the 32-caliber muzzleloader, and only 8 grains weight serves to give 22 Long Rifle starting velocities. No matter how we look at it, the 32 is very cheap to fire. When I use my own 32 for small game hunting, I often buy the swaged lead ball from the gunshop. Even with that expense added in, a day of enjoyable muzzleloading still costs but a small price for the "ammo."

The 32 offers plenty of ballistics for the task it is designed to handle. Below is an example of a 32-caliber rifle with various loads. The reader can easily see that there is plenty of punch for tin can rolling, small game shooting, and in fact the harvesting of wild turkeys and similar game. I would bet that a good shot could cleanly bag game up to the size of *javelina,* the small "wild pig" of the Southwest, provided that the ball was placed correctly.

Thompson Center 32-Caliber Cherokee Rifle (24-Inch Barrel/45-Grain, .310-Inch Round Ball)

10 grains volume FFFg—1120 fps MV/125 fpe ME
20 grains volume FFFg—1649 fps MV/272 fpe ME
30 grains volume FFFg—1871 fps MV/350 fpe ME

Naturally, the ballistics of a small-caliber round ball fall off rapidly and at 100 yards from the muzzle, the 32-caliber projectiles in the above test look like this:

100-Yard Velocity and Remaining Energy

10-grain volume charge = 538 fps/29 fp remaining energy
20-grain volume charge = 775 fps/60 fp remaining energy
30-grain volume charge = 879 fps/77 fp remaining energy

The 32-caliber, then, is a fine choice. Sure, it is wind-sensitive, being a little round ball of not much mass and momentum, but I have found no big problem in plinking, informal target work and small-game hunting, which are the strong areas of the smallbore. I would recommend the 32-caliber highly, and I can say that as this is written the 32 is coming into its own. The aforementioned T/C Cherokee is a perfect example of a light, small, handy 32-caliber muzzleloader. Mowrey Gun Works has switched its Squirrel Rifle from 36-caliber to 32-caliber, and Navy Arms is planning to offer its fine Mule Ear rifle in 32-caliber.

The 36-Caliber

All that we said about the 32-caliber applies to the 36-caliber, but for the fact that it is a bit more expensive to shoot. I have yet to find truly fine accuracy in a 36-caliber using 10 grains of powder, though I am sure some 36s will group with this charge. I like 20 grains volume of powder, and that means we are now spending as much as 2 cents per shot for fuel. As for the lead ball, each weighs 65 grains in the .350-inch size, so we get about 107 shots for a pound of lead. Patching, lube and percussion caps stay close to the same here, very cheap.

If I had to select a 32 or a 36 for jackrabbits at 75 yards or so, and for wild turkey hunting, I would probably take the 36-caliber for its slightly heavier ball. But I remain firm in my conviction that a good shot can take wild turkeys with a 32-caliber, and we would be nitpicking to get into the wind drift advantages of the 36 over the 32. I like the 36, and I intend to keep right on using a 36-caliber, but if I were starting from scratch, and if my shooting were for plinking purposes, informal target work, and small game in the main, the 32 would be my pick.

Below are some figures for my 36-caliber flintlock. They give the reader some idea of 36-caliber ballistics.

Hatfield 36-Caliber Flintlock Squirrel Rifle (39.5-Inch Barrel/65-grain, .350-inch ball)

20 grains volume FFFg—1471 fps MV/312 fpe ME
25 grains volume FFFg—1653 fps MV/394 fpe ME
30 grains volume FFFg—1799 fps MV/467 fpe ME
40 grains volume FFFg—2023 fps MV/591 fpe ME

At 100 yards, here is what has happened to the 36-caliber round ball for the above loads:

100-Yard Velocity and Remaining Energy

20-grain volume charge = 794 fps/91 fp remaining energy
25-grain volume charge = 851 fps/105 fp remaining energy
30-grain volume charge = 882 fps/112 fp remaining energy
40-grain volume charge = 956 fps/132 fp remaining energy

The 36-caliber is another good one, then, for the smallbore fan. It is a fine small-game bore size, and it serves well for wild turkey. The 36 will also handle varmints of coyote size if the range is within black powder limits.

The 38-Caliber

The only 38-caliber black powder rifle readily available over the counter at the moment is the Richland Arms Plainsman model, or perhaps, the same exact firearm bearing another import name. The 38-caliber size is useful for those who feel that they want more power for hunting wild turkey or large varmints. It is not legal for deer or other big game where I live, and rightly so. The 38 uses the .375-inch round ball, which is very handy because a shooter can buy the popular swaged .375-inch ball meant mainly for revolver shooting.

Here is a ballistic glance at the 38-caliber longrifle.

Richland Arms Plainsman 38-Caliber Rifle (37-Inch Barrel/80-Grain .375-Inch Ball)

20 grains volume FFFg—1418 fps MV/357 fpe ME
30 grains volume FFFg—1686 fps MV/505 fpe ME
40 grains volume FFFg—1876 fps MV/625 fpe ME
50 grains volume FFFg—1930 fps MV/662 fpe ME

The Navy Arms Mule Ear rifle is a sidelock. This one is in 36-caliber and fires a 65-grain round ball at 2000 fps MV. It is an excellent choice for small game hunting and plinking and can be very economical to shoot.

This Navy Arms Cub muzzleloader is available in 45-caliber and is light in weight and fast-pointing. It is excellent for newcomers to the sport of muzzle-loading.

100-Yard Velocity and Remaining Energy

20-grain volume charge = 851 fps/129 fp remaining energy
30-grain volume charge = 944 fps/158 fp remaining energy
40-grain volume charge = 1013 fps/182 fp remaining energy
50-grain volume charge = 1051 fps/196 fp remaining energy

The 40-Caliber

Although not very popular today, the 40-caliber (.395-inch ball) is a big favorite of mine. It is fine for target work. It will take small game if head shots are used to save the meat (body hits even with a 32-caliber ruin too much meat), and it falls at the very bottom of deer calibers under certain circumstances. Ozark Mountain Arms still offers the 40-caliber as this is written, and Green Mountain Rifle Barrel Company has a 40-caliber in its lineup of drop-in barrels for, in the main, the Thompson/Center firearm.

I know of a tight little thicket resting on a private ranch which is loaded with whitetail deer. The little spot is unique in that the habitat of these whitetails is such that they only exist along this narrow strip of land. A 50-yard shot in that tangle is a long one. Under these circumstances, a little 40-caliber is adequate with good shooting. I have taken antelope with a 40-caliber, too, but only where I knew the shot would be close. I do not consider the 40-caliber ideal for any big game, but a well-practiced shot can make it do. The 40 is pleasant to shoot.

Here is a ballistic look at the 40-caliber rifle.

Ozark Mountain Arms 40-Caliber Muskrat Rifle (36-Inch Barrel/93-Grain .395-Inch Ball)

20 grains volume FFFg—1294 fps MV/346 fpe ME
30 grains volume FFFg—1584 fps MV/518 fpe ME
40 grains volume FFFg—1813 fps MV/679 fpe ME
50 grains volume FFFg—1993 fps MV/820 fpe ME

100-Yard Remaining Velocity and Energy

20-grain volume charge = 828 fps/142 fp remaining energy
30-grain volume charge = 927 fps/177 fp remaining energy
40-grain volume charge = 981 fps/199 fp remaining energy
50-grain volume charge = 1017 fps/214 fp remaining energy

The smallbore muzzleloader is a joy to own, a pleasure to shoot, and the do-it-yourself shooter can fire the subbores for a very nominal cost, using home-cast round balls (see the chapter on casting) and caps made from discarded aluminum cans. A newcomer to the smokepole would do well to check out the little muzzleloaders, for he may find the 32- to 40-caliber range just right for his needs.

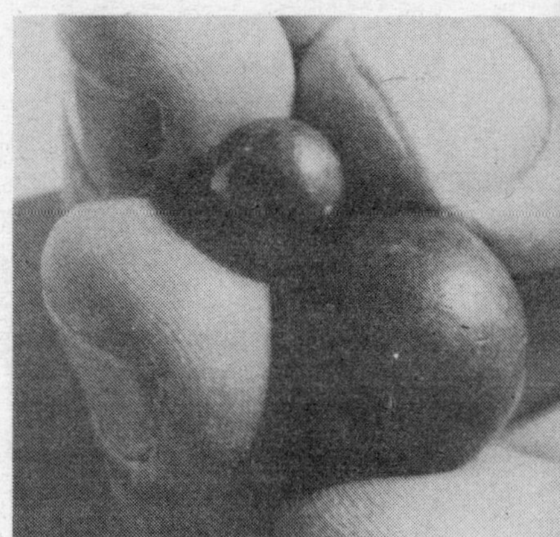

The round ball gains in mass far out of proportion with its diameter. For example, this little .350-inch round ball weighs 65.0 grains, but the .714-inch ball, about twice the diameter of the .350-inch, weighs 548 grains, over 8 times heavier!

The Big Bore

Big bore is a matter of comparison. In this modern world of high velocity, bores are actually quite small when compared with those of the past. A 30-caliber is a big bore to a modern shooter. Almost anything past 22-caliber seems to fit this niche. But in black powder shooting, a 32 is a smallbore and so is a 40-caliber. I would say, arbitrarily, that the big bore realm begins with 45-caliber in the frontloader, and that a 45 would have been laughed at as minuscule by the old-time shooter such as the Englishmen who hunted Ceylon, India and Africa. Their guns were measured in different terms indeed.

S. W. Baker had a 4-bore he hunted with. This equates to four projectiles per pound. In other words, four round ball for Baker's rifle equalled 1 pound in weight, each ball going 1,750 grains. The common 180-grain bullet for the 30-06 pales into the background in comparison as far as mass is concerned. However, since we are not facing too many charging elephants and rhinos these days, big bore black powder rifles are not quite so large. They begin at 45-caliber and actually end at around 58-caliber. Yes, it is very true that there are custom-made rifles in 60- and 62-caliber and a few semi-customs are also offered in larger-

This impala was harvested with one shot from a Navy Arms Mark I Hawken. In Africa, the conical was used by the author because it was difficult to tell what sort of game would be encountered at any given time, and the conical allowed for good mass out of a 50-caliber rifle.

This 58-caliber round ball (left) was recovered from test material. Note that it is quite deformed, but it weighed almost the same after recovery as before firing. The ball on the right is the 58-caliber in unfired condition.

than-58 size. But on the whole, 45 to 58 is the range of our big bores.

If the 40-caliber will take a deer at close range, then a 45 must be a real powerhouse, right? Not really. For general day-in and day-out deer hunting, I like a 50-caliber front-loader. We have here a 50-caliber ball, generally .490-inch to .495-inch in diameter, and it can be pushed along at 1800 to 2000 fps MV in a good rifle. My Navy Arms Ithaca Hawken in 50-caliber uses 110 grains volume of FFg black powder for a 2000 fps MV, for example. The .490-inch round ball weighs 177 grains. The ballistic story for the 50 Hawken looks like this:

Navy Arms Ithaca Hawken New Model 50-Caliber Rifle (34-Inch Barrel/177-Grain .490-Inch Round Ball)

50 grains volume FFg = 1355 fps MV/722 fpe ME
70 grains volume FFg = 1505 fps MV/890 fpe ME
90 grains volume FFg = 1889 fps MV/1403 fpe ME
110 grains volume FFg = 2000 fps MV/1572 fpe ME

100-Yard Remaining Velocity and Energy

50-grain volume charge = 879 fps/304 fp remaining energy
70-grain volume charge = 919 fps/332 fp remaining energy
90-grain volume charge = 1069 fps/449 fp remaining energy
110-grain volume charge = 1120 fps/493 fp remaining energy

One can see that the 50-caliber is pretty good in the power department when compared with other black powder calibers. I like the 50 and have taken several deer and antelope with it. All in all, however, I like the 54 the best for deer where I hunt because even with stalking, a 100-yard shot, and up to 125 yards or so, is not uncommon, due to the open terrain. I have two 54s which see a lot of service. One is a Dennis Mulford custom 54 which fires a .535-inch round ball of 230 grains weight at about 1975 fps MV. The other is a 54-caliber Ozark Mountain Arms Hawken, which shoots a .530-inch 224-grain round ball at 2025 fps MV. Either one will do a good job on deer, but I have also taken elk with this caliber, and if the shot is well-placed, the 54 is large enough for the job.

The latter was rated for a full 140 grains of FFg as a safe maximum (or optimum) hunting load, and it has the proper barrel twist so that the ball does not strip the rifling at over 2000 fps MV. The 54 seems to be a fine balance. I like the 58, too, especially with conicals. But with a round ball, I end up with about 1800 fps in most 58s by the time the law of diminishing returns takes over. To be sure, a .570-inch ball of 279-280 grains is certainly formidable, and at 1800 fps the muzzle energy is over a ton. The 54-caliber 224-grain ball at about 2000 fps is about the same.

Give me a good 54-caliber muzzleloader, and I will be fully confident in harvesting the biggest buck deer in the land at 100-125 yards. If I can get a 50- to 75-yard shot at a bull elk, that same ball will do the trick handily. I realize that many elk have been dropped with balls of smaller caliber, but we are talking about day-in and day-out hunting here, and having enough projectile mass is good insurance.

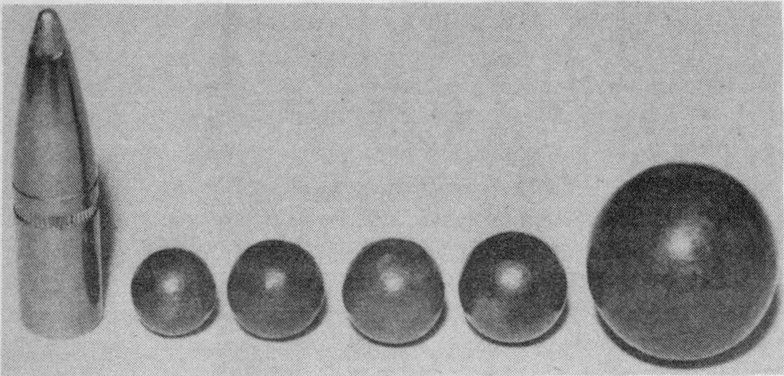

Various round ball sizes show the property of the round ball to increase in mass way out of proportion as the sphere grows greater in diameter. The big 12 gauge ball on the right will weigh almost 500 grains. The 180-grain 30-caliber bullet on the left is for comparison.

The ordinary round ball is quite remarkable in its ability to hang together. This 54-caliber ball made its way through the chest area of a large bull and retained almost all of its original weight.

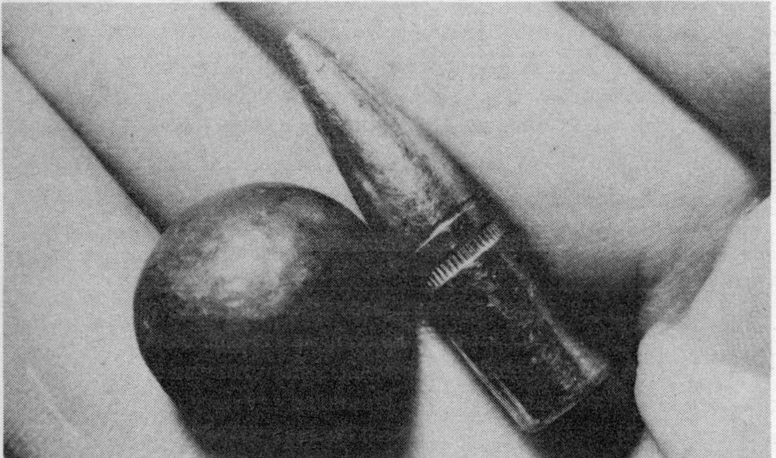

The black powder round ball looks terribly archaic up against a sleek 180-grain 30-caliber jacketed bullet, and it is. It is in no way as aerodynamic as the elongated missile. But if the muzzleloader hunter will get close, the old round ball, with its ability to hang together, will do the job neatly. And it is very accurate from an accurate rifle or pistol. Twist rates for these two projectiles are entirely different.

Remember, power in any firearm does come through velocity. Anyone who doubts this can take a bullet of any description and throw it as hard as he can at a clay bank. It probably won't even stick in the bank. Shoot it out at 2000 fps MV, and it will penetrate considerably. But . . . black powder shooting is not a game of ultra-high velocity, and remaining velocity with the smokepole, especially with the lead sphere, is pretty low. Going up in caliber is the answer when it comes to getting maximum punch from the muzzleloader. That is why the old-time hunters of large and dangerous game used those ponderous big bores—to get missile mass. Their muzzle velocities were actually very low by modern standards.

The modern big bore, then, ranges from 45- to 58-caliber. This black powder hunter, after harvesting considerable game with the smokepole, likes the 50 and 54 for deer and similar game. Others will prefer other calibers. The 45 is a good size, too, but a 133-grain pill at 2000 fps MV is not the same as a 224-grain ball at the same speed. And, though all round ball lose their velocity rapidly, the smaller the lead pill, the more rapid the shedding of speed. On the other hand, the more mass, the better for "carry-up."

Ball or Conical for Big Game?

I have taken more game with the ball than the conical because I have enjoyed the *type* of rifle which normally is created with a round ball in mind. But I have nothing against the conical. After all, it carries up better than the ball, and it penetrates very well. I have taken game with both ball and conical and find very little difference in the actual harvest of game with either one, unless a very small bore is used. If a 45-caliber rifle is going up against an elk, give me a conical. But a 45-caliber conical and a 54-caliber ball seem to do about the same at close black powder ranges. Want to shoot farther? Get a conical. Leave the round ball home. The conical will carry up and deliver a lot more energy at long range than a round ball will, but we do have to add that S. W. Baker used a ball and made shots at very long range.

How did he do that? First, he used huge ball, such as the 4-gauge already mentioned. Even though it was a lead ball, such a huge mass carried up fairly well. He shot completely through huge water buffalo in Ceylon at several hundred yards using a round ball, often breaking both shoulders of those large animals. But had he been using a small caliber, such shooting at 300, 400 and 500 yards would have been a disaster.

We do not recommend long-range shooting with either ball or conical, not because the latter is weak at long range, but because trajectory is close to the same with both in most cases. Given a 54-caliber rifle, the round ball will generally leave the muzzle at 1900-2000 fps if the rifle is made to withstand a good charge of powder, as is the case with the out-of-manufacture Browning, the T/C or the Ozark Mountain Arms Hawken. The conical will leave the muzzle at about 1500 fps. If a shooter sights the first load on the money at 13 yards, the ball will strike about 1-inch high at 25 yards and about 1-inch low at 100 yards from the muzzle. At 125 yards, the ball will have dropped by about 6 inches. The conical at 1500 fps will do just about the same thing, forming the same arc of pattern in its parabola. Therefore, for all practical purposes, the 54-caliber firing either ball or conical produces a trajectory which allows for big game hunting out to 125 yards without a lot of guesswork as where to hold on the target.

The only exception comes with special firearms using high-grade gun barrel quality steel, such as 1137M stress-relieved steel, and using very stout loads in order to gain *some* muzzle velocity advantage for the conical. In a moment, this sort of firearm will be discussed briefly for those who do want the ultimate in black powder power for hunting large game. However, for all practical purposes, a shooter will find that within normal black powder ranges, a ball of large caliber will perform well enough for the duties intended for muzzle-loading.

Many of the primitive shoots, most of them in fact, call for "ball only, with loading out of the bag." This means that the round ball is the only projectile allowed at the shoot, and that the shooter must produce all of his loads directly from his shooting bag (sometimes mistakenly called a possibles bag).

The Special Conical-Shooters

There are several special rifles used for the shooting of the conical. Their barrels are made with a rifling twist that's faster than the ball-shooting firearms. A prime example is the Whitworth. I tested a model produced as a replica of that famous 19th century English target rifle. The specific rifle I tested was from the Navy Arms Company, and it carried a 1:20 twist. At 50 yards, the 490-grain bullet backed by a charge of 50, 70 or 90 grains volume of FFg black powder created a 1-inch group measured center-to-center. With a scope sight, I would not be surprised to see this rifle do the very same thing at 100 yards. What's more, the long 45-caliber bullet has high sectional density, the resulting "carry-up" being very good. Using 90 grains volume of FFg black powder, that bullet leaves the muzzle at about 1300 fps. However, a full 100 yards from the muzzle, the bullet is still traveling at a little over 1100 fps. Muzzle energy with this load is over 1850 foot-pounds, and remaining energy at 100 yards is almost 1350 foot-pounds. Anyone can see that this "target" rifle is actually on par with the old 45-90, which was noted as a cartridge suitable for game larger than deer.

The conical-shooters cannot be ignored, then, for they do offer the black powder shooter a viable alternative to the "longrifle" which we normally think of as a muzzleloader, such as the "Kentucky" (Pennsylvania) rifle and the Hawken. If one wants a Hawken geared for conical accuracy, he can have it. Many of the so-called Hawken models do a pretty good job of grouping the Minie, Maxi or similar missiles. And the Navy Arms Mark I Hawken is offered

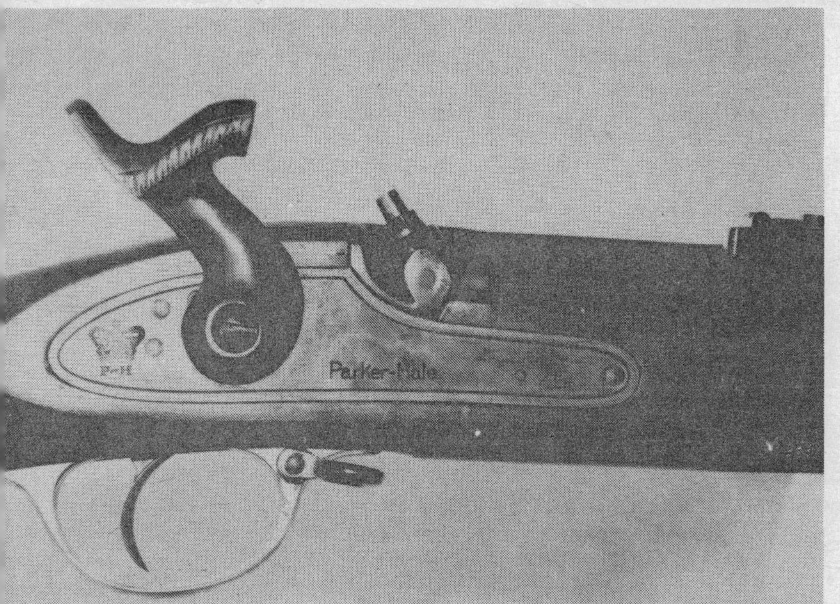

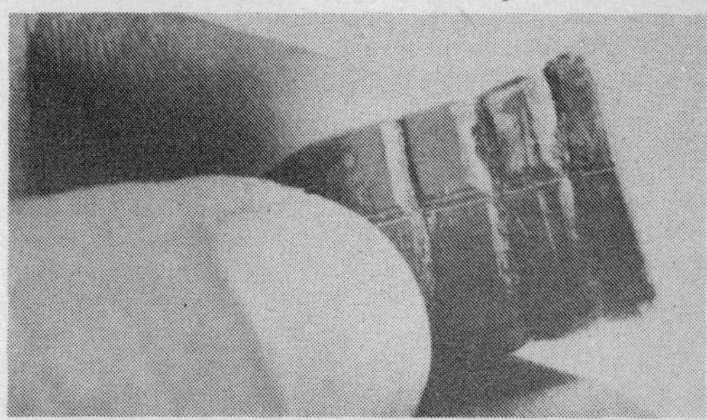

The conical projectile for the muzzleloader is elongated in form, and is more familiar to the modern shooter. Although we sometimes call the conical a bullet and the ball a "round ball," the latter is also a bullet by definition.

(Left) Navy Arms' beautiful Whitworth rifle is capable of excellent accuracy. It fires big 45-caliber cast bullets in the 550-grain class and is suitable for North American big game as well as target shooting.

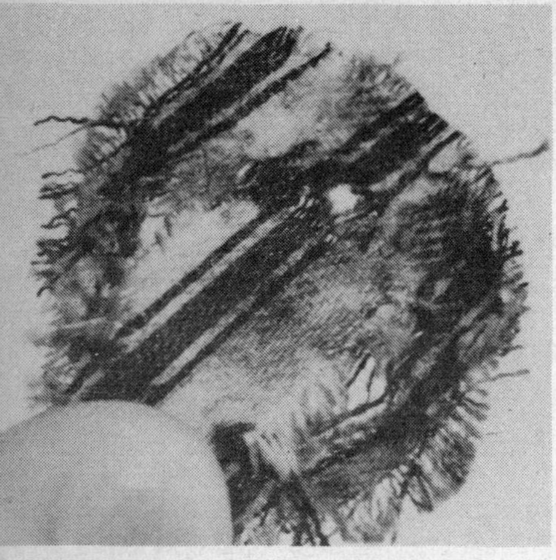

This patch shows holes from gas and/or rifling. It is wise to use a backer of some sort, such as hornet nesting material, if the patch is blown.

with a special 1:34 rate of twist in order to take advantage of the good conicals available for the muzzleloader.

I tested the latter rifle in Africa. During those tests I used the Buffalo Bullet Company projectile, and found accuracy excellent, often getting 1-inch groups at 50 yards, and there was plenty of punch using heavy charges of FFg black powder. This rifle is constructed of gun barrel quality steel and is capable of handling stiff charges of powder as long as the projectile is properly seated on the powder charge. This leads us to another important point: No missile, ball or any form of conical, should ever be allowed to slip up the bore and away from its powder charge. No one knows precisely why, but in some instances, a separated load is definitely the cause of trouble.

I have tested for this and have never been able to conclude *why* the separated charge/projectile is bad, only that it is. In some cases, the separated load has actually caused a barrel to burst. I have also seen several barrels which are said to have a "walnut" in them. This is a lump in the barrel itself, quite visible usually, and in all cases that I know of, the barrel was "short-started" (improperly loaded, the ball separated from the powder charge) and then fired. The lump appeared at the point where the base of the projectile rested in the bore. The latter has been true in 100 percent of the cases I have seen to date. Also, a "ring" may be seen after short-starting a load. This is just what the name implies, a ring or depression within the bore itself, again following short-starting. It is imperative that ball or conical be seated *firmly* upon the powder charge and that the load remain intact, unseparated, right up to the point of firing.

The Magnum

Today, every field of shooting, it seems, must have a magnum, from the 22 rimfire class to the elephant rifle. And the muzzleloader is no exception. My magnum was put together by two gunmakers. The metal work was done by Dale Storey and the stockwork by Dean Zollinger. The rifle actually resembles a late 19th century Hawken style quite closely, including the semi-pistol grip. But the reason it is a magnum lies not in the style, but primarily in a few other facts.

The barrel is 54-caliber and a full 1 1/8-inch across the flats. The barrel is made of gun barrel quality steel, its twist rate is one turn in 34 inches, 1:34. This will seem terribly *slow* to the modern shooter, who knows his 270 barrel, for example, wears a 1:10 rate of twist. But the big Minies and Maxis for the muzzleloader are still rather short for their caliber, hence a 54-caliber firing Minies or Maxis, and using a 1:34 twist, is considered stabilized.

The charges used in this rifle would be totally unwarranted in rifles of lesser construction. However, with big charges of FFg, the average muzzle velocity for the big 54 using the Buffalo Bullet Company 460-grain projectile, is 1700 fps. This renders a muzzle energy of close to 3000 foot-pounds. We have gone as high as 1800 fps using the same bullet for a muzzle energy of 3310 foot-pounds. However, even for elk or moose, I have a lot of faith in a 460-grain lead bullet at 1700 fps. This magnum is a special rifle and it is intended for a special purpose, hunting for game larger than deer where there is any chance that getting ultra-close is a problem. I still would not want to shoot past 150 yards with this rifle, but there is no denying its big power up to that range.

Twist

Now a word on twist. A conical bullet is stabilized on a line drawn through its axis by spinning on that line. The round ball is stabilized in the same way, but primarily because spinning allows the slight imperfections of the sphere to be averaged out on both sides of that imaginary axis. But spinning at any rate is hardly correct for all projectiles. As the projectile is more elongated for its diameter, more spin is needed. More spin gives the missile more RPS (revolutions per second).

RPS is a product of the rate of twist plus the muzzle velocity. If the latter is slowed, then the RPS is slowed. Also, as the mass of the projectile is increased it "automatically" becomes more stable, so we find that a small caliber will have, much of the time, more twist in the barrel than a large caliber. For example, we make the 270 or 30-06 with a 1:10 or 1:12 rate of twist, but the big 458 Winchester uses a slower rate of twist, from about 1:14 to about 1:16.

The ball requires very little spin for stabilization, and when too much twist is used, the ball can "strip" or "trip" over the lands instead of being contained and guided by the rifling. Therefore, we find *very slow* rates of twist in ball-shooting muzzleloaders. But remember mass. As the mass increases, stabilization is easier to obtain. So a ball of large caliber has a very, very slow rate of twist, while a ball of smaller caliber simply has a slow twist, but faster than a big bore has. Examples include a little 32-caliber with a good rate of twist of 1:40 or 1:48, but mov-

Black powder granulation is a very important aspect of muzzleloader shooting. For example, the FFFFg (4F) on the left is a very fine-grain granulation used for priming the pans of flintlocks. The popular FFg (2F) granulation on the right is much more coarse and is favored in hunting loads for big bore muzzleloaders of 45-caliber and larger.

ing up to a 50- or 54-caliber, we find knowledgeable barrelmakers offering twists in the very slow 1:70 rate of twist domain.

Now, that means a single turn of the projectile in 70 inches, but the key here is the word "rate." We are not interested in barrel length here at all. The rate of twist is established irrespective of the barrel length. A 1:70 twist in a 10-inch barrel has the same effect as a 1:70 twist in a 30-inch barrel, but the RPS is a factor of twist plus exit velocity, so the shorter barrel may not have enough MV to stabilize the projectile. That is why we see pistols with faster rates of twist than rifles, but *it is not* due to barrel length in and of itself.

We see these facts in action when looking at various rifles. The Whitworth, which uses a long bullet, has a 1:20 rate of twist, but the Green Mountain Rifle Barrel Company offers a 45-caliber ball-shooter with a correct 1:60 rate of twist. That same company offers a 1:48 rate of twist for its 32-caliber ball-shooting barrel. Navy Arms' New Model Ithaca Hawken is a 50-caliber ball-shooter that comes with a 1:66 rate of twist, but their Mark I Hawken, made for conical-shooting, comes with a faster 1:34 rate of twist.

The modern black powder shooter needs to have a handle on rate of twist, for he will then be able to determine if his own rifle is more suited to ball or conical shooting. Of course, exit velocity is a part of stabilization, so the shooter must often try various powder charges with ball or conical in his rifle to see which powder charge gives the exit velocity suited for stabilization. Obviously, this is generally a *range* of charges, not only one charge. But often, one specific charge will indeed give the very best possible accuracy from a given rifle. We test for this by shooting and keeping records. The slow twist seems to give a round ball a very wide range of accuracy. My custom 54-caliber muzzleloader is quite accurate with only 40 grains of FFFg black powder. But it shoots very well with 120 grains of FFg, too.

Though the most popular black powder in America today is G-O or GOEX brand, on the right, there are other black powders, such as Nobel brand on the left, still available to shooters in certain areas.

Which Powder Granulation?

The rate at which black powder burns is regulated in part by the size of the powder granulation, and the energy inherent in the fuel is released according to that granulation. Today, we find four major granulations in black powder. These are Fg, FFg, FFFg, and FFFFg, or 1-F, 2-F, 3-F, and 4-F. The smaller the number, the larger the kernel size of the powder, so Fg is big in each individual granule size and FFFFg is very small. The former burns slower, the latter faster. Here is how to apply this fact:

Fg Black Powder

Fg is useful in large gauge shotguns, 12-gauge and up. Even in a 16-gauge or 20-gauge, Fg can give good velocity, nice patterns and reasonable muzzle velocity. After all, even a 20-gauge shotgun is somewhat in the big bore realm, being over 60-caliber. But in any rifle we would normally use, Fg is not going to work out well in terms of muzzle velocity. I have tried Fg in a 54-caliber, and even with very big charges, muzzle velocity was low while recoil was high.

I use Fg exclusively in my 10-gauge shotgun, and patterns are beautiful, with good muzzle velocity. Fg is not used nearly enough in the shotgun. Fg will also render modest pressure in both the 12-gauge and 10-gauge shotgun—not much pressure, but plenty of performance.

FFg Black Powder

FFg is the proper black powder for most of our big bore rifle shooting. FFg gives the same MV with a lot less pressure in hunting loads for calibers of 45, 50, 54, 58 and up. In many tests, it has been shown that FFFg produces the same MV as FFg but with much higher pressures. Yes, it is true that it takes more FFg, perhaps as much as 40 percent more, to get the same muzzle velocity achieved with FFFg, but the fact remains that FFg reaches its velocity with less pressure than FFFg when it comes to hunting loads for rifles of 45-caliber and larger.

FFFg Black Powder

FFFg is at home in calibers under 45 in most cases. Of course, if the shooter wishes to use target loads in calibers 45 and over, FFFg is fine. My own 54 custom does well with 40 grains of FFFg for a 25-yard target and plinking load. But when it comes time to shoot heavy loads in that 54-caliber rifle, FFg is used, not FFFg.

FFFFg Black Powder

FFFFg is pan powder. It is meant for priming the pan of a flintlock firearm. Yes, in the past it has been used in some well-made revolvers, but most manufacturers recommend FFFg in the revolver. FFg or FFFg is also recommended for the pistol in most cases, but not FFFFg. If we think of FFFFg as pan powder, we are thinking along the right lines.

Pyrodex

Pyrodex is a replica black powder. Since it burns differently than black powder, the shooter, using Pyrodex, need not clean between shots. Because of the lack of bore fouling, pressures will not rise after a few shots with Pyrodex and the bore is "dressed" or stabilized. Pyrodex, at this point, is not recommended for most flintlocks, as it is a little harder to ignite than black powder.

Pyrodex is loaded by bulk. It is *not* loaded by weight. The same volume measure used for black powder loading is used for Pyrodex. This means that the volume of Pyrodex to black powder is the same, but the weight of the charge is not. Pyrodex is less dense than black powder; volume-for-volume, the Pyrodex charge is lighter. But Pyrodex is also a bit stronger than black powder, so volume-for-volume it gives the same general MV as black powder. Pyrodex is available in different granulations—P, RS and CTG. P stands for Pistol. Pistol Pyrodex is not only used in the handgun, but also in smallbore rifles of the 32-, 36-, 38- and 40-caliber range, and in reduced charges in some of the bigger bores. RS, which stands for Rifle/Shotgun, is used in the big-bore rifle, 45-caliber and up, for hunting and longer range charges, and also in the shotgun. RS is also at home in the big-bore pistol. "CTG" stands for Cartridge and it is used in many of the black powder cartridge loads, such as the Sharps series, the 45-120, and so forth. CTG is also useful in shotguns. Obviously, P is fine grain, with RS medium in granule size and CTG the most coarse of the group.

Patching

Important to round-ball shooting, the patch holds the lube and helps retain the ball firmly down upon the powder charge where it belongs. It also helps to maintain pressure on the load, which aids the burning characteristics of black powder, thus insuring shot-to-shot consistency, hence better accuracy. Tests show that where consistent pressure on the load is used that standard deviation from the mean velocity is better. Random pressure from one load to the next, on the other hand, means more variation in the muzzle velocity of each load, meaning the ball will not strike the same point of impact on the target due to the MV variation.

Tests have shown that the cloth patch is not a true gasket in spite of the thousands of words written to the contrary. It does not seal the black powder gases behind the ball. But this is an academic point. The patch is nonetheless vital to round ball shooting because it also helps impart rifling twist to the ball, since the ball does not directly touch the

This round ball was collected from a mule deer buck taken at a range of about 40 yards. The imprint of the patch can be clearly seen on the ball itself, a condition which seems to take place when stiff patching material is used in an unwashed state. That this harms anything is not at this point clear, and accuracy seemed good in spite of the imprinted ball. Note the flatness of this pure lead ball. Flat, yet the ball drove all the way across the chest cavity of an adult-sized mule deer buck and was stopped only by the elastic skin of the hide on the offside of the animal.

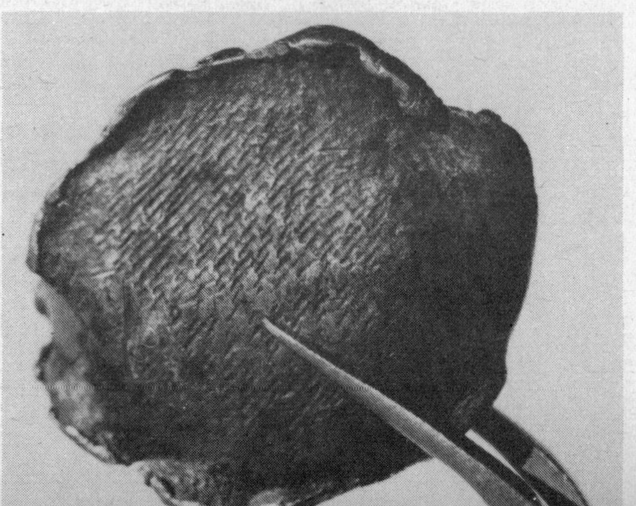

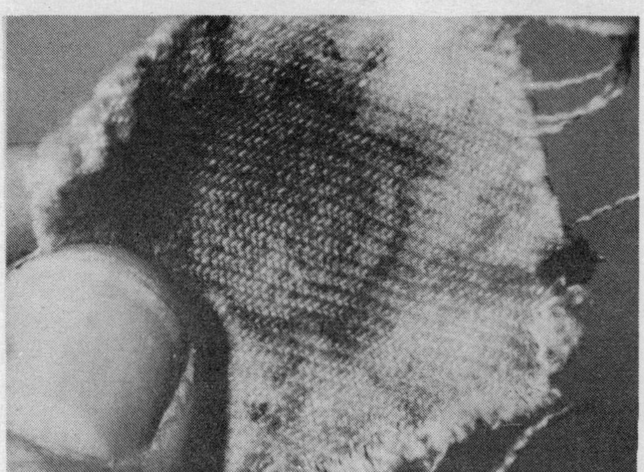

Reading patches is an important part of black powder shooting. This pure Irish linen patch has held up to the powder charge and is still intact.

rifling lands. It merely impresses into the rifling with the patch being squashed in between the ball and the rifling.

This effect is called obturation. Upon ignition the expanding powder gases push on the base of the projectile. The projectile, trying to remain at rest in the bore, swells out squeezing the patch into the rifling lands. The law of inertia is at work, trying to make the ball at rest in the bore stay at rest in the bore. When the expanding gases from the powder charge whack the ball on the base, it does not immediately fly forward, but in fact tends to remain at rest for a minute particle of time. It in fact slightly fore-shortens in the bore, gets "fatter" and tends to fill the bore to a degree. Nonetheless, the patch remains useful as a go-between here.

Because the patch is valuable we try to protect it. I use double patching for this purpose and have seen marked improvement in accuracy, but not in all cases. On the range, a smaller patch can be loaded down upon the powder charge prior to ramming home the patched ball. This extra patch will keep the main patch around the ball from burning out. In the field, I use a little piece of hornet's nest for the same purpose. Although hornet's nest will burn unconfined, for some reason it does a marvelous job of protecting the cloth patch in the bore. In my tests, even with 120 grains of FFg behind a .530-inch ball, the hornet nesting material kept the patch totally free of scorching. (Incidentally, "hornet's nest" is just that, a piece of the nest of the hornet.)

Lubes and Solvents

We ask much of the lube in a black powder firearm. First, it must facilitate the loading of the round ball. A patch without any lube can require sledge hammer force to ram home, especially if the gun has been fired several times with only cursory cleaning in between shots. So, we want the lube to make the patch "slick" enough to slide the load down the barrel. Next, we want the lube to lubricate. This is more than merely overcoming some of the friction in the loading process. We also expect a quality lube to aid in keeping that patch-to-bore relationship a good one, without the patch ripping to pieces in its journey.

We would like the lube to clean the bore, too, acting as a cleaning agent, softening the black powder residue as the new ball is rammed home. Finally, the lube, when applied to the patch for round ball shooting, must act as a fire retardant. This is a very important function, for hot gases are trying to eat the patch up before it clears the barrel, and if the patch does disintegrate, accuracy will suffer.

Modern black powder lubes and solvents are excellent, many serving double-duty as both lubricant and solvent. A good example is Young Country No. 103, the emulsified form of Falkenberry Juice and other similar products which offer the shooter more shots between cleanup because they reduce the effect of fouling in the bore.

The true double-duty lube/solvents have helped to minimize the frequency of my water/soap cleanups. Moose Milk®, Falkenberry Juice, Old Slickum and similar solvents/lubes are super for cleaning and I also use them as patch lubricants in the field, especially for small-game hunting with patched ball. The greases have excellent staying power and are good for big-game hunting where the rifle is carried a lot, but fired little.

One tip—after running a patched ball or conical downbore, it is wise to swipe the bore once or twice with a dry cleaning patch to remove excess lube clinging to the rifling. A wet or greasy bore can shoot off the mark. Shoot with a bore that's free of excessive lube; but, remember

Modern chemistry has given the black powder shooter many excellent cleaning and lubricating aids, such as Old Slickum, which serves as both cleaner and patch lube.

that a *thin* film of lube in the bore will not harm accuracy and this slight coating will aid in protecting the bore.

Making the Load

A lot of shooters fail to gain the best performance from their black powder rifles because they never really come up with the best loads for them. Loading the frontstuffer is as precise and scientific as loading for any modern firearm.

Here are some steps which will help you find the best load for your black powder firearm.

1. Find out what the manufacturer lists as the maximum safe or optimum load for the rifle he has made.
2. Start with about half that charge. If the maker says that his 50-caliber ball-shooter is good at 110 grains volume of FFg, then try 55 grains volume as a starter.
3. Go to the benchrest. Fire from 50 or 75 yards, many times with the various loads. Keep records. Work up at the rate of 5 to 10 grains volume of powder for each new attempt.
4. After learning which load is the most accurate, make a note of that load. Use that load for target work.
5. Never exceed the maximum listed by the gunmaker.
6. Juggle components. Try various round ball or conicals. Try different lubes, even percussion caps (but don't expect too much change in the latter's performance accuracy-wise). Try round ball closer to bore size with *strong* patches, but not always thick patches. I have several rifles which shoot their best groups with round ball close to bore size, such as .535-inch (as opposed to .530-inch) in a 54-caliber. I have a 40-caliber rifle which does its very best work with a bore-sized ball and a thin strong patch. In other words, the ball is .400-inch diameter and I use a .010-inch patch.

Go ahead and load by bulk. It is all right, as will be described below. *But be consistent*. I also use a chronograph because I can find that law of diminishing returns, the point where more powder gives very little additional MV. But loading for accuracy can be accomplished through the trial-and-error method, safely.

Black Powder Load Quality

The shooter can make remarkably high-quality loads if he observes some rules. Loading by bulk is acceptable with black powder. I have tried many tests weighing powder charges and tossing them with a measure, with accuracy the same in either case. How come? Because of the *inefficiency* of black powder. Yes, the lack of efficiency allows bulk loading. With smokeless powder, a half grain weight (and remember there are 7000 grains to a pound weight) can make a difference. But black powder is not that efficient, so a difference of a grain weight or two cannot even be detected by a sensitive chronograph. The idea is to load with *consistency*. In using the adjustable powder measure, I pour the powder to a point just slightly above the neck of the measure, tap the barrel of the measure a given number of times, from 5 to 10 usually, and then slide the funnel of the measure in place, leveling off the charge. The idea is to have a routine and observe it for accuracy. (For more information on loads and loading procedures see *The Gun Digest Black Powder Loading Manual,* DBI Books, Inc.)

Remember that smaller calibers are more sensitive to load variation. While it is true that black powder is not nearly as efficient as smokeless, the littler bores are more sensitive to powder changes because the volume of the bore is less and there is less area for pressure to act upon. Change the load from 70 to 75 grains of FFg in a 50-caliber and the chronograph has a hard time picking up the actual difference in muzzle velocity, but change from 20 to 25 grains in a 32-caliber and the chronograph shows it.

Loading Technique

Use the ramrod in the same manner each time, and do not use the wooden ramrod under the barrel for other than field loads. Get a good loading rod, such as the fine N&W model. This loading tool centers the rod in the bore so that the precious crown of the muzzle is undamaged. A muzzle protector is an important addition to a loading rod because damage to the crown of the muzzle can destroy accuracy.

When the loading rod is used haphazardly, the pressure upon the load can vary, and when the pressure varies load to load, shot-to-shot consistency is harmed. Cleaning between shots can also help consistency. Of course, some of the modern lubes help on this score, but if a bore builds up fouling it actually becomes effectively smaller. If the bore size is changing, then consistency is very difficult to obtain, and pressures can rise with a dirty bore. Recall that the smaller calibers are more prone to sensitivity in the powder charge. The smaller the hole in the barrel, the more pressure per load. This is why we obtain under 9,000 LUP (lead units of pressure) with a full 150 grains of FFg in a 58-caliber rifle using a round ball. But in a 45-caliber rifle shooting a round ball, 100 grains of the same powder can generate over 15,000 CUP (copper units of pressure).

Follow the basic instructions which attend the new muzzleloader. Never, under any circumstances, use any powder other than black powder or Pyrodex. In short, *smokeless powder can destroy the muzzleloader and injure the shooter*. Do not overload. Overloads usually waste powder, raise pressure, all with very little actual increase in muzzle velocity. In the flintlock, follow this procedure:

1. Insure that the firearm is totally clean, including the flashhole.
2. Place a nipple pick or pipe cleaner in the touchhole.
3. Pour the main charge and seat the patched ball.
4. Carefully remove the vent pick (same thing as nipple pick) or pipe cleaner.
5. Fill the pan half to three-fourths only, using FFFFg black powder, and only to the outside of the pan in the horseshoe shaped portion. Do not overload the pan with

Reloading the Muzzle-loading Flintlock Rifle Step-By-Step

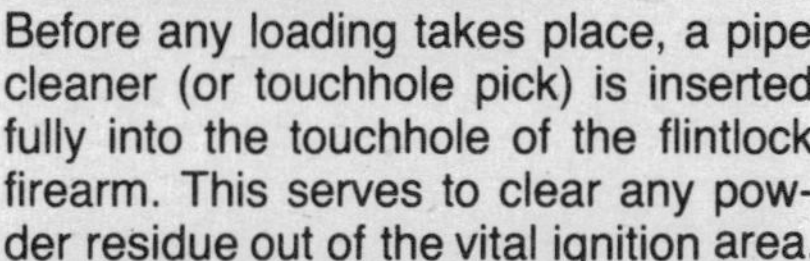

Before any loading takes place, a pipe cleaner (or touchhole pick) is inserted fully into the touchhole of the flintlock firearm. This serves to clear any powder residue out of the vital ignition area.

The powder charge is now poured down barrel, with the pipe cleaner or touchhole pick in place. In this case, a CVA flask is used to drop the charge.

Now a round ball is dropped into the shooter's hand. The author is using a homemade ball bag in this instance.

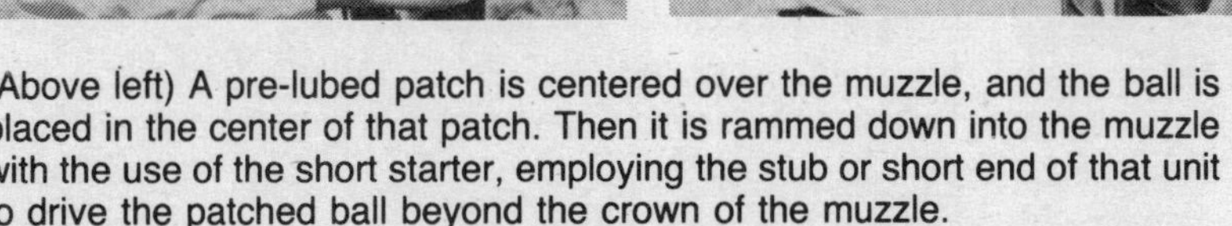

(Above left) A pre-lubed patch is centered over the muzzle, and the ball is placed in the center of that patch. Then it is rammed down into the muzzle with the use of the short starter, employing the stub or short end of that unit to drive the patched ball beyond the crown of the muzzle.

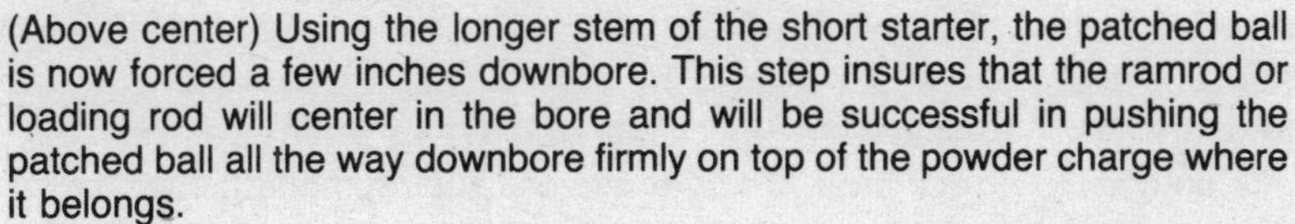

(Above center) Using the longer stem of the short starter, the patched ball is now forced a few inches downbore. This step insures that the ramrod or loading rod will center in the bore and will be successful in pushing the patched ball all the way downbore firmly on top of the powder charge where it belongs.

(Above right) Using the loading rod instead of a ramrod (a loading rod is excellent because of its stiffness and its self-centering muzzle protector), the patched ball is pushed firmly down on top of the powder charge down in the breech.

(Right) A small amount of pan powder is poured on the outer edge of the pan. The pan is half-filled with FFFFg powder only.

The long and the short of it: a Sile 12-gauge with 11-inch barrels, and a standard size double barrel black powder shotgun from Armsport. Both have a place in modern black powder shooting and both can be choked.

powder and try to avoid having the pan powder lying up against the entrance to the flashhole or vent.

A flintlock will tend to go off quite well with this method provided the lock is right in the first place and the rifle or pistol is correctly designed. The idea is to keep the flash channel clear so the spark or flash from the pan can quickly dart through the channel and into the main charge in the breech, rather than having to burn powder out of the path like a fuse.

The black powder rifle is king among muzzle-loading enthusiasts of the day, and that is why the great bulk of this chapter has dealt with that form of firearm. However, the shotgun and handgun deserve mention as well, for both are extremely interesting black powder shooting tools.

The Black Powder Shotgun

Sadly, the black powder shotgun has not been well received in the rebirth of the smokepole. That is really too bad, because the charcoal burner in scattergun form is a real treat to shoot. I would be very surprised if a shooter failed to enjoy busting clay pigeons with a black powder shotgun, and equally puzzled if a shooter failed to enjoy a day afield with the scattergun in frontloader fashion. The black powder shotgun is very easy to clean, too, due to the big smooth bores. And ballistics are superb, as is pattern, when the guns are properly choked.

Gauge & Style

I would suggest you buy a 12- or 10-gauge black powder shotgun. I use the latter mostly, for it is light and handy for its size, but the 12-gauge black powder muzzleloader is capable of shooting up to 1½ ounces of shot at very respectable muzzle velocities in the realm of 1200 fps MV. I use up to 1¾ ounces of shot in my own 10-gauge. Obviously, loads will vary with the shotgun, and the manufacturer will decide maximum powder and shot charges for his particular gun. I would not have a black powder shotgun which could not burn a good charge of powder safely behind a good charge of shot, and I mean something like 100 grains of Fg or FFg black powder and 1¼ ounces of shot in a 12-gauge.

Choke

The pity is that the ordinary black powder shotgun comes as free of choke boring as a shark is of guilt feelings. The shooter can count on patterns in about the 45 percent area, meaning just what that suggests, cylinder bore. With top quality components, and with special wads like those from Ballistic Products, Inc., the patterns can be tightened up to some degree. Choke was invented and accepted worldwide because it makes patterns many times more useful in the shotgun, and yet in the smokepole scattergun the makers give us tubes that spit out shot like a geyser spews out water.

My own 10-gauge, however, which I use for upland game, on sage grouse and pheasant, as well as waterfowl hunting, has its tubes choked full and full and gives nearly 80 percent patterns out of each barrel. I had the work done by Myron Olson, a student of U. M. Starr, the famous black powder choke specialist. Myron does the work from his shop in Watertown, South Dakota (605-886-9787). Dale Storey, another Starr pupil, is working with screw-in chokes for black powder shotguns. Dale works out of Casper, Wyoming (307-237-2414).

The black powder shotgun is a real joy to handle. Last season I was able to bag 12 sage grouse with my own 10-gauge in full choke, and I only fired 15 shots. Sage grouse are not hard to hit, but still, some of the birds were fairly spooky. I made a couple shots at what I thought to be 40 yards or better. The black powder shotgun can also be used, where legal, for deer hunting, especially with a buck-and-ball load, in this case loads consisting of a round ball of 494 grains (.690-inch diameter) in one barrel with about 80 grains of Fg pushing it in a 12-gauge, and a load of buckshot in the other barrel. It is quite a popular combination.

Reloading the Percussion Revolver Step-By-Step

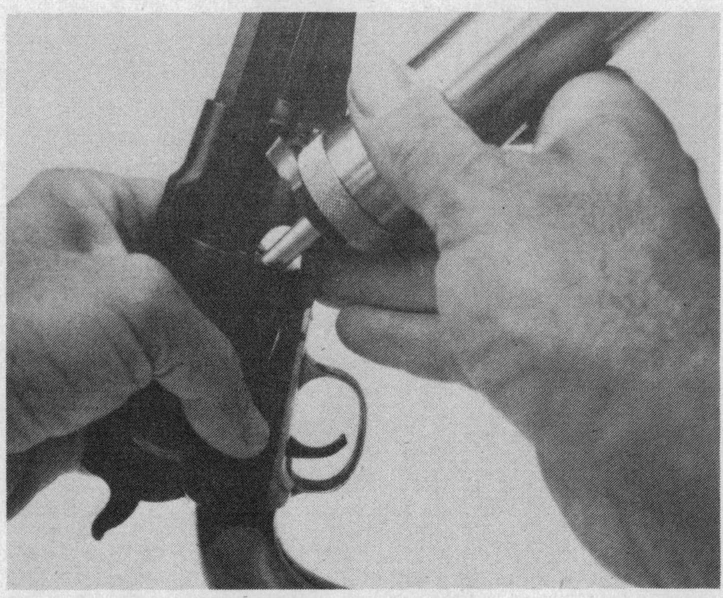

Using a CVA powder flask, 30 grains of FFFg is loaded into the chamber of this Navy Arms Remington 1858 replica revolver. Each of the six cylinder chambers receives its 30-grain charge.

The round ball is rammed home. A small ring of lead may be cut off the ball in the process. If the shooter wishes to avoid this situation, though it is not overly detrimental to accuracy, he can have each chamber mouth chamfered by a gunsmith.

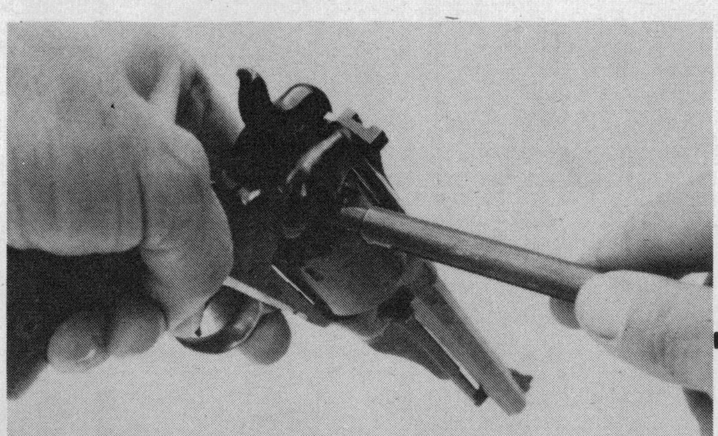

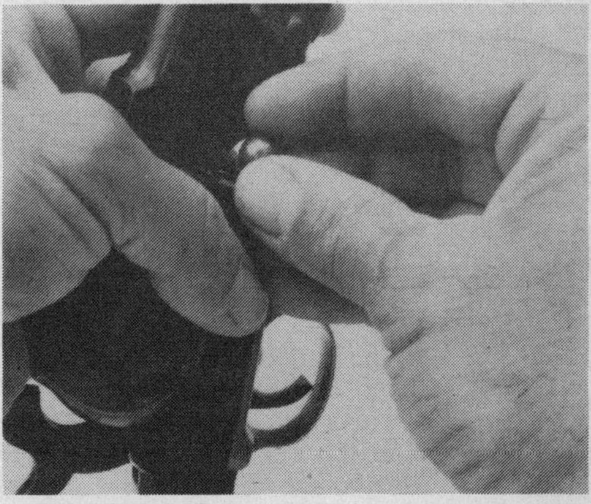

The round ball is introduced into the mouth of the chamber. Before inserting the ball, a felt disc can be placed on top of the powder charge. This *greased* felt disc will prevent a chainfire situation.

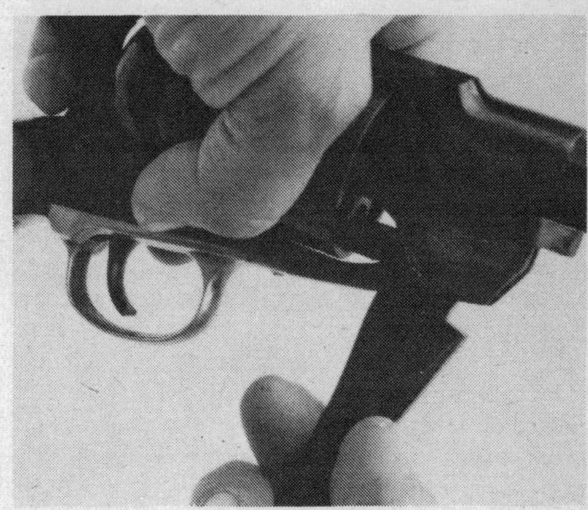

The ball is fully rammed down upon the powder charge, leaving about 1/16- to 1/8-inch area above the top of the seated ball. If the felt wad has not been used, then a layer of grease can be placed right on top of the seated ball. This is mainly a lubricating measure, but may also prevent chainfiring, where all of the chambers detonate at once.

(Left) Using a capper of the in-line type, this model from the Hawken Shop, the revolver's nipples each receive a percussion cap. On this model, there are safety notches between the cylinders so that the chamber and ball are not in line with the bore. On other models, only five of the six chambers should be loaded, with the empty chamber rotated to line up with the bore.

The Handgun

The black powder handgun is available in pistol or revolver and in far too many styles to mention here. In fact, it took an entire book to tell the story of the black powder handgun. *(The Black Powder Handgun,* DBI Books, Inc.) These are historical guns and very enjoyable to own and shoot. No black powder battery is complete without one or two soot-burning one-hand guns.

The Pistol

One of the most accurate single shot pistols I have fired is the Thompson/Center Patriot, using 35 grains volume of FFFg or the same volume of Pyrodex P behind a patched ball of either .440- or .445-inch diameter. Groups of 1-inch at 25 yards were no problem with either ball. And 35 grains of Pyrodex P with the patched 129-grain .440-inch ball gave over 1000 fps MV. There are also some very special dueling-type black powder pistols, such as the various Navy Arms offerings.

The pistols can have a lot of power, too. Lyman's Plains Pistols can push a 54-caliber round ball at over 950 fps MV. The Navy Arms J&S Hawken 54-caliber pistol also shoots a .530-inch round ball of 224-225 grains weight in the domain of 1000 fps. The Navy Arms 58-caliber Harper's Ferry Horse Pistol can fire a 500-grain Minie slug at over 800 fps or a 278-grain round ball at 975 fps MV.

The pistol in black powder form is a very interesting affair, and it loads just like the muzzle-loading rifle, using patched ball in most cases, with some taking the elongated missile. Most of these pistols are found in percussion form, with a few flintlocks available for flavor.

The Revolver

The black powder revolver covers a wide field of styles and purposes. Many importers have given us replica Colt and Remington models of very good workmanship and shooting quality both. Ruger offers its Old Army as a take-off on the Remington model, but in slightly different form. Many of these guns are very accurate and some are about like a 38 Special in power. The 44 Colt in the Walker style is quite a powerhouse, with some models holding as much as 60 grains of FFFg in each chamber of the cylinder.

Some hunters have used caplock revolvers for game up to deer-size and larger, but mostly the revolvers are for fun. They hold great historical interest, shoot well, and are usually a part of the black powder shooting match in one form or another. The revolvers make interesting shooting instruments for anyone, and there are some six-shooter fans who do not own any other form of black powder gun.

Black powder shooting never did die out in this land. Nor did the muzzleloaders fade entirely away. Yes, the cartridge guns took over, and we still have these represented wonderfully today, especially in the Sharps replicas of the old buffalo rifles as offered by the C. Sharps Company of Big Timber, Montana. But somewhere, usually in a small shop with many of the most basic tools, fathers and grandfathers passed on the skills of their gunmaking to their charges.

Today, we have general manufacture of the black powder gun once more, but I don't think this would be true if it were not for those dedicated gunmakers who never ceased to handcraft the beautiful and graceful longrifles out of our past. I like to think that modern shooters have three general domains of firearms, all highly worthwhile. There is the *modern firearm,* with all of its high class ballistic excellence. And there is the fine *muzzleloader* in one of many forms, offering a special challenge in a slower, more deliberate, hands-on style of shooting. It is highly rewarding, more so than some shooters would believe, and also not too hard to take care of with modern solvents on hand. And then there is an *in-between* type of firearm, a style born in the late 19th century, but never rendered defunct. These are most readily represented by the lever-actions of the Savage, Marlin and Winchester styles.

The originals which never found their way to the boneyard also helped instill in us, the modern shooters of America, a love for the classic style of the arms that won the country. Black powder shooting will never take the place of firing the fine modern shootables of our times. However, the shooter unfamiliar with the aroma of black powder smoke hanging on the air is missing an important part of the gunsports. Highly accurate, beautiful, balanced and graceful, the well-designed and properly constructed caplock or flintlock of yesteryear is still with us to the delight of those who know its ways, are willing to load it with care and respect, and who don't mind taking on the added challenge which comes with firing the old-time guns. When handled with know-how, the accuracy and effectiveness of the antique-type frontloader is plenty rewarding, too. These guns are still around because they deserve to be.

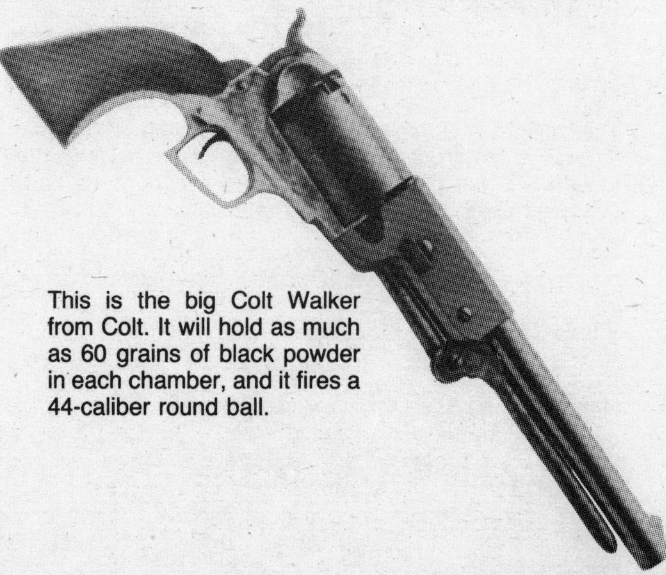

This is the big Colt Walker from Colt. It will hold as much as 60 grains of black powder in each chamber, and it fires a 44-caliber round ball.

Chapter 13
The Shooter's Stance

Note that in this informal stance, the shooter has dropped the right arm instead of using the target style stance in which the arm is held high. Also note that the left arm is not directly centered beneath the forearm in this informal pose. For target shooting or long-range shooting, the right arm would probably be held a little higher and the left arm would center beneath the forearm more.

THE FINEST GUNS in the world will do a shooter little good if he fails to observe the proper shooting stance, as well as basic firearms management, control, execution and follow-through. During a hunting trip in Canada, I met a newcomer to hunting who decided he was ready to tackle big game. His motive was a good one—a winter's supply of meat. He had the best firearms he could afford, with equally excellent ammo to go in them. He was *sure* he'd be successful. He wasn't.

Lack of hunting know-how and experience were major causes for failure, but mostly the fellow could not shoot straight. He had not learned the proper basics of shooting. Had he ingrained himself with those tenets, the shooter's stance, basic firearms management and control, as well as execution and follow-through, he would have had a freezer full of meat. He saw his game. He had good shots. But he did not connect. The only "food" he got was food for thought, with plenty of "track soup" tossed in for good measure.

The man had built a house without a foundation. He thought he had mastered the basics because he could put a few holes in and around the bull's-eye from the bench at the local target range. But the basics are more than that. Shooting basics, in fact, can be quite demanding, and they call for many exact functions all coming together at the same time. Basic shooting stance and firearms control, for example, do not follow as simple a path as some well-meaning shooting instructors may suggest. Some shooters have forgotten the separate components of the shooting skill, or they have never really identified them by breaking shooting down into its parts.

They have forgotten that they learned each segment individually, often a long time ago. Now it is second nature for them to mount the firearm, aim it, control it, and squeeze off the round when the sights are "glued" to the target. Their unconscious fashion leads them to believe that shooting is a very simple skill with few parts. If they were shown a slow-motion movie of themselves on the firing line, they would often be amazed at how many things they do, and do well, in order to consistently put 'em in the black. The shooting of any firearm is not a simple process —it has many concepts.

The shooter's stances shown here are: offhand (upper left), sitting (one style of the sitting stance), kneeling and prone. The author's individual stances vary from these; however, not by much. The individual shooter must take the stance which fits him best. Note use of the Uncle Mike's sling in all of these positions.

The Concept of Aim

We *learn* the concept of aim. There are no ''natural-born'' shooters. There are people who are blessed with ''steady nerves,'' the eyesight of an eagle, and superb hand-eye coordination. But there are no ''born'' shooters, and if there were, they would probably be women. Most women come to the sport with few pre-conceived ideas; they listen, apply the advice, trying each bit of instruction to see how it works for them personally. Then they modify where they have to, adjust the data to fit themselves, and merrily they procede to chew the center out of the target.

The concept of aim becomes more simplified as the sighting device becomes more sophisticated. With open iron sights we must focus on three objects, the notch in the rear sight, the front bead settled into that notch and the target, with the eye doing quite a bit of work in order to keep all three lined up. The peep sight reduces the focus problem somewhat. With the peep or aperture sight we simply look *through,* not at, the rear sight, put the front sight on target and squeeze off. Then comes the scope. The scope offers a flat two-dimensional sighting plane. Cross-wires seem attached to a target, as it were.

The shooter should understand that the concept of aim does include the eye doing what may be called ''visual accommodation,'' i.e., focusing back and forth to keep rear sight, front sight and target visually clear. Visual accommodation is used less with the aperture or peep sight and less yet with the telescopic sight and its length/width-only picture.

But there is something basic to all three sighting styles, and that is that the first tenet of sighting is to aim the *body*. This is where shooter's stance enters the picture, for it is the very first rule of good aiming. It is the body which is poised to the target first. Then the sights, sight picture and firearm control enter the situation. We point the body first, positioning it to allow the best chance of controlling the shooting situation.

No matter the firearm, the body is aimed first in rifle shooting, as well as in handgunning and shotgunning. A shotgun, for example, is ''pointed,'' not aimed, but the pointing is rather precise. The body instantly poises itself, following an assessment made by the brain. If the body moves haphazardly before the mind ''dopes out'' the shot, chances are a miss will be the result.

That we point a shotgun is quite easily seen, really. The story about a missing bead not being noticed by the shotgun owner is a true one. I have not personally experienced the situation of going a full season with a shotgun bead knocked off; however, I did spend one shooting season with a broken bead which amounted to almost the same thing. The gun was used in upland bird hunting, and the prominent white bead had been broken completely off, leaving only a metal lump which used to retain the bead. I used the shotgun all season. I have no way of knowing when the bead was broken off; however, at the end of the season I had as good a record of hits as ever, and it was well into the summer when I just happened to look down and see that the white bead was no longer in place.

We do not aim a shotgun when we use it with shot. We

point it. And in this chapter on shooter's stance, it is important to note that we point our body first, then the gun. In the concept of aim, then, we should make a mental note of thinking in terms of aiming our entire body and then our sights. It is a very basic truth in gunning.

The Concept of Hold

If all we had to do was somehow get the sight aligned, I think most of us would be world class shooters. In fact, the finest scope sight in the world will not hold the firearm stable and let off a clean shot. Aiming is but one part of hitting, and it is only one part of many important aspects of shooting. Holding is one of the major points of this chapter, for holding the firearm properly is to *control* it.

A shooter who has mastered hold and body control (which are intertwined), be he firing a handgun, a shotgun or a rifle, is on his way to becoming a truly fine shot. Each serious shooter must master control of his body as a simultaneous part of delivering that well-aimed or well-pointed shot. Sighting is much simpler than body control or stance. Sighting is mechanical, but body poise is both a physical and a mental endeavor. Being out of position is to invite a miss. Again, this factor holds true for the use of any firearm. Line up the sights with unerring accuracy. Squeeze the trigger so that your own mind does not know when the firearm is going to ''go off.'' Do these things and you will be on the road to straight shooting. But fail in stance and the two features mentioned above will not fully compensate for that mistake.

Sometimes the perfect footing for a shot is not available, and footing is very important to stance. This shooter has achieved the best position possible in the least amount of time. The right foot is planted firmly on the boulder, and the left foot has at least some grip with the rock. Also, note that the left arm is supported by the left knee.

The Concept of Trigger Control

While the trigger itself is simply a mechanical device, its mastery is actually a part of body control or stance, if we can use the latter word in a broad sense. Sighting, stance and trigger control may be thought of as separate, and they are in a way, for they are *parts* of shooting. But all three are interelated to the point of failure to hit the mark when one part is lacking in excellence of execution.

We point or aim our body at the same time we are aligning the sights. Then the trigger release comes to the fore. The crack shot has *learned* to do these things without conscious effort. He ties them together like a sheaf of straw. The brain sizes up the shot. The body moves and positions itself so that the firearm can be best aimed and controlled, and at about the same time the sight picture is developed. The trigger is activated to get the shot away, but the notion of the entire hand squeezing down is, to my way of thinking, a poor one. Do not squeeze the entire hand around the grip or there will be a chance of spoiling the hold/aim. Instead, use the trigger control commonly used by handgunners—''convince'' the trigger finger that it is an independent part of the hand. And force it to operate independently of the whole hand. The trigger finger ''sneaks'' into the guard and the soft pad of the forward joint does the pressing because it contains sensitive nerve endings.

Try this—have someone turn around, back to you. Now touch the person's back with your fingers, one finger, two, three, four or five. Sometimes put the fingers close together on the person's back, sometimes more spread apart. Ask that person to relate *how many* fingers are touching his back at any given time. A 50-50 response is a good one. In many cases if all five fingers are close together, the person may guess only ''one'' or ''two.''

But this is not true of the fingertips. The nerve endings are close together here. The fingertip is sensitive and in using it to touch off the trigger be sure to use it as independently of the hand as possible. Do not squeeze the whole hand around the wrist of the firearm in an attempt to squeeze the trigger with more control.

Control of the Body

Breathing

If a person holds his breath for a minute or so, his pulse rate will increase. When that occurs, it translates into more body tremor. In shooting, obviously, this is undesirable. The best way of controlling breathing for shooting is to draw in a full breath, exhale about half of it, and then hold that ''half breath'' until the shot is away. One learns to get a shot off without delay as his experience increases. The newcomer seems to take forever because he is tentative. There is nothing wrong with wanting to be very careful, but hesitation, remember, means raising the pulse rate and

Placement of the feet is just as important in the sitting stance as it is in any other stance. Dean Zollinger uses his feet to brace the knees, which in turn are used to anchor the elbows for a steady shot in the sitting position.

bringing on some sort of body tremor. Ideally, the shooter takes only a few seconds to actually pull the trigger after he has aligned himself and his sights in relation to the target.

The Feet

Even those of us who have been shooting for a very long time sometimes fail to position our feet properly for a shot. Although there is variation to be considered from one individual shooter to the next, we can make some good blanket statements concerning placement of the feet when shooting. Every shot from every firearm demands correct foot placement. Even from a solid benchrest shooting position, the feet need to be slightly spread and flat on the ground. I have opened up a group because I failed to observe this fact, raising a foot to rest on a toe.

All of our commentary will be based upon right-handed shooting here, so the left-handed reader needs to reverse the information for his purposes. When I say to put the left foot out in the general direction of the shot, the left-handed shooter reverses that, placing his right foot in the general direction of the shot.

Initial foot placement is more appropriate to shotgunning, but true for riflemen too. When it comes to rifle shooting, the shooter should shift his feet so that they are approximately at a 45-degree angle to the right of the target. The feet should be spread far enough apart to offer stability, yet with comfort. About 20 inches apart is my norm—it will probably be different for you. A quick rule of thumb is to spread the feet apart about the same width as your shoulders.

The shotgunner puts his left foot out in the direction of the target and his body is angled slightly to the right. Giving degrees here is rather pointless because the amount of angle differs with each shooter according to the *comfort* of the individual. Some shotgunners almost face the target squarely, while others seem to do all right with an almost 45-degree angle, an angle which is more suited to rifle-shooting.

In general terms, the shotgunner does almost face his target, but not quite as he will generally try to position his body so he'll be "ahead" of a moving target—commonly called body lead. In the case of a target moving from right to left or left to right the left foot will be pointed slightly ahead of the target by a few degrees. When it comes to shooting at a stationary target, the rifleman's left foot may easily point 45 degrees to the right of the target. And, of course, the feet are spread apart in either case. The handgunner positions himself much as the rifleman does, and his feet, too, are spread apart, sometimes a bit more than in rifle-shooting. How far should the feet be spread? That's a matter of personal comfort and variation in physical build. But it's not hard to determine how far to spread the feet. It's a matter of trial-and-error. I found that I spread my feet *most* in handgunning. I feel more solid that way and much steadier. I have spread my feet as much as 3 feet apart in handgunning and scored well at the target (I am a bit under

Spreading the legs gives the body a more solid stance. Here, Gene Thompson spreads his feet apart slightly wider than his shoulders for a good steady offhand shot.

6 feet tall). In rifle-shooting, my foot spread is more like 18 inches and in fast-handling shotgun-shooting, such as found in upland gunning, my feet may spread but a foot apart. But spread they do, for any shooter. I have watched newcomers with a feet spread of only a few inches. They are unsteady.

Shifting Foot Pressure

I find in analyzing the situation, I shift my foot pressure, that is the "weight on each foot" in shooting the shotgun, but I am not aware of much if any shifting in handgunning or rifle-shooting. Being a right-hander, I am certain that the weight of my body is shifted to the left foot before I fire a shotgun. I do know that this allows me to *pivot the hips* in shotgunning. The upland gunner along with, I suspect, any shotgunner, spots the target, sets his body for whatever amount of body-lead he wants, positions his feet with the left foot "aiming" slightly ahead of the target, and then pivots his upper body at the hips for his swing. *He does not pivot by shifting his feet.*

Stay loose. Do not tense up. In shifting the weight from both feet to the left foot in shotgunning, it is a gentle pressure which is felt on the left foot. Sure, you can feel that you have shifted your weight. You feel more pressure on the left foot than the right, but if excessive weight is shifted to the left foot, you lose balance. Balance is, quite obviously, paramount to good shooting.

A two-hand hold is used to control this 44-caliber black powder revolver. The two-hand stance is coupled with a kneeling posture for a bit of added steadiness.

The Knees

Never lock the knees in shotgunning. *Never*. In fact, the knees should be *broken,* meaning that the hunter assumes a *very slight* crouch stance. If the knees are locked up, swinging and pivoting for that smooth flow and good hit are impaired tremendously. I learned that when I missed shots on upland birds, the miss was almost always accompanied by knees which were *not bent* and a left hand which was putting too much pressure on the forearm of the shotgun.

If the knees are locked up, even slightly (and there are degrees of locking the knees), that smooth swing is gone. Also, try pivoting at the hips when the knees are locked. It's difficult to do smoothly. I find that if I *lean* slightly forward, I tend to force my knees to relax instead of lock up. Try this—mount the shotgun. Break the knees (unlock them). Lean slightly forward. Now pivot. It's smooth and fast. Your upper body flows in the direction you want it to move in. The lower body, waist down, rocks gently. Now lock the knees. Try the same swing. It's ragged at best.

With knees unlocked and in a very slight crouch, the problem of left-swing/right-swing lessens, though it is still there to be sure. These factors pertain mostly to shotgunning, but are not untrue in rifle-shooting. As you swing or follow on a moving shot your weight does not stay on the left foot. In shooting left to right, as the barrel of the shotgun swings to the right, the weight of the body changes from left foot accent to right foot accent. It is natural as breathing air. The body pivots at the waist, and the weight of the upper body or torso moves to the right foot, in the direction of the pointed shotgun barrel. This applies to rifle-shooting at a moving target as well.

The management of the knees is important to all phases of shooting where motion of the body is necessary. As in shotgunning, the knees should not be fully locked up in rifle-shooting at a stationary target either. There is no body crouch here, but the knees are unlocked, the legs supported in a normal standing position. In handgunning this stance is also accepted. The knees are not locked up, but there is *generally* not much crouch. In combat shooting, the handgunner may lean forward, bending his knees, in a crouch, squarely facing the target.

The Hands

The left hand directs the swing of the shotgun or the rifle when a moving target is presented. The left hand also balances either firearm, maintaining the horizontal position of the muzzle. In shotgunning, when that left hand is too close to the receiver or lock of the gun, the shot is likely to strike low. The left hand should push forward to that point which allows an easy balance of the gun.

The right hand controls the shot. We have eye-brain-

Note the placement of the elbow directly beneath the forearm for steady support of the rifle. Also note the gentle grasp of the forearm with the left hand of this right-handed shooter.

hand cooperation here. The eye has seen a target. The message reaches the brain. The brain dictates the action to be taken. That right hand is going to fire the gun at what we hope to be the correct instant of time. When gripping the forearm of either rifle or shotgun, the left hand applies only gentle pressure. It does not put a strangle hold on the forearm. If the left hand squeezes down with white-knuckle force, a likely miss is in the making.

Elbows

In rifle-shooting, the left elbow should be fairly well underneath the forearm for reasons of *support*. This position in target-shooting is vital. The left elbow is almost, if not directly and perfectly, underneath the forearm of the rifle. In shotgunning, the left elbow is not so rigidly placed and is slightly out from under the center of the forearm. This is also true of informal rifle shooting. This allows a comfortable posture for swinging either rifle or shotgun. In formal rifle shooting the right elbow is held high. It is at *least* horizontal to the ground if not higher, but in informal rifle shooting, the elbow is generally below that horizontal line. Locked elbows are taboo. Locked elbows, as with locked knees, cause two major problems. First, any sort of swing is impeded when the elbows are locked up. Second, locking any joint in the body can produce body tension, and that tension can eventually culminate in body tremor. The locked elbow problem is a very small one, however, because locked elbows are unnatural to us. Generally, we have to *consciously* lock up our elbows.

In shotgunning, the elbows are not held the same as in rifle-shooting. Of course, the left elbow supports and balances the gun, but it is not held directly beneath the forearm. The right elbow, in my opinion, should be held at a *comfortable* level, comfortable to the *individual shooter*, for good shotgun stance.

In one-hand handgunning, the left elbow for a right-handed shooter has very little to do with the firing of the piece. But the left arm/hand should be rested against the body, which of course means that the movement in the elbow joint is nil. One can place the off hand on the hip or in the front or back pocket. The off arm is a balancing factor in traditional handgunning. Of course, there is the two-hand hold, which now incorporates the left arm and the left elbow, and the only advice is, once again, not to lock up an elbow. The shooter can see for himself the damage done in handgunning if he will consciously lock up an elbow. With a right-hand hold on the handgun, lock up the right elbow and watch the sight picture of the handgun change. Unlock the elbow and a steadier picture is possible.

The Eyes

Shoot with both eyes open. This pertains to all forms of shooting, even benchrest, and it holds up quite well as advice. However, it is not to be considered the best advice for every shooter. There are some shooters who shut the non-aiming eye an instant before firing the gun, any gun, and they hit the target with consistency. I still suggest that these shooters try to learn the two-eye "stance," but I won't argue with success. If a shooter has tried the two-eye method and finds he can hit better by squinting, let him squint.

Shooting with both eyes open is a reality for many shooters. It's natural, regardless of the sight being used.

What I do not like about one-eye shooting is the fact that some muscle tension is introduced into an otherwise controlled body stance. It is not natural to us. We do not go around closing one eye when we are normally looking at things, and we should not introduce the one-eye squint into our shooting if we can help it.

The second factor against the squint is that of visual perspective. No longer do we have a true three-dimensional view of the target. Oh yes, it seems that we do. We can close an eye and the scene changes but little because of "learned perception." We have learned to relate the position of objects through size and shape. But in fact, the one-eye view does not offer the same visual perception as that with both eyes open.

Sometimes a shooter will find that he has a lot of trouble adapting to the two-eye shooting stance. When he does, the problem may sometimes be traced to the master eye. A right-handed person will usually have a master right eye, and the opposite is true of a left-handed person. However, there are some people who are right-handed but who have a left master eye and vice versa. A few may have been trained in school to avoid the use of the left hand in favor of the right hand. However, the master eye remained as intended by nature.

To test for the master eye, hold a pencil vertically out at arms length. With both eyes open, hold the pencil tip like a front sight on an object in the room about 10 or 20 feet away. Now close the left eye. If the *right* eye is the master eye, then the point of that pencil will remain right on target. Now shut the right eye. If the right eye is the master eye, the pencil will optically take a jump to the right. It will no longer be aiming on target.

Sometimes we do things in shooting which are not truly observable under normal circumstances. If we try to *catch ourselves* in the act of shooting to see if we have developed undesirable habits, we can correct the problem. This is something like trying to find out if we hold our breath at the moment of firing the gun. In shotgunning, for example, it is wise to hold the breath an instant before firing. I do. I found out by trying to catch myself at it. The same holds true for closing one eye before firing. If you catch yourself doing it, you can then try to consciously correct the situation.

The Shoulders

The main point to remember here is to nestle the butt of the shotgun or rifle well into the shoulder, not out on the arm. With my older rifles which have the crescent-shaped buttplate, I tend to put the butt of the rifle out away from the shoulder slightly and can find no damage to my shooting because of this. However, a rifle with a shotgun-style buttplate, which most rifles have today, is another story. The soft shoulder area is the correct place to position the butt of the rifle or shotgun stock with this style of buttplate or recoil pad.

The Face

Simply, the face should rest upon the comb of the stock. When the face is not *comfortably* nestled against the comb or the cheekpiece, good shooting is unlikely to occur. The position of the face dictates the position of the head which in turn, dictates the position of the eyes. In shotgunning, the face's position on the stock should allow the shooter to see the rib of the shotgun, *but not consciously*. When he mounts the shotgun, he should not be conscious of seeing the whole rib, but if he looks for the rib, he can see it *without* raising his face/head upward to do so. The face should stay down upon the stock until the shot is away.

Physical Health and Shooting

I have known shooters who complained that no matter what they tried, they could not climb out of a shoooting slump they had entered into. In some cases, I have found that this shooting slump is coupled with a change in physical health. As an important part of the shooter's stance, we must include overall physical welfare. A shooter who does

Keep your face down on that comb! This advice is very important in both rifle-shooting and shotgunning.

not feel well may often see that lack of physical well-being in his markmanship. We must ask ourselves if a change in our shooting ability comes from a general feeling of ill health.

An eye checkup is essential from time to time. Shooters sometimes learn that the connection between a drop in their scores and their ability to see the target clearly is the entire answer to the problem. A doctor must make a thorough examination of the eyes in order to determine how we are doing visually.

Developing Shooting Muscles

The body in general is used in shooting, not merely the eyes and hands. And when the body is lacking in muscle tone, shooting can suffer. We can build up certain "shooting muscles" by doing a few minor exercises or for general health purposes embarking on a total exercise program. But before undertaking a rigid program of exercising, consult your doctor.

Toe stands which can help build the shooter's lower legs do not take stringent body exercise. During the day, we can simply remember to stand up on our toes a dozen times or so a day. Lifting weights is not for everyone. But lifting *light* weights will help build the arms, which is an aid to any shooting, especially handgunning. Holding a small weight, even as little as 2 pounds, out in the right hand, straight out from the body, can greatly aid the handgunner in his ultimate control and steadiness of his handgun.

We can hike, bicycle, or walk to build up our wind. A good brisk walk is not going to damage anyone who is in good physical health. I like to walk with a packframe on, the pack holding a modest weight. This, I think, helps to build up the legs and steady legs mean a lot in any kind of shooting which takes place without a rest. Squeezing a rubber ball or squeezing a hand spring will strengthen the hand, which aids a great deal in firing the sidearm.

Self-Analysis

The best form of self-analysis is a series of high-speed photos. Anyone can take such photos as long as he or she observes the rules of safety and, of course, has a camera with a motor-drive. The shooter should try to fire his gun using his most natural form, with someone taking pictures with a 35mm camera with a telephoto lens of about 135mm length. I suggest black and white film of 400 ASA or similar speed.

A series of high-speed photos will capture the shooter and his stance and form forever. This is especially helpful in shotgunning, and I have had my brother, Nick, photograph me shooting upland game birds. I learned a lot. I learned that when I locked my knees, I missed. I found out that when I gripped the forearm too tightly I missed. Those high-speed photos caught me off-balance, too. I found out that when I unlocked my knees and crouched slightly I swung better and hit better.

The presence of a competent shooting coach can be another form of analysis which can lead to shooting improvement. A coach can detect problems and then help the shooter correct these problems for himself. A coach can also teach you a lot about how to analyze your own shooting stance and form. You can carry on from there, improving your own ability.

Toe-stands can be helpful in building the muscles of the lower leg and gaining greater shooter stability and steadiness. Shooter strength can play a role in marksmanship.

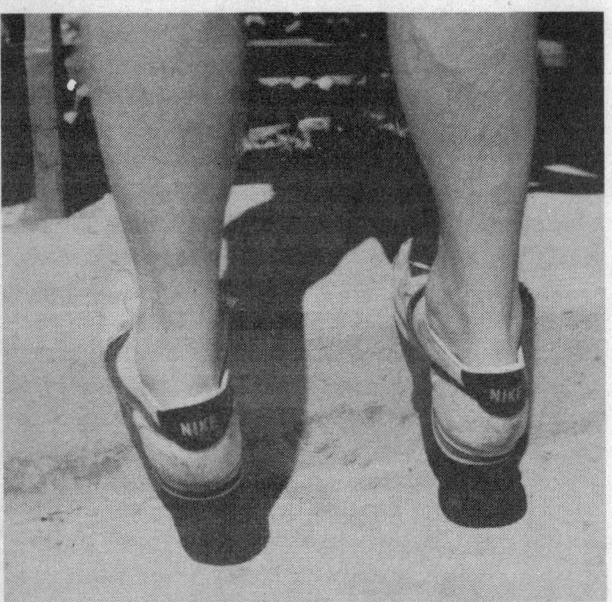

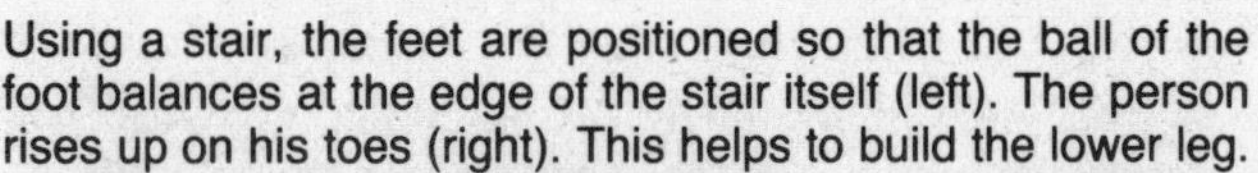
Using a stair, the feet are positioned so that the ball of the foot balances at the edge of the stair itself (left). The person rises up on his toes (right). This helps to build the lower leg.

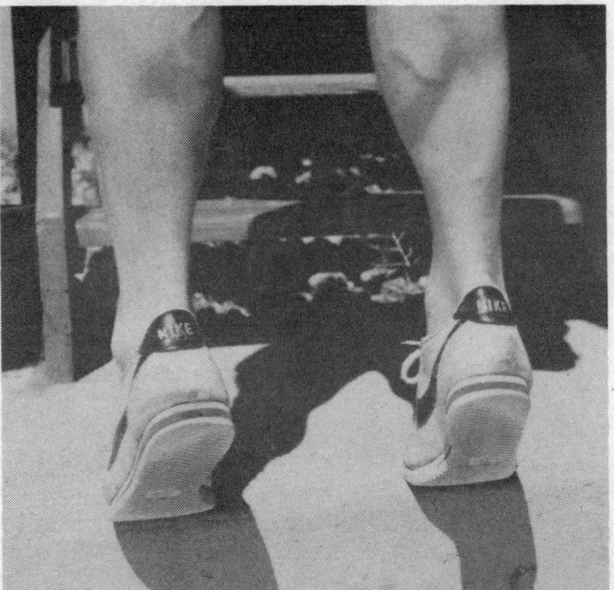

Mini Shooting Lessons

The pursuit of excellence in marksmanship of any type requires the complete interest of the shooter. But that is not enough. Shooting is a precise activity. We *learn* how to master the firearm through basic techniques, analyzing our own shooting, having others help us analyze it, and then working to improve upon our faults. We learn a basic set of shooting principles first, and then we modify those principles to suit our own needs and our own personal abilities. The rest of this chapter is devoted to those important shooting rules. Other shooters will offer other rules, but the rules listed here have worked for me for many years and have been applied to many other shooters with good results. They are not rules which should be called "beginner's" regulations. They are "truths." They apply to all shooters of any age or experience level in the shooting world.

Review of Some Shooting Points

The following is a list of a few basic but all-important shooting points, a brief review of what we have said above, necessary to repeat before getting into the specifics of the shooting lessons themselves.

1. Aim the *body* as well as the firearm.
2. *Control* the body as well as the firearm.
3. Treat aim as a *concept* as well as a mechanical procedure.
4. Learn how each part of the body functions in the *act* of shooting.
5. Treat trigger pull as an *individual* entity of shooting.
6. Hold the half-breath *before* the instant of firing, no matter the gun.
7. Position the feet *precisely,* until it becomes habit.
8. *Never* lock the knees.
9. Observe the position of the *elbows,* changing that position according to the *type* of shooting being done.
10. Shoot with *both eyes open,* if possible.
11. Use the *shoulder* to maintain control of the buttstock, not the arm.
12. Keep the face *down* upon the stock.
13. If you experience a shooting slump, *check your physical* health in general to see if that is part of the problem—get an eye examination.
14. *Develop* your shooting muscles.
15. *Analyze* your own shooting or have someone help you analyze it.

The Rifle

There are a few basics worth discussing in rifle-shooting before going into the specifics in our mini lessons. First, treat the rifle according to its physical factors, such as weight, recoil-per-caliber/load, shape of the stock, sight radius, sight type and so forth. One does not handle a little light Model 94 carbine and a big bolt-action 375 Magnum

Before taking any stance with a rifle, "get the feel of it." Balance the rifle in both hands. See how it settles into the hands. Move the rifle about. Get to know its balance point. This is a first step to good marksmanship with the longarm.

Configuration of the firearm often dictates the hold. In this case, a very wide forearm gives the impression that the shooter's left hand is choking down firmly in its grip, but this is not the case. No matter the style of the forearm, a comfortable but modest grip is preferred over an overly strong hold. Of course, heavy-recoil firearms dictate a grip commensurate with that recoil.

in the same fashion. That may seem painfully obvious, but I have observed that some shooters try to handle each firearm in the same manner. I recall a guide who wanted to try out a client's 600 Nitro Express double rifle. He held it as he would a 28-gauge shotgun, and he got bashed for it.

Mounting the Rifle

The rifle comes to the shooter. The shooter does not go to the rifle. I have learned to shoot rifles of somewhat shorter length of pull for my own personal "reach" measurements. I could use a 14¼- to even 14½-inch length of pull, but I don't. I have gone to about 13⅞ inches length of pull in my personal rifles. This allows me to *maintain a better stance*, bringing the rifle smoothly to my shoulder without having to worry about the buttstock catching on my clothing. I "push" the rifle out in front of me, then draw it slightly back and into my shoulder. I recommend this procedure. The main point, however, is to bring the rifle to you; do not bring the rifle up and then step forward in order to settle the buttstock into the shoulder.

Do Not Force the Position

Do not force the rifle into position. By this, I mean do not find that your stance is wrong and then try to correct it by forcing the rifle to fit the body. *Position the body first*. Then the rifle will move naturally, fitting into the right position. If the shooter learns to aim his body first, he will find that when the rifle is mounted it all but points itself in the direction of the target. If the shooter has to move the rifle considerably after he has mounted it, then his body stance is off the mark.

This shooter knows how to control the rifle without choking it. The right hand is maintaining a grip, but the trigger finger is relaxed. The left hand is controlling the elevation of the rifle, but it is loosely gripping the stock. It is not throttling the forearm. This latter point is important to good marksmanship with the rifle.

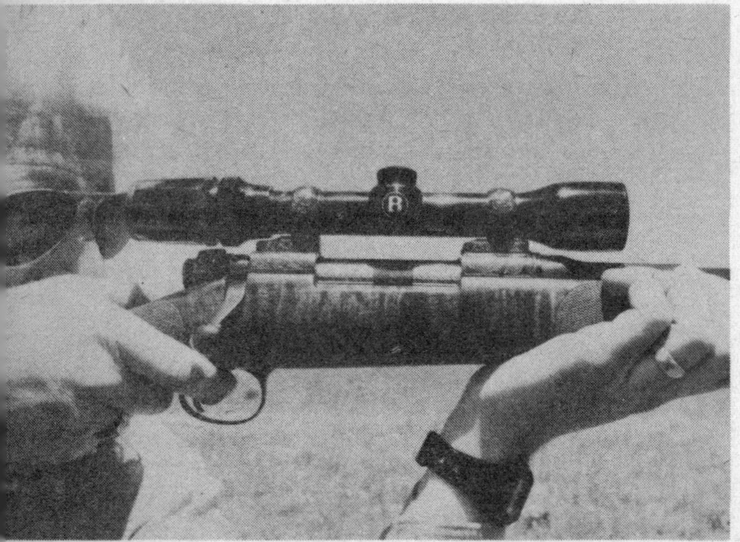

There must be flexibility in firearm handling and control. For example, a big game rifle, even of the 30-06 to 300 Magnum class, need not be gripped with full force at the forearm, nor should it be. But with the 458 Winchester, shown here as fired by the author's son, Bill Fadala, a good grip on the forearm is advisable.

Follow-Through

As in shotgunning or handgunning, the shooter must maintain his shooting position *after* the shot is away. This practice precludes the bad habit of dropping the stance at the moment of firing. Again, the shooter must hold his proper stance all the way through, from the mounting of the rifle to the sight picture and trigger activation, and even *after* the rifle has been fired.

Aim-Hold-Fire

The shooter must observe the tenets of firearm control until they become habit. He learns to position his body, and then aim, hold and fire with proper follow-through. Sight picture, be it a 6-o'clock hold using iron sights, with the front bead held just below the intended point of impact, or with the bead held dead on the point of impact, must be *controlled* along with stance. Part of this is the length of time the sight picture is held. My suggestion is to hold that sight picture only long enough to master a *steady* picture. Then squeeze the trigger.

The Prone Shooting Position

The prone position is the most steady for field shooting of the rifle. The shooter lies down on his stomach, flat on the ground, for this position. Here are the points of consideration:

1. Spread the legs comfortably, toes outward. Be sure to spread the legs wide enough to offer good balance. This can be felt by the shooter. He can feel a steadiness in the torso of the body. Some shooters will use a wider spread than others. That is fine. Be comfortable.

2. The left elbow should be positioned directly beneath the forearm of the rifle. This allows for the pressure from the weight of the rifle to be directed in a straight line through the left arm (right for a left-handed shooter) to the ground. It offers steadiness.

3. The left hand should be extended out on the forearm to a point of comfort. It is unwise to hold the left arm too close in because this is not as steady as holding the forearm farther out toward the end. The shooter can tell if he puts his left hand too far out on the forearm; it feels awkward and the steadiness of the rifle is visibly impaired.

4. Rest the forearm on the heel of the hand, not the palm of the hand. Again, we have a situation of controlling the rifle with the left hand, while not choking it down. There should be little or no actual pressure exerted directly upon the forearm in terms of *squeezing*. *Do not squeeze the forearm*. Allow the forearm to *rest* on the heel of the hand.

5. Grip loosely with the right hand. The right hand does not control the rifle in the prone position. The rifle is controlled because it is balanced upon the left hand with the buttstock firmly pressed into the shoulder. In fact, it is not unwise to place the thumb against the palm side of the wrist of the stock rather than around the wrist of the stock. Doing this precludes gripping the pistol grip area too tightly.

6. Insure that the buttstock is firmly into the shoulder. The rifle should actually stay pretty much on target even if the right hand is removed entirely from the wrist. In fact, I often remove my right hand after attaining the prone position as a check. If the rifle stays on target, then my left hand and shoulder are controlling the rifle, as they should.

7. Relax; draw in a breath; hold that breath for 10 seconds; let out half of it; hold again; *squeeze the trigger*. Relax. Tenseness of any kind will increase body tremor.

The prone position is *not* advisable for rifles of extremely heavy recoil. I have fired a 375 H&H Magnum from the prone—it is not pleasant. The body's extensive area of coverage on the ground means that there is very little "give" and the shoulder is going to absorb the recoil full force, your body not being able to "roll with the punch."

The shooter who wishes to be expert in the prone position should try placing his body at various angles to the target. Definitely, the body should *not* lie in a straight line with the target. The legs should be extended in a line which angles to the left of the target (southpaws reverse this), and the degree of this angle depends upon the comfort of the position for the shooter. You merely need to try various angles to see which works best. As in all shooting, aim the *body,* as well as the *firearm* in prone shooting.

The Sitting Position

If the prone position holds the honor of being the steadiest of rifle-shooting stances, barring the benchrest of course, then the sitting position is next in line for steadiness. As a hunter, I have taken quite a bit of game from the sitting postion. In fact, in most of my western hunting for big game, I assume the sitting postion as a rule. The game is sighted, and I immediately plop to the ground for a shot if I want to harvest that game. The sitting position allows a shooter to see over low brush, whereas the prone does not. The sitting position can be assumed in seconds. Although a practiced shooter can fall into the prone position quickly, the sitting position is going to be faster to achieve.

If a shooter knows how to use the sitting position he can do some fine work in the area of marksmanship, too. And it is not difficult to learn this stance. Here are the steps:

1. Sit with knees bent and comfortably spread. Do not lean to one side or the other.

2. Remember that as in all shooting stances, the body is aimed as well as the firearm. Learn to sit down in position. Do not sit first and then squirm into position.

3. Maintain about a 45-degree angle to the target, with the feet pointed about 45 degrees to the right of the target for a right-handed shooter.

4. Place the left elbow firmly to the inside of the left knee. Place the right elbow on the lower thigh just above the knee.

Using a walking staff united with the sitting position, the shooter manages to create a very sturdy and steady stance. The walking staff is wedged solidly underneath the right lower leg, with the left hand holding the middle of the stick and the forearm of the rifle. It works very well.

In hunting, the sitting position is far better than the standing or offhand position, and the sitting shot is easy to get in any sort of open terrain. Make no mistake. A hunter should know the offhand stance inside and out. But it is the sitting shot which should be used when possible.

A kneeling shot is often useful when high brush or other obstacles preclude the sitting shot. This is a hastily taken stance, but solid enough to allow for a hit. The right elbow is comfortably low. The major support comes through the left elbow on the left knee and the right hand on the grip of the rifle's wrist. Even though the left hand is supporting the rifle in this stance, it does not throttle the forearm.

5. The left hand is again used as a rest to maintain the rifle on the horizontal. Again, very little pressure is applied by the left hand.

6. The right hand controls the firearm.

7. In order to change the point of aim, the body is shifted. The body is, itself, aimed at the target.

The Kneeling Position

Not as rock-steady as the sitting position, the kneeling position is more flexible in allowance for movement by the shooter. It is not as steady because the right elbow is unrested. However, it puts the hunter up a little higher if he is in the brush, and it does offer speed. The kneeling shot is a fast one. In terms of making a good group on target without a benchrest, the prone wins easily, but the kneeling posture has its place. It is an important part of rifle-shooting stance. Here is how to do it:

1. Kneel on the right knee if you're a right-handed shooter.

2. Place the left elbow on the lower thigh just above the left knee.

3. Shift the weight of the body on the right knee.

4. The left hand controls the aim; it can be shifted in order to change the direction of aim. But again the left hand does not squeeze the forearm of the rifle.

5. The body can be shifted forward or backward to make the stance more comfortable for the shooter. If the shooter slides back a bit, he can often give the left arm a little more contact with the left leg for a steadier hold, but this action can cause an imbalance, too. The shooter can shift his body until he is comfortable *and* steady.

6. Timing is very important to the kneeling shot, for it is not a position easily maintained over an extended period of time. The right elbow is out in space, as it is with the standing shot.

Standing or Offhand

Shooting "off the hind legs" must be mastered by all riflemen. While it is wise to achieve a prone or sitting position for the sake of better hitting, it is not always possible. The hunter of woods and brush often must take his shot from the standing stance. And he should know how to get the most from this position.

1. Again the body is aimed before the rifle is aimed.

2. The moment the shooter decides on his target, he shifts his feet so that they are at *about* a 45-degree angle to the right of the target for a right-handed shooter.

3. The feet are spread apart. How far? Far enough to offer stability with comfort. No one can say exactly how far that is. For me, the distance comes to about 20 inches.

Here is an offhand stance. The feet are spread apart. They are about as widely set apart as the width of the shooter's shoulders. The left arm is fairly well centered directly beneath the forearm of the rifle. The right elbow is comfortably held, not in the full formal target position, but not bent downward either. The face is fully in contact with the comb of the rifle.

Dale Storey demonstrates a fast offhand pose using a 30-30 rifle. Dale's left hand holds the forearm like the neck of a violin. His right elbow is a little lower than horizontal, comfortable, but steady. His left elbow is just about directly underneath the forearm. His feet are spread apart just a little less wide than his shoulder width, and they are pointed to the right of his intended target by about 45 degrees.

Try spreading the feet the width of your shoulders.

4. The left hand should be positioned far enough forward to offer good support. Again, the shooter can tell where this is on the forearm by shifting the left hand back and forth until the rifle is most stable (and again comfortable for the individual).

5. The left elbow is held directly underneath the forearm. It may angle outward a little if a direct in-line hold with the forearm is uncomfortable.

6. The right elbow is held as close to the horizontal as possible for the shooter to maintain.

7. The left hand controls the movement of the rifle. The right hand of course activates the trigger, but it also keeps the gun on a vertical plane, not "canted." Canting means to twist the firearm to right or left. Canting also means throwing the bullet off target. It is to be avoided by maintaining the buttplate in a vertical position, straight up and down. The right hand controls this factor.

The good shot can score remarkably well from the offhand posture, but he absolutely must master all of the steps above before this is possible. The standing position is, after all, the least steady of the stances shown here in our mini shooting lesson phase.

Running Game

The offhand stance is generally used in taking a shot at

(Right) Author uses the Moses Stick for a hasty offhand shot. The staff will help support the rifle. Note that the forearm is not actually gripped but rests on the left hand, and the left hand grips the staff.

a moving target, for it allows the most freedom of motion for the shooter, which is necessary in order to swing the rifle, to maintain the swing for purposes of proper lead, and to get off a shot at the best possible second. Shooting running game is sometimes quite difficult. But in our mini shooting lessons here are a few pointers:

1. Swing the rifle smoothly, like a shotgun, from the offhand stance, but maintain the tenets of the offhand position as stated above.

2. It is impossible to hit a running target with a stationary rifle unless the target moves into the perfect position and the trigger is pulled at that instant—highly unlikely. The rifle must be in motion in order to hit running game *with regularity*.

3. One way to make a running shot is to first hold directly on the target. This establishes the proper aiming point, especially in terms of the horizontal hold. Then the sights are moved out ahead of the moving target. The trigger is pulled when the sights are far enough ahead of the target to allow for a meeting of the target and the bullet. How far? That depends upon the distance and speed of the game. How is this learned? Experience. Lots of time spent in the game field.

4. The rifle must maintain its lead and motion when the trigger is pulled. To stop the swing is to hit behind the moving target. The trigger is pulled while the rifle is *in motion* only.

5. The face must remain upon the cheekpiece of the rifle. Some shooters try to make a quick snapshot and in doing so, they lift the face from the stock, which destroys aim.

Running Game from Other Stances

The running shot is made from the offhand position most of the time, but not all of the time. When game is very far out, and the shooter must recognize when it is too far to shoot at, the swing can be much less pronounced because of the angle of departure of the bullet. Therefore, from a sitting or kneeling position, a running shot at over 100 yards or so is quite possible and oftentimes the sitting position is the way to go because of the steadiness that position affords. Remember, if the swing is stopped prior to trigger pull, chances are the bullet will strike behind the moving target. Once again, the swing is maintained; the sights are well ahead of the target, and the trigger pull is made while the rifle is in motion.

The Sling

A sling can be used in all of the shooting stances mentioned in the rifle mini lesson section. A sling adds greatly to the steadiness of the hold. Of course, it is not used for close-range brush shots at moving targets, but in the offhand position, the sling makes for a much steadier shot. Instead of the military-style sling, I use a carrying strap. I simply loop my left arm through this strap, as shown in the illustration, and that does wonders for the holding stability of the rifle.

The Rest

The shooter should rely on a rest whenever possible. If he is in the field, he can rest the rifle over many different things without harming it. The forearm, *not* the barrel, is rested. Placing the barrel over a hard object can cause the bullet to fly off the mark, generally high on the target. A barrel vibrates as the bullet rushes downbore. To alter that vibration is to change point of impact of the bullet.

The shooter can rest his rifle over a rock or smooth boulder, but he should pad the hard spot with his hat, gloves or other cushioning item. And, as stated, the forearm goes on top of that cushion, not the barrel. I have carried a walking staff for many years in my treks into the outback. I use it as a rest. Sometimes I take an ''offhand'' shot by standing and using the rest, but often I sit and lock my body up with the shooting staff as illustrated. I have produced groups at 100 and 200 yards with this stance which rivaled the best groups I have obtained from the prone position. Fence posts, trees, tree limbs, boulders—they're all potential field rests, regardless of the firearm used.

When it comes to handgun hunting and using a rest, the

An offhand stance using the sling—the right elbow, not visible, takes a military/target-type position, quite high. The sling is used in the "hasty" fashion, with only one loop through the left arm. The left hand, as always, supports the rifle but does not choke the forearm. Both eyes are open, in spite of the use of a scope sight.

shooter should take advantage of any rest that's presented, i.e., tree limbs, fence posts, etc. The shooter should also make every effort to plant his feet firmly, brace his body against a firm object and, if possible, utilize any available support for his forearms.

At best, a handgun is much less steady than a long gun. As a result, a solid rest is imperative when it comes to accurate shot placement. It should be employed whenever possible. Like our advice to riflemen, handgunners should avoid placing the handgun barrel on the rest. Rest the butt (on a hat or other soft object); or, if you assume a two-hand hold, rest the hands on a solid object. When it comes to autoloaders, be sure the gun isn't rested in a fashion that would impede the slide during rearward travel—a jam may result.

The Benchrest

A benchrest is vital to a rifleman. He sights his firearm in off the bench, and he checks the rifle before each shooting season by using the bench. A benchrest is simple to use, but it requires a certain approach just as the other aspects of shooting do. Here are some of them:

1. Keep feet flat on the ground. Do not allow your feet to rest on the toes.

2. Make the sandbags point toward the target. Do not try

When using a hard object as a rest, be certain to support the forearm, even if nothing but the hand is used to do this. Obviously, recoil would damage the forearm with this abrasive boulder for a rest, but even if the rest were softer, the idea is to keep the forearm away from a very hard rest. It can alter barrel vibration and where the bullet will strike the target.

The handgunner can also use a rest such as the walking/shooting stick shown here. Groups will shrink amazingly with such a rest.

A rest is a welcome addition to the shot whenever a rest can be obtained. In a hunting situation, there are often available rests as part of the landscape, such as the boulder in this photo. As a part of a big game stalk, a hunter may plan ahead, looking at the terrain in front of him as he approaches his game, and hoping to find something to rest that rifle on for one sure shot.

(Left) This shooter's face is down on the comb of the stock, not uplifted. His own stance calls for an elbow at an outward position, almost rifle-style, but not in the high-hold of the target rifleman. Note the position of the offhand on the forearm—too far back? It's a matter of shooter preference.

This is an ideal benchrest setup. The bench has been properly constructed for either right- or left-handed shooters. The shooter has positioned himself at the bench, has the rifle supported at the butt and forearm, and has placed his feet flat on the ground, comfortably spread.

The shotgunner bends his knees slightly to relax them and insure that they are not locked up, which would impede his swing. The left hand grips the forearm lightly. The elbow need not be underneath the forearm for support, as this slows the swing of some shooters. The face is down on the stock. The other shooter waits his turn, already in the process of relaxing the left hand and bending the knees.

to jockey the rifle around on the sandbags.

3. Rest the rifle's forearm, not the barrel, on the sandbags for the reasons stated above.

4. Be certain that you are comfortable. Make sure that your chest is far enough from the bench to allow you to breath easily. If your feet do not rest firmly on the ground, then find something to rest them on.

5. The elbow should rest on something soft when shooting a rifle of high recoil. Such a rifle can skin the elbow along the surface of the benchrest, which is oftentimes rough wood.

6. Be certain to rest the buttstock of the rifle as well as the forearm on sandbags. A great many shooters rest the forearm, but hold the butt aloft instead of solidly resting the buttstock on a sandbag.

The Shotgun

Of course much of what has been said above pertains to shotgun shooting in those sections prior to our mini lessons. However, here are a few particulars which can aid the shotgunner in hitting more often.

1. As always, point the body first. As the target presents itself, the body goes into action.

2. The feet are slightly spread apart, as previously described.

Good stance starts before the shotgun is even lifted to the shoulder. The dogs are on point and a bird is about to rise. The shotgunner grips his gun loosely. Note that the right hand is not fully enclosed upon the grip. Note that the trigger finger is not in the trigger guard. These will be taken care of as the bird rises, in one smooth flow of movement.

3. Crouch slightly. Limber up the knees. Bend them very slightly.

4. Bring the shotgun to you. Do not put the gun up and move the body forward into the gun.

5. Do not grip that forearm. Caress it. Gently guide the muzzle with the left hand on the forearm, but allow that forearm to nestle into the hand.

6. Keep your face on the stock the entire time.

7. Never stop the swing. Follow through. Fire while the barrel is in motion. To stop and then shoot is to shoot behind the moving target.

8. Remember the "philosophy" of that shot string. Think about how it looks out in front of you.

9. Push the buttstock *into* the shoulder, not *out* on the arm.

10. Be light on your feet. Observe rhythm. Do not jerk the shotgun up. Bring it up smoothly.

The many previous statements pertaining to the position of the body have explained shotgunning for success, and these points will not be recounted here. Shooting the shotgun means closely observing the many principles laid down in this chapter, added to a lot of experience. The good shotgunner may get caught out of position, but he doesn't shoot from that stance. He moves his body quickly into position before firing. His body flows. His knees bend slightly. He never grips the forearm with a death hold. He treats the shotgun as a fine instrument, pointing it instead of aiming, but always firing when the gun is on the swing.

The Handgun

Mini lessons in handgunning can be somewhat involved in that there are many different paths to success in sidearm management. All of the stances discussed under the rifle can be maintained with the handgun. Using a two-hand hold a handgun can be shot from the prone position, or sitting or kneeling, or, of course, from the offhand stance. Shooters know these things. But I have not seen all shooters observe some of the finer points of one-handed sidearm shooting and these will be the subject of our mini shooting lessons here.

1. Begin by holding the handgun in the off hand. (This means the left hand for the right-handed shooter.)

2. Now, the gun is handed from left to right hand. The right hand closes down upon the grip so that grip *pressure* becomes the same each time. Practice will insure this. The grip is fitted into the shooting hand in the same *position* each time.

3. With each finger of the hand in the same location on the grip each time, the trigger finger is held out independent of the rest of the hand for a moment.

4. The trigger finger then moves into the guard slowly. The trigger finger acts in an almost separate fashion. The idea is to try to gently touch off the trigger without adding pressure to the rest of the fingers which are gripping the handgun.

5. Maintain the sight picture and squeeze the trigger simultaneously. The gun must "go off" during that sedentary period when the sights are optically glued to the target.

Once again, we have covered many aspects of stance

The grip of the handgun is essential to good marksmanship. The hand proper maintains the control over the Navy Arms Silhouette Pistol here. The thumb aids in control, too, but is not applied with much force. And the trigger finger "sneaks" into the guard as an independent part of the hand, squeezing with gentle pressure until the firearm goes off almost without the rest of the hand knowing what the trigger finger is doing.

The Uncle Mike's swivel and sling set for the Contender 14S can be used to steady the handgun very nicely. Stance of this sort aids in the scoring department.

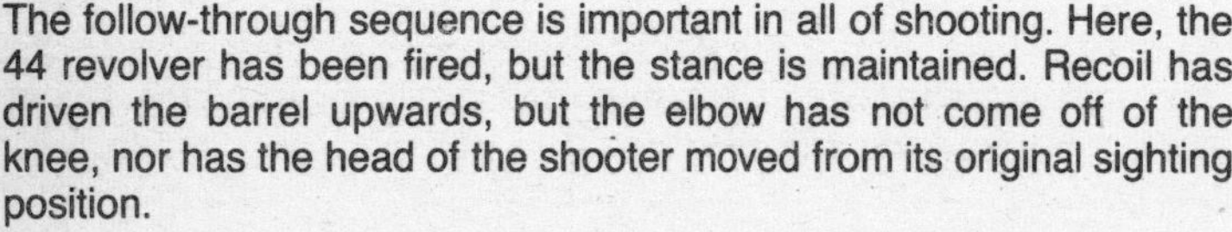

The follow-through sequence is important in all of shooting. Here, the 44 revolver has been fired, but the stance is maintained. Recoil has driven the barrel upwards, but the elbow has not come off of the knee, nor has the head of the shooter moved from its original sighting position.

and shooting in the previous material and repetition is not our aim here. However, we do observe the good rules of shooting by not locking up the elbow of the shooting arm holding the handgun. We position the feet to point to the left of the target for a right-handed shooter. I suggest a 45-degree pivot, even a bit more. The feet should be spread apart for comfort and stability.

Again, the breath control we learned for the rifle is upheld, holding the breath just prior to squeezing off the shot. If the shooter will put into practice all of the notations made previously, he will find that they work admirably for the handgun. It's a matter of control, a matter of controlling our bodies while also putting into practice the basic, but not always simple, rules of good shooting practice.

The Two-Hand Hold

Today's handgunner is likely to treat the sidearm as a handsgun, plural, instead of a handgun. That is, he will want to control the piece with both hands, not just one. In fact, most of what has been stated or will be stated on the management of the sidearm with one hand pertains to two-hand holds, including the fact that the firearm is mainly controlled by the trigger hand, with the trigger finger acting as independently as possible. The other hand, in the two-hand hold, is a steadying device. We have illustrated a couple of two-hand holds photographically, especially the two-hand grip used from the kneeling position.

The two-hand hold can also be used in a standing pose, with the feet spread apart and the gun held out in front of the shooter with both hands. From the sitting position, the handgun can be controlled with two hands also. And there have been handgun hunters who found that lying prone with both hands mastering the sidearm is one of the better ways to achieve stability. I have used this hold several times with a Thompson/Center 30-30 pistol in the taking of antelope.

The complete shooter must be a student of his sport. He needs to know a great deal about the activity in order to gain the most from it. Stance is just as important as firearm accuracy and reliability. Learning stance can make a fine marksman of a shooter who might otherwise hit the mark with haphazardness.

Chapter 14

Practice for the Practical Shooter

Good practice can be obtained with the 22 rimfire rifle and very informal shooting. Using her own Browning 22 lever-action rifle, Nancy Fadala does a little tin can rolling. Shooters can learn all of the basic precepts of good marksmanship with a 22 rimfire rifle.

PRACTICE for any sport is a simulation of sorts. The participant is trying to create a situation which closely resembles "the real thing." If he were doing that particular event "for real," then it wouldn't be practice. A shotgunner may run a round of Skeet, actually performing the exact shooting situations he would perform in competition, but even at that, he is practicing for he is not under the pressure of the actual competition. The duck hunter shoots a round of trap. The deer hunter practices on a moving target. The small game hunter plinks with a 22-caliber rifle or pistol.

It would be possible to simply list various types of practice in order to give the complete shooter a compilation to work from. But there is more to practice than simply firing and making note of hits and misses. Haphazzard shooting is not practice. Shooting without distinct goals is not practice, and failing to work toward self-improvement is not practice either. Practice is an organized (even when plinking) activity with a goal in mind—improved markmanship—and the goal is reached through specific activities.

There Are No Born Shooters

I have said it before, but it bears mentioning again. There are no born shooters. There are coordinated people with good eyesight and a steady hand, but nobody is a marksman without learning proper stance and then practicing to retain and enhance the highest level of achievement for the individual shooter. I have told the story before of my friend John Doyle and his basement target range. John and I used to shoot 22 rifles in the safety of that range. Then my friend moved to a larger taxidermy shop, one without a basement range, however. Our shooting slumped. We could not figure out why, because both of us agreed we were good, "natural shots." Well, we weren't; we were practiced shots. That frequent aiming and firing in the basement range kept our ability honed to a razor's edge. Once the practice was gone, so was our sharpness as marksmen.

Practice with firearms need not be on a regular basis, though it should be. But it must be regulated. To merely fire at a tin can, which can be practice, without noting the exact point of impact of the bullet is a waste of time unless the can is hit every shot. In other words, if a shooter does

In practicing, the shooter should always use his best stance. In the sitting position, this shooter practices the correct stabilization of the rifle.

not know where he is hitting on a target, he's not practicing. He's just shooting. Obviously, in much of our field firing, such as on small game or varmints, good transfer of ability is there, transfer from being a good small game/varmint shot to being a good big game shot. In the field, we may not always see where the misses go. But in any circumstance which allows us to fire on any type of target, we should know where the misses go as well as the hits. Even in firing at a "running deer target," the shooter needs someone behind him to at least try to determine, often through binoculars, just where the bullet hits.

Dry Firing

In dry firing, the shot should be "called." A called shot means simply the ability of the hunter to note at the instant he pulls the trigger just where the hit is going to be. I have seen good marksmen call a shot a few inches high on the target, or to the left, right, or low, as well as calling a bull's-eye. How do they do this? They have *control* of the firearm and their shooting. At the instant of firing, they know where the sight picture is pointing. They won't always hit the mark, for nobody can always squeeze off with total precision. But they know where they were aiming when the gun did fire, and that is calling the shot.

Dry firing is very important in the process of learning to call a shot and is superb practice with any firearm, including the shotgun. Dry firing means shooting without ammunition in the chamber or magazine. In order to protect a gun, a shooter may opt to use a Snap-Cap or a fired, empty cartridge in his firearm to prevent any damage to the firing pin. However, the point in dry firing is to determine where you were pointing or aiming at that split second when the firing pin fell.

The average shooter will learn to do this with live ammo, as a direct result of his dry-firing practice.

Dry Firing the Rifle

Using Snap Caps or a fired, *empty* cartridge case where applicable, the shooter should pick his target and maintain all of the tenets of good shooting posture and stance. (Again, the magazine and chamber of the rifle must be *entirely empty* as far as *live ammunition* is concerned.) The idea is to select the target, aim the body toward the target in the proper manner already discussed, mount the rifle, take careful aim and control the trigger through squeeze-off. This form of practice is just like any serious shooting of the rifle, albeit without live ammo; yet, there is one other big factor at work. Because there is no report, no recoil, nothing to cause the shooter to move a muscle during the dry-fire session, two good things happen. First, the shooter can tell exactly where the sight picture was when the trigger was pulled. He can quickly "call his shot," knowing whether he hit or missed.

Second, the shooter can *correct* his errors. It is a rather simple matter to detect improper shooting form, trigger control or sight picture, even stance and canting of the rifle, during the dry-fire session. The shooter can now learn to call his shots on the range and in the field. Through dry firing he can actually train himself to control and manage the firearm with professional skill. He may learn things through dry firing he can never find out during actual shooting sessions. Dry firing a rifle can also show a shooter a specific bad habit, one he may never detect while firing live ammo.

Dry Firing the Handgun

There is little difference in the philosophy between dry firing the handgun and dry firing the rifle. Again, a sight picture is taken, the firearm fully controlled and the trigger mastered. Again, the shooter sees exactly where his sight picture was optically "pasted" when the fall of the striker

Dry firing can be an important part of any practice session. This youngster is in the process of learning the basics. Dry firing is a natural place to start.

was heard. And again he can learn to be a superb handgunner through dry firing because he can detect his problems and correct them, all the while building the best possible shooting habits in a situation free of recoil or noise.

Dry Firing the Shotgun

If anything, the matter of shotgun control is a bit more involved than rifle/handgun control. The latter are more rigid, more ordered. You mount the rifle or raise the handgun, maintain proper overall stance and squeeze off. Of course there's more to it than that, but with a shotgun there are matters of balance to consider, matters of swing, follow-through and total control of the body through fluid motion and unlocked joints. Dry firing can improve the shotgunners score by allowing him to snap off many hundreds of practice "shots" without so much as one pellet leaving the barrel.

An off-season walk through the fields with shotgun in hand is an ideal setup for some dry-fire practice. The gun can be carried in a natural hunting posture and quickly brought to the shoulder to track a bird on the wing.

With the shotgun, however, you will have to concentrate on your target in a different manner. You may, in fact, have no actual target. To pick out a stationary object and swing on it is somewhat counterproductive, for you may learn to stop your swing in order to "click off" at the instant the bead or barrel is pointing at the target.

Instead, the shooter may have to use his imagination, swinging the gun and firing when he has properly led a target which exists only in his mind or in the reality of a sparrow winging its way through your backyard. A shotgunner could also have targets of one sort or another tossed for him. But he is more likely to use dry firing as something he can do at the spur of the moment, perhaps daily for a mere few moments a session.

One of the advantages of dry firing the shotgun is the fact that you'll learn to *coordinate* all of the important individual components of good shotgunning—the matter of body form, handling the gun itself, placement of the feet, swing, continued swing, follow-through and even sight picture, for there is a sight picture with shotgunning, even if it is pointing instead of aiming. You will also learn how a particular shotgun fits your body. Sometimes recoil actually blots out a tiny problem with shotgun fit. But in dry firing that recoil factor is nil. Dry firing the shotgun will keep a shooter in tune when he cannot get out to do the real thing. And even if he can get out and fire live ammo, the shotgunner should still use the dry-fire method when it

Games make practice fun. This shooter is trying to split a black powder round ball on the edge of an axe imbedded in a log. If he does split the lead ball in two, the two pieces will break the clay pigeons on either side of the blade. Shoots such as this one offer practice as well as competition.

comes to learning more about his gun and about how he handles it.

Plinking

Plinking is thought of as 22 rimfire work, and I suppose the term best fits that activity. But, in fact, plinking is simply informal shooting, with a rifle, handgun, or even shotgun at various objects which are not official targets; that is, targets with bull's-eyes and scoring rings. Any safe background is a good plinking spot as long as the setting is correct, away from occupied buildings and anyone who would be bothered by the noise. Plinking is live-ammo work of course.

Most plinking, I think, takes place on the common tin can. A tin can is a pretty good target. It won't always jump when hit, but it usually will from a 22 rimfire strike. And it is easily picked up and discarded after a plinking session. On the other hand, glass items are wrong for plinking. They can shatter in all directions, and they amount to litter. The major caution, however, aside from the all-important safety aspects of this mini-sport, is having order maintained. Random firing does not teach a shooter much, and learning is the reason for practice, as well as keeping ourselves in fine tune as marksmen. Random plinking, then, is, to me, relatively worthless. When I am plinking, I insist that the targets be set up in such a way that I can actually see where I hit, or to be more accurate about it, where I missed. Tossing tin cans in the brush and plinking away at them can be all right for learning to pick a spot through the brush, but at the very least, I want to know how many holes are in those targets so I can see how many hits I made for sure, all guesswork aside.

One afternoon a friend had a good idea concerning a plinking session. He brought along a couple of metal stakes, put them opposite each other with a safe backstop behind them, and then he tied a string at the top of each stake so that it stretched out straight. To this string, he attached a series of charcoal briquets, hanging by individual strings. The briquets easily indicating a hit.

The only problem was actual background. It was safe, but too far away to show us where the misses landed. The next time we set up a similar series of targets, we did so with a clay wall a couple of feet behind the targets. With 22 rimfire ammo it was easy to see where the bullets struck —we could instantly determine if we were hitting high or low, left or right, rather than noting a miss as a miss and nothing more.

Games

Actually, even Skeet and trap amount to shooting games, even though both can be highly serious competition. Trying to distinguish between a shooting game and a shooting event might be fruitless, but I consider a game to be non-official. A target match has awards and, stringent rules, which can only be altered by consent of a committee in charge. The ordinary shooting game for the sake of practice may contain plenty of competition, but it's a friendly affair and certainly not official in any sense.

Shooting games are limited by two things, safety and imagination. All shooting is to be conducted with good backstops, of course, and in an appropriate setting. As for imagination, that can run wild as long as the rules of safety are adhered to. Draw a circle in the sand with a stick. Put a bunch of tin cans in the center of the circle. Taking turns, two or more shooters can try to skip the tin cans out of the circle (rim shots on the cans work best) using 22 rimfire rifles or the new and powerful air rifles. That's a shooting game. Is there any transfer value in such a game? I think so, and transfer value is essential to all practice. In this case, the shooter learns to take aim at a small, specific point, and he must use good stance and firearm control if he is going to win. Sloppy shooting won't do it, though of course, a good run of luck might help.

At very close range, as close as 20 or 30 feet, line up a series of spent 22 rimfire cases, preferably on a log or other platform. The shooter who can snap these little cases off the log by scoring a direct hit and not by "barking them off," is doing quite well for himself. He has to master trigger control, for example, because he won't do very well by jerking the trigger when the sight picture looks right. The target is too small to allow for sloppy shooting.

We have slipped a series of kitchen matches, the wooden matches with the tips that ignite easily, in a row, into the tiny crevices of a downed tree's bark. The winner will ignite the most matches by skimming a bullet, usually a 22 rimfire slug, across the head of the match without blowing the match to pieces. Few riflemen will strike many matches, but it's not impossible to light those matches without hitting them solidly, as long as the distance remains at 20 feet or so.

Gather up some strips of wood. They should be thin, maybe 1/4-inch or so in thickness, and fairly narrow, possibly 2 inches across. These little stakes are placed firmly into the ground. They are identical and the shooters compete by trying to cut those stakes in half with bullets. The shooters can either fire as many times as they wish as rapidly as they can, provided they have similar firearms (a fellow with a single-shot would be at a distinct disadvantage), or they can insure that all shooters take the same number of shots. Either way, it takes good bullet placement to cut a stake in half.

Balloons make good targets. If a person wants to go through the trouble, he can have the balloons filled with helium so they will rise. These are simply set at a distance, such as 100 yards using the 22 rimfire rifle or 50 yards for handguns, and the shooter who breaks the most balloons with the least shots wins the game. The same game can be played with a shotgun, except in shotgunning the balloons, the helium-filled targets are allowed to drift skyward. This is safe, of course, in the right area.

I'm sure the reader gets the idea. Cans filled with water tend to explode when hit by a bullet, even a bullet fired from the 22 rimfire round. Water-filled cans make interesting targets for shooting games. Clay pigeons are meant for shotgunning, but they are also interesting rifle and handgun targets. The good 22 rimfire rifleman (even some exceptional handgunners) can draw figures on flat pieces of tin or other metal by the use of the bullet placement. The famous Indian head silhouettes fired by various exhibition shooters comes to mind, but other outlines are also possible. Another game I have a good deal of fun with, and it must be termed a game, is placing dirt-filled empty beverage cans at a full 200 yards and firing on them with a 22 rifle. Wind drift is a problem, a problem fun to solve in this little game. And drop is not easily figured either. Sometimes an entire box of 22 rimfire ammo will be gone before a mere half dozens cans are toppled.

This Federal Champion clay target is much more sophisticated than may meet the eye. It is made of a special construction to break easily when struck by a pellet from a shotgun, but not to break into bits during transportation. It is aerodynamic as well. And it comes in colors, all-orange for high visibility, black for a desert or grey/brown background, white for nighttime shooting and orange dome only for a clear blue sky background. A box full of "clays" and a simple hand trap makes for excellent practice.

Clay Pigeons

The shotgunner has a fine target available to him. It sails neatly through the air and it breaks easily when hit. This is the clay pigeon or clay target. It's a simple disc, at first glance, but there is more to it than that. The Champion brand clay target, for example, has a bright upper center portion for visibility and pointing purposes. The clays come with blaze orange, yellow, white or black centers for good contrast depending upon the background. Champion

Skeet or trap shooting are often formalized affairs. However, if the local range isn't too busy the shotgunner may be able to run a round of Skeet or trap *alone*. Opportunities like these allow a shooter to sharpen his game-field shooting positions.

has what is known as a Hi-Thin dome for easy breakability. The rim is designed to feed smoothly in hand trap units or sophisticated trap or Skeet machines.

Clay birds are smooth so they fly uniformly from one bird to the next and are uniform one batch to the next in form, shape, and weight. Clays come in large or small packs. I purchase them by the case, 135 clays to the case. The clay target is a sophisticated unit with very special characteristics, and the shotgunner can enjoy practice on these "birds" with the use of a simple hand trap or a full-fledged machine. Obviously, the clay bird can be tossed under full regulation procedures and distances at a trap or Skeet club, or simply winged into the sky with the hand trap. With the latter, we can toss the targets out at a grass-skimming level to simulate quail shooting, for example. The clay target is a shotgunner's practice medium, as well as an interesting rifle/handgun target.

Air Gun Practice

The air rifle or air pistol makes splendid target practice possible for the shooter on a daily basis. We are all busy these days, but no shooter is too busy to take 10 minutes after work so that he can pop off a handful of pellets in the basement. The air gun is just about as close as you are going to get to dry firing. Indeed, recoil is so minimal and blast nonexistent that, with a decent scope sight from close range, one can see the hole(s) produced in the target.

I met the famous shooter Colonel Charles Askins on a flight to South Africa not long ago and learned from him that he tries to make that African trip on an annual basis. What's more, the Colonel practices with an air rifle as a *major* means of getting ready for his hunt. When he leaves for Africa, he feels confident that he can hit a mark without a hitch, and that confidence is built on a solid foundation of regular air gun practice. I think this speaks highly for the idea of practicing with air power. Askins practices *every day* with either a 22 rimfire target rifle or an air gun. *Every day*. If a shooter of his ability feels that daily practice is necessary, I believe the rest of us can take heed and practice a bit, too.

Askins often fires a routine with his air rifle. He will fire 10 times from the sitting position and 10 times in the offhand stance. He practices on a 50-foot indoor range using targets with a bull's-eye measuring 1.75 inches across and a 10-ring of 3/32-inch. He feels that the more formal target beats any kind of plinking because the shooter can tell *precisely* where he hit. Plinking at a tin can may mean firing 10 times, missing four of those shots, but not truly knowing where those four shots went. Nor, for that matter, will a shooter often closely note where his hits registered on the tin can. This is not to knock plinking. Plinking is fine, but the Colonel has a point—practice at least part of the time on the type of target that will show you precisely where you hit (and missed).

I said that the Colonel practices in the sitting position and in the offhand posture. What about the kneeling or prone stances? The Colonel feels both are fairly useless to the shooter practicing for big game hunting, and he is right. Once in a while, a prone position shot is possible, and now and then a kneeling shot may be called for, but the sitting shot is going to be easy to assume and useful most of the time in open terrain, while the standing shot is generally the norm in the brush and woods.

Let's not lose sight of the fact that we practice for transfer value. We want to learn how to do "A" so that "B" is more easily accomplished. In this case, the Colonel wants to be a fine air gun marksman so that this ability will transfer into the field during big game hunting. And it works. The idea is to *consciously* assume your practice positions so that you are making good habits all the while. Sloppy practice, I think, is about next to worthless. Simply "listening" to the *crack* of a 22 rimfire never made a shooter of anyone. With the air-powered rifle or handgun, the shooter can practice "calling the shot."

Small Game and Varmints

Transfer value. That, again, is the name of the game when we hunt small game or varmints as practice. When I was growing up in Arizona, a young shooter almost automatically took to the desert in pursuit of jackrabbits. There were a great many rabbits and the ranchers and citizens of the area knew full well that management of the hares was as good as the practice it provided for the youngsters learning to harvest those hares. I believed then and still maintain that if a marksman can consistently hit a running jackrabbit at even 100 yards, a target as large as a deer is a cinch for him.

As a kid, I would often assume the sitting position and cleanly drop a jackrabbit at 300 yards, and there is no exaggeration in the statement, but rather a bit of understatement. Quite often I would pace 400 long steps over fairly flat terrain to retrieve a dead jack. I'd call 400 long steps at least 300 true yards. I learned to shoot with a sling during those hunts and learned to dope out the wind. I found out how to sustain a lead and, conversely, learned that to stop the swing usually meant a miss on a running jackrabbit.

Small game hunting has many transfer traits, too. The hunter who can regularly bag a cottontail on the run, at any range, even 20 yards, with a 22 rimfire is on his way to becoming a remarkable big game shot. Even when the requirement is not so stringent, such as a sitting shot at a cottontail or squirrel at 40 or 50 yards, remember that with a rifle it's the head shot that counts, and the head, a target roughly 2 inches across, is no easy mark. You bet. If a person can take small game under all small game hunting situations, he is going to be fairly well practiced for big game hunting and its shooting problems.

Of course, seasons for small game are not open year around. Varmints generally are huntable year around but may not be available. So the previously mentioned practice sessions, as with the air gun, is still vital to continued sharpness in marksmanship. Varmints and small game, however, often provide the most difficult shots in all of field shooting. They are generally small targets and often on the move. A rifleman or handgunner can sharpen his eye considerably on these targets. The varminter who can reduce the prairie dog or woodchuck population from 300 yards and farther knows his rifle, its trajectory and how to dope out the wind. All of these are going to transfer into the big game dominion.

Off-season varminting has great transfer value when the hunting season rolls around. Dropping a woodchuck at 300 yards, or more, serves to build the shooter's confidence in both himself and his equipment.

Moving Target Practice

Small game and varmints often provide moving targets. But they are not always available. There are two ways, however, and probably many more, to gain confidence on moving marks. The first is to set up a moving deer target at the local shooting range. The fun here is in the form of competition, and many clubs have running deer shoots at which prizes are given. The running deer target is set up in

The better (read that, "more organized") private and public ranges often have a moving-target field. If you have access to, for example, a running deer setup, take advantage of it. The practice may make the difference between success and failure in the field.

various ways. The one I shot at was at the Tucson Rod & Gun Range in Tucson, Arizona. Basically, it amounted to a small deer cutout with an old plate attached to it. The deer slid on a down-angled wire with a pulley. It not only sped along, but it sped along at a downward angle, making the shot pretty difficult from the 200-yard range offhand. Also, "hitting the deer" was considered a miss. You had to hit the dinner plate attached to the side of the deer, representing a hit in the vitals.

I have also heard of running deer targets being set up on a pulley arrangement with a bicycle type unit powering it. The deer's speed of motion was dictated by how fast the pedals of the bike were churned. This type of running target could be set up on the horizontal and the speed altered.

Another means of practicing the running shot is to paste or wedge a target into the open middle area of an old car tire. The tire can be rolled down an incline with a safe backstop, the shooter seeing how well he can do in placing his shots in the moving bull's-eye. The person who rolls the tire is protected because he does so from behind a hill. Under no circumstances would it be allowable for the tosser to stand out in the open and roll the tire. But from behind a hill he's safe from a bazooka, let alone a deer rifle or 22 rimfire.

The Benchrest

Unfortunately, most shooters fail to think of the benchrest as a practice place, but it can be. A solid bench setup can allow a shooter to practice many phases of the shooting art. He must learn to maintain a good stance, even if it is a sedentary one, and he must master his breathing and other body controls, as well as firearms management. Oftentimes, good trigger pull is learned at the benchrest, and I think a lot about trajectory and actual bullet flight can also be found out from the bench. Certainly, the shooter learns much about sighting and holding a sight picture from the benchrest as well. He also finds out a lot about recoil and recoil management from the bench. These phases of shooting all transfer to the target range or the field. The benchrest is indeed a good place to practice from.

The Formal Target Shoot

The shooter who practices on a formal target range is certainly doing himself some good, although I think the major "good" he attains is in the area of winning

Practice from the bench is well-advised. However, even from the bench, all good points of stance are adhered to. And use hearing protection whenever possible.

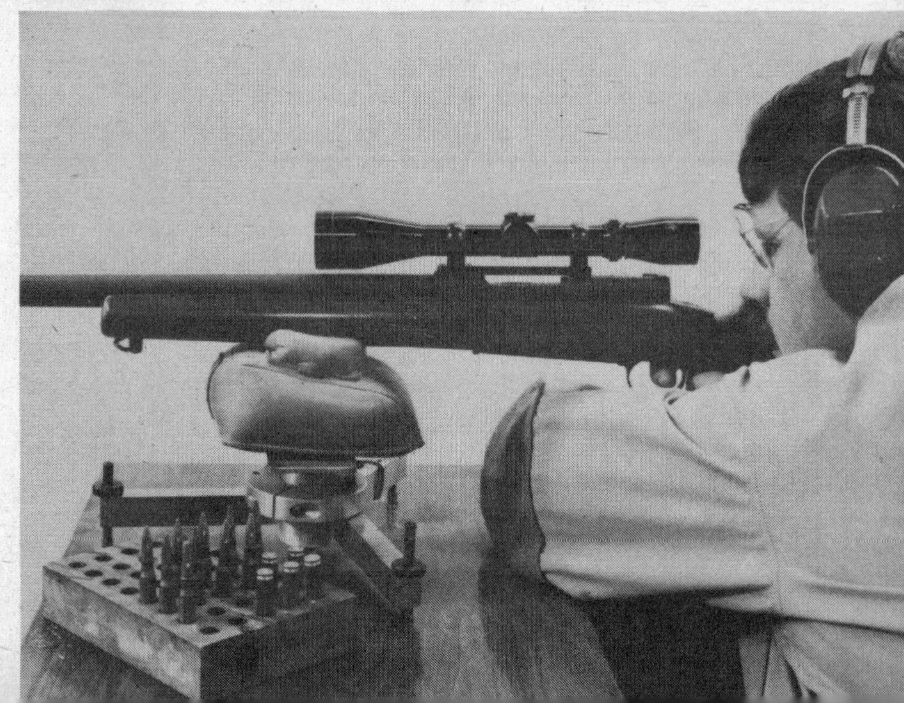

Even if the session is for practice only, the shooter must use the proper rests and position at the bench for best results. Note that the forearm, not the barrel, is placed upon the pads, and the shooter is comfortable as well as stable.

matches. For reasons I will never understand, I have found that all good target shots are not necessarily good game shots. I happen to know three men who have taken world marksmanship titles of one sort or another with the rifle. None of these three is a good big game shot. I have seen them shoot. They miss more than they hit in the field, but perhaps this has to do with factors other than direct shooting reasons.

Let's face it. If a man can shoot, *he can shoot*. I think that the three marksmen I mentioned above actually "talk" themselves out of the game hits. Being methodical competitors, they need to find out what is causing a miss in the field, which would, otherwise, be a cinch on the range. And they need to correct that problem. I have watched some of those world-class marksmen take a stance which seemed perfect, only to witness another miss on big game. I sometimes think they have learned to master the steady stance so well that they fail to "stay loose" on big game.

Proof, I have none, but the formal target shooter misses big game because he is applying the stringent rules of the range to the field. Basically, shooting is shooting. Body control is body control. Trigger squeeze is trigger squeeze. Sight picture is sight picture, and it matters not what the target is, a painted bull's-eye or the side of a deer. But there are differences between formal marksmanship and good field shooting. The formal target shooter may be missing because he is too rigid, too regimented, too formal and too stiff. But I also feel that good target shooting is a boon to good field shooting. The big difference is the type of target. A formal bull's-eye type target isn't going anywhere at all. It's stationary. It's also not "the real thing." The game animal, on the other hand, is a coiled spring ready to charge out of sight with the flick of an eyelash. Formal target shooting makes my heart pound. I get shy and self-conscious on the range, with dozens of other shooters and spectators looking on. But I don't seem to choke up on game. I think, perhaps, that the opposite may be true for some very fine target shooters.

My advice—do all of the formal target shooting you desire to do. Do not feel that knowing how to put holes in paper bull's-eyes will hamper your ability to hit a game animal. I do not see how it could. But be aware, too, that shooting game is very different from shooting targets, and the expert target shooter may not be an expert game shot. Game can be seen at any angle, in motion or as still as a buried city, very close to the hunter or very far away, in the brush or out in the open. The good game shot works the angles like a fine billiards player deals with the angles on his table. The bullet travels a line which intersects that point where the game is or is going to be. Shoot paper all you want. But keep in tune with some practical practice, too. A little small game hunting, of course, never did a shooter any harm in sharpening the eye.

The Silueta

Following our formal target shooting at paper bull's-eyes comes the game out of Mexico which is now an international competition, *silueta,* born in Mexico, shared with American shooters and now adopted by the latter as their very own shooting sport. I covered the first national *silueta* competition in Tucson, Arizona on assignment for *Gun World* magazine, and knew the sport would overtake us. The reason for the silhouette's popularity is two-fold. First, the game offers a real challenge. There is nothing overly simple about hitting that small metallic target at ranges up to 500 meters from the offhand posture or stance. Second, the game promotes shooting interest. It is much more interesting for bystanders to watch a metal target fall than to guess at where the bullet went on the paper, not knowing, usually, until told by the score-keeper. As opposed to for-

Those who pursue formal target shooting, like this military competitor will become extremely proficient at "doping" out windage and elevation at specific ranges. It must be said, however, that the ability to hit the bull's-eye, under formal shooting conditions, doesn't always transfer well to the game fields.

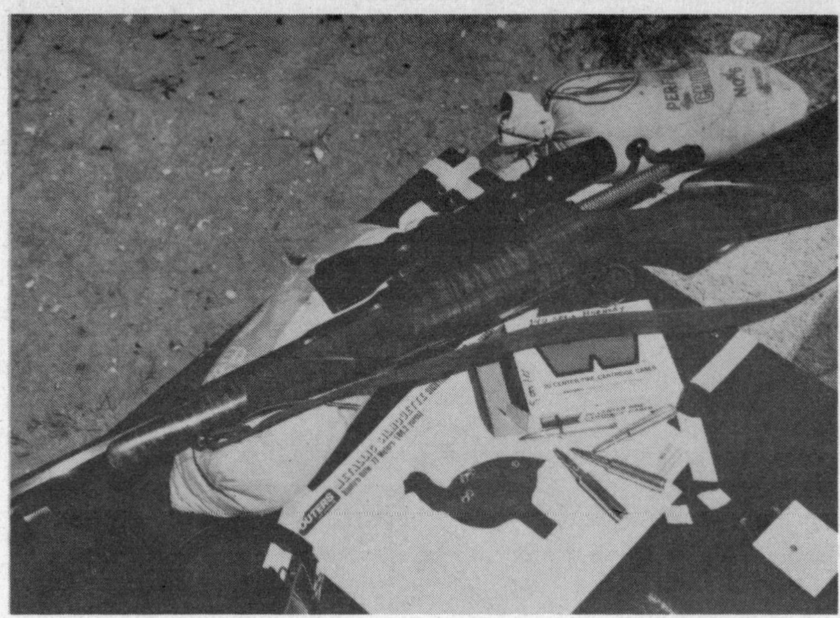

Practicing with your favorite rifle will make all the difference when the hunting season rolls around. The shooter will know the firearm inside and out, and he will be able to handle the rifle smoothly and efficiently. The man using this rifle is sighting in for some informal silhouette shooting. It's an excellent way to sharpen the eye for big game.

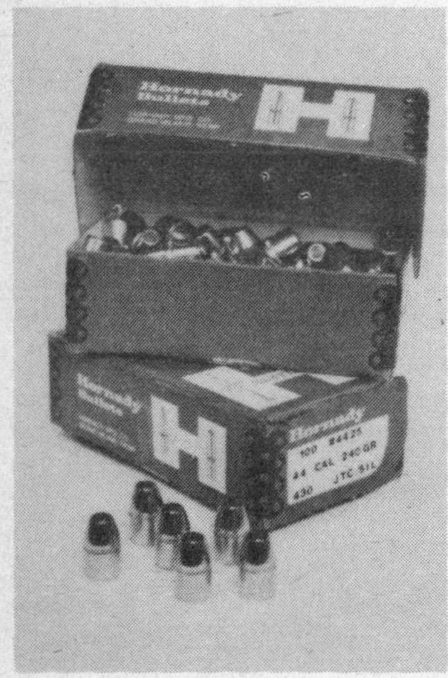

The silhouette handgunning game has brought about new bullets, such as these Hornady 44-caliber 240-grain jacketed truncated cone silhouette bullets. Interestingly, the harder core of these bullets make them good for big game hunting, too, especially where added penetration is desirable.

mal paper punching, silhouette shooting is animated.

Briefly, the idea of the *siluetas metalicas,* Spanish for metal silhouettes, is to fire a big game, hunting-weight scoped rifle, oftentimes chambered for the 308 Winchester at metal animal silhouettes. The shooting is from offhand only. The targets are: *gallina* (chicken) at 200 meters, *javelina* (peccary) at 30 meters, *guajolote* (turkey) at 385 meters and *borrego* (sheep) at 500 meters. The shooter gets 10 shots at each type for a total of 40 rounds in the match, not counting sighting-in shots of course. Although the sport waned in Mexico, it is flourishing here and is an NRA sanctioned activity, complete with a set of rules.

Silhouette shooting promotes big game hunting accuracy. In order to hit a silhouette the shooter must of course be very good with his rifle, knowing it inside and out, so to speak. His sighting must be superb, and he must be able to switch sight-settings for the various ranges, from 200 meters all the way out to 500 meters, taking bullet drop into consideration. He needs to be a master at doping the wind, too, for the breezes drift a bullet easily off target at long ranges. His silhouette loads need to be excellent as well, because hitting the metal target does not count. It must be knocked over. Because of this, the bullet companies have brought out a good many projectiles designed for optimum performance in silhouette shooting. Accuracy, obviously, must be top notch, with half-minute groups called for. Again, the scope manufacturers have catered to the silhouette shooter by offering him special optics for the sport.

The original big bore silhouette competition has branched out into handguns and 22 rimfires. The former is really going wild. There is a special group called the IHMSA, International Handgun Metallic Silhouette Association, and the membership has reached thousands. Handgun silhouette targets range from the chicken cutout at 50 meters to a ram at 200 meters, with a *javelina* at 100 meters, a turkey silhouette at the 150-meter mark. There are "production" and "unlimited" classes, the first being for factory-made guns, the second for any type of hand-held firearm. Limitations, of course, are imposed so that the sport can continue with good regulation. The area of 22 rimfire silhouette shooting is going to grow rapidly, because it is a game which can be played without the ultra long range necessary for the big bore event.

Siluetas metalicas is one of the most interesting shooting sports ever devised, not only for participants, but also for onlookers. It offers some of the most fantastic hunting practice yet devised. The challenge is so great that few

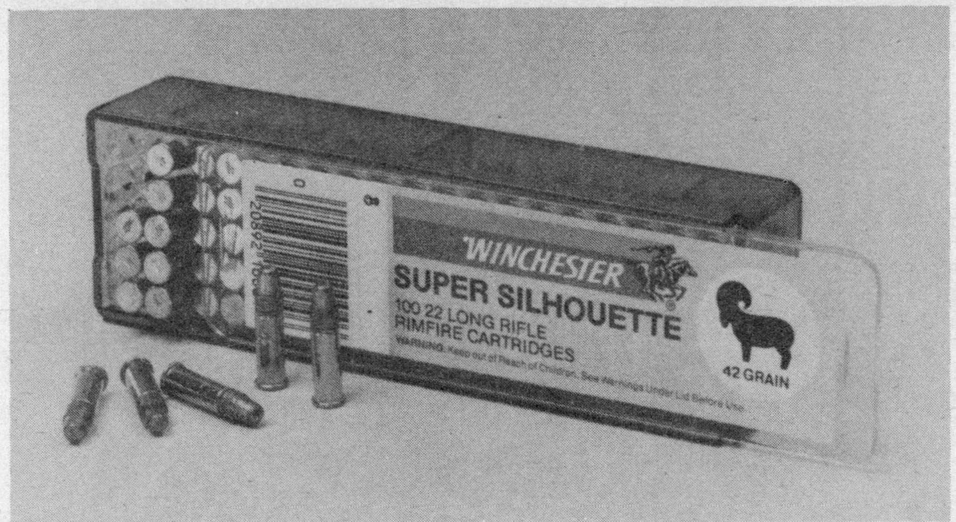

Winchester was well aware that of the excellent interest in silhouette shooting in the rimfire class, and the company has offered these special 22 Long Rifle loads for the purpose. They are loaded with a 42-grain truncated cone bullet.

shooters could ever grow bored of this sport. And anyone who can consistently score well in a silhouette match would simply have to be very good on game. After all, this is not a sport of bull's-eyes, but of animal shapes. The targets are, of course, sedentary and they do not include that special excitement which comes only in the harvesting of real game, but they do offer fine practice for the hunter. In fact, the sport was started by hunters, for hunters, when it originated in Mexico.

Keep It Up

Practicing any skill means work and dedication. The high jumper does not rely on his raw ability to win the track meet. He practices. The football quarterback does not rely on his strong arm alone to win the game. He practices. And practice is the byword for all other sports as well. Shooting is a sport in the best sense of the term. It requires skill. It requires knowledge. It demands the use of the body in a very special way, where numerous functions must be mastered and used simultaneously and in synchronization. And it is a sport that demands *practice*.

The practice cannot be done for you, of course. You have to do it for yourself. Generally speaking, the more you practice, the better you are going to get. In my youthful days it was my ability to shoot straight, which helped lead me into the profession I hold today as "gunwriter." I truly felt blessed with an ability to fire a gun, which especially thrilled me because I was uncoordinated and not much good in most other sports, except for tennis and soccer. My friends shot well, too.

We often repaired to a tall dirt bank near our neighborhood. That big bank was a safe backstop for our shooting and we used to fire at tossed tin cans, the can-thrower standing behind the shooter of course. It took some pretty good marksmanship to knock tin cans out of the air with a 22 rimfire rifle, and I managed to do that in the 7-out-of-10 category. Today, I do not feel confident that I could come close to repeating that particular type of shooting demand. It was a feat demanding fine tuning of the shooter and that fine tuning came because we practiced on a *daily* basis or close to it. Confidence grew out of that practice, and confidence is the reward of shooting practice no matter the branch of the sport.

If I said that shooting practice was meant to improve marksmanship, the reader would chalk that statement up as the redundancy of the century, and yet I see a great deal of practice; informal shooting would be a better term for it, which is really not conducive to improvement of the shooting skill. Most shooters have not *structured* the practice session so that it: A.) teaches them what they were doing wrong; B.) helps correct the faults.

Good practice is structured practice. It has a goal. The shooter sets up a condition, no matter how informal the shoot is, right down to the simple shooting of tin cans in a circle scratched into the dirt. He consciously goes about firing his guns so that he can record the results, if not formally, at least mentally. If he shoots at clay birds with a shotgun, he works on stance all the while. He keeps track of his scores, noting the misses as well as the hits.

He might discover that he hits under certain specific circumstances with certain specific firearms, while missing more than he thinks he should with other guns and in other situations. The shooter has to take note of these facts and do something about them. The shooter says to himself, "I am shooting for a reason. I want to know my shooting faults. I want to correct them. I want to strain the most from my own innate ability to coordinate myself, control my firearms, make them work for me." With this attitude, the shooter is going somewhere. He's going toward better and better marksmanship. He will be limited only by those physical attributes which pertain to shooting, such as eyesight, and he will be limited, too, by his own willingness, or lack of willingness to practice—a lot.

Chapter 15
Aiming Devices

CAPTAIN JOHN DILLIN, in his well-known book, *The Kentucky Rifle*, NRA, 1924, researched many flintlock rifles of early America and found that hunters used the plain open sight more than any other. That's no surprise, but the Captain also learned that those early sights, fixed into dovetail grooves with only windage adjustment, were so constructed as to insure the bullet/ball would strike the bull's-eye at 50 to 75 yards or so, falling about 3 inches below the line of sight at 100 yards. This would be called a "point blank" sight adjustment for about 100 yards, meaning that the shooter would not aim high or low on a target from zero to 100 yards, even if the target were only 3 or 4 inches high.

We see right away that sights and sighting had reached a certain level of sophistication rather early in shooting history. Gunpowder was not in wide use, actually, until the 1600s and we have to call the 1700s a good starting point in any discussion of modern shooting. And yet, in the 1700s, the concept of sighting devices was very well established. In those days the target models in flintlock form used a very fine pinhead front sight, a sight which I have used to this day on the Navy Arms Whitworth replica, and a sight which provides a very clear, fine picture. It seems to stand almost alone when the sight radius is long.

In the same era, it was not impossible to find the rear sight in "peep" form. A tiny hole was cut into a disc which was mounted so that the shooter could peer through it and see the front sight, which was often of the "globe" type. With this sight picture the globe appears as a ball all but suspended in mid-air. The combination is called, quite simply, "peep-and-globe sights." The globe is back today, offered by Freeland and Redfield. It's an excellent set-up for target shooting.

Before long there was the "tube sight." Old photographs show the long tubes, often running the entire length of the gun barrel. They appear to be scope sights and are often mistaken as such, but there was no glass inside of those tubes. They were metallic sights, aiming devices about 3/8-inch to 5/8-inch in diameter. The tube would sport a globe in front with a peep aperture mounted in an eyecup affair at the rear. Unfortunately, I have no photos of original tube sights, but the reader can see the advantage of isolating the light within the tube itself. Some very fine shooting was accomplished with the tube sight. Telescopic sights were known in the Civil War era, too, so our major ideas on modern sights are not really new ones, though they are certainly refined in many respects.

The Open Iron Sight

Sights are for alignment. I know that sounds painfully simplified, but it's a great starting point for an open sight discussion. No matter the experience of the shooter, if he does not actually *think* of the open sight system in terms of alignment, he's probably never going to be truly expert with the open sight. A good comparison can be made using the shotgun. The shooter who has a good concept of shot string is going to have a much better chance of pointing the gun in order to intercept the target. The open sight shooter who thinks in terms of aligning the rifle or handgun via the open sight system is like the shotgunner, well on his way to hitting the mark. Sight alignment is extremely important to good open sight shooting, and in my opinion, there is still a lot of room for the "old-fashioned" open sight in modern shooting.

Essentially, the open iron sight is no more than a post or bead up front with a notch at the back part of the gun for that bead to optically rest in. Sound simple? It is simple. But many modern shooters do some poor work with the open sight. There are a few things to consider. In order to hit the target with the open sight arrangement, there must be a *specific* alignment of that front sight within the open notch of the rear sight. The reason for so many dozens of variations in open iron sights, both front and rear, is the fact that shooters disagree upon what is most easily aligned and most easily seen as sights.

Basically, what we want is a highly visible front sight which fits into the configuration of the rear sight notch. When we align these two with near perfection, we are pointing the barrel in such a manner that the bullet can strike what the sights are holding on optically. The muzzle points upward because the sights are fixed to the barrel in such a manner as to cause that situation.

It would be a simple matter, then, to align the front sight into the rear sight notch and then pull the trigger when these two aligned sights were optically held upon the tar-

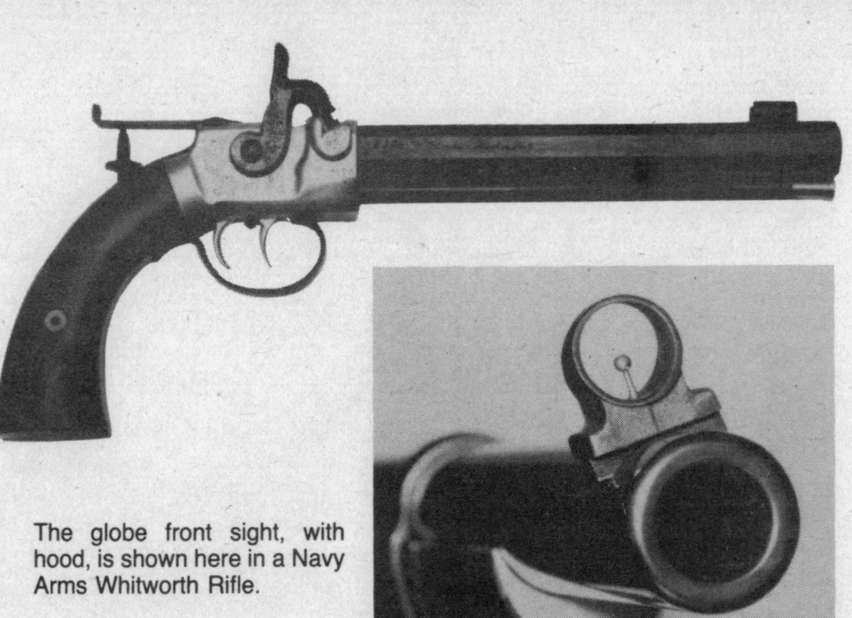

Many variations in sights have been established over the years. This rear sight has an elevation device located in the upper grip of the pistol. A threaded shaft forces the sight upward in order to raise the point of impact. Of course, the rear sight is also adjustable in that it can be lowered to a point where the shank of the rear sight is about in plane with the top barrel flat. This is a Daniel Baird Wesson Pistol from Garrett Imports.

The globe front sight, with hood, is shown here in a Navy Arms Whitworth Rifle.

(Below) Detonics offers a special Combat Selector adjustable sight for the 45 pistol, fitting military and commercial models. Note the two white dots. These form reference points for the shooter to go by.

The open sight is hardly obsolete. Handguns enjoy the use of open sights primarily, and they work well for many shooters. Here is a gold bead front sight for the Ruger Redhawk. Note how the front sight fits into the dovetail slot. It can be changed to a different style with little trouble.

This Thompson/Center Patriot Pistol wears a post front sight with an open hood.

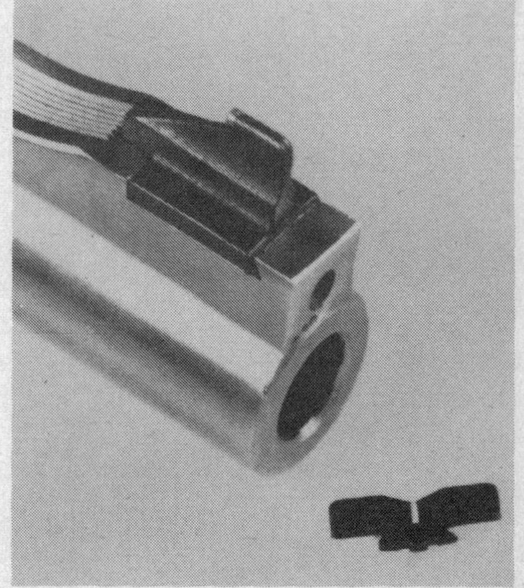

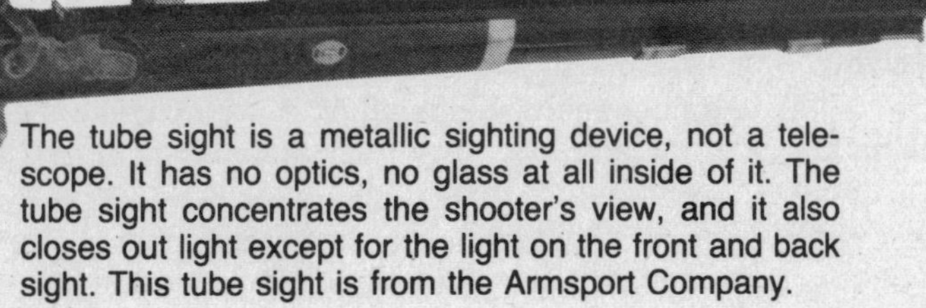

The tube sight is a metallic sighting device, not a telescope. It has no optics, no glass at all inside of it. The tube sight concentrates the shooter's view, and it also closes out light except for the light on the front and back sight. This tube sight is from the Armsport Company.

get. The problem is *frame of reference*. It is not enough to put the front sight into the notch of the rear sight and then aim at the target and pull the trigger. There must be a clearly understood frame of reference in operation here. And that is why the front sight must fit *properly* into the rear sight notch so that the shooter can achieve the same frame of reference over and over again. I have seen sighting arrangements whereby the front sight post or bead literally filled the entire notch of the rear sight, optically speaking. No good.

If the front sight literally fills up the notch, a frame of reference is *lost* to the shooter. The shooter must be able to determine *when* he has achieved alignment. Therefore, it is well for the front sight to rest within the rear sight notch in such a manner that *light* can be seen on both sides of that front sight bead or post. The side light is necessary because it provides you with a shot-to-shot frame of reference. With some light on both sides of the bead as its rests within the rear sight notch, you can quickly determine that there *is* alignment. If the bead gets lost in the notch, we can never tell, shot-to-shot, just how to hold our sight picture.

Shooters have to watch for this when buying a firearm with open iron sights. I have seen sights that had no light on either side of the bead, even though those sights were made with an apparent attempt to match the bead and notch. As a result, the shooter has to guess when the front bead is truly aligned with the rear sight notch. If the shooter finds that his open-sighted rifle (or even handgun) has this problem, he must opt for a thinner post or a smaller bead up front.

Bead Size

The topic of bead size is important not only for alignment purposes, but also for individual situations. First, of course, is the fact that the bead must *fit* the rear notch. Does it seem that it's a foregone conclusion that it would? Well it is not certain that the bead/notch fit will suit us all in factory style. I have, more than once, removed a front sight and replaced it with one carrying a smaller bead so I could get that vital frame of reference advantage mentioned. Also, bead size depends upon particular use. A good big bead is fine for woods shooting where the game is close. Some shooters find that with a large bead, especially an ivory colored bead, speed in "getting on the game" is enhanced for close-range work. Maybe it is. I have never found it any sort of problem getting a rather fine bead on target, even in deep woods. The shooter who needs good fast open iron sights for whatever purpose should consider looking into the larger bead. But never should the bead be so large as to totally fill the rear sight notch, thereby destroying the frame of reference.

Two good bead sizes are 1/16-inch and 3/32-inch width. I have the 1/16-inch bead size on rifles of mine that have open iron sights, and which are modern. (My muzzleloaders wear blade sights.) I like the finer bead. I see it well enough in poor light, and up close in brush and woods. It shows up just fine, under any shooting circumstances I have thus far encountered. But, remember, the bead size should be selected upon the basis of personal need and preference as well as sheer fit. So in some instances a 3/32-inch or even larger bead may be correct. I like the 1/16-inch size because I can get light around it easily in any rear sight notch I have tried, and yet it is not "sloppy" in optical fit.

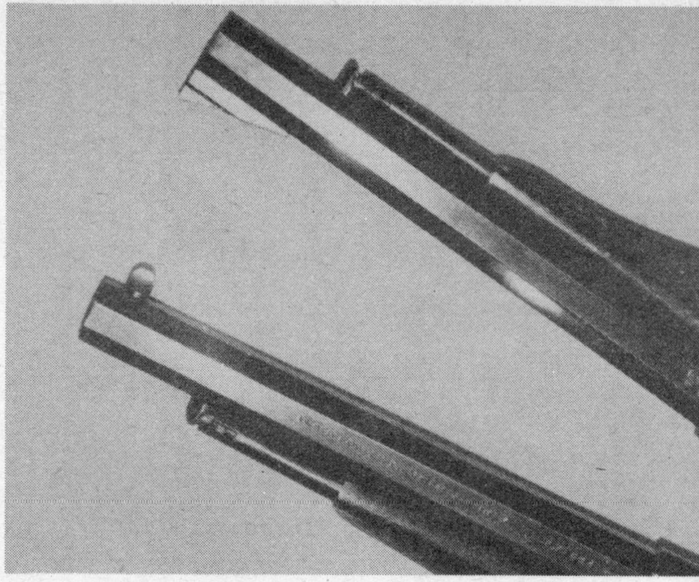

Two very different front sights are shown here. The rounded sight is mounted directly into the barrel via a dovetail slot. It's more for pointing than aiming, and it couples with a notch in the topstrap of the revolver—no actual rear sight. But the other sight is fixed on a ramp. It appears as a square-topped post and, is coupled with a target rear sight.

I shoot a lot of Model 94 30-30 rifles these days, and I have had the front sights switched over to the flat-faced gold bead of 1/16-inch size, both on the 20-inch barreled carbine and the 26-inch barreled rifle model. I have also opted for the 1/16-inch bead on my Storey Conversion which is a beautiful custom rifle based upon the Model 94 Winchester action and chambered for the 30-30 Improved. This rifle wears iron sights because it is used for close work. Let the shooter and the situation decide, but for me a flat-faced bead of gold in the 1/16-inch dimension has proved a winner.

Bead size must also be dictated in part by sight radius. Sight radius is the distance between the notch of the rear sight and the face of the front sight's bead. This distance makes a great deal of difference in sight picture. The above-mentioned 30-30s, for example, all have different barrel lengths. My over-the-counter carbine wears the 20-inch tube. My very old take-down rifle, made around 1899, has the 26-inch barrel, and the Storey Conversion, from DGS, Inc., has a 24-inch octagon barrel. This means they all have different sight radius measurements, of course, not only based upon the barrel length factors, but also *where* the sights are placed on the barrel. My Model 94 rifle with the 26-inch barrel has a 21-inch sight radius. My 20-inch barreled carbine has a sight radius of about 16.5 inches. Optically, the long-barreled rifle gives me a slightly sharper ''picture,'' mainly because my own visual accommodation is less strained by the longer sight radius. And the sight picture is plenty good enough to do big game work at up to as much as 200 yards distance, which is none-too-far for the excellent handloads found in Lyman's handbook.

Bead Color

Beads not only come in various sizes, but also in various colors. A bead can be found in gold, silver, ivory, white, black and many other hues. Red beads, for example, are somewhat popular. I have seen beads of blaze orange, too. The darker colors, such as red, seem to do quite well in bright light. They appear bold and dark and also stand out well against a white or light background. The lighter-colored beads, ivory or white, are better in poor light or against a darker background, such as the deep woods. But there's no free lunch here. The dark bead, though it is good in bright light, may not be as clearly defined when used in the woods, and those light beads so good in the deep woods get all but lost in bright light. The gold bead is a good compromise. It seems to work well under most shooting light conditions, though I suppose as with all compromises, it's not the very best for either very dark or very light situations.

In hunting situations, I have found the gold bead to be good because it's a fairly decent color for shade or sun. The hunter simply must experience many lighting conditions because he is always going to be venturing into different terrain. Even if he remained on one stump for the entire season, the lighting would change with the position of the sun and condition of the sky. Light filtered through clouds is quite different, for example, from light shining directly down on the sights from a blue sky.

From my experiences the brighter sight is more prone to sighting problems as the sun directly strikes the sight. Bright sun shining on the left-hand side of the sight tends to make me shoot to the right. The opposite is, of course, equally true. And bright light from directly overhead can make me shoot a bit low as that light plays down on the bead. Given the gold bead, I feel that these tendencies are somewhat more in control.

Bead Shape

Basically, we have the round-faced bead and the flat-faced bead. I'm sure there are other shapes; there have been so many different sight configurations over the years that nothing surprises me. I recently saw a front sight which was in fact an aperture. Standing up on a narrow stem, it was a small metal circle with a hole in it. Yet it was coupled with a standard open notch rear sight. The idea was to center the metal ring in the rear sight notch and then put the target in the center of the ring itself.

The full, round-faced bead seems a bit better in poor light than the flat-faced bead. It tends to gather more light due mainly to its larger surface area and its angled-dome construction. At the same time, if light is going to bounce at all, it will bounce off of that round-faced bead. The flat-faced bead, I think, is better in bright light because it tends to retain the same *optical shape*. The round-faced bead, under some lighting conditions, looks eliptical to me. But the flat-faced bead seems to remain round to the eye no matter the light. Can I prove this? I'm not sure I can, but I'd suggest you try both kinds before you make your decision.

Bead-type front sights are available in a number of sizes and colors. This Williams ramp front sights wears a Williams gold bead. In case you hadn't noticed, this type of sight comes as standard fare on many of today's factory rifles.

Coarse Bead/Fine Bead

I believe in using the bead's optical placement in the rear sight notch to best advantage. The old-time shooters used to gain a bit more flexibility from the open iron sight by taking what is called either a *fine bead* or a *coarse bead*—the terms referring to aspects of the sight picture. I find that my standard sight picture *is the ''fine bead.''* In short, I nestle the bead well down into the notch of the rear sight. How does this look? Picture it like this if you can: The front sight consists of a nice round bead with a flat face. It is gold in color. It rests on a stem, optically, though in fact it could be sitting upon a strong ramp with a good stout front sight body. But it appears to be a round bead resting upon a rather slender stem. The bead is placed in the rear sight notch so that there seems to be equal light on both sides of it. The bead rests deeply in the notch so that a slight trace of light shines *underneath* it. That is important for frame of reference. If the shooter does not allow for a tiny bit of visible light underneath the bead, how does he know, shot-to-shot, where the bottom of the bead rests in relation to the notch? He doesn't.

That is the "fine bead." Sighted in properly, that bead posture should be used for all normal shooting. The "coarse bead," and remember, that is an optical term having nothing to do with the actual size of the bead, is then used for more distant shots, the bead being placed (by comparison) higher in the rear sight notch. It works. I use open sights a lot; I like them. They are totally appropriate on my muzzleloaders, of course, but equally at home on several of my other rifles, especially the above-mentioned Model 94s. The open sight is fast and can be quite accurate, more accurate than some shooters would believe. Under normal shooting conditions and normal ranges, shots from under the nose to maybe 200 yards, that standard sight picture (fine bead) is the one used.

My 30-30 load may often be a 150-grain bullet at almost 2550 fps from a 20-inch barrel, and that is with an H-335 load from Lyman's excellent reloading manual and chronographed not only on my machine, but a backup machine as well. From the 26-inch barrel, the same load achieves over 2600 fps MV. This is, of course, a very easy 20-yard trajectory. The standard sight picture, the "fine bead," allows a dead-on hold at 200 yards. In fact, it allows for a dead-on hold from zero to *over* 200 yards on a deer with no hold-under for the closer-than-200-yard shots. If, for some odd reason, I felt the need to shoot at more than 200 yards distance with the above 30-30 handload, I would then take the "coarse bead" sight picture, meaning that more light would be seen underneath the bead as it rested within the rear sight notch. Simply, this picture lifts the barrel upward, the bullet thereby striking higher.

Other Front Sights

Beads are the front sight aiming devices often seen on rifles today, but my muzzleloaders do not generally wear bead front sights if they are true replicas. Then we have a blade sight. The blade sight works quite well, too. Simply, the blade front sight rests in a notch, the same as the bead, and gains its frame of reference in much the same way. Light is only presented on either side of the blade as it rests in the rear sight notch, the *top* of the blade being brought to optical rest *even* with the top of the rear sight notch. That is the proper frame of reference. In a way, fine bead/coarse bead sighting is almost simpler with the blade sight. For very small targets at very close range, I can squeeze that blade optically down until the tip shows in the rear sight notch. For far shots, the top of the blade will stand *higher* than the top of the rear sight notch.

The blade front sight was very popular in the old days. It was often called a German silver front sight because it was made of German silver, which is a white alloy of copper, nickel and zinc. It had and still has other names. Some call it nickel-silver. Others called it albata or electrum, in days gone by. It is bright, but does not always appear bright during the sighting process. I like the German silver front sight on the older guns. Another good front sight is the simple post; its flat top rests neatly in the rear sight notch. The sight picture is quite clear and precise. In theory, the post is best suited to the 6-o'clock hold, where the target optically rests atop the post. In fact, the post can be used with the "hunting sight" picture, in which case it is simply placed where the bullet is intended to strike.

From a modern-day perspective, those old-time iron open sights are considered to be about as useful as a girdle on an elephant. Today, the opinion is often sounded that those sights are crude and no better than the bead on a shotgun for fine aiming. Don't you ever believe it! My prowess with the rifle is all right, but I am no champion target shooter. However, I can do no more than hope when I aim my iron-sighted rifles. As an example, I was at the range with a good friend of mine. He was sighting in a 7mm Magnum at 100 yards, using a black bull's-eye of 6 inches in diameter that featured a 1-inch white circle in the center. I had along my 54-caliber longrifle.

When front sights are found on factory rifles, they are usually of the ramp variety, as seen here in this example from Williams Gun Sight Co.

To be sure, I could never match the 1½-inch groups my friend's 7mm Magnum was making. He was using a 3x-9x scope set at maximum power. He suggested we move up on the target when it came time for my turn with the old round-ball muzzleloader. I said I figured I could at least hit the black from the 100-yard bench. I fired and the ball cut the white circle. I could not see that circle, of course, but I did aim for the center of the black and the ball went there, by chance putting a hole in the white center. I shot twice more and hit the white circle one more time (more luck than skill), a third shot falling about 3 inches from the white center. With the same rifle I later produced a 2½-inch group for three shots, center-to-center, again at 100 yards from the bench. Good iron sights do allow for excellent groups, nothing like the scope will do, of course, but hardly a chance situation.

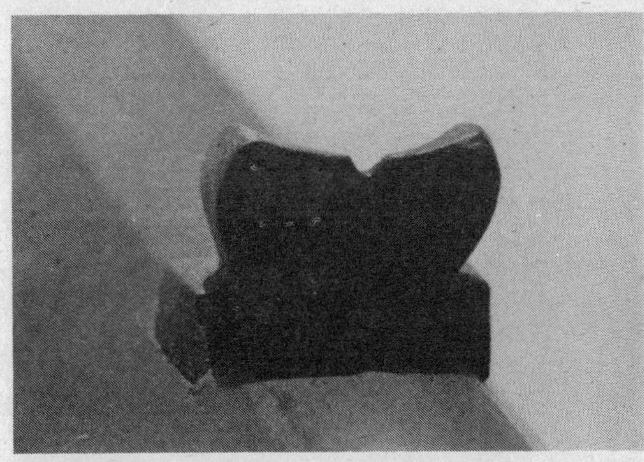

The semi-buckhorn sight shown here is almost without the "horns" of the original style buckhorn. The notch is somewhat interesting because it resembles the V-type, but is rounded in the bottom, like a U-notch. The frame of reference here might be settling the bead in the notch so that the top of the bead is even with the top of the notch.

Open iron sights are still favored by many hunters in many different areas. The man on the left, Ivon DuPlesses, prefers the open iron sights of his Manlicher 30-06, a rifle which was used by the author to harvest this African warthog. Ivon likes the speed of the open sight, and feels that it is a useful sight for Africa, where most shooting is done within a range of 100 yards.

The Ramp

Many front sights rest upon ramps commonly adorning the barrels of handguns or rifles. The ramp is one way of offering a sturdy platform for a front sight. Instead of having a high front sight, which could be easily bent, the ramp allows the same sight height, with the front sight now dovetailed into the strong ramp. Not fitting for truly replica old-time frontloaders, the ramp is just fine on our modern iron-sighted rifles and provides a good means of getting sight height without having to use a tall, delicate, front sight blade.

The Rear Sight

There are so many rear sight styles that a book could be written on the subject. Gunmakers from the beginning of the art must have all felt that they individually had the answer when it came to the proper shape and style of the rear sight and its notch. This brief look will give the complete shooter a basic guide to go by, as well as some out-and-out opinions of mine to accept or refute. I have used dozens of various rear sight styles, and I admit to having my own ideas about them.

1. Notches: Generally speaking, there is the U-notch, V-notch, square notch and the shallow V-notch. The U-notch, as its name implies, is shaped like a U. The actual "U" cutout is quite wide, the front bead actually having a chance to settle into position with light admitted on both sides of the bead. The "u" resembles the lower case letter, rather than a capital "U." This means the sides are not so high, the front sight generally resting into the U-notch so that the top of the bead is somewhat close to the top of the notch. The V-notch is just that, a "v" shape to gain a better perspective of the walls of the notch. Yes, a bead does fit into the V-notch all right, in spite of what seems an optical problem. The square notch is most often coupled with a post sight up front. This gives a very easy-to-manage sight picture. There is light on both sides of the square and the post (which also appears square), rests evenly with the top of the square notch. The shallow V, though a fast sight, is not as good for longer-range shooting. But what a fine sight picture it gives for close-in (under 100 yards) work.

When I spoke with a few professional African hunters, I was told over and over again that the sight they liked for dangerous game was the shallow V notch. They often coupled this with what would be a blade-type front sight. In order to get the proper sight picture, the blade was held so that it matched with the top of the V to form a "W" in appearance. They also liked a bead front sight, but did not want it to be small. I concede. For that shooting, often at 20 to 100 yards distance on animals that look like the side

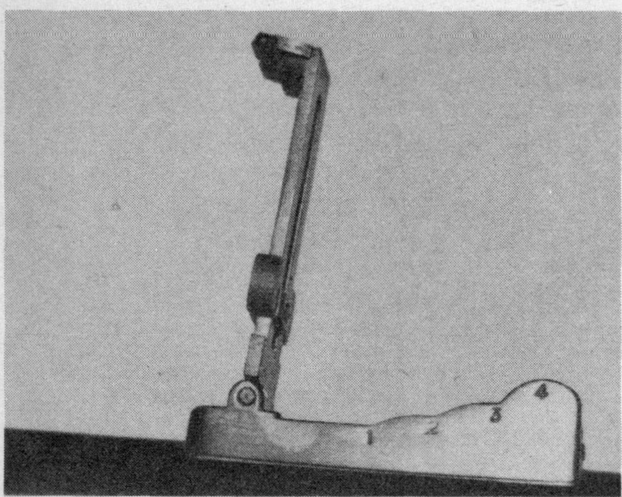

The Navy Arms Whitworth Rifle's sights are military in design, with the flip-up feature allowing for very long-range sighting.

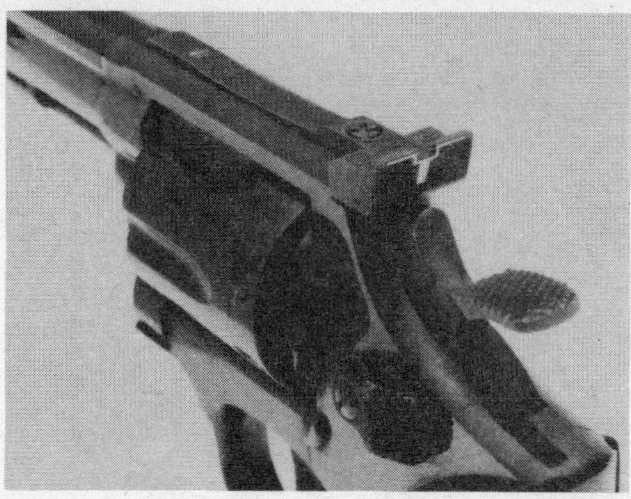

The Millett adjustable revolver sight is shown here. It has the high visibility outline which can aid the shooter in keeping good alignment between rear and front sight.

of a barn, a heavy bead would be fine. For North American shooting, however, I want the finer bead.

On a handgun, the square notch is super. I prefer it. On the rifle, I prefer the U-notch. If I had a rifle made up for big game hunting where dangerous animals were pursued, the shallow V would be all right with a stout bead as the front sight. By the way, I would not at all mind a peep sight with a very large aperture for dangerous game. It's very fast, and very accurate.

2. Aiming aids: It is customary for nice white diamonds or triangles or other neat shapes to be on the back of the rear sight blade with the point of the shape leading to the center of the notch. In very dim light, these are all right. Most of the time, they are simply useless add-ons which do not need to be there. Do they cause a problem for the shooter? I wish I knew. I have felt at times that the added white diamond, for example, was more hindrance than boon. They are, for me, distracting. As a result, I don't have them on my rear sights. When that "add-on" shape is on a sight, I simply scratch it off.

3. Folding sights: Folding rear sights would be just wonderful if they would refrain from accidentally doing one thing, *folding*. I recently tried a nice lever-action rifle which had a folding rear sight, and in the brush I found the sight folded, without any assistance from yours truly, about half the time. It was a very large pain in the neck. This particular folding sight had no direct, firm means of holding it rigidly in the upward position. It was folded flat against the barrel as often as it was standing up.

I replaced a rear sight on a fine old Remington Model 12,22 rimfire pumpgun and the only sight that fit the dovetail notch was a folding rear sight. Again, I found myself fighting the rear sight. I then took the rifle to a local gun-

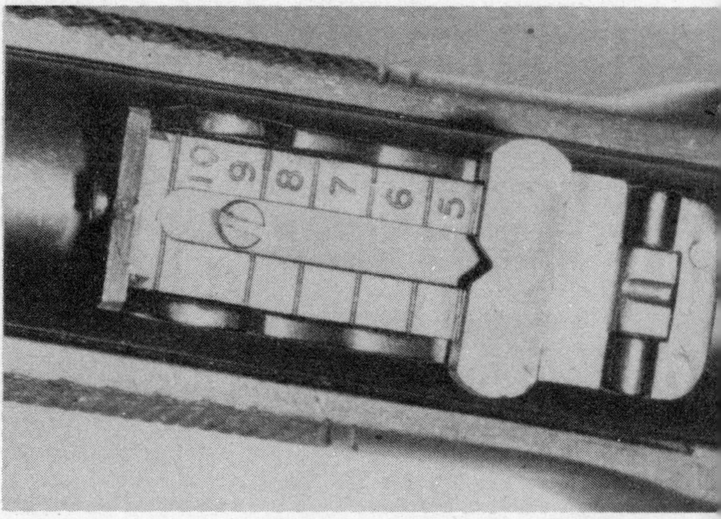

Military-type open rear sights are adjustable for elevation. The numbers indicate 100-yard increments, right on up to "10," or 1000 yards.

smith and told him to weld, pin, glue or solder that rear sight so that it would never again fold for any reason. He did it, and the sight hasn't threatened to fold on me since. A folding rear sight is all right when needed if it is an auxiliary sight only and if it must fold out of the way. But for a rear sight which is meant to serve as a *full-time* rear sight, unfold my folding sight, please, and make it stand up rigidly forever.

Zeroing the Open Sight

One may think it inappropriate to spend so much time on open iron sights. Aren't they finally on the way out? I should say not, and the complete shooter cannot call himself that without knowing how to manage the open iron sight, to include sighting it in. There are two kinds of open

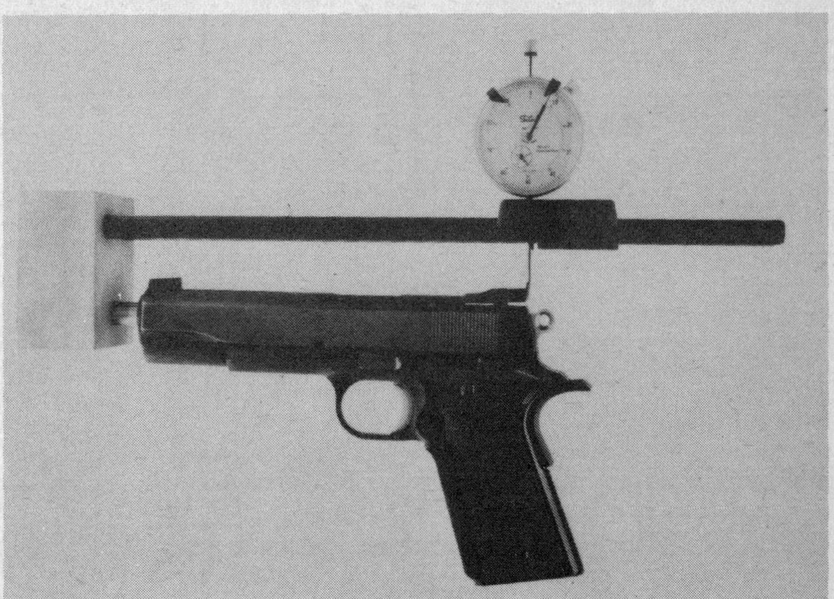

The Millett Handgun Boresighter Gauge is a unit which accurately determines the height difference between front and rear sight relative to the bore. It allows sighting in of handguns in much less time.

iron sights in use today, the "fixed" sight and the "adjustable." We are leaving out all of the fine and fancy target sights available and staying with the open sight used for hunting because this is the open sight of the hour. Target work is seldom accomplished with open irons except for certain types of competitive shooting which require that sight system as part of the rules.

The fixed sight means that the front sight is fitted via a dovetail slot, generally featuring a "blade" on a very small base. The rear sight is fitted directly to the barrel via a dovetail slot also. What this means is that there is available lateral movement of either front or rear sight in the fixed-sight system, but no vertical movement. In other words, windage adjustment is accomplished by drifting the front or rear sight within its dovetail slot, with no provision for elevation adjustment.

Hopefully, the fixed sight rifle comes to the shooter either pre-sighted by the gunmaker, and I am thinking mostly of replica longrifles now, or it comes to the shooter with an overly *high* front sight. With the high front sight, the rifle, using full throttle loads, is very likely to shoot low, in spite of the highest velocity obtainable from it. But that is no problem. In order to make that rifle shoot higher, the shooter (or competent gunsmith) merely files, very carefully, until he shortens the front sight blade. I use a fine toothed file and touch up the job with emery paper, ever so little at a time. The process is quite simple. After establishing windage by drifting the rear sight (usually) in the direction we want the bullets to strike on the target, we file down the front sight until elevation is also correct. It's a matter of cut-and-try.

If the rear sight is to be drifted right or left in the dovetail slot, be sure to use a light mallet with a small wooden dowel—you don't want to damage the sight. Also, be sure to drift the rear sight in the direction you want the next shot to land on the target. If the rifle is shooting to the left, you drift the rear sight to the right in order to make the next shot hit to the right. When it comes to adjusting the front sight, you'll be drifting it in the *opposite* direction. If the rifle is shooting to the left, for example, and you want the next shot to go to the right, drift the front sight to the left. If the rifle is shooting low, cut the front sight down (lower it) a bit at a time, until the bullets impact at the proper height.

That's all there is to fixed sights. By the way, once your fixed sights are sighted in, the edges of the dovetail slot can be peened down a bit by using a brass punch—they

Sighting-in means paying attention to the particular sighting style of the firearm of course, and this is why handgun hunters should be especially mindful of the sights their firearms wear. This Ruger has good adjustable sights which one might call target style, just right for hunting where open iron sights are preferred.

won't wander out of adjustment. Fixed sights are not bad, nor outmoded, actually. But it is the *adjustable* sight which is king today. The sighting-in adjustment of the open iron sight with adjustable features means, in the main, moving the rear sight only, though every now and then a shooter may have to actually change a front sight (from higher or lower, or lower to higher) in order to attain the desired degree of elevation. I had to do this with my Model 94s which were shooting high because my handloads shot so much faster than the loads used in the original model. Higher (taller) front sights allowed me to correct the problem on all three of my '94s. The mechanical aspects of rear sight adjustments can vary, of course, from maker to maker. The older style of rear sight was usually mounted on a springy base which was slotted for an elevator bar. The elevator bar was, and still is to this day, notched. If the shooter wanted the bullet to strike higher on the target, he moved the elevator bar into the next higher notch so that the rear sight was raised. If he wanted the next shot to strike lower on the target, he moved the elevator bar to a lower notch, thereby lowering the rear sight.

The full buckhorn sight is supposed to be quite useless and ineffective according to many modern day shooters who say that the horns of the sight blot out the target. The author has made many head shots on squirrels and rabbits with this sight style and has never known of the horns to blot the target out.

There are now many methods used to raise or lower the rear sight, but mainly we still have the old elevator bar and/or the sliding rear sight panel. That panel, or blade, can be moved up and down in the rear sight leaf by use of a small screwdriver. A screw (or pair of screws) holds the blade in place. You simply loosen the screw(s), move the bar up or down, and then re-tighten the screw(s). It's very easy. There are also rear sights which have a screw in the shank of the ramp itself. This screw presses against the barrel. If the screw is turned clockwise, it raises the rear sight. If turned counterclockwise, the rear sight drops downward. The Williams Guide open sight has interchangeable blades so that a shooter can select the blade style he prefers for the task at hand, SQ (square notch), U, V or B, the latter being a shallow V. But windage and elevation are incorporated into this rear sight on dovetails within the makeup of the sight itself. A screw allows movement of the sight, and the same screw locks the sight in place with gib locks.

Choose Your Own Open Sight

I have heard for years that the "buckhorn" style of rear sight is an "abomination." Maybe it is. Many shooters feel the little wings on either side of the notch serve no useful purpose. Those same shooters in fact, will call the buckhorn's ears a "hindrance," serving only to blot out the target. I went into my own buckhorn sights with that sort of prejudice. Today, I have taken many a fine game animal with buckhorn sights. Of course the wings do not hide the game, they "frame" game, and quite nicely. If they did "hide the game," the old-timers would have torn them off faster than a race horse leaves the starting gate.

The shooter should certainly obtain open sights which present a good picture. But he should also select his type and style with an open, inquisitive mind. I learned, through experience, that the old-time buckhorn sight with the nice, small U-notch worked very well for me. I currently have several rifles which wear this type of rear sight. I found that with a small bead front sight, such as the 1/16-inch model mentioned earlier, I could get a good sight picture with the buckhorn rear sight. I also learned that the longer sight radius of the longer barrel meant a clearer picture for my eyes, but that the short barrels with iron sights also worked out well, at least for me.

One afternoon, I was hunting with my friend John Kane, who is a professional hunter and guide. John and I were hunting for ourselves that day; the object was meat. We parted on a ridge and separated by about 100 yards. A whitetail buck broke cover and sped along through a series of small trees with pretty good gaps between them. The shot was John's. He upped his rifle and fired once. The bullet from his iron-sighted 30-30 saddle ring carbine took the buck through the shoulders and the animal was harvested with instant results. The shot was from about 150 yards out. There was no luck to it. I had watched John do it many times before.

The open sight is still viable. It's a greater challenge than the other sight styles to be sure. In pure terms of sightability, the iron open is inferior to the fine aperture or peep sight and vastly inferior to the scope sight. Yet, there remains a place for the open iron sight, not only in the hands of the 5 million shooters who are currently enjoying black powder arms, but also among the millions of hunters who use carbines in the brush and woods to harvest their venison. Today's shooter needs to know about these old-style sights, because though they may be old, they are not obsolete, not by a long shot.

The Peep Sight

The peep sight, or aperture sight, is nothing new. I have read accounts which suggested that aperture sights came along to replace the open iron sight, and that they did not truly make a hit because the scope sight entered the scene and eclipsed them. In fact, the peep sight never did replace the open iron sight. Many are the reasons. First among these then is expense. The aperture sight costs more than the open sight; therefore, manufacturers stayed with the open sight. If shooters wanted to move to the peep, they had to buy the sight and install it or have a gunsmith install it for them.

This Lyman receiver (peep) sight offers fine adjustment capability. Note the small disc, about a third of an inch OD (outside diameter). It uses a larger .10 aperture for fast sighting.

Advantages of the Peep Sight

The rear-mounted peep sight has a number of advantages over the open ''notched'' sight. But before going into these, I want to justify the time and reverence spent on the open sight one more time, briefly. The plain open sight is still fitting on certain rifles. They are ''trim'' in both appearance and construction. Conversely, most of the receiver sights, or ''peeps'' as they are commonly called, are appendages by comparison. And the open sight can get the job of aiming accomplished quite well. But the peep is ''better'' than the open in many respects. let's see why:

1. More Accurate: No, a peep sight will not make a rifle shoot better. Good shooters, good loads and good barrels do that. But we can say that the aperture sight is more accurate than the open sight because its adjustments are usually much more refined.

2. Faster: There can be some question on this one, but all in all, the peep sight with a large aperture is hard to beat in terms of fast *accurate* aiming. Even John Taylor, the famous ivory hunter of Africa, stated that the peep sight with a large aperture was faster than open iron sights. The eye has less work to do.

3. Easier to Use: In fact, the peep is easier to use than an open iron sight. The open sight must be managed very carefully in order to align it. There must be equal amounts of light entering on both sides of the front sight as it rests optically in the notch of the rear sight, and the shooter must be very careful to settle the front sight image the same way in the notch. If he does not, he will shoot higher or lower than his last shot. But the peep simply requires looking through the aperture, centering the front sight within the aperture and putting the front sight on the target.

4. Longer Sight Radius: We talked about sight radius earlier and the advantage of greater distance between the back sight and the front sight. Since the peep sight is mounted on the receiver (or upper tang, on some rifles) this automatically provides for a longer sight radius when compared to barrel-mounted irons.

5. Better in Poor Light: The peep sight is better than the open sight in poor light. In fact, it presents the shooter with a front sight that's bathed in available light, whereas the open sight does not, at least not as generously as the peep does.

6. Easy to Adjust: The peep is generally easier to adjust accurately than the open sight. Once a shooter knows the actual value of the clicks on a micrometer peep sight, for example, he can quickly alter the point of impact on the target with a fast adjustment. Furthermore, the peep is more versatile than the open sight. By merely screwing in a new aperture, the peep changes its picture immediately.

The Tang-Mounted Peep Sight

The tang sight was one of the early peep styles. On my often-mentioned older Model 94 Winchester 30-30, there is

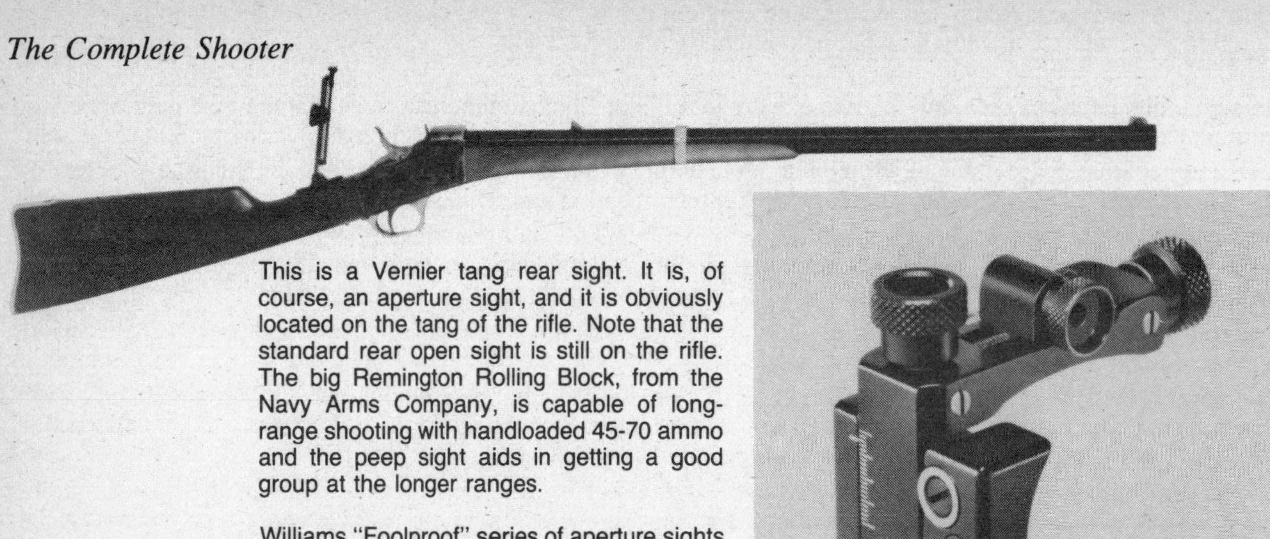

This is a Vernier tang rear sight. It is, of course, an aperture sight, and it is obviously located on the tang of the rifle. Note that the standard rear open sight is still on the rifle. The big Remington Rolling Block, from the Navy Arms Company, is capable of long-range shooting with handloaded 45-70 ammo and the peep sight aids in getting a good group at the longer ranges.

Williams "Foolproof" series of aperture sights are available for a broad range of rifles. Varying aperture sizes are also available to meet the needs of both the target shooter and hunter.

a tang peep sight. This sight is an auxiliary to the open iron sight on that rifle and meant for longer range shooting. Since it is an auxiliary, it folds out of the way. The only time I use it is for 200-yard shots. It is sighted for 200 yards, in fact. When I feel the range is about 200 yards, and I want the advantage of the peep sight, I simply lift the tang sight in place. These flexible tang sights were made by Marble and Lyman, to name two companies, and can still be found (not commonly) from time to time.

The Vernier tang sight is still available. I have one from the Navy Arms Company, and I have seen them also offered by Thompson/Center. Such a sight is easily and quickly adjusted in the field for windage and elevation. The Vernier tang sight was commonly used for target work, as well as hunting. It is used today on black powder cartridge rifles and black powder muzzleloader rifles. It's very easily mastered.

The Receiver Sight

Commonly called a "peep sight," the receiver sight is just that, a sight which attaches to the receiver of the firearm. It can have target-type or hunting-type adjustments, though, of course, the latter will also work at the target range. I call a target receiver sight one which allows click adjustments via knobs. These can be quickly manipulated at the range for fast resighting. There is now a Silhouette Foolproof receiver sight from Williams. It has the fine internal micrometer adjustments for windage and elevation, with target knobs that have an audible "click" when used. This sight also offers positive internal locking so the sight setting can be maintained. It is often used on Contender pistols and is a very good sight.

The micrometer adjustment common to receiver sights is just that, an *extremely* accurate vertical or horizontal adjustment of the aperture itself. A shooter moves the fixture on the sight and the aperture moves accordingly, usually in 1/4- or 1/2-minute clicks. I have used a micrometer receiver sight on a very accurate Pre '64 Model 70 Winchester and could easily put the group precisely where I wanted it to go. That sight had 1/4-minute clicks. For each click, the point of bullet impact was moved about 1/4-inch at 100 yards. Naturally, we are dealing with variables here other than the sight itself, but the capability of that micrometer receiver sight is without question. It is accurate to 1/4-minute of angle. This means that one click on that particular sight would change the point of impact about 1/2-inch at 200 yards.

The receiver sight with micrometer adjustments would be my choice if I were putting iron sights on a new, modern rifle. Again, appropriateness is the rule. My custom Storey Conversion is, in fact, modernized, but it is not modern in the sense of being a bolt-action model in a high-speed caliber. Therefore, open irons have been used on it. But the same Storey Conversion model built for another shooter was in fact fitted with a peep sight featuring micrometer adjustment. It's a matter of personal choice.

Size of Aperture

In my opinion, there has been much confusion concerning disc/aperture size of the peep sight and accuracy. Target discs are generally larger than hunting discs and have very minute apertures. In fact, I have tested these against discs with slightly larger apertures and cannot discern enough actual aiming advantage for the tiny aperture to make it worth the while. For hunters, however, the use of tiny apertures is all wrong. In fact, a large disc with a very small "peep hole" is the opposite of what I want for hunting purposes.

I have often totally removed the disc, using only the screw-in hole in the sight and my accuracy did not fall off in terms of hunting. For my money, the best type of hunting disc is small in overall diameter and possesses a good-sized aperture. The small disc will allow the shooter to see all around his target. The big disc is designed to obscure all but the target. That may be fine for precision target shooting, but it's not the best choice for most of our shooting. For target work, the big disc, in the 7/8-inch diameter size works well. The actual aperture in a target disc may be as small as 0.46-inch or similar. Redfield offers a Sure-X Disc which fits the Redfield target micrometer peep sight, and this disc is adjustable in increments of .004-inch, going from .030-inch to .058-inch. The Merit adjustable disc runs from .022-inch to .125-inch. But the Merit No. 4 Hunting Disc (a good one, too) runs from .025-inch to .155-inch. Outside diameter of the No. 4 is 1/2-inch. Since this is an adjustable model, the 1/2-inch diameter of the Merit No. 4 is necessary to accommodate the mechanical elements of the disc. My favorite hunting disc, however, has an outside diameter of 1/3-inch, the aperture running about 1/10-inch. It allows for fast, accurate sighting. This particular size allows for the disc to appear as a thin black circle around the front sight and not much more, depending, of course, upon how close the eye is to the disc itself.

Since we never have to consciously try to center the front sight in the aperture of the peep sight, it's easy to see just how fast and slick the peep sight is for hunting. With the open iron sight, the eye must focus upon the rear sight notch, the front sight and the target—three different planes. And the eye must continually keep all three visually sharp if possible, plus making certain that the front sight is perfectly aligned in that notch, not sloppily resting in the notch just any old way. But with the peep sight, the shooter merely looks *through* the hole, not at it, never trying to center the front sight in it, and then he places the front sight upon the target and squeezes off the shot. The disc and its aperture is forgotten in the sighting process because the human eye will *automatically center* the front sight at the highest point of light, which happens to be dead in the center of the peep, *dead center*. Now we have but two planes to consider, the front sight and the target. Older eyes do better with a peep sight than with open sights for this reason, since visual accommodation is less stringent with the peep sight.

Sighting In

Sighting in with the peep sight is quite simple. Recall that with the open sight, the front sight moved in the opposite direction from where we wanted the next shot to strike. The same holds true for the peep sight, but we can just about forget the front sight since it all but takes care of itself. The actual peep sight itself, especially in the case of the true receiver micrometer sight, usually has more than enough adjustment necessary for sighting in. And again we find that where the rear sight goes (right, left, up or down), so goes the next bullet. It's that simple. The peep sight's adjustment knobs are also generally marked with arrows to show the "up, down, left or right" settings. Here is the step-by-step procedure for sighting in the peep sight.

1. Get close for initial sighting-in. A distance of 25 yards or less is recommended.
2. Fire a group of at least 5 shots (or as many as 10 shots) to determine the average center of impact on the target.
3. Measure the distance from the center of this group to where you want the next group center to strike the target. For example, if the center of the group is 3 inches to the right of where you want to group on the target, and 3 inches low, you must move the point of impact 3 inches to the left and 3 inches up.
4. Make your windage and elevation adjustments. At only 25 yards, the adjustment values will be 4 times what they would be at 100 yards. You must move the sight 4 times more than your values say for 100 yards. With 1/4-minute clicks, if you wanted to move the point of impact over to the left 1 inch, then you would move the sight to the left 4 clicks . . . at 100 yards remember. But at only 25 yards, you must now move the sight 16 clicks to the left in order to gain that inch change in point of impact.
5. After hitting on target at 25 yards, move out to 100 yards and shoot another group of 5 to 10 shots. Measure the center of this group and determine what further adjustments are necessary.
   Example: If the rifle is still shooting 1 inch to the right and 1 inch low, then you'll need four more clicks left and four more clicks up.
6. If you wish, you can now move back to 200 yards and shoot further groups. Remember, at 200 yards, the values of the sight are cut in half. In order to change point of impact by 1 inch at 200 yards, the 1/4-minute clicks are only two, two clicks per 1 inch of movement instead of the four clicks required at 100 yards.

Sighting-in with the micrometer receiver sight is a snap. But there can be two problems. First is the problem of understanding the actual values of the clicks or calibrations on the sight. Again, it's imperative you remember that a 1/4-minute click translates into 1/4-inch for each click at 100 yards, but only half that at 200 yards and four times that at 25 yards. The second problem is one of grouping shots. If the group is random, you may have an inaccurate rifle which cannot be properly sighted in. The group must be *reliable*. Levels of reliability vary from rifle to rifle, but rifles which shoot less well than 4-inch groups at 100 yards (regardless of the sights used) are very difficult to sight in with precision. Fortunately, there are few of these around. Use the Weighted Average for Groups: The 10-shot sighting-in groups can actually save you time because the "fliers" can be tossed out. In other words, if a shooter fires 10 well-aimed shots at the target, he may find seven

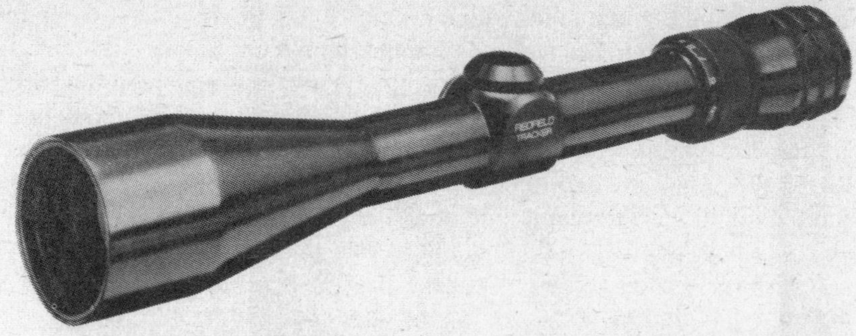

Scope prices have increased along with all other prices, but the Redfield company added the Tracker scope to the lineup as a lower cost alternative. It is a warranted product with the Redfield name to back it up.

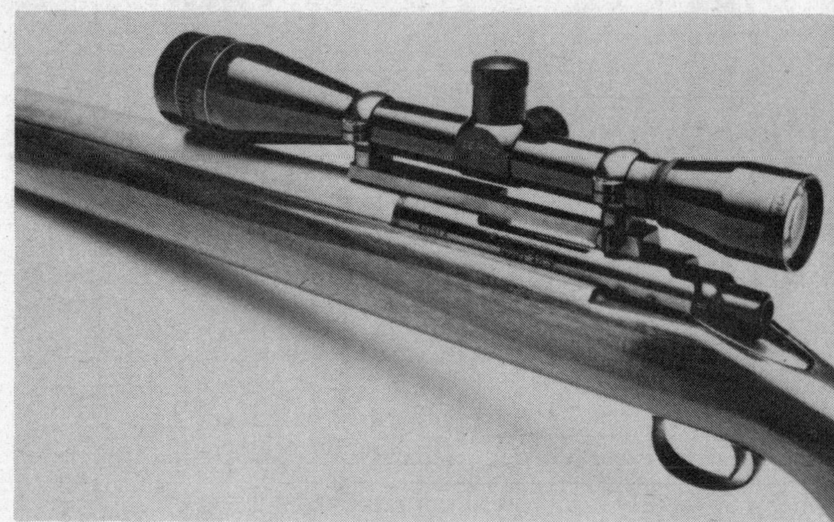

Scope power is a matter of need. This is a 24x Leupold, a scope designed with competition in mind. It is under 14 inches long and weighs but 14.5 ounces. Eye relief is 3.2 inches. It has a focusing objective. It also has a sunshade. Scopes have come a long way in the past 100 years, with most of the true refinements arriving quite recently.

shots clustered nicely, while three are away from the cluster. In a "weighted" group, these three shots are actually tossed out and forgotten. Only the seven clustered shots are measured center-to-center. This means from the center of the bullet hole to the center of the other bullet hole of the two most extreme holes in the cluster. This center-to-center group measurement is the one to use when it comes to sighting-in.

The Telescopic Sight

To date the telescopic sight is the finest sighting instrument ever devised for firearms. Obviously, the scope sight magnifies the target. But it does a lot more. It isolates the target, not severely, but just enough to improve the concentration of the shooter. It also offers a single sighting plane, with width and height only. The eye does not have to work hard here. It merely sees one flat image, the target, with the crosswires pasted flat to that target. Also, the scope allows for a very clear view of the target, another benefit of magnification. And a scope is really helpful in sighting in, not only because of its obvious advantage in very simplified sighting adjustments, but also because the scope generally allows for more precise shooting and grouping. So the better the group, the easier it is to find the group's center of impact. Therefore, the scope-sighted firearm is easier to sight in. Yes, a scope does a lot more than magnify the target. In fact, as the sophistication of the sight advances, it is easier and easier to use. An open iron sight is more difficult to master than an aperture sight or scope. The scope is the easiest sight to use of the main sight styles in vogue today.

The telescopic sight is older than we think, just as the peep sight is hardly anything new. During the Civil War, scope sights were in use, and even before that, the mountain men of the Far West had a few scope sights available to them. The buffalo hunters (or "buffalo runners" as they preferred to be called) also had scope sights. Frank Mayer, an original buff hunter who lived on into this century, described his favorite Sharps rifle as "scope-sighted." In fact, it carried a 20x target-type scope with stadia wires. Stadia wires consist of two horizontal wires in the crosshair instead of one. If a hunter knows how much the two wires cover at a given distance, he can determine the range of his target. In other words, if the distance between the stadia wires translates into a couple of feet at 200 yards and a mature mule deer buck fills that space, he's *about* 200 yards out (a mule deer buck will have a chest depth of about 18 inches). It's not exact, but it's useful for approximate gauging of shooting distances.

Over the years not everyone has been in favor of the scope sight. The following comments are from a gunwriter airing his opinions in 1946. It's a laundry list, if you will, of scope-sight negatives:

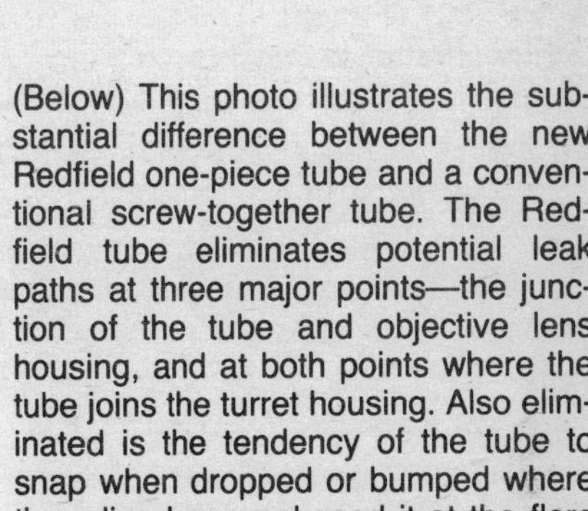

Concern about the elements fogging a scope is wasted these days. Of course, no one suggests that a scope should be abused. But if a shooter does get caught out in bad weather, it's unlikely that a well-made scope will fog up. Of course, it's still wise to leave the scope out of a hot area after a while in the rain. This is a Leupold variable standing up to the rain.

(Below) This photo illustrates the substantial difference between the new Redfield one-piece tube and a conventional screw-together tube. The Redfield tube eliminates potential leak paths at three major points—the junction of the tube and objective lens housing, and at both points where the tube joins the turret housing. Also eliminated is the tendency of the tube to snap when dropped or bumped where threading has weakened it at the flare of the objective lens housing.

1. Too delicate, easily damaged
2. Snow, leaves and other debris will collect on the lenses
3. If kept capped, it's unready for use, so it must be exposed to elements
4. It may fog or ice over
5. Will not fit into a scabbard well
6. Limited field of view, too slow to use
7. Magnifies unsteadiness

At this point, I want to deal with that writer's list of "faults," one by one:

1. I have carried scope-sighted rifles from Mexico to Alaska to Africa and have never had one break on me. I did knock one out of line by having it strike a rock, but the same blow may have bent an iron sight totally out of whack.

2. I have never had "snow, leaves or other debris," cause me a miss because I could not see out of the scope. It is true that snow can gather on the lenses, but it takes quite a storm. Incidentally, on the other hand, I have had peep sights and even open iron sights clog up with snow.

3. There are lens caps today (Supreme lens covers, to be precise) which are spring loaded and do snap up out of the way, instantly.

4. Current scopes have little problem when it comes to fogging. But, to be fair to that writer, it should be said that some of the early commercial scopes did tend to fog up under certain circumstances. I have not seen a fogged scope for about 10 years, maybe longer.

5. Scabbards are now readily available for scope-sighted rifles.

6. There are scope sights which have immensely wide fields of view. I just mounted a 1.5–6x Bausch & Lomb scope on a 458 Win. Mag. rifle which was to be used in Africa. At the 1.5x setting, the scope has over 75 feet field of view!

7. Of course the scope magnifies our shake. And that is good, for it helps us correct this error in shooting. It certainly does not, however, make us shake more.

Scope Attributes

1. Construction: The scope sight's construction is very important. We can have a big clear picture, but without good scope construction, the unit may not serve the shooter very well at all. Top quality means top construction, not merely good glass. The good news is that the better scopes today are very well constructed of the finest materials.

2. Optics: Just because a scope has magnification does not mean that it's a quality sighting instrument. Top quality

The Bushnell 3x-9x Banner Lite-Site scope offers a bright dot as a reticle when the shooter feels the need for added definition of sight picture. It works especially well in the latter part of the hunting day and in deep woods on overcast days.

scopes have the best in optical glass, ground to precision. Good optics mean that there will be *fine* definition—a *clear* picture. Definition can be scientifically calculated, but for us, definition means being able to define a target, see it clearly, distinguish its elements.

3. *Magnification:* While the simple term "scope" usually indicates some presence of magnification, a 1x, or no-power scope, can be useful as it is still a sighting instrument, and one with a very wide field of view. A 1x scope can be placed upon a shotgun, for example, or any firearm where magnification is not needed, but a clear view with a very distinct aiming point is desired.

4. *Aberration:* Aberration is the distortion which one finds in low-quality optical instruments. The glass lenses tend to bend light. Distortion can result. But quality lenses are *achromatic,* that is, there are two (or more) lenses cemented together so that distortion is greatly minimized. No need to worry. Today's better scopes use these lenses which, along with other features, provide the shooter with an optical product possessing minimal (if any) aberration.

5. *Field of View:* Today's scopes have plenty of field of view, and, field of view is determined at the 100-yard mark and expressed in feet. A good example would be a 30-foot field of view at 100 yards for a 4x scope. I recently placed a Bushnell Scopechief 2.5-8x on a custom 6.5mm rifle. That scope has a 45-foot field of view at the 2.5x setting and a 14-foot field of view at the 8x setting. In short, there is a wide field of view at low power, hence I carry the scope on the 2.5x setting in the woods. When cranked up to 8x, that means I'm shooting either at a small or distant target, the 14-foot field of view presenting no problem at all.

6. *Eye Relief:* Eye relief is the optimum distance between the eye of the hunter and the external surface of the scope's ocular lens. Again, the variation is great. There are low-power scopes which can be used on handguns or mounted forward of the receiver on rifles because the eye relief is generous—usually 18 inches or so. Normally, eye relief measures in the 2.5- to 5-inch range for receiver-mounted big game scopes. You should mount a scope in such a way that it's as far forward as it will fit on the rifle while still giving you a full sight picture (no blackout at the edges). Too little eye relief can mean getting whacked in the head by the ocular lens, depending of course on the recoil potential of the rifle.

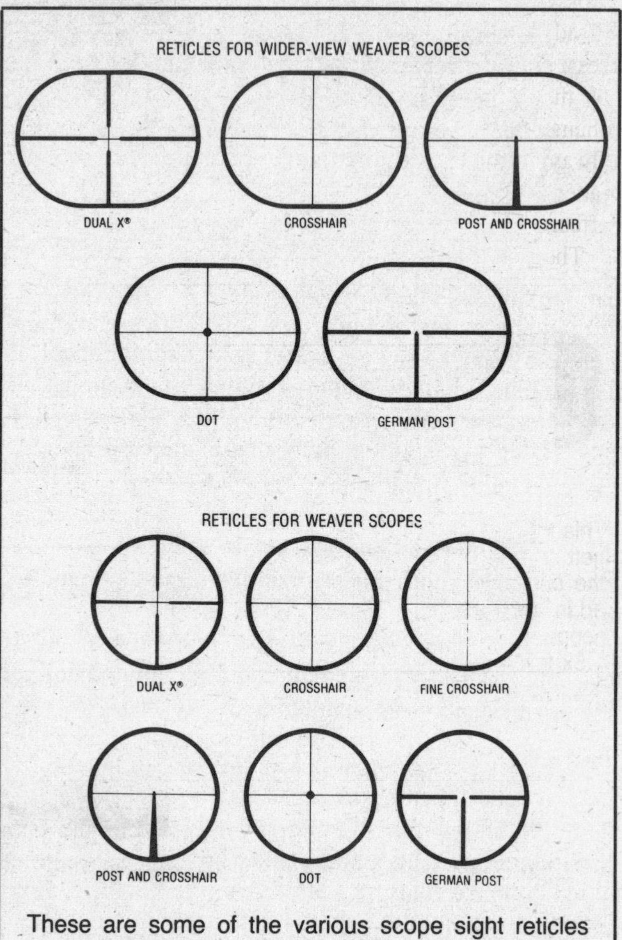

These are some of the various scope sight reticles available for the shooter. The author prefers the Dual-X, upper left-hand model. However, there are many shooters who prefer other styles and they have a wide selection to choose from.

7. *The Reticle:* Over the years there have been so many different types of reticles used in scopes that it would take pages to review them all. Most of them were dreamed up as miracle workers, but they failed to produce anything special at all. For my part, give me a crosswire that is either tapered or of the type called 4-Plex (Redfield's name) or Multi-Plex (Bushnell's name). What this means is that the outer construction of the reticle's crosswires is quite thick (so they can be seen in dim light) while the aiming center is finer. I prefer this type of reticle.

The good news is that the reticles remain centered in today's scopes. In earlier times, it was not uncommon to sight in a scope and end up with a sight picture that had the crosshairs intersecting well off center. But today, the crosswires always appear well centered, even after plenty of adjustment has been made during the sighting in process. Our variables have the reticle placed at the focal point of the scope's eyepiece. So changing power does not change the apparent optical size of the reticle. This was not always true. In some of the old variables, the reticle got fatter as the power went up, just the opposite of the desired effect. Today, that's all corrected.

There used to be some excitement over fancy reticles in terms of posts, tapered posts, posts and crosswires, dots of all sizes, dots with crosswires and about everything in between. The dots were well-liked by many for hunting purposes, but it is the original, traditional crosshair which has survived, though more commonly in the "Plex" style with the fine aiming center.

What about rangefinders and wind drift calculators and other built-in gadgets? In fact, they are just fine. When it comes to big game, I opt for traditional scopes, free of those gadgets, but I am not against them. I simply find that with the modern cartridge, one can generally sight in for about 275 yards, roughly speaking, and this means that from zero to 300 yards, you simply hold right on a big game animal. Varmints constitute a different story, however. I like built-in rangefinders and other aids when a scope is used for shooting at small targets very far away.

I also like some of the newer reticle advantages such as the Bushnell Banner Lite-Site. Many fine big game trophies have been taken at the latter part of the hunting day. The Lite-Site has a battery which powers a little red dot which lights up in the center of the scope, providing a very positive aiming point for dusky conditions or overcast days in the deep woods. The march continues toward more and more innovations in shooting scopes, and a good many of these innovations are going to make the scope sight more and more useful as time goes by.

Much is happening. There are scopes with matte finishes for those hunters who do not care for the bright, reflective finish. There are fine scopes for silhouette shooting, with quick-adjust turrets. There are wide-angle scopes. There are superb handgun scopes. There are very economical scopes for 22 rimfire rifles and scopes especially made for air gun use. There are scopes with adjustable objective lenses. The modern telescopic sight, I feel, will continue to evolve. It is already remarkable in what it can do, but I have a feeling "we ain't seen nothing yet."

(Left) Scopes have reached high levels of sophistication. This Bushnell 4-12x Banner riflescope has a Bullet Drop Compensator built into it along with a Primsatic Rangefinder. It is also available in a wide angle model.

This rifle, belonging to hunter Val Forgett, was used in Africa. Because of the close-range opportunities presented in the bush, Val mounted a variable scope with wide angle, the Bushnell 1.5x to 4x Banner.

The Variable Scope

My scope choice is the variable which was once less than perfect in many ways, but lacking little today. The variable can be very light and small, too. My aforementioned 2.5-9x Bushnell is about the same size as a 4x scope, and yet I have all that range of power. A variable is extremely useful on a big game rifle or a rifle which doubles for varmints and deer, too.

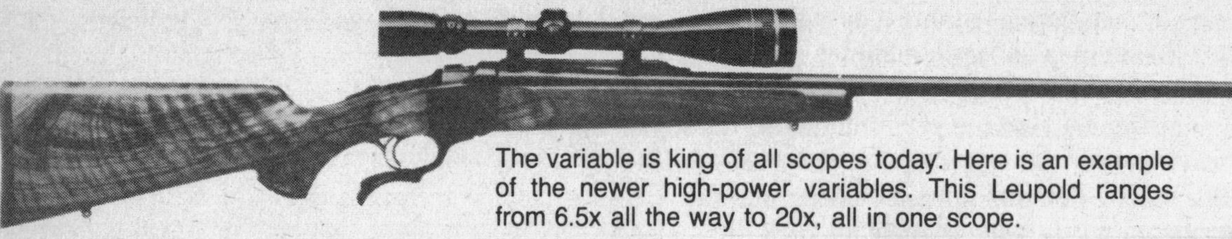

The variable is king of all scopes today. Here is an example of the newer high-power variables. This Leupold ranges from 6.5x all the way to 20x, all in one scope.

This is the H&R Model 904 22 Long Rifle swing out model. Note the excellent mounts which allow the H&R Model 435 Hunting-Silhouette scope to fit the revolver perfectly.

Scopes can take plenty of recoil these days without the least bit of internal problem. This includes the handgun scope. This Leupold handgun scope is mounted on a Colt 45 auto pistol. Note how the scope fits the slide as an integral part of the pistol.

Some shooters say they don't use the variable feature much. They end up setting it at a certain power, such as 4x, and leaving it there. That is like buying a car with 50 features and using only three of them. The variable is to be used *as a variable*. Even in open country, I carry my rifle with the scope on low power, 2.5x to maybe 3x. You never can tell when a game animal is going to pop right up in front of you, even in wide open terrain. At the lower setting, the field of view is wonderfully wide. Let a big buck get up across a canyon, however, and by the time the seat of my pants meets with the ground I will have my scope cranked up in power. Even for a running shot at long range, a little more power is good for precision in aiming. Give me a feeding buck at long range and a good rest, and I will wind the power up all the way for the most precise aiming point possible.

The variable feature is the best thing that ever happened to scopes. But use its potential. The variable offers a lot of power in one package. Take advantage of that reservoir of optic power. Switch the power to suit the need at hand, and always sight in at the highest power of the variable. If I could gain only the advantage of sighting in at high power, the variable would be worth having. But it does so much more.

Scope Mounts

Talking scopes is fine. Picking a good scope is wise. But no matter what the scope or the purpose for that scope, it must be securely mounted on the firearm. Many are the systems used, actually. But the old nightmares, those huge ugly monsters which were used to attach scopes to firearms, are gone. Today, the scope mount is sleek and strong and light in weight.

There is no point in going into great detail here. A properly dimensioned one-piece base is a good investment for high power, high recoil rifles. The two-piece base unit is plenty for most rifles, even the high recoil numbers. As for looks, I suppose the two-base is better to the eyes. But that's a matter of opinion. I say pick the scope mount which is most appropriate and handsome for the rifle in question. The gunsmith can show the prospective buyer a lot of ring/base styles, and so can the gunshop clerk. Catalogs are also good places to shop for mounts. See what's available to fit your particular firearm and then choose on the basis of strength required and of beauty.

Mounting the Scope

Pre-drilled and tapped rifle receivers, as well as some sidearms, make home-mounting of scopes possible. When the gun is not drilled and tapped for the proper mount, a good gunsmith is the answer to the problem. Choose your mount and make sure that it fits correctly and tightly. Also, be sure to follow precisely the installation instructions that come with your rings and base(s). Place the scope as far forward on the rifle as it will go and still allow for proper eye relief and clearance of the bolt handle. How far forward the scope is mounted is based upon how an individual shooter places his face on the comb of the stock.

Mount the scope loosely and try it over and over again. A good way to do this is to mount the rifle with the eyes shut, and then after the rifle is firmly against the shoulder with the face on the comb, open your eyes. Where are you looking? If the shooter mounts the scope rigidly and then tries to look through it, he may actually force himself into an uncomfortable shooting position in order to make him fit the scope, instead of making the mounted scope fit him and his shooting style.

Sighting the Scope

Sighting in your scope sight is not difficult. Here are the five steps.

1. Bore sight: Any gunsmith can bore sight a scope. This usually means lining the scope's crosshairs up with an optical boresighter such as that offered by Bushnell. The boresighter is afixed to the muzzle of the gun prior to reticle adjustment. By matching the scope's crosshairs with the optical grid system of the boresight, the shooter is assured of hitting the paper at least at close range. It's a real time and ammo saver.

2. Focus: Shooters often forget that a scope can be focused. I take a newly scoped firearm to the range and mount it with my eyes shut. Then I look through the scope. If the picture is the least bit unclear, I focus the scope (directions on focusing come with the scope). This means loosening a small lock ring at the front of the ocular bell and actually turning the eyepiece in or out until visual clarity is achieved.

3. Start Close: Once again, that 25-yard starting point is used. It saves time and ammo.

4. Sighting In: Removing the caps from the scope's windage and elevation turrets, there is bound to be an indication of how much movement value each increment or "click" has. If there is no indication within the scope cap itself, then the instruction sheet that came with the scope will have that information. As an example, the inside of the turret caps on my Bushnell ScopeChief VI, reads, "One Click 1/4 inch at 100 YD." That's all I needed to know.

As for direction, the scope tells you that, too. An arrow on the adjustment knob will indicate the correct direction to go, be it up, down, left or right. If, for example, my rifle were shooting 4 inches to the left at 100 yards, my ScopeChief would require 16 clicks *to the right* to correct that problem. Some scope mounts also have adjustment in them, of course, and the shooter may wish to take up major adjustment, especially for windage, within the mount before working with the scope's internal adjustments.

5. Summary: Instead of going into further detail concerning the sighting in of a rifle, in terms of where the bullet should strike at 100 yards in order to be "on" farther out, we have designed a whole, and important, chapter around that topic. For specifics on correctly sighting your own firearm *to gain the most from its potential trajectory,* turn to the next chapter.

Other Sight Devices

Millet Sights makes a custom device for firearms which does not fall into the class of open iron sight, peep iron sight or scope. They call it the Cyclops 22 Reflex Sight. It wears integral mounts and fits quickly into any 22 rimfire

Redfield has offered the one-piece base for a very long time. It now offers the same type of setup for the handgun. The mount in the foreground is a JR double dovetail suited for the Ruger Mark I and Mark II pistols. A rugged pistol mount is as important as a rugged scope mount on a rifle.

style dovetail slot. The crosshair, dot or pyramid reticle (your choice) is bright fluorescent, but there is no battery or electrical device within the Cyclops. It's a reflex sight because it uses a mirror system. The Cyclops gathers light and concentrates it through the reticle module onto the mirror and then this image is reflected to the shooter's eye. Reticles are interchangeable in seconds, using only a coin. The unit only weighs a bit under 5 ounces.

The "Aimpoint" is a non-magnifying, optical device designed to fit shotgun, rifle, handgun or bow. If you want magnification for the Aimpoint, there are optional 3x or 1.5x-4x variable devices that provide a boost. When you look through the Aimpoint, you'll see a red dot dead in the center of the sight picture. It's electronically displayed. The red aiming point will vary in intensity according to the background, this accomplished with a rheostat control. You simply place the dot on the target and squeeze off the shot.

Almost from the beginning of shooting, the marksman has continued to invent device after device for the purpose of aiming the firearm. Of course, it's no wonder. Given the finest gun in the world, that gun is no better than its sights. A rifle, for example, may be capable of ½-inch groups at 100 yards, but without the proper sights, it will never approach its actual capability. Both shooters and manufacturers have spent a lot of time, effort and money designing sighting devices, but the effort has been worth it. Today, we have fine sights all the way from open irons to peeps to scopes and a few modern units which don't even fall into the traditional categories of sights. The complete shooter needs to be aware of the options. He must select the sights which suit his arms and his needs. Then he has to sight in to take advantage of the trajectory potential of the gun/cartridge those sights are mounted on.

The Millett Cyclops is a 22 rimfire aiming device which cannot be called a scope sight. It is in fact a reflex sight system which offers three quick-change reticles, all of which stand out brightly and require no battery power.

The Aimpoint sighting device offers a bright red dot as its reticle. There is also an optional scope attachment in 3x and another in 1.5x-4x. The latter is shown here with the Aimpoint.

Chapter 16

Trajectory Charts

GETTING CLOSE to the target, especially when that target is a game animal, is my policy. Harvesting of game for food is an important part of the game management system, and the hunter owes it to himself (and the game) to perfectly place one shot for a swift dispatch of the animal. If I can get a 100-yard shot instead of a 200-yard shot, I prefer it. If I can get even closer, I prefer that. Getting close is often the key to sure bullet placement.

But there are times when it is legitimate to shoot at longer ranges, and there are occasions when the only opportunity is going to be a longer shot. We have the ammunition which will do the job at long range, very cleanly and humanely. The 7mm Remington Magnum handload has more punch at 300 yards than many of the popular "deer rounds" possess at the muzzle.

Furthermore, shooting at long-range targets is a very rewarding sport. You do not have to be a hunter to enjoy firing at silhouettes at 200 or even 500 meters. And you don't have to be shooting in a formal contest to enjoy safe long-range shooting either. I have placed targets against a dirt bluff, backed off 300 or 400 yards and learned much from the shooting experience, especially concerning bullet drift and drop.

The "trick" to hitting at longer range, however, is knowing where to hold. No rifle ever made shoots "flat." That would be impossible. Even the scintillating 220 Swift at 4000 fps MV does not shoot "flat." In fact, firing a 50-grain 22-caliber bullet out of the Swift at 4000 fps MV nets a bullet drop of more than 1 foot at 300 yards providing the barrel is perfectly horizontal to the landscape. The 30-06 using a 180-grain bullet at a MV of 2700 fps will drop 2 feet at 300 yards under the same conditions. If we could get rid of gravity and atmosphere, things would be different, but we are stuck with both of these physical powers and both work hard to thwart the flight of the bullet, gravity "pulling" the bullet down and atmosphere creating drag.

The complete shooter simply has to learn how to sight in

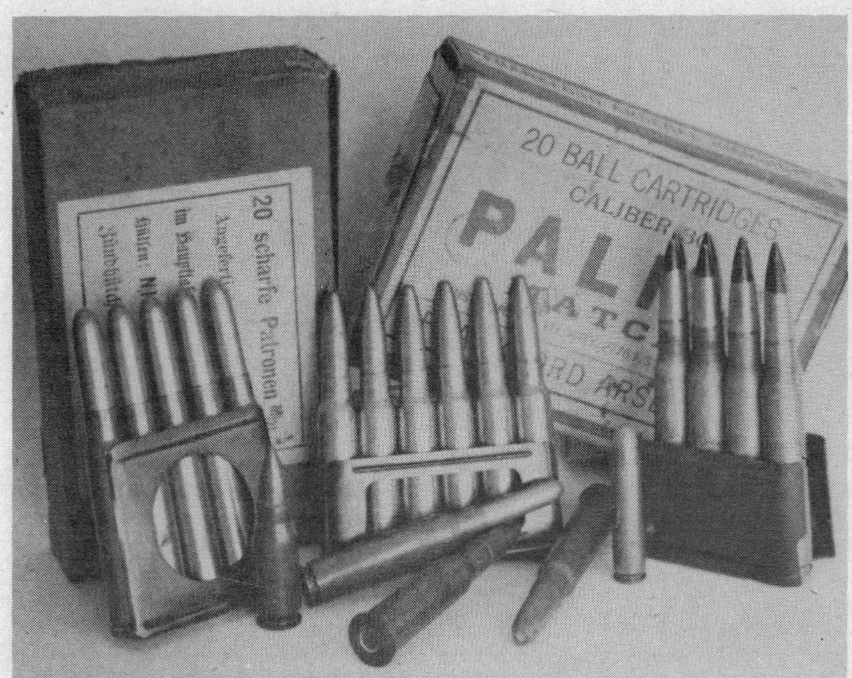

Ammunition, be it military or sporting, is designed for different tasks, each caliber having its own peculiar internal and external set of ballistics. Every shooter should make a sincere attempt to understand the ballistic attributes of the cartridges/shotshells his firearms are chambered for.

his particular firearm and load to gain the very most of the potential trajectory pattern from that load. I was hunting in Wyoming one season when I came across a fellow who had bagged an antelope buck. My son had also downed a buck. The fellow looked into the back of the pickup truck and admired my son's prize, and we admired his. Then he said, "He sure got a nice buck, but I bet he didn't have to shoot as far as I did." I asked the man how far he had to shoot in order to get his antelope. "I shot this buck at 700 yards," he informed me

He was using a 30-06 with 150-grain factory loads. I have chronographed 150-grain 30-06 factory loads at about 2800 fps, but let's say this load was doing 2900 fps out of the man's 22-inch barrel. I asked how the rifle was sighted in and how high he had to hold. He told me that the rifle was sighted in for 200 yards and that he had held a few inches over the back of the antelope, because, after all, the 30-06 is relatively flat-shooting, and it is. However, if our friend had actually held only a couple of inches over the back of an antelope at 700 yards, shooting a 30-06 with a 150-grain bullet starting out at 2900 fps MV, he would have missed that antelope clean as new snow. In fact, the bullet would have struck somewhere in the neighborhood of 100 inches or over 8 feet *low!* An antelope buck is lucky to be 14-inches tall in the chest. Holding a few inches over his back, that bullet would have plowed earth before it ever got to the buck. Our shooter certainly did *not* have a 700-yard shot. He probably shot from something like 250 yards out, given the position of the entrance wound.

Had that man known something about judging range, he would not have thought he had taken an antelope at 700 yards. He knew nothing about it, however. Had he known something about the actual trajectory of his load, he still would not have been so badly fooled as to think he had dropped a pronghorn at 700 yards. The complete shooter owes it to himself to know the trajectory pattern of his firearm, and that goes for everything from the 22 rimfire to the rifled slug. By knowing the capabilities and limitations of his firearm, the shooter can sensibly manage his own long range attempts, not only at game, but also on less animate targets.

We must sight the rifle in such a way as to gain the *most* from its ballistic potential. Sighting a 270 Winchester for 100 yards is castrating the load and reducing it from the long-range round that it is, down to an also-ran. Think about this: Let's say that a shooter sights his 270 Winchester in dead on at 100 yards. He's using the 130-grain bullet at 3100 fps MV. His bullet will strike *about* a foot low at 300 yards with this sighting. That fine flat-shooting 270 Winchester is striking 1-foot low at 300 yards because it has not been sighted-in *correctly*.

Using Our Charts

The following information is based upon mathematical construct in part, but I did not stop there. I fired many of the loads myself (over the years) and the data reflects my own findings. That there are problems here, I am the first to admit. The big problem is group size and along with that problem we also have firearm individuality. Call it a difference in bedding and barrel vibration, chambering, bore drag and many other factors, but two 30-06s of identical brand, style and barrel length may shoot quite differently in spite of the fact that they are using the same exact load. Moreover, when considering drop, we must also consider group size. If a rifle groups into 4 inches at 300 yards, then part of the drop can be considered inherent in the group

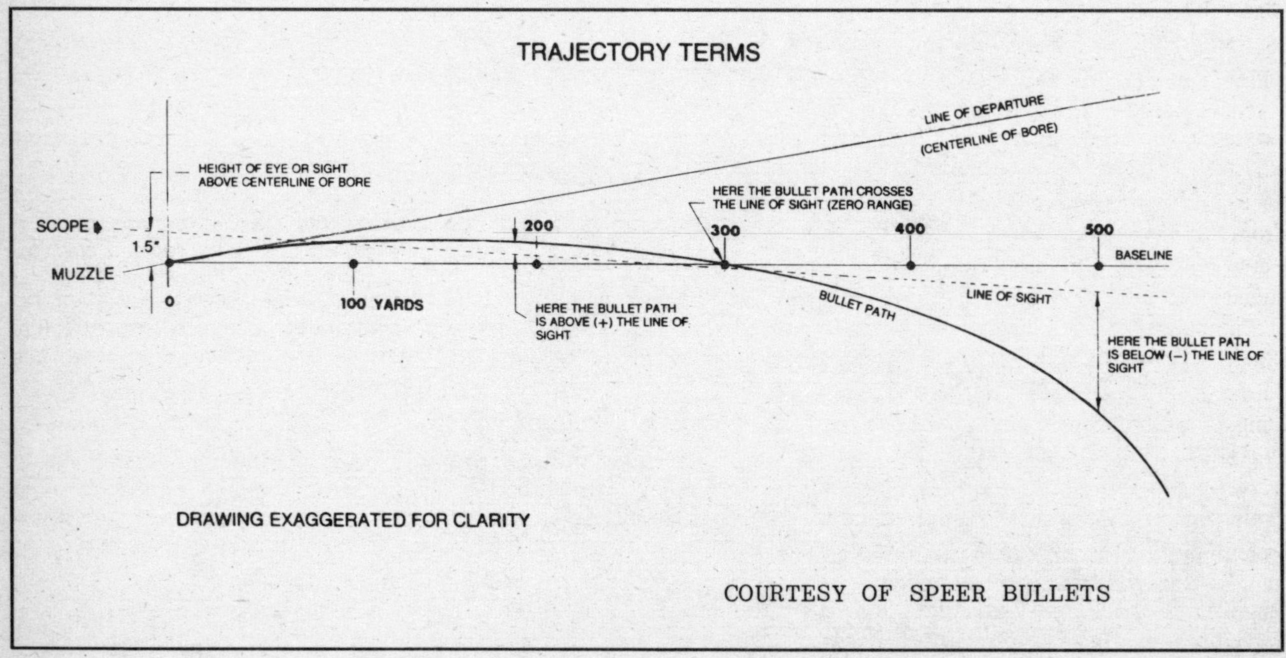

COURTESY OF SPEER BULLETS

These four rounds are more alike than they are different. On the left is the 264 Winchester Magnum, followed by the 270 Winchester, the 7mm Remington Magnum and finally the 30-06. All make fine all-around cartridges, but the 7mm Remington Magnum was selected by the author as the best of the bunch *for that purpose,* though better by a small margin only. (See trajectory chart comparing the four rounds, as well as remaining energy chart.)

size itself. I tried to get a center-to-center group size first so that I could better determine the actual drop of a load as opposed to the opening of the group itself.

Also, it's not possible to put the findings into neat little boxes. In short, if we show that a rifle chambered for the 257 Roberts drops X-inches at 200 yards, that means little to us because we have sighted the rifle to gain the *most* from *its* trajectory potential. Therefore, it's important to show a lot more information than that. And this set of tables does have much more information than that.

First, the shooter is going to find out where to start shooting from in yards. All of our loads describe a parabola, a curved flight, with the bullet rising up and then dropping down. This means that the bullet strikes the *line of sight twice,* once when it's on the way up and once when it is on the way down. The bullet must go up first. If we fire it on the horizontal, that kills all chances of gaining the potential of the trajectory. So we want to know at what range a bullet strikes the first time on the line of sight so that we can *start our sighting-in there*. For example, it may be wise to start firing a 270 at only 25 yards, because the bullet hits the line of sight at 25 yards first and then hits again at about 275 yards, being a bit low at 300 yards.

Line of Sight

Line of sight is in fact that line described by the eye as it looks at the target. It is perfectly *flat*. The line of sight is perfect from the eye to the target with no drop or rise, of course. It's only imaginary as compared with the bullet, which actually does wing its way to the target, but the line of sight is very real because it is a true line from the eye to the actual destination of the bullet. What we need to know is how much, up or down, the bullet departs from that perfect line of sight. After all, no bullet shoots "flat." So no bullet matches the line of sight.

Ideally, we want four basic figures. The first is the distance at which the bullet initially crosses the line of sight—it will be close to the shooter. This is when the bullet is on the way "up" at the beginning of its parabola. Next, we want to know where the bullet hits the line of sight the second time, on its way down, near the end of the parabola. That is two of our four major pieces of information. We also want to know *how high* the bullet hits at 100 yards, and how low it hits *after* it has crossed the line of sight for the second time.

If the rifle is sighted-in correctly, a "flat-shooting" rifle will initially cross that line of sight quite close to us, maybe only 25 yards out. It will then climb until it strikes a little *high* at 100 yards and perhaps a little *high* at 200 yards as well, sometimes a bit higher than it hit at 100 yards. As the bullet travels towards the "down-side" of the parabola it will strike right on the line of sight again, and of course will proceed to drop after it strikes the line of sight for the second time. Our job is to determine both of those bullet-intersection points along the line of sight. A 270 Winchester firing a 130-grain bullet at 3100 fps MV will hit the line of sight at about 25 yards. It will climb until it strikes 3-inches high at 100 yards. It will still be climbing at 200 yards, hitting about 4 inches above the bull's-eye's center. Now it begins to fall. It crosses the line of sight again at 275 yards, and it's about 3 inches low at 300 yards.

Let us not concern ourselves with mid-range trajectories. The mid-range trajectory is the height of a specific bullet's trajectory at some point precisely *halfway* between the muzzle of the gun and the aiming point or where the line of sight cuts through the center of the bull's-eye. It can be an interesting figure, but I want to know other things. I want to know where to start my sighting-in. I want to know how high the rifle bullet is going to strike at 100 yards and at 200 yards. I want to know where that bullet is going to hit the line of sight again. And I want to know how much it is going to drop (in inches) after that point. Remember, the rifle is sighted in for that point where the bullet hits the line of sight *for the second time*. The above 270 load was sighted in for 275 yards. If someone asked me, "Where should

I sight my 270 with a 130-grain bullet at 3100 fps MV so I can gain the most from the trajectory?,'' I would say to sight in for 275 yards. But that's a problem. Public shooting ranges are not laid out that way. So I would add that he should start shooting at the first bullet-intersection point, about 25 yards. Once the rifle has been sighted-in at 25 yards, he should shoot so that the center of the group hits 3 inches high at 100 yards. Even if he quit shooting right there, I would be confident that his 270 was fairly well sighted for its best advantage. But he should try to find a 200-yard and 300-yard range if possible, for the sake of verifying the initial sighting in. As we get farther and farther down-range, the angle of departure of the bullet means that being off ½-inch at 100 yards can magnify itself considerably at 300 yards. I have worked with a long-range rifle, trying to get it to group at 300 yards so that I would thwart the problem of angle of departure. In short, refine the sighting-in of your rifle on a long-range target if possible. But remember that the group is going to open up at long range. Be sure to take that factor into account. Also, there is a small tendency for a bullet to drift (even in dead calm) in the direction of the rifling twist. So a right-hand twist means a drift to the right for the bullet. Sighted perfectly at 100 yards for windage, a bullet may drift slightly right in this case at 200 and 300 yards and beyond. I like to sight in at longer range, knowing that I may in fact strike very slightly left of target at 100 yards. The variation is not important to big game hunting, but should be taken into account for target shooters, who should sight in for the specific range of the match.

Rifle Trajectory Charts

Rimfires

1. 22 Long Rifle/40-grain bullet/1300 fps MV

0	+1″	0	−2.5″	−7.5″
20 yards	50 yards	85 yards	100 yards	125 yards

Interpretation: Sight in for 20 yards initially. Refine at 50 yards for a 1-inch high group average, or measure off 85 yards and shoot right on target at that range. In this test, which was an actual shooting test, the results were as shown above. However, 22 ammunition can vary slightly. Also, elevation above sea level does affect accuracy; therefore, the results would vary slightly at other elevations, though not by any great degree. All of our tests were taken at about 6,000 feet above sea level.

2. 22 Hyper-Velocity Long Rifle/33-grain bullet/1500 fps MV

0	+2.5″	0	−6.0″	−9.25″
25 yards	50 yards	100 yards	125 yards	150 yards

Interpretation: It's like the 22 LR, only better. Stingers, Yellow Jackets, Spitfires, etc., attain their extra velocity via a slightly longer case and slow burning powders. It is better suited for medium range varmint shooting than 22 LR high speed hollow points. Zero it for 25 yards and you'll be on at 100, only 6 inches low at 125 yards. Hyper velocity rimfires, and their light (and normally hollow-pointed) bullets can destroy meat on small game. Pick your shots accordingly.

3. 22 Winchester Rimfire Magnum HP/40-grain bullet/1900 fps MV

0	−1″	0	−6.0″	−20″
25 yards	50 yards	100 yards	150 yards	200 yards

Interpretation: Sighting in for 100 yards gives the shooter a ''point blank'' range of about 150 yards for varmint-shooting. This is not bad, considering that the 22 WMR is losing much of its steam at about 150 yards anyway. If a shooter does feel a need for gaining more potential from this round, he can sight in for 150 yards on the money. This will put the bullet 3 inches high at 50 yards, 4 inches high at 100 yards, and about 11 inches low at 200 yards.

17-Caliber Centerfires

1. 17 Mach IV (221 Jet necked with change in shoulder)/25-grain JHP bullet/3700 fps MV

0	+1″	+3″	+4″	0	−.75″
25 yds.	50 yds.	100 yds.	200 yds	290 yds.	300 yds.

Interpretation: The little wildcat 17-caliber Mach IV is best sighted as above because the energy level has fallen off, even for varmints, at the 300-yard range. However, in terms of trajectory, the round is only ¾-inch low at 300 yards in our tests. Even a small varmint can be hit at 325 yards with this sighting.

2. 17 Remington/25-grain JHP spitzer bullet/4100 fps MV

0	+1″	+2″	+3″	0
25 yards	50 yards	100 yards	200 yards	300 yards

Interpretation: The hot little Remington 17-caliber flattens the trajectory sufficiently to allow for a mere 3-inch rise at 200 yards in order for a sight-in at a full 300 yards. Although the small bullet will drift badly in a strong wind, it shoots remarkably well in the calm. Furthermore, accuracy is very good if the bore is kept clean. At least one barrel maker has turned to a 3-groove bore in order to reduce fouling.

22-Caliber Centerfires

1. 22 Hornet & 218 Bee/50-grain JHP spitzer bullet/2800 fps MV

0	+3″	0	−9″.
25 yards	100 yards	225 yards	300 yards

Interpretation: The 22 Hornet and 218 Bee can be sighted dead on at 225 yards. This gives a good pattern of trajectory out to a solid 250 yards plus. In my opinion these little 22 centerfires are best held to 250 yards in terms of power for clean dispatch of varmints.

2. 222 Remington (222 Remington Magnum and 223 Remington)/50-grain JHP spitzer bullet/3300 fps MV

0	+3″	+4″	0	−2″	−15″
25 yds.	100 yds.	200 yds.	285 yds.	300 yds.	400 yds.

Interpretation: The fine 222 Remington and its near cousins the 223 and 222 Magnum do very well with a sight-in of about 285 yards. Note that the drop is only 2 inches at 300 yards. But by the time the bullet has reached 400 yards, it is dropping so rapidly that we find more than a foot loss. This shows us that the 222 class is best limited to shots under 350 yards.

3. 220 Swift, 22-250 Remington, 224 Weatherby/50-grain JHP spitzer bullet/3900 fps MV

0	+2.5″	+3.5″	0	−8.5″
25 yards	100 yards	200 yards	310 yards	400 yards

Interpretation: The flat-shooting Swift and its counterparts make fine varmint rounds out to 350 yards. A knowledgeable shooter who can either guesstimate or calculate the range fairly exactly could probably make hits at 400 yards without undue strain. In my own experience, I found that on jackrabbit-sized targets, the Swift or 22-250 was excellent up to 400 yards on a calm day.

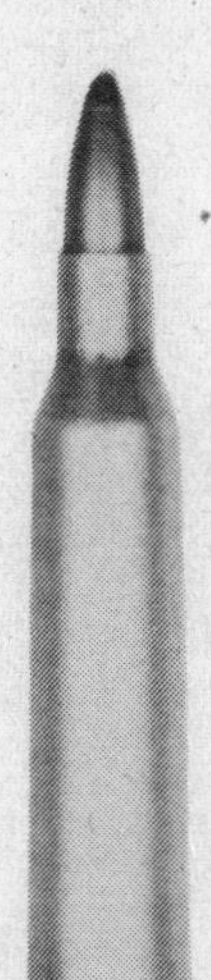

High speed cartridges like the 220 Swift either flirt with or beat the 4000 fps mark. Cartridges like the Swift, 22-250 Remington and 224 Weatherby are well suited for varmints at longer ranges.

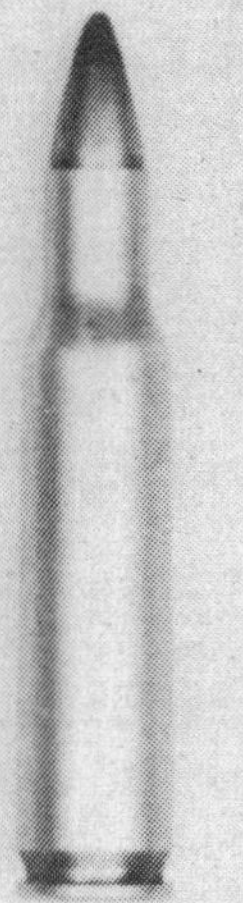

Sighted in for 25 yards, the 222's 50-grain slug drops about 2 inches at 300 yards. As varmint rounds, this class of cartridge is best limited to ranges of 350 yards, or less.

243-Caliber Centerfires

1. 243 Winchester & 6mm Remington/100-grain JHP spitzer bullet/3100 fps MV

0	+3″	+4″	0	−3″	−13″
25 yds.	100 yds.	200 yds.	275 yds.	300 yds.	400 yds.

Interpretation: The 243 Winchester and 6mm Remington are near ballistic twins. They sight in very much the same as the 270 Winchester, and in my tests I found that the mean figures for both were nearly identical and so close as to be called *the same*. The 270 sighted for 275 yards also dropped 13 inches at 400 yards with the 130-grain bullet starting at 3100 fps MV.

2. 240 Weatherby/100-grain JHP spitzer bullet/3400 fps MV

0	+3″	+3.5″	0	−9″
25 yards	100 yards	200 yards	300 yards	400 yards

Interpretation: The hot 240 Weatherby did pick up some yardage in terms of trajectory flatness. I could theoretically sight the 240 Weatherby dead on at 300 yards, and it would still have sufficient flatness of trajectory for a hold-right-on hit at up to 400 yards on an 18-inch tall target. In practical terms, one could shoot at a deer-sized target at up to 350 yards with a dead-on hold, and by holding directly level with the spine, a deer-sized target could be hit at a full 400 yards. This is not to advocate 400-yard shooting, but to merely point out that it's a possibility considering the 240's trajectory pattern.

25-Caliber Centerfires

1. 250 Savage & 257 Roberts/100-grain SP spitzer bullet/3100 fps MV

0	+3″	+4″	0	−3″	−10″
25 yds.	100 yds.	200 yds.	275 yds.	300 yds.	400 yds.

Interpretation: The 250-3000 Savage and 257 Roberts, both with their best handloads, pushed the 100-grain .257-inch bullet at a MV of 3100 fps for a trajectory pattern very much like the 243 Winchester and 6mm Remington rounds. As best as could be established, those two rounds shot very slightly lower at 400 yards.

2. 25-06 Remington/120-grain SP spitzer bullet/3200 fps MV

0	+3″	+4″	0	−10″
25 yards	100 yards	200 yards	300 yards	400 yards

Interpretation: I used the 120-grain bullet at a chronographed muzzle velocity of 3200 fps. The load consisted of 64.0 grains of H-870 in Winchester cases. In three separate tests, drop was 9 inches, 10 inches and 10 inches, so the mode of 10 inches was recorded for 400 yards with a dead-on 300-yard sighting. This is a flat-shooting round indeed and the 120-grain bullet can be recommended.

3. 257 Weatherby/100-grain SP spitzer bullet/3600 fps MV

0	+2.5″	+3″	0	−8″
25 yards	100 yards	200 yards	300 yards	400 yards

Interpretation: Sighted for 300 yards, the fast 257 Weatherby bullet landed only 3 inches high at 200 yards. One could experiment with this round by sighting-in his rifle to hit 4 inches high at 200 yards, which would put the bullet on at about 325 yards and about a 1/2-foot low at 400 yards. The 100-grain bullet was selected over the 120-grain bullet in this test because our own 257 Weatherby shot the 100-grain bullet more accurately.

264-Caliber Centerfires

1. 264 Winchester Magnum/140-grain SP spitzer bullet/3200 fps MV

0	+3″	+4″	0	−9″
25 yards	100 yards	200 yards	300 yards	400 yards

Interpretation: The 264 Winchester Magnum was the only 6.5mm tested because the .264-inch diameter bullet has not seen great popularity among American shooters. With full-power charges, the 140-grain bullet does manage 3200 fps from a 26-inch barrel, and the round is very flat-shooting for big game, with good retention of initial energy.

270-Caliber Centerfires

1. 270 Winchester/130-grain SP spitzer bullet/3100 fps MV

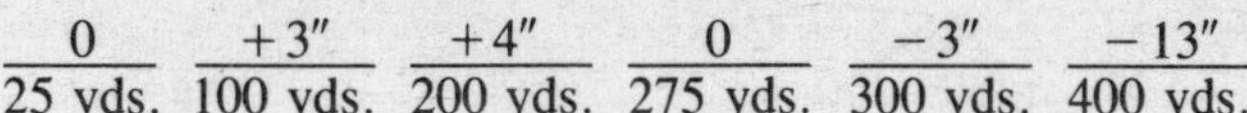

0	+3″	+4″	0	−3″	−13″
25 yds.	100 yds.	200 yds.	275 yds.	300 yds.	400 yds.

Interpretation: As popular as the 270 Winchester has been, and it is a world-class cartridge known in many countries, it has not sired an extensive list of .277-inch calibers. Therefore, only the 270 Winchester is listed here. Note that the 270's 130-grain bullet at 3100 fps MV (which can be gained from a 22-inch barrel), is quite flat-shooting for big game. Shots at 350 yards would require little guesstimation of hold. Again, this is not an advocation of long-range shooting, but rather a statement of the facts.

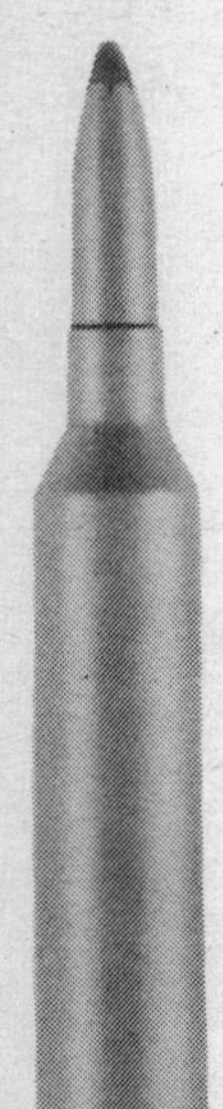

While the 264 Winchester Magnum has not seen great popularity with shooters, it's a flat-shooting round that possesses good retention of initial energy.

If the shooter/hunter takes the 7mm/08's drop chart into consideration, he will realize this round will serve nicely on deer-class game up to 300 yards. It's not an ultra-long range proposition.

7mm (.284-inch) Centerfires

1. 7mm/08 Remington/150-grain SP spitzer bullet/2600 fps MV

0	+2.5″	0	−6″	−10″
25 yards	100 yards	200 yards	250 yards	400 yards

Interpretation: The sensible 7mm/08 shoots quite flat enough for most big game hunting, in fact for all big game hunting if the outdoorsman will simply stalk instead of trying for long shots. However, it is clearly not flat-shooting much beyond the 240- to 275-yard mark. With sensible calculation, however, this round would serve for 300-yard shooting on game of the antelope class.

2. 7x57 Mauser & 284 Winchester/150-grain SP spitzer bullet/2900 fps MV

0	+3″	+4″	0	−4″
25 yards	100 yards	200 yards	270 yards	300 yards

Interpretation: The grand old 7mm Mauser, or 7×57, same thing, and the fine 284 Winchester can be sighted very much like the 270 Winchester, which was determined through testing. My wife's Dean Zollinger custom 284 with 22-inch barrel easily achieved 2900 fps MV with the 150-grain bullet and 3100 fps with a 125-grain Remington Core-Lokt bullet. The "standard" sighting (3 inches high at 100 yards) allowed for dead-on holding out to a solid 325 yards on big game with the weight of bullet and muzzle velocity shown above.

3. 7mm Remington Magnum & 7mm Weatherby Magnum/139-grain SP spitzer bullet/3400 fps MV

0	+3″	+4″	0	−9″
25 yards	100 yards	200 yards	300 yards	400 yards

Interpretation: The 139-grain bullet happens to be a handload we tried in the 7mm Remington Magnum with older Hornady data. Cases lasted well and case-head expansion was well within safe limits with the 3400 fps MV figure. Note that this round is as flat-shooting as most of the other calibers regarded as long-range numbers. The 160-grain bullet at 3100 fps MV is also flat-shooting. The

7mm Remington and Weatherby Magnums are quite the same ballistically which is why both are shown under one trajectory setup.

30-Caliber Centerfires

1. 30-30 Winchester/170-grain flat-point bullet/2200 fps MV

0	+1.5″	+2″	0	−5.5″
15 yards	50 yards	100 yards	150 yards	200 yards

Interpretation: In spite of its reputation as a close-range only proposition, the old 30-30 shoots flat enough to offer dead-on hold from zero to at least 200 yards, even with a very standard 170-grain flat-point loading. Out of the standard 30-30, velocities of 2500 fps MV have been achieved using H-335 powder with good case life, this being with the 150-grain bullet. This load allows for sighting dead-on at 200 yards, the bullet only rising about 2½ inches at 100 yards. My own 30-30 improved Model 54 Winchester bolt-action fires the same 150-grain spitzer or spire point bullet at 2700 fps MV, meaning a shooter can sight in only 2 inches high at 100 yards for a dead-on at 200 yards. (Pointed bullets are, of course, *never* to be loaded in ammo intended for use in rifles with tubular magazines.)

2. 300 Savage & 308 Winchester/150-grain SP spitzer bullet/2800 fps MV

0	+2.5″	0	−7″
25 yards	100 yards	225 yards	300 yards

Interpretation: One can readily see that a good shot with the ballistically similar 300 Savage or 308 Winchester can sight in for 225 yards, or a mere 2.5 inches high at 100 yards, and thereby have a point blank range for big game on up to 300 yards or a bit better.

3. 30-06 Springfield/150-grain SP spitzer bullet/3100 fps MV

0	+3″	+4″	0	−4″
25 yards	100 yards	200 yards	270 yards	300 yards

Interpretation: One can see that the venerable 30-06 is a flat-shooting round with the modern powders, such as Winchester 760 at work. With 63.0 grains of 760 in the Winchester case, we achieved 3100 fps MV from a 24-inch barrel. This allows the 30-06 to shoot just about as flat as a 270 Winchester with its 130-grain bullet at 3100 fps MV.

4. 300 H&H Magnum, 300 Winchester Magnum, 300 Weatherby Magnum/165-grain SP spitzer bullet/3200 fps MV

0	+3″	+4″	0	−10″
25 yards	100 yards	200 yards	290 yards	400 yards

Interpretation: These similar cartridges all have tremendous power at long range. The 300 Weatherby, for example, will fire a 150-grain bullet at a MV of 3500 fps. This means that with this load a shooter could sight in 3 inches high at 100 yards while striking the bull's-eye at about 325 yards! At 300 yards, the remaining energy of this load would be 2351 foot-pounds; the remaining energy of the 165-grain bullet with a MV of 3200 fps being 2251 foot-pounds at the same distance.

338-Caliber Centerfires

1. 338 WinchesterMagnum/225-grain SP spitzer bullet/2900 fps MV

0	+3″	+4″	0	−3″
25 yards	100 yards	200 yards	265 yards	300 yards

Interpretation: The 338 Winchester is the only highly popular round in that caliber at the moment, and the only one listed here. It is easy to see that the big 338 shoots quite flat and can be used on big game up to 350 yards with very little concern for severe hold-over measures when firing the 225-grain bullet at a MV of 2900 fps. Remaining energy with this load is 2620 foot-pounds a full 300 yards from the muzzle.

35-Caliber Centerfires

1. 35 Remington/200-grain round nose SP bullet/2000 fps MV

0	+2″	+3″	0	−7″
25 yards	50 yards	100 yards	150 yards	200 yards

The 300 Winchester Magnum (left), the 300 Holland & Holland (right) and the 300 Weatherby Magnum (not seen) all have good reputations when it comes to stopping big game at long range.

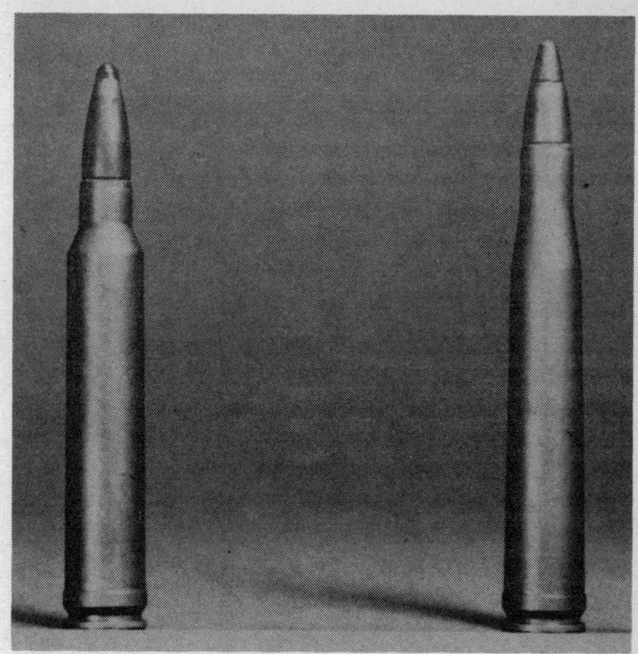

Interpretation: With the round nose bullet, the 35 Remington will sight well at 150 yards, making the rifle useful to the 200-yard mark on big game without undue hold-over concern. The 35 Remington should remain, however, in the 200 yards-or-less category for big game as the retained energy isn't much to brag about at longer distances.

2. 358 Winchester/200-grain SP spitzer bullet/2500 fps MV

0	+3″	0	−12″
25 yards	100 yards	200 yards	300 yards

Interpretation: The fine 358 Winchester makes a perfectly adequate round for up to 250-yard shooting. The 200-grain spitzer or spire point bullet delivers good energy at a starting velocity of 2500 fps, and though the round is not greatly popular today, it's easy to see that it is a good one.

3. 35 Whelen/200-grain SP spitzer bullet/2700 fps MV

0	+2.5″	0	−10″
25 yards	100 yards	200 yards	300 yards

Interpretation: The 35 Whelen is a wildcat round, but is quite common and very easily made from 30-06 cases; therefore it is rightfully included here. With the 200-grain pointed bullet at a starting velocity of 2700 fps, the 35 Whelen is certainly good for 250 yards without undue hold-over on big game. Over the years, many shooters have called for commercializing of this popular wildcat. It delivers about a ton of big-game killing energy at 200 yards.

4. 358 Norma Magnum/200-grain SP spitzer bullet/2900 fps MV

0	+2.5″	0	−8″
25 yards	100 yards	225 yards	300 yards

Interpretation: At a range of 300 yards, the big 358 Norma Magnum delivers 1797 foot-pounds of energy. In fact, the 7mm Remington Magnum with a 175-grain bullet at 3000 fps (my own handload) ends up with about 2240 foot-pounds of remaining energy. With heavy bullets at close range, the 358 Norma would be superior to the 7mm Magnum on big game, I believe, but at longer ranges the 7mm Magnum is hard to beat. One can, however, shoot point blank on big game out to 300 yards with a 358 Norma Magnum loaded with a 200-grain bullet.

45-Caliber Centerfires

1. 45-70 Springfield (loads for 1895 Marlin rifle only)/ 350-grain round nose SP bullet/1900 fps MV

0	+2.5″	+3	0	−8″
25 yards	50 yards	100 yards	150 yards	200 yards

Interpretation: The grand 45-70 is still around and seems to be looking forward to a continued tenure with the shooting fraternity. Note that out of the handsome Marlin rifle, one can sight dead on for 150 yards without undue hold-under at close range. At 200 yards a good shot who knows his Marlin 1895 should be able to easily connect with big game. Energy is down to 1100 foot-pounds at 200 yards with this load, but still adequate for deer.

2. 458 Winchester Magnum/500-grain full-metal-jacket bullet/2100 fps MV

0	+1.5″	+2″	0	−5″
25 yards	50 yards	100 yards	150 yards	200 yards

Interpretation: Although it probably has no right to its popularity among American shooters, the big 458 Winchester is enjoyed by a good many arms enthusiasts, many of whom simply want to experience its tremendous power. The round has become a standard in modern African hunting as well. With the 500-grain "solid" at 2100 fps, it is no trick to sight-in for 150 yards. The bullet rises a mere 2 inches at 100 yards to achieve this and is actually shooting flat enough for any big game out to 200 yards with no problem. Its point blank range on big game is more like 225 yards in fact. Many African hunters sight the big 458 for 100 yards or less, fearing too much hold-under at close range if they sight for a longer range. As can be seen, sighting for 150 yards takes much better advantage of this big bore's potential trajectory, and on dangerous game at close range, the slight 1- to 1.5-inch rise of the bullet will make no difference.

Summary of Rifle Section

Early on in the testing of trajectory patterns and proper sight-in measures, several facts made themselves clear. First, it became very obvious that approximations had to be made. Some of the test rifles would do no better than 5-inch groups at 300 yards, in spite of good scope sights. In other words, there was a potential 2.5 inches to consider here as "drop" if one takes the group from its center point. I simply averaged things out and made a *specific point of impact* by using the center of the group. Then my actual test data was compared with a mathematical construct based upon the use of the ballistic coefficient of the bullet. At this point, a sensible compromise was made again, splitting the difference between minute degrees between actual drop and theoretical drop.

All in all, the tests were very satisfactory, especially considering the fact that an inch or so of actual difference at long range would not make a *true* difference for the big game hunter in practical terms, and not even for the varmint or target shooter, the latter sighting in always for the exact range of his competition targets anyway.

Another happy fact emerged. I was initially very concerned that if a rifle were sighted for its flattest-shooting load, it would be terribly off the mark with heavier bullets for the same cartridge. For example, if the 7mm Remington Magnum were sighted with the 139-grain bullet at 3400 fps MV, we might have to resight the rifle when using the 160-grain bullet at 3100 fps MV. With most modern cartridges, this situation did not arise. Except for sighting in with the very lightest varmint bullet, the rifles were on the mark with both modest-weight and heavy-weight bullets per each respective caliber. The reason is clear. With the heavier bullets, close-range shooting is the rule, so it did not matter that the heavier bullet would strike lower at long range, for the heavy bullet was *not used at long range*. Going to the heavier bullet was for more penetration and close-range punch.

This concept is important and worth an example. I sighted a 30-06 to strike 3 inches high at 100 yards when loaded with the 150-grain bullet at 3100 fps MV. This put the bullet back on at 270 yards. Then the 30-06 rifle in question went on an African trip. It was loaded with a 220-grain bullet at 2600 fps MV. Should the rifle have been resighted? No. The rifle was no longer on the money at 270 yards, as it had been with the 150-grain bullet sighted 3 inches high at 100 yards. Now the 220-grain bullet at 2600 fps was just about on target at 200 yards *with the same sight setting,* which was right for bush hunting.

Also, it became very plain that many shooters who were sighting in at an arbitrary 100 yards with flat-shooting modern big game or varmint rounds were not even coming close to the trajectory potential of those rounds. Even the "lowly" 30-30 with everyday factory-type loads, such as the flat-nosed 170-grain bullet at 2200 fps MV, turned out to be quite adequate for 200-yard shooting in terms of its trajectory. Shooters should be very aware that the parabola of the modern rifle catridge deserves a lot of consideration.

Finally, another factor came out of the testing. In fact, it was possible to standardize our procedure, giving us a basic starting point to work with. Most of the big game cartridges, as well as some of the varmint rounds, were sighted initially for a flat 25 yards. This not only allowed us to easily "get on paper," but also provided us with a surprisingly close approximation of the long-range potential of the round being tested. Another number which came up often was "3," and that was in sighting to print the center of the group "3 inches high" at 100 yards with modern flat-shooting rounds, such as the 264 Winchester Magnum, 7mm Remington Magnum, 270 Winchester, 30-06 and many other rounds. So these two standardizations could help the shooter. As a general rule, sight-in your rifle to strike right on at 25 yards for starters, and then move on to 100 yards, insuring your rifle prints about 3 inches high.

Short-Range Handgun Trajectory Charts

The following deals with those handgun calibers considered common in revolvers and pistols for close-range shooting. (The next section will attend to those rounds suited for longer range handgun work.)

9mm .355-Inch Centerfires
1. 9mm Luger/115-grain JHP bullet/1250 fps MV

0	+.5"	0	−3"	−7.5"
15 yards	25 yards	50 yards	75 yards	100 yards

Interpretation: The 9mm Luger is for short-range shooting. It always was. It is interesting to note that if sighted for 50 yards, the little 115-grain jacketed hollow-point bullet, for example, is only ½-inch high at 25 yards and 3 inches low at 75 yards. If a shooter wished to do some field work with the 9mm Luger as a small-game pistol, he could probably bag his quarry at 50 to 60 yards without any problem.

38-Caliber Centerfires
1. 38 Special/125-grain JHP bullet/1100 fps MV

0	+1"	0	−3"	−9"
15 yards	25 yards	50 yards	75 yards	100 yards

Interpretation: The popular 38 Special, loaded with the fast moving 125-grain jacketed hollow point, is quite useful to 75 yards in terms of trajectory. Anyone interested in firing at 100 yards with an accurate 38 Special would have no problem sighting for that distance. The round is, however, a short-range number for close-in uses.

2. 357 Magnum/158-grain JSP bullet/1300 fps MV

0	+.5"	0	−2.5"	−7"
15 yards	25 yards	50 yards	75 yards	100 yards

Interpretation: The shooter can see that the 357 Magnum is no long-range round out of the normal barrel. However, it does allow for sighting at 50 yards with only ½-inch hold-under at 25 yards. And at a full 75 yards from the muzzle, the 158-grain jacketed soft point bullet has only dropped 2½ inches.

Back in the '30s the 357 Magnum was the first handgun cartridge to bear the "Magnum" designation. It was then, and is now, a popular choice for whitetail-class game.

41-Caliber Centerfires

1. 41 Remington Magnum/210-grain JSP bullet/1400 fps MV

0	+.5″	0	−2″	−6″
15 yards	25 yards	50 yards	75 yards	100 yards

Interpretation: Although there have been several 41-caliber rounds offered in the history of handgunning, today only the 41 Magnum stands out as "popular," and just barely at that. It has, however, a lot of power potential and good penetration. Sighted for 50 yards, it shoots very flat to 75 yards. However, with a 4- or 6-inch barreled 41 even the best shot should recognize that this round's power is limited to 100 yards.

44-Caliber Centerfires

1. 44 Remington Magnum/240-grain JSP bullet/1400 fps MV

0	+.5″	−2″	−6″
15 yards	25 yards	75 yards	100 yards

Interpretation: For all practical purposes, the tests disclosed no load-for-load difference in trajectory between the 41 and 44 Magnums. (Incidentally, a Hornady 265-grain jacketed soft point bullet was pushed at 1300 fps MV in our 6-inch test barrel. This bullet is designed for the 444 Marlin, and it serves well for deep penetration on big game out of the 44 Magnum, but does not expand well on deer and antelope. Used as a backup, where bone-breaking or deep penetration is desired, the 265-grain Hornady bullet is worth looking at.

45-Caliber Centerfires

1. 45 ACP/230-grain Full Metal Jacket bullet/950 fps MV

0	+1.5″	0	−5″	−14″
15 yards	25 yards	50 yards	75 yards	100 yards

In the eyes of many the 41 Remington Magnum is a close ballistic twin to the 44 Rem. Mag. Using a 210-grain slug, the 41's drop chart is identical to the 44 Mag. (240-grain slug) chart seen here. Like the 44, the 41 is well suited for handgunning big game.

Interpretation: This close-range powerhouse defense round is not at home past 75 yards in the trajectory department, nor should it have to be for the type of work demanded of it. Past 75 yards, the bullet is on a definite downhill path.

2. 45 Colt/250-grain JHP bullet/1000 fps MV

0	+1″	0	−4″	−11″
15 yards	25 yards	50 yards	75 yards	100 yards

Interpretation: Sighted for 50 yards, this strong handgun round is 4 inches low at 75 yards. It is at home from zero to 50 yards, and after that it begins a definite downhill trend. A good shot can do well on targets at 75 yards with the big 45 Colt, however. (Often called the 45 Long Colt, there is no historical evidence to support that commonly used title.)

Long-Range Handgun Trajectory Charts

22-Caliber Centerfires

1. 22 Hornet/45-grain SP spitzer bullet/2400 fps (10-inch Contender)

0	+1.0″	+1.5″	0	−4.5″
25 yards	50 yards	100 yards	150 yards	200 yards

Interpretation: Since the 22 Hornet round in the fine Contender handgun is meant for modest-range shooting, the above sighting allowing for a hold-on, even on smaller varmints, is a good compromise.

2. 22 Remington Jet/45-grain SP spitzer bullet/2500 fps MV (10-inch Contender)

(Closely follows the trajectory pattern of the Hornet—sight 1-inch high at 50 yards.)

3. 221 Remington Fireball/50-grain SP spitzer bullet/2700 fps MV (10.75-inch XP-100 barrel)

0	+2.5″	0	−13″
25 yards	100 yards	200 yards	300 yards

Interpretation: Pushing the 50-grain bullet at 2700 fps MV allows for a 200-yard sighting out of the Remington XP-100 pistol. Of course, after the 200-yard mark, the bullet is describing a fairly sharp downward path. With the fine handgun scopes available today, an expert with this pistol could hit the bull's-eye at 250 yards without a lot of holdover problems. Confine the Jet and Hornet to shots under 200 yards.

4. 222 Remington/50-grain HP spitzer bullet/2500 fps (10-inch Contender Barrel)

0	+1.5″	+2.0″	0	−3″
25 yards	50 yards	100 yards	150 yards	200 yards

Interpretation: Very accurate shooting at 200 yards is easily accomplished with the fine 222 Remington round out of the 10-inch Contender. However, the bullet is on the way down at 200 yards and beyond 225 yards the shooter begins to experience hold-over problems.

7mm (.284-inch) Centerfires

1. 7x45mm Ingram (7x223 Improved)/154-grain SP spitzer bullet/2150 fps MV (14.5-inch Remington XP-100 barrel)

0	+2″	+2.5″	0	−3.5″	−6″
25 yds.	50 yds.	100 yds.	150 yds.	200 yds.	225 yds.

Interpretation: The 7x45 mm Ingram is another of the wildcat rounds which has boosted the handgun from close-range to longer-range tool. Up to 225 yards, with our sighting, a shooter can merely hold dead on for a target of appropriate height, since bullet drops is only 6 inches at that distance. Good shots can use such a sighting for deer hunting.

2. 7mm BR Remington/154-grain SP spitzer bullet/2100 fps (15-inch Remington XP-100 barrel)
(same data as for 7×45mm Ingram)

30-Caliber Centerfires

1. 30 Herrett & 30-30 Winchester/150-grain SP spitzer bullet/2000 fps MV (10-inch Contender barrel)

0	+2.5″	+3″	0	−4″	−6.5″
25 yds.	50 yds.	100 yds.	150 yds.	200 yds.	225 yds.

Interpretation: The 30 Herrett or 30-30 Winchester in the 10-inch barrel gives a shooter a point blank sighting of at least 225 yards on big game animals or varmints of the larger class. These rounds have worked well on big game when shooters have gotten close for sure bullet placement.

357-358-Caliber Centerfires

1. 357 Herrett/158-grain JSP bullet/2000 fps MV (10-inch Contender barrel)

0	+3″	+4″	0	−6″
25 yards	50 yards	100 yards	150 yards	200 yards

Interpretation: Once again, the point blank sighting here is 200 yards, very impressive out of a handgun. In order to arrive on target at 150 yards, the bullet should impact 4 inches high at 100 yards. On smaller targets, at ranges between 50 and 100 yards, the shooter would have to take this into account and use hold-under to insure a hit.

2. 35 Remington/200-grain SP spitzer/(14-inch barrel) at 1800 fps MV

0	+3″	+3.5″	0	−6″
25 yards	50 yards	100 yards	140 yards	200 yards

Interpretation: The 35 Remington was a surprising cartridge as tested in 14-inch barreled Thompson/Center Contender. It allows a point blank sighting, on larger game, of 200 yards, with a dead-on sighting of 140 yards (bullet struck a bit low on the average at 150 yards with this sight setting). The rise of the bullet was only 3.5 inches at 100 yards in order to achieve the 6-inch drop at 200 yards. It would be a good choice for those who hunt big game with the handgun.

44-Caliber Centerfires

1. 44 Remington Magnum/240-grain JHP bullet/1700 fps MV (14-inch Contender barrel)

0	+2″	0	−8″
25 yards	50 yards	140 yards	150 yards

Interpretation: The 44 Magnum firing a 240-grain bullet at 1700 fps has a point blank sighting of about 125 to 150 yards, depending upon the size of the target. The slight rise of only 2 inches at 50 yards allows a hunter to hold right on target (big game or varmints) from 25 to 100 yards.

45-Caliber Centerfires

1. 45 Winchester Magnum/250-grain JSP bullet/1500 fps MV (14-inch Contender barrel)

0	+3″	0	−10″
25 yards	50 yards	100 yards	150 yards

Interpretation: The big 45 Winchester Magnum out of the Contender serves well for use at 100 yards with a 3-inch hold-under at 50 yards. It is not among the more flat-shooting of the long-range pistol rounds, but a dedicated hunter would do well with it all the same if he stalks for shots of the 100-yard domain.

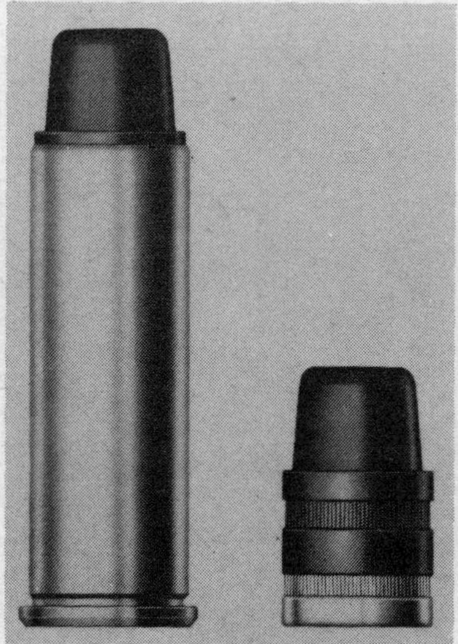

With a 240-grain slug, the 44 Magnum steps out at about 1400 fps. Given the energy, drop and muzzle velocity, it's no surprise the big 44 Magnum is generally the cartridge of choice when it comes to handgunning big game.

Summary of Long-Range Pistol Trajectory Charts

It is very clear that the long-range handgun is here, substantially overshadowing standard handguns and their attendant cartridges. If compared with the ballistics of the standard sidearm calibers, the above numbers show a point blank sighting in the 100 to 200-225-yard range. The owner of a handgun chambered for a long-range round must sight in with the idea of gaining the most from that round's trajectory potential.

Rifled Slug Trajectory Charts

Many shooters use the rifled slug in their shotguns for big game hunting purposes. In some areas, this is a matter of the law, which states that rifles are not allowed. In other situations, it may be a matter of hunter choice. Most important, of course, is the fact that the rifled slug is not always a highly accurate missile when fired from the standard shotgun. Although trajectory patterns indicate that the slug can be sighted for 75 yards, my tests show that dispersion at 50 yards (in some barrels, through some chokes) tends to limit its practical use to 50-yard shooting.

Only two gauges were tested for trajectory, those being the 12 in the 1¼-ounce weight and the 20 in ⅝-ounce slug.

1. 12-gauge/1¼-ounce slug (547 grains weight)/1500 MV

0	+.5″	+1″	0	−2.5″	−7″
15 yds.	25 yds.	50 yds.	75 yds.	100 yds.	125 yds.

Interpretation: In terms of drop, the 12-gauge rifled slug is a hold-on proposition out to 100 yards, or even 125 yards, on a target about the size of a whitetail deer. Shooters should try to sight for 75 yards. However, they should also be aware of problems in longer range slug shooting. Our chapter on slug shooting discusses a few of these problems. I refer you to it.

2. 20-gauge slug ⅝-ounce

0	+1.5″	+1.25″	0	−3″	−7.5″
15 yds.	25 yds.	50 yds.	75 yds.	100 yds.	125 yds.

Interpretation: While the 20-gauge rifled slug is not my favorite in comparison to the 12-gauge on big game of the deer class, there is no denying that the modern version of this load is definitely superior to its former loading. Today, the major difference in rifled slug shooting in 20-gauge is additional projectile weight, and since we cannot gain high velocity with a slug, going up in projectile mass is the way to increase effectiveness. A ¾-ounce slug is obtainable in the 20-gauge rifled slug load.

Black Powder Trajectory Charts

Today's reported 5,000,000 black powder shooters need to know just as much about trajectory and sighting-in patterns as do those shooters who use modern arms. In fact, the shorter-range muzzleloader requires care in sighting so that it is not further handicapped by its innate short-range ballistic qualities. Below is a summarization of tests which show the proper sight-in characteristics for most muzzleloaders used today.

Black Powder Handguns

1. 44-Caliber Revolver/141-grain round ball/1100 fps MV

+1″	0	−4.5″
25 yards	50 yards	75 yards

Interpretation: Todays 44-caliber black powder revolvers, using full-throttle loads, will be sighted-in to print on at 50 yards. This allows for shooting up to 75 yards on relatively small targets. Beyond 75 yards, the ball is dropping quite rapidly.

The Federal Super Slug line includes a 10-gauge load with a slug weighing a full 1¾ ounces, as well as a Magnum 12-gauge slug which goes 1¼ ounces in weight. This means that the 10-gauge slug is a full 766 grains, while the 12-gauge slug weighs 547 grains.

2. 50-54-Caliber Pistol/225-grain round ball/900 fps MV

+1″	0	−4″
25 yards	50 yards	75 yards

Interpretation: Much the same as for the 44-caliber revolver.

Black Powder Rifles (32- to 58-caliber)

1. 32- and 36-caliber/45- and 65-grain round balls/1500 fps MV

+1″	0	−2″
25 yards	50 yards	75 yards

Interpretation: These smallbores can be loaded to produce about 1500 fps MV for small game hunting and plinking. When so loaded, a sight-in of 50 yards is excellent, giving the shooter no hold-under problems at 25 yards and only 2 inches of drop at 75 yards. Since black powder shooting dictates close-range work, this arrangement works out very well.

2. 38- to 40-caliber/80 grains to 93-96 grains weight round balls/about 2000 fps MV.

+.5″	0	−1″
25 yards	50 yards	75 yards

Interpretation: The 38s to 40s are also close-range calibers, best suited for game of the wild turkey size, but the 40s have taken a great number of deer, even in recent times. When used for larger game, the shooter should get *very close* with these small calibers and their attendant lightweight projectiles. Hence, sighting-in at 50 yards is appropriate.

3. 45- to 58-caliber/133 to 279 grains weight round balls/at 2000 fps MV area. (The conical in these calibers, at about 1500 fps MV, produces about the same trajectory curve, hence these figures are for top loads for *both* ball and conical missiles.)

0	+1″	−1″	−6″
13 yards	50 yards	100 yards	125 yards

Interpretation: This sighting allows a big game hunter the option of starting at a mere 13 yards in order to get on the paper. He can then work on a group which is a little high at 50 yards, perhaps only 1-inch high if he can manage to manipulate his sights that well, and he probably can with care. Then the rifle of big-bore stature, using a top end load, is on the money between 50 and 100 yards, being only 1-inch low at 100 yards. At a full 125 yards, which is plenty of distance for a dedicated muzzle-loading enthusiast, the ball or minie (Maxi, too) will have dropped about 1/2-foot. This means that the black powder big-game hunter can shoot from zero to 125 yards without too much concern about his trajectory pattern. At 125 yards, the round ball is very "tired" anyway, with over 50 percent loss of MV—this range should be considered *maximum* for shooting at game.

Sighting in haphazardly or at some common distance, such as 100 yards for all rifles or 25 yards for all handguns, is not the route to follow. The complete shooter wants to get the most from his firearm, and getting the most means, in part, sighting for optimum trajectory benefit.

Chapter 17
Modern Factory Ammunition

LITTLE HAS CHANGED for shooters over the past 100 years or so. In the Wild West, for example, when a shooter walked into his gunshop he could not simply say, "Give me some rifle or handgun fodder" any more than we can today. About 100 calibers were sold back in those "good old days," about the same number of rounds offered to us today. Our old-timers also faced the same problem with older ammunition in terms of cartridges which had become obsolete. Today, we have a rather large number of old calibers which are defunct on the one hand, but still in use on the other. We are going to discuss, later on in this chapter, how to find or perhaps we should say "procure" some of that obsolete ammo.

The modern dedicated shooter handloads his own ammunition on a wide scale. The ammo companies are offering the cartridge cases, and the primers and even the powder in the instance of Winchester, which manufactures its own line of propellants for the handloader. But the modern shooter uses factory ammo as well as handloads. Yes, I custom load much of my own ammunition, but certainly not all of it. I like the convenience of walking into my gunshop and buying a box of "ready-made" when I want it. Furthermore, the most dedicated handloader finds that in certain instances he simply does not have the time to build his own ammo. Then factory ammo is selected.

Factory Ammunition Benefits

Total Reliability/High Quality Control

Today's factory ammunition is totally reliable. In more than 35 years of shooting, I have had but one round of factory big game ammunition fail me, and it was a fluke, a round which simply ended up with a dead primer. As for rimfire ammo, having fired thousands upon thousands of rounds, I can recall only twice when new ammo did not "go off." In fact, I once ran into a bargain on 1,000 rounds of 22 rimfire ammunition which had been stored for many years. The ammo was oily to boot. But the lot contained less than 10 misfires.

Factory ammunition can be counted on. This is not to say that handloaded ammunition cannot be counted on. That isn't the situation at all. But factory ammo is one thing for sure—it is new. The brass is not going to be stretched, too soft, or have loose primer pockets. Carefully loaded custom ammo is not going to suffer from any of these bad traits either, but the point remains—factory ammo is brand new, shiny, sized to fit the chamber with no problems and simply ready to go.

Accuracy

I believe that the most accurate ammunition in the world is handloaded, but factory ammunition is accurate enough for almost any task. I recently pulled bullets on five sample rounds taken from a new box of factory 307 Winchester ammunition loaded with 180-grain Power Points. Here are the results of weighing the five sample powder charges and five sample bullets:

Powder Charges	180-Gr. Power Point Bullets
40.3 grains, 40.2 grains, 40.2 grains, 40.2 grains, 40.1 grains 179.8 grains.	179.8 grains, 179.8 grains, 179.7 grains, 179.6 grains, 179.8 grains

With this kind of superb uniformity, ammo accuracy is insured.

Bullet Selection

I happen to like Winchester's Silvertip, as well as Remington's Core-Lokt, for certain applications. But if I want to use these bullets, I basically have to shoot factory ammunition today. They are not available from the companies for reloading purposes. I may lament the fact, and I do, but the point is this: If I want to use these fine bullets I have to buy factory ammunition.

Convenience

Another reason for buying factory-loaded ammunition is the convenience. It's a very obvious reason, but also a very important one, especially when a shooter finds himself a long way from home on a hunting trip and for one reason or another needs additional ammo. How nice it is to walk into a store and buy factory fodder. In fact, some shooters select a big game caliber on the basis of availability. If a store does not have a box of 30-30 or 30-06 ammo in stock, it probably has no big game ammunition at all.

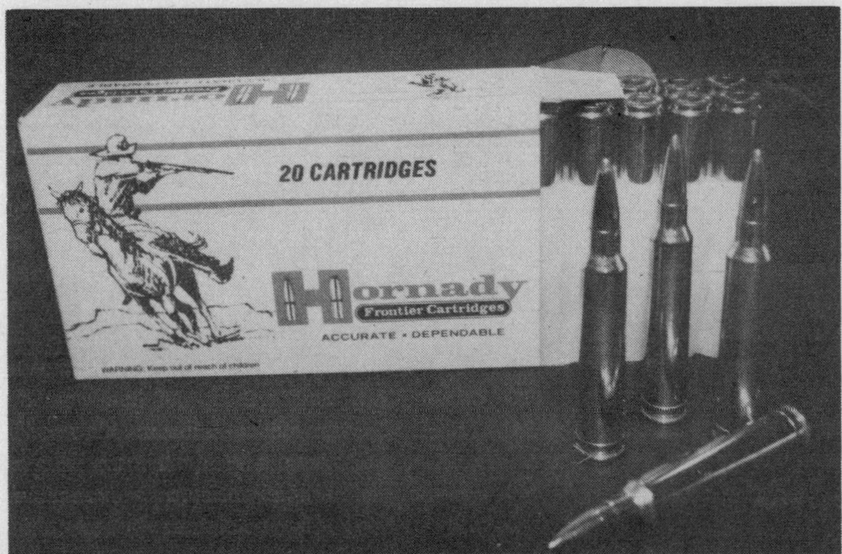

Loaded ammunition saves a shooter *time.* There is simply nothing more convenient than dropping into the gunshop and picking up a box of "ready-mades." These Hornady 300 Winchester Magnum loads feature a 190-grain bullet.

Remington's Viper 22 rimfire ammunition is a good example of the hyper-velocity school. MV with this ammo is about 266 fps more than with 22 Long Rifle rounds in standard velocity and 155 fps more than the 22 Long Rifle in the high-velocity loading. These loads shoot 14 percent to 23 percent flatter at 100 yards than 22 LR high velocity or standard velocity loads. The Viper comes with a 36-grain solid bullet.

(Left) Federal offers its Premium brand round with Sierra bullets. Here is the Federal 30-06 firing the Sierra 150-grain boat-tail soft-point bullet. This Federal offering has an excellent reputation for accuracy.

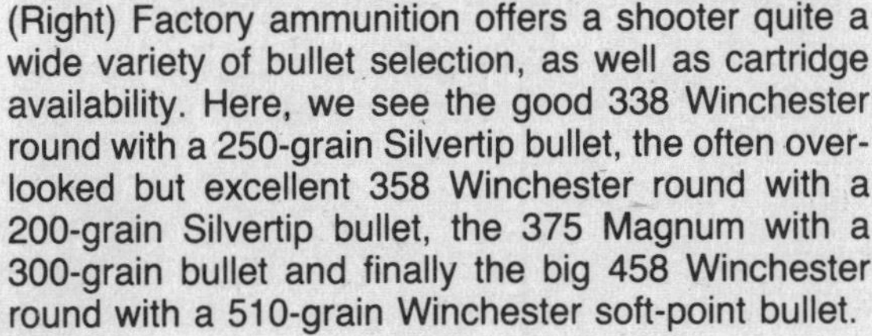

(Right) Factory ammunition offers a shooter quite a wide variety of bullet selection, as well as cartridge availability. Here, we see the good 338 Winchester round with a 250-grain Silvertip bullet, the often overlooked but excellent 358 Winchester round with a 200-grain Silvertip bullet, the 375 Magnum with a 300-grain bullet and finally the big 458 Winchester round with a 510-grain Winchester soft-point bullet.

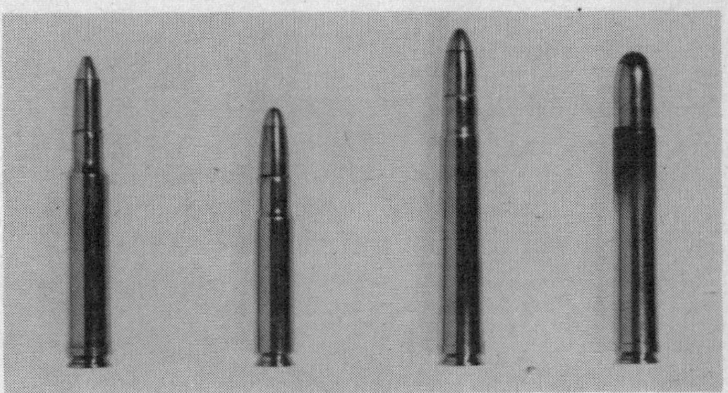

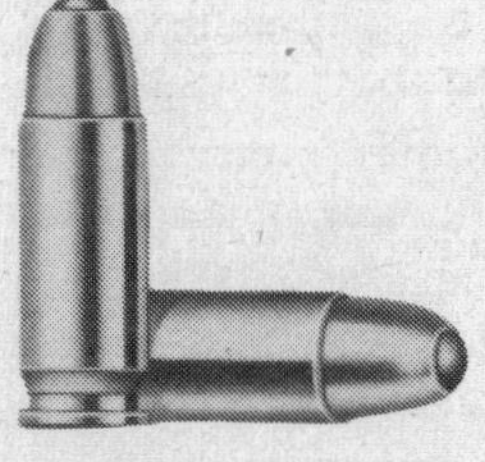   

Here is an improved loading of the little 25 Auto round. Winchester loads this one with a 45-grain bullet with a tiny steel ball inbedded in the hollow point of the nose. This allows for perfect feeding in the auto pistol coupled with expansion. This bullet achieves a MV of 835 fps. Note expansion of bullet as taken from test materials (right).

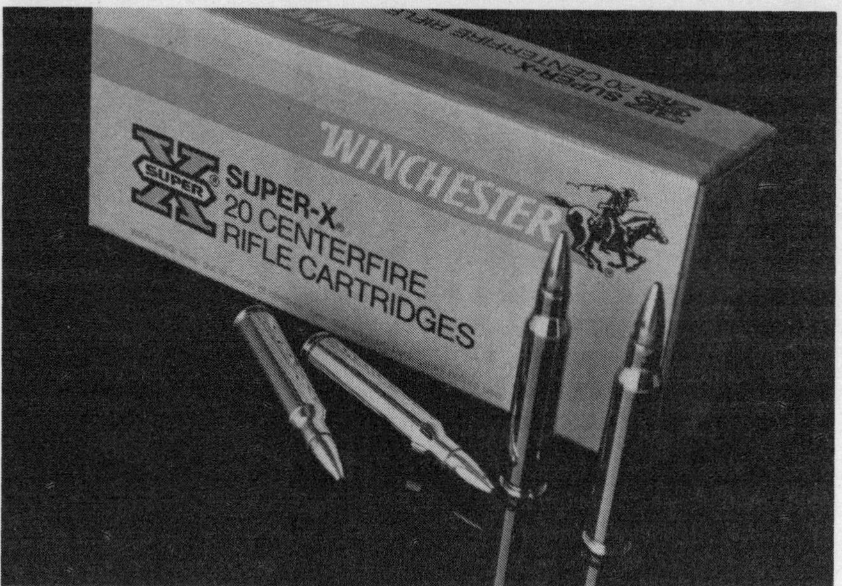

No industry in America can boast better quality control than the ammunition industry. These Winchester varmint loads are for the 223 Remington cartridge. From initial materials selection to packaging, every step has been taken to insure a reliable product. The quality is actually visible to the shooter.

Uniformity

I'm not talking about uniformity in terms of accuracy and quality of one particular lot of ammo. I'm talking about uniformity of a load, lot after lot, year after year. I have fired tests with factory ammo made several years ago along with the same ammo made today and the "formula" stays close to the same. Sure, ammo companies will improve a load's ballistic force when a new powder becomes available. But all in all, if a fellow shot a good group with Brand X factory ammunition in 1975, he's likely to experience very much the same results with the same brand and load in 1985. In other words, the shooter can count on factory ammo remaining *uniform*.

Wide Selection

One of the main reasons for reloading, in my opinion, is the increased versatility available from a given round, and I'll include shotgun shells in that statement. I can make a 30-06 behave like a turkey gun or a near magnum in factory terms, all with careful *and safe* reloading tactics. At the same time, however, modern factory ammunition has taken on some of that same quality of versatility. A brief walk through the newest Remington ammunition catalog proves this to me.

In centerfire, I can have loads from the 22 Remington Jet and Fire Ball all the way to 458 Winchester Magnum, with the tiny 17 Remington tossed in for good measure. Many of those rounds are even available in myriad bullet styles and weights. In the 30-30, I can even buy an "Accelerator" load from Remington; it features a 55-grain 22-caliber bullet loaded in a sabot that exits the muzzle at 3400 fps MV. Or I can obtain the old traditional 170-grain Remington Core-Lokt if I need a 30-30 slug with lots of penetration and retention of mass. But at the same time, if I so choose, I can buy 170-grain hollow point Core-Lokt ammo for that same 30-30 round.

Remington also has an Accelerator round in 30-06—it fires a sabot-encased 55-grain 22-caliber bullet at 4080 fps MV. But I can also get a 125-grain bullet in that caliber, or even the popular 150-grain Core-Lokts or Bronze Points. I believe I've made my point. Yes, I reload for the 30-06, but I must say that the selection in this caliber is plenty broad enough from the factory, with the exception of a light load for plinking and wild turkey hunting.

Regardless, the loading companies continue to *serve the shooter*. Federal, for example, immediately offered the 7x30 Waters round for the new Winchester Model 94 rifle in that caliber. On the other end of the spectrum, you can still buy ammo for cartridges which, truly, have lost their popularity. The ammo companies offer less-than-popular cartridges for the convenience of the shooter mostly. Sure, they make a profit from this ammunition, but in terms of volume sales, it simply may or may *not* be there. I can, as an example, still purchase 25-20 ammo. A rifle for the 25-20 has not been around for ages in new form. I can also buy 30-40 Krag, or 303 British, or 44-40 rounds. None of those cartridges are setting any sales records, but I'm sure there are a lot of shooters who are happy to be able to buy them.

Performance

I have no intention of painting a picture too rosy here. In many instances, my handloads simply overtake and pass up the factory equivalent of the same round. Oftentimes, I am in fact very unhappy with my chronograph readings of certain specific, albeit isolated, cases of ammo from the factory. As one example, I have tested 300 H&H Magnum factory ammo which provided 30-06 ballistics. I recently fired some 7mm Remington Magnum factory ammo which gave a 175-grain bullet a velocity in the area of 2800 fps and another brand which showed even less punch. A muzzle velocity of 2800 fps is like that from a 30-06, *not* a 7mm

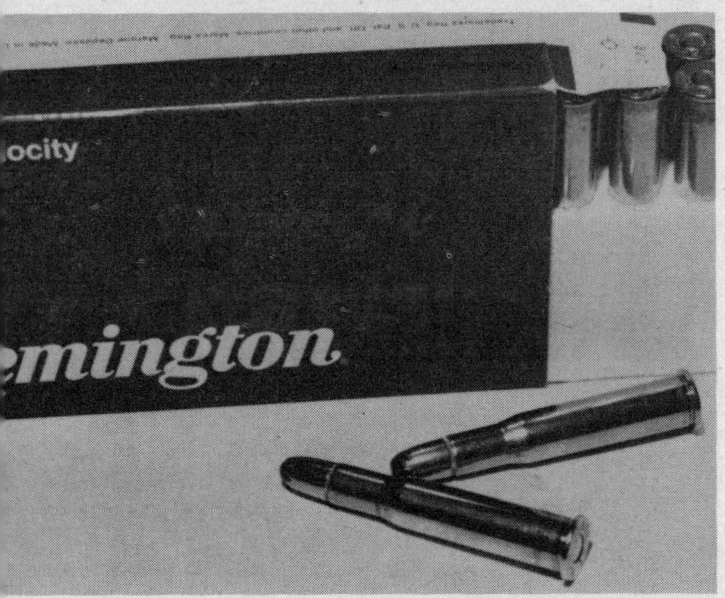

Choosing factory ammo means selecting a given load for a given purpose. These Remington 170-grain Core-Lokt 30-30 round nose bullets stay together for deep penetration. But if a hunter wanted a faster-opening bullet, he might look at the Remington 170-grain hollow point Core-Lokt type.

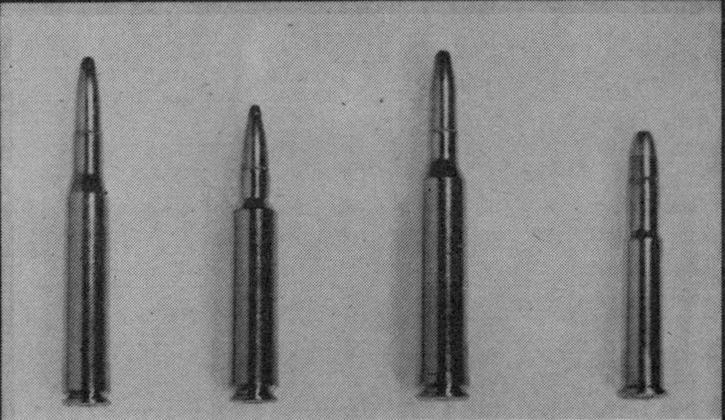

Shown here is a variety of Olin-Winchester ammo. This ammunition is, of course, available over the counter for the shooter wishing ready-made ammo for his rifle. (Above) On the far left is a 270 Winchester round with 150-grain Power Point bullet, a controlled expansion projectile. The 284 Winchester is a very good round, here loaded with a 150-grain Power Point. The 7mm Remington Magnum is offered with a 175-grain Power Point Winchester bullet as shown here, and then there is the famous 30-30 round, here shown with the deep-penetrating 170-grain Silvertip bullet. Below (left to right) is the popular 308 Winchester with a 200-grain Silvertip, a good choice for high penetration on big game at close range. The excellent 30-06 is shown here with a 220-grain Silvertip, a bullet of excellent properties for big game. The same bullet is loaded into the 300 Winchester Magnum, albeit at higher velocity. And on the end is the 300 H&H Magnum with the same bullet at a little less than 300 Winchester Magnum muzzle velocity.

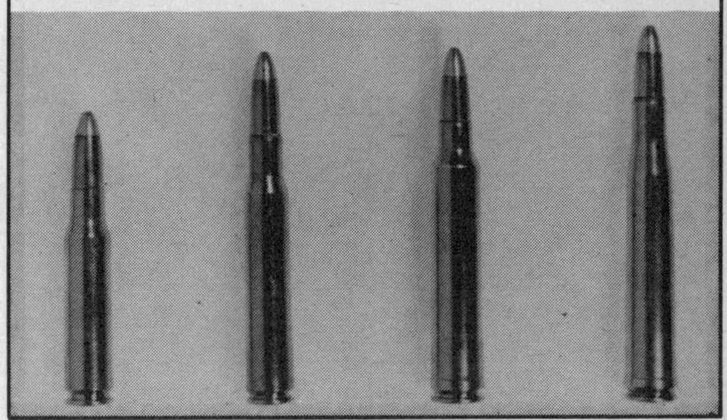

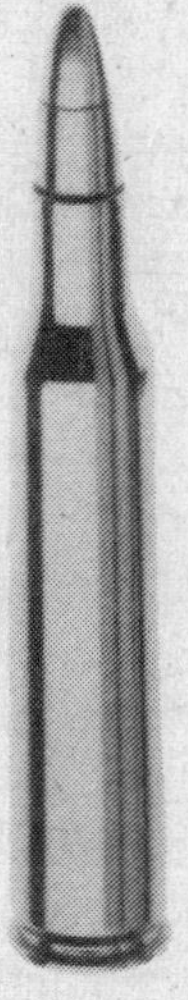

Factory ammunition changes with shooter's needs and demands. Winchester has offered a special loading for the 257 Roberts to help reach the full potential of that round. They call it the Winchester Plus-P, and it is available in the 100-grain Silvertip bullet (shown) or a 117-grain round nose Power Point bullet. This ammo provides greater muzzle velocity than achieved previously from factory loads.

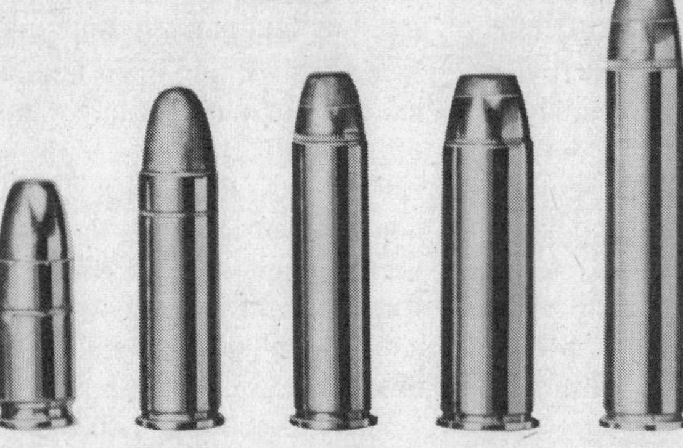

The wide variety of ammunition available to the modern shooter continues its trend. New cartridges are always on the horizon and old ones continue to be used. Most of these rounds are old in origin. (From left) The 9mm Parabellum was introduced in 1902, and it is still going strong. The 38 Special is a 1906 round. The 357 Magnum came along in 1935. The 44 Magnum was born in 1955. The much newer 357 Maximum round, a 1983 offering, has not yet jelled into a standard, and it remains to be seen what will happen to the round in the future.

Remington Magnum. My very safe handloads push a 175-grain bullet at 3000 fps from a 24-inch barrel, with even a mundane handload providing 2900 fps at the very least with the "Big-7" round.

On the other hand, I recently fired some 44 Magnum factory ammunition which ballistically surpassed the handloads I had been making up. So the factory does not always offer the milder load in a given round. We must understand, of course, that the factory has to leave a margin for those older rifles in less than pristine condition. The factory can only load for the least common denominator. If there were no 30-06 rifles around, for example, except those built on absolutely modern actions of top strength, factory ammo would push a 180-grain bullet at 2800 fps+ as the handload does.

In some cases, I feel certain loads could be kicked up a bit. I have, for example, fired 300 Winchester Magnum ammunition which I felt could have delivered more punch, and there is no excuse here. No weak 300 Winchester Magnum rifles have been made to date that I know of. The 300 Winchester Magnum is a comparatively new round, invented only in the era of high-strength actions and offered only in rifles of top quality. The potential of that round should be realized, I feel.

All in all, however, factory ammunition has plenty of power. I recently tested a couple boxes of Winchester ammunition in 30-30 caliber. Two things came very clear. First, the ammo was up to level in power. Second, it was loaded to perfection. The standard deviation from the mean (or average) velocity was wonderfully low, as low as my *best* handloads have been in the same round.

Here is a look at the results of this test:

Winchester 30-30 Factory Ammunition (170-grain Power Point soft-point bullet)

Lowest Velocity	Highest Velocity	Extreme Spread	Average MV	Standard Deviation
2146 fps	2150 fps	4 fps	2148	2 fps

(Fired from a Model 94 Winchester, 20-inch barrel)

The test made me curious, so I began to look into two other major brands, Remington and Federal, and I found that the 30-30 ammo they offered was also of superb quality. You simply don't handload any better than this in terms of consistency. Of course, a low standard deviation of only 2 fps is not the rule with lots of ammunition, but further testing of Winchester ammo revealed standard deviations of 7 fps, 3 fps, 8 fps, and so forth. A batch of Remington ammo revealed deviations of 8 fps, 5 fps and similar. Some Frontier ammunition gave 12 fps, 8 fps, 9 fps and 4 fps. These are *all* quite remarkable. To be fair, I have found that 30-30 ammo is sometimes ahead of other rounds in the area of standard deviation. Perhaps it's due to the fact they produce so much of the stuff. But no matter. There is no denying the quality of the above ammunition, and it's from the factory.

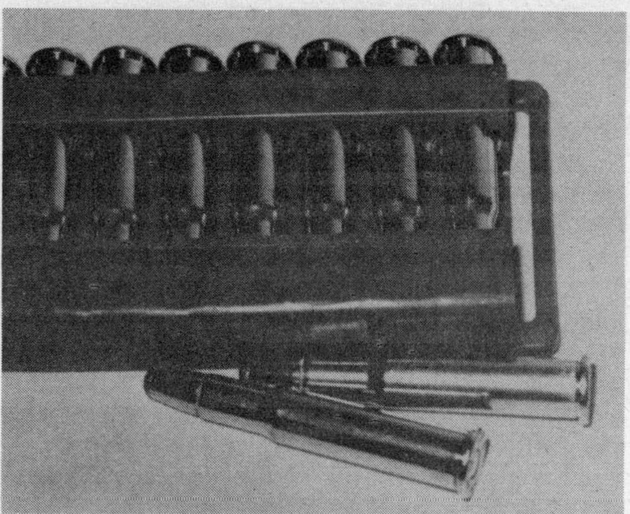

Typical of the factory innovations in ammo, Federal has these 30-30 rounds loaded into a container which can be slipped on the belt and carried that way.

How to Choose Factory Ammunition

I use a chronograph to test all of my ammo, handloads or factory. If, as an example, a company says it is offering a 30-06 load with a 180-grain bullet at a muzzle velocity of 2700 fps, I can find out what the load does from *my* rifle with its particular barrel length, and I can also learn something of the quality of that ammo.

Not everyone will want to buy a chronograph. But a well-equipped shooting club should certainly have one. In the event you can't get to a chronograph, then I suggest shooting your selected factory ammo in order to determine which brand/load provides the best accuracy in your particular firearm. Remember, firearms differ in many ways. I have often found that Brand X is more accurate than Brand Y in a certain rifle. A session at the benchrest will help you determine which brand/load provides the best accuracy.

Furthermore, I feel a shooter can use the trial-and-error field method when it comes to bullet selection. For example, through hunting and postmortems on big game, I found that the 130-grain Remington Bronze Point offered more explosiveness than I wanted on white-tailed deer out of my 270 Winchester. At the same time I discovered that the 130-grain Remington Core-Lokt offered more penetration, but without nearly the expansion of the Bronze-Point. On the other hand, the Bronze Point proved to shoot a bit flatter than the Core-Lokt, due to the fact that the point did not upset in the atmosphere as the bullet exited the muzzle of the rifle.

So I learned that I should choose one bullet over the

other for specific tasks. If I wanted to absolutely drop a thin-skinned game animal in its tracks, and employ the lung shot for reasons of minimal meat loss, the Bronze-Point would do that. The Core-Lokt still offered very fast expansion, but it did so with less explosiveness. Furthermore, I learned that certain factory bullets had special characteristics that literally performed "as advertised." For example, Winchester's Silvertip has always pleased me with its ability to hang together. I found Silvertips to be excellent out of the 30-30 when I wanted to put a big game animal down with a shoulder shot. Conversely, Silvertips seemed a bit too tough for small deer or antelope. So I turned to the Power Point in the 30-30 and found expansion on lighter big game a bit more sure. This does not mean that the Silvertip is better than the Power Point or the Power Point better than the Silvertip. It's simply indicative of what you can learn through field experience. It's how you use that knowledge that counts.

It means that the factory has offered two different types of bullet *construction,* each with a special purpose in mind. Given a chance to hunt big mule deer bucks in the woods, I will happily take along a 170-grain Silvertip bullet out of the 30-30. Change that hunt to whitetails in the brush, and I would prefer the Power Point. Give me an opportunity to hunt antelope with the neat little 30-30, and I do just that, and Federal's 125-grain hollow point load is going to put this game down nicely. On the other hand, I would opt for the Federal 170-grain Soft Point Hi-Shok bullet for larger game at closer range. You see, the factories are offering these various selections for a purpose. Versatility cannot reach the plateau enjoyed by handloading, of course, but the factory ammo being offered is wide enough to allow the shooter an opportunity to *learn* how to choose the right fodder for the task he wants performed.

In shotgunning, I have learned that too many shooters don't take full advantage of the tremendous variety of loads offered by the ammo companies. For example, a target load of No. 8s might be perfect for quail. However, the shooter turns, instead, to a magnum load, perhaps with buffered shot at that, intended for geese, not quail. It's only commonsense application, but some shooters seem to forget that they can buy a box of 12-gauge ammo which uses a mere ounce of shot for those close-in targets. These pleasant-to-shoot loads are extremely effective when long-range punch is not necessary. A 12-gauge shotgun has tremendous versatility because the factory offers such a wide range of loads for the shooter to pick from. It's just a matter of selecting the right load for the right job.

I pick my shotgun shells on the basis of how they pattern in my shotguns. I pick them also on the basis of the game

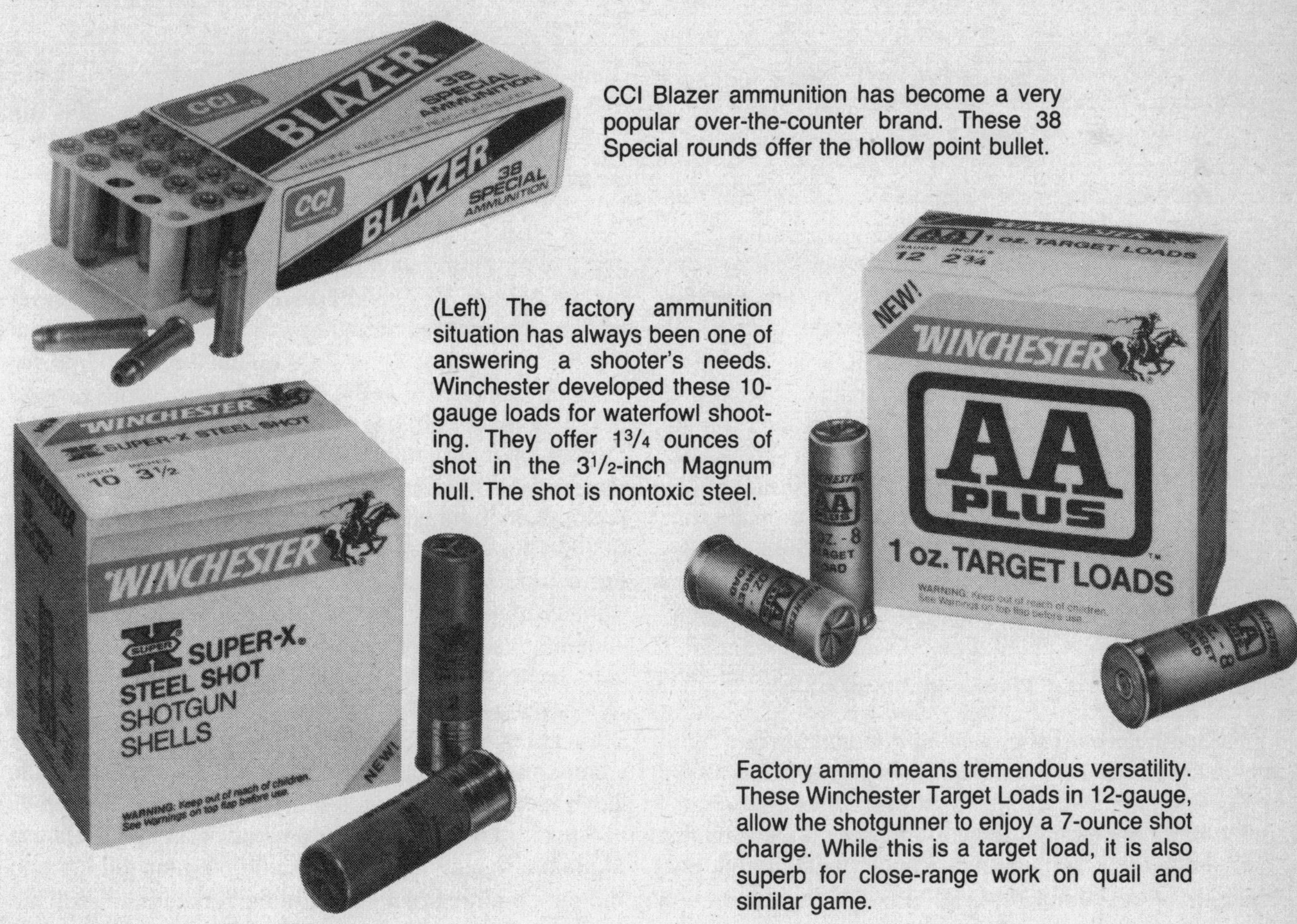

CCI Blazer ammunition has become a very popular over-the-counter brand. These 38 Special rounds offer the hollow point bullet.

(Left) The factory ammunition situation has always been one of answering a shooter's needs. Winchester developed these 10-gauge loads for waterfowl shooting. They offer 1$^{3}/_{4}$ ounces of shot in the 3$^{1}/_{2}$-inch Magnum hull. The shot is nontoxic steel.

Factory ammo means tremendous versatility. These Winchester Target Loads in 12-gauge, allow the shotgunner to enjoy a 7-ounce shot charge. While this is a target load, it is also superb for close-range work on quail and similar game.

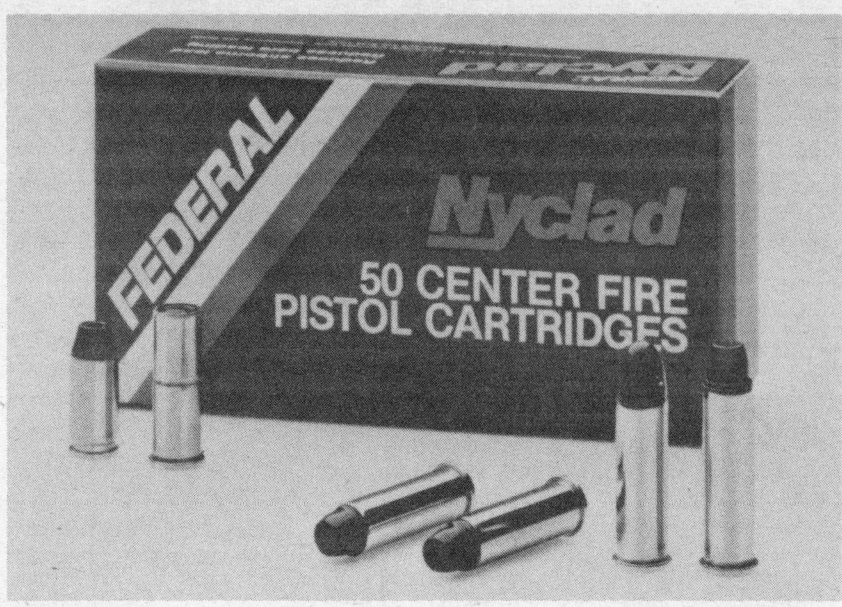

New innovations are part of the factory ammo business and have been from the start. These are Federal's Nyclad loads, with nylon-coated lead bullets. These bullets reduce bore leading and help in the prevention of bullet fragmentation.

CCI's 38 Special/357 Magnum shotshells offer a small shot charge that provides a useful pattern at close range.

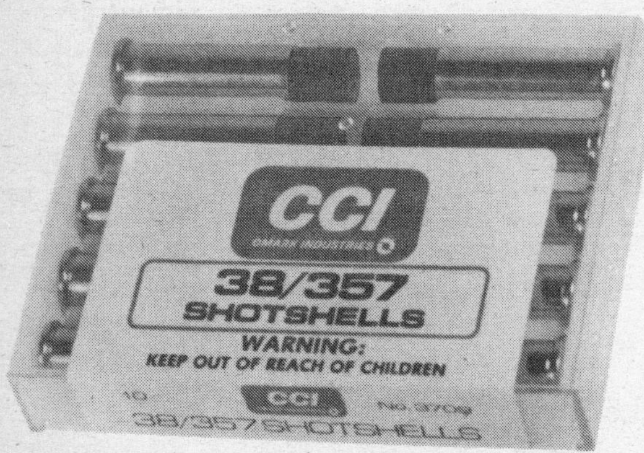

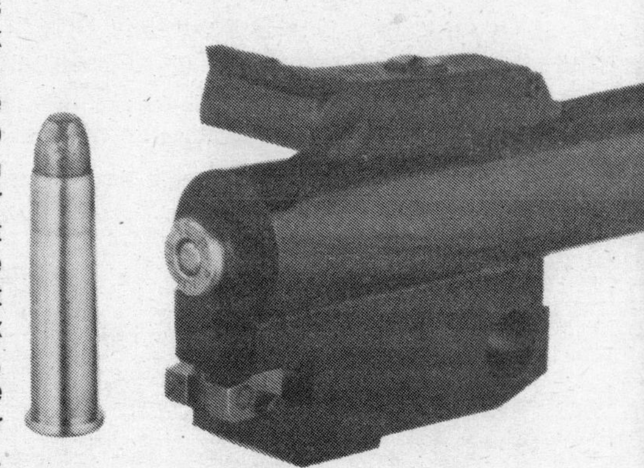

Outdated ammo is often brought back for various reasons. Though not obsolete as such, the 32-20 round has not seen much action for many years. Yet, it is currently on the scene again, not only in some six gun chamberings, but also in the fine Thompson/Center single shot pistol.

to be hunted. And, of course, there are other factors. But in the main, a shotgunner should look for optimum performance. Remember, "optimum performance" does not always mean obtaining the most punch. It means suiting the load to the hunting situation.

I pick my rifle ammo based upon accuracy and appropriateness for the game being hunted. The same goes for the handgun. I chronographed some 240-grain handloads at 1400 fps MV out of the 44 Magnum; those loads were what I considered to be truly hot. I later tested a factory load with a 220-grain bullet at over 1600 fps, a fine round for deer and similar game within the range of the 44 Magnum.

Changing Trends in Ammunition

All for the good, I feel, are the changing trends in factory ammo. I also believe that, perhaps, the handloading public has had at least a minor influence upon that trend. I see further influence on the horizon, not only in straining the most from a given round, with total safety, but also from the standpoint of offering "less" in some cases. An example of the former would be a reload I worked up for for my Model 94 30-30. That handload achieves *higher* velocity at *lower* pressure than my previous loads. Ammo manufacturers currently tend to head in directions like this—reloaders have, for years. As for the lower-power end of the factory-ammo spectrum, I feel that the shooting fraternity would appreciate the availability of some less-expensive loads in the target domain, even the plinking area. Handloaders have been doing this for a long time. Omark/CCI has made some inroads, in this area, with their Blazer line of aluminum cased (non-reloadable) handgun ammo.

Another changing trend in factory ammo is the presence of ammo designed for special needs. For example, in some areas hunters must harvest deer with the shotgun. Today, factory ammunition for big game hunting with the shotgun is far ahead of its former state. Today's rifled-slug loads are more accurate than those I tested many years ago, and the buckshot is better-grouping. Also, both have been boosted in power. Given the presence of slug barrels and adjustable sights, the current crop of slug/buckshot ammo will enable cleaner harvesting of deer.

I do not think that factory ammo has ever been as accurate as it now is. Yes, factory ammo has always been "good," at least as long as I have tested it, and this includes tests using old, oftentimes out-of-print loads. However, today's ammo is simply more accurate than what was offered a few years ago—my tests prove it. Also, I think we have to hand it to the ammo manufacturers for the better bullets and shot available in component form to handloaders. The newer trend in the "big game bullet" is certainly due in part to the fact that factory bullets, for many years, possessed excellent hang-together qualities. I distinctly recall the fact that, for too many years, most of the bullets from components manufacturers (Nosler excepted) were a bit on the soft side. Not now. We also have rounder shot, and copper coated shot, and buffered shot. These trends are all for the good. Factory ammo has been good from the start. It's just getting better.

Finding Ammo for Obsolete Cartridges

Today, there is great interest in the "collectible" firearm. However, a great many of these old-time pieces are not just for show, and not quite ready to adorn the wall. They are for *shooting*. On the other hand, trying to find obsolete ammo for these guns can be a real problem at times. Factory ammunition is, fortunately, still available for many rounds which are truly obsolete in the sense that a firearm has not been built for them for years. For example, the only rifle I know of chambered for the fine 348 Winchester round was the Model 71 lever-action rifle. That rifle has not been around since 1958! Yet, ammunition is still available for it. Why? Because shooters still like the 348 (and its case is frequently used by handloaders in the construction of other obsolete calibers). Today, a Model 71 Winchester lever-action rifle may be worth a good five times more than its original asking price. But it is not a collector's item in the same sense that a fine old Colt percussion revolver or an old "Kentucky" longrifle might be. In short, it doesn't really hurt the value of this rifle to shoot it, except in the rare case of locating one in the box in unfired condition. (I would not fire a new "in-the-box" Model 71 at all.)

In the case of the Model 71, then, a shooter can buy 348 Winchester ammo. He can also reload for it. Hornady, for example, offers a 200-grain flat-point bullet especially for the 348 Winchester cartridge. The 32-20 is another hang-on. Not only that, but newly spurred interest in the round has brought its rechambering in a couple of six-guns. It always was a very fine cartridge in the handgun for light-duty work, and factory ammo is available.

Finding Ammo for Obsolete Calibers

Lastly, we have literally dozens of rifles and handguns which are still in shootable condition with no commercial ammo being readily available for them. These guns are the object of our interest. I ran across, for example, a beautiful Model 81 Marlin lever-action in 40-60 caliber. How in the world would a shooter get ammo for that one? I found a 45-90 Model 86 Winchester at a good price. This one is less a problem because a 45-70 case will chamber here. But if a shooter wants to use the 45-90 load, he can. We will discuss how in a moment. One might expect the 45-120-550 Sharps to be as defunct as the old buffalo runners themselves, but it isn't. If you have or come into possession of an old-time firearm still in shootable condition and want to fire it, please take the following precautions.

1. Do Not Trust Markings on the Rifle

First, do not trust the markings on the barrel. I had a rifle which stated 38-72 on the rifle itself, but this lever-action box magazine rifle was not chambered for the 38-72, not any longer. Many old guns were often rechambered. Some had sleeves put in their bores or chambers; some were simply rebored and rechambered. Do not trust the markings on the gun itself.

Modern factory ammunition has many distinct traits. A semi-rimmed case has an indentation at the head of the case as in a rimless case, but the rim protrudes past the case body. In the rimmed case, the rim itself protrudes past the walls or body of the case. The 30-30 is an example of a rimmed case. The rim of a rimless case is even with the body or walls of the case, the indentation allowing for an extractor to function. There are many rimless type cases today. This is a 45 Auto pistol case.

The belted magnum rifle case is rimless in effect, but the belt makes the head area quite strong. When handloaders mike this case for case head expansion they mike it on the belt (upper left). To its right is the rimless rifle case, and lower left is the rimmed pistol or revolver case. On the right is a semi-rimmed pistol or revolver case.

Reloaders need not worry about finding or making brass for most of the cartridges they will come across these days, even rounds which are not popular, nor loaded in America. Here, the B.E.L.L. company offers the shooter brass cases for reloading in a cartridge which would be considered very rare in America, the 500 Nitro Express 3¹/₄-inch case. John Taylor stated that this round was loaded with a 480-grain metal-cased bullet at a MV of 2175 fps for an energy rating of 5043 foot-pounds.

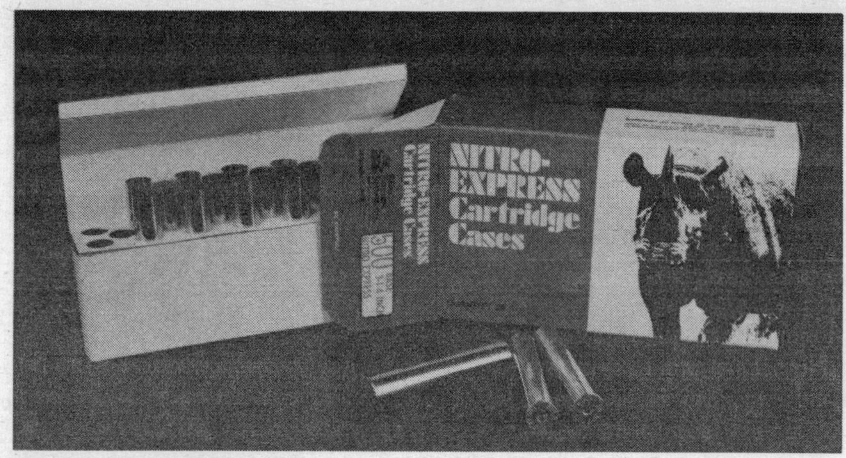

Never attempt to guess the identity of a cartridge or chambering. You'll only be playing with dynamite. Enlist the service of a *qualified* gunsmith—he'll help sort things out, properly.

2. How to Test for the Correct Caliber

Get help—take your rifle to a competent gunsmith and have him help decide which ammo the rifle truly shoots. A gunsmith can, if necessary, make a chamber cast, mike the bore and also check for headspace problems. Headspace is the fit of the cartridge within the chamber of the gun, and it is the distance from the breech face to that point where the round would normally halt in the chamber. This varies. Some cases "headspace on the shoulder," meaning that the shoulder of the case is the measuring point. But some cases headspace on the neck of the case, or the mouth. A rimless 45 ACP round is a good example of this. A case may headspace on the cartridge case rim, too, or on the belt of the magnum type case. At any rate, the gunsmith can check to see if the firearm is in proper shooting order. Get help. Good help can pay off big if a rifle is not worthy of service.

Be aware that there have been some very significant differences in some of the bore and chamber dimensions of some of the old-time rounds. For example, some 38-55s actually have a bore diameter which require a cast bullet of .377-.380-inch for accurate shooting. Though no damage will be done by shooting a .376-inch jacketed bullet in those barrels, accuracy is going to be better with the proper projectile fit.

"Slug" the bore—it's an old practice. Slugging the bore is a measure which any knowledgeable gunsmith can do for a shooter. A light lube, such as WD-40, is used in the bore first, and a pure lead bullet of approximate bore size, is carefully forced through the bore. Obviously, this slug will show the size of the bore. Micrometer calipers will be used to measure the "slugged" lead ball to determine depth of groove as well as land-to-land width. Also, your gunsmith can determine if the bore is oversize, or in a few cases actually undersize, which can be bad. As mentioned earlier, a knowledgeable gunsmith can also provide a *chamber cast,* which will precisely show the dimensions of the chamber of the gun. The guesswork is now over—you have verified (or determined) the cartridge your gun's chambered for.

Finding Obsolete Ammo

Once the cartridge is known, the shooter can go about his business finding the correct ammo for his firearm. Here are a few hints:

Ammunition Availability Table

(Courtesy of the National Rifle Association)

Code Key to Availability Table
(From: The American Rifleman Magazine April, 1983)

1. **Winchester Div., Olin Corp., Shamrock St., East Alton, Ill. 62024**
2. **Remington Arms Co., Inc., P.O. Box 1939, Bridgeport, Conn. 06601**
3. **Federal Cartridge Corp., 2700 Foshay Tower, Minneapolis, Minn. 54402**
4. **CCI/Speer, Omark Ind., Inc., P.O. Box 856, Lewiston, Idaho 83501**
5. **Midway Arms, Inc., Rt. 5, Columbia, MO 65201**
6. **Weatherby, Inc., 2781 Firestone Blvd., South Gate, Calif. 90280**
7. **Dynamit Nobel of America, Inc., 105 Stonehurst Ct., Northvale, N.J. 07647 (RWS and GECO ammunition)**
8. **T&C Enterprises, 5218 Pine Hills Rd., Box 15652, Orlando, Fla. 32858 (Obsolescent factory ammunition)**
9. **Outdoor Sports Headquarters, Inc., Box 1327, Dayton, Ohio 45401 (Norma ammunition)**

A. **James B. Stegall, Box 148B, Forest Road, Wallkill, N.Y. 12589**
B. **Anthony F. Sailer, Box L. Owen, Wisc. 54460**
C. **Ballistek Weapon Systems, 2014 Sunray Ave., Odessa, Tex. 79763**
D. **The Old Western Scrounger, 3509 Carlson Blvd., El Cerrito, Calif. 94530 (Factory and custom made)**

Cartridge	Code
.17 Rem.	2
.17 Wildcats	C
.20 Wildcats	C
.218 Bee	1
.219 Mashburn	A
.219 Zipper	8,A,B,C,D
.22 Caseless Daisy	8,D
.22 Hornet	1,2,7,9
.22 Rem. BR	C
.22 Rem. Jet	2
.22 Savage H.P.	7,9,A,B,C
.22 W.C.F.	A
.22 Wildcats	C
.220 Swift	9,C
.221 Rem. Fire Ball	2
.222 Rem.	1,2,3,9
.222 Rem. Mag.	2
.223 Rem.	1,2,3
.224 Wby. Mag.	6
.225 Win.	1
.22-.250 Rem.	1,2,3,9
.228 Wildcats	C
.23 Wildcats	C
.240 Apex	B
.240 Gibbs	C
.240 Wby. Mag.	6
.240 Wildcats	C
.242 Rimless Nitro	C
.243 Win.	1,2,3,7,9
.243 Wildcats	C
.246 Purdey Flanged	C
.25 ACP	1,2,3,7
.25 Rem.	A,B,C
.25 Rimfire Short	8
.25 Stevens Rimfire	8
.25 Wildcats	C
.250 Savage	1,2
.25-'06 Rem.	1,2,3
.25-20 Single Shot	A,B
.25-20 W.C.F.	1,2
.25-35 W.C.F.	1
.25-36 Marlin	A,B,C
.256 Gibbs Mag.	C
.256 Newton	A,B,C
.256 Win. Mag.	1
.257 Roberts	1,2
.257 Wby. Mag.	6
.257 Wildcats	C
.260 A.A.R.	C
.263 Wildcats	C
.264 Wildcats	C
.264 Win. Mag.	1,2
.270 Wby. Mag.	6
.270 Wildcats	C
.270 Win.	1,2,3,7,9
.275 H&H	B,C,D
.275 Rigby	C
.280 Rem.	2,9
.280 Ross	C
.280 Wildcats	C
.284 Win.	1
.30 Carbine	1,2,3,7,9
.30 Gibbs	A,C
.30 Herrett	C
.30 Newton	C
.30 Rem.	1,2
.30 Wildcats	C
.30-'06 Spr.	1,2,3,7,9
.30-30 Win.	1,2,3,9
.30 H&H Mag.	1,2
.300 Savage	1,2,3
.300 Wby. Mag.	6
.300 Win. Mag.	1,2,3
.303 British	1,2,9
.303 Savage	1
.30-40 Krag	1,2
.307 Win.	1
.308 Norma Mag.	9,C
.308 Win.	1,2,3,7,9
.310 Cadet	C
.318 Westley Richards	C
.32 ACP	1,2,3,7,9
.32 Long Colt	1,2
.32 Rem.	1,B,C
.32 Rimfire Long	8
.32 Rimfire Short	8
.32 S&W	1,2,7
.32 S&W Long	1,2,7,9
.32 Short Colt	1,2
.32 Win. S.L.	8,A,D
.32 Win. Spl.	1,2,3
.320 Revolver	C
.32-20 W.C.F.	1,2
.32-40 Rem. Hepburn	A,C
.32-40 Win.	1,A,B,C
.33 Newton	C
.33 W.C.F.	8,A,B,C
.33 OKH	C
.333 Jeffery	C
.338 Win. Mag.	1
.338 Wildcats	C
.340 Wby. Mag.	6
.348 Win.	1
.35 G&H Mag.	C
.35 Newton	C
.35 Rem.	1,2,3
.35 S&W Auto	C
.35 Whelen	B,C
.35 Wildcats	C
.35 Win.	8,A,B
.35 Win. S.L.	8,A,B
.350 Rem. Mag.	2
.350 Rigby	C
.351 Win. S.L.	1
.35-40 Maynard	C
.357 Auto Mag	C
.357 Herrett	C
.357 Maximum	3
.357 S&W Mag.	1,2,3,4,7,9
.358 Norma Mag.	9,C
.358 Win.	1
.360 Nitro	C
.369 Purdey Nitro	C
.375 H&H Flanged	C
.375 H&H Mag.	1,2,7
.375 Win.	1
.375 Wildcats	C
.378 Wby. Mag.	6
.38 ACP	1,2
.38 Long Colt	1
.38 Short Colt	1,2
.38 S&W	1,2,7
.38 S&W Spl.	1,2,3,4,7,9
.38 Super	1,2
.380 ACP	1,2,3,4,7
.38-40 Ballard	A
.38-40 Rem. Hepburn	A
.38-40 W.C.F.	1
.38-45 ACP	C
.38-45 Bullard	A,C
.38-50 Ballard	A,C
.38-50 Maynard	A,C
.38-50 Rem.	A
.38-55 Win.	1,A,B,C,D
.38-56 Win.	A,B,C
.38-70 Win.	B,C
.38-72 Win.	A,B,C
.400 Whelen	C
.400 × .375 Belted	A

continued page 226

Cartridge	Code	Cartridge	Code	Cartridge	Code
.401 Win. S.L.	8,A,B,C	.44-70 Sharps & Rem.	C	.50-95 W.C.F.	A,B,C
.404 Jeffery	7,C,D	.44-90 Sharps $2\frac{7}{16}$"	A,C	.50-100 Maynard	A
.40-40 Maynard	A	.44-90 Sharps $2\frac{5}{8}$"	A	.50-100 W.C.F.	A,C
.40-45 Rem. Straight	A	.44-100 Rem. Straight	A	.50-105 W.C.F.	C
.40-45 Sharps Straight	A	.45 ACP	1,2,3,4,7	.50-110 W.C.F.	A,B,C
.405 Win.	A,B,C	.45 Auto Rim	2	.50-140 Sharps	A,C,D
.40-50 Sharps Straight	B,C	.45 Colt	1,2,3	.577 Nitro	B,C
.40-60 Bullard	A	.45 S&W	B,C	.577 Snider	B,C
.40-60 Marlin	A,B,C	.45 Win. Mag.	1	.577-.450 Martini	A,B,C
.40-60 Maynard	A	.45 Wildcats	C		
.40-60 W.C.F.	A,B,C,D	.450 Adams Revolver	C	**METRIC**	
.40-65 W.C.F.	A,B,C,D	.450 Alaskan	C	4mm Zimmerstutzen	D
.40-70 Maynard	A	.450-.400	C,D	6 mm Lee Navy	A,B,C
.40-70 Rem.	A,C	.454 Casull Mag.	C	6 mm Rem.	1,2,3
.40-70 Sharps Bottleneck	A,C	.455 Webley	8,A	6 mm Wildcats	C
.40-70 Sharps Straight	A,B,C	.45-50 Peabody Martini	A,C	6.5 Rem. Mag.	2
.40-70 W.C.F.	A,B,C	.45-60 W.C.F.	A,B,C,D	6.5×48R	A
.40-72 W.C.F.	A,B,C	.45-70 Government	1,2,3,A,B,D	6.5×50 Arisaka	9,A,B,C
.40-75 Bullard	A,C	.45-75 Sharps $2\frac{1}{10}$"	A,B,C	6.5×52 Carcano	9,A,B,C
.40-80 Sharps Bottleneck	A	.45-75 W.C.F.	A,B,C	6.5×53	A
.40-82 W.C.F.	A,B,C,D	.458 Win. Mag.	1,2	6.5×53R	8,B
.40-90 Bullard	A,C	.45-82 W.C.F.	A,C	6.5×54 Mauser	B
.40-90 Sharps Straight	A,C	.45-85 Win., Marlin	A,B,C	6.5×54 M.S	8,A,B,C
.41 Long Colt	8,A,B,C	.45-90 W.C.F.	A,B,C,D	6.5×55 Swedish	9,A,B,C
.41 Rem. Mag.	1,2	.45-100 Ballard	A	6.5×57	7,A,B,C
.41 Rimfire Short	8,D	.45-100 Sharps Straight 2.4"	A,B,C	6.5×57R	7,A,B,C
.416 Rigby	C	.45-100 Sharps Straight 2.6"	A,B,C	6.5×58	8,B
.42 Russian	A	.45-100 Sharps Straight 2.71"	A,B,C	6.5×58R	A,B
.425 Westley Richards	B,C	.45-100 Sharps Straight 2.87"	A,B,C,D	6.5×68	7,A
.43 Egyptian	C	.45-120 Sharps Straight $3\frac{1}{4}$"	A,C,D	6.5×68R	7
.43 Spanish	8,A,C,D	.460 Wby. Mag.	6	6.5 Wildcats	7
.44 Auto Mag	8,9,C	.470 Nitro	B,C	7 mm Baby Nambu	C
.44 Rem. Mag.	1,2,3,4,9	.475 A&M Mag.	C	7 mm B.R.	C
.44 S&W American	C	.476 Nitro	C	7 mm Express Rem.	2
.44 S&W Russian	8,A,B,C	.50 Browning M.G.	D	7mm H&H Rimmed Mag.	C
.44 S&W Spl.	1,2,3	.50 Government Carbine	A	7 mm Rem. Mag.	1,2,3,9
.444 Marlin	2	.500 Nitro	B	7 mm Wby. Mag.	6
.44-40 Extra Long	A	.500-.450 H&H	C	7 mm-08 Rem.	2
.44-40 W.C.F.	1,2	.500-.465	B,C	7mm Wildcats	C
.44-60 Creedmoor	A,C	.505 Gibbs Mag.	D	7×57 Mauser	1,2,3,7,9
.44-60 Maynard	A	.50-50 Maynard	A	7×57R	7,9,A,B,C
.44-60 Sharps	A,C	.50-70 Government	A,B,C	7×61 S&H	A,B,C
.44-70 Maynard	A,C	.50-90 Sharps $2\frac{1}{2}$"	A,C	7×64	7,9,A,B,C

1. Do not trust the store clerk to help you unless that clerk also has a reputation as a very knowledgeable gun expert. I was waiting in line in a department store one afternoon, close enough to the sporting goods section to overhear a clerk trying to sell a shooter a box of 7mm Remington Magnum ammunition for a 7mm Mauser rifle! Well, they both were 7mm, weren't they? Of course, this situation would present no problem because the big 7mm Magnum would not chamber in the 7mm Mauser anyway, but I repeat that department store clerks are not always "reliable" when it comes to finding, recommending or even identifying guns and ammo.

2. While this is a chapter on factory ammo, we must state here that some of the old-time ammunition can be handloaded for. One can buy dies for obsolete cartridges from an outlet such as Huntington Die Specialties, P.O. Box 991, Oroville, CA 95965. Furthermore, special bullet moulds can be made up by experts such as Richard Hoch (62778 Spring Creek Rd., Montrose, CO 81401).

3. Obsolete brass can be obtained often through companies dealing in hard-to-find ammo. A good example would be Huntington Die Specialties or Brass Extrusion Laboratories, Ltd. (B.E.L.L.), 800 W. Maple Lane, Bensenville, IL 60106. Also, special factory or ready-made ammo is sometimes available through these outlets.

4. Watch for ammo sales. In the *Shotgun News,* for example, a large firearms tabloid, I have located many bargains in out-of-print ammo. Once located, I'd suggest the shooter buy all the ammo he can afford.

5. Keep an eye on rounds which are obsolete and yet still in production. For example, one can still buy 303 Savage ammo from Winchester, loaded with the excellent 190-grain Silvertip round nose bullet. Will this ammo always be available? I would like to think so, but would not guarantee it. If I owned a 303 Savage, I would buy as much as I could store safely and legally.

6. Barrel liners are a possibility, too. They can work well. I have fired a rifle with a barrel liner from Bauska

Cartridge	Code	Cartridge	Code	Cartridge	Code
7×65R	7,A,B	8×64S	C	9.3×74R	7,A,B
7×66	C	8×68R	A	9.3×82	A
7×72R	A,B	8×68S	7,C	9.5×47R	C
7×75R	C	8×72R	A,B	9.5×56 M.S.	A,D
7.35 Carcano	8,A,B,C	8.15×46R	A,B,C	9.5×57	A,B
7.5 Swedish Nagant	C	9 mm Bergmann Bayard	5	9.5×60R Turkish	C
7.5 Swiss Revolver	C	9 mm Browning Long	5,C	9.5×72	A
7.5×54 French	8,B,C	9 mm Glisenti	C	10 mm Bren D&D	C
7.5×55 Swiss	9,A,B,C	9 mm Japanese Revolver	5	10.3×60R Swiss	C
7.62 Nagant Revolver	C	9 mm Luger	1,2,3,4,7,9	10.75×68	7,B,C
7.62 Tokarev Pistol	5	9 mm Makarov	C	10.75×73	7
7.62×39 Russian	5,A,B,C	9 mm Rimfire	D	11 mm French Revolver	C
7.62×54R Russian	9,A,B,C	9 mm Steyr Hahn	5,C	11 mm German Revolver	A,C
7.63 Mauser Pistol	5	9 mm Win. Mag.	1	11 mm Mannlicher	8
7.65 Borchardt	C	9×18 Ultra	7,C	11 mm Mauser	A,C,D
7.65 French Auto.	C	9×56 M.S.	A,B,C	11 mm Werndl	8
7.65 Luger	1,7,9	9×57 Mauser	8,A,B,C,D	11.15×50R	A
7.65 Mannlicher	8,C	9×63	C	11.15×60R	A
7.65 Roth-Sauer	C	9.3×53R	8	11.2×60 Shuler	A
7.65×53 Argentine	9,A,B,C	9.3×57	9,A,B	11.2×72 Shuler	A
7.7×58 Arisaka	9,A,B,C	9.3×61	A	11.3×50R Beaumont	C
7.92×33 Kurz	C	9.3×62	7,9,A,B,C,D	11.75 Montenegrin Revolver	C
8 mm Gibbs	C	9.3×64	7	11.75×51R Danish	A
8 mm Lebel Revolver	8,A,C	9.3×72R	7,B,C		
8 mm Nambu	5,B				
8 mm Rast-Gasser	C				
8 mm Rem. Mag.	2				
8 mm Roth-Steyr	8,C				
8 mm Wildcats	C				
8×48R Sauer	A				
8×50R Lebel	8,A,B,C				
8×50 Mannlicher	A,B				
8×52 R Siamese	A,B,C				
8×56R	A,B,C				
8×57 Mauser	1,2,3,7				
8×57J	9,A,B				
8×57JR	A,B				
8×57JRS	7,A				
8×57JS	9,A				
8×58R Krag	A				
8×58R Straight	A				
8×60R	8,A,B				
8×60S	7,B,C				

Suppliers of Collectors' Cartridges

Chas. E. Duffy, Williams Lane, West Hurley, N.Y. 12491	**No lists**
Tom M. Dunn, 1342 So. Poplar, Casper, Wyo. 82601	**List $4.00**
W. F. Gaines, Box 22, Buffalo Lakes, Minn. 55314	**No lists**
Idaho Ammunition Service, 410 21st Ave., Lewiston, Idaho 83501	**No lists**
Gary R. Reusze, Box 362, Crown Point, Ind. 46307	**List $4.00**
San Francisco Gun Exchange, 124 Second St., San Francisco, Calif. 94150	**No lists**
James C. Tillinghast, Box 27A, Hancock, N.H. 03447	**List $1.50**
Lewis Yearout, 308 Riverview Dr., E., Great Falls, Mont. 59404	**No lists**

When selecting factory ammo, the author prefers to employ a chronograph to determine precise velocity. While every shooter may not own a chronograph, local gun clubs and commercial ranges often have them available.

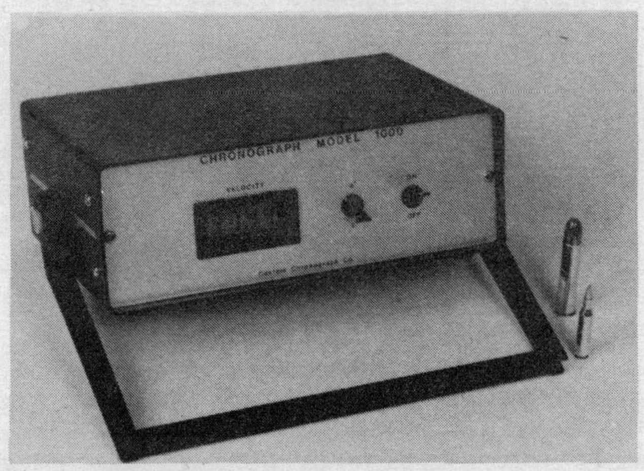

Rifle Barrel Co., Inc., 105 9th Avenue West, Kalispell, MT 59901. Accuracy was excellent. A shooter may wish to restore an old gun with a bore liner (barrel liner) to improve accuracy or to switch over to another round which is more readily available.

Ammunition in factory form is widely available in a number of calibers which have gone defunct. However, there are few guarantees that such ammo will always be on hand. I have often suggested that instead of storing a lot of live ammo, a shooter could save a good number of brass cases. Clean them first, and that means in a case tumbler. Store them in a dry place and check them often. If they start discoloring, clean them again. Also store some bullets if the caliber is an odd one and slugs are hard to come by.

In summary, we find that factory-loaded ammo in rimfire, centerfire handgun and rifle, and shotgun is of super quality and wide distribution. The complete shooter who uses the resources available to him, will have little to worry about when it comes to finding his favorite ammunition.

Chapter 18

Modern Handloading

AMERICAN SHOOTERS have been handloaders from the start. After all, a black powder load was made by hand, literally, one at a time and with the full attention of the shooter. The cartridge was not in wide general use until the very end of the 19th century, yet even into the 20th century, some shooters remained with the muzzleloader. In muzzle-loading, it was the responsibility of the shooter to pour a correct powder charge down into the breech, followed by a properly fitted patched ball, or conical, which he rammed down on top of the charge. Then the shooter had to insure the ignition of his piece either by priming the pan of the flintlock or by fitting a percussion cap to the nipple of his firearm. It was all done by hand.

Handloading continued with the advent of the metallic cartridge, at first with black powder, then with smokeless. For several years, it was the 44-40, 38-40, 45-70, 38-55 and rounds such as the 50-110 which were used by hunters in this country. The first number designated the caliber, the second number represented the amount (in grains weight) of black powder used. Handloading tools were readily available very early in the cartridge-shooting era, too. I have a reloading tool which carries a Winchester patent from 1884. My sample, in caliber 44-40 Winchester, the tool itself stamped "44 W.C.F.," is equipped with a mould section to cast a bullet. This simple tool decaps, resizes, reprimes and even has a built-in bullet mould. It still functions to this day.

The old-timer, that is, the hunter of the late 19th century, could, with that one simple tool, reload his ammo even on the trail. Since lead melts at 621 degrees Fahrenheit, the hunter could mould his own projectiles in the outback over a campfire, or at home with some hot coals and perhaps, but not necessarily, a bellows. By carrying a few primers and some lead, along with a supply of black powder, the reloader was all set. Black powder did not yield the high energy ratings that the later smokeless powder would, and it was perfectly fine to build a charge by simply using a scoop to measure out powder for the load. In fact, with a 44-40 or a similar round, the hunter could get by without a measure by filling the case with Fg black powder to that point where a bullet would be normally seated.

The reloader has the option of making up ammunition for guns which are chambered for rounds no longer manufactured. These cases from B. E. L. L., Brass Extrusion Laboratories, Ltd., make the loading of antique ammunition a reality.

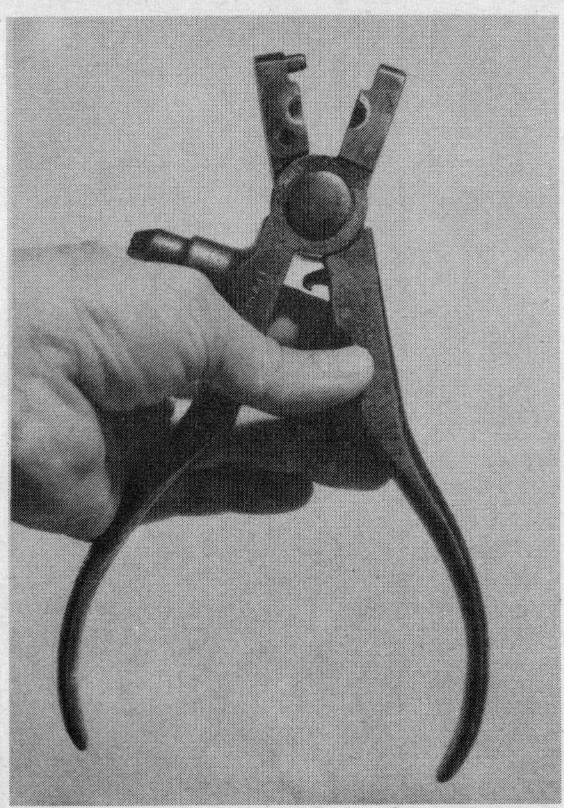

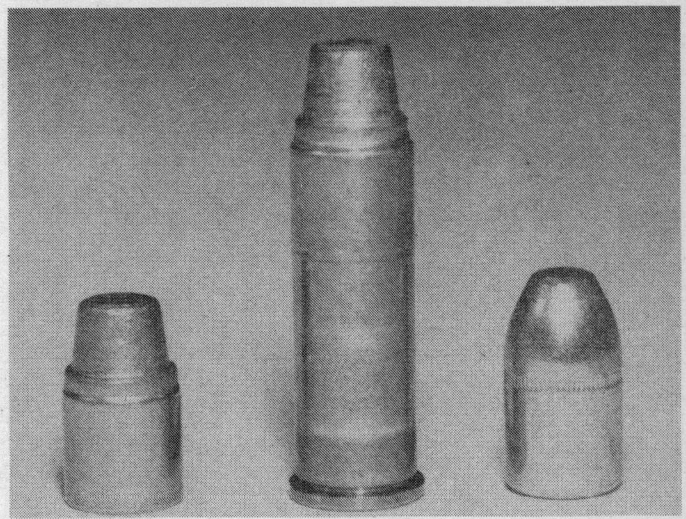

The reloader has a choice. The 44 Magnum round here can be loaded with a 240 grain soft nose bullet, left, or with the 265 grain bullet on the right. The tough 265 grain Hornady bullet will not readily upset at 44 Magnum velocities, but it is accurate from the 44 Magnum handgun and it does penetrate admirably. It can be loaded to over 1300 fps MV.

(Left) This Winchester pattern reloading tool goes back to the 19th century. Reloading has been a part of the shooting game from the beginning.

The tradition of handloading has lived on and on and is extremely popular today. Shooters can still buy (from Lyman) tools as simple as the one described above. Or they can invest in much more elaborate reloading outfits. Most handloaders today have determined that the investment in fine reloading tools is actually realized in a couple of years, the cost of the equipment being amortized in short order. Of course, this is true for shooters who fire more than a couple of boxes of ammo annually. For the shooter who does not use his firearms much, then it would take much longer for the entire outfit of reloading tools to pay for itself.

Why Reload?

I can think of several reasons for reloading our own ammo, but to capsulize those reasons, I'll list only three prime forces in handcrafting ammunition. They are:

1. Increasing versatility
2. Customizing a load for supreme accuracy and power
3. Saving money (up to perhaps 70 percent).

Versatility and Custom Loading

A shooter can turn a shotgun, handgun or rifle into many different guns all wrapped up into one by handloading. The simplest example of this would be the 30-06 Springfield. The 30-06 can be handloaded for rabbits and squirrels, using light bullets, including cast lead alloy missiles, at modest velocities, and also handloaded for really big game by going all the way up to a 300-grain bullet. That big 300-grain '06 slug is the Elk Mountain Alaskan bullet which is partially made of tungsten alloy. It's for big, *big* dangerous game.

Sure I could pick the 30-06 for all of my hunting chores, but I don't. There is another cartridge—one that I'm fond of—which handloaders use widely. That cartridge has maintained its popularity over much of the world since about 1895, and that is the famous 30-30, often maligned these days as an underpowered round. Can a handloader really turn the old 30-30 round into a versatile cartridge? Some detractors claim that this is not possible, that the 30-30 case is so puny it will not handle a wide range of bullets. But just watch.

Small Game Loads for the 30-30: I use a 30-30 for small game hunting and even for mountain grouse. I truly enjoy packing old "Slab Side" into the mountains with me, and I am highly confident in the models I own, especially an old original Model 94 rifle and a custom Model 94 dubbed the "Storey Conversion." The old rifle, with its 26-inch barrel, was made in 1899, and the Storey Conversion is a 24-inch barrel rifle with "button" magazine, actually chambered for the 30-30 Improved, but also handles the standard 30-30 round, including my small game loads. It shoots 1-inch 3-shot groups all day from the bench at the 100-yard range. Since the 30-30 is legal for mountain grouse where I live, as well as cottontail rabbit and other game, here is what I use in my 30-30s:

A very fine example of handloading flexibility is seen in the famous 30-30 Winchester round. The loads shown here are but a few of the many which can be made, and these do not even include the excellent cast bullet loads for the 30-30. On the left is a 110 grain bullet loaded down to only 1500 fps MV for small game. Then a 125 grain HP for varmints, a 130 for fast-stepping deer round, a 150 grain general load, a 165 boat-tail for long-range shooting (in bolt actions *only)*, the all-around 170 grain load, a deep-penetrating 180 grain bullet and finally a long 190 grain Silvertip load.

30-30 Small Game Load

Bullet: 120-grain Cast Bullet (No. 2 Alloy) Lyman No. 311441 (gas check)
Powder: 7.0 grains of PB smokeless powder
MV: 1300 fps

Remarks: This load is found in the *Lyman Reloading Handbook,* 45th edition, page 93. It's accurate and mild and the report is minimal. Recoil? The shooter hardly knows he's shot a rifle with this little load. It will not destroy the valuable meat of a rabbit, squirrel or grouse.

Plains Game Loads for the 30-30: I also hunt antelope and desert mule deer with my 30-30s, and I am totally confident that I can cleanly harvest any antelope at 200 yards with my handloads. The 130-grain Speer Flat Nose, made for the 30-30, will shoot very accurately from my rifles and will deliver enough punch at 200 yards to drop game mule deer in size. Here is my 130-grain Speer bullet load.

30-30 Load for Plains Game

Bullet: 130-grain Speer Flat Nose
Powder: 38.0 grains of H-335
MV: 2650 fps MV out of a 26-inch barrel

Remarks: Out of my Storey Conversion using the 30-30 Improved load, the 24-inch barrel gives me an average muzzle velocity of 2780 fps, with improved loads. However, even from the standard 30-30, this fine bullet does the job remarkably well on plains game, which means, mostly, antelope for me. I usually use another bullet for mule deer hunting, but might consider this load for Coues deer in the Southwest as well as plains game. The load comes from page 157 of *Hodgdon's Data Manual Number 24*.

General Deer Hunting Loads for the 30-30: I like to get close to my game when possible. Hunting with a muzzleloader has aided me in thinking about a stalk instead of a long shot, and my 30-30 is truly a long-range number in comparison with my round ball rifles, so I always feel very well armed when hunting deer with the venerable 30-30.

30-30 Load for Deer

Bullet: 170-grain Speer Flat Nose
Powder: 38.0 grains of W-748 powder
MV: 2300 fps

Remarks: I found this load in the *Hornady Handbook of Cartridge Reloading,* Third Edition, page 211. However, it was listed as 39.0 grains of W-748. I worked up from about 35 grains and my chronograph actually showed 2300 fps MV with 38.0 grains so I stopped there. For a flat nose bullet, the Speer has good ballistic coefficient and the bullet holds together well for supreme penetration on deer-sized game. This is a very adequate deer round for up to 200 yards.

Varmint Loads for the 30-30: I am throwing this one in as varminting with this cartridge *is* a reality. In fact, many ranchers where I live use the 30-30 for varmints ranging from prairie dogs to coyotes and larger. The 30-30 is hardly an ideal varmint round, but for the hunter who is at work, who is not able to tote a big long-range scope-sighted rifle, that little 30-30 can account for considerable varminting.

30-30 Load for Varmints

Bullet: 125-grain Sierra Flat Point Hollow Point
Powder: 38.0 grains of H-335
MV: 2650 fps

Remarks: This is no hotrock varmint number by any means, but when a shooter has mastered a 30-30 carbine, he can put a varmint down at reasonably long range, depending upon the sights he uses. Many a Marlin Model 336 wears a scope, and the new Model 94 Side Eject wears one, too, without any hitch at all. The load is to be found on page 157 of the *Hodgdon Data Manual No. 24*.

The Cast Bullet in the 30-30: There should be special interest in shooting the cast bullet in the 30-30 because the cast bullet works extremely well in this cartridge. Just to round out our story on versatility, here are a couple more cast bullet loads for the shooter to look at. Remember, a cast bullet was used for small game hunting. It is extremely economical, as are the following loads with their heavier bullets.

Cast Bullet Loads for the 30-30

Bullet: 170-grain, #2 Alloy, gas check, Lyman No. 311441
Powder: 35.0 grains of Win. 748
MV: 2270 fps

Bullet: 180-grain, #2 Alloy, gas check, RCBS No. 30-180 Flat Nose
Powder: 23.0 grains of H4198
MV: 2032 fps

Remarks: These loads are entirely suitable for deer hunting at close range. The lead bullet will penetrate well in such game. The 170-grain load is from the *Lyman Reloading Handbook, 46th Edition,* page 283. The 180-grain load is from the *Hodgdon Data Manual No. 24,* page 211.

The picture is clear. The facts are in. The little 30-30 becomes quite versatile when handloaded, and just think of what happens to other rounds, such as the 308 Winchester, or the aforementioned 30-06. The big 7mm Remington Magnum can be tamed down or made to roar like a lion by a handloader, with a 160-grain bullet at 3100 fps or a cast bullet of 147 grains at less than 1600 fps MV.

As for the shotgun shell, I have 12-gauge reloads which push a mere ounce of shot at about 900 fps MV, and others which throw a full 1½ ounces of shot at over 1200 fps MV. That is customizing your ammo. But more importantly, the reloader can work on patterns from his own personal shotguns, using data provided by the component/tool companies. There are many different tested loads offered, so the choice is great.

Saving Money

The fine Cabela catalog of useful shooting and outdoor items, fall of 1984, lists a chart that shows the savings that can be realized through handloading. Of course, these figures are current only for the moment, and will change. But I suspect they will hold up for a very long time to come in terms of percentages. After all, the most expensive part of a metallic cartridge is the case itself and the shotgun shell hull is not exactly worthless either. Here are Cabela's figures.

Cost to Reload a Box of Rifle or Pistol Shells

357 mag. 158 gr.	Per 50	22-250 55 gr.	Per 20	270 Win. 130 gr.	Per 20
Primer	$.55	Primer	$.55	Primer	$.55
Powder	$.86	Powder	$1.26	Powder	$1.76
Bullets	$4.50	Bullets	$1.30	Bullets	$1.90
Reloads/50	$5.81	Reloads/20	$3.01	Reloads/20	$4.21
Factory/50	$14.30	Factory/20	$7.20	Factory/20	$9.80
You Save	**$8.49**	**You Save**	**$4.19**	**You Save**	**$5.59**

Cost to Reload A Box of Shotgun Shells

	12 ga. 1⅛ oz. Trap	12 ga. 1¼ oz. Field	12 ga. 1½ oz. Mag.	12 ga. 1⅞ oz.-3″ Mag.	10 ga. 2 oz.-3½″ Mag.
Shot	$1.05	$1.77	$1.41	$1.99	$2.12
Primers	45¢	45¢	45¢	45¢	45¢
Wads	42¢	42¢	42¢	42¢	42¢
Powder	77¢	98¢	$1.18	$1.38	$1.76
Reloads per 25	$2.69	$3.02	$3.46	$4.24	$4.75
Factory Box 25	$6.60	$6.50	$11.60	$12.85	$16.20
You Save	**$3.91**	**$3.48**	**$8.14**	**$8.71**	**$11.45**
% You Save	**59%**	**53.5%**	**70%**	**67%**	**70.6%**

I have taken a close look at my own reloading costs, and it is without a doubt that Cabela's figures are right. I have saved up to a possible 70 percent in my own reloading. But I do not consider cost factors to be the most important ones in handloading. If handloaded ammo cost me more money than factory fodder, I would still reload. My commentary on the 30-30 round certainly stands as powerful testimony to the fact that as a reloader I have taken a rifle I like a lot and made its rather mundane cartridge do workhorse labor for me.

I like to reload when I can use the activity as a relaxation session. There are times not to reload, too, and these are when a shooter is pressed and hurried. There is no sense in rushing an enjoyable project to begin with, but the shooter who does hurry his work may also find that he has made a *mistake*. Handloading is a precise hobby. It requires concentration and care.

Omark/CCI has compiled a few notes on handloading myths which I am paraphrasing here with permission. I think these are points well taken and they deserve telling over and over again. There have always been myths surrounding the handloading process, and the modern complete shooter might as well know what they are so he can understand them.

Myths About Handloading

Myth 1: "Handloading Is Complicated"

The actual act of safely building reloaded ammunition is not complicated. In fact, it is rather simple. Now, the advanced handloader has indeed entered a domain of interior ballistics and fine scientific points which would make a mathematician weep. But the actual act of putting ammo together in reloaded form is not difficult to accomplish.

Myth 2: "Handloading Doesn't Save That Much Money"

The brass case is about 65 percent of the original cost of a cartridge, and it can be reloaded safely several times before the brass itself "gets tired." Speer calculated the cost of a 30-06 factory round as 12¢ for the bullet, 6¢ for the powder, a penny for the primer and 41¢ for the case.

Myth 3: "Handloading Requires a Bunch of Costly Equipment"

Speer calculates that one can get started off right for about $150. A shooter who uses his guns will get this back very rapidly.

Myth 4: "Handloaded Ammunition Doesn't Measure Up to Factory Ammo"

I think we successfully buried this myth earlier. Handloaded ammo is very fine when prepared with care and understanding. Factory ammo is darn good, too. Make no mistake. But the factory cannot offer every little nuance of variation a shooter may want in his particular ammunition. The handloader can.

Myth 5: "Only a Few Kinds of Cartridges Can Be Handloaded"

There is almost no end to the number of rounds which can be reloaded, including obsolete ammo! RCBS offers dies for many of the rounds long since out of production. Shooters who cannot buy ammo can often make it for those older guns, or rare and exotic arms as well. Case-forming dies are available so that, for example, a hard to find cartridge can be built up from a more common piece of brass. Wildcat dies are also available. My wife's 6mm/222 uses RCBS dies which were simply purchased over the counter.

Myth 6: "Handloading Is Dangerous"

Handloading is not as dangerous as taking a bath. Sure, if a person loads a heap of pistol powder into a rifle case he can get hurt. But somewhere along the line we must realize that in order to enjoy any activity we must assume responsibility for our own actions. Driving is dangerous, but I have no intention of remaining within the four walls of my home because I might be hurt on the highway. I will do my best to drive safely and watch out for traffic instead. Handloading is no more dangerous than any activity which requires care and alertness.

The Reloading Area

A clean and well-lighted place is just what is needed for a reloader's working area. I also like a place which can be locked if powder and primers are to be stored, but sometimes this is not a possibility. You do not need much space. I have seen converted closets which were certainly adequate for handloading. It is nice if the reloading room is private enough to allow for concentration. I really do not care for kitchen table reloading if it can be prevented.

Tools for Reloading

The Reloading Manual and Finding a Load

The reloading manual is a tool—the foundation of reloading. These are not the days of heavy black powder cartridge loading. Smokeless powder is very efficient fuel; in some cases, a mere grain weight of difference can show a statistically significant response in both velocity and pressure. It is the reloading manual which gives the shooter those tried and tested load chains of the correct powder bullet and primer, all in the correct case.

I don't tamper with the data taken from a reloading manual because each load has been compiled as a result of extensive pressure testing. In the main, two methods are used by ballistics labs to determine the chamber pressures created by the firing of a specific load chain. One method is the crusher system, a piston device, driven by the expansion of powder gases, which squashes a copper pellet. The degree of pellet deformation is then translated into a figure and expressed as CUP (copper units of pressure). The other commonly used method is the piezo-electric transducer. The transducer is an electrical device which uses the property of its crystals to provide pressure readings. These crystals give off an electrical response to pressure, the response expressed in psi, or pounds per square inch. Though both systems have been in use for many years, controversy as to which system is better for measuring chamber pressures still abounds. The important point for handloaders to keep in mind is that the two systems measure chamber pressures differently and the resulting pressure figures for one given load in CUP and psi will be different. The two are *not* interchangeable.

Knowing the pressures a cartridge creates inside the chamber of your firearm is extremely important to the reloader. On the one end of the spectrum, without safe, manageable pressures a bullet or shot charge would never leave the muzzle of a firearm. On the other end is where the problems arise. When the handloader starts to go beyond a reliable manual's suggested maximum powder charge, pressure problems arise. Higher-than-acceptable pressures in a firearm can spell disaster, the result often being a blown-up firearm. Over the years, shooters have lost more than their guns by firing over-loaded cartridges.

In order to build a load, I always consult several different loading manuals before settling on anything. Suppose we want the most punch we can derive from a 30-06 for

A loading manual is a must, and the author suggests collecting several such manuals, mainly to search out the best loads for a given shooting purpose. Never get rid of old manuals.

long-range shooting. First, we can settle on the projectile. From consulting the reloading manuals we can see that the 150-grain bullet will be driven faster than a 165-grain bullet, and it may shoot a little flatter, but will not have the energy of the heavier slug at long range. So we settle on the 165-grain bullet. Now the manuals are searched for a load chain.

After going through several manuals, I finally find a load utilizing the 165-grain bullet in the current *Lyman Reloading Handbook*. I see one with a maximum load of 61.5 grains of H-4831 for a MV of 2881 fps, and with a pressure listed at 45,900 CUP average. My newer Remington Model 700 is capable of that with ease.* That is a load worth considering.

While looking through several other manuals, I also came across a 165-grain bullet, 30-06 load featuring a maximum charge of 60.8 grains of Winchester 760 powder for a muzzle velocity of 3000 fps. That load came from the Third Edition of the Hornady manual, page 230. Admittedly, this is only 100 fps faster, roughly, than the previous load, but I wanted to try it anyway. As you can see, the first step in my reloading process was bullet selection and my second was to find a powder charge which gave the high velocity I wanted. But there is more. I must study the entire load chain, not just the bullet and powder type/charge. In the Hornady load the case used for testing was a Frontier. The primer listed was a Federal 210. So my load chain is a 165-grain boat-tail bullet, with a Frontier case and a Federal 210 primer and a *max listing* of 60.8 grains of Winchester 760 powder.

I never start with a maximum load. I load from below first, but not very far below, 10 percent at most. Some powders do not take well to vast underloading. I might start with 59.0 grains of 760, then 60.0 and maybe then will I go to 60.8 grains as a maximum, providing the pressure signs indicate that potential. Each load you try, from 59.0 to 60.8, should be accuracy tested. I would suggest that you head for the bench to see how each load stacks up against the known accuracy levels of your rifle. It so happened that in my 30-06, the top load of 60.8 grains of 760 with the 165-grain bullet was most accurate. I now have the long-range powerhouse load I wanted for my 30-06. To test the velocity of your load you'll need access to a chronograph. Your local gun club should be able to help you out.

The Reloading Press

There are a number of loading press types on the market today, all having certain advantages for the shooter. First there is the C-type press. I have reloaded many rounds of metallic ammo with such a press. However, the C-type press is not as popular today as the O-frame model. The reason is the added rigidity of the O-frame. However, the

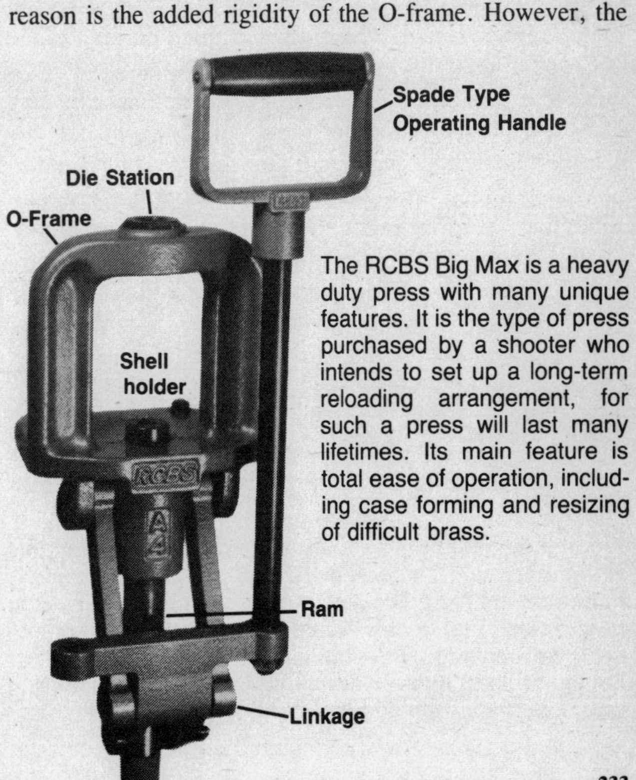

The RCBS Big Max is a heavy duty press with many unique features. It is the type of press purchased by a shooter who intends to set up a long-term reloading arrangement, for such a press will last many lifetimes. Its main feature is total ease of operation, including case forming and resizing of difficult brass.

*SAAMI (Sporting Arms and Ammunition Manufacturers' Institute) is the arm of the firearms industry responsible for setting pressure specification standards for centerfire, rimfire and shotshell ammunition. Firearms manufacturers, using the SAAMI information, test every firearm at levels exceeding those specs—it's called proof testing. However, the presence of a proof mark on a firearm doesn't mean you can haphazardly approach the hobby of reloading. Safe pressure levels must *always* be maintained. That means, for the handloader, never exceeding maximum loads found in reliable loading manuals.

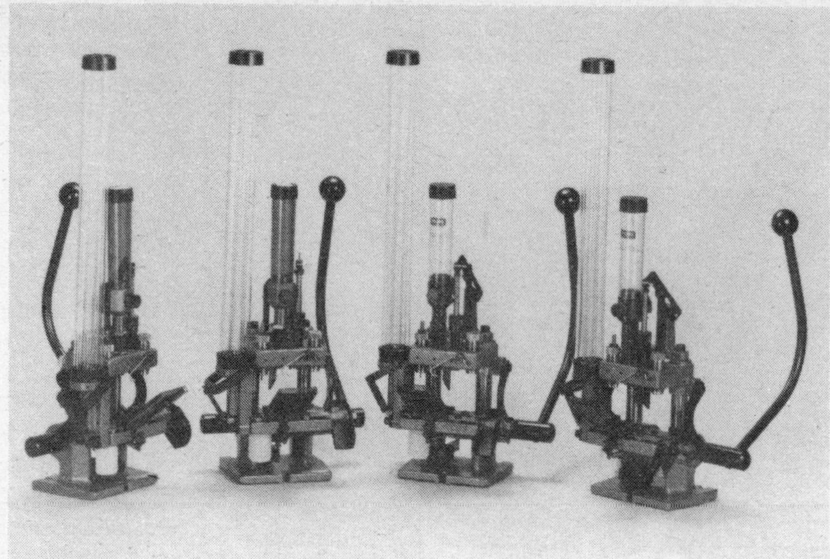

The GREEN MACHINE from RCBS was originally set up for 38 Special and 357 Magnum reloads for speedy mass production. The popularity of the Green Machine led to the addition of the 9mm 45 ACP (Automatic Colt Pistol) and 44 Magnum/Special.

question is one of need—does a reloader need the rigidity of the O-type press? On the face of it, no. However, because of the excellent alignment of the ram as well as no discernible spring in the frame, the O-type press has gained in popularity and the situation is most likely permanent.

The turret press is still with us. It is an option worthy of consideration, especially for the handgun ammo reloader. The turret press allows several dies to be inserted in a revolving wheel. The dies are then rotated into position as they are needed. In handgun loading, where many rounds could be necessary for practice, any expedition is nice to have and the turret press does give the shooter somewhat greater speed of operation.

Also fast are any of the production type reloading presses. These are offered in various price ranges and, as one would guess, the very high-priced production presses turn out a great deal of ammo in very little time. Shooting clubs are especially fond of these production models because of the time-saving factor. One can spend a great deal of money setting up a precision production-type press for super high-speed reloading. However, there are other production type models which do fall into a more modest price range for individual handloaders. Press selection, quite often, is simply a matter of deciding upon the amount of money you want to spend.

The Scale

Even if a shooter gets a powder measure, he will need a scale to verify and regulate his loads. In fact, I most often use a scale to *make my loads,* especially for top end handgun and rifle rounds. For plinking and informal practice work, I might simply use a powder measure, of course. (Nobody wants to hand-weigh 200 rounds of practice fodder for a 38 Special.) The scale is a precision instrument. Because my interest in handloading has always been high, I have elected for the RCBS Model 304. It does everything except talk, and it has a large capacity. It's worth the cash outlay, but the smaller scales are also accurate and very fine. I see reloading equipment as an investment which will last a lifetime, so the initial dollar spent is never lost.

The Huntington Compact Press is one of the reloading tool types which can be carried into the outdoors for making rounds on the spot. The author often uses such an outfit in building loads for a new firearm, taking along the components he wants to use in making various loads for testing. But the compact type reloading tool is also useful on hunting trips, especially extended one.

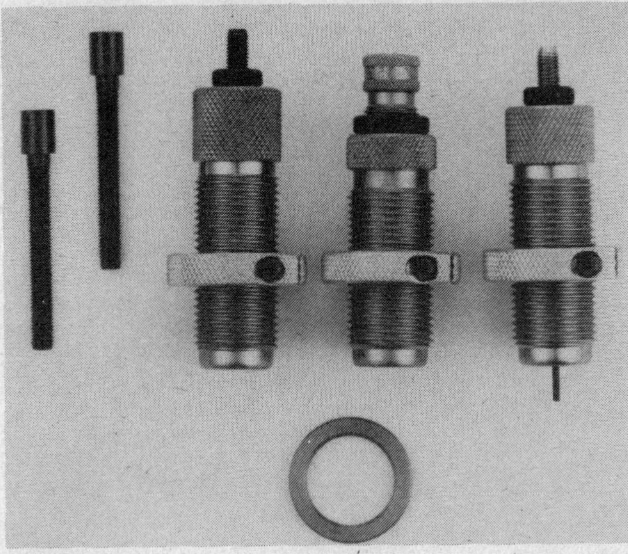

The pistol die set is of the three-piece variety here, as explained in the text. The three-piece die set may also be used with some straight-case rifle rounds.

Dies

When it comes to rifle dies, a standard set consists of two dies—the sizing die and the seating die. The three-die set is used with some straight-wall rifle cartridge cases, as well as all handgun cartridge cases. The third die is for expansion or ''belling'' of the case mouth so that the bullet will be accepted better.

There are also carbide die sets. The carbide dies eliminate any need for lubricating cases. While they are expensive, carbide dies are very time-saving, especially when it comes to sizing a large batch of handgun brass. Though normally associated with handgun calibers, custom *(very* expensive) carbide dies have even been made for bottleneck rifle calibers. Of course, for pistol, revolver or rifle, we must select the proper set of dies, which is merely a matter of matching the caliber to the die. Loading for the 270 Winchester? Ask your local dealer for 270 Winchester dies. That's it.

A powder measure is a fine addition to any reloading setup. This RCBS Little Dandy measure is for pistols/revolvers and it has optional preset fixed charge units.

The Powder Measure

Powders can be measured by bulk. This is what a powder measure actually does—it drops a specific charge of powder by volumetric means. A simple powder measure is found in black powder shooting, being simply a tube of a certain diameter and length. The small dippers for metallic cartridge smokeless powder reloading are really the same thing. They come in various sizes and one dips out a given amount of powder by bulk/volumetric means.

The press-mounted or bench-mounted powder measure used by today's metallic reloading enthusiasts is, in effect, not much different from the earlier bulk-loaders, except for its obvious sophistication. With these measures, the shooter simply loads the hopper and sets a threaded unit in or out depending upon the amount of powder he wants dropped each time the handle is activated. One can load some pretty accurate ammo with a powder measure, but a scale must be used to set things up.

Trial-and-error adjustments of the modern powder measure will soon bring about a charge which fits the amount of powder needed for the load. Again, the powder/bullet scale must be used to set the powder measure to this exacting amount. Once the amount is determined, the reloader can go on with his loading. But he must observe a fairly rigid routine if he wants the powder measure to dump the same amount of powder each throw. If the shooter works the handle rapidly a few times and then slowly a few times, he could find significant differences in the weight of the charges of powder dropped.

Be consistent. That is the rule. Learn to operate the handle of the powder measure the same each time. And set the measure to drop a bit less charge than needed, using the scale to top off the load to perfection for those loads which require the full accuracy potential of the round. I often set my powder measure to drop a charge a few grains weight lighter than I want, and then employ an RCBS powder trickler to top off the charge. By using the measure, and the trickler, the shooter will actually end up with precise, scale-weighed charges every time.

Case Trimmer

A case trimmer is a must. Brass stretches. Cases have to be trimmed back. A rotary, bench-mounted case trimmer is

Every handloader should have a case length gauge like this one from McKillen & Heyer. A case length gauge will tell you when your brass is too long. It also lets you know when your case trimming job is right on the money.

The rotary case trimmer is an important tool in reloading. It may be replaced by case trim dies, of course, but this unit is universal in use and will handle all normal cartridges in trimming.

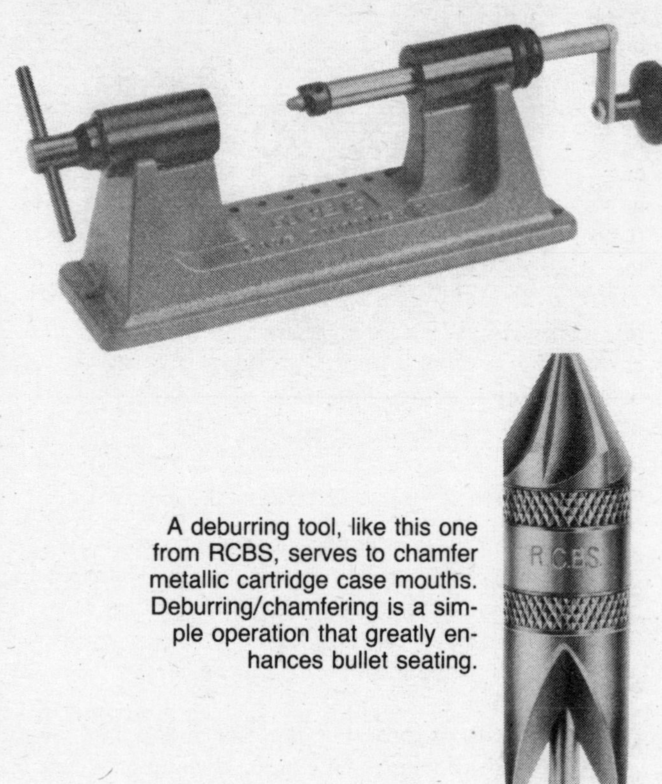

A deburring tool, like this one from RCBS, serves to chamfer metallic cartridge case mouths. Deburring/chamfering is a simple operation that greatly enhances bullet seating.

excellent, but RCBS also offers a comparatively inexpensive trim die which allows the cartridge to be run up into it, the mouth of the case protruding past the die face if it is too long. Then it is trimmed back with a file, flush with the die face. You can't go wrong. Case trimming is a common reloading chore. The trimmer makes the task easy.

Deburring Tool

This cheap little tool is a must. It removes any burrs or other irregularities at the mouth of the case, but it also performs another important function. The deburring tool chamfers the mouth of the case giving it a bevel which allows easy seating of the bullet. After trimming my 30-30 cases, I often cannot seat a bullet into the case unless that case has been chamfered. Failure to chamfer a case neck often leads to a destroyed piece of brass, the destruction always taking place during bullet seating. Save your cases —chamfer the mouths.

Case Length Gauge

This gauge measures the length of the case, which is no surprise, since that's what the name implies. But the service is a good one. It tells us right away if our case is too long. A long case is no good. Pressure can rise if the upper end of the neck protrudes too far into the leade* of the bore.

Case Tumblers

Get one of these. They are *very* useful. A case is cleaned to perfection in a top quality case cleaner. Both tumbler or vibrator types are available—they're excellent. The larger units will hold several boxes of brass, the "cleaning" accomplished through a medium of crushed walnut shells and rouge polish. All you have to do is toss in the cases and turn on the machine. Those cases will be vibrated shiny clean. A case tumbler, in my opinion, beats the pants off dip-type liquid cleaners.

Other Tools

It's nice to have a *primer pocket swager* to bring to correct size the crimped primer pockets normally found on military surplus brass. The *primer pocket brush* is also useful when it comes to cleaning up the primer residue found in the pockets. Shooting some of the foreign calibers may

*The chamber leade is that portion of a firearm's bore which is just forward of the chamber itself. Its purpose is to allow the bullet, with a greater-than-bore diameter to fit into the bore.

mean Berdan primers, and you can get a *Berdan decapping tool* from RCBS—it works. Also, a separate *decapping unit* is useful when it comes to removing crimped-in primers from military brass. A crimped primer will usually break the decapping pin in the sizing die sooner or later. It is much easier to knock the military primer out with a sturdy decapping tool, then using a primer pocket swager to clear out the pocket and size it up for commercial primers. A *stuck case remover* is also very nice. One should not get cases stuck in the resizing die, but it happens anyway (usually as a result of no lube on the case), and this little tool does a fine job in getting those stuck cases free.

A *loading tray* is necessary. This holds the cases being reloaded. And a *powder funnel* is needed to pour the charge into the case, except when the powder measure is being used by itself without the scale. There are all kinds of other devices, and I suggest that a reloader check into his local gunshop to see what is available. He may want an *automatic primer feeder*, or he may want a separate *priming tool*, or a *primer tray*, or a *primer catcher* or *case lube pad* or *case neck brushes* or an *accessory kit* of one sort or another.

Steps in Reloading the Metallic Cartridge Case

Step 1: Clean and Lube the Cases

Clean cases not only work through the reloading dies better, they look better, which is important to the handloader because he is making a product he can be proud of. My reloads look factory fresh and they shoot like mad. A clean case works better in the firearm, and also is easier on the fine polished interior of the die. After a case is cleaned any problems such as a split neck, ruptured case wall or unwanted bulge will show up better. One more advantage of cleaning your cases is that a fired case is easier to find after it has been ejected from the firearm. After all, those cases are worth cash. We like to pick them up and use them again. A clean case means clean on the inside as well as the outside. Any contamination within the case is removed in the tumbling process.

To lube the cases I use my fingers and palms of my hands, but there are more civilized methods. I dab a bit of lube on the palm of my left hand and then roll a few cases together between both hands. I touch up the neck area with a finger and sometimes dab the smallest touch of lube inside of the neck. I want an expander plug to function, but I also want friction at work in that area. No heavy lube goes on the inside of the case neck. If you use your hands like I do, just be sure to thoroughly wash them before going near live primers—grease only serves to kill a primer, a dud round being the eventual result. If you want to avoid these problems, get a case lube pad.

Step 2: Full-Length Resize and Decap

I have used the neck-size only method. It works out fine, but I think it should be reserved for benchrest or, perhaps, varmint shooting. In fact, in some very fine rifles of high

STEP-BY-STEP RELOADING OF METALLIC CARTRIDGES

STEP ONE

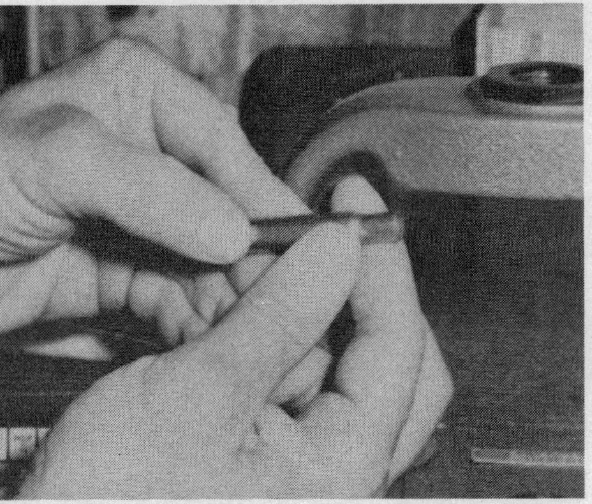

The cartridge has come from the case tumbler clean and bright. Now it can be lubed. The author prefers to lube by hand, rubbing a small amount of lubricant onto the case—not too much on the shoulder area, as this may cause an "oil dent."

STEP TWO

Full-length resize and decap the case now. The lubed 30-30 case has been inserted into the shell holder and forced up into the full-length resizing die all the way. The spent primer is forced out of its pocket by the decapping pin and on my press drops through the hollow ram into a primer catcher.

accuracy potential, I have used full-length resized loads and neck-only resized loads and I never could see a difference. The fully resized case, because it's subjected to so much stress, probably does not last as long as the neck-sized, and if a person wants ultimate case life, then neck sizing is fine. I do not neck-size only because I want a cartridge to get into the chamber of a hunting rifle as smoothly as possible. Also, in some firearms, full-length resizing is the only way to obtain a reload which will function as new. My Model 94 lever-action arms require full-length resizing, for example.

Nothing said here is meant to discourage neck-only sizing of cases if that is the reader's desire. It is true that there can be a slight gain in actual case capacity by neck-sizing only instead of full-length resizing. And some shooters seem to desire this modest gain in volume, using full-throttle safe loads for the very slow-burning, case-filling types of powders. Also, cases do seem to last a bit longer when necked only because the brass is not worked so much. However, as for accuracy gains, if they exist, they must be very slight. In my own tests, I cannot *prove* actual accuracy enhancement by neck-sizing only, at least not for sporting rifles that produce groups well under 1 inch, at 100 yards, after full-length resizing.

A case is resized by simply placing the case head into the shell holder and running the case up into the resizing die all the way. I set my resizing die so that the upper part of the ram barely touches the base of the die. This insures full-length resizing. In fact, I can feel a slight spring in the lever of the press when I set the die because there is definite contact between its base and the shell holder, though, again, only a contact of the smallest degree.

Decapping has taken place in this step. The decapping pin is an integral part of the resize die, and it forces the

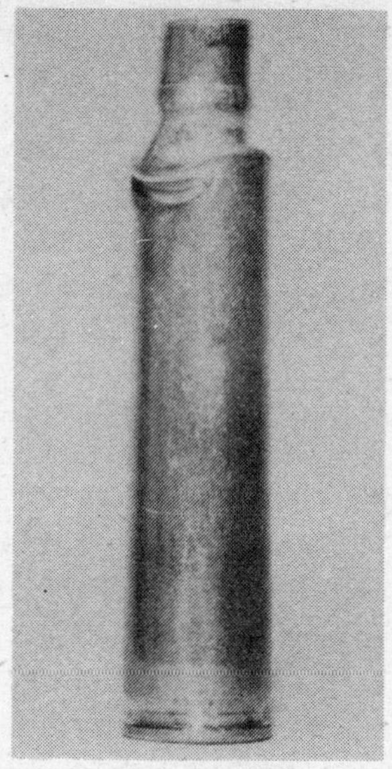

This totally destroyed, but brand new cartridge case, shows what can happen when the case is haphazardly driven up toward the reloading die. In this instance, the case struck off center and was smashed. The reloader who does not have time, at that moment, to practice his art should stop the process and wait until he can slow down and enjoy his reloading. Haste has made waste of this case.

STEP THREE

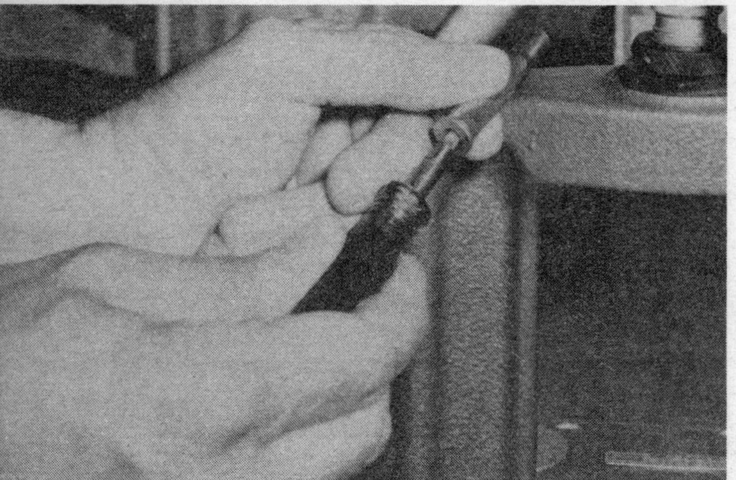

The primer pocket brush will remove any fouling left behind from previous firings. After this operation, tap the case gently on the bench surface to insure that no metal filings are stuck in the case or in the primer pocket. The flash hole should be *clear.* Use a pin or needle to dislodge any small particle stuck in the flash hole.

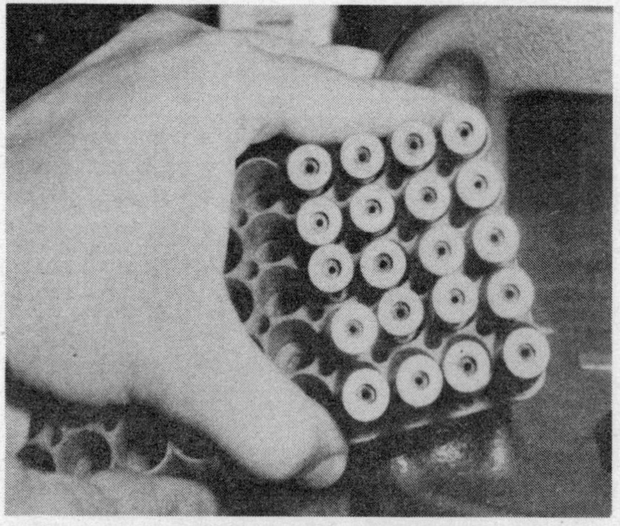

The primer pockets are cleaned, not to shiny bright, but certainly to the point of having all obvious fouling removed. A reloading block is used to contain the cartridge cases. They should be inserted with the primer pocket up at this stage and so they will remain until they are charged with powder.

used primer out of its pocket. On my press, the primer drops down through the hollow ram and into a primer catcher. The dead primers are, of course, discarded later. So we now have, in a few seconds actually, a fully resized case with the old primer knocked out.

Step 3: Clean Primer Pockets and Check Flash Hole

If the primer pockets are dirty, and they will be, a primer pocket brush is used to clean the pocket out. This only takes a few twists of the wrist with the brush.

At this point check for *grossly* off-center flash holes and discard any cases suffering from this condition. Many reloaders experience broken decapping pins during sizing as a result of this problem, but fail to understand "what happened." Be assured, broken decapping pins are usually the result of off-center flash holes, assuming, of course, the case was fully seated in the shell holder during sizing. The condition is more commonly associated with, but not confined to, military brass.

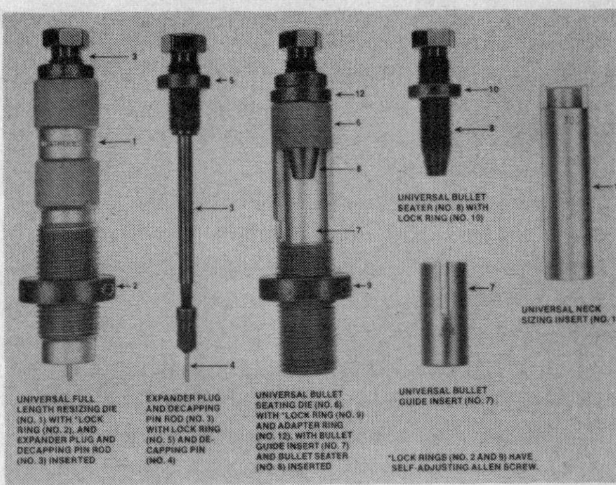

This Weatherby photo allows us to see the mechanical elements of a 2-die rifle set. The adjustment possibilities on any set of dies is extensive.

Step 4: Trim the Case

Using a rotary trimmer or the trim die, the case is brought back to proper overall length. This is important because as the brass stretches it can get too long, meaning it can retard the escape of the bullet and raise pressures. When using a trim die, it is wise to remove any type of adjustable, spring-loaded shell holder and use the standard shellholder as brass filings will eventually clog up the cam-operated claws. If those claws do get loaded with filings, a small punch or pin will quickly remove them.

Step 5: Deburr the Case Mouth

With the pointed end of the deburring tool, the inside of the case mouth is chamfered out and beveled. Then with

STEP FOUR

Using the RCBS Trim Die, the 30-30 case is inserted all the way up into the die as far as it will go. The die works simply by allowing any excess neck length to protrude up above the face of the die itself. Since the die is very hard, the reloader simply files away the excess length of cartridge neck with an ordinary metal file. Be sure to tap the case to remove metal bits after trimming.

STEP FIVE

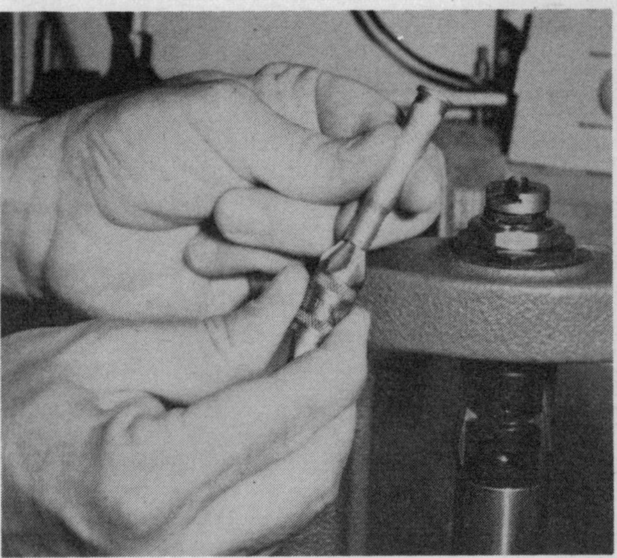

The trimmed case is now chamfered with the deburring tool. The end shown reams out the inside of the mouth. By turning the deburring tool around, the outside of the cartridge case neck is smoothed up with a twisting motion of the wrist to rotate the deburring tool.

the opposite end of the same tool fitted over the outside of the case neck mouth, a few twists of the wrist will remove any exterior burrs. Now the case neck mouth is smooth, beveled and ready to accept a bullet. Tap the case a few times on the loading bench to insure that any metal filings from trimming or deburring have been removed.

Step 6: Reprime

The new primer is now inserted. This operation is handled in many ways. A good method is with a separate priming tool, as the shooter can get a good feel of the seating itself. But I like the built-in priming unit that's an integral part of every reloading press. I can feel the seating of the primer very well with it. At any rate, the new primer is to be inserted so that it is slightly below the level of the primer pocket. You don't smash the primer, of course, but a primer must not protrude! It is not entirely impossible that a protruding primer could be set off prematurely.

Also, do not substitute primers, i.e., a Large Pistol primer for a Large Rifle primer. Large Pistol primers feature a thinner cup that insures positive ignition under the (typically) light hammer (firing pin) fall of a handgun. The heavy fall of a rifle's striker may pierce the cup of a handgun primer. The resulting escape of gas (under tremendous pressure) is potentially dangerous.

When working with maximum loads calling for a "standard" primer, don't substitute a "magnum" primer. Pressures could rise enough to create problems. In short, stay with the primer that's recommended for the cartridge/powder you are working with.

Primer selection is an important part of handloading. Choosing the magnum primer simply because it is a magnum, however, is not prudent.

Step 7: Charge the Case

Using the scale or scale/measure combination, or in some instances only the measure, the primed cartridge case

STEP SIX

Now the cartridge case is primed. The RCBS Big Max press uses a system whereby the priming tool is inserted into the top of the press. This is called the Positive Priming Unit. The ability to feel the primer's insertion is excellent with this unit. Shown is the primed case next to the priming unit.

STEP SEVEN

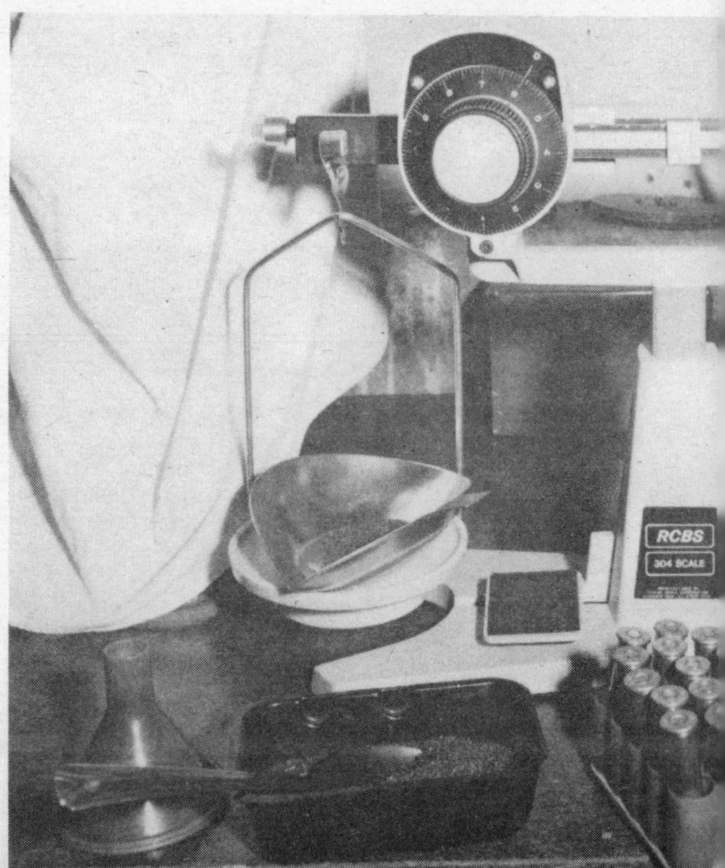

is now loaded with the powder charge. Remember—the charge used should be the one which the loading manuals have recommended. The powder is generally transferred into the case with a powder funnel.

If you use a powder measure to toss your charges, be sure you throw the lever in a consistent fashion. To fail to do so will only mean inconsistent charges. Also, be sure to verify the measure's setting by weighing every tenth charge. If you find your measure is off, return the thrown charges to the measure and reset and reverify the measure with the aid of a powder scale.

It's also wise to use a loading tray when charging cases with a powder measure. It helps eliminate life-threatening "double charges." Simply look into the mouths of all of the cases in the loading block. You'll notice tremendous uniformity in terms of how high (or low) the powder charges stand in each case. Excessively low or high standing powder charges should be returned to the measure, *immediately;* the measure should then be checked and reverified with the aid of a powder scale.

The magnum small pistol primer is another example of handloader's choice. The handloader selects his primer on the basis of information listed in loading manuals. Primers can make a difference in the pressure/velocity relationship, and this is especially true of shotgun shells. These No. 550 small pistol primers are of the magnum type, used especially where a hot flame is desired.

Step 8: Seat the Bullet

The bullet must be seated to the proper depth and that means setting the die correctly. This is a simple matter, but an important one. I generally set the seater die in the same manner as described for the resizing die, with the bottom of the die touching the shell holder, and then I back off a

STEP EIGHT

Using a powder funnel, the weighed charge is dropped into the primed, fully sized and trimmed 30-30 case. Note the rounds which have received powder are upright in the tray, but the cases yet to be charged are case head up in the tray. This insures against double charging.

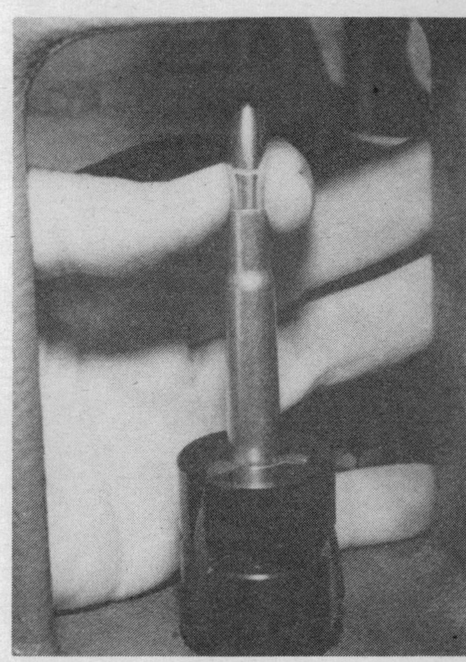

The case has been charged with powder and it is now ready for the seating of the bullet. The bullet is centered on the mouth of the case and then rammed into the seater die for proper bullet depth.

◀(Opposite page) The powder scale is used to weigh the powder charge.

little so that there is no contact at all. Now, for those cases which require crimping, it is wise to look at this another way.

If the case is to be crimped, I put an empty case into the shell holder and run it up into the seater die, which is resting in the frame, but not set. In other words, it can still be screwed up or down. In this case, the seater die is screwed downward a little bit at a time. As I make adjustments on the seater die, I check the neck of the case to find out at what point it is being crimped. When the neck is taking a crimp, just at the mouth of the neck only, I then set the seater die right at that point.

With the seater die set in place and locked in, the stem is screwed out most of the way (but not until it comes out of the die). Now a loaded round of correct overall length is placed in the shell holder and run up into the die. The stem is slowly screwed downward until it touches the tip of the bullet and then it is set in place, locked up.

The crimp is very important, by the way. In an autoloading handgun round, it may in fact make the difference as to the ammo functioning at all. In a revolver, the same is true. A bullet may in fact work its way out of the case and prevent the cylinder of the revolver from turning if the bullet is not properly crimped into the case.

In theory, crimping also aids the load due to added "bullet pull weight" (BPW). BPW is the force it takes to pull a bullet from its seated position in the case. Supposedly, there will be increases in breech pressure without increases in velocity with tightly crimped bullets. I have tried to test for this, but to no real conclusion. I think you should crimp only those loads which will go into tubular magazines or handguns and which require crimping for those reasons, BPW notwithstanding.

As for seating the bullet, a shooter wants to do this correctly. Even if the loaded round fits the magazine (and this is one way to gauge the overall length for a cartridge), the overall length may not be correct. The leade or throat of the bore, which is not the same on all guns, should also be considered when determining a cartridge's proper overall length. If a bullet is seated to *engage* the rifling ahead of the leade, pressures can go up. BPW is supposed to mean a lot, even to ignition problems. Though I do not worry about it much, I do worry about bullets being seated too far out. The attendant pressures may simply be too great.

Some rifles have "freebore," a lot of leade in other words, and some rifles, for reasons I do not fully understand, are very short of leade. In theory (again) the short leade (where the bullet does not have to jump into the rifling) creates the best accuracy. Maybe for world record benchrest shooting this is right, but for hunting rifles, that super short throat is to no avail. I recently loaded ammo for a 270 bolt-action rifle and then I ran a little test. I painted a bit of black with a felt tip pen right on the front portion of a couple bullets and then ran the rounds home into the

STEP NINE

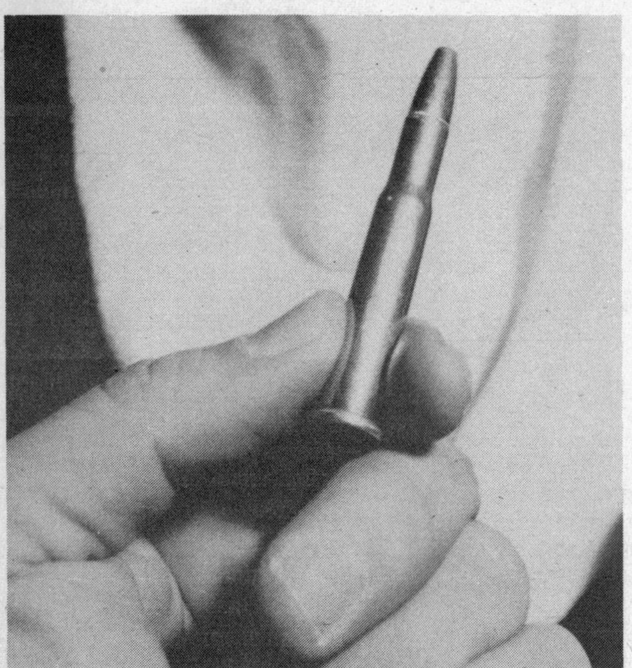

STEP ELEVEN

The finished product should be protected by a good cartridge container like this RCBS plastic unit.

(Left) The finished product—a fully formed case, ready to use. This particular case uses a crimp which was applied during the bullet seating operation. Crimping is not essential for bolt-action rifles, but this 30-30 round will be used in a tubular magazine. This is a proper crimp, with the neck of the case slightly engaged into the cannelure of the bullet.

chamber of the rifle, closing the bolt on them, and then extracting the rounds.

There were marks in the fresh ink, showing me that the bullet was being driven into the lands of the rifling. I reseated the bullets and had to push them into the case neck to the point where the cannelures were no longer visible. The shooter should check his own rifle's leade by doing the same test. Of course, once you've determined the best seating depth, the seating die is set. However, remember that the depth of seating will change with different bullet shapes.

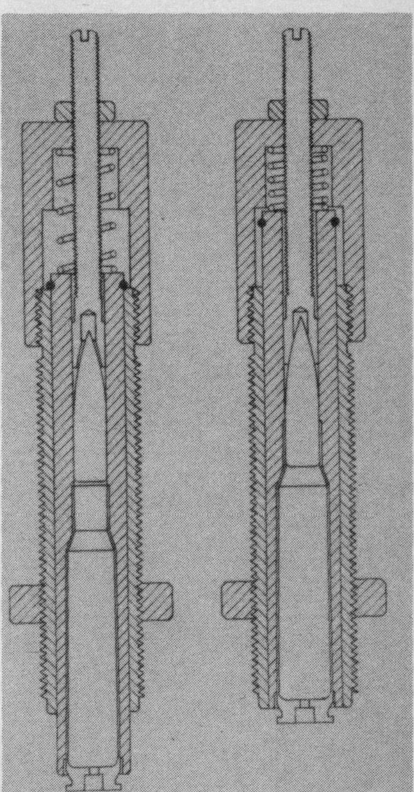

This illustration, courtesy of Bonanza, shows how a bullet is seated in the seater die. On the left is the unseated bullet and on the right, the bullet has been seated into the case to the proper depth. The key to proper bullet seating is to set the length according to safety practices first and accuracy practices second.

Step 9: The Finished Product

In the final step, the new round should be wiped clean of any lubrication. This is important because of case cling in the chamber. A greasy case is not going to cling to the walls of the chamber as well as a dry case. Also, a greasy case can hold debris which might scratch the chamber walls. The presence of grease on a cartridge will also raise pressures, sometimes dangerously.

Step 10: Testing

Head for your local range and check your loads in your gun. I run my reloads into my rifles or my revolvers to see that they actually fit the chambers and feed reliably. Sure, it's unlikely that they won't fit, but it can happen. A tired case may not respond to full-length resizing, and it could actually balk at entering the chamber. It's better to find out now and pull the bullet than find out in the field, especially in the hunting field. Even in the auto pistol, rounds can be worked through the gun in order to see that they fit. Of course, this operation is done with care and with the firearm pointed in a totally safe direction, a solid backstop present the entire time.

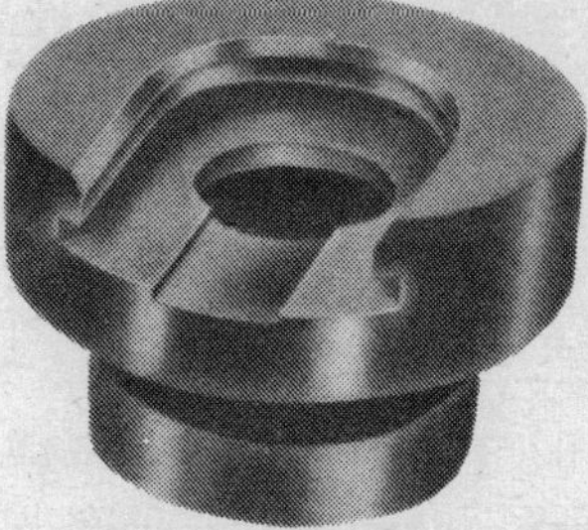

The modern shell holder is easy to insert and easy to remove, and it is available in many cartridge head sizes.

Step 11: Package Your Ammo Properly

I like good plastic boxes intended for holding ammo, though I sometimes use the original cardboard box which held the unprimed brass or ammo. Identify that box of ammo, with a label, right down to the primer and, of course, the powder and charge weight and the exact bullet used. Don't say "150-grain bullet," but rather, for example, "150-grain Speer boat-tail."After all, the load is unique and if it is to be duplicated later, all of the data must be known.

Reloading the Handgun Case

Handgun ammo is loaded very much as described above so we will not go into a step-by-step process concerning the reloading of ammunition for the pistol or revolver. But there can be a few differences.

First, there are tungsten carbide handgun dies which do not require lubrication. There are, to be fair about it, custom rifle dies of similar structure, but it is the handgun die which is more popular in this area.

Second, there may be a difference in how we treat the handgun case. Three- or four-die sets are common in reloading for the handgun. These dies prevent working the brass excessively. The first die sizes and decaps. The second die expands the case mouth so a bullet is easily seated and the third die seats the bullet and crimps the neck of the case into the cannelure of the bullet. The fourth die, if present, and used, is called a "taper-crimp" die. It's used as the final step and serves to very slightly taper the case and improve the friction fit of the bullet. It's commonly used, for example, in loading for the 45 ACP.

"Oil Dents" and Stuck Cases

A case can bind and gall in the sizing die. Improper lubing of the case is generally the cause. Lube *every* case, not every third case or so. Some shooters follow the latter procedure to prevent excessive lube from making "oil dents" in the shoulder area of bottleneck cases. I don't overlube, and I don't use too much lube on the shoulder. I lube the body of the case sparingly but all over and the same for the neck and, generally, I'm not troubled with oil-dented cases. If an oil dent arises, so be it. It is ugly, but I have never heard of a minor oil dent causing a problem in shooting.

Quite often, oil dents result from two other factors: 1) a build-up of lube in the die as a result of doing a lot of case resizing; 2) a combination of over-lubing coupled with the failure to periodically clean out the sizing die.

If a case should become stuck in the sizing die, an RCBS stuck case remover can get that case out. So all is not lost. Instructions are clearly explained with the unit and it would seem somewhat pointless to go over them here. The unit is not expensive and it does work.

The Bullet Puller

The inertia-type bullet puller from RCBS is an optional tool which can come in very handy. One reason for bullet pulling is a change of mind. I have loaded up 40 or 60 rounds of ammo only to learn later on that a better load was available. It's somewhat annoying, but it's easier to pull those bullets and start over than to go out and buy new cases and components and start from scratch, especially when you no longer want those loads anyway. An example of this condition just happened to me. I had some 6.5mm wildcats loaded up and then I learned that with Accurate Powder Companies MR-3100 I could get more velocity with a perfectly safe load. I had 40 rounds loaded up, pulled the bullets and reloaded them with the MR-3100.

One of the most common uses of the bullet puller is for the purpose of tearing down ammo the handloader feels is unsafe due to an excessive (or incorrect) powder charge. Frankly, I believe the inertia-type bullet puller is used for this purpose more than any other.

A tip in using the bullet puller is to whack the inertia type "hammer" on a hard surface until the bullet begins to come out of the case. And then gently tap the bullet puller so that the bullet nose is not deformed when it breaks free. What if the nose is deformed? Nothing. From a hunting-accuracy standpoint it will still shoot into the group with the rest of the bullets, but being a reloader enthusiast, I like my loads uniform, neat and without bent or blunt tips. You can avoid the problem by putting a bit of cloth rag down into the bottom of the puller so the bullet will have a soft landing site.

Studying the Spent Case

There is much to be learned from a fired cartridge case, and the handloader should pay special attention to his cases so he can learn from them. Here are a couple of things to do and look for:

1. Case Head Expansion

After the first firing (called fire-forming) of five or ten brand new cases, mike the cases at the head area, just above the base for a rimmed or rimless case, and right on the belt itself for a belted, magnum-type case. Take an average of these measurements. Remember, do not mike new cartridge cases out of the box which have never been fired. Use only once-fired (fire-formed) cases.

Then, after handloading, check that measurement again. If there is so much as .001-inch expansion at the head or on the belt, that means trouble. This is called case-head expansion and it implies quite a lot of pressure in the chamber. It means that the brass has been forced to *flow*. Cut back a bit on that load. But do not be fooled. I was once shooting my 30-30 Improved wildcat and discovered that some of the cases were rather soft, even mild loads showing some expansion!

2. Check the Primer

After firing, a primer will have a crater where the firing pin hit it. If the walls of that crater are so high that you can feel it as a sharp projection, the pressure may be up too high in that load. Some primers may be soft and fool the shooter, but usually a badly cratered primer is a *bad* pressure sign. Also, there should be no leaking around the primer. Black marks indicating escaping gas around the primer through the primer pocket are no good. Of course, there is also the pierced primer. Obviously, if there is a

A gas leak at the primer pocket has revealed itself here by the discoloration around the headstamp area. This handload is obviously too hot and must be cut back. Handloading is a precise operation and the shooter who experiments may be moving away from the domain of safety. The loading manuals offer so many good loads that it is seldom that a shooter has to invent his own, though in some instances individual shooters have produced fine handloads.

Bullet pullers like this inertia-type from RCBS are handy when it comes to correcting handloading errors or tearing down large quantities of ammo for the components.

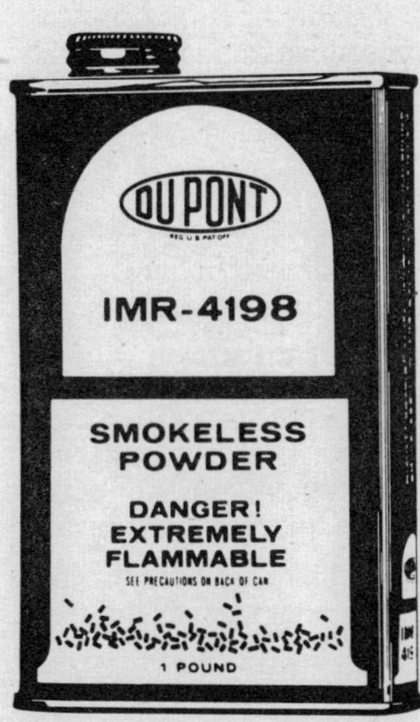

All powders are *not* the same. While two different brands of gun powder may carry the same numerical designation, you can be sure their burning rates are different. All reliable loading manuals will call for a *specific* brand and type of powder for each specific load. *Never substitute.*

hole through the primer, that load is too much. And there is also the primer which will fall out by simply tapping the case, another indication of high pressure. When the fired case is reloaded, the primer should go back in snugly. If it just about falls out, that, too, is a sign that the case is used up or that a load which is too hot has been used.

3. Check the Headstamp Area

Check the face of the headstamp area of the cartridge, where the name of the round is stamped into the metal. A hot load will produce an engraving on this area. One can see the actual irregularities of the bolt face metal stamped into the brass in some cases. If this is clearly visible, the load may be too hot. All of the above conditions should be heeded and powder charges reduced, immediately, any remaining ammo discarded or broken down in an effort to determine what went wrong.

Powders

We are blessed with a world of fine powders. And, of course, each is designated clearly, by the maker, with name or number so there is never an excuse for mixing up powders kept in their original, factory containers. Even when a *number* is the same, the company designations clearly distinguish one from the other. How? H-4831 and IMR-4831, for example, are two different fuels. The H-4831 is a Hodgdon powder. IMR-4831, Improved Military Rifle, is from Du Pont. The latter is faster burning than the former, and each has its own use. Both are superb. But *different*.

Powder selection is very important for reasons beyond the simple and obvious. It is entirely possible to get less velocity with more pressure, and this is why we try to find the powder which will give us the most velocity for the least pressure. Where the loading manual indicates pressure tests, it is always wise to at least try the best combination of powder/bullet in terms of the most velocity for the least pressure, with accuracy checks of course.

Loading density is another factor to consider, though I think of the situation as somewhat over-stated at times. The idea is to use the powder which fills the case as much as possible without compressing the powder charge. For example, if one looks at a loading manual, he may find a 270 Winchester load with a 130-grain bullet which shows 60.0 grains of H-4831 for 3213 fps MV and 48,500 CUP. In the same column, you may find a load of 54.0 grains of H-414 pushing the 130-grain bullet at 3100 fps MV for a pressure of 50,300 CUP. The 60-grain load is a 100 percent density situation, while the 54.0 grains of H-414 is not quite 100 percent in loading density. In fact, I shot these two loads in one rifle and the latter was, or seemed to be with rather limited testing, slightly more accurate. But that was *one* shooting session with *one* rifle. Yes, trying for 100 percent loading density is one method of looking for an accurate load. Knowing that it won't always pan out is simply acknowledging one of the realities of the reloading game.

Some Fine Points

1. In looking for a really reliable load, one means of testing is to use a chronograph which has a "standard

This illustration shows what can happen when a die is incorrectly set up. The cartridge on the far right is a 30-30 Improved with a 180 grain Speer bullet. It is fine, no problems. Next to it is a 30-30 handload with the same bullet, also fine. On the far left is a 30-30 bolt-action handload using a 165-grain Speer bullet and it is also all right. But the load second from the left shows a problem at the shoulder from a die which was not correctly set in the press.

Winchester offers components for shotgun shell reloaders, including the powder. Shotgun shell powders are not extruded, and this ball powder is very workable in the shotgun shell. Some powders designated for the shotgun do work in metallic cartridges. Check your loading manual.

deviation'' reading. The standard deviation from the mean or average velocity should be very low for a reliable uniform load. For example, a standard deviation of 10 to 25 fps, maybe even 40 fps, is not so bad, but I have found that very high deviations in the 100 fps domain usually spell accuracy trouble at the target.

2. A bullet should fit into the neck of a fired, unsized case. If it does not, the metal of the case neck could be too thick, a result of brass flowing into the area after repeated firing and sizing. A thick neck can compress in the chamber area upping the pressures. You have two choices: 1) discard the case; 2) purchase an inside neck reamer and have at it. Remember, a bullet should fit into a fired and unsized case, *without* force.

3. Size new brass which has never been fired. Yes, it's unnecessary most of the time, but in some rifles it can make a difference. I always size the new case. It trues up the necks and insures the right fit, especially in my Model 94s which are a little touchy about case fit.

4. Check your reloading scale for accuracy from time to time. A small set of weights can be purchased from Lyman for this work. Sometimes a scale can get out of whack. If you don't have an accurate scale, you won't be able to load an absolutely correct powder charge.

5. Be consistent. Use the same good methods of loading your ammo all the time. Establish a routine.

6. While reloading, don't smoke, drink or tolerate distraction. Be safe.

Shotgun Shell Reloading

When it comes to shotshell reloading, the tools are different than those used for metallic cartridges, even though the goal is the same. Before going farther, it's only right to admit that there have been many different types of shotgun shell reloading devices from the beginning, and we still have handy little tools which will all but fit into a coat pocket. These kits are easily found, easily mastered, and well worth the buying. But this brief discussion of shotshell reloading will mainly revolve around the modern, bench-mounted reloading press.

The functions necessary to rebuild the spent shotgun shell are not complicated. However, making shotgun ammunition is not without its fine points. Thanks to many dedicated reloaders and experimenters, as well as the technicians at the loading companies, todays shotshells are

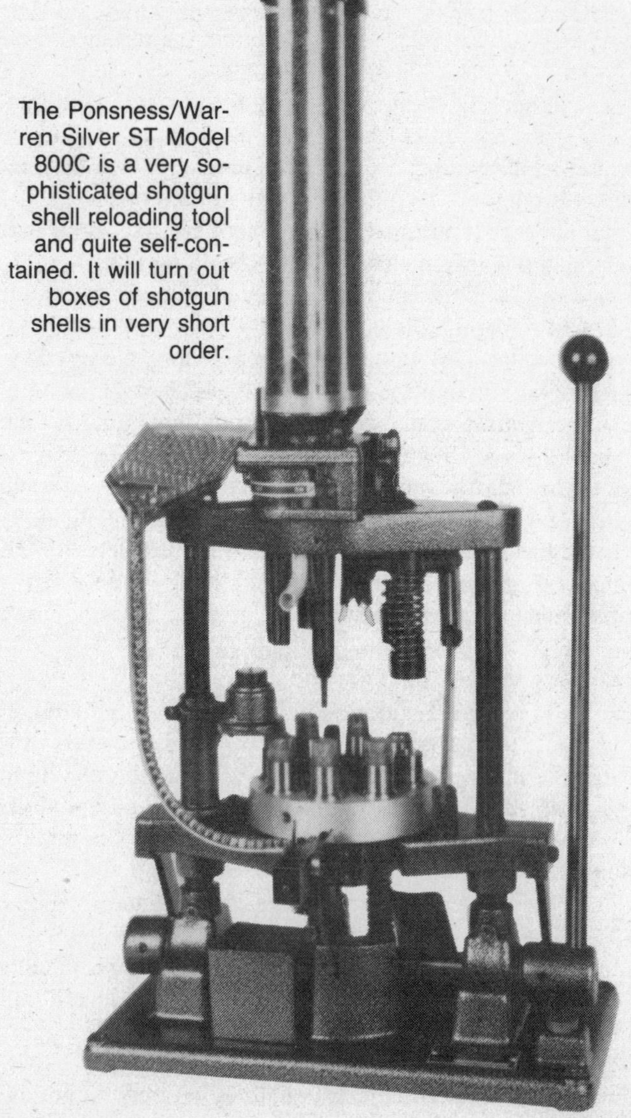

The Ponsness/Warren Silver ST Model 800C is a very sophisticated shotgun shell reloading tool and quite self-contained. It will turn out boxes of shotgun shells in very short order.

The art of shotgun shell reloading is often enhanced by the smaller accessory tools. The Taper Crimp Kit from Ponsness/Warren is an example of this statement.

Shotgun shell primers are quite different from rifle or handgun cartridge primers in their structure, but not in their general function. The loading of shotgun shells requires strict adherence to the use of tested loads, meaning that shotshell primers must not be switched around at will. Use the primer which the approved load calls for.

highly efficient and much better than ammo of the past. The reloader of scattergun ammo, therefore, has a lot of incentive to make the best ammunition possible, and for the same reasons established earlier, increased versatility from a particular shotgun and gauge, uniform and well-patterning loads and of course realized savings.

The modern shotgun shell reloading tool differs from model to model, the function of individual stations varying from one press type to the next. But the shell is being treated to the same general reconstruction. Here are the steps necessary to make a fired shotshell into a new one. The presentation, in this instance is designed to give the novice a simple, general idea as to what it takes to load a shotshell. Of course, these steps may vary somewhat, depending on the brand of press.

1. Resize the Hull

The principle is the same here as with the metallic rifle or handgun round, to put the case back to the dimensions it had before it was fired.

2. De-Cap

Of course the spent primer must be ejected from the case. Usually accomplished during resizing.

3. Prime

A new primer is inserted.

4. Charge

Charge the shell with the proper amount of powder.

5. Wads

The proper wad is inserted and seated firmly in the hull.

6. Shot Charge and Crimping

The proper shot charge is dropped into the hull. The mouth of the case is crimped for at least three important reasons. First, the contents of the shell would tend to fall out if the crimp were anything less than correct. Second, the crimp aids in sealing the contents, especially the powder charge, from moisture. Third, the crimp helps to retain the pressure with which the wad was seated, which is important.

The modern shotgun reloading press provides for all of these of course, and with speed. Many of the presses will turn a completed box of shells out in just moments. Furthermore, there is built-in adjustment which the reloader can take advantage of, such as crimping variations. And the pressure put upon the wad column is also adjustable. This pressure determines to some degree how the powder will burn, especially in terms of ignition, though this factor also depends upon the powder being used. In the eyes of many reloaders, Mayville Engineering Company (MEC) offers some of the finest shotshell presses ever made. The photo sequence on the following pages is a step-by-step look at the reloading of a shotshell on a MEC 600 Jr. press.

STEP-BY-STEP RELOADING OF SHOT SHELLS

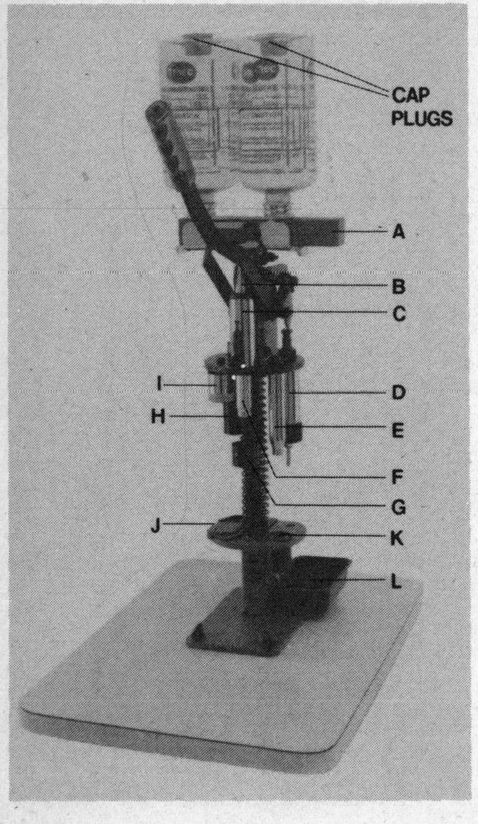

SHOT SHELL PRESS KEY

A. The **CHARGING BAR** is located just under the powder and shot containers. Moving the bar to the left charges the powder. Moving the bar to the right charges the shot. Make sure shot and powder containers are placed correctly.

B. WAD HEIGHT INDICATOR used to disclose improper wadding.

C. WAD PRESSURE INDICATOR gives the exact amount of pressure actually being applied to wad column at bottom of handle stroke.

D. RECONDITIONING DIE—The spent primer is ejected, the shell mouth is ironed and the metal base is resized with one stroke of the handle.

E. REPRIMING PUNCH—seats new primer into shell from PRIMER SEATING ASSEMBLY (K).

F. RAMMER TUBE—through which powder and shot are dropped into the shell. This tube is used also to seat the wad column.

G. ADJUSTA-GUIDE WAD FEED—permits quick and accurate seating of wad column.

H. CRIMPING STATION—containing the exclusive cam-operated two-stage crimping apparatus. Die is completely adjustable for depth of crimp.

I. CRIMP STARTER—8-point, 6-point, (smooth cone optional for paper shells).

J. SHELL HOLDER—holds shell down on handle upstroke.

L. PRIMER CATCHER—secure in position by tilting so that notched edge slips under tab provided in the base.

STEP ONE

Take an empty shell in your right hand and place it into the deprime resize station (left). With your left hand depress the handle to the bottom of its stroke. You will feel resistance as the resize ring starts resizing the brass, also you may feel the primer being ejected. Make sure that the handle is depressed to the full bottom of its stroke or you will not remove the primer or completely resize the shell. Now lift the handle to the full top of its stroke. As you come up you will feel resistance as the shell is pushed from the resize ring. Again with your right hand remove the shell from the resize station and place this shell onto the reprime punch (right).

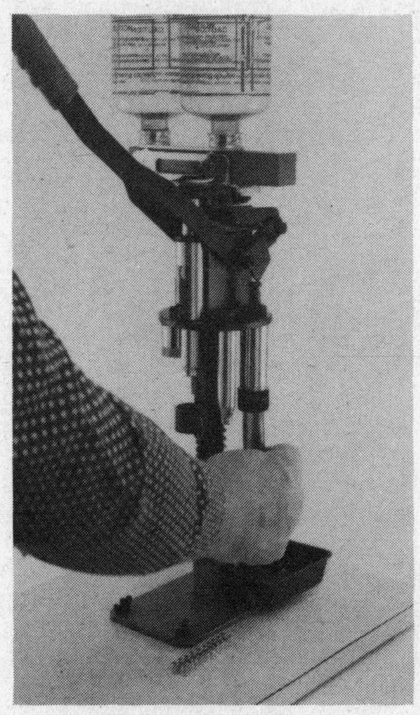

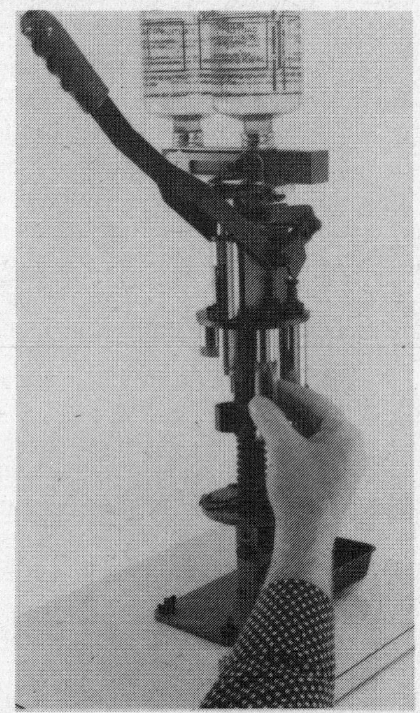

STEP TWO

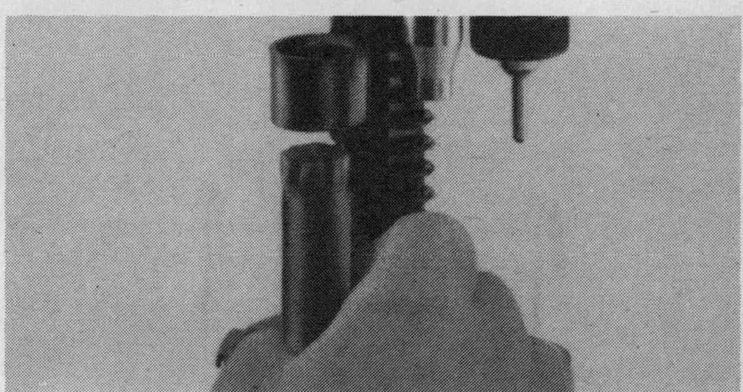

At this time take a primer with your right hand and place it into the reprime pocket (top). Again with your left hand depress the handle until the primer is firmly seated. Use no more pressure than is needed to seat the primer level with the bottom of the shell. While raising the handle with your left hand remove the reprimed shell from the reprime punch with your right hand and place it into the shell holder (bottom).

STEP THREE

Now depress the handle with your left hand. It is only necessary to depress the handle until the rammer tube enters the shell. Hold the handle in this position and with your right hand move the charging bar to the left thus charging with powder.

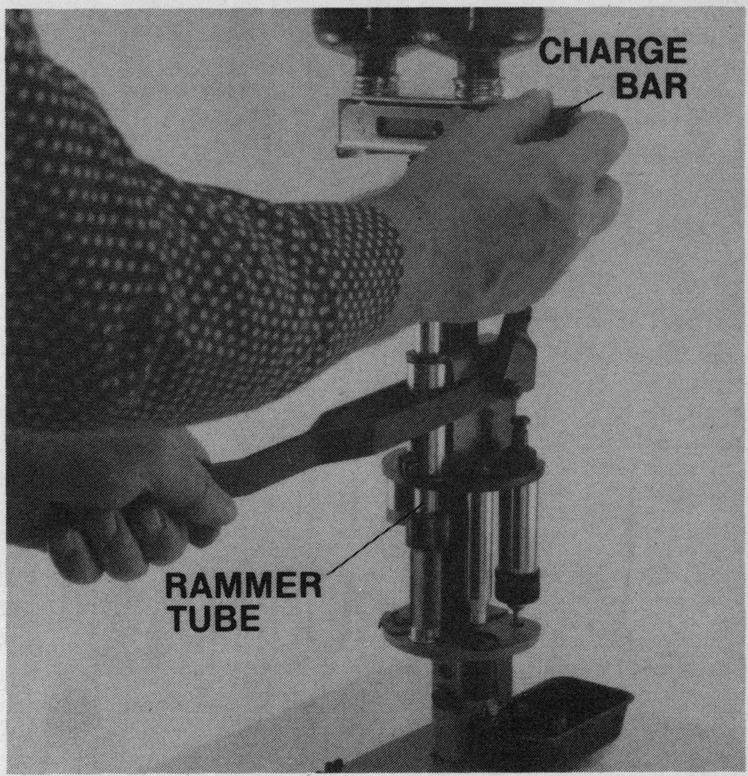

STEP FOUR

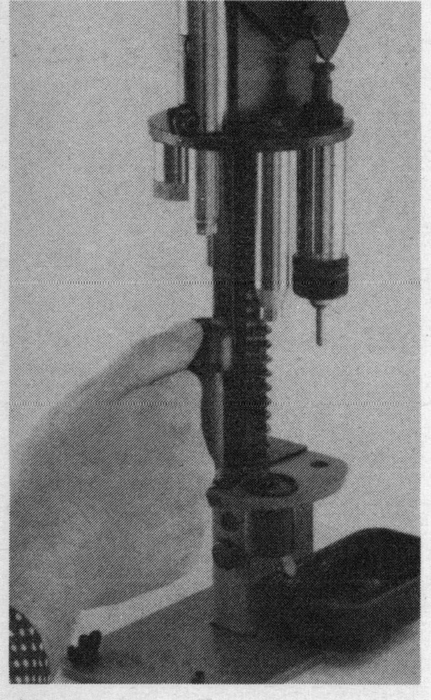

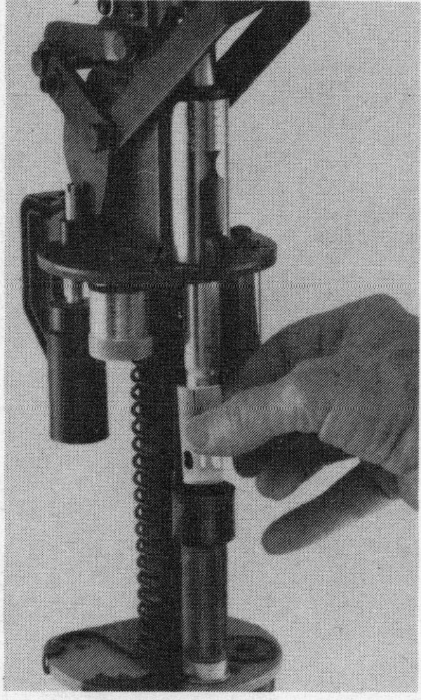

Now with your left hand lift the handle to the top of its stroke. With your right hand push the wad guide down to the bottom of its travel so the fingers enter the shell (left). Now place a wad on the rammer tube (right). With your left hand again depress the handle to the bottom of its stroke.

STEP FIVE

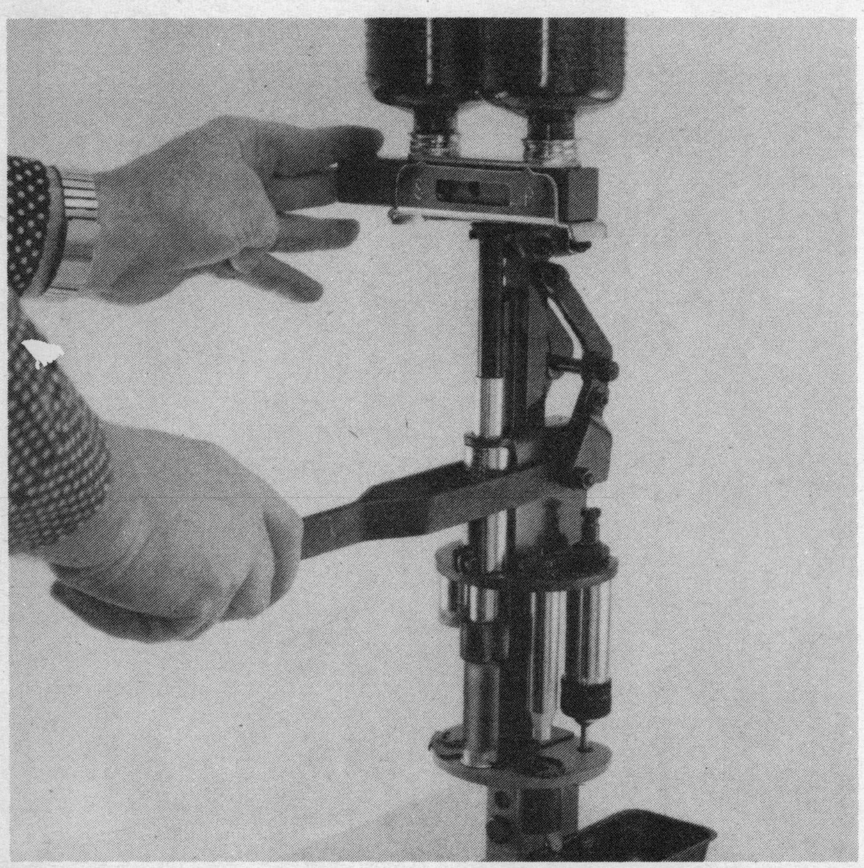

At this point change from your left hand to your right hand and lift the handle so the reprime tube is still in the shell. Now with your left hand move the charging bar to its full right position, thus charging with shot.

STEP SIX

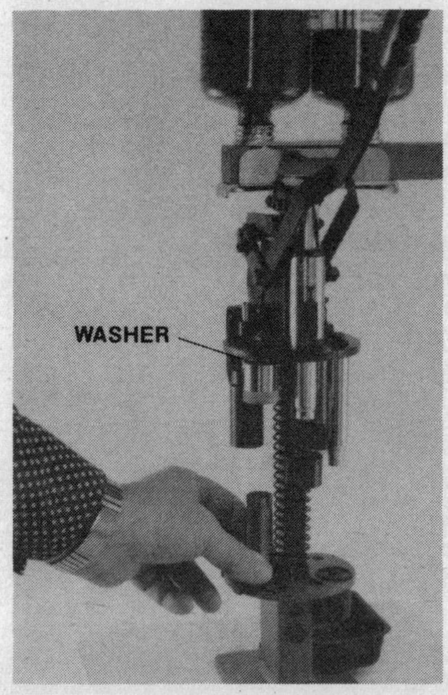

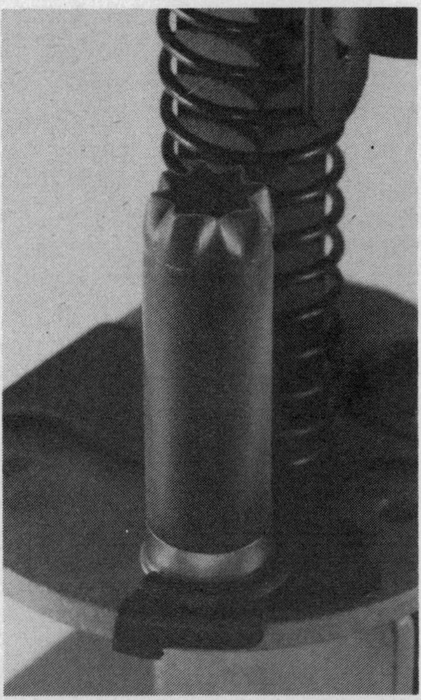

Now lift the handle to the top of its stroke and with your left hand place the shell into the crimp start station (left). With your right hand again depress the handle to its full bottom position starting the crimp. Note this crimp starter should be shimmed up or down by adding or removing a washer so that the crimp looks like the one in the photo at right. The adjustment as it came from the factory should be correct for most shells. Most Skeet and trap loads except for 28-gauge and .410 are 8 point crimp. Many field loads may be 6 point. It is important that shells are crimped with the same crimp as original. Paper shells are best crimped with a smooth cone.

The Shotshell Reloading Manual

The proper reloading manual is just as much a bible for the shotshell reloader as it is for the metallic cartridge reloader. The strongest advice I can give you is to use the data *as it is written, by the manufacturer, without further experimentation*. I am the first to admit that experimentation improved the shotgun shell tremendously, and I am not suggesting that there is no more room for improvement. But working with reloads in an experimental fashion takes equipment—sophisticated equipment.

For example, it does very little good for the citizen shooter to concoct what he thinks is a heller of a load, unless that person can professionally chronograph and pressure test the load and show *with proof* what is really being gained in muzzle velocity. Getting kicked hard or seeing birds drop cleanly does not tell us about muzzle velocity, and it could just be that we have plenty of recoil and that we are hitting well so the shell's load seems to be very fine. It may not be. It may not be due to pressure levels. If an experimenter has no access to a pressure gun, then he can only guess as to the actual pressure being developed by his load.

For example, let's take a look at two 12-gauge handloads. Both are entirely safe and useful. That's not the point. Neither is excessive in pressure, and of course pressure is not bad. Guns wouldn't work without it. But this shows how pressure and velocity may not spiral upwards hand in hand.

Load 1:
35.5 grains of SR 4765 powder
Federal 399 primer
Winchester No. WAA12R wad (one)
1¼ oz. of shot
Muzzle Velocity: 1410 fps
Muzzle Energy: 9,900 LUP

Load 2:
30.5 grains of Blue Dot
Federal 209 primer
Pacific Blue Verelite wad (one)
1¼ oz. of shot
Muzzle Velocity: 1290 fps
Muzzle Energy: 10,430 LUP

The above clearly shows that velocity and pressure can vary with the load. Without a chronograph and especially a pressure gun, the reloader cannot say what his experimental load is getting. This is why experimentation is not totally worthwhile for the average shooter. Of course, there is patterning to do. It is not impossible that Load 2 will pattern better than Load 1 in a particular shotgun. However, this is an example for the reader that serves to prove that velocity does not tell of pressure, and of course pressure does not tell of velocity. It is pressure which forces the case out to seal the chamber area and pressure which drives the load of shot, but our aim here is *knowing* what a load's

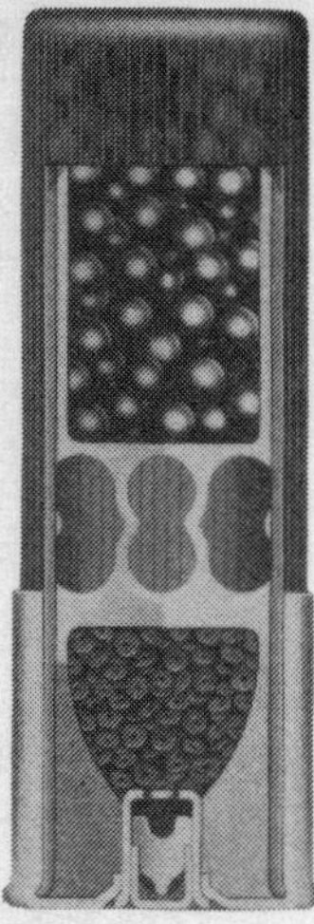

This cutaway of a Remington Express shotgun shell shows the general makeup of this type of ammunition. There is the brass head and the base wad at the "bottom" of the shell. In other words, it is standing on the head portion. Note the primer pocket with the seated primer in it. The powder charge is obvious as is the one-piece plastic wad and the shot, which is all contained by the hull.

pressure is. A high-pressure load is harder on the gun in the long run.

The Shotshell Hull

The hull must be selected exactly according to the prescription of the loading manual. Sure, there are exceptions and there is some interchangeability. But all in all, the word of the manual should be *"the law."* There are plenty of options in a manual such as the *Lyman Shotshell Handbook,* so the shooter is not hurting for variations. The point is, shotshell hulls vary enough so that a specific load which fits into one 12-gauge shell would not fit into another one of a different type.

High Base Hull: The high-base shell is often thought of as the one with the most powder capacity. This is false. The base is that portion of the hull inside and at the bottom within the head area. As the base gets higher, it takes up more space in the hull and this is exactly what it is supposed to do in order to balance the space for specific loads and wad columns.

Low Base Hull: This type of shell has a smaller base wad as an integral part of its construction. In other words, the base is down low in the bottom of the hull.

High Brass: In the high-brass shell, the external brass head is high up on the bottom part of the shell.

Low Brass: The low-brass shell is just the opposite. The external brass head is low, much lower than that of the high-brass shell. The low base/high base and low brass/high brass situation can be in combination. There can be a low brass shell with a high base, this hull being right for a target load, for example.

Checking the Hull

The reloader must make it his business to check the base of a hull before reloading the case. The base must be intact. When there are bits of the base missing, the hull has to be discarded. It is fairly easy to see down into the hull, so this visual inspection is all that is necessary. If the shooter does not have sufficient light to see the base, he should use a flashlight to take a look inside of the hull.

There are some shells in which the base wad and the case body are formed in one piece. These vary considerably from other shells where the base wad structure is of different material than the case, the wad actually being inserted into the head area of the hull. Winchester's compression formed 1-piece hulls are built this way, as are Federal's Plastic Champions.

Also, be sure to discard any hull that's split or otherwise so excessively deformed that it can't be "ironed out" through resizing.

Building a Load

The handloader turns to his manual and selects that load which fits his needs in terms of velocity and shot charge. He also must sometimes select his load upon the basis of the hulls he happens to have in stock, building his loads around them. He should also pattern that load in order to find out which works best in his particular shotgun with its specific choke arrangements. Actually, there is not much more to it than this. And the product from a modern shotshell press is beautiful. It looks great and functions beautifully.

Primer Substitutes

Switching primers can raise pressures when going from a cooler to a hotter primer, but without the benefit of much increase in velocity. Ignition can suffer, too, in a primer switch. The loading company has done plenty of study in order to determine which primer is matched for a load.

The sophisticated one piece plastic wad from Ballistic Products, Inc., is used along with a plastic cup which helps to seal the gases from the powder charge behind the wad and of course behind the shot charge. When a particular brand and type of wad is indicated in a reliable loading manual, stay with that recommendation—never substitute wads.

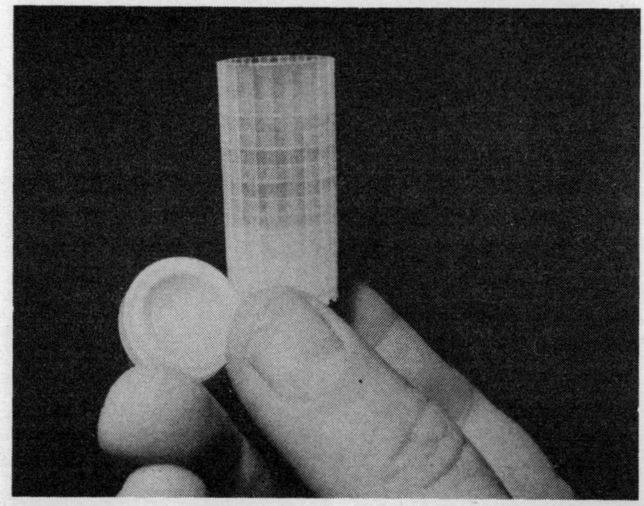

Switching primers around can also bring an overall lack of performance. *Do not substitute primers.*

Substituting Wads

A wad which is not correct for the selected load and hull may alter the pressure of the load and can also cause problems in terms of the wad escaping upbore in a normal unimpeded manner. Also, the wad substituted may not fit correctly for the crimp, meaning the shot will be either too low in the hull or too high in the hull. Wads vary for a reason. They do different work. They must be selected accordingly. *Do not substitute wads.*

Ultra High Velocity Loads

In the past, patterns were *blown* with most ultra high velocity loads. We used to call this condition a "doughnut," for the pattern often looked like a doughnut, shot in a circle with the critical center missing in the pattern. In order to bring the pattern back, the velocity was reduced. Goodbye high-speed load. Today, the story has changed. Why? Largely because of the new wads and discontinuance of the roll-crimp and its attendant over-shot wad. It is my feeling that the old wads were partly destroyed by the tremendous gases exerted from the powder charge necessary to propel the shot at high speed. Also, the wads seemed to be fired right through the shot.

Today's modern wads eliminate this problem to a great degree and probably altogether. For example, Ballistics Products, Inc., lists a velocity of 1,400 fps with a pressure rating of an acceptable 9,900 LUP in a 12-gauge hull pushing a full 1¼ ounces of shot and using the AA Winchester hull, the Winchester 209 primer and 26.0 grains of Herco. The wad is the Ballistics Products, Inc., BPGS+BP12. I tried this load, and patterns in my 12-gauge were excellent.

Some loads have surpassed 1500 fps MV while still retaining good patterns, though generally with 1⅛ ounces of shot in the 12-gauge, not 1¼ ounces. With the latter, speeds of about 1400 fps seem to be tops, though there are exceptions. An increased velocity does mean more impact per pellet, of course. As to the shooter determining the proper lead, we are talking about inches here. So to claim that a 1400 fps load is going to cut the necessary lead on a fast flying bird is true, when compared with the 1200 fps MV load, but to think that you simply hold right on or even just a bit in front of a fast flying bird or clay pigeon just because the velocity has been increased by 200 fps is a mistake. However, waterfowlers, especially goose hunters, have benefitted from the high-speed loads of the day. For example, how about a 10-gauge load which pushes 2 ounces of shot at over 1300 fps?

Shot

The high-speed load generally requires hard shot. Normal soft shot is going to deform when being slammed by the blast of a big powder charge. And deformed shot does not fly true. High antimony shot can help, and, of course, there is nickel-plated shot and copper-plated shot. These are excellent, but costly. However, ultra high velocity loads are for special purposes anyway, so not too many loads need be made up generally.

It's Worth It

Reloading, be it for metallics or shotshells, is worth it. It's a very interesting activity and one which allows a shooter to get more "bang" for his buck. It also provides for great versatility in all respects for the rifle, handgun or shotgun. Some metallic cartridge reloaders have taken the game one giant step forward. They are true experimenters and they deserve an award for their work. Usually, they have the equipment it takes in order to *safely* experiment, of course. We are grateful for their work which is recognized in the next chapter on wildcats.

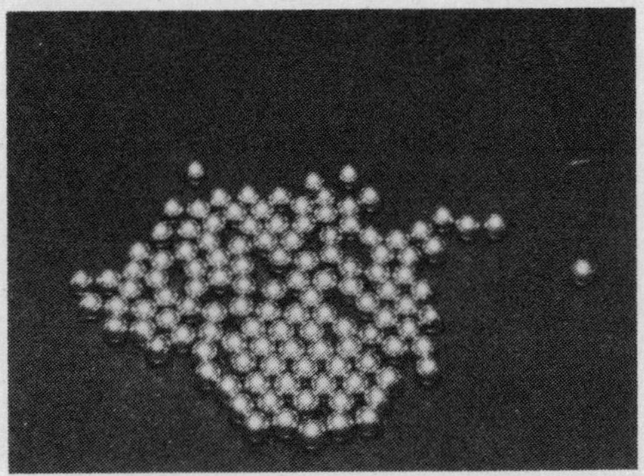

The shotgun shell reloader may wish to employ some highly sophisticated shot. Shot may be coated with nickel or copper. It is a very worthwhile addition to the shot because coating helps to prevent deformity.

A one-piece plastic wad, such as this 10 gauge number from Ballistics Products, Inc., can be highly versatile. This wad can be cut back with slits using scissors. The amount of cutting will change the pattern of the shot.

Chapter 19

The Wildcat

THE COMPLETE SHOOTER may own a wildcat at some time in his shooting career, and even if he doesn't, he should know what the wildcat world is all about. This is and always has been a very interesting phase of handloading, and it is both intellectual (most of the time) and interesting. Furthermore, the wildcatters from about the 1930s to the present have always given us at least a few rounds which have "gone factory" and have proved to be some of the better rounds in existence.

A wildcat is simply a cartridge which you can't buy commercial ammo for at your local gunshop. However, even this simplified definition, though basically accurate, won't hold up totally because some wildcats shoot factory ammunition, but when the case is extracted after firing, the case suddenly has a brand new shape. It usually ends up with a dramatic change in shoulder and neck dimensions. And it will no longer fit into the rifle for which it is designated on the headstamp.

30-06 Improved

A good wildcat example would be a 30-06 Improved. A standard factory round can be fired in a rifle chambered for the 30-06 Improved but there will be some significant changes. These changes will preclude the newly formed case from fitting into a rifle chambered for the standard 30-06 ever again. Here are some dimensions to consider:

***Standard* 30-06 Springfield Dimensions:**
Overall Length = 2.494″
Diameter of shoulder = .441″
Shoulder angle = 17° 30′

30-06 *Improved* Dimensions
Overall length = 2.494″
Diameter of shoulder = .453″
Shoulder angle = .40°*

*Subject to minor variation depending upon the gunsmith who performed the conversion.

Looks like a standard 30-30 Winchester Model 94 rifle, and it is, except it is now chambered for the 30-30 Improved. With the 26-inch barrel, this rifle rendered some interesting velocities. It achieved about 2600 fps with a 150-grain bullet, for example.

So it is easy to see by these dimensions what has happened here. The walls of the case have been blown out straighter

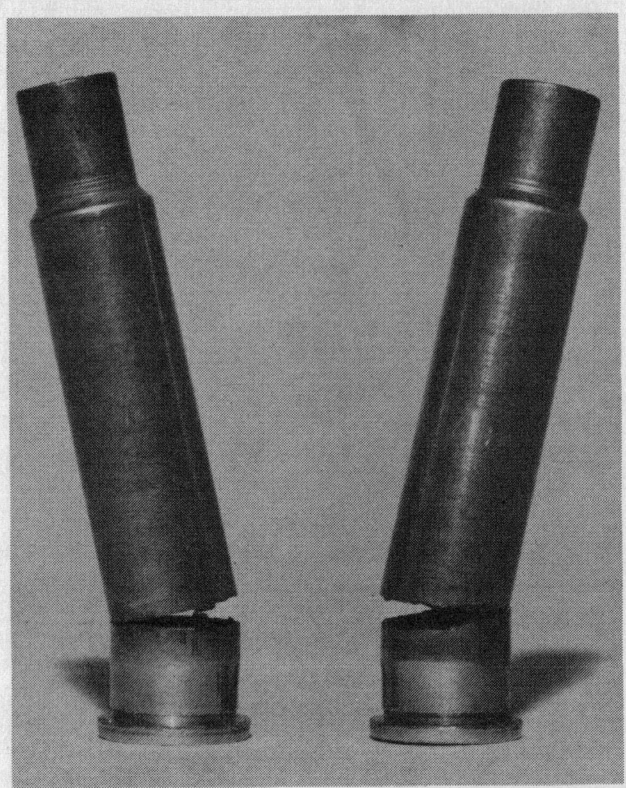

Wildcats do have some problems at times. This is a case of severe case head separation. However, it is more the fault of nickel-brass cases than it is of the round being fireformed. Hundreds of brass cases were fireformed in the same rifle without a loss. Extraction was no problem with these two cases, but case head separation is a problem to be watched for when fireforming cases.

than the walls of the original 30-06 case and the diameter of the shoulder change shows it. Furthermore, the shoulder angle has been made sharper, much sharper.

In fact, case capacity has been increased, and that, in essence, is what gives the 30-06 Improved its "improved" stature. Just how improved is the round? In a moment we will see. But if the improved is so "improved," why didn't the case designers at the turn of the century, make it that way to start with? Answering the last question first, those designers stayed with the then-current trend in the 30-06's dimensions. This meant a sloping wall for ease of extraction along with a neck that held the bullet firmly in place. I should say immediately that I have used the 30-06 Improved and never had a case fail to extract and I certainly never had a bullet fall out. I think, in fact, that the sharp-shoulder design and straight walls are just fine in this round or any other improved cartridge I have used.

We know that with the correct powder, a standard 30-06 case can push a 150-grain bullet at 3100 fps MV, even from a 22-inch barrel. The 30-06 Improved can drive the same bullet at 3200 fps MV. We know that a hot load in the 30-06 will propel a 165-grain bullet at a flat 3000 fps MV. The 30-06 Improved will give that same 165-grain bullet a muzzle velocity of 3100 fps. The standard 30-06 will go 2800 fps with a 180-grain bullet. The Improved will do almost 3000 fps with the 180-grain bullet. I have been able to get about 2600 fps with a 220-grain round nose bullet in a standard 30-06, while obtaining about 2650 fps in the Improved.

Is the conversion worth it? I suppose that is going to be an individual matter in the final analysis. Using 22-inch barrels in both the standard and the Improved, the latter pushes a 180-grain bullet at near-magnum velocities. Certainly that is something worth considering from a standard-cum-wildcat case. And yet, it is "only" 200 fps faster than the standard 30-06 with the same bullet. The question, really, has to do with the increase in velocity. Is 200 fps worth a lot?

A "blown out case" is the same as a fireformed case. The cartridge is fired in a chamber which has been reamed out to the new dimensions established for the wildcat cartridge. Since the case is brass, it stretches out to fill the inside of that chamber, thus changing the shape of the case. On the left we have a 7mm Mauser case which has been necked to hold a .264-inch bullet. On the right is the same case/bullet combination after being fired in a 6.5 (.264-inch) D.G.S. custom rifle. We now have a new cartridge with sharp shoulder and increased case capacity.

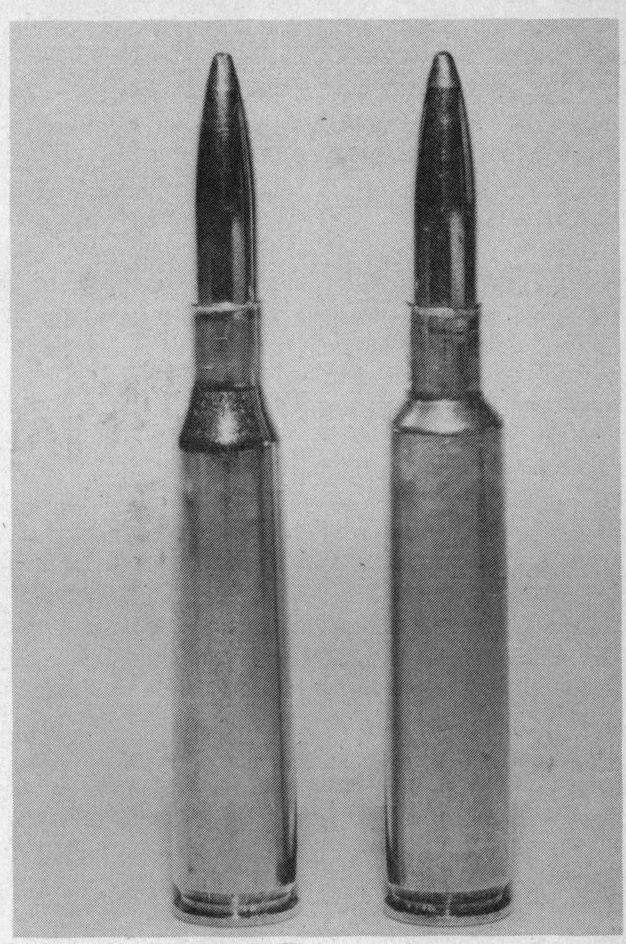

If we believe in kinetic energy ratings, then the improved version of the 30-06 does offer a worthwhile advantage. The standard 30-06, with its 180-grain bullet at 2800 fps MV, earns a muzzle energy of 3134 foot-pounds. The 30-06 Improved with its 180-grain bullet at 3000 fps MV gains 3598 foot-pounds of muzzle energy.

There is another consideration. Trajectory. Will the improved version shoot a lot flatter than the standard 30-06? Since the 180-grain bullet shines in the Improved, it will be used as an example, to give the wildcat a fair and even more than fair chance at proving itself. The standard 30-06 with the 180-grain bullet at a MV of 2800 fps can be sighted in to strike 3 inches high at 100 yards. The bullet will then be on the money at about 225 yards and about 7 inches low at 300 yards. These figures are from one test only, but they are close if not exact. On the other hand, the same 180-grain bullet leaving the muzzle at 3000 fps can be sighted 3 inches high at 100 yards, and it will be on target at about 250 yards and about 6 inches low at 300 yards. Again, this is from one test, but it is not too far off.

So, the gain of 200 fps has given us about 1 inch, roughly speaking, in trajectory flatness over 300 yards. And certainly, 300 yards is plenty far enough to be shooting at most game and getting a whole lot closer is a whole lot better. I would consider the trajectory gain not very impressive for the Improved '06. As for the energy increase, it is there and no denying it. Men who have successfully employed the 30-06 for years without a single failure will not be impressed by this wildcat, but those who want more punch from a standard 30-caliber case might well want to consider having their rifles opened up to 30-06 Improved.

30-30 Improved

Another example of an improved round is the 30-30 Improved. It is cavalier these days to knock the 30-30, and the 30-30 Improved gets little more respect than its parent round in most of the gun magazines. It was not easy to work up superior loads for the 30-30 Improved in the beginning, and when I had a Model 94 Winchester switched over to the Storey Conversion, I had to consult my own loading tables, literally hundreds of 30-30 and 30-30 Improved loads, before I could fully make up my mind whether to have the Storey Conversion chambered for the 30-30 or the wildcat. I went with the wildcat because I finally found the improvement that I was hoping for from the blown-out case. Besides, I could still buy factory 30-30 ammo anywhere and it would feed and fire perfectly in my 30-30 Improved.

The 30-30 Improved is, after all, no more than the standard 30-30 case blown out in the Improved chamber. The shoulder is made sharper and the powder capacity is somewhat increased. In the Marlin Model 336, we achieved over 2700 fps MV with a 150-grain bullet from the 20-inch barrel with the 30-30 Improved and H-335 powder. I found no standard load for the 30-30 that would do that.

In my Model 94 Winchester, in fact in two test rifles, the best MV was 2660 fps average from the Storey Conversion with its 24-inch barrel. I also found that the 30-30 Improved would easily push the 180-grain bullet (which was pulled from 307 Winchester factory ammo) at 2222 fps MV. The 190-grain flat point Silvertip (which I pulled from 303 Savage factory ammo) chronographed at an average of 2092 fps MV. I have read of standard 30-30 loads which do the same, but in all of my testing I have not found these velocities to be possible out of my own standard 30-30 rifles.

I continued to work with the 30-30 Improved, even though at first I did not achieve the results I was hoping for. I found that I could load in standard 30-30 cases and achieve higher than 30-30 velocities in the Improved chamber as well, and with easy extraction in the Model 94. Accuracy in using the standard 30-30 case was the same as using the blown-out case. With some loads, such as the 180- and 190-grain bullets, the Improved case gave better velocity than the standard case did when using the same

The 190-grain Silvertip bullet, shown in the middle of the two cartridges, was extracted from a 303 Savage factory round. It had been loaded into the 30-30 Improved (left), a wildcat, as well as the standard 30-30. Tests with an Oehler chronograph showed that the bullet could be pushed at from 2095 fps MV to 2175 fps MV from a 24- to 26-inch barrel in the wildcat 30-30 Improved. This certainly puts it on par with the 35 Remington.

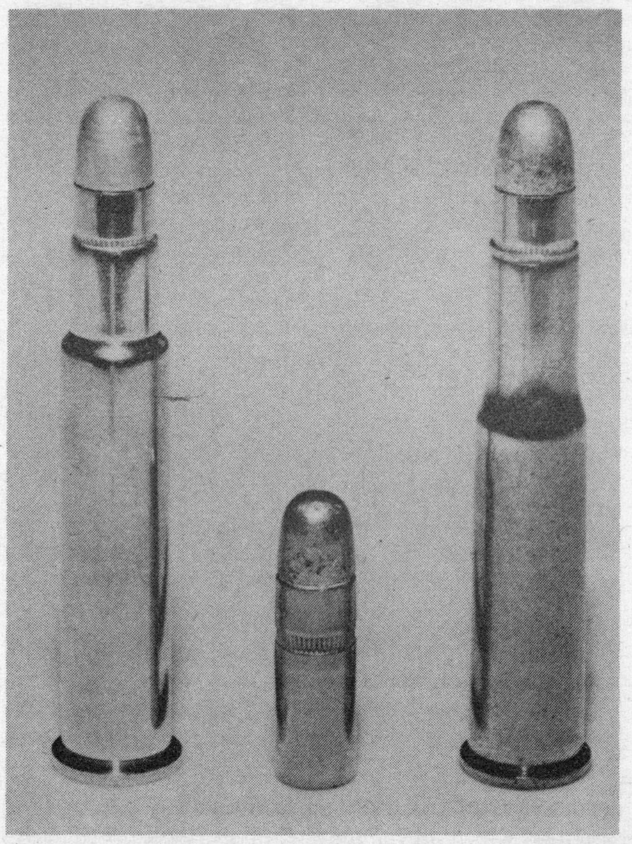

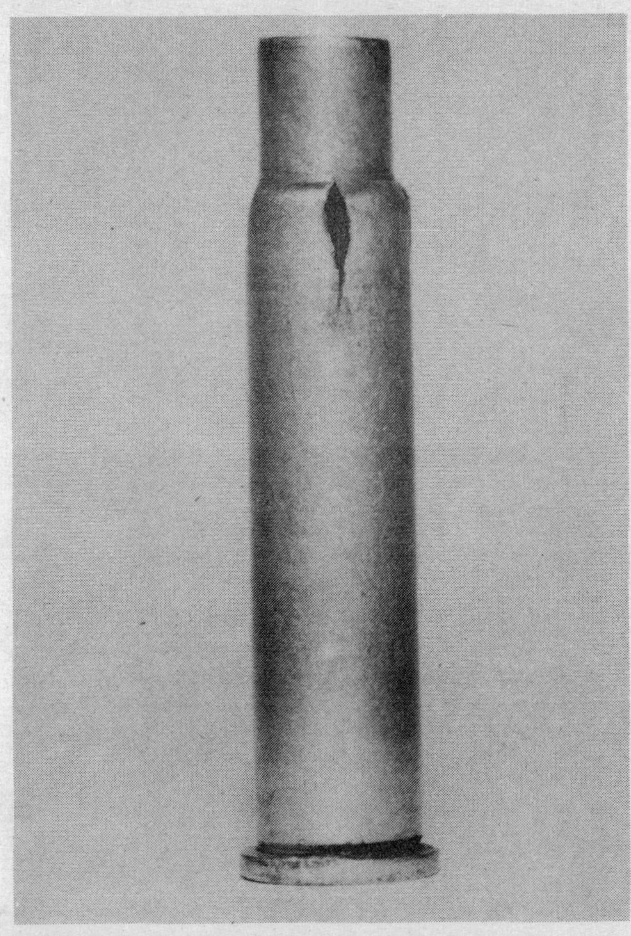

Fireforming this 30-30 Improved brought on a blown shoulder. If the reader will look very carefully, he will see that the left side of the shoulder is not filled out to chamber size. This is an incident of trying to fireform with a light load. Most fireforming is best with modest to normal loads.

charges. A lot more study of this round is in store for me, but I am content that the 30-30 Improved is quite a round in my rifles.

I am going to say "yes" to the 30-30 Improved, and my reasons are not totally ballistic. I like the Model 94 for its flat-sidedness and easy packing and "feel." And my Storey Conversion puts 'em in a 1-inch group at 100 yards all the time, day-in and day-out, with its peep sights. (This accuracy is from the 24-inch octagon barrel as made by the Bauska Rifle Barrel Company of Kalispell, Montana.)

I wanted the improved ballistics of the 30-30 Improved case in that custom rifle, and I am convinced that I got them. The proof resides in my chronographed loads, of course. And though I do use a 24-inch barrel in my 30-30 Improved, the round has also done very well out of the 20-inch barrel.

The highest MV I have achieved in the standard 30-30 with a 20-inch barrel is about 2400 fps. I can get almost 2500 fps with the best load for the 150-grain in the 24-inch barrel. But in the Improved, that 150-grain bullet is leaving the muzzle at 2660 fps average.

What is more, the 165-grain bullet, with a load I picked up from the *Hornady Handbook of Cartridge Reloading,* Third Edition, shows a MV of 2504 fps with easy case extraction and good case life. The load, in fact, was listed for the 170-grain bullet, and I did not go up in powder charge. What is rather interesting is the fact that I can sight in 3 inches high at 100 yards with this load and hit the bull dead-on at 200 yards. At a full 300 yards from the muzzle, the 165-grain bullet hits about 9 inches low in my tests.

Know what else? That last load reaches 200 yards with a retained energy of almost 1600 foot-pounds. There are a lot of "deer cartridges" which don't do that. I truly admire the fine 257 Roberts, but with a 100-grain bullet starting at 3000 fps the retained energy at 200 yards is about 1325 foot-pounds. The 30-30 Improved whips it for energy at 200 yards, with that load. The best velocity I've been able to get with an approved 100-grain bullet load from the 257 Roberts was 3100 fps, and this means a retained energy at 200 yards of about 1425 foot-pounds, but the old 30-30 Improved still wins. It beats anything you can put through a 243 or 6mm, too, for retained energy at 200 yards.

Here is a wildcat I like. My workhorse rifle is a Model 94 with some changes, via the Storey Conversion, and it is a 30-30 Improved. Those who have Marlin Model 336s can gain even more from the 30-30 Improved. In fact, the 30-30 Improved very closely approximates the first 30-06 loads. Of course, the 30-06 is a lot more round today with modern powders. I merely point this fact out because people found the early 30-06 quite a good round for game. I think they found it more than good. Today, I have those old-time 30-06 ballistics in a handy lever-action rifle by using a wildcat round.

257 Improved

Another of the blown-out neck series is the 257 Improved. It, too, requires no more than fireforming to change it from the parent 257 Roberts to the wildcat offspring. And factory ammo can be used in the 257 Improved. While I would elect for the 30-06 Improved only if

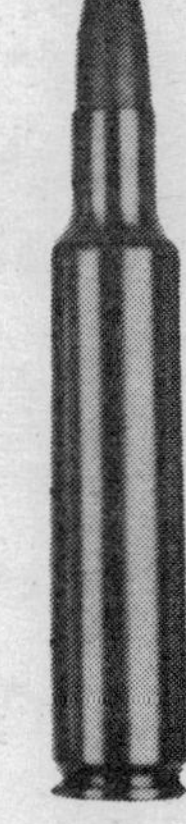

The 257 Ackley Improved is a 257 Roberts case with blown-out shoulder and reduced body taper. The author has gotten 3250 fps MV from a 24-inch barreled 257 Ackley Improved.

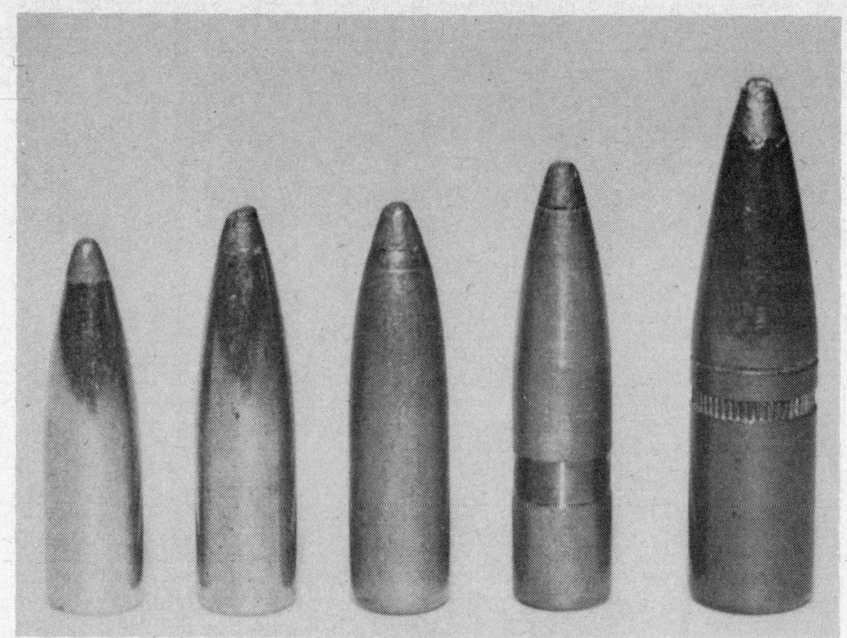

Wildcatting can often lead to a great deal of experimentation. The 80-, 85-, 90- and 95-grain bullets presented here from left to right, were all good in the 6mm/222 wildcat, but the 85- to 90-grain class worked out best. (The 30-caliber 180-grain bullet on far right is for comparison.)

my rifle were intended for game larger than deer, and while I admire the 30-30 Improved for my own specific uses, I think the 257 Improved is a wildcat I can say good things about with a clear conscience.

Again, shoulder angle is increased and body taper is reduced in the 257 Improved. Remember, this task requires the mere firing of the standard 257 Roberts in a 257 Improved chamber in order to achieve the new case. Velocity, by the way, will be a bit lower when the standard 257 Roberts is fired in the Improved chamber.

The 257 Improved or 257 Roberts Improved, to be more specific, is another brainchild of the reknowned P. O. Ackley. As my 30-30 is the Ackley Improved version, so is the 257 Roberts Improved version. My tests have shown up to 3250 fps with a 100-grain bullet for the 257 Roberts Improved using a 24-inch barrel. The 120-grain bullet whipped out at 2950 fps MV. No, this is not the 25-06. But it is still a nice jump ahead of the 257 Roberts.

6mm/222 Remington

One wildcat of very simple design is the 6mm/222 Rem. I vouch for it. I have seen a 6mm/222 in use for over 10 years and it has *never* failed on game of deer/antelope size out to 200 yards plus. It has produced more one-shot harvests than any other rifle we have had in the house. A possible exception may be my Storey Conversion in 30-30 Improved, but the latter has not dropped enough game yet to compare with the little 6mm/222.

There are reasons for certain rounds doing so well on game. The 30-30 Improved seems to do well for two big reasons. First, the velocities imparted to the 150-grain and 165-170-grain bullets I have been using seems about right for bullet upset and penetration. Second, because it is not a big powerful long-range brute of a round, I think that I, and others who have used the rifle, tend to get closer with the intention of putting one well-placed shot perfectly into

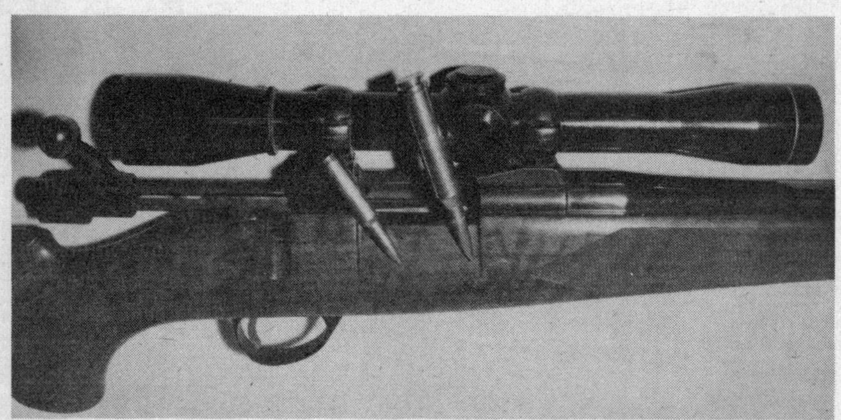

By going to the little 6mm/222 wildcat, this rifle was made in small dimensions for the lady shooter. Note the difference in size between the 6mm/222 cartridge (left) and the 30-06 (right) used for comparison

This custom rifle, in 6mm/222 caliber, has accounted for numerous one-shot harvests on game of the deer/antelope size. The 6mm/222 is a standard 222 Remington case necked up to accept 6mm (.243-inch bullets).

the shoulder/chest region, if not a neck shot.

The 6mm/222 does so well because it shoots about like a cap gun. Literally, there is no felt recoil from the rifle we have. Frank Wells built it on a Sako action and it made up into a very petite and handy rifle for my wife. But Frank did not make it into a super lightweight job. He did not want it much under 8 pounds with scope and sling. I have a custom 6.5 which weighs 7.5 pounds with scope and sling. The little 6mm/222 round fires a bullet in the 87-grain class at 2875 fps, and 2900 fps for the 85-grain bullet.

If this seems puny, remember that we have duplicated, very closely, the ballistics of the original 250 Savage load, and it is very handy to have those ballistics from a tiny case. Because of the tiny 222 Remington case, Frank Wells was able to build the rifle on the short Sako action. It made for a well-balanced rifle for my wife, but she has had to loan her little 6mm/222 many times to her husband, who simply wanted to fill a second antelope tag and preferred doing so with the absolutely positive force of the tiny round.

Anyone who can shoot at all can shoot the 6mm/222. It is the mild report and recoil which allow the round to be so deadly, plus its obvious decent ballistics. The previous rounds have been blown-out jobs, but this little 6mm/222 is not that at all. In fact, it is necked up and that is *it*. I simply run standard 222 Remington brass into my full-length resizing die (dies for the 6mm/222 are commercially available from RCBS) and there you have it. A 6mm bullet is seated over a suitable powder charge and away we go.

I do not like bullets beyond 90 grains weight with the 6mm/222, mainly because the tiny capacity of the case will not drive them at higher velocities. But with a bullet in the 80- to 90-grain class, we have dropped up to large mule deer bucks (weighing perhaps 170 pounds dressed) with one shot each. I will say this—give me a broadside shot at

Wildcatting can oftentimes lead to interesting searches. A search for a good powder for the 6mm/222 wildcat ended up with BL-C-2 as the best of those powders tried, and many were tried. Other powders failed to achieve the MV obtained with BL-C-2.

On the left is the standard 222 Remington case with a 22-caliber bullet standing by it. On he right is the 6mm/222 wildcat case with a 90-grain 6mm bullet standing by it. Not all wildcats work out as hoped for. This one did.

up to 200 yards on a deer, and one shot will take him down with the 6mm/222. It has never failed us.

But we are, to be fair about it, very careful hunters and we hunt a lot. I would not put the 6mm/222 into the hands of a hunter who felt he had to try for 'em at much over 200 yards. The round is not made for that. It is not intended for that. It is intended for deer-sized game *up to* about 200 yards. The 222 Remington case is a strong one and our loads are good and stout, but we reload the cases up to 10 times and I have *never* had a 6mm/222 case split, not even after 10 reloadings with our hottest combinations of bullet and powder. Only one powder works best for us so far, and that is Ball C-2 from Hodgdon's.

So here is a wildcat which will not accept a standard factory round. It is not a matter of improving a case. It is a matter of simply necking a case up to hold a larger bullet.

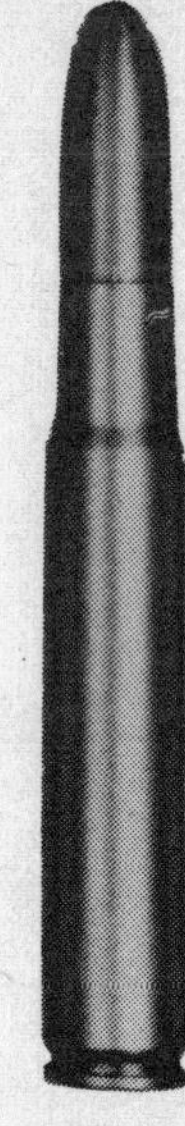

The 35 Whelen is named after the late Colonel Townsend Whelen. It's a simple wildcat, a 30-06 case only having its neck bumped up to 35-caliber.

35 Whelen

The 35 Whelen is named, obviously, for the well-known shooter, the late Colonel Townsend Whelen. The 35 Whelen is, in fact, nothing more than the 30-06 round with the case necked up to hold a 35-caliber bullet. Whelen developed the round in 1922. He was, indeed, ahead of his time here, for the 35 Whelen is a fine round for larger game at medium range. As with our 6mm/222, the 35 Whelen is made by simply running the 30-06 brass into a 35 Whelen resizing die. The expander plug forces the neck out to 35-caliber, and there you have it. Simple, yes, but for those who wanted a larger bullet, the switch was a good one, and the 35 Whelen would work through the action of any rifle which was long enough to contain the 30-06 round, for they are, of course, the same length.

The 35 Whelen will propel a 250-grain 35-caliber bullet at 2500 fps MV. My own tests with the 35 Whelen have produced a muzzle velocity of 2575 fps with the 250-grain bullet from a 24-inch barrel. This was with IMR-4320 powder. The muzzle energy here is 3682 foot-pounds. The 30-06 with the fine 220-grain bullet at 2600 fps MV gives a muzzle energy of 3303 foot-pounds. So here is another fine wildcat round for anyone who wants more bullet weight than normally found in 30-caliber, and yet also desires a standard length case.

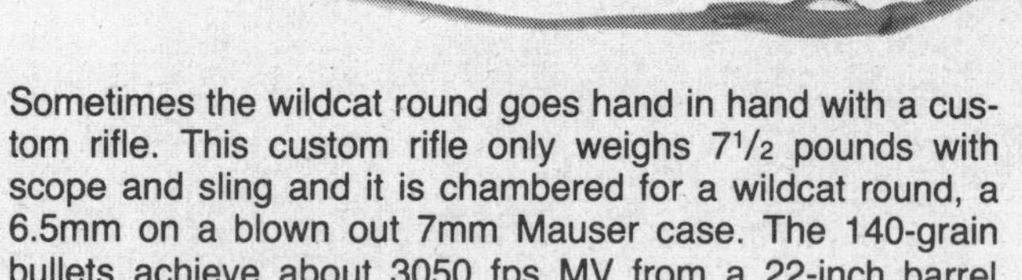

Sometimes the wildcat round goes hand in hand with a custom rifle. This custom rifle only weighs 7½ pounds with scope and sling and it is chambered for a wildcat round, a 6.5mm on a blown out 7mm Mauser case. The 140-grain bullets achieve about 3050 fps MV from a 22-inch barrel using MR-3100 powder.

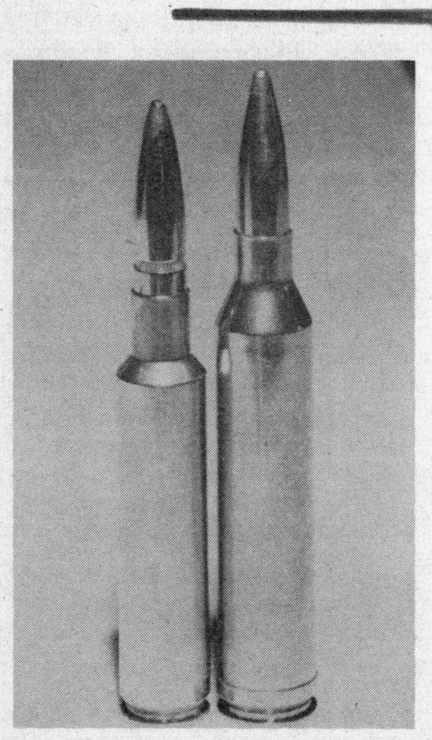

In the smaller bores, a big case can indeed be overbore capacity; that is, containing more powder than can actually be burned behind a bullet of that smaller diameter, dependent in part on barrel length, of course. On the left is a 6.5mm DGS, a round built on a blown out 7mm Mauser case necked to .264-inch. In a 22-inch barrel, the average muzzle velocity in the author's rifle is 3015 fps out of a 22-inch barrel. The big 264 Magnum, an overbore capacity round, will do little to no better out of a 22-inch barrel.

6.5mm DGS

Then there are wildcats which take just a little more effort in the handcrafting, though not a great deal more. One does not simply fireform these rounds, nor is it a matter of necking up a standard case. The example I will name is the 6.5 DGS from DGS, Inc. It is, in fact, a 7mm Mauser, necked down to 6.5mm (.265-inch bullets) and then the case is blown out straight complete with a sharp shoulder. One must neck the 7mm Mauser case down about half to three-fourths the length of the neck. The fireforming works best when the round seats with some resistance. After it is fired, the neck is often somewhat tilted, but this is no problem, for it is easily trued up in a standard case trimmer of the rotary type.

In a rifle with a mere 22-inch barrel, the 6.5 DGS has delivered 3050 fps MV average consistently, using a 140-grain .263-inch Speer bullet and an appropriate charge of MR-3100 smokeless powder from Accurate Arms Company. Sure, the pressure is there, but I have been reloading the brass five times without any problem, and my micrometer shows no case head expansion after the fireforming shot. The round has proved itself very adequate in that it duplicates the ballistics we were able to generate from a big 264 Magnum with a 22-inch barrel. And accuracy from the custom rifle has been remarkable, 1/2-inch groups at 100 yards for three shots, and even some smaller groups. Plus, a 140-grain .263- to .265-inch bullet at 3060 fps MV is certainly strong ballistically. It's a fine long-range number.

The More Sophisticated Wildcats

The previous wildcats are truly simple in their forming. There are many very fine rounds which are simply existing calibers necked down or necked up, for example. We have mentioned the 35 Whelen as a round which is simply the 30-06 necked up. Of course, the 30-06 can also be necked down to make some fine calibers. The 25-06, for example, was so good that it went "commercial," the round now wearing the Remington label. We have a 25-06 in our battery, and it drives a 120-grain Nosler bullet at 3200 fps MV using 64.0 grains of H-870 (source: *Pacific Rifle/Pistol Cartridge Reloading Manual,* 1967 edition, page 156).

Neck a 30-06 down to 6.5-caliber and you can fire .263-.264-caliber bullets at superb velocities. A 140-grain bullet will leave the muzzle at 3066 fps using 57.0 grains of H-4831 powder (previously mentioned Pacific manual, page 173). Neck the 30-06 down to 7mm and you have, *essentially,* the 280 Remington, and, of course, the famous 270 Winchester, which actually shoots 7mm bullets if the truth be known for .277 inches *is* 7mm.

We have also talked about slightly more sophisticated loads through fireforming, and there is also necking up or down, *plus* fireforming so that a new case is born from the original. And now, how about some wildcats of more sophistication? The 30 Herrett is a good example of a wildcat

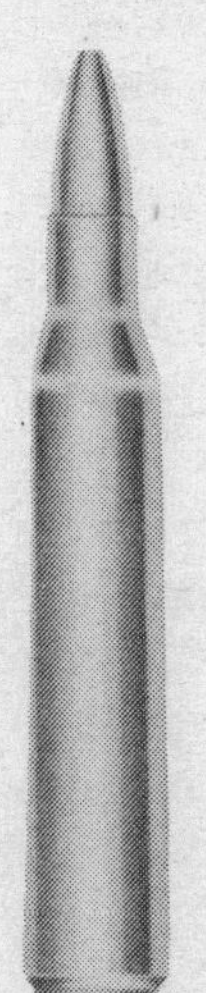

The 25-06 Remington was a wildcat before it went commercial. In fact, it is one of our older wildcat rounds.

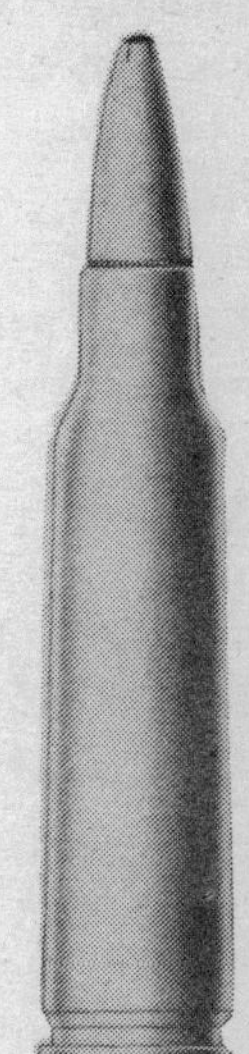

The 280 Remington is basically a 30/06 case necked down to 7mm caliber, but when it went commercial, the factory round came out with a longer neck.

or more sophistication than merely necking a round up or down. The 30 Herrett starts out as a 30-30 case, but it ends up only 1.605 inches long, whereas the standard 30-30 case is 1.976 inches long.

The 30 Herrett, then, is a shortened version of the 30-30 round. And it is made by shortening the overall length of the 30-30 case and then working the brass into 30 Herrett dimensions. In the Hornady Handbook, Third Edition, there is a description of the 30 Herrett and also some advice concerning the manufacture of the round. The quote below, from that excellent manual, will give the reader an idea concerning how this type of wildcat can be much more sophisticated than those previously mentioned. Note that the shooter must work carefully with this cartridge or he will not gain the results he is looking for.

> Cases for the 30 Herrett are formed from 30-30 cases. Sizing is a critical step in proper forming of 30 Herrett cases. If the case is not sized enough and closing is difficult, accuracy will suffer and pressure signs will appear prematurely. If the case is sized too much, excessive head space creates misfires and unnecessary case stretch, which diminishes case life. To eliminate the aforementioned problems, the size die should first be adjusted so the action will not close on the sized case. The reloader must then turn the die in approximately a sixteenth of a revolution at a time, checking the sized case in the action after each adjustment. When the action clicks shut easily, the die is properly adjusted.

This is a very important statement for the reader to examine, for he can make up his mind about the more sophisticated wildcats by asking himself if he truly wants to get involved in case forming and tinkering. I will say this right up front—the end result can be *super*. Properly made 30 Herrett rounds work with excellence. Why did the 30 Herrett come into existence?

The wildcat 30 Herrett exists because the 30-30 did not

offer much, ballistically, in a very short barrel, and shooters wanted to have 30-30 power from the single shot pistol. The shorter case of the Herrett has better loading density for those powders better suited to short barrel lengths. A stark example of this fact would be 30 Herrett ballistics from a Thompson/Center Contender pistol with a 10-inch barrel. The little case gives 2400 fps MV with a 110-grain bullet, 2200 fps MV with a 130-grain bullet and 2000 fps MV with a 150-grain bullet.

Ah, you say, those are not 30-30 ballistics. You can bet your Rolls Royce they aren't. But they are quite impressive from a one-hand gun all the same. Now put the 30-30 into a T/C Contender with a 10-inch barrel. The best velocities obtained by Hornady were 2200 fps for the 110-grain bullet, or 200 fps less than the Herrett obtained for the same bullet, and 2100 fps MV for the 130-grain bullet, 100 fps less than the Herrett managed. But with the 150-grain bullet, the 30-30 gives 2000 fps, the same as the Herrett managed.

There is, however, one more part to this story. The 30-30 has not proved as accurate out of the pistol as the Herrett has, mainly because the 30-30 is a rifle round designed to be used with barrels of 16 to 26 inches. (Actually, the 20-inch barrel produces optimum velocity with some bullets in the 30-30, but the longer barrels of 24- and 26-inch length do offer velocity increases with some bullets and loads). In my own tests, standard deviation from the mean velocity was quite poor with most of the 30-30 loads I tried out of the Contender.

So the 30 Herrett has a place. It is more accurate than the 30-30 out of a pistol barrel of 10-inch length. It is not going to whip the 30-30, even in the 10-inch barrel, if bullets of the 150-grain class are used, for muzzle velocity with both rounds will be quite similar. The reloader now has a choice. He can form the Herrett cases and gain accuracy, or he can use the standard 30-30 with similar ballistics but not, perhaps, the accuracy. Finally, he can hope that further experimentation with 30-30 loads in the 10-inch barrel will produce accuracy with that round. I selected the 30-30 round in my T/C, but with a longer barrel. Also, I had the pistol rechambered for the 30-30 Improved and standard deviations improved, as did MV to a small degree.

I made a choice. I did not wish to form cases for the T/C Contender because I shot the pistol very often and I wanted the convenience of being able to use standard ammo. At the same time, I desired better accuracy than I was obtaining, so I ended up with a wildcat anyway, but a wildcat which would allow me to shove in 30-30 factory ammo whenever I wanted to, or to load up the fireformed cases in my own special way. That is wildcatting for you. It can give a wider range of choice, and in my own 30-30 Contender I have that choice by going to a wildcat which is merely a fireforming situation.

What About Those Sharp Shoulders?

The idea of the wildcat with the sharp shoulders is to gain efficiency within the case. Some shooters feel that "turbulence" builds up within the case when the shoulder is sharp, thus allowing for the powder to burn better *within* the case itself, rather than allowing the powder granules to burn in the bore as they follow the bullet out towards the muzzle. I simply have no proof that this works. I have had, I think, fine bore life with a couple of my sharp-shouldered wildcats, perhaps indicating that there is some truth to the postulation. Proof? I have none.

We must understand that we are not going to move very far away from the raw basics of cartridge function, even with our sharp shoulders. You simply have a container for powder and this is the cartridge case. Then you have a bore with a certain size hole, the projectile pushing its way through that hole. Expanding gases push on the bullet to give velocity. The gas also pushes some powder around, and we see blast and flame. The gas also has to work against the friction created by the rifling as the bullet rotates through the barrel. There is also heat from powder gas

The Thompson/Center pistol is a good example of a handgun which has used many rounds of wildcat stature. Today, some of these wildcat rounds are headed for possible factory manufacture.

This incipient crack in the shoulder indicates trouble, and the case is to be tossed away of course. Wildcatters, as with all reloaders, should always check their brass for signs of trouble.

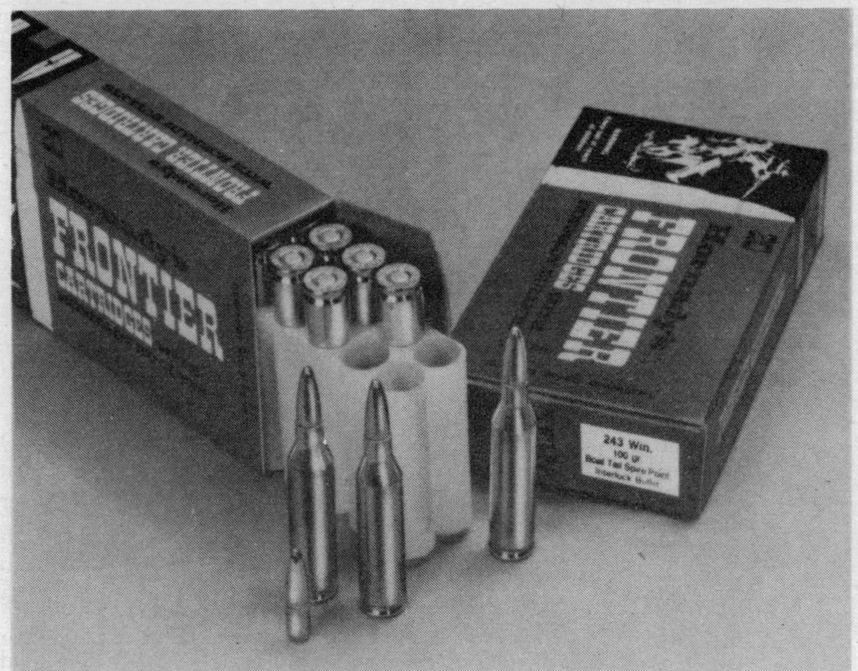

The 243 Winchester is another example of a cartridge which began its life as a wildcat. The 243 Winchester is the 308 Winchester necked down to hold 6mm bullets.

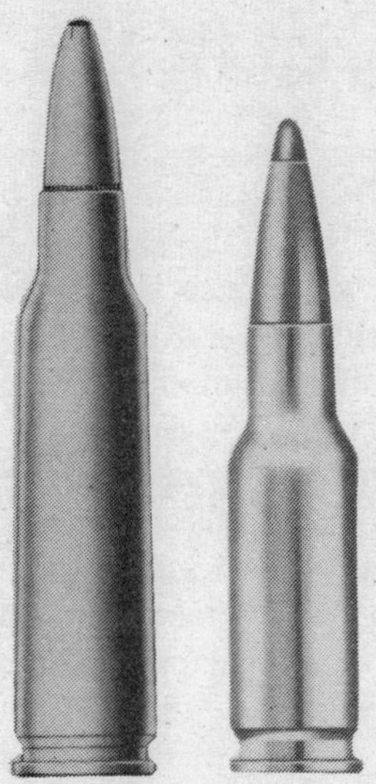

(Left) Some 30 years after the 250-3000 was necked down to 22-caliber by the wildcatters, Remington finally legitimized the round. It sometimes happens that way with wildcats.

(Right) The 7mm BR (Bench Rest) Remington starts life as a 308 Winchester case that features a small rifle size primer pocket. As you can see, things get small quite quickly in the game of wildcatting.

and from bullet friction. We can assume for our discussion that perhaps 30 percent of the power from the expanding gas is lost to these factors which *do not* contribute to MV.

So we try to gain as much efficiency as we can by making certain case capacities for certain calibers. We call a round overbore capacity when the case holds more powder than will efficiently burn through the particular bore size being used. The sharp shoulder may improve combustion and therefore efficiency. By how much? We do not truly know. Gas dynamics pertaining to firearms is very interesting, and complicated.

So we end up wildcatting a round and then trying it out with the old trial-and-error method. This may be archaic, but it ends up being the proof of the pudding. Theory is lovely, but it does not push bullets. Gas pushes bullets, and we need to generate the most push for the longest period of time in order to gain the highest velocity. Some of our sophisticated wildcats seem to do this.

What about the sophisticated wildcat then? Is it worth the bother? Only if the shooter truly wants a certain and specific result which cannot be obtained either by a factory round or a simpler wildcat. Since the 30 Herrett has been our example here, I will continue with it by saying that a shooter should select the Herrett if he wants fine accuracy and power from a 30-caliber bullet in a 10-inch pistol barrel, and then the work involved in forming cases is well worth the effort.

The Factory and the Wildcat

Wildcat cartridges have made a great deal of difference in American shooting. The factories have darn well listened to the wildcatters. Thirty years after the 250 Savage was necked down to form the 22-250 round, Remington decided to offer the 22-250 as a standard loading. It has surpassed the famous 220 Swift to the point of eclipsing that round from a shooter-popularity standpoint. So this is one example of a wildcat becoming a factory number.

While the 280 Remington is, on the surface, a 7mm/06, the factory 280 case is actually longer than the 30-06 case. Nonetheless, the origin of the 280 Remington is certainly seen in the wildcatting of the 30-06 necked down to 7mm caliber. No, the 280 Remington is not a 7mm/06. It is a unique round all its own, but the influence of the original 7mm/06 is seen in this factory round.

A very interesting round is the 7mm BR ("Bench Rest") Remington. The 7mm BR is a 308 Winchester case to start with, but it is shortened and the primer pocket is changed to accommodate a small rifle primer in place of the normal large rifle primer. So Remington offers special 7mm BR brass that has thinner walls to aid reforming of the case. But the cases still have to be made, essentially, by the handloader. The 7mm BR is made by first running the brass into a form die, which moves the shoulder *back*, but neck size still remains the same 308 Winchester size. Then a trim die is used with a file to cut off the long neck to proper length. The caliber is also changed (through necking down) to accommodate .284-inch bullets. Then the case is run into a full-length die for final forming to the 7mm BR round.

The 243 Winchester and 6mm Remington certainly followed on the heels of wildcatted rounds. The 257 Roberts was in fact a wildcat first. The 25-06 was most certainly a wildcat before it was a factory round. The latter was thought up by A. O. Niedner, Remington commercializing the round 49 years after its inception.

Those of us who like to sit around thinking about wildcat possibilities can always come up with some notion which we think is a grand idea. I would like to see, for example, a 6mm based on the 220 Russian case. I feel the round could be made to push 85- to 90-grain 6mm bullets at 3000 fps MV or so. A round like this would be adequate for careful hunters who would refrain from taking shots over 200 yards. The round would be good for young or recoil-sensitive shooters.

The factory is not finished with the wildcat. We would not, perhaps, have the fine 7mm Remington Magnum if it were not for wildcatters, for this round was most certainly a wildcat before it became a world standard. The wildcatter is not finished by a long shot, and the factories are going to watch his progress as they apparently always have. On the one hand, it seems that we already have all of the rounds we can use, but we must not have, because many new ones crop up only to become favorites of modern shooters.

Where fireforming the reloaded wildcat case is necessary, trimming the case after the first shot is indicated often by a slanted neck, as can be seen on this wildcat round on the right.

Will the Factory Round Eliminate the Wildcat?

I sometimes think that we will reach a point where we can get it all from the factory. After I obtained my custom Model 94 in 30-30 Improved, Winchester introduced a Model 94 chambered for the new 307 Winchester round, a cartridge that's more potent than the 30-30 Improved and yet available in the handy and trim lever-action Model 94. I still see a lot of shooters taking their standard Model 94s from years gone by and remaking them into something like the Storey Conversion, and in 30-30 Improved, but there is much to be said for the 307 Winchester round all the same.

Someone came up with the idea of necking a 30-30 up to 35-caliber. The 356 Winchester is that and more. While the 35 Whelen is a dandy round, the 350 Remington Magnum is just as good in the same barrel lengths. I would not work up a 35 Magnum on a wildcat basis. The existing 358 Norma Magnum is already with us in factory form. Nor would I play much with a 33-caliber on a magnum case, for the 338 Winchester is already here.

Some wildcatting is an absolute waste of time as far as you and I are concerned, of course. But such tinkering is not a waste of time to the fellow doing the tinkering. A friend of mine built a wonderful 7mm on a big magnum case and after a great deal of trouble and more than a little expense in barrels and custom gunsmithing work and special dies, he ended up re-creating the standard 7mm Remington Magnum you and I can buy at the hardware store. A waste? Not really. The inventor enjoyed his experimentation and if these creators did not learn by such *failures* we might not have their *successes* either.

Wildcatters will continue to neck cases down, neck cases up, fireform brass, create new cases with case forming dies and, all in all, change the dimensions of brass cases to various sizes. While plenty of the so-called improved rounds are little to no improvement over the standards of the day, there have been some very bright creations which have arisen from the fertile minds of the wildcatter. The complete shooter must at least recognize the fact that the wildcatter is at work, because we are already enjoying the fruits of his labor, and will probably see many more useful innovations from this field in the future.

Chapter 20
Casting Bullets

LEAD PROJECTILES are extremely effective. They are accurate, accurate enough to win prizes, and they work quite well on game in certain situations. There is no way a lead projectile will hold up to the velocities modern arms can attain, and the jacketed bullet is far superior here. But make no mistake—load up a lead bullet of good weight, modest muzzle velocity, and head for the woods; place that lead bullet in the shoulder/chest area of a deer, and you have meat on the table. My own interest in modern lead projectiles does not extend to big game hunting. Instead, I like lead missiles because I can make them for very little cash outlay and they're accurate.

Furthermore, being a black powder shooter, I can cast my own round ball or conicals for a very modest cost. Here, the all-lead ball or conical does shine, for it is just right at black powder velocities. Lead is a fine product for these missiles with plenty of mass for its volume. That is, a lead ball weighs a lot more than a ball of iron or steel. One of the properties of lead is its high molecular cohesion. I have used all-lead projectiles on big game, even bull elk, with only a percent or two of grain weight loss; that is, a black powder lead pill or conical will weigh just about as much after passing through the chest cavity of a big game animal as it did before firing. This allows for very good penetration and an adequate wound channel.

Casting for modern bullets or old-time missiles is not quite the same, so these two areas will be broached separately, but, hopefully, without too much undue repetition. The major difference lies in the fact that for modern lead projectiles, an alloy is desired. The alloy is simply lead with some tin and/or antimony blended into that lead. Black powder projectiles do not require this alloy and therefore we try to make them of pure lead. Obviously, the word ''pure'' is used advisedly. There is *no* pure lead, not totally pure. But you can clean lead up to reach the 99 percent + mark and you can buy Lawrence brand lead (at your local gunshop) which is beyond the 99 percent pure mark.

The Tools

Whether for black powder projectiles or modern bullets, the tools for casting are much the same. Some sort of pot or furnace is needed to melt the lead. A dipper of some sort is always needed, even if the furnace has a pouring spout. And an ingot mold is nice for storing quantities of pot-ready lead; be sure to clean up that mold for black powder usage—your goal is as pure a ''melt'' as possible. After casting a bullet for a modern cartridge, a sizer/lubricator will be used, but is not necessary for casting black powder projectiles. And, of course, a bullet mold must be obtained.

A molder's hammer is also a nice tool to have for casting projectiles, black powder or modern. Also, a bullet caster must think of safety gear. The safety gear I am thinking of consists of a long-sleeve shirt, safety glasses and a good pair of leather boots or shoes, just in case some molten lead should drop on the feet. Gloves are nice, too. Better to burn gloves than hands.

Using the Tools

The Mold

The mold should be prepared properly before use. If the mold is new, all of the packing grease should be removed. (Degreasers are available in spray cans and work well for this purpose). It is sometimes useful to lay a coating of carbon inside of the mold, this being done with a common match, and lubricate the hinge pin with grease. The mold is generally of iron or aluminum. Both have advantages and disadvantages. Iron molds last longer generally, though I have aluminum molds which are as new, and they are 20 years old. Also, aluminum molds heat up faster. I have cast fine projectiles in two or three tries with an aluminum mold, but often an iron mold must cast a great number of projectiles before it is heated just right.

The Pot or Furnace

A melting pot is all right for the shooter who only occasionally casts bullets, but the serious caster is going to be better off with a furnace. A furnace offers variable temperatures, and it has a pouring spout. I like the large, heavy-duty furnaces best. They stay put and they are professional in the way they work. RCBS makes a good one, as does SAECO. These, of course, are electric.

My furnace holds 11 pounds of lead, and the molten lead will flow in accord with how I operate the pouring handle. It's a bottom-pour model, so I can, if I want to, hold the mold beneath the furnace and let the lead flow into the

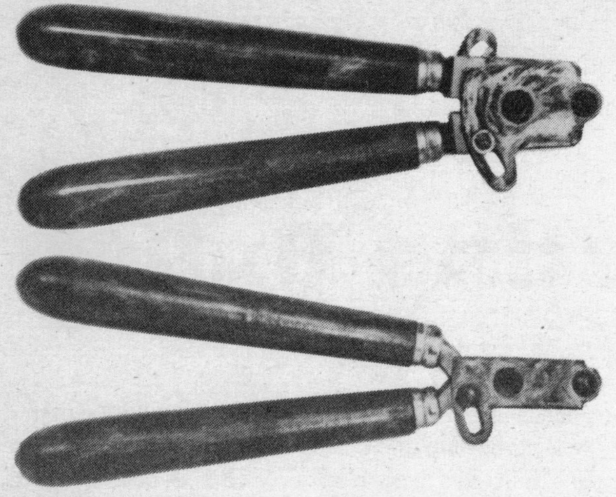

These replica molds from Armsport Company are closely patterned after the original molds used by shooters of the past. Oftentimes, tradition-minded shooters cast their bullets in the outdoors, using the campfire coals for melting the lead.

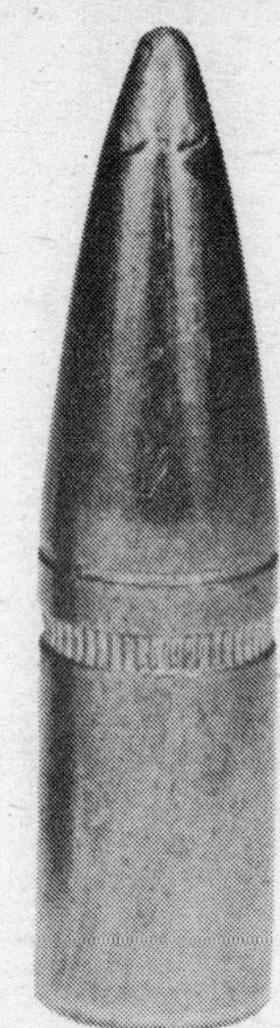

The tremendous contrast between the cast bullet and the modern jacketed bullet can be seen here. The jacketed bullet allowed for the greater potential inherent in smokeless powder. However, the cast projectile can be very accurate and surprisingly effective on game.

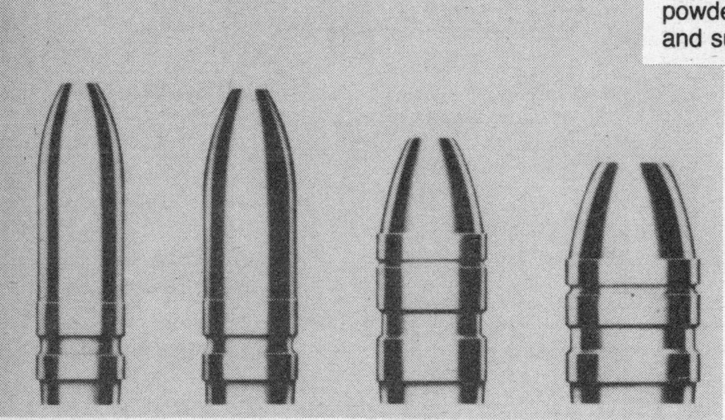

The cast bullet may take various forms. These bullets, made from RCBS molds, all use a gas check, but grease grooves vary considerably here. Note plenty of bearing surface on the two rifle bullets (left), which, after proper sizing, aids in cast-bullet accuracy.

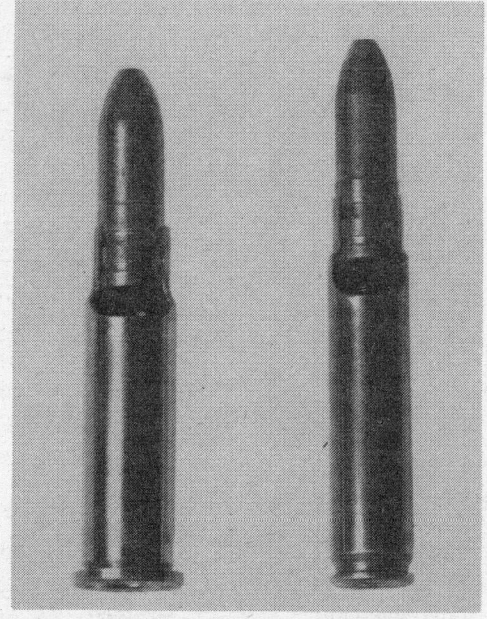

(Right) This cutaway shows the seating of the cast bullet. These bullets are made of Alloy No. 2, which is lead plus tin and antimony. The *antimony hardens the bullets,* but antimony will not stay in combination with lead unless tin is added to help the alloy structure.

mold itself directly, without any ladle or dipper. The furnace has 1000 watts in the heating element, and can melt down 11 pounds of lead in 10 minutes.

Ladle or Dipper

A ladle or dipper is necessary if the lead is melted in a plain pot and can also be used with a bottom-pour furnace. For some casting, especially a few round ball sizes, I have used the dipper instead of the bottom pour of the furnace, finding that it worked better for me. The ladle is like a large spoon with a crease in it for the lead to flow out of; the dipper is more enclosed with a spout. I like the dipper better than the ladle.

Ingot Mold

This simple device is no more than a metal container, but it is quite useful for the caster. Use the mold to provide ingots of varying weights and alloys. I store those ingots for future use. Most ingot molds are sectioned—the RCBS ingot mold, for example, having four sections.

A fine furnace is a wise investment for the shooter truly interested in casting uniform and excellent projectiles. One of the features to look for is a good range of heat choices, as well as an ability for easy pouring of molten lead. This RCBS Pro-Melt unit has it all.

This excellent Lyman mold casts a 525-grain Minie ball. It is of iron construction. Though the iron molds take longer to heat, they retain their heat very well.

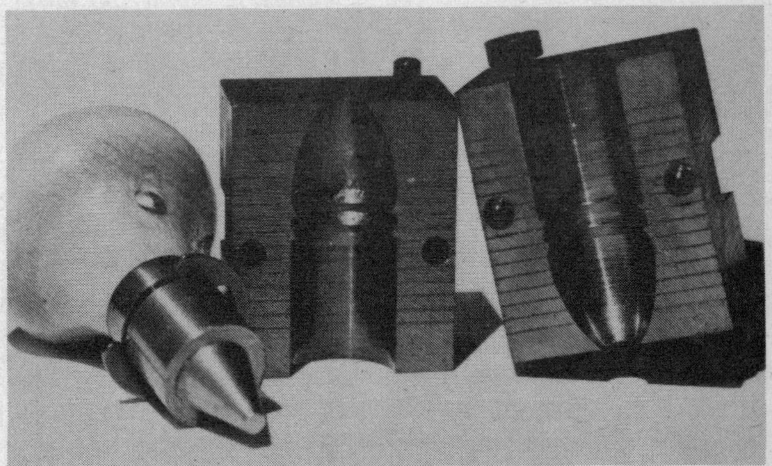

Molder's Hammer or Mallet

The molder's hammer has a nylon head on one end and a sharp pick on the other. Mine is from the Navy Arms Company, and I use it all the time. The nylon head is used to gently tap aside the sprue plate cutter, and the pointed end is used to *carefully* pick out a stubborn projectile which will not exit the mold, something which does not happen very often, fortunately.

Sizer-Lubricator

This is a very useful tool and somewhat essential for bullets of modern type used in centerfires. This unit swages the bullet to the correct size. Swaging is not new. In the fine old book, *The Muzzle-Loading Cap Lock Rifle,* by Ned Roberts the author, describes swaging projectiles to be used in rifles of the day, muzzleloaders at that. I do not swage my conicals for my muzzleloaders, but I do swage bullets which will be used in handguns and rifles of modern design.

The sizer-lubricator not only swages the cast projectile to the proper dimension, but it also lubricates the bullet. This step is actually a part of the operation, and this tool does the job in an automatic fashion. The bullet is inserted into the sizing die and the handle of the machine is pulled down (on the RCBS model). As the handle is raised back up, the sized and lubricated bullet is ejected automatically. Lube flow is adjustable, too.

The machine requires bullet sizing dies which are inserted into the sizer-lubricator machine. The RCBS die couples with an automatic lube system. Lube is forced through in the sizing die side holes and into a retaining ring which then fills lubricant grooves in the bullet. The die uses an ejector pin to force the bullet out of the unit after it has been sized and lubed. There is also a top punch designed to fit the shape of the nose of the bullet being sized. Remember, the bullet sizing die is a swager; it does not remove metal. It forces metal to change form, so the bullet weight is the same after sizing.

To be quite accurate, the bullet should be sized to truly fit the bore dimensions of the firearm. This means "slugging" the bore first. To slug a bore, a soft lead core (or pure lead bullet of approximate bore size) is virtually hammered through the bore itself, and then the resulting core (or bullet) is measured to determine exact bore size, groove-to-groove. The next step is to find a mold which matches that groove-to-groove diameter. The projectiles you eventually swage will be oversize, perhaps, by a couple thousandths of an inch. A competent gunsmith can slug the bore of any gun, incidentally, and he can do it without damage to the firearm.

Procedures

The world of casting projectiles can be very involved. Books have been written on the subject, because the subject deserves such coverage. However, this chapter can get both the black powder and modern shooter into casting. From this beginning, the complete shooter can go forward to whatever levels he wishes to attain. For myself, I am content in making superlative black powder projectiles and what I would call very good modern missiles. A shooting partner of mine is quite the opposite. He has, in fact, mastered the manufacture of modern lead projectiles and he hunts with a 45-70 rifle, shooting his own 455-grain bullet made from a Northeast Industrial, Inc. (2516 Wyoming St., El Paso, TX 79903) mold.

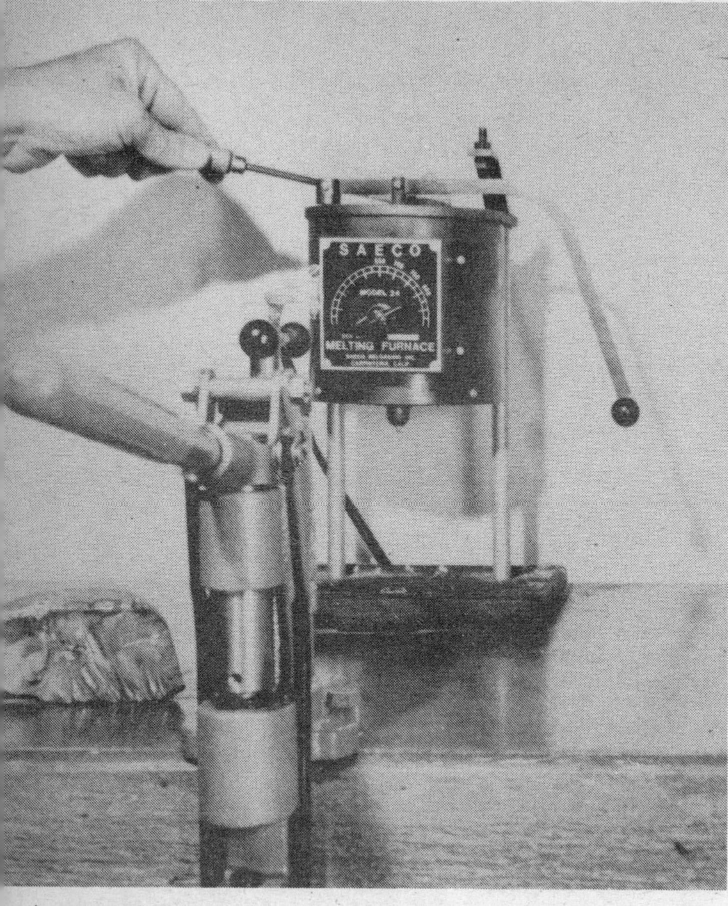

The lead alloy is stirred with a long-handled spoon or in this case a long-handled dipper. Then the dross is carefully skimmed from the top of the lead. This means only the debris, usually dark in color. Do not skim off the silvery surface as this surface will often be the lighter elements used in making an alloy, such as tin.

Steps for Making the Modern Bullet

Actually, the raw basics of making a modern lead projectile are terribly simple. You get some lead, melt it, pour it into a mold, let it harden a few seconds, tap it out of the mold and then size/lube it and load it into the cartridge. Simple. However, there are a few more wrinkles to consider.

In the first place, the shooter must consider which style and weight bullet he wants to shoot. Fine bullet molds are available from several reliable sources. Lyman offers so many bullet styles and weights that it takes a couple pages of small print to list them. The same can be said of Lee and RCBS. There are bullets for the pistol, starting with a little 25-caliber number of 51 grains cast weight and going to a big 255-grain bullet for the 45 Colt. When it comes to long guns, Lyman offers a little 49-grain 22-caliber bullet with a couple grease grooves and a gas check, all the way up to a 475-grain 12-gauge rifled slug.

SAECO is another maker of excellent molds. There is an interesting 85-grain 6mm cast bullet, for example, or a 6.5mm 140-grain number or a 140-grain bullet for the 270. SAECO has some fine 7mm bullets, too, along with a good line of 30-caliber offerings. For 45-caliber, SAECO goes up to a 500-grain bullet, and the company also has molds for obsolete calibers, such as .359-inch bullet of 250 grains which could be used in the 35 Winchester cartridge.

Lee Precision, Inc., offers bullet molds which provide a 93-grain slug for the 32-20. That bullet is a good one for this all but obsolete (but still useful) round. Or you can find a 170-grain bullet for your 30-30 here. RCBS molds are in keeping with the rest of that firm's product line, quite complete and totally reliable. Bullets from 22- to 45-caliber are offered, including a line of bullets especially designed for silhouette shooting. There is also an excellent 250-grain bullet for 44 Magnums and many more.

Another consideration is how fast the shooter wants to propel these bullets. My own suggestion is that the bullet should wear a gas check at about 2000 fps MV. I see nothing wrong with a gas check even for speed-of-sound muzzle velocities. The gas check is only a small metal cup which attaches to the base of the bullet, but it prevents undue gas erosion at this highly important ''steering'' portion of the bullet.

Step 1: Prepare the Metal

Ideally, an alloy is required, and the alloy is going to consist of lead, tin and possibly some antimony. The problem is that the actual size of the projectile and its weight will depend in part upon the alloy used. For example, a 22-caliber bullet may way 47 grains in *pure* lead. However, that same mold will toss a 46-grain bullet when a No. 2 Alloy is employed. Linotype with its alloys will drop the same bullet to a 44-grain weight. So it's obvious that there is a big difference in mass with different bullet materials. Dimensions change, too. The above-mentioned 22-caliber bullet will be .2237-inch in pure lead, but .2240-inch in No. 2 Alloy.

No. 2 Alloy is a time-honored ''melt'' that can be made in various ways. Lyman recommends the following two examples:

Alloy No. 2

Formula A

9 pounds of wheelweights
1 pound of 50/50 solder (bar solder)

Formula B

4 pounds of Linotype
1 pound of 50/50 solder (bar solder)
5 pounds ''pure'' lead

Of course, there are several other combinations which work. Lyman further lists these for comparison purposes:

Composition & Hardness of Common Bullet Metals

Alloy	Lead	Tin	Antimony	BHN*
Linotype	86%	3%	11%	22
#2 Alloy	90%	5%	5%	15
16-1	94%	6%	0%	N/A
10-1	91%	9%	0%	11.5
Wheelweights	95.5%	0.5%	4%	9
Pure Lead	100%	—	—	5

* Brinell Hardness Number
Courtesy of the Lyman Products Corporation

And then there are bullets cast of very hard alloy. I am totally in disfavor of these. Reasons for my disfavor will be stated soon, but I think a definition is in order first. For our purposes, we will think of three divisions in cast bullets, the lead bullet (or round ball), which is mainly lead and in fact an attempt at ''pure'' lead, the Hard Cast bullet, which would be represented by Alloy No. 2 with its Brinell number of 15, and then the Extra Hard Cast bullet. Following our information here, with a step-by-step approach to making our own bullets, we will then talk about the Extra Hard Cast bullet.

Step 2: Melting Down the Lead

With the metal proportions established above, in one alloy or another, the caster goes ahead with the heating process. I set my furnace at 800 degrees Fahrenheit for the initial melting of the lead and alloy products. The 800-degree temperature insures that any other metal such as foreign metals or tin (along with antimony) melt with the lead.

Step 3: Fluxing the Lead

Fluxing combines the metals and removes any impurities in the melt. In order to mix lead and its fellow metals, we use a flux which can be as simple as plain paraffin or as complex as a commercial product offered strictly for fluxing. I like the latter better, but will use wax quite often, too. NEI Flux is excellent (from Northeast Industrial, Inc.). If I'm using wax, I break off a hunk about the size of a thumbnail and toss it into the molten lead. The amount of wax will vary with the capacity of your furnace. A match is immediately struck and touched to the fumes rising off the pot or furnace. The gas will ignite.

With a ladle (or a long metal spoon) the lead alloy is stirred and stirred at least until the flame goes out, indicating all the wax is used up. The same stirring occurs with the commercial fluxing material. The idea is to combine the metals into an alloy. A true alloy is not all that easy to

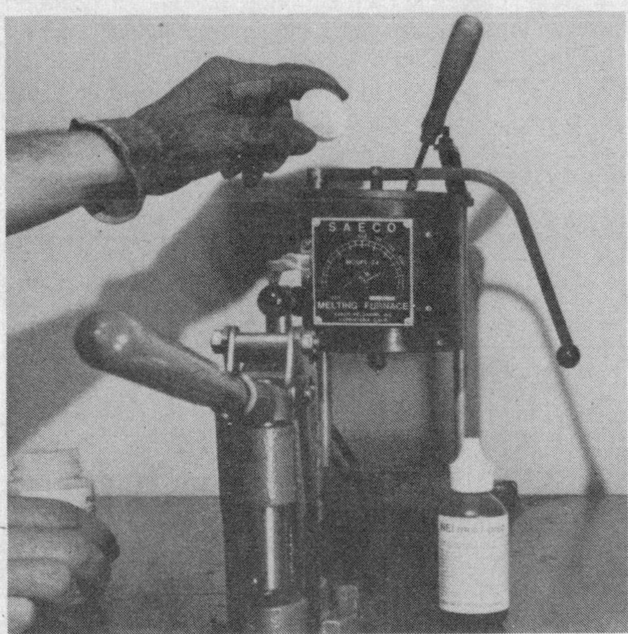

NEI fluxing flakes are sparingly added to the ~~10~~ pounds of molten lead in the pot. Three or four flakes will do, but fluxing of the lead must be done often during the process of casting. You can't flux too much, but you can flux too little.

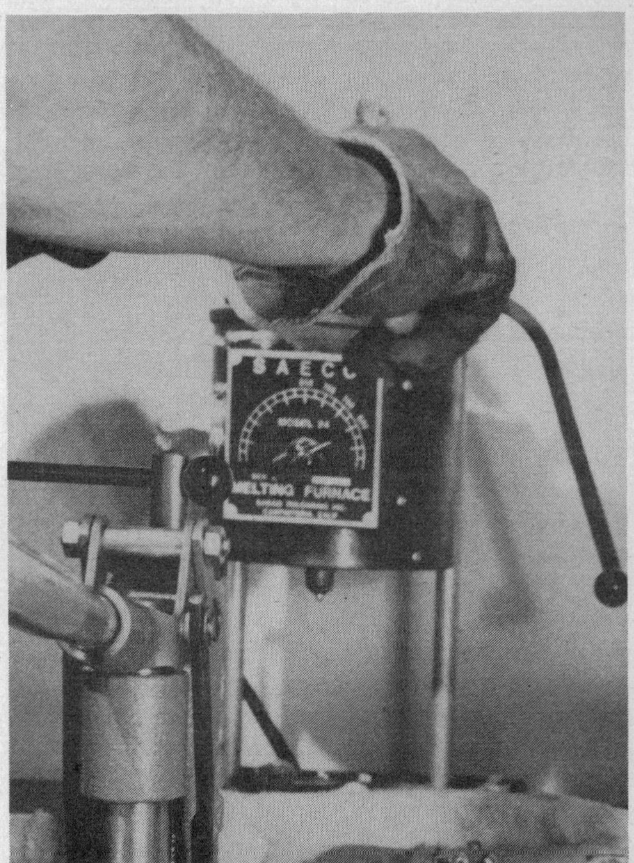

(Right) The lead is stirred again after the fluxing agent has been added to it. The idea is to form as uniform an alloy as is possible.

make and the above method is not perfect, but it will produce a consistency which is totally useful for bullet-making. (This is only the first fluxing, there's more to come and for different reasons.)

Step 4: Prepare the Mold

The mold should be free of oil, as described earlier. If the solvent method does not remove all of the oil, the mold can be boiled in soapy water. But be sure to lube the hinge pin. An unlubed hinge pin can gall and may even warp the mold's handles or do some damage to the mold itself.

Now bring the mold up to proper heat for casting. Iron molds, unlike those made of aluminum, can indeed be warped, so *do not* dip a corner of the mold into the molten lead. Always set iron mold blocks on the top edge of the furnace and let them slowly heat up for a few minutes.

Step 5: Flux Again

That first fluxing was just for a warmup. This time, we are going to clean the lead as best as possible. Fluxing is a process of combining. I think, however, that we should also think of fluxing as a cleaning process. The impurities (called "dross"), which exist in our would-be alloy will rise to the surface. That first fluxing was in hopes of mixing the important tin and/or antimony back into the lead. Now we want to flux again, with more fluxing material, and I do mean *more*.

If using wax, then nip off a hunk about the size of a quarter or 50 cent piece and drop it in the melt, lighting up the gases as before. Stir and stir with ladle or spoon. Watch for the dross to rise to the surface. You'll be treated to an eyeful of lighter-than-lead metals, even dirt. Skim it off with the ladle or spoon and get rid of it safely. I suggested earlier that true alloy-making, through fluxing, was not terribly likely in the sense of making a totally "mixed" metal. But this fluxing will clean the lead and the resulting bullet will be, or at least can be, very superior in homogeneity.

Step 6: Casting the Bullets

The 800-degree setting on the furnace should now be reduced to 700 degrees Fahrenheit. Be sure this step is taken just prior to putting the mold into service. The 800-degree temperature will drop down to 700 soon enough and, meanwhile, the extra heat will serve to get the mold ready for some good casting. We never want the lead to reach 900 degrees, for it will give off dangerous vapors. The iron mold should now be warm, but will probably not make good bullets right away. However, cast away. This is an enjoyable activity, and I suggest caution and a no-rush posture. The first projectiles may be wrinkled. This indicates a cold mold. Later, the bullets may come out "frosty." This indicates a mold which is too hot. In the first case, keep on casting as it will bring up the temperature of the blocks. In the second instance, stop casting and let the mold cool off a while.

Using the mold is rather easy. The cavity is filled and the molten lead is allowed to harden for a few seconds. The bit of sprue, that little glob atop the mold, will harden soon and at that point, the mold can be opened up by first tapping the sprue plate aside gently. The bullet should fall out. Give it a good landing site; it's soft. I like corrugated

Predicted Physical Characteristics of Bullets Cast in Various Lead Alloys (Courtesy Lyman Products Corporation)

		Predicted As-Cast Characteristics									Predicted Dimensions - Sized			
		Lead		Wheelweights		#2 Alloy		Linotype		H&I Sizing				
Caliber	Bullet Example	Wt. grs.	Dia.	Wt. grs.	Dia.	Wgt. grs.	Dis.	Wt. grs.	Dia.	Die	Lead	Wheel-weights	#2 Alloy	Lino-type
Rifle														
.22	#225415	47	.2246″	46	.2246″	45	.2250″	44	.2252″	**.224**	.2237″	.2237″	.2240″	.2240″
.243, 6mm	#245496	87	.2437″	85	.2441″	83	.2445″	81	.2447″	**.243**	.2427″	.2427″	.2430″	.2430″
.25	#257464	92	.2576″	91	.2581″	88	.2585″	87	.2588″	**.257**	.2567″	.2567″	.2570″	.2570″
.270	#280473	129	.2776″	127	.2781″	123	.2785″	121	.2788″	**.277**	.2765″	.2767″	.2770″	.2773″
.280, 7mm	#287308	170	.2846″	167	.2850″	162	.2855″	158	.2858″	**.284**	.2836″	.2837″	.2840″	.2844″
.30	#311291	176	.3095″	173	.3100″	168	.3105″	163	.3108″	**.308**	.3076″	.3077″	.3080″	.3081″
8mm	#323470	167	.3234″	165	.3240″	160	.3245″	155	.3248″	**.323**	.3226″	.3227″	.3230″	.3233″
.35	#358315	215	.3578″	212	.3584″	206	.3590″	200	.3594″	**.357**	.3566″	.3567″	.3570″	.3573″
.375	#375449	276	.3773″	272	.3779″	264	.3785″	256	.3789″	**.376**	.3756″	.3757″	.3760″	.3763″
.45/70, 458	#457193	439	.4575″	433	.4583″	420	.4590″	407	.4595″	**.457**	.4566″	.4567″	.4570″	.4574″
Pistol														
.25	#252435	53	.2522″	53	.2526″	51	.2530″	49	.2533″	**.251**	.2507″	.2507″	.2510″	.2510″
.32	#311252	80	.3125″	79	.3130″	77	.3135″	75	.3138″	**.309**	.3086″	.3087″	.3090″	.3100″
9mm	#358242	96	.3558″	95	.3564″	92	.3570″	89	.3574″	**.356**	.3556″	.3557″	.3560″	.3563″
.38/357	#358156	156	.3578″	153	.3580″	149	.3590″	144	.3594″	**.357**	.3566″	.3567″	.3570″	.3573″
.41	#410610	225	.4101″	221	.4108″	215	.4115″	209	.4119″	**.410**	.4096″	.4097″	.4100″	.4103″
.44	#429421	256	.4296″	252	.4303″	245	.4310″	238	.4314″	**.429**	.4286″	.4287″	.4290″	.4294″
.45	#452374	235	.4515″	232	.4523″	225	.4530″	218	.4535″	**.451**	.4506″	.4507″	.4510″	.4514″

cardboard, at a sloping angle so the bullet slowly rolls down the cardboard and onto some clean lintless cloth.

If the bullets seem to stick, try smoking the interior of the mold with a candle flame or a flame from a match, the idea being to deposit a thin film of carbon on the mold cavity. NEI also has a product which will aid this problem. It is called NEI Mold Prep, and it works well.

Easy on the mold! It is hot, and it can be damaged. I squeeze the mold handles together enough to ensure the blocks are mated, but I do not "clack" them together or squeeze beyond that first level of "springiness."

Step 7: Check Your Bullets

Toss away the bad bullets; they are generally obvious. A well-cast bullet is shiny and bright, but not frosty and never wrinkled. It has no pock marks in it and also, does not look like it was made in two separate halves, as though glued together. It is a one-piece affair only. If the bullets are for hunting or target work, the shooter may want to weigh them one at a time on the bullet/powder scale. Light ones should be tossed out, as they may have impurities or air pockets.

If cast correctly, the bullets should be very uniform. I

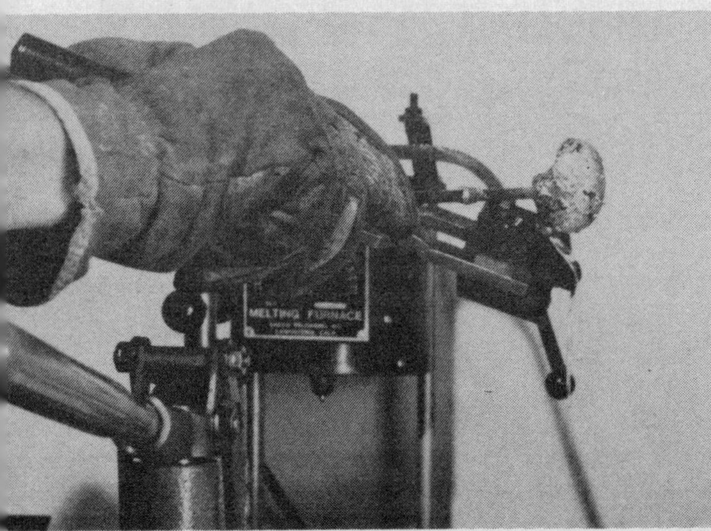

(Left) With a dipper, a quantity of molten alloy is removed from the melting furnace and the nose of the dipper is pressed up against the sprue hole of the hot mold. With a turning motion of the wrist, the molten lead is allowed to flow down into the sprue hole. The caster holds the dipper in place for a few seconds, then rotates the wrist again so the the remaining contents of the dipper will not flow out of it.

(Below) Now that the cavity is filled with alloy, the bullet must be extricated from the mold. With a Navy Arms molding hammer, the sprue plate is gently tapped aside; the handles of the mold are pulled apart, and the bullet drops out onto a protective surface. If the bullet does not freely fall from the mold, the mold blocks should not be struck. Rather, the hinge pin area can be tapped with the nylon head of the molder's hammer.

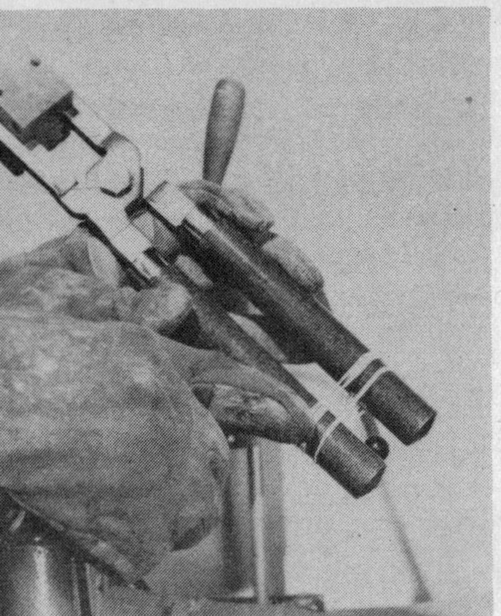

(Left) After using the mold, the author prefers to place a rubber band around the handles to hold the two halves of the mold together firmly. It should be placed where it will not be damaged.

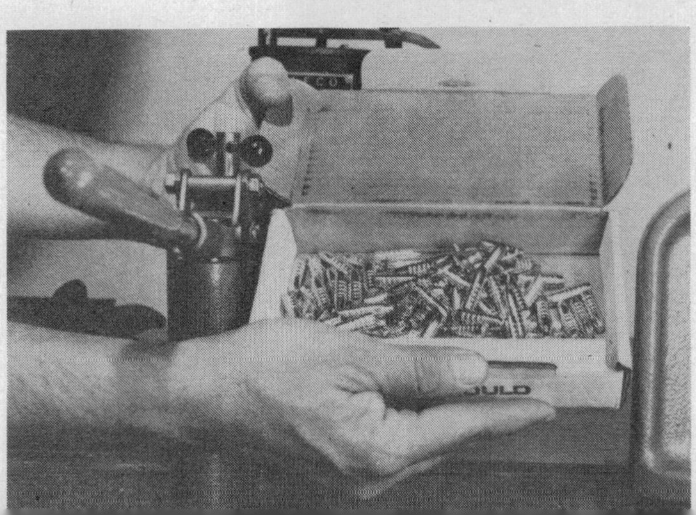

Here are some examples of cast bullets, these being 180-grain 30-caliber bullets from a double cavity RCBS iron molding block. They will be loaded into the 30-30 Winchester round at over 2000 fps MV. They have been checked for uniformity, bad slugs being returned to the pot.

mean *very* uniform. I was making bullets for a 30-30, to be used primarily for small game hunting, and I wanted them to be consistent in weight. I discarded bullets which were ½-grain weight off the norm. I have cast both black powder and modern projectiles which have sampled out at ±.1-grain. Not all the time. No. But I have had this type of success in casting.

Step 8: Size the Bullet

Now use the sizer-lubricator. The bullet should have grease grooves. When sized, the grooves will also be filled with lube. Now the bullets are ready for use.

When initially selecting a bullet weight for your cartridge, I would suggest that you opt for heavier bullets and not the lighter ones, caliber for caliber. After all, high velocity is not in the picture anyway, and I like plenty of bearing surface and a good bore fit in my cast bullets. By the way, those nice pointed jobs are OK, but I will take a round nose or similar bullet without that long ogive. I have obtained groups of under one minute of angle, for example, with an NEI 30-caliber bullet in my 30-30 Storey Conversion. This is with the 178-grain bullet at about 1700 fps MV.

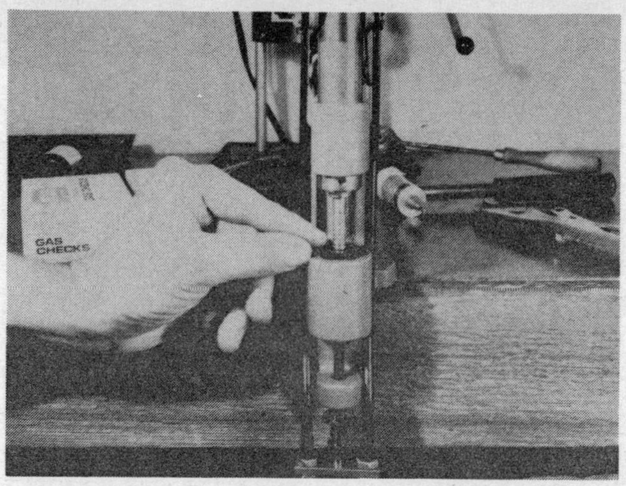

After placing the gas check on the base of the bullet, or into the top of the sizing die, the bullet is located in the Lube-A-Matic with the top punch carefully centered on the bullet's nose.

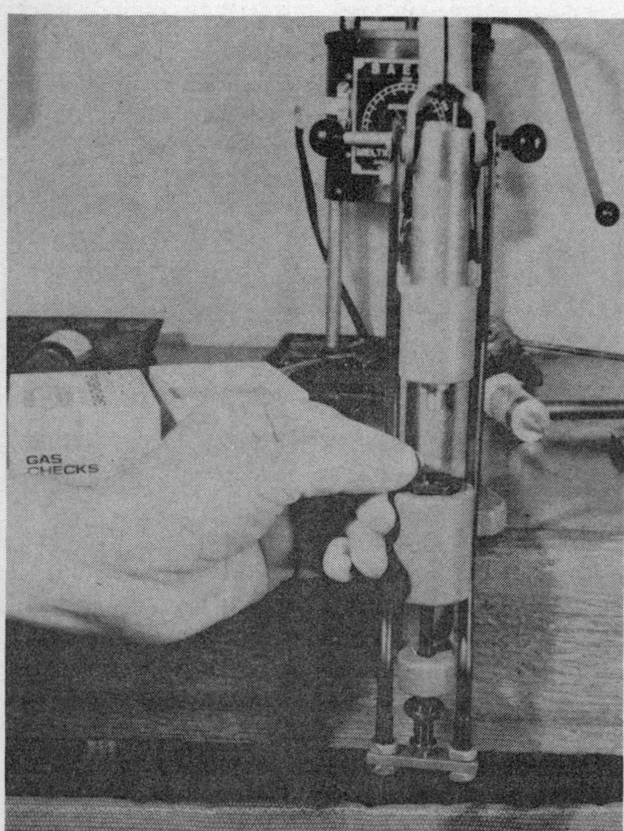

Using the RCBS Lube-A-Matic 2, a gas check is placed down on the face of the sizer die. This is an often-used method and works well enough, but the author prefers to hand-place the gas check on the base of the bullet, tapping the gas check on with the nylon face of the molding hammer.

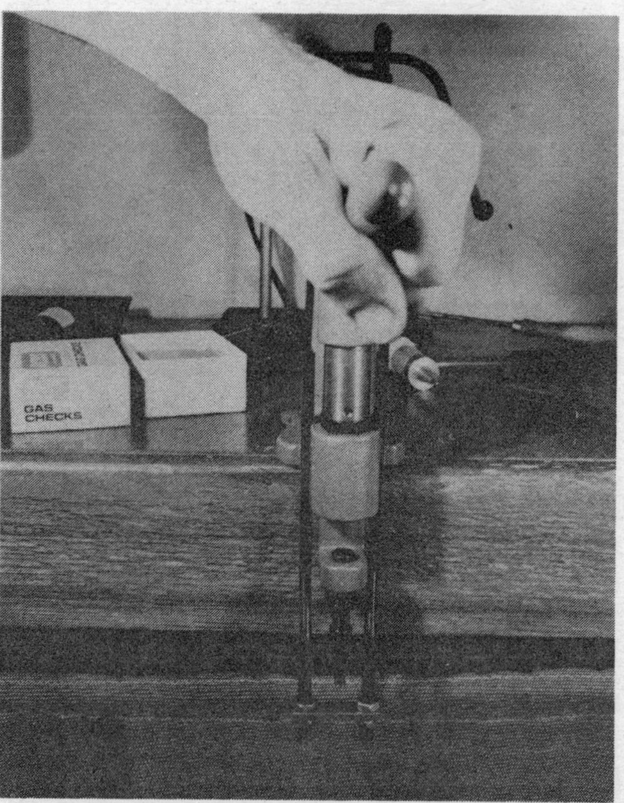

The handle of the Lube-A-Matic is pulled downward, which forces the bullet into the sizing die. This function, of course, swages the bullet to a uniform and exact diameter. This step does not require a great deal of pressure. Shooters who are used to sizing stretched brass cases may apply more pressure than required here. Once the bullet is driven into the sizing die all the way, that is all that is required. Do not exert force after the bullet is fully seated in the sizing die.

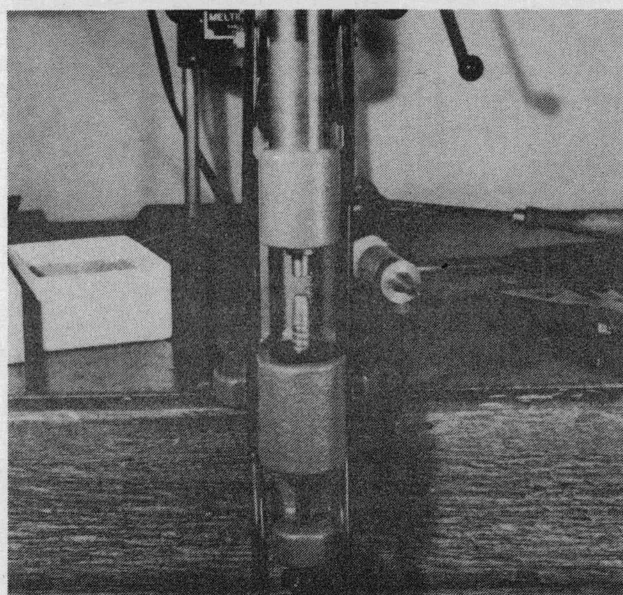

By simply pulling up on the handle of the Lube-A-Matic, the bullet appears again, fully sized and lubed. Follow the directions provided with your particular machine in order to lubricate a bullet's grease grooves only. The crimping groove is not lubed.

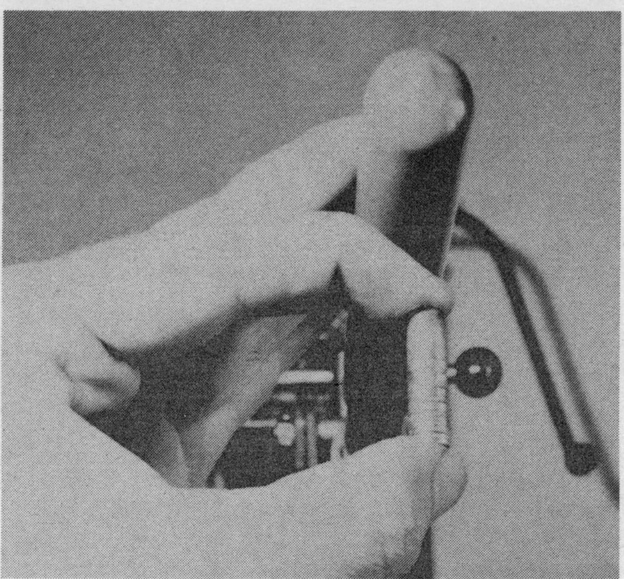

There are many different types of cast bullets for various applications. This bullet, the 180-grain .308-inch from an RCBS mold, is excellent in the 30-30 using full power loads. From the author's 24-inch and 26-inch barrel 30-30 rifles, this bullet hits over 2100 fps MV.

Here is a fully loaded 30-30 round using a 180-grain cast bullet. Some cast bullets are used for money-saving plinker loads; others for small game hunting. But this is a full-fledged deer load. Cast bullets do well on thin-skinned game of modest size when using bullets of 30-caliber or similar size.

The cast projectile in the center is a 625-grain Minie from a Shiloh mold. Compared with a 140-grain 7mm bullet on the left and a 500-grain 458 bullet on the right, the all-lead projectile seems primitive, but it does shoot accurately from an accurate barrel.

Casting Black Powder Projectiles

The modern swaged ball and the ready-made conicals available from various manufacturers have taken away much of the intensity of projectile-making for muzzleloaders, but there are many of us who still mold *some* of our black powder missiles because casting is enjoyable. As stated in the black powder chapter, if the projectile can be obtained for little or no cost, the smallbore squirrel rifle can be fired for less than the cost of a 22 rimfire round.

Also, "running ball," as the old-timers called casting, is a part of the muzzle-loading tradition, and the modern downwind shooter should know how to make up his own

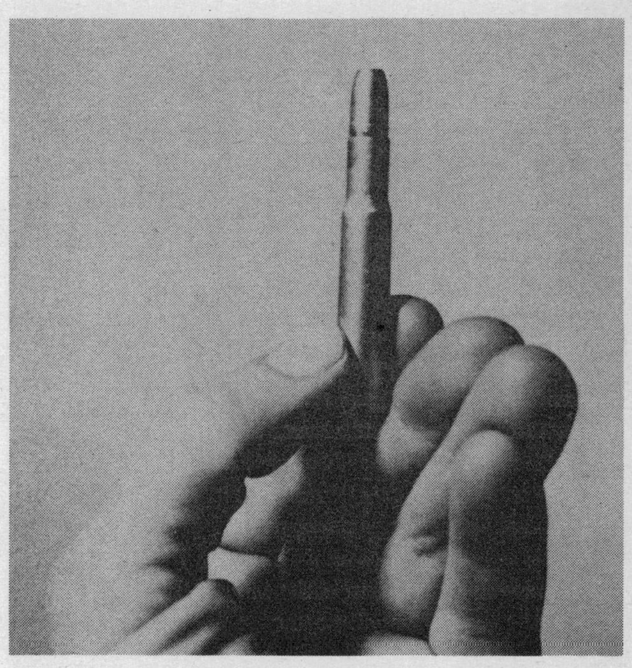

"ammo" and in top form at that. Also, as noted above, the all-lead missile works extremely well. Modern shooters may doubt the ability of a lead ball or conical because modern shooters are used to the sleek jacketed projectile of the day. The lead pill seems overly soft, about like shooting a wad of chewing gum, but in fact the results are quite extraordinary as long as there is sufficient mass to work with. So, for reasons of economy, the history of the sport, and for the fact that the lead ball or conical works so well, the black powder shooter should consider making at least some of the missiles he fires.

Anyone who considers the all-lead projectile a failure should remember that they were used on *all game* at one time, and with pretty good effect. No, the modern jacketed missile is better, but think of Samuel Baker, the Englishman who hunted places like Ceylon and who dropped many elephants, probably in the hundreds, with plain lead missiles. Baker, with witnesses looking on, shot completely through water buffalo in Ceylon using lead round balls of large caliber.

Step 1: Prepare the Metal

There is a difference here. In preparing metal for the modern projectile, the caster had to be very careful not to skim away some of the silvery metal "floating atop the lead." These seemingly impure parts of the lead are often tin or antimony and are essential to making the alloy needed for the higher velocities of the modern round. However, the black powder shooter does *not* concern himself with keeping these metals in his lead. He wants to get rid of them! So instead of skimming only the dross away, the black powder caster also tries to eliminate all metals in the pot except the lead.

Step 2: The Melting Process

In the stage of lead preparation, the furnace is initially set at 800 degrees Fahrenheit and then reduced to about 700 degrees for actual casting.

Step 3: Skimming

The difference here has been alluded to above. *Before* adding any fluxing agent, such as wax or a commercial product, it is a good idea to take spoon or ladle and thoroughly skim the surface of the melt to remove *anything* which is not lead; this includes tin, antimony and other agents which float to the surface due to their lighter atomic weight.

Step 4: Prepare the Mold

There is no essential difference here as compared with casting modern projectiles. The idea is to get the mold as clean as possible, with a touch of lube at the hinge pin. Again, a light coating of carbon on the interior of the bullet cavity may be advisable if fresh-cast projectiles are sticking to the blocks.

Step 5: Flux

In fact, for black powder work, this is the first fluxing session. The other step was simply a skimming task designed to remove the bulk of any non-lead metals which may have existed in the melt. This time, with a nice big gob of fluxing agent, such as wax, the lead is stirred and stirred. Of course, the same idea exists as before, an attempt to promote dross to rise to the surface. Skim away that dross, making the remaining molten lead as pure as possible.

Step 6: Casting the Projectile

The mold is again warmed up by allowing the furnace itself to do the heating, at least in the case of the iron mold. The corner of an aluminum mold may, as mentioned earlier, be dipped in the molten metal to heat it up. Then casting proceeds as before. The furnace should be set at about 700 degrees. I have found that as projectiles grow in caliber, which some black powder missiles tend to do (a 625-grain 58-caliber missile for example), it may be best to keep the lead hotter than it was with smaller projectiles.

Step 7: Check your Bullets

In checking the black powder missile, the first step is to follow the same procedures as before, insuring that the missiles are clean and shiny and neither wrinkled nor frosted. Occlusions can be checked for with the scale, the lighter-than-normal slugs being tossed back in the pot. But there is another check here. With our modern missiles we wanted to insure that they were uniform. This is obviously important here, too. But we may also want to check for lead purity with the all-lead round ball or conical.

First, check for the theoretical perfect weight of the lead ball. This is simple to do with a calculator and a micrometer. First, using the micrometer, obtain the actual dimensions of the sphere. As an example, let's use a .535-inch round ball. With this information, .535, it is simple to determine what the ball should weigh *in pure lead*.

Here is the simple formula to use: $D^3 \times .5236 \times 2{,}873.5$. It is the diameter of the round ball cubed, times a constant for the volume of a sphere, times the weight of one cubic inch of *pure* lead. The .535-inch round ball would work out in this way:

$.535^3 = .1531303$
$.1531303 \times .5236 = .080179$
$.080179 \times 2{,}873.5 = 230.39436$

The latter figure is the weight of a .535-inch led ball in *pure* lead. Rounded off we have 230 grains. Now it is a simple matter to take some sample weights of the actual .535-inch round ball which have been cast. They should weigh 230 grains. If they average out much lighter, this shows impurities in the lead or voids in the casting.

With a conical, one good way of establishing lead purity is to make some samples out of known pure lead, or as

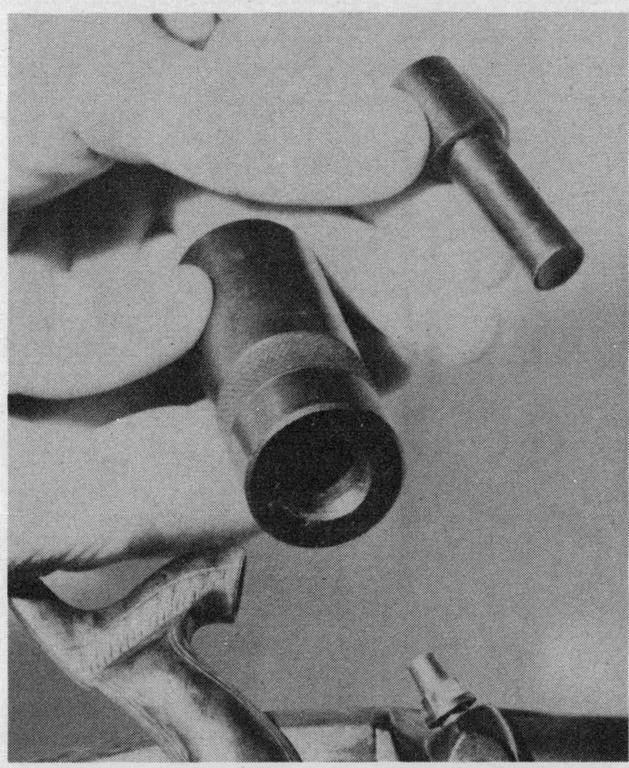

This is a swaging unit for the Whitworth Navy Arms rifle. Navy Arms Company supplies a kit with the Whitworth target rifle, and the sizer is included. The cast bullet is inserted into the sizer body and driven through with the metal rod shown here.

close to pure lead as possible. To do this obtain some of the pure Lawrence brand bar lead for this operation and cast your samples from a clean pot or furnace. That sample conical will serve as a model for further conicals out of the same mold. Why not simply use the weight figure provided with the mold? Because these are not always calculated in pure lead. In one instance, a mold marked "500 grains" produced pure lead missiles which weighed 525 grains average. In another instance a mold marked "600 grains" made Minies which actually averaged at 624 grains. Yet another mold marked "570 grains" produced a product of 600 grains weight.

Some shooters may wish to size conicals for black powder guns. For target work, this is all right, and there are some sizers available from time to time, though certainly not on a large scale basis. I do not size my own black powder conicals. I trust obturation in the bore to "true up" the conical. Of course, sizing a Minie would be somewhat pointless, since the Minie is intentionally made to be about a caliber "undersize." The Maxi could be sized, but the idea of the Maxi is to have a driving band which will engrave upon seating the projectile downbore with the loading rod. All in all, I would not concern myself about sizing any of the black powder missiles, with one possible exception.

The "exception" would be some of the frontloaders firing projectiles essentially identical to bullets used in modern guns. A good example of this is the Whitworth rifle. I tested a Whitworth from the Navy Arms Company, and I

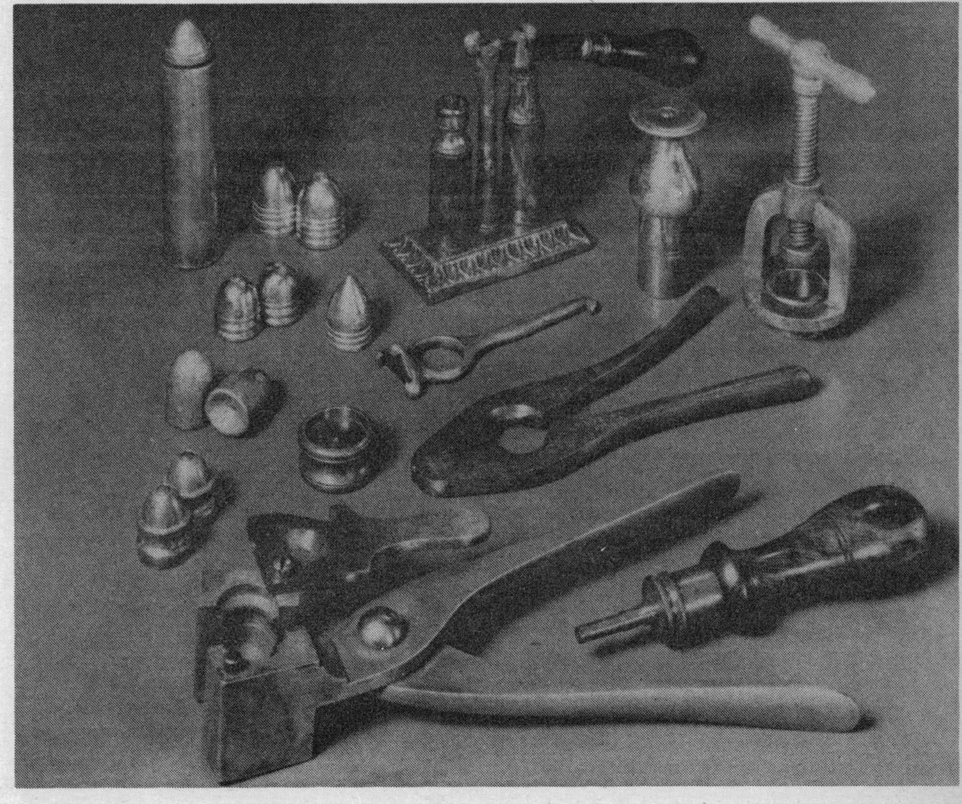

Oftentimes, and with a little perseverance, the modern handloader can come across appropriate loading tools for long out-of-print calibers. In this instance you're looking at reloading and casting gear designed for the loading of a Paradox-bored double rifle. Sources for out-of-print reloading gear include Huntington Die Specialties in Oroville, California, and Creekside Gun Shop in Holcomb, New York.

Today, many shooters seek out molds, sizers and other casting gear to accommodate their need for ammo for older calibers. Outfits like RCBS, Lee, SAECO, NEI and Lyman stand ready to meet the needs of the modern bullet caster.

sized the bullet after it was cast. Furthermore, this particular bullet features grease grooves designed to be filled just prior to loading. With the standard Minie or Maxi, the lubing can take place just before loading, and often amounts to no more than applying some grease or lube of some type to the Maxi or Minie just prior to running it downbore.

Extra Hard Cast Bullets

In recent times, there has been considerable interest in what is called a Hard Cast Bullet, but which is more accurately the Extra Hard Cast bullet. There is nothing wrong with a hard cast bullet. It minimizes leading and is very accurate. Therefore, our argument is certainly not with the bullets referred to above as normal alloys, such as No. 2. The term Extra Hard Cast bullet refers to casting with lead which is made into an alloy of extreme hardness, considering the Brinell Hardness Number of pure lead. Refer to the Lyman table in this chapter for these hardnesses. The "BHN" number on the far right of the table means Brinell Hardness Number. Note that pure lead is a 5. Lyman No. 2 Alloy is a 15; that is pretty hard lead in shooting terms. Remember, some bullet bore upset is sought after for proper function of the projectile, and at low velocity, a super hard bullet may not upset into the grooves of the rifling. Linotype, incidentally, has a Brinell Hardness Number of 22 and Monotype, which is 9 percent tin and 14 percent antimony, has a BHN of 28.

First problem to note with extra hard bullets is the possibility that they will fail to upset in the bore. A second problem may be noted at the range, especially an indoor range with a backstop of metal. The extra hard bullet may tend to fragment and splatter around the place. Hard bullets may not be, and probably will not be any more accurate than softer ones. As for leading, though a harder bullet may save some of that problem, the way to take care of leading is to clean the bore, not turn to Extra Hard Cast bullets to prevent the problem.

Safety

Casting lead projectiles is not a dangerous hobby, but it can be practiced in a dangerous fashion. First, in my book, is to look at the casting process as a serious business, because, of course, molten lead is being used here. Severe burns are quite possible, but need not ever occur. I have been casting bullets for many years and have never had one burn of any type and I can name several other bullet casters who can say the same thing. Here are some safety points:

1. Location

Cast bullets in a proper place. If the kitchen stove is the only area available for casting bullets, then insure that the area is clear of any clutter. Use a metal sheet to work on, possibly covering part of the stove with it or at least the counter. Insure against burning the counter. *Stay away from any water source*.

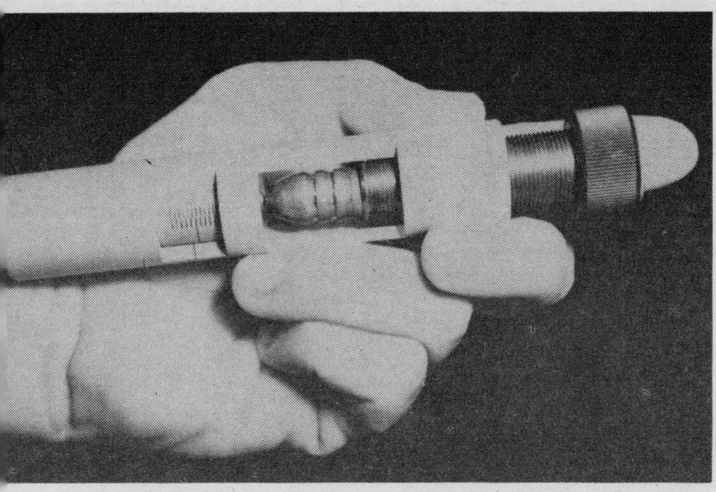

This tool from the SAECO Company is used to test the hardness of lead projectiles. A bullet hardness tester of this type is very useful for the shooter who wants to know how hard his alloy is. Alloy which is much beyond Alloy No. 2 in hardness can often give problems to shooters.

2. Fumes

Insure that there is proper (sufficient) ventilation. Lead gives off fumes at about 900 degrees Fahrenheit and the fumes *are poisonous*. Even though the bullet caster may never set his furnace beyond 800 degrees, still the area must allow for good fresh air at all times. If an exhaust fan is handy, use it.

3. Water

Casting outdoors or anywhere where water may land in the melting pot or furnace is asking for big trouble. Water landing in hot lead can cause an eruption and you could be severely burned.

4. No Food, No Drink

Concentrate on the task at hand. Eating a sandwich between casting or worse, during casting, can mean trouble, and drinks can spill into the molten lead. Even smoking can indirectly cause a problelm. When casting projectiles, *cast projectiles*. Save other things for later. Lastly, don't drink any alcoholic beverage before or during the casting process.

5. Protective Clothing

Wear leather shoes or boots preferably. A caster's glove and safety glasses are also advised. A pair of yellow or clear-lens shooting glasses will serve here. Don't forget the long-sleeved shirt.

6. Time

Insure that there is time to cast bullets. If there is not, save the task for later. Rushing the job can cause problems, especialy in terms of safety. Casting is a relaxing hobby as well as a useful by-product of shooting. The caster should enjoy himself. Take your time.

7. No Kids

Children should be kept away from the casting operation until they are old enough to be responsible for their motions and actions around the casting equipment. In one instance, a child was playing in the room where an adult was casting bullets, and the child tossed a ball which landed smack in the molten lead. Nobody was hurt, but somebody could have been.

8. No Gun Powder or Flammables

Never do your casting in a loading room where gun powder is present. Keep any heat source away from powder or anything which will explode. If you must cast in your loading room, remove all primers and powder.

The art of casting excellent projectiles for both modern and old fashioned arms is an art well worth learning and passing on to others. It can become a very involved practice, and there are casters who have experimented (safely) with many different bullet styles and loads and who have provided improvements for all of us. A cast bullet can bring even more versatility to the hobby of reloading, too, for a cast load can be used for practice and small game hunting, even for big game hunting in some instances.

The complete shooter should look into a bullet casting outfit. He should also consult manuals on the subject of casting. Books such as the *RCBS Cast Bullet Manual* will help the caster become an expert in this enjoyable sideline to shooting. With accuracy of the first order possible from a cast bullet, and a lot of potential economy as well, coupled with increased versatility for a firearm, bullet casting makes a lot of sense.

Good Casting!

Chapter 21

The Big Game Bullet

THE BULLET can make all of the difference in big game hunting. A good bullet can cleanly harvest game, while a bullet ill-designed or constructed can leave the shooter with the worst problem he can have, wounded game. The good news is that the big game bullet has advanced so far in the past few decades that it is far easier to find a superior missile than it is an inferior missile. This chapter could be eliminated because of this fact, with one exception. While the big game bullet has improved steadily, to a point of near perfection, the current choices of bullets have also increased vastly. The complete shooter seeking a bullet to handle a specific big game hunting task has a big selection to choose from, and he has to know the inside story on projectiles if he's to do a good job picking the best bullet for the task at hand.

The jacketed bullet came along because velocities increased with the advent of smokeless powder. There was no hue and outcry concerning lead bullets. I have read many documented hunting chronicles from the 19th century, and the lead projectile did a fine job. The way to make it perform on big game was to make the lead bullet large. We consider some of the old-time rounds as "mundane" in the power department because of a velocity which matches the speed of the tortoise. But even these slowboats had some bullet mass to work with. I think of the 44-40 Winchester as a very lightweight performer, even on deer, but the fact remains that a 44-40 will cleanly harvest deer-sized game at close range. A friend uses one. He has never lost a deer. I don't think he ever will. His 44-40 fires a lead bullet of 215 grains weight at a muzzle velocity of 2000 fps. Many of the old-timers liked rounds such as the 45-90 or even the 50-110 Winchester. Bullet weight was the key to success because velocity was not yet the big issue. It could not be. Black powder would not allow it.

The shooter soon learned that if he wanted to drive lead bullets at 2500 fps MV, he'd better start protecting that lead. The bulletmakers came out with an answer. It was our old friend German silver, some sources say, which was first used as bullet jacket material. Other sources suggest that the better term is "cupro-nickel," and I think I would buy that. German silver is a combination of copper, nickel and zinc. Maybe the first jackets contained zinc. Maybe not. It doesn't matter, but the complete shooter should recognize the fact that the first metal jackets attached to lead cores were the forerunners of the great bullets of today.

One problem—the old-time jackets left part of themselves in the bores of the rifles, and this meant a cleaning task for the shooter. There were various solvents used to get the "wash" out of the bore, and I suspect plenty of elbow grease tossed in for good measure, with bristle brushes scrubbing the bores. The base of the bullet was not metal-covered in the beginning. A few shooters (and writers) felt that a bullet going through a bore at such tremendous velocity would get the bullet so hot that the lead would melt, and you would have, in effect, a "bottle of molten lead" for a bullet. This is not quite right. Today, we have fine bullets with the lead exposed at the base and the lead stays right where it is, even at well over 3000 fps MV. The reason is time. The bullet is in the bore for too short a time to melt its core of lead.

So the old jackets worked. They protected the lead core to allow for high velocity. The military jacketed bullets were of the "full patch" or full metal jacket variety, with no lead exposed at the nose.

As time passed, it was the soft point bullet which took hold. The soft point was simply a jacketed bullet with some of the lead core exposed at the nose. The idea was this—the soft exposed lead, and thin jacket, would smash back upon impact and hopefully continue back to form what we know now as the "mushroom" shape. Soft points caught on because full metal jacketed bullets with sharp points provided inconsistent performance on game. One time they might zip through a game animal making a neat round hole, while the next time these bullets would (presumably) tip, tumble and go end-over-end and wind up ripping a hole as bad or worse than a hollow point would.

In Africa, a companion decided to collect a few small species for preserving purposes. He chose a 223 Remington using a 55-grain full metal jacketed bullet. I suggested to him that the bullet might tear a gaping hole in these small and thin-skinned creatures, but he said a full patch bullet would make a neat small hole. He brought back a couple small animals which looked as if they had been hit on the freeway. Those full metal jacketed bullets had blown gaping holes in their hides. As a result of this sort of

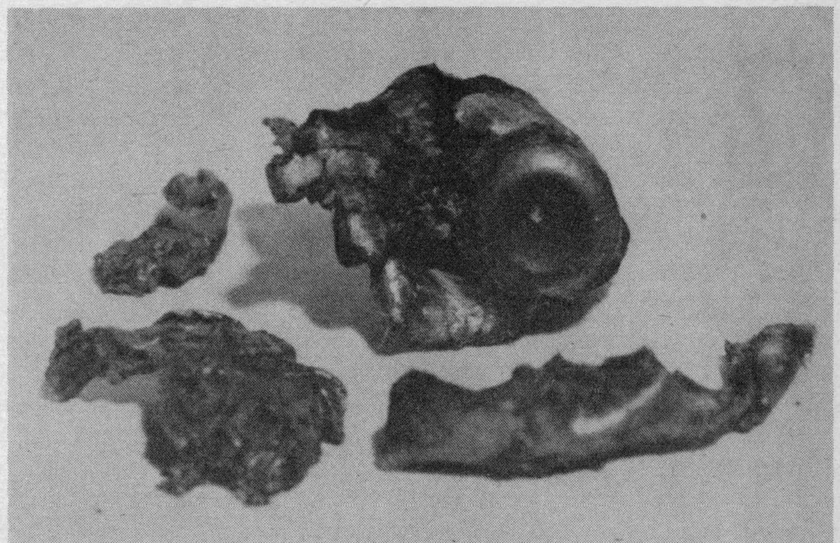

This is a 156-grain Norma bullet after extraction from a greater kudu bull. The bullet struck in the shoulder, not behind the shoulder, and the animal fell instantly to the single shot. Although there was some bullet breakup, the projectile did penetrate well in this case. The author prefers bullets which do not break up and fragment, thinking them best for big game hunting.

Here are four bullets of very different construction. Upper left is a soft-point jacketed spitzer for long-range rifle shooting. On the upper right is another rifle bullet, this one a full metal jacket, used for deep penetration and breaking of bone in large and dangerous game, and in smaller calibers for salvation of pelts or meat. Lower left is a full metal jacket bullet for the pistol, this one a 45-caliber and on the far right is a lead projectile for the handgun, this one used for target work. (Photo Courtesy of Remington)

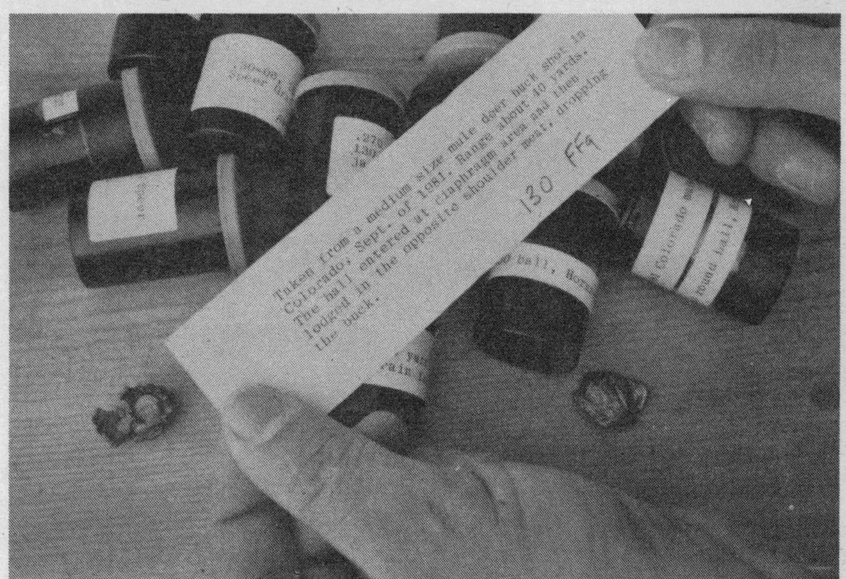

Retaining bullets taken from game is one way of keeping a record of field experiences with various bullets. The shooter must include a note detailing the harvest so that he will always maintain the correct information concerning a specific bullet. The author shows here a small part of his own collection, which he keeps in empty plastic 35mm film containers.

inconsistent performance, bulletmakers wanted to produce a hunting projectile possessing much more reliability. Going forth with this idea in mind, those bulletmakers headed toward the soft-point bullet. As a result, today's soft point bullet is available in many different designs.

We were then, and are now, asking a tremendous number of things for one bullet to do. The bullet must first hang together so that it can reach the target. And it must hold together well enough to be stable and accurate. But at the same time, the bullet must not be so hard that it merely punches a hole through the game. It *must* expand. Meanwhile, it should also *penetrate*. It would do little good if the bullet expanded on the hide of the game. Not only must the bullet expand, but it must expand in a certain way. If the bullet blows up a bunch of meat, hunters become angry, and I do not blame them. But if the animal does not drop in its tracks or almost in its tracks, hunters also become angry.

Colonel Townsend Whelen summed it up nicely in his 1940 book, *The Hunting Rifle*. My edition, from Wolfe Publishing of Prescott, Arizona, has this well-known statement on page 236, the beginning of Chapter 10 on "Killing Power." The Colonel said, "The killing power of a bullet in flight depends entirely upon the average size of the wound channel it makes in the animal, and upon nothing else. The size of the wound in turn depends upon the size, weight, construction, and shape of the bullet, and the velocity with which it strikes, and upon no other details."

What the first part boils down to is that tissue has to be disrupted in order for a clean harvest. It's interesting that when the 270 Winchester came out, hunters were delighted with the fact that deer dropped as if struck by lightning. They were delighted until they hit a deer through the hams, and then they were no longer blissful—they were hot under the collar! And they complained! The factories listened and brought out a 150-grain bullet that hummed along at maybe 2800 fps MV. You guessed it. The hunters got madder than hornets because the 270 was no longer dropping deer in their tracks.

The compromise which has ensued has been a very interesting one, and the complete shooter should be well briefed on this information in order to deal with hunting bullets. In fact, it takes know-how to select the right bullet for the big game hunting situation. After all, not only must a bullet do all of the things named above, but it must also do them at varying ranges. It is supposed to hold together at close range, where velocity is high, and yet it is expected to expand at long range, when velocity has dropped off.

Bullet Factors

Colonel Whelen's concise statement encompasses many important aspects of bullet performance. Breaking these down in a paraphrased sort of way, we have:

1. The caliber of the projectile
2. The weight of the bullet
3. Construction of the bullet
4. Shape of the bullet
5. Velocity of the missile
6. Sectional density of the bullet (my addition)

Caliber

While we may not think about it a lot, the fact is, an expanding bullet actually increases its caliber somewhere in the wound channel, depending upon how fast it expands. Because a bullet starts out at 30-caliber does not mean it will end up at 30-caliber after bullet upset. This bullet upset is not the same as the upset spoken of in internal ballistics, where the projectile changes shape in the bore due to the forces of inertia at work and the gases from the powder charge. This upset is the shape change of the bullet upon striking the target, and it does represent *expended energy*. Changing the shape of the missile takes energy, so some of the bullet's energy is used in this process.

If a bullet starts out as a large caliber, obviously, the wound channel Colonel Whelen spoke of will have a correspondingly large entrance hole. The size of the exit hole depends upon factors such as the striking energy of the bullet, bullet construction, and so forth, as well as caliber. A hard bullet of large caliber may leave a smaller exit wound than a smaller bullet which is more fragile in its construction. While caliber is important to this wound channel, we must also recognize that bullets in and of themselves do not always make exit holes.

In front of, and surrounding the bullet is a shock wave set up by the projectile as it strikes the target—it's responsible for part of the wound channel. If this were not so, then it would be impossible to have exit holes larger than the caliber of the bullet that hit the target. Yet, this factor is prevalent. I have seen exit holes of teacup size from a 25- to 30-caliber bullet. No 25- to 30-caliber bullet could be smashed out to that diameter. It was not the bullet, then, which made the hole. It was the *force* created by the bullet.

One season I was hunting with my son Bill. Bill and I were after antelope. My tag had been filled, so it was Bill's hunt. We found some antelope, including a mature buck we wanted to harvest. I remained behind and let Bill stalk the buck, using my 7mm Frank Wells rifle. I was watching the buck through a Bushnell 20x spotting scope when Bill made his shot.

Actually before I heard the shot I saw a strange sight. The offside of the buck, the side away from the shooter, expanded out to what seemed to be a couple feet. I was probably overly impressed and it may have been only ½-foot to a foot, but it was a remarkable occurrence. My surmise is that I was witness to the shock wave ahead of the bullet forcing that hide outward. The buck dropped instantly, and the entrance and exit hole were as normal as ever, with about a 2-inch diameter for the exit. Caliber does mean something when it comes to killing power, and it means a great deal if the velocity is too low to effect a great shock wave, such as it is with muzzleloaders. Using the latter for hunting, the big bore is better than the small bore for large game because of projectile diameter as well as projectile mass.

Weight

We can look at this factor as momentum (velocity times mass) if we wish. But the bullet does function on the basis of its mass as well as other factors mentioned here. A larger bullet is used for big dangerous game because the weight factor allows for greater penetration and an ability to break bones. Another factor attributed to weight is retention of energy. The heavy bullet is better at this than the lighter one. So a bullet's weight is very important in connection with performance.

Construction

Now comes the fun. There are so many different types of jacketed big game bullets that the best we can do here is hit the major styles. This is a very important consideration, too, for bullet construction can make all the difference in bullet performance on big game. Furthermore, the construction of the bullet will dictate how that bullet changes shape when it upsets in flesh.

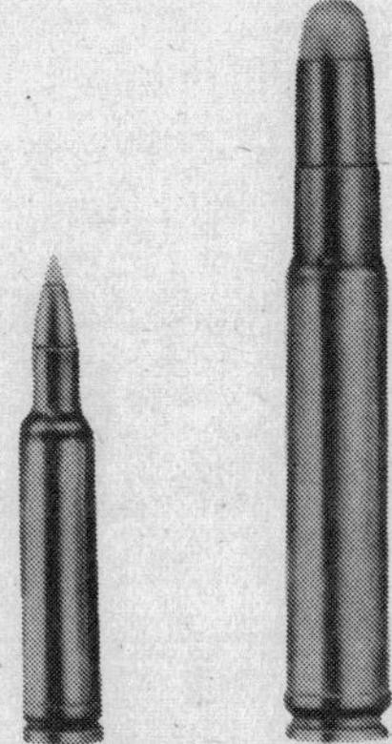

Bullet construction must coincide with the muzzle velocity of the round as well as many other factors. The Weatherby line of cartridges uses bullets of varying hardness dependent upon MV, and also dependent upon function. The 224 Weatherby (left) would use a bullet of rapid expansion for varmints, but the 460 Weatherby bullet (right) would be geared for maximum penetration.

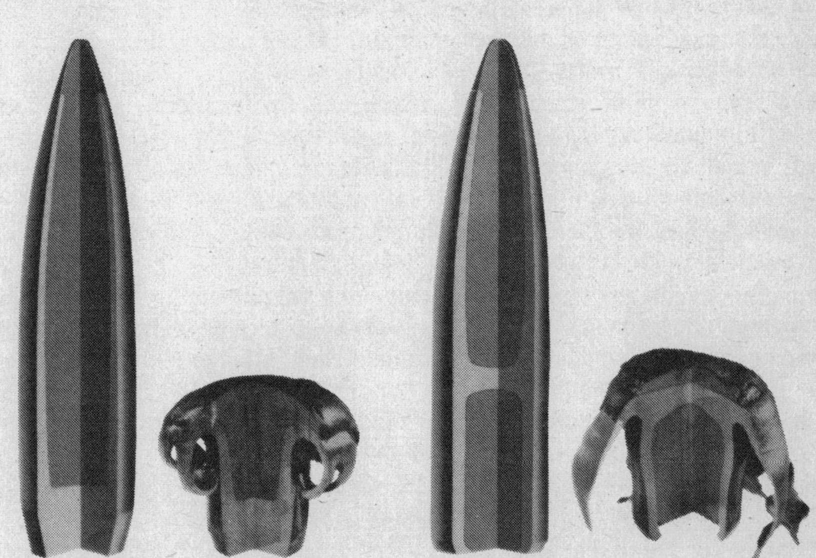

Nosler has two prominent bullet designs, the Solid Base, on the left, and the Partition. The Solid Base works on the principle of retaining the core through a cup effect at the base of the missile, while the Partition uses a division of metal to keep core and jacket together.

I know what I want in a big game bullet. And I know what I do not want. I want *penetration,* and that means the bullet has to hold together. The other side of the street calls for the bullet to ''blow up'' within the game animal. After all, why use the energy of the bullet on the hillside behind the animal? The theory is fine. It is true that a bullet which holds together and exits the game is going to use up energy on the landscape, but I want just that. I am willing to forego a part of that bullet's energy in order to achieve an exit hole.

In the first place, the exit hole means that in the unlikely event of the animal being wounded instead of dropped on the spot, there will be a greater chance for body fluids to leave through the hide if there are both entrance and exit holes. Secondly, the exit hole means a complete wound channel. Remember that Colonel Whelen suggested that all a bullet can really do is create a wound channel. If the bullet goes half-way into the animal and stops there, the wound channel is less than it could be.

Of course, if the strike has been in the chest/lung area, then it may not matter if the bullet comes apart on the inside of the animal. But I do want the bullet to remain wedded for life, the jacket to the core. I want no stripped jackets, no shrapnel to speak of, and no breakup of the bullet. The classic mushroom shape is, to me, still the best for big game harvesting.

Very generally speaking, we can look at bullet construction in a couple of ways. Either a bullet is so constructed as to hold together upon impact and even well after impact in the creation of the wound channel, or it is not so constructed. There are many different methods of keeping the jacket and core together, of course, including the bonding process. A bullet can actually be soldered together, core to jacket. Also, a bullet can be constructed in such a manner that the lead core is poured into the jacket hot, so that it has to cool and ''stick'' to the jacket. Cannelures can help hold jacket and lead together, too. A bullet can also be constructed so that its base is filled with a hard alloy lead while the upper portion uses a soft lead, the lower section of the bullet resisting expansion.

Of course, there is also the partition-type bullet made famous by Nosler. In a way, it does the same task as stated above with the last bullet style mentioned, but it does so via a sturdy metal partition that separates the front half of the bullet from the rear half of the bullet. The front part, generally considered about half of the length of the bullet, can easily ''peel back'' now, but the back half is going to remain intact, period. Also, there are jacket thickness variations. A thick jacket is obviously less fragile than a thin one, the best bet being a combination of thick and thin—thin up front for expansion, thick at the base to offer hold-together power. There are solid-base bullets which take this theory a step further, the base of the projectile being solid jacket. There are also construction differences which are really material differences. Bullets with pure copper jackets and pure soft lead cores also tend to hang together, so it is the materials used in this case which make the difference.

Jacket design can make a difference, too. The jacket can be shaped so that it bulges inwardly at about the middle of

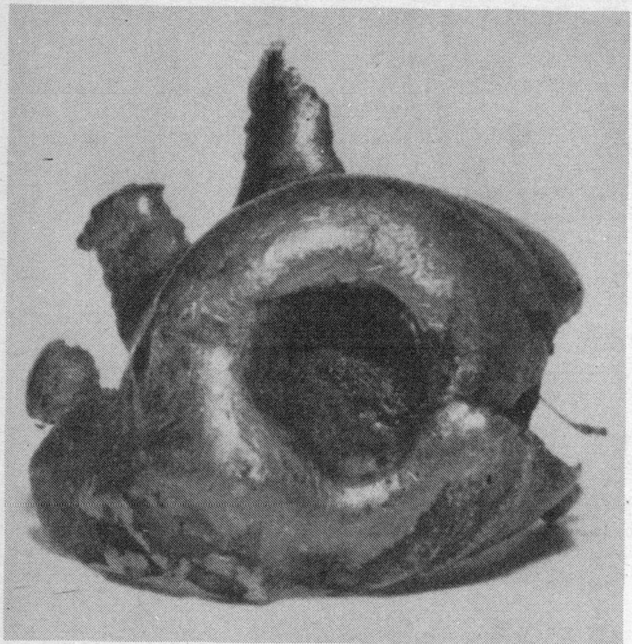

This is a 120-grain bullet from a 25-06, recovered from the carcass of a coyote taken at about 25 yards. The entire core is missing from the bullet. Interestingly, it is a bullet design which usually retains its core, but the high velocity strike at close range probably offered too much force upon the bullet. A coyote is a very thin-skinned and small animal in reality and the bullet should have held together in this instance, even at near muzzle velocity.

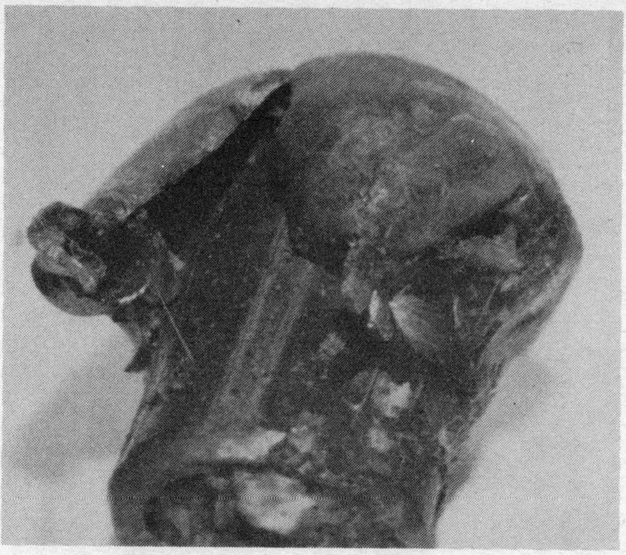

This is a 140-grain Nosler bullet extracted from a greater kudu bull taken at about 75 yards. The bullet struck in the rear of the shoulder and dropped the animal instantly with the one shot. The Nosler Partition bullet is designed so that the rear portion simply cannot break up.

This bullet is a 300-grain "solid" or full metal jacket made by hand by the RWS factory. It was used on a Cape buffalo from 25 yards distance. The bullet made a frontal chest hit and ended up under the backbone after traveling about 4 feet through the bulk of the buffalo bull.

the bullet. If this occurs, then there is likely to be a situation of the lower half of the bullet holding together, with less chance of the core stripping out and away from the jacket. Jackets can also be tapered in such a way as to promote retention of the lead core of the bullet, too.

Remember, one of our criteria for bullet performance was *weight*. The bullet which stays together keeps more of its weight working to create a wound channel. This is not, to be sure, a perfect situation at all times. Sure, if a bullet goes to pieces after totally eliminating the contents of the chest cavity of a big game animal, let it go to pieces. The problem is that this same bullet may, next time, strike a shoulder, and then its fragile traits will not be so appreciated.

There is nothing new about elaborate designs in bullets. Construction variations have gone on for a very long time. I like to cite the example of the DWM "Strong Jacket" bullet. This bullet can be found in catalogs prior to 1932. The jacket of that bullet was strong. It was thick at the base and thin at the nose. The bullet was designed to upset at the nose, but not shed its jacket. It also had, at least in some versions, a thin cap over the lead nose so that the bullet was not so easily deformed, and the cap also aided penetration, I would think. In fact, the lead nose was hollow-pointed beneath that cap for sure expansion, but *not* disruption.

I will include the hollow point here, under construction, for it really isn't a shape. The hollow point bullet has been with us and used successfully for a very long time. It can be a useful style of bullet construction, especially when it comes to varmints, but I am not overly fond of it for most big game hunting. In the high-speed numbers, and I will include the 308 Winchester and up in this class, the hollow point can tend to come apart all too fast and too much for my liking. I prefer a controlled expansion design instead, rather than the almost instantaneous disruption a hollow point provides in the big game field. In a moment, however, when discussing actual bullets by name, I will bring up a particular hollow point bullet which I do like very much.

For a long time, I was shaky in my conviction that the best bullet was one which would hang together. I had, to be sure, dropped big game cleanly with bullets that did not remain intact. I had a chance to see a softer bullet in use in Africa on about 15 head of big game, however, and my dislike for bullets which come apart was cemented. If one or two of these harvests had been poor, I would not place any faith in the situation, but the soft bullet from a 30-caliber magnum proved lousy, without exception, on everything it hit. Expansion was there, all right, but penetration was just too little. I collected bullets from about 50 head of game in Africa and those soft bullets usually amounted to nothing but bits and pieces of core and jacket. In contrast, the bullets which stayed together did far better work on game ranging from small to large antelope. Of course, solids were used on the really big boys and that's another story.

The solid is a full metal jacketed bullet. I saw a few so-called solids literally blow up on big game of the Cape buffalo type. The idea of using the solid is not to create a big wound channel so much, but rather to break a dangerous animal down by crunching bones and through *penetration*. One solid from a big game rifle penetrated only a few *inches* of a Cape buffalo. That is not what a solid is supposed to do. Our good old American Hornady solid, incidentally, remained totally intact and penetrated as it should have.

All in all, the soft-point bullet of a controlled expansion design is my choice for American hunting. It works well enough for chest hits on big game, but if the chest is not the target, at least good penetration can be counted on. Shoulder shots do, of course, ruin some meat. But on an animal such as a bull elk, the shoulder shot can often be far more effective than a chest strike. Lung tissue can close up to some degree and unless plenty of disruption has been the case, a big animal hit by a modest bullet in the lung area may go a distance before dropping. On game smaller than elk, moose and big bears, it's preferred, mainly because the tissue which is lost is not edible. However, on a big tough animal, a strong bullet through the shoulder area where the spine is also a possible target is highly effective.

Shape

Bullet shape is also important to performance. The round nose truly does offer a good wound channel. The flat point seems to smack a big game animal very hard, indicating, perhaps, a transfer of energy which is all but instantaneous. If range is not a big consideration, I would just as soon have a round nose or flat point bullet. And, of course, these are the only types allowed in the tubular magazine, since a pointed bullet might set off the primer of the round in front of it.

The spitzer or spire point, or any other pointed shape, is much better at bucking the atmosphere than a round nose or flat point. These bullets are far and away the most popular today because they shoot considerably flatter than the blunter varieties. For example, if a 180-grain round nose 30-caliber bullet is fired at 3100 fps MV out of a magnum cartridge, and if sighted to strike about 4.5 inches high at 100 yards, it will hit about 5.5 inches high at 200 yards, dead on at 300 yards and 14.5 inches low at 400 yards. Now, with the same weight bullet, 180 grains, at the same muzzle velocity, 3100 fps, but with a sharp profile, one may sight in about 3.5 inches high at 100 yards, landing about 4.5 inches high at 200 yards, on at 300 and about 10 inches low at 400 yards.

So shape does matter. In fact, the differences above might be greater but for an important factor. The sharp-nosed bullet does not stay sharp-nosed on its way to the target. As a bullet exits the muzzle, the nose of the bullet on contact with the atmosphere is smashed back to a degree, blunting it somewhat. The shape of the spitzer or spire point still gives it quite an edge over long range when compared with a round nose or flat nose bullet, but it does not arrive downrange with its pretty, pointed profile intact.

In order to stave off this problem, bullets with very hard noses have been designed. There are a few ways of doing this. One way is to forget the exposed lead tip, bring the jacket all the way out to the nose, and then put some slits in the jacket so it can peel back and allow expansion. Another way is to make a wedge and stick it in the nose of the bullet. Remington's Bronze Point is just this, a metal wedge of sharply pointed design. It will not deform in the atmosphere and it will shoot flatter, all other things being equal, than the usual soft point with exposed lead. Another bullet of similar design is the Nosler Ballistictip. It, too, has a wedge-type point, very sharp, and without any tendency toward deformation. If a shooter wants the flattest possible trajectory, these last two bullet types will offer it, though we are talking only inches of difference. The shooter must make up his own mind about these bullet styles. They do not act as a controlled expansion bullet in all cases.

Velocity

Obviously, the striking velocity is very important to bullet performance. One of the big problems in bullet design

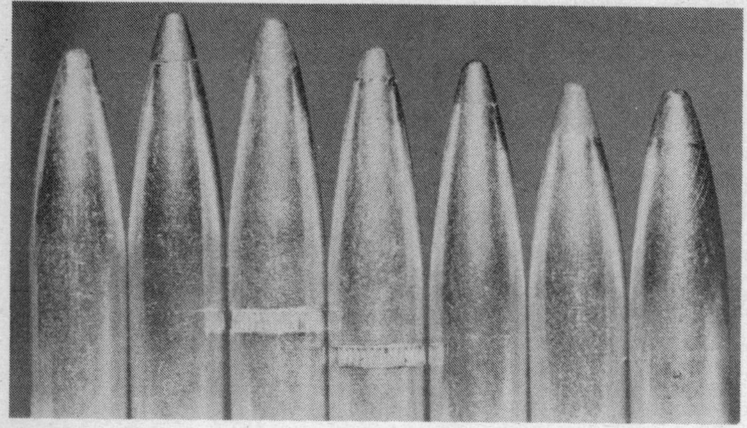

An excellent example of the various bullets offered in a given caliber is seen in the 6.5, or .264-inch diameter. These are actually only a few of the different bullets a handloader can select for his .264-caliber (6.5mm) cartridge. From left to right the 140-grain Speer, the 140-grain Nosler Partition, the 140-grain Hornady Interlock, the 129-grain Hornady Interlock, the 120-grain Nosler Solid Base, the 120-grain Sierra Spitzer bullet, and finally the Speer .263-inch 120-grain bullet.

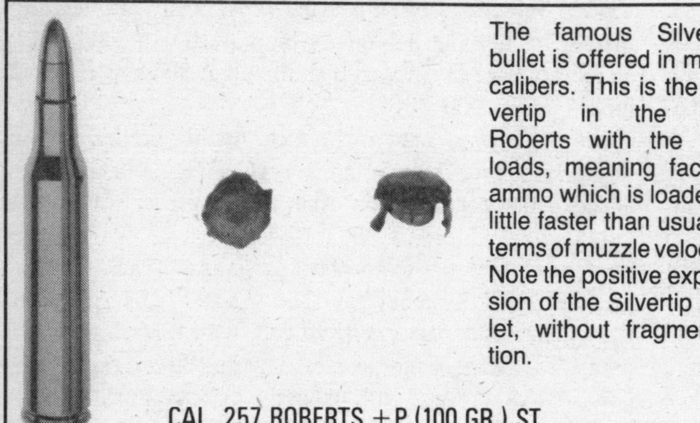

The famous Silvertip bullet is offered in many calibers. This is the Silvertip in the 257 Roberts with the +P loads, meaning factory ammo which is loaded a little faster than usual in terms of muzzle velocity. Note the positive expansion of the Silvertip bullet, without fragmentation.

CAL. 307 WIN. (150 GR.) PP

CAL. 307 WIN. (180 GR.) PP

The Power Point bullet is extremely useful in calibers such as the 307 Winchester, chambered in the Model 94 Winchester carbine. Here we see the flat point design in both 150- and 180-grain weights in recovered form. Good expansion with intact core/jacket is the byword for the Power Point.

over the years has been a quesiton of controlling the expansion of a bullet at various velocities. If the velocity remained the same from muzzle to game, the problem would be nil, but a big game bullet may start out at 3000 fps and strike the target at 2000 fps. A means of control has been to insure expansion through a fragile nose and, at the same time, offer a base or shank section which will hold together for penetration.

Sectional Density

Given a 120-grain 6.5mm bullet and a 140-gain 6.5mm bullet, the latter should offer more penetration, velocity for velocity, than the former. While this is the case, given bullets of the exact same design and construction, it does not mean that bullets of low sectional density fail in penetration. I have driven a .530-inch 224-grain round ball of pure lead totally through a bull elk at about 70 paces. And the sectional density of a pure lead round ball is downright pitiful.

A Few Famous Bullets

I have used many different types of bullets throughout my hunting life, and it is appropriate to mention a few of them here, as well as a couple bullets I have not had personal hunting experience with, but have used in test media. It is not my aim to condemn nor praise any particular bullet, because a bullet I do not think well of may be used with great authority by another shooter, and a bullet I admire could be less than desirable for some other shooter. But a brief list of a few famous bullets gives the reader an overview he can agree with, disagree with, or use for his own benefit.

The Silvertip

The Winchester Silvertip has been a fine bullet for many years. The entire idea of the Silvertip design is controlled expansion. The tip is lead, all right, but it is covered with a thin jacket. The entire construction changes according to the intended use of the bullet, and a Silvertip for a 30-30 is less rigid than one used in a 30-06.

I have used the Silvertip bullet on big game. Hunting the little white-tailed deer of Arizona, I found the 170-grain Silvertip to be slightly too strong for expansion on a ribcage shot. But the bullet from the same 30-30 was fine on the much larger mule deer. If I were to use the 30-30 on small deer, I might elect for a softer-nosed bullet. But the Silvertip holds together and it's a good penetrator.

The Power Point

Winchester's Power Point bullet is a soft-point of high reliability. It is probably a better choice than the Silvertip in the less speedy rounds on smaller, thin-skinned game. Jackets and cores of the Power Point tend to hold together well. It is a fine big game choice. While slits in the jacket, at the nose, tend to aid early expansion, Power Points do not fly apart.

The Bronze Point

When I was a young man, I had a chance to hunt in Mexico. For a few dollars, a license was procured and it was common to be allowed a couple deer and six *javelina* (peccaries). A hunter could get quite a bit of experience, too, because the license, issued for the state of Sonora, was also good in any other contiguous state. One season, I decided to try a different bullet in my 270 Winchester. It was the Bronze Point.

I finally had my chance. Two deer were moving out of a canyon and I got them both. The destruction made me blink. There was an exit hole in one you could toss a cherry pie through and I felt lucky that I hit the other one a little too far back. At least, not much meat was gone, and I did not have to dress the deer very much for the bullet had done most of the work for me.

This is not a total condemnation of a fine bullet. The Bronze Point has a very flat trajectory, and if the shooter will keep his hits confined to the ribcage, the Bronze Point will certainly perform in a most dazzling way. In fact, Tom Bolack took, what was at the time, a new world-record Polar bear with a 270 Winchester firing the 130-grain Bronze Point bullet. One shot did it. Remington's Bronze Point is an innovative bullet design. On smallish deer, however, I would prefer something less dramatic.

Core-Lokt

Remington's Core-Lokt bullet has found its way into my loads for many years. When Remington discontinued the sale of bullets as a component, I went so far as to buy factory ammo for the sole purpose of extracting the bullet so I could load it my way for my specific purposes. I also bought Remington factory ammo with the Core-Lokt bullet and used the ammo in its over-the-counter form with total success.

I have never had a Remington Core-Lokt bullet fail me in any way. I have never found the jacket in one place and the core in another place in many animal autopsies in the field. There is not much more to add. As I said in the beginning of this discussion, it's not my place to praise nor to condemn, but this bullet is hard not to praise.

Core-Lokt Hollow Point

The 170-grain Core-Lokt hollow point bullet for the 30-30 has proved itself admirably in test media. And I will use it for deer this season, because of my tests. The design is

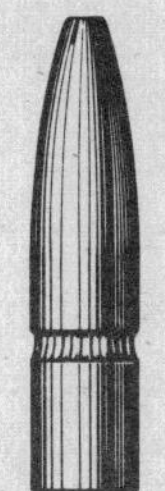

Pointed Soft Point "Core-Lokt" Rifle Bullet

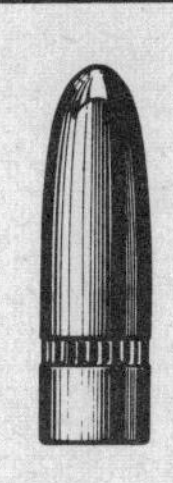

Soft Point "Core-Lokt" Rifle Bullet

These two Core-Lokt bullets are characterized by good penetration qualities and controlled expansion with minimal separation of core from jacket. However, the style on the left, a spitzer in design, is for long-range shooting, while the round nose is best at closer ranges. The round nose bullet makes a good straight wound channel in most cases and tends not to veer off course.

Tapered Heel Metal Case Rifle Bullet

Lead Pistol & Revolver Bullet

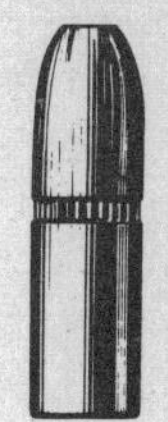

Hollow Point "Core-Lokt" Rifle Bullet

The bullet on the upper left is called a tapered heel full metal jacket spitzer, but it is also known more popularly as a boat-tail. It loads easily, and at very long range its aerodynamics take over. On the upper right is a lead round nosed bullet used in handgun cartridges, and in the lower right a hollow point Core-Lokt bullet, this one a 170-grain missile used in the 30-30 cartridge. It offers fast expansion initially, and then the bullet holds together for penetration.

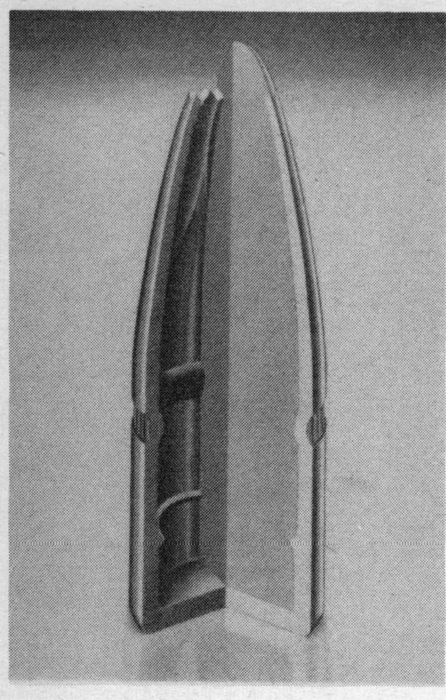

The Hornady Interlock bullet features a sharp ring inside the bullet jacket which extends into the lead core of the bullet. This is designed to hold core and jacket together, a situation the author is in favor of in a big game bullet.

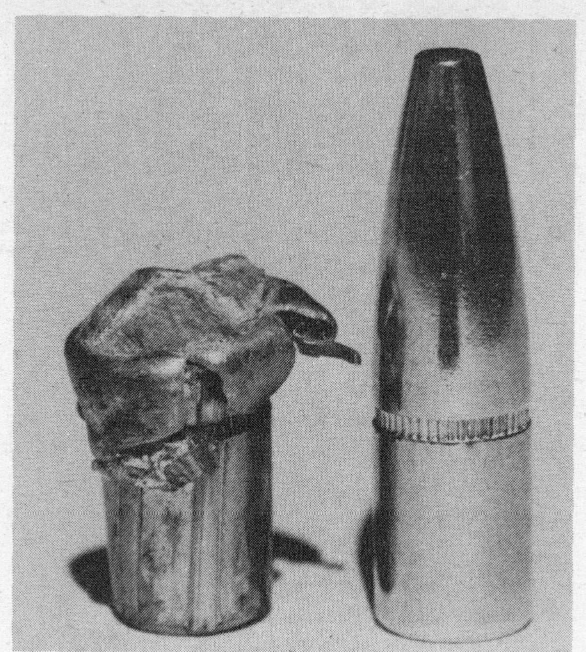

This 165-grain Speer Grand Slam bullet was tested with a 200-yard remaining velocity from a 30-06. Note that the bullet still expanded almost up to the cannelure, but that the core and jacket remain intact as a unit. The bullet penetrated well.

excellent for the modest velocity of the 30-30, and though we have a hollow point design, I did not find shrapnel in the test box from the Core-Lokt Hollow Point 30-30 bullet.

Hi-Shok

I have only used the Federal Hi-Shok bullet in factory loads, those being the Federal 30-30 Winchester round with the 170-grain bullet. This is a soft-point bullet in what seems, from an exterior glance, to be quite ordinary in design. It is basically a round nose bullet with minute slits at the nose to aid expansion. This bullet hangs together, too, and is a true controlled expansion number.

GameKing

I have used the Sierra GameKing bullet in the 140-grain 6.5mm version at a muzzle velocity of 3050 fps. This is a streamlined and accurate bullet of the controlled expansion type. In a couple of big game animals the bullet was recovered, and it retained about 80 percent of original weight. Penetration was excellent. The GameKing is not well known as a "premium" big game bullet. It should be.

Pro-Hunter

I have experience only with the .307-inch 170-grain Pro-Hunter from Sierra. This bullet is suited to the 30-30 Winchester round, and it's slightly undersize, .307-inch instead of .308-inch. That reduced diameter makes this bullet ideal in my very old Model 94 rifle, built in 1899, because it provides a little less bore drag which means a little less breech pressure. This bullet does *not* fly to pieces. It is a good choice for the 30-30. The Pro-Hunter is a flat-base.

InterLock

This is the best move that Hornady has made in terms of a premium big game bullet at a modest price. The InterLock is very reliable. I have had the pleasure of using it and have enjoyed its topflight performance. The InterLock has a sharp ring inside the bullet jacket, near the base, which extends out into the lead core, preventing the core from separating from the jacket. I do not have an InterLock bullet in my collection of retrieved missiles from game because they have all gone through with good exit holes but not undue destruction.

The Speer Grand Slam bullet is an example of a modern day attempt to insure that jacket and core remain together. It is in the general realm of "premium" or "big game" bullets. Here are some of its features: **1.** The lead below the cannelure is harder alloy than the lead above the cannelure. **2.** This is the heel fold to help retain core with jacket. **3.** The lead in front of the cannelure is softer in alloy composition than the lead behind the cannelure. **4.** The cannelure also aids in keeping jacket and core together. **5.** The metal in the nose area is thinner than the jacket metal in the base area. **6.** The spitzer shape helps in retention of velocity. **7.** The nose is slightly flat because the exposed lead has been eliminated.

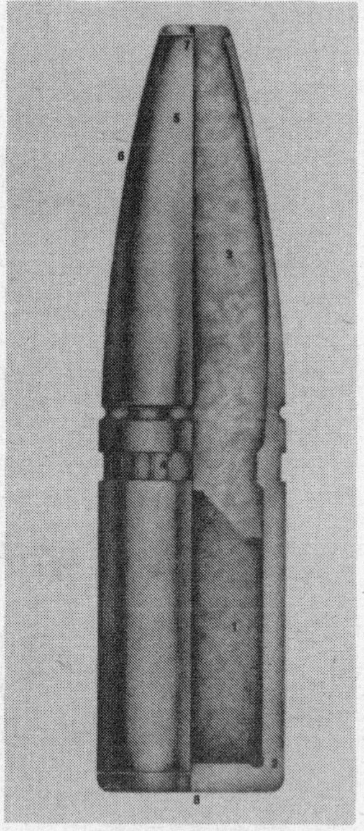

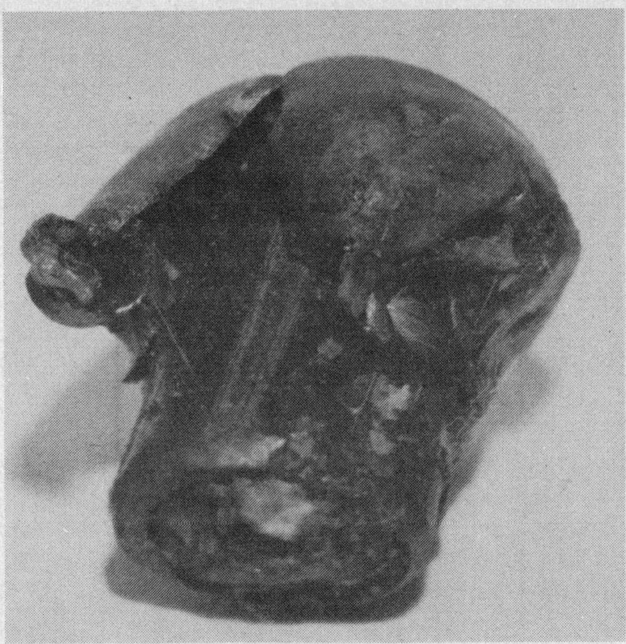

The Nosler Partition bullet shown here was extracted from a kudu bull taken at about 75 yards distance. It is a 6.5mm (.264-inch) bullet fired from a 264 Winchester Magnum.

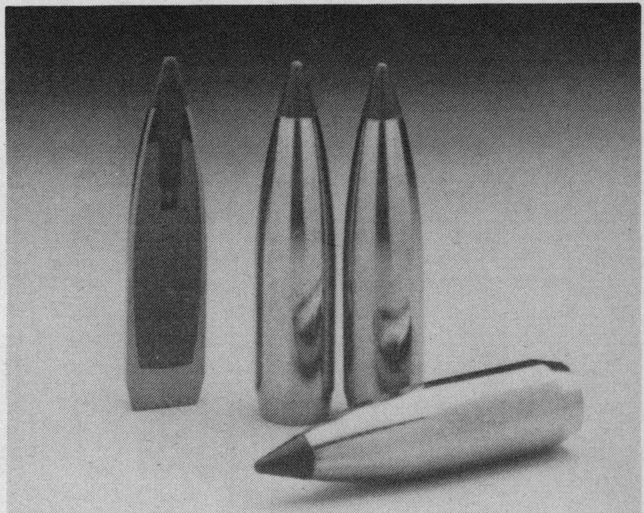

Nosler's Ballistictip is a bullet based on their Solid Base design, but using a polycarbonate tip. Nosler states that the chief reason for Ballistictip is to keep the point from deforming in the magazine and feed ramp. Actually, the Ballistictip's main function is to maintain ballistic coefficient by keeping the point "sharp" all the way to the target, thereby maintaining the shape that the bullet's ballistic coefficient was based upon to begin with.

The Grand Slam

Speer's Grand Slam is a true premium bullet in its sophistication. The core in the base of the jacket is of harder alloy than is the lead in the forward portion of the jacket. The core is poured via the HotCor process to help bond jacket and lead core. There is a heel fold at the base of the jacket to help grip the core. There is also a cannelure that provides additional grip. The jacket is fluted and softened in the nose. The nose is slightly flat, which is fine because any exposed lead at the tip would flatten from contact with the atmosphere anyway. The Grand Slam is a good bullet.

Speer Flat Nose

Brief mention of the 170-grain Speer Flat Nose is in order. The ballistic coefficient of this bullet is .304, and yet it works fine in the tubular magazine. I have never known one of these 170-grain bullets to strip a jacket when fired in the 30-30 at 2000 to 2200 fps or in the 30-30 Improved at up to 2350 fps.

The Nosler Partition

The Nosler Partition is a favorite of many shooters. The partition design, with its metal band separating the front of the bullet's core from the back of the bullet's core, insures that it simply has to stay together. A friend of mine, John Kane of Colorado, has taken several bull elk with the 160-grain Nosler Partition with superior success. He has recovered a few bullets, and they have always been intact as they should be, fired from the 7mm Remington Magnum at over 3100 fps MV.

Ballistictip

The Ballistictip bullet from Nosler features that firm's Solid-Base design with an insert at the nose of the bullet. The insert is of super sharp profile and is made of polycarbonate. It maintains ballistic coefficient admirably. Of course, the bullet will probably do considerable tissue damage, as my tests in media seem to indicate. In my opinion, Ballistictips should work beautifully when it comes to putting game down quickly and humanely. This coming season will be my first in testing the Ballistictip on game, but my tests using the "bullet box" referred to below, show this missile to be an interesting one indeed.

Other Bullets

The preceding has dealt with the modern jacketed projectile, but it is only fair to say that some fine big game

Hornady recognizes that some of our modern shooting is best accomplished with the lead bullet, and this is why the company offers its lead pistol bullet line. Reloaders who do not cast can use these lead projectiles at a modest cost.

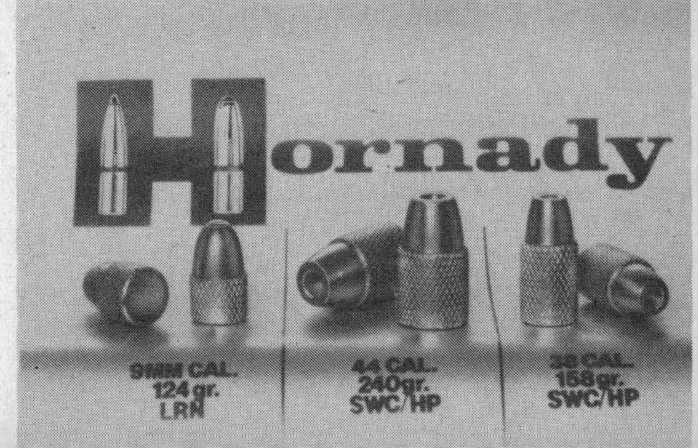

These big 460-grain 54-caliber bullets of pure lead are intended for the muzzleloader. They are prelubed with a wax coating. They are offered by the Buffalo Bullet Company.

The Maxi ball is shown here in a before and after pose. Note that the projectile has upset so that it is hardly recognizable from the unfired Maxi. But the fired sample weighs about as much as the unfired sample.

Handgun bullets require as much care in manufacture as rifle bullets when they are expected to perform in a specific manner. These are Winchester's Silvertip hollowpoint bullets in 357 Magnum, 38 Auto and 45 Colt. Note the excellent expansion in test media, the type of expansion sought by the bulletmaker.

bullets are not of the jacketed variety. Using the muzzleloader, I have taken a reasonably large number of big game animals with the round ball, both home-cast and also of the fine commercial variety. The Speer and Hornady swaged round balls are remarkably accurate and well-made. They "weigh out" as well as modern bullets.

Also, there are some commercial conicals well worth considering. The Buffalo Bullet Company Pre-Lubricated Maxi Bullet is one such conical. I have used it extensively in a big magnum muzzleloader of mine built by Dale Storey and Dean Zollinger, and in this powerhouse the 460-grain Buffalo Bullet Company Maxi exits the muzzle at over 1700 fps. It is a very accurate projectile as well and it comes ready to load and shoot.

Test Your Own Bullets

Before the hunting season, the shooter can readily test his own bullets and/or factory ammo as well as handloads for big game. The testing is rather simple and quite reliable. I use what I call a "bullet box," a compartmentalized wooden box which has a clay filler, a water balloon and some department store catalogs as backups to catch bullets which will get through both the clay and the water. But a shooter can also get by with wet newspaper. Simply fill a large cardboard box full of newspapers and then soak them. They will catch bullets securely if enough newspaper is used. Also, damp sawdust in a box will serve to catch bullets.

The idea is to study the recovered bullet for various

This is the author's bullet box, a compartmentalized affair which uses clay, water and other materials in order to upset and retain bullets for study.

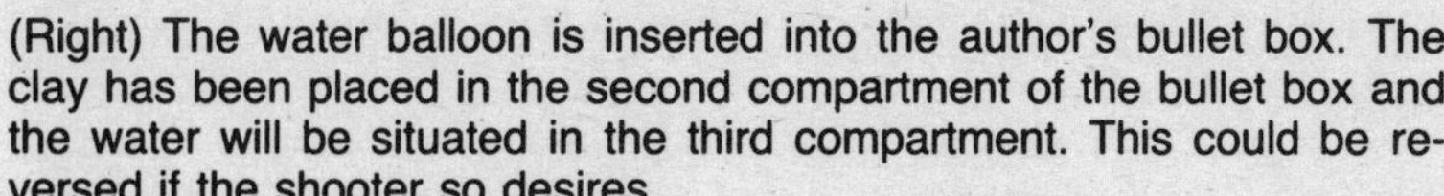

(Right) The water balloon is inserted into the author's bullet box. The clay has been placed in the second compartment of the bullet box and the water will be situated in the third compartment. This could be reversed if the shooter so desires.

traits. In my bullet box, I have found that if jackets strip, they will strip in game. If jackets and cores hang together in the box, these bullets will hold together in the field. In fact, I would consider my bullet box highly reliable as a test element. I have run across a few bullets which did not upset nearly enough. In fact, I kept one batch of 150-grain 270 bullets because they were so hard as to be useless for deer hunting in terms of ''instant'' harvests, but those same bullets were very good on larger-than-deer game.

The bullet is the workhorse. The most accurate rifle in the world will not always drop game cleanly if the bullet fails to perform properly. It is the bullet, after all, which harvests the game. Today, we have an array of fine bullets to work with in the big game field. These bullets are capable of doing something which was thought for a long while to be nearly impossible—they do not explode on game at close range, and yet they open up on game at long range.

While it seems that the bullet makers have come up with the last word in design to handle a variety of tasks, from ultra-long-range shooting to breaking down a big and dangerous mean-eating beast at point blank range, I would assume that they won't stop here. I am not sure what will come next, but I am sure that the bulletmakers will think of something new. They always do.

Chapter 22
"Brushbusting" in Theory and Practice

BULLETS in the brush have been an important concern to shooters for a very long time. Ever since I can remember, shooters have believed in certain rounds as out-and-out brushbusters. That is, certain rounds gained the reputation for staying on track through the brush and reaching the target. Over the past 3 years, I have tried to test the brush-busting ability of certain projectiles at certain velocities.

My tests should really be called "demonstrations," because a true test has a control and certain built-in parameters which I did not have to work with. All the same, I think that the data presented here is of value to the complete shooter who wants to know the why and how when it comes to choosing rounds for shooting in the brush. Obviously, any part of the country can offer such shooting situations. Even the "wide open West" has plenty of ecological niches which abound in brush. And the high country timberlands are also loaded with brushy draws and ridges.

My tests, if I may use the term as an expedient here, were designed around setting up targets behind screens of brush. Of course, the brush varied, and this is where the "science" got knocked out of my plan. At the same time, certain rounds did give very similar results over and over again, so something *was* learned. Mostly I found out that brushbusters are more theory than fact, but on my third series of "tests," I compiled a rather impressive list of data and had to change my mind *to some degree* on that score. It seemed that indeed a few rounds were better in the brush than other rounds, and the long-talked-about notions of brushbusting cartridges was not all puff and talk after all.

Avoid the Brush If You Can

First, I would like to state one conclusion which arrived after a lot of testing and quite a bit of field experience—avoid shooting *through* the brush if you can. You may not be able to avoid this situation if you want to fire a round, but on the other hand, I have been in several situations where it was entirely possible to pick spots or holes in the brush to shoot through.

So, if the shooter remains conscious of the fact that he may indeed be able to avoid the brush, even when he's in it, I think this attitude is well worth holding onto. I found out the hard way that even the most powerful round can be diverted by the brush, and this is why I ask that the shooter try, at least, to pick a hole to shoot through if possible.

One of the most interesting "brush-hunting" situations I ever found myself in was during my recent safari in Africa. I had been looking hard, very hard, for an eland, the largest antelope in the world. Prior to leaving for Africa, I had heard that under "some circumstances," the eland could be difficult to hunt.

Unfortunately, I found myself in those "circumstances." There was no great abundance of eland in the bushveld of Africa where I was hunting, and the beasts seemed to slip in and out of the thick brush like fast-moving snakes. There would be a patch of eland one minute and nothing but brush the next. I was on foot the entire time and walking most of the day. Every time I tried to get close to these big antelope my reward would be a pinkish-looking shadow.

Bill Edwards, the professional hunter I was with, saw me hesitate a couple of times. I had not, at that time, missed a shot on perhaps 8 or 10 head of game (though I missed a waterbuck a little later), and he wondered why I was not taking a try on the eland. "Too much brush," I retorted. "Can't get a decent shot." In his fine and carefully spoken English, Bill explained to me that if I waited for a clear shot on an eland in that brush, I might be waiting a long time indeed.

Nine eland were spotted from a high *kopje*. I found the animals in my glasses, but they were much too far away to shoot at. We decided to stalk. Nothing. Then I spotted a kudu bull and held sight of it while a companion tried to get a shot at him. But that did not work out either. However, as I was pointing the kudu out to my friend, one of the trackers pointed and said "Mhofu (eland)!" And it sure was. There were several of them, and as usual they were slipping through the brush like ballet dancers in spite of the fact that a bull eland can weigh 1500 to 2000 pounds on the hoof. We took off after them.

This time, I was going to get my shot. We slipped ahead of them as much as possible, and after an hour were still on the tracks or trying to move ahead of where we thought they might be traveling. Then my chance came. I let the cows slip by. (The only way I could tell they were cows in

The test target behind a screen of brush. Note that there is not really all that much brush in the path of the bullet, but with this situation, the bullets tested by the author were affected. Few bullets hit the target as if the brush were not there.

brush without deflection, the other rounds we normally shoot are probably not true "brushbusters."

Bullet Shape

After the first session of shooting at targets through brush, I was ready to state flatly that *no round* could be counted on to break through the bush and hit a target. I am happy that I went back for tests two and three, because I have changed my mind by a small degree. I still do not think that there is any shoulder-fired rifle which will propel its missile through a lot of brush without deflection, but the last two sessions, especially the most recent, has brought me around to thinking that *some* rounds are indeed going to be better in the brush than others.

One of the factors that affect a bullet's brushbusting abilities is bullet shape. Using the 30-06 cartridge, I tried various pointed bullets against various sharp-pointed bullets, at the same muzzle velocities. For example, I used a 180-grain spitzer loaded to 2812 fps MV average and a 180-grain round nose loaded to about the same velocity level. I tried 20 shots with each from the same distance, alternating so that the two bullets would have *about* the same amount of brush to shoot through.

The differences were not overly dramatic. I shot from 50

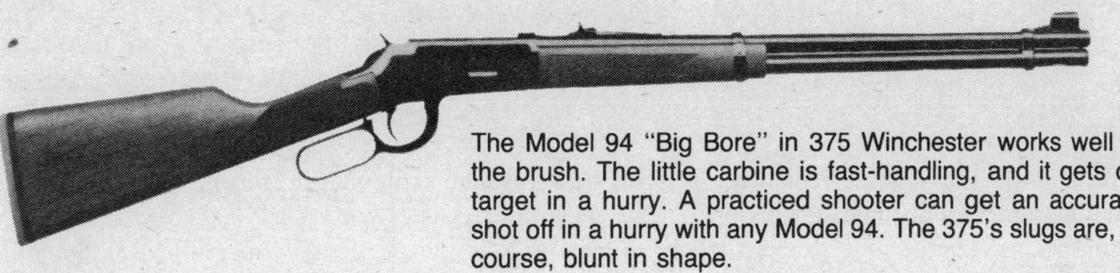

The Model 94 "Big Bore" in 375 Winchester works well in the brush. The little carbine is fast-handling, and it gets on target in a hurry. A practiced shooter can get an accurate shot off in a hurry with any Model 94. The 375's slugs are, of course, blunt in shape.

that brush was by their size—the bull was much larger than the others.) Then it happened. The bull stopped for that split second, and only 75 yards away by my calculations. I sent a 300-grain bullet from my 375 Weatherby straight for the chest.

That big strong bullet hit a few twigs on the way and whacked the eland in the hip. We had to track it a bit—then I got another shot. This time the shot was clear. I put another 300-grain bullet out, this one landed squarely in the bull's chest. Away he went. We tracked. Again I got a clear shot and put the third 300-grain bullet into the chest area and down he went. Typical of Americans, I had used the *behind*-the-shoulder shot. My really big game from here on out, whether foreign or domestic, is going to get the *on*-the-shoulder shot, in the scapula area, up front, where there are some bones. Deer and other like-sized game will still be harvested with the *behind* the shoulder shot, into vitals not eaten by most of us. However, back to the real point of this story—the brush. If a big 300-grain bullet from a 375 Weatherby has trouble getting through

This is a 150-grain Nosler Partition bullet taken from a mule deer buck. The buck was partially hidden behind a light screen of brush at the time, but the bullet obviously found its way through the brush and to its destination. No doubt, shooting through holes in the brush is better than any attempt at brushbusting.

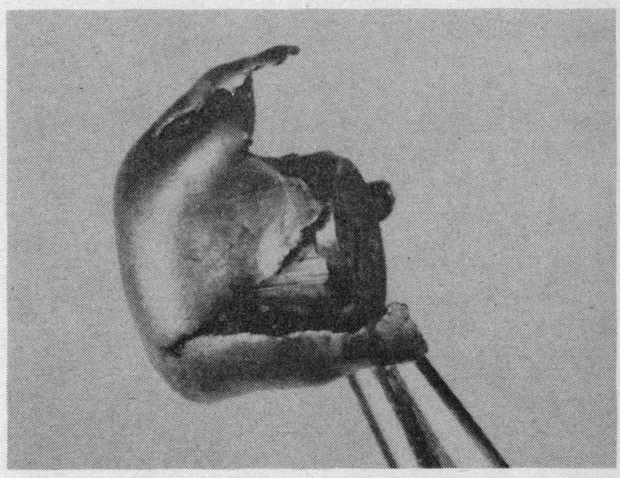

The target seems to have been hit by a shotgun, and at least one of the bullets has tipped and struck the target sideways. This is a graphic illustration of what can happen when a bullet must break through brush to reach a destination. Some of the tiny holes represent bullet fragments and others are made from bits of brush blowing through the target.

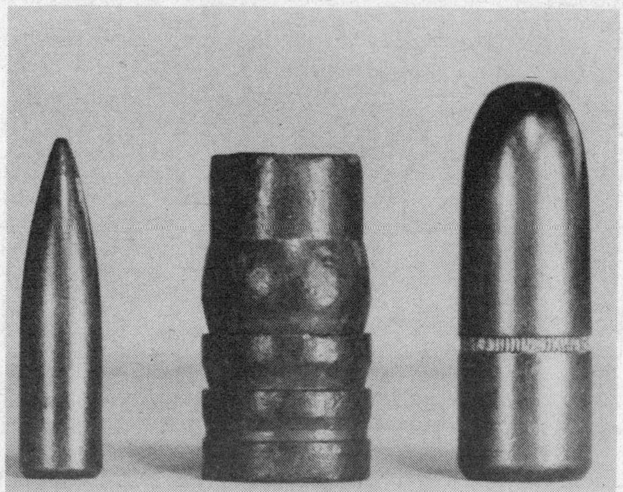

Three entirely different bullet shapes are shown here. On the left is a spitzer, and then a big flat-point bullet, and finally a round nose. In tests, the center bullet did best in bucking brush, but its weight and momentum may have been the contributing factors. The 500-grain round nose from a 45-70 also did better than the spitzer, but the spitzer was not that far behind. Load to snuff, however, even with the spitzer bullet, for brush. Loading down won't help.

yards and from 200 yards, and in both cases, deflection was obvious. In the final analysis, however, I would have to go with the round nose bullet, because it seemed a *little better* at getting to the target point-on, there being less evidence of keyholing. In some cases, the round nose was more centered in the bull's-eye than the spitzer, suggesting, perhaps, that it had stayed on course a bit better.

Hoping to gain *true, consistent* brushbusting performance by using the round nose bullet, however, is not in the cards. I do like blunt bullets for close-up shooting because, I feel, blunt bullets deliver more immediate shock value to the animal than pointed bullets do. Of course, I use pointed bullets for anything to be taken at long range, as they retain their energy better than blunt bullets and shoot flatter, too. But if all of my shooting were going to be from 50 or 100 yards, or perhaps 150 yards plus for that matter, I would opt for the blunt-nose projectile first.

Full Metal Jacket

I also had a chance to try some full metal jacket bullets in the brush. I am well aware that it is wrong to use full metal jacket bullets on game. I never do. It is even against the law on big game in most states. But I wanted to satisfy my curiosity and at the same time see if it would buck brush better. If so, then perhaps going to *stronger* jacketed soft points might be the answer to the age-old brushbusting problem. In the final analysis, I would say that the 220-grain full metal jacket slug got through brush *slightly* better than the 220-grain round nose of the same make. As far as turning to heavy jackets, I don't think my full metal jacket test proved much. However, as a result of this test, I went a bit further. I turned to a 45-70 with 400-grain soft nose bullets of fairly heavy jacket thickness and 405-grain soft nose bullets of light jacket thickness. The heavy jacketed bullet hit point-on more than the light jacket bullet. Enough to make a difference? Not really.

Caliber and Brushbusting

We always think of a big caliber bullet as being better than a small caliber bullet in terms of getting through brush. In a way the thought is not a bad one, but I am not sure it is caliber alone which allows for enhanced brushbusting. In *all* of my tests the super high-speed cartridges such as the 22-250 did not penetrate the brush as well as

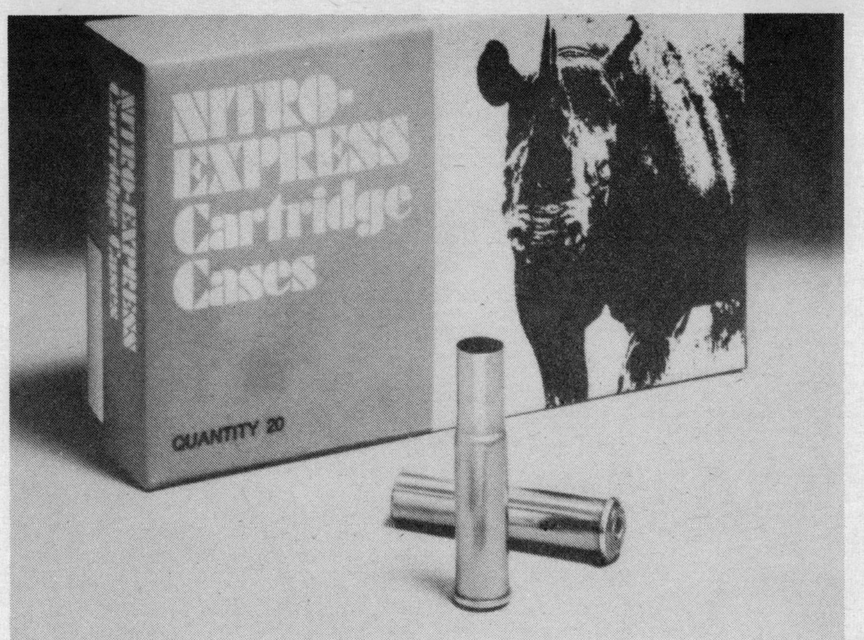

The 11mm (.43-inch Mauser Base Case) is offered by B.E.L.L. for handloaders. Such a round is good for close-range shooting and would serve in the brush. Load up to snuff, however, as underloading this round will not improve its brushbucking ability.

(Below) Obstacles in the path of the bullet can force the bullet to do some strange things. This 130-grain .277-inch bullet fired from a 270 Winchester, hit a prickly pear pad at close range, turned sideways, and slammed into a *javelina,* dispatching the wild pig instantly. The bullet hit the pig sideways, however. Brush can also deflect a bullet in the same manner.

the 35-caliber numbers such as the 356 Wincheser, which I tested with a 250-grain bullet out of a Model 94 Winchester.

We may actually be looking at other factors without knowing it, however. Does a larger bullet get through the brush better because it is a *larger* bullet, or because it wears a tougher jacket? Or we might ask the question the other way around. Does the small caliber bullet fail in the brush because its light jacket, often intended to go to pieces on the landscape when varmint hunting, busts up easily? Either way, one of the factors here might be jacket toughness, and I go with the latter manner of looking at the problem. The thin-jacketed bullets go to pieces on the brush. This is why they don't reach the target very well. I found, in some cases, that the target looked as if it had been struck by a shotgun when a 50-grain bullet was launched at the target through a screen of brush, the bullet doing about 3800 fps MV.

Kinetic Energy

In an earlier brushbusting test, I concluded that kinetic energy might not be much of a factor because a 35 Remington whipped a 270 Winchester, the former using a 200-grain round nose bullet, the latter using a 130-grain spitzer or a 150-grain round nose. My later tests, plus a little more time to mull over earlier findings, suggest my conclusions were wrong. There can be an increase in brushbusting ability with an increase in energy. I think now that the reason the 35 Remington got through more brush better at the time in comparison with the 270 was one of bullet construction, very blunt nose and other factors. But energy did not play a role here.

I went back to the 30-06. This time, I loaded 220-grain

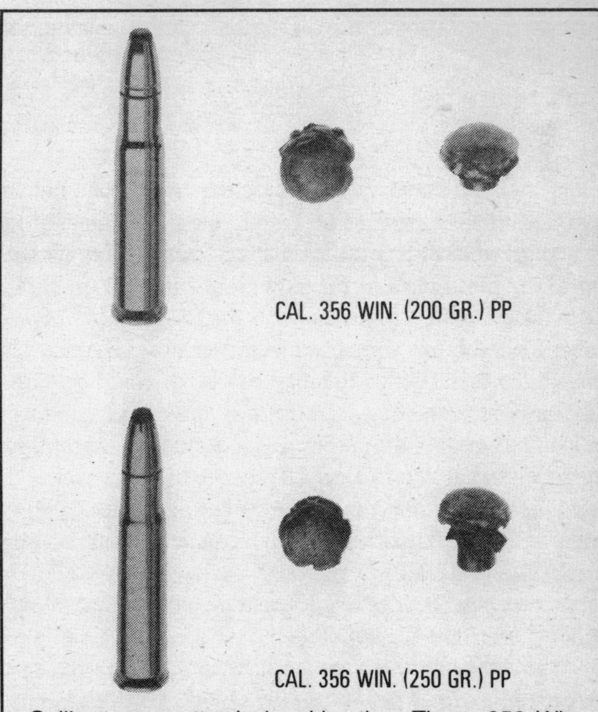

Caliber can matter in brushbusting. These 356 Winchester rounds are served up by the factory with 200-grain and 250-grain bullets of high momentum. They do well in the brush compared with a very light bullet which might fragment more.

These two missiles are almost opposites. The 30-caliber sharp-pointed bullet on the left holds up much better to long-range shooting, but in the brush, the big 54-caliber bullet on the right was the winner. Drive any bullet at optimum velocity for brushshooting. Do *not* underload.

Here is a 58-caliber Shiloh-molded Minie, the Stakebuster, with an original weight of 625 grains in "pure" lead. The bullet nearly destroyed the bullet box in testing and its momentum is very high. At 1400 fps, the momentum figure would be 87.5, against a 30-06/180-gr. bullet/2800 fps of 50.4. It penetrated brush better than many other bullets of lower momentum quality, and it retained its mass weight very well. The recovered 625-grain bullet on the left is almost as heavy as the unfired bullet on the right.

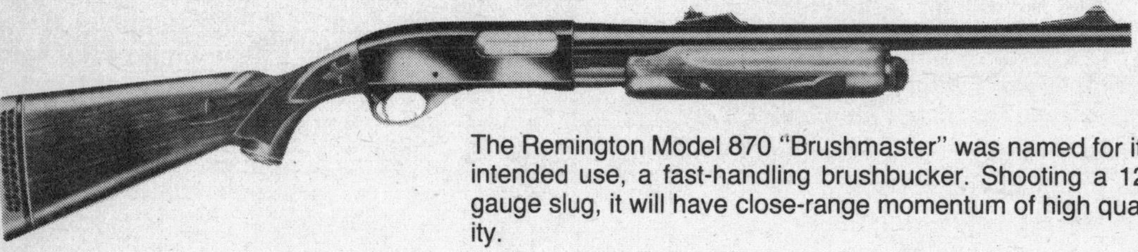

The Remington Model 870 "Brushmaster" was named for its intended use, a fast-handling brushbucker. Shooting a 12-gauge slug, it will have close-range momentum of high quality.

round nose bullets at various velocities for various muzzle energies. If energy were no factor, then it seemed to me that there would be no difference between the faster-moving 220-grain bullets or the slower-moving 220-grain bullets. Furthermore, some shooters had suggested *loading down* for the brush, because the slower projectile had less chance for deflection. That may be. There could be something to that, but I could not back it up with my findings.

The 220-grain bullet seemed to penetrate better at 2600 fps MV than at 2200 or even 1800 fps MV. Furthermore, there were fewer incidents of keyholing with the 220-grain bullet at 2600 fps than with the same bullet at 2200 or 1800 fps MV. At 50 yards, where the faster bullet would, by some theories, be deflected much more than the slower bullets, the 2600 fps bullet won over the slower samples.

Once again, conclusions are difficult. We are trying to isolate one factor when in fact we cannot. In order to make a valid test, all other variables would be held in check, but while in the act of shooting 220-grain bullets, we were also dealing with the changes in the actual brush being penetrated, as well as other extraneous variables. All of this notwithstanding, it seemed that the extra velocity did not destroy the 220-grain bullet in the brush.

One may conclude, though not on entirely firm ground, that increased energy would not harm penetration of brush. Increased kinetic energy increases penetration in other media. An arrow will penetrate well due to many factors, but all things being kept the same, the arrow of higher kinetic energy will penetrate better than the same arrow at lower kinetic energy. Same with the bullet, I think. However, we might have to add that increased energy helps penetration as long as the increase in MV (in order to get that energy) does not mean that the bullet will bust up right on the brush. In other words, the jacket and overall construction of the bullet must allow for the extra velocity and energy.

Momentum

Momentum is simply mass (bullet weight) times velocity. If a 30-06 with the 180-grain bullet at 2800 fps has 3134 foot-pounds of energy, then the same bullet at the same MV would have a momentum rating of 504,000, but the figure is rather meaningless without further interpretation. However, it can be used strictly as a comparison number. In order to make things simpler, let's divide the resulting momentum figure by 10,000 in each case. The resulting number will then be used for purposes of comparison.

Why compare at all? Because I think there just might be something valuable here, not as important as the sun's continuance to warm the planet, but interesting all the same. In fact, let's make a "pumpkin roller" such as the 45-70 and compare it with the 270 Winchester, one of the high-rollers of our time in spite of its advanced age.

Kinetic Energy

270 Winchester, 130-grain bullet at 3100 fps = 2775 foot-pounds ME.

45-70 Govt., 405-grain bullet at 1600 fps = 2,303 foot-pounds ME.

Momentum

270 Winchester, 130-grain bullet at 3100 fps = 403,000 ÷ 10,000 or 40.3

45-70 Govt., 405-grain bullet at 1600 fps = 648,000 ÷ 10,000 or 64.8

Obviously, the 270 Winchester round wins handily in the kinetic energy department. But the old 45-70 wins in the momentum department, even at a mere 1600 fps MV. Which is better at bucking brush? Without getting too carried away with this notion, I would go with the 45-70 in the brush by a small margin in terms of getting through to the target. In test shooting the 45-70 along with the 458 Winchester, and then later shooting the 270, I felt that the 45-70 did a little better job of getting through the brush. I picked the 1600 fps MV figure because that was the actual velocity of the particular load tested with a 405-grain Winchester bullet.

Does this mean that momentum will always win in terms of brush penetration? Do bullets of higher momentum get through more brush with less deflection than bullets of lower momentum? It's a very unscientific postulation, but again I suggest there may be a little something to it. I tested two other cartridges which pose similar comparison. This was the 300 Winchester Magnum *vs* the 45-70 with a 500-grain bullet at 1700 fps out of a Ruger Number One carbine. Actually, more velocity can be gained from the Ruger with the 45-70, but this was an accuracy load as well as power load. Here're the results.

Kinetic Energy

300 Winchester Magnum, 180-grain bullet at 3000 fps = 3,598 foot-pounds ME

45-70 Govt., 500-grain bullet at 1700 fps = 3,209 foot-pounds ME

Momentum

300 Win. Magnum, 180-grain bullet at 3000 fps = 54

45-70 Govt., 500-grain bullet at 1700 fps = 85

In the kinetic energy domain, the 300 Winchester Magnum wins over the 45-70 with the above load, but in the

Another good brush rifle is the Marlin 1895S. Despite a 24-inch barrel, the rifle handles well in the brush and the big 45-70 round can be loaded to fair velocity with pretty hefty bullets.

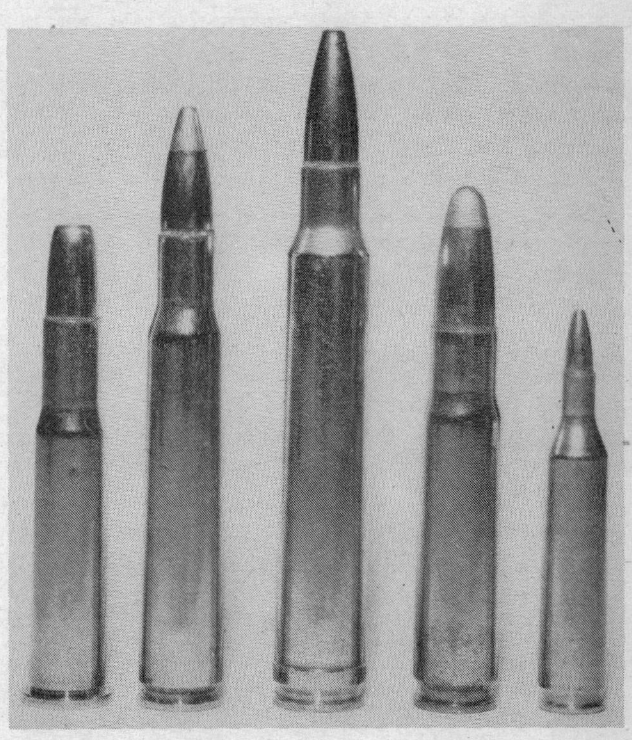

Various cartridges send their respective bullets into the brush with varying results. On the far left is the 30-30 Winchester with flat-point bullet. It's not bad in the brush. Next to it is the 30-06 with its 180-grain Silvertip bullet, another decent round for brush. The big 8mm Remington Magnum will break some brush, too, though with the heavier bullets it shines in the brush, and its high velocity does not seem to harm its brushbucking ability. The fine 358 Winchester round is another good one for close-up work, and then for comparison is the little 17 Remington. It did not make it through much brush at all, not with a 25-grain bullet at about 4000 fps MV.

momentum arena it is the 45-70 which wins, and by a good margin. The 45-70 with the 500-grain bullet also outdid the 300 Winchester Magnum in the little brushbusting demonstration, and once again, there was not a huge and obvious difference.

Does this mean that we can tell how well a bullet will do in the brush by examining its momentum? Partly, yes. I think it can tell us a little about the brushbusting ability of a bullet at a certain velocity, but it's too unscientific to call a fact. It's a notion, a thought, an idea, a surmise, but not a fact. In terms of momentum, an automobile with more momentum than another automobile will be harder to stop, so it is not too far-fetched to assume that a bullet with more momentum than another bullet will also be harder to stop. The problem lies in those extraneous variables. All the same, let us agree that the idea of momentum and brushbusting is not totally without merit until proved to be.

Velocity and Brushbusting

In effect, information about kinetic energy and momentum is directly related to velocity, but all the same, I wanted to see what would happen with the same exact bullet at different muzzle velocities in terms of brushbusting. First, I loaded down, in recognition of the old saw that states a brushbusting projectile should be rather slow. I took my 45-70 and cut the velocity. Funny thing here is that it did not seem to hurt in terms of the bullet getting through the brush, so I question that demonstration to some degree. Of course, it did not help either, and perhaps this is the more important point.

Next, I took some 500-grain jacketed bullets and loaded these into both the 45-70 and the 458 Winchester, the former doing 1700 fps and the latter doing 2100 fps. The 458 won 10 out of 10 shots. I hope that there is some significance in this. Ten out of 10 is good. But it is not proof, for the reasons stated all along. Nonetheless, the 458 got through the brush better than the 45-70, and the holes near or in the bull's-eye were more numerous than those tallied up by the 45-70. Perhaps we are actually talking in terms of momentum again without overtly stating the fact.

Revolutions Per Second (R.P.S.) and Brushbusting

Revolutions Per Second (R.P.S.), among other factors, is responsible for the stabilized flight of a projectile. For example, a 45-70 400-grain bullet may be stabilized at X R.P.S. while a 140-grain 6.5mm bullet would require X-plus R.P.S. to stabilize it, yet both bullets would be fully stabilized. So the old saw of R.P.S. (and it's touted brush-drilling benefit) had to be approached in another way. I tried to dispel or prove the R.P.S. and brushbusting theory from the standpoint of bullets with high R.P.S. versus bullets of lower R.P.S. I don't think a thing was proved. Mainly, the problem actually reverted itself to another question. Since the R.P.S. of some bullets is higher than others when stabilization has been achieved, then aren't we merely comparing bullet shapes and the R.P.S. required to stabilize them? In other words, we were probably comparing long and heavy bullets with bullets of less sectional density. The little tests did not prove much. My 6.5mm at higher R.P.S. fired a 140-grain bullet through a bit more brush than my 270 did with its 130-grain bullet, test problems aside. In my opinion, R.P.S. (be it high or low) only serves to stabilize bullets, it doesn't create any discernible "brush-drilling" benefit.

Sectional Density

This was another consideration born from the idea of looking at R.P.S. Will bullets of high sectional density get through more brush than bullets of less sectional density. One would think so, but the 35 Remington firing a 200-grain bullet did a bit better than the 270 firing a 130-grain bullet, and the sectional density of the 200-grain 35-caliber bullet is .223; the sectional density of the 130-grain 270 bullet is .242. Perhaps these bullets were too close in sectional density to test the theory, and perhaps it is true that bullets of higher sectional density, all other things being equal (such as shape of point), will go through more brush than bullets of lesser sectional density.

I suspect the notion is not a bad one, and I think that shooters should consider sectional density if a clear choice is presented in terms of caliber/bullet weight selection. I suspect that in a 35-caliber rifle, if the 200-grain bullet and the 250-grain bullet can both be fired at reasonable MV, then the latter with both more sectional density and more mass would be the "suggested" choice for brush. Going beyond the point of "suggesting" is not possible at the moment.

A Few Samples From the Field

A few samples from the field might be in order. I wish I could compile the experiences of 20 well-seasoned shooters who have fired hundreds of rounds at game in the brush, but I am not prepared to do that. I am, however, prepared to relate a couple of incidents, though, both from the personal side and through comments from hunters about their own brush-shooting incidents.

The 44 Magnum

My 44 Magnum is a favorite of mine and from it I drive 240-grain bullets at about 1400+ fps MV and a 265-grain bullet at 1300 fps+ MV. I have used both in the brush, not in a very formal way, but in general shooting situations. The latter bucks more brush, incidentally, but the real point is that in neither tests nor field experiences has the 44 Magnum proved to me it can eat its way through brush like boiling water through soap bubbles.

In fact, I would have to say that my 30-30 whips my 44 Magnum in terms of getting through brush. I say this with the thought in mind that slower, more squat bullets were supposed to be best in the brush according to many sources I have read over the years. But in this case at least, 30-30 *vs* 44 Magnum, it seems not so.

The 30-06

Much of my brushbusting test shooting was with a 30-06, and in this particular instance, I think I would go along with the popular notion that the 220-grain bullet of round nose design is best in the brush. It could be that further testing might turn that verdict around, but if I were to take to the brush tomorrow with close-range brush shooting in mind, and if I were to tote a 30-06, I'd just as soon have the 220-grain bullet as anything I have tried in that cartridge.

The 30-30

As a matter of fact, I found a flat-nosed 170-grain 30-30 bullet about as reliable as most other ammo when it came to putting the bullet through a pile of brush on the way to a target. It did *not* beat the 30-06, but it wasn't too far behind that great cartridge. Using the 170-grain bullet at about 2250 fps MV, neat round holes in the target were often the rule. Also, boosted to about 2325 fps in a 30-30 Improved, brushbusting was about the same if not slightly better.

20 paces, and then miss it by a foot.

That ball, I am convinced, took a bounce from the twig. I was lucky it bounced downward. Had it bounced the other way, there would have been no meat for me. I later tried a round ball, a 54-caliber sphere, and found it not very great at getting through brush. In a very recent test, a .690-inch or 12-gauge round ball was fired through some brush, and it did not get through any better than a 180-grain bullet from a 30-06. This little test had been run previously with about the same results.

I concluded that the round ball was simply no good in the brush, or better stated, the round ball was not good in getting through a lot of brush. I have dropped several deer with a round ball muzzleloader in brush country and hope to do the same again and again. Actually, as the ball grew in diameter, its performance certainly did improve in the brush. The .690-inch was better than the .530-inch ball, for example. I imagine that the ponderous round ball missiles of the old elephant rifles, with lots of momentum going for them, did get through more brush.

The Ideal Bullet for Brushbusting

There may, in fact, be an ideal bullet and/or load for the brush. I'll try to talk about it in general and even specific

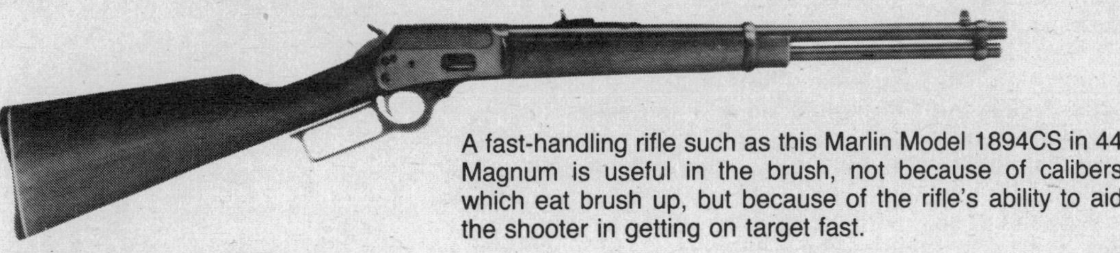

A fast-handling rifle such as this Marlin Model 1894CS in 44 Magnum is useful in the brush, not because of calibers which eat brush up, but because of the rifle's ability to aid the shooter in getting on target fast.

The 35 Remington

The 35 Remington has long been noted as a brush round. I agree. It is a good deer cartridge for the woods and other places of heavy vegetation. But in one little shootout, the slightly faster 358 Winchester was tried with the 250-grain factory load and I felt it was better than the 35 Remington with the 200-grain round nose bullet at about 2000 fps MV. Nonetheless, our tests indicate the 35 Remington is still a fine one for deer in brushy places.

The Black Powder Round Ball

I once had a shot at a mule deer buck at 20 yards, after a long stalk which was taken after my son located the buck way up a narrow canyon. The aim was held for that spot where head and neck join, and from only 20 paces, it would be no trick to place the round ball exactly at that juncture. But that's not where the ball went. It struck a twig on the way to this target and plunked directly into the chest of the buck. The results were about the same as they would have been with the other sighting, but it was somewhat disconcerting to miss the target, as it were, from only

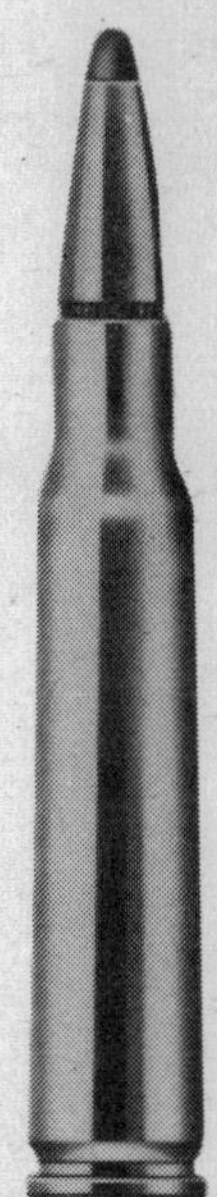

The little 7mm Mauser (7x57) was tried in the brush and did about as well as some of the other similar rounds, and not too far behind the 30-06 in ability to find the target through a screen of brush. It was bettered by the 358 Winchester and some of the larger-calibered rounds.

The standard 30-06 Springfield round is as good at brush-breaking as many other rounds thought of as brushbusters, to include the 35 Remington. A blunt, heavy bullet is a good choice for brush.

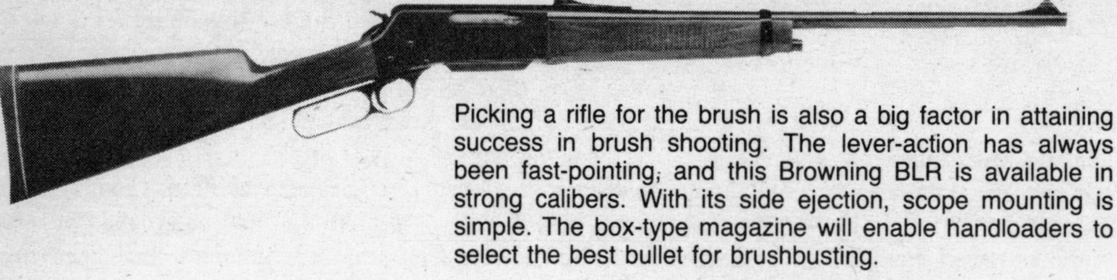

Picking a rifle for the brush is also a big factor in attaining success in brush shooting. The lever-action has always been fast-pointing, and this Browning BLR is available in strong calibers. With its side ejection, scope mounting is simple. The box-type magazine will enable handloaders to select the best bullet for brushbusting.

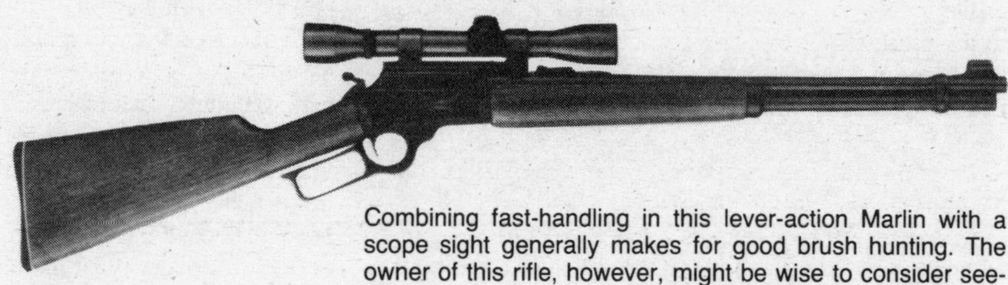

Combining fast-handling in this lever-action Marlin with a scope sight generally makes for good brush hunting. The owner of this rifle, however, might be wise to consider see-through mounts to take advantage of the iron sights.

Although a shooter would not buy a big 8mm Remington Magnum specifically for brush shooting, it is difficult to downgrade the ability of a cartridge of this type to stay on track in the brush. A big bullet at high speed means momentum advantages, which in turn means that a bullet will be hard to stop.

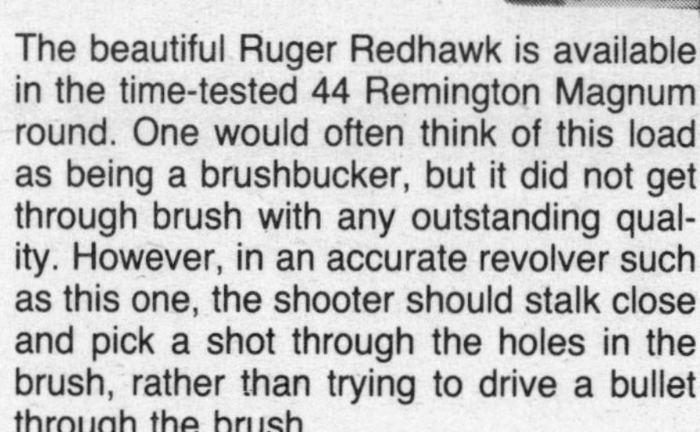

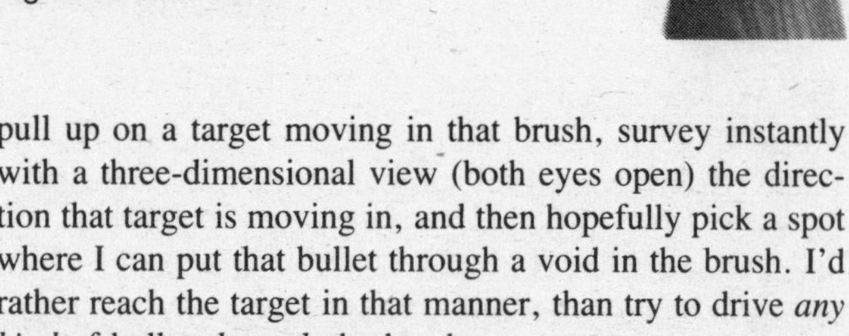

The beautiful Ruger Redhawk is available in the time-tested 44 Remington Magnum round. One would often think of this load as being a brushbucker, but it did not get through brush with any outstanding quality. However, in an accurate revolver such as this one, the shooter should stalk close and pick a shot through the holes in the brush, rather than trying to drive a bullet through the brush.

terms. Furthermore, my ideal bullet is not totally mythical. There are no doubt bullet *types* which do fall in the "ideal" bracket, even if no one single bullet is the total answer in trying to shoot through brush. The ideal bullet looks like this:

1. It has a blunt, not sharply pointed nose.
2. It is a heavy bullet rather than a light one.
3. It has plenty of momentum.
4. Its caliber is larger rather than smaller, i.e., 30-caliber on up.

The Answer to the Problem of Brush Shooting

The answer lies, then, in picking a round and rifle which fit the above picture. I say rifle as well as round because I want a brush rifle which fits me like my shirt and which handles, for me, with tremendous pointability. And I want close-range accuracy. You bet. That's the answer. I want to be able to take that rifle and shoot rapidly with supreme accuracy at brushland ranges. In fact, I want to be able to pull up on a target moving in that brush, survey instantly with a three-dimensional view (both eyes open) the direction that target is moving in, and then hopefully pick a spot where I can put that bullet through a void in the brush. I'd rather reach the target in that manner, than try to drive *any kind* of bullet *through* the brush.

So my brush rifle will be accurate, or at least accurate at close range. This may sound too demanding, but I would not mind if the rifle were capable of putting three-shot groups center-to-center, inside an inch at 50 yards. I want as much firearm margin of error removed as possible, in other words.

All bullets will be deflected. Live by that fact, and you will do well. There is no bullet which can be counted on to bust through a lot of brush and center a target, point-on, at the other end—this includes even the 458 Winchester and its ilk. Look to accuracy and fast, accurate shooting with a rifle of high pointability instead of thinking that any gun can push bullets through much more than a light brush screen without deflection.

Shots in brush like this are always dicey. Look for "holes." Deer on left is most open—it's the best choice in this herd.

Sights

I think the brush rifle should wear the sights which the shooter has total confidence in and has mastered so that he can put a bullet in a precise spot through the holes in the brush. If I had to pick but one sight type for all of us to use, I guess it would have to be a scope. I would prefer low power, and I would get that lower power from a variable. We can talk about the worst brush country we have ever seen, but most of us will have to admit that even in that brush, there were *some* openings, even meadows. So my variable will drop down to as low as 1.5 power, but I won't mind if it can jump back up in power for that concentrated shot across a meadow.

I also have a taste for peep sights. My Model 94 Winchester wears one. The disc in that sight's slide is small in diameter and features a large ''hunting'' aperture. It is fast and accurate. I have also found plain open sights fine for close-range accuracy, and some not-so-close-range accuracy, too. The scope is king here, though. A wide-angle scope gives plenty of field of view, and a lot of pinpoint accuracy potential.

A time ago, I had a chance to harvest a nice white-tailed buck in a very brushy situation. The rifle was a 30-30, and I recall my handload used Silvertips at about 2000 fps MV. The buck's antlers seemed almost detached from the rest of the animal when he jumped. And I knew it was a trophy specimen. The sights came up and I was about to fire, when some good little guardian angel told me to, ''Hold it! Wait for a second. The buck is going to hit that open patch just 20 steps ahead.'' I listened to the little voice and waited, and put one bullet on the mark for a swift and clean harvest. I think brush shooting is mainly that, controlling the shot so that the bullet seeks an open path to the target. Millions of us shoot in the brush, and we should remain aware that certain ballistic traits do aid brush shooting, but the most important trait is shooting *straight*.

Chapter 23
The Rifled Slug and Buckshot

THE WORLD of deer hunting has expanded for the complete shooter. The reason is population—the *deer* population. Whereas the mighty elk is a creature of the quiet, wilderness-oriented places, the deer, especially the whitetail, can set up housekeeping on a lawn and raise a fawn in the garage, to overstate the case. Seriously, white-tailed deer are living at this very moment within hearing distance of a farm house or other dwellings.

But there's a problem in this very positive situation. Without a harvest, the deer's population would continue to grow until the deer destroyed their own habitat. Also, the rancher and farmer demands some relief from deer eating, literally, into their profits. Therefore, the deer are hunted and, hopefully, numbers will be controlled, just as numbers are controlled in the harvesting of any farm or ranch animal.

Over the years, as deer herds across the country increased in numbers, it was recognized that those herds had to be intensively harvested. However they had moved right into areas quite populated and the hunting problem was one of safety. Since hunters could not fire big game rifles in settled areas, the shotgun came to the rescue. If loaded with buckshot or rifled slugs, the range of the shotgun would be far less than the range of a modern rifle, even of the modest calibers such as the 30-30 Winchester or 35 Remington. The only problem was one of possible effectiveness. Would rifled slugs or buckshot prove humane on game of the deer class? Would the slug be accurate enough for deer hunting? Would the buckshot loads pattern well enough for the same task?

The questions were not asked too loudly at first. After all, the use of buckshot and slugs had been a tradition in America long before the population density skyrocketed. The problem, however, arose when hunters actually took to the field with these two shotshell types loaded into their shotguns. At the time, there wasn't any solid information available as to slug/buckshot accuracy. Questions arose. How far should a hunter attempt to hit a deer-sized target with a load of buckshot or a rifled slug? Also, how much punch did these loads have at 30, 40, 50 yards or more?

As with most phases of shooting, the complete shooter of the day who uses a shotgun with buckshot or rifled slug is better off than ever, and this chapter is aimed at explaining why this is a fact. But another objective is to discuss the actual accuracy level and authority of the buckshot load and the rifled slug. The two are covered in one chapter because they belong together. Hunters sometimes have a choice, in fact, between buckshot or rifled slug, and this discussion may help them make a decision.

General Information on the Slug

The rifled slug followed round ball use in the shotgun. A shotgun was, and still is, capable of using a round ball, the same type of round ball found in muzzleloaders. In my tests, I have loaded lead round balls of about .690-inch diameter into modern 12-gauge shotgun hulls using current loading information, and I have found these loads to be useful in terms of accuracy and power for close-range shooting, in the 50- to 75-yard bracket.

But somebody wanted something different. Enter the rifled slug. It turns out that the first rifled slug, as well as some of those used today, was not indeed an elongated missile at all. In fact, it was a squat affair with little better potential than a round ball. For years, the 12-gauge rifled slug, factory style, was 7/8-ounce in weight. This is a slug of 383 grains weight. The simple .690-inch round ball weighed 494 grains, so where the big gain was supposed to lie is hard to tell now. The slug would not be accurate at long range anyway, so the motive did not lie there, or at least shouldn't have.

Sectional density of these rifled slugs was certainly poor, and loss of initial MV was commensurate with this low sectional density. Ballistic coefficient was nothing to rave about either. But these detriments were in one respect the salvation of the rifled slug. After all, long range was *not* the goal of slug shooting. So what if the rifled slug did not shoot a mile. Its safety in populated areas was based upon the fact that the slug would not shoot far. However, deer hunters had to recognize the fact that trajectory-wise and energy-wise, the slug would not better a good 12-gauge lead round ball by much if anything worth talking about at all.

Somebody came up with the idea that accuracy would be enhanced, however, if the slug were rifled. So rifling of

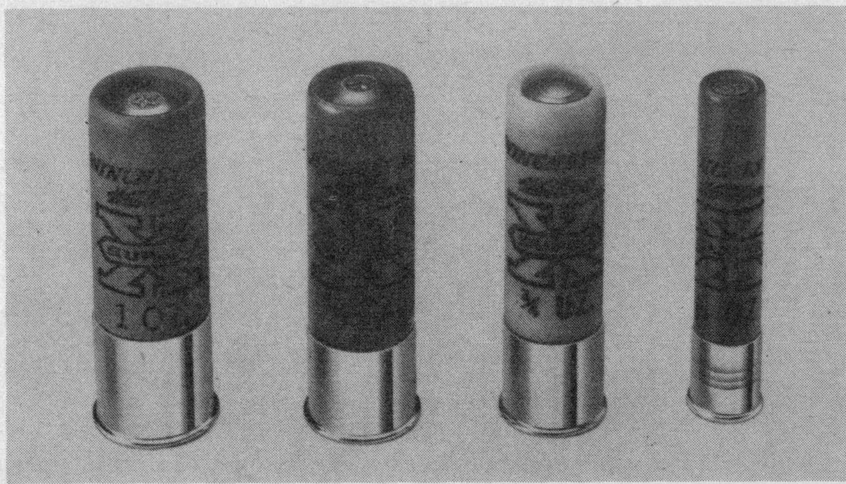

Winchester's line of rifled slugs is quite interesting in that the company has made significant strides in increasing accuracy of their factory-loaded slugs. Continued effort along these lines mean that rifled slugs may someday in the near future offer increased range potential in the terms of accuracy.

(Below) For many, the slug gun is the only "legal" firearm for deer. At ranges under 75 yards, a 12-gauge slug is effective deer medicine. This fat doe was taken with a single 12-gauge slug in the neck.

Thick terrain does not belong to the East alone, nor to the South. This heavily brushed country in Colorado proves that even western outdoorsmen may have to shoot in the brush.

sorts was imprinted on the outside of the slug to make it spin in order to stablize it just as if it had been fired from a rifled bore. Would that it were true. Some problems arose. First, the slug had to fit the bore. Obturation (bullet upset in the bore) was going to be high in rifled slugs, but bore fit could not be ignored anyway. Second, the slug had to remain centered in the bore. If a projectile is blasted downbore in a cockeyed fashion, it's very unlikely to shoot well in terms of accuracy. Third, there was wadding to consider. Unlike the cloth patch in the muzzleloader, a wad system could be a gas seal, but a wad could ruin the base of the slug, and if that happened, accuracy would suffer as the light, skirt-like base of an elongated projectile does help steer it.

Also, there was choke to consider. Fire a rifled slug in a shotgun, and the slug, most obviously, had to make contact with a choke. It sounds nice to think of the choke as a forcing cone here, just swaging that soft lead bullet beautifully and making it shoot straighter than a good ramrod. It never happened. In spite of obturation, the slug did not always reach the muzzle of the shotgun in uniform shape, and contact with the choke might be different each shot. Accuracy is not obtained by putting pressure on the missile in different places shot after shot. Incidentally, with even a modified choke barrel, my recent tests showed fliers, and one would ask if those fliers were due to the above-mentioned problem.

Also, if the base of a slug helps steer it, what happens to the rifled slug when the wads bang into it as it rides upbore? It deforms. A deformed projectile is not the best way

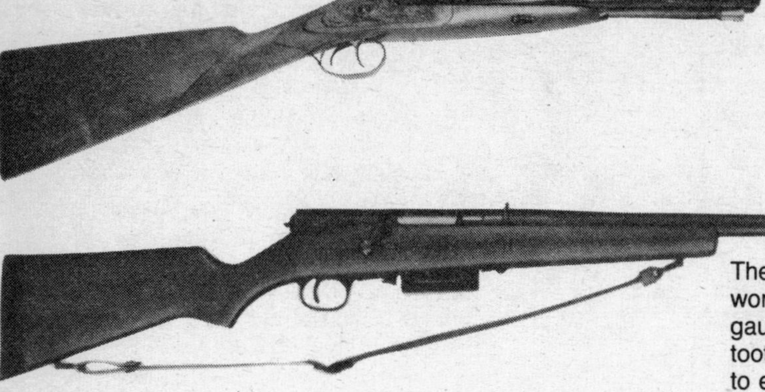

The black powder shotgun is not without ability in the use of single projectiles or buckshot. This little Navy Arms Texas Terry Range 12-gauge can handle buckshot loads and it can also shoot a single 12-gauge round ball out of each barrel.

The big Marlin 5510 goose gun in 10-gauge would work as a deer hunting gun with the 1³/₄-ounce 10-gauge factory slug load. Admittedly a bit "long in tooth," the big Marlin still has its place when it comes to economically priced 10-gauge slug tossers.

to gain accuracy. Interestingly, the hollow base of the rifled slug would not work in the same manner as the hollow base of the Minie, mainly because the Minie is rammed down-bore without wads. At this point, I know of no slug tests where wads were not used. But wads were attached to the slug in a permanent way in some cases to ease the deformation problem.

So the slug remained. But it did not remain the same. In 1980, the weight of the 12-gauge slug was increased from ⁷/₈-ounce to 1-ounce. Now the weight went from 383 grains to approximately 437.5 grains. Further development by the ammo companies brought about a hollow point slug, along with some changes in the aerodynamic design. The slug was and still is being improved.

Power of the Rifled Slug

On the face of it, a rifled slug is very formidable looking. The new 10-gauge factory slug is of pure lead and hollow point design. The Federal "Super Slug" series includes the 10-, 12-, 16-, 20-, 28-gauges and the .410, all of hollow point design. The 10-gauge 3¹/₂-inch Magnum Super Slug can be sighted for 75 yards. These are all rifled slugs. Authority? A 12-gauge slug can be pushed at good muzzle velocity considering its heft.

As an example, Lyman's cast slug of 445 grains weight, a bit more than an ounce, can leave the muzzle at 1565 fps according to the *Lyman Shotshell Handbook,* Second Edition, page 271. This would render a muzzle energy of 2421 foot-pounds. However, in order to present a fair and honest picture, such a load will also lose velocity within a relatively short range to the tune of half its energy. In the first 50 yards, the 12-gauge slug will lose roughly 50 percent of its velocity. Consider the above load, a 445-grain slug at 1565 fps MV. At 50 yards, this slug would be down to about 939 fps with a remaining energy of 871 foot-pounds.

I have no argument with 871 foot-pounds of deer-killing energy assuming good bullet placement, especially if the missile is large enough to create a good wound channel. Furthermore, as will be seen in a moment, the rifled slug may penetrate a little better when it is slowed down slight-

Federal has upgraded its offerings for slug-shooters. The slugs are now in hollow-point form and are heavier than before. The 10-gauge, far left, weighs 1³/₄ ounces, followed by the 12-gauge Magnum slug at 1¹/₄ ounces, the 16-gauge at ⁴/₅-ounce, the 20-gauge at ³/₄-ounce, a 28-gauge slug and the .410-inch slug.

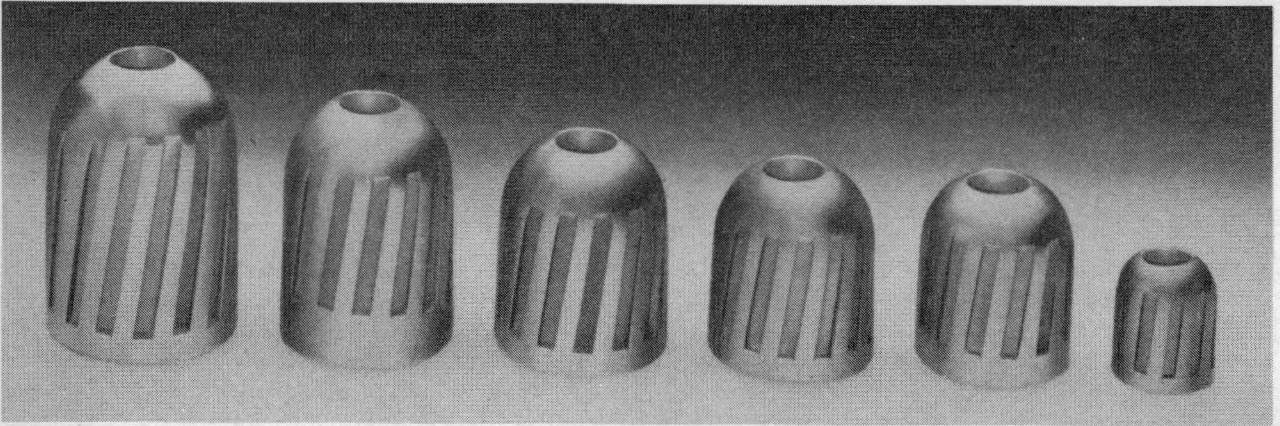

The 20-gauge rifled slug is considered by many to be a minimum size for deer hunting, but as in all generalities, there are exceptions. Some prefer the 20-gauge due to its lightness, and the fact that it can be sighted in for 75 yards with a trajectory pattern very similar to that of the 12-gauge with 1-ounce slug.

ly. I have taken a number of larger deer, weight-wise, with a 12-gauge and .535-inch round ball ammo starting out at 2000 fps. At 100 yards, this ball will be down to roughly 1100 to 1200 fps. Given 1200 fps, the 230-grain ball will have a remaining energy at 100 yards of 736 foot-pounds. As I say, I have cleanly dropped a number of deer with that level of energy.

However, we still have to talk about a few other factors before we can ascertain the range at which the shotgun slug loses its ability to truly harvest deer-sized game cleanly. A factor is the gauge, of course. Most of us agree that for deer the 16, 12 and 10 gauges are suitable, and that a 20-gauge is getting into the borderline area. Remember, when velocity of any stupendous nature is out of the question, we turn to mass of the projectile to help make up for the lack of speed. With velocity of the rifled slug being low, then we want the larger gauges with their subsequently heavier projectiles.

For example, the bullet caster can make a Lyman 20-gauge slug which weighs 341 grains cast in pure lead. I recommend it. This 341-grain slug can be pushed at 1635 fps MV according to the *Lyman Shotshell Handbook,* Second Edition, page 281. The muzzle energy isn't so bad. We have 2025 foot-pounds to work with. But the 20-gauge slug, being of less mass than the 12-gauge slug, may lose 45 percent of its original velocity in a span of 50 yards. Now we have 899 fps left for a remaining energy of 612 foot-pounds at 50 yards from the muzzle.

Yes, many deer have been dropped with a lot less than 612 foot-pounds of energy, but guidelines have to be drawn. I try to get as close as I can with my 54-caliber muzzleloader because I realize the ball loses its velocity, hence its energy, rapidly. Therefore, to equate the situation, one would surely want to be very close to his deer when using a 20-gauge slug, maybe only 30 yards or so to be on the safe side. There is no margin for error built into the 20-gauge slug load in terms of excess energy.

The damage done by modern hollow point 12-gauge slugs can be seen on the left. The can on the right was hit with a conventional, 12-gauge, solid slug. The difference in destruction is obvious.

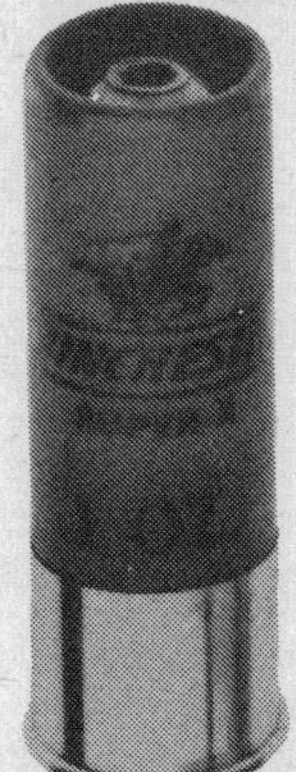
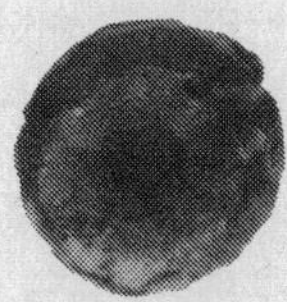

The 12-gauge rifled slug from Winchester uses the hollow point design. This is the 1-ounce version, which would weigh about 437-438 grains. At close range, there is no question concerning its effectiveness.

Power? Up close, there is no doubt that the "power" is there for a 10- or 12-gauge slug, possibly a 16-gauge as well, with the 20-gauge good only for *extremely* short-range work. The big 10-gauge factory load from Federal proved that it could be sighted for 75 yards, of course, with a trajectory pattern which would give a shooter 90 to 100

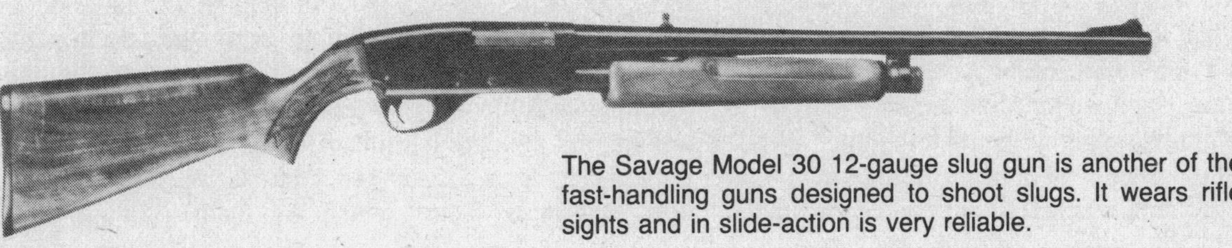

The Savage Model 30 12-gauge slug gun is another of the fast-handling guns designed to shoot slugs. It wears rifle sights and in slide-action is very reliable.

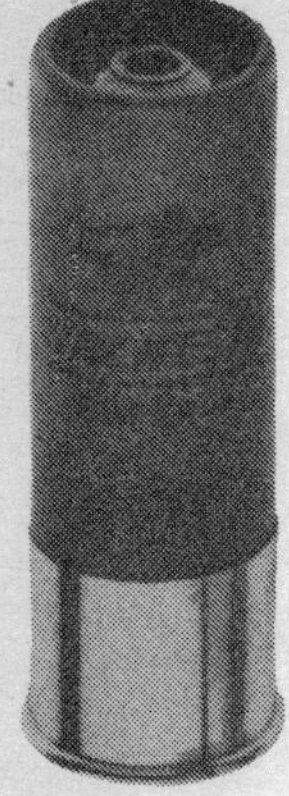

The 12-gauge rifled slug with the 1-ounce slug can be sighted in for 75 yards. The slug will then drop about 2.5 inches at 100 yards. Most authorities agree that 75 yards and under is better in rifled slug shooting for deer than is longer range.

(Right) Accuracy with slugs is not gilt edged. At 50 yards, a pattern like this could, indeed, harvest deer. However, by switching to a slug barrel, or a barrel with something more loose than a Full or Modified choke, groups will generally improve. Generally speaking, maximum slug accuracy will be found in guns wearing Improved cylinder or Cylinder bores.

yards of range to work with, but the shooter might want to consider even this big boy on the block a 75-yard proposition.

Range

Obviously, range is dictated by power and accuracy. So we will keep this short here. The conclusion I came to is that I would prefer to keep my own slug-shooting down to about 75 yards with a 10- or 12-gauge load. In the next commentary on accuracy, the reader will see why. I might add that the range of shotgun slugs could very well increase as the factories continue to upgrade slug performance. We will have to wait for the results of tests going on, at this moment, in most of the major ammo factories. If the ammo makers can advance another giant step forward, as they have in the past few years, effective range will increase for shotgun slugs.

Accuracy

The accuracy of the rifled slug is nothing to get excited about, not when compared with the modern rifle, or for that matter, the rifle of 200 years ago! Smoothbores are smoothbores. (I have, in fact, increased the accuracy of single projectile shooting from my black powder shotguns by loading a round ball, just one in each barrel, of course, with a cushion wad and an over-powder wad downbore. The wad was soaked with a paste such as Falkenberry Juice, emulsified version, or Young Country Lube 103. Then the round ball is run downbore patched, as one would patch a rifle ball in a muzzleloader.)

When it comes right down to it, the accuracy of slugs in the modern shotgun is simply no better than ''OK.'' While I have managed to make some center-to-center groups for three shots at 40 yards which fell into the 2-inch area, I cannot say with confidence that I could do that all the time. The slug is an interesting projectile. Obturation is very complete, which is certainly not bad in itself, but it almost seems that the obturation goes beyond that point of normal bullet upset with the shotgun slug ''trying'' to deform during obturation.

Sure, the slug is soft. But so are black powder missiles, and yet I have tested a 12-gauge rifled slug in my bullet box against a 58-caliber 500-grain Minie, and the latter totally eclipsed the rifled slug when it came to penetration. In fact, I have destroyed a bullet box with 58-caliber loads in a muzzleloader, while actually capturing a 12-gauge rifled slug after only a few inches of penetration.

Accuracy? I think part of the problem lies in the above facts, and I wish I knew exactly what to do about this. If the slug is combined with a strong wad which will not deform the base of the slug itself, accuracy improves. However, in my tests, I simply cannot report any tackhole accuracy, even with slugs which have the wads attached firmly to the base of the slug. I would have to admit to three-shot groups of about 4 to 5 inches, center-to-center, at 50 yards for most of my shotgunning. Those have been the *good* ones. My *worst* groups in a series of tests were in the 9-inch realm at 50 yards for three shots, these from a full-choke gun.

Previously, I thought I was having better luck with a modified choke over a cylinder or improved cylinder bore, but when I challenged myself to prove the statement, I found my data lacking. I did *not* get best accuracy with the modified choke, and I got worse with the full choke when testing was done with a lot of group averages. The improved cylinder was a bit better in this last series of tests using Winchester factory ammo, and the best groups of all

If your own shotgun does not wear a modern slug barrel, complete with adjustable sights, consider going over to a scope. The author likes a 1.5 × 4 variable for slug shooting.

The H&R Single Shot Magnum Shotgun in the Model 176 Slug Gun style is available in 10-gauge Magnum. Using the Federal slug, this gun will put out a missile of 1 3/4-ounce heft. It is cylinder bore and wears rifle sights.

came from the cylinder bore of a slug barrel. I admit that the adjustable sights on that slug barrel would have had something to do with this, but not this time. I interchanged barrels and used the same sights with all choke types.

At this juncture, I would like to state that the full choke is definitely not as good as the modified, the modified not as good as the improved cylinder and the latter not as good as the cylinder bore. My only problem is that with a few *combinations* of certain shotguns and certain loads, this factor was bent a little. My best advice is for the shooter deeply interested in shotgun slug shooting to buy a small quantity of each of several different brands of slugs, and if he's a handloader, then he might even consult the loading manuals and put a few of these combinations together. The shooter should then try them all in his own shotgun, trying to find a specific load which will shoot with the most accuracy from that specific shotgun.

Fliers were also a part of my tests. When I had a group of some sort going for me at 50 yards, there would suddenly be a nice big hole off in the corner of the target somewhere, or even off the paper altogether. Having spoken on accuracy of slugs, my suggestion is to find the best combination for the shotgun of the individual shooter, and then to consider using slugs at 50 yards or so. Sighted at 50 yards, the 12-gauge rifled slug will fall into the earth at roughly 200 yards, so trajectory is not terribly flat.

What about the rifling on the rifled slug? I have my doubts that these vanes act to spin the slug with much R.P.S. (revolutions per second), and I think the slug flies because it is nose heavy, the way a playing dart at the pub flies true because its center of gravity is well forward. The vanes might help hold the slug better centered in the bore, but I cannot prove that either.

Sights for Slug Guns

If a shooter wants to shoot bullets in a shotgun, then he might consider sights meant for shooting bullets. I have a friend who can take his shotgun, a side-by-side, and hit a 6-inch bull at 50 yards just about every time, and he uses the bead on the shotgun. I suppose a shooter can learn to master his own shotgun in this fashion, but my suggestion is to shoot the slugs with "real sights."

The variable telescopic sight of 1.5x4x is one of the choices I would make. If not, then the open sight as found on today's slug barrels would be the answer. Why a scope? After all, the accuracy of the slug, or lack of it, may not be enhanced by the aforementioned scope, even at the 4x setting. I'll agree with that up to a point, but if I had a shot at even 75 yards and had "the drop" on a buck, I would as soon have a view of the buck at 4x for best aiming, even with the rifled slug.

Reloading

Already touched on, is the fact that there are some good reloading opportunities for the slug-shooter. As this is written, Lyman offers a couple of molds for slugs (smooth, not rifled). I have tried the Slugmasters from Ballistics Products, Inc., with satisfaction. These are offered in 12-gauge, 410 grains weight; 16-gauge, 339 grains; and 20-gauge at 275 grains. Information from Ballistics Products, Inc., shows that these are "fracture-type slugs," and that they are designed to break up on impact. I have not tested this feature. The above-named company is in the process of providing additional information on slug-loading, however, and their work will be worth looking at and keeping abreast of.

Buckshot has been, and continues to be, popular in certain areas of the U.S. Federal Cartridge is currently offering buckshot in their Premium lineup. Federal Premium buckshot loads feature copper plated shot and buffered plastic filler.

Buckshot

Buckshot has always been popular in our country. "Buck-and-ball" loads were used in doubles in the black powder days—one barrel carried a patched round ball and the other carried a load of buckshot. A man was ready for 'most anything with that combination.

Today, the buckshot situation still rides high with deer hunters in certain areas of the U.S. Some shooters even live in areas where they must, by law, use buckshot for deer.

Buckshot should be viewed as a load of individual pellets. Sure, a load of buckshot is formidable because it carries multiple projectiles, but no matter how that fact stands up, another fact stands just as tall, and that's the individual pellet punch. Yes, a lot of pellets may hit the target. But maybe they won't. Maybe only a couple will find the deer. If so, what does a shooter have going for him? I will tell you what he has going for him—less than the power of a single round ball from a squirrel rifle.

Black powder shooting was discussed earlier and the squirrel rifle was mentioned. Nobody got excited about hunting deer with the sub-bores, though surely deer have been taken with tiny round balls, especially in early America on the eastern seaboard. The fact stands that a 00 buckshot pellet is only 33-caliber, or .330-inch in diameter.

In the casting chapter the formula for figuring the weight of a round ball was worked out, being $D^3 \times .5236 \times$

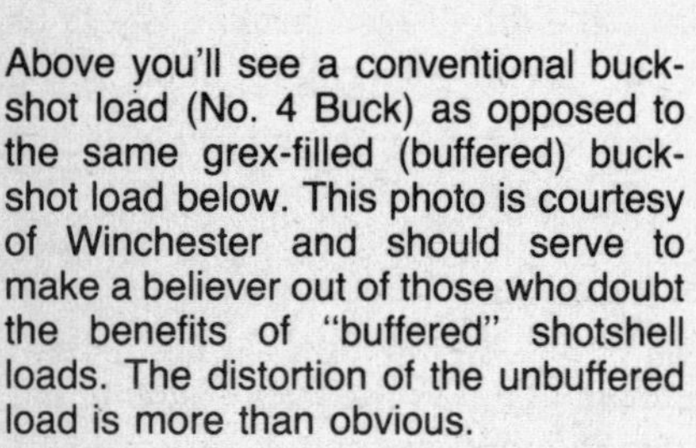

Above you'll see a conventional buckshot load (No. 4 Buck) as opposed to the same grex-filled (buffered) buckshot load below. This photo is courtesy of Winchester and should serve to make a believer out of those who doubt the benefits of "buffered" shotshell loads. The distortion of the unbuffered load is more than obvious.

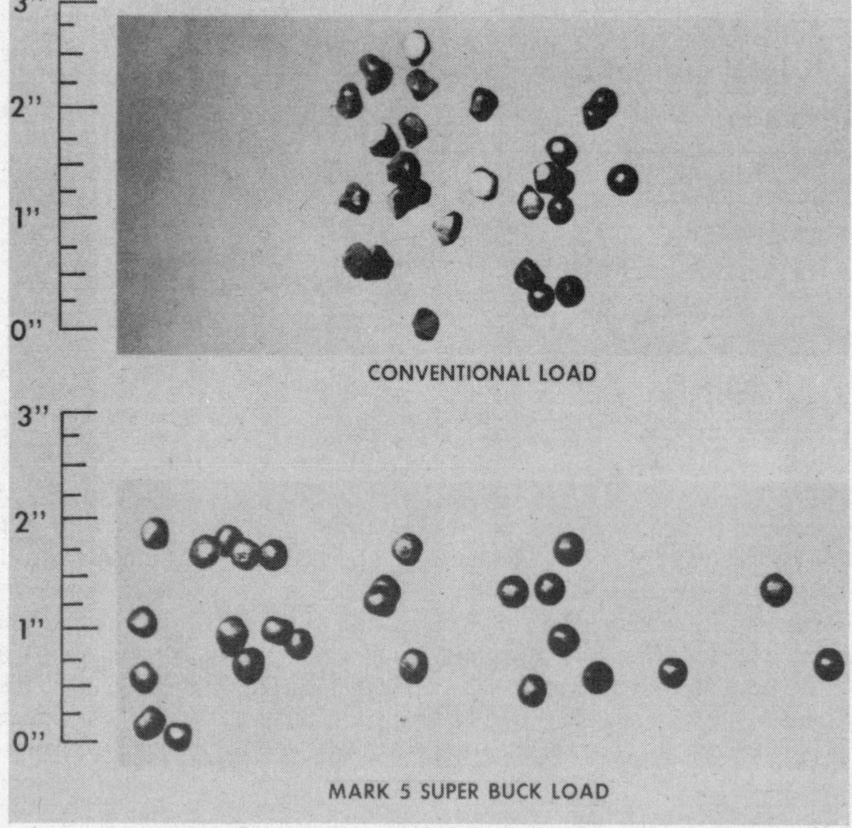

2,873.5. Using this formula for the .330-inch pill, we find that the 00 buckshot pellet weights 54 grains. A round ball for the 36-caliber squirrel rifle weighs 65 grains in the .350-inch size and darn few shooters would be recommending the 36-caliber for deer. And there's more. The little .350-inch ball from my Hatfield squirrel rifle leaves the muzzle at over 2000 fps with a very safe charge of black powder. I know of *no* buckshot load which leaves the muzzle at 2000 fps.

A look at individual pellet energy reveals that the 54-grain 00 buckshot will go about 1300 fps MV out of the common buckshot shotshell. This means an individual pellet energy of 203 foot-pounds. Note that well—203 foot-pounds of energy per 00 pellet at 1300 fps. Now more reality—that pellet won't hit at 1300 fps. At 50 yards, that 00 pellet will be lucky to be going along at 1000 fps. If so, the energy has now dropped to only 120 foot-pounds per pellet.

Multiple Pellet Strikes

But let's get back to the whole idea of buckshot, which is multiple strikes. It's not one pellet hitting, but several. A common 12-gauge buckshot load consists of an even dozen 00 pellets per shell. If all of the pellets hit at the same time, that's a force to be noted. Let's see, those dozen 00 pellets will weigh a total of 648 grains. At 1300 fps, the muzzle energy here is 2432 foot-pounds. Pretty good. At 50 yards, the energy rating for the entire mass of 00 pellets would be 1439 foot-pounds, still a real power—*if every pellet hit*.

Ah, there is the rub, and it's a two-way rub, about like an itch you can't get to. In the first place, every pellet is *not* going to hit the target at 50 yards. The 00 buckshot load is a cluster up close. But move back 15 yards and see what happens. At 30 yards, it's quite unlikely that every pellet in the 00 load will strike the chest area of a deer. Beyond 30 yards, it becomes more doubtful yet. And I don't care what choke is used.

Buckshot Range

For the reasons stated above, I view the range of buckshot, even in the larger gauges with larger pellets, as about 30 yards for surefire deer-taking, with maybe another 5 yards tacked on if the shooter will remember to keep on shooting. In the course of researching buckshot, aside from my personal tests, I spoke with a few hunters who had taken several deer each with buckshot of the 0 to 000 size, and each hunter agreed that the idea was to keep right on shooting—even if the buck drops, in other words, shoot again, put more pellets on target.

The pattern of buckshot is not nearly as even and well-dispersed at one might think. We speak about shotgun patterning, and I urge the shooter to get out and do some buckshot patterning for himself. He may be very surprised at 40 yards when he finds that instead of a central concentration of pellets, the big 0 to 000 buck have pretty well splattered over the pattern board.

My most recent work with patterning of buckshot showed best results with a particular modified choke barrel. I am convinced, however, that there are various factors which contribute to buckshot patterning and though it seems like passing the buck, I suggest that the shooter go afield with his own shotgun and a few different types of buckshot loads and pattern for himself.

Buckshot Reloading

Of course the buckshot load can be a reloading proposition for those who care to do so. Ballistic Products, Inc., is now working on various methods of improving buckshot patterning, in fact, and the information will be passed on to shooters in that outfit's next catalog. I look forward to their findings. Since buckshot loads are used on deer in many areas, it will be all the better to have the most efficiency possible from them. At this point, I am much more concerned with pattern than with anything else in buckshot shooting. If I were able to put every 00 or 000 pellet from a heavy load into a 1-foot circle at 40 yards, I would speak highly of buckshot loads for use at 40 yards or so.

Also, it might not be a bad idea for the shotgunner to consider a 10-gauge if he is going to do extensive deer hunting with buckshot. Lyman's aforementioned shotshell handbook shows 10-gauge loads of 18, 00 buck, and this is with a 1200 fps MV. There are 12-gauge loads which will handle 12, 00 buckshot, too. And the fine 3-inch 12-gauge hull can handle 16, 0 buckshot, which is impressive.

In Summary

Without a doubt, the buckshot load is a very powerful one, but it is certainly not on par with the rifled slug, and the rifled slug is not exactly a long-range number at the present time. The complete shooter is a person who tunes his loads to the highest point, and in the case of buckshot and rifled slugs, that point is finding, by trial and error, the buckshot or slug which works best in the individual shotgun. And then it's a matter of using each within its range in terms of both power and accuracy.

Chapter 24

Pattern Your Shotgun

While most riflemen go into the game fields knowing the accuracy, trajectory and general ballistics of a particular rifle/caliber combo, most shotgunners leave their success or failure up to the "fates of the hunt." All shotgunners would do well to follow in the tracks of the knowledgeable rifleman, i.e., "pattern" that firearm before you head for the game fields.

THE KNOWLEDGEABLE SHOOTER would not think of going into the field without sighting in his rifle. After finding out which load works best in terms of accuracy and power, he not only wants to sight it in with great care, but he also wants to know the trajectory of the bullet over a specific range, such as zero to 300 yards. Somewhat surprisingly, these very same shooters may take to the field with shotgun in hand, never having the slightest idea where the pattern strikes "the target," nor, for that matter, having the slightest notion of what the pattern looks like with various loads.

It doesn't make sense. A shotgun is not the precise shooting instrument which the rifle or handgun definitely is, but neither is it a smokestack designed to spew shot out in random fashion. In fact, the shotgun can be very sensitive to various load changes. In some instances, I have noted *greater* differences between two 12-gauge shotguns than I would find between two 270 Winchester rifles. Therefore, to treat the shotgun as a generalized work tool which does not require testing and adjustment, is to treat it wrongly.

Testing and adjustment in shotgun language comes in the form of *patterning*. The loads are fired at a pattern board, and though it would be nice to have an elaborate setup here, the pattern board can be no more than a mere sheet of butcher paper set up on a flat surface to face the shooter. The idea is to fire into the paper so that the pattern made by the shot is clearly visible. I have used paper as basic as the butcher-shop variety, a flattened out refrigerator carton, sheets of wrapping paper, all about 5 feet × 5 feet in size, all stretched out and tacked down to a wooden frame.

Reasons for Patterning

1. Determining the Actual Choke of Your Shotgun

The manufacturer cannot afford the time to check each and every shotgun leaving the factory, except for those very expensive, special-order guns. If someone fired each shotgun to see how it actually patterned, the cost of each would rise considerably. Therefore, the gun goes out unchecked, which is certainly understandable and not that bad. However, a shotgun is as individual in its mechanical nature as other arms, and each shotgun will vary in how it

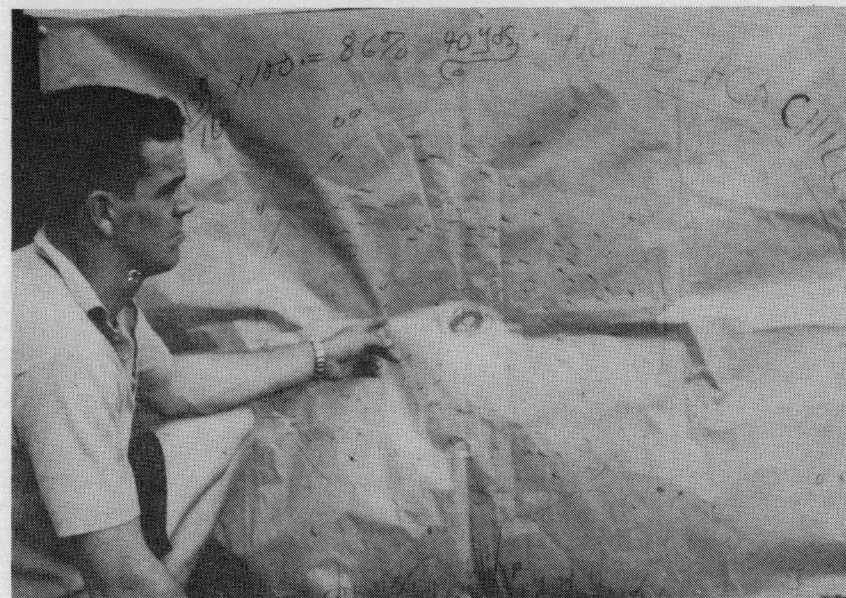

One of the prime reasons for patterning your shotgun is to determine the actual degree of choke (regardless of what's stamped on the barrel) with a specific charge and shot size. This shooter just got an 86 percent (Full choke) pattern using a Browning A5 3-inch Magnum and No. 4 shot.

patterns. After all, changes occur throughout manufacture, and one bore will never be the same as the next, not even when both guns have the same brand name on them and the same choke value.

The prime reason for patterning is to determine what *your* shotgun choke really is. A sample case comes to mind. An Arizona friend, who hunted quail and dove as an occupation it seemed, bought a brand new over/under 20-gauge shotgun, choked improved cylinder/improved cylinder, just right for quail. He also bought a spare set of barrels choked modified/improved modified, perfect for doves. He shot lousy with that gun. In spite of his deep interest in shotgunning, this fellow had never patterned any of his guns. One day, after about a box of shells and but a few birds in his game bag, I suggested we pattern his shotgun. "Do you think we will find something wrong with the gun?," he asked in disbelief. After all, he paid a bundle for it.

I said we might not find anything wrong, but another trip to the optometrist was more expensive than a little time and a few shells, so we headed for an open spot, with lots of sheet paper in tow. The gun shot, with the improved cylinder/improved cylinder barrels, about 65 percent in one barrel and about 60 percent in the other. I would call it improved modified and modified. How did it get that way? I have no idea, but that wasn't the first time I had seen a gun shoot tighter or more open patterns than the stated choke on the barrel.

2. You Can Choose Your Best Load from Patterning

It is very common for a given shotgun to shoot nice patterns with one load and maybe not so great patterns with another load. In fact, it is more common for this condition to exist than it would be locating a shotgun which simply shot all sizes of pellets to the same pattern style in density. So, in a trial and error manner, the shotgunner takes his tubegun to the range, and he carries along a variety of ammo for it. The handloader has it made here, for he can whip up all kinds of variations to play with. But the non-handloader can still scrounge around and locate different shells in terms of shot size, load, brand and so forth. Besides, it is so worthwhile knowing what a shotgun will do with what ammo that buying a few different types of shells just for patterning is well worth the expense. Generally, the patterning session per gun will occur but once.

3. You Can Choose a Best Load for the Specific Game Being Hunted

Not only can a shotgunner select the very best load for his gun, but he can also work up specific loads around one

Shooters have found that a fine target load, such as this Winchester AA Plus, with its 1 ounce No. 8 shot charge in 12-gauge, is often just right for upland game birds such as quail. The reason is pattern, a well-distributed, dense pattern for close-range work.

Without proper stock fit, patterns won't always center as nicely as you would like them to. In other words, where your shot charge impacts the pattern board isn't always a function of shot size, charge and choke. Also, as you can see, the pattern board needn't be elaborate. A 4-foot by 4-foot square of butcher paper tacked on to a simple frame is all it takes.

given shot size. Example: I don't care if No. 8 shot patterns to near perfection in a shotgun of mine, I still won't use it for geese. I want larger shot *where I hunt*. So I would take my No. 4 shot, No. 2 shot and so forth, and load it in various ways, trying to find out how to make the "best pattern" in my goose gun *with that shot*. This is different from the last search, which was for a load or loads which simply patterned nicely in the gun.

4. Stock Fit

You'd better believe it! I have learned about stock fit through patterning a shotgun. The method is easy enough. And I suppose one could use other than the standard patterning board, but with the patterning board, the shooter aims quickly at a center point on the pattern sheet. The idea is to get a nice natural shot off, aimed right at the dot in the center of the pattern board in hopes of putting the shot all over that aiming point. You'd be amazed. I have seen patterns which struck so high that a bird would be hit only if it flew straight up out of the grass. I have hit way left, way right, too, and too low.

Obviously, the idea is to shoot a few times to determine for sure that there is a strong continuance of a certain *trend*. One shot won't do it. The fit of gun-to-shooter can allow a shooter to think he is putting his pattern in a certain area, when he is not. Therefore, the patterning of the shotgun can teach a fellow just where he is actually putting the bulk of his shotgun's pattern. Yes, an upland game gun may be stocked to shoot a little high. We have to bear that in mind. But the pattern should still strike the pattern board somewhere at 40 yards, and I don't mean fringing along the very top of the paper.

5. A Bent Barrel

A bent barrel or other fault can be determined from patterning. Unfortunately, some shooters have taken a gun into a gunsmith for adjustment when in fact the gun fit them fine. The barrel was bent. Not often will this occur, but it can happen. I shot one factory gun which came with this barrel problem. Generally, the bent barrel is going to be a situation of damage somewhere in the gun's life. When a pattern hits way off, look for a bent barrel before suggesting that the stock does not fit. If the barrel is OK, then look to stock fit as a possible problem.

The Pattern Board

The pattern board may be no more than a nice big sheet of butcher paper 4 by 4 feet or larger. It must be supported so that it faces the shooter squarely. It's nice to staple the paper onto two vertical thin boards about 2 inches wide and tall enough so that the center aiming point is about level with the shooter's eye. Before putting it up, put a nice 6-inch diameter black aiming point in the center of the pattern sheet.

Some shooters will prefer to shoot while simply standing up and letting fly. I always try this method first, and then if I think I am not getting a good center hold, I may use a rest of some sort. I have even used a portable benchrest in a couple of cases, so that I knew that the bead of the shotgun was indeed pointed to the center of the pattern sheet. A shotgun is not much fun to shoot from a bench when high-velocity, heavy-shot loads are used, so pad your shoulder.

The Pattern

A pattern is also needed to make a 30-inch diameter circle on the sheet after the shot. Cut out a circle from a piece of paper 30 inches in diameter. Use this as a template to make a cardboard cutout. If the circle is a problem, find something to draw it with. I usually forego the paper pattern and look for a lid which is 30 inches in diameter. It's not easy to find, but I found one. It was the top of a wastepaper basket.

This is an important tool in the process of patterning, and it is well worth taking a few moments to find stiff cardboard and to make a neat 30-inch pattern. It will be used over and over again.

This shooter has just counted up the number of pellet strikes in a 30-inch circle at 40 yards. His old Marlin 20-gauge over/under, using 3-inch shells, just dropped 140 No. 6 shot into the circle. Given an average of 168 No. 6 shot in this type of load, the number of pellet strikes indicates 83 percent—a Full choke pattern, indeed.

Range and Shot Pattern

Shoot from 40 yards away. This is critical. I don't mean critical to the inch, but try to arrange for a distance of 40 yards between the muzzle of the shotgun and the paper pattern board. The 40-yard range is a standard used by all shotgunners. I've seen shooters firing from 30 yards or 20 yards because "that's where I do most of my shooting." Fine, do that some other time, but for now, choose a 40-yard range without fail or you will not learn what you must learn about the pattern of your shotgun.

Fire a single shot aimed directly at the center of the pattern board using the dot as a guide. Now walk up to the board and place your 30-inch cardboard cutout over the most prominent part of that pattern. This is just eyeball work. It won't be difficult to see where the most dense part of the pattern lies. With a marking pencil, trace a line all around the edge of the 30-inch cardboard disc. Now when the disc is removed, the dark line will encompass the most shot in the pattern. The reason we shoot from 40 yards and use a 30-inch measure is that now we have a standard to work from that we can *interpret*. By using this method, we can actually see what our choke is in terms of full, modified, and so forth. The 20- and 30-yard distances are not standard, but they can be used later on.

Count the Shot

Count the number of shot within that 30-inch circle. Jot down the number. To find your shotgun's pattern percentage, it's a simple matter of division, which a hand calculator does for us in a second. Divide the total number of holes in the 30-inch circle by the number of shot contained in that shotgun shell. How do you know the number of shot in the load? Easy. Just read the charge of shot on the hull or box and then refer to the chart below.

Example: I have just fired on my pattern board. I have traced around the densest part of the pattern and within the 30-inch circle, my shotgun has made 276 holes. My load was 1¼ ounces of No. 7 shot. What is my percentage pattern? My percentage pattern is 74 percent.

By the chart below, we see that there are 299 pellets in an ounce of No. 7 shot. In 1¼ ounces of No. 7 shot, we find a total of 374 pellets. If we divide 276 by 374 we get .73796. And rounded off, that is 74 percent. In that load,

Shot Chart

Number of Shot Pellets Per Ounce

BB	=	50 pellets	**No. 7**	=	299 pellets
No. 2	=	88 pellets	**No. 7½**	=	350 pellets
No. 4	=	136 pellets	**No. 8**	=	409 pellets
No. 5	=	172 pellets	**No. 9**	=	585 pellets
No. 6	=	223 pellets	**No. 12**	=	2,385 pellets

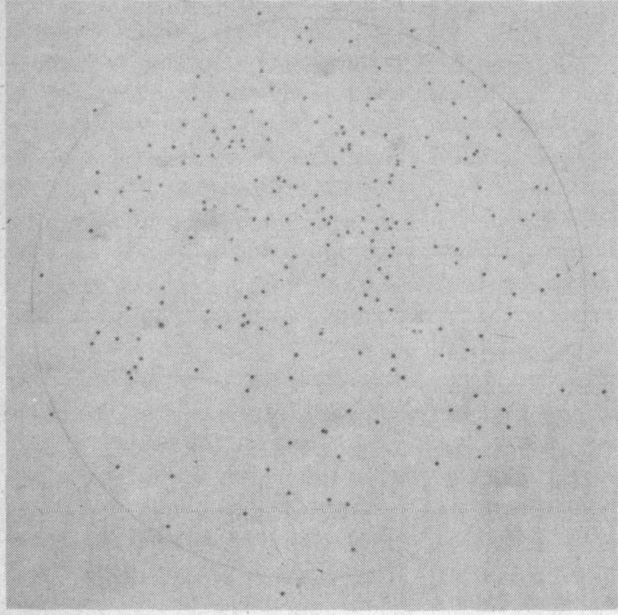

While this particular pattern is very high in shot count, you can see "holes" at 4, 5, 6, 7 and 8 o'clock. In other words, small birds such as quail, dove, etc., might escape unscathed. Try various, appropriate shot sizes for the game you're hunting and settle on a load that provides the best possible density and distribution of the shot charge.

the gun patterned full choke. Great. Now we know that our barrel is full choke and that we can expect all of our following loads to produce full choke patterns, right? Wrong. The next time around a charge of 1¼ ounces of No. 5 shot may pattern 65 percent. I have seen it happen before.

Let's try another example. This time we have our favorite 20-gauge bird gun at the pattern board. Standing 40 yards away, we shoot for the center of the pattern paper. Again, the 30-inch circle is traced around the most dense part of the pattern. We are using 1 ounce of No. 8 shot in the gun, and we find that there are 212 pellets in our 30-inch circle. Since there are 409 pellets in an ounce of No. 8 shot, we divide 212 by 409, and the percentage of that pattern is 52 percent. This would be Improved Cylinder or Improved Cylinder I. Here are the ratings:

Extra Full Choke	80 percent or better
Full Choke	70 to 79 percent
Improved Modified Choke	65 to 69 percent
Modified Choke	55 to 64 percent
Improved Cylinder I	50 to 54 percent
Improved Cylinder II	45 to 49 percent
Cylinder	under 45 percent

Variations

I have seen many variations within one shotgun. For example, I tried three different shot sizes in an over/under full choke barrel with 1¼ ounces of shot in each case. With 1¼ ounces of No. 8 shot, the pattern was 80 percent. With 1¼ ounces of No. 6 shot the pattern was 70 percent (still full choke). But with 1¼ ounces of No. 4 shot, the pattern was 84 percent, getting into the extra full choke range. I have seen larger differences, too, and in the other direction, with smaller shot making the fuller choke pattern.

Pattern Distribution

There is more to studying a shot pattern on a pattern board than determining the choke percentage. In fact, I consider another factor more important than choke percentage, and to use the vernacular, this is the aspect of "holes in the pattern." No pattern will perfectly cover a 30-inch circle at 40 yards. But the holes I am speaking of are problems. I have seen a shotgun throw a fine well-distributed pattern of No. 7 shot, while at the very same time putting No. 4 shot into such a splotchy distribution pattern that a big bird would have been missed if that bird happened to occupy that portion of that pattern.

The cure? Try other loads until the gaps in the pattern disappear. If the gaps never do go away, then a good checkup of the barrel is in order; there is something wrong. I have never had a shotgun barrel in good order which would not shoot *some* load and shot size with good pattern density. One of the biggest reasons for patterning is this one—find that load with the right shot that makes a nice evenly distributed pattern. We know, for example, that we should choose certain shot sizes for certain game, and for specific target situations as well, but when those shot sizes leave holes, go to another shot size.

Remember, of course, when studying holes in the pattern, or when looking at an evenly distributed pattern, that the shot did not arrive in a sheet. The pellets did not get to the paper at the same time. The pattern is very important as a study, but never get the idea that it represents what actually happens in the air with a shot string. The word string is used because that is how a bunch of shot flies from a shotgun. Not in a cloud, but in a string, the shorter the better, theoretically.

Small shot wins the distribution contest generally due to the fact that the many pellets of a small-shot string have a better mathematical chance of even distribution, so the pattern must be studied with this fact in mind. I have, however, seen lousy distribution with small shot in some barrels. I recall one improved cylinder gun which blew small shot around on the pattern board badly. That gun, meant as an upland bird gun to begin with, did better on quail with No. 6 shot than with No. 8 shot.

Shot Size Choices

Generally, we want a compromise. The compromise is between a good pattern with shot size adequate for the game being taken or the target being broken. Examples are

American Standard

No.	Chilled Shot No. in Oz.	Drop Shot No. in Oz.	Diam. in Inches	Diameter in Millimeters
Dust	....	4565	.04	1.02
No. 12	2385	2326	.05	1.27
11	1380	1346	.06	1.52
10	868	848	.07	1.78
9	585	568	.08	2.03
8	409	399	.09	2.28
7½	345	338	.09½	2.41
7	299	291	.10	2.54
6	223	218	.11	2.79
5	172	168	.12	3.02
4	136	132	.13	3.30
3	109	106	.14	3.53
2	88	86	.15	3.78
1	73	71	.16	4.06

No.	Drop Shot No. in Oz.	Diameter in Inches	Diameter in Millimeters
B	59	.17	4.32
Air Rifle	55	.17½	4.44
No. BB	50	.18	4.57
BBB	42	.19	4.83
T	36	.20	5.08
TT	31	.21	5.33
F	27	.22	5.59
FF	24	.23	5.84

Shotgunners have always had a generous selection of shot sizes to choose from. The smaller shot always carries the largest numercial designation, i.e., No. 12 (or "dust") is generally the smallest available shot size.

Pattern derives from the actual shot wad column as well as the choke in the barrel. As shown in this cutaway of a Remington shotgun shell, the one-piece plastic wad offers a cushioned effect for the shot, aiding in keeping the shot rounder for fewer fliers.

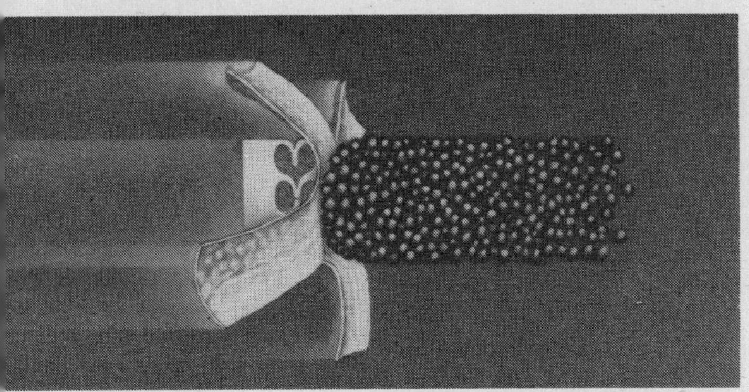

This is a superb demonstration of how a shot charge escapes its one-piece plastic wad. Patterns have improved considerably with the advent of plastic shot wads.

rampant. I have read samples of correct shot sizes per application all of my life, and there's something to the recommendations. The problem is as stated above—pick the right size shot for the task at hand, but hope that it patterns with good distribution on the target.

The reason for concern with shot size is the fact that each pellet is indeed a little round ball and the principles which govern the round ball from the muzzleloaders apply to the shot used in a shotgun. The sphere is not an ideal shape for aerodynamic excellence. In short, shot loses its initial muzzle velocity in a hurry. And the smaller the shot, the worse the problem. Penetration and kinetic energy are related. Let the shot energy dissipate and penetration is poor. This is why hunters will choose No. 2 or BB shot for geese or wild turkey. More on this in our upcoming ballistics chapter, but the point is, patterning a shotgun is more than finding out what truly patterns best in shot size and charge at what velocity. It is also a matter of compromise, finding the pattern plus right shot size to make for a powerful force at shotgun ranges. Some shooters will choose pattern over shot size; others will select shot size over pattern. In the next chapter, the shooter will see a few figures on this, and he can make up his own mind.

Wads and Patterns

The handloader has a wonderful opportunity to try various wad systems in order to enhance patterns. In fact, I have often decided upon a shot size which I wanted to use for a specific reason, such as No. 5 shot for pheasants or sage hens, and then worked on handloads which would give a good pattern with that shot size. One company which has specialized in making wads for various performance levels is Ballistics Products, Inc. of POB 488, Long Lake, Minnesota 55356. In BPI's catalog one will find all sorts of information concerning variations in shotshell reloading. I have used some of the BPI wad combinations to virtually change my patterns with a specific shot, rather than going from shot size to shot size to get the holes out of the pattern or produce the percentage I was after.

The above company offers a gas seal which they call the BPGS unit. The gas seal, a plastic cup, can aid a pattern to a degree. Coupled with the company's BP12 Magnum Shotcup, more improvement in pattern may be noted. It takes a few tries, and the BPI company does offer variations with their own wads. The point is, wad columns can make a difference, and the shooter must recognize that fact.

Factories have known it for a long time. They got rid of the old top wad. I'm dating myself, but I was a young lad when the star crimp came into being, and in the 1950s, it was not impossible to walk into a sporting goods store and buy a box of shells with the old roll crimp and a top wad over the shot charge. These wads, it is pretty sure, got in the way of the shot and did the pattern no good at all.

Shooters who do not reload may wish to try various factory loads which offer different setups in the actual composition of the shotshell, variations mostly in wad column. So, the point is, do not give up on a shot size right away. Try some different brands and some handloads with different types of wad systems to see if a shot size will pick up in pattern quality by this means.

Shot Hardness

Another aspect which can be clearly seen in patterning is the difference that shot hardness can make on a pattern. This fact is very easily discovered if the shooter will try various shot hardnesses in his own gun. I like to first find the very best load for my gun with "standard shot." By standard I mean the shot which we normally buy in the sporting goods shop, not hardened beyond the average. When I have a load which patterns nicely with this shot, I then turn to testing harder shot with *the same* wad column, hull and load. Here are a few choices:

Chilled Shot

This is the "normal" shot mentioned above. It is not pure lead, but neither is it as hard as many other types of shot.

Magnum Shot

I prefer the term "high antimony," for that is what this shot is, a lead alloy with more antimony than the chilled shot had, making it harder, in some cases much harder.

Nickel Plated Lead Shot

This shot is just plain excellent. I use it on some of my

Unlike most upland game gunners, the waterfowler will require 70–80 percent (full-choke) patterns for long-range work. One of the waterfowler's best bets is shotshell ammo loaded with copper or nickel plated shot. Such shot, by virtue of its plating, deforms less in its flight down the bore, thereby providing top-quality patterns. Federal, Remington and Winchester all offer shotshell ammo featuring copper plated shot. Lawrence Lead, and Hornady, offer copper plated shot as components for reloaders.

bird hunting trips because it's worth the extra money, and it will not be used up nearly as rapidly in bird hunting as it would be for target work anyway. The core of this shot is softer than copper plated shot.

Copper Plated Shot

Fine, fine patterns can be gleaned out of this hard shot.

Steel Shot

Due to the hazard of lead poisoning of waterfowl, (the birds dive down into the bottom of the water and scoop up the lead shot and ingest it), steel shot has come into being. I am not wild about steel shot. It is hard, all right, almost too hard. And steel shot requires very special care. I will recite some of the hazards of steel shot here for the benefit of the reader:

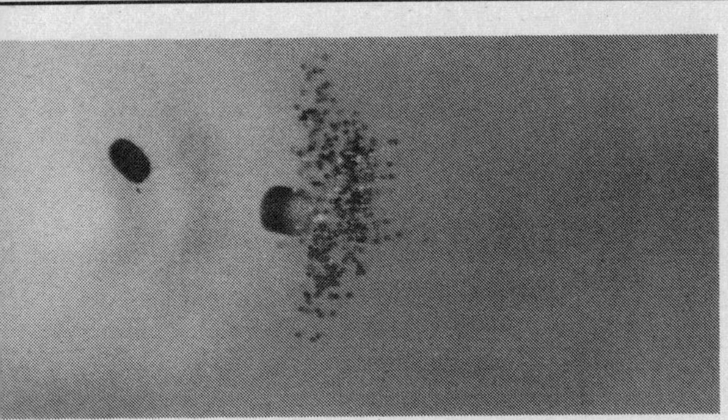

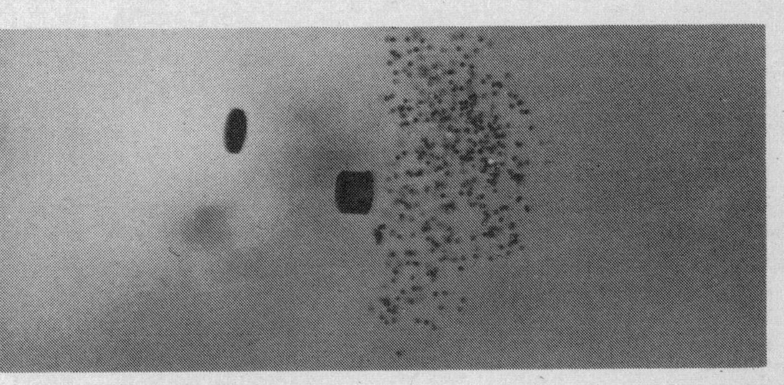

Fresh out of the muzzle of a 12-gauge. From left to right, in sequence you can see the pattern open up. The wad system is of the old type, the shell itself featuring a star (not "roll") crimp. The over-powder wad is to the rear, the shot wad in the center, the shot to the right. Today's modern wads serve to more adequately protect the shot charge. The result is less damaged pellets, hence fewer "flyers" and greatly improved patterns.

1. If you have ever crunched down on a hot pellet while in the act of enjoying the beautiful meat of a game bird or animal, then get ready for a whole new experience with steel shot. It will bring a person to attention in a hurry.

2. The density of steel is less than lead, and a steel pellet is less able to retain its velocity compared with a lead pellet. In short, steel shot is less effective. Some shooters select at least one shot size larger to compensate for this.

3. Use only steel shot data with steel shot. Do not think that you can turn to standard loading data for lead shot and get away with the same data in steel shot. It won't always work out.

4. Use steel shot components. Steel shot has special problems in the bore, and these problems are countered in some respects by the use of special wads and plastic collars. BPI company does offer a few components which will serve for steel shot and lead both, but the shooter is urged to check the loading data with care before plunging into steel shot reloads.

5. Steel shot can ricochet easier than lead shot. The lead shot tends to deform and lose its ability to travel on.

6. Use only that steel shot which is made for shotguns. Other steel pellets may be entirely damaging to the bore.

Patterns and High Velocity Loads

The general concensus of opinion for years held that a high-velocity pattern would be a "blown" pattern. The wads driving the shot would be propelled so fast, with such force, that these wads would almost push right through the shot charge, thereby scattering the shot out. A blown pattern would be the result. The problem is that many of us, and I certainly include myself in this, could "prove" the fact that high-speed shotgun shells had poor patterns.

I loaded many high-speed shotgun shells and fired them at pattern boards, and each time the pattern would be less

Steel shot has been a very controversial issue in recent times. However, improvements in factory-loaded steel shot ammo continue apace. These Winchester steel shot loads are for the 10-gauge shotgun and a full $1^1/_3$-ounce of BB or No. 2 shot is loaded into these shells, which aids pattern in sheer terms of additional pellets on target. Steel shot, while it's less dense than lead shot, is much harder. As a result, patterns with steel shot have always been quite good.

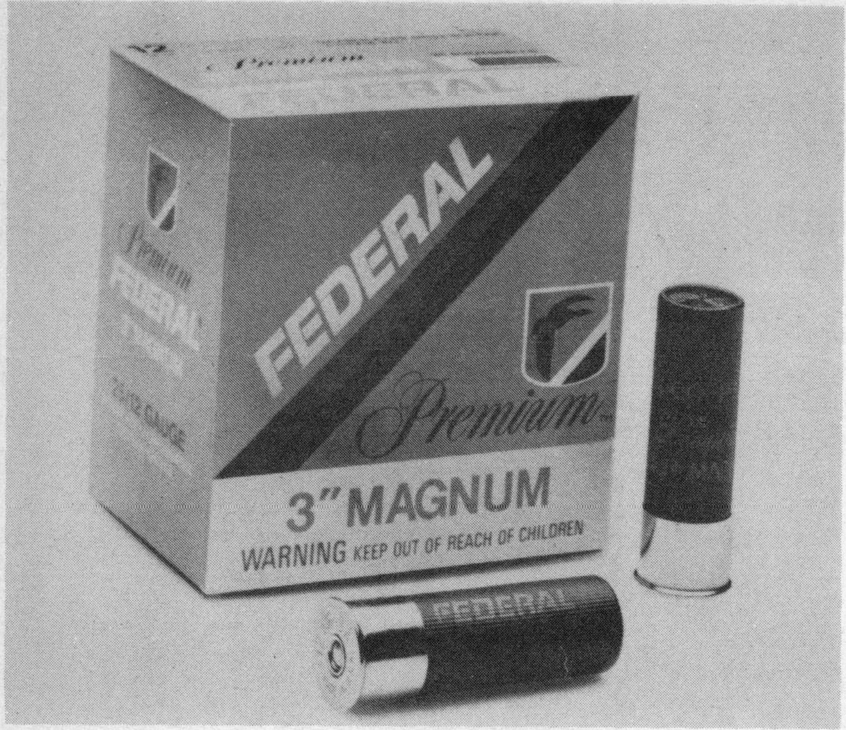

One of the improvements in the modern shotgun shell has been the addition of granulated plastic (it's called "grex") to many commercial loads. In the author's tests, these grex-buffered Federal 3-inch Premium shotgun shells produced excellent full-choke patterns at 40 yards using No. 6 shot. In fact, at 40 yards, the load would be efficient for wild turkey hunting using the head shot, and wild turkey hunting was Federal's reason for producing this shell.

evenly distributed than with a lower velocity load. It seemed very logical to blame the high-speed load for the problem. The facts, however, were not in tune with our thinking. Sure, with the ordinary wad system, the wad might either go to pieces, thereby no longer pushing on the shot with uniformity, or it might actually burst into the shot charge. Then components of the "modern" school came along. These components were plastic. They were often in one- or two-piece form and could be cushioned.

Today, high-speed shotgun shells are possible without blown patterns. My suggestion, as always, is to try the high-speed loads, just once, on a pattern board, to insure that they do function in the individual shotgun. But to make a blanket statement that high-speed shells do not have good patterns is, today, false. BPI has tested high-speed shotgun loads, and they offer special components designed for giving good patterns at high velocity.

High velocity in the shotgun shell is 1200 to 1400 fps with a few exceptional loads making a bit more than 1400 fps in my chronographing. So, the pattern board comes through again. For those wishing to load the higher velocity shotgun shell, patterning is the only sensible means of determining exactly what the pattern is for those loads in the personal shotgun. Remember—the pattern seen, however, is not a perfect replica of what is occurring with that shot string in the air on the way to the target. But it is a lot better than nothing at all to study and learn from.

Buffered Shot

The patterning of the shotgun is also essential, to my way of thinking, when buffered shot loads are used. I turn again to BPI company because they have run extensive tests with their own buffering agents with considerable success. On the other hand, buffered shot loads are not needed for every shotgunning application. The pattern can tell the story. If shooting at close-range targets or upland birds, the buffer may not be necessary.

Also, buffers must be used according to prescription, and not in a haphazard fashion. Buffer, being a plastic material (polyethelene) finely ground, can change the pressure in a shotgun hull, raising the pressure as much as 1500 LUP. Buffer, then, is an addition which is to be used the same as all shotgun components—with the rules as stated in a loading manual.

In my tests, I have seen some lead shot loads improve in distribution markedly at 40 yards, with the shot pellets more evenly spread over the pattern paper. I can't give a percentage of improvement from my tests, but consistency seems excellent. I am convinced that buffers work when they are needed for longer range shooting, and the patterning of the shotgun is once again the best indicator we have of the value of a buffered shotgun load. The buffer material minimizes the deformation of the pellets, especially during ignition, I am told. Deformed shot is always a problem, of course, so keeping the shot round is going to improve patterns.

Other Pattern Tests

In my opinion the best situation for testing shotgun patterns is the pattern board. I have read about many other means such as making cardboard cutouts of quail and I am

Shotgunners should check both the patterns and 40-yard barrel regulation of their double-barreled shotguns, be they side-by-sides or over/unders. Generally, doubles have their barrels regulated to impact at the 40-yard mark. Failure to meet this, or asked-for custom performance level, may well call for a trip back to the factory or custom maker.

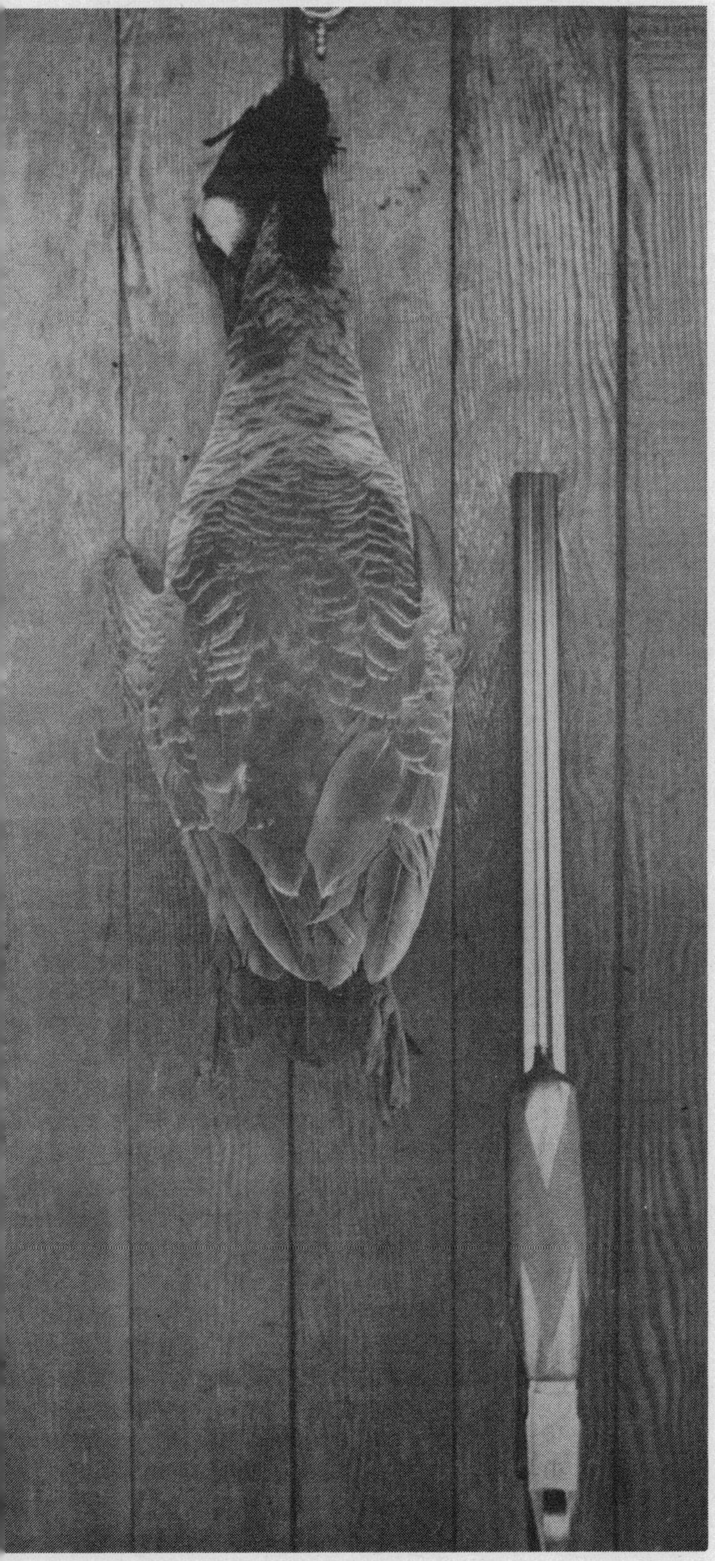

Today there are even handgun cartridges loaded with shot. Primarily, the distribution of the shot is for close-range (15 yards or less) only, but after all, shot in the metallic round is meant for close-range work. The handgunner interested in using this type of ammo should pattern it and see what sort of performance he gets out of his own handgun.

never satisfied with them. While there is nothing wrong with such test tools, the pattern board is a constant. It is a standard. And it gives us choke percentages to work with as well as distribution sample.

I have used other methods, of course. I have shot at old decoys which were going to be thrown away, just to see how the pattern of a particular load reacted in terms of the number of hits on these decoys. I have placed clay targets at various ranges, shooting at them from a benchrest so that I could see the results of breakage. But these are haphazard. The pattern board is not perfect by a long way in showing the exact pattern because it actually does not give an indication of the length of the shot string, nor the particular manner in which the string flies through the air.

Patternboard and Range Variations

There are many different styles of pattern boards. I like a plain sheet of clean paper, period, in conjunction with the cardboard 30-inch diameter cutout. I do not like to shoot into any pre-drawn circles or anything of that nature. Some shooters also divide the 30-inch circle into quadrants or even smaller divisions in order to determine "more scientifically" how the shot is distributed. This is all right. But in the main, it's quite easy to determine how the shot is

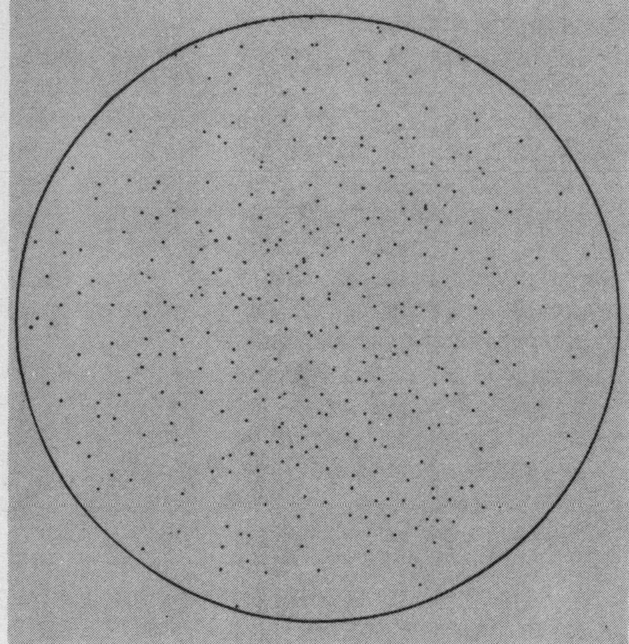

This is a near-perfect, short-range (25-yard) pattern. Note the superb distribution, excellent density and centered aspect of the pattern. Hunters who, for example, pursue upland game in thick cover, might consider trying a 25-yard pattern. Full-choke, under these conditions, will not provide best performance.

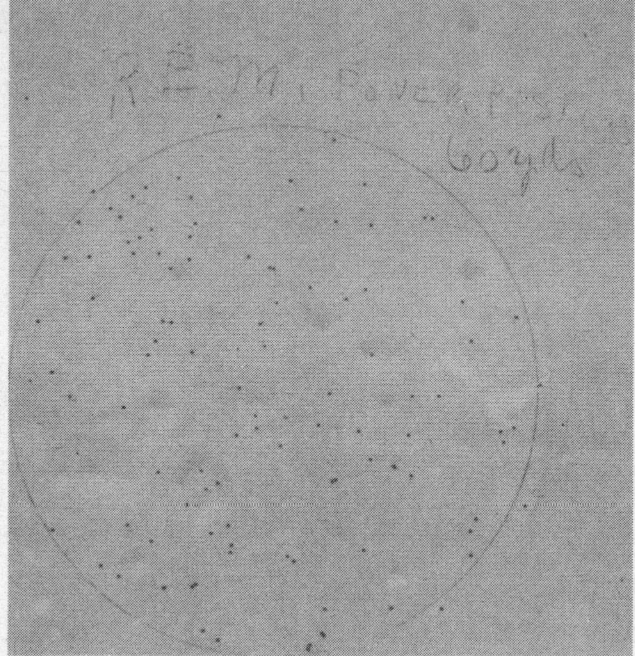

At longer ranges, patterns tend to open up—sometimes quite dramatically. This 12-gauge pattern was fired at 60 yards using No. 4 shot out of a full-choke barrel. The pattern runs about 52 percent, at that range, providing improved cylinder performance.

being distributed from a given load. You can see it. Either there are holes all over the circle, well-distributed or there are not. The shooter who wants to know more about a given load shoots more. One shot won't always tell the story. Several shots, repeating a pattern over and over again, do tell a story, especially if the shot pellets are always well distributed,

Forty yards is the right range for the patterning operation, with the exception of the .410 shotgun, which is fired at 20 yards and which uses a 20-inch diameter circle cutout instead of the 30-inch. With all other gauges, *after* the 40-yard pattern has been established, then the shooter is free to fire at any range he wishes. In fact, he should shoot at other ranges. I often finish up with a load, determining my pattern percentage and shot distribution, and then moving on to other patterning ranges.

It is nice to know just what a pattern looks like at 20 yards and at 30 yards, even though we know what it looks like at 40 yards. And there are a few cases where specially loaded shotgun shells are capable of farther than 40-yard shooting, so it is also good to take a look at patterns beyond the 40-yard range. The 40-yard setting is a standard, and for figuring choke percentages is the range to use, with the .410 being an exception. But yes, other ranges for patterning are useful.

The shotgun patterning operation is an important one. All of the reasons previously mentioned support that statement, and as we have wound our way through the many advantages of shooting shotgun loads at a paper, I think more reasons for patterning have cropped up. But I leave the complete shooter with the original idea presented at the beginning of this chapter. And that idea says that it is just as logical to know, by test, what a shotgun is doing for us as it is to know what a rifle is doing. To go out into the field with an untested shotgun is a little bit like heading for the shooting range or field with an unsighted rifle.

Chapter 25
Understanding Basic Ballistics

THE MOTION of projectiles . . . *that* is ballistics. The student of ballistics tries to discover what happens to a projectile in motion. The study breaks down into two major parts, both of interest to the complete shooter, because we all deal with ballistics in one way or another in our everyday shooting. The two parts are *internal ballistics* and *external ballistics*. (These can also be called *interior* ballistics and *exterior* ballistics.) Studying a bullet in flight through the atmosphere is obviously the exterior part, while studying the same bullet's action in the bore of the gun is internal (or interior) ballistics.

The study of ballistics is hardly new. Several hundred years ago, students of ballistics worked for their governments. These men tried to ascertain the flight of wartime projectiles so that those projectiles would strike the enemy with reliability. Their learnings were often passed on to other ballisticians, who held the findings secret, for the information was very valuable. Understanding the actual characteristics of a bullet's flight was not yet a part of man's knowledge, and little discoveries were jealously guarded.

Quite a few ballisticians and military men felt that the trajectory of a missle was a flat line, until the energy ran out, and then the object fell to the earth, out of steam, as it were. But a man by the name of Tartaglia described a different sort of shape for trajectory, not a flat line with a big nose dive in it, but rather a parabola, a curve. He felt that if a gun were aimed at a 45-degree angle, it would assume its farthest flight. He was right, too.

The famous Galileo was experimenting with cannon balls about this time and he, too, described a curve, a parabola, as the arc taken by the projectile in flight. Galileo determined that the acceleration of a falling body by gravity is a constant. He figured that if you dropped a feather and a cannon ball off a tower and there was no air resistance, gravity would attract each to the same degree. We use a constant of gravity to this day in some formulas. The two big forces which act to slow a bullet down are gravity and the air flow around the bullet, and both of these ideas were in Galileo's mind, though not proportionally correct at the time.

Galileo, armed with the bore elevation angle, the parabola and the range, could now figure muzzle velocity. He would have been quite accurate in his figures, too, but he was not giving the atmosphere enough credit. He knew air was a problem, but did not realize that it was worse on a bullet's flight than gravity. But by the 1700s, a man by the name of Benjamin Robbins invented the ballistic pendulum. It was a simple pendulum with a large, heavy wooden bob. To make a velocity measurement both the bullet and bob were weighed. Then a bullet was fired at the motionless hanging bob. The height of pendulum swing resulting from the bullet striking the bob was measured. The higher it swung, the faster the projectile's velocity. Of course, the weight of the missile was taken into account, and the entire basis for the ballistic pendulum was mathematical. But it worked. Even more important, Robbins' pendulum demonstrates dramatically the impact air drag

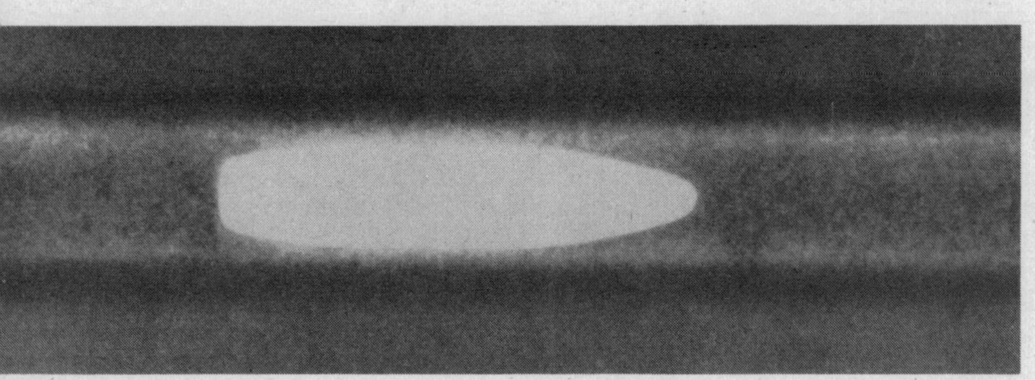

Internal ballistics can now be studied with the X-ray photograph. This is a Sierra 180-grain Spitzer boat-tail bullet inside of a rifle barrel. In about 2 more inches of bore it will exit the muzzle of the rifle. As you can see, the entire shank section of the bullet is in contact with the bore. (Courtesy of Sierra Bullets)

The boat-tail bullet offers an advantage in easy loading into the mouth of the case. It also aids in trajectory patterns at very long range due to the lesser amount of drag during flight.

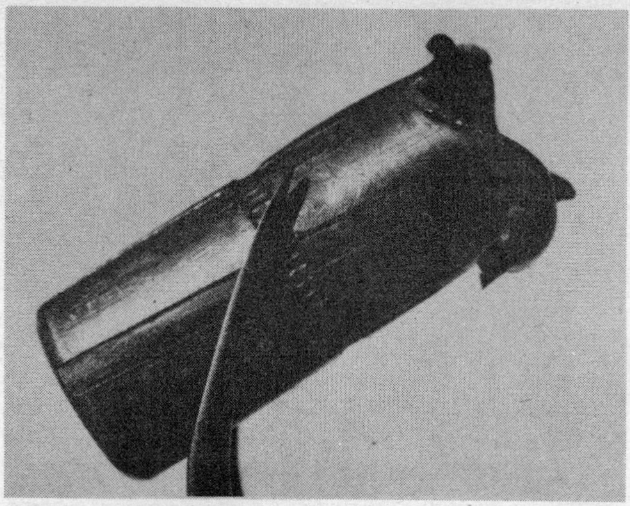

Exterior ballistics includes the study of projectiles after recovery. This is a very fine bullet which has always proved itself to be excellent. Although it did the job of harvesting well in this instance, note that the front part of the core is gone and the nose of the jacket has not expanded back.

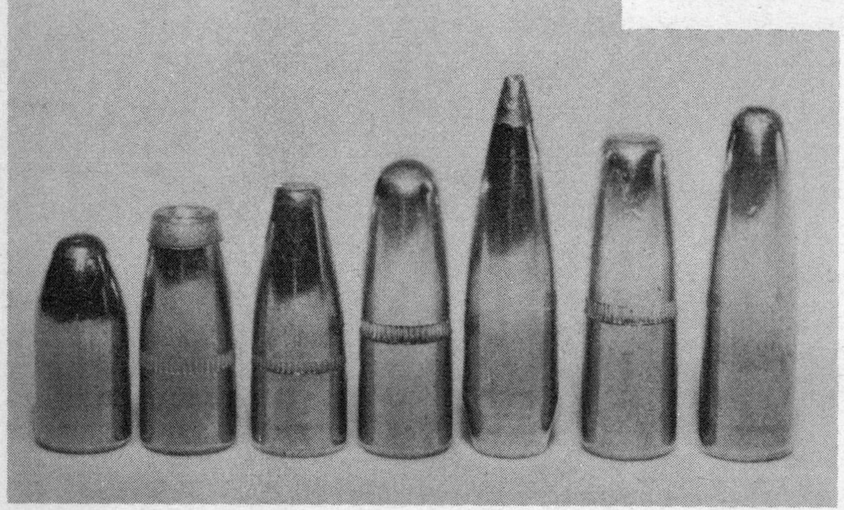

Many bullet shapes exist and each one must be computed as to a form factor before the formula for C can be applied. This array of 30-caliber bullets shows the flat-point in hollow-point form, a round nose configuration, a boat-tail spitzer, and the round nose, including a spitzer-shaped bullet with a flat point.

has on bullet flight by measuring the flight of a bullet at different ranges from the muzzle.

In 1850, the concept of a *standard bullet* came into being. This was a wonderful move, because it gave a *model* of a bullet in flight, and all other bullets in flight could be compared with that standard model. It opened the door for ballistic coefficient, the single most valuable tool we have today when it comes to telling us how a bullet will react in the atmosphere and to gravity.

Ballistic coefficient is called "C" for coefficient, and this C was and still is based upon that standard bullet concept. In other words, if we know the drag deceleration of a standard bullet, and we divide by the drag deceleration of an actual bullet, we end up with a fraction of a number. The higher that number is, the better off we are in terms of the bullet flying "flat." By that we mean the better the bullet will stay close to the *line of sight*.

Today, we use a coefficient of form compared with the standard bullet so that we can determine how a bullet will fly according to its shape. It is no big surprise that sharp-pointed bullets describe a flatter trajectory than round or flat nosed bullets. If we look at a few ballistic coefficient numbers we can grasp the meaning of these numbers fairly easily. For example, we can look at some 30-caliber bullets. In the *Speer Reloading Manual Number Ten,* on pages 209 to 210, several Speer 30-caliber bullets are reviewed.

Bullet	Ballistic Coefficient
100-grain Plinker	.124
110-grain HP Varminter	.136
110-grain round nose	.144
110-grain Spire Point	.273
130-grain HP (spitzer)	.263
130-grain flat point	.248

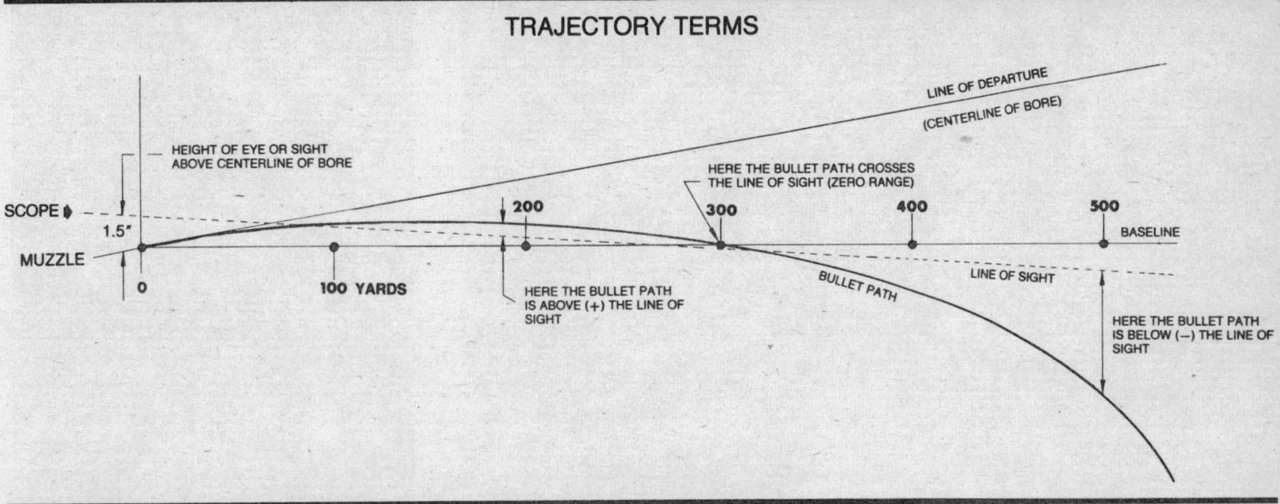

(Above) A bullet's path is not as it may seem. This illustration, courtesy of the "Good Old Boys" at Speer, shows in somewhat exaggerated terms, the flight of a bullet from the muzzle on out to 500 yards. Note that the bullet actually crosses the line of sight at two points—the first time at about 80 yards, the second time at 300 yards which is the distance this particular rifle was sighted in for.

The shooter who becomes interested in ballistics generally ends up testing his own firearms. However, he can only test within the guidelines of established loads, since he usually does not have pressure-reading apparatus to guide his way. Nonetheless, he can find out a great deal about his own guns through personal shooting.

Bullet	Ballistic Coefficient
150-grain flat nose	.268
150-grain round nose	.266
150-grain Spitzer boat-tail	.423
150-grain Spitzer	.389
150-grain Mag-Tip	.301
165-grain round nose	.274
165-grain boat-tail	.477
165-grain Spitzer	.459
165-grain Grand Slam	.393
170-grain flat nose	.304
180-grain round nose	.304
180-grain boat-tail	.540
180-grain Spitzer	.500
180-grain Mag-Tip	.352
180-grain Grand Slam	.436
200-grain Spitzer	.556

Interpretation is necessary. For example, we must remember that the atmosphere truly plays hob with our missile, trying to retard its flight. In fact, a high-speed bullet smashing into the atmosphere will actually be blunted, compressed, if the nose is designed for expansion. In other words, a soft point with that lovely sharp tip of lead will no longer have that lovely sharp tip after the bullet is a minute distance from the muzzle.

So we look at a 180-grain Spitzer and its C is .500, but a 180-grain Mag-Tip, with its blunter nose, has a C of only .352. Part of the reason for this is the fact that we must use the coefficient of form of the *unfired* bullet in our testing. An unfired 30-caliber 180-grain Speer Spitzer bullet, with its sharp tip of lead, comes up with a C of .500, while the blunter 180-grain Mag-Tip in unfired form has a C of .351. However, if we fired both of these bullets through the air and caught them intact downrange, they would be much closer in terms of C than they were before they were fired,

The shape of the bullet is tantamount to how it will buck the ravages of the air it must pass through. However, this factor cannot mean that all bullets be constructed with an aerodynamic purpose alone. The .357-inch 180-grain full metal jacket bullet on the left has a far different purpose in comparison to the 139-grain 7mm bullet on the right.

It is ballistic force which causes the collapse of the bullet, of course. This Federal 180-grain .357-inch bullet fired from the 357 Magnum can also be used in carbines of the same caliber because of the bullet construction. Remember that the high shock of the air can destroy a bullet before it ever gets to the target, so this bullet has been designed to expand at handgun velocities while holding together at rifle velocities.

Bullet design and construction is a matter of ballistics, too. On the far right is a 180-grain bullet designed for high velocity from the 30-caliber rifle. The bullet on the far left is a 375-caliber 235-grain with a blunted point. It's designed for the 375 H&H Magnum, but through the 375 Winchester it offers tremendous penetration. Ballistics will force the bulletmaker to construct a bullet to do a specific job from a specific cartridge.

because the Mag-Tip's strong nose does not smash back nearly as much as the Spitzer's lead nose. The Mag-Tip looks closer to its unfired form than the Spitzer would look when compared with its unfired form. More about ballistic coefficient and its little brother, sectional density, in a moment. For the moment, let's continue our look at general ballistic information.

So the world of ballistics experts had C to work with now. And they actually had a forerunner of the chronograph, the ballistic pendulum to advance ballistic knowledge. Then in 1884 the famous Ingall's Tables were developed by a U.S. Army colonel of the same name. The ballistics of a standard bullet shape were charted here with accuracy and great usefulness and application.

More was learned. Ballistics experts found out that there was a big difference in how a bullet flew through the air at the speed of sound (about 1120 fps) and how it flew when the velocity was higher than the speed of sound. In fact, the pounding a bullet took from the air it went through was much greater when the speed of sound was exceeded. Ballisticians also knew by now that the air was much more devastating on the projectile than gravity, perhaps as much as 70 times worse than the acceleration due to gravity.

As studies advanced, the idea of *shock waves* came into

This spark photograph clearly shows the turbulence in the wake of the Sierra 180-grain 30-caliber bullet. Until such high technology as spark photography and shadowgraphing became possible, technicians had a difficult time seeing what they knew to be there from tests. (Courtesy of Sierra Bullets)

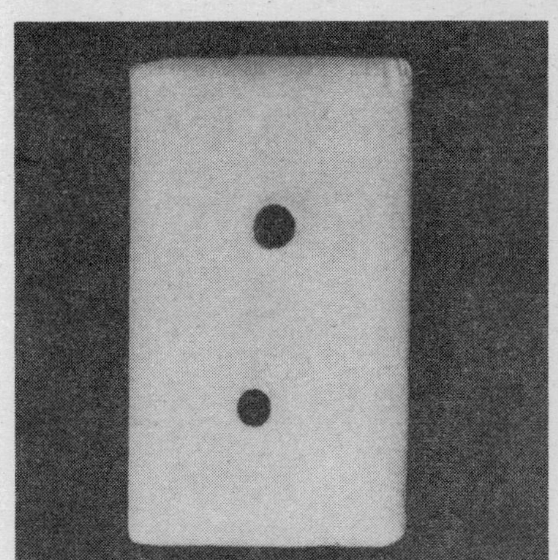

The bar of soap shows the effect of the hollow point design. The entrance and exit sides are obvious. The mushrooming of the bullet changes the shape of the shock wave in front of the bullet; the result is a wider "wound channel." The 22 rimfire, even with its relatively low velocity benefits considerably here from the hollow point factor.

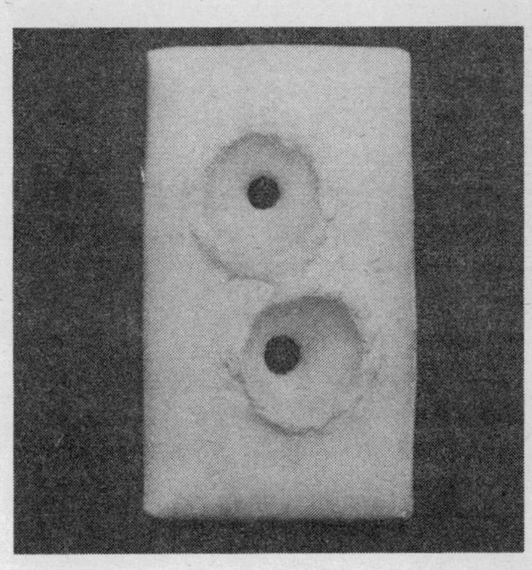

This high speed spark photograph shows the interesting shock wave patterns which attend the flight of this Sierra 180-grain Spitzer boat-tail bullet. The base of the bullet is very sensitive as a steering element of the projectile. Damaged bases cause inaccuracy. (Courtesy of Sierra Bullets)

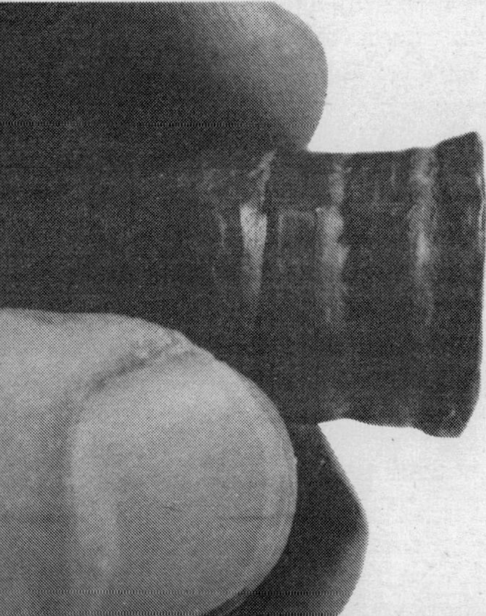

Interior ballistics, in a sense, is at work here. Although the actual flaring of this black powder Minie ball's skirt could not take place until the projectile was clear of the muzzle, the fact is, flaring was precipitated within the bore of the gun from the pressures exerted upon it. A flare of this degree could be slightly harmful to accuracy.

being. It was found that shock waves indicated drag and that the bullet pushes this shock wave in front of and around the bullet. There is turbulence behind the bullet, too. Ballisticians think of air as a substance now, not as something which has little to do with retarding the flight of the bullet. The bullet does have some *lift,* but the degree of lift is nothing when compared to the amount of projectile retardation created by the atmosphere. In short, the simple presence of atmospheric pressure will affect a bullet's flight. The tester sees that at high altitudes, where the air is less dense, the bullet is somewhat less bothered by the atmosphere.

While interior ballistics provides a look at what happens to a bullet as it races down the barrel, it is exterior ballis-

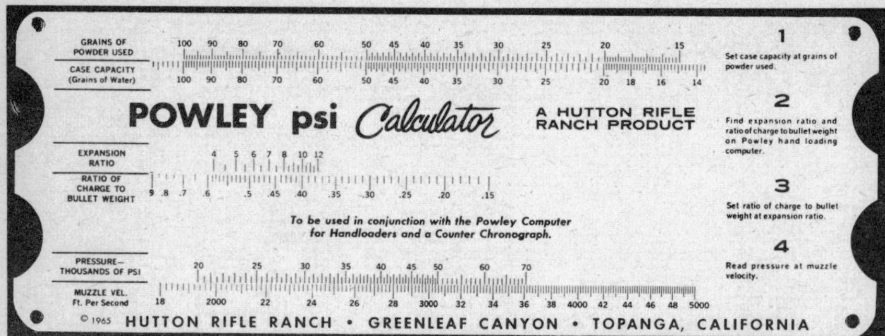

The modern shooter's interest in ballistic knowledge has led to instruments such as this Powley PSI Calculator.

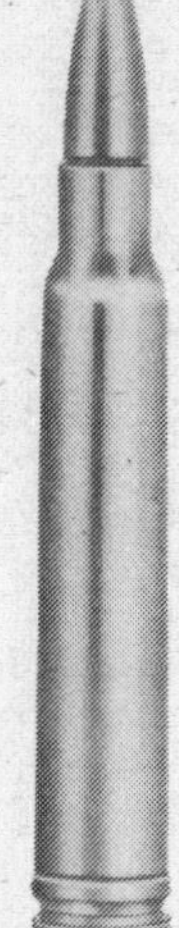

Ballistics interest created rounds such as the 8mm Remington Magnum, which is an example of good bullet weight at high velocity. Obviously, when both bullet mass and velocity are good, energy ratings are very high.

The modern chronograph has made a vast difference in how data is learned in ballistics because any shooter who really wants to can get his hands on a chronograph. Note the screens. Properly set up, a shooter can fire through them at long range from the bench, obtaining actual remaining velocities.

tics which gives the shooter hard information about drop of the bullet, about wind drift and losses in velocity and energy over the ranges.

Uphill and downhill shooting also comes into the exterior ballistics picture, and shooters will also see that shooting at angles makes a difference as well. The bullet strikes higher at *either* a steep *uphill* angle or a steep *downhill* angle, not because the bullet tends to do better in its parabola, but because the gun is actually aimed higher at these angles. Careful shooters recognize that on steep angles, either up or down, they should be careful not to shoot *over* the mark.

The study of modern ballistics gives the complete shooter a scientific look at his world. The old wives' tales die hard, but they do die. Most shooters who bother to read stop saying things about shotguns shooting "harder" because they are longer-barreled. They realize that energy is relative to that gun's actual velocity and charge. They no longer talk about the bullet "gaining speed." When I was a lad, I was given a long lecture about not shooting a deer at 25 yards because the bullet did not have time to get moving, and it wasn't going very fast only 25 yards from the muzzle. In fact, the lecturer was not the only one to believe that this notion was a "truth." It was not a matter of being foolish at all. Ideas were changing, but it takes time to develop a new way of thinking on a subject.

Power

Ballistics turned out to be the sounding board for "power." Shooters wanted to know which cartridge or load was more powerful than the other, and *why*. And they got their answers because of ballistics, *external* ballistics. Ballistics formulae would provide the shooter with a mathematical computation. Shooters eventually got their ballistic "hardware" as well—the modern chronograph. The chronograph is the modern shooter's counting machine, of sorts—it is capable of instantly providing muzzle velocity readings.

The Formula for Kinetic Energy

The only formula used for power today which is acceptable to the world of ballistics is the kinetic energy model. No other model is accepted. This is the Newtonian idea of energy at work, and it takes velocity into account in a special way. The formula is very easy to use, especially today with modern hand calculators.

Given: 200-grain bullet at 2900 fps MV

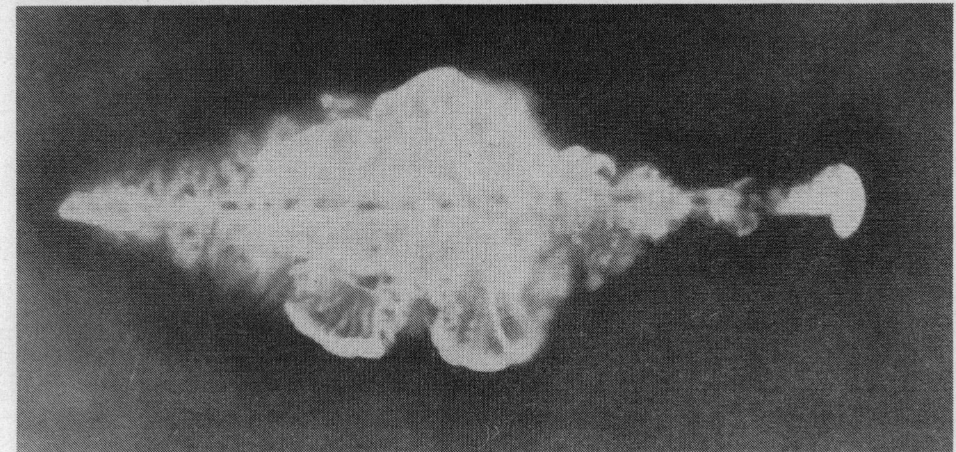

The Sierra 180-grain Spitzer boat-tail bullet has completely penetrated a block of test gelatin. The bullet is visible on the right-hand side in its mushroomed form. It retained over 80 percent of its weight, an indication of a true premium bullet. Note the pattern of disruption. The exit hole is much larger than the diameter of the bullet. Shock waves have been at work here, and this high speed photograph reveals their actions to a great degree. (Courtesy of Sierra Bullets)

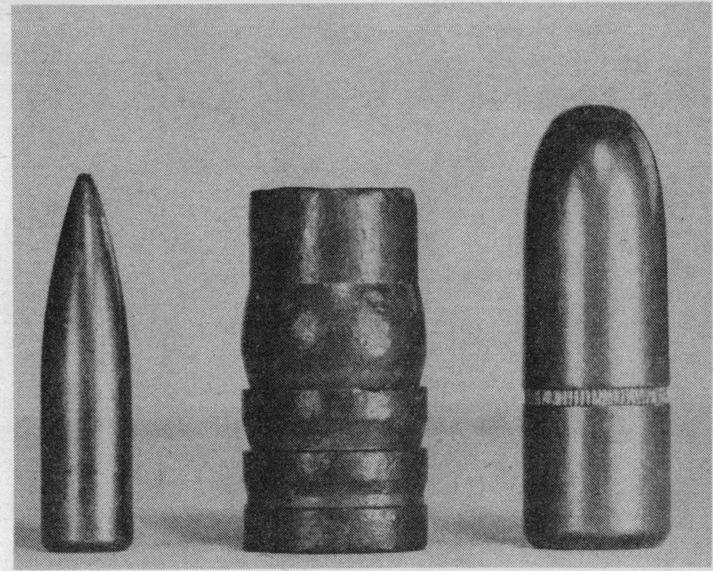

Sectional density plays an important role in ballistics, for it is incorporated into the ballistic coefficient formula. However, looking at a bullet will not always reveal the comparative value of that bullet in terms of sectional density. The 140-grain bullet on the left will have a sectional density of about .248. The big 58-caliber 625-grain bullet in the center will have a sectional density of about .265. But the 45 caliber 500-grain round nose on the right has a sectional density of .341. In terms of C, the 7mm bullet wins.

We have a 200-grain bullet at 2900 fps muzzle velocity. This is all we need to know to calculate our energy in foot-pounds. The ''foot'' part is due to Newton's idea of work and the energy that it would require to lift mass so many feet. What it actually does for us today is offer a whole world of *comparisons*. For the average shooter, the comparison is more important than the actual statement of foot-pounds of energy.

So, the 200-grain bullet at 2000 fps ends up with a muzzle energy of 3,736 foot-pounds. How is that derived? Newton showed us how to do it. Here it is:

1. Square the velocity
2. Divide the figure by 7,000 to reduce to grains (there are 7,000 grains weight in a pound weight)
3. Divide by 64.32, twice the acceleration of gravity, a *constant*.
4. Multiple the figure by the weight of the bullet in grains.

This is all there is to it. Given a different set of facts, we will take a 300-grain bullet at 2500 fps MV. Will this load have more or less energy than our previous 200-grain bullet at 2900 fps? This is what we find:

1. 2500 × 2500 = 6,250,000
2. 6,250,000 ÷ 7,000 = 892.8571429
3. 892.8571429 ÷ 64.32 = 13.88148543 (this figure is the foot-pounds in one grain weight, so we must multiply times the bullet weight next)
4. 13.88148543 × 300 grains (weight of bullet) = 4164.445629. This is rounded off to 4,164 since the figure after the decimal point is under 5.

So now we have a verdict. The 300-grain bullet at 2500 fps is more powerful than the 200-grain bullet at 2900 fps. It is about 10 percent more powerful. How meaningful is this? In my opinion, it is quite meaningful, but it does not offer the last word. Too many other factors must enter in, but only if we want to talk about ''killing power.'' If contented with raw power *figures,* then there is no arguing with this formula. The 300-grain bullet at 2500 fps MV is more powerful than a 200-grain bullet at 2900 fps MV.

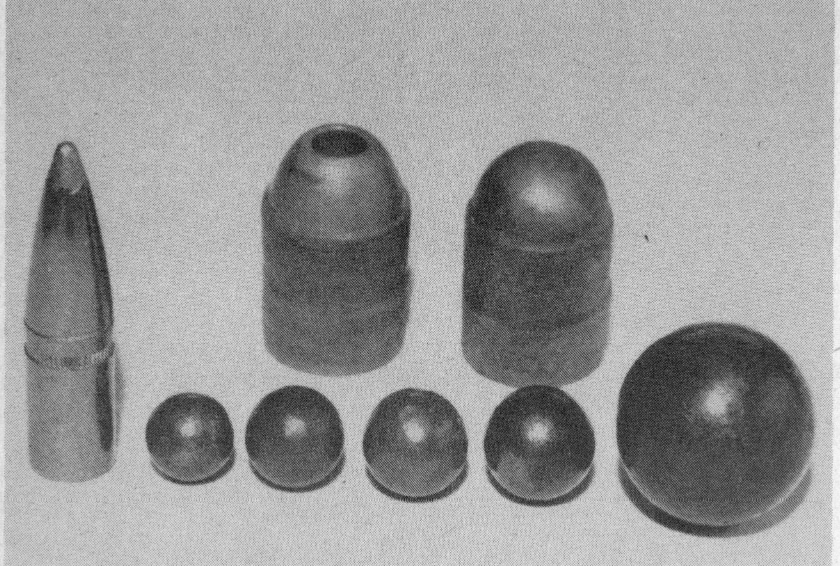

The student of ballistics readily understands that C is the force to consider in the carry-up ability of these missiles. The sharply pointed 180-grain 30-caliber jacketed bullet on the left will win handily in terms of ballistic coefficient and will be the choice for long-range shooting. Also, the large round ball on the right will beat the rest of the lead balls in carry-up due to mass, and the conicals in the background will have what some shooters think of as high momentum ability.

Killing Power

The problem with any such formula enters in when the gun is used to harvest big game. Then things get sticky, at least to some degree. For example, let's pretend for a moment. Let's pretend that we are in the alders up in Alaska after a man-eating grizzly bear. Which gun of the above two would you take? Why, the one shooting the 300-grain bullet—the muzzle energy is greater. So would I. But enter a few more variables. The selected 300-grain bullet is a very soft-jacketed number. We have tested this bullet and determined it would blow up on the wing of a butterfly, let alone penetrate to the vitals of a big bear or break a shoulder bone.

On the other hand, the 200-grain bullet features strong jacket construction and will not come apart. Even though its energy is less by 10 percent, it might be the best choice. And then we come to "caliber." Caliber *does* matter. We already talked about that in our chapter on bullets. You can get a 200-grain bullet in 30-caliber and a 45-caliber 300-grain bullet. So the shooter may want to choose the 300-grain bullet just because of caliber and not because of 10 percent difference in energy.

Downrange Energy

The fact is, energy at the muzzle is far less meaningful than downrange energy. We could start a 250-grain bullet at 2900 fps and a 200-grain bullet at 2900 fps and find that at longer ranges the lighter bullet has more energy left than the heavier bullet. Remember C (ballistic coefficient). Remember the shape of that bullet. And there is sectional density to consider, too.

Sectional Density

I always think of sectional density as a stepping stone to C, ballistic coefficient, and not as important as C by any means. But sectional density is worth looking at. The idea that sectional density is a comparison between the diameter of a bullet and the length of the bullet is a bad one. Many shooters think of a bullet's sectional density as meaning only, "long for its caliber."

Sectional Density is: The ratio of a bullet's weight in pounds to the square of its diameter in inches.

Now this does suggest that the idea of a bullet's length-to-caliber is included, in the matter of mass per diameter. But it is better to work the formula. Just because our eyes *see* a graceful, long, slender beautiful bullet, or one that does not look quite so long for its caliber, does not mean our eyes are telling the truth.

A truly good example would be a 140-grain Hornady 6.5mm bullet, .264-inch diameter. When I load that bullet into the case of my 6.5mm wildcat, the bullet seems to stick out like a church steeple. I have had people ask if there is any bullet seated in the neck. They respond, almost disbelievingly, when the bullet is seated into the neck right to the beginning of the powder space in the case.

In short, the 6.5mm 140-grain bullet looks wildly long, and it is. It has a darn good sectional density, too. The sectional density of the 140-grain 6.5mm bullet is .287. Now let's look at another bullet. This one is also from Hornady. It's loaded into my 45-70 round at the moment, and it is the 500-grain number. Looking at the 45-caliber 500-grain bullet compared with the 140-grain .264-inch bullet, one would think that the streamlined .264-inch bullet would be far and away ahead of the 45-caliber 500-grain bullet. The two have a very different profile, but the 500-grain, 45-caliber bullet has a sectional density of .341, considerably better.

This is important, because it shows that sectional density is not merely a matter of looking at a bullet and proclaiming that it will have a high sectional density just because it

The bullet manufacturer is also up against another ballistic problem, that of retained velocity at various ranges. This Hornady 140-grain 357-caliber bullet is shown after striking test media at 1100 fps and 1500 fps. A good bullet is designed to withstand a *range* of impact speeds.

is apparently, to the eye, long for its caliber. Think of sectional density in terms of the *formula,* (the ratio of the bullet's weight to the square of its caliber) not in terms of "long for caliber."

Ballistic Coefficient

Ballistic coefficient is the *ratio of the bullet's weight to the square of its diameter, plus a "form factor."* The first part of the formula is, in fact, sectional density. So, we can say that ballistic coefficient (C) is sectional density plus a form factor. The form factor is based upon the standard bullet which was discussed earlier. Knowing a bullet's ballistic coefficient is highly meaningful to us, for it shows what a bullet can do against the ravages of the atmosphere. It tells us how well the bullet will overcome the resistance that the air presents to the bullet in flight.

Let us look again at the two above bullets. If we simply cast our eyes on them, the 6.5mm bullet, in spite of the fact that it loses in terms of sectional density, looks better than the 45-70 slug in terms of ballistic coefficient. Is it? You better believe it! The .264-inch 140-grain Hornady has a ballistic coefficient of .441, while the 500-grain .458-inch Hornady bullet has a ballistic coefficient of .320.

The true value of C comes to bear when a shooter is looking for a long-range missile. Here is a perfectly legitimate comparison of trajectory first, using two popular bullets. Then we will go on and see how these two bullets do in terms of retained energy, also based upon C, because it is ballistic coefficient which allows for the "carry up" or retained velocity which gives us the energy figure.

Two 30-caliber bullets (both 3000 fps MV)

150-grain Spire point bullet Trajectory(w300-yd. zero)

Sectional Density: .226	**100 yds.**	**200 yds.**	**300 yds.**
Ballistic Coefficient: .358	+4.1″	+4.9″	0

150-grain round nose bullet Trajectory(w300-yd. zero)

Sectional density: .226	**100 yds.**	**200 yds.**	**300 yds.**
Ballistic Coefficient: .185	+5.8″	+7.3″	0

We are again going to start both of these bullets off at a muzzle velocity of 3000 fps. See what happens (from *Hornady Handbook,* Third Edition):

150-grain Spire Point

MV	**100-yd.**	**200-yd.**	**300-yd.**	**400-yd.**
3000 fps	2729 fps	2473 fps	2234 fps	2012 fps

150-grain round nose:

MV	**100-yd.**	**200-yd.**	**300-yd.**	**400-yd.**
3000 fps	2489 fps	2040 fps	1653 fps	NA

We can see what a tremendous difference there is between the remaining velocities at 100, 200 and 300 yards between the 150-grain spire point and a 150-grain round nose. At 300 yards, the 150-grain pointed bullet is going almost 25 percent faster than the 150-grain round nose, and the shape of the projectile is the reason. After all, the sectional densities of the two bullets are identical, and both started at 3000 fps MV.

What would happen if the spire point were actually a full metal jacket bullet? Hornady has a full metal jacket 150-grain 30-caliber bullet, so it is only a matter of looking at the manual to find out. Of course, the 150-grain full metal jacket bullet is the same in sectional density, .226, but in ballistic coefficient the bullet is .453, and it is this high C rating which does the following:

30-caliber Hornady bullet 150-grain full metal jacket

MV	**100-yd.**	**200-yd.**	**300-yd.**	**400 yd.**
3000 fps	2785 fps	2578 fps	2383 fps	2197 fps

The 150-grain full metal jacket bullet whips the spire point by a fair margin, but totally eclipses the round nose. Of course, this is why ammunition manufacturers have concerned themselves with providing a bullet which would not set back upon striking the atmosphere. The Bronze Point and Ballistictip are two such styles discussed in the bullet chapter. But there is always a trade-off. The trade-off here is that some of the bullets which have these sharp metal or polycarbonate points can tend to open large wound channels. This may not be a problem. It may even be desirable. It depends upon the situation.

Furthermore, don't knock the round nose or the flat nose bullet. Neither will keep up with the nice keen profile of the spitzer or other pointed bullet, but for good wound channels, the round nose and flat point do all right. They also provide for very immediate transfer of energy to the target. They are suitable bullets for a great deal of hunting, for in spite of our mania for long-range energy, the fact is, most game is shot far closer than 200 yards, and a round nose bullet does very well at these closer ranges.

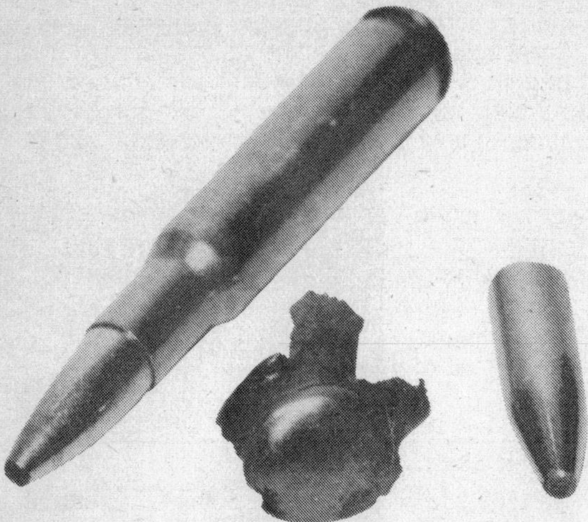

Sometimes the shooter uses his knowledge of ballistics and bullet construction to make a bullet do something which it was not truly intended to do. This 80-grain bullet was made for quick expansion out of a 243 Winchester or 6mm Remington cartridge. In the 6mm/222, however, it becomes a very fine deer/antelope bullet with good expansion and *no* blowup. Why? Less muzzle velocity is the answer.

(Right) The end result of ballistic force is shown in a big game harvest. This buck was taken from close range with a 54 caliber round ball from a muzzle-loader. The actual wound channel is far different from the wound channel made by a high speed modern bullet, much less disruptive but still quite extensive.

Long-Range Energy

Having stated that the round nose and flat point are fine bullets, we do have to concede that when long-range punch is desired it will be the sharper profile bullets which provide this. With the above bullets, at 300 yards the round nose 150-grain bullet was left with 910 foot-pounds of energy. At the same time, the 150-grain spire point still had 1663 foot-pounds of energy remaining. That is a big difference, in the 45 percent range.

Momentum

Momentum cannot be used in comparison with the kinetic energy figures which we have been employing here. Momentum is not recognized as a scientific means of looking at the energy rating of a bullet. The trouble is that some very prominent hunters over the years have not always bought the kinetic energy theory as the only one in terms of the effect of a bullet at the target. I also doubt some of the story. But I cling to kinetic energy because I do not have anything better to offer the reader. No matter how we might feel, kinetic energy is king today in talking effectiveness of the bullet at the target.

However, for comparison measures, let's take a look at a few points. Momentum is very simply velocity times mass. So, as discussed in our bullet chapter, we multiply the weight of the bullet times the velocity of the bullet, and then I divide by 10,000 so the figure is smaller to work with. Given two very different types of rifles, it might be enlightening to see what happens when momentum is applied as an energy statement compared with kinetic energy. The 50-110 Winchester round was chambered into the Model 86 Winchester rifle, and the cartridge was well thought of by many of the old-time shooters. In fact, in some of my texts from the 19th century, the 50-110 is considered the finest big game round of the day. In many accounts, the shooter would drop his game with one shot with this rifle, and this means moose and elk as well as other game.

But watch out on paper. The 50-110 does not set the world ablaze. The standard 50-110 loading was with a 300-grain bullet. I do not know the original velocity of the load, but Frank Barnes lists it as 1605 fps as a factory load, so I doubt that the black powder handloaders of the 19th century did much if any better than this. That means a muzzle energy of 1716 foot-pounds. Not very good. To give the round a much more fair appraisal, another Barnes load, from the same *Cartridges of the World* book, page 128 of the 4th edition, shows a 450-grain bullet at 1475 fps

MV for a muzzle energy rating of 2174 foot-pounds.

Some shooters still feel that a 50-caliber bullet of 450 grains, even with a "lowly" muzzle velocity of 1475 fps, would stomp all over some of the hotrock rounds of our time. A 6mm Remington round with a 100-grain bullet at 3100 fps has a muzzle energy rating of 2134 foot-pounds.

I won't jump to any conclusions. Instead, I will ask the reader to ponder over this conundrum. Surely, all of the factories and bulletmakers and armsmakers in the world cannot be wrong. They all use the kinetic energy figure to talk punch. But here we have a 50-caliber bullet of 450 grains at 1475 fps, and its energy rating is 2174 foot-pounds. The little 6mm Remington's energy number is 2134 foot-pounds, for all practical purposes much the same. Are these two really the same?

If a moose stepped out of the timber at 50 paces and there was a choice between hitting the moose with a 6mm Remington or a 50-110, each loaded as described above, I am inclined to think, after more than a passing acquaintanceship with harvesting game animals, that I would as soon drive the 450-grain 50-caliber bullet into the moose, and I'd think hard about putting it into, not behind the shoulder. I further believe that if a bone were hit, the shoulder in this case, by a 6mm bullet *vs* a 50-caliber bullet, the latter would do a better job of breaking that bone. That's my opinion, and it's based on seeing game decked with a fair number of various rounds and bullets over the years.

We can carry this another step. The 25-06 would soundly whip the 50-110 in a duel for power. A well-loaded 25-06 will shove a 120-grain bullet at 3200 fps MV for a muzzle energy of 2729 foot-pounds. I know the 25-06 is a fine round, and one of my all-time favorites, but even though it uses those fine long bullets, at 50 yards, I am not so sure the 50-110 wouldn't be more positive, especially in the bone-breaking department.

What about momentum? I don't believe momentum is the answer either. I do not feel it is better than, nor even as good as kinetic energy in talking about authority of a given load. But some hunters do not agree. One thing is certain, the 50-110 will shine under the laws of momentum. A 50-110 with the 450-grain bullet at 1475 fps is worth a momentum figure (our figuring) of 66. The 6mm with the 100-grain bullet at 3100 fps is worth 31. The 25-06 with a 120-grain bullet at 3200 fps is going to show a figure of 38 momentum-wise. The 50-110 beats 'em both.

As another means of looking at ballistic power, the momentum story is all right, but just as I do not believe that the 6mm Remington is on par with the 50-110 for a moose at 50 yards, I don't believe that the 50-110 is about 30 percent stronger than the 25-06. Look at momentum. Talk about it. But don't try to replace kinetic energy figures with momentum figures. It just won't work.

Big Bore *vs* Smallbore

This old argument is also one from the ballistic arena, and in a way, an offshoot of the above commentary. The argument really asks: Which is better, a small caliber bullet at high speed, or a larger caliber bullet at lesser velocity? The answer? I think the best answers come from experience, and not from tables or ballistic talk. Make no mistake, ballistics is still the topic here and I am not downgrading the superior position modern ballistics holds with shooters the world over. I merely state that the big bore has its place and that this place is clearly delineated by means of experience.

Mainly, the experience lies in other lands. It is in Africa that dangerous game of the elephant, lion and Cape buffalo class are encountered, and in Africa, there's no question. No African professional hunter uses a small caliber high-speed projectile to stop the charge of an elephant. The big bore is the ticket. Given the choice between a 30-caliber bullet at 3000 fps or a 45-caliber bullet at 2000 fps, the latter is the pick.

Appropriateness is the key. In breaking down a beast which wants to eat you for lunch, the right thing to do is smash into that animal's bone structure in order to stop its charge. While the little high-speed pill is not at home here, the big bore with a strong bullet *is*. Ideally, big strong bullets at high velocity would be an answer, but the fly in the ointment here is recoil. Some shooters can handle such recoil; others cannot. Given a 375- or 458-caliber bullet pushed in the 2700 to 3000 fps range, power is abundant. So is the kick. (See the rifle cartridge ballistics charts at the end of this chapter.)

The Shotgun Shell

The modern shooter knows full well that he must understand basic ballistics if he is to gain the most from his rifle or handgun. But it is sometimes forgotten that shotgun ballistics teach the scattergun fan a great deal about that type of gun. We may look at the amount of shot and the velocity at which that shot charge leaves the muzzle, but more often

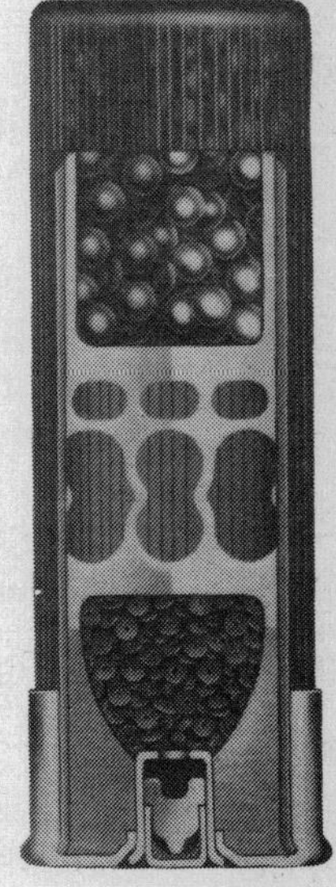

The internal ballistics of the shotgun shell include the fact that most of the pressure is going to be exerted within the hull. Therefore, the hull must contain a proper wad column that has the ability to escape the bore without undue friction.

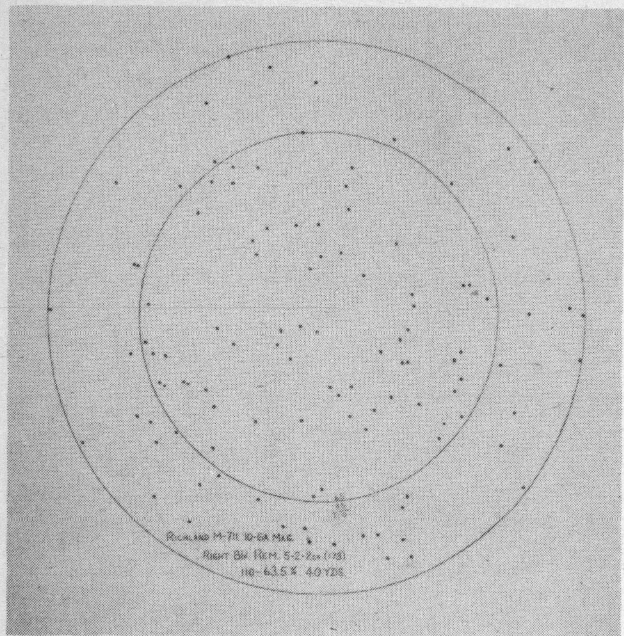

This 40-yard, 10-gauge pattern with No. 2 shot indicates a Modified choke. The pattern a shotgun makes, at whatever yardage, is part of a shotgun's ballistic make up. The physical presence of a 40-yard pattern, and the story it tells, is also part of the external ballistics picture.

Shotgun shell manufacturers had to cope with internal ballistics when steel shot was demanded along certain waterfowling areas. The steel shot reacted very differently from lead shot, and it was no easy matter to overcome some of the most basic ballistic problems, such as mass-per-pellet.

than not, we trust to decent components, hopefully, and take to the field. There is more to shotgun shell ballistics than tossing a heap of pellets toward the target.

Effective Shotgun Range

Perhaps the most important study in the field of day in and day out practical shotgun ballistics is that of effective range, that range in which a certain target will be struck with enough force to cleanly harvest it. The study of effective range includes at least two major areas, the shot itself, and its ballistic properties, and the pattern. We end up with an idea of individual pellet energy at a given range, and then we couple that with the pattern available from the given shotgun to see if enough pellets of this energy will strike the target with reasonably good probability.

Pattern

The pattern becomes a part of the ballistic story in shotgunning because each pellet is a unit of delivered power. Hit a target with one pellet and you have one unit of delivered power. Hit with two pellets and you have two units of delivered power. And so forth. Ballistics experts have tried to determine how many pellets of a given size at a given range it would take to cleanly harvest a bird of a specific size.

Sometimes these figures see print. I have read that it takes an average of five No. 4 pellets to cleanly harvest a mallard-size duck at 40 yards. This supposes a high-velocity load with the pellet energy commensurate with the remaining or striking velocity. I have heard that it also takes about five No. 6 pellets to cleanly drop a cottontail rabbit. These are very broad statements, of course.

The interesting spreader load has come into being because of this ballistic theory. While it is useful to have a full choke boring for long-range shooting so that a good number of shot gets into the target, the same is true in reverse. The full choke may either "feather" a bird at very close range or do a job of overkill, ruining some of the edible portions. The spreader load does two things. It does aid the hunter in hitting his target at close range with a gun of modified or full choke, and it also allows for more pellets to strike the target if the pattern is not properly centered.

How far to shoot? I consider the shotgun a short-range tool. I am not in favor of skybusting. But the shotgun is effective at more than under-the-nose ranges. It is my considered opinion based upon both testing and experience that if a shooter wants to do well on game birds with a shotgun at ranges *over* 40 yards, he'd best rely on full choke patterns to deliver the desired energy through multiple hits.

A choke which is giving 70 percent at 40 yards will likely give 50 percent patterns at 50 yards. For normal 12-gauge shooting, even with 1½ ounces of shot, this might not be good enough to truly drop certain upland game. The pattern looks like a cone. The farther out, the wider the cone becomes. If I were to look for a shotgun for 50-yard shooting on upland game, I would try for a choke

The photo on the right shows a successful crow hunter. The photo on the left is indictive of the type of long-range shooting a duck hunter will encounter. The ranges for both types of shotgunning are usually quite different; the duck hunting usually being a longer-range affair. The type and amount of shot and the powder charge will vary tremendously for each type of shooting. As you can see the external ballistic requirements will be quite different.

of 80 percent. This would give about 50 percent at 50 yards and could be lived with in terms of pattern density.

I look at ''killing power'' as a combination of pellet energy and pattern, and this is why pattern becomes a part of the ballistic story in the shotgun shell. The second part of our story, shot size, is worth looking at very closely because shot size is all in terms of retention of original energy. It is highly unlikely that we are going to greatly increase shotshell velocity in the near future. Therefore, we won't be able to rely on that attribute for more striking energy at longer range.

Shot

Shot loses speed rapidly because it is, after all, no more than a tiny round ball. Even buckshot is small when compared with the round ball recommended for muzzleloaders for game larger than rabbits. The shot is treated ballistically as nothing more than a tiny round ball. Quite simply, pellets increase their ability to retain energy as the shot size increases.

But all shot loses original MV very rapidly in shotgunning. My best efforts have come up with a loss of velocity to the tune of 30 percent at 50 yards for small shot.

Just as with rifle ballistics, it's the energy of the projectile at the target that counts. And too few shotgunners may stop to consider the fact that though their load develops 1300 fps at the muzzle, at 50 yards, that per-pellet velocity could be more like 900 fps. Looking at a No. 8 pellet, we find a diameter of .09-inch. In pure lead this would be a weight of 1 grain. The muzzle energy of a 1 grain projectile at 1300 fps is 3.75 foot-pounds. Given a remaining velocity at 50 yards of 900 fps, the No. 8 pellet would be 1.8 foot-pounds. So, for 50-yard shooting, one could not pick the No. 8 pellet as a result of sound ballistic reasoning.

A No. 4 pellet would be .13-inch in diameter and a .13-caliber round ball would weight 3.3 grains. At 1300 fps the energy per pellet would be 12 foot-pounds. At 50 yards, the larger pellet would be moving along with better retained velocity than its smaller cousin, perhaps 1100 fps to 1150 fps. Given the latter velocity figure, the No. 4 pellet would arrive at 50 yards with a retained individual pellet energy of about 9.7 foot-pounds.

Now the shooter can see why some shotgunners who have studied shotgun shell ballistics prefer larger shot for larger targets. Of course, the story appears too grim when looking at individual pellet power. After all, the whole idea of pattern is to offer multiple hits. So we do not have a mere 9.7 foot-pounds of retained energy from that No. 4 pellet at 50 yards, but rather 9.7 times the number of pellets striking, and if enough pellets do hit the target, even at 50 yards from the muzzle, there will be an effective harvest of an upland game animal.

As the shot size increases, so does energy, of course. A No. 2 shot is .15-inch and a BB size is .18-inch. The former would have a pellet weight of 5 grains, while the latter would go 8.8 grains. This is a far cry from the 1 grain pellet spoken of earlier, but of course the trade-off is in the fact that the load will contain far fewer No. 2 or No.BB pellets than it will No. 8 or similar size shot.

Shot Trajectory

Of course the shotgun pattern drops as the distance from the muzzle increases. It must. Ballistics tell us that these little round balls lose velocity rapidly and therefore describe quite a curve as they go from muzzle to destination. But when the destination is but 20 or 30 yards, there need be no real concern for drop. If a shooter intends to do 50-yard shooting or beyond for whatever reasons, hopefully target shooting or curiosity satisfaction, then he should remember the drop of the pattern.

I think in terms of "shot drop" even for 40-yard shooting, and I am sure that such consideration has paid off for me. I shoot a full choke black powder shotgun with a good charge of Fg black powder quite often, and when I go for grouse or pheasants at 35 to 40 yards, I try to take into consideration the trajectory of the pattern. This may seem like a small point to consider but the shooter must consider *drop* as a part of the story.

Shotgun Pressures

As a part of shotgun shell ballistics, pressures are an important subject. Pressure has almost gotten a bad connotation because we are told over and over again, "Watch out for the pressure!" And we darn well must. But we all know that without pressure, the gun would be no gun at all. Projectiles would sit still without pressure to push them away from the bore. In the shotgun, pressure situations differ from the rifle or handgun round.

In a rifle or handgun, pressures vary on many counts. For example, a rough bore can raise pressures in a metallic cartridge firearm. So can a bore size too small for the projectile. Harder jacketed bullets do not render the same pressure as softer jacketed bullets. Cast bullets differ again. The rate of twist can alter pressure, due to more bore friction in the faster twists. And, of course, the condition of the throat and its length matter in pressure a good deal.

Naturally, many things can change black powder pressure. Shell length is one. We never want to use a shell too long for the chamber. If a gun is chambered for 2¾-inch shells, that means the shell is 2¾ inches *after* firing it in the gun. The shell is not 2¾ inches long in loaded form, and the same goes for the 3-inch shell. It is 3 inches long only after it is opened up to full length, not 3 inches long in unfired form.

Mainly, the difference with the black powder shotgun shell is that a bulk of the pressure takes place within the shell itself instead of in the bore. Remember that black powder loads tend to use small charges when compared to a rifle round of any size, such as a 30-06. It is common to see charges of 60 grains of slower burning smokeless powder in a 30-06, but charges of 30 grains of black powder, by volume, for a 12-gauge are not uncommon. It should also be said that modern, smokeless shotshell powder is generally faster burning than the smokeless powder used in full-power rifle loads, too.

So, for the shooter this means remembering that if he is to reload he must be careful not to experiment with components. Leave that up to the boys in the test labs. Since the pressures seem to center in the hull, then fooling around with components can often change pressures dramatically in that hull. Over the years, as the shotgun shell became more efficient, individual experimentation was virtually eliminated. Stick with the good information found in the current loading manuals.

Dram Equivalent

In keeping with the black powder days, shotgun shells have retained the dram equivalent designation. Ballistically, this means, at least in theory, that a modern shotgun shell of 3 drams equivalency would be something like an old-time shotgun shell loaded with about 80 to 82 grains weight (by volume) of black powder. A 4-dram equivalent would be like an old-time black powder shell loaded with about 100 to 109 grains (by volume) of black powder. Today, the modern shooter should look at dram equivalent only for its comparison value. The larger the dram equivalent of the modern round, the more powerful the load generally speaking.

The world of ballistics is a fascinating one and a very useful one for the complete shooter. The complete shooter wants to know what makes his firearms tick, and ballistics addresses that issue by showing us what happens to a bullet as it travels through the bore and onto its final destination. The study of ballistics is far too deep to dive to the bottom of that well of knowledge here, but at least we got our feet wet.

CENTERFIRE RIFLE CARTRIDGES—BALLISTICS

(R) = REMINGTON; (W) = WINCHESTER-WESTERN); (F) = FEDERAL; (H) = HORNADY-FRONTIER; (PMC) = Patton & Morgan Corp.

Cartridge	— BULLET — Wt. Grs.	Type	Bbl. (in.)	— VELOCITY (fps) — Muzzle	100 yds.	200 yds.	300 yds.	— ENERGY (ft. lbs.) — Muzzle	100 yds.	200 yds.	300 yds.	— BULLET PATH† — 100 yds.	200 yds.	300 yds.
17 Remington (R)	25	HPPL	24	4040	3284	2644	2086	906	599	388	242	+0.5	− 1.5	− 8.5
22 Hornet (R) (W)	45	PSP,HP, OPE	24	2690	2042	1502	1128	723	417	225	127	0.0	− 7.7	− 31.3
218 Bee (W)	46	OPE	24	2760	2102	1550	1155	778	451	245	136	0.0	− 7.2	− 29.4
222 Remington (R) (W) (F) (H)	50	PSP, SX	24	3140	2602	2123	1700	1094	752	500	321	+2.2	0.0	− 10.0
222 Remington (R)	50	HPPL	24	3140	2635	2182	1777	1094	771	529	351	+2.1	0.0	− 9.5
222 Remington (W) (R) (PMC)	55	FMC	24	3020	2675	2355	2057	1114	874	677	517	+2.0	0.0	− 8.3
222 Remington (F)	55	MC BT	24	3020	2740	2480	2230	1115	915	750	610	+1.9	0.0	− 7.7
222 Remington Magnum (R)	55	PSP	24	3240	2748	2305	1906	1282	922	649	444	+1.9	0.0	− 8.5
222 Remington Magnum (R)	55	HPPL	24	3240	2773	2352	1969	1282	939	675	473	+1.8	0.0	− 8.5
223 Remington (R) (W) (F) (H) (PMC)	55	PSP	24	3240	2747	2304	1905	1282	921	648	443	+1.9	0.0	− 8.5
223 Remington (R)	55	HPPL	24	3240	2773	2352	1969	1282	939	675	473	+1.8	0.0	− 8.2
223 Remington (R) (H)	55	MC	24	3240	2759	2326	1933	1282	929	660	456	+1.9	0.0	− 8.4
223 Remington (W) (F) (PMC)	55	FMC, MC BT	24	3240	2877	2543	2232	1282	1011	790	608	+1.7	0.0	− 7.1
225 Winchester (W)	55	PSP	24	3570	3066	2616	2208	1556	1148	836	595	+1.2	0.0	− 6.2
22-250 Remington (R) (W) (F) (H) (PMC)	55	PSP	24	3730	3180	2695	2257	1699	1235	887	622	+1.0	0.0	− 5.7
22-250 Remington (R)	55	HPPL	24	3730	3253	2826	2436	1699	1292	975	725	+0.9	0.0	− 5.2
22-250 Remington (F) — Premium	55	BTHP	24	3730	3330	2960	2630	1700	1350	1070	840	+0.8	0.0	− 4.8
220 Swift (H)	55	SP	24	3630	3176	2755	2370	1609	1229	927	686	+1.0	0.0	− 5.6
220 Swift (H)	60	HP	24	3530	3134	2763	2420	1657	1305	1016	780	+1.1	0.0	− 5.7
243 (W) (R) (F) (H) (PMC)	80	PSP, HPPL, FMJ	24	3350	2955	2593	2259	1993	1551	1194	906	+1.6	0.0	− 7.0
243 Winchester (F) — Premium	85	BTHP	24	3320	3070	2830	2600	2080	1770	1510	1280	+1.5	0.0	− 6.8
243 Winchester (W) (R) (F) (H) (PMC)	100	PPSP, PSPCL, SP	24	2960	2697	2449	2215	1945	1615	1332	1089	+1.9	0.0	− 7.8
243 Winchester (F) — Premium	100	BTSP	24	2960	2760	2570	2380	1950	1690	1460	1260	+1.4	0.0	− 5.8
6mm Remington (R) (W) (Also, 244 Rem.)	80	PSP, HPPL	24	3470	3064	2694	2352	2139	1667	1289	982	+1.2	0.0	− 6.0
6mm Remington (R) (W) (F)	100	PSPCL, PPSP	24	3130	2857	2600	2357	2175	1812	1501	1233	+1.7	0.0	− 6.8
25-20 Winchester (W) (R)	86	SP	24	1460	1194	1030	931	407	272	203	165	0.0	−23.5	− 79.6
256 Winchester (W)	60	OPE	24	2760	2097	1542	1149	1015	586	317	176	0.0	− 7.3	− 29.6
25-35 Winchester (W)	117	SP	24	2230	1866	1545	1282	1292	904	620	427	0.0	− 9.2	− 33.1
250 Savage (W)	87	PSP	24	3030	2673	2342	2036	1773	1380	1059	801	+2.0	0.0	− 8.4
250 Savage (W)	100	ST	24	2820	2467	2140	1839	1765	1351	1017	751	+2.4	0.0	− 10.1
250 Savage (R)	100	PSP	24	2820	2504	2210	1936	1765	1392	1084	832	+2.3	0.0	− 9.5
257 Roberts (W)	100	ST	24	2900	2541	2210	1904	1867	1433	1084	805	+2.3	0.0	− 9.4
257 Roberts (W) (R)	117	PPSP, SPCL	24	2650	2291	1961	1663	1824	1363	999	718	+2.9	0.0	− 12.0
25-06 Remington (R)	87	HPPL	24	3440	2995	2591	2222	2286	1733	1297	954	+1.2	0.0	− 6.3
25-06 Remington (W) (F)	90	PEP, HP	24	3440	3043	2680	2344	2364	1850	1435	1098	+1.2	0.0	− 6.1
25-06 Remington (R)	100	PSPCL	24	3230	2893	2580	2287	2316	1858	1478	1161	+1.6	0.0	− 6.9
25-06 Remington (F)	117	SP	24	3060	2790	2530	2280	2430	2020	1660	1360	+1.8	0.0	− 7.3
25-06 Remington (R) (W)	120	PSPCL, PEP	24	3010	2749	2502	2269	2414	2013	1668	1372	+1.9	0.0	− 7.4
6.5mm Remington Magnum (R)	120	PSPCL	24	3210	2905	2621	2353	2745	2248	1830	1475	+1.3	0.0	− 6.6
264 Winchester Magnum (W) (R)	100	PSP, PSPCL	24	3320	2926	2565	2231	2447	1901	1461	1105	+1.3	0.0	− 6.7
264 Winchester Magnum (W) (R)	140	PPSP, PSPCL	24	3030	2782	2548	2326	2854	2406	2018	1682	+1.8	0.0	− 7.2
270 Winchester (W) (R)	100	PSP	24	3480	3067	2690	2343	2689	2088	1606	1219	+1.2	0.0	− 6.2
270 Winchester (W) (R) (F)	130	PPSP, BP, SP	24	3110	2849	2604	2371	2791	2343	1957	1622	+1.7	0.0	− 6.8
270 Winchester (W) (R) (H) (PMC)	130	ST, PSPCL	24	3110	2823	2554	2300	2791	2300	1883	1527	+1.7	0.0	− 7.1
270 Winchester (F) — Premium	130	BTSP	24	3110	2880	2670	2460	2790	2400	2050	1740	+1.6	0.0	− 6.5
270 Winchester (W) (H)	150	PPSP	24	2900	2632	2380	2142	2801	2307	1886	1528	+2.1	0.0	− 8.2
270 Winchester (F) — Premium	150	BTSP	24	2900	2710	2520	2350	2800	2440	2120	1830	+1.6	0.0	− 7.0
270 Winchester (R) (F)	150	SPCL, SP	24	2900	2550	2225	1926	2801	2165	1649	1235	+2.2	0.0	− 9.3
270 Winchester (F) — Premium	150	NP	24	2900	2630	2380	2140	2800	2310	1890	1530	+2.1	0.0	− 8.2
7mm Mauser (R) (W)	175	SP	24	2440	2137	1857	1603	2313	1774	1340	998	0.0	− 6.8	− 23.7
7mm Mauser (F)	175	SP	24	2470	2170	1880	1630	2370	1820	1380	1030	0.0	− 6.6	− 23.0
7mm Mauser (F)	140	SP	24	2660	2450	2260	2070	2200	1865	1585	1330	+2.4	0.0	− 3.2
7mm-08 Remington (R)	140	PSPCL	24	2860	2625	2402	2189	2542	2142	1793	1490	+2.1	0.0	− 8.1
280 Remington (R)	150	SPCL	24	2970	2699	2444	2203	2937	2426	1989	1616	+1.9	0.0	− 7.8
280 Remington (R)	165	SPCL	24	2820	2510	2220	1950	2913	2308	1805	1393	+2.3	0.0	− 9.4
284 Winchester (W)	150	PPSP	24	2860	2595	2344	2108	2724	2243	1830	1480	+2.1	0.0	− 8.5
7mm Remington Magnum (W)	125	PPSP	24	3310	2976	2666	2376	3040	2458	1972	1567	+1.2	0.0	− 6.5
7mm Remington Magnum (R) (W) (F)	150	PSPCL, PPSP, SP	24	3110	2830	2568	2320	3221	2667	2196	1792	+1.7	0.0	− 7.0
7mm Remington Magnum (F)—Premium	150	BTSP	24	3110	2920	2750	2580	3220	2850	2510	2210	+1.6	0.0	− 6.2
7mm Remington Magnum (F)—Premium	165	BTSP	24	2860	2710	2560	2420	3000	2690	2410	2150	+1.6	0.0	− 6.9
7mm Remington Magnum (R) (W) (F) (H)	175	PSPCL, PPSP	24	2860	2645	2440	2244	3178	2718	2313	1956	+2.0	0.0	− 7.9
7mm Remington Magnum (F)—Premium	160	NP	24	2950	2730	2520	2320	3090	2650	2250	1910	+1.8	0.0	− 7.7
30 Carbine (R) (W) (F) (H)	110	SP, HSP, SP, RN	20	1990	1567	1236	1035	967	600	373	262	0.0	−13.5	− 49.9
30 Carbine (W) (F) (H) (PMC)	110	FMC, MC, FMJ, FMC	20	1990	1596	1278	1070	967	622	399	280	0.0	−13.0	− 47.4
30 Remington (R) (W)	170	SPCL, ST	24	2120	1822	1555	1328	1696	1253	913	666	0.0	− 9.7	− 33.8
30-30 Accelerator (R)	55	SP	24	3400	2693	2085	1570	1412	886	521	301	+2.0	0.0	− 10.2
30-30 Winchester (F)	125	HP	24	2570	2090	1660	1320	1830	1210	770	480	0.0	− 7.3	− 28.1
30-30 Winchester (W) (F) (PMC)	150	OPE, PPSP, ST, SP	24	2390	2018	1684	1398	1902	1356	944	651	0.0	− 7.7	− 27.9
30-30 Winchester (R) (H)	150	SPCL	24	2390	1973	1605	1303	1902	1296	858	565	0.0	− 8.2	− 30.0
30-30 Winchester (W) (R) (F) (PMC)	170	PPSP, ST, SPCL, SP, HPCL	24	2200	1895	1619	1381	1827	1355	989	720	0.0	− 8.9	− 31.1
300 Savage (R)	150	SPCL	24	2630	2247	1897	1585	2303	1681	1198	837	0.0	− 6.1	− 21.9
300 Savage (W)	150	PPSP	24	2630	2311	2015	1743	2303	1779	1352	1012	+2.8	0.0	− 11.5
300 Savage (W) (F) (R)	150	ST, SP, PSPCL	24	2630	2354	2095	1853	2303	1845	1462	1143	+2.7	0.0	− 10.7
300 Savage (R) (W)	180	SPCL, PPSP	24	2350	2025	1728	1467	2207	1639	1193	860	0.0	− 7.7	− 27.1
300 Savage (R) (W) (F)	180	PSPCL, ST	24	2350	2137	1935	1745	2207	1825	1496	1217	0.0	− 6.7	− 22.8
30-40 Krag (R) (W)	180	SPCL, PPSP	24	2430	2098	1795	1525	2360	1761	1288	929	0.0	− 7.1	− 25.0
30-40 Krag (R) (W)	180	PSPCL, ST	24	2430	2213	2007	1813	2360	1957	1610	1314	0.0	− 6.2	− 21.1
303 Savage (W)	190	ST	24	1940	1657	1410	1211	1588	1158	839	619	0.0	−11.9	− 41.4
308 Accelerator (R)	55	PSP	24	3770	3215	2726	2286	1735	1262	907	638	+1.0	0.0	− 5.6
308 Winchester (W)	110	PSP	24	3180	2666	2206	1795	2470	1736	1188	787	+2.0	0.0	− 9.3
308 Winchester (W)	125	PSP	24	3050	2697	2370	2067	2582	2019	1559	1186	+2.0	0.0	− 8.2
308 Winchester (W)	150	PPSP	24	2820	2488	2179	1893	2648	2061	1581	1193	+2.4	0.0	− 9.8
308 Winchester (W) (R) (F) (H) (PMC)	150	ST, PSPCL, SP	24	2820	2533	2263	2009	2648	2137	1705	1344	+2.3	0.0	− 9.1
308 Winchester (PMC)	147	FMC-BT	24	2750	2473	2257	2052	2428	2037	1697	1403	+2.3	0.0	− 9.1
308 Winchester (H)	165	BTSP, SPBT	24	2700	2520	2330	2160	2670	2310	1990	1700	+2.0	0.0	− 8.4
308 Winchester (W) (R)	180	PPSP, SPCL	24	2620	2274	1955	1666	2743	2086	1527	1109	+2.9	0.0	− 12.1
308 Winchester (W) (R) (F) (PMC)	180	ST, PSPCL, SP	24	2620	2393	2178	1974	2743	2288	1896	1557	+2.6	0.0	− 9.9
308 Winchester (W)	200	ST	24	2450	2208	1980	1767	2665	2165	1741	1386	0.0	− 6.3	− 21.4
30-06 Springfield (W)	110	PSP	24	3380	2843	2365	1936	2790	1974	1366	915	+1.7	0.0	− 8.0
30-06 Springfield (W) (R) (F)	125	PSP, PSP, SP	24	3140	2780	2447	2138	2736	2145	1662	1269	+1.8	0.0	− 7.7
30-06 Springfield (W)	150	PPSP	24	2920	2580	2265	1972	2839	2217	1708	1295	+2.2	0.0	− 9.0
30-06 Springfield (W) (R) (F) (H) (PMC)	150	ST, PSPCL, SP, SP	24	2910	2617	2342	2083	2820	2281	1827	1445	+2.1	0.0	− 8.5
30-06 Springfield (R)	150	BP	24	2910	2656	2416	2189	2820	2349	1944	1596	+2.0	0.0	− 8.0
30-06 Springfield (PMC)	150	FMC (M-2)	24	2810	2555	2310	2080	2630	2170	1780	1440	+2.2	0.0	− 8.8
30-06 Accelerator (R)	55	PSP	24	4080	3485	2965	2502	2033	1483	1074	764	+1.0	0.0	− 5.0
30-06 Springfield (R)	165	PSPCL	24	2800	2534	2283	2047	2872	2352	1909	1534	+2.3	0.0	− 9.0
30-06 Springfield (F) (H)	165	BTSP	24	2800	2610	2420	2240	2870	2490	2150	1840	+2.1	0.0	− 8.0
30-06 Springfield (R) (W) (PMC)	180	SPCL, PPSP	24	2700	2348	2023	1727	2913	2203	1635	1192	+2.7	0.0	− 11.3

CENTERFIRE RIFLE CARTRIDGES—BALLISTICS (continued)

Cartridge	— BULLET — Wt. Grs.	Type	Bbl. (in.)	— VELOCITY (fps) — Muzzle	100 yds.	200 yds.	300 yds.	— ENERGY (ft. lbs.) — Muzzle	100 yds.	200 yds.	300 yds.	— BULLET PATH† — 100 yds.	200 yds.	300 yds.
30-06 Springfield (R) (W) (F) (H) (PMC)	180	PSPCL, ST	24	2700	2469	2250	2042	2913	2436	2023	1666	+2.4	0.0	−9.3
30-06 Springfield (R)	180	BP	24	2700	2485	2280	2084	2913	2468	2077	1736	+2.4	0.0	−9.1
30-06 Springfield (F)	200	BTSP	24	2550	2400	2260	2120	2890	2560	2270	2000	+2.3	0.0	−9.0
30-06 Springfield (W) (R)	220	PPSP, SPCL	24	2410	2130	1870	1632	2837	2216	1708	1301	0.0	−6.8	−23.6
30-06 Springfield (W)	220	ST	24	2410	2192	1985	1791	2837	2347	1924	1567	0.0	−6.4	−21.6
300 H & H Magnum (W) (R)	180	ST, PSPCL	24	2880	2640	2412	2196	3315	2785	2325	1927	+2.1	0.0	−8.0
300 Winchester Magnum (W) (R)	150	PPSP, PSPCL	24	3290	2951	2636	2342	3605	2900	2314	1827	+1.3	0.0	−6.6
300 Winchester Magnum (W) (R) (F) (H)	180	PPSP, PSPCL, SP	24	2960	2745	2540	2344	3501	3011	2578	2196	+1.9	0.0	−7.3
300 Winchester Magnum (F) Premium	200	BTSP	24	2830	2680	2530	2380	3560	3180	2830	2520	+1.7	0.0	−7.1
303 British (R)	180	SPCL	24	2460	2124	1817	1542	2418	1803	1319	950	0.0	−6.9	−24.4
303 British (W)	180	PPSP	24	2460	2233	2018	1816	2418	1993	1627	1318	0.0	−6.1	−20.8
32-20 Winchester (W) (R)	100	SP	24	1210	1021	913	834	325	231	185	154	0.0	−32.3	−106.3
32-20 Winchester (W) (R)	100	L	24	1210	1021	913	834	325	231	185	154	0.0	−32.3	−106.3
32 Winchester Special (F) (R)	170	SP	24	2250	1920	1630	1370	1911	1390	1000	710	0.0	−8.6	−30.5
8mm Mauser (R) (W)	170	SPCL, PPSP	24	2360	1969	1622	1333	2102	1463	993	671	0.0	−8.2	−29.8
8mm Mauser (F)	170	SP	24	2510	2110	1740	1430	2380	1670	1140	770	0.0	−7.0	−25.7
8mm Remington Magnum (R)	185	PSPCL	24	3080	2761	2464	2186	3896	3131	2494	1963	+1.8	0.0	−7.6
8mm Remington Magum (R)	220	PSPCL	24	2830	2581	2346	2123	3912	3254	2688	2201	+2.2	0.0	−8.5
338 Winchester Magnum (W)	200	PPSP	24	2960	2658	2375	2110	3890	3137	2505	1977	+2.0	0.0	−8.2
338 Winchester Magnum (W)	250	ST	24	2660	2395	2145	1910	3927	3184	2554	2025	+2.6	0.0	−10.2
348 Winchester (W)	200	ST	24	2520	2215	1931	1672	2820	2178	1656	1241	0.0	−6.2	−21.9
351 Winchester S.L. (W)	180	SP	**20**	1850	1556	1310	1128	1368	968	686	508	0.0	−13.6	−47.5
35 Remington (R)	150	PSPCL	24	2300	1874	1506	1218	1762	1169	755	494	0.0	−9.2	−33.0
35 Remington (R) (F)	200	SPCL, SP	24	2080	1698	1376	1140	1921	1280	841	577	0.0	−11.3	−41.2
35 Remington (W)	200	PPSP, ST	24	2020	1646	1335	1114	1812	1203	791	551	0.0	−12.1	−43.9
358 Winchester (W)	200	ST	24	2490	2171	1876	1610	2753	2093	1563	1151	0.0	−6.5	−23.0
350 Remington Magnum (R)	200	PSPCL	**20**	2710	2410	2130	1870	3261	2579	2014	1553	+2.6	0.0	−10.3
375 Winchester (W)	200	PPSP	24	2200	1841	1526	1268	2150	1506	1034	714	0.0	−9.5	−33.8
375 Winchester (W)	250	PPSP	24	1900	1647	1424	1239	2005	1506	1126	852	0.0	−12.0	−40.9
38-55 Winchester (W)	255	SP	24	1320	1190	1091	1018	987	802	674	587	0.0	−23.4	−75.2
375 H & H Magnum (R) (W)	270	SP, PPSP	24	2690	2420	2166	1928	4337	3510	2812	2228	+2.5	0.0	−10.0
375 H & H Magnum (W)	300	ST	24	2530	2268	2022	1793	4263	3426	2723	2141	+2.9	0.0	−11.5
375 H & H Magnum (W) (R)	300	FMC, MC	24	2530	2171	1843	1551	4263	3139	2262	1602	0.0	−6.5	−23.4
38-40 Winchester (W)	180	SP	24	1160	999	901	827	538	399	324	273	0.0	−33.9	−110.6
44-40 Winchester (W) (R)	200	SP, SP	24	1190	1006	900	822	629	449	360	300	0.0	−33.3	−109.5
44 Remington Magnum (R)	240	SP, SJHP	**20**	1760	1380	1114	970	1650	1015	661	501	0.0	−17.6	−63.1
44 Remington Magnum (F) (W)	240	HSP	**20**	1760	1380	1090	950	1650	1015	640	485	0.0	−18.1	−65.1
444 Marlin (R)	240	SP	24	2350	1815	1377	1087	2942	1755	1010	630	0.0	−9.9	−38.5
444 Marlin (R)	265	SP	24	2120	1733	1405	1160	2644	1768	1162	791	0.0	−10.8	−39.5
45-70 Government (F)	300	HSP	24	1810	1410	1120	970	2180	1320	840	630	0.0	−17.0	−61.4
45-70 Government (W)	300	JHP	24	1880	1559	1294	1105	2355	1619	1116	814	0.0	−13.5	−47.1
45-70 Government (R)	405	SP	24	1330	1168	1055	977	1590	1227	1001	858	0.0	−24.6	−80.3
458 Winchester Magnum (W) (R)	500	FMC, MC	24	2040	1823	1623	1442	4620	3689	2924	2308	0.0	−9.6	−32.5
458 Winchester Magnum (W) (R)	510	SP, SP	24	2040	1770	1527	1319	4712	3547	2640	1970	0.0	−10.3	−35.6

*Price for 50. †Bullet Path based on line-of-sight 0.9" above center of bore. Bullet type abbreviations: BP—Bronze Point; BT—Boat Tail; CL—Core Lokt; FN—Flat Nose; FMC—Full Metal Case; FMJ—Full Metal Jacket; HP—Hollow Point; HSP—Hollow Soft Point; JHP—Jacketed Hollow Point; L—Lead; Lu—Lubaloy; MAT—Match; MC—Metal Case; NP—Nosler Partition; OPE—Open Point Expanding; PCL—Pointed Core Lokt; PEP—Pointed Expanding Point; PL—Power-Lokt; PP—Power Point; Prem.—Premium; PSP—Pointed Soft Point; SJHP—Semi-Jacketed Hollow Point; SJMP—Semi-Jacketed Metal Point; SP—Soft Point; ST—Silvertip; SX—Super Explosive. PMC prices slightly less.

WEATHERBY MAGNUM CARTRIDGES—BALLISTICS

Cartridge	— Bullet — Wt. Grs.	Type	Bbl. (in.)	— Velocity (fps) — Muzzle	100 Yds.	200 Yds.	300 Yds.	— Energy (ft. lbs.) — Muzzle	100 Yds.	200 Yds.	300 Yds.	— Bullet Path† — 100 Yds.	200 Yds.	300 Yds.
224 Weatherby Magnum	55	PE	26	3650	3214	2808	2433	1627	1262	963	723	+2.8	+3.6	0.0
240 Weatherby Magnum	70	PE	26	3850	3424	3025	2654	2305	1823	1423	1095	+2.2	+3.0	0.0
240 Weatherby Magnum	87	PE	26	3500	3165	2848	2550	2367	1935	1567	1256	+2.8	+3.6	0.0
240 Weatherby Magnum	100	PE	26	3395	3115	2848	2594	2560	2155	1802	1495	+2.8	+3.5	0.0
240 Weatherby Magnum	100	NP	26	3395	3068	2758	2468	2560	2090	1690	1353	+1.1	0.0	−5.7
257 Weatherby Magnum	87	PE	26	3825	3470	3135	2818	2827	2327	1900	1535	+2.1	+2.9	0.0
257 Weatherby Magnum	100	PE	26	3555	3256	2971	2700	2807	2355	1960	1619	+2.5	+3.2	0.0
257 Weatherby Magnum	100	NP	26	3555	3242	2945	2663	2807	2335	1926	1575	+0.9	0.0	−4.7
257 Weatherby Magnum	117	SPE	26	3300	2853	2443	2074	2830	2115	1551	1118	+3.8	+4.9	0.0
257 Weatherby Magnum	117	NP	26	3300	3027	2767	2520	2830	2381	1990	1650	+1.2	0.0	−5.9
270 Weatherby Magnum	100	PE	26	3760	3341	2949	2585	3140	2479	1932	1484	+2.4	+3.2	0.0
270 Weatherby Magnum	130	PE	26	3375	3110	2856	2615	3289	2793	2355	1974	+2.8	+3.5	0.0
270 Weatherby Magnum	130	NP	26	3375	3113	2862	2624	3289	2798	2365	1988	+1.0	0.0	−5.2
270 Weatherby Magnum	150	PE	26	3245	3012	2789	2575	3508	3022	2592	2209	+3.1	+3.8	0.0
270 Weatherby Magnum	150	NP	26	3245	3022	2809	2604	3508	3043	2629	2259	+1.2	0.0	−5.4
7mm Weatherby Magnum	139	PE	26	3300	3037	2786	2546	3362	2848	2396	2001	+3.0	+3.7	0.0
7mm Weatherby Magnum	140	NP	26	3300	3047	2806	2575	3386	2887	2448	2062	+1.1	0.0	−5.4
7mm Weatherby Magnum	154	PE	26	3160	2928	2706	2494	3415	2932	2504	2127	+3.3	+4.1	0.0
7mm Weatherby Magnum	160	NP	26	3150	2935	2727	2528	3526	3061	2643	2271	+1.3	0.0	−5.8
7mm Weatherby Magnum	175	RN	26	3070	2714	2383	2082	3663	2863	2207	1685	+1.6	0.0	−7.5
300 Weatherby Magnum	110	PE	26	3900	3465	3057	2677	3716	2933	2283	1750	+2.2	+3.0	0.0
300 Weatherby Magnum	150	PE	26	3545	3248	2965	2696	4187	3515	2929	2422	+2.5	+3.2	0.0
300 Weatherby Magnum	150	NP	26	3545	3191	2857	2544	4187	3392	2719	2156	+1.0	0.0	−5.3
300 Weatherby Magnum	180	PE	26	3245	3010	2785	2569	4210	3622	3100	2639	+3.1	+3.8	0.0
300 Weatherby Magnum	180	NP	26	3245	2964	2696	2444	4210	3512	2906	2388	+1.3	0.0	−6.0
300 Weatherby Magnum	220	SPE	26	2905	2578	2276	2000	4123	3248	2531	1955	+1.9	0.0	−8.6
340 Weatherby Magnum	200	PE	26	3210	2947	2696	2458	4577	3857	3228	2683	+3.2	+4.0	0.0
340 Weatherby Magnum	210	NP	26	3180	2927	2686	2457	4717	3996	3365	2816	+1.3	0.0	−6.2
340 Weatherby Magnum	250	SPE	26	2850	2516	2209	1929	4510	3515	2710	2066	+2.0	0.0	−9.2
340 Weatherby Magnum	250	NP	26	2850	2563	2296	2049	4510	3648	2927	2331	+1.8	0.0	−8.2
378 Weatherby Magnum	270	SPE	26	3180	2796	2440	2117	6064	4688	3570	2688	+1.5	0.0	−7.3
378 Weatherby Magnum	300	SPE	26	2925	2564	2234	1935	5700	4380	3325	2495	+1.9	0.0	−9.0
378 Weatherby Magnum	300	FMJ	26	2925	2620	2340	2080	5700	4574	3649	2883	+4.9	+6.0	0.0
460 Weatherby Magnum	500	RN	26	2700	2395	2115	1858	8095	6370	4968	3834	+2.3	0.0	−10.3
460 Weatherby Magnum	500	FMJ	26	2700	2416	2154	1912	8095	6482	5153	4060	+2.2	0.0	−9.8

†Bullet Path based on line of sight 1.5" above center of bore. Bullet type abbreviations: FMJ—Full Metal Jacket; NP—Nosler Partition; PE—Pointed Expanding; RN—Round Nose; SPE—Semi-Pointed Expanding.

Chapter 26

The Custom Rifle

THE COMPLETE SHOOTER may be fortunate enough at some time in his shooting career to own a fine personal rifle—a handmade, *custom rifle*. The term has changed in meaning over the years, and probably needs re-evaluation today, but it conjures up the same picture in the minds of dedicated shooters which has been projected for many decades—one of a handsome function, accuracy with beauty, and that personal touch that says, "this one is mine and there isn't another one quite like it anywhere."

What is a custom rifle? Once upon a time in America, a custom rifle was almost the rule. There were military muskets about and these were abundant, and there were shotguns which came from overseas in numbers, but when the American shooter wanted his own rifle to hunt with, to protect his life with, he had a man make it. Today we might call that man a *custom* gunsmith, but he was just a gunsmith in the 1800s.

In those days the shooter contracted with his gunsmith to build a rifle, the resulting product far and away ahead of the muskets and factory-type guns of the day. I am talking about the so-called Kentucky rifle—that graceful, accurate beauty which repelled the British and put meat on the table, and which is viewed today as a collector's treasure. It should be called the Pennsylvania rifle, perhaps or at least the Pennsylvania/Kentucky rifle, but that doesn't matter. What does matter is the fact that the tradition of having a rifle made just for you was born in this country a great time back.

The gunsmith of the 18th and 19th centuries had to often work from scratch or near scratch. He was obliged often to fashion a part. Perhaps he took a hunk of metal and shaped it into a tumbler for the lock, or he handcrafted some other metal piece. He made the furniture of the rifle from metal flatware, probably, and of course the stock began life as a big hunk of wood with no more contour than a railroad box car. He finished everything. He browned the barrel, and the furniture, if iron. He polished up the brass parts of the rifle. He even cut the rifling in the bore of the barrel, and probably worked the barrel steel into shape as well.

Certainly, the old-time gunsmith set the sights, created the lines of the rifle and finished the wood. There wasn't much that our early gunsmith didn't do. But he did not always use his own locks. Even then, it was not at all uncommon for the lock of a fine handmade rifle to be fashioned by someone other than the gunmaker, or for it to be imported from overseas. This is important to know, because it helps us decide today the criteria for a custom rifle.

The Custom Rifle Today

What is a custom rifle? Must it be handmade from scratch? Is a custom rifle no longer considered "custom" if high technology machines are used to shape its stock or to cut the rifling of the barrel? The whole question gets sticky in a big hurry. Earlier, we hinted that the custom rifle was unique in some way, that there would not be another just exactly like it anywhere. And yet, many a gunmaker today has a "trademark," and it is not always a problem to spot the work of a particular craftsman. This does not mean that the style of the smith turns a rifle into a factory-form type of rifle. But it does mean that we have to bend our ideas of uniqueness from time to time.

Although it may be impossible to define the term custom to everyone's satisfaction, there are a few points which can be made about today's custom rifle. We can even define that rifle so the complete shooter can go out and have one built for himself. Here are some points.

1. The rifle is *individually* made. This does not mean that the gunmaker never crafts another like it in his career. It means that the gunsmith does not set up 10 rifles by getting 10 identical barrels and trying to make 10 identical stocks, fitting each with the same embellishments until he has 10 rifles which look like peas in the proverbial pod. No. A custom rifle is *individually* made. And the buyer should be able to expect just that. His rifle will be unique in that there will not be another *exactly* like it, but here may be many of the same general *style*.

2. The custom rifle is designed for a purpose, even if the purpose is "show." Both gunmaker and gun owner set out to have something specific made up, and that something must have some sort of function. The function itself may be just plain show. A fine rifle is a work of art. And art is to show, to appreciate with our senses. I can always

Custom work often means innovation. This is an escutcheon on a Model 700 custom rifle by Dale Storey. Note the wood-to-metal fit. The escutcheon has also been embellished with a bit of engraving, by the maker.

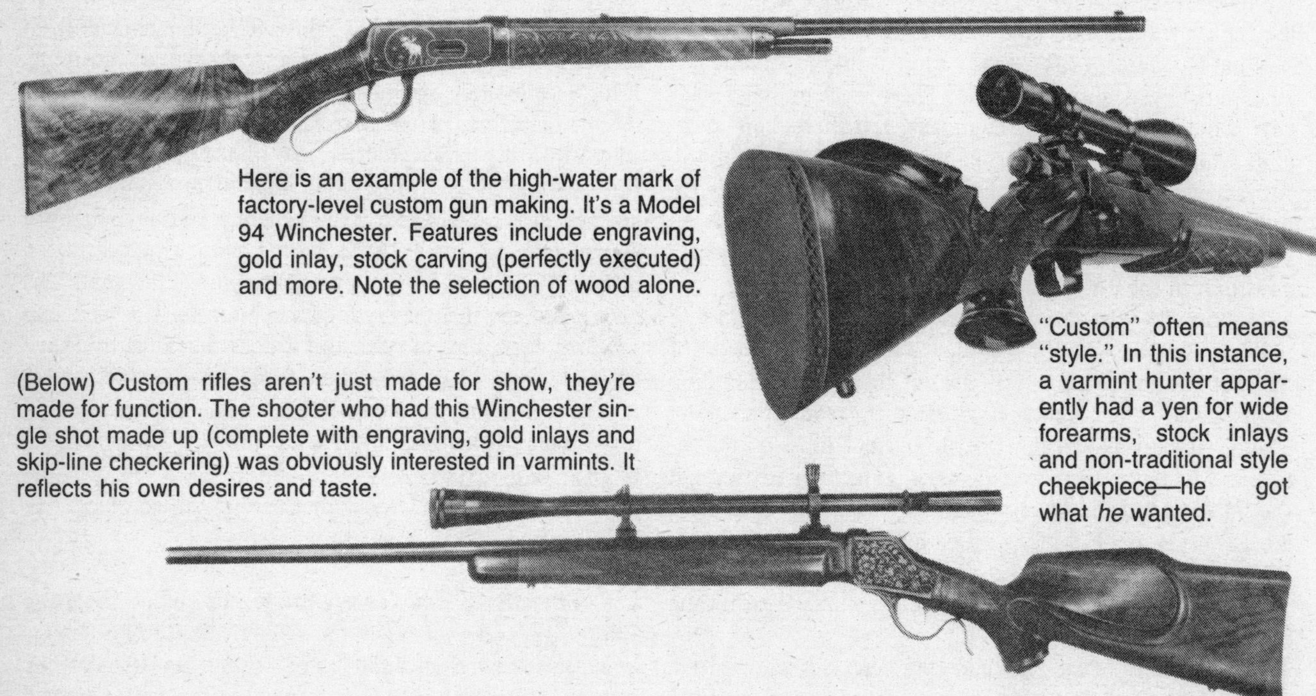

Here is an example of the high-water mark of factory-level custom gun making. It's a Model 94 Winchester. Features include engraving, gold inlay, stock carving (perfectly executed) and more. Note the selection of wood alone.

"Custom" often means "style." In this instance, a varmint hunter apparently had a yen for wide forearms, stock inlays and non-traditional style cheekpiece—he got what *he* wanted.

(Below) Custom rifles aren't just made for show, they're made for function. The shooter who had this Winchester single shot made up (complete with engraving, gold inlays and skip-line checkering) was obviously interested in varmints. It reflects his own desires and taste.

tell a lover of fine rifles for when he examines a custom rifle of merit he not only looks at the piece; he also works it in his hands, testing the mechanical smoothness as well as inspecting the finish and fit.

One of my gunmaker friends, who specializes in fine collectible longrifles, claims that one out of three of his currently made custom muzzleloaders goes to someone who mainly wants to own the rifle for its beauty. He wants to collect it, not shoot it. Sometimes, my friend says, it is very frustrating to know that a rifle built with accuracy and handling in mind may never be fired.

It should also be said that the custom rifle is often expected to do something special. When there is no factory rifle made to take care of a certain task (in the mind of the shooter at least), then that shooter goes forth seeking a custom rifle. A very good example is a custom rifle I own. I wanted a fine-grade lever-action, and it had to be the older style, such as the Model 94, but I also wanted a round chambered into that rifle which was slightly hotter than the 30-30, but not much more in punch. I wanted a little flat-sided piece, hence the Model 94, but I wanted a 24-inch barrel on it, for sight radius, balance and my own sense of what looks good to *my* eye. I also desired peep sights and a built-in sling with a sling eye built right into the barrel. I wanted a front sight with a ramp which was integral with the barrel, too. And I desired accuracy not generally obtained from a standard off-the-rack 94.

I wanted a better hunk of wood than normally found on the factory rifle. I wanted balance not always associated with the Model 94, at least not the type of balance suited to a long-armed person. The finish had to be something special, and the metal had to have a soft luster and sheen, not a high blue. In short, I wanted what *I wanted!* And I got it. When my desires and my gunmaker's expert knowledge were melded together into one, the Storey Conversion was born, a rifle which is the result of the ideas of a shooter *and* the ideas of a gunmaker.

3. Investment—the custom rifle can be a great investment, and I am not speaking only in terms of dollars. Sure, a truly fine custom rifle may end up making money for its owner when he sells it. As an example, try to buy a Bob Owen custom rifle today. Believe me, it will cost a great deal more than it cost when it was made. Inflation is partly

A custom rifle means getting what you want. This rifle was designed by the author and by the gunmaker, Dale Storey. It is a superbly constructed piece, weighing a well-balanced 7.5 pounds with scope and sling. It handles beautifully and is highly accurate and fast-pointing. It is built on the time-tested Model 700 Remington action and wears a Bushnell Scopechief variable sight, 2.5×-8×.

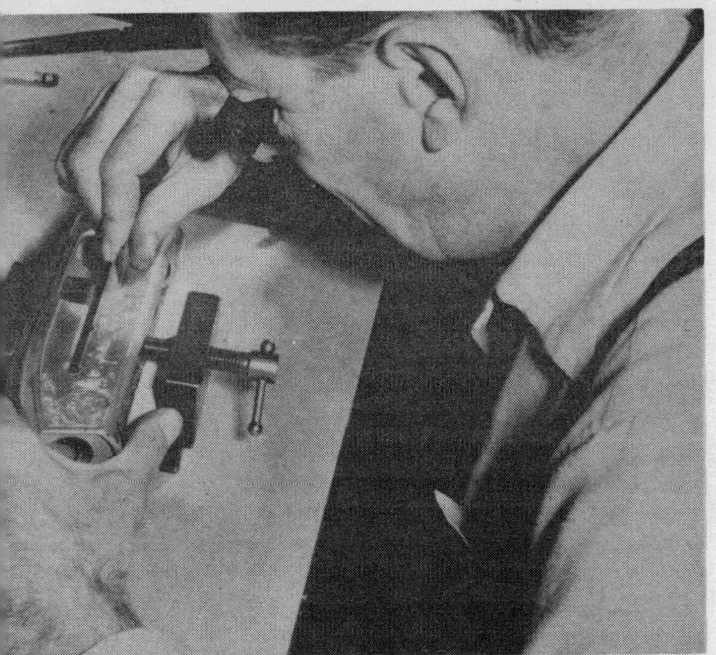

A custom job of engraving usually requires the services of someone other than a custom gunsmith. Good engraving should only be done by qualified, expert engravers. When you pay for top engraving, you're buying both art and workmanship.

the reason, but that Owen custom rifle not only kept up with inflation, which few possessions can do, it also gained in value. I should hastily add that this is not always the case. Some custom firearms, even though well-made, may not gain in dollar value. It would be nice if they were always worth more as time passed, but investment is more than money.

There is nothing wrong with giving dad's rifle to a son or daughter way down the road. Passing on a fine rifle is a good tradition. And there is nothing wrong if that rifle is a factory job, probably no longer made at that. There is plenty of value here. But handing down a custom rifle, one made just for you, is also an investment value in its own class. The aforementioned Storey Conversion will find its way into the hands of a son or daughter down the line, and he or she will have a very personal possession. That was truly Dad's rifle. He even had a part in its development. And this last statement is a very important one—the shooter should have a part in the development of his own personal custom rifle if he's contracting for one.

4. Workmanship—I also feel that a custom rifle is really not a custom if it lacks professional workmanship. Sadly, there are smiths out there who do not have great talent. They should confine their labors to installing buttplates and scopes, but they don't always do that. One so-called custom rifle I saw not long ago fell far short in the workmanship department. It was just a homemade rifle. Nobody wants to pay a custom price for a homemade rifle. "Homemade" does not mean *custom*.

I think a custom is a rifle built by a pro. He's a trained craftsman, either from a gunsmithing school or as a result of years of learning on his own. And the latter case is generally one of learning from others, too. I know a young gunmaker who has not been to a gunsmithing school, but he is forever looking and learning. He has worked with an older gunmaker, and he has even purchased custom rifles to study them.

5. Materials—the custom is made from the *best* materials. And great attention is paid to the details when using those materials. There is precision of fit. A custom rifle shows that it was fitted by an expert. There are no obvious gaps between wood and metal, for example. And the fine fit is also finished correctly. It's a tuned rifle, too. I would not consider any custom rifle correct if the mechanics of the rifle were faulty. In short, the action should be polished and balanced, the parts functioning together in smoothness of operation.

That's a custom rifle, or at least some of the criteria to look for. Obviously, you can't buy a custom rifle off the rack in the same manner you buy a factory rifle. It is not put out in production-line form, though certainly a smith may be making several rifles at the same time. Mostly a custom is a rifle which is born from the ideas and desires of the shooter as well as the knowledge and skills of the gun-

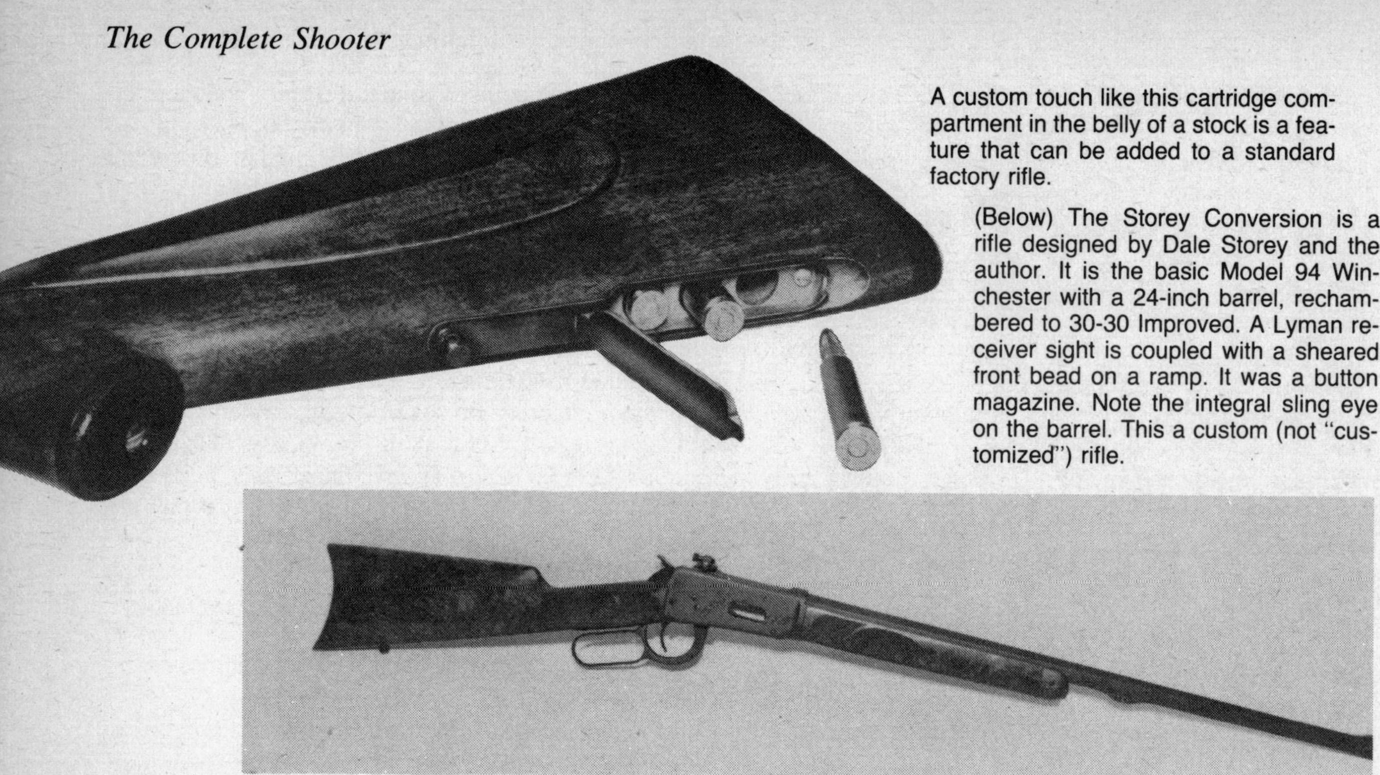

A custom touch like this cartridge compartment in the belly of a stock is a feature that can be added to a standard factory rifle.

(Below) The Storey Conversion is a rifle designed by Dale Storey and the author. It is the basic Model 94 Winchester with a 24-inch barrel, rechambered to 30-30 Improved. A Lyman receiver sight is coupled with a sheared front bead on a ramp. It was a button magazine. Note the integral sling eye on the barrel. This a custom (not "customized") rifle.

maker. A man *knows* when he has a custom rifle. The criteria which make it a custom rifle are his own.

Custom Versus Customized

This can be a touchy area, but the distinction between *custom* and *customized* has to be made. Today, a custom rifle may certainly not be a product of pure handwork. The riflesmith could never afford to sit there cutting a floorplate out by hand and filing it smooth with simple tools. It's simply not that kind of economy any longer, though a few black powder smiths come pretty close to doing just that. I have seen an octagonal barrel which was made with a drawfile.

A *customized* rifle is a standard factory model which has had work done to it; I said this division would be touchy. My wife owns a 284 Winchester Model 77 Ruger. I call it a custom rifle. It certainly began life as a sound and worthy Model 77, but it is hardly that today. The contour of the barrel has been changed so that the rifle bears featherweight proportions. The stock is one which was cut from a blank and totally *hand*-inletted by Dean Zollinger. If you want to pull barrel/action from stock, you'd best be careful. The two go together like bacon and eggs. The dimensions have been matched to my wife's needs, though this can be accomplished *in part* through customizing an existing rifle. I am not talking about that. I mean the rifle fits in every line because it was engineered to fit. The bedding job, I suspect, has brought some accuracy with it, for the rifle shoots better than ever, though it was always accurate, as the Ruger 77 is known to be.

However, there is a rifle which is truly a *customized* model instead of a custom. The customized rifle is a factory number with changes. Here are some of the "customizing" features possible:

1. Add checkering. Checkering of a handcrafted quality is a mark of the custom rifle, but it can be added to any production rifle which has no checkering on the wood.

2. Remove the sights. Sights can be removed in an effort to smooth the lines of a rifle, giving it a more custom appearance. At the same time, a very fine finish can be added to the metal. This means a lot of metal polishing before the bluing—a custom touch.

3. Glass bed the barrel and/or action. While this may seem to be an expedient, it may not be at all. An existing rifle can be glass bedded to make a more perfect fit between wood and metal.

4. Change the balance. The rifle's barrel can be shortened, as can the stock's length of pull. The wrist of the rifle can be made more trim, and the comb of the stock changed.

5. Change sights. New iron sights can be added to a rifle, or as stated above, the sights can be removed in the case of irons and a scope installed. This is considered a customizing feature only if original sights were removed, which certainly takes a professional touch. If the front sight is integral with the barrel, a new blue job will probably follow its removal.

6. Fill holes or slots in the metal. There are often holes of the drilled and tapped variety, or the removal of a rear sight may leave a dovetail slot. The latter can be filled in with a blank and then polished up. Other holes can be filled prior to a rebluing effort.

7. Change the safety. For those who prefer smoother-looking safeties, changes can be made on various models. For example, I like the wing-type safety found on the Model 70 Winchester. I have this type of safety on my Model 700 Remington.

8. Reduce weight. This can be work done with the stock, but it can also mean turning a barrel down and rebedding, or it can mean many other methods which will trim a rifle down.

9. Triggers—a new, more fully adjustable trigger is often added to the customized rifle.

10. Restocking. A whole new stock can be added to an existing factory rifle. This is "customizing," but it is not making a custom rifle. The rifle will still be that same factory model, but with a custom stock.

Glass Bedding

Not long ago, I had a fine lightweight rifle made up in a 6.5mm wildcat round. The idea was accuracy without weight. I wanted a rifle under 8 pounds total with sling and scope. I got a rifle which went right on 7.5 pounds with sling and scope. Accurate? It was and is superb. I have had witnesses at the range check a target for its three-shot group at 100 yards to find that what I said about the lightweight putting 3 shots into 1/2-inch center-to-center was not in my imagination.

And the rifle is glass-bedded. When the gunmaker told me he wanted to glass the barrel and action into the stock, I shuddered. The wood came from a blank and now the fellow was going to glass-in the barrel and action? I had come along in the time when glass bedding was considered a crutch for those too lacking in skill to mate wood with metal. But the man explained to me that with such a light stock, the glass bedding would offer *stability*. I consented to the bedding job.

What I should have considered was the fact that this man was a pro. He glass-bedded the stock all right, but I defy anyone to see the glass. It's there, but the wood of the barrel channel is what a person sees, not glass. And the glass bedding, in this case, is probably wise due to the light weight of the stock.

Is glass bedding taboo for a custom? I imagine that a lot of gunmakers and not just a few custom gun buyers consider a glass bedding job anything but a custom touch. I will agree that a finely-fitted stock without glass is a touch of class, but at the same time, we must admit that if done properly, the fiberglass bedding job can look all right and it may function better than a pure wood/metal fit. When glass is used to cover up inletting errors, it fails. Glass work does not cover up very much to the discerning eye. Also, if the smith is using glass because he cannot perform a good job of inletting without it, chances are he is also unskilled in other matters of the custom rifle and his work will show it. The above gunmaker made another rifle for me and this time there was no glass bedding. It was a different situation.

The Semi-Inletted Stock

Here is another point which should be aired. Is the semi-inletted stock a true "custom" job? I imagine a number of people will say no. I have switched my thoughts on the subject up to a point. This is not the 19th century. Things have changed. A person who wants to make handcrafted things must also add enough automation to allow enough productivity to afford a living. The semi-inletted stock may seem to be a total contradiction to the concept.

But is it? I suggest that it is if the gunmaker uses that type of stock to cover up his own lack of stock-making ability. But anyone who thinks a semi-inletted stock can be fitted perfectly by the layman should give the job a try. It might be an enlightening experience, as well as a frustrating one. I feel that the gunmaker should be fully able to inlet a stock from a hunk of wood that resembles a railroad tie, but if he can use a semi-inletted stock in a custom fashion, then let him do so. The end result will tell the tale.

High Technology and the Gunmaker's Art

Another situation has changed since the days when a man contracted for a longrifle which was truly made by hand from the trigger guard to the rifling. High technology has arrived, and though this factor is thought of as electronic, which it is, there are also a few things happening in the world of mechanics which were not possible but a short time ago. A stock duplicator is one of these interesting tools. It is an automated means of shaping a stock.

There are many other tools which are certainly more than handtools. Yes, there is some balking when it comes to the use of these tools in a "handsome custom rifle." One gunsmith I know builds old-style rifles only, and he does so *by hand*. He has even duplicated a workshop which he saw in Pennsylvania. I can assure you his tools are not plugged into electrical sockets. They are run by human power only. His guns are beautiful and I admire how he works them up. But his income is, at this point, poor at best, and it may never get better. Gunmakers eat, too. And though I admire handwork, I feel that the handwork may have to take place in the finish more than in the more basic manufacturing steps of gunmaking.

Contracting for a Custom Rifle

There are some rules, I think, in going about looking for a custom riflemaker. True custom guns do not come cheaply, and it would be very disappointing to plunk down some big dollars and later end up with something which could have been made in your own basement and by you at that. Fortunately, today's artisan is really good. There are few gunmakers who would last long if they were not good. There are simply too many critics out there who would blow the whistle on a fraud. But here are a few things to look at when planning your own custom rifle.

1. Shop around. Look at various custom rifles and look

Here is a custom rifle in the raw. The stock has been rough-shaped and the parts which will one day be a rifle lie below the stock. Note the custom octagonal barrel made by the Bauska Barrel Company, Bushnell 2.5-8 scope, Remington Model 700 action, Ken Jantz replacement safety, strap from Uncle Mike's, sling swivel also Uncle Mike's, fine standard Model 700 trigger, and Conetrol scope mounts.

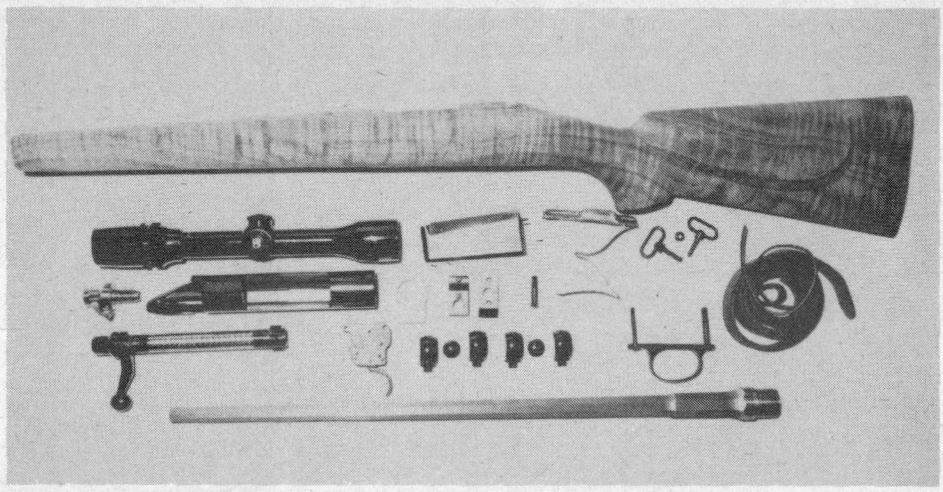

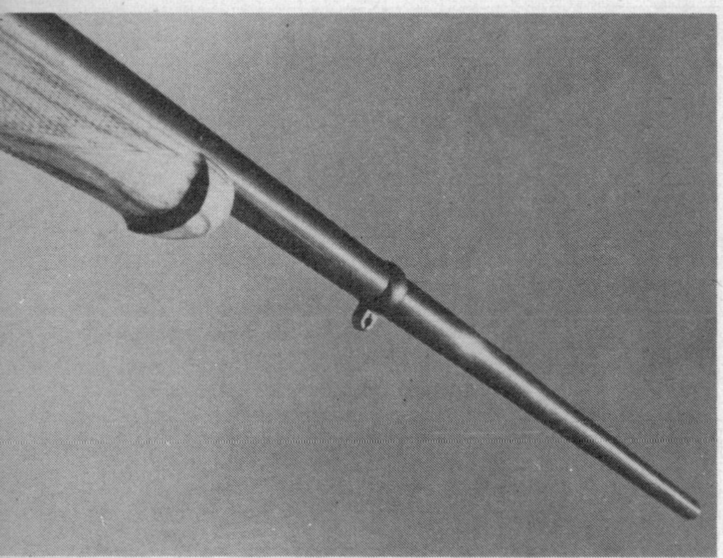

This custom rifle wears the sling eye on the barrel, which allows for the barrel to ride lower when the rifle is carried on the shooter's shoulder with a sling. Also, this style prevents damage to the hand from recoil which might cause the sling/sling swivel to strike the left hand of a right-handed shooter. It's a small touch. However, "small touches" can add up quickly. In short, it's *your* money—spend it wisely, on what *you* want.

hard. Check the wood-to-metal fit, the finish, the function of the rifle, the lines, the workmanship in general, the embellishments, the balance, the feel. If a smith is going to build a rifle for you, look at his work before you sign up with him.

2. References. Ask for them. There is nothing wrong with this. But be careful, too. A smith may make a particular type of firearm. There are gunmakers today who do make showpieces and there are gunmakers who handcraft practical hunting rifles. A person may not have understood that, and when he gets his practical hunting rifle after expecting a showpiece, he may be *wrongly* angry. Check references, but try to get at least three opinions.

3. Gun shows. I have seen plenty of custom work at gun shows. I have made up my mind, sometimes very quickly, about a smith after seeing his display at a gun show. These shows take place all over the country, and while custom work is not always on display, it usually is.

4. Advertisements, brochures and journals. Some gunmakers advertise. There is nothing wrong with finding a good gunmaker through an ad. In fact, some of the very best gunmakers in this country put ads in the gun magazines or other outlets. Look for them. Brochures can be worthwhile, too. They can relate prices and attitudes as well as showing pictures of the work the smith does. And magazines often include the work of gunsmiths, as do certain annuals and books.

5. Money. Custom guns cost money. There is no way around that. The buyer who expects to pick up a custom rifle at a factory price had best forget it. Is the custom rifle worth the bucks? I say yes indeed. Most of us will not own numerous custom rifles. We may own one, two or three in a lifetime. Is a custom rifle necessary? Of course not. Neither are well manicured lawns necessary, nor good cars, nor fine furniture.

For the shooter who truly appreciates the custom rifle, the gunmakers price will be entirely reasonable. However, I must hasten to say that I know of no rich gunmakers. Owning a hot dog stand can make a lot more money for a man than building custom rifles. So what should we, as buyers, be prepared to pay for a custom rifle? Obviously, the sky is the limit. If the buyer wants gold inlays of tigers and lions leaping and cavorting all about the rifle, then he has to pay for them. If the buyer wants full-coverage engraving, he must be prepared to reach into his wallet to own them.

There are other considerations in price, too. Wood is one of them. Wood is expensive. It is not outrageous these days to pay $300, even $400, or *much, much* more for a blank. That is a blank, just a hunk of wood, but it won't be just any hunk of wood. It will be a carefully selected piece of wood, with good to outstanding grain—the better the grain, the higher the price, usually. Also, it will be cut for the building of a stock. Just because a piece of wood is pretty does not mean it is stock material. The grain direction has to be correct, not to mention the stability of the wood and its weight (density) factors.

Laying out $2,000 for a custom rifle is no fancy trick today. Let's be specific. I made mention of a specific rifle, the Model 94 Storey Conversion. That rifle can be purchased for $950 as I write this. This means that a Model 94 Winchester is provided for the gunmaker, of course. The Black Velvet finish is used, as DGS, Inc., calls their soft-look blue. And all workmanship is guaranteed professional, with good fit and function. The sling eye is an integral part of the barrel, and the barrel is custom made by the Basuka Rifle Barrel Company, Inc., of Kalispell, Montana. The sling stud is installed in the wood and the swivels are the locking style from Uncle Mike's. The wood is at least semi-fancy grade. DGS won't use less. Of course, they will use a higher grade if the buyer wishes.

The same $950 brings some engraving, a few touches here and there, very appropriately executed, and the stocks are checkered with a very nice pattern. The checkering pattern alone probably amounts to about $250 of the overall cost, but it is a part of the Storey Conversion rifle and unlikely to be omitted. I opted for a more luxurious pattern costing in the $400 range.

Again, I ask, is the price worth it? I again answer my own question with a big affirmative. The rifle should gain, not lose in value, but more than that, it will last a lifetime —no, many lifetimes-and it will be used very often. If the cost is broken down over the useful life of the rifle, it comes to a few bucks a month. The buyer is usually asked to lay 50 percent down before work commences, which is only fair. The gunmaker needs an assurance that the work will be paid for, and he has to buy parts, materials and pay his overhead, well as provide a living for self and others while he is building the rifle.

6. How long to wait. I believe in reasonableness. There are a few gunmakers out there who have gotten totally possessed by their own self-worth and they are not only rude to their customers, but they also think that their labors are so wonderful that a buyer should wait for several years after plunking down his hard cash. About 8 years ago I planned a custom longrifle and began scouting around for a builder. I ran into a couple of these guys. Their prices were high, which did not bother me—I am willing to pay for quality—but they were rude and wanted me to understand that they were doing me a great favor by taking my money. The customer is not always right. But he is always the customer. These boys did not see any of my folding green. They never will.

The Customer's Input

I wanted a rifle, a muzzleloader, with a 30-inch barrel. A custom. The gunmaker looked me in the eye and said, flatly, No! He would not do it. I could take my money elsewhere, but I was not going to get that particular rifle with a 30-inch barrel. I conceded, thank goodness. When the rifle was finished, it wore a barrel of 34 inches, and it balanced like a teeter-totter with two identical twins on it. Had I gotten my way, the rifle would have been wrong.

It is the customer's money, and it is his duty to get what he wants. It is unfair to a gunmaker to build a rifle for a shooter only to find out later that the end product was not really what the shooter wanted. That is defeating to the whole idea of custom rifle building. But the buyer must also work with the judgment of the expert building his rifle. As custom rifle maker Dale Storey said, "It is unethical of me to give you something I know is wrong." Dale said another thing which bears repeating, "I will advise you, but I will also draw the line." And I think that sums it up very nicely.

The custom arms maker simply must retain some of the decision-making power for himself. He has to. If the customer were as expert as the gunmaker, then maybe he would be handcrafting his own custom rifle, and he would not need the gunsmith's services. On the other hand, the customer has the right to plenty of input.

It is up to the customer to decide on the wood quality and price. There are a few exceptions, and I agree with them. One is the exception a gunmaker will take when a customer picks the wrong wood for the job. The other is when a customer wrongfully demands a cheaper grade of wood which will detract from the finished product.

The gunmaker may also veto a buyer's wishes if his own sense of historical correctness is being violated. I have seen this happen among some of the muzzleloader makers. It

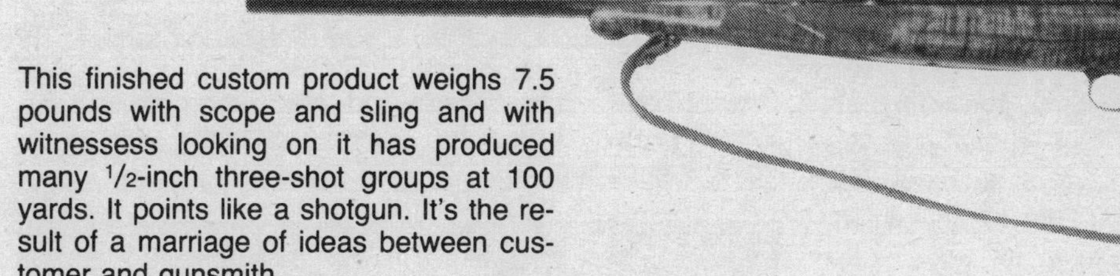

This finished custom product weighs 7.5 pounds with scope and sling and with witnessess looking on it has produced many 1/2-inch three-shot groups at 100 yards. It points like a shotgun. It's the result of a marriage of ideas between customer and gunsmith.

usually happens when the customer wants a cross between a longrifle and halfstock. It's wrong. If the customer insists upon creating something which does not look right, should he be responsible for it? He should. But will he? When asked, "What happened to that rifle? It's all wrong." Will he admit that he wanted it that way, or will the gunsmith take the blame? The answer should appear obvious.

The Parts of the Custom Rifle

1. The Action

The action is the heart of the custom rifle. Today, it is going to be a commercial action, of course, except for some gunmakers, such as Fred Wells of Arizona, who will actually make the action as well as the other parts of the custom rifle. The bolt-action is king, of course, but some nifty custom rifles have been made on other action types. The lever-action was already mentioned. Pumpguns can be custom made, as can autos and single shots, too. All I ask is that the custom rifle maker insure that whatever action he uses, that action is polished up to function smoothly, perfectly and in as quiet a manner as possible.

2. The Wood

Never try to save a few bucks on the grade of the wood. Go for stability and figure. The bulk of stock cost is in the labor of the gunmaker. To save a few dollars by going to a lower quality wood is a waste because the gunsmith's efforts will still be there, and paid for, but all that work has been put into a product which will never be up to snuff.

The finish should be *in* the wood, not *on* the wood. Although I am definitely not a gunsmith in any sense of the term, I have worked with finishes. I have seen some otherwise beautiful custom rifles saddled with finishes anyone could put on in an hour. Some smiths work very hard at looking for the best finish. Frank Wells of Tucson, Arizona, is one of these, as is Deal Zollinger of Rexburg, Idaho. Both search endlessly for the finest finish and both are putting a very good finish on their stocks.

What about the fiberglass stock? For a special purpose that calls for a rugged lightweight rifle, the customer has a right to select such a stock. I doubt that a fiberglass stock can ever enhance a rifle's beauty and my rifles do not have such stocks at this time. It's a point for both the customer and custom gunsmith to come to agreement on.

3. The Barrel

I have seen some fine custom rifles built around factory barreled actions. This means that a factory barrel and action were used as the beginning of the rifle. On the other hand, custom barrels are also very popular. Custom barrels are very accurate, the ones I have owned and tested, hav-

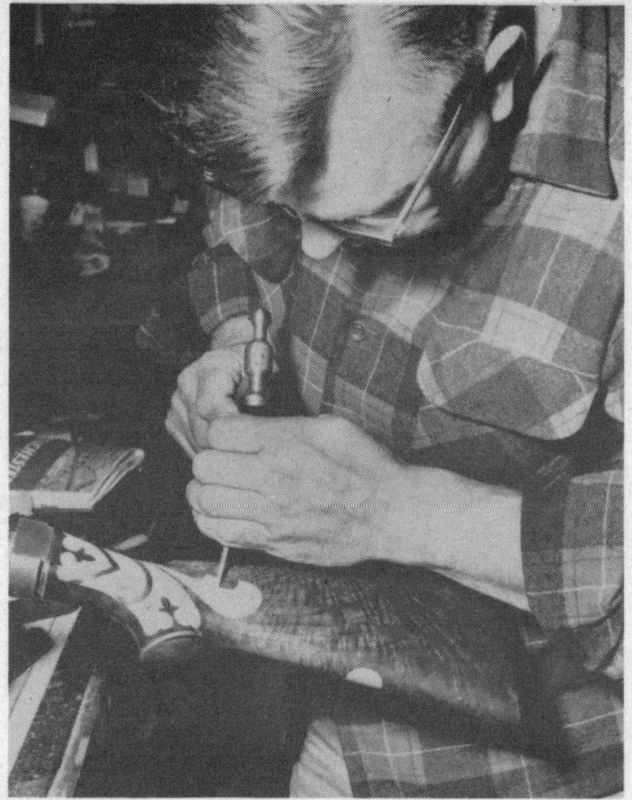

When it comes to selecting wood, go for the best you can afford—you won't be sorry. Note the beautiful grain structure in this custom shotgun stock.

Even scope bases can be altered for a custom rifle. Instead of a rectangular design, these bases will wear a beveled edge, at the customer's request.

The Completion of a Custom Stock

1. The barrel channel and action have been inletted. An excellent fit is insured here by gunmaker Dale Storey. Note that the stock has been roughed out only at this stage.

2. The cheekpiece is further shaped.

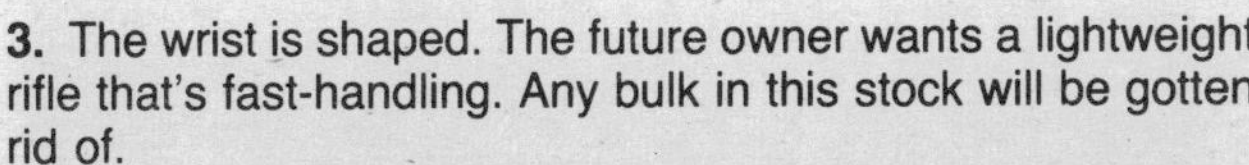

3. The wrist is shaped. The future owner wants a lightweight rifle that's fast-handling. Any bulk in this stock will be gotten rid of.

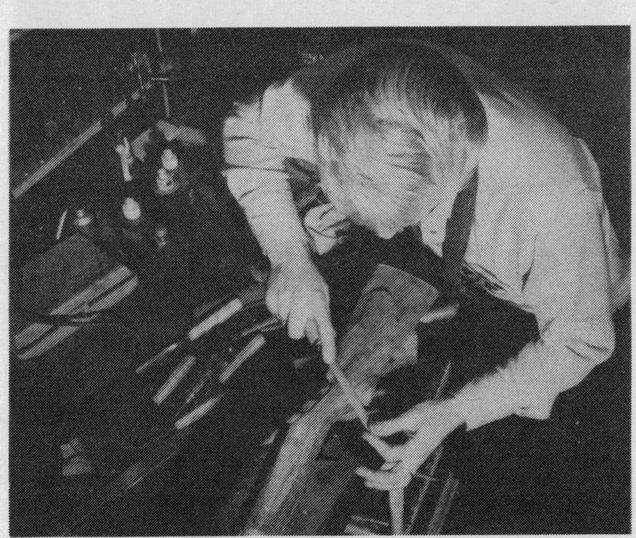

4. Removing the flatness from the forearm is imporant to the handling characteristics of this rifle. Dale Storey is blending the lines of the stock with the trigger guard here.

Completion of a Custom Stock (Con't.)

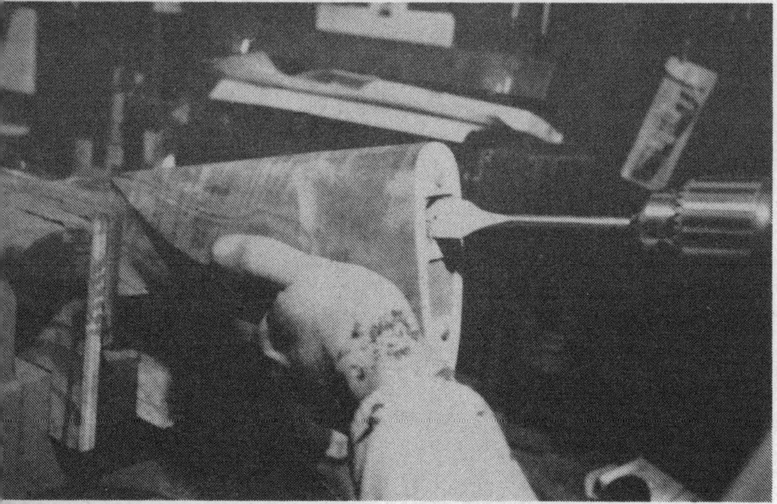

5. In a move to balance the rifle and to lessen its weight at the same time, wood is removed from the buttstock.

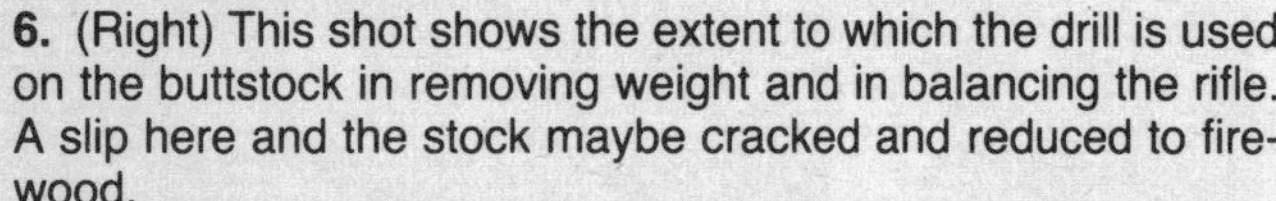

6. (Right) This shot shows the extent to which the drill is used on the buttstock in removing weight and in balancing the rifle. A slip here and the stock maybe cracked and reduced to firewood.

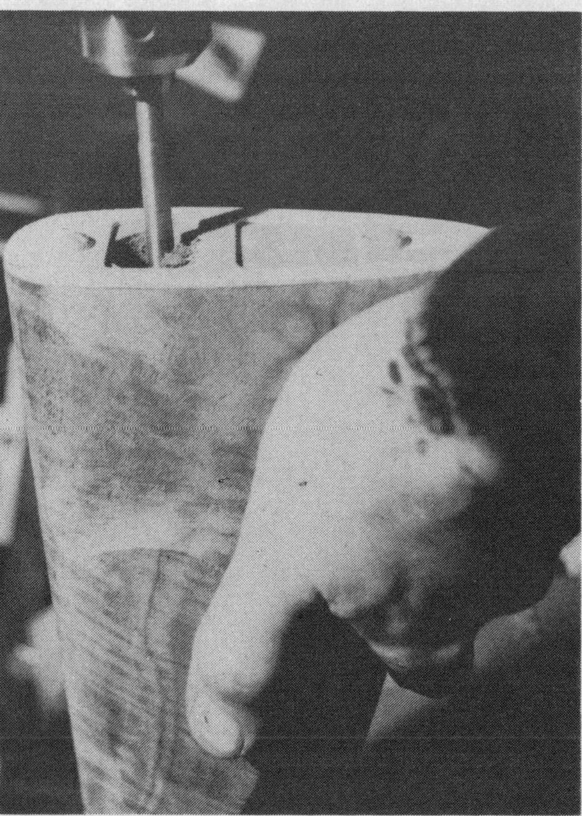

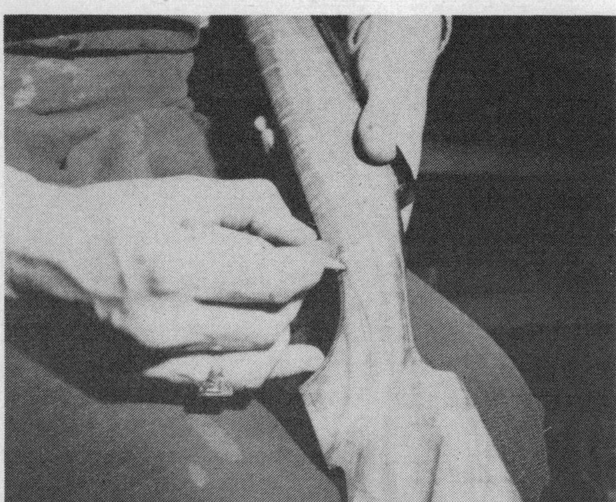

7. The lines for checkering are placed with a soft lead pencil. Patterns will be drawn on the unfinished stock until one is selected.

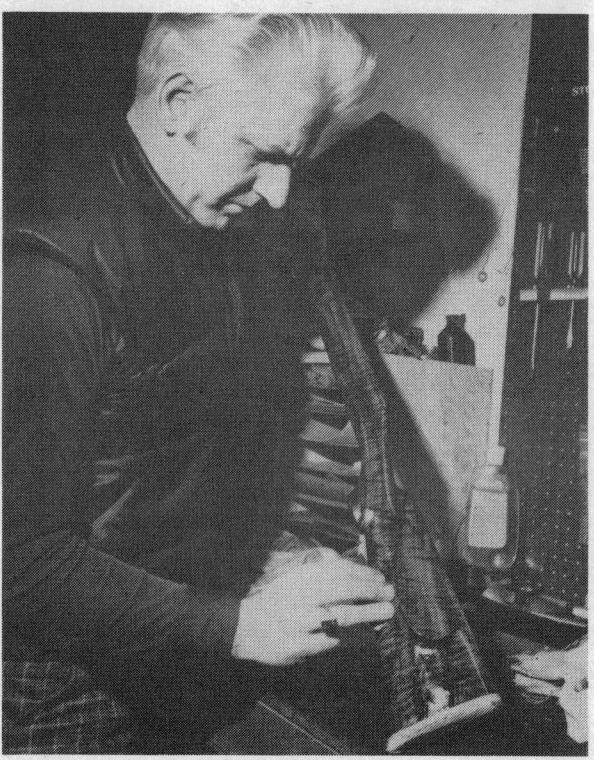

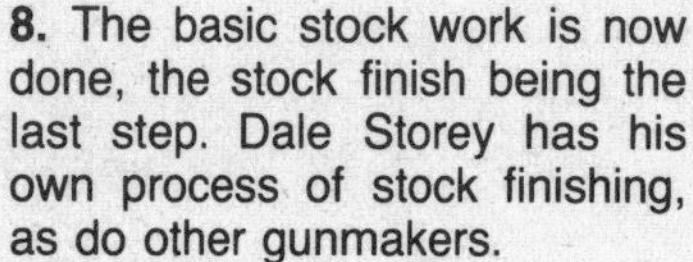

8. The basic stock work is now done, the stock finish being the last step. Dale Storey has his own process of stock finishing, as do other gunmakers.

ing been prepared with tremendous skill. Also, a custom barrel can be custom ordered, which is important. For example, I found in tests that a 6.5mm 140-grain bullet would be stabilized with a 1:10 rate of twist at 3000 fps MV, and I had no desire to shoot heavier bullets in my own 6.5mm wildcat, so the 1:10 was used. Results: 1/2-inch groups at 100 yards from the muzzle.

4. Metalwork

Bolt handles can be customized if necessary, especially when it comes to bolt handle angle. The blue should be appropriate. I have a bright blue-black finish on a custom bolt-action rifle, while a lever action model has a softer finish. The tang can be altered and contoured for better lines. Trigger guards maybe changed in shape or custom trigger guards may be used. The magazine floorplate can be fitted nicely. Magazine floorplate releases are also candidates for custom work. And the blind magazine can be used in some cases, no floorplate at all.

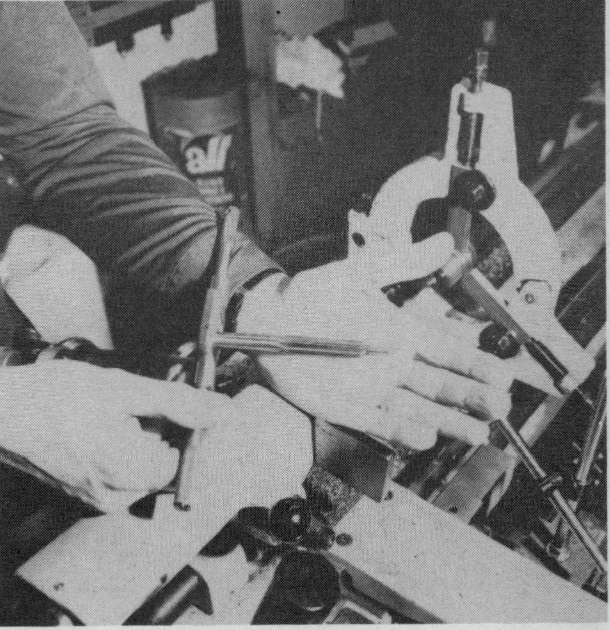

1

1. This custom rifle is going to be chambered in the 6.5mm DGS cartridge. The reamer is ready.

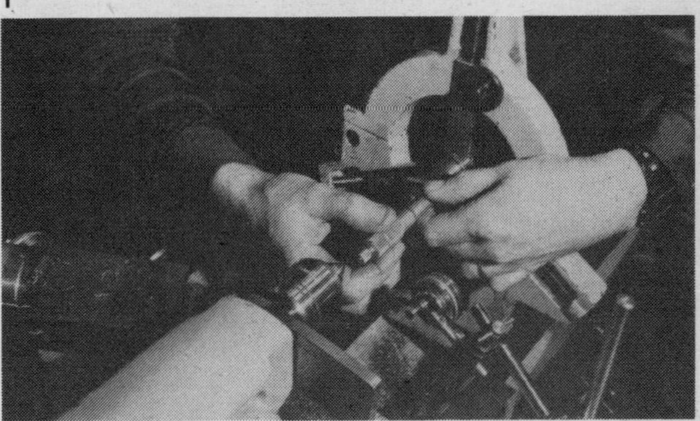

2

2. Careful alignment by the custom smith insures that the chamber is cut accurately. The barrel is held steadily. Note the breech end by the gunmaker's hands.

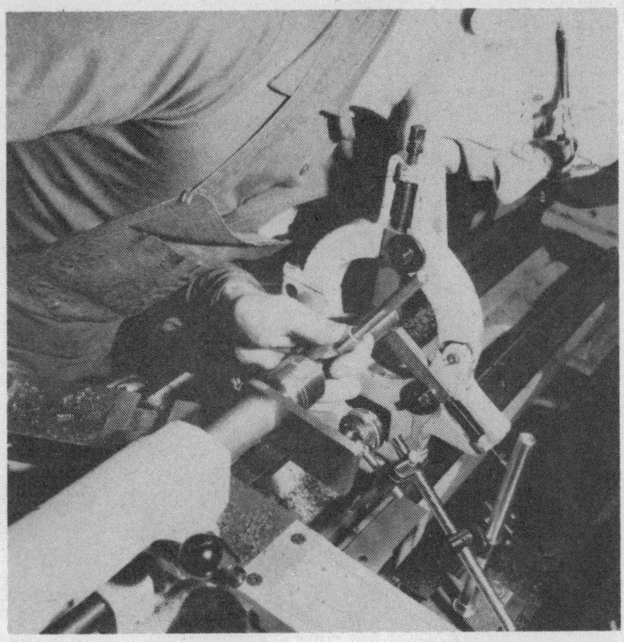

3

3. With continual measurement, the reamer creates the shape of the cartridge case in the breech section of the custom rifle.

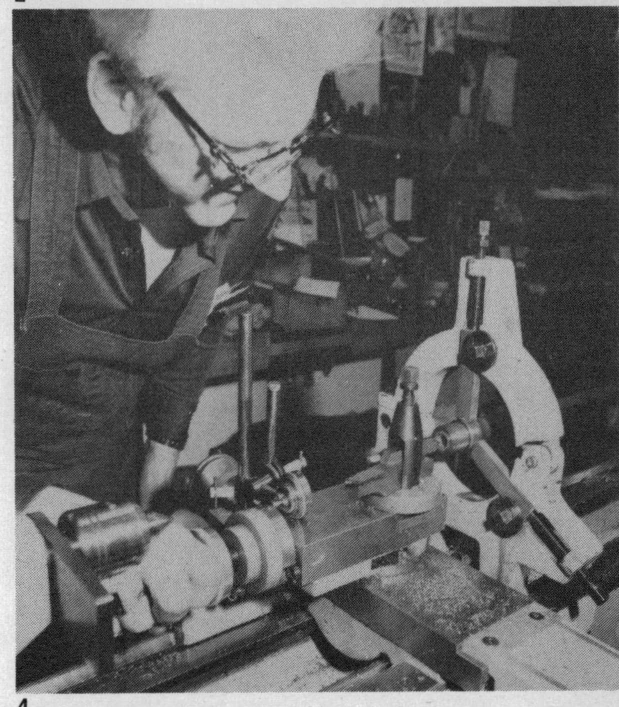

4

4. The chamber has been reamed and is dimensioned finally here. The full-fledged custom armsmaker has many skills, as demonstrated by gunsmith Dale Storey.

5. Embellishment

A great many custom rifles are embellished in one way or another. When this treatment gets out of hand, the result is a nightmare. I have seen checkering which went everywhere except the recoil pad, and I think that would have been checkered, too, if the smith could have managed it. Insets are nice sometimes, but inlayed diamonds and ovals and rectangles and triangles all over the place are, in my opinion, sad additions to good wood. Carving is OK, too, except when it gets carried away. Most craftsmen will admit that it takes special talent to carve a deer into wood and still have it recognized as a deer. I once saw a scene all over the buttstock of a rifle which was supposed to be a mountain lion catching a deer. It looked like an alley cat pouncing on a mule.

Engraving is another fine embellishment to a custom rifle. If the engraver is good, he can get away with quite a lot of it. If he is not, he should content himself with a couple scratches here and there and let that suffice. In fact, before accepting an engraving job on a custom rifle, I would want to see several samples. I do not own customs with heavy engraving, but I have seen both good and bad examples of the engraver's art.

Checkering is a definite part of the custom rifle scene, and it should be. The excuse given for checkering is to offer a better grasp on the rifle. I have never picked up a rifle in my life which I feared would fall from my hands because it lacked checkering. Checkering is an embellishment and a nice one. Again, the lines per inch should be appropriate with the stock. A softer stock may be well off with 18 lines to the inch. Twenty lines to the inch might be considered a medium area, with a hard wood taking 24 or more lines to the inch.

Precious metals, gold inlays, diamond-shaped rare wood stock inlays, and all other such additions are good embellishments when not overdone, or when accomplished so tastefully that these additions seem to become a part of the rifle. When such inlays and additions are appendages, they are best left off of the work. Always ask to see completed examples of such work *before* buying them.

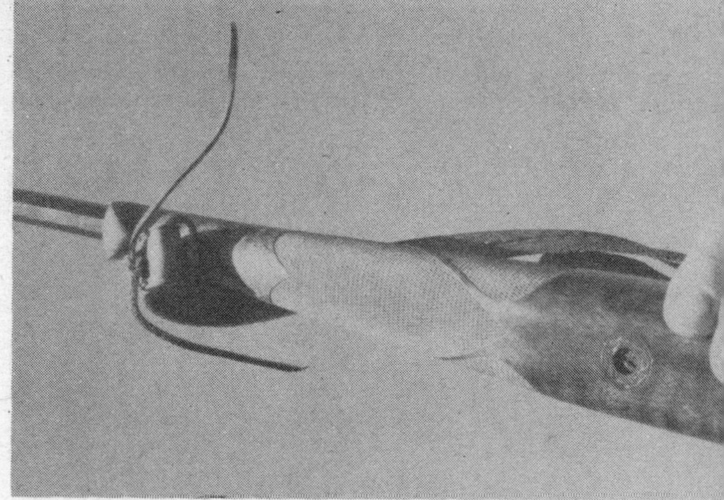

The fine checkering pattern shown on the forearm of this rifle reveals the diamond effect which top quality checkering is meant to display.

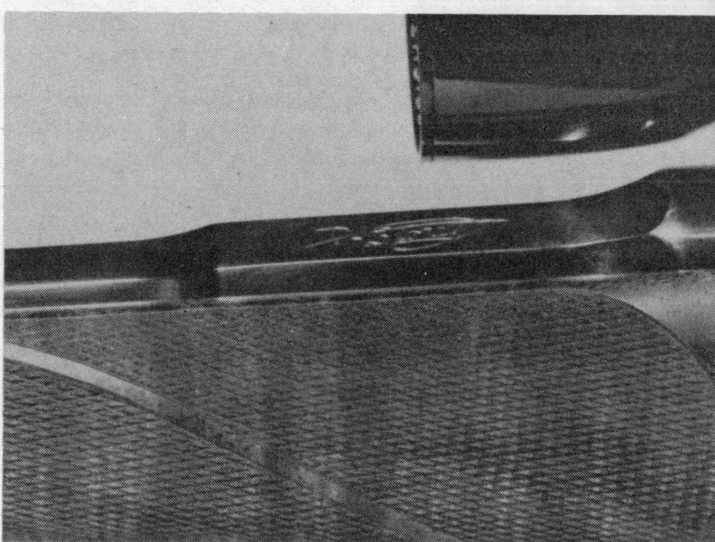

Checkering by hand is a mark of the custom. The amount of checkering and its fineness dictate price, but lines-per-inch should be selected upon the basis of appropriateness.

The Trade Mark

A custom arms maker's "style" often ends up as his trademark. This is good because it gives the buyer a starting point to work from. The gunsmiths I know of, and can vouch for, all have distinctive styles, trademarks if you will, though I sometimes wonder if they know it. A thumbhole stock says Harry Lawson to me. A custom action handling a big caliber on a well-made handsome rifle says Fred Wells. When I see classic lines which flow from beginning to end like a smooth-running river, I again think of Frank Wells. The lines of the American classic belong to Dean Zollinger who is now coming to the custom gunmaking fore. A customized Model 94 Winchester spells out DGS, Inc., to me, with Dale Storey doing the building.

Then there is the world of custom black powder gunsmithing, with men such as Bivens and Dangler standing tall, and even here there are style trademarks. Given a Lancaster school rifle with a fine graceful appearance, Bill Kennedy or Dennis Mulford might be responsible for the work. The black powder gunmaker is often interested in the historical correctness as well as the actual product he's making.

The Semi-Custom Rifle

There is another brand of custom rifle available these days. I call it a *semi-custom*. The term has to be used because the rifles in question are not truly custom, but they are certainly not off-the-press factory models either. In the

This is a good example of the semi-custom. It is a Hatfield Squirrel Rifle in 36-caliber flintlock, and it has a great deal of fine handwork in it.

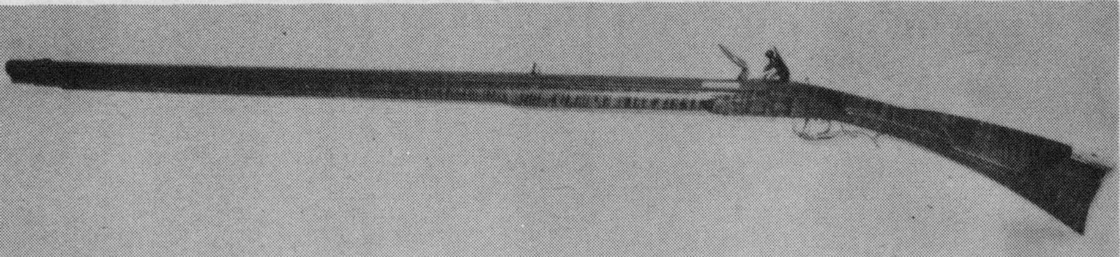

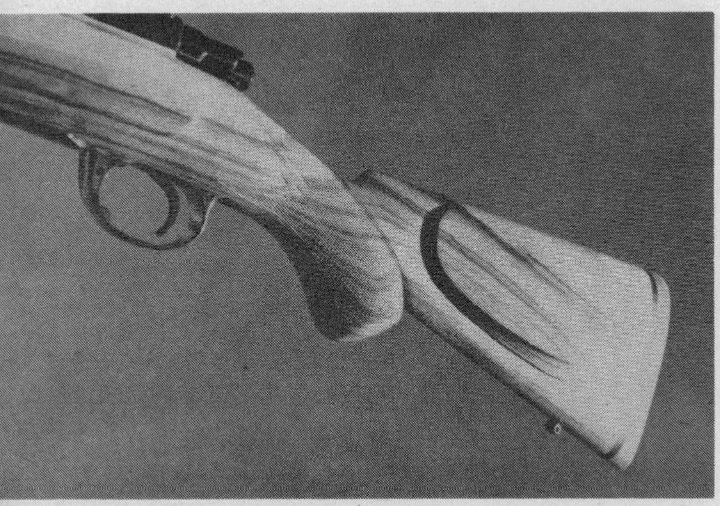

(Left) This English walnut stock is found on a Bishop custom rifle. The clean lines of the stock are strictly classic. Note the cheekpiece. The rifle comes up fast and points well. The grip is smooth-flowing, almost a semi-pistol grip.

This is a Bishop custom rifle. Note the excellent checkering pattern of the grip.

black powder world, these semi-customs are represented by companies such as Hatfield Rifle Works and Ozark Mountain Arms. The Hatfield rifle certainly looks like a Hatfield rifle, but each one has too much handwork in it to be considered a factory model. And just about any amount of custom additions can be made on the Hatfield. The Ozark Mountain Arms Muskrat or Hawken do represent a certain look, especially the Hawken because it is patterned after an actual J&S Hawken original. But these, too, are far too handworked to call them factory rifles.

Bishop should be mentioned here, but with a special note. The well-known E. C. Bishop & Son stock company of Warsaw, Missouri, is offering a custom rifle now, and it *is* a custom. It comes from an established company and therefore may seem to be a semi-custom, but the buyer can actually select most of the components, and the workmanship is of the handcrafted variety. The prices here are bargain-rate, too. I saw one Bishop custom made rifle which sold for about $1200, but it certainly bore the mark of a custom rifle costing more. The Bishop offering, then, is from a company, but it is still a custom rifle.

The Specialized Custom Rifle

A specialty of a specialty is the custom rifle fitted to the shooter for a particular individual reason. Of course, it is the duty of the gunmaker to fit a custom rifle to its owner. That is not the question here. I speak of special physical differences. For example, one well-known gun editor has a bad right eye, but he's right-handed. He has a few custom rifles with bent stocks so that he holds the rifle in a normal right-handed fashion, but it is his left eye which looks into the scope sight.

Another shooter I know has a permanently injured left arm. He can only shoot by turning at an abrupt angle and then allowing the fore-end to rest on the hampered left arm. He has had special custom rifles built so that there is a very short fore-end with a pronounced schnable on the end which physically aids his shooting.

Also, many personal accommodations can be met with the custom rifle. A shooter who wants a certain balance can have it. He can also have a *customized* rifle instead of a full-blown custom rifle to take care of this, but often the full custom is the only answer because it can be made to balance correctly from scratch. A barrel-heavy rifle can be built, or a rifle with butt-heavy tendencies. And so forth.

The Custom Rifle in Your Life

The custom firearm in your life can also be a handgun, though not much is done here, or a shotgun. The rifle, however, is far and away king of the customs.

The modern shooter could live a lifetime and never own a custom firearm, of course. But I would recommend at least a look at the world of the custom so that the complete shooter has some idea as to what is available to him. He may find that for his taste and desire, there is one particular style which suits him. Then it is time to find the right custom arms crafter and strike up a contract with him. It won't be cheap and the rifle will not appear in a few days, but the end result can be a shooter's rifle of a lifetime.

Chapter 27

Gun Fit

THE COMPLETE SHOOTER knows that if the gun does not fit him, his ability to hit the mark, be it with rifle or shotgun, even the handgun in some respects, will be impaired. Gun fit was discussed as a part of the chapters on stance and practice, but it was not covered in the detail it deserves. A firearm may be the finest available, and yet if the shooter does not find that firearm a well-fitting instrument, he cannot do his best with it. There are ways of discovering improper fit and ways of improving the problem.

The shooter heads for the range at the beginning of the shooting season, and he may first check the sighting of his rifle. He sits at the bench, adjusts himself fully, and then insures that there is a comforting pad between buttplate and shoulder. Of course, some light-recoiling rifles will be fired without the buffer. But no matter how we set up at the bench for rifle-shooting, it is a contrived position and the rifle does not fit us the same as it will when we assume the offhand, prone, sitting or kneeling positions.

If a shooter can take the time, he can in fact make an ill-fitting rifle fit his frame. He squirms, wiggles, pushes his head and face back and forth on the comb of the stock, and pretty soon he can see through the scope sight. The problem with ill rifle fit comes to the fore when a shooter needs to gracefully mount his rifle and fire an accurate shot without a lot of delay.

It is not my intent to downgrade the rifle stock which comes with the standard rifle sold over the counter. Most of the time those stocks come close enough to fitting the majority of men (not women and not children) that few complaints are registered against them. Furthermore, some shooters don't even know that they crawl the stock or pull back the head so that they can shoot a given rifle with accuracy. They have crawled stocks or reared back for so long with so many different rifles and shotguns that the act has become a part of shooting for them.

This chapter is designed strictly as an awareness report. The object here is to alert the complete shooter, who wishes to get the most from his guns, and explain in basic terms why a given firearm may not fit him, along with some ideas on how to make that firearm fit correctly. A lifetime's worth of shooting with firearms that don't fit is about as sensible as wearing shorts two sizes too small for the same period of time. Either way, the person is uncomfortable without good reason, because the problem can be corrected.

One aspect of stock fit which is very obvious is that of thumb placement. Even from the bench, where "stockcrawling" is more prominent, this shooter still fits into his rifle in terms of thumb placement. There is plenty of distance between thumb and nose for this 22-250's recoil.

When the Gun Fits

First, the shooter knows his gun fits when he puts either rifle or shotgun to shoulder and the rifle sights or shotgun bead are aiming/pointing at the object the shooter has se-

Changes in posture may dictate changes in how the gunstock is held. Normally, this shooter would control the forearm by putting his hand farther out on it, but in this position, the hand slides back so that the left elbow makes full contact with the left knee.

ing for me and I photographed him at one thousandth of one second. Here is what he did. He mounted the gun by pushing it out as far as he could. There is nothing wrong with pushing out and bringing back. But this was different. He had to *strain* to get the gun out far enough just so he could slip the buttpad up to his shoulder.

Next, this gentleman held his face in the only place he could hold it, way back on the comb of the stock. His head was up too high. And finally, his left hand (he was a right-handed shooter) was way toward the back of the forearm. That in itself is not necessarily bad, if that's the comfort point for a shooter. But in this case, it was not a matter of comfort. The shooter's left hand was way back toward the action of the gun because he could not *reach* to get a good comfortable grip on the forearm.

All of these things were revealed by high-speed photos. I have not used the method for a while, but it does work, especially today with motor drives being all but standard on so many 35mm cameras. So, the first point here is to have a rifle or shotgun which comes up *naturally*. The shooter should not have to squirm around in order to see through his rifle's sights or pull his head back or push it forward in order to see the correct amount of shotgun barrel or rib.

The lady shooter attempts to fire a man-sized Ruger Model 77 in 7mm Remington Magnum. She simply cannot shoot this rifle successfully. It does not fit her. Length of pull is much too long. It's all too obvious.

lected. Some shooters have used ill-fitting guns for so long that testing for the above can be very tricky. I took high-speed photos of a shooter, several years ago, who was doing a horrible job with his shotgun. I had asked him if he felt the gun fit him, because he was heavily-built and short-armed and the shotgun had a good 14-inch length of pull. The man said he thought the fit was excellent.

At the time, I was using a 35mm camera to learn more about shotgun shooting. So I had my friend do some shoot-

Testing for Fit

I have already mentioned the high-speed photo. Now there is another test for gun fit which any shooter can do in his own home. This is to take the *empty* rifle or shotgun and hold it in his two hands in a relaxed manner. Now the shooter looks at an object, possibly in his backyard, 15 or 20 yards distant. Look at the object. Concentrate on it. Now, without moving the head, the idea is to *close the eyes* and quickly, but smoothly mount the rifle or shotgun.

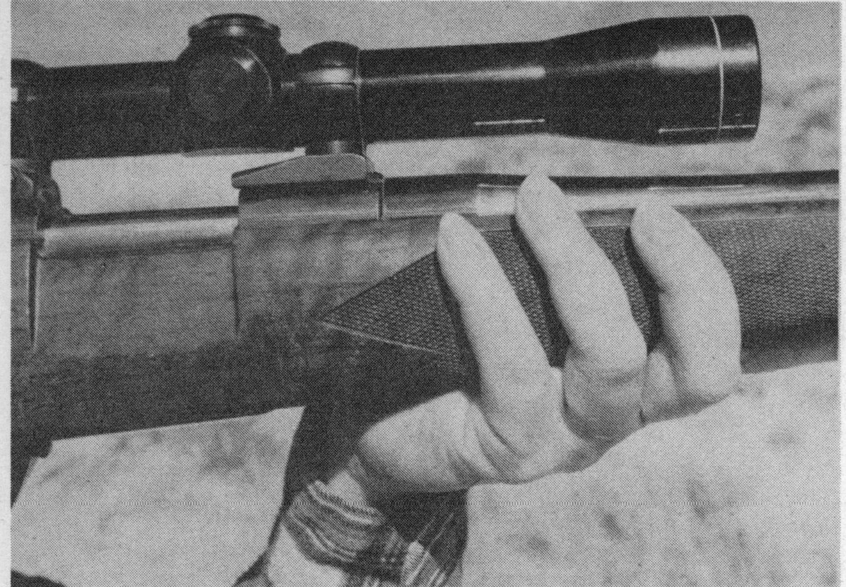

While the hand grasps this forearm a bit far back, the position is a part of the shooter's individual style. The offhand group fired by this shooter was excellent and rifle management was very fine.

(Below) In this instance, the best balance for this lady shooter with the rifle shown here was with the left hand all the way back to the magazine's floorplate. This is not usual and not necessarily desirable. She did shoot good offhand groups with this rifle and this position. It is hard to argue with success, but one should seek a normal stock fit whenever possible.

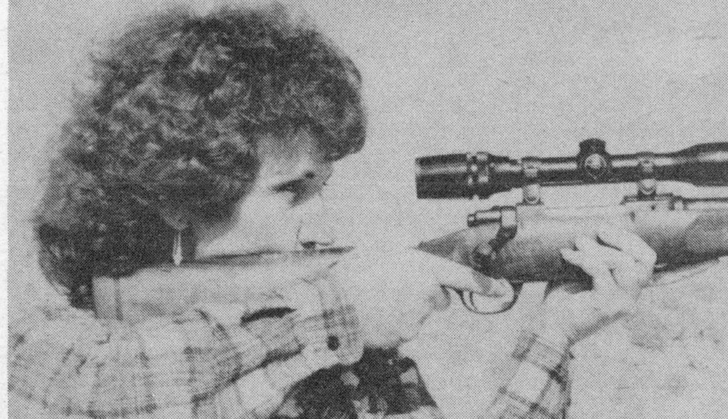

(Left) Stock fit also means that the hands are positioned comfortably and correctly. The right hand makes full contact with the grip, but does not overlap it. The left hand lightly balances the forearm. This stock fits the shooter.

If the gun fits, this is what will happen. When he mounts the gun and then snaps his eyes open, a well-fitted gun will be pointing at least close to the target. This means that the rifle sights will be aiming in the vicinity of the target; the shotgun will be pointing in such a manner that if the gun were loaded, which it should not be of course, a trigger pull would probably result in a hit.

Secondly, the shooter knows his gun fits when it is relatively pleasant when shot. I think the term "relatively" has to be put in here because a lightweight 375 Magnum is going to belt the shooter no matter how fine gun fit is. However, in a general way, the well-fitted gun truly does not hurt to shoot. In fact, if fit is just right, I would rather fire a lightweight big bore than I would a heavier rifle with a totally wrong fit. That is how much gun fit can mean to felt recoil.

Proving this one out is a matter of personal study. I suggest some normal shooting from the offhand stance. By normal, I mean smooth flow. The shooter should be able to just stand there without trying to perform any special task other than hitting a target with a rifle or busting a claybird with the shotgun. Now the shooter fires a number of times, possibly 20 times with a rifle or 25 with the shotgun. Sure, we know when we have fired a 12-gauge shotgun 25 times, but if the gun fit is decent and target ammo is being used,

Before putting a rifle to your shoulder, you should attempt to balance it in your hands. This shooter found that the rifle felt best when the left hand was fairly far back on the forearm.

a shooter should not be battered by 25 shots from a 12-gauge. The same goes for a rifle even of the 30-06 class with common loads. Yes, you'll know you shot 20 times, but the cheekbone should not hurt. The shoulder area should not ache either. Also, proper gun fit means that the parts of the firearm are out of the way of recoil. I just got through testing a customized single shot rifle which allowed the lever to smash into the second finger of my right hand with every shot. The grip was wrong on that rifle.

Third, the shooter knows his gun fits when he can control it easily. If a person has to move the hand to get a true control over the trigger after the gun is mounted, I would question the fit of that gun. If the left hand of a right-handed shooter has to push the forearm around in order to control the rifle or shotgun, I would question fit.

The Try Stock/Try Gun

Every good gunshop should have one, but try stocks are about as common as pieces of eight lying on the bar room floor. In fact, the average shooter would not know what a try stock was if one came up and hit him. The try stock or try gun is a device used to fit the shooter into his future rifle or shotgun stock. The grip comb and length of pull are all adjustable to a very fine degree. Angle of the butt is also adjustable.

First, the shooter should find out what his proper length of pull is. I have changed my mind so much on this score in the past several years that I am now a crusader, asking shooters to evaluate length of pull in a different fashion. I used to believe that length of pull was no more a problem than simply holding the shotgun or rifle in the shooting hand with finger in place on the trigger, and then bringing the buttplate of the stock into the crook of the arm, the side of the stock lying against the forearm. If the buttstock fit into the crook of the arm, it was fine. If it would not fit into the folded arm at all, the stock was too long. And if there was more than 1/4-inch of space between the buttplate and the upper arm then the stock was too short.

The use of "try guns" or "try stocks" has long been associated with first-quality double barreled shotguns. However, many custom smiths or custom-oriented shops (Pachmayr comes to mind) either have these guns available or are capable of *correctly* fitting a stock (shotgun or rifle) to a customer's needs.

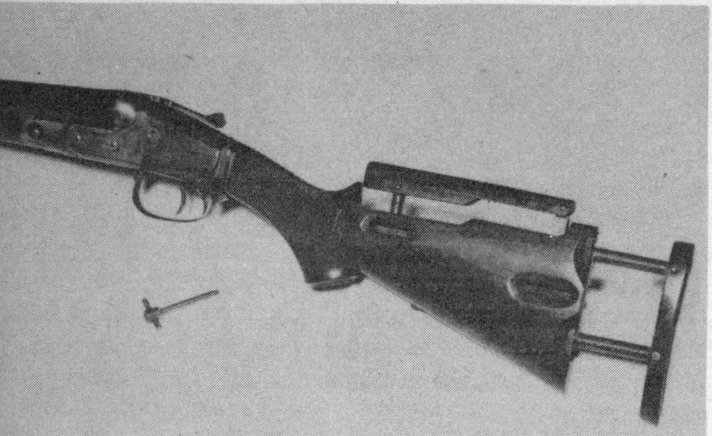

Here's a better look at a try gun with its buttplate extended and comb raised. Note the articulated area at the front of the pistol grip, just above the rear trigger. Adjustment of this portion of the gun results in the presence of cast-off or cast-on.

The test above can give the shooter a crude idea of stock length, too short or too long. But I lean toward the type of fit which means *smooth operation* of the gun, and I want my stocks a *little bit* (not much) shorter than would be indicated by the old crook-of-the-arm test. I can now mount a shotgun with a length of pull a tad shorter than what I once used, much faster than I can mount a shotgun which fits snugly into the crook of my arm.

With the try stock, length of pull and cast at the heel of the stock for the toe are adjusted and locked in place. A gunmaker with a try stock can do this in a few moments for the shooter. Then the comb is adjusted. But be careful getting that length of pull first. Measuring from the trigger to the center of the buttstock is right, but remember that the trigger/hand relationship varies from shooter to shooter. What happens is this: A person uses a try gun (or some other means) to determine his proper length of pull, but he fails to bear in mind that with another gun the actual placement of the finger on the trigger may vary. Be careful. Get that length of pull as close to comfortable trigger management as you can. And if in doubt, go a 1/2-inch too short.

One big point—do not do as I have done for years. I have very long arms, so I have always believed that length of pull for me should be very great. Measuring my "reach" alone, one could put me into a rifle with a 15-inch length of pull. But my stance does not call for a 15-inch length of pull on a rifle. I much prefer about 13-7/8-inches, as a general rule. With certain rifles, this could vary slightly for me. So the shooter must not be fooled into thinking he can determine correct length of pull by the length of his arms, or his height, or his broad or narrow shoulders, or any other single physical attribute of his body.

Also, the scope must be mounted far enough in front of the shooter's eye to prevent the ocular lens from making contact with the shooter's forehead or eye (usually the orbit of the eye is struck) through recoil. This does not mean that we build stocks to accommodate scopes, necessarily. We want to adjust the scope in such a manner as to fit the stock which fits us. But all the same, it is important to remember that the scope does require some leeway. A rap in the eye from a scope mounted on a high-power rifle is one rap nobody needs.

The drop at the heel of the stock can be determined very nicely with the try stock. Ever own a rifle where the buttplate caught your shoulder with the toe? Ever own a rifle where the upper portion of the buttplate, the "heel," struck the "meat" of the shoulder? Ideally, the center of the buttplate should firmly contact the center of the shoulder area when the gun is mounted. Too much drop-at-heel can bring too much of the upper portion of the stock into contact with the shoulder muscles, while too little drop-at-heel can mean that the toe of the buttplate makes too much contact with the shoulder muscle.

We spoke of "pitch" before. The pitch of the gun is the angle the muzzle takes when the buttstock is placed on a flat surface, such as the floor. The muzzle should pitch

In checking for stock fit, the observer should take several angles. One is this angle from below. Note how the left hand positions itself on the forearm. See how the face fits the comb of the stock, which is *very* important. This last item is very clearly seen from below, as shown here. Note how the right hand fits the grip.

With the shotgun stock cut down to a correct length of pull for the lady shooter, she will no longer be bothered by the recoil of the gun using field loads for upland birds (7/8-ounce 20-gauge loads in this case).

forward, away from the flat surface to some degree. In other words, if a rifle or shotgun is placed buttstock on floor with the barrel up against a wall, the barrel would not make contact with the wall even if the scope or sights were not in the way, because the barrel would pitch forward away from the wall.

Drop at comb is very important. I think a lot of shots are missed, both with rifle and shotgun, because a shooter forgets to paste his cheek *down* on the comb. His head is actually held off of the comb of the stock, which ruins his chances of sighting correctly with open sights. That position does nothing to help him find the picture in the scope sight, and puts a shotgun pattern off the mark as well. The comb should allow the shooter to mount the gun so that the sight picture, be the firearm a rifle or shotgun, is right there. *The head should not have to be moved again after the face contacts the cheekpiece or comb of the stock.*

Then there is "cast-off" and "cast-on." This is the angle of the buttstock in relation to the bore's center, or a line drawn through the center of the bore perpendicular to the buttstock. If there were no cast-on and no cast-off, this line would be center to the bore and center to the middle of the buttplate. A lot of rifles will have the latter situation, and this is not too bad, but a shotgun with no cast-on or cast-off may lead a person to assume a rifle-shooting stance. Cast-off or cast-on may assume a very minute degree, but an important one. Cast-off may be 1/8-inch at the comb to 1/4-inch at the butt. Cast-off is to the right. Cast-on is to the left.

The Shotgun

I want to concentrate for a moment on the shotgun because if anything, shotgun stock fit is even more important than the fit of a rifle stock. Of course, both are very important to good shooting, but with a chance to be more deliberate when rifle-shooting, a person can bend himself to fit the rifle. But shotgunning is a fast-pointing affair and when a shotgun does not fit correctly, hitting with consistency is difficult at best. I wonder how many shooters have been discouraged from shotgunning because they were led to believe that they lacked talent, when in fact, "the lack" was only in "gun fit?"

This little foray into proper shotgun stock fit may seem slightly repetitive, since a lot of the terms are the same ones we have been using, but I ask the reader to bear with me for a few moments, because the following could change his shotgunning forever. First, note that the drop at the comb positions not only the face, but of course *the eyes*. The eyes are positioned in relation to where the pattern is going to strike. A high comb will usually make the shotgun pattern land *too high,* all other things being accounted for, such as the shooter's face being truly down upon the comb. A low comb will generally have the opposite effect.

How high? In some cases, the pattern can fly a good foot high at 40 yards. A goose could be missed with this type of problem. A pattern should hit about two-thirds above the point of aim and one-third below the point of aim, so that drop of the shot column is accounted for. In addition this type of patterning allows for the shot to better meet a bird which is on the rise from a jumped covey. If the eye is about 3/8-inch above the plane of the rib in the way it sees the rib, this will help achieve the two-thirds high pattern effect.

Again, the way to test for this is to mount the gun with the eyes closed. Then pop the eyes open and try to get an optical measure of the above. It's not easy, and approximations are about the best we can do. But even with approximations, I have definitely improved shotgun fit through the closed-eye, open-eye method.

Another way to observe the impact point of a shotgun pattern is to simply employ a pattern board. Using a pattern board, I shoot at a big dot in the center of a pattern sheet from the normal 40-yard distance. Shooting once or twice tells us something, but shooting a half dozen times tells more. One can eventually see a trend, and the trend should show the pattern hitting about two-thirds above center, one-third below center.

The Standard Stock

A look at dimensions for the standard-dimensional factory stock will help the shooter recognize where he stands if he owns such a shotgun. If the shooter will get to a try gun,

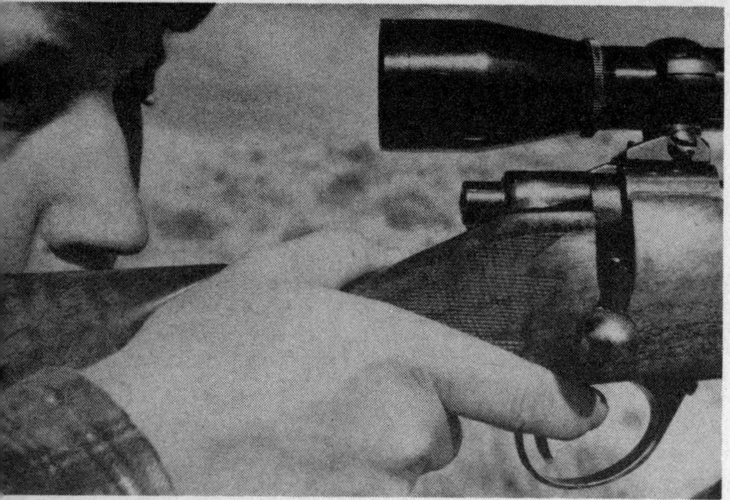

This grip fits the lady shooter's hand. She can reach the trigger with no problem and the right hand is wrapped comfortably around the grip. The grip is not too large for her hand.

he can then compare what the professional gunsmith tells him about what he *should* have in shotgun stock dimensions, and this can be compared with what he does have in the standard shotgun. The standard shotgun will have a length of pull of just about 14 inches. It will have 2.5 inches drop at heel. There may be no cast-off. There may be no cast-on. The ''standard'' stock is a compromise, as it must be. It is made for that elusive ''average'' shooter, and yet it is not so bad for a lot of us. Nothing said here is meant as a detrimental remark concerning the dimensions of factory shotgun stocks. But the shooter owes it to himself to see how the standard stock he owns compares with the results of the try stock. Changes can be made in the fitting of the standard stock, by the way. I had Frank Wells of Tucson, Arizona, change a shotgun stock for me, and I can vouch for the fact that a standard stock can be successfully altered by a competent gunsmith.

Patterning

We have a chapter on this subject because patterning is as important to shotgunning as sighting-in is for rifle shooting. However, there are, perhaps, a few points that can be made here. Mount and shoot at the pattern board in a smooth, fast style. Do not aim the shotgun as a rifle. Now watch for the pattern strike on the paper.

1. High hit—comb too high.
2. Low hit—comb too low.
3. High hit—too much upward pitch
4. Low hit—too much drop at comb, too much downward pitch
5. Hitting to the left of the mark—stock may be too long (this is for a right-handed shooter)
6. Hitting to the right of the mark—stock may be too short (this is for the right-hand shooter)

Here's an additional tip: a thin-faced shooter may get by with zero cast on a shotgun, but many shooters will find from try gun measurement that some cast-on or cast-off is useful to them.

General Gun Fit

The lines of either rifle or shotgun may conflict between two desirable and valuable things. These are eye appeal and gun fit. Not every fine-looking rifle or shotgun mounts ideally for the shooter. I have a rifle with lines not always admired by some of the more knowledgeable shooters. They feel that the lines are not quite legitimate.

And they are right. What I ask them to do is take the little lightweight rifle and mount it to the shoulder. They do. Generally, they are silent on the subject of that rifle's lines from that point forward. That big game rifle points like a shotgun. When mounted, chances are awfully good that the sight picture in the scope will appear right where the shooter was looking *before* the rifle was mounted. I don't mind when someone tells me that the lines of a rifle are not quite proportional with the way things are supposed to be in a rifle stock. I chuckle and say that this may be true, but when it comes time to place a shot swiftly and accurately, the lines of that rifle will afford me the best chance of doing just that.

The Handgun

We have concentrated on the rifle and shotgun for most obvious reasons here. But the handgun does deserve at least some mention. The fact is, handgun grips are not all created equal. And many shooters have turned to custom grips for better handgun control. The custom grip works because it is engineered with gun handling in mind.

The specialized grip usually means different contours, contours designed to do certain things. When the handgun recoils, these lines allow for the gun to come back smoothly in the hand without any part of the hand being ''picked on'' by recoil. Also, grip design can include ''texture,'' or lack of it. Some grips will have checkering in an effort to increase the friction between the hand and the grip, but high-recoil handguns may in fact be smoother in texture so that the grip will slide back in the palm of the hand instead of rasping the hand.

Also, the use of gloves in handling a hard-kicking large caliber sidearm is advised. The gloves need not be terribly heavy. Even soft-tanned leather gloves help out in saving the hand from the bite of a handgun.

Gun fit, or stock fit to be more specific, is one of the most important areas of concern for the complete shooter. We shoot to hit a mark, and hitting a mark, be it a black bull's-eye or a quail, very often hinges on the way a firearm fits the shooter. The intelligent shooter is aware of the fact that his misses may be the result of shooting a firearm which does not fit him. Once he finds this out, he should make every effort to correct the situation.

Chapter 28

Storage and Travel

THE GLASS FRONT display case for firearms may never have been the best idea in the first place, but it was a popular means of storing firearms when I was getting started in shooting. I always wanted one of those handsome, handmade cabinets. The firearms were placed inside in a dust-free environment and one could get a quick look at the contents through the glass front. Of course, that was one of the problems with these nice gun cabinets. Anyone could instantly take stock of the owner's supply of firearms.

Ammunition was often kept in the same cabinet, usually in a separate drawer that was secured with lock and key. Or the ammo was stored in another place altogether. Today, these glass-front gun cabinets are not considered the best way to store firearms. In fact, whether a display type cabinet or closed front, valuable firearms should not be stored in such a way as to readily attract attention.

Today's shooter has some other options. We will explore a few of those possibilities and then explore ways and means of transporting guns correctly. The two go hand in hand, for the whole idea is to safeguard our firearms when they are stored and also to safeguard them while in transit. Furthermore, there are several legalities to consider in the latter. One does not simply tote his guns through state after state without some previous knowledge of individual state laws.

The Vault

Not too long ago vaults were pretty much out of the question because they were generally of a special order nature, quite costly and also not necessarily made for firearms. All that has changed. Today's shooter can buy a steel-constructed firearms vault, designed especially for gun storage and protection. A gun vault is not impenetrable, but it is a deterrent. A deterrent may be good enough to thwart a would-be thief.

Today's security chests are well-made. Not only do they provide security from thieves but more important provide a safety factor in terms of children getting a hold of those firearms. It simply is not possible for anyone without tools and some knowledge to break in without a key or combination.

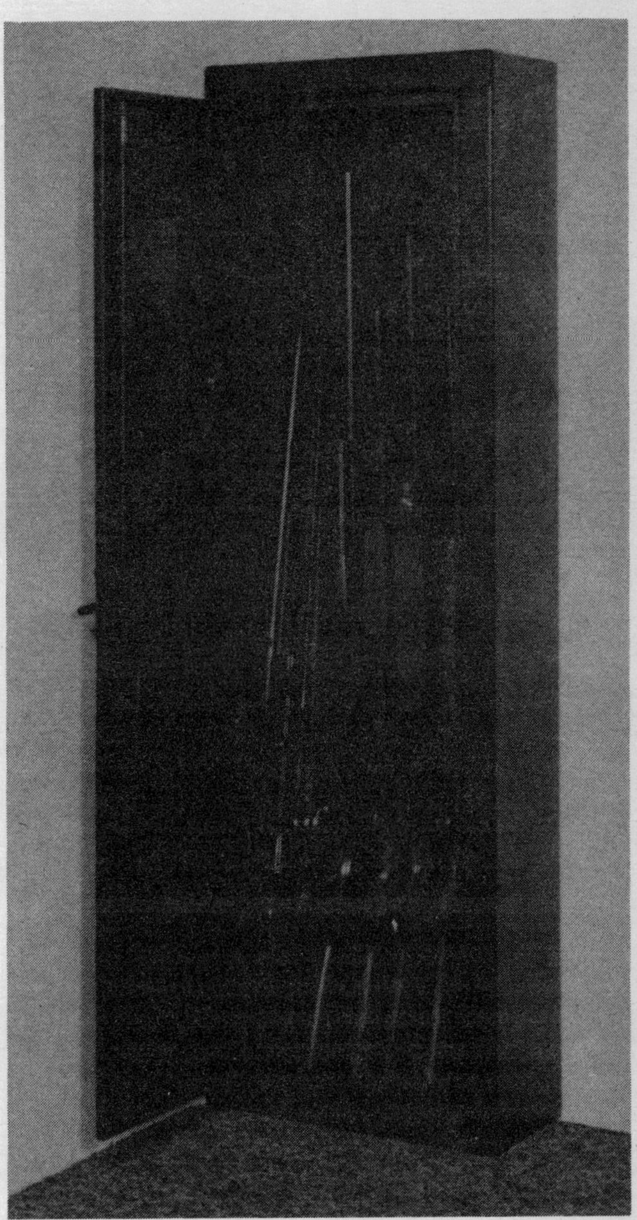

Omark Industries new line of steel, vault-type safes is designed for maximum home security for firearms and valuables. This Omark offering is the vertical type and is fully lined to add additional gun protection.

The Tread Corporation also offers vertical-type vaults. This unit features optional racks and shelving for handguns, shooting accessories or personal valuables.

Therefore, the safety element of the security vault is even more important than the anti-theft aspect. A curious child will remain safe from contact with firearms that are secured inside a vault. Furthermore, crime *prevention* is a viable aspect of the security vault. Guns locked in a vault usually cannot be stolen and used for illegal activities.

The good gun vault is a heavy-duty proposition complete with heavy gauge steel construction, continuous welding, and a locking system that may include steel bolts in a dead-bolt lockup. Also, the inside of many vaults is nicely padded for protection of firearm finish. For added security the gun vault can and should be bolted to the wall or floor.

Along with the upright models, there are also horizontal vaults which can be used where space provisions allow. The horizontal vault is often more spacious and is used by those who have both guns and valuables (jewelry or family heirlooms) to store. Even some of the larger vaults will weigh under 150 pounds empty, and though they will be loaded with firearms, it's not impossible for a thief to carry the vault and its contents out of a door, so bolt 'em down or sacrifice some storage space and toss in several 25-pound bags of lead shot—the weight adds up quickly and deters the man who wants to haul your safe out the back door.

There are also security vaults which fit across the pickup

The Tread Corporation's line of Treadlok gun safes led the way in home-security for firearms. This Tread offering is a horizontal unit designed to hold a dozen long guns with room left over for handgun storage. When filled with guns and bags of lead shot, a unit like this is tough to move, at the very least. For maximum security a safe such as this could be bolted to the floor. When closed (below) and covered with pillows, etc., the horizontal unit tends to "blend in," often being overlooked by burglars.

truck bed toward the cab end of the truck. Both of my sons have gone to this type of vault. While in transit, guns and other gear are relatively safe. Of course, the vault is securely attached to the truck body via bolts.

The Gun Case

In days gone by, hard-type portable gun cases were usually made of leather. There are still some magnificent leather gun cases to this day. But there are also the hard plastic models and aluminum models. The high-impact plastic case is a good one. I have used several, and they have kept my guns from being scratched and bruised on long treks, or any trip which would include bumpy rides over rough terrain.

The whole thrust of the plastic gun or sport case is to offer a lot of protection at a modest price. These come in various sizes, of course, and one I've tried, the Outers Two-Gun Rifle or Shotgun Case 41106, proved very rugged. I punished that case just to convince myself that such an item would hold up—it did. These are made of high-impact styrene with a connected aluminum frame, the inside being foam cushioned. These plastic cases can be locked. They really are well worth the investment, and they will protect a firearm from considerable bumps and bangs, especially since the guns are protected by the cushioning foam within.

Storing firearms in the Outers' wall safe means not only the security of a strong built-in vault, but also an opportunity to conceal the hideaway.

This is the Kolpin Gun Boot 007 gun case, brought back by popular demand after it had been dropped from the Kolpin line. The Kolpin separates into two parts, both of the same rugged construction. The lower half can be used as a saddle scabbard. Or, the whole case can be carried on the horse in scabbard fashion. This case locks up for air travel. The inner part of the case is pile-lined with thick material for cushioning and shock absorption. The scope is not likely to become knocked out of line with a case like this one.

The aluminum gun case, however, is another step upward in firearms protection. The Outers Silverline was a model I tested pretty rigidly. In fact, I placed the case in an open pickup truck bed for a season of rugged driving. The case got banged, scratched, and abused. In one instance, a Handyman jack came crashing down on the Silverline. It scarred the case, but the guns inside were kept totally safe.

The aluminum case costs more, but I like it because though truly rugged, it can be carried with about the same ease as a plastic case. It will weigh a little more, but not that much more. In transporting firearms on an airplane especially, I like the locked aluminum case very much. The Silverline caught my attention because the price tag was not all that much higher than some plastic models I had looked at.

Cases such as these serve their purpose well. However, soft-type gun cases are *not* ideal when it comes to *maximum* firearm protection.

This particular case opened and closed very reliably and easily. It had a well-matched upper and lower half, and was hinged well. When locked it has a mini-vault type of protection, especially from curious children who might, conceivably, try to open the case. The Silverline comes in many sizes to accommodate most needs. The foam egg-crate style inner protection was just right in this case as far as being able to insert a couple rifles and still close the case down with ease.

Travel

Traveling with firearms is not a simple matter of tossing the guns into the vehicle or handing them over to the airline counterman and letting it go at that. There are laws to consider here and there are also rules to consider. Just because your state allows free and easy transportation of firearms from one point to the other does not mean that a contiguous state has the same laws.

In fact, my best advice for the shooter going on a tour with a personal vehicle is to contact the state police of those states through which you will pass. Learn the laws pertaining to *those areas*. Below, a few samples of various state laws pertaining to firearms transportation will convince any shooter that he cannot drive off into the sunset without knowing the laws of the states he will pass through. It just isn't smart.

After learning the exact rules and regulations pertaining to firearms transportation, my next advice is for the shooter to travel a route selected on the basis of those laws. If I can travel through a state or area which will give me better access than another in terms of firearms transportation, I will go somewhat out of my way to bend my route in that direction. It's often worth the additional expense in time and gasoline.

Here are a few examples of states taken from a study done by the National Rifle Association. First, a look at the state of New York is in order. One does not transport a firearm at will here, not if he's smart. It is illegal for non-residents to transport handguns in the state of New York. A jail sentence of up to 7 years is possible for this offense. The resident can transport a handgun in New York state—

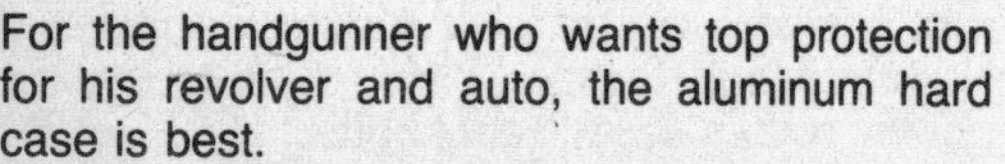

For the handgunner who wants top protection for his revolver and auto, the aluminum hard case is best.

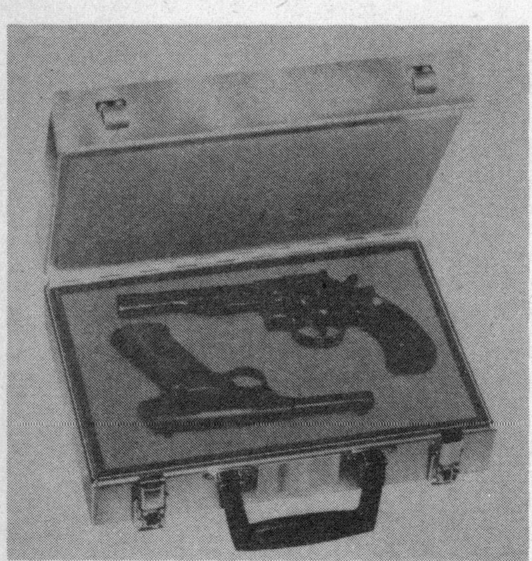

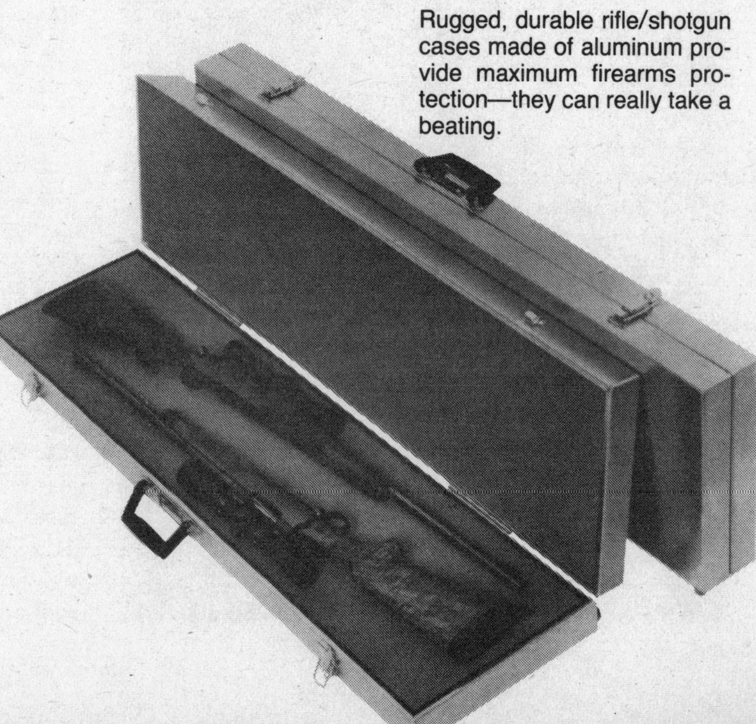

Rugged, durable rifle/shotgun cases made of aluminum provide maximum firearms protection—they can really take a beating.

New York City excluded—if he has a valid New York license permitting him to do so. Rifles and shotguns, however, may be transported through the state of New York by both resident and non-resident. The rifles and/or shotguns must be completely unloaded while in transit.

The one exception to handgun transportation is for *certain,* legitimate shooting matches. But even here, the carrier of the target handgun must possess a pistol license or a firearms registration card in accordance with the laws of his home state, and must also be on his way to an NRA-sanctioned shooting match with proof that he is a participant in that match. The handgun must be unloaded and locked up and can be brought into this state for only a specified time period. A shooter simply must check with the authorities before attempting to transport a handgun into New York state even though it is for an NRA-sanctioned match.

New York City has a few laws of its own in regard to the transportation of handguns. Residents of New York state had best take heed of the rules. If the handgun carrier intends to stay around New York City for a while, he will need a city handgun permit. The NRA reports that persons going through New York City, even to an NRA-sanctioned match, should perhaps think of another route if possible. Even with the NRA-sanctioned match being the obvious reason for transporting a handgun through this city, lawyers warn that there could still be trouble.

Unloaded shotguns and rifles in a closed container being transported through New York City are all right if the shooter will be on his way out of the city within 48 hours. The shooter who plans to stay longer than that must obtain a city registration for his guns.

Massachusetts may jail a person for a year if he fails to follow the rules in transporting a firearm through this state. A valid handgun carrying permit must be in the possession of the person transporting a handgun through this state, the permit being issued in that person's home state. Not only that, but the state which issued the handgun permit must have the same handgun restrictions as Massachusetts. That would eliminate many permits right there.

Anyone transporting rifles or shotguns through Massachusetts must have them completely unloaded, cased and locked in the trunk of the vehicle. Massachusetts does allow non-resident hunting, so it is very important that the prospective non-resident hunter going into Massachusetts learn all he can about the gun laws pertaining to transportation and possession.

New Jersey non-residents must get a Firearms Identification Card from the superintendent of state police *prior to* arriving in the state of New Jersey. The hunting gun must be unloaded and cased and must be secured in the trunk of the vehicle or kept in another inaccessible place in the vehicle.

Washington, D.C. prohibits the transportation of a firearm through its city unless the travel is to or from a special lawful, recreational, firearms-related function in the District or to a similar function in another district. The transporter needs proof of ownership and proof of the use intended for the firearm. The gun, further, must be unloaded, wrapped up securely, and the wrapped container must be carried in open view.

The above are only a few samples. They are cited because it is very important for the complete shooter, who might very well transport his firearms for shooting matches and for hunting trips, to be totally aware that firearms transportation is a state-by-state consideration. Before taking a trip, know *ahead of time* where you may encounter problems in arms transportation.

Traveling with handguns through some states could turn a perfectly lovely trip into a nightmare of legal entanglements. *Never* transport a handgun into another state (even municipality) without knowing the handgun, and handgun-transport laws of that area. The jail sentence you save could be your own!

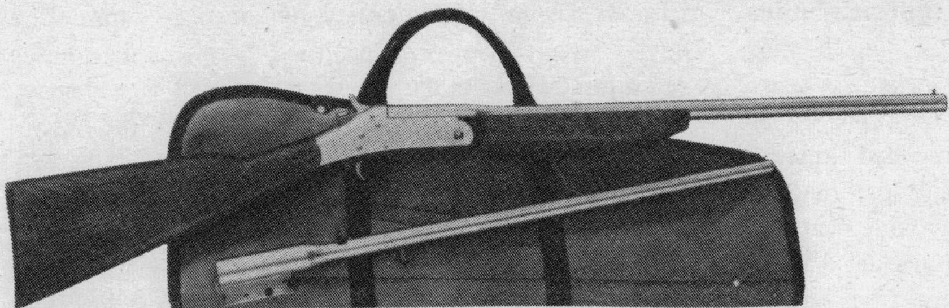

Traveling by car (with firearms) through different states will require a thorough check of each state's gun-transport laws. Some states will require a case, locked or unlocked, the firearm unloaded, stripped, unstripped, bolt open or bolt closed and the list could go on and on. Be safe—check with the authorities before you start crossing state lines with firearms in your possession.

When it comes to transporting firearms on airlines, soft gun cases won't do the trick. A hard aluminum gun case like this Saf-T-Case offering is a must. It's durable, lockable and designed to get those guns to your destination in one piece.

Flying

I have transported my firearms through the air a number of times without a hitch. It's only recently that I ran across a fellow who could state otherwise, and this particular case happens to be that of transporting ammunition, not firearms. The report came to me that the ammunition was not allowed as it was packaged. Therefore, my suggestion, a rather obvious one, is for the shooter to call the airline on which he intends to travel and to get the exact information needed in order to package both guns and ammo correctly for air travel.

Upon arriving at the airport, I always go directly to the ticket counter where the baggage is going to be tagged and loaded onto the aircraft. My guns are, most obviously, unloaded and there is no ammo in the gun case with the gun. Furthermore, I use good hard gun cases, locked, to transport my firearms. The ticket agent will quite probably apply a tag which reads something like "unloaded firearm" and that is about it. In some instances, the shooter may not own a hard gun case, so the airline *may* provide one for a fee. Your firearms will be placed in the airplane's cargo area where passengers cannot get at them in flight.

The Train

Federal law allows firearms to be transported on board trains, but Amtrak rail line does not. There you have it. As this is written, Amtrak may back off of its restriction to some degree by allowing dismantled firearms to travel, provided the firearm is accompanied by its owner. In addition, Amtrak will not transport a firearm to someone from someone else. Amtrak advises they will notify the public of any changes affecting transported firearms.

The Bus

Federal law allows firearms in transport on buses, but the bus companies do not. There you have it. There seems to be no change in this policy for the near future. Both Greyhound and Trailways disallow firearms on their buses, even if turned over to the driver, or if placed in the luggage compartment beneath the passenger section of the bus.

The Mail

If a shooter must travel across country by bus or train, and if he wants to have his firearms when he arrives at a certain location down the pike, then the suggestion is for

Most airlines (American Airlines in this instance) will tag and identify any type of case being used to transport firearms via air. Because each air carrier has its own interpretation of Federal regs, you *must* call ahead to see what your selected airlines' gun-transport policy is. Don't arrive at the ticket counter uninformed—you may never make your flight.

the shooter to mail his guns. Mail them? Isn't that against the law, too? Yes and no. It is against the law for the average shooter to mail his firearm to another party, either by United Parcel Service or United States Postal Service. But a couple options are possible. First, the shooter can check with air freight. He *may* be able to air freight his firearm, unloaded of course and in a hard locked case without ammo, to a certain destination, *there to be held* until the shooter himself goes to claim the rifle or shotgun. A hunter traveling by train or bus could look into this option. I called one airline spokesman who said that it would be legal for a firearm to be shipped air express to another party. There could be inspection privileges by the airlines, of course.

Another option is to have a firearm mailed ahead by the United States Postal Service or the United Parcel Service or other carrier. This can be accomplished by taking your firearms to the local gunshop, where a FFL (Federal Firearms License) holder can send your arms to another FFL holder at your destination. Then you travel by bus or train and your firearm is there waiting for you, quite legally. Ammo? You buy your ammo where you are going to hunt.

This brief discussion of storing firearms in a safe and safeguarded manner, along with transporting them in a legal fashion is meant to open a door for the reader. The many ramifications of firearms storage would never fit into our alloted space, and the many variations in transportation legalities seem to be in a continual state of flux. But the shooter must be aware of keeping his guns safe from theft, and even more important, safe from the grasp of curious hands. In transit, we want to be legal. Store safely, and travel legally. These are the watchwords.

Chapter 29

Gun Care and Cleaning

CLEANING AND MAINTAINING firearms is an art all its own. It should not be a haphazard operation, even in this enlightened day of non-fouling ammunition and miracle cleaning agents. The gun owner wants to preserve his firearms, and yet it's probably true that some types of cleaning ruin more guns than shooting can ever wear out. A 22 rimfire is a good example. I have witnessed shooters working a cleaning rod up and down rimfire bores, *far to vigorously,* from the muzzle end of the barrel. Once the muzzle of any rifle is worn down, gilt-edged accuracy is quite unlikely. So this is but one example of improper cleaning, and it's stated here to convince the complete shooter that part of the shooting operation is the follow-up, the cleaning and maintainance tasks.

Modern Firearms Cleanup

The actual method of cleaning a modern firearm is a rather simple one. This has not always been the case, and we are going to talk about black powder cleanup in a while because there are 5,000,000 shooters using muzzleloaders. That cleaning the modern firearm is "simple" is a boon. But cleaning and maintaining a firearm is a bit more than simply running a solvent-soaked patch through the bore a couple of times.

1. Dismantling the *Unloaded* Firearm

Dismantling is a very individual task. There are bolt-action 22 rimfire rifles which require no more than the withdrawal of the bolt, often through a release mechanism which functions with the rearward pull of the trigger. After the bolt is out, cleaning is a simple chore indeed, and we will go through the basic steps in a moment. But there are also firearms which require much more dismantling, at least for an occasional in-depth clean-up. A good example would be the semi-automatic shotgun. Every now and then, the shooter should dismantle his semi-auto, according to instructions, for the purpose of a careful cleaning job of the "works" inside of that gun.

Giving detailed examples of firearms break-down is not the purpose here. The shooter receives a schematic with his new firearm that teaches him how to field strip it, which is all he's required to do for cleaning. For those who have a firearm which was not purchased with such information, the information is available, not only through manufacturers, but also through texts on the subject.

Our aim here is to give some broad and general, but important, advice on dismantling or field-strippng a firearm for cleanup. Here it is: First, use tools that *fit*. In some cases, special tools are provided for break-down of a specific firearm. Leave the pliers in the toolchest. Use the special tool provided for the job. Use screwdrivers that fit, too. Damaged screw heads are ugly, and eventually they may have a slot so wide and sloppy that actually getting the screw or bolt tight (or out) is impossible.

Second, don't field-strip haphazardly. The term "field-strip" refers to a simple dismantling of the firearm. Just be sure to put a clean cloth or even a newspaper down, not only to keep from losing parts, but also to keep table or counter surfaces free of gun oil. Third, from time to time, do go into a more thorough dismantling, in accord with the instructions for the gun. Check for powder fouling in the action. See if moisture has built up between the barrel and barrel channel. Find out if there's dirt in the ejector channel or other crevices. See if the bolt face is clean. Fourth, put the gun back together *correctly*. Field-stripping is not a detailed dismantling of the firearm. It is merely a basic take-down for cleaning. But shooters do fail to reassemble correctly at times.

In the process of reassembling the firearm, use proper pressure on the right screws and bolts. On a bolt-action big game rifle, it is imperative to tighten the bolt which aligns with the recoil lug, but go easy on the bolt which attaches upper tang with the lower tang or rear of trigger guard. As for bedding screws, the shooter should know how tight these need to be for accuracy. The pre-'64 Model 70 Winchester bolt-action rifle had the bedding screw on the fore-arm section of the stock, and the screw (bolt) ran into a tapped and threaded unit on the underside of the barrel. My own pre-'64 Model 70 shot best with this bolt turned one-fourth out. It was turned in all the way first, then backed out a quarter turn. Tighten enough so that a bolt or screw will not shoot loose, but do not tighten so much that a screw head is stripped. This sounds like impossible advice.

How can one tell a head will strip until it is stripped? My suggestion is to tighten a screw with one hand with the firearm supported. If it takes two hands with the gun in a vice, stripping is around the corner.

Make certain that "takedown" shotguns are broken down into their proper sub-groups. For example, a double gun should be broken down into its three major sub-groups for cleaning—forearm, barrels and buttstock/action. This enables easy cleaning. Also, a gun taken down into its basic parts is quite unlikely to fire. The bolt removed from the bolt-action rifle has the same effect.

The leverguns pose a different situation. I use the pull-through cleaning device, to be discussed, for my lever-action rifles. Takedown is almost impossible with today's leverguns.

As was said in the beginning, the cleaning process starts with an *unloaded* firearm. Be sure the chamber is empty and magazine removed or fully unloaded. During cleaning, remember the tenets of safe gun handling, i.e., always keep the muzzle pointed in a safe direction.

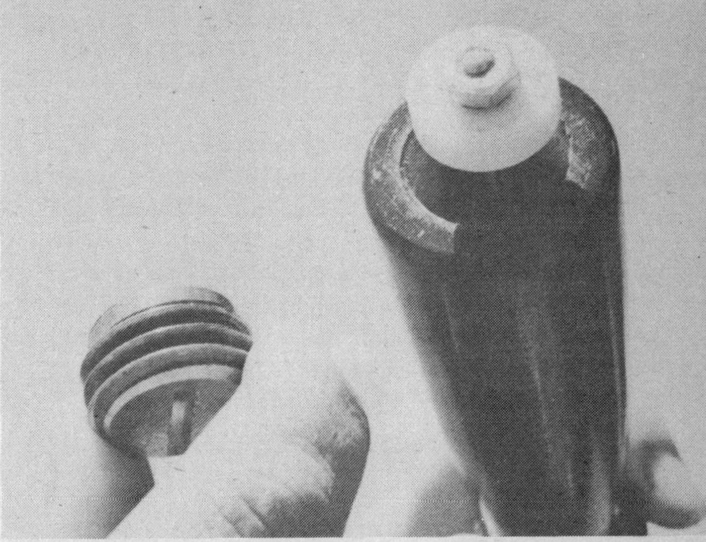

The Outer's Imperial cleaning rod has a hollow handle in which rests a nylon insert. This constuction allows the rod to swivel.

The modern cleaning rod is the best ever. These Outers cleaning rods are sturdy and come in various sizes and lengths. They are designed to clean a firearm without damaging it.

2. The Tools

There are many fine tools used in the process of cleaning a firearm. Here are the basics. It's my advice for the new shooter to invest in a cleaning kit. Then he will have all of the tools he needs in one box. The shooter eventually adds to this kit, of course, though he never outgrows it.

The Modern Cleaning Rod: The modern cleaning rod comes in various forms. Today's rod is the best I have ever seen, and I have used cleaning rods for well over 30 years. There is the solid or one-piece rod, which is fine for the stay-at-home tool. It is always ready to go without put-together, and it's strong and straight. The take-down rod is handier. It is also very rigid when assembled and it goes wherever the shooter wants to take it in a very compact way. The pull-through rod is a flexible cleaning cable, so it probably falls out of the realm of "rod" at all, but it serves the same cleaning function. The latter is available today in the fine Outers Pocket Pak. The pull-through is my choice for the lever-action, since it's impossible to insert a rigid cleaning rod from the breech end.

Some modern cleaning rods wear muzzle protectors. I

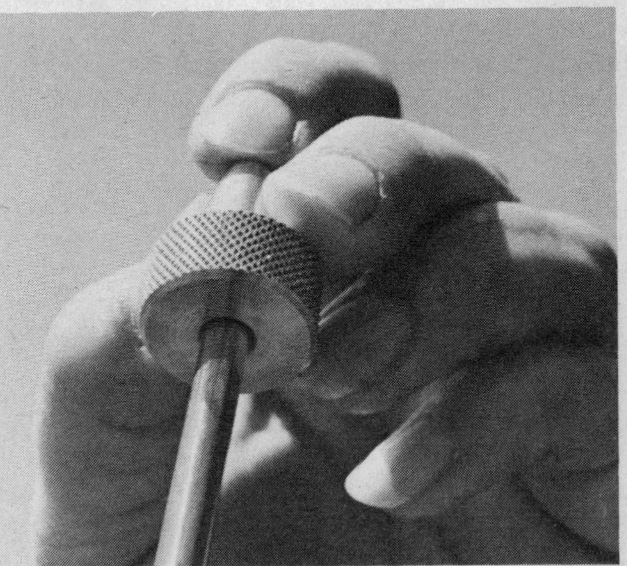

The muzzle protector, on an Outer's Imperial cleaning rod, slides along the shaft of the cleaning rod, centering the shaft in the bore and keeping the rod from scraping against the lands at the muzzle of the gun.

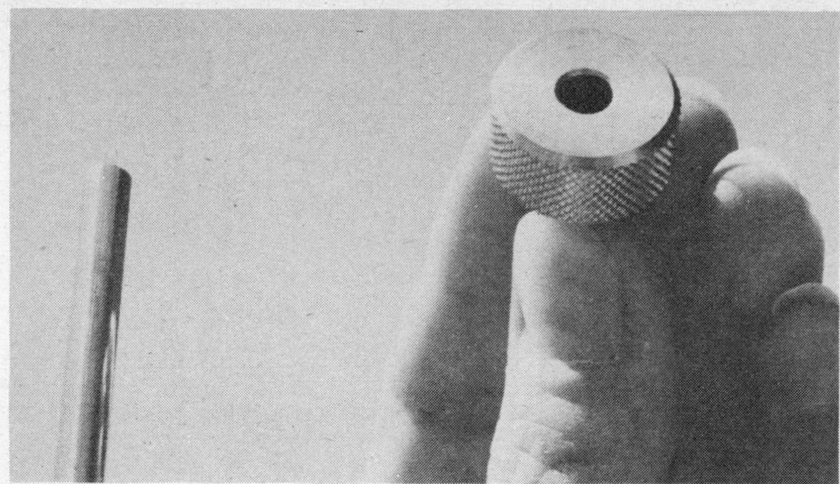

The Outer's Imperial cleaning rod is a stainless steel model with a very small diameter. The small diameter per caliber works quite well in conjunction with a muzzle protector. The muzzle protector slips over the tip of the rod and remains on the rod throughout use.

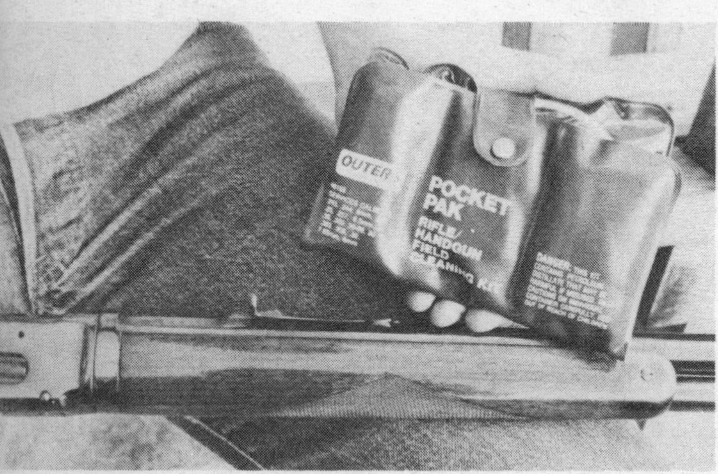

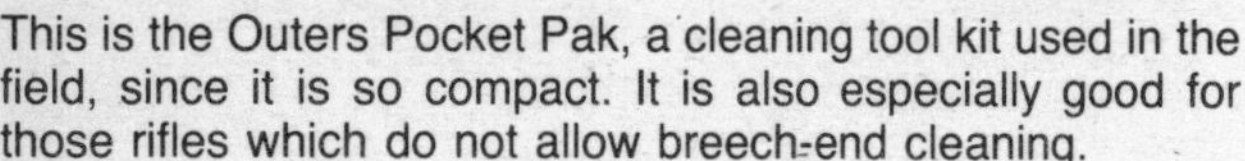

This is the Outers Pocket Pak, a cleaning tool kit used in the field, since it is so compact. It is also especially good for those rifles which do not allow breech-end cleaning.

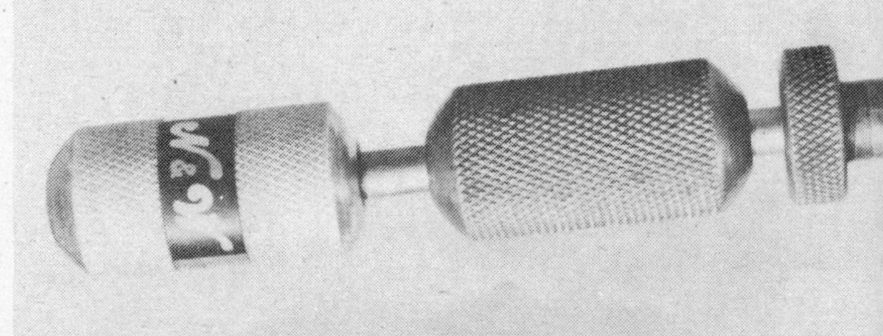

The N&W Cleaning rod is well-suited to black powder shooting because it doubles as a loading rod as well.

Even in camp, cleaning a gun is no big problem. This frontloader is being prepared for elk hunting in the morning.

would suggest you purchase that type of rod. The muzzle protector is a cone-shaped device which slides along the rod. The small end of the cone fits into the muzzle of the gun. This means that the cleaning rod itself cannot damage the precious muzzle area because it does not touch it. Also, the muzzle protector insures that the cleaning rod is centered in the bore while in use. For guns which must be cleaned from the muzzle, the protector is an excellent device.

The black powder cleaning rod is more than a ''cleaning rod.'' It also serves as a loading rod, and it's more reliable than the ramrod secured underneath the barrel of the gun. The N&W model comes with a muzzle protector and is strong and rigid. Also, it will accept the worm, a corkscrew affair used to withdraw a stuck patch, the screw, which is just like a screw and can be used to extract a stuck ball, and many different jags for cleaning.

The Cleaning Tip: A jag is a cleaning tip. It's a metal screw-in device which hangs onto a patch so that it can be

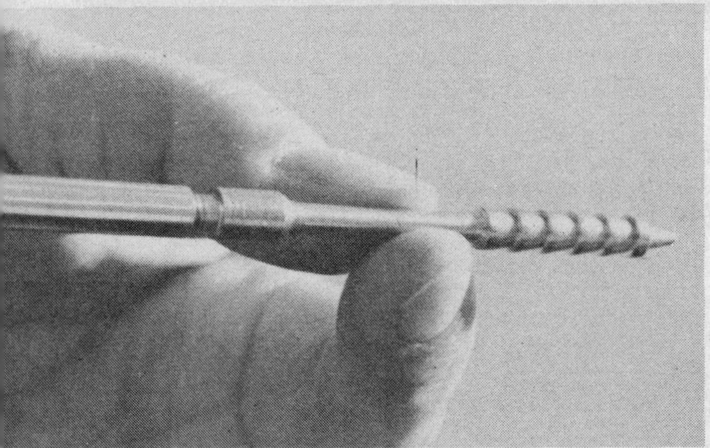

The Outer's Imperial cleaning rod accepts a jag. The jag guides a cleaning patch downbore and will aso retract the patch if necessary.

withdrawn as well as forced down the bore. The jag is most useful with the black powder gun, but has also found its way into modern gun cleaning to quite a degree. There is also the standard cleaning tip complete with its patch-holding loop. Each has a place, but each has the same function, too, to send a patch downbore and retract it.

The Bristle Brush: The bristle brush is just that, a brush fitted on one end with a threaded shank so it can screw into a cleaning rod. It is run up and down the bore to loosen fouling and minor leading. Today, there are several kinds of bristle brushes, including those of nylon as well as those of traditional bronze.

The Patch: Simple that it may be, the patch does a lot of work. One may buy patches pre-cut, simply looking for the correct size to match his gun, or he may cut them himself. Either way, the material must be kept clean. If you're buying patches, keep them clean, for they will arrive that way. If you choose to cut them from scratch, use clean flannel cloth and then put the patches in a plastic bag to keep dirt and grit away.

Adaptors: Today, there are many metal adaptors which screw into the tip of the cleaning rod. These allow for interchange of cleaning items, such as various bore brushes and other fixtures.

Rifle Cleaning

1. With bore brush attached, dampen the brush in solvent and scrub the bore from chamber to muzzle. A few strokes should do the job. This will loosen up jacket fouling, or even remove a bit of cast bullet lead if the lead has not been heavily worked into the grooves of the rifling as a result of extensive cast bullet shooting.

2. Attach a cleaning tip with patch in the slot. Soak the

STEP-BY-STEP RIFLE CLEANING

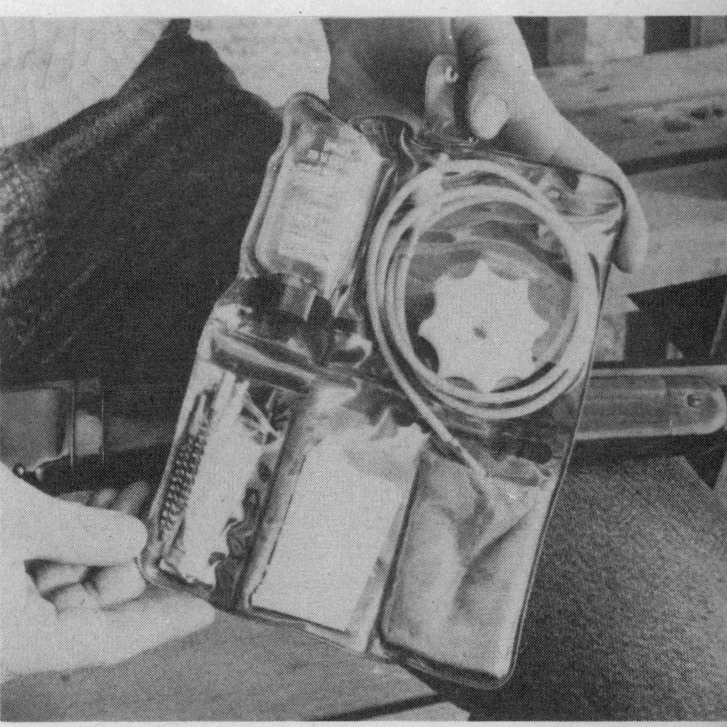

The Outer's Pocket Pak cleaning tool kit contains a swivel cleaning cable plus handle, gun oil and solvent, two phosphor bronze bore brushes, two cleaning tips, and adaptor, a silicone cloth and cleaning patches.

The handle attaches to the swivel cleaning cable.

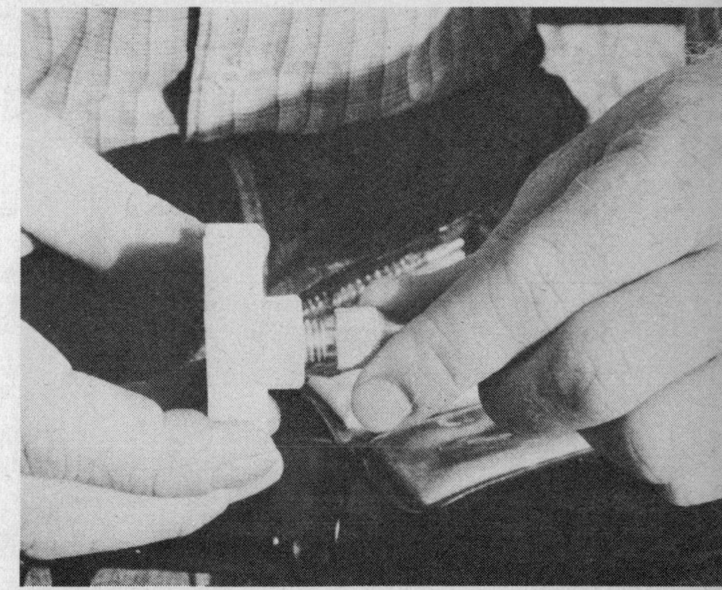

Step-By-Step Rifle Cleaning (Con't.)

(Left) After running the Outers cable-type rod down the muzzle of this lever-action centerfire, a solvent-soaked brush was attached and drawn through the chamber and bore of the rifle.

(Below) Removing the brush, the cable-type rod was again run down the muzzle, a looped-tip then attached.

(Bottom) Next, insert a solvent-soaked patch in the looped tip and drag it through the bore. Follow this up with a series of dry, clean patches.

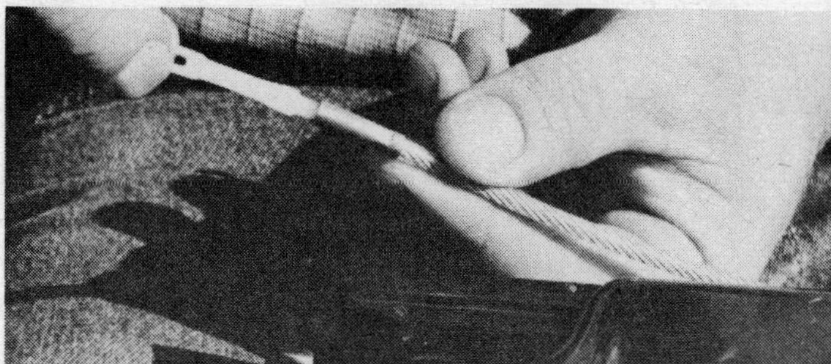

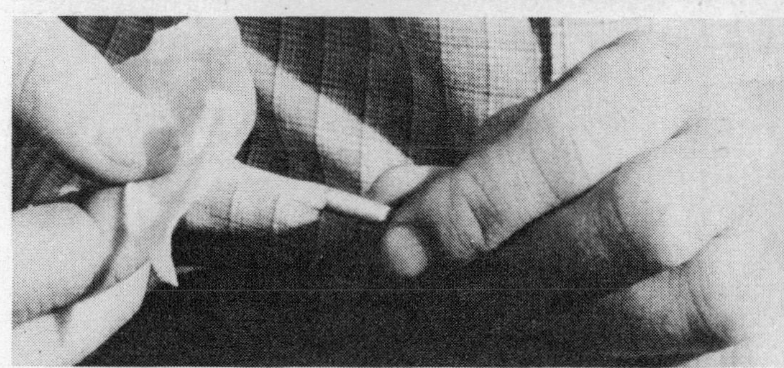

patch with solvent. Run the solvent-soaked patch through the bore several times. The spillage can be taken up by old rags or newspapers beneath the muzzle of the rifle. If the patch is too snug, it will squeeze out much of the solvent. The patch should be a good fit, but not requiring heavy pressure to get it through the bore.

3. Remove the solvent-soaked patch and replace it with a clean dry patch. Run this patch up and down the bore a few times. Do it again. The second patch may get the dampness out. If not, use a third or even fourth clean dry patch.

4. Repeat the solvent treatment if the bore still shows dark places in it or streaks. With the bolt removed, it's easy to see through the bore, from both the muzzle and breech ends. With a gun which requires cleaning from the muzzle, use a bore light. These can be bought through a gunshop. They are tiny bulbs with long cords, battery operated, and they allow the shooter to see inside of the bore fairly well. Dry the bore with clean patches before checking for cleanliness of course.

5. After the bore is clean and dry, apply a light film of oil to the bore itself. This is accomplished with a clean patch and a touch of oil.

6. Clean the bolt or other parts of the mechanism with a clean cloth lightly dabbed with solvent. When these parts are clean, oil them lightly. Get to all parts, as much as the field-stripping will allow.

7. Wipe the entire gun down—the metal with a silicone gun cloth, and the wood with a clean cloth dabbed with a touch of inedible linseed oil. Use *very little* of the latter, just enough to pick up the dirt. (Those guns with modern, heavy, synthetic stock finishes are, perhaps, more easily cleaned with a soft rag and furniture polish. Once again, use a small amount.)

8. Before shooting the rifle again, run one dry cleaning patch through the bore. An oily bore will not shoot to the same point of impact as a dry bore, and all shooting should be done with a relatively dry bore. Excess oil in the bore can damage the bore as well. This is an important step and must be observed.

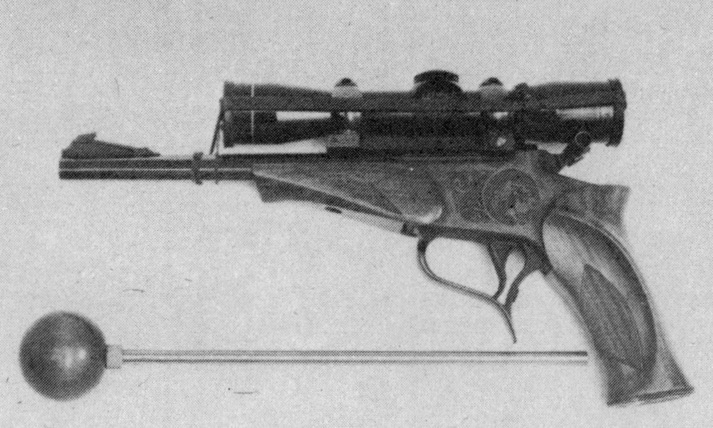

This tough cleaning rod is offered by Uncle Mike's. It is a heavy duty stainless steel model for silhouette handguns mainly, in calibers .357 and larger. It was originally designed as a muzzleloader cleaning and loading rod, but it works perfectly for heavy duty cleanup.

Handgun Cleaning

When it comes to "cleaning" guns, it's probably safe to say that more handguns end up on the gunsmith's bench for "reassembly" than any other type of firearm. Unlike long guns, handguns are, by necessity, small—their "smallness" fairly inviting the owner to tear it down as far as possible.

Rule No. 1: Tear a handgun down only as far as the manufacturer recommends. Rule No. 2: If you're not sufficiently competent to fully disassemble a handgun, and you fail to observe Rule No. 1, you're in for a trip to the gunsmith. Rule No. 3: If you have a long term mechanical understanding of firearms in general, and feel up to fully "detailing" a handgun be sure you have reliable assembly/disassembly data at hand *before* you proceed.

Double-Action Revolvers

With the muzzle pointed in a safe direction, open up the cylinder and make sure that all the chambers are empty.

Using a sturdy pistol-type cleaning rod of proper caliber, install a bronze brush (again of proper caliber). Dip the brush in solvent and thoroughly scrub out each chamber. Letting the scrubbed, solvent-laden chambers soak on their own, re-dip the brush and scrub out the bore, from the muzzle just as thoroughly. If you hadn't already guessed, the cleaning of a revolver barrel requires the entry of a cleaning rod at the muzzle. Don't go at it in an aggressive ham-fisted fashion. Remember, damage to the crown of the muzzle will only result in lost accuracy. If the damage is severe, barrel replacement may be necessary. And I can assure you that replacing that barrel isn't going to be cheap.

Now, remove the brush from the rod, install a looped tip, insert a solvent-soaked patch and run it through the chambers of the cylinder. Remove and discard the patch, insert a fresh solvent-soaked patch and run it down the muzzle of the barrel.

Repeat the process until the patches are clean.

Sometimes a bore is going to end up with some metal fouling from the bullet jacket (very seldom happens these days) or some lead fouling. The latter is usually found in a handgun firing lead projectiles, but it can also be found in rifles using cast bullets. Generally, the problem can be dealt with by running a solvent-soaked bristle brush through the bore several times, perhaps up to 20 or more swipes, followed by a cleaning with JB Compound or similar product. Pistol leading can be easily taken care of with the Lewis Lead Remover for handguns of 357-caliber and larger.

When cleaning your D/A revolver, be sure to raise the star-type ejector and thoroughly remove as much powder residue and/or lead shavings as possible. An over accumulation of this type of debris will only serve, at some point, to tie the revolver up entirely.

If your D/A revolver is an S&W and it wears an adjustable rear sight, be sure to check the small, forward mounted sight retaining screw for tightness. Extended recoil tends to loosen things up a bit; and, I'm sure there are those of you who have even "lost" an entire S&W rear sight assembly just because of this. Colt/Eliason adjustable rear sights are held in place by a simple cross-pin—make sure the pin isn't walking its way out of its slot.

After you're through cleaning your D/A revolver, a few drops of quality gun oil on the ejector rod, hammer and trigger (and adjustable sight) should do the trick. I can hear you now—"What about all those screws on the side of the frame." You are again referred to Rules 1 through 3.

With the gun cleaned, *unloaded*, and the muzzle pointed in a safe direction, cock the hammer. If the cylinder fails to fully cycle and go into proper alignment, *don't shoot the gun*—it's probably out of time. Take it to a competent gunsmith or factory service center—they will be happy to re-time it for you, usually at reasonable cost.

STEP-BY-STEP REVOLVER CLEANING

Making sure the revolver is unloaded, run a solvent-soaked brush down the muzzle (several times) and through each chamber in the cylinder.

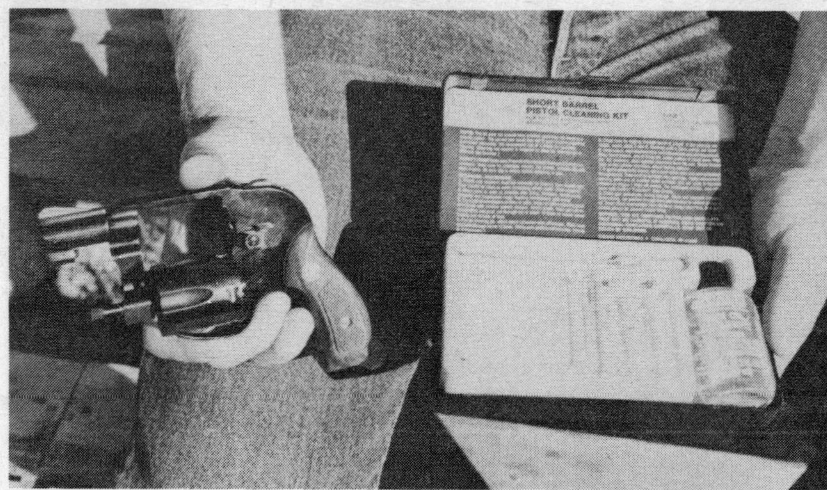

Next, install a looped tip on the rod and run a solvent-soaked patch/patches through the bore and each chamber.

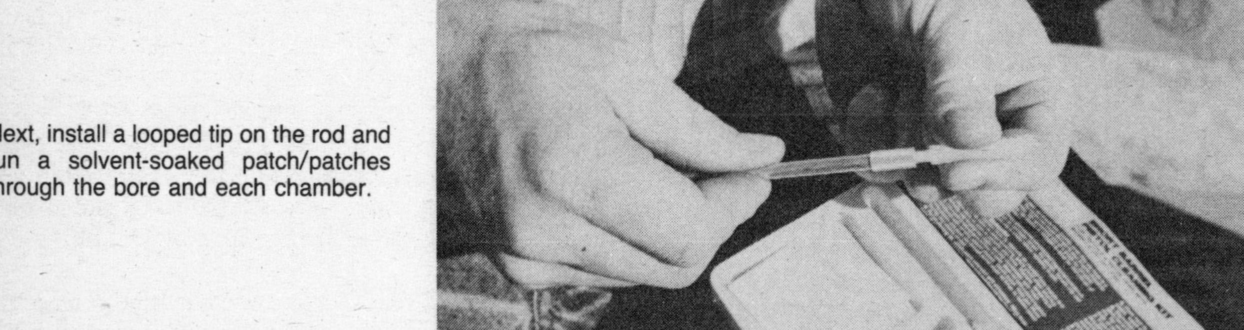

Lastly, run a series of clean, dry patches through the bore and chambers of the cylinder. If the patches come out dirty, repeat the cleaning process.

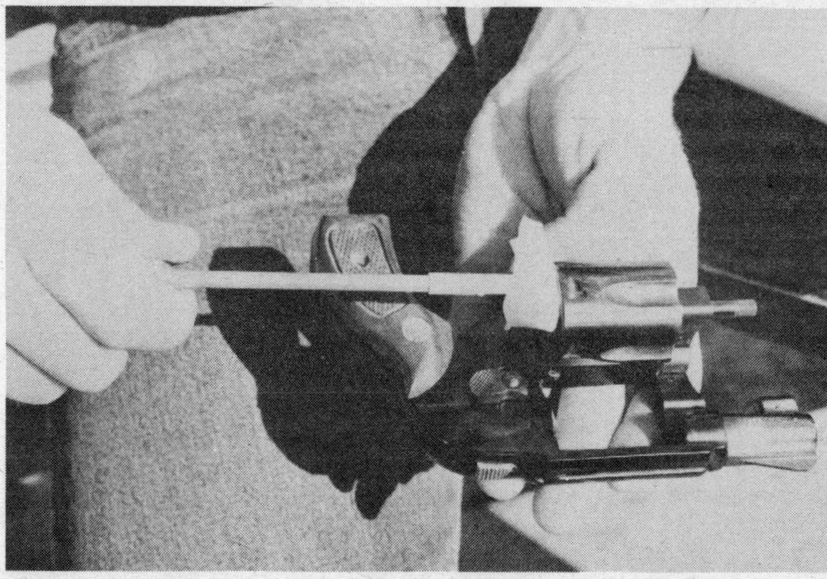

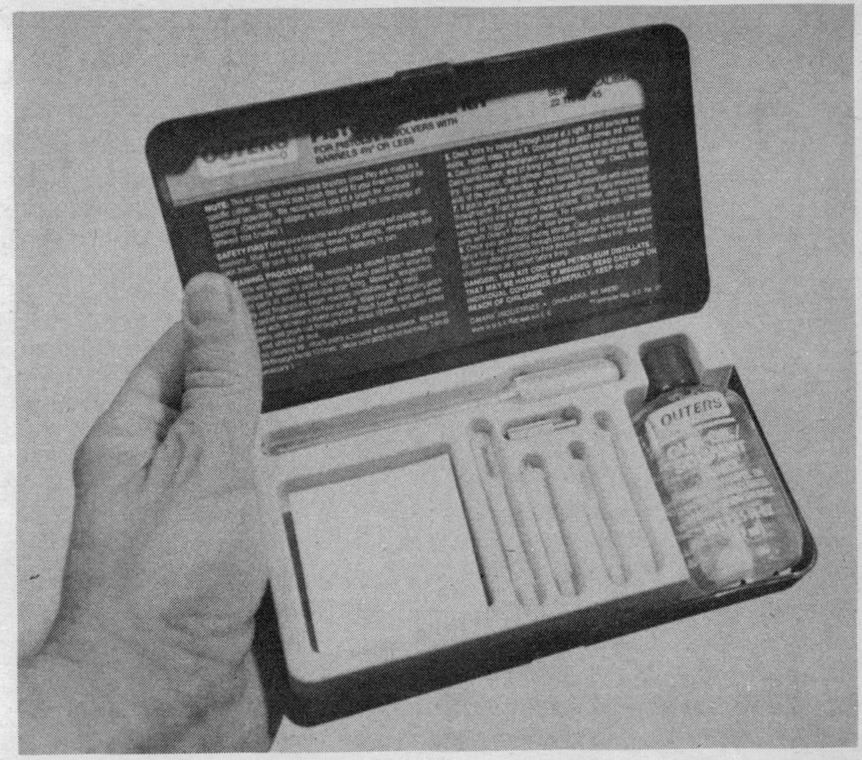

Outers Pistol Cleaning Kit is a compact unit which serves to clean short-barreled handguns. With patches, solvent, and accessories, as well as rod, encased in a compact box, this handgun cleaning kit is small enough to go anywhere.

Single-Action Revolvers

With the muzzle of the pistol pointed in a safe direction, open the loading gate, put the hammer on half cock (if your S/A is of the "old" type) and rotate the cylinder making sure *every* chamber is empty.

Cleaning for the single-action revolver is basically the same as for the double-action revolver, with only a couple of exceptions.

The prime exception is in the way the cylinder is cleaned. On a D/A revolver the cylinder *swings out* on the crane; on an S/A revolver, the cylinder is fully *removed* from the frame. The removal of the cylinder is usually quite simple; however, I will refer you to the manufacturers instructions for cylinder removal on your own S/A revolver.

S/A ejection of loaded ammo or fired brass is usually accomplished one-at-a-time via the barrel mounted ejector rod. During cleaning be sure to blow out the ejector rod and ejector rod housing with an aerosol degreaser. After you re-lube the ejector rod, be sure to check its housing for any obvious looseness. The ejector-rod housing is usually married to the barrel, at or near the muzzle, with a single screw. Extended shooting and the resulting recoil tends to loosen that screw—check it for tightness.

Semi-Auto Pistols

Semi-auto pistols, rimfire or centerfire, are unique in their construction and operation. When it comes to cleaning the semi-auto handgun, field stripping, as recommended by the manufacturer is the first step in cleaning. Disassembly beyond basic field stripping is not recommended.

With the muzzle pointed in a safe direction, remove the magazine, pull the slide to the rear and remove any chambered ammo. If the magazine was loaded now's the time to remove that ammo.

Using a solvent-soaked brush of proper caliber, scrub out the barrel starting at the chamber end. Yes, in a pinch a shortened rifle cleaning rod can work; however, that approach is awkward at best and potentially rod damaging at the worst. Obviously, the use of the littler handgun-type cleaning rod (of proper caliber) is the best most efficient approach. Once the bore has been brushed, run a solvent-soaked patch down the barrel followed by additional passes with clean patches.

Setting the barrel aside, turn your attention to the slide. The slide, so it seems, usually gets quite filthy, even with minimal shooting. With moderate to heavy shooting, the build-up of powder residue gets even worse. I would suggest using a piece of cloth or a large size cleaning patch soaked in Marksmans Choice bore cleaner for the slide clean up. Marksmans Choice removes deposited powder residue like no other cleaner on the market. Take that patch and wipe down the guide rail recesses, locking-lug recesses and the face of the slide. Also clean out the extractor hook and any other nook or cranny that's reachable.

Setting the slide aside, take up the frame and wipe it down as you did the slide. Concentrate on the "male" guide rails, their recesses and the feeding ramp. The latter will usually show a build-up of jacket wash, lead, bullet

STEP-BY-STEP SEMI-AUTO PISTOL CLEANING

Field stripping and cleaning is an individual thing, the shooter being best advised to follow the manufacturer's instructions. Seen here is the Ruger Mark II, the latest version of, and quite similar to, the old Ruger Standard Auto.

The first step in cleaning the pistol, in this case a Ruger Mark II 22 semi-auto pistol, is to insure that the gun is unloaded. The clip is removed first. Then the chamber is inspected visually to see that no round is hung up at this point. Only after the gun has been totally checked out to guarantee that it is *fully unloaded* does take-down and cleaning begin.

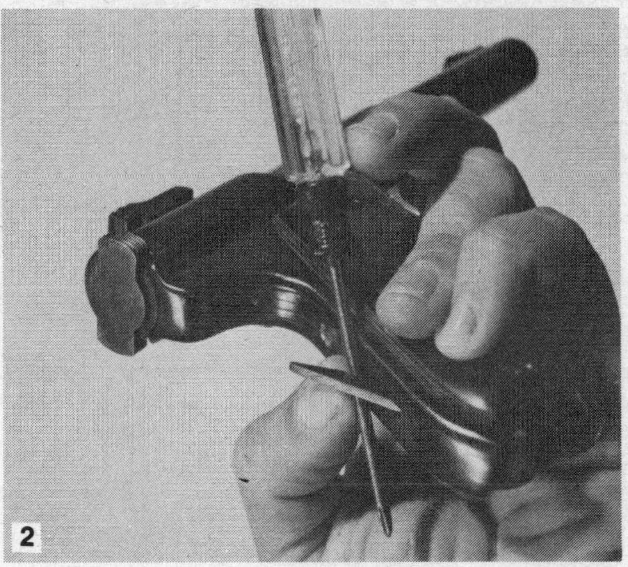

Using a narrow instrument, in this case a small screwdriver, the mainspring housing is swung outward.

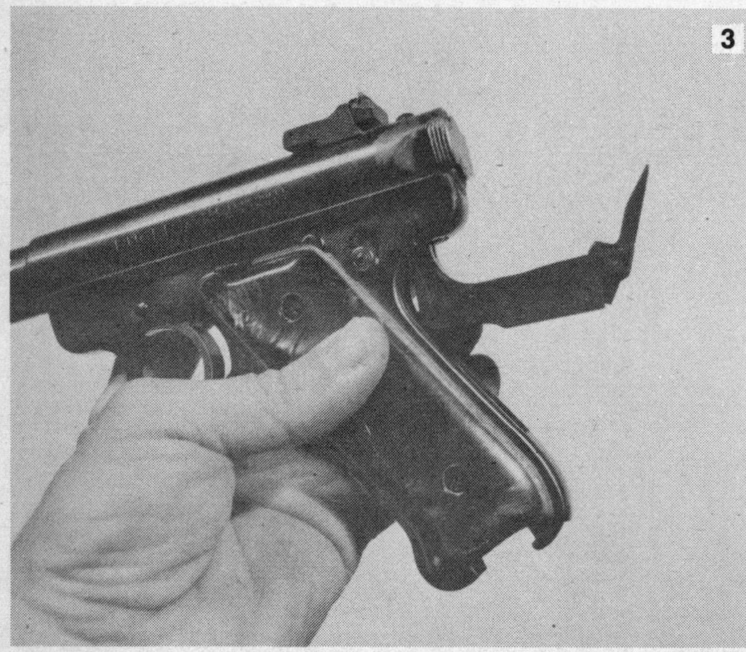

The mainspring housing is pulled fully away from the rear of the pistol grip. It will pivot upward with hand pressure.

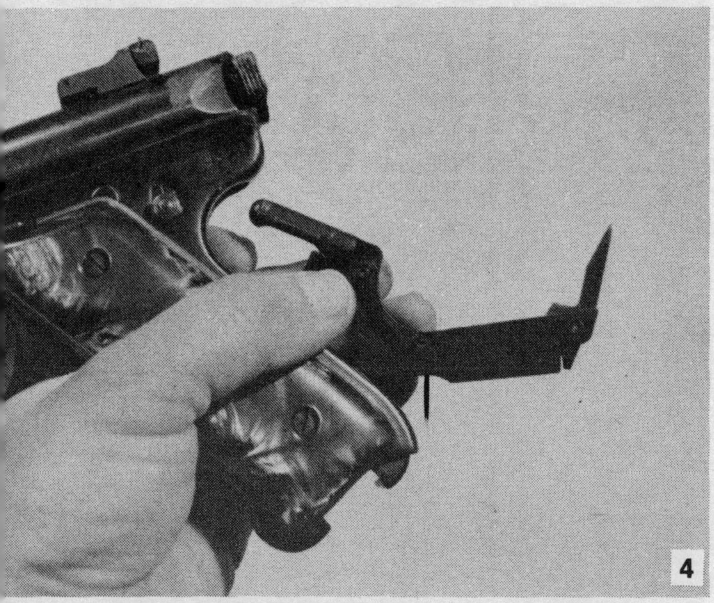

At this point, the mainspring housing is entirely removed, by hand, from the pistol.

Now the bolt is removed by simply tipping the gun upward. The bolt will fall out on its own volition. And now the gun can be cleaned from the breech end by using a small cleaning rod with brush, patches and solvent, after which the bore is dried and lightly oiled.

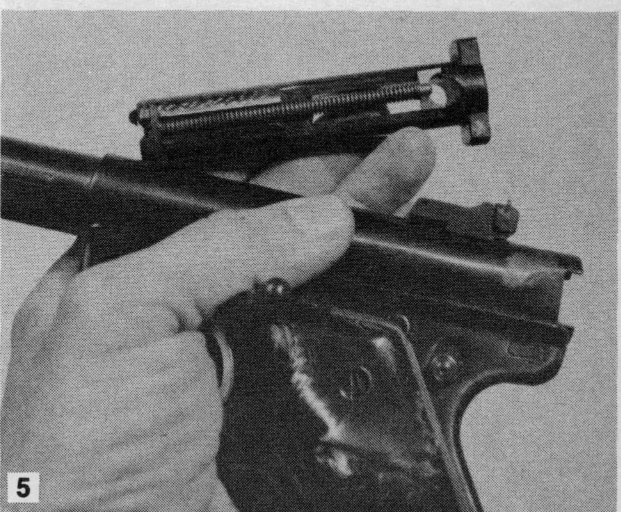

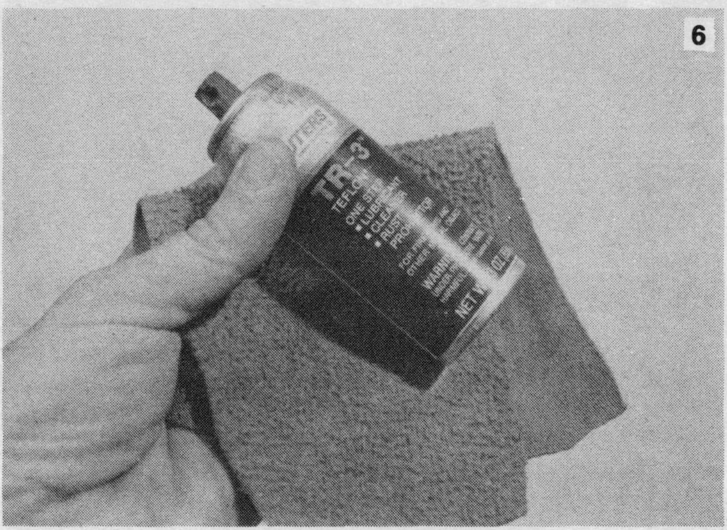

Using a soft rag doused lightly with a spray of Tri-Lube, a Teflon-based aerosol lubricant, the pistol will be wiped down before storing.

lube or a bit of all of the above. Again, I would recommend Marksmans Choice for the chore. Once you're satisfied that the frame is clean, move on to the magazine(s) and repeat the Marksmans Choice cleanup. Because of the magazine construction, an aerosol degreaser (RIG III works well) will help "blow things out." Have at it. Using that same aerosol degreaser, I would suggest you now blow out the barrel, slide and frame (grips removed, please).

You are now ready to relube, *sparingly*, your pistol. I recommend Outers Tri-Lube as its Teflon additive truly smooths things up. And that's what you're after with a semi-auto pistol. Lube the slide rails, hammer, trigger, extractor and any other obvious bearing surface. Again, use that Tri-Lube sparingly—don't drown the gun in lube. Believe me it won't enhance (and may hinder) proper function.

Lastly, check the pistol and its components carefully. Look for dented magazines as they, more than any other problem, can quickly tie up a semi-auto. Reliable feeding is your goal, and a dented magazine can really foul things up. If the main recoil spring is badly kinked, consider replacing it—the same advice applies to badly dented magazines. Check the extractor hook and ejector for any cracks, chips or breaks. If something doesn't come up to snuff,

STEP-BY-STEP PUMP SHOTGUN CLEANING

Field stripping and cleaning is an individual thing, the shooter being best advised to follow the manufacturer's instructions. Seen here is the Remington 870 pump, one of the most popular shotguns ever made in the U.S.

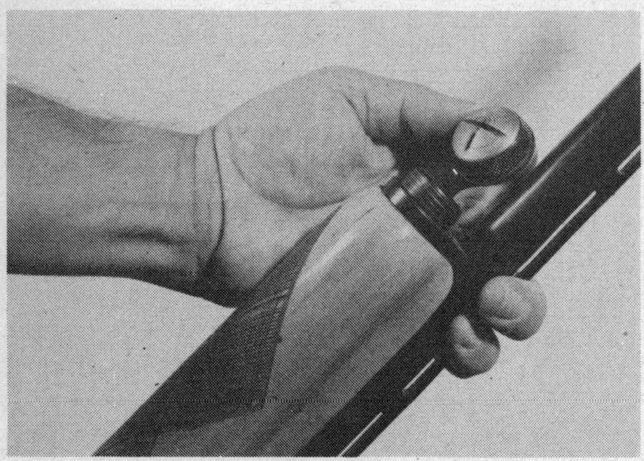

Making sure the gun is fully unloaded, remove the barrel. In this instance, barrel removal is easily accomplished by unscrewing the cap at the end of the tubular magazine. The barrel will now slide away from the receiver.

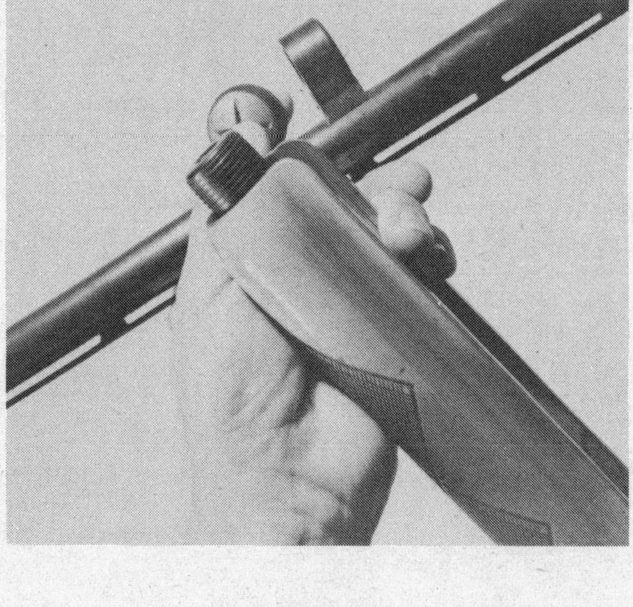

(Right) After the cap has been unscrewed, the barrel easily slides out and away from the receiver.

(Below) Cleaning devices such as this bore brush and mop work well in removing powder residue from the bore of the shotgun.

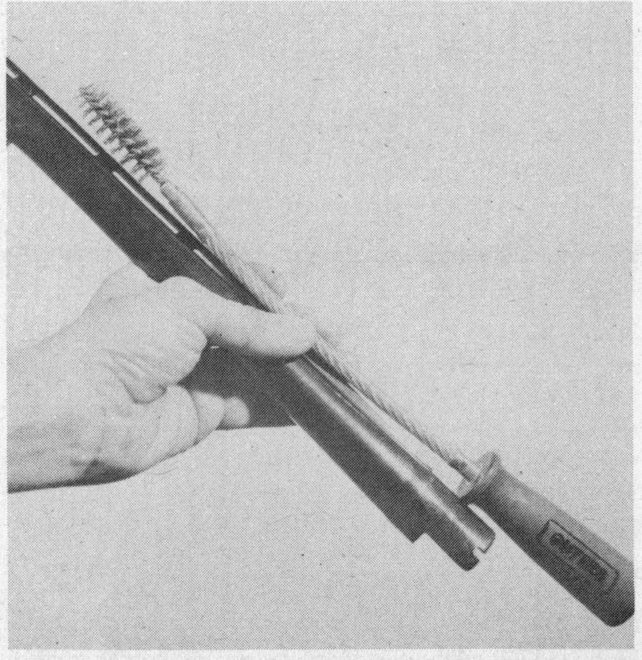

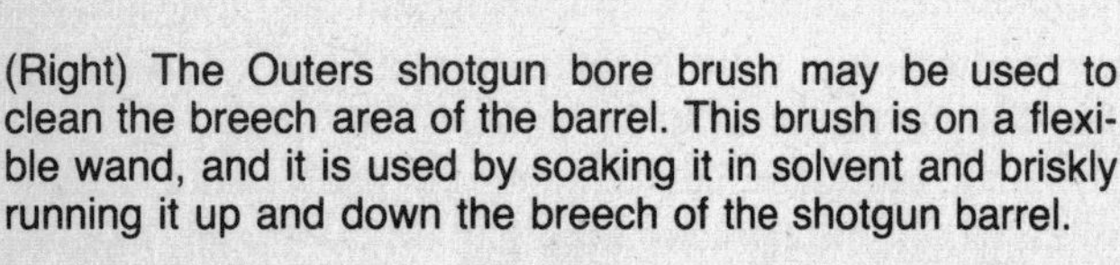

(Right) The Outers shotgun bore brush may be used to clean the breech area of the barrel. This brush is on a flexible wand, and it is used by soaking it in solvent and briskly running it up and down the breech of the shotgun barrel.

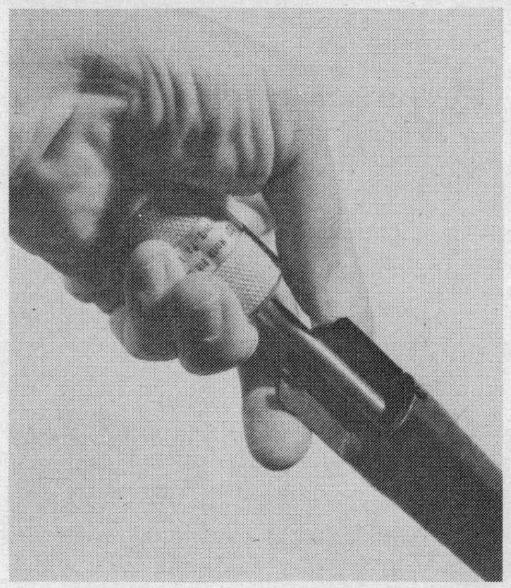

A regular cleaning rod may be used to clear the bore of powder residue. A cleaning patch can be soaked in solvent and run up and down the bore several times, followed by dry patches and finally a patch lightly doused in oil.

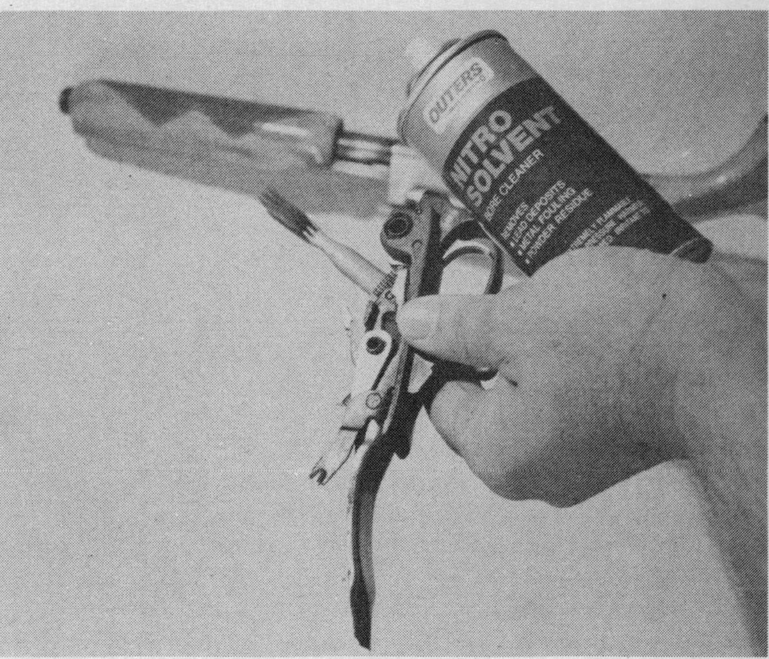

The trigger housing on the Model 870 is removed very quickly and simply by merely drifting out the cross pins located at the rear of the receiver. A toothbrush and solvent can be used to free this area of powder residue.

After the bore is clean, the outside of the gun should be wiped down with a light lube such as Outers TR-3 (now called Tri-Lube).

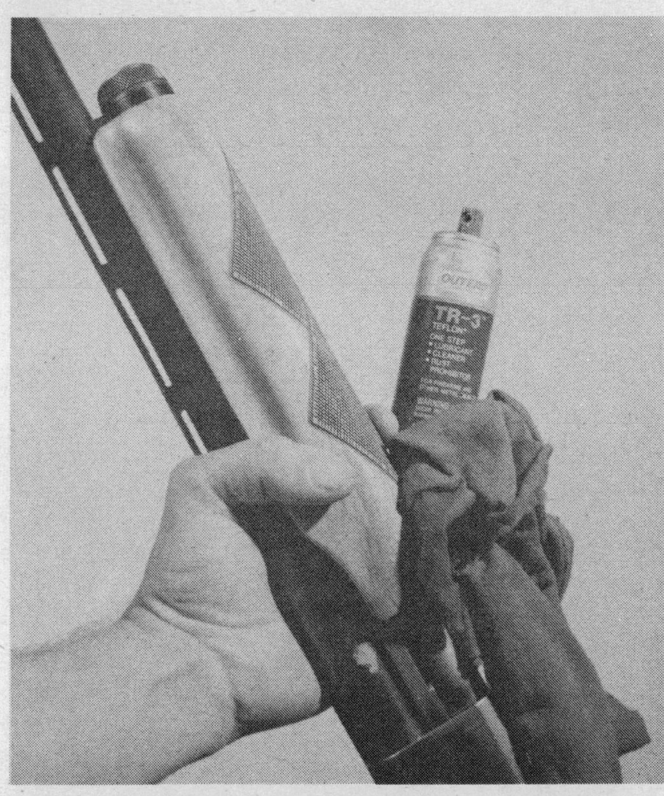

enlist the services of a competent gunsmith.

Reassemble your pistol and check out every safety feature on that pistol for proper function. Any failure of a safety should be brought to the attention of a competent gunsmith, *immediately*.

Generally speaking, failure to feed, fire, extract or eject can be directly traced to 1) a dirty gun; 2) ammo; 3) a damaged magazine; 4) all (or a combination) of the above.

Shotgun Cleaning

In the main, shotguns are even easier to clean than rifles. When it comes to cleaning out a shotgun's bore, just be sure to use a quality cleaning rod of the correct size for the gauge of shotgun to be cleaned. Outers and RIG come to mind when I think of reasonably priced, quality shotgun cleaning rods.

First, with the muzzle pointed in a safe direction, make sure the chamber and magazine are empty.

Today's shotshells and their plastic wad columns leave a plastic residue in both the chamber and bore. Failure to recognize this fact, and deal with it, in the cleaning process, can only lead to rusted bores and chambers. The cure is simple. Using a good solvent (Marksman's Choice is recommended), thoroughly clean out the bore and chamber with a bronze brush. Don't be shy about it—make about 6 or 8 good passes through the chamber, and down the bore with that solvent-soaked bronze brush.

Next, run a solvent-soaked patch of proper size down the bore. Now run a couple of dry patches through the barrel. Lastly, put little bit of Outers Tri-Lube on a patch and swab the bore—your gun's almost ready for storage.

Your next step should be to remove any powder residue from the action and/or face of the breech bolt. At this point, guns like Remington's 870/1100 series should have their trigger groups removed (as they were intended to be) by driving out the side-mounted pins in the receiver. Using an aerosol degreaser (RIG III works well) you can now "blow-out" the trigger group and even give the now "open" action the same treatment. Shake or wipe off any excess degreaser of remaining residue, lightly lube the inner workings and reassemble the trigger group to the receiver.

When it comes to gas-operated semi-autos, don't fail to overlook the gas port(s) (they're quite small) usually found inside (or in the area of) the barrel mounted magazine guide ring. Using a pipe cleaner soaked in solvent, lightly swab out those gas ports and then degrease them. The same vigorous cleaning should also be applied to any attendant gas rings or neoprene gas seals, not to mention the external areas of a gas-operated auto's magazine tube. You will be amazed at the amount of carbon that comes off of these parts.

Single shots or double-barreled shotguns (O/U or side-by-side) should have their ejectors or lifters carefully cleaned and lightly lubed—there's nothing quite as aggravating as a stuck lifter or ejector, in the field.

Things to Look For

If, during a hunting trip, you noticed an unusual amount of jams or failures to extract and eject that were not related to "bad" ammo, the clean-up is the time to look for the answers. I once had a Remington 1100 in 28-gauge that, during a pheasant hunt, started tossing out empties in an "odd" fashion—empty hulls would fly out normally, or, just barely clear the ejection port. During cleaning I discovered that the hook of the extractor had sheared off flush with the face of the bolt. A quick trip to the gunsmith cured the problem.

During your shotgun cleaning, look for barrel bulges, barrel dents, cracks in the wood, loose ribs, missing bead-type sights, etc. All of these problems can, usually, be easily repaired or attended to by a competent gunsmith.

Before putting that "clean" shotgun away, be sure to give the external metal a light coat of quality gun oil or a nice coat of RIG grease—that's the final step, the step that will insure your gun will be ready the next time you want it.

Wear and Cleaning

There is no doubt that cleaning can aid in the wearing process. As stated earlier, there are probably some 22 rimfire guns which have been worn out by cleaning, especially improper cleaning. Also, as stated several times, cleaning from the muzzle doesn't help this problem. Yes, it is wise to clean a firearm soon after shooting, but it is unwise to get too vigorous in the use of the cleaning hardware. Go slowly. The process should only take about 10 pleasant minutes. Maybe 10 swipes with the solvent dampened bristle brush and five to 10 swipes with the solvent soaked cleaning patch. Clean 'em up right, but don't wear 'em out.

Modern Chemicals for Cleaning and Preserving

These following modern chemicals do really work. I urge shooters to use them. They are not as expensive as one may think because they do a lot of work in small amounts. In fact, I believe some shooters tend to overuse these chemicals.

1. Solvent

The modern solvent is easy on the bore and tough on fouling. Hoppes No. 9 is still cleaning guns as well as ever, and though this is an older solvent, it has modern

Modern chemicals make cleaning easier than ever. And they also help the shooter maintain the life of his firearm.

RIFLE CLEAN-UP WITH THE JOINTED CLEANING ROD

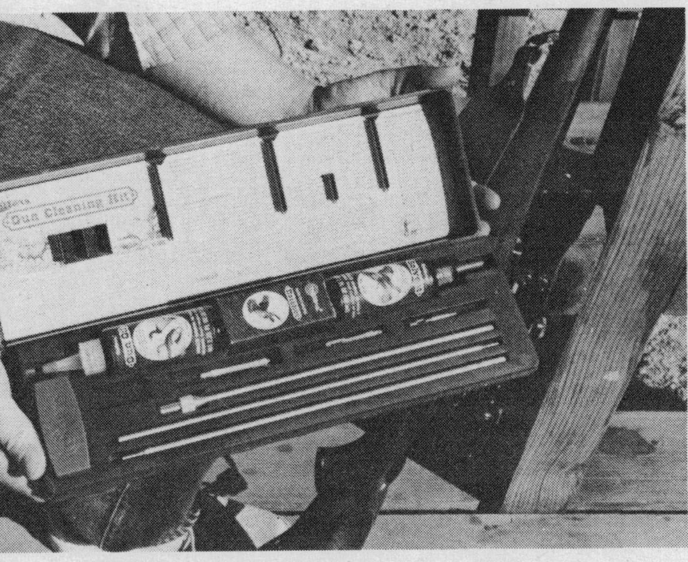

The Outers Gun Cleaning Kit is a compact outfit that comes complete with a jointed cleaning rod and all of the chemicals and patches necessary for most cleaning of guns.

(Right) The jointed cleaning rod is assembled. It has an optional insert which allows various cleaning tips to be inserted.

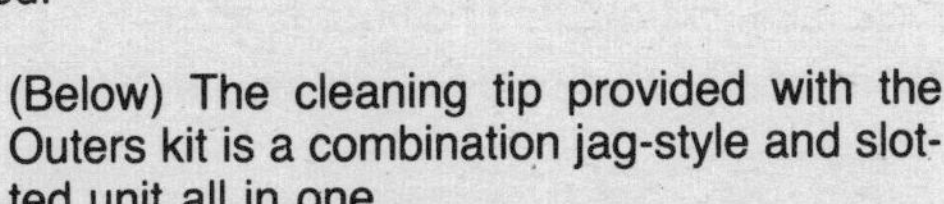

(Below) The cleaning tip provided with the Outers kit is a combination jag-style and slotted unit all in one.

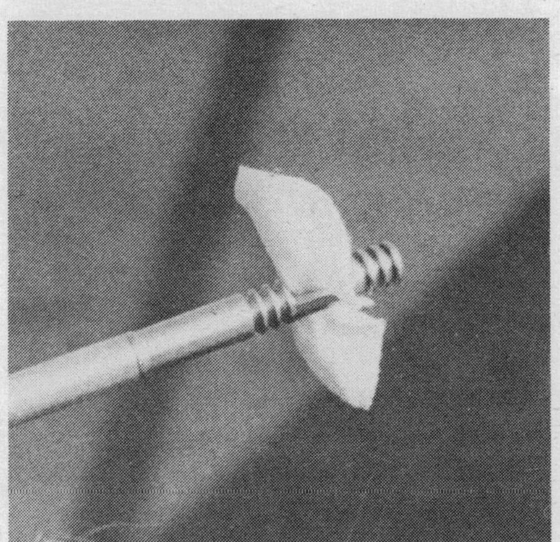

The rifle should then, if possible, be cleaned from the breech end. Always avoid cleaning a barrel from the muzzle end whenever possible.

These Birchwood/Casey gun wipes are handy and they work well.

properties. Outers solvent is tough on crud. And speaking of crud, Outers also has "Crud Cutter," a very fine degreaser that *works* and leaves no trace of itself. It dries like magic after having knocked the gunk away. Nitro Solvent from Outers is also excellent and I like the fact that it's available in a spray can. Another *superior* bore solvent is Marksmans Choice. It removes carbon and powder residue (and bore fouling) instantly. I can also recommend RIG III degreaser—it works.

Birchwood/Casey has several good chemicals for the modern shooter, including a Cleaner-Degreaser, Blue and Rust Remover (it removes old blue, so don't use it on that new gun!), and more. Another Outers product which is truly fine is their Tri-Lube, a Teflon-based Lube/solvent. It cleans fouling nicely and leaves protection behind.

Black powder solvents are also up to date. Moose Milk[R] from Winchester Sutler does a good job of cleaning as does Falkenberry Juice from the Oak Gun Shop. Blue and Gray Muzzle Loader Bore Cleaner is another good one, and there are many other modern chemicals designed to remove black powder fouling very quickly.

2. The Oils

Oils are still popular. They should be. Today's gun oils are very refined and engineered specifically for firearms. I never use any other type of oil on a gun other than *gun* oil, so specified on the container. The selection is broad; the choice is yours.

3. Metal Protectors

These are many today. Tri-Lube already mentioned, cleans up nicely, but its Teflon base also protects and lubricates. Good old RIG, over 50 winters used by gunners, is still a fine protector, and the truly modern refinements such as Accragard and Accralube are very valuable in keeping a firearm in top form, these two products from the J&A Enterprises people in Hinckley, Ohio.

Modern greases, sprays and oils are designed to aid metal protection. Some oils are non-gumming to 30 degrees below zero today. All in all, the chemicals designed to keep guns new do work. They are not simply sales oriented. And they cost very little when used properly. Considering that they can also help a gun last not only one lifetime, but many lifetimes, the modern chemicals are a bargain.

Cleaning and Accuracy

But does a clean firearm really shoot better than a dirty one? The problem here may stem from a little misunderstanding. I have been told that it's no use cleaning a rifle because accuracy is not as good as when it was fired with a dirty bore. This is not exactly true. What can happen is this—a rifle is cleaned and oiled. The bore is left oily. The rifle shoots off the mark. But no, a clean barrel is not an inaccurate barrel.

With some rifles, especially the smallbores in the little 17-caliber class, cleaning is paramount. Accuracy truly does suffer when the bore is fouled. Also, I have seen accuracy drop off when using certain powders. Some pow-

Birchwood Casey's Gun Scrubber is one of the various spray-can cleaners available to gunners now.

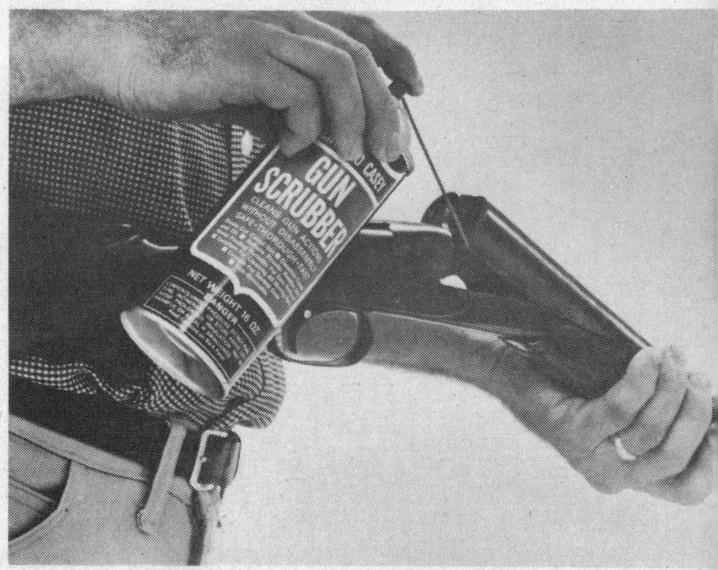

STEP-BY-STEP BLACK POWDER CLEAN-UP

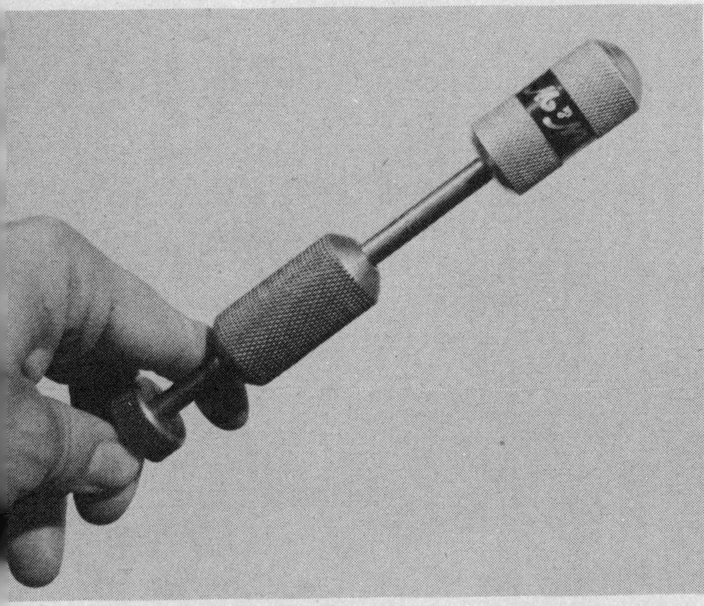

Using the correct rod is important in cleaning the muzzle-loading rifle. This N&W rod is for both cleaning *and* loading. It has a muzzle protector and also a brass knocker which is used to withdraw the rod if it is stuck downbore, or to extract a ball when using a screw.

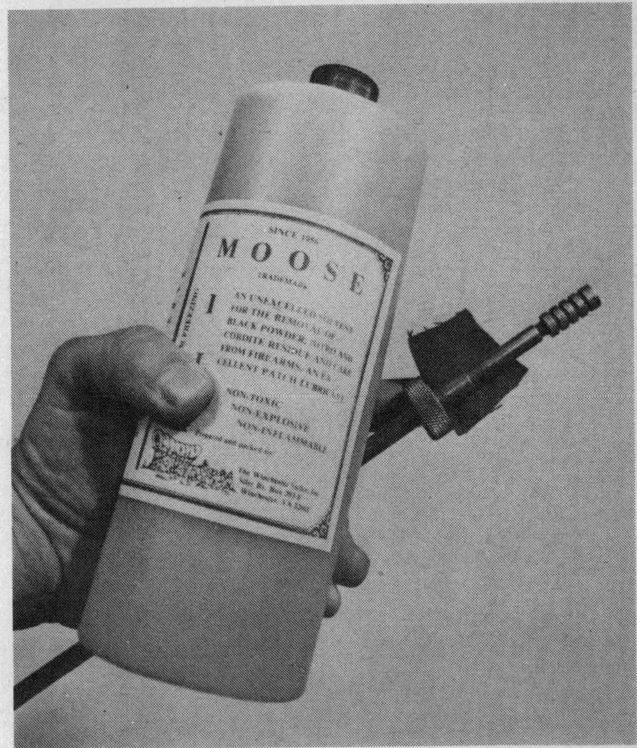

In the no-water cleanup, a modern black powder solvent, such as Falkenberry Juice, or (shown here) Moose Milk [R] is used. With a cleaning jag in place and patches soaked in the lube, the fouling is removed from the bore of the rifle.

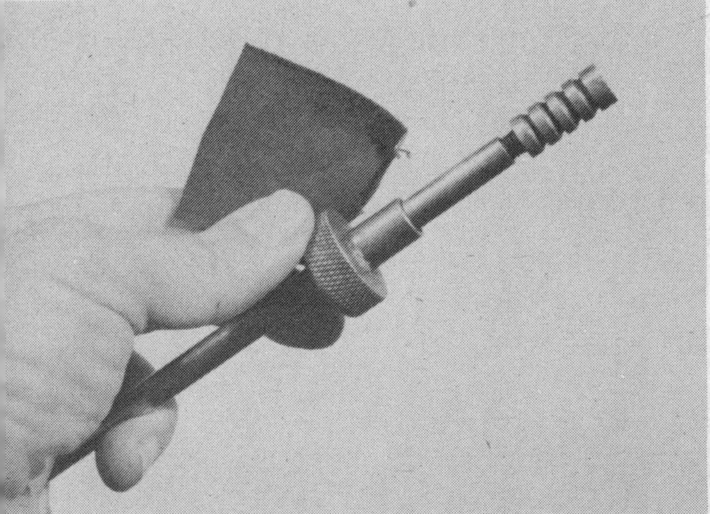

The cleaning jag is not screwed all the way onto the shank of the cleaning rod. This prevents jag lock up on the cleaning rod threads. (Note the muzzle protector, and cleaning patch.)

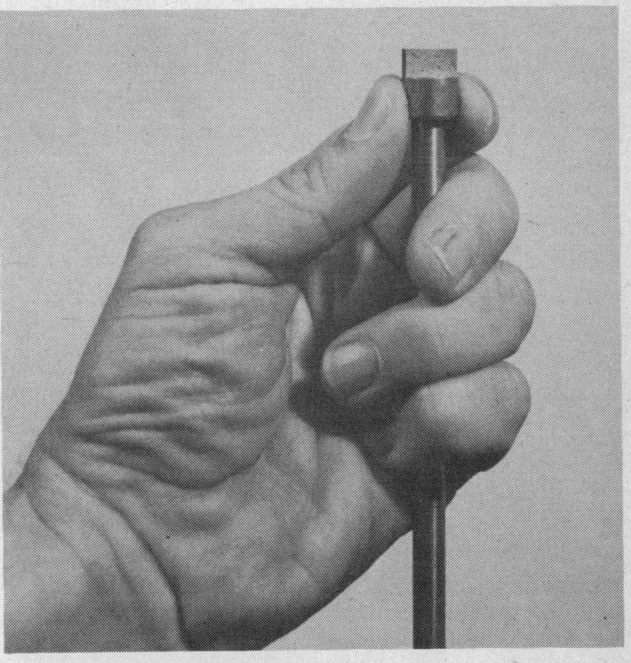

(Right) After a few wet patches have been run downbore, the shooter may wish to use a scraper to clean the face of the breech plug. With a scraper a rotating motion is applied to the rod.

Step-By-Step Black Powder Clean-Up (Cont.)

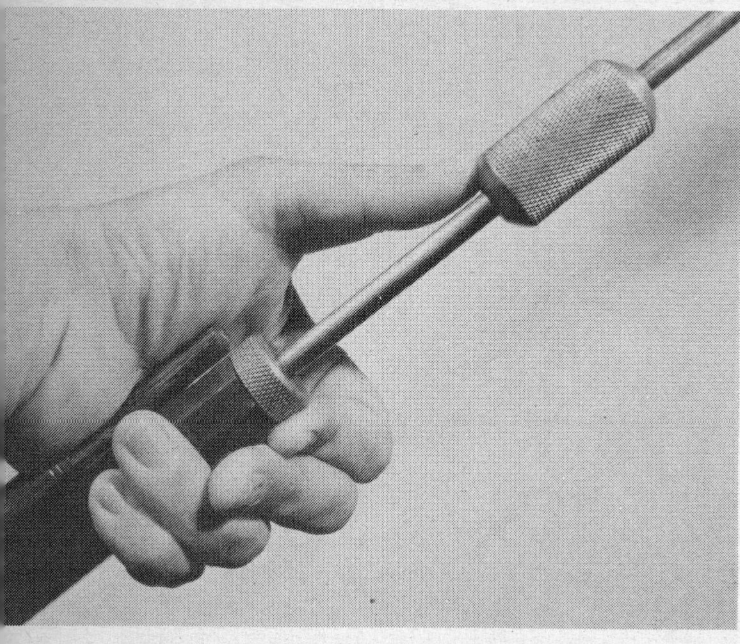

Here, the jag of the rod, with damp cleaning patch in place, has been inserted into the bore. With up-down motion, the damp patch will remove black powder fouling. Also note that the muzzle protector is in place in the crown area. This centers the cleaning rod so that it cannot scrape the lands of the rifling, which could harm accuracy.

After the patches emerge clean, instead of dirty, a final patch may be run downbore. This patch should hold a small amount of protective oil, such as this Accragard. Apply sparingly as a little goes a long way. Be sure to remove oil prior to the next shooting session.

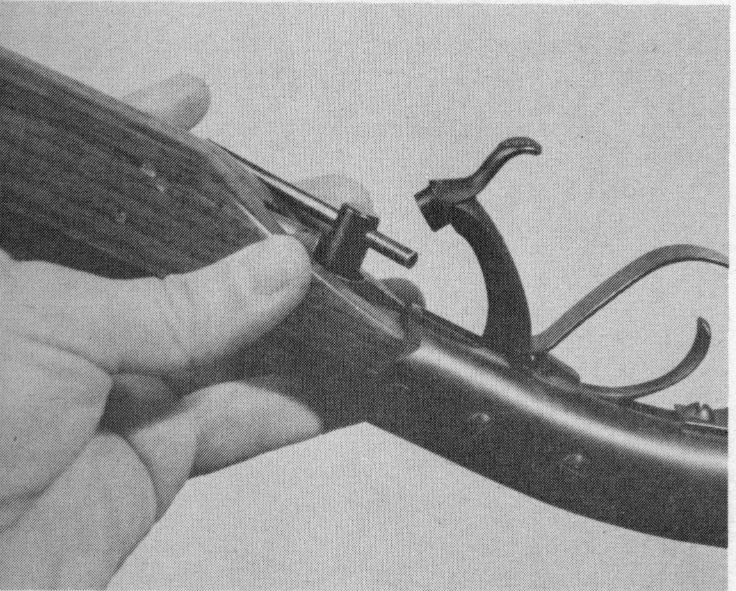

As a part of the black powder cleaning process, the nipple is removed using a nipple wrench, as shown here. The wrench should fit the nipple properly and not harm it. Also, do not over-tighten the nipple. This will not help hold the nipple in its seat and the thread may be ruined.

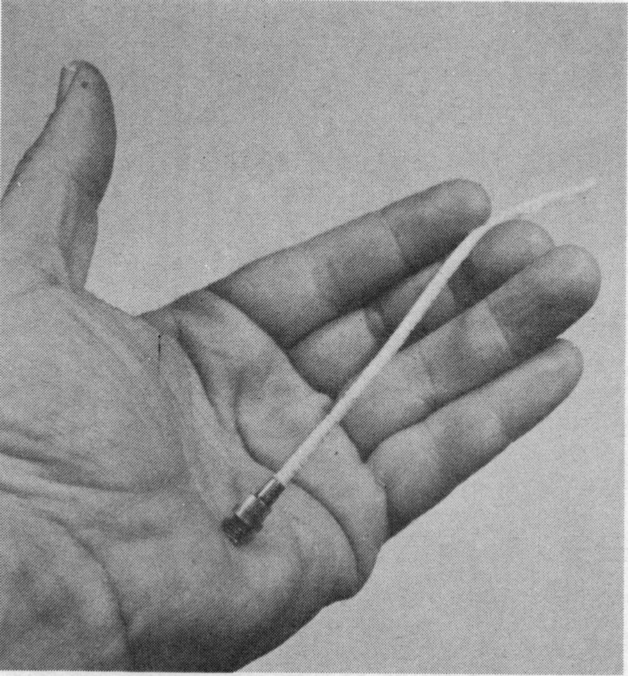

After the nipple has been removed with the nipple wrench, it should be cleaned with a pipe cleaner soaked in solvent.

ders tend to leave a bit of fouling which does nothing for the bullet/rifling relationship.

Black Powder Cleanup

The big news here is with the modern solvents. I have abandoned the hot water cleanup for most (not all) of my muzzleloader cleaning. I use the solvent method. There are a few differences here as compared with the cleaning methods described above, however. Therefore, we'll go through the paces quickly with a few fast steps to better black powder cleaning.

1. Soak a patch in solvent, such as Falkenberry Juice, and run this patch downbore. Use plenty of solvent here.

2. Wait for about 5 minutes.

3. With a dry patch, sop up some of the solvent in the bore. This may take a few patches.

4. Soak another patch in solvent and work this patch up and down the bore several times. Do not hurry. Let the solvent do most of the work.

5. Follow up with dry patches.

6. Try a few damp patches, just dabbed with solvent, in order to see how clean the bore is at this point.

7. Using a bristle brush, especially one which fits quite tightly to the bore, scrub the bore with several good strokes, being sure to touch bottom and also to catch the muzzle end of the bore. Use a dry brush unless the bore is very dirty, in which case some solvent on the brush may be needed. If so, be sure to follow up with dry cleaning patches again.

8. Remove the cleanout screw if there is one. Also remove the nipple from the nipple seat. Solvent will have gotten to the threads by now and this operation should not be difficult.

9. With the pipe cleaner soaked in solvent, clean out the nipple seat and the cleanout screw hole.

10. With a toothbrush and solvent, scrub out the hammer nose and the lock area.

11. Dry these areas with clean pipe cleaners and a rag.

12. Using Accragard or Tri-Lube or similar product, soak a pipe cleaner and use this to swab the lock areas, hammer nose, nipple seat and cleanout screw hole.

13. The bore is dried again, and then a clean patch with Tri-Lube or Accragard is run down. A light film is all that we want here.

14. Spray Tri-Lube or similar product on the lock plate and metal surfaces and wipe down well. Insure that all of the metal, not just the barrel, is free of fouling and lightly coated with protective agent.

15. Be sure to wipe the bore out prior to the next shooting session for the same reasons stated earlier, an oily bore does nothing for accuracy.

Use a hot water flush, per the old way, when the gun is truly filthy or on a routine basis. I try to clean my muzzleloaders with the hot water flush every now and then just to insure that I am getting into the little crevices and pock-

A solvent-soaked pipe cleaner is also used to clean the threads of the nipple seat.

Black powder fouling is removed from any and all locations of the firearm, and then the gun is wiped down with an oily cloth.

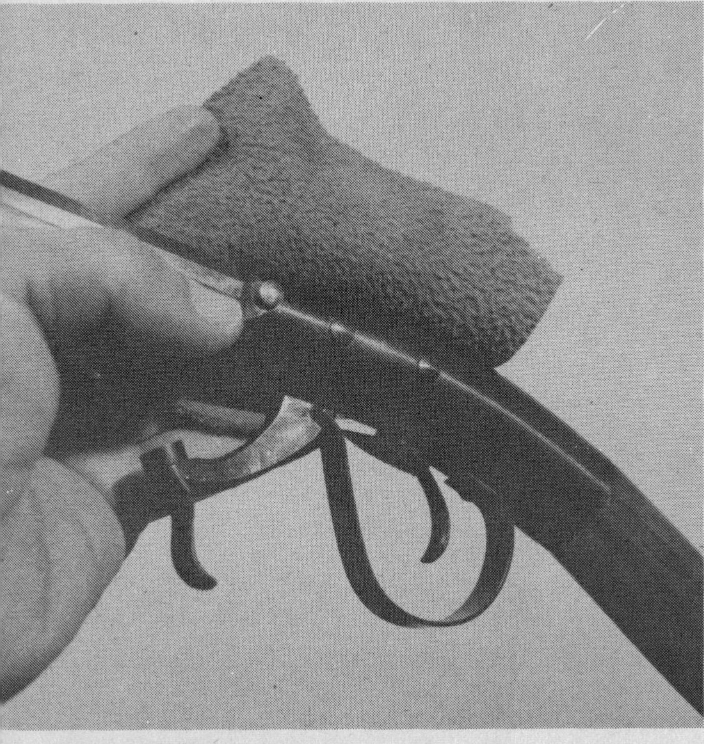

ets with my solvent-only method. I have no evidence of firearm deterioration with the solvent-only cleaning method.

The black powder handgun in pistol form is cleaned just as above. The revolver is broken down and cleaned with solvent, and the shotgun is easiest to clean of all, for it usually operates on the hooked breech system, the barrels coming right off for easy cleaning.

Maintenance

The idea of cleaning a firearm is maintenance in itself, but there are a few other ideas which apply, too. First, it is always well to safeguard a firearm from abusive action, so that extensive repair and refurbishing will not be necessary later. In other words, don't scratch a stock up, and the stock won't have to be refinished. But a gun is a tool, and a tool will be worn with use. So here are a few ideas concerning maintenance.

1. Keep the screws snug. Loose screws can cause excessive wear and sometimes in the wrong places. A loose bolt or screw on a big game rifle may allow the barrel and action to recoil in the bedding, thereby breaking down some of the edges of the bedding structure, perhaps even damaging the stock.

2. Use a bore light if the interior of the bore cannot be seen by removing a bolt. Check from time to time to see if there has been a buildup of leading or other fouling and if so get rid of it as stated above.

3. Keep the gun in a good case. And even though it is in

Alaskan Big Game Guide and outdoor writer Prof. Charles Keim uses a ramrod in a demonstration of black powder field cleaning when the wiping stick or cleaning rod is not available.

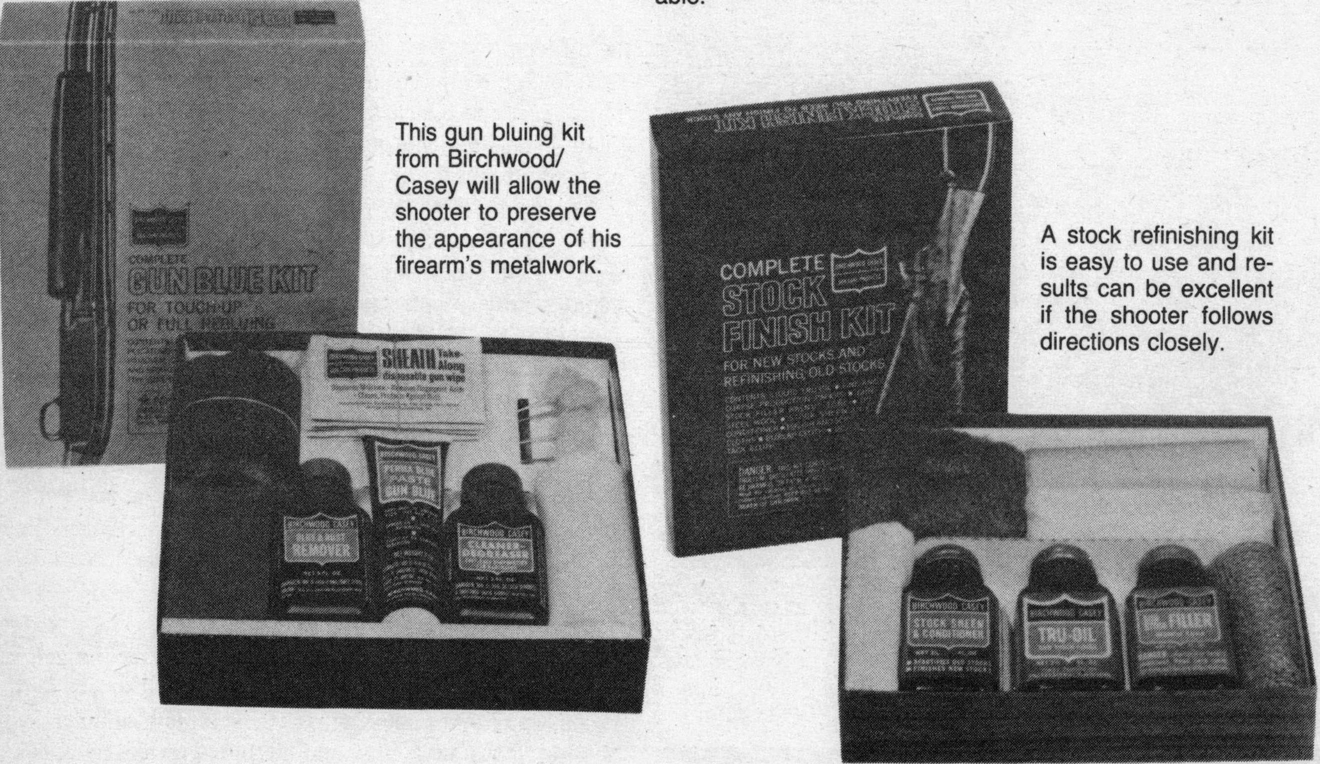

This gun bluing kit from Birchwood/Casey will allow the shooter to preserve the appearance of his firearm's metalwork.

A stock refinishing kit is easy to use and results can be excellent if the shooter follows directions closely.

a case, protect it with a silicone-treated gun sleeve.

4. Consider buying a gun maintenance kit, such as the one offered by Birchwood/Casey.

5. Refinish the stock yourself. You can do this. I am against some home gunsmithing, but a stock refinish job can be accomplished by the shooter and without danger. In fact, although I am not a gunsmith, I have refinished stocks myself to a reasonably high level of appearance. There are a number of stock refinishing kits to choose from. I like the Birchwood/Casey offering.

6. Blue your own gun, too, but do not expect to have a fully professional job. A nice touch-up can be accomplished on a small worn area with the new cold blue solutions. The newest of these formulas is really much better than the older types. It will take the shine off of an abused area very nicely. Today, there are also immersion style bluing kits available, such as the Birchwood/Casey Perma Blue[R] Immersion Kit. The kit contains sufficient chemical to do about 10 gun barrels and it comes with a plastic tank for gun barrel immersion.

Again, there is no blue like that provided by a full-blown professional gunsmith, but there are some instances when touch up bluing is just fine and other times when a shooter can do his own immersion blue job, too. The kit here is a good way to go because it will contain the necessary chemicals and a supply of everything needed for bluing, including good instructions.

The entire gamut of gun care and cleaning is conducive to firearms always being in tip top shape for the full life of the firearm, which is to say a very long time. Firearms are made to last all but forever, but they are subject to wear. Keeping the gun clean is one way to slow the wearing process and a reasonable maintenance schedule is another. Finally, it never hurts to occasionally have a professional gunsmith take a look at a favorite firearm. He should be checking for points of excessive wear and also checking to see how well our own maintenance methods are working for us.

Chapter 30

Shooting Safety

THE ONLY GOOD SHOOTING is *safe* shooting. The experienced shooter may feel that he knows all about safety, and that this chapter is a good one to skip. I have been shooting the vast majority of my life, including professionally, and would be the first person to admit that I do not know all there is to know about firearms safety. The material here has been garnered over many years. Some of it is very basic, and perhaps some of it is not. All of it is vital to good shooting—*safe shooting*.

Ten Commandments of Safety
(Courtesy SAAMI)

1. Don't rely on your gun's safety. Treat every gun as if it were loaded and ready to fire.
2. Never cross a fence, climb a tree or jump a ditch with a loaded gun.
3. Never load or carry a loaded gun until you are ready to use it.
4. Watch your muzzle so the other fellow doesn't have to.
5. Keep guns and ammunition separately and in locked storage.
6. Don't shoot unless absolutely sure of your target and what is beyond it.
7. Know the range of your gun. Remember, even a 22 rimfire can travel over 1 mile.
8. Always wear eye and ear protection when shooting.
9. Always be sure the barrel is clear of obstruction and only carry ammunition specifically intended for the gun you are using.
10. Always carry handguns with the hammer down on an empty chamber.

The Unloaded Gun

An unloaded firearm never shot anybody. In fact a loaded firearm never shot anybody. It takes a loaded firearm directed in some manner by an outside force in order for a gun to "go off," and yet people get hurt while cleaning or handling an "unloaded gun." The first tenet of good gun safety practice is to take any firearm picked up or handed to you and, with the muzzle pointed in a safe direction, check the gun for the presence of any ammo and remove it if found.

Really check it. If you are not familiar with the function of the firearm, then leave it alone until shown how the gun operates. For example, people have checked the auto pistol by pulling the clip and pronouncing the gun unloaded. Of course, there was "one up the snout," one round in the chamber. With a bolt-action big game rifle I learned to pull the bolt open and stick a pinky finger into the chamber. There could be a loaded round stuck in there! The extractor may not be able to pull it, but it could be there. I want to *feel* that there is nothing in the gun.

The tubular magazine, especially on the 22 rimfire rifle, is another which takes careful checking. One may pull the tube and allow the ammo to slide out, but it is very common for a round to be stuck at the end of the tube. The best idea is to slide the tube open or pull it out, emptying the contents of the magazine. Then put the tube back in and work the action several times while aiming the rifle in a safe direction. Very often a round or more will eject.

Cleaning Guns

Along the same train of thought, only unloaded guns should be cleaned. Really unloaded. Also, in the cleaning process, even though the gun is field stripped, continue to handle it as if it were a loaded gun. The idea of pointing a gun barrel *sans* action all about the room seems harmless enough, but safety is often a matter of habit. The habit needed here is one of being safe to the point of super-safety. Nobody can be *too safe* in any endeavor.

Loading the Gun

Some firearms are more awkward to load than others. I have watched people pinching a rifle between their legs while rabbit hunting as they tried to put new ammo into a clip or into the tubular feed port. In the process of loading the firearm, consider safety aspects by positioning the body

Loading the 22 rimfire rifle with tubular magazine is accomplished safely by getting into position first. The shooter is solid and he can manage the rifle as he loads it. Also, with rifle leaning back against the shoulder, 22 ammo can be held in one hand and loaded in with the other hand instead of fumbling.

in a solid manner and handling the ammo in a safe way. Of course, the gun must be aimed in a safe direction the entire time it is being loaded. Finally, the chamber is left empty until firing is to commence. On the range, there is no reason to be waiting for a shot while having a round in the chamber.

Tubular Magazines

Big game rifles with tubular magazines should not be loaded with pointed-bullet ammo. Although I have only heard of one actual case of a detonation with tubular magazines and spitzer ammo, this rule is a hard and fast one with no exceptions. As an example, a handloader might load some spitzer ammo for a Model 94 or Marlin 336,

Keeping the firearm clean is part of the rules of safety. This black powder revolver will receive a good cleaning. The method, as described in our care and cleaning chapter, is really very simple.

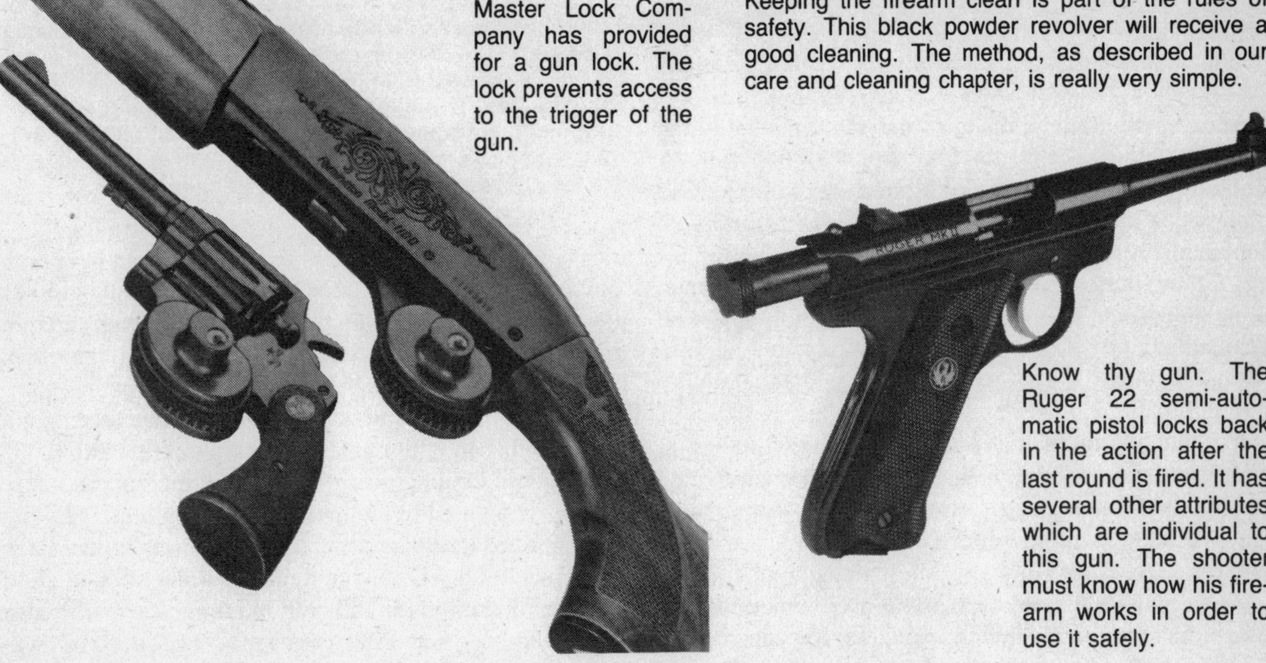

Master Lock Company has provided for a gun lock. The lock prevents access to the trigger of the gun.

Know thy gun. The Ruger 22 semi-automatic pistol locks back in the action after the last round is fired. It has several other attributes which are individual to this gun. The shooter must know how his firearm works in order to use it safely.

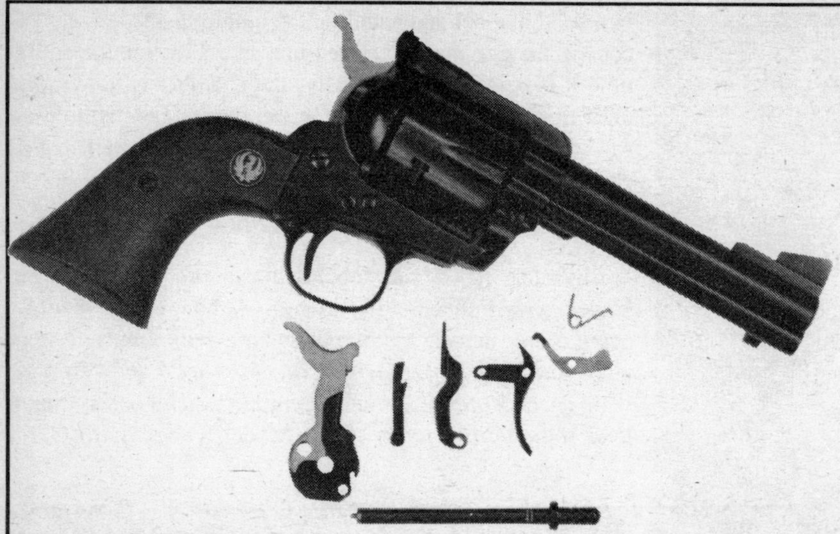

Here is the Old-Style Ruger revolver with the transfer bar conversion kit shown below it. Ruger offers a program whereby the owner of an Old-Style Ruger revolver can have the new transfer-bar system installed for mailing fees only. This system improves an already safe design. All Old-Style single-actions (regardless of make) should be carried with only five rounds in the cylinder; the hammer down and resting on the remaining, empty chamber.

trying to flatten the trajectory a bit. *This is wrong in the tubular magazine*. The point of one bullet may drive into the primer of the cartridge in front of it, setting that cartridge off in the magazine. Therefore, one must *never* load pointed bullets of any type in a tubular magazine.

Five Shots or Six?

A six-shooter without a safety block to prevent the accidental discharge of a cartridge lined up with the bore, should load only five of the six cylinder chambers. One chamber should be left without a cartridge in it at all, and this must be the chamber which is in line with the bore. This way if the hammer is whacked from being dropped or knocked, it will fall upon an empty chamber. The old style six-shooter, then, should be considered a five-shooter.

Fast Draw

Fast draw is fine for TV and for TV cowboys . . . and for the experts. There are trained experts in the art of fast draw. But the average shooter, the shooter who is not trained, should refrain from the practice altogether. A friend of mine, back in the days when a lot of people were interested in pretending to be Billy the Kid, fast-drew a 22 rimfire revolver and sent a bullet through the calf of his leg. He was lucky. No permanent damage. But the point is, it can happen, to anyone . . . forget the fast draw with a loaded gun.

Shooting Range Safety

The shooting range is designed to be safe. It has good strong backstops and the lanes are clear and unobstructed from the bench to the target. However, every shooter must obey the rules of the range for safety reasons. Each range that I have been to has these rules posted, and there is going to be a rangemaster around to give commands and insure that safe gun-handling practices are adhered to.

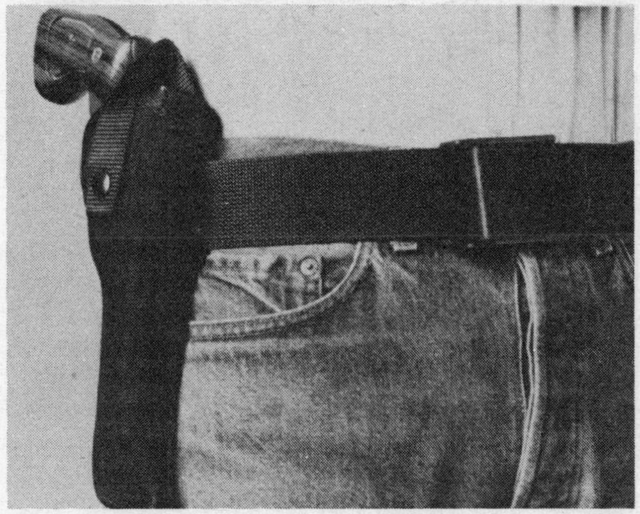

This Uncle Mike's Sidekick holster keeps the sidearm snug to the body. The topstrap prevents the gun from falling out of the holster as well. Note that the gun is worn up on the hip, not low-slung. This is where it belongs for ease of shooter movement. Fastdraw? Never! The art of fastdraw, with blanks (not loaded ammo) should be left to the experts who use specialized gear.

Obviously, targets have to be replaced, and without rules governing every aspect of changing these targets and other aspects of shooting, the range could become a dangerous place to shoot.

Also, only firearms in good repair should be used on the range with any questionable firearms kept away. Of course, questionable firearms in terms of mechanical safety should not be used in the first place, the owner not having any right to jeopardize other shooters. I was at the range one day when a fellow with a muzzleloader stepped up to the line. He shot once and with the *Bang!* there was also *Whiz!* The bang was the gun going off, but the whiz was

Range etiquette calls for all shooters to be ready before anyone attempts to set up new targets. If one person is not yet prepared to leave, the rest wait until he is. It is also good manners to stay attune of what's happening on the range so every shooter will be ready to set up targets at the same time. *Obey the range officer.*

Leave the "experimenting" to those professionals who have the testing equipment at their disposal.

the drum and nipple exiting the rifle at an obvious high rate of speed. Nobody was hurt but someone could have been. The fellow admitted that this was the second time that rifle had blown a drum and nipple.

Testing and Experimenting

Much grassroots testing by laymen is of dubious value. The fact is, I personally would not think of developing a new load with untested powders without having a lab do some pressure testing for me. I want to know what I am dealing with. Yet, shooters run tests all the time, sometimes dangerous tests, not only with reloading, but in trying to make things work when they were never meant to. For example, I know of shooters who have intentionally tried ammo in a firearm which was *not* chambered for that type of ammunition. That sort of "testing" is only a short cut to disaster.

Handloaders sometimes seem to feel that if they don't work up their own experimental loads, they are not really taking advantage of the handloading experience. That is false, and working up loads can be very dangerous, even when they are *underloads*. In one case, a handloader decided to make up some 270 Winchester ammo using the 130-grain bullet and about half of a called-for charge of H-4831 powder. He ruined his rifle. Loading with that slow-burning powder required a greater loading density and the underload was not safe. Handloading offers great versatility with safety. Just use reliable handloading manuals and leave the experimenting to the boys with the pressure guns.

Altering Ammunition

Another good way to get into trouble is to alter ammo. Not long ago, one could obtain a larger quantity of military ammunition, mostly 30-06, but plenty of 7mm Mauser, too, for a modest cost. Some shooters decided to alter this ammo, and its full metal jacketed bullets, into dum-dum rounds. It had been done before, they argued. Of course, it worked out in some cases, but in a few cases it did not pan out. It was possible to strip the jacket of the bullet in the bore, in fact. Leaving a jacket "somewhere in the rifle's bore" was not conducive to good pressure relationship with the next round fired.

It is best to leave ammo the way it was intended to be. Filing bullets down for expansion purposes is actually illegal for big game hunting in most areas. If the shooter has

Benchrest safety is partly a matter of obeying range rules. However, even when using a private benchrest setup, the rifle should never be left unattended with a round chambered.

Ammunition boxes carry many warnings which should be heeded. The warning Keep Out of the Reach of Children is well-taken. One will also find admonitions concerning extreme range. The "Dangerous up to the range of one mile," (or longer) statements are accurate, not an optimistic wish of the ammo company. Fired with the muzzle at about a 45-degree angle, a 22 Long Rifle can travel more than a mile.

some full metal jacket ammo, he should use it for practice at a range that has a good backstop. Non-expanding, full metal jacketed ammunition not only tends to penetrate, it tends to ricochet.

Incendiaries

The tracer bullet is useful for military purposes, but, with limited exception, tracer ammo is not necessary in sport shooting. However, at times the tracer round falls into the hands of sport shooters. The dangers of firing tracers in the field should be obvious—they present a tremendous, life threatening fire hazard. Tracer ammo, if it's not already illegal in your locale, should be shunned. It should also be said that the incendiary mixture in the base of the tracer bullet (that which gives off the bright flame) does the bore of the rifle no good at all.

Benchrest Safety

In my opinion, single-loading should be the rule at the bench. A bench setup is meant to give the shooter a solid rest. Firing in semi-auto mode from the bench is quite pointless. Also, there have been cases of a shooter preparing to fire and then changing his mind. He gets up from the bench, but leaves the rifle settled on the bags, still loaded. If a shooter leaves his rifle unattended for any amount of time, he should unload it always. *Never walk away from a loaded gun.*

Pellet Gun Traps

When using a pellet gun trap, stay with the heavy paper stock target usually provided. Do not switch to pieces of typing or notebook paper with a target drawn on it. There can be some fragmenting of the pellet in the trap, and the standard, heavy paper stock target will aid in stopping those bits of lead from flying back toward the shooter, whereas the thinner paper may not contain them. Also, keep your distance when firing the pellet gun into the pellet trap. Usually, a minimum of 30 feet is suggested. Wear eye protection.

Ammo Storage

Do not store ammunition in hot places. In fact, it's not terribly smart to store ammo in extremely cold places. The powder can change its characteristics after a while. Although the powder may actually weaken, it could also change into a more powerful fuel. And the breech pressure could go upward. Ammo should be stored in a *cool* (not cold) *dry* place.

While it is very obvious, we should also add that ammo must be stored where children won't be able to get to it. There may be curious and dangerous experimentation with the ammunition if kids have easy access to a supply of it.

Powder Storage

Powder itself must be stored with care. Powder of the smokeless variety is very stable. So is black powder when kept within the right environment, but no powder should be stored where it can get very hot or very cold, and of course, powder must be kept away from any open flame or excessive heat source. Never fool around with powder of any type. One shooter decided to show his neighbor that you could whack smokeless powder with a hammer and it would not go off. He adjourned to his driveway, poured out a very small quantity of powder and proceeded to "have at it" with a hammer. It blew up. Nobody was hurt, but somebody was sure surprised. Percussion will, indeed, detonate some powders.

Breech Heat

Forget about shooting long strings. Firing time after time with a big game rifle simply wears the bore. The breech gets very hot. But by all means, do not fire several fast shots and then load a round into the chamber and let it sit there. The heat from the chamber could, at the very least change the way the powder in the case reacts to combustion. At the very worst, excessive chamber heat could "cook-off" a round, your hand never having a chance to get near the trigger. So after shooting a string, let the rifle cool off and keep the chamber unloaded.

Train Newcomers for Safety

Children and all new shooters must be trained in firearms safety. Adults coming to the sport in later life are often given less safety training than necessary because they are "grown up." Being grown up does not mean that a person has firearms experience or knowledge. *All* shooters must be trained in firearms safety. Nobody is born knowing firearms safety. This chapter is geared to help in that training.

Gun Fit

It may not seem logical, but improper gun fit can be a safety hazard. I have seen young shooters trying to manage a firearm too large and too heavy for them. The muzzle may sway around and in fact point where it should not be pointed. Also, when a gun does not fit correctly, it can injure the shooter, not only with minor knicks and cuts, but also through improperly received recoil. If the stock of a rifle or shotgun is too long, the shooter may catch the heel of the stock on his clothing as he shoulders the gun. This can often lead to a fast, reflexive manipulation of the stock in an attempt to correct the problem. If this happens in the hunting field, and the safety has been moved to the "off" position in preparation to fire, that fast reflexive manipulation can lead to a life threatening accidental discharge. The gun should fit the man behind it.

Handling any type of powder requires respect. Although gunpowder in general is less dangerous than many other common items in use, such as gasoline, it is a substance which must always be regarded with respect.

Bore Obstructions

Few things will blow a gun barrel faster than a bore obstruction. Never, ever try to shoot anything free of the bore! Any amount of mud or snow could ruin a gun barrel if that gun is fired with the obstruction in the bore. Use good shotgun shells, too, to avoid obstruction from bits of base wad which could become lodged in the bore. In a recent test, I constructed simulated barrels under test conditions with supervised test methods. These barrels were very thin and made to show signs of pressure. They actually held up fairly well, but never to bore obstructions. Bore obstructions destroyed the test barrels instantly.

Extreme Range of Ammunition

Until a very short time ago, comparatively, the 22 rimfire round had a warning printed on the box. The warning stated that the ammo was dangerous to within a mile. Now the boxes for 22 Long Rifle ammo state that the ammo is dangerous to within 1¼ miles. And yet, the ammunition is not really faster in muzzle velocity. But the shape of some of the 22 rimfire bullets has been improved and the factory considers that when the muzzle is elevated from level with the ground to a 45-degree angle, a fired bullet could go the distance of $1^1/_4$ miles.

Big game ammo goes *much* farther. It is not uncommon for the bullet from a big game rifle to travel a full 3 miles in flight when the gun barrel is at a 45-degree angle. Because of this extreme-range situation, shooters must be constantly aware of their backstop or lack of it. Shooting should be done so that the final destination of the bullet is, as much as possible, fore-known. The dirt bank or hill without an angle to it will usually stop any bullet fired into it. *Use backstops.*

Shooting at Water

No rifle or handgun should be shot at or over any body of water. The reason is the obvious glancing of the bullet from the surface of the water. This "skipping" of the bullet is the same thing that happens when we toss a flat stone across water. The water's surface tension keeps the stone from sinking. A bullet striking a body of water is an unknown. The bullet may deflect and strike an unintended target.

Shooting at Rocks or Hard Ground

Bullets can ricochet off rocks or hard ground, too. The whine of a bullet which has not met with a proper backstop is a warning sign which nobody wants to hear. Ricochets are *very* dangerous. Shoot at no hard surfaces and in no rocky locales. Use a backstop that will absorb the fired bullet.

Know the extreme range of the ammunition you use. This shooter's Weatherby Mark XXII is capable of launching a 22 Long Rifle slug out to better than one mile.

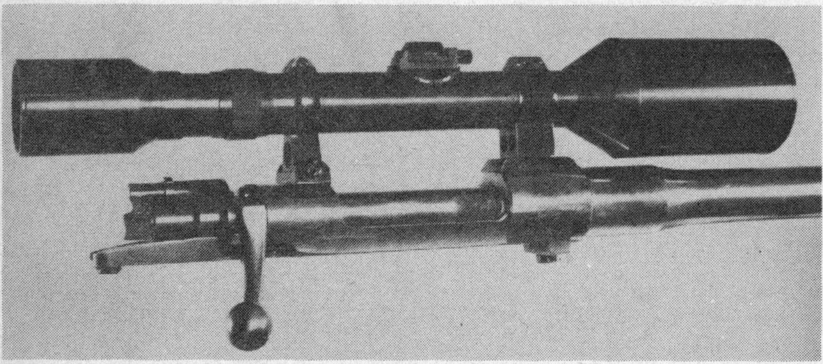

If you have any doubts about a new or old rifle's headspace, take it to a professional gunsmith.

Headspace Problems

The shooter should inspect his fired cases, even if he is not a handloader, to see if those cases show headspace problems. He's checking to see if the case is stretched, which is sometimes easy to see with a simple glance, or if there is a bulge at the head of the case or even a case head separation underway. Excessive headspace poses a serious problem, and a gunsmith can quickly determine the headspace of a rifle by running proper "go" and "no-go" gauges through the chamber. If in doubt on the headspacing of your firearm, take the gun to a professional gunsmith and have him check it out.

Never take any type of gun powder and store it in a can bearing the designation of a different propellant. At a later date, the resulting confusion could lead to a disastrous situation.

Overloads

The handloader who dabbles in overloads is playing with dynamite. The modern firearm gains all the ballistics it needs for its intended uses. If a shooter should require more punch, he should go up in cartridge size or buy a bigger-gauged shotgun. Trying to make a magnum out of a standard round is folly. Good safe handloading can bring out a lot of power from a cartridge case or hull. But the shooter should not try to strain out of a round what was not meant to be there. Stay with those loads found in reliable, current loading manuals.

Powder Identification

Handloaders must always insure that they do not remove handloading powders from their proper containers and store them in something else. Also, never pull bullets from factory ammo with the intention of using the powder within for other reloading purposes. Nobody can be certain that he will always recognize a powder by sight alone. There are some powders which look alike, but which do not burn at all alike. It is dangerous to assume from the looks of a powder that it is a particular number. Besides, factory-ammo gun powder is compounded to meet the needs of the ammo maker, not the handloader, i.e., the burning rates are known only to the maker—you won't find any loading data for it.

Handloading Safety

Load in a safe manner. This refers not only to the overload, which was already warned against, but also to other aspects of loading. If too busy to reload, save the task for later on. Don't load when distracted. Don't drink alcoholic beverages. Don't smoke while loading. Be sure not to mix powders. Don't substitute components.

Holster Safety

The holster is made to secure the handgun while it is being carried by the shooter, but somewhere along the line this fact was forgotten by a few designers and shooters alike. Even law enforcement officers, who might legitimately need their handguns in a hurry try to secure them so they won't fall out or be grabbed out of their holsters. Sportsmen should consider the same sort of protection. The holster need not always wear a strap, but it should be deep enough to insure that the gun will not fall out.

The Mechanics of the Firearm

All firearms should be maintained in top working order. I was in my gunsmith's shop a while ago and he showed me a rifle a person wanted repaired. The muzzle of the barrel had literally disintegrated through neglect. The outside of the rifle was rusty and pitted, and the bore totally abused. The gunsmith looked at it and declared that the only way he would fix the rifle was through rebarreling. Firearms are no longer safe when so abused.

The holster is a very important safety item. It allows for protection of the firearm, but mostly it keeps the gun from falling or being knocked out of the control of the shooter. This Uncle Mike's holster has the topstrap for added safety.

Knowing the firearm means studying the firearm's mechanical operation. This schematic shows the Ruger New Model Single-Six in its component parts.

Triggers are one mechanical element of a firearm which should be adjusted by an expert, with the exception of some triggers that do allow for owner-adjustment to some degree. Read your firearm's instruction booklet before attempting *any* trigger adjustment. If you aren't sure about the adjustment instructions, or encounter any problem, head for a professional gunsmith.

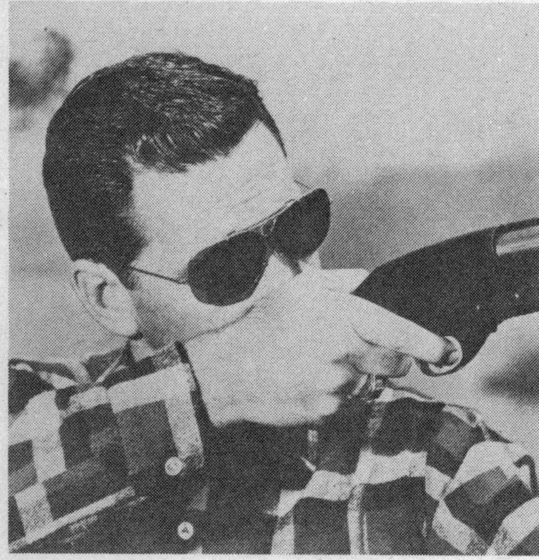

Bausch & Lomb glasses protect the shooter's eyes from gas ejection or other mishap.

Proper assembly as well as takedown is necessary for safety. This fine Weatherby 22 semi-auto rifle has been broken down for inspection and cleaning, and it must be put back together correctly, which is very simple on this model.

The Mechanical Safety

A safety is not always a safety. A safety, in some mechanical form, blocks the means of firing the gun. However, a safety is only a man-made device. Of all things that bother me at any range, it is the fellow who is not as careful with his firearm as he could be because "the safety is on." Incidentally, the half-cock notch so familiar on many, many firearms is not a safety in the strict sense of the term. It is only a notch in the hammer, a spot where the sear may be caught in a specific location so that the hammer will not fall forward upon the trigger being activated. It's fine and I have no qualms with the half-cock "safety," but as with any safety, the firearm should be handled as if it was ready to fire.

Also, a safety should be *used*. One prominent gunwriter once wrote that he did not use the safety because he wanted to know that his firearm was ready to shoot at all times, and he treated it so. *Use the safety*. Put it on and keep it on until you're ready to fire. Handle any firearm, loaded or unloaded, as if it had *no* safety, but always engage that safety catch or half-cock notch.

Assemble the Firearm Correctly

There have been instances of gun failure through incorrect gun assembly. If in doubt about "how the gun goes back together," take the piece to a competent gunsmith and have him reassemble it and instruct you as to the proper assembly/disassembly of the piece. Incorrect firearms assembly can cause problems. Generally, the guns simply won't work, which is not so bad, but sometimes incorrect assembly can cause real trouble. There was one rifle whose bolt could fly back at the shooter if not correctly assembled. That's one surprise nobody needs. It's also the sort of "surprise" that, under the wrong set of circumstances, could lead to bodily injury or worse.

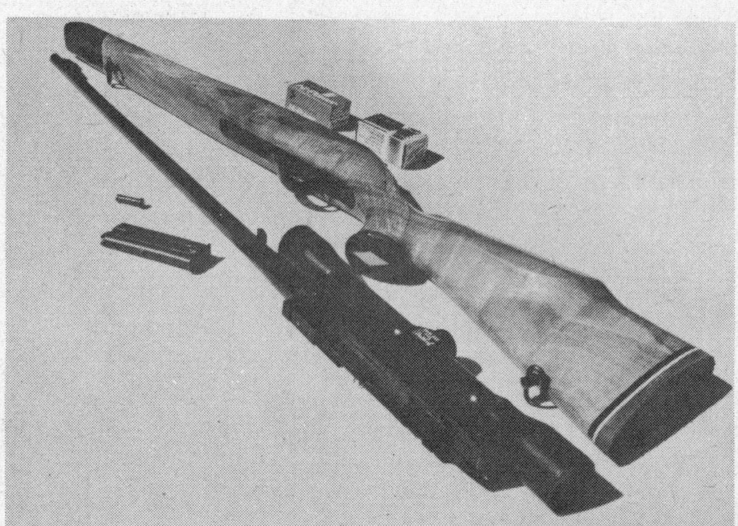

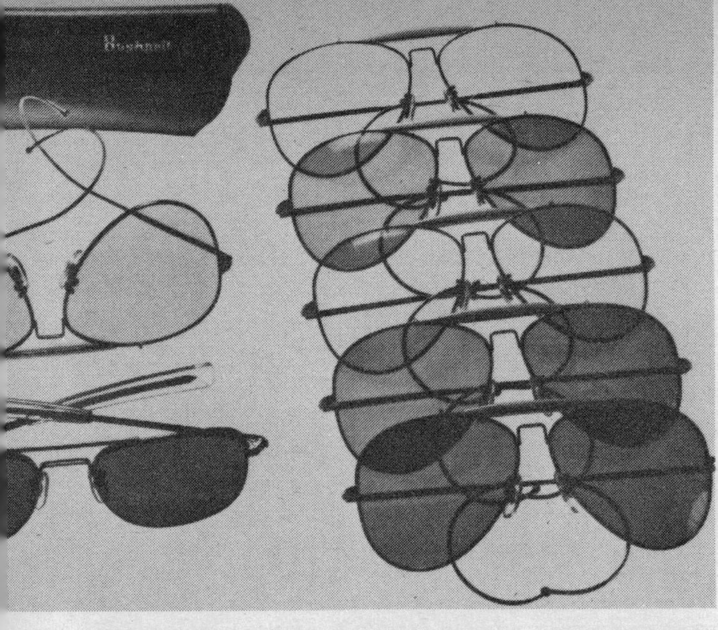

These Bushnell Sportview glasses are available in shooter's yellow, but also in gray and other colors. The entire point of the glass is having a barrier in front of the eye to ward off scratching brush or anything which could damage our sight.

Silencio offers a compact folding muff which only weighs 5 3/4 ounces. It is called the Silencer and will fit into small places, especially in the shooting box. Protect your ears now—not later.

Ear protection is vital. Use muffs or muffs coupled with ear plugs for good protection.

Eye Protection

Wear shooting glasses. Protective eyeglasses, even with clear safety lenses, serve to prevent eye damage in many pursuits. Take care of your eyes. Shoot with good quality safety glasses.

Ear Protection

Ear protection was no big deal in the earlier part of American shooting history. People did not fully realize that the ringing ears and unpleasantness from being bombarded with noise could result in, or lead to, permanent damage. Now we know. Unfortunately, it's too late to save full hearing in some of us who have spent a lifetime shooting without ear protection. Everyone should wear either muffs and/or plugs for shooting.

In the field, management of the firearm means having full control over it. Be prepared. If you sense a fall coming up, be ready to control the direction of the gun's muzzle away from a partner.

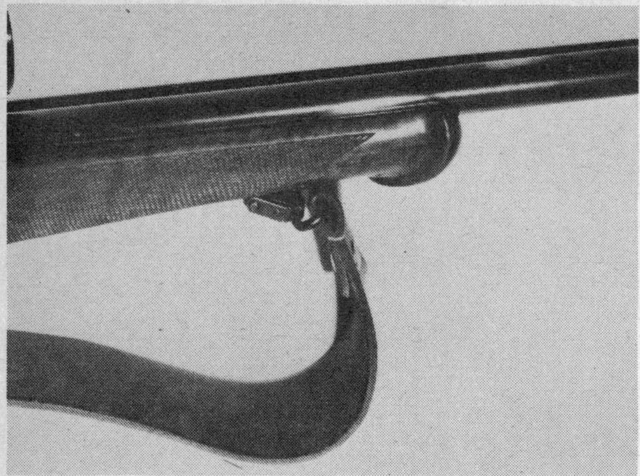

The sling should be attached in such a manner as to prevent it from ever coming free. The rifle could be dropped and damaged—or someone seriously hurt—if a sling swivel should fail to hold in the wood.

The Kap Kover is a device used to prevent a black powder muzzleloader from firing, even if the hammer is dropped on the nipple.

Firearms Management

The shooter must learn to manage his firearm(s) fully. The gun should fit, as we explained earlier. If a shooter cannot fully manage his firearm for *any* reason, he should get another gun. I watched a frail shooter firing a heavy, large caliber semi-auto rifle. At shot number three, the gun was really out of control. That shooter should have refrained from rapid semi-auto shooting with that rifle and/or considered the purchase of a rifle better suited to his build.

The shooter should also know his firearm inside and out. Fumbling around with feeble lines such as, "Now where is the safety on this gun?" will not do. It is up to the shooter to learn how his firearm functions, how it loads and unloads safely and what makes it tick.

Sling Swivels

Good sling swivels, properly installed, are not likely to fall off. And good sling eyes or studs are not likely to fail. But I have seen a rifle take a tumble due to the sling swivel literally falling off. In fact, the rifle was a handsome piece and it fell backwards in relation to the position of the shooter, the barrel smashing down hard on a boulder. Sling swivels should be sturdy and should be well anchored to the firearm.

Black Powder

Use black power or Pyrodex® only in the black powder gun. *Never* use smokeless powder in any muzzleloader or any type of black powder firearm. For added safety, try the Kap Kover, a device explained in the accessories chapter. Treat the powder horn as if it were a container for powder, because that is just what it is. Avoid sparks and heat and keep any container that holds black powder away from any sort of open flame. Do not pour powder directly from the horn into the muzzle of any gun. Watch your loads. Overloading is foolish and wasteful. Follow prescribed loading methods.

Chapter 31

Starting the New Shooter

TRAINING new shooters is much more than taking them to the range with a 22 rifle and telling them to plink the tin cans you have set up. In fact, the training of a shooter follows along the same lines as any other learning. There must be a method, with most if not all of the haphazardness removed from the teaching process. Also, keep in mind that the student is learning about tools and how to manage those tools. Give a person a power saw without any training and that person is dangerous to himself, and others. A firearm is also a tool, a tool with no mechanical problems almost all of the time. Firearms seldom fail in such a manner as to hurt anybody, unlike a few other tools.

When used without discretion, firearms are tools which can cause damage. The aim of the teacher is to prepare his future shooters so that they will be both safe and successful. The trained shooter will treat all firearms with great respect and endanger no one in his use of those guns. That trained shooter will also be able to gain the most good from his guns. He will know their function. He will hit the mark with regularity. This chapter offers a few hints for starting the newcomer.

The Guns

It's my belief that the best beginner's firearm is not a ''firearm'' at all. I'm talking about air guns, a subject we will address in a moment. If a true firearm is to be used as the ''first gun,'' I can only encourage you to start off with the *correct* firearm. If the shooter is very young, find or modify a rifle in an effort to provide the beginner with a gun that fits from the start. Yes, I feel the newcomer's first firearm should be a rifle. Why? The handgun is much harder to master than the rifle, and the rifle is easier to maintain control over when compared to to either the handgun or shotgun. But to give a new shooter a 22 rimfire or even an air gun which does not fit is just asking for a problem. Kids can start shooting *safely* at a very early age if *totally supervised*. I would not think of letting a six-year-old youngster handle a firearm *alone*. But I believe in starting young, albeit on a big proviso—start young *but right,* with safety measures always at the 100 percent mark. When it comes to gun handling, the best place to start is with the Ten Commandments of Safety as seen in our chapter on that subject. I now refer you to it.

Beginning with airpower is a good way to start. Young shooters do not have to cope with either recoil or blast with the air gun.

The Air Rifle

I still like the air rifle as a beginner's shooting instrument. Overall dimensions are manageable. Recoil is nil. Noise is no problem. Accuracy with the modern BB gun is acceptable and with the pellet rifle it can be superb. Neither the BB gun nor the pellet rifle is a toy in any sense. Both are serious shooting tools and must always be handled as such. The first point I make when teaching newcomers how to fire a rifle, and I have taught quite a number to date, is the fact that *I consider the BB gun or pellet rifle to be a very serious shooting tool*. In other words, the teacher should not convey the idea to his student that the BB gun or pellet rifle is actually a mere beginner's sample and not the real thing at all. It is the real thing.

The first lesson has to do with familiarizing the newcomer to the nomenclature of the air gun and its basic internal function. It is sometimes a little beyond the youngest shooter to grasp just how air forces projectiles from a BB gun or pellet rifle with such speed, but older beginners do understand the basics of pneumatics very well. Also, each part of the gun is explained, and I use the word "gun" here because by definition the air-powered shooting instrument is not a *firearm*. Tell your new shooter how each part of "the gun" works.

No shooting takes place before the newcomer has been fully versed in, and understands, the 10 Commandments of Safety. Before shooting, the newcomer must be able to identify his own gun's safety, how to use it, how the firearm is loaded and unloaded, the sights and their function, and the major parts of the gun. A newcomer who does not have enough interest to learn these raw basics had best wait a while (perhaps a *long* while) before doing any shooting at all.

Using the air rifle, I set up standard targets first. I want the new shooter to gain a sense of "group placement" right from the start. Shooting at tin cans, clay birds and water balloons is wonderful, but the first target should be clear bull's-eyes so the shooter can see precisely where every bullet has struck. Hit or miss is not the whole story. So with the air gun in hand, targets are used, basic targets with bull's-eyes.

If necessary, try to fit the air gun to the shooter. In spite of the fact that recoil is no problem, it is uncomfortable to force the fit. Fortunately there are models made to fit the smaller shooter. At the same time, the beginner is not always a child of course, as many adults take up shooting as a new hobby. Today, it is quite common for women to be interested in the shooting arts. Women shoot very well, of course, and in some instances I have found ladies new to the shooting sports to be better shots than beginning men. My older daughter took her first 13 head of big game with only 13 shots. I never had that kind of record to boast about. I told this to a visting greenhorn hunter and he laughed. I offered to lay a crisp $100 bill down for him to enter into a shooting contest with my daughter. He shut up.

The ladies can shoot, and if started with air-powered guns, then the guns should fit. They should be accurate enough so that the new shooter, young or old, will be encouraged and not discouraged by the results obtained. I start my BB gun shooters at 30 feet, shooting on bull's-eyes up to a full 6 inches in diameter. The newcomer does not often consider that the bull's-eye is too large for such close-in shooting. He or she simply gains confidence as the holes cut into the bull. But always stress quality results, i.e., tight groups.

The 22 Rimfire Rifle

The 22 rimfire rifle is my second choice when it comes to a firearm for starting the new shooter. It costs a bit more to shoot than the air gun and this can limit practice sessions, but it is very accurate and in some cases, perhaps, a bit better than an air gun because the shooter seems to respect the report and results on the other end more than he does the mild plunk of a pellet or BB hitting the target or the backstop.

The first thing I do with a 22 rimfire in showing a new shooter the ropes is fill up some aluminum beverage cans with water and set these 20 or 30 yards away in front of a good back stop. I then hit these cans with a 22 rimfire hollow point, especially of the hyper-velocity type. This is a lesson in *respect*. The exploding water and huge gaping hole in the can will convince anyone that the light recoil

Starting the new shooter with an ill-fitting rifle is a poor practice. This fine 22 rimfire rifle is of the full-sized pattern. It will be fine later on, but is simply too long for this shooter right now.

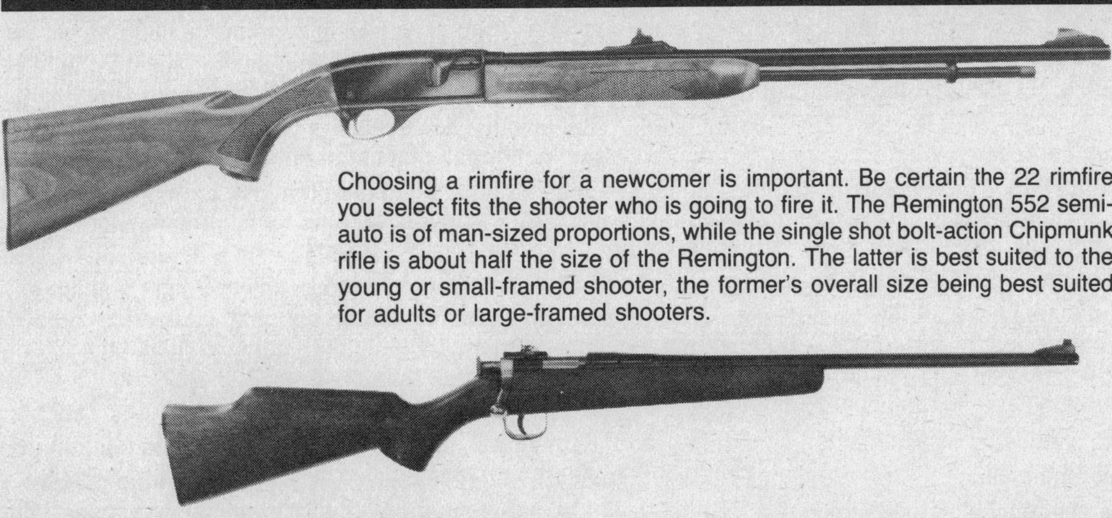

Choosing a rimfire for a newcomer is important. Be certain the 22 rimfire you select fits the shooter who is going to fire it. The Remington 552 semi-auto is of man-sized proportions, while the single shot bolt-action Chipmunk rifle is about half the size of the Remington. The latter is best suited to the young or small-framed shooter, the former's overall size being best suited for adults or large-framed shooters.

and soft report of the 22 rimfire is no indication of inadequacy of the round.

Again, choose a rifle which fits. This is easy today. There are rifles made to order for the smaller shooters and of course the standard full-sized 22 rimfire rifles for the larger beginners. Sights? I truly like to begin with iron sights. If time is no problem, I will begin with the open iron sight and progress to the aperture sight and then to the scope sight. I do not, however, hold this last statement as "the law." In fact, I fight myself on this because there are two ways to look at the situation.

If we start the shooter with a scope sight, he will immediately have success. He can see the target better, after all, and the aiming point is just plain obvious. Also, it is easier to teach arms control when using a scope because lessons in shooting can be confined to gun management, trigger control and hold, rather than iron-sight alignment. Calling the shot is much easier when using the scope sight. But . . . there is something to using the more basic sights first, too. I like the fact that the shooter can gain the concept of two-eye shooting much easier with open sights.

It is really too bad that so many newcomers try to squint an eye shut as do the actors on TV and in the movies. It is the wrong way to shoot for most situations and anyone who thinks otherwise should try shotgunning grouse with one eye shut. Now, as already stated in this book, there are some shooters who must squint. If it works for them, fine. But do not teach this to a new shooter. Give the newcomer a chance to learn two-eye shooting first. If he or she must close one eye in order to shoot, then fine. So be it. But do not prejudice the new shooter toward squinting.

The Big Game Rifle

Graduation to the big game rifle from the 22 rimfire or air gun is always a big step up because the shooter now has to deal with recoil in both of its factors, *real* recoil, or felt recoil, and the other type of recoil which is just as important, *apparent* recoil or that which bothers our senses and makes us flinch. Because recoil and blast are such big factors in teaching the newcomer his first big game rifle lessons, I *always* start with underloads.

Cast bullet shooting is accurate and in many cases can offer big game punch, but in this instance the cast bullet is especially helpful in producing squib loads for the beginner. There is no end to the fine, light, but accurate loads

When graduation from rimfire to centerfire takes place, the new shooter shouldn't be treated to full-blown, powerhouse loads. The instructor who handloads has a unique opportunity in that he can tailor-make light loads for his pupil; and, at the same time, the instructor has a chance to introduce his student to the world of reloading.

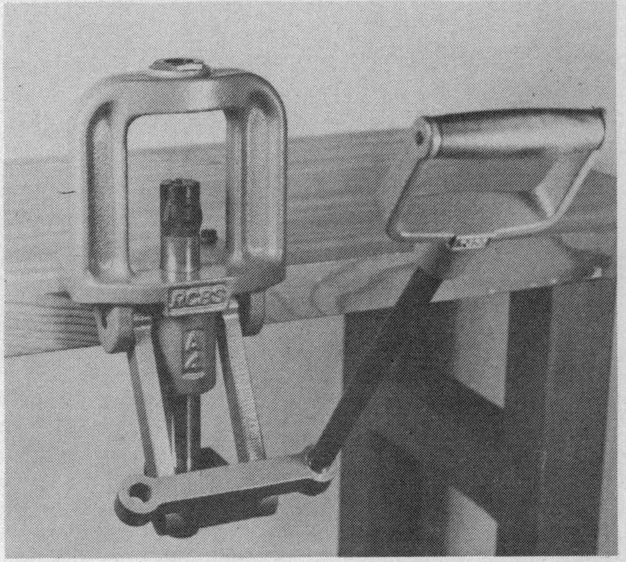

which can be made with cast bullets, and those offered here are a mere sample to show the reader what is possible.

243 Winchester
100-grain gas check bullet (Alloy No. 2)
H4227 powder/12.0 grains
Velocity: 1660 fps MV

6mm Remington
100-grain gas check bullet (Alloy No. 2)
H4227 powder/12.0 grains
Velocity: 1664 fps MV

270 Winchester
115-grain gas check bullet (Alloy No. 2)
H4227 powder/15.0 grains
Velocity: 1613 fps MV

308 Winchester
150-grain gas check bullet (Alloy No. 2)
H4227 powder/19.0 grains
Velocity: 1699 fps MV

30-06 Springfield
115-grain gas check bullet (No. 2 Alloy)
H4227 powder/14.0 grains
Velocity: 1358 fps MV

All of these loads were taken from the *Hodgdon Data Manual No. 24* in the lead bullet section. There are many other loads listed in this book using the lead cast bullet, and the reader may wish to check into them. The point is, recoil and report are both very low with the loads shown above and others of a like nature. The newcomer gets to learn his big game rifle without also learning to be afraid to shoot it. Later on, handling recoil can become a part of the shooter's experience and ability.

As for sights on the newcomer's big game rifle, I say go with the actual sights the person will use for big game hunting, which these days will probably be a scope. I do want my new shooters to know how to manage open sights and peep sights as well as scopes, so I use the 22 rimfire for teaching the use of iron sights.

What rifle to start with? The Model 94 30-30 has been famous as a first rifle for the deer hunter. It was my first rifle and at first I couldn't hit a Brahma bull in the backside with it from 10 paces. Today, one of my favorite rifles, and I have had a chance to shoot virtually hundreds of different rifles in my line of work, is the Winchester Model 94 lever-action.

I think of the Model 94 as a firearm for the veteran. Watch out for the dedicated hunter who owns and knows how to use it because he will come home packing the venison, and his cartridge belt will most often be but one cartridge shy when he does. I lived and hunted with some old-time shooters on the Arizona/Mexico border when I was young, and every one of them had a 30-30 Model 94. Every one of them got deer with this carbine, too, with no problem whatever.

But buy that new shooter a big game rifle which takes a scope sight, and I would start with the lever-action new Model 94 called the Angle Eject. Put a scope on it and the newcomer will have plenty of sighting power. Also consider the Marlin 336. It's a centerfire lever-action which has always been able to wear a scope sight without any special mount. And look to the 6mm class of cartridge in both bolt- and lever-action.

The Shotgun

Fit is most important. A 20-gauge is a good one for the beginner, too, but I would rather see a newcomer shoot a 12-gauge shotgun that fit rather than a 20-gauge which did not fit. Also, remember that there are plenty of light loads available for the shotgun, too. The reloader can make them, and there are some factory light loads as well. Give these to the newcomer. Forget the heavy loads until they are absolutely necessary for cleanly harvesting game.

What choke? I say straight cylinder or improved cylinder. It's tough enough getting the hang of putting that shot string on target without having a narrow pattern to work with to boot. Give the newcomer a chance by using up-close targets and light loads, with enough spread to the pattern to allow for some hits.

Under full supervision, a youngster has a chance to sight with a 22 rimfire Chipmunk rifle. No ammo yet. While this youngster is still at the air rifle stage, the wise instructor will take time to *familiarize* the young shooter with firearms.

By getting started at a very early age, John Fadala has been able to enjoy successful hunting in several states and in Africa. Here, he poses with a 36-caliber squirrel rifle.

Methods of Teaching

Teach the Mechanics First

Among the very first lessons should be those dealing with the mechanical aspects of the firearm. I want the new shooter to have some understanding of what makes the gun work, not only in terms of firearm function, but also in terms of internal and external ballistics. The very young shooter will not understand comments on pressure and rifling, but even the youngest shooter can learn two things—how to operate the safety (and the importance of the safety) and how to load/unload the gun. Before firing a single round, the newcomer should be able to clearly demonstrate proficiency in these two general areas. I have seen 6-year-olds do it—under strict supervision at all times, of course.

Teach Control of the Firearm

This means control in actually managing the gun, holding it, aiming it, keeping the muzzle in a safe direction at all times. This also means trigger control. Enough has been said about dry-firing already, but this is a reminder—teach trigger control with a snap cap or other protector, but do teach trigger control with a dry-fire method first. The shooter will learn the meaning of that all-important concept of "calling the shot" with the dry-fire method.

Instill Confidence

The teacher has a very important task in helping the new shooter develop his confidence. Praise the good shots. Talk about the bad ones, but only in light of improvement. Don't make the shooter feel incompetent. "Not bad!," is a lot better than, "Well, you shoot pretty poorly, but maybe there's some hope for improvement." This is important. It may seem trivial, but I know that the new shooter learns faster with praise than with belittlement.

Encourage

This is not the same as instilling confidence, for this particular aspect of teaching firearms management and marksmanship usually comes at the end of each session. With the adult or teenager, even the 8- or 9-year-old student, go over the high and low points of the shooting session, starting with the low points, but always end each criticism with a statement telling how to improve that specific problem which the shooter has. When the session is at an end, then encourage the shooter toward the next lesson. "You show promise. I'm looking forward to the next time we can shoot" is the way to go.

Patience

Always exhibit patience, even when you truly feel that the student should be way ahead of where he or she is. Flying off the handle is anti-teaching. It is counterproductive, too. Be patient. It may take a while longer, but if the shooter has no problems of a physical nature, there is certainly a 99 percent chance that he or she will be proficient.

Look for Physical Problems

I once taught a shooter who simply exhibited no aptitude for marksmanship. He could not hit a 6-inch bull's-eye at 40 paces with a scoped 22 rimfire rifle. It took me a while to catch on to the fact that the boy could not see well. I finally had him read the letters on the target at 20 feet distance, and he could only make out a few of them. Watch for any physical problem which may be hampering progress.

Teaching Stance

A whole chapter was devoted to this very important shooting topic. Without proper stance the shooter is certainly not going to do his best work. As for teaching

Start them young, but start them right. Nicole Fadala was on the hunt and in the field when this antelope was stalked and harvested with a muzzleloader. She took part in the work of field dressing by helping to hold onto the harvested buck for her father. The two hunted alone on the prairie—a good experience for a youngster.

stance, the coach should start by working on relaxation methods. Have the student sit down for 5 minutes before the session. Talk about relaxing each part of the body, starting with the hands and then the arms and head and legs. Then get started with the lesson.

Shotgunners simply have to learn to bend those knees. After the shooter has gained some confidence, I don't mind shouting out a command or two as a reminder. I have a new shotgunner in tow right now and we both understand that I am proud of his progress and if I say something of a negative nature, it's only to help. Because we have a solid teacher/student relationship built, I will toss the clay bird, and if I see stiff legs, I will scream out "Bend those knees!" at the top of my lungs.

When to Start 'Em Out

Very often the question of age enters into shooting lessons. At what age should a young shooter begin to learn the art of marksmanship? I wish there were a magic starting place, but there is not. Nobody can say that 10 years old is just right. I like that age OK, but I have seen 6-year-old kids who were very serious about shooting, and though they were always under full control of the teacher, they never exhibited a single dangerous move. And I have seen 12-year-old children who simply were not yet prepared to handle guns, even under strict supervision. There are some things to look for.

Interest

Please don't force a child (or anyone) to learn to shoot. It is really a waste of good time for both of you. Sure, try to instill the love of shooting. You should. Our task as parents is to pass on our beliefs and culture. So I have taught my children to shoot. But had they not wanted to learn, they wouldn't have been cajoled into lessons.

Aptitude

Just as interest can come along later, so can aptitude. If a teacher of shooting sees that his pupil simply is not ready in terms of aptitude, he is better off waiting until that person is ready. Everyone can't be a great shot, and perhaps some people can't even be good shots, though I have not actually met anyone in the latter category.

Responsibility

If a youngster cannot even handle simple chores without being told each time not only to do them, but also how to do them, I would hold off on shooting lessons. Even a 6-year-old can learn to pick up toys regularly or give the dog water. I would train no young shooter who completely lacked a sense of responsibility.

Maturity

This is more difficult to check out at times, but in general, we can see traits of maturity in a young person. A boy or girl may be 12 or more and not show these traits. I would be wary of handing anyone a rifle, except in a fully controlled situation, if that person did not show signs of maturity. In children, we see maturity grow with responsibility and with *training*. As an example of a lack of maturity, I was once offered the tutorship of a 13-year-old boy who would have public temper tantrums if he did not get his way and who expected to have everything done for him. I turned the offer down.

Oftentimes the "instructor" is the only person capable of determining a newcomer's aptitude, maturity and level of responsibility. Parents, and adults newcomers should choose their teachers wisely. Local, N.R.A. affiliated clubs are often the best place to look to for proper instruction.

Physical Coordination

This one is not too hard to see. The girls generally have better coordination than boys at those early ages. They can jump rope and play hopscotch and jacks very well in the earliest school grades. But the trainer should be aware of the student's level of coordination, especially for shotgun shooting.

Starting the New Hunter

The vast majority of shooters in this country will hunt at some point in time. In this society, procuring meat with a firearm is far from defunct. But hunting is a responsibility, and as a part of beginning shooting, it's well to take a brief look also at beginning hunting.

Teach Ethics First

Long before the young shooter goes hunting he should know why he is going. Reasons will be many, but in general I like to teach that the hunt is honorable and worth doing if done right, meaning stalking, shooting well and then knowing what to do with what you get, from field to table. Game cannot be stockpiled. It must be harvested. And it will be, in one way or another. Hunters can take a share in this harvest without any damage to the population. That is what game laws are all about.

Small Game

Start with small game first. Teach finding and stalking where applicable. Show how to lead with a shotgun. Concentrate on safety in the field, both in firearms and all other ways. Also show the newcomer how to care for the small game taken. He may not do the job the first time around, but after a few hunts, he should begin to field dress his own game.

Birds

Upland game birds and waterfowl are good possibilities for the beginner, with proper supervision. Field ethics are very important, too. Manners in the field will be appreciated by your hunting partners. The newcomer should know

Newcomers to the world of shotgunning should: 1) be started out with a gun that fits their general physical make-up; 2) be started with light-recoiling target loads. The more open the choke, the better.

Upland bird hunting is a good place to start a new shooter. The instructor will have an opportunity to teach the newcomer about the ethics of hunting and field manners.

that you don't shoot at another hunter's jumped bird and you don't give commands to his dog.

Big Game

This comes later. The new shooter must be able to manage a big game rifle with big game loads, and he should be able to handle himself in the field. Set good examples by not taking long distance shots at game and by making sure that no game meat is wasted. The new shooter should understand enough about the trajectory of his rifle/cartridge combination to know when not to shoot. And he should also understand that bullets don't break trees down on the way to the target. Get a clear shot.

Starting the Lady Shooter

These days a number of women are getting into shooting. They are very good, not only at the target range, but also in the game field. Mostly, gun fit seems to be a big problem as far as I can tell. Too many ladies are expected to begin a career in shooting by starting out with the wrong gun, especially the wrong big game rifle.

The same chain of lessons can take place here as mentioned above for the young shooter. Of course, there will be no problems in teaching the basics of firearms function, nor ballistics to the adult lady, but nobody comes to the sport knowing all about it, and it is right to relate the basics

Getting started in the field of hunting larger game than rabbits and birds is often best accomplished with pronghorn antelope. Antelope are plentiful (in areas of the west) and offer a good opportunity for the new hunter. The best way to start a new hunter is, however, on small game.

first, even to an adult beginner.

If ever there was a need for custom or customizing, here it is. Far too many of today's guns are simply too large for their owners, especially their lady owners. I had Frank Wells of Tucson, Arizona, put together a 6mm/222-caliber on a short-action Sako for my wife. The rifle has been super in the field. It is also the object of a joke on me. For years, right up to this book's writing, and for more than 13 years of ownership of the little Sako, I have said that it weighed 8 pounds with scope. In fact, this is the weight given in the 1977 edition of *Gun Digest*. It turns out that when Frank Wells and I weighed that rifle, the scale was off and the rifle was not weighed again, until now. It only weighs 7 pounds with scope, and that is on a calibrated scale.

So the lady shooter deserves a gun which fits, not only in weight, but also in other dimensions. I bought my wife a 284 Winchester for larger game, and it was purchased in the fine Ruger Model 77. But it weighed too much. Dean Zollinger of Rexburg, Idaho, had the barrel turned down to Winchester Model 70 Featherweight dimensions, and he restocked the rifle from scratch. It now weighs 7³/₄ pounds with scope and it is still very accurate.

Now that the featherweight rifle is again prominent from the gunmakers, I might start there if looking for a big game rifle for a lady shooter. The stock could be cut down by a professional gunsmith. Remember, cutting the stock back can change other measurements as well. A professional who does cut some length of pull off had also best check for comb alterations, too, and even for pitch. It's not a simple matter of chopping some of the buttstock off to make the stock shorter.

With the shotgun, the lady shooter simply must be fitted into the right model. It's bad enough to attempt to squeeze into the wrong rifle, but trying to get on target with a shotgun that does not fit is a terrible problem for any shooter. We men shooters would not like it if we were forced into shooting guns which did not fit us. Just imagine your rifle suddenly growing on you. Instead of a 14-inch length of pull, it is suddenly 17 inches long. Instead of 8 or 9 pounds, the rifle suddenly weighs 15 pounds. Our good shooting would be altered. The lady shooter deserves a rifle or a shotgun which fits first.

The lady shooter can also become a lady hunter. Nancy Fadala, far right, poses with antelope she harvested from over 200 yards with her Frank Wells custom 6mm/222 rifle. Daughter Nicole is already in the field with her mother. Onlooker is David Right, professional hunter in Zimbabwe, Africa, a visitor on the hunt. He was very pleased with Nancy's shooting.

The Handgun

The handgun has been left for last because it is, in my opinion, more difficult to master than the rifle and perhaps even more difficult to master than the shotgun in terms of doing truly fine shooting with either. All safety precautions are doubled here with new shooters because the handling/shooting aspects are decidedly different. One little flick of the wrist and the muzzle is pointing somewhere else.

So I suggest taking up handgun work only after rifle and shotgun have been mastered, and this goes for the lady shooter as well as the youngster. Today's many handguns are very safely made for the most part and highly reliable. The new shooter, however, should work up to the handgun after mastery of the rifle and shotgun.

Getting the new shooter involved in this sport is no big problem. It takes a method, however, not a haphazard approach. There is special joy in teaching anyone to do any worthwhile task, and shooting is no exception. With some careful training, the newcomer is soon hitting the mark with regularity. Just give the beginner a chance by putting good firearms of proper fit into his or her hands.

Chapter 32
Accessories For Shooters

THE COMPLETE SHOOTER requires and deserves a good many tools to go along with his firearms, and he gets them in many forms. This look at shooting accessories cannot cover every item a shooter may wish to consider as an accoutrement, but it is a look into a world almost as fascinating as the guns themselves, a world of equipment designed to enhance the interesting sport of marksmanship.

The Kolpin Gun Boot was dropped from production and then brought back by shooter demand. Its hard-case design makes it a good choice for those who want a scabbard-type gun case.

Gun Cases

Our chapter on firearms storage and travel covered the gun case to a degree, and this segment will not tread upon the same ground. The gun case, however, has been built in many styles for many purposes and the shooter should look to the hard case for ultimate protection. The aluminum body is expensive, but worth the price, and many plastic models are very rugged and more economical. A form-fitted hard plastic case is available in the Kolpin Gun Boot, brought back by popular demand after it was dropped from the line of good Kolpin products.

Soft cases offer protection from scratches and usually these are sufficient to safeguard a fine gun. There is also the leather gun case, very beautiful and a fine piece of artwork in itself in some instances. The scabbard is generally used to give the horseman a place to secure his rifle, but I have seen good leather scabbards used mainly for general protection. Then if the shooter needs to attach his gun to a horse, he simply grabs his rifle-in-scabbard, and he has it.

Today, the complete shooter has such a wide range of choices in gun cases that it would be impossible to list them all here. The idea is to decide what is needed, a hard case, soft case, a formed hard case, such as the Kolpin Gun Boot, or a scabbard. There are also cases for handguns, and for take-down models. The world of the gun case has never been more complete.

Glassware

As important as any attending item to shooting is the glassware. The hunter uses both binoculars and spotting scope in the field to spot his game. The spotting scope is also employed at the range where the shooter need not move from his bench in order to tell where the bullets

The Outers aluminum gun case accommodates two long guns. It is ideal for the hunter who wishes to take his standard rifle or shotgun along with a spare.

This is more than a tripod. It is the Bushnell Shooter's Stand, a solid unit designed for benchrest holding of the spotting scope.

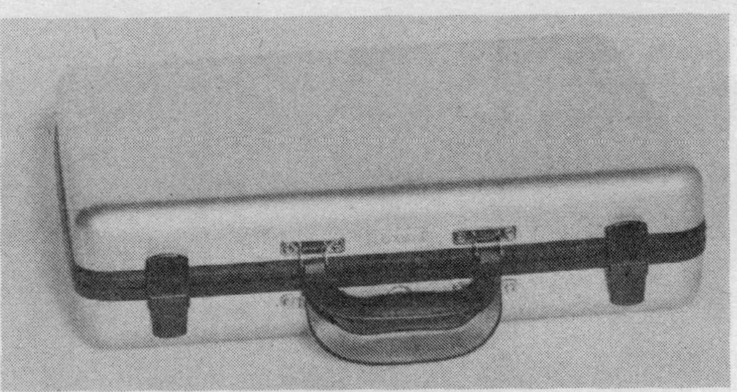

Outers offers an aluminum gun case to accept the handgun and its accoutrements. Some gun cases will also contain the takedown rifle or shotgun very nicely.

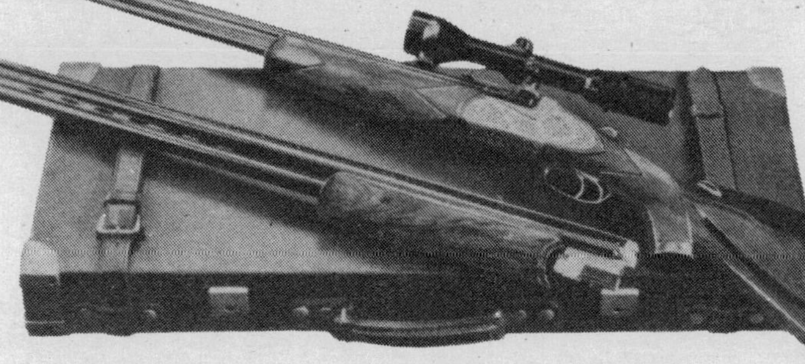

Note the fine leather gun case which comes as a part of the Emperor set from Armsport Company.

The Bushnell Banner Navigator 7×50 binocular is rubber armored with a built-in compass for the outdoorsman. There is also an internal rangefinder scale.

Variable power spotting scopes are quite popular today. Here is the B&L 15-60× Discoverer.

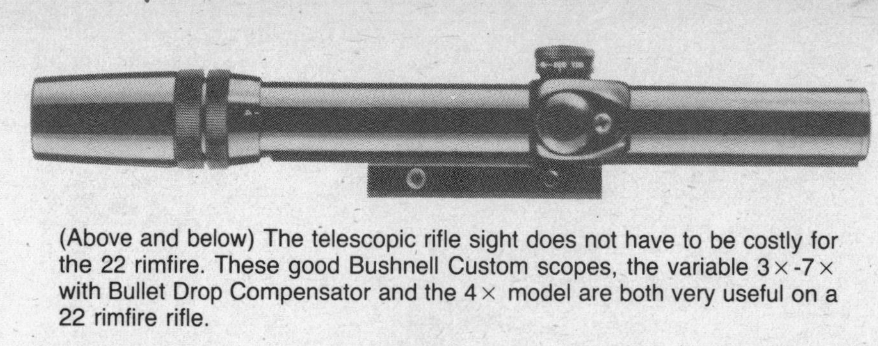

(Above and below) The telescopic rifle sight does not have to be costly for the 22 rimfire. These good Bushnell Custom scopes, the variable 3×-7× with Bullet Drop Compensator and the 4× model are both very useful on a 22 rimfire rifle.

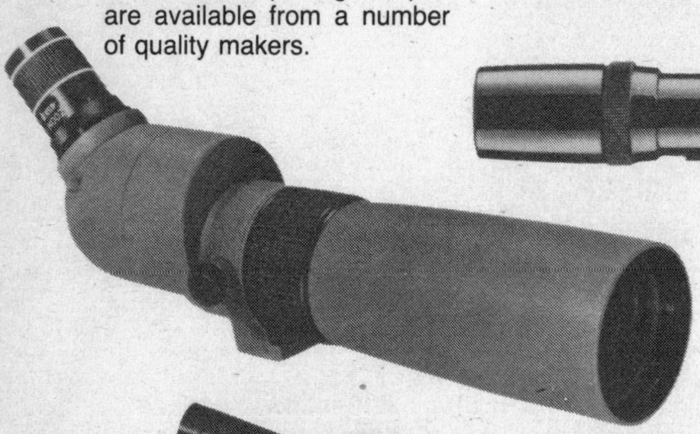

The 45 degree telescope is often useful at the shooting bench-rest. Spotting scopes are available from a number of quality makers.

Redfield led the way in Wide-Field scope designs. The models seen here have the Wide-Field feature and are available in fixed or variable power models.

Shooters who are also hunters find the good binocular a definite boon to their outdoor activities. These binoculars are from the Aimpoint people. They are 8×, 30mm objective lens, rubber armored and waterproof.

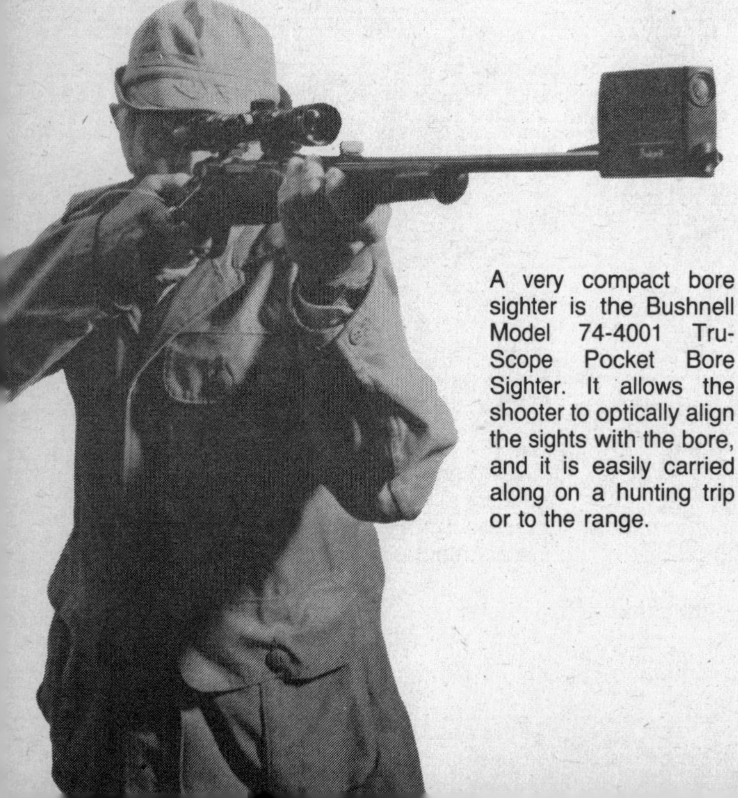

A very compact bore sighter is the Bushnell Model 74-4001 Tru-Scope Pocket Bore Sighter. It allows the shooter to optically align the sights with the bore, and it is easily carried along on a hunting trip or to the range.

entered the target. A good spotting scope, somewhere in the range of 15x up, will show bullet holes at 200 yards and more without much trouble, especially if the optical quality of the scope is up to par. There is also an instrument for bore sighting which is an optical aid and another member of the glassware family. Shooting glasses with protective lenses keep dust and debris from getting into the shooter's eye, and of course, there is the riflescope which has been expanded in recent times to find its way atop the handgun as well. The older pistol shooter who opts for a scope will have an optical aid when it comes to focusing at pistol-range distances. There are the mounts which attach the scopes to the guns as part of the glassware accessory system and tripods for spotting scopes.

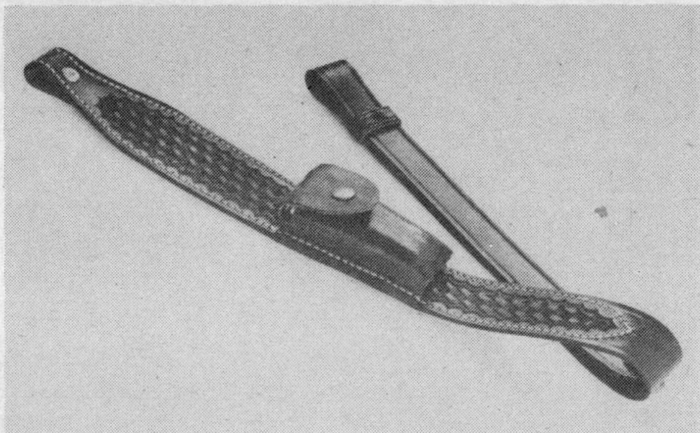

Many of today's "slings" aren't slings at all. Seen here is a Bianchi Cobra Rifle Strap complete with ammo pouch. The generous width of the strap makes for comfortable carrying.

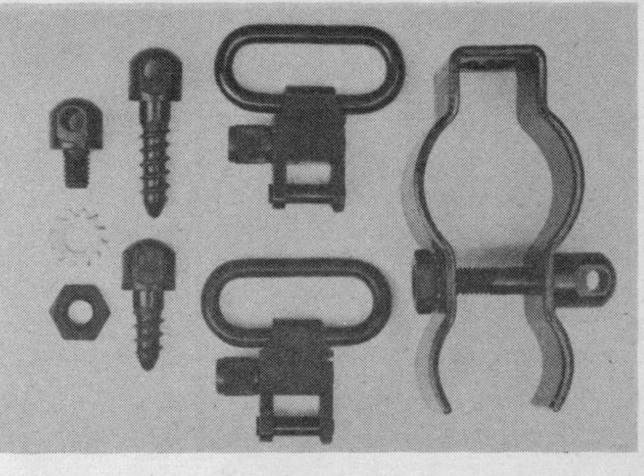

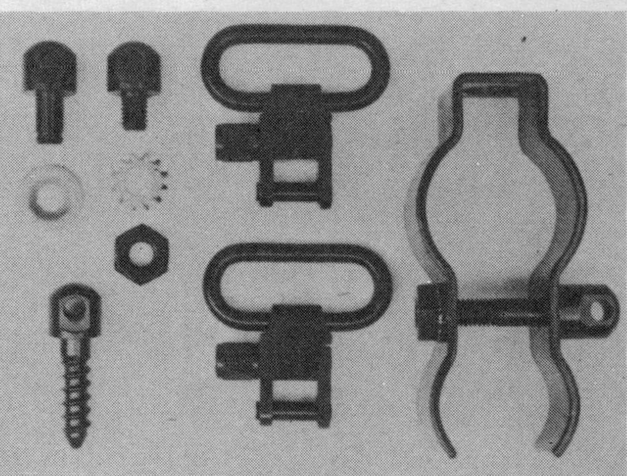

(Upper right and right) The shotgun has not been left out of the swivel picture. Uncle Mike's Universal Sling Swivel Set accommodates law enforcement type shotguns. Uncle Mike's also offers swivel sets for slug guns.

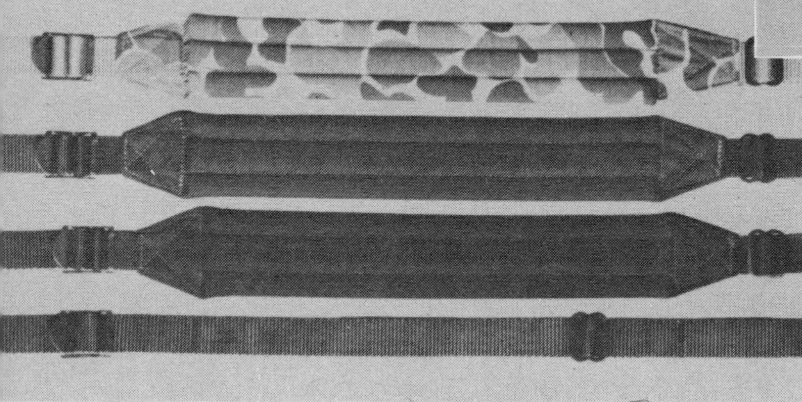

Michaels of Oregon is offering these nylon web gunslings. These are reasonably priced, long-lasting and they are also available in padded models.

Michaels of Oregon offers the Super Swivel, which has a positive locking system. It is a fine, secure unit for the big game rifle.

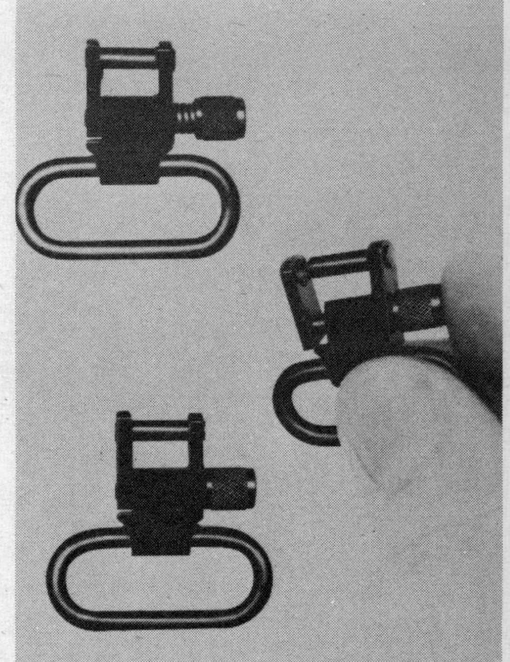

Slings and Swivels

The firearm must be carried, and toting it in the hand is not always the comfortable way to go, nor the safest way if the shooter is trying to negotiate rough terrain. There are literally dozens of variations among sling styles and quite a number of variations among swivels as well. The obvious choice is that which fits both the sling and the firearm in question. But a shooter does have to look at a few other avenues, too.

Carrying sling or military type sling? I think that the everyday shooter should look to the carrying sling. If it is not too elaborate, it can be made to serve as a shooting device by simply slipping the left elbow through the sling

Some of the finest and most reasonably priced slings on the market come from the Hunter Leather Company. Hunter makes a wide selection of slings. Seen here is a modified military-type sling. It works.

for a right-handed shooter. This puts tension on the sling and steadies the rifle. As for swivels, all I ask is that they hold. I can recall a fine rifle falling and hitting a boulder because a sling swivel gave way. Not terribly long ago, it was difficult to find slings and swivels for a few guns, but today the variety is very good.

Black Powder Guns

The black powder firearm is attended by more accessories than an old king was in his court. There are tools for almost anything you can think of, from priming horns to nipple and vent picks. One way to obtain very fine and authentic-looking accoutrements for black powder shooting is through a custom-maker, such as William Knight, who is at 541½ Moss St., Reading, PA 19604. Bill makes museum quality black powder accessories. So do other black powder artisans.

In the main, a loading rod is going to be needed for the black powder frontloader. The loading rod is much stronger than the normal ramrod which is held in the pipes underneath the barrel of the muzzleloading rifle or shotgun, and it is a cleaning rod as well. I insist that mine have special muzzle protectors, and that is not a heavy demand these days, for many of the newer cleaning rods do have these. Beware that the rod is strong enough to act as an actual loading rod, however. Putting a good load down the bore of a longrifle is a pressure-push if ever there was one.

A rod made especially for black powder shooting is desirable. A particularly good one is the N&W rod from N&W Products, RR 1, Box 38, Philipsburg, PA 16866. The reason I am giving the reader addresses here and seldom elsewhere is the fact that many times fine black powder articles are *not* for sale at the local gunshop, and yet the reader owes it to himself to obtain these items. Therefore, a few addresses are included here.

Another handy accoutrement is the Kap Kover. This is an item of safety more than dress, believe me. It is designed to keep water out of the nipple area, which it does through a neoprene ring. It also prevents the hammer from falling upon a percussion cap. Therefore, its safety function is very high on my list. The Kap Kover is for sale from K&M Industries, Inc., Box E, Elk River, ID 83827.

The short starter is necessary, too, for those tight projectile loads. There are many good short starters, such as the Uncle Mike's unit, which can often be found at the local gunshop, and there is also the Forster model with muzzle protector, made by Forster Products, 82 E. Lanark Ave, Lanark, IL 61046. The same company produces the Tap-

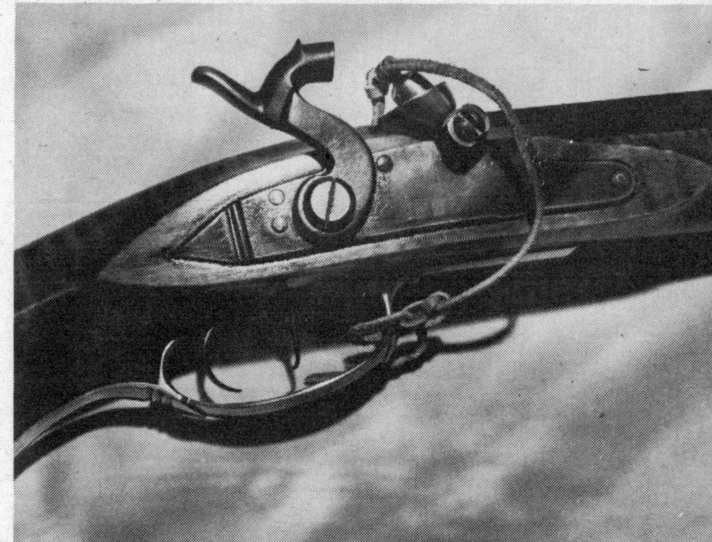

The Kap Kover is a device offered by the K&M Co, Box 151, Elk River, ID 83827. It is one of the most foolproof means of making certain that water does not enter the nipple area and create a misfire or hangfire. Also, the Kap Kover is a safety device, for with it properly in place, the hammer nose will not make contact with the percussion cap on the nipple.

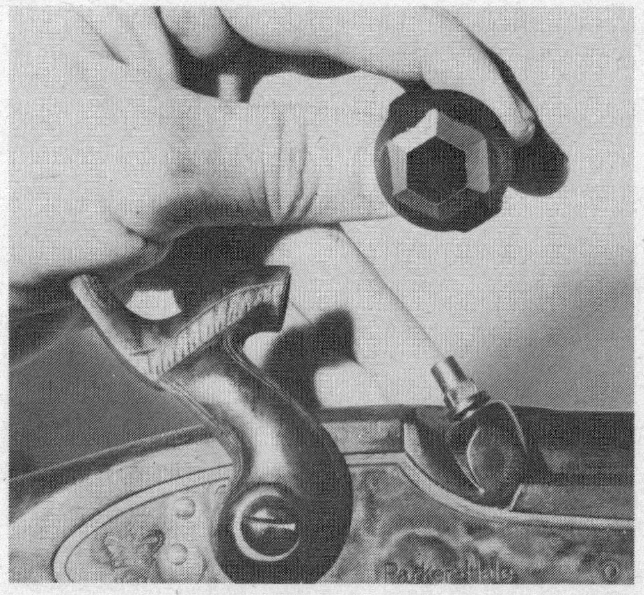

This well-made patch cutter for the fine Parker-Hale Whitworth target rifle comes from the Navy Arms Company, as does the accurate Whitworth.

The patch cutter is from Forster. It has a very sharp cutting edge which, when rotated, slices out a cloth patch.

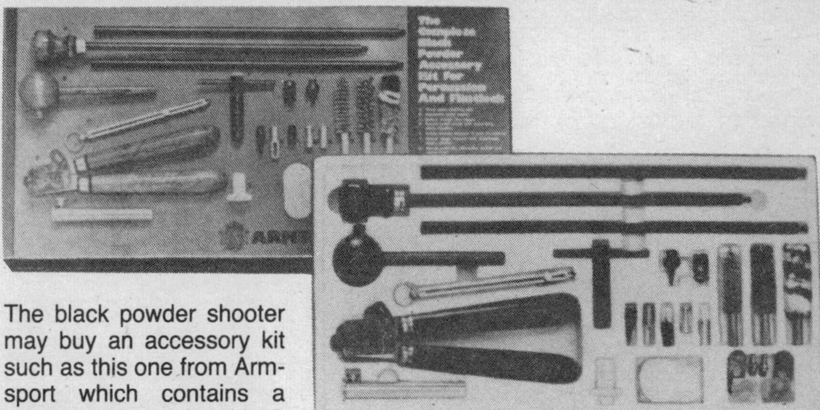

The black powder shooter may buy an accessory kit such as this one from Armsport which contains a number of useful black powder shooting accessories, including cleaning apparatus.

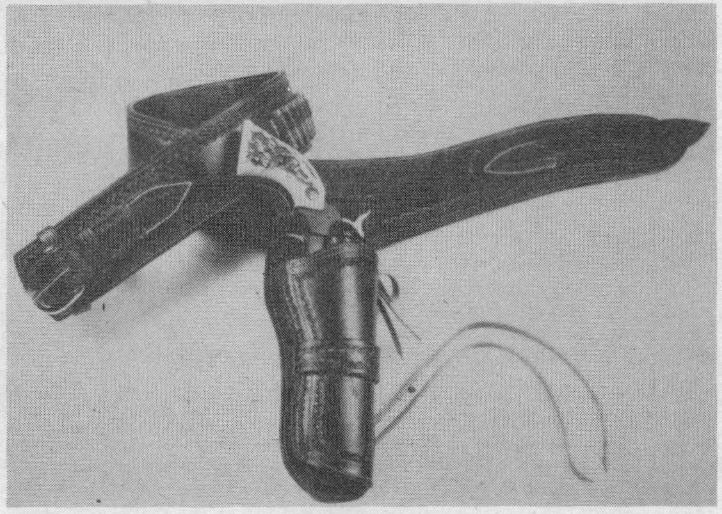

The western type holster is a very beautiful leather design. It can allow for safe carrying as long as the handgun is inserted properly. However, it is advised that a loop of leather lace be attached over the hammer spur to insure that the gun will not fall out of the holster.

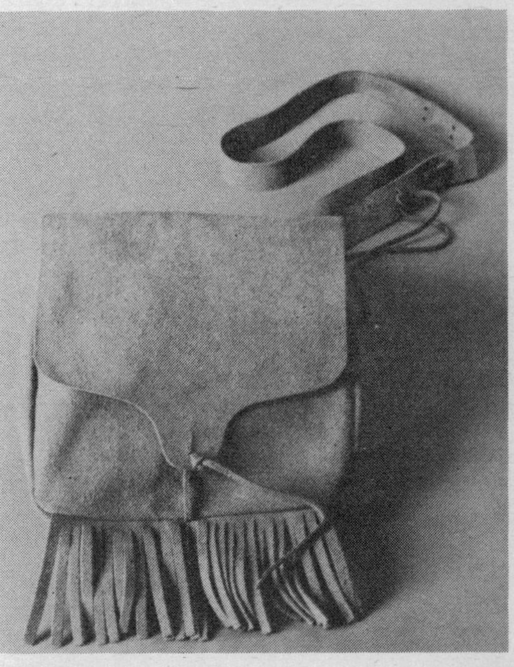

The "Possibles Bag" from Uncle Mike's is a shooting pouch designed to hold a good number of black powder shooting accessories.

O-Cap unit which is an instrument for making percussion caps out of toy caps and aluminum beverage cans. Also from Forster is the patch cutter. I would look at their Muzzleloader Kit, which contains the short starter, patch cutter and loading block.

Navy Arms Company has more accoutrements than Bayer has aspirin tablets it seems. If there is any desired accessory for black powder shooting, from a small handsome powder horn, to a special shotgun flask, Navy Arms has it, and in good quality, too. They are located at 689 Bergen Blvd., Ridgefield, NJ 07657.

Everything from special powder measures to cappers and patches and nipples can be obtained from Armsport, Inc., POB 523066, Miami, FL 33122. Retail black powder shops which specialize in muzzleloading accoutrements are also fine places to locate special gear. I picked up a very good flash cup recently, which is a device that attaches to the base of the nipple. It diverts sparks from the wood on the rifle. Powder horns may be obtained at the local shop, or may be special handmade items.

The list simply goes on, because the black powder shooter may need a worm to extract a stuck patch, or a screw to withdraw a stuck ball. A shooting pouch may also be needed. The world of black powder shooting is replete with accoutrements and the shooter should gather up those tools which make muzzleloading easier and safer.

Holsters

The holster is much more than a carrying device for the handgun. It is also a safety device. Today's holsters are

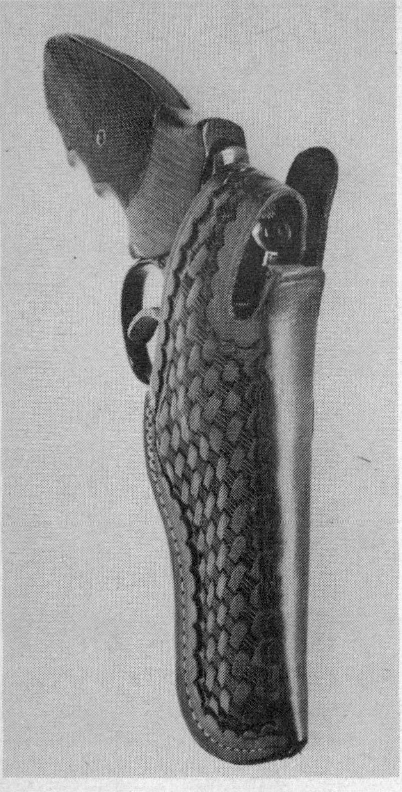

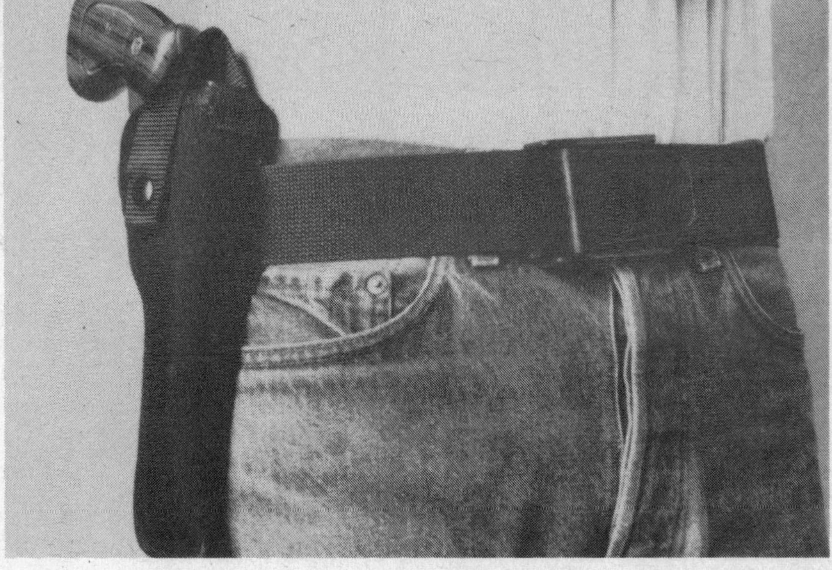

Using a matching belt of nylon material, the Uncle Mike's holster is positioned for safety and ease of withdrawl.

Bianchi offers a complete, beautifully made line of holsters. Seen here is a Thumb Snap model for revolvers. The Thumb-Snap feature is also available in many Bianchi holsters made for semi-autos.

(Right) Although this holster seems to allow a good deal of handgun to remain uncovered, it is a very secure arrangement because of its design, and yet it offers rapid withdrawal of the revolver.

(Left) Ruger's holster offers a flap and a good safety catch.

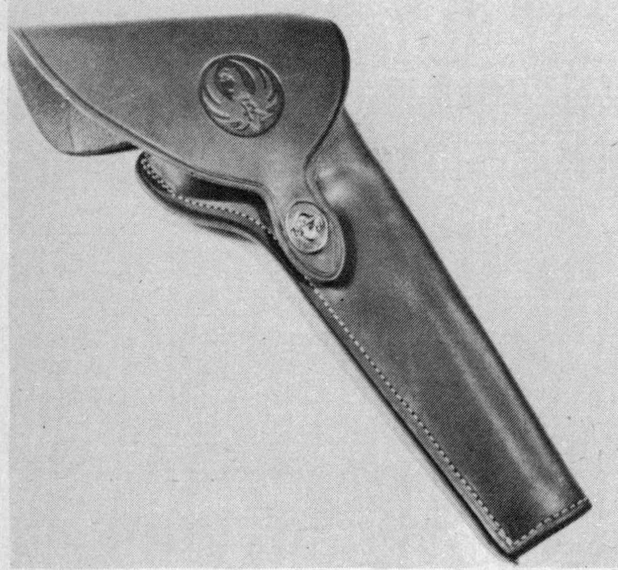

well-made and well-designed, not only for allowing easy access to the firearm, but also for securing the handgun. As always, appropriateness is the key to picking the right holster. First, and most obvious of all, is the fact that the holster has to be of the right size and shape to fit the handgun. But it must also be of the right style depending upon what the shooter wants to do with the handgun. A shoulder holster can be just right, even for a big hunting handgun. Or a closed-type holster with a flap might be just right for another shooter's needs. Pick the holster to do the job, of course. It's that simple, and that complicated, because there truly are many different holsters these days to select from, even in terms of materials. It was once a case of "leather-only." Now it is still leather, but there are some fine nylon holsters available, too, non-scratch and tough.

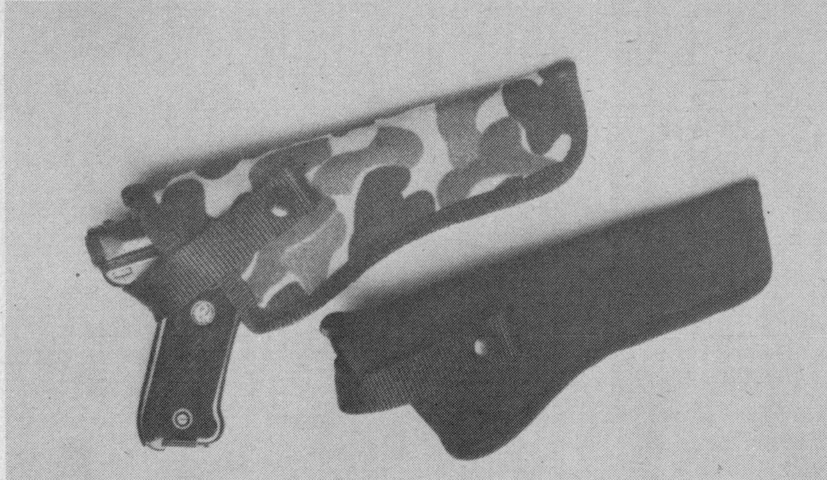

The Unlce Mike's Sidekick holster, offered in camouflage design or black, is made of nylon. It's a modern design and a good one.

(Right) The Tour de Force shooting bench allows a shooter to go to his favorite spot and still have benchrest solidity with him. It is very portable.

Oehler offers the Chronotach chronograph with a new set of Skyscreens which allows for ease of use. It's a fine model for anyone who really wants to know what his loads are obtaining ballistically from his own firearms.

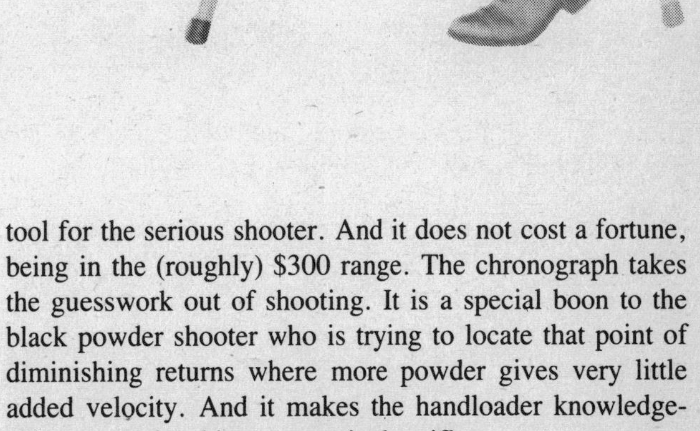

Miscellaneous Accessories

We could easily list another 200 items. As stated early in this chapter, the sport of shooting is attended by a great many accessories. However, instead of trying to name all of the available shooting accessories, I will close with a select few items of note, items which have proved noteworthy to a great many of us over the years.

1. The Tour de Force Shooting Bench is included because it gives the shooter an option he may truly enjoy, that of having truly portable benchrest which can go along to a favorite shooting site. It is made of good materials and it's sturdy. Contact Tour de Force at POB 82, Williams, OR 97544.

2. The Oehler Model 33 Chronotach is a particularly fine tool for the serious shooter. And it does not cost a fortune, being in the (roughly) $300 range. The chronograph takes the guesswork out of shooting. It is a special boon to the black powder shooter who is trying to locate that point of diminishing returns where more powder gives very little added velocity. And it makes the handloader knowledgeable concerning his own particular rifles.

3. The Sugar Creek Handgun Rest has been in my use for several years and its rugged construction has helped it survive the rough roads which lead to some of my favorite shooting spots. It is a very well made outfit and comes from the company of the same name at Highway 34 East, Ottumwa, Iowa 52501.

4. Hoppes is offering a number of fine shooting rests and bags. These are well-distributed and need no address at-

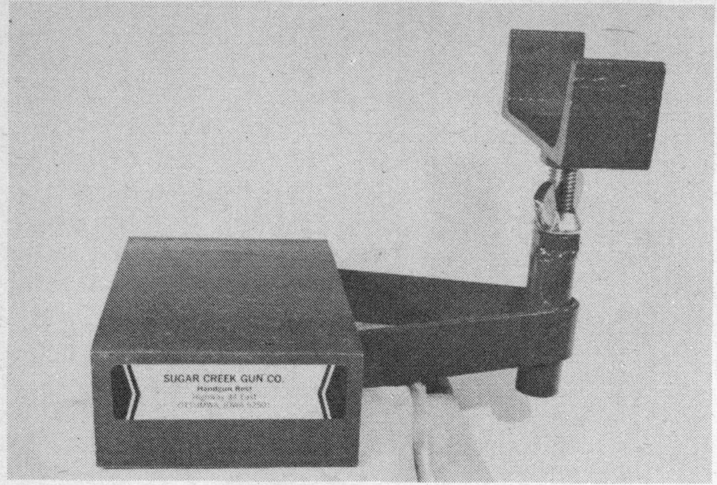

The Sugar Creek Handgun Rest is a model which has held up very well for the author. It allows good steady handgun shooting.

The RCBS Pistol Ammo-Crafter is another of the kits which gives the reloader a number of useful items at a good price.

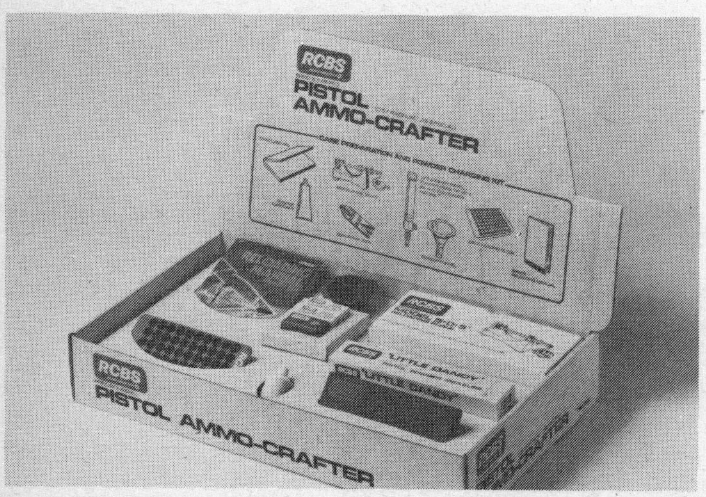

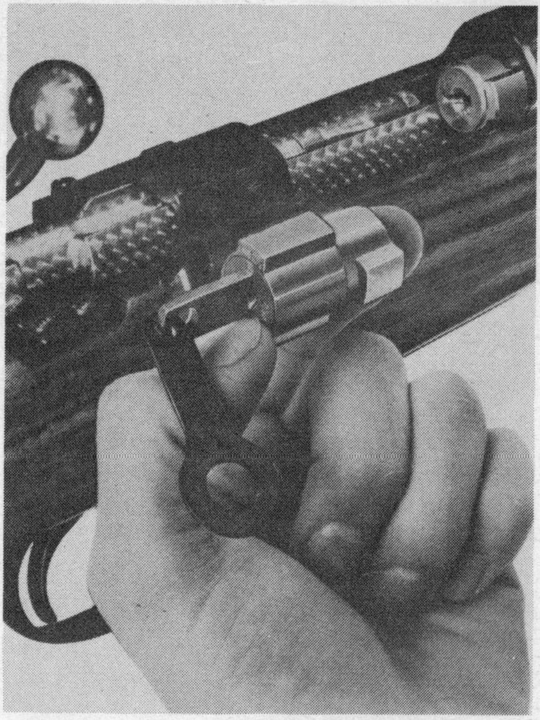

A gun lock is one safety device well worth the investment. This is Uncle Mike's Cease Fire action lock.

(Left) Hoppes, famous for its fine cleaning products, has this lineup of rests and pads to aid the shooter.

The LL Bean packframe is shown here with the author's added hook, over which the rifle's sling attaches securely. A frame allows the shooter considerable hand freedom in the backwoods and mountains.

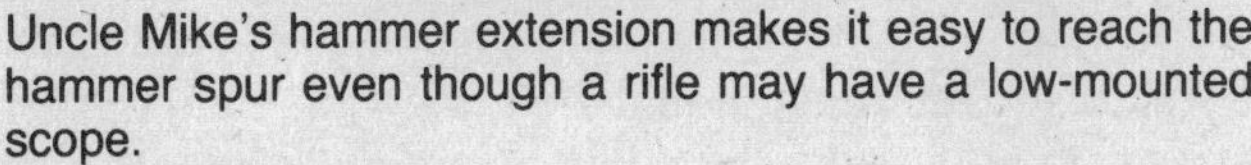

Uncle Mike's hammer extension makes it easy to reach the hammer spur even though a rifle may have a low-mounted scope.

Extra magazines make continued semi-auto shooting a lot easier. Every maker of semi-auto handguns offers spare magazines—buy some!

A trigger pull gauge will tell you how many pounds of let-off your own trigger has. But take trigger problems to a qualified gunsmith.

tached, but the shooter should be aware that they exist.

5. Uncle Mike's "Cease Fire!" gun lock is a safety device worth looking for. There are several good safety locks for both rifle and handgun, as well as shotgun. These are particularly welcomed in the home with young children.

6. Even though it seems to be a non-shooting item, I'd like to mention a tool which in fact has helped me enjoy out-of-the-way shooting localities many times—the pack. A very good one is the L. L. Bean model with the shelf unit, and my pack has a special hook which retains the rifle via the sling. I also pad the sides of the packframe so the rifle will not be scratched.

7. The RCBS Accessory Kit II is a particularly nice addition to the loading bench. It includes a powder trickler, a most useful item which dribbles out a granule of powder at a time to balance the scale off. The kit also contains a powder measure stand and other useful items.

8. The RCBS Pistol Ammo-Crafter is a reloading accessory kit of note. It contains the Little Dandy pistol powder measure, a powder funnel, a deburring tool, lubricant and other items of importance for reloading. It's all in one box.

9. Uncle Mike's hammer extension unit makes it easy to manipulate the hammer on a rifle with a low-mounted scope. Currently, the unit is made for Marlin rifles.

10. Extra clips are very nice to have for various firearms which use the clip feed. I especially like an extra clip for my semi-auto 22 rimfire pistol because I often like to concentrate on my practice with this firearm and the added clip means I can shoot 20 rounds (30 with two extra clips) with concentration, and without a break in the action.

11. A trigger pull gauge is an instrument which a number of shooters really should have. I believe that lousy trigger pulls mean misses for a good many of us, but shooters do not take the opportunity to test their own trigger pulls. The firearm should be tested *empty* in all cases.

Good shooting is more than good guns. The complete shooter must have the tools which attend his sport. And the list of good and worthwhile accessories continues to grow. Remember that there are also many custom-crafted shooting accessories as well as those offered over the counter. Also remember that good shooting equipment may double as good safety equipment.

Chapter 33

Practical Gun Collecting

MANY MODERN SHOOTERS are gun collectors in one way or another. The realization of gun values grew rapidly after World War II and is still growing today. Collectors have always appreciated the values inherent in things old, of course, and it is only right to add that they have also helped to establish matters of excellence as well. Appreciation is as much learned as anything else, and many of the learned, advanced collectors have shown us what to appreciate and how to appreciate it.

These advanced collectors do not need a primer on what to look for and how to look for it, but there is another level of gun collecting which fits the complete shooter like the hand in the proverbial glove. I call it practical collecting. It is practical because it does not include those super rare and exotic pieces. It is practical because this type of collecting can be done by anyone with a firearms interest and a modest cash account to work from.

Reasons for Collecting

The major reason for firearms collecting is a love of firearms, and don't let the big time collectors say otherwise. I have known a couple of these fellows and they consider themselves horsetraders of the most erudite class. They love to recount tales of great deals, where they located a rare and wonderful firearm, bought it for the price of a good hat and then turned around and sold it for a small fortune. They generally leave out all of the stories in which they found great bargains, bought them and then couldn't give the guns away for what they had in them.

Sure, there is money to be made in guns. But in the main, I suggest that anyone who is vastly interested in seeing his money grow, buy an investment of some other nature. For the fun of it, I had a computer program built up concerning a basic investment over a 20-year period in a tax sheltered annuity. This I put against a possible excellent buy in firearms. Believe me, the profit on the money package was the better deal by a good margin.

So I put love of firearms and firearms history, along with appreciation of fine things, as first on the list for collectors, even though there is no doubt that many collectors do make some money at their hobby. Before being taken to task on this matter, I promptly admit that there are so-called collectors who make a living in the gun trading world. But they are not collectors. They are businessmen. One of these fellows studies the newspaper every day. Do you know what he studies first? The obituaries. If he finds that a Mr. Jones, age 86, has departed us, he contacts Mrs. Jones to see about any guns left behind. He has come upon some buys that would astound anyone who knows guns, but he, in all fairness, pays just as much as the local gunshop would give for the guns and just as much or more than a hock shop would pay. So he, in a way, does a service, but the service is mostly to himself.

Is he a gun collector? Not at all. He's a *businessman*. So I don't see the owners of major gun houses as "collectors." If they were collectors they would covet what they find. They don't covet these guns. They sell them, *for a profit*. It's pure buy and sell. And they have every right to continue the practice.

The dedicated collector is usually looking for a specific thing. He may specialize, in fact, in certain firearms. Sure, he will trade. I sometimes think the urge to trade is a desire to expand the collector's experience. If he finds a firearm he wants to enjoy, he does so, much as a connoisseur of art appreciates a picture, studying the detail, learning more of its history or the history of the painter. The gun collector does the same thing, and then he trades that firearm for another. This gives him yet one more gun to enjoy, to learn and to study.

In summary, it is my opinion that the *gun collector* collects because he loves firearms. The *dealer* in firearms collects for profit motives mainly. With this definition, which is my perspective only, of course, it's easy to see that the general shooter can be a collector. He can collect what he likes, be that 22 rimfire rifles of days gone by, or lever-actions, or double barrel side-by-side shotguns, and these guns do not have to be remarkable collector values, as such. They are simply those firearms which the individual himself enjoys.

Any shooter who has visited the famous Winchester Collection, which is now housed in the Buffalo Bill Historical Center in Cody, Wyoming, will quickly catch collecting fever. I am not a collector. I have no firearms which are not practical in the shooting sense. Basically, if it won't

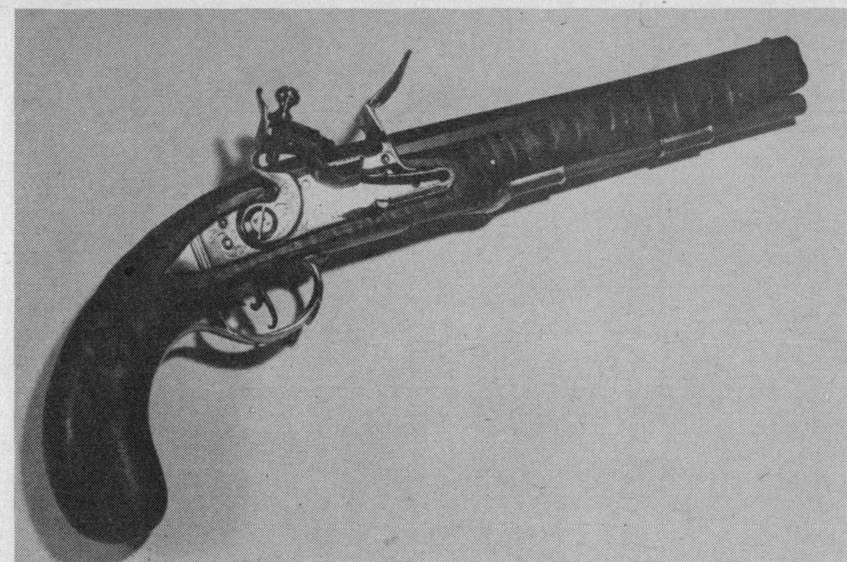

The black powder pistol in handmade form is a collectible item, as are quality custom firearms of other types.

(Right) This unique powder dispenser is one of the many interesting items on display at the Buffalo Bill Historical Center in Cody, Wyoming. Note the ornate carving of this fine item.

The famous Winchester Collection is housed in the Buffalo Bill Historical Center in Cody, Wyoming. It is one of the most interesting gun collections in the world, and a visitor can learn much about firearms history in a tour of this collection.

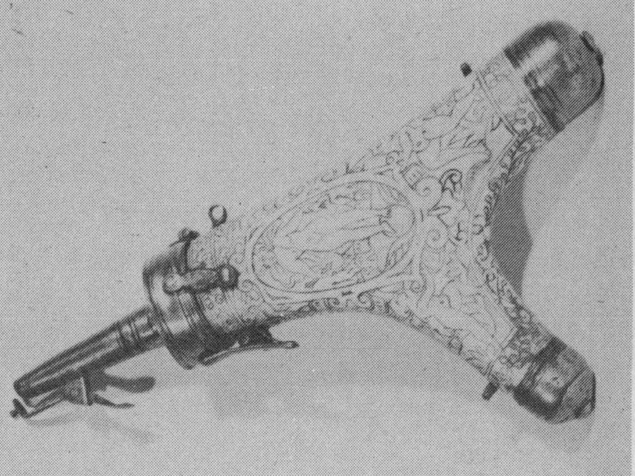

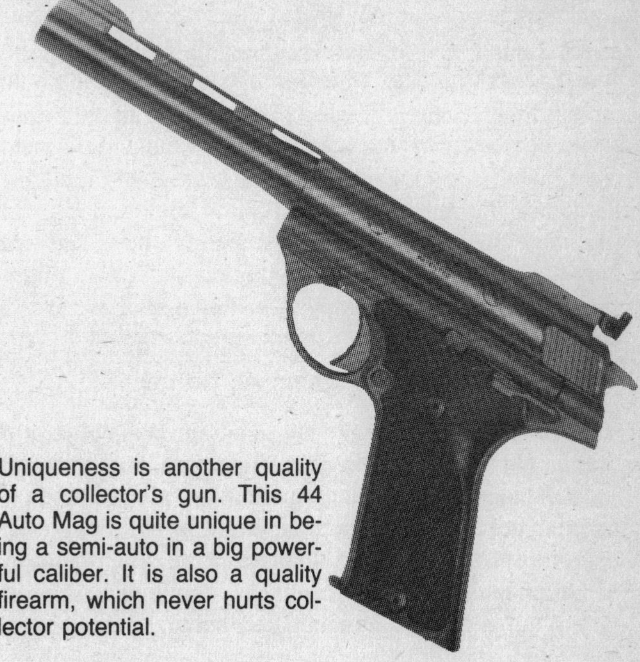

Uniqueness is another quality of a collector's gun. This 44 Auto Mag is quite unique in being a semi-auto in a big powerful caliber. It is also a quality firearm, which never hurts collector potential.

Some collectors like to specialize. One way to go is the older 22 rimfire rifles, such as these two Remingtons, both out of production. On top is the Model 121, while the Model 12 is the other rifle.

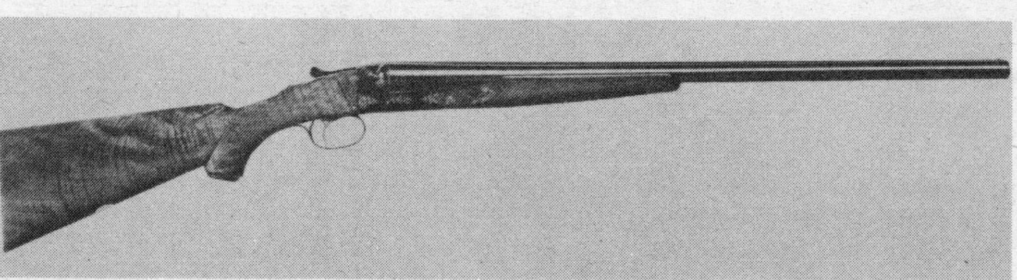

The fine Model 21 Winchester shotgun is a collector's item of the highest rank and order. This beautiful shotgun was once priced only slightly higher than some of the more ordinary shotguns. But today it commands a high price.

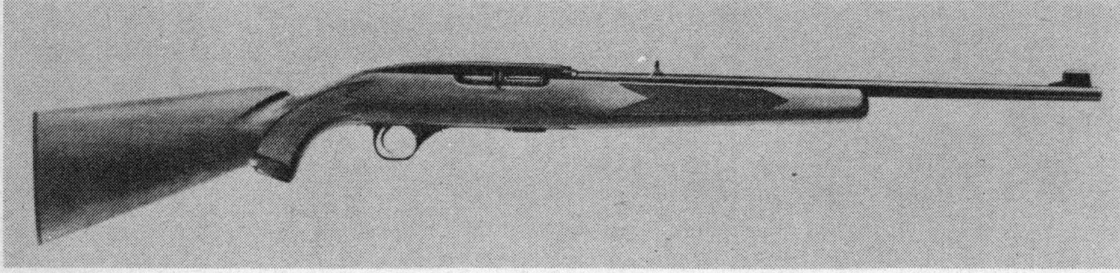

Another discontinued rifle is the Winchester Model 490 and it has collector status because it is no longer made, although it does not warrant the price tags found on some of the earlier Winchester rifles.

shoot, I don't want it. But when looking at the wonderful Winchester Collection, I can readily see that it is not only the firearms on display, but a history lesson in hardware. Every firearm there has a story to tell, and I want them right there. Had I the chance to own some of those fine heirlooms, I'd rather leave them on display. And if I had my way, I would enjoy shooting some of these fine old guns—which would be like drinking out of George Washington's favorite crystal water goblet as part of my everyday supper service.

Are the Bargains All Gone?

No, the bargains are not all gone, but don't expect to find an old Winchester Model 61 pumpgun complete with original hanging tags for a hundred bucks. It is not likely to happen. But it could. That's the world of collecting. The collector/shooter may have to adjust his thinking today. A bargain I ran into a number of years ago was an original Colt S.A. revolver for a hundred bucks. I could have bought a few bushel baskets full of these for that price. In fact, I can remember where they were. There was a fellow dealing in used guns in Tucson, Arizona, and he had a case of original Colt revolvers. Prices were thought to be fair, but stiff at a hundred bucks on the average. This was in the early 1950s.

The true bargains are those firearms which are not sought after today, but will be sought after in the future. And the shrewd buyer will have a crystal ball which tells him what guns these are. Imagine the shooter in 1950 buying up Model 70 Winchesters. He could have had them for just a bit over $100. I bought a brand new Model 70 Winchester 270 in 1958 for $120. Today, if that rifle were in the original box with all of the tags and maybe even a box of ammo purchased at the time the rifle was bought, it would be worth many hundreds of dollars.

But nobody knew Winchester was going to change the Model 70 Winchester and drop the Model 69, the Model 71, the Model 72, the Model 62, the Winchester Model 21

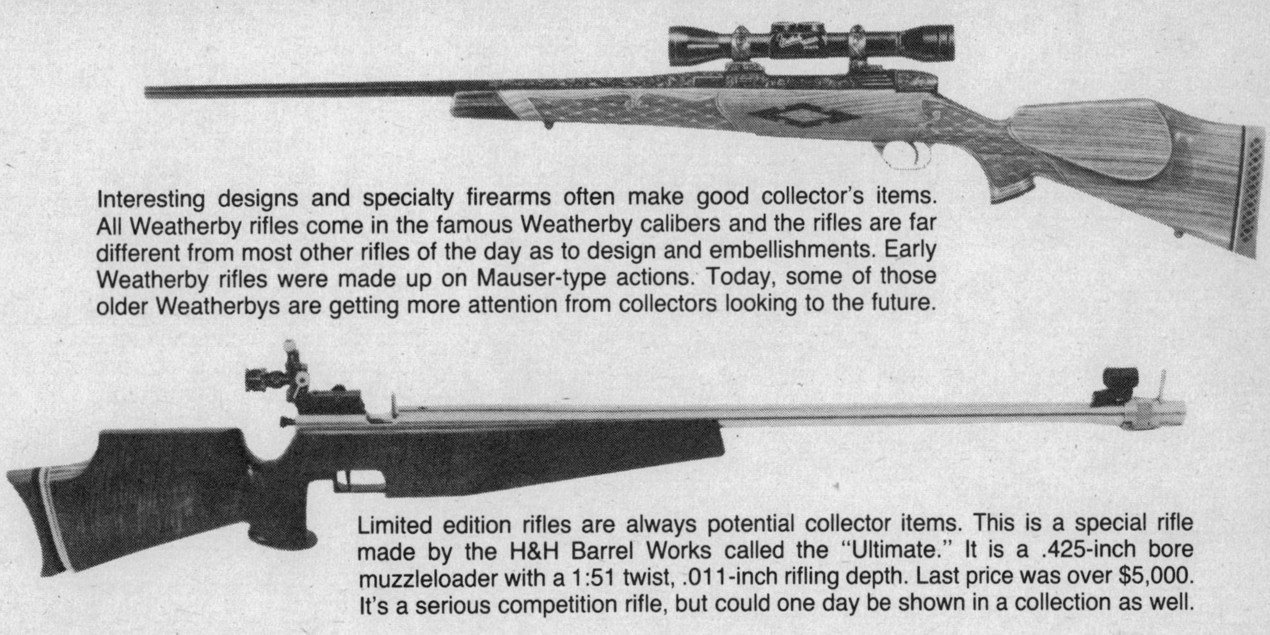

Interesting designs and specialty firearms often make good collector's items. All Weatherby rifles come in the famous Weatherby calibers and the rifles are far different from most other rifles of the day as to design and embellishments. Early Weatherby rifles were made up on Mauser-type actions. Today, some of those older Weatherbys are getting more attention from collectors looking to the future.

Limited edition rifles are always potential collector items. This is a special rifle made by the H&H Barrel Works called the "Ultimate." It is a .425-inch bore muzzleloader with a 1:51 twist, .011-inch rifling depth. Last price was over $5,000. It's a serious competition rifle, but could one day be shown in a collection as well.

Collecting ammunition is a very interesting side-hobby of shooting. While this box of ammo is not terribly old, it is old enough to bear the Express title. Note that the buyer is told that the ammunition is loaded with smokeless powder. One day in the future, it could be an interesting addition to a collection.

shotgun and so forth. So there was no great rush to the gunshop to buy up Model 70s or any of the other now-coveted Winchesters. In fact, the post-1964 Winchester was heralded as a better rifle than the pre-1964 Winchester, at least in the famous Model 70, and this proclamation was made by some pretty famous gunwriters. They may have been right, too, in terms of mechanics. Maybe the newer Model 70 was better, but it certainly wasn't (and isn't) worth as much money as the older one.

I think that the individual collector of the day, our practical collector who simply wants to own a few nice guns from the past (and even the present), should look at "a bargain" from the standpoint of how much he wants that firearm. It may indeed be a case of paying too much for a certain gun, but the money is soon forgotten.

What To Collect?

Collectors not only go for guns. They also go for just about everything which attends guns. Knives make good items for collection. They are small and some are very interesting. And they do go along with shooting. Remington's old folding "Bullet Knife" is a perfect example of a blade that shooters want to collect. And there are currently many handmade, custom knives which are certainly not made to cut with. Many are pieces of art and are to be *collected,* not used.

Cartridges are very nice collector's items. A cartridge collection makes one of the most interesting arms-related conversation pieces I have ever seen. The wonder of it all is in the fact that there were and are so many different cartridges. If we think we are "caliber crazy" today, all we need do is look at a cartridge collection to realize that those who preceded us were as bad as we are or worse. Books have been written on the various cartridges offered over the years. A look at a 40-50 Sharps shows a necked round of 1875. There is a 40-65 Ballard Everlasting and a 45-70 Van Choate and a 22-15-60 Stevens round. The list seems endless and the potential is equally "endless."

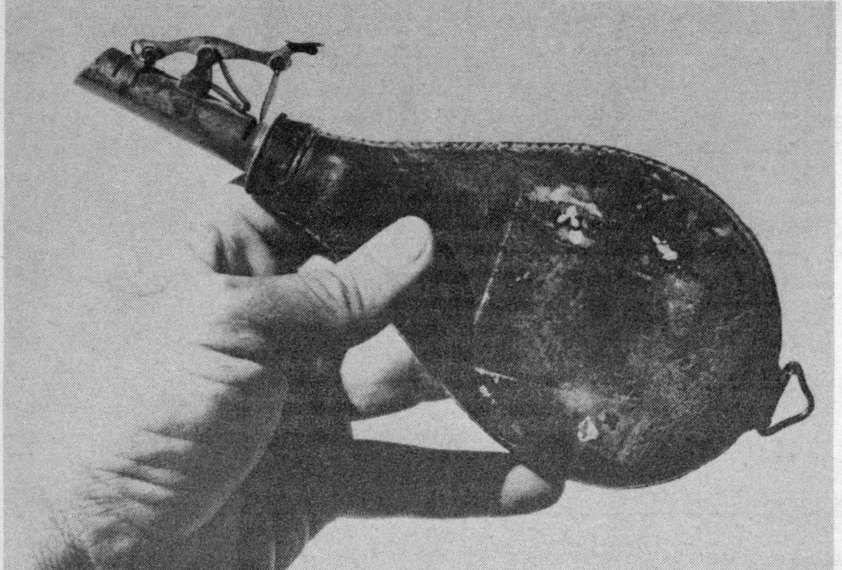

An original shot pouch is a nice addition to a black powder collection.

Shotguns are things of beauty with collector value. Here is a fine Winchester 101 Diamond Grade over/under Skeet gun. Its beauty is apparent, and its value is quite likely to grow in time. As this is written, it comes in 20-gauge or 12-gauge for about $1400 and in .410 or 28-gauge for about $1450.

Reloading equipment is also interesting. The old Winchester tools and many items from even earlier times are a part of shooting history and deserve to be preserved and enjoyed as well as studied. Books are also very collectible, and they are a lot of fun to look for. Any bookstore dealing in old titles could have a very precious gun book for a shooter. This is one area in which there are still a few bargains because not every book dealer in the land is keen on gun titles. Old reloading manuals can sell for 50¢ sometimes.

Accoutrements of all types are collectible. Some of the old powder horns are highly valuable. There are many with dates and scenes and other markings which give them historical dating. There are shotgun flasks and leather goods and shooting pouches and no end to the gear which can be collected in the accessories vein. In a way, the accessories area is broader than gun collecting.

(Below) Discontinued about a dozen or so years ago, the Winchester lever-action Model 88 is *very* popular with shooters—and collectors. It was the last, pre-'64-introduced Winchester centerfire lever-action. The Model 88 seen here is distinctly pre-'64 in production. Why? The hand checkering—later 88s had machine "impressed checkering."

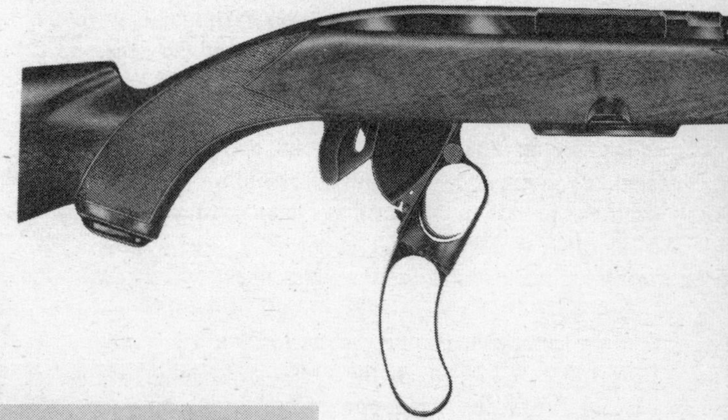

General and Specialty Collections

A friend of mine is gathering up lever-action rifles, but they are not Winchesters. He has found some big bargains in non-Winchester lever-action rifles. A fine Marlin 40-60 in Very Good condition came his way recently for $250. And he has a number of other lever-action rifles of the 19th century which may someday escalate in value. If they don't, he does not care. He is collecting for that reason I named earlier, love of firearms. To him, these working rifles of the past represent what was happening with the *average shooter*. They are not embellished. They are plain.

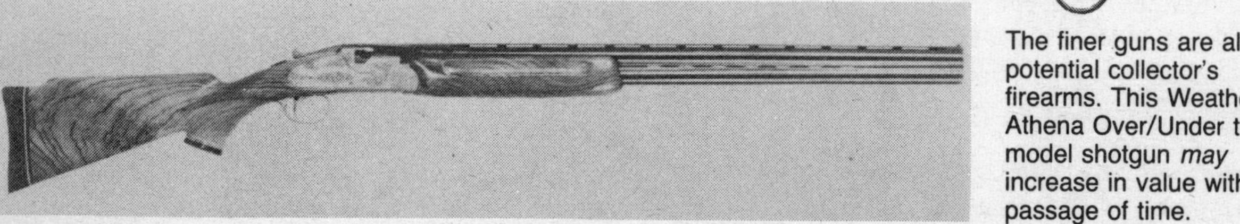

The finer guns are always potential collector's firearms. This Weatherby Athena Over/Under trap model shotgun *may* increase in value with the passage of time.

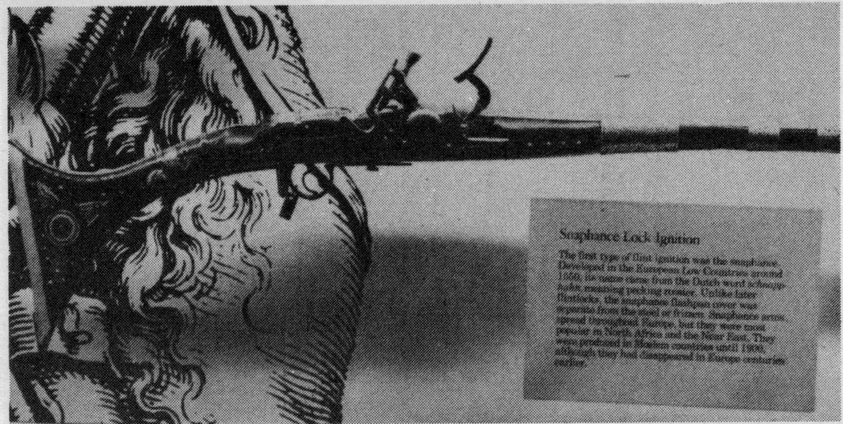

Educationally, the Winchester Collection in the Buffalo Bill Historical Center in Cody, Wyoming, is one of the best collections ever put together. Here is a display of a snaphance lock.

But they are functional and actually pretty nice to look at.

This is an example of what often happens to a collector. He tends to specialize. The enjoyable fact is that we who might enjoy a little practical collecting can also specialize. I call my friend's lever-action collection very practical. The guns are not museum pieces. They are not of great monetary value. He can afford to do his collecting with a few dollars worth of capital. And it will not harm a thing if he wants to shoot his collection, making the guns even more practical to own.

The general collector would be just that, a person who buys a firearm because he likes it, not because it fits into some niche in his collection. He might find a beautiful Kentucky/Pennsylvania rifle this month and next month he could be buying a Model 21 Winchester shotgun or a military firearm. The specialist may like all guns but he looks for particular ones only. He may even become ultra-specialized. A specialty could be muzzleloaders, meaning that a person would collect caplock revolvers as well as flintlock rifles. But this can narrow itself considerably.

The muzzleloader collector may decide that he wants only longrifles. And then he may decide that the only longrifles he really wants are those of the Pennsylvania type. Or he may look for the earlier Jaeger models. To be more specific, he could end up collecting Pennsylvania rifles only of one school, such as the Lancaster or Bedford school. Another fellow may be collecting Model 70 Winchesters only. A collection consisting only of Model 70s may indeed seem narrow, but it isn't at all. The great variety of calibers chambered in the Model 70 will keep a person busy—for a long time. And then there were plenty of modifications to the Winchester Model 70 line, including Featherweights, Carbines, Super Grades and Westerners—and that is just scratching the surface.

Collecting by brand is not quite as specialized as the collection of a particular model, but it can be fairly narrow. A shooter may find himself interested in Smith & Wesson handguns, and though there were and are many, many different models, there are not so many that a collector would find it impossible to become an expert on the Smith & Wesson line. Other brands could offer a wider search for the collector, but even those lines which were very expansive are, after all, finite. There were only so many models and no more.

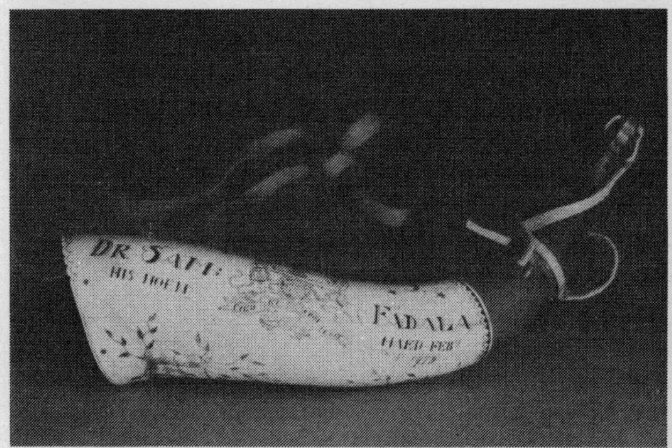

The handmade powder horn has become quite a collectible item of the day. This powder horn, handmade by Vince Poulon, is a high-grade horn of personal value. Other horns are more collectible if they tend to copy a horn of the past.

The Rare Firearm

This type of gun, I think is beyond the realm of most "practical" gun collectors. Some of these rare guns are one of a kind, or almost so. Mainly, they are firearms which were made in limited numbers to begin with, though it is surprising that some firearms made in numbers of several thousand or so are equally difficult to find. On the other hand, there are models with production runs of *under* 1000 which *have* been located, the extremely valuable Colt Walker being a good example of this.

Some rare guns are showpiece items. There are guns presented to dignitaries which are indeed "one of a kind" and in no way can that one firearm ever be replaced. There are also firearms used by famous and infamous people which are one of a kind only. Teddy Roosevelt's "Big Medicine" would be an example of the former, and Booth's assassination pistol an example of the latter.

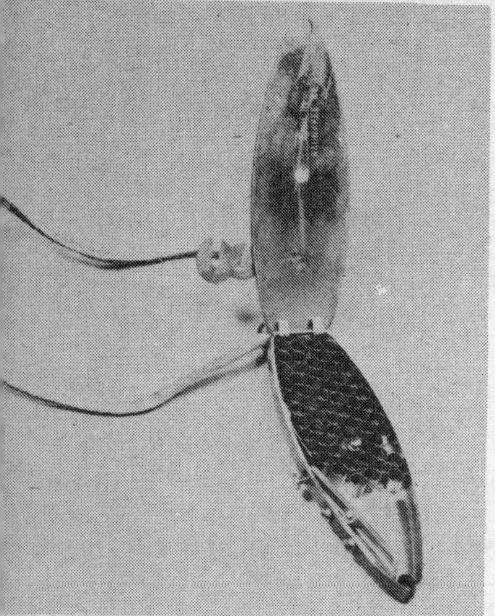

A shooting item need not be custom-crafted in order to enjoy collector status. This Tedd Cash magazine capper is a quality replica which would enhance a black powder collection.

Handmade beauty is often collectible. This is a rifle made by Dennis Mulford. It is a custom of collectible value.

Replicas and Museum Copies

A friend of mine makes accoutrements and sometimes firearms for museums. These tools and guns are often used as examples to fill in a niche where the real thing is missing. He is an artist of the highest order, and it's a good thing that he's ethical. He could certainly fool some people, most of us I think, with his copies. The replica is not totally uncollectible, but only the passing of time will tell us just how valuable these copies really are. I can't guess at the way this will work out. It's quite conceivable that some day in the future, a rifle handmade in the year 1985 as a copy of a Hawken or Jaeger or Lancaster will be very valuable, worth more than its original price and well beyond whatever inflation level exists at the time of future sale.

One custom arms maker I know tells me that the *majority* of the fine flintlock custom arms he makes these days are *not* fired by their owners. People are buying these guns to hold them. They are enjoying the artwork and the fact that these firearms are historically correct, not to mention just plain beautiful. They are showpieces. So the modern replica is indeed collectible, but as to its worth in the future, only time will tell us.

Replicas do not stop at rifles, and I am happy that they don't. There are a good number of items I would enjoy owning, but either could never find or would not want to invest in to a great sum. Also, there are items from the past which I would like to use. A replica is the answer. There are replicas of just about every famous shooting item from the past that can be named.

The powder horn is a perfect example of a replica because today's hornsmiths are just as good as those of yesteryear. I would not take an original 18th century powder horn into the mountains with me to use on a hunting trip, but I might take certain replicas of this horn. I have to qualify here because I have seen modern powder horns I

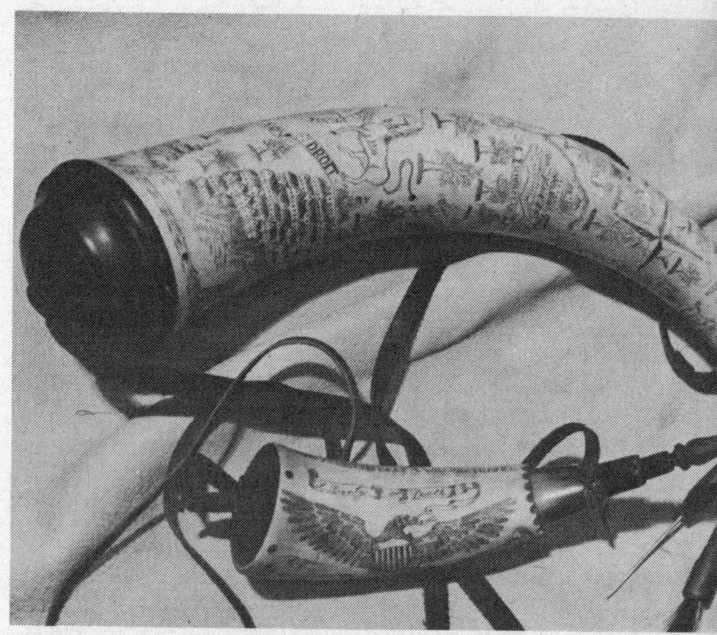

These handmade powder horns are very collectible. They are made by Dennis Mulford, a custom black powder gunmaker and hornsmith. Note the detail on the horns.

would encase and preserve against harm. I would not take these into the outback any more than I would take an original to the shooting range.

Replica powder horns are just a start. There are replica knives which duplicate famous models from the past. There are so many black powder items that a book could be done on that subject. And there are in fact replica books, for which I am personally grateful. I have a copy of *The Rifle and the Hound in Ceylon*, for example. It has the same words and illustrations as the original, but it cost far less than an original copy would cost and it offers me what I want—the information that Sir Samuel Baker put down.

There are replica gun catalogs which are very interesting and enjoyable to read. These are priced right and they always make me daydream about the days when a fellow could buy a fine rifle for $30. Of course, it was probably pretty tough getting the $30, but it's fun to dream. If Wells time machine worked, I would travel back to the early days and bring back a time capsule full of fine old guns, starting with a batch of Winchester Model 21 shotguns for $76.50, the 1932 price tag.

Fine Guns

Fine guns can be old or new. There are plenty of fine guns being made right now, and there is no reason to think that these firearms will not gain appreciably in value, but there is also no guarantee that they will keep up with inflation. The fine gun is almost easier to spot than it is to describe. A veteran shooter who has been buying and looking at firearms for a long time can pretty easily tell the difference between a utility rifle and one that makes it into the ''fine'' realm. The lines and style of the fine firearm, shotgun or rifle, are fairly telltale.

The fine replicas of the old-time rifles are quite collectible in modern custom-made form. These rifles are the products of the skillful hands of professional gunmaker William Kennedy. The quality matches that of the early day gunsmiths.

Unfortunately, Remington no longer offers their man-sized "40-XB Rimfire Sporter." The rifle was dropped just a couple of years ago. Used specimens are bringing between $750 and $1200, depending upon condition and who's doing the selling and buying. All 40-XB Sporters were produced in Remington's Custom Shop.

Unusual, finely crafted factory pieces will always command top dollar. This Old Browning A-5 has fine checkering in a non-standard pattern. It also has gold-wire inlay work. *Very* collectible.

The gun may also enjoy tasteful engraving. I am not a fan of all sorts of engraving on the metalwork, but there are some fine guns which have such high-quality engraving that even though the metal is covered with scrollwork, I like it. The work is simply too good to detract from the gun itself. Inlays and overlays don't thrill me a whole lot either, but again, they can be done with taste and skill and I have to concede that they do enhance a firearm.

Carvings are just about as poor as they are good in terms of the odds. I will bet that 50 percent of the carvings I have seen were not helpful to the overall looks of the firearm. Sometimes a fine gun will have carving, and when it does, chances are the carving will be limited in coverage but very nicely executed. Checkering can also be an art. On super fine rifles I have seen checkering of 32 lines to the inch. This is really not very practical, and I suppose it was never meant to be. That type of checkering is for show, and I like it—to look at.

The fine gun is simply one which left the realm of utility and is now a part of the realm of artwork. If the gun is of the finest workmanship, but does not have the luxury wood or the artisan's touch in terms of checkering and engraving and other additions, then it's probably not going to fall into the category of "fine gun," no matter how nicely made.

Today, one means of collecting fine guns is to have a professional make one for you. In other words, we are talking about the custom firearm. There are collectors who seek out certain builders whom they, the collectors, find talented. Then they have the builder put two or three or more firearms together for them. Object? To collect. Sometimes the rifles may be used as tools, in other words on hunts or at the range, and sometimes these rifles—seldom handguns, but black powder pistols are fine for collecting—are simply salted away for the future.

Restoration

Quite often a shooter will get his hands on an older rifle of collector value and enjoy that firearm so much that he has an urge to restore it to original condition. A good piece of advice is to leave the gun alone unless it is truly at the lower end of the list in collector value. Often, restoring a firearm of true collector value will ruin it or at least damage its worth. A perfect example comes to mind, a Winchester '76 which had been restored. It was not a rifle of super value to begin with, but when I saw it, the rifle had character. When the restoration was done, it was a lot prettier, but all the history was all gone. Some guns do take to restoration. Another Winchester did. It was a takedown Model 94 rifle in 30 WCF (30-30) caliber. It did not have character. It was just plain scratched up. But the metalwork was sound and the wood better than average. In fact, it was probably a special rifle to someone in the past (made in about 1899 according to records) because it was of the "Special Order" type. Refinished, the rifle showed its original beauty, and it was used as a hunting piece and enjoyed deeply. Even in this instance, however, it is impossible to say that restoration brought the value of that rifle up. It may have lowered the value. The key to *restoration* is finding the right "artisan" to do the work. Believe me, local gunsmiths, even those of good repute, will *never* cut the mustard when it comes to restoration.

Factory Refinished

Factory refinishing is not the same as having a professional restoration specialist work on a firearm. An example of a factory refinish job would be a Model 21 Winchester I saw. It had been renewed at the Winchester factory to "new" condition. Yes, it was back to its original condition, but that restoration was acomplished by the manufacturer. This is not to say that the company was better than a professional armsmaker, but it's a matter of propriety. Factory refinished models can retain their value, while professionally refinished firearms usually don't.

I would look for refinishing signs on a rifle if I were a collector. One way to find out if a firearm has been refinished or is simply in fine condition is to look very closely at the wood of the stock. Sometimes it is possible to find tiny scratches *underneath* the new finish. In other words, those scratches were finished over. Look at the barrel for signs it has been reblued. On modern firearms, a reblue can give itself away on several counts: the presence of rounded (normally sharp) edges; the presence of pits under the new blue; the presence of white, powder-like bluing salts residue at the juncture of the barrel and breech (or barrel extension in the case of some shotguns); ovaled screw head recesses; over-buffed, barely ledgible barrel legends; the lack of correct buffing texture; the absence of "correct" color in the blue.

But there are some modifications and options which are acceptable to collectors. A good many fine orginal black powder longrifles were switched from flintlock to percussion, as a matter of fact. These rifles are still excellent and still of high value. The rifles were switched over with the drum and nipple conversion. This meant that a threaded unit was inserted where the touchhole had been. This unit, the drum, screwed right into the flat of the barrel and usually had a cleanout screw on the end of it. Then screwed

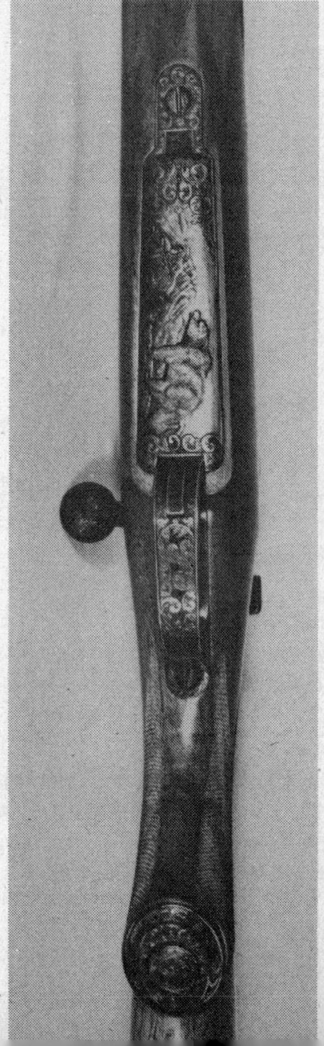

Well done, quality engraving, will always command a premium when it's found on a custom firearm. The name of the engraver will *always* be the determining factor when it comes to the question, "How collectible is it?"

Older firearms will show varying degrees of "patina." There is, indeed, a distinct difference between "patina" and "heavy rust." Note the extensive stock carving. Beauty or beast?

rial numbers always mean a great deal in gun collecting d some serial numbers end up on firearms of very special ture. The one millionth Model 94 Winchester, for exam-, would be such a firearm. This is the three millionth Rem-ton Model 1100 autoloading shotgun. There will never ain be a Model 1100 with serial number 3,000,000, of urse, and therein lies part of the collector interest. This arm is indeed a *one-of-a-kind.*

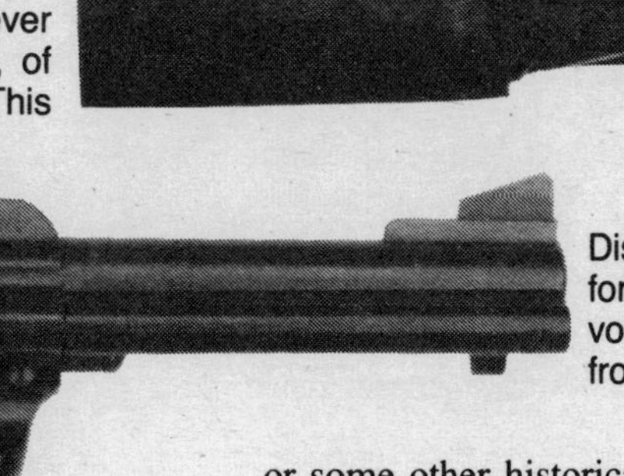

Discontinued models are always prone for collector status. Old Style Ruger revolvers are now getting more attention from collectors. *Now* is the time to buy.

into the drum was the nipple itself. Fire went from the nipple, through the drum and into the breech. I have a couple drum-and-nipple rifles of modern manufacture and the system works well in terms of ignition.

Aging and Patina

Patina is a type of rust or *aerugo*, which does not sound very good, but which can be very handsome. It is, in many cases, the very basis for that old or antique look which metal can have. The collector will not think of trying to clean such metal, for patina is a sign of *honest* aging and not a bad sign at that. It does not mean that the rifle is rusted out like an old car. Now, a gun can be rusty, too. I can assure you that heavy, scaley rust is *not* the patina. Patina is light, very even in distribution—a sort of graying effect which usually adds to the aging appearance rather that detracting from it.

Commemoratives

Another collector's firearm is the commemorative. These consist of modern rifles, handguns and even shotguns. The commemorative is a limited edition model and it must ''commemorate'' something such as our Bicentennial or some other historical event.

There may be a special firearm limited edition commemorating statehood or the gold rush or any number of events. Are these really valid? Some collectors feel they are. Others do not. I find myself mostly in the first camp with a few reservations, but being a practical gun owner, would only find an interest in the commemoratives which appealed to my sense of good shooting.

Some commemoratives I have seen were not nearly as appealing to me as orginials of similar design. In fact, in some instances I would prefer having the old-time original instead of a commemorative. The idea is to buy one of these and put it away. It is more a showpiece than a working gun and that is probably where my full appreciation for some of the commemoratives falls short.

Buying a Collector's Firearm

Since our approach is from the practical nature, I would say that the ''average'' shooter might want to look at *general* collecting rather than *specific* collecting. In other words, if you come across a fine pre-war Model 99 Savage for a decent price, and you truly want it, go ahead and buy it. Perhaps the next purchase will be that custom rifle long desired. And later on, a nice double barrel shotgun may show up. But to delve into guns of the Civil War period is going to take time, concentration and at least a fairly good outlay of dollars.

Timing is all-important. I mentioned the pre-war Savage 99 above because I see what I think of as ''good buys'' on these all the time. At this time, a pre-war Savage Model 99 is not going to command what some other rifle will warrant, even though it may be every bit as well constructed and certainly a part of American shooting history. So tim-

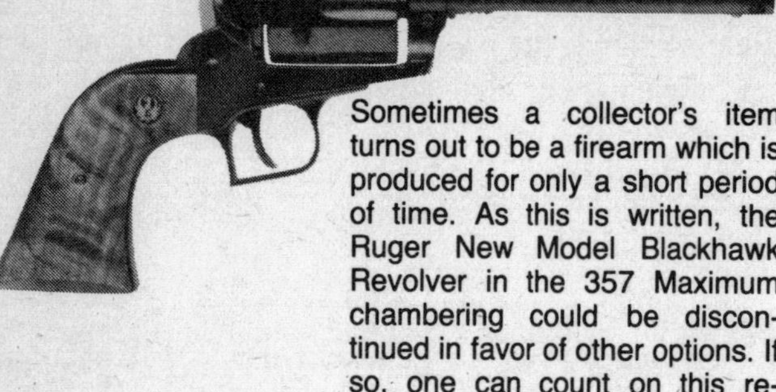

Sometimes a collector's item turns out to be a firearm which is produced for only a short period of time. As this is written, the Ruger New Model Blackhawk Revolver in the 357 Maximum chambering could be discontinued in favor of other options. If so, one can count on this revolver to enjoy collector status.

This old L.C. Smith is in N.R.A. Excellent (plus) condition and would command top price from an L.C. Smith collector.

ing is important. If this country's body of collectors suddenly decide that Savage 99s should be worth more, they *will* be worth more.

Look at a book of gun values. It will give you an idea of used gun values and a range of figures to study for the various models so that a shooter will have an idea of what he should pay for a certain firearm.

Gun shows are very fine outlets for good collector's guns. The visitor to a gun show can walk the area, check the booths and see not only plenty of used guns, but there may be custom work on display as well. There usually is. The local paper is not a bad place to begin looking casually for used guns. Also, there are special gun-oriented newspapers, such as *Shotgun News*, which deal strictly in firearms and related items, to include good gun books and magazines. Auctions can be all right even if they don't always attract the best firearms, but good buys *are* possible.

Of course, gunshops also deal in used firearms, often of some collector value. I located a pre-64 Model 70 Winchester Featherweight, in very good condition, at a local gunshop for $350. I did not want the piece, but a friend did. I have seen quite a number of excellent used firearms at gunshops. Sometimes there are guns on consignment in these establishments, too. "Consignment" amounts to the seller giving his own personal firearm to a local shop, the shop taking a percentage of the sale price established by the gun's owner. Hock shops sell guns, too. Sometimes there are bargains here.

Condition Standards for Antique Firearms

Basic to understanding the monetary value of an antique firearm is knowing the condition of the firearm being bought or sold. As a result a set of rules has been established by the NRA for antique firearms. Many dealers will use these guidelines. If a collector buys a firearm advertised in the *The Shotgun News,* for example, he will find the NRA guidelines in use. They are presented here as a guideline for the readers to use.

Factory New—all original parts; 100 percent original finish; in perfect condition in every respect, inside and out.

Excellent—all original parts; over 80 percent original finish; sharp lettering, numerals and design on metal and wood; unmarred wood; fine bore.

Fine—all original parts; over 30 percent original finish; sharp lettering, numerals and design on metal and wood; minor marks in wood; good bore.

Very Good—all original parts; none to 30 percent original finish; original metal surfaces smooth with all edges sharp; clear lettering, numerals and design on metal; wood slightly scratched or bruised; bore disregarded for collectors firearms.

Good— some minor replacement parts; metal smoothly rusted or lightly pitted in places, cleaned or reblued; principal lettering, numerals and design on metal legible; wood refinished, scratched, bruised or minor cracks repaired; in good working order.

Fair—some major parts replaced; minor replacement parts

may be required; metal rusted, may be lightly pitted all over, vigorously cleaned or blued; rounded edges of metal and wood; principal lettering, numerals and design on metal partly obliterated; wood scratched, bruised, cracked or repaired where broken; in fair working order or can be easily repaired and placed in working order.

Poor— major and minor parts replaced; major replacement parts required and extensive restoration needed; metal deeply pitted; principal lettering, numerals and design obliterated, wood badly scratched, bruised, cracked or broken; mechanically inoperative; generally undesirable as a collectors firearm.

Insurance

The collector is faced with losing quite an investment if his arms are lost to theft, flood, fire or any other catastrophe. The homeowner's policy may or may not offer enough coverage for some gun collections, and some insurance agencies do offer *Fine Arts Floaters* which can be investigated. These will often insure a collection, along with the insurance company maintaining a record of the arms for the owner.

A gun owner may be asked to have appraisals made of his firearms before they can be insured. This will include the name and caliber of the gun, the serial number and a statement by a professional gunsmith or seller of arms as to the value of the particular gun(s). A bill of sale may also be useful, and the person buying a custom firearm should always ask for such. This can establish the value of a fine rifle rather well, because non-shooters in insurance companies usually balk when told that a firearm was worth a couple thousand dollars.

The NRA has offered an insurance plan for *members only* for some time and it covers the member's guns for a few hundred dollars up to several thousands of dollars. Any member can get all the information he needs on this plan by writing to the NRA headquarters, 1600 Rhode Island Ave., in Washington, D. C. 20036.

Things Change

The practical collector who is simply looking for a few modest firearms which interest him for his own personal reasons may be quite surprised one day when he learns that those old guns have increased markedly in value. A practical collector in Nebraska showed me his own set of firearms when I was on a visit there. They were simple guns, all right, nothing much to brag about, he said.

What the gentleman had were utility grade guns, but they were primarily pre-64 Winchesters, enough of them to fill a good-sized bathtub. There were Model 70s and a couple Model 71s and a few Model 63s and so forth. He had bought them all new or near new and had not paid all that much for them. Some he had fired. Others he simply kept around to enjoy from the visual and textural standpoint. But they were certainly worth more than he paid for them.

One never knows when a gun company is going to make a drastic engineering or model change. When changes do take place, some of the most mundane firearms of the hour may turn out to be worth something down the pike. But I don't worry about that. And the practical collector doesn't either. He buys what he likes and often what he likes to shoot. Even if they are never worth a lot of money to other people, they are certainly worth a great deal to the owner.

Chapter 34

The Law and Your Guns

FIREARMS OWNERSHIP is not the same as owning a home, car, boat or television set. In a sense, all of these may be "registered" or at least documented in ownership, and the firearm may or may not be, depending upon many circumstances, including the laws which pertained at the time of the firearm's purchase. Whether the gun is registered or not, many laws pertain to its use and/or possession and the complete shooter should at least have an understanding of the more important laws having to do with his firearms. The old saw, "Ignorance of the law is no excuse," may turn into a lot more than a saying if a shooter fails to comply with the rules governing his firearms.

In our chapter on transportation of firearms, the reader found that laws varied tremendously from state to state. This situation is very important for the shooter to understand, for he must always remember that as he moves about the country, the gun laws he knows in his home state may not at all apply in the state he is visiting. In order to comply with the law, the shooter must learn the gun laws of the state he intends to visit. Also, there may be county or parish regulations to consider. Laws pertaining to firearms vary, then, not only from state to state, but may also vary from county to county or city to city.

How Can I Know the Law?

The gun-owning citizen must take it upon himself to know the law pertaining to his firearms. There are many books and booklets on the subject of gun laws, many of which are available through the local library in the first instance and through the NRA in the second. The library will have books such as *The Rights of Gun Owners* by Alan Gottlieb, though I would recommend buying this good, but inexpensive book so it can be used as a handy reference. There are also books in the library by writers such as Bill Davidson, these books dealing with gun ownership. Pamphlets such as "Ten Myths About Gun Control" and "The Right to Keep and Bear Arms" are offered through the NRA.

But these are not always enough. The gunowner must always check into the laws for his own home state and even smaller geographical locale. If there is ever any doubt, *ask*. As for asking, I suggest the local police as a starting point. But do know the law. Do not try to rely on ignorance of the law as an excuse for failing to obey it. No one source can provide all of the gun law information available, either. This chapter, for example, is designed to start the shooter in the direction of finding out about the gun laws of his specific area, but it is not designed to answer all of the gun law questions which could possibly be asked.

The Second Amendment

There has always been quite a controversy over the Second Amendment to the Constitution of the United States. On September 25, 1789, this law was put into effect. Since that time, detractors claim that it was meant to give the country an army of sorts *(a militia)*, made up of citizens, much like our National Guard today. In my opinion, that is not so. There are countless quotes from George Washington, as well as other prominent U.S. statesmen pertaining to this amendment. Any reasonable legal interpretation of the Second Amendment, indicates that the "citizen" was the person being spoken of, not an army. So, in the opinion of many, the Second Amendment does hold up, even under legal scrutiny. It says, "A well-regulated militia, being necessary to the security of a free state, the right of the people to keep and bear arms, shall not be infringed." The *people. Not the army*. The documentation in the records further indicates that this is just what the law means, that citizens of this free country shall have the right to bear arms.

Of course, it is not that simple. One does not, truly, have the right to grab up a firearm and trudge off through town with it. As a matter of fact, a person does not have the right, these days, to simply buy a gun from a gun store without following procedures outlined by federal, state or local laws. Our *basic right* to own firearms as free American citizens is intact. But it is a right absolutely replete with rules and regulations! Gottlieb, in the aforementioned book, states that there are about 20,000 gun laws in America, or "gun control ordinances" to quote his book.

The BATF

With the presence of over 20,000 gun laws, a chapter in a book is not going to even begin to scratch the surface, but we can talk about some major gun laws and firearm control organizations. As to the latter, the BATF must be mentioned. The BATF is a part of the United States Department of the Treasury. BATF stands for Bureau of Alcohol, Tobacco and Firearms. In the past, the firearms part was not included here. Now, it is the firearms portion of that bureau which accounts for a large percentage of that outfit's work load. In short, the BATF is the major governmental body dealing with Federal gun laws and the administration of Federal Firearms Licenses (FFLs).

The FFL

Just about every serious shooter in the land has heard of the FFL. As just mentioned, FFL stands for Federal Firearms License, and this license is directly related to the BATF and the resulting prohibitions created by the Gun Control Act of 1968. The latter is often referred to as the "GCA of '68." It is very important to *all* gunowners, and you should have an idea of what this law means to you.

To recite the entire Gun Control Act of 1968 would require a book in itself to simply cover the ramifications of that law. We can scratch the surface, however, and in a very important way, giving some highlights of this law. The law immediately changed many things about gun ownership. My very first rifle was purchased through the mail. Today, ordering and receiving a firearm through the mail is no longer legal, although it certainly was legal prior to 1968. In other words, mail-order guns are out now due to the Gun Control Act of 1968. Here are some points pertaining to this law.

1. No Mail Order

As just stated, a gun store cannot honor a "mail-order" request for a firearm from a citizen. As an obvious result of the GCA of '68 one will no longer find advertisements in the popular gun or outdoor magazines pertaining to the mail-order sale of guns. Younger readers may see these ads by going to the local library and checking into some older gun or outdoor magazines, those which are prior to 1968. An ad for a firearm stated simply to mail the amount to the dealer, after which the dealer sent gun to the buyer through the U.S. mail. This is no longer legal.

2. Old Guns

However, if the gun was made before 1899, or if it is a black powder original or replica, or earlier, then the above statement does not apply. Today, for example, one may see an advertisement for an original black powder firearm or a replica that dates back to, perhaps, the 1800s. These may be mailed. One will notice that this is the case because the ad may suggest sending a check or money order, after which the black powder muzzle-loading firearm will be sent to the door of the buyer. So there is an exception to the rule of mail-order, and that exception, again, pertains to firearms either made prior to 1899 or of a design which is generally black powder in origin. The reader does not have to concern himself as to which guns these are. The seller, however, *must* concern himself and does.

3. Obtaining an FFL

The FFL will be required for various reasons. Not just anyone can purchase the FFL from the BATF. The FFL, Federal Firearms License, is for those who sell firearms or deal in firearms in some legitimate form. A holder of the FFL may mail a firearm to another holder of an FFL. While a citizen may not mail a firearm to another citizen, he may mail a firearm *for repair* to an authorized dealer or repair center which has the FFL. And the firearm will be mailed back to him by that company. I say "may" because there are specific license restrictions here. A citizen who has a repair need on a firearm may send it to a licensed repair center only, but never to a non-FFL-holding friend who happens to know how to fix guns.

At this point in time, the FFL situation is an interesting one. Many retailers, for example, feel that the FFL is held by too many people. They want further restrictions. The reason is one of protection, business-wise. For example, if the citizen wishes to buy a firearm from a discount center which advertises in a gun paper or other advertising medium, he can go to anyone who holds the FFL and have that person get the gun for him. A Federal document will have to be signed (mentioned next), and this would constitute a federally legal transaction as far as the BATF is concerned. Generally, the FFL holder will charge about 10 percent of the value of the transaction for his services.

4. Keeping Records

The Gun Control Act requires the keeping of records. As stated above, if the buyer of the firearm goes through an FFL holder, the holder of the FFL must have the buyer sign a document known as *Form 4473*. This form asks pertinent character questions of the buyer concerning matters of the law, such as conviction of crimes or other similar factors. In other words, the transfer of a firearm from a dealer to a buyer would require the completion and signing of Form 4473.

5. Age Limits

The Gun Control Act has established age limits for ammunition and firearms purchase. A person under the age of 18 may not buy ammunition. In fact, a person of 18 may only buy ammo for a rifle or shotgun. He may not purchase ammunition for a handgun. Handgun ammo can be purchased only by a person 21 years of age or older. A person 18 years or older can buy a rifle or a shotgun, but he cannot buy a handgun. One must be 21 years of age or older in order to buy a handgun.

6. Residency

Furthermore, the Gun Control Act provides that the resident of one state cannot enter another state and buy a gun.

He must be a resident of the state if he is to buy a firearm in that state, *or* he must hold an FFL. If an FFL holder is traveling through a state other than his home state and decides he wants to buy a firearm at a local gunshop, he cannot buy it unless he has signed a copy of a current FFL in his possession. If the person is *not* an FFL holder, he would have to have an FFL holder in his state buy the rifle from the FFL holder in the state which has the gun.

7. Dealers and Manufacturers

Actual dealerships and manufacturers must be licensed. This does not affect the citizen gun owner directly, but it is another point of the Gun Control Act of 1968. A manufacturer, in other words, must have a special license in order to manufacture firearms.

8. Selling of Firearms

A citizen may sell a firearm to another citizen if both are residents of the same state. These are some of the rules and regulations which have been included under the Gun Control Act, that 1968 law which is so prominent today in the transactions between gun owners. It would be redundant to try to include more on this law, because the onus falls upon the seller of firearms to comply with this regulation. It is the dealer's responsibility to inform the buyer of the laws which pertain and to insist upon the compliance of the laws before selling ammunition or guns to anyone. However, given some of the documented negative BATF encounters experienced by some gun owners, always exercise extreme caution in buying guns or ammo, i.e., know your seller. If you ever encounter a gun-selling situation that raises serious questions in your own mind, check with your local authorities (or nearest BATF office) for complete clarification, *before you buy*.

Self-Defense and the Law

It is imperative that this issue be addressed briefly here. No chapter can cover all of the laws pertaining to self-defense in America, of course. In fact, no small book could do it. But there are some general thoughts which must be shared on the topic so that the complete shooter has an idea of when he can and cannot employ a firearm in the act of what he may construe as self-defense.

1. The laws of self-defense vary from state to state. No shooter is prepared in knowledge of this topic unless he knows the laws pertaining to *his home area*. One must never assume that the laws of his home area will be similar to the laws of another area.

2. Your life must be threatened, or the life of someone else, with the latter being a questionable situation. Imagine being in court and actually proving that you saved another's life through the use of a firearm.

3. Do not think that you can protect property by wielding force via a firearm. If your auto is being looted, call the police. If your neighbor's house is being carried off bit by bit, call the police. Do not attempt to save property from either theft or vandalism by use of a firearm. In other words, self-defense does not, *generally*, mean property defense.

4. One may not use a firearm because of "threats." A person may even threaten your life, but the force of a gun is not the way to answer that threat. Life itself must be at stake.

5. The citzens arrest—for the most part, forget it. It is legal to perform a citizen's arrest, but only if a very serious crime (generally a felony) is underway. If you see a crime in progress, your first response should be to call the police.

6. Never use a firearm to frighten away a person or persons who might be stealing your property. The only justified use will be in saving your life, and the court may not construe this as a life-saving measure. The simple firing of a gun to warn off intruders could be illegal.

7. You won't be a hero—do not believe for a moment that you will be a hero, even if you save a life through the use of your firearm. Use that firearm only when there is no other resort. The court will not consider the situation as heroic even though the firearm may have been used to thwart a crime.

8. Self-defense is for real. In spite of all of the above warnings, self-defense is still viable in America. If a person is about to lose his life, or if the situation is definitely life-threatening, a citizen of our land does have a right to defend himself. Incidentally, records clearly show that the use of a firearm has saved thousands of innocent lives in this country in modern times.

The world of firearm law is just as complex as the world of business law, and even more complex in a few instances. It is a world of local application and interpretation, too. The complete shooter is obliged to study the gun laws of his home area so that he will be familiar with them. Although our very constitution provides for firearms ownership, it has not provided for a simplification of the laws pertaining to that ownership.

Chapter 35

The Shooter's Library

RAIN, SLEET, SNOW, the cold of winter or the heat of summer may keep me from getting to the shooting range or into the field to fire my guns, but none of these will prevent my enjoying firearms as long as I have reading material on the subject. The complete shooter should begin to collect immediately, if he has not already started, written matter on the sport, be that material in the form of books, pamphlets, magazines or personal notes.

Gathering the written word on the topic of shooting is a very important aspect of the shooting sports. Without a dissemination of information on shooting, the sport would never have grown in richness the way it has. It would be a shame to have to wait until "word of mouth" got around for a shooter to find out what is new in the way of arms and ammo, or in the manner either is loaded or used.

There are many ways to successfully build a library for shooting, and this part of the sport need not be at all expensive or even time-consuming. Most of my own library building is incidental. I approach the matter seriously, but without strain. While not a book collector, as such, and while my investments are monitarily very small, I have still managed to gather up a sizable collection of material for reference and for enjoyment. Sometimes, quite often at that, the two mix, and I enjoy reading reference material.

The Magazine

The magazine is just about the most current source of shooting material. Since the magazine is usually a monthly or bimonthly affair, it is going to be fairly up-to-date in its information. To teach and to delight—those two reasons have often been cited as reading's main thrust. And the magazine is capable of teaching and delighting the reader. Shooting magazines have changed a lot over the years, and they will again change, but they continue to present updated information to the shooter.

Today, the "how-to" aspect is still strong. It has been a major avenue in magazines for at least 10 if not 15 years, preceded by an aim to delight more than to teach. I like a mix of the two in some magazines, pure research in others. When I pick up an *Outdoor Life* magazine, I expect to be entertained while being shown some of the latest information on shooting and hunting, and that's the way the magazine works. When I look at a *Sports Afield* magazine, the same is true, although I also expect that journal to present some art-oriented material each month. In *The Rifle* magazine, I know I am going to find a technical approach to shooting, with plenty of useful information.

Some magazines are for saving. *The Rifle* or *The Handloader* will be saved each month by me because they always contain superb, technical reference material. This means shooting data I can turn back to again and again in the future. Other magazines will have some of the same sort of data, and with these I employ the "tear sheet" method of saving information. This means removing the pages which hold the information I'm interested in and putting these pages into a notebook. This works well as long as the shooter remembers to attach a title page to his notebook so that he can find what he has so carefully saved.

The Book

Generally thought of as more permanent, the gun book is simply another means of presenting gathered material. What we hope for in a book is a lot of information and interesting material put together in a somewhat organized fashion so that there is considerable "meat" between the two covers. Then we have a source to return to time and again.

If a book is mine, I like to mark in it. I realize that we are taught in school that it's sacrilegious to make marks in books, but on the inside cover of my books, I will have a list, and the list will tell me that on page such and such I can find a statement on a given topic. I was just rereading a book entitled *Three Against the Wilderness* by Eric Collier, making notes, and when Mr. Collier gave his capsulized view of game management, I turned to the inside cover and made a note of it. Now I can find that reference again easily.

Collecting Books

A book does not have to be a collector's item to be collected. Books are collected because they make up a personal shooter's library and that library is used hundreds of times by the complete shooter who cares enough to continually update and refresh his knowledge. But books can be collected, too. And it's a hobby all its own. Over the

The used book store is an excellent place to find many good titles, such as Ruark's *Use Enough Gun* and Stewart Edwards White's text on *The Mountains, The Cabin The Forest.* But *The Rights of Gun Owners* is a book which would not likely be located in a used rack. It is too current for that.

years, there have been hundreds of superb books written on the shooting sports, and it is not impossible to locate these books to this day, often in excellent condition. Here are a few ways:

1. Library Sales

Libraries have to update their collections from time to time. My own local library not only annually releases a certain number of books to make room for newer texts, but it also has a library sale as well. Each year, citizens from the community donate old books to the cause. The library sells the used books at a reasonable price and uses the proceeds to help buy new books. This past year, I found an old Speer loading manual for 50 cents.

2. Mail-Order Book Dealers

A more positive way to find excellent books on the shooting sports is through a specialty house which deals in them. For example, I just, today, received a listing from Blacktail Mountain Books, 42 1st Ave. West, Kalispell, MT 59901. The list included dozens of fine shooting titles, most of them at very modest prices. And there are several such outlets for this type of used book. Are all of these books collector's copies? Not by any stringent standards of the collecting game. For example, I would not call a modern title which is still in print a collector's copy, but you darn well would collect that book in order to build a library. So instead of worrying about definitions, let's be positive and continue looking into how to build a library.

3. The Search

Booksellers may often put on a search for a book. I have wanted a particular book by Hornaday, the naturalist, so I had a bookseller search out a copy for me. Yes, this may mean a few extra dollars for the bookseller. After all, why should a person spend time looking for a title without being compensated for it?

4. Bibliography

Sometimes we can find fine books on the shooting sports listed in bibliographies found in other books. I have located information on many good books as I was reading a shooting text. Also, there is *Guns and Shooting—A Bibliography,* by Ray Riling (6844 Gorsten St., Philadelphia, PA 19119) and this text lists many gun books. The point is, look to lists of books located in various sources, for these lists are available and they do help in locating good shooting volumes.

5. The Book Shop

Obviously, the new or used book shop is a fine place to locate shooting titles. Look under various categories in the new/used book shop, including *natural history, travel, technical* as well as *sports*. New shooting titles emerge all of the time, and the bookstore will often have copies or can order them for you. Ask your local bookstore if you can look through a list of their titles to see if they have anything you want to order. Also, you might leave your phone number with the bookstore owner, telling him to call you if he finds certain gun titles.

6. Flea Markets

The flea market is an outlet for sporting books, too. I have seen a number of shooting texts in such places. Also, an antique show may provide a good place to find such books. Look in thrift shops, too. Gun shows also have shooting texts from time to time as do junk shops and sporting goods stores.

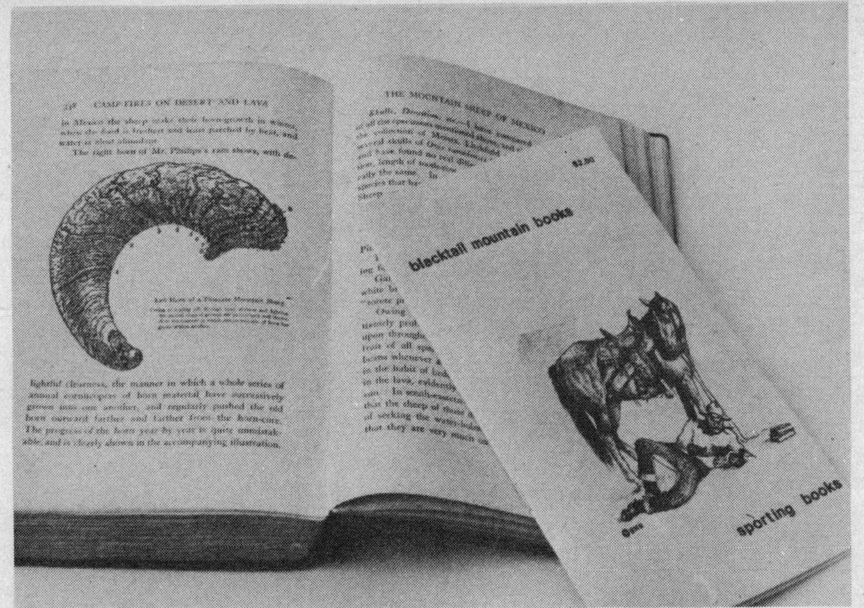

A brochure on the right shows a listing of books on shooting and related topics. This list is from Blacktail Mountain Books, and behind the listing is a fine book by Hornaday, the naturalist. Although out of print for years, this book can still be found through book dealers who specialize in gun and outdoor titles.

7. Classified Ads and Gun Papers

Classified ad sections in various papers may advertise used books, and among these used books may be found several good gun titles from time to time. Sporting or gun papers also have books for sale. *The Shotgun News,* (Box 699, Hastings, NE 68901), a paper for those who are looking for guns and equipment, carries a listing of gun books each and every issue.

8. The Reprint

Another source for a grand old book is the reprint. I have, for example, a copy of *The Gun and Its Development* by W. W. Greener. It is not a collector's item, because it is a modern version of that 1910 edition. Also, there are some very fine special editions being offered these days. Wolfe Publishing Co. of Prescott, Arizona, offers several, including a series of limited edition titles from their Wolfe Classics Limited Edition publications. This last series begins with *The Hunting Rifle* by Colonel Townsend Whelen, a reprinting of the 1940 edition.

9. The Book Club

A book club, such as the Outdoor Life Book Club, can be an excellent resource of good gun books. The argument that one will buy books he does not truly want when he belongs to a book club is not the case. One must keep up

The *Gun Digest* has been with us for 40 years and is one book the author picks up annually. Not only does it update the shooter on current ammo, trends, hardware and so forth, but it also contains many ideas worthy of application.

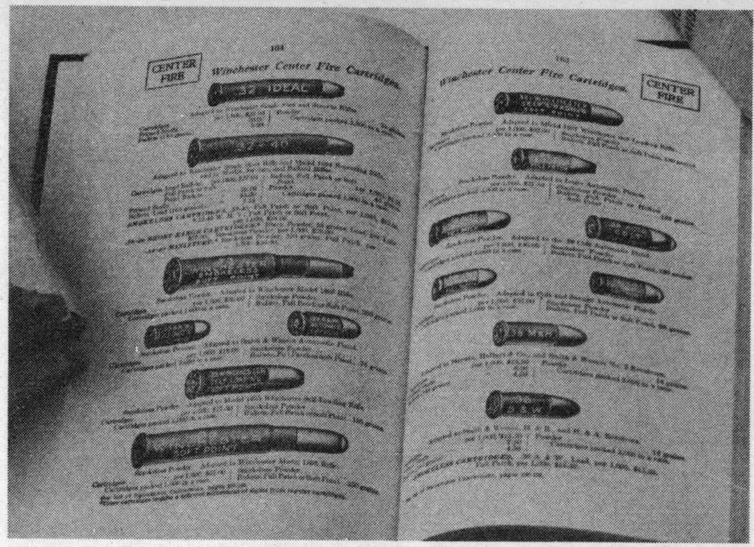

The 1916 Winchester catalog reprint is loaded with interesting data on cartridges, such as the 32 Ideal and the 38 M&H. Such information is not likely to be found in current writing, at least not to any great extent.

(Left) Reprints have allowed the return of some very interesting firearms texts at a modest price. This is the Winchester 1916 catalog of arms, which is an excellent addition to the library of a shooter who likes the older Winchesters.

with the selections, but a shooter only orders what he wants and he need not ever end up with unwanted titles.

10. Gun Digest

This is an excellent resource book and a title I buy every year. However, there is another benefit in the *Gun Digest* for those building a library of arms books. In the back of *Gun Digest,* one can find the ''Arms Library for Collector Hunter/Shooter/Outdoorsman,'' which is ''A selection of books—old, new and forthcoming . . .'' It's a fine place to locate good books on shooting.

Condition of Used Gun Books

The shooter looking into a collection of used firearms texts will find that many of the bookstores and mail-order outlets use a code which helps the reader understand the actual condition of the book. This code does vary among bookstores, but here is a common set of rules to go by when buying a used book:

Fine

Fine means that the book is close to new. It has no defects at all and would all but pass as brand new—collectors enjoy finding a rare book in Fine condition, of course.

Very Good

Very good means little wear. There will be no torn pages, no defect(s) in the cover or any other significant damage, but one can see this is not a brand new book.

Beautiful books are available today as well as from the past. This is a Wolfe Publishing Company text (Prescott, Arizona) of *The Hunting Rifle* by Colonel Whelen. Wolfe will print a series of fine older gun books all in this collector's edition style.

The shooter's library should include several good reloading handbooks. One just won't do usually, as testers use different loads and a certain manual may have a load which works best in a given rifle.

Good

Good means that all of the pages are intact. The book is readable and not torn, but may show definite signs of use.

Fair

Fair suggests that the pages are intact but the book could have some stains and perhaps a repair or two.

Poor

A poor book is generally a reading copy only. It is, probably, dirty and may even have some large stains. It is not a bad book in some cases, but is seldom going to be the kind of condition a collector would want.

There may also be an *Ex-Lib* book classification, which means Ex-Library. This book was once the property of a public library, but the library no longer wanted it. Now it is in personal ownership. Usually, there will be a notation in the ex-library book stating that the book is no longer the property of that library.

Technical Manuals

Manuals also make super library additions for shooters. The most obvious manual is the handloading book, and as stated earlier, a shooter should never sell an "outdated" loading manual. There are often some very interesting articles included in these books, as well as loads which may not be in general use at the moment, but which are all the same very good for certain tasks. There are also Army manuals and many other manuals which contain shooting information. Even the manuals which come with new firearms are worth keeping though the owner of the firearm may have all but memorized them.

Catalogs

Shooters often enjoy catalogs well enough to keep them. In fact, replicas of old catalogs are sold these days, and some original old-time catalogs are fairly valuable. I have a couple of older Herter's catalogs which represent good reading for sheer fun, and I have replicas of 19th century and early 20th century catalogs which are actual sources of information.

Personal Notebook

The shooter's library may include personal notebooks. I wish I had gotten started much earlier with my own, for I would have thousands of recorded loads and other data at my disposal if I had. I urge the shooter to think about compiling personal shooting notes. These days, there are small books with hard covers, the pages inside being blank. They are perfect for the shooter who wishes to start a diary of his shooting experiences.

Letters

Files of letters are often valuable to a library. There are often a number of shooters who continually send letters back and forth explaining rifle tests and accuracy loads and various other aspects of the sport, and these letters can play a role in giving some good information down the line. I have such a collection, and have often turned to it to find out what another shooter did about a certain cast bullet load or other such bit of information. The shooter's letters can be a good library addition.

I am convinced that a shooter should have a library at his disposal. He may bend that library toward shooting history or technical data, or he may wish to collect books which pertain to hunting or some other aspect of shooting. And he may in fact turn out to be a collector, building a library of books which are valuable not only for the information they contain, but actually in and of themselves as collector's items. No matter the particular reason, the fact is, a library is very important to the complete shooter.

Chapter 36

A Shooter's Dictionary

THIS ABRIDGED dictionary of shooting language is geared to help the reader find his way through the maze created by the world of shooting jargon. There are many terms which need clarification and that clarification is the aim of this chapter.

Sayings which many of us use today originated from shooting terminology. For example, if you buy something ''lock, stock and barrel,'' you buy it all. Naturally, the *lock, stock* and *barrel* are the component parts of the muzzle-loading firearm. He's a ''straight shooter'' if he's a fair person. You really ''hit the mark'' if you got everything right. And so forth. But there are also many terms which pertain in a more technical manner to the world of shooting, and the complete shooter should have a grasp of these terms, understanding their meaning, so he can deal with them. These terms do not amount to a mere ''flash in the pan.'' And knowing some of these terms means we won't ''go off half-cocked'' in an arms discussion.

A

Accoutrements

These are all of the incidental devices for shooting. Some shooters include all but the firearm as the meaning of this term. Accoutrements are the accessories to shooting.

Accuracy

Accuracy refers to a firearm's ability to group its projectiles on a target. Today, an accurate big bore rifle is one which will group into a minute of angle, meaning it will keep 3 to 5 shots roughly inside 1 inch at 100 yards, 2 inches at 200 yards, 3 inches at 300 yards, and so forth.

Action

The action is the mechanical device in any rifle which consists of the receiver, bolt or breech block, feed mechanism and firing mechanism. The working portion of a firearm that actually contains the round. A breech bolt or locking block, in the action, serves to lock a round in the barrel's chamber prepatory to, and during, firing. Action types include the bolt, lever, pump, auto and single shot.

Airspace

In the cartridge case that space not taken up by the powder is called airspace. We say that a round has 100 percent loading density if all of the space in the case is taken up by the powder charge.

Angle of Departure

The angle of departure is the angle above the horizontal at which a bullet departs the muzzle.

Anneal

The process of making brass more malleable, less brittle and tougher. We find annealing on the necks of some cartridge cases, such as the 458 Winchester. To anneal is to rapidly heat the neck (of the cartridge case in this example) and then douse the case in a liquid coolant. This makes the brass less likely to split. Also used in forming cases, sometimes. Excluding the above example, and a few others, the bluish hue left on case necks by the annealing process is polished off of commercial ammo. The bluish hue of annealing is commonly seen on the necks of military ammo.

Aperture Sight

This is the same as a ''peep'' sight, a disc of some sort with a hole in its center. The eye automatically focuses in the very middle of this hole because that is where the most light is concentrated. Therefore, the aperture sight is very accurate, and all the shooter has to do is look *through* the hole, without consciously trying to center anything, but rather simply placing the front sight on the target. The aperture is not new, examples having been found on 19th century guns.

B

Backlash

Backlash refers to the continued motion of the trigger in a rearward direction after the sear has been released. Ideally, at the instant the sear is released, the trigger movement should halt.

Aperture Sight: This Winchester Model 94 Big Bore has a Williams aperture (or "peep") sight mounted on the receiver

Ball

Actually a term used to refer to a projectile fired from a gun, but today this term is mainly a reference to the "round ball" of old, the lead sphere used in muzzle-loading firearms. One may still hear of "ball ammunition" however, and this will refer usually to military ammo with a full metal jacket bullet. Of course, the lead ball is undersized for muzzleloaders and it uses a cloth patch to take up the windage in the bore. This is referred to as a "patched round ball." Although "round ball" is a redundancy, the term hangs on for the sake of history.

Ballistic Coefficient

This term is used to explain the ability of a bullet to overcome the ravages of the atmosphere. It is a ratio between a standard bullet and the actual bullet itself, and it is expressed as a number. The higher the number the better the ability of the bullet to retain its original muzzle velocity and energy. As an example of C (ballistic coefficient is denoted by the letter C) we can see that a 180-grain 30-caliber round nose bullet might have a C of .239 while a 180-grain 30-caliber pointed bullet might have a C of .431. The shape of the bullet, then, has a lot to do with how the bullet "bucks the atmosphere."

Ballistics

Ballistics is the study of a projectile's performance upon ignition inside and outside the barrel of a firearm. When the projectile is still in the bore, the study is called *internal ballistics*. After the bullet leaves the muzzle and from there to its final destination, the study is called *external ballistics*. Ballistics includes many aspects of a projectile's flight, including delivered energy.

Ball Powder

Ball powder is a spherically shaped propellant, as opposed to extruded powder, and was developed by Olin (Winchester). It is a double-base powder, that is, it is made with both nitrocellulose and nitroglycerine.

Barleycorn Sight

This is a very plain simple front sight which presents to the shooter the image of a truncated triangle. It's early in design, and usually mounted low on the barrel. It is rounded in appearance (from the side view) and looks like an individual grain of barley in shape, hence its name.

Ballistics: The study of ballistics can be "internal" or external. The simple examination of a bullet's expansion characteristics (after firing) would be an example of external ballistics.

Base Wad

This is that inner portion of the shotgun shell which rests within the head of the hull. It aids in supporting the walls of the hull (brass), and it also serves as an *integral* part of the hull, unlike those wads which comprise the wad column and are fired away through the bore.

BB

The BB-size shot pellet measures 17-caliber (.177-inch, to be precise). It takes approximately 55 BB pellets to make an ounce.

Bead

A bead is an aiming device on a rifle/or handgun and a point of reference on a shotgun. There are various types of beads for the cartridge gun, but their purpose is the same, to form a portion of the front sight. A shotgun may have two beads, the normal one mounted on the front of the barrel and a center bead on the rib, used for alignment purposes, since the lining up of the two beads will prevent canting the shotgun. Beads are cylindrical in appearance and generally made of materials such as brass, gold or ivory.

Bearing Surface

This is the portion of the bullet which makes contact with the rifling in the bore. Bore fit and accuracy go hand in hand. The amount of bearing surface also affects pressure.

Beavertail Forearm

The beavertail forearm is large, wide and flat in construction. While more normally found on rifles, they can also be found on shotguns.

Bedding

In reference to the action and barrel as fitted to the stock of the firearm. A barrel and action are bedded into the wood via appropriate channels and mortices. Fiberglass is often used to enhance bedding.

Belted Case

The band commonly found ahead of the extactor groove on cartridge cases bearing a "magnum" designation. Belts are found on rounds such as the 7mm Remington Magnum, 300 H&H Magnum and others. Cartridges with belts actually headspace on that area of the case.

Berdan Primer

European cartridges may have this system of ignition, where the primer has no anvil. The anvil is integral with the base of the primer pocket. The base of the primer pocket in this type of cartridge usually has two or more flash holes instead of one. A regular decapper will not remove a spent primer from a Berdan-primed case.

Boat-Tail Bullet: This is an example of a boat-tail bullet. The tapering at the heel of the bullet adds stability during flight.

Bluing

The process of changing the metal parts of a firearm from "the white" stage to a blue-colored condition is termed bluing. It is a form of oxidation. While there are cold processes for altering the metal's color, permanent bluing is generally accomplished with salts in a hot process with bluing tanks. There are various types of bluing finishes, the soft, or bead-blasted look being a very popular type among shooters today.

Boat-Tail Bullet

The heel of the boat-tail bullet is tapered, thereby reducing drag and giving the projectile excellent stability at long range.

Bolster

A lump of metal which may be welded or screwed onto the breech of the black powder caplock gun, or it may be a contiguous part of the breech itself. The nipple screws into it. A strong unit.

Boot

Originally, a leather covering for a flintlock, often treated with some form of weatherproofing agent, which is fitted over the lock itself for bad weather protection. Often, the word is used for the weatherproof covering on a caplock as well.

Bolt Thrust

This is the force presented to the face of the bolt caused by the pressure in the cartridge case upon firing the gun.

Bore Sighter

An instrument used to align the bore with the line of sight by viewing a target through both the sight and bore. A bore sighter is also known as a collimator (usually an optical instrument). A gunsmith will bore sight a firearm in his shop.

Bore Diameter

Generally, the diameter of the bore of a firearm is measured from land-to-land. A 270 Winchester, for example, would have a bore diameter of .27-inch, but the groove diameter would be .277-inch, .007-inch larger than bore diameter. A bullet for the 270 Winchester would generally be .277-inch, to correspond with the groove diameter so that the lands would impress upon the bullet.

Boxer Primer

This is the primer common to American shooting. The cup contains priming compound and an anvil. The flash from this type of primer travels through a single flash hole centrally located in the base of the cartridge's primer pocket.

Breech

The rearward portion of the barrel which contains the cartridge or in the case of black powder, the load itself.

Breech Plug

This is a threaded plug of metal which is screwed into the breech as a seal at the rear of the chamber. The barrel tang is often an integral piece with this plug.

Bullet Pull

The force measured in pounds, necessary to extract a seated bullet from a loaded cartridge.

Bullet Upset

Specifically, bullet upset is the expansion of the bullet within the bore of the gun due to the push of the gases on the one hand, and the inertia of the bullet on the other. See "obturation."

Burning Rate

The rate at which powder is changed from the solid to the gaseous state is the burning rate. Comparatively, we have fast-burning and slow-burning powders. For example, H-4831 would be considered a slow-burning powder, while Bullseye would be considered a fast-burning powder. The application of these two powders would be very different because of their diverse burning rates.

Buttplate

The portion of the rifle stock upon which the shooter's face rests is the buttstock, the rearmost portion of that buttstock being (usually) covered with a buttplate. Quite often, the buttplate is nothing more than a metal or plastic piece fitted to the contour of the back of the stock. When made of softer-than-metal materials, such as rubber, this area is usually called a *buttpad*.

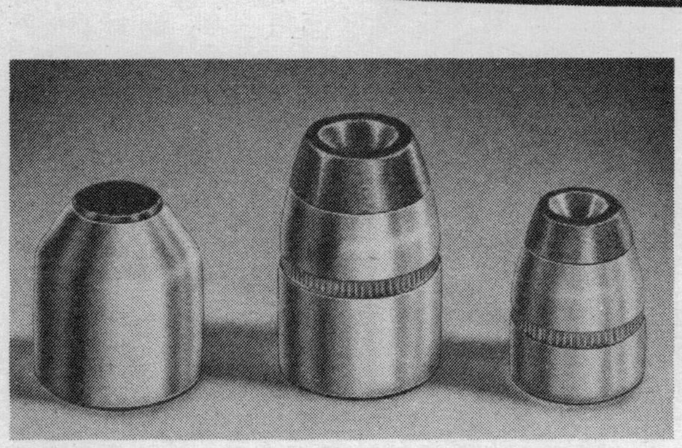

(Above) **Buttstock:** In this instance the buttstock is that portion of the overall stock from the rear of the pistol grip back to the recoil pad.

Cannelure: The bullet on the far left has no cannelure while the bullets to the right of that slug both possess cannelures. In these cases the cannelures serve as crimp grooves.

Brinell Hardness

Surface hardness of metals, surface only, using a scale where the higher the number, the harder the surface of the metal.

Bullet Core

This is the lead of the jacketed bullet. In other words, the jacket covers the lead core.

Bullet Diameter

The diameter of a bullet is commonly expressed in decimals of an inch, or millimeters. A .264-inch bullet would be 264 thousandths of 1 inch across. That same diameter of projectile is also commonly expressed, in metric terms, as 6.5mm.

Buttstock

The latter or rearward part of the rifle or shotgun stock upon which the face is rested.

C

Caliber

The original definition of the word correctly means the diameter of the *bore*. Today, however, the conversational usage of the term is used to designate "cartridge." Most shooters, when asked what "caliber" their rifle is, respond, "30-06 Springfield, 243 Winchester," etc.

Cannelure

Cannelures are found on both cartridge cases and bullets. In the case of the bullet, the cannelure is a groove around the bullet into which the lip or leading edge of a cartridge case neck is crimped. A bullet cannelure also acts to retard the mushrooming of the bullet upon impact. The current 220-grain 30-caliber Silvertip bullet has a double cannelure. In these factory loads, the topmost cannelure is used as a crimping groove, the lower cannelure serving to retard bullet expansion. Case cannelures are generally found on handgun ammunition and serve to more rigidly grasp the seated bullet, preventing the bullet from moving rearward in the case as a result of heavy recoil.

Cant

Tilting the firearm, left or right, off of the prescribed vertical holding position.

Case Capacity

The amount of powder that can be held by the cartridge case. Case capacity may differ depending upon the brand of the case even though the cartridge is the same. For example, a military 30-06 case will generally hold less powder than a commercial 30-06 case, especially of Winchester brand. Therefore, the reloader must pay attention to and not mix, brands of cases.

Centerfire: The centerfire cartridge has its source of priming centrally located in the head of the cartridge. In this instance you're viewing a fired 244 (6mm) Remington case, the primer having been fully indented by the firing pin.

Case Cling

During firing a cartridge swells out to fill the chamber. The force against the chamber walls is case cling.

Case Forming

Case forming is accomplished through the use of reloading dies in which case shape is altered.

Case Trimming

It is very important that a case be short enough so that the neck does not drive up into the leade of the chamber. If it does, higher than normal pressures may result upon firing. Cases are trimmed, using rotary or trim die tools, to keep them at a safe overall case length.

Centerfire

As opposed to rimfire, where the detonating materials are retained all along the rim of the cartridge case, the centerfire, once called "central fire," uses a primer which is located in the center of the case head.

Chamber

The chamber is the rearmost portion of the barrel which opens up to accept a cartridge or shotshell of specific dimensions. In the black powder vernacular, chamber refers to the section of the breech that contains the powder charge.

Chamber Pressure

A cartridge functions because of pressure from expanding gases forcing a projectile or projectiles from the bore. The actual measurement of this pressure in the breech or chamber area is called chamber pressure.

Chamfer

To bevel the edge of a revolver's cylinder chamber or to bevel the edge of a cartridge case mouth is known as chamfering.

Charger

This is a black powder measure (sometimes used to designate a shot measure, too) which is non-adjustable, throwing just one particular volume only; and, it can be made of a section of horn, drilled out antler, or many other materials.

Choke

In the shotgun, the choke is generally a constricted area in the forward portion of the barrel, the degree and construction of which will determine pattern percentage tightness at a range of 40 yards. There are degrees of choke. From "tight" to "loose" they are as follows: full, improved modified, modified, improved cylinder, cylinder and "Skeet."

Chronograph

An electronic instrument used to measure the velocity of

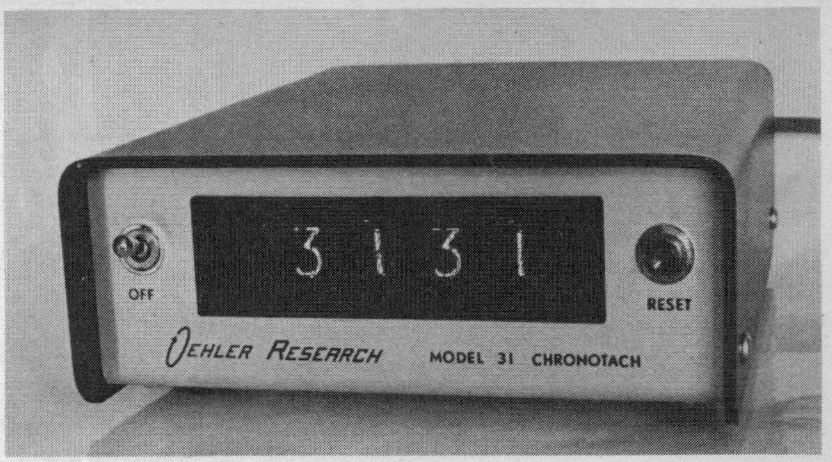

Chronograph: Modern, electronic chronographs are used to measure the velocity of a projectile or shot charge in flight. The speed of the bullet just measured by this chronograph was 3131 fps.

a bullet or a shot charge.

Collimator (see Bore Sighter)

Comb

The comb of the stock is the top edge of the upper half of the buttstock. In shooting, the shooter's face rests on the comb.

Compensator

Specifically, this is the Cutts Compensator. The "Cutts", as used on shotguns, is a muzzle-mounted device into which a variable choke device or specific choke tube is screwed. The Cutts Compensator also serves to reduce muzzle jump and, for some shooters, felt recoil. Sans the choke feature, the original "Cutts" was first used as a muzzle break on Thompson Submachineguns.

Creep

Creep refers to slack in the trigger. When the trigger is pulled, instead of crisp disengagement with the sear, the trigger moves excessively to the rear before the sear is disengaged.

Crimp (metallic round)

The crimp is the inward folding of the cartridge case mouth into the bullet's cannelure or crimp groove.

Crowning

The muzzle crown on a rifle or pistol barrel may be one of many types, including the flat crown, which is basically a polished surface. Normally, the interior portion of the crown is recessed so that the rifling is protected at the muzzle. The removal of this metal, to form a concave section at the muzzle, is termed "crowning."

Cup

This stands for Copper Units of Pressure. A copper section is placed in a crusher unit, and the copper is smashed to a very specific point. The pressure gun is used with this device to tell just how much force a particular load develops. CUP is used for pressures over the number of 10,000 generally, with LUP used for pressures under 10,000. The figure is not directly related to pounds per square inch of pressure, and cannot be interchanged with it; but, CUP (and LUP) give a very accurate indication of the pressures created by a given load.

D

Detent (see Fly)

Double Action

A revolver is double action if it may be fired by simply pulling the trigger, or by cocking back the hammer for each consecutive shot fired.

Drachm

Drachm is a synonym for *dram*. A dram is 27.34 grains by weight, and a drachm should be considered the same weight. In the past, there was an apothecary term for drachm which was 60 grains weight. The apothecary definition is *not* applied to the firearms hobby.

Dram

A dram is equal to 27.34 grains by weight.

Dross

Dross is the waste which collects on the surface of molten lead during the process of preparing lead for casting. Dross is skimmed away, as it is often mostly dirt. However, do not confuse separated metals, such as tin, with dross.

Dry Fire

Firing the gun without any ammo as a practice measure. Also used in testing a gun's function.

Duplex Load

The term has application to both black powder shooting

and metallic cartridge reloading with smokeless powder. Often, black powder shooters used to drop in a small dose of finer granulation powder to "kick off" the main charge. The practice led to putting in a little bit of smokeless powder, too. Duplex refers to the two different powders being used in the *one* load. It is *NOT* recommended practice, especially with smokeless powder. In the world of smokeless powder, metallic cartridge reloading, the approach is almost the same, the hoped-for results being higher velocity and lower working pressures. Smokeless duplex loads feature, usually, a small amount of fast burning powder separated from (and underneath) a larger charge of slow burning powder. The late Elmer Keith experimented extensively with smokeless duplex loads. The technique is not recommended to the hobbyist, its practice being appropriately confined to firearms industry labs.

E

Ejector
The mechanical device which expels the loaded round or empty case from the firearm is the ejector.

Escutcheon
On a black powder firearm the metal inlay which has a hole in its center, normally rectangular in shape, to accept and hold the barrel key. The barrel key slips through the escutcheon, then the wood of the stock, the tenon next, more wood, and comes out on the opposite side of the forearm and into a second escutcheon. These escutcheons are screwed into both sides of the stock.

Extractor
A mechanical device on a firearm which pulls the loaded or spent case or hull from the breech as the action is opened.

Extreme Range
This is the farthest a given bullet at a given velocity can fly regardless of accuracy.

F

Field of View
The width of the view as seen through an optical device, such as a firearm telescopic sight or a binocular or telescope is the field of view and is measured generally in feet in the USA. For example, a scope sight may have a 30-foot field of view at 100 yards, meaning that the encompassing vision through the scope will be 30 feet wide at 100 yards.

Fireforming
Expanding a case to fit a larger or differently shaped chamber. When a cartridge is fired in a modified chamber or when a modified cartridge is fired in a standard chamber, the resulting case will emerge with the new shape. Fireforming is commonly used in wildcatting.

Firing Pin
The mechanical device which actually collides with the detonating part of the cartridge is the firing pin.

Flinching
This amounts to involuntary shooter motion which takes place as the gun is fired or in anticipation thereof. This motion deflects the gun off target.

Floorplate
The bottom covering of the magazine in a bolt-action rifle, made of metal and usually spring-activated so it can drop down to allow the emptying of the magazine.

Flux
An agent used, in bullet-casting, to help clean lead. Wax is a fluxing agent in this context.

Fly
On a black powder firearm, this tiny protrusion in the

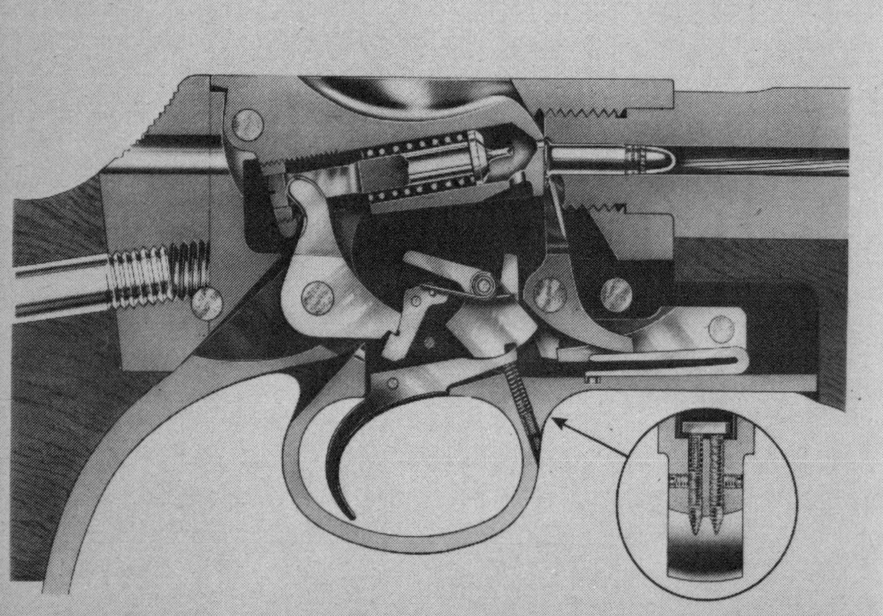

Firing Pin: In this cut-away rendering, the firing pin (or "striker") of a falling block rimfire single shot is poised, ready to strike the rim of the chambered, rimfire cartridge.

lock, also called a detent, forces the sear nose down so that while the rifle is being fired there is no chance of the tumbler getting hung up in the half-cock notch. The fly allows the tumbler to flow smoothly, which gives much more postitive action.

Forcing Cone
In a modern shotgun that portion in the forward part of the chamber which is reduced in diameter. The forcing cone allows shot to pass into the bore easier.

Fouling Ring
This is a literal ring of fouling in the bore of the black powder gun. It builds up right in front of the load and can often be felt by a cleaning patch on a jag. If a shooter is going to test various loads, he is better off beginning with the light ones. This way, the fouling ring will be low in the barrel and consequent loads won't be caught on it. If the heavier loads are run down, the ball and patch will not have to be forced past this ring.

Freebore
A portion of the barrel, just ahead of the chamber, which is not rifled. A barrel may have a lot of freebore or a little. Freebore can ease chamber pressure, but some shooters believe that the pressure of freebore and a normally seated bullet will prove less accurate than having the bullet just touching the rifling. The latter has not been proved.

Freshening
Also "fresh out," the act of recutting the rifling of a barrel a little bit deeper to effectively create a new bore for a gun that has been shot out or pitted from failure to clean properly.

Frizzen
Found on black powder firearms and also called a "hammer" or known, too, as "battery" or "steel." It is a hard piece of metal that pivots in place on the flintlock so that the flint must strike its surface, thereby giving off sparks which hit the pan powder and set it off.

Furniture
In muzzle-loading guns, this is the metal trim, the brass, German silver or iron decorative pieces.

G

Gang Mold
This is a mold for making ball or bullet which contains more than one cavity, so that several projectiles can be made at one time.

Gas Check
A metallic cup which fits snugly on the base of the cast bullet, allowing higher velocity with less leading.

Gas Cutting
Actual barrel throat erosion or bullet distortion brought about by the melting away of portions of the bullet's surface. Gas cutting is caused by high-pressure impact gases escaping between the bullet and the bore of the firearm. Normally associated with revolvers.

Gas Port
A gas port is an orifice or hole in the barrel of semi-auto firearms which allows a portion of the expanding gases from the fired round to be bled off into a gas cylinder which gives the power for the function of the action.

Gauge
A means of measuring the bore diameter of a shotgun. Initially, gauge had to do with the number of round lead balls it would take to constitute 1 pound of weight. So a 12-gauge shotgun required 12 round balls to equal 1 pound; 20-gauge would need 20 round lead balls to make a pound.

German Silver
Also known a nickel silver, this is an alloy of 60 parts copper, 20 parts zinc and 20 parts nickel. It's very popular for black powder furniture or accoutrements, such as magazine cappers, tobacco tins and tinder boxes.

Glass Bedding
Glass bedding is the use of a fiberglass compound to make a seat for the barrel or barrel and action so that those elements are resting on the fiberglass instead of directly upon the wood channel or mortices in the stock. Often used for strength as well as ability to resist warpage.

Globe Sight
A very tiny front sight with a thin shank, the bead is small and quite precise, often has a cover over it to protect that bead from breakage.

Go-No-Go Gauges
These are precisely made cartridge-like chamber inserts which measure the headspace of a firearm. They serve as *standards* with which to check the headspacing of a firearm. The "Go" gauge *should* fit into the chamber, while the "No Go" should *not*.

Grain
In shooting, a unit of measure to designate the weight of a bullet or powder charge. It takes 7000 grains to make 1 U.S. pound. There are 437.5 grains in 1 U.S. ounce.

Grooves
The groove is the spiral cut in a bore which in turn creates the land. The land is impressed into the projectile, thereby *engraving* the projectile and making that missile spin in order to stabilize it.

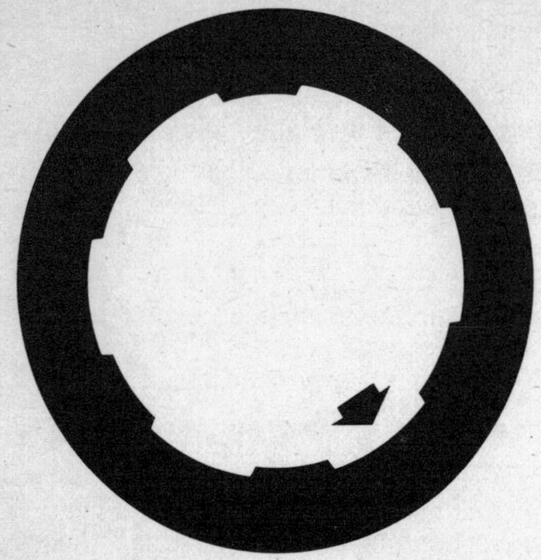

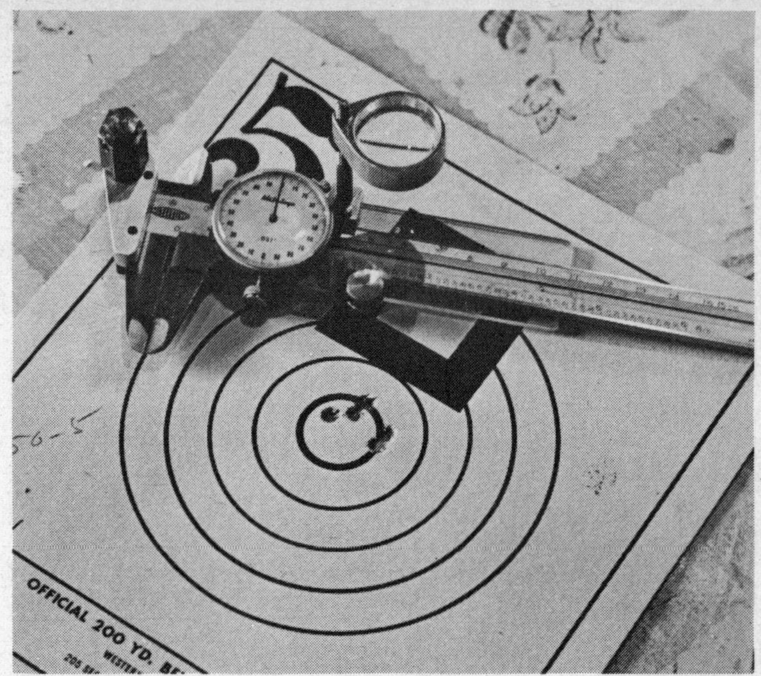

Groove: The "groove" (arrow) portion of the rifling can be seen in this artist's rendering of the rifling of a barrel. (The "lands" are found in between each groove.)

(Right) **Group:** The "group" fired here measures .664 inch, center-to-center.

Group

The pattern of distribution made by consecutive shots fired upon the target at a specific distance is a group. It should be measured at the widest point from the center of one hole to the center of another hole.

H

Half-Jacket

A half-jacketed bullet is one which is a swaged lead bullet with a thin copper jacket covering much, if not all, of the bearing surface of a projectile. It prevents leading associated with cast bullets.

Hammer

The device which delivers the blow to the firing pin. Sometimes a firing pin may be an integral part of the hammer.

Hammer Cup

On a black powder firearm the indented part of the hammer nose. On a percussion gun the hammer cup is supposed to be deep enough to contain at least most of the cap debris, if not all of it.

Hammer Nose

The forward portion of the hammer, the part that protrudes downward and does the striking.

Hangfire

Not a *misfire*, a hangfire *does* go off. It's a situation whereby the primer, percussion cap or pan charge does not *instantly* explode and ignite the main powder charge. In other words, a "perceived" misfiring may turn into a hangfire several seconds after the firing pin has impacted the primer, or the hammer inpacted the percussion cap or frizzen. Whenever an "apparent" misfire takes place, keep the muzzle pointed safely downrange for a full 60 seconds —you may, as the seconds tick off, be treated to a hangfire.

Headspace

In a gun, it is the distance from the breech face or bolt face to that part of the chamber which stops the forward movement of the case. In some rounds, the shoulder of the case stops the forward movement, so we say this round headspaces on the shoulder. In some rounds, the rim of the case stops the forward movement, and we say that this type of case headspaces on the rim. In the latter, the headspace would be determined by the thickness of the rim.

Hollow Point

A cavity in the nose of a bullet constitutes a hollow point projectile.

I

Ignition

In a modern round, the detonation of the primer compound and the resultant burning of the powder. In a muzzleloader, a percussion cap or in the case of flintlocks priming powder supplies the initial spark to ignite the main charge in the breech.

Ingalls' Tables

These tables, created by Colonel James Ingalls, allows

the computation of remaining velocities and trajectories of sporting rounds.

IMR

This stands for Improved Military Rifle and refers to duPont's line of single-base powders.

Inletting

The channels in the gunstock into which the metal portions of the gun fit.

J

Jacketed Bullet

As opposed to an all-lead projectile, the jacketed bullet consists of the lead core with a wrapping of gilding metal, the later being the jacket itself.

Jag

A metal unit that screws into a tip or wiping stick tip, as well as a cleaning rod tip; and, with its many ridges, it hangs onto the cleaning patch as that patch is run up and down the barrel to clean the bore.

K

Kentucky Windage

An imprecise estimation of how to aim the rifle in order to make a hit downrange.

Key

On black powder firearms a flat, wedge-shaped piece of metal that holds the barrel to the forend of the stock. It fits through the escutcheons. If not put into place carfully, the key can knock out an escutcheon on the opposite side of the stock.

Keyholing

When the bullet loses its rotational stability, it may tumble. The tumbling is called keyholing, which may also be looked at as a condition of the RPS falling off too much to stabilize the bullet. (RPS is revolutions per second.)

L

Lands

In a rifled barrel, the raised ribs left by the cutting of the rifling grooves. The grooves and the lands together are called rifling.

Magazine: This lever-action rifle features a "tubular magazine" located directly under the barrel. It runs from the muzzle back to the action.

Leade

The leade, also known as "throat", is a slightly enlarged conical shaped portion of the bore just ahead of the chamber.

Leading

Depositing of lead within the bore is known as leading of the bore.

Lock Plate

This is the metal base, or plate which holds the screws, pins and other attachments of the lock. Bolts enter from opposite the lock side and thread into the plate.

Lock Time

This is the actual time elapsed from the release of the sear (pulling of the trigger) to the firing pin impact on the primer.

LUP

This is "Lead Units of Pressure." It does not correspond directly with pounds per square inch; but, the lead being crushed to various degrees does tell quite accurately how much force is being exerted by the particular load being tested.

Hollow Point: This is an excellent example of a hollow point Speer pistol bullet (357 caliber, 158 grains). The dotted line indicates the internal configuration and depth of the hollow cavity.

M

Magazine

That section of the firearm which contains the rounds is the magazine of the gun.

Mid-Range Trajectory

The highest point reached by a bullet from the muzzle to the target is the mid-range trajectory.

Minute of Angle

In layman's terms, and for shooting purposes, a minute of angle is approximately 1 inch at 100 yards, 2 inches at 200 yards, 3 inches in 300 yards and so forth. More specifically, it is 1/60th of one degree.

Misfire

Total failure of a loaded cartridge to "go off" is a misfire, as opposed to a "hangfire," in which the firearm does detonate, but in a delayed fashion. (See Hangfire.)

Monte Carlo Comb

Essentially, this is the condition of raising the comb of the stock toward the butt of the stock, and then dropping that comb severely to form a notch or sloped contour.

Monte Carlo Comb: This Weatherby Mark V features a stock with a Monte Carlo Comb.

N

Nipple

The coned device, metallic in composition, which holds the black powder percussion cap and also allows the spark to travel from the cap into the breech area, is the nipple.

O

Obturation

This is the same as bullet upset, the condition which exists when the bullet is struck by the full power of the detonated powder charge. The projectile tends to remain in its position in the bore (inertia) for a very minute portion of time, which foreshortens the projectile and actually "fattens" it out, which makes the bullet better fit the bore of the gun.

Ogive

This is the curved, rounded or pointed forward portion of the bullet; that which is forward of the bearing surface.

Oil Dent

An oil dent is an actual "dent" impressed into the metallic catridge case during the process of resizing the fired case. It is caused by excessive lube which is trapped between the case and the inner walls of the die. Oil dents are commonly found in the shoulder area of bottleneck cartridges. Oil dents aren't generally assoicated with cases of straight-wall construction.

P

Partition Bullet

The partition bullet has an inner division between the rearward and forward portions of the bullet. This division prevents the stripping of the jacket upon impact in flesh.

Patent Breech

A construction feature of some black powder firearms, the breech plug and nipple seat having been cast as a single unit.

Patina

This is the yellowing, or golden effect that comes from the aging of metal. It is seen on many old-time original guns. Some shooters try to create patina on black powder firearms by never shining brass parts or overdoing the cleaning of lock plates, and so forth. Especially on the old originals, the patina should be left alone, rather than cleaned.

Peep Sight

The peep sight uses an aperture or hole through which the shooter views the front sight. Since the human eye will concentrate its focus at the highest point of light, it will center the front bead in the peep sight hole for accurate aiming. Also known as an "aperture sight," or a "receiver sight" when mounted on the receiver of the gun.

Percussion Cap

The forerunner of the modern primer, a percussion cap is a metal cup which contains the detonating charge which creates the spark which sets off the main charge in the breech of the muzzleloader and some breechloaders.

Pin

Usually found on full-stock black powder rifles (but also

on some halfstocks), this is the metal rod of very small dimension which holds the barrel and the stock together. It does the same service as the key; and, it must be removed (carefully) from the correct side of the stock so as not to split out any wood.

Pipes

On black powder firearms, short metal tubes attached to the barrel and into the stock forend, too, through which the ramrod is seated. Also called a "thimble," although some particular shooters prefer to separate the two terms. (See "thimble.")

Pitch

The angle which the butt of a firearm makes in relation to the line of sight. It can be seen quickly by resting the gun on its buttplate and seeing whether the barrel pitches backward or forward. A gunsmith can change the pitch, which often helps (especially with shotguns) in obtaining a better fit for the shooter.

Powder Residue

Although modern smokeless powder is very clean-burning, the change from solid to gaseous state is not totally complete. What remains in the bore after combustion is powder residue.

Pressure Gun

A test device used to determine breech pressure of a given load is a pressure gun.

Primer

This is the device which contains the detonating materials which ingnite the powder charge in the metallic cartridge or shotgun hull. It is, in fact, a container which holds not only the charge of detonating chemicals, but also the means for setting off that chemical. The modern primer consists of the cup itself plus the priming mixture as well as an anvil, a metal wing which rests above the priming mixture. The blow of the firing pin crushes the priming mixture between the base of the cup and the anvil, setting off the priming mixture. The resulting detonation creates an intense jet of flame that serves to ignite the powder charge in a metallic cartridge of shotgun shell.

R

Recoil

Recoil is a phenomenon of Newton's Third Law of Motion in which every action has an opposite and equal reaction. The propulsion of a missile from the bore of a firearm gives a rearward thrust which forces the firearm back toward the shooter. This rearward action is known as recoil.

Recoil Pad

This is a buttplate which is made of a soft agent for the absorption of recoil.

Reticle

This is the sighting device within the telescopic sight. It may consist of crosshairs or a dot or any number of other arrangements (to include combinations) which allows for sighting.

Rifling

The rifling consists of lands and grooves in the bore. The former are created when grooves are cut into the bore. Because the rifling is arranged as a spiral, it imparts a twist to the bullet. The proper amount of rifling twist serves to stabilize a bullet's flight.

Rimless Case

A cartridge case with the head diameter the same dimension as the body of the case. An extractor groove is cut into this type of case since there is no rim to be grabbed by an extractor. The 30-06 case is a rimless case.

Rimmed Case

A cartridge case with the head diameter larger than the body diameter. A typical example is the 30-30. Extraction is acomplished via this rim.

Rimfire

A cartridge which has the priming mixture distributed all around the rim of the case. The firing pin can strike anywhere along this rim for detonation.

Ruptured Case

A cartridge case (as well as shotgun hull) may actually burst, leaving a division or void in the metal or plastic/paper of the round. This opening constitutes the ruptured case and may be a sign of overly high pressure and/or very weak case/hull construction.

S

SAAMI

An acronym for the Sporting Arms and Ammunition Manufacturer's Institute. The organization is responsible for standardizing the measurements of the industry, to include chamber dimensions and other vital specifications.

Safety

The safety is a mechanical device which prevents the firing of a gun by, usually, blocking the sear, the hammer, the trigger or a combination of these three elements.

Scabbard

Generally of leather, the scabbard is a container for a rifle or carbine which is usually fastened to a saddle and which is often called a "saddle scabbard." It allows quick removal of the firearm when the gun is carried via horseback. Some scabbards do have covers or "boots." Others are open.

Scope Mount
The device through which the telescopic sight is attached to the firearm is the scope mount.

Screw
In black powder shooting a "screw" is just like a regular wood screw, except that the shank is threaded so that it can be inserted into the tip of a ramrod, wiping stick, or cleaning rod. It is used for the removal of a stuck ball, but it must be centered or damage to the rifling is possible.

Sear
The sear is a bar or piece of metal which engages the hammer notch or other portion of the trigger system. It is essentially a link between trigger and firing pin. Pulling the trigger trips the sear, which results in the firing pin striking the primer.

Sectional Density
The ratio of a bullet's weight in pounds to the square of its diameter in inches. This is used as a part of the C or ballistic coefficient function.

Sighting In
The process of aligning the sights so that the gun is capable of putting a bullet on target is called sighting in. This altering of the sights is essential in compensating for the arc of the bullet's flight.

Sight Radius
This is the distance between the rear sight and the front sight of a metallic sighted firearm.

Single Action
As opposed to the double-action, a single-action gun requires that the hammer be earred back (cocked) each and every time the gun is to be fired.

Sizing
The term sizing can have several definitions, depending upon the area of the shooting sports being addressed. Most commonly, the term sizing (or resizing) refers to the step in the reloading process where a fired case (or shotshell) is brought back to original dimensions via the use of a reloading press and resizing die of proper caliber/gauge. "Sizing" can be "Full Length" or "Neck-Only" when metallic cartridges are involved. In the world of black powder shooting, the term "Sizing" refers to a coating or glaze, sometimes a type of starch, soaked into material so that the cloth can be more easily woven, and to make the fabric look better in the store for sales appeal and handling. The sizing must be removed by soaking or washing before patches are cut from it.

Soft Point
Instead of drawing the bullet jacket all the way out to the tip or nose of the projectile, the forward potion of the bullet allows for a protrusion of the lead core. The presence of that small amount of lead indicates that the bullet is of soft point construction.

Single-Action: The Colt Single Action Army must have its hammer cocked each time the gun is to be fired.

Sprue: The sprue is seen here as a white blob of solidified lead found directly on top of the sprue-cutter plate.

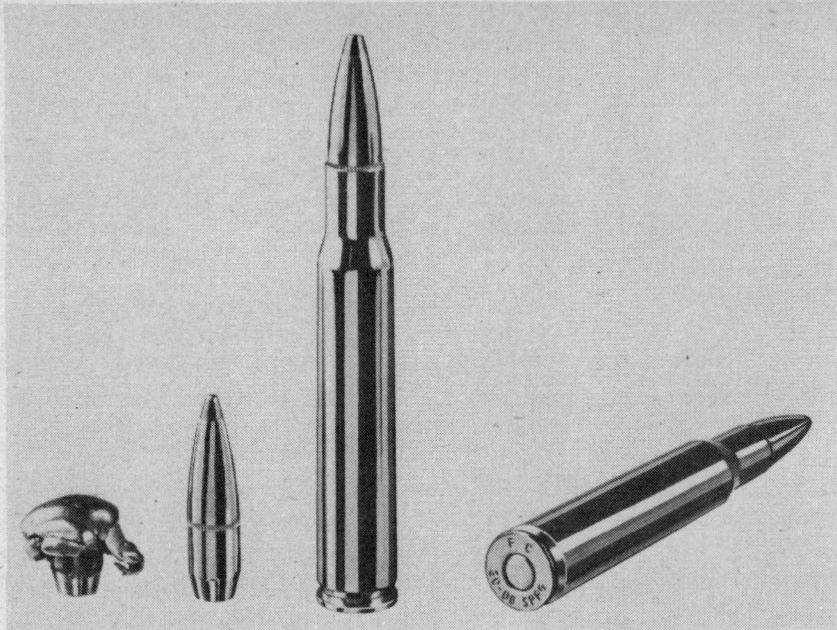

Soft Point: Soft point bullets are identified by the small amount of exposed lead at the tip of the bullet. Seen here is a Federal 30-06 loaded with a Sierra boat-tail, soft point bullet. The soft point bullet is designed to expand upon impact. A fully expanded soft point bullet can be seen at the left.

Spitzer

In general terms, this is a pointed bullet as opposed to a flat nose or round nose bullet.

Sprue

The small amount of excess lead attached to a cast ball or bullet which is left behind by the sprue cutter plate during the process of casting.

Squib Load

This is, in effect, a light load. But it usually refers to a cast bullet load with a light powder charge, used for various functions, including practice and small game hunting with a firearm of big game caliber.

Star Crimp

Replacing the old "roll crimp" with its over-shot wad to hold the shot inside of the shotgun hull, the star crimp is the folding of the forward portion of the hull to retain the shot. It derives its name from the fact that the folds resemble the pattern of a star.

Swaging

Swaging is the shaping of a bullet by forcing the bullet through a sizing die. This is accomplished "cold" and in no way relates to the casting of a bullet. The process reduces the diameter of the bullet slightly and produces uniformity of projectiles.

T

Takedown

Takedown refers to that type of firearm which may be broken down. For example, the takedown rifle generally breaks around the forward part of the action, allowing the buttstock and the barel to separate into two parts.

Tangent Ogive

As opposed to the secant ogive, this bullet shape has the surface of the cylindrical part of the bullet tangent to the curve of the bullet's point.

Tenon

On a black powder firearm this is the metal loop or hunk of flatwork that is fitted to the bottom of the barrel. The keys or the pins go through this tenon to hold the stock and the barrel together.

Tenon Pin

(This is another term for tenon—see "Tenon.")

Thimble

Sometimes called a "ferrule," the thimble is found on black powder firearms and is a small metal loop that usually wraps around the entire barrel and stock. A thimble secures and helps store a ramrod in the stock.

Throat (see Leade.)

Time of Flight

This is the time it takes for a bullet to exit the muzzle and then "land." Time of flight will vary depending upon the distance between the muzzle and the intended target. For example, we can compute the time of flight of a 180-grain bullet starting at 2800 fps and traveling 200 yards.

Wad: This is an example of the modern, one-piece plastic shotshell wad. The lower half of the wad serves as an over-powder seal, the top half of the wad holding the shot charge.

Trajectory

The parabola (arc) described by a bullet from the muzzle of the gun to the end of the bullet's flight is the trajectory of that missile.

Transducer

This is, in effect, an electronic means of calculating chamber pressure as opposed to LUP or CUP measurements. Because some crystal types emit an electical impulse upon being crushed, a quartz crystal can be attached to an oscilloscope to get a reading of a particular load. The chamber pressure is expressed in PSI, pounds per square inch.

Triplex Load

Similar to Duplex Load (see same) with the exception that a third propellant type is added to the charge.

Try Gun

A try gun is a model of a firearm rather than an actual firearm. It allows for many moveable parts so that the shooter can be fitted for drop at comb, drop at toe or heel, length of pull, cast-on, cast-off and so forth. A gunsmith uses a try gun in order to fit his customer into the stock which will match that shooter's style and physical makeup.

Twist

This is the spiral shape of the rifling as it turns in the bore. The more turn, the more twist. The ''twist rate'' will change depending on the bullet used. ''Twist rate'' is expressed, for example, as ''1 in 10,'' meaning one complete revolution of the bullet per each 10 inches of barrel.

W

Wad

The wad is a unit which rests between the powder charge and the shot charge in the shotgun hull. Today, the plastic one piece wad is most prevalent.

Wadcutter

The wadcutter bullet is cylindrical in shape with a flat or beveled base and a flat nose. It is used for target shooting, as its sharp-edged flat nose cuts a very neat hole in the target, making scoring much easier.

Windage

In a muzzle-loading firearm it is the space between the bare ball and the inside of the bore, which is taken up by the patch.

Worm

The worm is a corkscrew-shaped tool used to extract a stuck patch from downbore in the muzzleloader.

Chapter 37

Shooting Groups and Organizations

SHOOTING ORGANIZATIONS have been very important to American firearms enthusiasts for well over 100 years. For one thing, shooting organizations have made many fine matches available to target shooters who would not have otherwise had opportunities to display their skill. Furthermore, several shooter's organizations have been responsible for safeguarding the rights of gun owners. This short offering is calculated to give the reader a brief introduction to some of the national shooting organizations with addresses.

Although shooters are often characterized as individualists, there are certain groups which promote the sport for all of us. Of course, the major shooting organization in America is the NRA (National Rifle Association) and this body of official rulemakers and guardians of shooter's rights began in 1871. Fifteen National Guard officers, all of them veterans of the Civil War, got together and decided to build a club which would be much more than a club. They had a "pattern" to follow, that pattern being the National Rifle Association of Great Britain. With the NRA of Great Britain as a model, the men went about designing a group which would affect policy-making for American shooters. Today, that group is 2.25 million strong in membership. The NRA is the official sounding board for many target matches. It gives awards to hunters, too, for trophy-sized game. It sponsors Voluntary Practical Firearms Programs to provide basic instructions in shooting handguns for personal and home protection. And the NRA offers a pair of magazines to its subscribers, *The American Rifleman* and *The American Hunter*. A member gets his choice with his membership.

While there are several extremely worthwhile shooting organizations for American marksmen, the NRA must be noted as the largest and most important in terms of legislative involvement. Located in Washington, D.C., the NRA is watchful of proposals which will curtail the use and private ownership of firearms by the American people.

Addresses of Major American Shooting Organizations

American Association of Shotgunning
P.O. Box 3351
Reno, Nevada 89505

American Police Pistol & Rifle Association
1100 N.E. 125th St.
So. Miani, FL 33161

American Single Shot Rifle Association
987 Jefferson Ave.
Salem, OH 44460

American Society of Arms Collectors
6550 Baywood Lane
Cincinnati, OH 45224

Boone & Crockett Club
205 South Patrick
Alexandria, VA 22314

Cast Bullet Association
14193 Van Doren Rd.
Manasses, VA 22111

Citizens Committee for the Right to Keep and Bear Arms
Nat'l. Headquarters
12500 N.E. Tenth Place
Bellevue, WA 98005

Deer Unlimited of America, Inc.
P.O. Box 509
Clemson, SC 29631

Ducks Unlimited
One Waterfowl Way
Long Grove, IL 60047

Experimental Ballistics Association
110 Kensington
Trenton, NJ 08618

Handgun Hunters International
P.O. Box 357 Magnum
Bloomingdale, OH 43910

International Benchrest Shooters
411 N. Wilbur Ave.
Sayre, PA 18840

International Cartridge Collectors Association
1211 Walnut St.
Williamsport, PA 17701

National Benchrest Shooters Association
5735 Sherwood Forest Dr.
Akron, OH 44319

National Deer Hunters Association
1415 Fifth St.
Hopkins, MN 55343

National Muzzle Loading Rifle Association
P.O. Box 67
Friendship, IN 47021

National Reloaders Mfgs. Association
4905 S.W. Griffith Dr.
Suite 101
Beaverton, OR 97005

National Rifle Association of America (NRA)
1600 Rhode Island Avenue, N.W.
Washington, D.C. 20036

National Shooting Sports Foundation
1075 Post Rd.
Riverside, CT 06878

Sporting Arms and Ammunition Manufacturer's Institute (SAAMI)
P.O. Box 218
Wallingford, CT 06492

Safari Club International
5151 E. Broadway
Tucson, AZ 85711

Second Amendment Foundation
12500 N.E. 10th Pl.
Bellevue, WA 98005